Cite This Volume:

38 USCS §—

LEARNING RESOURCES CENTER
Southwestern Community College
Sylva, NC 28779

★ ★ ★ ★ **UNITED STATES CODE SERVICE** ★ ★ ★

Lawyers Edition

All federal laws of a general and permanent nature arranged in accordance with the section numbering of the United States Code and the supplements thereto.

38 USCS
Veterans' Benefits
§§ 3001 – 4300
1998

LEXIS®
LAW PUBLISHING

701 East Water Street
Charlottesville, VA 22902

Copyright © 1998 by
LEXIS® Law Publishing,
a division of Reed Elsevier Inc. All rights reserved.

Copyright is not claimed in any works of the United
States Government.

LEXIS is a registered trademark of Reed Elsevier Properties
Inc., used under license.

Library of Congress Catalog Card Number 72-76254

ISBN 0-327-06107-3

4703911

PUBLICATION EDITOR:
Derrick R. Wilborn, J.D.

CONSULTING EDITOR:
Martin M. Heit, J.D.

CONTRIBUTING EDITORS:
Michele D. Ferrara, J.D.
Gary Knapp, J.D.
Julie L. Riethmeier, J.D.
Stacey M. Romeo, J.D.

TECHNICAL SUPPORT STAFF:
Sheri Ashton
Mary Carey
Julie Lisciandro
Dolores Marlowe
Jennifer Nealon

ABBREVIATIONS

Reporters, Texts, Etc.

A	Atlantic Reporter
A2d	Atlantic Reporter, Second Series
ACMR	Army Court of Military Review
AD	Appellate Division Reports (NY)
AD2d	Appellate Division Reports, Second Series (NY)
AdL2d	Pike and Fischer Administrative Law, Second Series
ADVA	Administrator's Decisions, Veterans' Administration
AFCMR	Air Force Court of Military Review
AFTR	American Federal Tax Reports
AFTR2d	American Federal Tax Reports, Second Series
AGBCA	Department of Agriculture Board of Contract Appeals
Ag Dec	Agriculture Decisions
ALAB	NRC Atomic Safety and Licensing Appeal Board
ALR	American Law Reports
ALR2d	American Law Reports, Second Series
ALR3d	American Law Reports, Third Series
ALR4th	American Law Reports, Fourth Series
ALR5th	American Law Reports, Fifth Series
ALR Fed.	American Law Reports, Federal
Am Bankr NS	American Bankruptcy, New Series
ADD	Americans With Disabilities Decisions
AMC	American Maritime Cases
Am Disab	Americans With Disabilities: Practice and Compliance Manual
Am Jur 2d	American Jurisprudence, Second Edition
Am Jur Legal Forms 2d ...	American Jurisprudence Legal Forms, Second Edition
Am Jur Pl & Pr Forms (Rev ed)	American Jurisprudence Pleading and Practice Forms, Revised Edition
Am Jur Proof of Facts	American Jurisprudence Proof of Facts
Am Jur Proof of Facts 2d ..	American Jurisprudence Proof of Facts, Second Series

Abbreviations

Am Jur Proof of Facts 3d	American Jurisprudence Proof of Facts, Third Series
Am Jur Trials	American Jurisprudence Trials
Am Law Prod Liab 3d	American Law of Products Liability, Third Edition
App DC	United States Court of Appeals for the District of Columbia
Appx	Appendix
ASBCA	Armed Services Board of Contract Appeals
ATF Qtrly Bull	Quarterly Bulletin, Alcohol, Tobacco and Firearms Bureau, U.S. Dept. Treas.
ATR Rul	Ruling of Alcohol, Tobacco and Firearms Bureau, U.S. Dept. Treas.
BAMSL	Bankruptcy Reporter of the Bar Association of Metropolitan St. Louis
BCA	Board of Contract Appeals
BCD	Bankruptcy Court Decisions
Bd Imm App	Board of Immigration Appeals
BIA	Board of Immigration Appeals
Bkr L Ed	Bankruptcy Service, Lawyers Edition
BLR	BRBS Black Lung Reporter
BNA EBC	Employee Benefits Cases
BNA FEP Cas	Fair Employment Practices Cases
BNA IER Cas	Individual Employment Rights Cases
BNA LRRM	Labor Relations Reference Manual
BNA OSHC	Occupational Safety and Health Cases
BNA WH Cas	Wage and Hour Cases
BR	Bankruptcy Reporter
BRBS	Benefits Review Board Service
BTA	Board of Tax Appeals
BTA Mem	Board of Tax Appeals Memorandum Decisions
CA	United States Court of Appeals
CAB Adv Dig	Civil Aeronautics Board Advance Digest
CAD	Customs Appeals Decisions
Cal Rptr	California Reporter
CB	Cumulative Bulletin of the Internal Revenue Service
CBC	Collier Bankruptcy Cases
CBD	Customs Bulletin and Decisions, Customs Service, Department of the Treasury
CCG	Consumer Credit Guide
CCH Bankr L Rptr	Bankruptcy Law Reporter
CCH BCA Dec	Board of Contract Appeals Decisions
CCH CCG	Consumer Credit Guide
CCH Comm Fut L Rep	Commodity Futures Law Reporter
CCH EEOC Dec	Decisions of the Equal Employment Opportunity Commission
CCH EPD	Employment Practice Decisions
CCH Fed Secur L Rep	Federal Securities Law Reporter

Abbreviations

CCH FERC	Federal Energy Regulatory Commission Reports
CCH Lab Cas	Labor Cases
CCH LC	Labor Cases
CCH NLRB	National Labor Relations Board Decisions
CCH OSHD	Occupational Safety and Health Decisions
CCH TCM	Tax Court Memorandum Decisions
CCH Trade Cas	Trade Cases
CCH Trade Reg Rep	Trade Regulation Reports
CCH Unemployment Ins Rep	Unemployment Insurance Reporter
CCPA	Court of Customs and Patent Appeals
CD	Customs Decisions
CDOS	California Daily Opinion Service
CFR	Code of Federal Regulations
CFTC	Commodity Futures Trading Commission
CGCMR	Coast Guard Court of Military Review
CGLB	Coast Guard Law Bulletin
CIT	Court of International Trade
CLI	Commission Licensing Issuance
CMA	Court of Military Appeals
CMR	Court-Martial Reports
COGSA	Carriage of Goods by Sea Act
Comm Fut L Rep	Commodity Futures Law Reporter
Comp Gen	Decisions of the U.S. Comptroller General
Comp Gen Unpub Dec	Unpublished decisions of the U.S. Comptroller General
Comr Pat	Commissioner of Patents and Trademarks
CPD	Customs Penalty Decisions
CPSC Advisory Op No	Consumer Product Safety Commission Advisory Opinion Number
CRD	Customs Rules Decisions
CR L	Criminal Law Reporter
CSD	Customs Service Decisions
Ct Cl	Court of Claims
Cust Bull	Customs Bulletin and Decisions, US Department of Treasury
Cust Ct	Customs Court
Cust & Pat App (Cust)	U.S. Court of Customs and Patent Appeals (Customs)
Cust & Pat App (Pat)	U.S. Court of Customs and Patent Appeals (Patents)
DC	United States District Court
DCAB	Department of Commerce Contract Appeals Board
DCO	Department of Commerce Orders
Dist Col App	District of Columbia Court of Appeals
DOA	Department of Agriculture
DOC	Department of Commerce

Abbreviations

DOE	Department of Energy
DOHA	Department of Defense Office of Hearings and Appeals
DOT CAB	Department of Transportation Contract Appeals Board
DPRM	Denial of Petition for Rulemaking, NRC Decision
EBC	Employee Benefits Cases
EBCA	Department of Energy Board of Contract Appeals
ECAB	Employees' Compensation Appeals Board, U.S. Department of Labor
EEOC DEC	Equal Employment Opportunity Commission Decisions
ELR	Environmental Law Reporter
Em Ct App	Emergency Court of Appeals
EMP COORD	Employment Coordinator
ENG BCA	Corps of Engineers Board of Contract Appeals
EPD	Employment Practices Decisions
ERA	Economic Regulatory Administration
ERC	Environmental Reporter Cases
ERISA Op Letters	Employee Retirement Income Security Act Opinion Letters
Ex Or	Executive Order
F	Federal Reporter
F2d	Federal Reporter, Second Series
F3d	Federal Reporter, Third Series
F Cas	Federal Cases
FCC	Federal Communications Commission
FCC2d	Federal Communications Commission Reports, Second Series
FCSC	Foreign Claims Settlement Commission
FCSC 1981 Ann Rpt	FCSC Annual Report for 1981
FCSC Dec & Anno (1968)	FCSC Decisions and Annotations, 1968 edition
FDA	Food and Drug Administration
FDA Dec	Food and Drug Administration Decisions
FEA	Federal Energy Administration
Fed Cl	Court of Federal Claims Reporter
Fed Evid Rep	Federal Rules of Evidence Service
Fed Proc, L Ed	Federal Procedure, Lawyers Edition
Fed Procedural Forms, L Ed	Federal Procedure Forms, Lawyers Edition
Fed Reg	Federal Register
Fed Rules Evid Serv	Federal Rules of Evidence Service
Fed Rules Serv	Federal Rules Service
Fed Rules Serv 2d	Federal Rules Service, Second Series
FEP Case	Fair Employment Practice Cases (BNA)
FEPC	Fair Employment Practice Cases
FERC	Federal Energy Regulatory Commission Reports
Fed Secur L Rep	Federal Securities Law Reporter

Abbreviations

FHLBB	Federal Home Loan Bank Board
FLRA	Federal Labor Relations Authority
FLRA GCO	Federal Labor Relations Authority, General Counsel Opinions
FLRC	Federal Labor Relations Council
FMC	Federal Maritime Commission
FMSHRC	Federal Mine Safety and Health Review Commission
FOIA	Freedom of Information Act
FPC	Federal Power Commission
FR	Federal Register
FRB	Federal Reserve Bulletin
FRCP	Federal Rules of Civil Procedure
FRCrP	Federal Rules of Criminal Procedure
FRD	Federal Rules Decisions
FRE	Federal Rules of Evidence
FRS	Federal Reserve System
FSIP	Federal Service Impasses Panel
F Supp	Federal Supplement
FTC	Federal Trade Commission
GAO	General Accounting Office
GSBCA	General Services Administration Board of Contract Appeals
HEW	Department of Health, Education and Welfare
HHS	Department of Health and Human Services
HUD	Department of Housing and Urban Development
HUD BCA	Department of Housing and Urban Development Board of Contract Appeals
IBCA	Interior Department Board of Contract Appeals
IBIA	Interior Board of Indian Appeals (Dept. of the Interior)
ICC	Interstate Commerce Commission
ID	Decisions of the Department of the Interior
I & N Dec	Immigration and Naturalization Service Decisions
ILS	Immigration Law Service
INS	Immigration and Naturalization Service
IRB	Internal Revenue Bulletin
IRS	Internal Revenue Service
ITRD	Internal Trade Reporter Decisions
JAG	Judge Advocate General
Jud Pan Mult Lit	Rulings of the Judicial Panel on Multidistrict Litigation
LBCA	Department of Labor Board of Contract Appeals
LC	Labor Cases
LD	Land Decisions
L Ed	Lawyers Edition U.S. Supreme Court Reports
L Ed 2d	Lawyers Edition U.S. Supreme Court Reports, Second Series

ABBREVIATIONS

LRRM	Labor Relations Reference Manual
MA	Maritime Administration
MCC	Motor Carrier Cases (decided by ICC)
Mich	Michigan Reports
Mich App	Michigan Appeals Reports
Misc	Miscellaneous Reports (NY)
Misc 2d	Miscellaneous Reports, Second Series (NY)
MJ	Military Justice Reporter
MSB	Maritime Subsidy Board
MSPB	Merit Systems Protection Board
MSPR	United States Merit Systems Protection Board Reporter
Mun Ct App Dist Col	Municipal Court of Appeals for District of Columbia
NASA BCA	National Aeronautics and Space Administration Board of Contract Appeals
NCMR	Navy Court of Military Review
NE	North Eastern Reporter
NE2d	North Eastern Reporter, Second Series
NLRB	Decisions and Orders of the National Labor Relations Board
NLRB Advice Mem Case No	National Labor Relations Board Advice Memorandum Case Number
NMCMR	U.S. Navy—Marine Corps Court of Military Review
NOAA	National Oceanic and Atmospheric Administration
NRC	Nuclear Regulatory Commission
NTSB	National Transportation Safety Board
NW	North Western Reporter
NW2d	North Western Reporter, Second Series
NY	New York Reports
NY2d	New York Reports, Second Series
NYS	New York Supplement
NYS2d	New York Supplement, Second Series
nt	note
nts	notes
OAG	Opinions of the Attorney General
OCSLA	Outer Continental Shelf Lands Act
OFCCP	Office of Federal Contract Compliance Programs
Op Atty Gen	Opinions of Attorney General
Op Comp Gen	Opinions of Comptroller General
ORW	Ocean Resources and Wildlife Reporter
OSAHRC	Occupational Safety and Health Review Commission (Official Reports)
OSHRC	Occupational Safety and Health Review Commission
P	Pacific Reporter

Abbreviations

P2d	Pacific Reporter, Second Series
PBGC Op No	Pension Benefit Guaranty Corporation Opinion Number
PRD	Protest Review Decisions
Proc	Proclamation
PSBCA	Postal Service Board of Contract Appeals
PS Docket	Postal Service Docket
PTE	Prohibited Transaction Exemption Decisions of The Office of Pension and Welfare Benefit Programs, Department of Labor
PUR3d	Public Utilities Reports, Third Series
PUR4th	Public Utilities Reports, Fourth Series
RD	Reappraisement Decision, U. S. Customs Court
RESPA	Real Estate Settlement Procedures Act
Rev Proc	Revenue Procedure
Rev Rul	Revenue Ruling
RIA	Research Institute of America.
RIA Corp Capital Trans Coord	RIA Corporate Capital Transaction Coordinator
RIA Employee Ben Comp Coord	RIA Employee Benefits Compliance Coordinator
RIA Employment Coord	RIA Employee Coordinator
RIA Employ Discrim Coord.	RIA Employment Discrimination Coordinator
RIA Estate Plan & Tax Coord	RIA Estate Planning & Taxation Coordinator
RIA Exec Comp & Tax Coord	RIA Executive Compensation & Taxation Coordinator
RIA Fed Tax Coord 2d	RIA Federal Tax Coordinator 2d
RIA Partnership & S Corp Coord	RIA Partnership & S Corporation Coordinator
RIA Pension Coord	RIA Pension Coordinator
RIA Real Estate Coord	RIA Real Estate Coordinator
RIA Tax Action Coord	RIA Tax Action Coordinator
RIA TC Memo	Tax Court Memorandum Decisions
RICO	RICO Business Disputes Guide
RRRA	Regional Rail Reorganization Act
R.S.	Revised Statutes
RUSCC	Rules of United States Claims Court
S Ct	United States Supreme Court Reporter
SE	South Eastern Reporter
SE2d	South Eastern Reporter, Second Series
SEC	Securities and Exchange Commission, also SEC Docket
So	Southern Reporter
So 2d	Southern Reporter, Second Series
Soc Sec LP	Social Security Law and Practice
Soc Sec & Unemployment Ins Rep	Social Security and Unemployment Insurance Reporter

Abbreviations

Sp Ct RRRA	Special Court, Regional Rail Reorganization Act
SSA	Social Security Administration
SSR	Social Security Rulings
Stat	Statutes at Large
SW	South Western Reporter
SW2d	South Western Reporter, Second Series
TC	United States Tax Court Reports
TCM	Tax Court Memorandum
T Ct	United States Tax Court
TD	Treasury Decisions
TD ATF	Treasury Decisions concerning matters of Alcohol, Tobacco and Firearms Bureau
TIAS	Treaties and International Agreements Series
TMT & App Bd	Trademark Trial and Appeal Board
TNT	Tax Notes Today
UCCRS	Uniform Commercial Code Reporting Service
US	United States Reports
USC	United States Code
USCMA	United States Court of Military Appeals
USCS	United States Code Service
USEPA GCO	United States Environmental Protection Agency, General Counsel Opinions
USEPA RCO	United States Environmental Protection Agency, Regional Counsel Opinions
USEPA NPDES	United States Environmental Protection Agency, National Pollutant Discharge Elimination System
USLW	United States Law Week
USPQ	United States Patents Quarterly
USSG	United States Sentencing Guidelines
UST	United States Treaties and Other International Agreements
USTC	United States Tax Cases
VA CAB	Veterans Administration Contract Appeals Board
VA GCO	Veterans Administration, General Counsel Opinions
Vet Apps	Court of Veterans Appeals Reporter
Vet App R	Rules of Veterans Appeals
WAB	Wage Appeals Board Decision, Dept. of Labor
WGL	Warren Gorham Lamont
WGL Employee Ben Comp Coord	WGL Employee Benefits Compliance Coordinator
WGL Employment Coord	WGL Employee Coordinator
WGL Employ Discrim Coord	WGL Employment Discrimination Coordinator
WH Cases	Wage and Hour Cases
WH2d	Wage and Hour Cases, Second Series
WH Op Letter	Wage and Hour Opinion Letter

Abbreviations

Legal Periodicals

ABA J	American Bar Association Journal
AFL Rev	Air Force Law Review
Adelphia LJ	Adelphia Law Journal
Admin LJ	Administrative Law Journal
Admin LJ Am U	Administrative Law Journal of American University
Admin L Rev	Administrative Law Review
Advoc Q	Advocates' Quarterly
AILPA QJ	AILPA Quarterly Journal
Akron L Rev	Akron Law Review
Akron Tax J	Akron Tax Journal
Ala L Rev	Alabama Law Review
Alaska L Rev	Alaska Law Review
Alb L Rev	Albany Law Review
Am Bankr Inst L Rev	American Bankruptcy Institute Law Review
Am Bankr LJ	American Bankruptcy Law Journal
Am Bus LJ	American Business Law Journal
Am Crim L Rev	American Criminal Law Review
Am Indian L Rev	American Indian Law Review
Am J Comp L	American Journal of Comparative Law
Am J Crim L	American Journal of Criminal Law
Am J Fam L	American Journal of Family Law
Am J Int'l L	American Journal of International Law
Am JL & Med	American Journal of Law and Medicine
Am J Tax Pol'y	American Journal of Tax Policy
Am J Trial Advoc	American Journal of Trial Advocacy
Am Soc'y Int'l L Proc	American Society of International Law Proceedings
Am UJ Int'l L & Pol'y	American University Journal of International Law and Policy
Am U L Rev	American University Law Review
Ann Rev Banking L	Annual Review of Banking Law
Antitrust Bull	Antitrust Bulletin
Antitrust LJ	Antitrust Law Journal
Arb J	Arbitration Journal
Ariz J Int'l & Comp L	Arizona Journal of International and Comparative Law
Ariz L Rev	Arizona Law Review
Ariz St LJ	Arizona State Law Journal
Ark L Rev	Arkansas Law Review
Army Law	Army Lawyer
BC Envtl Aff L Rev	Boston College Environmental Affairs Law Review
BC Int'l & Comp L Rev	Boston College International and Comparative Law Review
BC L Rev	Boston College Law Review
BU Int'l LJ	Boston University International Law Journal

Abbreviations

BU L Rev	Boston University Law Review
BYU J Pub L	Brigham Young University Journal of Public Law
BYU L Rev	Brigham Young University Law Review
Banking LJ	Banking Law Journal
Banking L Rev	Banking Law Review
Baylor L Rev	Baylor Law Review
Benefits LJ	Benefits Law Journal
Bridgeport L Rev	Bridgeport Law Review
Brook J Int'l L	Brooklyn Journal of International Law
Brook L Rev	Brooklyn Law Review
Buff Envtl LJ	Buffalo Environmental Law Journal
Buff L Rev	Buffalo Law Review
Bus Law	Business Lawyer
Cal Bankr J	California Bankruptcy Journal
Cal Intl Prac	California International Practitioner
Cal L Rev	California Law Review
Cal W Int'l LJ	California Western International Law Journal
Cap U L Rev	Capital University Law Review
Cardozo Arts & Ent LJ	Cardozo Arts and Entertainment Law Journal
Cardozo L Rev	Cardozo Law Review
Case W Res J Int'l L	Case Western Reserve Journal of International Law
Case W Res L Rev	Case Western Reserve Law Review
Cath U L Rev	Catholic University Law Review
Chi-Kent L Rev	Chicago-Kent Law Review
Clearinghouse Rev	Clearinghouse Review
Clev St L Rev	Cleveland State Law Review
Colo J Int'l Envtl L & Pol'y	Colorado Journal of Environmental Law and Policy
Colum Bus L Rev	Columbia Business Law Review
Colum J Envtl L	Columbia Journal of Environmental Law
Colum JL & Soc Probs	Columbia Journal of Law and Social Problems
Colum J Transnat'l L	Columbia Journal of Transnational Law
Colum L Rev	Columbia Law Review
Colum-VLA JL & Arts	Columbia-VLA Journal of Law and the Arts
Com LJ	Commercial Law Journal
Comm & L	Communications and the Law
Comp Lab LJ	Comparative Labor Law Journal
Computer LJ	Computer Law Journal
Computer Law	Computer Lawyer
Conn J Int'l L	Connecticut Journal of International Law
Conn L Rev	Connecticut Law Review
Copyright L Symp	Copyright Law Symposium
Copyright World	Copyright World
Cornell Int'l LJ	Cornell International Law Journal
Cornell JL & Pub Pol'y	Cornell Journal of Law and Public Policy
Cornell L Rev	Cornell Law Review

Abbreviations

Corp & Bus LJ	Corporate and Business Law Journal
Creighton L Rev	Creighton Law Review
Crim Just J	Criminal Justice Journal
Crim L Bull	Criminal Law Bulletin
Crim LJ	Criminal Law Journal
Crim LQ	Criminal Law Quarterly
Crim L Rev	Criminal Law Review
Cumb L Rev	Cumberland Law Review
Current Legal Probs	Current Legal Problems
Def Couns J	Defense Counsel Journal
Denning LJ	Denning Law Journal
Denver J Int'l L & Pol'y	Denver Journal of International Law and Policy
Denv U L Rev	Denver University Law Review
DePaul Bus LJ	DePaul Business Law Journal
DePaul L Rev	DePaul Law Review
Det CL Rev	Detroit College of Law Review
Dick J Int'l L	Dickinson Journal of International Law
Dick L Rev	Dickinson Law Review
Drake L Rev	Drake Law Review
Duke J Comp & Int'l L	Duke Journal of Comparative and International Law
Duq L Rev	Duquesne Law Review
Emory Int'l L Rev	Emory International Law Review
Emory LJ	Emory Law Journal
Empl Rel LJ	Employee Relations Law Journal
Envtl & Plan LJ	Environmental and Planning Law Journal
Envtl Claims J	Environmental Claims Journal
Envtl L	Environmental Law
Fed B News & J	Federal Bar News and Journal
Fed Comm LJ	Federal Communications Law Journal
Fla J Int'l L	Florida Journal of International Law
Fla L Rev	Florida Law Review
Fla St L Rev	Florida State University Law Review
Food Drug LJ	Food and Drug Law Journal
Fordham Intell Prop Media & Ent LJ	Fordham Intellectual Property, Media & Entertainment Law Journal
Fordham Int'l LJ	Fordham International Law Journal
Fordham L Rev	Fordham Law Review
Ga J Int & Comp L	Georgia Journal of International and Comparative Law
Ga L Rev	Georgia Law Review
Ga St U L Rev	Georgia State University Law Review
Geo Immigr LJ	Georgetown Immigration Law Journal
Geo LJ	Georgetown Law Journal
Geo Mason U L Rev	George Mason University Law Review
Geo Wash L Rev	George Washington Law Review
Glendale L Rev	Glendale Law Review

Abbreviations

Golden Gate U L Rev	Golden Gate University Law Review
Gonz L Rev	Gonzaga Law Review
Hamline J Pub L & Pol'y	Hamline Journal of Law and Public Policy
Hamline L Rev	Hamline Law Review
Harv CR-CL L Rev	Harvard Civil Rights and Civil Liberties Law Review
Harv Envtl L Rev	Harvard Environmental Law Review
Harv Int'l LJ	Harvard International Law Journal
Harv JL & Pub Pol'y	Harvard Journal of Law and Public Policy
Harv JL & Tech	Harvard Journal of Law and Technology
Harv J Legis	Harvard Journal on Legislation
Harv L Rev	Harvard Law Review
Hastings Comm & Ent LJ	Hastings Communications and Entertainment Law Journal
Hastings Const LQ	Hastings Constitutional Law Quarterly
Hastings Int'l & Comp L Rev	Hastings International and Comparative Law Review
Hastings LJ	Hastings Law Journal
High Tech LJ	High Technology Law Journal
Hofstra L Rev	Hofstra Law Review
Hofstra Lab LJ	Hofstra Labor Law Journal
Hous J Int'l L	Houston Journal of International Law
Hous L Rev	Houston Law Review
How LJ	Howard Law Journal
Idaho L Rev	Idaho Law Review
ILSA J Int'l L	ILSA Journal of International Law
Ind Int'l & Comp L Rev	Indiana International and Comparative Law Review
Ind L Rev	Indiana Law Review
Ind Rel LJ	Industrial Relations Law Journal
Int'l & Comp LQ	International and Comparative Law Quarterly
Int'l Law	International Lawyer
Iowa L Rev	Iowa Law Review
J Bankr L & Prac	Journal of Bankruptcy Law and Practice
J Copyright Soc'y USA	Journal of the Copyright Society of the USA
J Corp Law	Journal of Corporate Law
J Corp Tax'n	Journal of Corporate Taxation
J Energy & Nat Resources L	Journal of Energy and Natural Resources Law
J Energy Nat Resources and Envtl L	Journal of Energy, Natural Resources and Environmental Law
J Envtl L	Journal of Environmental Law
J Envtl L & Litig	Journal of Environmental Law and Litigation
J Health & Hosp L	Journal of Hospital and Health Law
JL & Com	Journal of Law and Commerce
J Mar L & Com	Journal of Maritime Law and Commerce
J Nat Resources & Envtl L	Journal of Natural Resources and Environmental Law

Abbreviations

J Pat & Trademark Off Soc'y	Journal of Patent and Trademark Office Society
J Real Est Tax'n	Journal of Real Estate Taxation
J S Corp Tax'n	Journal of S Corporation Taxation
J Tax'n	Journal of Taxation
J Transp L Logist & Pol'y	Journal of Transportation Law, Logistics and Policy
La L Rev	Louisiana Law Review
Lab LJ	Labor Law Journal
Lab Law	Labor Lawyer
Land & Water L Rev	Land and Water Law Review
Law & Contemp Probs	Law and Contemporary Problems
Litig	Litigation
Loy LA Ent LJ	Loyola of Los Angeles Entertainment Law Journal
Loy LA Int'l & Comp LJ	Loyola of Los Angeles International and Comparative Law Journal
Loy LA L Rev	Loyola of Los Angeles Law Review
Loy L Rev	Loyola Law Review
Lo U Chi LJ	Loyola University Chicago Law Journal
Marq L Rev	Marquette Law Review
Mass L Rev	Massachusetts Law Review
Mass LQ	Massachusetts Law Quarterly
Md J Int'l L & Trade	Maryland Journal of International Law and Trade
Md L Rev	Maryland Law Review
Me L Rev	Maine Law Review
Mem St U L Rev	Memphis State University Law review
Mercer L Rev	Mercer Law Review
Mich J Int'l L	Michigan Journal of International Law
Mich L Rev	Michigan Law Review
Mil L Rev	Military Law Review
Minn L Rev	Minnesota Law Review
Miss C L Rev	Mississippi College Law Review
Mo L Rev	Missouri Law Review
Mont L Rev	Montana Law Review
NC Cent LJ	North Carolina Central Law Journal
NC J Int'l L & Com Reg	North Carolina Journal of International Law and Commercial Regulation
NC L Rev	North Carolina Law Review
ND L Rev	North Dakota Law Review
N Ill U L Rev	Northern Illinois University Law Review
N Ky L Rev	Northern Kentucky Law Review
NM L Rev	New Mexico Law Review
NY Int'l L Rev	New York International Law Review
NYL Sch J Int'l & Comp L	New York Law School Journal of International and Comparative Law
NYL Sch L Rev	New York Law School Law Review

Abbreviations

NYU Envtl LJ	New York University Environmental Law Journal
NYU J Int'l L & Pol.	New York University Journal of International Law and Politics
NYU L Rev	New York University Law Review
Nat Resources & Envt.	Natural Resources and Environment
Nat Resources J.	Natural Resources Journal
Nav L Rev	Naval Law Review
Neb L Rev	Nebraska Law Review
New Eng L Rev	New England Law Review
Notre Dame L Rev	Notre Dame Law Review
Nova L Rev	Nova Law Review
Nw J Int'l L & Bus	Northwestern Journal of International Law and Business
Nw U L Rev.	Northwestern University Law Review
Ohio NU L Rev.	Ohio Northern University Law Review
Ohio St LJ	Ohio State Law Journal
Oil & Gas Tax Q.	Oil and Gas Tax Quarterly
Okla City U L Rev	Oklahoma City University Law Review
Okla L Rev	Oklahoma Law Review
Or L Rev	Oregon Law Review
Pac LJ	Pacific Law Journal
Pace Envtl L Rev	Pace Environmental Law Review
Pace Int'l L Rev	Pace International Law Review
Pace L Rev	Pace Law Review
Pat World.	Patent World
Pepp L Rev	Pepperdine Law Review
Prac Law	Practical Lawyer
Prac Litig	Practical Litigator
Prac Real Est Law.	Practical Real Estate Lawyer
Prac Tax Law	Practical Tax Lawyer
Pub Cont LJ	Public Contract Law Journal
Pub Land L Rev	Public Land Law Review
Real Prop Prob & Tr J.	Real Property, Probate and Trust Journal
Rev Litig.	Review of Litigation
Rutgers Computer & Tech LJ	Rutgers Computer and Technology Law Journal
Rutgers LJ.	Rutgers Law Journal
Rutgers L Rev.	Rutgers Law Review
SC L Rev.	South Carolina Law Review
S Cal L Rev.	Southern California Law Review
SD L Rev.	South Dakota Law Review
S Ill U L Rev	Southern Illinois University Law Review
S Tex L Rev.	South Texas Law Review
SU L Rev.	Southern University Law Review
San Diego L Rev	San Diego Law Review
Santa Clara Computer & High Tech LJ	Santa Clara Computer and High Technology Law Journal

ABBREVIATIONS

Santa Clara L Rev	Santa Clara Law Review
Sec Reg LJ	Securities Regulation Law Journal
Seton Hall Const LJ	Seton Hall Constitutional Law Journal
Seton Hall L Rev	Seton Hall Law Review
SMU L Rev	SMU Law Review
Software LJ	Software Law Journal
St John's L Rev	St John's Law Review
St Louis U LJ	Saint Louis University Law Journal
St Mary's LJ	St Mary's Law Journal
St Thomas L Rev	St Thomas Law Review
Stan Envtl LJ	Stanford Environmental Law Journal
Stan J Int'l L	Stanford Journal of International Law
Stan L Rev	Stanford Law Review
Stetson L Rev	Stetson Law Review
Suffolk Transnat'l LJ	Suffolk Transnational Law Journal
Suffolk U L Rev	Suffolk University Law Review
Sw U L Rev	Southwestern University Law Review
Syracuse J Int'l L & Com	Syracuse Journal of International Law and Commerce
Syracuse L Rev	Syracuse Law Review
Tax L Rev	Tax Law Review
Temple Envtl L & Tech J	Temple Environmental Law and Technology Journal
Temple L Rev	Temple Law Review
Tenn L Rev	Tennessee Law Review
Tex Intell Prop LJ	Texas Intellectual Property Law Journal
Tex Int'l LJ	Texas International Law Journal
Tex L Rev	Texas Law Review
Tex Tech L Rev	Texas Tech Law Review
Thomas M Cooley L Rev	Thomas M Cooley Law Review
Tort & Ins LJ	Torts and Insurance Law Journal
Touro L Rev	Touro Law Review
Trademark Rep	Trademark Reporter
Trademark World	Trademark World
Transp LJ	Transportation Law Journal
Trans Prac J	Transportation Practitioners Journal
Tul Envtl LJ	Tulane Environmental Law Journal
Tul L Rev	Tulane Law Review
Tul Mar LJ	Tulane Maritime Law Journal
Tulsa LJ	Tulsa Law Journal
U Ark LJ	University of Arkansas Law Journal
U Balt J Envtl L	University of Baltimore Journal of Environmental Law
U Balt L Rev	University of Baltimore Law Review
UC Davis L Rev	UC Davis Law Review
U Chi L Rev	University of Chicago Law Review
U Cin L Rev	University of Cincinnati Law Review
U Colo L Rev	University of Colorado Law Review

ABBREVIATIONS

U Dayton L Rev	University of Dayton Law Review
U Det Mercy L Rev	University of Detroit Mercy Law Review
U Fla JL & Pub Pol'y	University of Florida Journal of Law and Public Policy
U Haw L Rev	University of Hawaii Law Review
U Ill L Rev	University of Illinois Law Review
U Kan L Rev	University of Kansas Law Review
U Miami L Rev	University of Miami Law Review
U Pa L Rev	University of Pennsylvania Law Review
U Pitt L Rev	University of Pittsburgh Law Review
U Puget Sound L Rev	University of Puget Sound Law Review
U Rich L Rev	University of Richmond Law Review
USF L Rev	University of San Francisco Law Review
USF Mar LJ	University of San Francisco Maritime Law Journal
US-Mex LJ	United States-Mexico Law Journal
U Tol L Rev	University of Toledo Law Review
U West LA L Rev	University of West Los Angeles Law Review
UCLA J Envtl L & Pol'y	UCLA Journal of Environmental Law and Policy
UCLA L Rev	UCLA Law Review
UCLA Pac Basin LJ	UCLA Pacific Basin Law Journal
Utah L Rev	Utah Law Review
Va Envtl LJ	Virginia Environmental Law Journal
Va J Int'l L	Virginia Journal of International Law
Va L Rev	Virginia Law Review
Va Tax Rev	Virginia Tax Review
Val U L Rev	Valparaiso University Law Review
Vand J Transnat'l L	Vanderbilt Journal of Transnational Law
Vand L Rev	Vanderbilt Law Review
Vill Envtl LJ	Villanova Environmental Law Journal
Vill L Rev	Villanova Law Review
Vt L Rev	Vermont Law Review
W New Eng L Rev	Western New England Law Review
W St U L Rev	Western State University Law Review
W Va L Rev	West Virginia Law Review
Wake Forest L Rev	Wake Forest Law Review
Wash & Lee L Rev	Washington and Lee Law Review
Wash L Rev	Washington Law Review
Wash U LQ	Washington University Law Quarterly
Washburn LJ	Washburn Law Journal
Wayne L Rev	Wayne Law Review
Whittier L Rev	Whittier Law Review
Widener J Pub L	Widener Journal of Public Law
Wis Int'l LJ	Wisconsin International Law Journal
Wis L Rev	Wisconsin Law Review
Wm & Mary L Rev	William & Mary Law Review
Wm Mitchell L Rev	William Mitchell Law Review
Yale J Int'l L	Yale Journal of International Law

ABBREVIATIONS

Yale Law & Pol'y Rev .....   Yale Law and Policy Review
Yale LJ ....   Yale Law Journal

Auto-Cite®: Cases and annotations referred to herein can be further researched through the Auto-Cite® computer-assisted research service. Use Auto-Cite to check citations for form, parallel references, prior and later history, and annotation references.

TABLE OF CONTENTS

TITLE 38 – VETERANS' BENEFITS

[Chapters 30 through 41 of Part III are contained in this volume.]

PART I-GENERAL PROVISIONS

Chapter		Beginning Section
1.	General	101
3.	Department of Veterans Affairs	301
5.	Authority and Duties of the Secretary	501
7.	Employees	701
9.	Security and Law Enforcement on Property Under the Jurisdiction of the Department	901

PART II-GENERAL BENEFITS

11.	Compensation for Service-Connected Disability or Death	1101
13.	Dependency and Indemnity Compensation for Service-Connected Deaths	1301
15.	Pension for Non-Service-Connected Disability or Death or for Service	1501
17.	Hospital, Nursing Home, Domiciliary, and Medical Care	1701
18.	Benefits for Children of Vietnam Veterans Who Are Born With Spina Bifida	1802
19.	Insurance	1901
21.	Specially Adapted Housing for Disabled Veterans	2101
23.	Burial Benefits	2301
24.	National Cemeteries and Memorials	2401

PART III-READJUSTMENT AND RELATED BENEFITS

30.	All-Volunteer Force Educational Assistance Program	3001
31.	Training and Rehabilitation for Veterans with Service-Connected Disabilities	3100
32.	Post-Vietnam Era Veterans' Educational Assistance	3201
34.	Veterans' Educational Assistance	3451
35.	Survivors' and Dependents' Educational Assistance	3500
36.	Administration of Educational Benefits	3670
37.	Housing and Small Business Loans	3701
39.	Automobiles and Adaptive Equipment for Certain Disabled Veterans and Members of the Armed Forces	3901
41.	Job Counseling, Training, and Placement Service for Veterans	4100

TABLE OF CONTENTS

42.	Employment and Training of Veterans	4211
43.	Employment and Reemployment Rights of Members of the Uniformed Armed Services	4301

PART IV-GENERAL ADMINISTRATIVE PROVISIONS

51.	Claims, Effective Dates, and Payments.......................	5101
53.	Special Provisions Relating to Benefits......................	5301
55.	Minors, Incompetents, and Other Wards	5501
57.	Records and Investigations.................................	5701
59.	Agents and Attorneys	5901
61.	Penal and Forfeiture Provisions............................	6101

PART V-BOARDS, ADMINISTRATIONS, AND SERVICES

71.	Board of Veterans' Appeals	7101
72.	United States Board of Veterans' Appeals....................	7251
73.	Veterans Health Administration-Organization and Functions	7301
74.	Veterans Health Administration-Personnel....................	7401
76.	Health Professionals Educational Assistance Program	7601
77.	Veterans Benefits Administration	7701
78.	Veterans' Canteen Service	7801

PART VI-ACQUISITION AND DISPOSITION OF PROPERTY

81.	Acquisition and Operation of Hospital and Domiciliary Facilities; Procurement and Supply; Enhanced-Use Leases of Real Property	8101
82.	Assistance in Establishing New State Medical Schools; Grants to Affiliated Medical Schools; Assistance to Health Manpower Training Institutions	8201
83.	Acceptance of Gifts and Bequests...........................	8301
85.	Disposition of Deceased Veterans' Personal Property............	8501

THE CODE OF THE LAWS

OF THE

UNITED STATES OF AMERICA

TITLE 38 — VETERANS' BENEFITS

PART III. READJUSTMENT AND RELATED BENEFITS

Chapter	Sec.
30. All-Volunteer Force Educational Assistance Program	3001
31. Training and Rehabilitation for Veterans with Service-Connected Disabilities	3100
32. Post-Vietnam Era Veterans' Educational Assistance	3201
33. [Repealed]
34. Veterans' Educational Assistance	3451
35. Survivors' and Dependents' Educational Assistance	3500
36. Administration of Educational Benefits	3670
37. Housing and Small Business Loans	3701
39. Automobiles and Adaptive Equipment for Certain Disabled Veterans and Members of the Armed Forces	3901
41. Job Counseling, Training, and Placement Service for Veterans	4100
42. Employment and Training of Veterans	4211
43. Employment and reemployment rights of members of the uniformed services	4301

HISTORY; ANCILLARY LAWS AND DIRECTIVES

Amendments:

1965. Act June 24, 1965, P. L. 89-50, § 1(b), 79 Stat. 173 (effective 7/1/66, as provided by § 1(d) of such Act), deleted item 43 which read: "43. Mustering-Out Payments . . . . 2101".

1966. Act March 3, 1966, P. L. 89-358, §§ 4(c), 6(b), 80 Stat. 23, 27 (effective 3/3/66, as provided by § 12(a) of such Act), deleted item 33 which read: "33. Education of Korean Conflict Veterans . . . . 1601"; added items 34 and 36; and substituted new item 41 for one which read: "41. Unemployment Benefits for Veterans . . . . 2001".

1968. Act Oct. 23, 1968, P. L. 90-631, § 2(h)(2), 82 Stat. 1333 (effective 12/1/68, as provided by § 6(a) of such Act), substituted item 35 for one which read: "35. War Orphan's Educational Assistance . . . . 1701".

1971. Act Jan. 11, 1971, P. L. 91-666, § 2(b), 84 Stat. 2000, substituted item 39 for one which read: "39. Automobiles for Disabled Veterans . . . . 1901".

1972. Act Oct. 24, 1972, P. L. 92-540, Title V, §§ 502(b), 503(b), 86 Stat. 1097 (effective 90 days after 10/24/72, as provided by § 601(b) of such Act), substituted item 41 for one which read: "41. Job Counseling and Employment Placement Service for Veterans . . . . 2001"; and added item 42.

1974. Act Dec. 3, 1974, P. L. 93-508, Title IV, § 404(b), 88 Stat. 1600 (effective 12/2/74, as provided by § 503 of such Act), added item 43.

Act Dec. 31, 1974, P. L. 93-569, § 7(d), 88 Stat. 1866 (effective 12/31/74, as provided by § 10 of such Act), substituted item 37 for one which read: "37. Home, Farm, and Business Loans . . . . 1801".

1976. Act Oct. 15, 1976, P. L. 94-502, Title IV, § 405, 90 Stat. 2397 (effective 1/1/77, as provided by § 406 of such Act), added item 32.

Act Oct. 15, 1976, P. L. 94-502, Title III, § 309(b), 90 Stat. 2391, (effective 10/15/76, as provided by § 703(b) of such Act), substituted item 35 for one which read: "35. War Orphans' and Widows' Educational Assistance . . . . 1700".

1980. Act Oct. 17, 1980, P. L. 96-466, Title I, § 101(b), 94 Stat. 2186 (effective 4/1/81, as provided by § 802(a)(1) of such Act), substituted item 31 for one which read: "31. Vocational Rehabilitation . . . . 1501".

1981. Act Nov. 3, 1981, P. L. 97-72, Title III, § 302(b)(2), 95 Stat. 1059 (effective as provided by § 305 of such Act, which appears as 38 USCS § 1841 note) substituted item 37 for one which read: "37. Home, Condominium, and Mobile Home Loans . . . . 1801".

1982. Act Oct. 12, 1982, P. L. 97-295, § 4(35), 96 Stat. 1307, substituted item 31 for one which read: "31. Training and Rehabilitation for Veterans with Service-Connected Disabilities . . . 1,500"; and substituted item 34 for one which read: "34 Veterans' Educational Assistance . . . 1650".

Act Oct. 14, 1982, P. L. 97-306, Title III, § 301(b)(2), 96 Stat. 1437, in item 41, substituted "2000" for "2001".

1984. Act Oct. 19, 1984, P. L. 98-525, Title VII, § 702(a)(2) in part, 98 Stat. 2563, added item 30.

1991. Act March 22, 1991, P. L. 102-16, § 9(c)(2), 105 Stat. 55, in item 42, deleted "Disabled and Vietnam era" following "Training of".

Act Aug. 6, 1991, P. L. 102-83, § 5(b)(2), 105 Stat. 406, revised the analysis of this Part by amending the section numbers in accordance with the redesignations made by § 5(a) of such Act (see Table III preceding 38 USCS § 101).

1994. Act Oct. 13, 1994, P. L. 103-353, § 2(b)(1), 108 Stat. 3169 (effective and applicable as provided by § 8 of such Act, which appears as 38 USCS § 4301 note), amended the analysis of this Part by substituting item 43 for one which read: "43. Veteran's Reemployment Rights . . . 2021".

Nov. 2, 1994, P. L. 103-446, Title XII, § 1201(h)(1), 108 Stat. 4688 purported to amend the analysis of this Part by substituting "42. Employment and Training of Veterans . . .4211" for existing item 42; however, the amendment was not executed because the existing item was identical.

Other provisions:

Application and construction of the Oct. 12, 1982 amendment of this

READJUSTMENT BENEFITS 38 USCS § 3001

Part analysis. For provisions as to the application and construction of the Oct. 12, 1982 amendment of this Part analysis, see § 5 of such Act, which appears as 10 USCS § 101 note.

CHAPTER 30. ALL-VOLUNTEER FORCE EDUCATIONAL ASSISTANCE PROGRAM

SUBCHAPTER I. PURPOSES; DEFINITIONS

Section
3001. Purposes.
3002. Definitions.

SUBCHAPTER II. BASIC EDUCATIONAL ASSISTANCE

3011. Basic educational assistance entitlement for service on active duty.
3012. Basic educational assistance entitlement for service in the Selected Reserve.
3013. Duration of basic educational assistance.
3014. Payment of basic educational assistance.
3015. Amount of basic educational assistance.
3016. Inservice enrollment in a program of education.
3017. Death benefit.
3018. Opportunity for certain active-duty personnel to withdraw election not to enroll.
3018A. Opportunity for certain active-duty personnel to enroll before being involuntarily separated from service.
3018B. Opportunity for certain persons to enroll.
3018C. Opportunity for certain VEAP participants to enroll.
3019. Tutorial assistance.

SUBCHAPTER III. SUPPLEMENTAL EDUCATIONAL ASSISTANCE

3021. Supplemental educational assistance for additional service.
3022. Amount of supplemental educational assistance.
3023. Payment of supplemental educational assistance under this sub chapter.

SUBCHAPTER IV. TIME LIMITATION FOR USE OF ELIGIBILITY AND ENTITLEMENT; GENERAL AND ADMINISTRATIVE PROVISIONS

3031. Time limitation for use of eligibility and entitlement.
3032. Limitations on educational assistance for certain individuals.
3033. Bar to duplication of educational assistance benefits.
3034. Program administration.
3035. Allocation of administration and of program costs.
3036. Reporting requirement.

HISTORY; ANCILLARY LAWS AND DIRECTIVES
Amendments:
1984. Act Oct. 19, 1984, P. L. 98-525, Title VII, § 702(a)(1) in part, 98 Stat. 2553, added this chapter and analysis.

1986. Act Oct. 28, 1986, P. L. 99-576, Title III, Part A, § 301(d)(2), amended the analysis of this chapter by substituting item 1432 for one which read "Limitation on educational assistance for certain individuals".
1988. Act Nov. 18, 1988, P. L. 100-689, Title I, Part A, § 101(b), 102 Stat. 4162, effective July 1, 1985, as provided by § 101(c) of such Act, which appears as 38 USCS § 3017 note, amended the analysis of this chapter by adding item 1417.
Act Nov. 18, 1988, P. L. 100-689, Title I, Part A, §§ 103(c), 107(a)(3), 102 Stat. 4166, 4168, amended the analysis of this chapter by adding items 1418, 1419.
1990. Act Nov. 5, 1990, P. L. 101-510, Div A, Title V, Part F, § 561(a)(2), 104 Stat. 1573, amended the analysis of this chapter by adding item 1418A.
1991. Act June 13, 1991, P. L. 102-54, § 14(c)(2), 105 Stat. 285, amended the analysis of this chapter, in item 1423, by substituting "subchapter" for "chapter".
Act Aug. 6, 1991, P. L. 102-83, § 5(b)(1), 105 Stat. 406, revised the analysis of this Chapter by amending the section numbers in accordance with the redesignations made by § 5(a) of such Act (see Table III preceding 38 USCS § 101).
1992. Act Oct. 23, 1992, P. L. 102-484, Div D, Title XLIV, Subtitle A, § 4404(b)(1), 106 Stat. 2706, amended the analysis of this chapter by adding item 3018B.
1996. Act Oct. 9, 1996, P. L. 104-275, Title I, § 106(b)(1), 110 Stat. 3329, amended the analysis of this chapter by adding item 3018C.

Other provisions:
Effective date of subchapter III of this chapter. Act Oct. 19, 1984, P. L. 98-525, Title VII, § 702(b), 98 Stat. 2563, which appears as 38 USCS § 3021 note, provides that subchapter III of this chapter [38 USCS §§ 3021 et seq.] shall take effect on July 1, 1986.

SUBCHAPTER I. PURPOSES; DEFINITIONS

§ 3001. Purposes

The purposes of this chapter [38 USCS §§ 3001 et seq.] are—

(1) to provide a new educational assistance program to assist in the readjustment of members of the Armed Forces to civilian life after their separation from military service;

(2) to extend the benefits of a higher education to qualifying men and women who might not otherwise be able to afford such an education;

(3) to provide for vocational readjustment and to restore lost educational opportunities to those service men and women who served on active duty after June 30, 1985;

(4) to promote and assist the All-Volunteer Force program and the Total Force Concept of the Armed Forces by establishing a new program of educational assistance based upon service on active duty or a combination of service on active duty and in the Selected Reserve (including the National

Guard) to aid in the recruitment and retention of highly qualified personnel for both the active and reserve components of the Armed Forces;

(5) to give special emphasis to providing educational assistance benefits to aid in the retention of personnel in the Armed Forces; and

(6) to enhance our Nation's competitiveness through the development of a more highly educated and productive work force.

(Added Oct. 19, 1984, P. L. 98-525, Title VII, § 702(a)(1) in part, 98 Stat. 2553; June 1, 1987, P. L. 100-48, § 5, 101 Stat. 331; Aug. 6, 1991, P. L. 102-83, § 5(a), 105 Stat. 406.)

HISTORY; ANCILLARY LAWS AND DIRECTIVES

Explanatory notes:
A prior § 3001 was redesignated by Act May 7, 1991, P. L. 102-40, Title IV, § 402(b)(1), 105 Stat. 238. For similar provisions, see 38 USCS § 5101.

Amendments:
1987. Act June 1, 1987, deleted "and" at the end of para. (2), redesignated paras. (2) and (3) as paras. (4) and (5) respectively, substituted "; and" for a period at the end of para. (5) as redesignated, and added new paras. (2), (3), and (6).

1991. Act Aug. 6, 1991, redesignated this section, formerly 38 USCS § 1401, as 38 USCS § 3001.

CODE OF FEDERAL REGULATIONS
Department of Veterans Affairs—Adjudication, 38 CFR Part 3.

RESEARCH GUIDE
Am Jur:
77 Am Jur 2d, Veterans and Veterans' Laws §§ 132–134, 137, 139–145.

§ 3002. Definitions

For the purposes of this chapter [38 USCS §§ 3001 et seq.]—

(1) The term "basic educational assistance" means educational assistance provided under subchapter II of this chapter [38 USCS §§ 3011 et seq.].

(2) The term "supplemental educational assistance" means educational assistance provided under subchapter III of this chapter [38 USCS §§ 3021 et seq.].

(3) The term "program of education"—

(A) has the meaning given such term in section 3452(b) of this title, and

(B) in the case of an individual who is not serving on active duty, includes (i) a full-time program of apprenticeship or of other on-job training approved as provided in clause (1) or (2), as appropriate, of section 3687(a) of this title, and (ii) a cooperative program (as defined in section 3482(a)(2) of this title).

(4) The term "Selected Reserve" means the Selected Reserve of the Ready Reserve of any of the reserve components (including the Army National Guard of the United States and the Air National Guard of the United States)

of the Armed Forces, as required to be maintained under section 10143(a) of title 10.

(5) The term "Secretary of Defense" means the Secretary of Defense, except that it means the Secretary of Transportation with respect to the Coast Guard when it is not operating as a service in the Navy.

(6) The term "active duty" does not include any period during which an individual (A) was assigned full time by the Armed Forces to a civilian institution for a course of education which was substantially the same as established courses offered to civilians, (B) served as a cadet or midshipman at one of the service academies, or (C) served under the provisions of section 12103(d) of title 10 pursuant to an enlistment in the Army National Guard or the Air National Guard, or as a Reserve for service in the Army Reserve, Naval Reserve, Air Force Reserve, Marine Corps Reserve, or Coast Guard Reserve.

(7) The term "active duty" includes full-time National Guard duty first performed after June 30, 1985, by a member of the Army National Guard of the United States or the Air National Guard of the United States in the member's status as a member of the National Guard of a State for the purpose of organizing, administering, recruiting, instructing, or training the National Guard.

(8) The term "educational institution" has the meaning given such term in section 3452(c) of this title.

(Added Oct. 19, 1984, P. L. 98-525, Title VII, § 702(a)(1) in part, 98 Stat. 2554; Oct. 28, 1986, P. L. 99-576, Title III, Part A, § 301(a), 100 Stat. 3267; Nov. 18, 1988, P. L. 100-689, Title I, Part A, §§ 108(a)(1), 111(a)(1) 102 Stat. 4169, 4170; Dec. 18, 1989, P. L. 101-237, Title IV, § 423(b)(3), 103 Stat. 2092; Nov. 5, 1990, P. L. 101-510, Div A, Title V, Part F, § 563(a), 104 Stat. 1575; Aug. 6, 1991, P. L. 102-83, § 5(a), (c)(1), 105 Stat. 406; Oct. 5, 1994, P. L. 103-337, Div A, Title XVI, Subtitle D, § 1677(d)(2), 108 Stat. 3020; Nov. 2, 1994, P. L. 103-446, Title VI, § 603(b), 108 Stat. 4671; Oct. 9, 1996, P. L. 104-275, Title I, § 107(a), 110 Stat. 3329.)

HISTORY; ANCILLARY LAWS AND DIRECTIVES

Explanatory notes:

A prior § 3002 was redesignated by Act May 7, 1991, P. L. 102-40, Title IV, § 402(b)(1), 105 Stat. 238. For similar provisions, see 38 USCS § 5102.

Amendments:

1986. Act Oct. 28, 1986, substituted para. (3) for one which read: "The term 'program of education' has the meaning given such term in section 1652(b) of this title.".

1988. Act Nov. 18, 1988, in para. (3)(B), substituted "in the case of an individual who is not serving on active duty, includes" for "includes".

Such Act further (effective Jan. 1, 1989, as provided by § 108(c) of such Act, which appears as a note to this section), in para. (3)(B), inserted "(i)" and inserted ", and (ii) a cooperative program (as defined in section 1682(a)(2) of this title)".

1989. Act Dec. 18, 1989, substituted para. (5) for one which read: "The term 'Secretary' means the Secretary of Defense with respect to members of the Armed Forces under the jurisdiction of the Secretary of a military department and the Secretary of Transportation with respect to the Coast Guard when it is not operating as a service in the Navy.".

1990. Act Nov. 5, 1990 (applicable as provided by § 563(b) of such Act, which appears as a note to this section), added para. (7).

1991. Act Aug. 6, 1991, redesignated this section, formerly 38 USCS § 1402, as 38 USCS § 3002, and amended the references in this section to reflect the redesignations made by § 5(a) of such Act (see Table III preceding 38 USCS § 101).

1994. Act Oct. 5, 1994 (effective 12/1/94 as provided by § 1691 of such Act, which appears as 10 USCS § 10001 note), in para. (4), substituted "section 10143(a) of title 10" for "section 268(b) of title 10" and, in para. (6), substituted "section 12103(d) of title 10" for "section 511(d) of title 10".

Act Nov. 2, 1994 added para. (8).

1996. Act Oct. 9, 1996, in para. (7), substituted "June 30, 1985" for "November 29, 1989".

Other provisions:

Effective date of amendments made by § 108 of Act Nov. 18, 1988. Act Nov. 18, 1988, P. L. 100-689, Title I, Part A, § 108(c), 102 Stat. 4170, provides: "The amendments made by this section [amending this section and 38 USCS §§ 3032, 3202, 3231] shall take effect on January 1, 1989.".

Application of para. (7). Act Nov. 5, 1990, P. L. 101-510, Div A, Title V, Part F, § 563(b), 104 Stat. 1575; Aug. 6, 1991, P. L. 102-83, § 5(c)(2), 105 Stat. 406, provides: "The amendment made by this section [adding para. (7) of this section] shall apply only to individuals who before the date of entry on active duty, as defined in section 3002(7) of title 38, United States Code [para (7) of this section] (as added by subsection (a)), have never served on active duty as defined in section 101(21) of that title.".

Application of Oct. 9, 1996 amendment of para. (7). Act Oct. 9, 1996, P. L. 104-275, Title I, § 107(b), 110 Stat. 3329, provides:

"(1) An individual may only become eligible for benefits under chapter 30 of title 38, United States Code [38 USCS §§ 3001 et seq.], as a result of the amendment made by subsection (a) [amending para. (7) of this section] by making an election to become entitled to basic educational assistance under such chapter. The election may only be made during the nine-month period beginning on the date of the enactment of this Act and in the manner required by the Secretary of Defense.

"(2) In the case of any individual making an election under paragraph (1)—

"(A) the basic pay of an individual who, while a member of the Armed Forces, makes an election under paragraph (1) shall be reduced (in a manner determined by the Secretary of Defense) until the total amount by which such basic pay is reduced is $1,200; or

"(B) to the extent that basic pay is not so reduced before the individual's discharge or release from active duty, the Secretary of Veterans Affairs shall collect from an individual who makes such an election an amount equal to the difference between $1,200 and the total amount of reductions under subparagraph (A), which amount shall be paid into the Treasury as miscellaneous receipts.

"(3) In the case of any individual making an election under paragraph (1), the 10-year period referred to in section 3031 of such title shall begin on the later of—
"(A) the date determined under such section 3031; or
"(B) the date on which the election under paragraph (1) becomes effective.".

CROSS REFERENCES

This section is referred to in 38 USCS § 3011.

RESEARCH GUIDE

Am Jur:
77 Am Jur 2d, Veterans and Veterans' Laws § 134.

SUBCHAPTER II. BASIC EDUCATIONAL ASSISTANCE

§ 3011. Basic educational assistance entitlement for service on active duty

(a) Except as provided in subsection (c) of this section, each individual—
  (1) who—
    (A) after June 30, 1985, first becomes a member of the Armed Forces or first enters on active duty as a member of the Armed Forces and—
      (i) who (I) serves, as the individual's initial obligated period of active duty, at least three years of continuous active duty in the Armed Forces, or (II) in the case of an individual whose initial period of active duty is less than three years, serves at least two years of continuous active duty in the Armed Forces; or
      (ii) who serves in the Armed Forces and is discharged or released from active duty (I) for a service-connected disability, for a medical condition which preexisted such service on active duty and which the Secretary determines is not service connected, for hardship, or for a physical or mental condition that was not characterized as a disability and did not result from the individual's own willful misconduct but did interfere with the individual's performance of duty, as determined by the Secretary of each military department in accordance with regulations prescribed by the Secretary of Defense or by the Secretary of Transportation with respect to the Coast Guard when it is not operating as a service in the Navy; (II) for the convenience of the Government, in the case of an individual who completed not less than 20 months of continuous active duty, if the initial obligated period of active duty of the individual was less than three years, or in the case of an individual who completed not less than 30 months of continuous active duty if the initial obligated period of active duty of the individual was at least three years; or (III) involuntarily for the convenience of the Government as a result of a reduction in force, as determined by the Secretary of the military department concerned in accordance with

regulations prescribed by the Secretary of Defense or by the Secretary of Transportation with respect to the Coast Guard when it is not operating as a service in the Navy; or

(B) as of December 31, 1989, is eligible for educational assistance benefits under chapter 34 of this title [38 USCS §§ 3451 et seq.] and was on active duty at any time during the period beginning on October 19, 1984, and ending on July 1, 1985, continued on active duty without a break in service and—

    (i) after June 30, 1985, serves at least three years of continuous active duty in the Armed Forces; or

    (ii) after June 30, 1985, is discharged or released from active duty (I) for a service-connected disability, for a medical condition which preexisted such service on active duty and which the Secretary determines is not service connected, for hardship, or for a physical or mental condition that was not characterized as a disability, as described in subparagraph (A)(ii)(I) of this paragraph; (II) for the convenience of the Government, if the individual completed not less than 30 months of continuous active duty after that date; or (III) involuntarily for the convenience of the Government as a result of a reduction in force, as determined by the Secretary of the military department concerned in accordance with regulations prescribed by the Secretary of Defense or by the Secretary of Transportation with respect to the Coast Guard when it is not operating as a service in the Navy;

(2) who, except as provided in subsection (e) of this section, completed the requirements of a secondary school diploma (or equivalency certificate) not later than—

(A) the original ending date of the individual's initial obligated period of active duty in the case of an individual described in clause (1)(A) of this subsection, regardless of whether the individual is discharged or released from active duty on such date; or

(B) December 31, 1989, in the case of an individual described in clause (1)(B) of this subsection;

except that (i) an individual described in clause (1)(B) of this subsection may meet the requirement of this clause by having successfully completed the equivalent of 12 semester hours in a program of education leading to a standard college degree, and (ii) an individual described in clause (1)(A) of this subsection may meet such requirement by having successfully completed the equivalent of such 12 semester hours before the end of the individual's initial obligated period of active duty; and

(3) who, after completion of the service described in clause (1) of this subsection—

(A) continues on active duty;

(B) is discharged from active duty with an honorable discharge;

(C) is released after service on active duty characterized by the Secretary concerned as honorable service and is placed on the retired list, is transferred to the Fleet Reserve or Fleet Marine Corps Reserve, or is placed on the temporary disability retired list; or

(D) is released from active duty for further service in a reserve component of the Armed Forces after service on active duty characterized by the Secretary concerned as honorable service;
is entitled to basic educational assistance under this chapter [38 USCS §§ 3001 et seq.].

(b) The basic pay of any individual described in subsection (a)(1)(A) of this section who does not make an election under subsection (c)(1) of this section shall be reduced by $100 for each of the first 12 months that such individual is entitled to such pay. Any amount by which the basic pay of an individual is reduced under this chapter [38 USCS §§ 3001 et seq.] shall revert to the Treasury and shall not, for purposes of any Federal law, be considered to have been received by or to be within the control of such individual.

(c)(1) An individual described in subsection (a)(1)(A) of this section may make an election not to receive educational assistance under this chapter [38 USCS §§ 3001 et seq.]. Any such election shall be made at the time the individual initially enters on active duty as a member of the Armed Forces. Any individual who makes such an election is not entitled to educational assistance under this chapter [38 USCS §§ 3001 et seq.]

(2) An individual who after December 31, 1976, receives a commission as an officer in the Armed Forces upon graduation from the United States Military Academy, the United States Naval Academy, the United States Air Force Academy, or the Coast Guard Academy is not eligible for educational assistance under this section.

(3) An individual who after December 31, 1976, receives a commission as an officer in the Armed Forces upon completion of a program of educational assistance under section 2107 of title 10 is not eligible for educational assistance under this section if the individual enters on active duty—

(A) before October 1, 1996; or

(B) after September 30, 1996, and while participating in such program received more than $2,000 for each year of such participation.

(d)(1) For purposes of this chapter [38 USCS §§ 3001 et seq.], any period of service described in paragraphs (2) and (3) of this subsection shall not be considered a part of an individual's initial obligated period of active duty.

(2) The period of service referred to in paragraph (1) is any period terminated because of a defective enlistment and induction based on—

(A) the individual's being a minor for purposes of service in the Armed Forces;

(B) an erroneous enlistment or induction; or

(C) a defective enlistment agreement.

(3) The period of service referred to in paragraph (1) is also any period of service on active duty which an individual in the Selected Reserve was ordered to perform under section 12301, 12302, 12304, 12306, or 12307 of title 10 for a period of less than 2 years.

(e) For the purposes of subsection (a)(2) of this section, an individual who was on active duty on August 2, 1990, and who completes the requirements of a secondary school diploma (or equivalency certificate) before October 28, 1994, shall be considered to have completed such requirements within the individual's initial obligated period of active duty.

(f)(1) For the purposes of this chapter [38 USCS §§ 3001 et seq.], a member referred to in paragraph (2) of this subsection who serves the periods of active duty referred to in that paragraph shall be deemed to have served a continuous period of active duty the length of which is the aggregate length of the periods of active duty referred to in that paragraph.

(2) This subsection applies to a member who—
   (A) after a period of continuous active duty of not more than 12 months, is discharged or released from active duty under subclause (I) or (III) of subsection (a)(1)(A)(ii) of this section; and
   (B) after such discharge or release, reenlists or re-enters on a period of active duty.

(g) Notwithstanding section 3002(6)(A) of this title, a period during which an individual is assigned full time by the Armed Forces to a civilian institution for a course of education as described in such section 3002(6)(A) shall not be considered a break in service or a break in a continuous period of active duty of the individual for the purposes of this chapter [38 USCS §§ 3001 et seq.].

(h)(1) Notwithstanding section 3002(6)(B) of this title, a member referred to in paragraph (2) of this subsection who serves the periods of active duty referred to in subparagraphs (A) and (C) of that paragraph shall be deemed to have served a continuous period of active duty whose length is the aggregate length of the periods of active duty referred to in such subparagraphs.

(2) This subsection applies to a member who—
   (A) during an initial period of active duty, commences pursuit of a course of education—
      (i) at a service academy; or
      (ii) at a post-secondary school for the purpose of preparation for enrollment at a service academy;
   (B) fails to complete the course of education; and
   (C) re-enters on a period of active duty.

(Added Oct. 19, 1984, P. L. 98-525, Title VII, § 702(a)(1) in part, 98 Stat. 2554; Nov. 8, 1985, P. L. 99-145, Title VI, Part F, § 674(1), 99 Stat. 665; Oct. 28, 1986, P. L. 99-576, Title III, Part A, §§ 303(a)(1), 307(a)(1), 321(1), Title VII, § 702(8), 100 Stat. 3268, 3269, 3277, 3302; June 1, 1987, P. L. 100-48, § 3(a), 101 Stat. 331; Nov. 18, 1988, P. L. 100-689, Title I, Part A, §§ 102(a), 103(b)(1), 104(a), 111(a)(2)(A), (3), 102 Stat. 4162, 4165, 4166, 4170, 4171; Dec. 18, 1989, P. L. 101-237, Title IV, §§ 409, 423(b)(1)(A), 103 Stat. 2084, 2092; Nov. 5, 1990, P. L. 101-510, Div A, Title V, Part F, § 562(a)(1), (2), (b), 104 Stat. 1573; March 22, 1991, P. L. 102-16, § 10(a)(1), 105 Stat. 55; Aug. 6, 1991, P. L. 102-83, § 5(a), 105 Stat. 406; Oct. 29, 1992, P. L. 102-568, Title III, §§ 302(a)(1), 303(a)(1), 304(a), 305(a), 306(a), 106 Stat. 4326–4328; Nov. 2, 1994, P. L. 103-446, Title XII, § 1201(e)(10), (f)(2), 108 Stat. 4685, 4687; Feb. 10, 1996, P. L. 104-106, Div A, Title XV, § 1501(e)(2)(A), 110 Stat. 501;

38 USCS § 3011   VETERANS' BENEFITS

Sept. 23, 1996, P. L. 104-201, Div A, Title V, Subtitle H, § 556(a), 110 Stat. 2528.)

HISTORY; ANCILLARY LAWS AND DIRECTIVES

Explanatory notes:
A prior § 3011 was redesignated by Act May 7, 1991, P. L. 102-40, Title IV, § 402(b)(1), 105 Stat. 238. For similar provisions, see 38 USCS § 5111. Another prior § 3011 (Act Sept. 2, 1958, P. L. 85-857, § 1227, 72 Stat. 1227; June 8, 1960, P. L. 86-490, 74 Stat. 161) was repealed by Act Oct. 15, 1962, P. L. 87-825, § 5(a), 76 Stat. 950. Such section provided for the effective date of an award of increased compensation, dependency and indemnity compensation, or pension.

Amendments:
1985. Act Nov. 8, 1985, in subsec. (a)(1)(B), deleted "and without a break in service on active duty since December 31, 1976," following "of this title".

1986. Act Oct. 28, 1986, in subsec. (a), in the introductory matter, inserted a comma following "section"; in para. (1), in subpara. (A)(ii)(II), inserted "continuous", and in subpara. (B)(ii)(II), inserted "continuous", in subpara. (B), inserted "and was on active duty on October 19, 1984, and without a break in service since October 19, 1984,"; and in subsec. (b), substituted "Any amount by which the basic pay of an individual is reduced under this subsection shall revert to the Treasury and shall not, for purposes of any Federal law, be considered to have been received by or to be within the control of such individual." for "Amounts withheld from basic pay under this subsection shall revert to the Treasury.".

1987. Act June 1, 1987, in subsec. (a)(1)(A), substituted "after June 30, 1985," for "during the period beginning on July 1, 1985, and ending on June 30, 1988,".

1988. Act Nov. 18, 1988, in subsec. (a), in para. (1), in subpara. (A)(i)(I), inserted ", as the individual's initial obligated period of active duty,", substituted para. (2) for one which read: "who, before completion of the service described in clause (1) of this subsection, has received a secondary school diploma (or an equivalency certificate); and"; in subsec. (b), substituted "chapter" for "subsection"; and added subsec. (d).

Such Act further (effective as provided by § 102(c) of such Act, which appears as a note to this section), in subsec. (a)(1), in subparas. (A)(ii) and (B)(ii), in item (I), inserted ", for a medical condition which preexisted such service on active duty and which the Administrator determines is not service connected," substituted "; (II)" for ", or (II)", and inserted "; or (III) involuntarily for the convenience of the Government as a result of a reduction in force, as determined by the Secretary of the military department concerned in accordance with regulations prescribed by the Secretary of Defense or by the Secretary of Transportation with respect to the Coast Guard when it is not operating as a service in the Navy".

1989. Act Dec. 18, 1989, in subsec. (a)(2), inserted "(i)" and ", and (ii) an individual described in clause (1)(A) of this subsection may meet such requirement by having successfully completed the equivalent of such 12 semester hours before the end of the individual's initial obligated period of active duty".

Such Act further, in subsec. (a)(1), in paras. (A)(ii) and (B)(ii), substituted "Secretary" for "Administrator".

1990. Act Nov. 5, 1990 (effective 10/19/84 as provided by § 562(c) of such Act, which appears as a note to this section), in subsec. (a)(1), in subpara. (A)(ii)(I), substituted "for" for "or for" preceding "hardship", and inserted ", or for a physical or mental condition that was not characterized as a disability and did not result from the individual's own willful misconduct but did interfere with the individual's performance of duty, as determined by the Secretary of each military department in accordance with regulations prescribed by the Secretary of Defense or by the Secretary of Transportation with respect to the Coast Guard when it is not operating as a service in the Navy", and, in subpara. (B)(ii)(I), substituted "for" for "or for" preceding "hardship" and inserted ", or for a physical or mental condition that was not characterized as a disability, as described in subparagraph (A)(ii)(I) of this paragraph"; and, in subsec. (d), in para. (1), substituted "paragraphs (2) and (3)" for "paragraph (2)", and added para. (3).

1991. Act March 22, 1991, in subsec. (a)(3), redesignated former subpara. (C) as subpara. (D), and substituted new subparas. (A), (B), and (C) for former subparas. (A) and (B), which read:

"(A) is discharged from service with an honorable discharge, is placed on the retired list, is transferred to the Fleet Reserve or Fleet Marine Corps Reserve, or is placed on the temporary disability retired list;

"(B) continues on active duty; or".

Act Aug. 6, 1991, redesignated this section, formerly 38 USCS § 1411, as 38 USCS § 3011.

1992. Act Oct. 29, 1992 (effective 10/28/86, as provided by § 302(b) of such Act, which appears as a note to this section), in subsec. (a), in para. (1), in subsec. (B), in the introductory matter, substituted "at any time during the period beginning on October 19, 1984, and ending on July 1, 1985, continued on active duty without a break in service and—" for "on October 19, 1984, and without a break in service since October 19, 1984, and—".

Such Act further, in subsec. (a), in para. (2), in the introductory matter, inserted ", except as provided in subsection (e) of this section,"; and added subsec. (e).

Such Act further (effective as if enacted on 6/30/85 and applicable to the payment of educational assistance for education or training pursued on or after 10/1/93, as provided by § 304(b) of such Act) added subsec. (f).

Such Act further (effective as if enacted on 10/19/84, as provided by § 305(b) of such Act) added subsec. (g).

Such Act further (effective as if enacted on 6/30/85 and applicable to the payment of educational assistance for education or training pursued on or after 10/1/93, as provided by § 306(b) of such Act) added subsec. (h).

1994. Act Nov. 2, 1994, in subsec. (e), substituted "October 28, 1994," for "the end of the 24-month period beginning on the date of enactment of this subsection"; and, in subsec. (f)(1), substituted "the length of which" for "whose length".

1996. Act Feb. 10, 1996 (effective as if included in Act Oct. 5, 1995, P. L. 103-337, as enacted on Oct. 5, 1994, as provided by § 1501(f)(3) of Act Feb. 10, 1996, which appears as 10 USCS § 113 note), in subsec. (d)(3), substituted "section 12301, 12302, 12304, 12306, or 12307 of title 10" for "section 672, 673, 673b, 674, or 675 of title 10".

Act Sept. 23, 1996, in subsec. (c), in para. (2), deleted "or upon completion of a program of educational assistance under section 2107 of title 10" following "Coast Guard Academy", and added para. (3).

Other provisions:

Application of Oct. 28, 1986 amendments. Act Oct. 28, 1986, P. L. 99-576, Title III, Part A, § 303(b), 100 Stat 3269, provides:

"The amendments made by subsection (a) [amending this section and 38 USCS § 3012(c)] shall apply to any reduction in basic pay made under section 1411(b) or 1412(c) [now § 3011(b) or 3012(c)] of title 38, United States Code, after December 31, 1985.".

Effective date of amendments made by § 102 of Act Nov. 18, 1988. Act Nov. 18, 1988, P. L. 100-689, Title I, Part A, § 102(c), 102 Stat. 4163, provides: "The amendments made by this section [amending 38 USCS §§ 3011–3013, 5303A] shall take effect—

"(1) as of July 1, 1985, with respect to individuals discharged or released for a medical condition which preexisted service on active duty or in the Selected Reserve and which the Administrator determines is not service connected; and

"(2) as of October 1, 1987, with respect to individuals involuntarily discharged or released for the convenience of the Government as a result of a reduction in force.".

Effective date of 1990 amendments. Act Nov. 5, 1990, P. L. 101-510, Div A, Title V, Part F, § 562(c), 104 Stat. 1575, provides: "The amendments made by this section [amending this section and 38 USCS §§ 3012 and 5303A] shall take effect as of October 19, 1984.".

Effective date of 1992 amendments made by § 302 of Act Oct. 29, 1992. Act Oct. 29, 1992, P. L. 102-568, Title III, § 302(b), 106 Stat. 4327, provides: "The amendments made by this section [amending subsec. (a)(1)(B) of this section and 38 USCS §§ 3012(a)(1)(B) and 3031(e)] shall take effect as of October 28, 1986.".

Act Oct. 29, 1992, P. L. 102-568, Title III, § 304(b), 106 Stat. 4328, provides: "The amendments made by this subsection (a) [amending this section] shall take effect as if enacted on June 30, 1985, and apply to the payment of educational assistance for education or training pursued on or after October 1, 1993.".

Act Oct. 29, 1992, P. L. 102-568, Title III, § 305(b), 106 Stat. 4328, provides: "The amendment made by subsection (a) [amending this section] shall take effect as if enacted on October 19, 1984.".

Act Oct. 29, 1992, P. L. 102-568, Title III, § 306(b), 106 Stat. 4328, provides: "The amendment made by subsection (a) [amending this section] shall take effect as if enacted on June 30, 1985, and apply to the payment of educational assistance for education training pursued on or after October 1, 1993.".

Notification of extension of period for completion of diploma requirement. Act Oct. 29, 1992, P. L. 102-568, Title III, § 303(b), 106 Stat. 4327, provides: "Not later than 60 days after the date of enactment of this Act, the Secretary of each of the military departments shall notify each individual who was on active duty in the Armed Forces on August 2, 1990, and who has not met the requirements of a secondary school diploma (or equivalency certificate), of the extension of the period for the completion of such requirements afforded by the amendments made by this section [amending subsec. (a)(2) and adding subsec. (e) of this section and amending subsec. (a)(2) and adding subsec. (f) of 38 USCS § 3012].".

CODE OF FEDERAL REGULATIONS
Department of Veterans Affairs—Adjudication, 38 CFR Part 3.

CROSS REFERENCES
This section is referred to in 10 USCS § 2006; 38 USCS §§ 3012, 3013, 3015–3018, 3018A, 3018B, 3021, 3031, 3232, 3462, 4214, 5303A; 42 USCS § 12603.

RESEARCH GUIDE
Am Jur:
77 Am Jur 2d, Veterans and Veterans' Laws §§ 134–138.

INTERPRETIVE NOTES AND DECISIONS

1. Generally
2. Under particular circumstances

1. Generally
Veteran was properly denied conversion from Chapter 34 to Chapter 30 benefits since he acknowledged that he did not qualify for conversion and statute was clear and unambiguous. Kelly v Derwinski (1992) 3 Vet App 171.

2. Under particular circumstances
Veteran was not eligible for educational benefits since his final discharge was general, March 1988 honorable discharge was not based on three years' continuous active service commencing after June 30, 1985, and remaining honorable discharges were granted prior to June 30, 1985. Carr v Brown (1993) 5 Vet App 2.

§ 3012. Basic educational assistance entitlement for service in the Selected Reserve

(a) Except as provided in subsection (d) of this section, each individual—
  (1) who—
    (A) after June 30, 1985, first becomes a member of the Armed Forces or first enters on active duty as a member of the Armed Forces—
      (i) serves, as the individual's initial obligated period of active duty, at least two years of continuous active duty in the Armed Forces, subject to subsection (b) of this section, characterized by the Secretary concerned as honorable service; and
      (ii) subject to subsection (b) of this section and beginning within one year after completion of the service on active duty described in subclause (i) of this clause, serves at least four years of continuous duty in the Selected Reserve during which the individual participates satisfactorily in training as required by the Secretary concerned; or
    (B) as of December 31, 1989, is eligible for educational assistance under chapter 34 of this title [38 USCS §§ 3451 et seq.] and was on active duty at any time during the period beginning on October 19, 1984, and ending on July 1, 1985, continued on active duty without a break in service and—
      (i) after June 30, 1985, serves at least two years of continuous active duty in the Armed Forces, subject to subsection (b) of this section, characterized by the Secretary concerned as honorable service; and

(ii) after June 30, 1985, subject to subsection (b) of this section and beginning within one year after completion of such two years of service, serves at least four continuous years in the Selected Reserve during which the individual participates satisfactorily in training as prescribed by the Secretary concerned;

(2) who, except as provided in subsection (f) of this section, before completion of the service described in clause (1) of this subsection, has completed the requirements of a secondary school diploma (or an equivalency certificate), except that (i) an individual described in clause (1)(B) of this subsection may meet the requirement of this clause by having successfully completed the equivalent of 12 semester hours in a program of education leading to a standard college degree, and (ii) an individual described in clause (1)(A) of this subsection may meet such requirement by having successfully completed the equivalent of such 12 semester hours before the end of the individual's initial obligated period of active duty; and

(3) who, after completion of the service described in clause (1) of this subsection—

(A) is discharged from service with an honorable discharge, is placed on the retired list, or is transferred to the Standby Reserve or an element of the Ready Reserve other than the Selected Reserve after service in the Selected Reserve characterized by the Secretary concerned as honorable service; or

(B) continues on active duty or in the Selected Reserve;

is entitled to basic educational assistance under this chapter [38 USCS §§ 3001 et seq.]

(b)(1)(A) The requirement of two years of service under clauses (1)(A)(i) and (1)(B)(i) of subsection (a) of this section is not applicable to an individual who is discharged or released, during such two years, from active duty in the Armed Forces (i) for a service-connected disability, (ii) for a medical condition which preexisted such service on active duty and which the Secretary determines is not service connected, (iii) for hardship, (iv) in the case of an individual discharged or released after 20 months of such service, for the convenience of the Government, (v) involuntarily for the convenience of the Government as a result of a reduction in force, as determined by the Secretary of the military department concerned in accordance with regulations prescribed by the Secretary of Defense or by the Secretary of Transportation with respect to the Coast Guard when it is not operating as a service in the Navy, or (vi) for a physical or mental condition that was not characterized as a disability, as described in section 3011(a)(1)(A)(ii)(I) of this title.

(B) The requirement of four years of service under clauses (1)(A)(ii) and (1)(B)(ii) of subsection (a) of this section is not applicable to an individual—

(i) who, during the two years of service described in clauses (1)(A)(i) and (1)(B)(i) of subsection (a) of this section, was discharged or released from active duty in the Armed Forces for a service-connected disability, for a medical condition which preexisted such service on active duty and which the Secretary determines is not service connected, or for a physical or mental condition not characterized as a disability, as described in section 3011(a)(1)(A)(ii)(I) of this title, if the individual was obligated, at the beginning of such two years of service, to serve such four years of service;

(ii) who, during the four years of service described in clauses (1)(A)(ii) and (1)(B)(ii) of subsection (a) of this section, is discharged or released from service in the Selected Reserve (I) for a service-connected disability, (II) for a medical condition which preexisted the individual's becoming a member of the Selected Reserve and which the Secretary determines is not service connected, (III) for hardship, (IV) in the case of an individual discharged or released after 30 months of such service, for the convenience of the Government, (V) involuntarily for the convenience of the Government as a result of a reduction in force, as determined by the Secretary of the military department concerned in accordance with regulations prescribed by the Secretary of Defense or by the Secretary of Transportation with respect to the Coast Guard when it is not operating as a service in the Navy, or (VI) for a physical or mental condition not characterized as a disability, as described in section 3011(a)(1)(A)(ii)(I) of this title; or

(iii) who, before completing the four years of service described in clauses (1)(A)(ii) and (1)(B)(ii) of subsection (a) of this section, ceases to be a member of the Selected Reserve during the period beginning on October 1, 1991, and ending on September 30, 1999, by reason of the inactivation of the person's unit of assignment or by reason of involuntarily ceasing to be designated as a member of the Selected Reserve pursuant to section 10143(a) of title 10.

(2) After an individual begins service in the Selected Reserve within one year after completion of the service described in clause (A)(i) or (B)(i) of subsection (a)(1) of this section, the continuity of service of such individual as a member of the Selected Reserve shall not be considered to be broken—

(A) by any period of time (not to exceed a maximum period prescribed by the Secretary concerned by regulation) during which the member is not able to locate a unit of the Selected Reserve of the member's Armed Force that the member is eligible to join or that has a vacancy; or

(B) by any other period of time (not to exceed a maximum period prescribed by the Secretary concerned by regulation) during which the member is not attached to a unit of the Selected Reserve that the Secretary concerned, pursuant to regulations, considers to be inappropriate to consider for such purpose.

(c) The basic pay of any individual described in subsection (a)(1)(a) of this section who does not make an election under subsection (d)(1) of this section shall be reduced by $100 for each of the first 12 months that such individual is entitled to such pay. Any amount by which the basic pay of an individual is reduced under this chapter [38 USCS §§ 3001 et seq.] shall revert to the Treasury and shall not, for purposes of any Federal law, be considered to have been received by or to be within the control of such individual.

(d)(1) An individual described in subsection (a)(1)(A) of this section may make an election not to receive educational assistance under this chapter [38 USCS §§ 3001 et seq.]. Any such election shall be made at the time the individual initially enters on active duty as a member of the Armed Forces. Any individual who makes such an election is not entitled to educational assistance under this chapter [38 USCS §§ 3001 et seq.].

(2) An individual who after December 31, 1976, receives a commission as an officer in the Armed Forces upon graduation from the United States Military Academy, the United States Naval Academy, the United States Air Force Academy, or the Coast Guard Academy is not eligible for educational assistance under this section.

(3) An individual who after December 31, 1976, receives a commission as an officer in the Armed Forces upon completion of a program of educational assistance under section 2107 of title 10 is not eligible for educational assistance under this section if the individual enters on active duty—

(A) before October 1, 1996; or

(B) after September 30, 1996, and while participating in such program received more than $2,000 for each year of such participation.

(e)(1) An individual described in subclause (I) or (III) of subsection (b)(1)(B)(ii) of this section may elect entitlement to basic educational assistance under section 3011 of this title, based on an initial obligated period of active duty of two years, in lieu of entitlement to assistance under this section.

(2) An individual who makes the election described in paragraph (1) of this subsection shall, for all purposes of this chapter [38 USCS §§ 3001 et seq.], be considered entitled to educational assistance under section 3011 of this title and not under this section. Such an election is irrevocable.

(f) For the purposes of subsection (a)(2) of this section, an individual who was on active duty on August 2, 1990, and who completes the requirements of a secondary school diploma (or equivalency certificate) before October 28, 1994, shall be considered to have completed such requirements within the individual's initial obligated period of active duty.

(Added Oct. 19, 1984, P. L. 98-525, Title VII, § 702(a)(1) in part, 98 Stat. 2555; Nov. 8, 1985, P. L. 99-145, Title VI, Part F, § 674(2), 99 Stat. 665; Oct. 28, 1986, P. L. 99-576, Title III, Part A, §§ 303(a)(2), 307(a)(2), 321(2), 100 Stat. 3269, 3277; June 1, 1987, P. L. 100-48, § 3(b), 101 Stat. 331; Nov. 18, 1988, P. L. 100-689, Title I, Part A, §§ 102(b)(1), 103(b)(1), 104(b), 105, 111(a)(2)(B), 102 Stat. 4162, 4165, 4166, 4171; Dec. 18, 1989, P. L. 101-237, Title IV, §§ 409, 423(a)(1), (b)(1)(A), 103 Stat. 2084, 2090, 2092; Nov. 5, 1990, P. L. 101-510, Div A, Title V, Part F, § 562(a)(3), 104 Stat. 1574; Aug. 6, 1991, P. L. 102-83, § 5(a), (c)(1), 105 Stat. 406; Oct. 23, 1992, P. L. 102-484, Div D, Title XLIV, Subtitle B, § 4419(b), 106 Stat. 2718; Oct. 29, 1992, P. L. 102-568, Title III, §§ 302(a)(2), 303(a)(2), 106 Stat. 4326, 4327; Nov. 30, 1993, P. L. 103-160, Div A, Title V, Subtitle F, § 561(m), 107 Stat. 1668; Nov.

READJUSTMENT BENEFITS 38 USCS § 3012

2, 1994, P. L. 103-446, Title XII, § 1201(f)(2), 108 Stat. 4687; Feb. 10, 1996, P. L. 104-106, Div A, Title XV, § 1501(e)(2)(B), 110 Stat. 501; Sept. 23, 1996, P. L. 104-201, Div A, Title V, Subtitle H, § 556(b), 110 Stat. 2528.)

HISTORY; ANCILLARY LAWS AND DIRECTIVES

Explanatory notes:
A prior § 3012 was redesignated by Act May 7, 1991, P. L. 102-40, Title IV, § 402(b)(1), 105 Stat. 238. For similar provisions, see 38 USCS § 5112.

Amendments:
1985. Act Nov. 8, 1985, in subsec. (a)(1)(B), deleted "and without a break in service on active duty since December 31, 1976," following "of this title".

1986. Act Oct. 28, 1986, in subsec. (a), in the introductory matter, substituted "subsection (d)" for "subsection (b), and in para. (1)(B) inserted "and was on active duty on October 19, 1984, and without a break in service since October 19, 1984,"; in subsec. (b)(1) inserted "such"; and in subsec. (c), substituted "Any amount by which the basic pay of an individual is reduced under this subsection shall revert to the Treasury and shall not, for purposes of any Federal law, be considered to have been received by or to be within the control of such individual." for "Amounts withheld from basic pay under this paragraph shall revert to the Treasury.".

1987. Act June 1, 1987, in subsec. (a)(1)(A), substituted "after June 30, 1985," for "during the period beginning on July 1, 1985, and ending on June 30, 1988,".

1988. Act Nov. 18, 1988, in subsec. (a), in para. (1), in subpara. (A)(i), inserted ", as the individual's initial obligated period of active duty," and in para. (2), substituted "completed the requirements of" for "received", and inserted ", except that an individual described in clause (1)(B) of this subsection may meet the requirement of this clause by having successfully completed the equivalent of 12 semester hours in a program of education leading to a standard college degree"; in subsec. (c), substituted "chapter" for "subsection"; and added subsec. (e).

Such Act further (effective as provided by § 102(c) of such Act, which appears as 38 USCS § 3011 note), in subsec. (a), in para. (1), in subparas. (A)(i) and (B)(i), inserted ", subject to subsection (b) of this section,"; and substituted subsec. (b)(1) for one which read: "The requirement of four years of service under clauses (1)(A)(ii) and (1)(B)(ii) of subsection (a) of this section is not applicable to an individual who is discharged or released from service in the Selected Reserve for a service-connected disability, for hardship, or (in the case of an individual discharged or released after three and one-half years of such service) for the convenience of the Government.".

1989. Act Dec. 18, 1989, in subsec. (a)(2), inserted "(i)" and ", and (ii) an individual described in clause (1)(A) of this subsection may meet such requirement by having successfully completed the equivalent of such 12 semester hours before the end of the individual's initial obligated period of active duty".

Such Act further, in subsec. (b)(1), in subparas. (A), (B)(i), and (B)(ii), substituted "Secretary" for "Administrator".

Such Act further, in subsec. (a)(1), in subpara. (A)(ii), substituted "and beginning within one year after completion" for "and after completion", in subpara. (B)(ii), substituted "and beginning within one year after completion" for "and after completion"; and in subsec. (b)(2), in the introductory matter, substituted "After an individual begins service in the Selected Reserve within one year after completion of the service described in clause (A)(i) or (B)(i) of subsection (a)(1) of this section, the continuity of service of such individual as a member of the Selected Reserve" for "Continuity of service of a member of the selected Reserve for purposes of such clauses".

1990. Act Nov. 5, 1990 (effective 10/19/84, as provided by § 562(c) of such Act, which appears as 38 USCS § 3011 note), in subsec. (b), in para. (1), in subpara. (A), substituted "(v)" for "or (v)" and inserted ", or (vi) for a physical or mental condition that was not characterized as a disability, as described in section 1411(a)(1)(A)(ii)(I) of this title", in subpara. (B), in cl. (i), substituted "for" for "or for" preceding "medical condition" and inserted ", or for a physical or mental condition not characterized as a disability, as described in section 1411(a)(1)(A)(ii)(I) of this title", and, in cl. (ii), substituted "(V)" for "or (V)" and inserted ", or (VI) for a physical or mental condition not characterized as a disability, as described in section 1411(a)(1)(A)(ii)(I) of this title".

1991. Act Aug. 6, 1991, redesignated this section, formerly 38 USCS § 1412, as 38 USCS § 3012, and amended the references in this section to reflect the redesignations made by § 5(a) of such Act (see Table III preceding 38 USCS § 101).

1992. Act Oct. 23, 1992, in subsec. (b)(1)(B), in cl. (i), deleted "or" following the concluding semicolon, in cl. (2), substituted "; or" for the concluding period, and added cl. (iii).

Act Oct. 29, 1992 (effective 10/28/86, as provided by § 302(b) of such Act, which appears as 38 USCS § 3011 note), in subsec. (a), in para. (1), in subpara. (B), substituted "at any time during the period beginning on October 19, 1984, and ending on July 1, 1985, continued on active duty without a break in service and—" for "on October 19, 1984, and without a break in service since October 19, 1984, and—".

Such Act further, in subsec. (a), in para. (2), inserted "except as provided in subsection (f) of this section,"; and added subsec. (f).

1993. Act Nov. 30, 1993, in subsec. (b)(1)(B)(iii), substituted "September 30, 1999," for "September 30, 1995,".

1994. Act Nov. 2, 1994, in subsec. (f), substituted "October 28, 1994," for "the end of the 24-month period beginning on the date of the enactment of this subsection".

1996. Act Feb. 10, 1996 (effective as if included in Act Oct. 5, 1995, P. L. 103-337, as enacted on Oct. 5, 1994, as provided by § 1501(f)(3) of Act Feb. 10, 1996, which appears as 10 USCS § 113 note), in subsec. (b)(1)(B)(iii), substituted "section 10143(a) of title 10" for "section 268(b) of title 10".

Act Sept. 23, 1996, in subsec. (d), in para. (2), deleted "or upon completion of a program of educational assistance under section 2107 of title 10" following "Coast Guard Academy", and added para. (3).

Other provisions:

Applicability of 1986 amendment to subsec. (c). For the application of the amendment to subsec. (c) of this section by Act Oct. 28, 1986, P. L. 99-576, Title III, Part A, § 303(a)(2), 100 Stat. 3269, see § 303(b) of such Act, which appears as 38 USCS § 3011 note.

Notification of extension of period for completion of diploma requirement. For notification provision relating to the extension, pursuant to 1992 amendments, of the period for meeting secondary school diploma or equivalency certificate requirements, see § 303(b) of Act Oct. 29, 1992, P. L. 102-568, which appears as 38 USCS § 3011 note.

CODE OF FEDERAL REGULATIONS

Department of Veterans Affairs—Adjudication, 38 CFR Part 3.

Department of Veterans Affairs—Vocational rehabilitation and education, 38 CFR Part 21.

CROSS REFERENCES

This section is referred to in 10 USCS § 2006; 38 USCS §§ 3013, 3016–3018, 3018A, 3018B, 3021, 3031, 5303A.

RESEARCH GUIDE

Am Jur:

77 Am Jur 2d, Veterans and Veterans' Laws § 134.

§ 3013. Duration of basic educational assistance

(a)(1) Subject to section 3695 of this title and except as provided in paragraphs (2) and (3) of this subsection, each individual entitled to basic educational assistance under section 3011 of this title is entitled to 36 months of educational assistance benefits under this chapter [38 USCS §§ 3001 et seq.] (or the equivalent thereof in part-time educational assistance).

(2) Subject to section 3695 of this title and subsection (d) of this section, in the case of an individual described in section 3011(a)(1)(A)(ii)(I) or (III) of this title who is not also described in section 3011(a)(1)(A)(i) of this title or an individual described in section 3011(a)(1)(A)(ii)(I) or (III) of this title who is not also described in section 3011(a)(1)(B)(i) of this title, the individual is entitled to one month of educational assistance benefits under this chapter [38 USCS §§ 3001 et seq.] for each month of continuous active duty served by such individual after June 30, 1985, as part of the individual's initial obligated period of active duty in the case of an individual described in section 3011(a)(1)(B)(ii)(I) or (III) of this title, or in the case of an individual described in section 3011(a)(1)(B)(ii)(I) or (III) of this title, after June 30, 1985.

(b) Subject to section 3695 of this title and subsection (d) of this section, each individual entitled to basic educational assistance under section 3012 of this title is entitled to (1) one month of educational assistance benefits under this chapter [38 USCS §§ 3001 et seq.] for each month of continuous active duty served by such individual after June 30, 1985, as part of the individual's initial obligated period of active duty in the case of an individual described in section 3012(a)(1)(A) of this title, or in the case of an individual described in section

38 USCS § 3013   VETERANS' BENEFITS

3012(a)(1)(B) of this title, after June 30, 1985, and (2) one month of educational assistance benefits under this chapter [38 USCS §§ 3001 et seq.] for each four months served by such individual in the Selected Reserve "after the applicable date specified in clause (1) of this subsection (other than any month in which the individual served on active duty).

(c)(1) Subject to section 3695 of this title and except as provided in paragraph (2) of this subsection, each individual entitled to basic educational assistance under section 3018 of this title is entitled to 36 months of educational assistance under this chapter [38 USCS §§ 3001 et seq.] (or the equivalent thereof in part-time educational assistance).

(2) Subject to section 3695 of this title, an individual described in clause (B) or (C) of section 3018(b)(3) of this title whose discharge or release from active duty prevents the reduction of the basic pay of such individual by $1,200 is entitled to the number of months of assistance under this chapter [38 USCS §§ 3001 et seq.] that is equal to the lesser of—

    (A) 36 multiplied by a fraction the numerator of which is the amount by which the basic pay of the individual has been reduced under section 3018(c) [38 USCS § 3018(c)] and the denominator of which is $1,200; or

    (B) the number of months the individual has served on continuous active duty after June 30, 1985.

(3) Subject to section 3695 of this title and subsection (d) of this section, an individual described in clause (B) or (C)(ii) of section 3018(b)(3) of this title (other than an individual described in paragraph (2) of this subsection) is entitled to the number of months of educational assistance under this chapter that is equal to the number of months the individual has served on continuous active duty after June 30, 1985.

(d) Subject to section 3695 of this title, each individual entitled to educational benefits under section 3018A, 3018B, or 3018C of this title is entitled to the lesser of—

    (1) 36 months of educational assistance under this chapter (or the equivalent thereof in part-time educational assistance); or

    (2) the number of months of such educational assistance (or such equivalent thereof) that is equal to the number of months served by such individual on active duty.

(e) No individual may receive basic educational assistance benefits under this chapter [38 USCS §§ 3001 et seq.] for a period in excess of 36 months (or the equivalent thereof in part-time educational assistance).

(f)(1) Notwithstanding any other provision of this chapter or chapter 36 of this title [38 USCS §§ 3001 et seq., 3670 et seq.], any payment of an educational assistance allowance described in paragraph (2) shall not—

    (A) be charged against any entitlement of any individual under this chapter; or

    (B) be counted toward the aggregate period for which section 3695 of this title limits an individual's receipt of assistance.

(2) Subject to paragraph (3), the payment of the educational assistance al-

lowance referred to in paragraph (1) is the payment of such an allowance to an individual for pursuit of a course or courses under this chapter if the Secretary finds that the individual—

(A) in the case of a person not serving on active duty, had to discontinue such course pursuit as a result of being ordered, in connection with the Persian Gulf War, to serve on active duty under section 672(a), (d), or (g), 673, 673b, or 688 of title 10 [10 USCS §§ 12301(a), (d), (g), 12302, 12304, 688]; or

(B) in the case of a person serving on active duty, had to discontinue such course pursuit as a result of being ordered, in connection with such War, to a new duty location or assignment or to perform an increased amount of work; and

(C) failed to receive credit or lost training time toward completion of the individual's approved education, professional, or vocational objective as a result of having to discontinue, as described in subparagraph (A) or (B), his or her course pursuit.

(3) The period for which, by reason of this subsection, an educational assistance allowance is not charged against entitlement or counted toward the applicable aggregate period under section 3695 of this title shall not exceed the portion of the period of enrollment in the course or courses for which the individual failed to receive credit or with respect to which the individual lost training time, as determined under paragraph (2)(C) of this subsection.

(Added Oct. 19, 1984, P. L. 98-525, Title VII, § 702(a)(1) in part, 98 Stat. 2557; Oct. 28, 1986, P. L. 99-576, Title III, Part A, § 321(3), 100 Stat. 3277; Nov. 18, 1988, P. L. 100-689, Title I, Part A, § 102(b)(2), 103(b)(2), 111(a)(4), 102 Stat. 4163, 4165, 4171; Dec. 18, 1989, P. L. 101-237, Title IV, § 423(a)(2), 103 Stat. 2091; Nov. 5, 1990, P. L. 101-510, Div A, Title V, Part F, § 561(b)(1), 104 Stat. 1573; Aug. 6, 1991, P. L. 102-83, § 5(a), (c)(1), 105 Stat. 406; Oct. 10, 1991, P. L. 102-127, § 2(a), 105 Stat. 619; Oct. 23, 1992, P. L. 102-484, Div D, Title XLIV, Subtitle A, § 4404(b)(2), 106 Stat. 2706; Oct. 9, 1996, P. L. 104-275, Title I, § 106(b)(2), 110 Stat. 3329.)

HISTORY; ANCILLARY LAWS AND DIRECTIVES

Explanatory notes:
The bracketed reference "10 USCS §§ 12301(a), (d), (g), 12302, 12304, 688" has been inserted on authority of Act Oct. 5, 1994, P. L. 103-337, § 1662(e)(2), 108 Stat. 2992, which transferred 10 USCS §§ 672, 673, and 673b to 10 USCS §§ 12301, 12302, and 12304, respectively.

A prior § 3013 was redesignated by Act May 7, 1991, P. L. 102-40, Title IV, § 402(b)(1), 105 Stat. 238. For similar provisions, see 38 USCS § 5113.

Amendments:
1986. Act Oct. 28, 1986, in subsec. (a)(2), inserted "after the date of the beginning of the period for which the individual's basic pay is reduced under section 1411(b) of this title, in the case of an individual described in section 1411(a)(1)(A)(ii)(I) of this title, or after June 30, 1985, in the case of an individual described in section 1411(a)(1)(B)(ii)(I) of this title"; in subsec. (b), in para. (1), inserted "after the date of the beginning of the

period for which such individual's basic pay is reduced under section 1412(c) of this title, in the case of an individual described in section 1412(a)(1)(A), or after June 30, 1985, in the case of an individual described in section 1412(a)(1)(B) of this title'', and in para. (2), inserted "after the applicable date specified in clause (1) of this subsection''.

1988. Act Nov. 18, 1988, in subsec. (a), in para. (2), substituted "Subject to section 1795 of this title and subsection (c) of this section, in'' for "In'', and substituted "continuous active duty served by such individual after June 30, 1985, as part of the individual's initial obligated period of active duty in the case of an individual described in section 1411(a)(1)(B)(ii)(I) or (III) of this title, or in the case of an individual described in section 1411(a)(1)(B)(ii)(I) or (III) of this title, after June 30, 1985.'' for "active duty served by such individual after the date of the beginning of the period for which the individual's basic pay is reduced under section 1411(b) of this title, in the case of an individual described in section 1411(a)(1)(A)(ii)(I) of this title, or after June 30, 1985, in the case of an individual described in section 1411(a)(1)(B)(ii)(I) of this title.''; and in subsec. (b)(1), substituted "continuous active duty served by such individual after June 30, 1985, as part of the individual's initial obligated period of active duty in the case of an individual described in section 1412(a)(1)(A) of this title, or in the case of an individual described in section 1412(a)(1)(B) of this title, after June 30, 1985, and'' for "active duty served by such individual after the date of the beginning of the period for which such individual's basic pay is reduced under section 1412(c) of this title, in the case of an individual described in section 1412(a)(1)(A), or after June 30, 1985, in the case of an individual described in section 1412(a)(1)(B) of this title, and''; and redesignated subsec. (c) as (d), and added a new subsec. (c).

Such Act further (effective as provided by § 102(c) of such Act, which appears as 38 USCS § 3011 note), in subsec. (a)(2), inserted "or (III)'' in both places it appears.

1989. Act Dec. 18, 1989, in subsec. (a)(2), substituted "subsection (d)'' for "subsection (c)'' and "1411(a)(1)(A)(ii)(I)'' for "1411(a)(1)(B)(ii)(I)'' the second place it appears; in subsec. (b), substituted "subsection (d)'' for "subsection (c)''; and in subsec. (c), in para. (1), substituted "paragraphs (2) and (3)'' for "paragraph (2)'', and added para. (3).

1990. Act Nov. 5, 1990, redesignated former subsec. (d) as subsec. (e); and added subsec. (d).

1991. Act Aug. 6, 1991, redesignated this section, formerly 38 USCS § 1413, as 38 USCS § 3013, and amended the references in this section to reflect the redesignations made by § 5(a) of such Act (see Table III preceding 38 USCS § 101).

Act Oct. 10, 1991, added subsec. (f).

1992. Act Oct. 23, 1992, in subsec. (d), inserted "or 3018B''.

1996. Act Oct. 9, 1996, in subsec. (d), substituted ", 3018B, or 3018C'' for "or 3018B''.

CROSS REFERENCES

This section is referred to in 38 USCS § 3031; 42 USCS § 12603.

RESEARCH GUIDE
Am Jur:
77 Am Jur 2d, Veterans and Veterans' Laws § 137.

§ 3014. Payment of basic educational assistance

The Secretary shall pay to each individual entitled to basic educational assistance who is pursuing an approved program of education a basic educational assistance allowance to help meet, in part, the expenses of such individual's subsistence, tuition, fees, supplies, books, equipment, and other educational costs.

(Added Oct 19, 1984, P. L. 98-525, Title VII, § 702(a)(1) in part, 98 Stat. 2557; Dec. 18, 1989, P. L. 101-237, Title IV, § 423(b)(1)(A), 103 Stat. 2092; Aug. 6, 1991, P. L. 102-83, § 5(a), 105 Stat. 406.)

HISTORY; ANCILLARY LAWS AND DIRECTIVES
Amendments:
1989. Act Dec. 18, 1989, substituted "Secretary" for "Administrator".
1991. Act Aug. 6, 1991, redesignated this section, formerly 38 USCS § 1414, as 38 USCS § 3014.

RESEARCH GUIDE
Am Jur:
77 Am Jur 2d, Veterans and Veterans' Laws § 144.

§ 3015. Amount of basic educational assistance

(a) The amount of payment of educational assistance under this chapter [38 USCS §§ 3001 et seq.] is subject to section 3011 of this title. Except as otherwise provided in this section, a basic educational assistance allowance under this subchapter [38 USCS §§ 3011 et seq.] shall be paid—

(1) at the monthly rate of $528 (as increased from time to time under subsection (g)) for an approved program of education pursued on a full-time basis; or

(2) at an appropriately reduced rate, as determined under regulations which the Secretary shall prescribe, for an approved program of education pursued on less than a full-time basis.

(b) In the case of an individual entitled to an educational assistance allowance under section 3011 or 3018 of this title and whose initial obligated period of active duty is two years, a basic educational assistance allowance under this chapter [38 USCS §§ 3001 et seq.] shall (except as provided in the succeeding subsections of this section) be paid—

(1) at the monthly rate of $429 (as increased from time to time under subsection (g)) for an approved program of education pursued on a full-time basis; or

(2) at an appropriately reduced rate, as determined under regulations which the Secretary shall prescribe, for an approved program of education pursued on less than a full-time basis.

(c)(1) The amount of basic educational allowance payable under this chapter [38 USCS §§ 3001 et seq.] to an individual referred to in paragraph (2) of this subsection is the amount determined under subsection (a) of this section.
(2) Paragraph (1) of this subsection applies to an individual entitled to an educational assistance allowance under section 3011 of this title—
    (A) whose initial obligated period of active duty is less than three years;
    (B) who, beginning on the date of the commencement of the person's initial obligated period of such duty, serves a continuous period of active duty of not less than three years; and
    (C) who, after the completion of that continuous period of active duty, meets one of the conditions set forth in subsection (a)(3) of such section 3011.

(d) In the case of an individual who has a skill or specialty designated by the Secretary concerned as a skill or specialty in which there is a critical shortage of personnel or for which it is difficult to recruit, the Secretary concerned, pursuant to regulations to be prescribed by the Secretary of Defense, may increase the rate of the basic educational assistance allowance applicable to such individual to such rate in excess of the rate prescribed under subsections (a), (b), and (c) of this section as the Secretary of Defense considers appropriate, but the amount of any such increase may not exceed $400 per month, in the case of an individual who first became a member of the Armed Forces before November 29, 1989, or $700 per month, in the case of an individual who first became a member of the Armed Forces on or after that date.

(e)(1)(A) Except as provided in subparagraph (B) of this paragraph and subject to paragraph (2) of this subsection, in the case of an individual who on December 31, 1989, was entitled to educational assistance under chapter 34 of this title [38 USCS §§ 3451 et seq.], the rate of the basic educational assistance allowance applicable to such individual under this chapter [38 USCS §§ 3001 et seq.] shall be increased by the amount equal to one-half of the educational assistance allowance that would be applicable to such individual under such chapter 34 [38 USCS §§ 3451 et seq.] (as of the time the assistance under this chapter [38 USCS §§ 3001 et seq.] is provided and based on the rates in effect on December 31, 1989) if such chapter [38 USCS §§ 3451 et seq.] were in effect.
(B) Notwithstanding subparagraph (A) of this paragraph, in the case of an individual described in that subparagraph who is pursuing a cooperative program on or after October 9, 1996, the rate of the basic educational assistance allowance applicable to such individual under this chapter shall be increased by the amount equal to one-half of the educational assistance allowance that would be applicable to such individual for pursuit of full-time institutional training under chapter 34 [38 USCS §§ 3451 et seq.] (as of the time the assistance under this chapter is provided and based on the rates in effect on December 31, 1989) if such chapter were in effect.
(2) The number of months for which the rate of the basic educational assistance allowance applicable to an individual is increased under paragraph (1) of this subsection may not exceed the number of months of entitlement to educational assistance under chapter 34 of this title [38 USCS §§ 3451 et seq.] that the individual had remaining on December 31, 1989.

(f) In the case of an individual for whom the Secretary of Defense made contributions under section 3222(c) of this title and who is entitled to educational assistance under section 3018A, 3018B, or 3018C of this chapter, the Secretary shall increase the rate of the basic educational assistance allowance applicable to such individual in excess of the rate provided under subsection (a) of this section in a manner consistent with, as determined by the Secretary of Defense, the agreement entered into with such individual pursuant to the rules and regulations issued by the Secretary of Defense under section 3222(c) of this title.

(g) With respect to any fiscal year, the Secretary shall provide a percentage increase (rounded to the nearest dollar) in the rates payable under subsections (a)(1) and (b)(1) equal to the percentage by which—
  (1) the Consumer Price Index (all items, United States city average) for the 12-month period ending on the June 30 preceding the beginning of the fiscal year for which the increase is made, exceeds
  (2) such Consumer Price Index for the 12-month period preceding the 12-month period described in paragraph (1).
(Added Oct. 19, 1984, P. L. 98-525, Title VII, § 702(a)(1) in part, 98 Stat. 2557; Nov. 18, 1988, P. L. 100-689, Title I, Part A, §§ 103(b)(3), 111(a)(5)(A), 102 Stat. 4165, 4171; Nov. 29, 1989, P. L. 101-189, Div A, Title VI, Part E, § 641, 103 Stat. 1456; Dec. 18, 1989, P. L. 101-237, Title IV, § 423(b)(1)(A), (5), 103 Stat. 2092; Nov. 5, 1990, P. L. 101-510, Div A, Title V, Part F, § 561(b)(2), 104 Stat. 1573; April 6, 1991, P. L. 102-25, Title III, Part C, § 337(a), 105 Stat. 90; June 13, 1991, P. L. 102-54, § 14(c)(1), 105 Stat. 284; Aug. 6, 1991, P. L. 102-83, § 5(a), (c)(1), 105 Stat. 406; Oct. 29, 1992, P. L. 102-568, Title III, §§ 301(a), (c), 307(a), (b), 106 Stat. 4325, 4328; Aug. 10, 1993, P. L. 103-66, Title XII, § 12009(a), (d)(1), (2), 107 Stat. 415, 416; Oct. 9, 1996, P. L. 104-275, Title I, § 106(b)(3), 110 Stat. 3329; Nov. 21, 1997, P. L. 105-114, Title IV, § 401(b), 111 Stat. 2293; June 9, 1998, P. L. 105-178, Title VIII, Subtitle B, § 8203(a)(1)–(3), 112 Stat. 493.)

HISTORY; ANCILLARY LAWS AND DIRECTIVES
Amendments:
1988. Act Nov. 18, 1988, in subsec. (a), substituted "The amount of payment of educational assistance under this chapter is subject to section 1432 of this title. Except" for "Subject to section 1432 of this title and except"; and, in subsec. (b), in the introductory matter, inserted "or 1418".
1989. Act Nov. 29, 1989, in subsec. (c), substituted "$400 per month, in the case of an individual who first became a member of the Armed Forces before the date of the enactment of the National Defense Authorization Act for Fiscal Years 1990 and 1991, or $700 per month, in the case of an individual who first became a member of the Armed Forces on or after that date" for "$400 per month".
Act Dec. 18, 1989, in subsecs. (a)(2) and (b)(2), substituted "Secretary" for "Administrator"; and in subsec. (c), substituted "prescribed by the Secretary of Defense," for "prescribed by the Secretary,", and inserted "of Defense", following "Secretary".

1990. Act Nov. 5, 1990, added subsec. (e).

1991. Act April 6, 1991, in subsec. (a), in the introductory matter, substituted ", (c), (d), (e), and (f)" for "and (c)"; in subsec. (b), in the introductory matter, substituted "Except as provided in subsections (c), (d), (e), and (f), in" for "In"; and added subsec. (f).

Act June 13, 1991, in subsec. (c), substituted "November 29, 1989," for "the date of the enactment of the National Defense Authorization Act for Fiscal years 1990 and 1991,".

Act Aug. 6, 1991, redesignated this section, formerly 38 USCS § 1415, as 38 USCS § 3015, and amended the references in this section to reflect the redesignations made by § 5(c)(1) of such Act (see Table III preceding 38 USCS § 101).

1992. Act Oct. 29, 1992, § 301(a), (c) (effective 4/1/93, as provided by § 301(e) of such Act, which appears as 10 USCS § 2131 note), as amended by § 12009(d)(1) of Act Aug. 10, 1993 (effective as if included in the enactment of Act Oct. 29, 1992, as provided by § 12009(d)(3) of the 1993 Act), in subsec. (a), in para. (1), substituted "$400" for "$300"; in subsec. (b), in para. (1), substituted "$325" for "$250"; and, in subsec. (f), deleted para. (1), which read: "During the period beginning on October 1, 1991, and ending on September 30, 1993, the monthly rates payable under subsection (a)(1) or (b)(1) of this section shall be $350 and $275, respectively.", redesignated para. (2) as new para. (1), and in such paragraph as so redesignated, substituted "shall provide a percentage increase in the monthly rates payable under subsections (a)(1) and (b)(1) of this section" for "may continue to pay, in lieu of the rates payable under subsection (a)(1) or (b)(1) of this section, the monthly rates payable under paragraph (1) of this subsection and may provide a percentage increase in such rates", and redesignated para. (3) as new para. (2), and in such paragraph as so redesignated, substituted "shall" for "may" wherever appearing.

Section 307(a), (b) of such Act (effective as if enacted on 6/30/85 and applicable to the payment of educational assistance for education or training pursued on or after 9/1/93, as provided by § 307(c) of such Act), as amended by § 12009(d)(2) of Act Aug. 10, 1993 (effective as if included in the enactment of Act Oct. 29, 1992, as provided by § 12009(d)(3) of the 1993 Act), in subsecs. (a) and (b), substituted "(f), and (g)" for "and (f)"; redesignated subsecs. (c)–(f) as (d)–(g), respectively, and added a new subsec. (c); and, in subsec. (d) as redesignated, substituted "(a), (b), and (c)" for "(a) and (b)".

1993. Act Aug. 10, 1993, in subsec. (g), deleted para. (1), which read: "With respect to the fiscal year beginning on October 1, 1993, the Secretary shall provide a percentage increase in the monthly rates payable under subsections (a)(1) and (b)(1) of this section equal to the percentage by which the Consumer Price Index (all items, United States city average, published by the Bureau of Labor Statistics) for the 12-month period ending June 30, 1993, exceeds such Consumer Price Index for the 12-month period ending June 30, 1992.", deleted "(2)" preceding "With respect to any fiscal year beginning on or after October 1, 1994,", redesignated subparas. (A) and (B) as new paras. (1) and (2), respectively, and in para. (2) as redesignated, substituted "paragraph (1)" for "subparagraph (A)".

Such Act further (applicable as if included in the enactment of Act Oct. 29,

1992, as provided by § 12009(d)(3) of such Act, which appears as a note to this section), amended the directory language of Act Oct. 29, 1992, without affecting the text of this section.

1996. Act Oct. 9, 1996, in subsec. (f), inserted ", 3018B, or 3018C".

1997. Act Nov. 21, 1997, in subsec. (e)(1), designated the existing provisions as subpara. (A) and, in subpara. (A) as so designated, substituted "Except as provided in in subparagraph (B) of this paragraph and subject to paragraph (2)" for "Subject to paragraph (2)", and added subpara. (B).

1998. Act June 9, 1998 (effective and applicable as provided by § 8203(a)(4) of such Act, which appears as a note to this section), in subsec. (a), in the introductory matter, deleted "subsections (b), (c), (d), (e), (f), and (g) of" preceding "this section" and, in para. (1), substituted "$528 (as increased from time to time under subsection (g))" for "$400"; in subsec. (b), in the introductory matter, substituted "In" for "Except as provided in subsections (c), (d), (e), (f), and (g), in" and inserted "(except as provided in the succeeding subsections of this section)", and, in para. (1), substituted "$429 (as increased from time to time under subsection (g))" for "$325"; and, in subsec. (g), in the introductory matter, substituted ", the Secretary shall provide a percentage increase (rounded to the nearest dollar) in the rates payable under subsections (a)(1) and (b)(1)" for "beginning on or after October 1, 1994, the Secretary shall continue to pay, in lieu of the rates payable under subsection (a)(1) or (b)(1) of this section, the monthly rates payable under this subsection for the previous fiscal year and shall provide, for any such fiscal year, a percentage increase in such rates".

Other provisions:

Accounts from which payments made; effect of 1992 amendments. For provision that amendments made to subsecs. (a)(1), (b)(1), and (f) (now (g)) of this section by § 301(a), (c) of Act Oct. 29, 1992, P. L. 102-568, shall not be construed to change the account from which payment is made for that portion of a payment under 38 USCS §§ 3001 et seq. which is a Montgomery GI bill rate increase and a title III benefit is paid, see § 301(e)(2) of such Act, which appears as 10 USCS § 2131 note.

Limitation of cost-of-living adjustments for Montgomery GI Bill benefits. Act Aug. 10, 1993, P. L. 103-66, Title XII, § 12009(c), 107 Stat. 416, provides: "The fiscal year 1995 cost-of-living adjustments in the rates of educational assistance payable under chapter 30 of title 38, United States Code [38 USCS §§ 3001 et seq.], and under chapter 106 of title 10, United States Code [10 USCS §§ 2131 et seq.], shall be the percentage equal to 50 percent of the percentage by which such assistance would be increased under section 3015(g) of title 38, and under [former] section 2131(b)(2) of title 10, United States Code, respectively, but for this section.".

Effective date of Aug. 10, 1993 amendments. Act Aug. 10, 1993, P. L. 103-66, Title XII, § 12009(d)(3), 107 Stat. 416, provides: "The amendments made by paragraphs (1) and (2) [amending this section] shall apply as if included in the enactment of Public Law 102-568 [enacted Oct. 29, 1992]."

Effective date and application of June 9, 1998 amendments. Act June 9, 1998, P. L. 105-178, Title VIII, Subtitle B, § 8203(a)(4), 112 Stat. 493, provides: "The amendments made by this subsection [amending subsecs. (a), (b), and (g) of this section] shall take effect on October 1, 1998, and shall apply with respect to educational assistance allowances paid for months after September 1998. However, no adjustment in rates of educational assistance shall be made under subsection (g) of section 3015 of title 38, United States Code, as amended by paragraph (2), for fiscal year 1999.".

CROSS REFERENCES
This section is referred to in 10 USCS § 2006; 38 USCS §§ 3018A, 3032, 3035; 42 USCS § 12603.

RESEARCH GUIDE
Am Jur:
77 Am Jur 2d, Veterans and Veterans' Laws § 144.

§ 3016. Inservice enrollment in a program of education

(a) A member of the Armed Forces who—
   (1) first becomes a member or first enters on active duty as a member of the Armed Forces after June 30, 1985, and does not make an election under section 3011(c)(1) or section 3012(d)(1) [38 USCS §§ 3011(c)(1), 3012(d)(1)];
   (2) completes at least two years of service on active duty after such date;
   (3) after such service, continues on active duty or in the Selected Reserve without a break in service (except as described in section 3012(b)(2) of this title); and
   (4) but for section 3011(a)(1)(A)(i)(I) or 3012(a)(1)(A)(ii) of this title would be eligible for basic educational assistance,

may receive educational assistance under this chapter [38 USCS §§ 3001 et seq.] for enrollment in an approved program of education while continuing to perform the duty described in section 3011(a)(1)(A)(i)(I) or 3012(a)(1)(A)(ii) of this title.

(b) A member of the Armed Forces who—
   (1) as of December 31, 1989, is eligible for educational assistance benefits under chapter 34 of this title [38 USCS §§ 3451 et seq.];
   (2) after June 30, 1985, has served the two years required by section 3012(a)(1)(B)(i); and
   (3) but for section 3012(a)(1)(B)(ii) of this title would be eligible for basic educational assistance,

may, after December 31, 1989, receive educational assistance under this chapter [38 USCS §§ 3001 et seq.] for enrollment in an approved program of education while continuing to perform the duty described in section 3012(a)(1)(B)(ii) of this title.

(c) A member of the Armed Forces who—
   (1) completes at least two years of service on active duty after June 30, 1985;
   (2) after such service continues on active duty without a break in service; and

READJUSTMENT BENEFITS 38 USCS § 3017

(3) but for section 3018(b)(3)(A) of this title would be entitled to basic educational assistance under this chapter [38 USCS §§ 3001 et seq.],

may receive such assistance for enrollment in an approved program of education while continuing to perform the service described in section 3018(b)(2) of this title.
(Added Oct. 19, 1984, P. L. 98-525, Title VII, § 702(a)(1) in part, 98 Stat. 2558; Oct. 28, 1986, P. L. 99-576, Title III, Part A, § 321(4), 100 Stat. 3278; Nov. 18, 1988, P. L. 100-689, Title I, Part A, § 103(b)(4), 102 Stat. 4165; Aug. 6, 1991, P. L. 102-83, § 5(a), (c)(1), 105 Stat. 406.)

HISTORY; ANCILLARY LAWS AND DIRECTIVES
Amendments:
1986. Act Oct. 28, 1986, substituted this section for one which read: "A member of the Armed Forces who has completed at least two years of service on active duty after June 30, 1985, has continued on active duty or in the Selected Reserve without a break in service (except as described in section 1412(b)(2) of this title) and who but for section 1411(a)(1) or 1412(a)(1) of this title would be eligible for basic educational assistance may receive educational assistance under this chapter for enrollment in an approved program of education while continuing to perform the duty described in section 1411(a)(1) or 1412(a)(1) of this title.".
1988. Act Nov. 18, 1988, added subsec. (c).
1991. Act Aug. 6, 1991, redesignated this section, formerly 38 USCS § 1416, as 38 USCS § 3016, and amended the references in this section to reflect the redesignations made by § 5(a) of such Act (see Table III preceding 38 USCS § 101).

§ 3017. Death benefit

(a)(1) In the event of the service-connected death of any individual—
   (A) who—
      (i) is entitled to basic educational assistance under this chapter [38 USCS §§ 3001 et seq.]; or
      (ii) is on active duty in the Armed Forces and but for clause (1)(A)(i) or clause (2)(A) of section 3011(a) or clause (1)(A)(i) or (ii) or clause (2) of section 3012(a) of this title would be eligible for such basic educational assistance; and
   (B) who dies while on active duty or within one year after discharge or release from active duty,
the Secretary shall make a payment, subject to paragraph (2)(B) of this subsection, in the amount described in subsection (b) of this section to the person or persons described in paragraph (2)(A) of this subsection.
(2)(A) The payment referred to in paragraph (1) of this subsection shall be made to the person or persons first listed below who is surviving on the date of such individual's death:
   (i) The beneficiary or beneficiaries designated by such individual under the individual's Servicemembers' Group Life Insurance policy.

(ii) The surviving spouse of the individual.

(iii) The surviving child or children of the individual, in equal shares.

(iv) The surviving parent or parents of the individual, in equal shares.

(B) If no such person survives such individual, no payment shall be made under this section.

(b) The amount of any payment made under this section shall be equal to—
(1) the amount reduced from the individual's pay under section 3011(b), 3012(c), or 3018(c) of this title, less
(2) the total of—
(A) the amount of educational assistance that has been paid to the individual under this chapter [38 USCS §§ 3001 et seq.] before the payment is made under this section; and
(B) the amount of accrued benefits paid or payable with respect to such individual in connection with this chapter [38 USCS §§ 3001 et seq.].

(c) A payment under this section shall be considered to be a benefit under this title and, for purposes of section 3035(b)(1), it shall be considered to be an entitlement earned under this subchapter [38 USCS §§ 3011 et seq.].

(Added Nov. 18, 1988, P. L. 100-689, Title I, Part A, § 101(a), 102 Stat. 4161; Dec. 18, 1989, P. L. 101-237, Title IV, §§ 423(a)(3), (b)(1)(A), 103 Stat. 2091, 2092; Aug. 6, 1991, P. L. 102-83, § 5(a), (c)(1), 105 Stat. 406; Oct. 29, 1992, P. L. 102-568, Title III, § 308, 106 Stat. 4329; Oct. 9, 1996, P. L. 104-275, Title IV, § 405(c)(2), 110 Stat. 3340.)

HISTORY; ANCILLARY LAWS AND DIRECTIVES

Amendments:

1989. Act Dec. 18, 1989, in subsec. (a)(1)(A)(ii), substituted "but for clause (1)(A)(i) or clause (2)(A) of section 1411(a) or clause (1)(A)(i) or (ii) or clause (2) of section 1412(a) of this title" for "but for section 1411(a)(1)(A)(i) or division (i) or (ii) of section 1412(a)(1)(A) of this title". Such Act further, in subsec. (a)(1)(B), substituted "Secretary" for "Administrator".

1991. Act Aug. 6, 1991, redesignated this section, formerly 38 USCS § 1417, as 38 USCS § 3017, and amended the references in this section to reflect the redesignations made by § 5(a) of such Act (see Table III preceding 38 USCS § 101).

1992. Act Oct. 29, 1992, in subsec. (a)(1), in subpara. (B), inserted "or within one year after discharge or release from active duty".

1996. Act Oct. 9, 1996, in subsec. (a)(2)(A)(i), substituted "Servicemembers" for "Servicemen's".

Other provisions:

Effective date of Act Nov. 18, 1988. Act Nov. 18, 1988, P. L. 100-689, Title I, Part A, § 101(c), 102 Stat. 4162, provides: "The amendments made by this section [adding this section] shall take effect as of July 1, 1985.".

§ 3018. Opportunity for certain active-duty personnel to withdraw election not to enroll

(a) Notwithstanding any other provision of this chapter [38 USCS §§ 3001 et seq.], during the period beginning December 1, 1988, and ending June 30, 1989 (hereinafter in this section referred to as the "open period"), an individual who—

(1) first became a member of the Armed Forces or first entered on active duty as a member of the Armed Forces during the period beginning July 1, 1985, and ending June 30, 1988;

(2) has continuously served on active duty without a break in service since the date the individual first became such a member or first entered on active duty as such a member; and

(3) is serving on active duty during the open period,

shall have the opportunity, in accordance with this section and on such form as the Secretary of Defense shall prescribe, to withdraw an election made under section 3011(c)(1) or 3012(d)(1) of this title not to receive educational assistance under this chapter [38 USCS §§ 3001 et seq.].

(b) An individual described in clauses (1) through (3) of subsection (a) of this section who made an election under section 3011(c)(1) or 3012(d)(1) of this title and who—

(1) while serving on active duty during the open period, makes a withdrawal of such an election;

(2) continues to serve the period of service which, at the beginning of the open period, such individual was obligated to serve;

(3)(A) serves the obligated period of service described in clause (2) of this subsection;

(B) before completing such obligated period of service, is discharged or released from active duty for (i) a service-connected disability, (ii) a medical condition which preexisted such service and which the Secretary determines is not service connected, (iii) hardship, or (iv) a physical or mental condition that was not characterized as a disability and did not result from the individual's own willful misconduct but did interfere with the individual's performance of duty, as determined by the Secretary of each military department in accordance with regulations prescribed by the Secretary of Defense (or by the Secretary of Transportation with respect to the Coast Guard when it is not operating as a service of the Navy); or

(C) before completing such obligated period of service, is (i) discharged or released from active duty for the convenience of the Government after completing not less than 20 months of such period of service, if such period was less than three years, or 30 months, if such period was at least three years, or (ii) involuntarily discharged or released from active duty for the convenience of the Government as a result of a reduction in force, as determined by the Secretary concerned in accordance with regulations prescribed by the Secretary of Defense;

(4) before completing such obligated period of service (i) has completed the requirements of a secondary school diploma (or an equivalency certificate), or (ii) has successfully completed the equivalent of 12 semester hours in a program of education leading to a standard college degree; and

(5) upon completion of such obligated period of service—

38 USCS § 3018   VETERANS' BENEFITS

    (A) is discharged from service with an honorable discharge, is placed on the retired list, is transferred to the Fleet Reserve or Fleet Marine Corps Reserve, or is placed on the temporary disability retired list;
    (B) continues on active duty; or
    (C) is released from active duty for further service in a reserve component of the Armed Forces after service on active duty characterized by the Secretary concerned as honorable service,
is entitled to basic educational assistance under this chapter [38 USCS §§ 3001 et seq.].

(c) The basic pay of an individual withdrawing, under subsection (b)(1) of this section, an election under section 3011(c)(1) or 3012(d)(1) of this title shall be reduced by—
    (1) $1,200; or
    (2) in the case of an individual described in clause (B) or (C) of subsection (b)(3) of this section whose discharge or release from active duty prevents the reduction of the basic pay of such individual by $1,200, an amount less than $1,200.

(d) A withdrawal under subsection (b)(1) of this section is irrevocable.
(Added Nov. 18, 1988, P. L. 100-689, Title I, Part A, § 103(a), 102 Stat. 4164; Dec. 18, 1989, P. L. 101-237, Title IV, §§ 423(b)(1)(A), (b)(4)(A) 103 Stat. 2092; March 22, 1991, P. L. 102-16, § 10(a)(2), 105 Stat. 55; Aug. 6, 1991, P. L. 102-83, § 5(a), (c)(1), 105 Stat. 406; Aug. 14, 1991, P. L. 102-86, Title V, § 506(b)(2), 105 Stat. 426; Oct. 29, 1992, P. L. 102-568, Title III, § 309(a), 106 Stat. 4329.)

HISTORY; ANCILLARY LAWS AND DIRECTIVES
Amendments:
1989. Act Dec. 18, 1989, in subsec. (b)(3)(B), substituted "Secretary" for "Administrator".
Such Act further, in subsec. (a)(3), inserted "of Defense".
1991. Act March 22, 1991, in subsec. (b)(4), substituted "(i)" for a comma, and inserted ", or (ii) has successfully completed the equivalent of 12 semester hours in a program of education leading to a standard college degree".
Act Aug. 6, 1991, redesignated this section, formerly 38 USCS § 1418, as 38 USCS § 3018, and amended the references in this section to reflect the redesignations made by § 5(a) of such Act (see Table III preceding 38 USCS § 101).
Act Aug. 14, 1991 (effective Dec. 18, 1989 as provided by § 506(b) of such Act), amended the directory language of Act Dec. 18, 1988, without affecting the text of this section.
1992. Act Oct. 29, 1992 (effective as if enacted on 12/1/88, as provided by § 309(b) of such Act, which appears as a note to this section), in subsec. (b)(3), in subpara. (B), substituted "(iii)" for "or (iii)", and inserted ", or (iv) a physical or mental condition that was not characterized as a disability and did not result from the individual's own willful misconduct but did interfere with the individual's performance of duty, as determined by the

Secretary of each military department in accordance with regulations prescribed by the Secretary of Defense (or by the Secretary of Transportation with respect to the Coast Guard when it is not operating as a service of the Navy)''.

Other provisions:
Effective date of amendments made by Act Oct. 29, 1992. Act Oct. 29, 1992, P. L. 102-568, Title III, § 309(b), 106 Stat. 4329, provides: "The amendment made by subsection (a) [amending this section] shall take effect as if enacted on December 1, 1988.''.

CROSS REFERENCES
This section is referred to in 38 USCS §§ 3013, 3015, 3016, 3017, 3021.

RESEARCH GUIDE
Am Jur:
77 Am Jur 2d, Veterans and Veterans' Laws § 134.

§ 3018A. Opportunity for certain active-duty personnel to enroll before being involuntarily separated from service

(a) Notwithstanding any other provision of law, an individual who—

(1) after February 2, 1991, is involuntarily separated (as such term is defined in section 1141 of title 10) with an honorable discharge;

(2) before applying for benefits under this section, has completed the requirements of a secondary school diploma (or equivalency certificate) or has successfully completed the equivalent of 12 semester hours in a program of education leading to a standard college degree;

(3) in the case of any individual who has made an election under section 3011(c)(1) or 3012(d)(1) of this title, withdraws such election before such separation pursuant to procedures which the Secretary of each military department shall provide in accordance with regulations prescribed by the Secretary of Defense for the purpose of carrying out this section or which the Secretary of Transportation shall provide for such purpose with respect to the Coast Guard when it is not operating as a service in the Navy;

(4) in the case of any person enrolled in the educational benefits program provided by chapter 32 of this title [38 USCS §§ 3201 et seq.] makes an irrevocable election, pursuant to procedures referred to in paragraph (3) of this subsection, before such separation to receive benefits under this section in lieu of benefits under such chapter 32 [38 USCS §§ 3201 et seq.]; and

(5) before such separation elects to receive assistance under this section pursuant to procedures referred to in paragraph (3) of this subsection,

is entitled to basic educational assistance under this chapter [38 USCS §§ 3001 et seq.].

(b) The basic pay of an individual described in subsection (a) of this section shall be reduced by $1,200.

(c) A withdrawal referred to in subsection (a)(3) of this section is irrevocable.

(d)(1) Except as provided in paragraph (3) of this subsection, an individual who is enrolled in the educational benefits program provided by chapter 32 of this title [38 USCS §§ 3201 et seq.] and who makes the election described in subsection (a)(4) of this subsection [section] shall be disenrolled from such chapter 32 program as of the date of such election.

(2) For each individual who is disenrolled from such program, the Secretary shall refund—

(A) as provided in section 3223(b) of this title, to the individual the unused contributions made by the individual to the Post-Vietnam Era Veterans Education Account established pursuant to section 3222(a) of this title; and

(B) to the Secretary of Defense the unused contributions (other than contributions made under section 3222(c) of this title) made by such Secretary to the Account on behalf of such individual.

(3) Any contribution made by the Secretary of Defense to the Post-Vietnam Era Veterans Education Account pursuant to subsection (c) of section 3222 of this title on behalf of any individual referred to in paragraph (1) of this subsection shall remain in such Account to make payments of benefits to such individual under section 3015(f) of this chapter.

(Added Nov. 5, 1990, P. L. 101-510, Div A, Title V, Part F, § 561(a)(1), 104 Stat. 1572; April 6, 1991, P. L. 102-25, Title VII, § 705(c)(1), 105 Stat. 120; Aug. 6, 1991, P. L. 102-83, § 5(a), (c)(1), 105 Stat. 406; Nov. 2, 1994, P. L. 103-446, Title XII, § 1201(d)(4), (i)(4), 108 Stat. 4684, 4688.)

HISTORY; ANCILLARY LAWS AND DIRECTIVES

Explanatory notes:
The bracketed word "section" has been inserted in subsec. (d)(1) as the word probably intended by Congress.

Amendments:
1991. Act April 6, 1991, in subsec. (a)(1), substituted "section 1141 of title 10" for "section 1142 of title 10".

Act Aug. 6, 1991, redesignated this section, formerly 38 USCS § 1418A, as 38 USCS § 3018A, and amended the references in this section to reflect the redesignations made by § 5(a) of such Act (see Table III preceding 38 USCS § 101).

1994. Act Nov. 2, 1994, in subsec. (a)(1), substituted "after February 2, 1991," for "after December 31, 1990, or the end of the 90-day period beginning on the date of the enactment of this section, whichever is later,"; and, in subsec. (d)(3), substituted "section 3015(f)" for "section 3015(e)".

CROSS REFERENCES
This section is referred to in 38 USCS §§ 3013, 3015, 3035, 4214.

RESEARCH GUIDE
Am Jur:
77 Am Jur 2d, Veterans and Veterans' Laws § 134.

§ 3018B. Opportunity for certain persons to enroll

(a) Notwithstanding any other provision of law—

(1) the Secretary of Defense shall, subject to the availability of appropriations, allow an individual who—
(A) is separated from the active military, naval, or air service with an honorable discharge and receives voluntary separation incentives under section 1174a or 1175 of title 10;
(B) before applying for benefits under this section, has completed the requirements of a secondary school diploma (or equivalency certificate) or has successfully completed the equivalent of 12 semester hours in a program of education leading to a standard college degree;
(C) in the case of any individual who has made an election under section 3011(c)(1) or 3012(d)(1) of this title, withdraws such election before such separation pursuant to procedures which the Secretary of each military department shall provide in accordance with regulations prescribed by the Secretary of Defense for the purpose of carrying out this section or which the Secretary of Transportation shall provide for such purpose with respect to the Coast Guard when it is not operating as service in the Navy;
(D) in the case of any person enrolled in the educational benefits program provided by chapter 32 of this title [38 USCS §§ 3201 et seq.] makes an irrevocable election, pursuant to procedures referred to in subparagraph (C) of this paragraph, before such separation to receive benefits under this section in lieu of benefits under such chapter 32 [38 USCS §§ 3201 et seq.]; and
(E) before such separation elects to receive assistance under this section pursuant to procedures referred to in subparagraph (C) of this paragraph; or
(2) the Secretary, in consultation with the Secretary of Defense, shall, subject to the availability of appropriations, allow an individual who—
(A) separated before October 23, 1992, from the active military, naval, or air service with an honorable discharge and received or is receiving voluntary separation incentives under section 1174a or 1175 of title 10;
(B) before applying for benefits under this section, has completed the requirements of a secondary school diploma (or equivalency certificate) or has successfully completed the equivalent of 12 semester hours in a program of education leading to a standard college degree;
(C) in the case of any individual who has made an election under section 3011(c)(1) or 3012(d)(1) of this title, withdraws such election before making an election under this paragraph pursuant to procedures which the Secretary shall provide, in consultation with the Secretary of Defense and the Secretary of Transportation with respect to the Coast Guard when it is not operating as service in the Navy, which shall be similar to the regulations prescribed under paragraph (1)(C) of this subsection;
(D) in the case of any person enrolled in the educational benefits program provided by chapter 32 [38 USCS §§ 3201 et seq.] of this title makes an irrevocable election, pursuant to procedures referred to in subparagraph (C) of this paragraph, before making an election under this paragraph to receive benefits under this section in lieu of benefits under such chapter 32 [38 USCS §§ 3201 et seq.]; and

(E) before the one-year period beginning on the date of enactment of this section, elects to receive assistance under this section pursuant to procedures referred to in subparagraph (C) of this paragraph,

to elect to become entitled to basic education assistance under this chapter [38 USCS §§ 3001 et seq.].

(b)(1) The basic pay or voluntary separation incentives of an individual who makes an election under subsection (a)(1) to become entitled to basic education assistance under this chapter [38 USCS §§ 3001 et seq.] shall be reduced by $1,200.

(2) The Secretary shall collect $1,200 from an individual who makes an election under subsection (a)(2) to become entitled to basic education assistance under this chapter [38 USCS §§ 3001 et seq.], which shall be paid into the Treasury of the United States as miscellaneous receipts.

(c) A withdrawal referred to in subsection (a)(1)(C) or (a)(2)(C) of this section is irrevocable.

(d)(1) Except as provided in paragraph (3) of this subsection, an individual who is enrolled in the educational benefits program provided by chapter 32 of this title [38 USCS §§ 3201 et seq.] and who makes the election described in subsection (a)(1)(D) or (a)(2)(D) of this section shall be disenrolled from such chapter 32 [38 USCS §§ 3201 et seq.] program as of the date of such election.

(2) For each individual who is disenrolled from such program, the Secretary shall refund—

(A) as provided in section 3223(b) of this title, to the individual the unused contributions made by the individual to the Post-Vietnam Era Veterans Education Account established pursuant to section 3222(a) of this title; and

(B) to the Secretary of Defense the unused contributions (other than contributions made under section 3222(c) of this title) made by such Secretary to the Account on behalf of such individual.

(3) Any contribution made by the Secretary of Defense to the Post-Vietnam Era Veterans Education Account pursuant to subsection (c) of section 3222 of this title on behalf of any individual referred to in paragraph (1) of this subsection shall remain in such account to make payments of benefits to such individual under section 3015(f) of this title.

(Added Oct. 23, 1992, P. L. 102-484, Div D, Title XLIV, Subtitle A, § 4404(a), 106 Stat. 2704; Nov. 2, 1994, P. L. 103-446, Title XII, § 1201(d)(5), (e)(11), (f)(3), 108 Stat. 4684, 4685, 4687.)

HISTORY; ANCILLARY LAWS AND DIRECTIVES
Amendments:
1994. Act Nov. 2, 1994, in subsec. (a)(2)(A), substituted "October 29, 1992," for "the date of enactment of this section"; and, in subsec. (d), in para. (1), substituted "(a)(2)(D) of this section" for "(a)(2)(D) of this subsection", and, in para. (3), substituted "such account" for "such Account", substituted "section 3015(f)" for "section 3015(e)" and substituted "this title" for "this chapter" preceding the concluding period.

CROSS REFERENCES
This section is referred to in 38 USCS §§ 3013, 3035.

RESEARCH GUIDE
Am Jur:
77 Am Jur 2d, Veterans and Veterans' Laws § 134.

§ 3018C. Opportunity for certain VEAP participants to enroll

(a) Notwithstanding any other provision of law, an individual who—
   (1) is a participant on October 9, 1996 in the educational benefits program provided by chapter 32 of this title [38 USCS §§ 3201 et seq.];
   (2) is serving on active duty (excluding the periods referred to in section 3202(1)(C) of this title) on such date;
   (3) before applying for benefits under this section, has completed the requirements of a secondary school diploma (or equivalency certificate) or has successfully completed the equivalent of 12 semester hours in a program of education leading to a standard college degree;
   (4) if discharged or released from active duty after the date on which the individual makes the election described in paragraph (5), is discharged or released therefrom with an honorable discharge; and
   (5) during the one-year period beginning on October 9, 1996, makes an irrevocable election to receive benefits under this section in lieu of benefits under chapter 32 of this title [38 USCS §§ 3201 et seq.], pursuant to procedures which the Secretary of each military department shall provide in accordance with regulations prescribed by the Secretary of Defense for the purpose of carrying out this section or which the Secretary of Transportation shall provide for such purpose with respect to the Coast Guard when it is not operating as a service in the Navy;

may elect to become entitled to basic educational assistance under this chapter [38 USCS §§ 3001 et seq.].

(b) With respect to an individual who makes an election under subsection (a) to become entitled to basic education assistance under this chapter [38 USCS §§ 3001 et seq.]—
   (1) the basic pay of the individual shall be reduced (in a manner determined by the Secretary of Defense) until the total amount by which such basic pay is reduced is $1,200; or
   (2) to the extent that basic pay is not so reduced before the individual's discharge or release from active duty as specified in subsection (a)(4), the Secretary shall collect from the individual an amount equal to the difference between $1,200 and the total amount of reductions under paragraph (1), which shall be paid into the Treasury of the United States as miscellaneous receipts.

(c)(1) Except as provided in paragraph (3), an individual who is enrolled in the educational benefits program provided by chapter 32 of this title [38 USCS §§ 3201 et seq.] and who makes the election described in subsection (a)(5) shall be disenrolled from such chapter 32 program as of the date of such election.

(2) For each individual who is disenrolled from such program, the Secretary shall refund—

    (A) to the individual, as provided in section 3223(b) of this title and subject to subsection (b)(2) of this section, the unused contributions made by the individual to the Post-Vietnam Era Veterans Education Account established pursuant to section 3222(a) of this title; and

    (B) to the Secretary of Defense the unused contributions (other than contributions made under section 3222(c) of this title) made by such Secretary to the Account on behalf of such individual.

(3) Any contribution made by the Secretary of Defense to the Post-Vietnam Era Veterans Education Account pursuant to subsection (c) of section 3222 of this title on behalf of any individual referred to in paragraph (1) shall remain in such account to make payments of benefits to such individual under section 3015(f) of this title.

(d) The procedures provided in regulations referred to in subsection (a) shall provide for notice of the requirements of subparagraphs (B), (C), and (D) of section 3011(a)(3) and of subparagraph (A) of section 3012(a)(3) of this title. Receipt of such notice shall be acknowledged in writing.

(Added Oct. 9, 1996, P. L. 104-275, Title I, § 106(a), 110 Stat. 3327; Nov. 21, 1997, P. L. 105-114, Title IV, 401(c), 111 Stat. 2293.)

HISTORY; ANCILLARY LAWS AND DIRECTIVES

Amendments:

1997. Act Nov. 21, 1997, in subsec. (a), in para. (1), substituted "October 9, 1996" for "the date of the enactment of the Veterans' Benefits Improvements Act of 1996", in para. (4), substituted "after the date on which the individual makes the election described" for "during the one-year period specified" and, in para. (5), substituted "October 9, 1996" for "the date of the enactment of the Veterans' Benefits Improvements Act of 1996".

RESEARCH GUIDE

Am Jur:

77 Am Jur 2d, Veterans and Veterans' Laws § 134.

§ 3019. Tutorial assistance

(a) An individual entitled to an educational assistance allowance under this chapter [38 USCS §§ 3001 et seq.] shall also be entitled to benefits provided an eligible veteran under section 3492 of this title, subject to the conditions applicable to an eligible veteran under such section.

(b) The amount of such benefits payable under this section may not exceed $100 per month, for a maximum of twelve months, or until a maximum of $1,200 is utilized. This amount is in addition to the amount of educational assistance allowance payable to the individual under this chapter [38 USCS §§ 3001 et seq.].

(c)(1) An individual's period of entitlement to educational assistance under this chapter [38 USCS §§ 3001 et seq.] shall be charged only with respect to the amount of tutorial assistance paid to the individual under this section in excess of $600.

(2) An individual's period of entitlement to educational assistance under this chapter [38 USCS §§ 3001 et seq.] shall be charged at the rate of one month for each amount of assistance paid to the individual under this section in excess of $600 that is equal to the amount of the monthly educational assistance allowance which the individual is otherwise eligible to receive for full-time pursuit of an institutional course under this chapter [38 USCS §§ 3001 et seq.].

(Added Nov. 18, 1988, P. L. 100-689, Title I, Part A, § 107(a)(1), 102 Stat. 4167; Aug. 6, 1991, P. L. 102-83, § 5(a), (c)(1), 105 Stat. 406.)

HISTORY; ANCILLARY LAWS AND DIRECTIVES

Explanatory notes:
A prior § 3020 was redesignated by Act May 7, 1991, P. L. 102-40, Title IV, § 402(b)(1), 105 Stat. 238. For similar provisions, see 38 USCS § 5120.

Amendments:
1991. Act Aug. 6, 1991, redesignated this section, formerly 38 USCS § 1419, as 38 USCS § 3019, and amended the references in this section to reflect the redesignations made by § 5(a) of such Act (see Table III preceding 38 USCS § 101).

RESEARCH GUIDE

Am Jur:
77 Am Jur 2d, Veterans and Veterans' Laws § 134.

SUBCHAPTER III. SUPPLEMENTAL EDUCATIONAL ASSISTANCE

§ 3021. Supplemental educational assistance for additional service

(a) The Secretary concerned, pursuant to regulations to be prescribed by the Secretary of Defense, may provide for the payment of supplemental educational assistance under this subchapter [38 USCS §§ 3021 et seq.] to any individual eligible for basic educational assistance under section 3011 or 3018 of this title who—

(1) services five or more consecutive years of active duty in the Armed Forces after the years of active duty counted under section 3011(a)(1) of this title without a break in such service; and

(2) after completion of the service described in clause (1) of this subsection—

(A) is discharged from service with an honorable discharge, is placed on the retired list, is transferred to the Fleet Reserve or Fleet Marine Corps Reserve, or is placed on the temporary disability retired list;

(B) continues on active duty without a break in service; or

(C) is released from active duty for further service in a reserve component of the Armed Forces after service on active duty characterized by the Secretary concerned as honorable service.

(b) The Secretary concerned, pursuant to regulations to be prescribed by the Secretary of Defense, may provide for the payment of supplemental educational assistance under this subchapter [38 USCS §§ 3021 et seq.] to any individual eligible for basic educational assistance under section 3012 or 3018 of this title who—

(1) serves two or more consecutive years of active duty in the Armed Forces after the years of active duty counted under section 3012(a)(1) of this title and four or more consecutive years of duty in the Selected Reserve in addition to the years of duty in the Selected Reserve counted under such section without a break in service; and

(2) after completion of the service described in clause (1) of this subsection—

(A) is discharged from service with an honorable discharge, is placed on the retired list, is transferred to the Fleet Reserve or Fleet Marine Corps Reserve, or is placed on the temporary disability retired list; or

(B) continues on active duty or in the Selected Reserve.

(c) Continuity of service of a member in the Selected Reserve for purposes of subsection (b)(1) of this section shall not be considered to be broken—

(1) by any period of time (not to exceed a maximum period prescribed by the Secretary concerned by regulation) during which the member is not able to locate a unit of the Selected Reserve of the member's Armed Force that the member is eligible to join or that has a vacancy; or

(2) by any other period of time (not to exceed a maximum period prescribed by the Secretary concerned by regulation) during which the member is not attached to a unit of the Selected Reserve that the Secretary concerned, pursuant to regulations, considers to be inappropriate to consider for such purpose.

(d) A period of active duty or duty in the Selected Reserve that occurs before the period of duty by which the individual concerned qualifies for basic educational assistance may not be counted for purposes of this section.

(Added Oct. 19, 1984, P. L. 98-525, Title VII, § 702(a)(1) in part, 98 Stat. 2558; Oct. 28, 1986, P. L. 99-576, Title III, Part A, § 321(5), (6), 100 Stat. 3278; Nov. 18, 1988, P. L. 100-689, Title I, Part A, § 103(b)(5), 102 Stat. 4166; Dec. 18, 1989, P. L. 101-237, Title IV, § 423(b)(4)(B), 103 Stat. 2092; Aug. 6, 1991, P. L. 102-83, § 5(a), (c)(1), 105 Stat. 406.)

HISTORY; ANCILLARY LAWS AND DIRECTIVES

Explanatory notes:
A prior § 3021 was redesignated by Act May 7, 1991, P. L. 102-40, Title IV, § 402(b)(1), 105 Stat. 238. For similar provisions, see 38 USCS § 5121.

Effective date of section:
Act Oct. 19, 1984, P. L. 98-525, Title VII, § 702(b), 98 Stat. 2563, which appears as a note to this section, provides that this section shall take effect on July 1, 1986.

Amendments:
1986. Act Oct. 28, 1986, in subsec. (a)(1), substituted "after" for "in addition to"; and in subsec. (b)(1) substituted "after" for "in addition to", and in subsec. (c) substituted "the member's" for "his".
1988. Act Nov. 18, 1988, in subsec. (a), in the introductory matter, inserted "or 1418"; and in subsec. (b), in the introductory matter, inserted "or 1418".
1989. Act Dec. 18, 1989, in subsec. (a) introductory matter, and in subsec. (b) introductory matter, inserted "of Defense".
1991. Act Aug. 6, 1991, redesignated this section, formerly 38 USCS § 1421, as 38 USCS § 3021, and amended the references in this section to reflect the redesignations made by § 5(a) of such Act (see Table III preceding 38 USCS § 101).

Other provisions:
Effective date of subchapter III as added by Act Oct. 19, 1984. Act Oct. 1984, P. L. 98-525, Title VII, § 702(b), 98 Stat. 2563, provides: "Subchapter III of chapter 30 of title 38, United States Code [38 USCS §§ 3021 et seq.], as added by subsection (a), shall take effect on July 1, 1986.".

CODE OF FEDERAL REGULATIONS
Department of Veterans Affairs—Adjudication, 38 CFR Part 3.

CROSS REFERENCES
This section is referred to in 10 USCS §§ 708, 2006; 38 USCS § 3022.

RESEARCH GUIDE
Am Jur:
77 Am Jur 2d, Veterans and Veterans' Laws § 138.

§ 3022. Amount of supplemental educational assistance

(a) The amount of payment of educational assistance under this chapter [38 USCS §§ 3001 et seq.] is subject to section 3032 of this title. Except as otherwise provided under subsection (b) of this section, supplemental educational assistance under section 3021 of this title shall be paid—

(1) at a monthly rate of $300 for an approved program of education pursued on a full-time basis; or

(2) at an appropriately reduced rate, as determined under regulations which the Secretary shall prescribe, for an approved program of education pursued on less than a full-time basis.

(b) In the case of a member of the Armed Forces for whom the Secretary concerned has provided for the payment of supplemental educational assistance who has a skill or specialty designated by the Secretary concerned, pursuant to regulations to be prescribed by the Secretary of Defense, as a skill or specialty in which there is a critical shortage of personnel, the Secretary concerned, pursuant to such regulations, may increase the rate of the supplemental educational assistance allowance applicable to such individual to such rate in excess of the rate prescribed under subsection (a) of this section as the Secretary concerned

38 USCS § 3022 — VETERANS' BENEFITS

considers appropriate, but the amount of any such increase may not exceed $300 per month.

(Added Oct. 1984, P. L. 98-525, Title VII, § 702(a)(1) in part, 98 Stat. 2559; Nov. 18, 1988, P. L. 100-689, Title I, Part A, § 111(a)(5)(B), 102 Stat. 4171; Dec. 18, 1989, P. L. 101-237, Title IV, § 423(b)(1)(A), (4)(C), 103 Stat. 2092; Aug. 6, 1991, P. L. 102-83, § 5(a), (c)(1), 105 Stat. 406.)

HISTORY; ANCILLARY LAWS AND DIRECTIVES

Explanatory notes:

A prior § 3022 was redesignated by Act May 7, 1991, P. L. 102-40, Title IV, § 402(b)(1), 105 Stat. 238. For similar provisions, see 38 USCS § 5122.

Effective date of section:

Act Oct. 19, 1984, P. L. 98-525, Title VII, § 702(b), 98 Stat. 2563, which appears as 38 USCS § 1421 note, provides that this section shall take effect on July 1, 1986.

Amendments:

1988. Act Nov. 18, 1988, in subsec. (a), in the introductory matter, substituted "The amount of payment of educational assistance under this chapter is subject to section 1432 of this title. Except" for "Subject to section 1432 of this title and except".

1989. Act Dec. 18, 1989, in subsec. (a)(2), substituted "Secretary" for "Administrator"; and in subsec. (b), inserted "of Defense".

1991. Act Aug. 6, 1991, redesignated this section, formerly 38 USCS § 1422, as 38 USCS § 3022, and amended the references in this section to reflect the redesignations made by § 5(a) of such Act (see Table III preceding 38 USCS § 101).

CROSS REFERENCES

This section is referred to in 38 USCS § 3032.

RESEARCH GUIDE

Am Jur:

77 Am Jur 2d, Veterans and Veterans' Laws § 144.

§ 3023. Payment of supplemental educational assistance under this subchapter

The Secretary shall increase the monthly basic educational assistance allowance paid to an individual who is entitled to supplemental educational assistance under this subchapter [38 USCS §§ 3021 et seq.] by the monthly amount of the supplemental educational assistance to which the individual is entitled.

(Added Oct. 19, 1984, P. L. 98-525, Title VII, § 702(a)(1) in part, 98 Stat. 2560; Dec. 18, 1989, P. L. 101-237, Title IV, § 423(b)(1)(A), 103 Stat. 2092; Aug. 6, 1991, P. L. 102-83, § 5(a), 105 Stat. 406.)

HISTORY; ANCILLARY LAWS AND DIRECTIVES

Explanatory notes:
A prior § 3023 was redesignated by Act May 7, 1991, P. L. 102-40, Title IV, § 402(b)(1), 105 Stat. 238. For similar provisions, see 38 USCS § 5123.

Effective date of section:
Act Oct. 19, 1984, P. L. 98-525, Title VII, § 702(b), 98 Stat. 2563, which appears as 38 USCS § 1421 note, provides that this section shall take effect on July 1, 1986.

Amendments:
1989. Act Dec. 18, 1989, substituted "Secretary" for "Administrator".
1991. Act Aug. 6, 1991, redesignated this section, formerly 38 USCS § 1423, as 38 USCS § 3023.

RESEARCH GUIDE

Am Jur:
77 Am Jur 2d, Veterans and Veterans' Laws § 144.

SUBCHAPTER IV. TIME LIMITATION FOR USE OF ELIGIBILITY AND ENTITLEMENT; GENERAL AND ADMINISTRATIVE PROVISIONS

§ 3031. Time limitation for use of eligibility and entitlement

(a) Except as provided in subsections (b) through (e), and subject to subsection (g), of this section, the period during which an individual entitled to educational assistance under this chapter [38 USCS §§ 3001 et seq.] may use such individual's entitlement expires at the end of the 10-year period beginning on the date of such individual's last discharge or release from active duty, except that such 10-year period shall begin—

(1) in the case of an individual who becomes entitled to such assistance under clause (A) or (B) of section 3012(a)(1) of this title, on the later of the date of such individual's last discharge or release from active duty or the date on which the four-year requirement described in clause (A)(ii) or (B)(ii), respectively, of such section 3012(a)(1) is met; and

(2) in the case of an individual who becomes entitled to such assistance under section 3011(a)(1)(B), on the later of the date of such individual's last discharge or release from active duty or January 1, 1990.

(b) In the case of any eligible individual who has been prevented, as determined by the Secretary, from pursuing a program of education under this chapter [38 USCS §§ 3001 et seq.] within the 10-year period prescribed by subsection (a) of this section because such individual had not met the nature of discharge requirement of this chapter before the nature of such individual's discharge or release was changed by appropriate authority, release was under conditions described in section 3011(a)(3) or 3012(a)(3) such 10-year period shall not run during the period of time that such individual was so prevented from pursuing such program of education.

(c) In the case of an individual eligible for educational assistance under the provisions of this chapter [38 USCS §§ 3001 et seq.] who, after such individual's last discharge or release from active duty, was detained by a foreign government or power, the 10-year period described in subsection (a) of this section shall not run (1) while such individual is so detained, or (2) during any period immediately following such individual's release from such detention during which such individual is hospitalized at a military, civilian, or Department of Veterans Affairs medical facility.

(d) In the case of an individual eligible for educational assistance under this chapter [38 USCS §§ 3001 et seq.]—

(1) who was prevented from pursuing such individual's chosen program of education before the expiration of the 10-year period for use of entitlement under this chapter [38 USCS §§ 3001 et seq.] otherwise applicable under this section because of a physical or mental disability which was not the result of the individual's own willful misconduct, and

(2) who applies for an extension of such 10-year period within one year after (A) the last day of such period, or (B) the last day on which such individual was so prevented from pursuing such program, whichever is later,

such 10-year period shall not run with respect to such individual during the period of time that such individual was so prevented from pursuing such program and such 10-year period will again begin running on the first day following such individual's recovery from such disability on which it is reasonably feasible, as determined under regulations which the Secretary shall prescribe, for such individual to initiate or resume pursuit of a program of education with educational assistance under this chapter [38 USCS §§ 3001 et seq.].

(e)(1) Except as provided in paragraph (2) of this subsection, in the case of an individual described in section 3011(a)(1)(B) or 3012(a)(1)(B) of this title who is entitled to basic educational assistance under this chapter, the 10-year period prescribed in subsection (a) of this section shall be reduced by an amount of time equal to the amount of time that such individual was not serving on active duty during the period beginning on January 1, 1977, and ending on June 30, 1985.

(2) In the case of an individual to which paragraph (1) of this subsection is applicable and who is described in section 3452(a)(1)(B) of this title, the 10-year period prescribed in subsection (a) of this section shall not be reduced by any period in 1977 before the individual began serving on active duty.

(f)(1) If an individual eligible for educational assistance under this chapter [38 USCS §§ 3001 et seq.] is enrolled under this chapter [38 USCS §§ 3001 et seq.] in an educational institution regularly operated on the quarter or semester system and the period of such individual's entitlement under this chapter [38 USCS §§ 3001 et seq.] would, under section 3013 [38 USCS § 3013], expire during a quarter or semester, such period shall be extended to the end of such quarter or semester.

(2) If an individual eligible for educational assistance under this chapter [38

USCS §§ 3001 et seq.] is enrolled under this chapter [38 USCS §§ 3001 et seq.] in an educational institution not regularly operated on the quarter or semester system and the period of such individual's entitlement under this chapter [38 USCS §§ 3001 et seq.] would, under section 3013, expire after a major portion of the course is completed, such period shall be extended to the end of the course or for 12 weeks, whichever is the lesser period of extension.

(g) For purposes of subsection (a) of this section, an individual's last discharge or release from active duty shall not include any discharge or release from a period of active duty of less than 90 days of continuous service unless the individual involved is discharged or released for a service-connected disability, for a medical condition which preexisted such service and which the Secretary determines is not service connected, for hardship, or as a result of a reduction in force as described in section 3011(a)(1)(A)(ii)(III) of this title.

(Added Oct. 19, 1984, P. L. 98-525, Title VII, § 702(a)(1) in part, 98 Stat. 2560; Oct. 28, 1986, P. L. 99-576, Title III, Part A, §§ 307(b), 321(7), 100 Stat. 3270, 3278; Nov. 18, 1988, P. L. 100-689, Title I, Part A, § 111(a)(6), 102 Stat. 4171; Dec. 18, 1989, P. L. 101-237, Title IV, §§ 420(a)(1), 420(b), 423(a)(4), (b)(1), 103 Stat. 2087, 2088, 2091, 2092; Aug. 6, 1991, P. L. 102-83, § 5(a), (c)(1), 105 Stat. 406; Oct. 29, 1992, P. L. 102-568, Title III, § 302(a)(3), 106 Stat. 4327.)

HISTORY; ANCILLARY LAWS AND DIRECTIVES
Amendments:
1986. Act Oct. 28, 1986, in subsec. (a), substituted "(e)" for "(d)"; in subsec. (b), deleted "subchapter II or III of" following "education under", substituted "of this chapter" for "of such subchapter", deleted "(1)" preceding "before", and deleted "or (2) with respect to educational assistance under subchapter II of this chapter, the Administrator determined, under regulations prescribed by the Administrator, that such discharge or release was under conditions described in section 1411(a)(3) or 1412(a)(3) of this title," following "authority,"; redesignated subsec. (e) as subsec. (f); and added a new subsec. (e).

Such Act further directed that subsec. (e)(2) be amended by inserting "not" after "educational institution"; however, such amendment was executed to subsec. (f)(2), as redesignated, to reflect the probable intent of Congress.

1988. Act Nov. 18, 1988, in subsec. (a), substituted "beginning on the date of such individual's last discharge or release from active duty, except that such 10-year period shall begin—" and paras. (1) and (2) for "beginning on (1) the date of such individuals last discharge or release from active duty, or (2) the last day on which such individual becomes entitled to such assistance, whichever is later.".

1989. Act Dec. 18, 1989, in subsec. (a), in the introductory matter, inserted ", and subject to subsection (g),"; in subsec. (e), substituted "(1) Except as provided in paragraph (2) of this subsection, in" for "In", and added para. (2).

Such Act further, in subsec. (f), in paras. (1) and (2), substituted", under section 1413," for ", under this section,"; and added subsec. (g).

Such Act further, in subsecs. (b) and (d), substituted "Secretary" for

"Administrator"; and in subsec. (c), substituted "Department of Veterans Affairs" for "Veterans' Administration".

1991. Act Aug. 6, 1991, redesignated this section, formerly 38 USCS § 1431, as 38 USCS § 3031, and amended the references in this section to reflect the redesignations made by § 5(a) of such Act (see Table III preceding 38 USCS § 101).

1992. Act Oct. 29, 1992 (effective 10/28/86, as provided by § 302(b) of such Act, which appears as 38 USCS § 3011 note), in subsec. (e), in para. (1), substituted "June 30, 1985" for "October 18, 1984".

CROSS REFERENCES

This section is referred to in 10 USCS § 16133.

RESEARCH GUIDE

Am Jur:

77 Am Jur 2d, Veterans and Veterans' Laws § 137.

§ 3032. Limitations on educational assistance for certain individuals

(a) In the case of an individual entitled to educational assistance under this chapter [38 USCS §§ 3001 et seq.] who is pursuing a program of education—

(1) while on active duty; or

(2) on less than a half-time basis,

the amount of the monthly educational assistance allowance payable to such individual under this chapter [38 USCS §§ 3001 et seq.] is the amount determined under subsection (b) of this section.

(b) The amount of the educational assistance allowance payable to an individual described in subsection (a) of this section is the lesser of (1) the amount of the educational assistance allowance otherwise payable to such individual under this chapter [38 USCS §§ 3001 et seq.], or (2) the established charges for tuition and fees that the educational institution involved requires similarly circumstanced nonveterans enrolled in the same program to pay.

(c)(1) Except as provided in paragraph (2) of this subsection, the amount of the monthly educational assistance allowance payable to an individual pursuing a full-time program of apprenticeship or other on-job training under this chapter [38 USCS §§ 3001 et seq.] is—

(A) for each of the first six months of the individual's pursuit of such program, 75 percent of the monthly educational assistance allowance otherwise payable to such individual under this chapter [38 USCS §§ 3001 et seq.];

(B) for each of the second six months of the individual's pursuit of such program, 55 percent of such monthly educational assistance allowance; and

(C) for each of the months following the first 12 months of the individual's pursuit of such program, 35 percent of such monthly educational assistance allowance.

(2) In any month in which an individual pursuing a program of education consisting of a program of apprenticeship or other on-job training fails to complete 120 hours of training, the amount of monthly educational assistance allowance payable under this chapter [38 USCS §§ 3001 et seq.] to the individual shall be limited to the same proportion of the applicable rate determined under paragraph (1) of this subsection as the number of hours worked during such month, rounded to the nearest eight hours, bears to 120 hours.

(3)(A) Except as provided in subparagraph (B) of this paragraph, for each month that an individual is paid a monthly educational assistance allowance under this chapter [38 USCS §§ 3001 et seq.], the individual's entitlement under this chapter [38 USCS §§ 3001 et seq.] shall be charged at the rate of—

(i) 75 percent of a month in the case of payments made in accordance with paragraph (1)(A) of this subsection;

(ii) 55 percent of a month in the case of payments made in accordance with paragraph (1)(B) of this subsection; and

(iii) 35 percent of a month in the case of payments made in accordance with paragraph (1)(C) of this subsection.

(B) Any such charge to the individual's entitlement shall be reduced proportionately in accordance with the reduction in payment under paragraph (2) of this subsection.

(d)(1)(A) The amount of the educational assistance allowance payable under this chapter [38 USCS §§ 3001 et seq.] to an individual who enters into an agreement to pursue, and is pursuing, a program of education exclusively by correspondence is an amount equal to 55 percent of the established charge which the institution requires nonveterans to pay for the course or courses pursued by such individual.

(B) For purposes of this paragraph, the term "established charge" means the lesser of—

(i) the charge for the course or courses determined on the basis of the lowest extended time payment plan offered by the institution and approved by the appropriate State approving agency; or

(ii) the actual charge to the individual for such course or courses.

(2) Such allowance shall be paid quarterly on a pro rata basis for the lessons completed by the individual and serviced by the institution.

(3) In each case in which the rate of payment to an individual is determined under paragraph (1) of this subsection, the period of entitlement of such individual under this chapter [38 USCS §§ 3001 et seq.] shall be charged at the rate of one month for each payment of educational assistance to the individual that is equal to the amount of monthly educational assistance the individual would otherwise be eligible to receive for full-time pursuit of an institutional course under this chapter [38 USCS §§ 3001 et seq.].

(e)(1) Notwithstanding subsection (a) of this section, each individual who is pursuing a program of education consisting exclusively of flight training approved as meeting the requirements of section 3034(d) of this title shall be paid an educational assistance allowance under this chapter [38 USCS §§ 3001 et seq.] in the amount equal to 60 percent of the established charges for tuition and fees which similarly circumstanced nonveterans enrolled in the same flight course are required to pay.

(2) No educational assistance allowance may be paid under this chapter [38 USCS §§ 3001 et seq.] to an individual for any month during which such individual is pursuing a program of education consisting exclusively of flight training until the Secretary has received from that individual and the institution providing such training a certification of the flight training received by the individual during that month and the tuition and other fees charged for that training.

(3) The number of months of entitlement charged in the case of any individual for a program of education described in paragraph (1) of this subsection shall be equal to the number (including any fraction) determined by dividing the total amount of educational assistance paid such individual for such program by the monthly rate of educational assistance which, except for paragraph (1) of this subsection, such individual would otherwise be paid under subsection (a)(1), (b)(1), (d), or (e)(1) of section 3015 of this title, as the case may be.

(4) The number of solo flying hours for which an individual may be paid an educational assistance allowance under this subsection may not exceed the minimum number of solo flying hours required by the Federal Aviation Administration for the flight rating or certification which is the goal of the individual's flight training.

(Added Oct. 19, 1984, P. L. 98-525, Title VII, § 702(a)(1) in part, 98 Stat. 2561; Oct. 28, 1986, P. L. 99-576, Title III, Part A, § 301(b), (d)(1); 100 Stat. 3267, 3268; Nov. 18, 1988, P. L. 100-689, Title I, Part A, §§ 108(a)(2), 111(a)(7)(A), (8), 102 Stat. 4169, 4172; Dec. 18, 1989, P. L. 101-237, Title IV, § 422(a)(2), 103 Stat. 2089; March 22, 1991, P. L. 102-16, § 10(a)(3), 105 Stat. 55; Aug. 6, 1991, P. L. 102-83, § 5(a), (c)(1), 105 Stat. 406; Oct. 29, 1992, P. L. 102-568, Title III, § 310(a), 106 Stat. 4329; Nov. 2, 1994, P. L. 103-446, Title XII, § 1201(d)(6), 108 Stat. 4684; Oct. 9, 1996, P. L. 104-275, Title I, § 105(a), 110 Stat. 3327.)

HISTORY; ANCILLARY LAWS AND DIRECTIVES

Amendments:

1986. Act Oct. 28, 1986, substituted the heading of this section for one which read: "Limitation on educational assistance for certain individuals", and added subsec. (c).

1988. Act Nov. 18, 1988, in subsec. (c), in para. (3), substituted "(A) Except as provided in subparagraph (B) of this paragraph, for" for "For", redesignated subparas. (A)–(C) as cls. (i)–(iii), respectively and added subpara. (B); and added subsec. (e).

Such Act further (effective 1/1/89, as provided by § 108(c) of such Act, which appears as 38 USCS § 1402 note), added subsec. (d).

1989. Act Dec. 18, 1989 (effective 9/30/90 as provided by § 422(d) of such Act, which appears as 10 USCS § 2131 note), added subsec. (f).

1991. Act March 22, 1991, in subsec. (f)(3), substituted "(c), or (d)(1)" for "or (c)".

Act Aug. 6, 1991, redesignated this section, formerly 38 USCS § 1432, as 38 USCS § 3032, and amended the references in this section to reflect the redesignations made by § 5(a) of such Act (see Table III preceding 38 USCS § 101).

1992. Act Oct. 29, 1992 (applicable to certain flight training received after 9/30/92, as provided by § 310(d) of such Act, which appears as 10 USCS § 2131 note), in subsec. (f), in para. (1), deleted "(other than tuition and fees charged for or attributable to solo flying hours)" following "for tuition and fees", and added para. (4).

1994. Act Nov. 2, 1994, in subsec. (f)(3), substituted "(d), or (e)(1)" for "(c), or (d)(1)".

1996. Act Oct. 9, 1996 deleted subsec. (d), which read:

"(d)(1) The amount of the monthly educational assistance allowance payable to an individual pursuing a cooperative program under this chapter shall be 80 percent of the monthly allowance otherwise payable to such individual under section 3015 and section 3022, if applicable, of this title.

"(2) For each month that an individual is paid a monthly educational assistance allowance for pursuit of a cooperative program under this chapter], the individual's entitlement under this chapter shall be charged at the rate of 80 percent of a month.";

and redesignated subsecs. (e) and (f) as subsecs. (d) and (e), respectively.

CROSS REFERENCES

This section is referred to in 38 USCS §§ 3015, 3022, 3034.

RESEARCH GUIDE

Am Jur:

77 Am Jur 2d, Veterans and Veterans' Laws § 144.

§ 3033. Bar to duplication of educational assistance benefits

(a)(1) An individual entitled to educational assistance under a program established by this chapter [38 USCS §§ 3001 et seq.] who is also eligible for educational assistance under a program under chapter 31, 32, or 35 of this title [38 USCS §§ 3100 et seq., 3201 et seq., or 3500 et seq.], under chapter 106 or 107 of title 10 [10 USCS §§ 2131 et seq. or 2141 et seq.], or under the Hostage Relief Act of 1980 (Public Law 96-449; 5 U.S.C. 5561 note) may not receive assistance under two or more of such programs concurrently but shall elect (in such form and manner as the Secretary may prescribe) under which program to receive educational assistance.

(2) An individual entitled to educational assistance under chapter 34 of this title [38 USCS §§ 3451 et seq.] may not receive assistance under this chapter [38 USCS §§ 3001 et seq.] before January 1, 1990.

(b) A period of service counted for purposes of repayment under chapter 109 of title 10 [10 USCS §§ 2171 et seq.] of an education loan may not also be counted for purposes of entitlement to educational assistance under this chapter [38 USCS §§ 3001 et seq.].

(c) An individual who serves in the Selected Reserve may not receive credit for such service under both the program established by this chapter and the program established by chapter 106 of title 10 [10 USCS §§ 2131 et seq.] but shall elect (in such form and manner as the Secretary may prescribe) the program to which such service is to be credited.
(Added Oct. 19, 1984, P. L. 98-525, Title VII, § 702(a)(1) in part, 98 Stat. 2561; Oct. 28, 1986, P. L. 99-576, Title III, Part A, § 306, 100 Stat. 3269; Dec. 18, 1989, P. L. 101-237, Title IV, § 423(b)(1)(A), 103 Stat. 2092; March 22, 1991, P. L. 102-16, § 10(a)(4), 105 Stat. 55; Aug. 6, 1991, P. L. 102-83, § 5(a), (c)(1), 105 Stat. 406.)

HISTORY; ANCILLARY LAWS AND DIRECTIVES
Amendments:
1986. Act Oct. 28, 1986, in subsec. (a)(1), substituted "chapter 31, 32, or 35 of this title, under chapter 106 or 107 of title 10, or under the Hostage Relief Act of 1980 (Public Law 96-449; 5 U.S.C. 5561 note) may not receive assistance under two or more of such programs" for "chapter 31, 34, or 35 of this title or under chapter 106 or 107 of title 10 may not receive assistance under both programs; and substituted subsec. (c) for one which read: "An individual who is entitled to educational assistance under chapter 106 of title 10 may not also receive educational assistance under this chapter based on entitlement under section 1412 of this title.".
1989. Act Dec. 18, 1989, in subsecs. (a)(1) and (c), substituted "Secretary" for "Administrator".
1991. Act March 22, 1991, in subsec. (b), substituted "chapter 109 of title 10" for "section 902 of the Department of Defense Authorization Act, 1981 (10 U.S.C. 2141 note),".
Act Aug. 6, 1991, redesignated this section, formerly 38 USCS § 1433, as 38 USCS § 3033.

RESEARCH GUIDE
Am Jur:
77 Am Jur 2d, Veterans and Veterans' Laws § 144.

§ 3034. Program administration

(a)(1) Except as otherwise provided in this chapter [38 USCS §§ 3001 et seq.], the provisions of sections 3470, 3471, 3474, 3476, 3482(a), 3483, and 3485 of this title and the provisions of subchapters I and II of chapter 36 of this title [38 USCS §§ 3670 et seq., 3680 et seq.] such chapter (with the exception of sections 3680(c), 3680(f), and 3687) shall be applicable to the provision of educational assistance under this chapter [38 USCS §§ 3001 et seq.].

(2) The term "eligible veteran", as used in the provisions of the sections enumerated in paragraph (1) of this subsection, shall be deemed to include an individual who is eligible for educational assistance under this chapter [38 USCS §§ 3001 et seq.].

(3) The Secretary may, without regard to the application to this chapter [38 USCS §§ 3001 et seq.] of so much of the provisions of section 3471 of this

READJUSTMENT BENEFITS   38 USCS § 3034

title as prohibit the enrollment of an eligible veteran in a program of education in which the veteran is "already qualified", and pursuant to such regulations as the Secretary shall prescribe, approve the enrollment of such individual in refresher courses (including courses which will permit such individual to update knowledge and skills or be instructed in the technological advances which have occurred in the individual's field of employment during and since the period of such veteran's active military service), deficiency courses, or other preparatory or special education or training courses necessary to enable the individual to pursue an approved program of education.

(b) Regulations prescribed by the Secretary of Defense under this chapter [38 USCS §§ 3001 et seq.] shall be uniform for the Armed Forces under the jurisdiction of the Secretary of a military department.

(c) Payment of educational assistance allowance in the case of an eligible individual pursuing a program of education under this chapter [38 USCS §§ 3001 et seq.] on less than a half-time basis shall be made in a lump-sum amount for the entire quarter, semester, or term not later than the last day of the month immediately following the month in which certification is received from the educational institution that such individual has enrolled in and is pursuing a program at such institution. Such lump-sum payment shall be computed at the rate determined under section 3032(b) of this title.

(d) The Secretary may approve the pursuit of flight training (in addition to a course of flight training that may be approved under section 3680A(b) of this title) by an individual entitled to basic educational assistance under this chapter [38 USCS §§ 3001 et seq.] if—

    (1) such training is generally accepted as necessary for the attainment of a recognized vocational objective in the field of aviation;

    (2) the individual possesses a valid private pilot's license and meets the medical requirements necessary for a commercial pilot's license; and

    (3) the flight school courses meet Federal Aviation Administration standards for such courses and are approved by the Federal Aviation Administration and the State approving agency.

(Added Oct. 19, 1984, P. L. 98-525, Title VII, § 702(a)(1) in part, 98 Stat. 2562; Oct. 28, 1986, P. L. 99-576, Title III, Part A, §§ 301(c), 302, 305, 308(a), 100 Stat. 3268–3270; Nov. 18, 1988, P. L. 100-689, Title I, Part A, §§ 106(a), 111(a)(7)(B), 102 Stat. 4166, 4172; Dec. 18, 1989, P. L. 101-237, Title IV, §§ 415(b), 422(a)(1), 423(a)(5)(A), (6), (b)(1)(A), 103 Stat. 2086, 2088, 2091, 2092; March 22, 1991, P. L. 102-16, § 2(b)(2), 105 Stat. 49; Aug. 6, 1991, P. L. 102-83, § 5(a), (c)(1), 105 Stat. 406; Oct. 29, 1992, P. L. 102-568, Title III, § 313(a)(4), 106 Stat. 4332; Nov. 2, 1994, P. L. 103-446, Title VI, § 601(a), 108 Stat. 4670.)

HISTORY; ANCILLARY LAWS AND DIRECTIVES

Amendments:

1986. Act Oct. 28, 1986, in subsec. (a), substituted "1683, and 1685" for "1683" and substituted "(with the exception of sections 1780(c), 1780(g), and 1787)" for "(with the exception of sections 1777, 1780(a)(5), 1780(b),

1786, 1787, and 1792 of such chapter)''; and substituted subsec. (b) for one which read:

"(b) An educational assistance allowance for any period may not be paid to an individual enrolled in or pursuing a program of education under this chapter until the Administrator has received—

"(1) from such individual a certification as to such individual's actual attendance during such period; and

"(2) from the educational institution a certification, or an endorsement of the individual's certificate, that such individual was enrolled in and pursuing a program of education during such period.''.

Such Act further redesignated subsec. (c) as subsec. (d) and added a new subsec. (c).

1988. Act Nov. 18, 1988, in subsec. (a), inserted "1786(a)"; deleted subsec. (c), which read: "When an eligible individual is pursuing a program of education under this chapter by correspondence, the individual's entitlement under this chapter shall be charged at the rate of one month's entitlement for each month of benefits paid to the individual."; and redesignated former subsec. (d) as subsec. (c).

Act Nov. 18, 1988 (effective 8/15/89, as provided by § 106(d) of such Act, which appears as a note to this section), in subsec. (a), designated the first sentence as para. (1) and designated the second sentence as para. (2), in para. (2) as so designated, substituted "the provisions of the sections enumerated in paragraph (1) of this subsection" for "those provisions", and added para. (3).

1989. Act Dec. 18, 1989, in subsec. (a)(1), deleted "1780(g)" following "1780(c),"; deleted subsec. (b) which read: "(b) The Administrator may, pursuant to regulations which the Administrator shall prescribe, determine and define enrollment in, pursuit of, and attendance at, any program of education by an individual enrolled in or pursuing a program of education under this chapter for any period for which the individual receives educational assistance under this chapter. Subject to such reports and proof as the Administrator may require to show an individual's enrollment in and satisfactory pursuit of such individual's program, the Administrator may withhold payment of benefits to such individual until the required proof is received and the amount of the payment is appropriately adjusted."; and redesignated subsec. (c) as subsec. (b).

Such Act further, in subsecs. (a)(3) substituted "Secretary" for "Administrator", wherever appearing and purported in subsec. (b) to substitute "Secretary" for "Administrator" wherever appearing but such amendment could not be executed as subsec. (b) was deleted by § 415(b)(2) of such Act.

Such Act further, in subsec. (a), in para. (1), inserted "1780(f),", in para. (3), substituted "employment during and since the period of such veteran's active military service)" for "employment)"; and added subsec. (c).

Such Act further (effective 9/30/90 as provided by § 422(d) of such Act, which appears as 10 USCS § 16131 note), added subsec. (d).

1991. Act March 22, 1991, in subsec. (a)(1), deleted "1663," following "sections".

Act Aug. 6, 1991, redesignated this section, formerly 38 USCS § 1434, as 38 USCS § 3034, and amended the references in this section to reflect the redesignations made by § 5(a) of such Act (see Table III preceding 38 USCS § 101).

1992. Act Oct. 29, 1992 (applicable as provided by § 313(b) of such Act, which appears as 10 USCS § 2136 note), in subsec. (a), in para. (1), deleted "3473," following "3471,"; and, in subsec. (d), in para. (1), substituted "3680A(b)" for "3473(b)".

1994. Act Nov. 2, 1994 (effective 10/1/94, as provided by § 601(d) of such Act, which appears as a note to this section), in subsec. (d), deleted para. (2), which read: "This subsection shall not apply to a course of flight training that commences on or after October 1, 1994.", deleted the designation for para. (1), and redesignated subparas. (A), (B), and (C) as paras. (1), (2), and (3), respectively.

Other provisions:
Effective date of amendments made by § 106 of Act Nov. 18, 1988. Act Nov. 18, 1988, P. L. 100-689, Title I, Part A, § 106(d), 102 Stat. 4167, provides: "The amendments made by this section [amending this section and 38 USCS §§ 3241, 3533] shall take effect on August 15, 1989.".
Determinations of status or character of service. Act Dec. 18, 1989, P. L. 101-237, Title IV, § 413(b), 103 Stat. 2085, provides: "Through July 1, 1990, no provision of law shall preclude the Department of Veterans Affairs, in making determinations of the active-duty or Selected Reserve status, or the character of service, of individuals receiving benefits under chapter 30 or 32 of title 38, United States Code [38 USCS §§ 3001 et seq. or 3201 et seq.], or chapter 106 of title 10 [10 USCS §§ 2131 et seq.], United States Code, from continuing to use any category of information provided by the Department of Defense or Department of Transportation that the Department of Veterans Affairs was using prior to the date of the enactment of this Act, if the Secretary of Veterans Affairs determines that the information has proven to be sufficiently reliable in making such determinations.".
Evaluation of providing assistance for flight training. Act Dec. 18, 1989, P. L. 101-237, Title IV, § 422(c), 103 Stat. 2090, effective Sept. 30, 1990, as provided by § 422(d) of such Act, which appears as 10 USCS § 2131 note, provides:
"(c) Evaluation of providing assistance for flight training.
  "(1)(A) The Secretary of Veterans Affairs shall conduct an evaluation of paying educational assistance for flight training under chapter 30 of title 38, United States Code [38 USCS §§ 3001 et seq.], and chapter 106 of title 10 [10 USCS §§ 2131 et seq.], United States Code.
  "(B) The evaluation required by subparagraph (A) shall be designed to determine the effectiveness of the provision of educational assistance referred to in such subparagraph in preparing the recipients of such assistance for recognized vocational objectives in the field of aviation.
  "(2) Not later than January 31, 1994, the Secretary shall submit to the Committees on Veterans' Affairs of the Senate and the House of Representatives a report on the evaluation required by paragraph (1). Such report shall include—
    "(A) information, separately as to payments made under chapter 30

38 USCS § 3034

of title 38, United States Code [38 USCS §§ 3001 et seq.], and payments made under chapter 106 of title 10, United States Code [10 USCS §§ 2131 et seq.] regarding—

"(i) the number of recipients paid educational assistance allowances for flight training;

"(ii) the amount of such assistance;

"(iii) the amount paid by the recipients for such training;

"(iv) the vocational objectives of the recipients; and

"(v) the extent to which the training (I) assists the recipients in achieving employment in the field of aviation, or (II) was used only or primarily for recreational or avocational purposes; and

"(B) any recommendations for legislation that the Secretary considers appropriate to include in the report.".

Ratification of use of certain information by the Department of Veterans Affairs. Act Aug. 15, 1990, P. L. 101-366, Title II, § 206(b), 104 Stat. 442, provides: "Any use by the Department of Veterans Affairs, during the period beginning on July 2, 1990, and ending on the date of the enactment of this Act, of any category of information provided by the Department of Defense or the Department of Transportation for making determinations described in section 413(b) of the Veterans' Benefits Amendments of 1989 (Public Law 101-237) [note to this section] is hereby ratified.".

Savings provision. Act Oct. 29, 1992, P. L. 102-568, Title III, § 313(b), 106 Stat. 4333, which appears as 10 USCS § 16136 note, provides that the amendments made by subsec. (a)(4) of such section [amending this section] are not applicable to any person receiving educational assistance for pursuit of an independent study program in which the person was enrolled on the date of enactment of such section for as long as such person is continuously thereafter so enrolled and meets the requirements of eligibility for such assistance for the pursuit of such program under title 38, United States Code, or title 10, United States Code, in effect on that date.

Effective date of amendments made by Act Nov. 2, 1994. Act Nov. 2, 1994, P. L. 103-446, Title VI, § 601(d), 108 Stat. 4671, provides: "The amendments made by this section [amending this section, 38 USCS § 3241(b), and 10 USCS § 2136(c)] shall take effect as of October 1, 1994.".

CROSS REFERENCES

This section is referred to in 38 USCS § 3032, 3680A, 3688.

RESEARCH GUIDE

Am Jur:

77 Am Jur 2d, Veterans and Veterans' Laws §§ 132, 133, 139, 140, 142–145.

§ 3035. Allocation of administration and of program costs

(a) Except to the extent otherwise specifically provided in this chapter [38 USCS §§ 3001 et seq.], the educational assistance programs established by this chapter [38 USCS §§ 3001 et seq.] shall be administered by the Department of Veterans Affairs.

(b)(1) Except to the extent provided in paragraphs (2) and (3) of this subsection, payments for entitlement earned under subchapter II of this chapter [38 USCS §§ 3011 et seq.] shall be made from funds appropriated to, or otherwise available to, the Department of Veterans Affairs for the payment of readjustment benefits and from transfers from the Post-Vietnam Era Veterans Education Account pursuant to section 3232(b)(2)(B) of this title.

(2) Payments for entitlements earned under subchapter II of this chapter [38 USCS §§ 3011 et seq.] that is established under section 3015(d) of this title at a rate in excess of the rate prescribed under subsection (a) or (b) of section 3015 of this title shall, to the extent of that excess, be made from the Department of Defense Education Benefits Fund established under section 2006 of title 10 or from appropriations made to the Department of Transportation, as appropriate.

(3) Payment for entitlements established under section 3018A or 3018B of this title shall be made—

(A) except as provided in subparagraphs (B) and (C) of this paragraph, from the Department of Defense Education Benefits Fund established under section 2006 of title 10;

(B) in the case of any individual described in section 3018A(a)(3), 3018B(a)(1)(C), or 3018B(a)(2)(C) of this title, from funds appropriated, or otherwise available, to the Department of Veterans Affairs for the payment of readjustment benefits; and

(C) in the case of the increase in payments made under section 3015(f) of this title, from the Post-Vietnam Era Veterans Education Account established pursuant to section 3222(a) of this title.

(c) Payments for educational assistance provided under subchapter III of this chapter [38 USCS §§ 3021 et seq.] shall be made from the Department of Defense Education Benefits Fund established under section 2006 of title 10 or from appropriations made to the Department of Transportation, as appropriate.

(d) Funds for the payment by the Secretary of benefits under this chapter [38 USCS §§ 3001 et seq.] that are to be paid from the Department of Defense Education Benefits Fund shall be transferred to the Department of Veterans Affairs from such Fund as necessary and in accordance with agreements entered into under section 2006 of title 10 by the Secretary, the Secretary of Defense, and the Secretary of the Treasury. Funds for the payment by the Secretary of benefits under this chapter [38 USCS §§ 3001 et seq.] that are to be paid from appropriations made to the Department of Transportation shall be transferred to the Department of Veterans Affairs as necessary. The Secretary and the Secretary of Transportation shall enter into an agreement for the manner in which such transfers are to be made.

(e) Payments for tutorial assistance benefits under section 3019 of this title shall be made—

(1) in the case of the first $600 of such benefits paid to an individual, from funds appropriated, or otherwise available, to the Department of Veterans Affairs for the payment of readjustment benefits; and

(2) in the case of payments to an individual for such benefits in excess of $600, from—

(A) funds appropriated, or otherwise available, to the Department of Veterans Affairs for the payment of readjustment benefits;

(B) the Department of Defense Education Benefits Fund established under section 2006 of title 10; and

(C) funds appropriated to the Department of Transportation,

in the same proportion as the Fund described in subclause (B) of this clause and the funds described in subclause (A) or (C) of this clause are used to pay the educational assistance allowance to the individual under this chapter [38 USCS §§ 3001 et seq.].

(Added Oct. 19, 1984, P. L. 98-525, Title VII, § 702(a)(1) in part, 98 Stat. 2562; Oct. 28, 1986, P. L. 99-576, Title III, Part A, § 321(8), 100 Stat. 3278; Nov. 18, 1988, P. L. 100-689, Title I, Part A, § 107(a)(2), 102 Stat. 4168; Dec. 18, 1989, P. L. 101-237, Title IV, § 423(b)(1), 103 Stat. 2092; Nov. 5, 1990, P. L. 101-510, Div A, Title V, Part F, § 561(b)(3), 104 Stat. 1573; Aug. 6, 1991, P. L. 102-83, § 5(a), (c)(1), 105 Stat. 406; Oct. 23, 1992, P. L. 102-484, Div D, Title XLIV, Subtitle A, § 4404(b)(3), 106 Stat. 2706; Nov. 2, 1994, P. L. 103-446, Title XII, § 1201(d)(7), 108 Stat. 4684; Oct. 9, 1996, P. L. 104-275, Title I, § 106(c)(2), 110 Stat. 3329.)

HISTORY; ANCILLARY LAWS AND DIRECTIVES

Amendments:

1986. Act Oct. 28, 1986, in subsec. (b)(2), substituted "subsection (a) or (b) of section 1415" for "section 1415(a)".

1988. Act Nov. 18, 1988, added subsec. (e).

1989. Act Dec. 18, 1989, in subsecs. (a), (b)(1), (d)(2) and (e), substituted "Department of Veterans Affairs" for "Veterans' Administration"; and in subsec. (d), substituted "Secretary" for "Administrator", wherever appearing.

1990. Act Nov. 5, 1990, in subsec. (b), in para. (1), substituted "paragraphs (2) and (3)" for "paragraph (2)", and added para. (3).

1991. Act Aug. 6, 1991, redesignated this section, formerly 38 USCS § 1435, as 38 USCS § 3035, and amended the references in this section to reflect the redesignations made by § 5(a) of such Act (see Table III preceding 38 USCS § 101).

1992. Act Oct. 23, 1992, in subsec. (b)(3), in the introductory matter, inserted "or 3018B" and, in subpara. (B), inserted ", 3018B(a)(1)(C), or 3018B(a)(2)(C)".

1994. Act Nov 2, 1994, in subsec. (b), in para. (2), substituted "section 3015(d)" for "section 3015(c)", and, in para. (3)(C), substituted "section 3015(f)" for "section 3015(e)".

1996. Act Oct. 9, 1996, in subsec. (b)(1), inserted "and from transfers from the Post-Vietnam Era Veterans Education Account pursuant to section 3232(b)(2)(B) of this title".

CROSS REFERENCES

This section is referred to in 38 USCS § 3017.

READJUSTMENT BENEFITS 38 USCS § 3036

RESEARCH GUIDE

Am Jur:
77 Am Jur 2d, Veterans and Veterans' Laws § 132.

§ 3036. Reporting requirement

(a) The Secretary of Defense and the Secretary shall submit to the Congress at least once every two years separate reports on the operation of the program provided for in this chapter [38 USCS §§ 3001 et seq.].

(b) The Secretary of Defense shall include in each report submitted under this section—
> (1) information including (A) the extent to which the benefit levels provided under this chapter [38 USCS §§ 3001 et seq.] are adequate to achieve the purposes of inducing individuals to enter and remain in the Armed Forces and of providing an adequate level of financial assistance to help meet the cost of pursuing a program of education, and (B) whether it is necessary for the purposes of maintaining adequate levels of well-qualified active-duty personnel in the Armed Forces to continue to offer the opportunity for educational assistance under this chapter [38 USCS §§ 3001 et seq.] to individuals who have not yet entered active-duty service; and
> (2) such recommendation for administrative and legislative changes regarding the provision of educational assistance to members of the Armed Forces and veterans, and their dependents, as the Secretary of Defense considers appropriate.

(c) The Secretary shall include in each report submitted under this section—
> (1) information concerning the level of utilization of educational assistance and of expenditures under this chapter [38 USCS §§ 3001 et seq.]; and
> (2) such recommendations for administrative and legislative changes regarding the provision of educational assistance to members of the Armed Forces and veterans, and their dependents, as the Secretary considers appropriate.

(d)(1) The first report by the Secretary of Defense under this section shall be submitted not later than January 1, 1986.
> (2) The first report by the Secretary under this section shall be submitted not later than January 1, 1988.

(Added Oct. 19, 1984, P. L. 98-525, Title VII, § 702(a)(1) in part, 98 Stat. 2563; Dec. 18, 1989, P. L. 101-237, Title IV, §§ 423(b)(1)(A), (b)(4)(D), 103 Stat. 2092; Aug. 6, 1991, P. L. 102-83, § 5(a), 105 Stat. 406.)

HISTORY; ANCILLARY LAWS AND DIRECTIVES

Amendments:
1989. Act Dec. 18, 1989, in subsecs. (a), (c) and (d)(2), substituted "Secretary" for "Administrator", wherever appearing; and in subsec. (b), in the introductory matter and in para. (2), inserted "of Defense".
1991. Act Aug. 6, 1991, redesignated this section, formerly 38 USCS § 1436, as 38 USCS § 3036.

RESEARCH GUIDE
Am Jur:
77 Am Jur 2d, Veterans and Veterans' Laws § 132.

CHAPTER 31. TRAINING AND REHABILITATION FOR VETERANS WITH SERVICE-CONNECTED DISABILITIES

Section
3100. Purposes.
3101. Definitions.
3102. Basic entitlement.
[3102A] [1502A. Repealed]
3103. Periods of eligibility.
3104. Scope of services and assistance.
3105. Duration of rehabilitation programs.
3106. Initial and extended evaluations; determinations regarding serious employment handicap.
3107. Individualized vocational rehabilitation plan.
3108. Allowances.
3109. Entitlement to independent living services and assistance.
3110. Leaves of absence.
3111. Regulations to promote satisfactory conduct and cooperation.
3112. Revolving fund loans.
3113. Vocational rehabilitation for hospitalized members of the Armed Forces and veterans.
3114. Vocational rehabilitation outside the United States.
3115. Rehabilitation resources.
3116. Promotion of employment and training opportunities.
3117. Employment assistance.
3118. Personnel training, development, and qualifications.
3119. Rehabilitation research and special projects.
3120. Program of independent living services and assistance.
3121. Veterans' Advisory Committee on Rehabilitation.

HISTORY; ANCILLARY LAWS AND DIRECTIVES

Explanatory notes:
The bracketed section number "3102A" was inserted to preserve numerical continuity following the section number redesignations made by Act Aug. 6, 1991, P.L. 102-83, § 5(a), 105 Stat. 406.

Amendments:
1962. Act Aug. 16, 1962, P. L. 87-591, § 2, 76 Stat. 394, added item 1502A.
1965. Act Aug. 28, 1965, P. L. 89-139, § 2(1), 79 Stat. 577, deleted item 1502A, which read" "1502A. Blinded veterans."; substituted item 1503 for one which read: "1503. Training and training facilities."; and added item 1511.
1980. Act Oct. 17, 1980, P. L. 96-466, Title I, § 101(a), 94 Stat. 2171 (effective 4/1/81, as provided by § 802(a)(1) of such Act), substituted analysis for one which read:
CHAPTER 31—VOCATIONAL REHABILITATION
Section
"1501. Definitions.

"1502. Basic entitlement.
" [1502A. Repealed]
"1503. Periods of eligibility.
"1504. Subsistence allowances.
"1505. Leaves of absence.
"1506. Medical care of trainees.
"1507. Loans to trainees.
"1508. Regulations to promote good conduct.
"1509. Books, supplies, and equipment.
"1510. Vocational rehabilitation for hospitalized persons.
"1511. Training and training facilities.".
1986. Act Oct. 28, 1986, P. L. 99-576, Title III, Part A, § 333(b)(7), 100 Stat. 3279, in item 1520, substituted "Program" for "Pilot program".
1991. Act Aug. 6, 1991, P. L. 102-83, § 5(b)(1), 105 Stat. 406, revised the analysis of this Chapter by amending the section numbers in accordance with the redesignations made by § 5(a) of such Act (see Table III preceding 38 USCS § 101).

§ 3100. Purposes

The purposes of this chapter [38 USCS §§ 3100 et seq.] are to provide for all services and assistance necessary to enable veterans with service-connected disabilities to achieve maximum independence in daily living and, to the maximum extent feasible, to become employable and to obtain and maintain suitable employment.
(Added Oct. 17, 1980, P. L. 96-466, Title I, § 101(a), 94 Stat. 2172; Aug. 6, 1991, P. L. 102-83, § 5(a), 105 Stat. 406.)

HISTORY; ANCILLARY LAWS AND DIRECTIVES
Amendments:
1991. Act Aug. 6, 1991, redesignated this section, formerly 38 USCS § 1500, as 38 USCS § 3100.

Other provisions:
Effective dates of amendments made by § 101(a)-(d) of Act Oct. 17, 1980. Act Oct. 17, 1980, P. L. 96-466, Title VIII, § 802(a)(1)-(5), 94 Stat. 2217, provided:

"(1) Except as provided in paragraph (2), the amendments made by subsections (a) and (b) of section 101 [adding 38 USCS §§ 3100, 3113, 3115, 3117 and amending 38 USCS prec. § 3100 and §§ 3101–3107, 3109, 3111] shall become effective on April 1, 1981.

"(2) The provisions of sections 1508, 1512, 1516, 1518, 1519, 1520, and 1521 of title 38, United States Code, as added by section 101(a) [now 38 USCS §§ 3108, 3112, 3116, 3118–3121], shall become effective on October 1, 1980.

"(3) Notwithstanding paragraph (2), the provisions of chapter 31 of title 38, United States Code, as in effect on the day before the date of the enactment of this Act [former 38 USCS §§ 1501 et seq.] (other than section 1504, relating to subsistence allowances, and section 1507, relating to loans [former 38 USCS §§ 1504, 1507]), shall continue in effect until March 31, 1981.

"(4) Effective on October 1, 1980, sections 1504 and 1507 are repealed [former 38 USCS §§ 1504, 1507]. During the period beginning on October 1, 1980, and ending on March 31, 1981, the provisions of sections 1508 and 1512 of title 38, United States Code, as added by section 101(a) [now 38 USCS §§ 3108, 3112], shall apply to veterans pursuing a program of vocational rehabilitation training under chapter 31 of such title in the same manner as sections 1504 and 1507 of such title, respectively, applied to veterans pursuing a program of vocational rehabilitation training under such chapter on September 30, 1980.

"(5) Subsection (c) of section 101 [adding 38 USCS § 3108 note] shall become effective on October 1, 1980. Subsection (d) of such section [adding 38 USCS § 3107 note] shall become effective on the date of the enactment of this Act.".

CODE OF FEDERAL REGULATIONS

Department of Veterans Affairs—Loan guaranty and vocational rehabilitation and counseling programs, 48 CFR Part 871.

RESEARCH GUIDE

Am Jur:
77 Am Jur 2d, Veterans and Veterans' Laws §§ 63, 72, 79, 108, 133, 139, 144.

INTERPRETIVE NOTES AND DECISIONS

1. Generally
2. Private actions

1. Generally

Fees charged by state or political subdivision, in connection with licensing trainee to engage in particular occupation, are payable as reasonable incidents of rehabilitation of trainee necessary to make him employable, and cost of transportation to required examination for license is payable as incident of program to attain employability; other fees required by law as condition to practice of profession are exactions conditioning practice of profession or vocation, as distinguished from preparation for admission to practice, and are not payable as part of training expense; fees and other charges prescribed by nongovernment organizations rather than by law such as labor union initiation fees and union membership dues which are incident to placement training are payable, provided there are no facilities for necessary training available without paying such charges as necessary incident of training; but union initiation fees and membership dues required to begin work following completion of training are not payable as necessary part of preparation for employment. 1944 ADVA 557.

2. Private actions

Veterans' Vocational Rehabilitation Act does not authorize private actions since there is no suggestion in language of act or legislative history that statute guarantees federal employment or provides for private enforcement actions, and creating private right of action to enforce VVR would not be consistent with overall legislative scheme. Harris v Adams (1989, CA6 Mich) 873 F2d 929, 1 AD Cas 1475, 49 BNA FEP Cas 1304, 131 BNA LRRM 2405, 50 CCH EPD ¶ 38973.

§ 3101. Definitions

For the purposes of this chapter [38 USCS §§ 3100 et seq.]—

(1) The term "employment handicap" means an impairment, resulting in substantial part from a disability described in section 3102(1)(A) of this title, of a veteran's ability to prepare for, obtain, or retain employment consistent with such veteran's abilities, aptitudes, and interests.

(2) The term "independence in daily living" means the ability of a veteran, without the services of others or with a reduced level of the services of others, to live and function within such veteran's family and community.

(3) The term "program of education" has the meaning provided in section 3452(b) of this title.

(4) The term "program of independent living services and assistance" includes (A) the services provided for in this chapter [38 USCS §§ 3100 et seq.] that are needed to enable a veteran to achieve independence in daily living, including such counseling, diagnostic, medical, social, psychological, and educational services as are determined by the Secretary to be needed for such veteran to achieve maximum independence in daily living, and (B) the assistance authorized by this chapter [38 USCS §§ 3100 et seq.] for such veteran.

(5) The term "rehabilitated to the point of employability" means rendered employable in an occupation for which a vocational rehabilitation program has been provided under this chapter [38 USCS §§ 3100 et seq.].

(6) The term "rehabilitation program" means (A) a vocational rehabilitation program, or (B) a program of independent living services and assistance authorized under section 3120 of this title for a veteran for whom a vocational goal has been determined not to be currently reasonably feasible.

(7) The term "serious employment handicap" means a significant impairment, resulting in substantial part from a service-connected disability rated at 10 percent or more, of a veteran's ability to prepare for, obtain, or retain employment consistent with such veteran's abilities, aptitudes, and interests.

(8) The term "vocational goal" means a gainful employment status consistent with a veteran's abilities, aptitudes, and interests.

(9) The term "vocational rehabilitation program" includes—

(A) the services provided for in this chapter [38 USCS §§ 3100 et seq.] that are needed for the accomplishment of the purposes of this chapter [38 USCS §§ 3100 et seq.], including such counseling, diagnostic, medical, social, psychological, independent living, economic, educational, vocational, and employment services as are determined by the Secretary to be needed—

(i) in the case of a veteran for whom the achievement of a vocational goal has not been determined not to be currently reasonably feasible, (I) to determine whether a vocational goal is reasonably feasible, (II) to improve such veteran's potential to participate in a program of services designed to achieve a vocational goal, and (III) to enable such veteran to achieve maximum independence in daily living, and

(ii) in the case of a veteran for whom the achievement of a vocational goal is determined to be reasonably feasible, to enable such veteran to become, to the maximum extent feasible, employable and to obtain and maintain suitable employment, and

(B) the assistance authorized by this chapter [38 USCS §§ 3100 et seq.] for a veteran receiving any of the services described in clause (A) of this paragraph.

(Added Oct. 17, 1980, P. L. 96-466, Title I, § 101(a), 94 Stat. 2172; Oct. 28, 1986, P. L. 99-576, Title III, Part A, § 333(b)(1), 100 Stat. 3279; Dec. 18, 1989, P. L. 101-237, Title IV, § 423(b)(1)(A), 103 Stat. 2092; Aug. 6, 1991, P. L. 102-83, § 5(a), (c)(1), 105 Stat. 406; Oct. 9, 1996, P. L. 104-275, Title I, § 101(a), 110 Stat. 3323.)

HISTORY; ANCILLARY LAWS AND DIRECTIVES

Explanatory notes:
A prior § 3101 was redesignated by Act May 7, 1991, P. L. 102-40, Title IV, § 402(b)(1), 105 Stat. 238. For similar provisions, see 38 USCS § 5301.

Effective date of section:
Act Oct. 17, 1980, P. L. 96-466, Title VIII, § 802(a)(1), 94 Stat. 2217, provided that this section is effective on April 1, 1981.

Amendments:
1986. Act Oct. 28, 1986, in para. (6) inserted "currently" and, in para. (9)(A)(i), inserted "currently".
1989. Act Dec. 18, 1989, in paras. (4) and (9)(A), substituted "Secretary" for "Administrator".
1991. Act Aug. 6, 1991, redesignated this section, formerly 38 USCS § 1501, as 38 USCS § 3101, and amended the references in this section to reflect the redesignations made by § 5(a) of such Act (see Table III preceding 38 USCS § 101).
1996. Act Oct. 9, 1996 (effective and applicable as provided by § 101(j) of such Act, which appears as a note to this section), in para. (1), inserted ", resulting in substantial part from a disability described in section 3102(1)(A) of this title,", in para. (6), inserted "authorized under section 3120 of this title" and, in para. (7), inserted ", resulting in substantial part from a service-connected disability rated at 10 percent or more,".

Other provisions:
Effective date and application of Oct. 9, 1996 amendments. Act Oct. 9, 1996, P. L. 104-275, Title I, § 101(j), 110 Stat. 3325, provides:
"(1) Except as provided in paragraph (2), the amendments made by this section [for full classification, consult USCS Tables volumes] shall take effect on the date of the enactment of this Act.
"(2) The amendments made by subsection (a) (other than paragraph (2)), subsection (d) (other than subparagraphs (A) and (B) of paragraph (1)), and subsection (i) [amending 38 USCS §§ 3101(1), (7), 3104(a)(12), (b), (c), and 3120(b)] shall only apply with respect to claims of eligibility or entitlement to services and assistance (including claims for extension of such services and assistance) under chapter 31 of title 38, United States Code, received by the Secretary of Veterans Affairs on or after the date of the enactment of this Act, including those claims based on original applications, and applications seeking to reopen, revise, reconsider, or otherwise adjudicate or readjudicate on any basis claims for services and assistance under such chapter.".

CODE OF FEDERAL REGULATIONS

Department of Veterans Affairs—United States Government life insurance, 38 CFR Part 6.

38 USCS § 3101

Department of Veterans Affairs—National Service life insurance, 38 CFR Part 8.
Department of Veterans Affairs—Vocational rehabilitation and education, 38 CFR Part 21.

CROSS REFERENCES
This section is referred to in 38 USCS §§ 1728, 3695.

RESEARCH GUIDE
Am Jur:
77 Am Jur 2d, Veterans and Veterans' Laws § 72.

Law Review Articles:
Benefits for Conscientious Objectors. 19 Catholic Lawyer 62, Winter 1973.

§ 3102. Basic entitlement

A person shall be entitled to a rehabilitation program under the terms and conditions of this chapter [38 USCS §§ 3100 et seq.] if—
  (1) the person—
    (A) is—
      (i) a veteran who has a service-connected disability rated at 20 percent or more which was incurred or aggravated in service on or after September 16, 1940; or
      (ii) hospitalized or receiving outpatient medical care, services, or treatment for a service-connected disability pending discharge from the active military, naval, or air service, and the Secretary determines that—
        (I) the hospital (or other medical facility) providing the hospitalization, care, services, or treatment is doing so under contract or agreement with the Secretary concerned, or is under the jurisdiction of the Secretary of Veterans Affairs or the Secretary concerned; and
        (II) the person is suffering from a disability which will likely be compensable at a rate of 20 percent or more under chapter 11 of this title [38 USCS §§ 1101 et seq.]; and
    (B) is determined by the Secretary to be in need of rehabilitation because of an employment handicap; or
  (2) the person is a veteran who—
    (A) has a service-connected disability rated at 10 percent which was incurred or aggravated in service on or after September 16, 1940; and
    (B) is determined by the Secretary to be in need of rehabilitation because of a serious employment handicap.

(Added Oct. 17, 1980, P. L. 96-466, Title I, § 101(a), 94 Stat. 2173; Dec. 18, 1989, P. L. 101-237, Title IV, § 423(b)(1)(A), 103 Stat. 2092; Nov. 5, 1990, P. L. 101-508, Title VIII, Subtitle C, § 8021(a), 104 Stat. 1388-347; March 22, 1991, P. L. 102-16, § 3(a), 105 Stat. 49; Aug. 6, 1991, P. L. 102-83, § 5(a), 105 Stat. 406; Oct. 29, 1992, P. L. 102-568, Title IV, § 404(a), 106 Stat. 4338; Oct. 9, 1996, P. L. 104-275, Title I, § 101(b), 110 Stat. 3323.)

HISTORY; ANCILLARY LAWS AND DIRECTIVES

Explanatory notes:
A prior § 3102 was redesignated by Act May 7, 1991, P. L. 102-40, Title IV, § 402(b)(1), 105 Stat. 238. For similar provisions, see 38 USCS § 5302.

Effective date of section:
Act Oct. 17, 1980, P. L. 96-466, Title VIII, § 802(a)(1), 94 Stat. 2217, provided that this section is effective on April 1, 1981.

Amendments:
1989. Act Dec. 18, 1989, in paras. (1)(B) and (2), substituted "Secretary" for "Administrator".

1990. Act Nov. 5, 1990 (applicable as provided by § 8021(b) of such Act, which appears as a note to this section), in para. (1)(A) and (B), inserted "at a rate of 20 percent or more".

1991. Act March 22, 1991, in para. (1)(B), substituted "or receiving outpatient medical care, services, or treatment for a service-connected disability pending discharge from the active military, naval, or air service, and the Secretary determines that (i) the hospital (or other medical facility) providing the hospitalization, care, services, or treatment either is doing so under contract or agreement with the Secretary concerned or is under the jurisdiction of the Secretary of Veterans Affairs or the Secretary concerned, and (ii) the person is suffering from a disability which" for "for a service-connected disability in a hospital over which the Secretary concerned has jurisdiction pending discharge or release from active military, naval, or air service and is suffering from a disability which the Secretary determines".

Act Aug. 6, 1991, redesignated this section, formerly 38 USCS § 1502, as 38 USCS § 3102.

1992. Act Oct. 29, 1992 (effective 10/1/93, as provided by § 404(b) of such Act, which appears as a note to this section) substituted the text of this section for text which read:

"A person shall be entitled to a rehabilitation program under the terms and conditions of this chapter if such person—

"(1)(A) is a veteran who has a service-connected disability which is, or but for the receipt of retired pay would be, compensable at a rate of 20 percent or more under chapter 11 of this title and which was incurred or aggravated in service on or after September 16, 1940, or

"(B) is hospitalized or receiving outpatient medical care, services, or treatment for a service-connected disability pending discharge from the active military, naval, or air service, and the Secretary determines that (i) the hospital (or other medical facility) providing the hospitalization, care, services, or treatment either is doing so under contract or agreement with the Secretary concerned or is under the jurisdiction of the Secretary of Veterans Affairs or the Secretary concerned, and (ii) the person is suffering from a disability which will likely be compensable at a rate of 20 percent or more under chapter 11 of this title; and

"(2) is determined by the Secretary to be in need of rehabilitation because of an employment handicap.".

1996. Act Oct. 9, 1996 (effective on enactment, as provided by § 101(j) of such Act, which appears as 38 USCS § 3101 note), in para. (1)(A)(i),

38 USCS § 3102

substituted "rated at 20 percent or more" for "which is, or but for the receipt of retired pay would be, compensable at a rate of 20 percent or more under chapter 11 of this title and", in para. (2), in subpara. (A), substituted "rated at 10 percent" for "which is, or but for the receipt of retired pay would be, compensable at a rate of 10 percent under chapter 11 of this title and", and substituted subpara. (B) for one which read: "(B) has a serious employment handicap.".

Other provisions:
Application of 1990 amendments of para. (1). Act Nov. 5, 1990, P. L. 101-508, Title VIII, Subtitle C, § 8021(b), 104 Stat. 1388-347, provides: "The amendments made by this section [amending para. (1) of this section] shall apply to veterans and other persons originally applying for assistance under chapter 31 of title 38, United States Code [38 USCS §§ 3100 et seq.], on or after November 1, 1990.".

Effective date and application of 1992 amendment. Act Oct. 29, 1992, P. L. 102-568, Title IV, § 404(b), 106 Stat. 4338; Nov. 2, 1994, P. L. 103-446, Title VI, § 602(c)(1), 108 Stat. 4671 (effective as of 10/29/92, as provided by § 602(c)(2) of such Act), provides: "The amendment made by subsection (a) [amending this section] shall take effect on October 1, 1993, but shall not apply to veterans and other persons who originally applied for assistance under chapter 31 of title 38, United States Code [38 USCS §§ 3100 et seq.], before November 1, 1990.".

CODE OF FEDERAL REGULATIONS

Fiscal Service, Department of the Treasury—General regulations governing U. S. securities, 31 CFR Part 306.

Department of Veterans Affairs—General provisions, 38 CFR Part 1.

Department of Veterans Affairs—Vocational rehabilitation and education, 38 CFR Part 21.

CROSS REFERENCES

This section is referred to in 38 USCS §§ 3103, 3106, 3113, 3120.

RESEARCH GUIDE

Am Jur:
77 Am Jur 2d, Veterans and Veterans' Laws § 72.

INTERPRETIVE NOTES AND DECISIONS

1. Generally
2. Requirement that disability be service-connected
3. Charge for vocational training

1. Generally
Veteran, receiving benefits for disability incurred in course of vocational rehabilitation training, is not entitled to further training on basis of such injury. 1951 ADVA 871.

2. Requirement that disability be service-connected
Claimant was no longer entitled to vocational rehabilitation training where disability on which vocational handicap and need and feasibility of training was predicated was erroneously determined to be service-connected. 1944 ADVA 600.

Regulation's requirement that veteran's service-connected disability must "materially contribute" to veteran's employment handicap is inconsistent with statute and therefore in excess of Secretary's statutory authority; neither language nor plain meaning of statute requires that there be causal nexus between veteran's service-connected disability and veteran's employment in order for veteran to be entitled to chapter 31 vocational rehabilitation. Davenport v Brown (1995) 7 Vet App 476.

READJUSTMENT BENEFITS 38 USCS § 3103

3. Charge for vocational training
Charge for instruction of trainees which exceeded charges paid by other students pursuing same course or courses and receiving identical services was payable so long as proposed rate was reasonable and proffered services practicable and necessary to proper purpose. 1944 ADVA 580.

[§ 3102A]. [§ 1502A. Repealed]

HISTORY; ANCILLARY LAWS AND DIRECTIVES

The bracketed section number "3102A" was inserted to preserve numerical continuity following the section number redesignations made by Act Aug. 6, 1991, P. L. 102-83, § 5(a), 105 Stat. 406.

This section (Added Act Aug. 16, 1962, P. L. 87-591, § 1, 76 Stat. 393) was repealed by Act Aug. 26, 1965, P. L. 89-138, § 2(3), 79 Stat. 578. It provided for the rehabilitation of blind veterans. For similar provisions, see 38 USCS § 3103.

§ 3103. Periods of eligibility

(a) Except as provided in subsection (b), (c), or (d) of this section, a rehabilitation program may not be afforded to a veteran under this chapter [38 USCS §§ 3100 et seq.] after the end of the twelve-year period beginning on the date of such veteran's discharge or release from active military, naval, or air service.

(b)(1) In any case in which the Secretary determines that a veteran has been prevented from participating in a vocational rehabilitation program under this chapter [38 USCS §§ 3100 et seq.] within the period of eligibility prescribed in subsection (a) of this section because a medical condition of such veteran made it infeasible for such veteran to participate in such a program, the twelve-year period of eligibility shall not run during the period of time that such veteran was so prevented from participating in such a program, and such period of eligibility shall again begin to run on the first day following such veteran's recovery from such condition on which it is reasonably feasible, as determined under regulations which the Secretary shall prescribe, for such veteran to participate in such a program.

(2) In any case in which the Secretary determines that a veteran has been prevented from participating in a vocational rehabilitation program under this chapter [38 USCS §§ 3100 et seq.] within the period of eligibility prescribed in subsection (a) of this section because—

(A) such veteran had not met the requirement of a discharge or release from active military, naval or air service under conditions other than dishonorable before (i) the nature of such discharge or release was changed by appropriate authority, or (ii) the Secretary determined, under regulations prescribed by the Secretary, that such discharge or release was under conditions other than dishonorable, or

(B) such veteran's discharge or dismissal was, under section 5303 of this title, a bar to benefits under this title before the Secretary made a determination that such discharge or dismissal is not a bar to such benefits,

the twelve-year period of eligibility shall not run during the period of time that such veteran was so prevented from participating in such a program.

38 USCS § 3103

(3) In any case in which the Secretary determines that a veteran has been prevented from participating in a vocational rehabilitation program under this chapter [38 USCS §§ 3100 et seq.] within the period of eligibility prescribed in subsection (a) of this section because such veteran had not established the existence of a service-connected disability rated at 10 percent or more, the twelve-year period of eligibility shall not run during the period such veteran was so prevented from participating in such a program.

(c) In any case in which the Secretary determines that a veteran is in need of services to overcome a serious employment handicap, such veteran may be afforded a vocational rehabilitation program after the expiration of the period of eligibility otherwise applicable to such veteran if the Secretary also determines, on the basis of such veteran's current employment handicap and need for such services, that an extension of the applicable period of eligibility is necessary for such veteran and—

(1) that such veteran had not previously been rehabilitated to the point of employability;

(2) that such veteran had previously been rehabilitated to the point of employability but (A) the need for such services had arisen out of a worsening of such veteran's service-connected disability that precludes such veteran from performing the duties of the occupation for which such veteran was previously trained in a vocational rehabilitation program under this chapter [38 USCS §§ 3100 et seq.], or (B) the occupation for which such veteran had been so trained is not suitable in view of such veteran's current employment handicap and capabilities; or

(3) under regulations which the Secretary shall prescribe, that an extension of the period of eligibility of such veteran is necessary to accomplish the purposes of a rehabilitation program for such veteran.

(d) In any case in which the Secretary has determined that a veteran's disability or disabilities are so severe that the achievement of a vocational goal currently is not reasonably feasible, such veteran may be afforded a program of independent living services and assistance in accordance with the provisions of section 3120 of this title after the expiration of the period of eligibility otherwise applicable to such veteran if the Secretary also determines that an extension of the period of eligibility of such veteran is necessary for such veteran to achieve maximum independence in daily living.

(Added Oct. 17, 1980, P. L. 96-466, Title I, § 101(a), 94 Stat. 2173; Oct. 28, 1986, P. L. 99-576, Title III, Part A, § 333(b)(2), 100 Stat. 3279; Dec. 18, 1989, P. L. 101-237, Title IV, § 423(b)(1), 103 Stat. 2092; May 7, 1991, P. L. 102-40, Title IV, § 402(d)(1), 105 Stat. 239; Aug. 6, 1991, P. L. 102-83, § 5(a), (c)(1), 105 Stat. 406; Nov. 2, 1994, P. L. 103-446, Title XII, § 1201(d)(8), 108 Stat. 4684; Oct. 9, 1996, P. L. 104-275, Title I, § 101(c), 110 Stat. 3324.)

HISTORY; ANCILLARY LAWS AND DIRECTIVES

Explanatory notes:
A prior § 3103 was redesignated by Act May 7, 1991, P. L. 102-40, Title IV, § 402(b)(1), 105 Stat. 238. For similar provisions, see 38 USCS § 5303.

Effective date of section:
Act Oct. 17, 1980, P. L. 96-466, Title VIII, § 802(a)(1), 94 Stat. 2217, provided that this section is effective on April 1, 1981.

Amendments:
1986. Act Oct. 28, 1986, in subsec. (d), inserted "currently".
1989. Act Dec. 18, 1989, substituted "Secretary" for "Administrator", wherever appearing, in the entire section.
1991. Act May 7, 1991, amended the references in this section to reflect the redesignations made by §§ 401(a)(4) and 402(b) of such Act (see Table II preceding 38 USCS § 101).
Act Aug. 6, 1991, redesignated this section, formerly 38 USCS § 1503, as 38 USCS § 3103, and amended the references in this section to reflect the redesignations made by § 5(a) of such Act (see Table III preceding 38 USCS § 101).
1994. Act Nov. 2, 1994, in subsec. (b)(3), substituted "section 3102(1)(A)(i)" for "section 3102(1)(A)".
1996. Act Oct. 9, 1996 (effective on enactment, as provided by § 101(j) of such Act, which appears as 38 USCS § 3101 note), in subsec. (b)(3), substituted "rated at 10 percent or more" for "described in section 3102(1)(A)(i) of this title"; in subsec. (c), in the introductory matter, substituted "current" for "particular" and, in para. (2), substituted "veteran's current employment" for "veteran's employment"; and, in subsec. (d), substituted "in accordance with the provisions of section 3120 of this title" for "under this chapter".

CODE OF FEDERAL REGULATIONS

Fiscal Service, Department of the Treasury—General regulations governing U. S. securities, 31 CFR Part 306.

Office of the Secretary of Defense—Discharge Review Board (DRB) procedures and standards, 32 CFR Part 70.

Department of Veterans Affairs—Vocational rehabilitation and education, 38 CFR Part 21.

RESEARCH GUIDE
Am Jur:
77 Am Jur 2d, Veterans and Veterans' Laws § 72.

§ 3104. Scope of services and assistance

(a) Services and assistance which the Secretary may provide under this chapter [38 USCS §§ 3100 et seq.], pursuant to regulations which the Secretary shall prescribe, include the following:

(1) Evaluation, including periodic reevaluations as appropriate with respect to a veteran participating in a rehabilitation program, of the potential for rehabilitation of a veteran, including diagnostic and related services (A) to determine whether the veteran has an employment handicap or a serious employment handicap and whether a vocational goal is reasonably feasible for such veteran, and (B) to provide a basis for planning a suitable vocational rehabilitation program or a program of services and assistance to improve

the vocational rehabilitation potential or independent living status of such veteran, as appropriate.

(2) Educational, vocational, psychological, employment, and personal adjustment counseling.

(3) An allowance and other appropriate assistance, as authorized by section 3108 of this title.

(4) A work-study allowance as authorized by section 3485 of this title.

(5) Placement services to effect suitable placement in employment, and postplacement services to attempt to insure satisfactory adjustment in employment.

(6) Personal adjustment and work adjustment training.

(7)(A) Vocational and other training services and assistance, including individualized tutorial assistance, tuition, fees, books, supplies, handling charges, licensing fees, and equipment and other training materials determined by the Secretary to be necessary to accomplish the purposes of the rehabilitation program in the individual case.

(B) Payment for the services and assistance provided under subparagraph (A) of this paragraph shall be made from funds available for the payment of readjustment benefits.

(8) Loans as authorized by section 3112 of this title.

(9) Treatment, care, and services described in chapter 17 of this title [38 USCS §§ 1701 et seq.].

(10) Prosthetic appliances, eyeglasses, and other corrective and assistive devices.

(11) Services to a veteran's family as necessary for the effective rehabilitation of such veteran.

(12) For veterans with the most severe service-connected disabilities who require homebound training or self-employment, or both homebound training and self-employment, such license fees and essential equipment, supplies, and minimum stocks of materials as the Secretary determines to be necessary for such a veteran to begin employment and are within the criteria and cost limitations that the Secretary shall prescribe in regulations for the furnishing of such fees, equipment, supplies, and stocks.

(13) Travel and incidental expenses under the terms and conditions set forth in section 111 of this title, plus, in the case of a veteran who because of such veteran's disability has transportation expenses in addition to those incurred by persons not so disabled, a special transportation allowance to defray such additional expenses during rehabilitation, job seeking, and the initial employment stage.

(14) Special services (including services related to blindness and deafness) including—

(A) language training, speech and voice correction, training in ambulation, and one-hand typewriting;

(B) orientation, adjustment, mobility, reader, interpreter, and related services; and

(C) telecommunications, sensory, and other technical aids and devices.

(15) Services necessary to enable a veteran to achieve maximum independence in daily living.

(16) Other incidental goods and services determined by the Secretary to be necessary to accomplish the purposes of a rehabilitation program in an individual case.

(b) A rehabilitation program (including individual courses) to be pursued by a veteran shall be subject to the approval of the Secretary.
(Added Oct. 17, 1980, P. L. 96-466, Title I, § 101(a), 94 Stat. 2174; May 20, 1988, P. L. 100-323, § 11(a)(3)(A), 102 Stat. 568; Dec. 18, 1989, P. L. 101-237, Title IV, § 423(b)(1)(A), 103 Stat. 2092; March 22, 1991, P. L. 102-16, § 3(b)(1), 105 Stat. 49; June 13, 1991, P. L. 102-54, § 14(c)(3), 105 Stat. 285; Aug. 6, 1991, P. L. 102-83, § 5(a), (c)(1), 105 Stat. 406; Oct. 9, 1996, P. L. 104-275, Title I, § 101(d), 110 Stat. 3324.)

HISTORY; ANCILLARY LAWS AND DIRECTIVES

Explanatory notes:
A prior § 3104 was redesignated by Act May 7, 1991, P. L. 102-40, Title IV, § 402(b)(1), 105 Stat. 238. For similar provisions, see 38 USCS § 5304.

Effective date of section:
Act Oct. 17, 1980, P. L. 96-466, Title VIII, § 802(a)(1), 94 Stat. 2217, provided that this section is effective on April 1, 1981.

Amendments:
1988. Act May 20, 1988 (effective on the 60th day after enactment, as provided by § 16(b)(2) of such Act, which appears as a note to this section), in subsec. (a)(7), designated the existing provisions as subpara. (A), substituted a comma for the period following "case" and added "and (B) job-readiness skills development and counseling under section 14(a)(2) of the Veterans' Job Training Act (29 U.S.C. 1721 note) for a participant in a program of training under such Act.".

1989. Act Dec. 18, 1989, in subsecs. (a) and (c), substituted "Secretary" for "Administrator", wherever appearing.

1991. Act March 22, 1991 (applicable as provided by § 3(b)(2) of such Act, which appears as a note to this section), in subsec. (a)(7), inserted the subpara. designator "(A)", redesignated former cls. (A) and (B) as cls. (i) and (ii) and, in cl. (i) as redesignated, substituted "handling charges, licensing" for "and licensing", and added subpara. (B).

Act June 13, 1991, in subsec. (b), substituted "(29 U.S.C. 296a)" for "(29 U.S.C. 296)".

Act Aug. 6, 1991, redesignated this section, formerly 38 USCS § 1504, as 38 USCS § 3104, and amended the references in this section to reflect the redesignations made by § 5(a) of such Act (see Table III preceding 38 USCS § 101).

1996. Act Oct. 9, 1996 (effective and applicable as provided by § 101(j) of such Act, which appears as 38 USCS § 3101 note), in subsec. (a), in para. (1), substituted "the veteran has an employment handicap or" for "such veteran's disability or disabilities cause" and inserted "reasonably", in para. (7)(A), deleted "(i)" following "including" and deleted ", and (ii) job-readiness skills development and counseling under section 14(a)(2) of the Veterans' Job Training Act (29 U.S.C. 1721 note) for a participant in a program of training under such Act" following "case," and, in para. (12), substituted "For veterans with the most severe service-connected disabilities who require" for "For the most severely disabled veterans requiring"; deleted subsec. (b), which read: "(b) A program of independent living services and assistance may include the types of services and assistance described in section 702 of the Rehabilitation Act of 1973 (29 U.S.C. 796a)."; and redesignated subsec. (c) as new subsec. (b).

Other provisions:
Veterans pursuing program of vocational rehabilitation under former 38 USCS § 1504. Act Oct. 17, 1980, P. L. 96-466, Title VIII, § 802(a)(4), 105 Stat. 238, which appears as 38 USCS § 3100 note, provides that during the period beginning on Oct. 1, 1980, and ending on Mar. 31, 1981, the provisions of 38 USCS § 3108 shall apply to veterans pursuing a program of vocational rehabilitation training under this chapter in the same manner as former 38 USCS § 1504 applied to veterans pursuing such a program under this chapter on Sept. 30, 1980.

Effective dates and application of May 20, 1988 amendments. Act May 20,1988, P. L. 100-323, § 16, 102 Stat. 575, provides:

"(a) In general. Except as provided in subsection (b), the provisions of and amendments made by this Act [for full classification, consult USCS Tables volumes] shall take effect on the date of the enactment of this Act.

"(b) Exceptions. (1) The following provisions of or amendments made by this Act shall take effect for all of fiscal year 1988 and subsequent fiscal years:

"(A) Clause (5) of subsection (b) of section 2002A [now 4102A] of title 38, United States Code, as added by section 2(a)(2) of this Act.

"(B) Subsection (a) of section 2003A [now 4103A] of such title, as amended by section 2(e)(1)(A) of this Act.

"(C) Paragraphs (1), (2), and (3) of section 2004(a) [now 4104(a)] of such title, as amended by section 3(a) of this Act.

"(D) Paragraphs (2) through (5) of section 1774(a) [now 3674(a)] of such title, as added by section 13(a)(1) of this Act.

"(2) The provisions of and amendments made by sections 4 through 11 [for full classification, consult USCS Tables volumes] shall take effect on the 60th day after the date of the enactment of this Act.".

Application of 1991 amendments of subsec. (a)(7). Act March 22, 1991, P. L. 102-16, § 3(b)(2), 105 Stat. 49, provides: "The amendments made by this subsection [subsec. (a)(7) of this section] shall apply only to payments made on or after the date of the enactment of this Act.".

CODE OF FEDERAL REGULATIONS

Fiscal Service, Department of the Treasury—General regulations governing U. S. securities, 31 CFR Part 306.

Department of Veterans Affairs—Vocational rehabilitation and education, 38 CFR Part 21.

CROSS REFERENCES

This section is referred to in 38 USCS §§ 1163, 1524, 3105, 3106, 3117, 3120.

RESEARCH GUIDE

Am Jur:
77 Am Jur 2d, Veterans and Veterans' Laws §§ 72, 73, 79.

INTERPRETIVE NOTES AND DECISIONS

1. Generally
2. Relationship with other laws
3. Subsistence allowances

1. Generally

Person who receives retainer pay is entitled to receive increased pension at same time, with retainer pay in such cases to be considered as a basic award of pension and any increase to consist only of difference between retainer pay and total amount payable. 1945 ADVA 656.

2. Relationship with other laws

Veterans given on-the-job training by Federal agencies without being paid salary or wage were not rendering gratuitous or voluntary services within meaning of former 31 USC § 655, and such training of veterans without compensation was proper; allowances paid to veterans while in training was not salary for purposes of former 5 USC § 58, and thus veteran is entitled to receive salary or wages from agency in which he was training while at the same time receiving allowances in form of increased pension benefits. 1944 ADVA 576.

Regulation precluding retroactive induction into chapter 31 vocational rehabilitation program for period in which veteran received educational benefits under another VA program is impermissibly restrictive to extent it imposes limits on veteran's receipt of such benefits to period that does not correspond to effective date of disability award, as language § 5113(a) clearly commands. Bernier v Brown (1995) 7 Vet App 434, app dismd without op (1995, CA FC) 73 F3d 377, reported in full (1995, CA FC) 1995 US App LEXIS 36579.

VA regulation stating that flight training could only be authorized in degree curriculums in field of aviation that included required flight training was not inconsistent with statute since it gives Secretary broad discretion in implementing vocational rehabilitation programs. Clarke v Brown (1997) 10 Vet App 20.

3. Subsistence allowances

Veteran whose right to receive compensation had been suspended for failure to report for physical examination requested for compensation purposes was not barred from continuing training; but so long as he persisted in refusal to report for physical examination, he was limited to amount of subsistence allowance available under applicable regulation without any compensation or other benefit. 1948 ADVA 784.

Veteran pursuing training, who was determined to be employable, was entitled at that time to 2 months' postrehabilitation subsistance allowance, and subsequent re-entry by veteran into active military service during 2-month period did not deprive him of right to 2 months' allowance. 1952 ADVA 893.

Female veteran pursuing vocational rehabilitation training is not entitled to claim her husband as dependent for purposes of receiving increased subsistance allowance. 1952 ADVA 900.

§ 3105. Duration of rehabilitation programs

(a) In any case in which the Secretary is unable to determine whether it currently is reasonably feasible for a veteran to achieve a vocational goal, the period of extended evaluation under section 3106(c) of this title may not exceed twelve months, except that such period may be extended for additional periods of up to six months each if the Secretary determines before granting any such extension that it is reasonably likely that, during the period of any such extension, a determination can be made whether the achievement of a vocational goal is reasonably feasible in the case of such veteran.

(b) Except as provided in subsection (c) of this section, the period of a vocational rehabilitation program for a veteran under this chapter [38 USCS §§ 3100 et seq.] following a determination of the current reasonable feasibility of achieving a vocational goal may not exceed forty-eight months, except that the counseling and placement and postplacement services described in section 3104(a)(2) and (5) of this title may be provided for an additional period not to exceed eighteen months in any case in which the Secretary determines the provision of such counseling and services to be necessary to accomplish the purposes of a rehabilitation program in the individual case.

(c) The Secretary may extend the period of a vocational rehabilitation program for a veteran to the extent that the Secretary determines that an extension of such period is necessary to enable such veteran to achieve a vocational goal if the Secretary also determines—

(1) that such veteran had previously been rehabilitated to the point of employability but (A) such veteran's need for further vocational rehabilitation has arisen out of a worsening of such veteran's service-connected disability that precludes such veteran from performing the duties of the occupation for which such veteran had been so rehabilitated, or (B) the occupation for which such veteran had been so rehabilitated is not suitable in view of such veteran's current employment handicap and capabilities; or

(2) under regulations which the Secretary shall prescribe, that such veteran has a serious employment handicap and that an extension of such period is necessary to accomplish the purposes of a rehabilitation program for such veteran.

(d) Unless the Secretary determines that a longer period is necessary and likely to result in a substantial increase in a veteran's level of independence in daily living, the period of a program of independent living services and assistance for a veteran under this chapter [38 USCS §§ 3100 et seq.] (following a determination by the Secretary that such veteran's disability or disabilities are so severe that the achievement of a vocational goal currently is not reasonably feasible) may not exceed twenty-four months.

(Added Oct. 17, 1980, P. L. 96-466, Title I, § 101(a), 94 Stat. 2176; Oct. 28, 1986, P. L. 99-576, Title III, Part A, § 333(b)(3), 100 Stat. 3279; Dec. 18, 1989, P. L. 101-237, Title IV, § 423(b)(1)(A), 103 Stat. 2092; Aug. 6, 1991, P. L. 102-83, § 5(a), (c)(1), 105 Stat. 406; Oct. 9, 1996, P. L. 104-275, Title I, § 101(e), 110 Stat. 3324.)

HISTORY; ANCILLARY LAWS AND DIRECTIVES

Explanatory notes:
A prior § 3105 was redesignated by Act May 7, 1991, P. L. 102-40, Title IV, § 402(b)(1), 105 Stat. 238. For similar provisions, see 38 USCS § 5305.

Effective date of section:
Act Oct. 17, 1980, P. L. 96-466, Title VIII, § 802(a)(1), 94 Stat. 2217, provided that this section is effective on April 1, 1981.

Amendments:
1986. Act Oct. 28, 1986, in subsec. (a), inserted "currently"; in subsec. (b), inserted "current"; and in subsec. (d), inserted "currently".
1989. Act Dec. 18, 1989, substituted "Secretary" for "Administrator", wherever appearing, in the entire section.
1991. Act Aug. 6, 1991, redesignated this section, formerly 38 USCS § 1505, as 38 USCS § 3105, and amended the references in this section to reflect the redesignations made by § 5(a) of such Act (see Table III preceding 38 USCS § 101).

1996. Act Oct. 9, 1996 (effective on enactment, as provided by § 101(j) of such Act, which appears as 38 USCS § 3101 note), in subsec. (c)(1), substituted "veteran's current employment" for "veteran's employment".

CROSS REFERENCES

This section is referred to in 38 USCS §§ 3106, 3108.

RESEARCH GUIDE

Am Jur:

77 Am Jur 2d, Veterans and Veterans' Laws § 72.

§ 3106. Initial and extended evaluations; determinations regarding serious employment handicap

(a) The Secretary shall provide any veteran who has a service-connected disability rated at 10 percent or more and who applies for benefits under this chapter [38 USCS §§ 3100 et seq.] with an initial evaluation consisting of such services described in section 3104(a)(1) of this title as are necessary (1) to determine whether such veteran is entitled to and eligible for benefits under this chapter [38 USCS §§ 3100 et seq.], and (2) in the case of a veteran who is determined to be entitled to an eligible for such benefits, to determine—

(A) whether such veteran has a serious employment handicap, and

(B) whether the achievement of a vocational goal currently is reasonably feasible for such veteran if it is reasonably feasible to make such determination without extended evaluation.

(b) In any case in which the Secretary has determined that a veteran has a serious employment handicap and that the achievement of a vocational goal currently is reasonably feasible for such veteran, such veteran shall be provided an individualized written plan of vocational rehabilitation developed under section 3107(a) of this title.

(c) In any case in which the Secretary has determined that a veteran has a serious employment handicap but the Secretary is unable to determine, in an initial evaluation pursuant to subsection (a) of this section, whether or not the achievement of a vocational goal currently is reasonably feasible, such veteran shall be provided with an extended evaluation consisting of the services described in section 3104(a)(1) of this title, such services under this chapter [38 USCS §§ 3100 et seq.] as the Secretary determines necessary to improve such veteran's potential for participation in a program of services designed to achieve a vocational goal and enable such veteran to achieve maximum independence in daily living, and assistance as authorized by section 3108 of this title.

(d) In any case in which the Secretary has determined that a veteran has a serious employment handicap and also determines, following such initial and any such extended evaluation, that achievement of a vocational goal currently is not reasonably feasible, the Secretary shall determine whether the veteran is capable of participating in a program of independent living services and assistance under section 3120 of this title.

(e) The Secretary shall in all cases determine as expeditiously as possible whether the achievement of a vocational goal by a veteran currently is reasonably feasible. In the case of a veteran provided extended evaluation under subsection (c) of this section (including any periods of extensions under section 3105(a) of this title, the Secretary shall make such determination not later than the end of such extended evaluation or period of extension, as the case may be. In determining whether the achievement of a vocational goal currently is reasonably feasible, the Secretary shall resolve any reasonable doubt in favor of determining that such achievement currently is reasonably feasible.

(f) In connection with each period of extended evaluation of a veteran and each rehabilitation program for a veteran who is determined to have a serious employment handicap, the Secretary shall assign a Department of Veterans Affairs employee to be responsible for the management and followup of the provision of all services (including appropriate coordination of employment assistance under section 3117 of this title) and assistance under this chapter [38 USCS §§ 3100 et seq.] to such veteran.

(Added Oct. 17, 1980, P. L. 96-466, Title I, § 101(a), 94 Stat. 2176; Oct. 28, 1986, P. L. 99-576, Title III, Part A, § 333(b)(4), 100 Stat. 3279; Dec. 18, 1989, P. L. 101-237, Title IV, § 423(b)(1), 103 Stat. 2092; Aug. 6, 1991, P. L. 102-83, § 5(a), (c)(1), 105 Stat. 406; Nov. 2, 1994, P. L. 103-446, Title XII, § 1201(d)(9), 108 Stat. 4684; Oct. 9, 1996, P. L. 104-275, Title I, § 101(f)(1), 110 Stat. 3324.)

HISTORY; ANCILLARY LAWS AND DIRECTIVES

Explanatory notes:
A prior § 3106 was redesignated by Act May 7, 1991, P. L. 102-40, Title IV, § 402(b)(1), 105 Stat. 238. For similar provisions, see 38 USCS § 5306.

Effective date of section:
Act Oct. 17, 1980, P. L. 96-466, Title VIII, § 802(a)(1), 94 Stat. 2217, provided that this section is effective on April 1, 1981.

Amendments:
1986. Act Oct. 28, 1986, in subsecs. (a)–(d), inserted "currently", wherever appearing.
1989. Act Dec. 18, 1989, in subsecs. (a)–(e), substituted "Secretary" for "Administrator", wherever appearing; and in subsec. (e), substituted "Department of Veterans Affairs" for "Veterans' Administration".
1991. Act Aug. 6, 1991, redesignated this section, formerly 38 USCS § 1506, as 38 USCS § 3106, and amended the references in this section to reflect the redesignations made by § 5(a) of such Act (see Table III preceding 38 USCS § 101).
1994. Act Nov. 2, 1994, in subsec. (a), substituted "clause (i) or (ii) of section 3102(1)(A)" for "section 3102(1)(A) or (B)".
1996. Act Oct. 9, 1996 (effective on enactment, as provided by § 101(j) of such Act, which appears as 38 USCS § 3101 note), in subsec. (a), substituted "rated at 10 percent or more" for "described in clause (i) or (ii) of section 3102(1)(A) of this title"; in subsec. (b), deleted "counseling in accordance with" following "provided"; in subsec. (c), substituted "with an extended" for "with extended"; redesignated subsecs. (d) and (e) as subsecs. (e) and (f), respectively, and added new subsec. (d).

CROSS REFERENCES

This section is referred to in 38 USCS §§ 1163, 3105, 3107–3109, 3118, 3120, 4211.

RESEARCH GUIDE

Am Jur:
77 Am Jur 2d, Veterans and Veterans' Laws § 72.

§ 3107. Individualized vocational rehabilitation plan

(a) The Secretary shall formulate an individualized written plan of vocational rehabilitation for a veteran described in section 3106(b) of this title. Such plan shall be developed with such veteran and shall include, but not be limited to (1) a statement of long-range rehabilitation goals for such veteran and intermediate rehabilitation objectives related to achieving such goals, (2) a statement of the specific services (which shall include counseling in all cases) and assistance to be provided under this chapter [38 USCS §§ 3100 et seq.], (3) the projected date for the initiation and the anticipated duration of each such service, and (4) objective criteria and an evaluation procedure and schedule for determining whether such objectives and goals are being achieved.

(b) The Secretary shall review at least annually the plan formulated under subsection (a) of this section for a veteran and shall afford such veteran the opportunity to participate in each such review. On the basis of such review, the Secretary shall (1) redevelop such plan with such veteran if the Secretary determines, under regulations which the Secretary shall prescribe, that redevelopment of such plan is appropriate, or (2) disapprove redevelopment of such plan if the Secretary determines, under such regulations, that redevelopment of such plan is not appropriate.

(c)(1) Each veteran for whom a plan has been developed or redeveloped under subsection (a) or (b)(1), respectively, of this section or in whose case redevelopment of a plan has been disapproved under subsection (b)(2) of this section, shall be informed of such veteran's opportunity for a review as provided in paragraph (2) of this subsection.

(2) In any case in which a veteran does not agree to such plan as proposed, to such plan as redeveloped, or to the disapproval of redevelopment of such plan, such veteran may submit to the person described in section 3106(f) of this title a written statement containing such veteran's objections and request a review of such plan as proposed or redeveloped, or a review of the disapproval of redevelopment of such plan, as the case may be.

(3) The Secretary shall review the statement submitted under paragraph (2) of this subsection and the plan as proposed or as redeveloped, and, if applicable, the disapproval of redevelopment of the plan, and render a decision on such review not later than ninety days after the date on which such veteran submits such statement, unless the case is one for which a longer period for review, not to exceed 150 days after such veteran submits such statement, is allowed under regulations prescribed by the Secretary, in which case the Secretary shall render a decision no later than the last day of the period prescribed in such regulations.

(Added Oct. 17, 1980, P. L. 96-466, Title I, § 101(a), 94 Stat. 2177; Dec. 18, 1989, P. L. 101-237, Title IV, § 423(b)(1)(A), 103 Stat. 2092; Aug. 6, 1991, P.

38 USCS § 3107 VETERANS' BENEFITS

L. 102-83, § 5(a), (c)(1), 105 Stat. 406; Oct. 9, 1996, P. L. 104-275, Title I, § 101(f)(2)(A), 110 Stat. 3325.)

HISTORY; ANCILLARY LAWS AND DIRECTIVES

Explanatory notes:
A prior § 3107 was redesignated by Act May 7, 1991, P. L. 102-40, Title IV, § 402(b)(1), 105 Stat. 238. For similar provisions, see 38 USCS § 5307.

Effective date of section:
Act Oct. 17, 1980, P. L. 96-466, Title VIII, § 802(a)(1), 94 Stat. 2217, provided that this section is effective on April 1, 1981.

Amendments:
1989. Act Dec. 18, 1989, in subsecs. (a), (b) and (c)(3), substituted "Secretary" for "Administrator", wherever appearing.
1991. Act Aug. 6, 1991, redesignated this section, formerly 38 USCS § 1507, as 38 USCS § 3107, and amended the references in this section to reflect the redesignations made by § 5(a) of such Act (see Table III preceding 38 USCS § 101).
1996. Act Oct. 9, 1996 (effective on enactment, as provided by § 101(j) of such Act, which appears as 38 USCS § 3101 note), in subsec. (c)(2), substituted "3106(f)" for "3106(e)".

Other provisions:
Vocational rehabilitation programs. Act Oct. 17, 1980, P. L. 96-466, Title I, § 101(d), 94 Stat. 2186 (effective 10/17/80, as provided by § 802(a)(5) of such Act), provided:
"With respect to veterans who are participating in a program of vocational rehabilitation under chapter 31 of title 38, United States Code [38 USCS §§ 3100 et seq.], on March 31, 1981—

"(1) individualized written plans of vocational rehabilitation shall be formulated under section 1507 of such title (as amended by subsection (a)) [this section] for such veterans to the extent that and at such times as the Administrator determines that the formulation of such plans is feasible and on the basis of such priorities for the formulation of such plans as the Administrator shall prescribe; and

"(2) extensions may be granted a veteran under sections 1503(c) and 1505(c)(2) [now §§ 3103(c) and 3105(c)(2)] of such title (as amended by subsection (a)) without regard to the requirement for a determination of a serious employment handicap.".

Veterans pursuing program of vocational rehabilitation under former 38 USCS § 1507. Act Oct. 17, 1980, P. L. 96-466, Title VIII, § 802(a)(4), 105 Stat. 238, which appears as 38 USCS § 3100 note, provides that during the period beginning on Oct. 1, 1980, and ending on Mar. 31, 1981, the provisions of 38 USCS § 3112 shall apply to veterans pursuing a program of vocational rehabilitation training under this chapter in the same manner as former 38 USCS § 1507 applied to veterans pursuing such a program under this chapter on Sept. 30, 1980.

CODE OF FEDERAL REGULATIONS

Fiscal Service, Department of the Treasury—General regulations governing U. S. securities, 31 CFR Part 306.

Department of Veterans Affairs—Vocational rehabilitation and education, 38 CFR Part 21.

READJUSTMENT BENEFITS　　　　　　　　　　　　　　　　38 USCS § 3108

CROSS REFERENCES
This section is referred to in 38 USCS §§ 1524, 3106, 3120.

RESEARCH GUIDE
Am Jur:
77 Am Jur 2d, Veterans and Veterans' Laws § 72.

§ 3108. Allowances

(a)(1) Except in the case of a veteran who makes an election under subsection (f) of this section and subject to the provisions of paragraph (3) of this subsection, each veteran shall be paid a subsistence allowance in accordance with this section during a period determined by the Secretary to be a period of such veteran's participation under this chapter [38 USCS §§ 3100 et seq.] in a rehabilitation program.

(2) In any case in which the Secretary determines, at the conclusion of such veteran's pursuit of a vocational rehabilitation program under this chapter [38 USCS §§ 3100 et seq.], that such veteran has been rehabilitated to the point of employability, such veteran shall be paid a subsistence allowance, as prescribed in this section for full-time training for the type of program that the veteran was pursuing, for two months while satisfactorily following a program of employment services provided under section 3104(a)(5) of this title.

(3) A subsistence allowance may not be paid under this chapter [38 USCS §§ 3100 et seq.] to a veteran for any period during which such veteran is being provided with an initial evaluation under section 3106(a) of this title or during which such veteran is being provided only with counseling or with placement or postplacement services under section 3105(b) of this title.

(b)(1) Except as otherwise provided in this section, the Secretary shall determine the subsistence allowance to be paid to a veteran under this chapter [38 USCS §§ 3100 et seq.] in accordance with the following table, which shall be the monthly amount shown in column II, III, IV, or V (whichever is applicable as determined by the veteran's dependency status) opposite the appropriate type of program being pursued as specified in column I:

Column I Type of program	Column II No dependents	Column III One dependent	Column IV Two dependents	Column V More than two dependents
				The amount in column IV, plus the following for each dependent in excess of two:
Institutional training: Full-time	$366	$454	$535	$39

Three-quarter time ...	$275	$341	$400	$30
Half-time	$184	$228	$268	$20
Farm cooperative, apprentice, or other on-job training:				
Full-time	$320	$387	$446	$29
Extended evaluation:				
Full-time	$366	$454	$535	$39
Independent living training:				
Full-time	$366	$454	$535	$39
Three-quarter time ...	$275	$341	$400	$30
Half-time	$184	$228	$268	$20

(2) With respect to the fiscal year beginning on October 1, 1994, the Secretary shall provide a percentage increase in the monthly rates payable under paragraph (1) of this subsection equal to the percentage by which the Consumer Price Index (all items, United States city average published by the Bureau of Labor Statistics) for the 12-month period ending June 30, 1994, exceeds such Consumer Price Index for the 12-month period ending June 30, 1993.

(3) With respect to any fiscal year beginning on or after October 1, 1995, the Secretary shall continue to pay, in lieu of the rates payable under paragraph (1) of this subsection, the monthly rates payable under this subsection for the previous fiscal year and shall provide, for any such fiscal year, a percentage increase in such rates equal to the percentage by which—

(A) the Consumer Price Index (all items, United States city average) for the 12-month period ending on June 30 preceding the beginning of the fiscal year for which the increase is made, exceeds

(B) such Consumer Price Index for the 12-month period preceding the 12-month period described in subparagraph (A).

(c)(1) In any case in which the vocational rehabilitation program for a veteran includes training on the job by an employer in any month, such employer shall be required to submit to the Secretary a statement in writing showing any wage, compensation, or other income paid (directly or indirectly) by the employer to such veteran for such month. Based upon such written statement, the Secretary is authorized to reduce the subsistence allowance of such veteran to an amount considered equitable and just in accordance with criteria which the Secretary shall establish in regulations which the Secretary shall prescribe.

(2) A veteran pursuing on-job training or work experience as part of a vocational rehabilitation program in a Federal, State, or local government agency or federally recognized Indian tribe under the provisions of section 3115(a)(1) of this title without pay or for nominal pay shall be paid the ap-

propriate subsistence allowance rate provided in subsection (b) of this section for an institutional program.

(d)(1) The Secretary shall, in accordance with regulations which the Secretary shall prescribe, define full-time and each part-time status for veterans participating in rehabilitation programs under this chapter [38 USCS §§ 3100 et seq.].

(2) A veteran participating in extended evaluation on less than a full-time basis may be paid a proportional subsistence allowance in accordance with regulations which the Secretary shall prescribe.

(e) In any case in which a veteran is pursuing a rehabilitation program on a residential basis in a specialized rehabilitation facility, the Secretary may (1) pay to such facility the cost of such veteran's room and board in lieu of payment to such veteran of the subsistence allowance (not including any portion payable for any dependents) payable under subsection (b) of this section, and (2) pay to such veteran that portion of the allowance for dependents payable, as determined by such veteran's dependency status, under subsection (b) of this section for a full-time institutional program.

(f)(1)(A) In any case in which the Secretary determines that a veteran is eligible for and entitled to rehabilitation under this chapter [38 USCS §§ 3100 et seq.], to the extent that such veteran has remaining eligibility for and entitlement to educational assistance benefits under chapter 30 of this title [38 USCS §§ 3001 et seq.], such veteran may elect, as part of a vocational rehabilitation program under this chapter, to pursue an approved program of education and receive allowances and other forms of assistance equivalent to those authorized for veterans enrolled under chapter 30 of this title [38 USCS §§ 3001 et seq.], if the Secretary approves the educational, professional, or vocational objective chosen by such veteran for such program.

(B) In the event that such veteran makes such an election, the terms and conditions applicable to the pursuit of a comparable program of education and the payment of allowances and provision of assistance under chapter 30 of this title [38 USCS §§ 3001 et seq.] for such a comparable program shall be applied to the pursuit of the approved program of education under this chapter [38 USCS §§ 3100 et seq.].

(2) A veteran who is receiving an allowance pursuant to paragraph (1) of this subsection may not receive any of the services or assistance described in section 3104(a)(3), (7), and (8) of this title (other than an allowance and other assistance under this subsection).

(g)(1) Notwithstanding any other provision of this title and subject to the provisions of paragraph (2) of this subsection, no subsistence allowance may be paid under this section in the case of any veteran who is pursuing a rehabilitation program under this chapter [38 USCS §§ 3100 et seq.] while incarcerated in a Federal, State, or local penal institution for conviction of a felony.

(2) Paragraph (1) of this subsection shall not apply in the case of any veteran who is pursuing a rehabilitation program under this chapter [38 USCS

§§ 3100 et seq.] while residing in a halfway house or participating in a work-release program in connection with such veteran's conviction of a felony.

(h) Notwithstanding any other provision of this title, the amount of subsistence allowance, or other allowance under subsection (f) of this section, that may be paid to a veteran pursuing a rehabilitation program for any month for which such veteran receives compensation at the rate prescribed in section 1114(j) of this title as the result of hospital treatment (not including post-hospital convalescence) or observation at the expense of the Department of Veterans Affairs may not exceed, when added to any compensation to which such veteran is entitled for such month, an amount equal to the greater of—

(1) the sum of—

(A) the amount of monthly subsistence or other allowance that would otherwise be paid to such veteran under this section, and

(B) the amount of monthly compensation that would be paid to such veteran if such veteran were not receiving compensation at such rate as the result of such hospital treatment or observation; or

(2) the amount of monthly compensation payable under section 1114(j) of this title.

(i) Payment of a subsistence allowance may be made in advance in accordance with the provisions of section 3680(d) of this title.

(Added Oct. 17, 1980, P. L. 96-466, Title I, § 101(a), 94 Stat. 2178; Oct. 14, 1982, P. L. 97-306, Title II, § 205(a), 96 Stat. 1434; Oct. 19, 1984, P. L. 98-525, Title VII, § 703(a), 98 Stat. 2564; Oct. 24, 1984, P. L. 98-543, Title II, Part A, § 201, 98 Stat. 2740; Dec. 18, 1989, P. L. 101-237, Title IV, §§ 402(a), 423(b)(1), 103 Stat. 2078, 2092; March 22, 1991, P. L. 102-16, § 3(c), 105 Stat. 49; Aug. 6, 1991, P. L. 102-83, § 5(a), (c)(1), 105 Stat. 406; Oct. 29, 1992, P. L. 102-568, Title IV, § 405(a), (b), 106 Stat. 4338; Nov. 2, 1994, P. L. 103-446, Title VI, § 602(b), 108 Stat. 4671; Oct. 9, 1996, P. L. 104-275, Title I, § 101(g), 110 Stat. 3325.)

HISTORY; ANCILLARY LAWS AND DIRECTIVES

Explanatory notes:

A prior § 3108 was redesignated by Act May 7, 1991, P. L. 102-40, Title IV, § 402(b)(1), 105 Stat. 238. For similar provisions, see 38 USCS § 5308.

Amendments:

1982. Act Oct. 14, 1982, in subsec. (g)(2), inserted "not" following "shall" and deleted "if the Administrator determines that all the veteran's living expenses are being defrayed by a Federal, State, or local government", following "felony".

1984. Act Oct. 19, 1984, in subsec. (f)(1), in subpara. (A), inserted "30 or" following "benefits under chapter", and substituted "either chapter 30 or chapter 34" for "chapter 34" following enrolled under, and in subpara. (B), inserted "30 or".

Act Oct. 24, 1984 (effective 10/1/84, as provided by § 205 of such Act, which appears as a note to this section), in subsec. (b), substituted the table for one which read:

READJUSTMENT BENEFITS 38 USCS § 3108

"Column I Type of program	Column II No depend- ents	Column III One dependent	Column IV Two depend- ents	Column V More than two dependents
				The amount in column IV, plus the following for each dependent in excess of two:
Institutional training:				
Full-time	$282	$349	$411	$30
Three-quarter-time	212	262	308	23
Half-time	141	175	206	15
Farm cooperative, apprentice, or other on-job training:				
Full-time	246	297	343	22
Extended evaluation:				
Full-time	282	349	411	30
Independent: living training:				
Full-time	282	349	411	30
Three-quarter-time	212	262	308	23
Half-time	141	175	206	15".

1989. Act Dec. 18, 1989 (effective 1/1/90, as provided by § 402(b) of such Act, which appears as a note to this section), in subsec. (b), substituted the table for one which read:

"Column I Type of program	Column II No dependents	Column III One dependent	Column IV Two dependents	Column V More than two dependents
				The amount in column IV, plus the following for each dependent in excess of two:
Institutional training:				
Full-time	$310	$384	$452	$33
Three-quarter-time	233	288	339	25
Half-time	155	193	227	17
Farm cooperative, apprentice, or other on-job training:				
Full-time	271	327	377	24

85

38 USCS § 3108 — VETERANS' BENEFITS

Extended evaluation:				
Full-time	310	384	452	33
Independent living training:				
Full-time	310	384	452	33
Three-quarter time	233	288	339	25
Half-time	155	193	227	17".

Such Act further, in the entire section, substituted "Secretary" for "Administrator"; wherever appearing, and in subsec. (h), substituted "Department of Veterans Affairs" for "Veterans' Administration".

1991. Act March 22, 1991, in subsec. (c)(2), inserted ", State, or local government".

Act Aug. 6, 1991, redesignated this section, formerly 38 USCS § 1508, as 38 USCS § 3108, and amended the references in this section to reflect the redesignations made by § 5(a) of such Act (see Table III preceding 38 USCS § 101).

1992. Act Oct. 29, 1992 (effective 10/1/93, as provided by § 405(c) of such Act, which appears as a note to this section), in subsec.(b), designated the existing provisions as para. (1), substituted the table for one which read:

Column I	Column II	Column III	Column IV	Column V
Type of program	No dependents	One dependent	Two dependents	More than two dependents
				The amount in column IV, plus the following for each dependent in excess of two:
Institutional training:				
Full-time	$333	$413	$486	$35
Three-quarter time	$250	$310	$364	$27
Half-time	$167	$207	$244	$18
Farm cooperative, apprentice, or other on-job training:				
Full-time	$291	$352	$405	$26
Extended evaluation:				
Full-time	$333	$413	$486	$35
Independent living training:				
Full-time	$333	$413	$486	$35
Three-quarter time	$250	$310	$364	$27
Half-time	$167	$207	$244	$18

and added paras. (2) and (3).

1994. Act Nov. 2, 1994, in subsec. (c)(2), inserted "or federally recognized Indian tribe".

1996. Act Oct. 9, 1996 (effective on enactment, as provided by § 101(j) of such Act, which appears as 38 USCS § 3101 note), in subsec. (a)(2), substituted "while satisfactorily following a program of employment services provided under section 3104(a)(5) of this title" for "following the conclusion of such pursuit"; and, in subsec. (f)(1), in subpara. (A), inserted "eligible for and", substituted "chapter 30" for "chapter 30 or 34" following "benefits under", and substituted "chapter 30" for "either chapter 30 or chapter 34" following "enrolled under" and, in subpara. (B), substituted "chapter 30" for "chapter 30 or 34".

Other provisions:

Applicability of subsection (g)(1) to apportionments made before Oct. 17, 1980. Act Oct. 17, 1980, P. L. 96-466, Title I, § 101(c), 94 Stat. 2186 (effective 10/1/80, as provided by § 802(a)(5) of such Act), provided: "The provisions of section 1508(g)(1) of title 38, United States Code [subsec. (g)(1) of this section], as added by subsection (a), shall not apply to an apportionment made under section 3107(c) [now section 5307(c)] of such title before the date of the enactment of this Act.".

Effective date; veterans pursuing program of vocational rehabilitation under this chapter. Act Oct. 17, 1980, P. L. 96-466, Title VIII, § 802(a)(2)-(4), 94 Stat. 2217, located at 38 USCS § 3100 note, provided that the amendment made to this section by Act Oct. 17, 1980, is effective on Oct. 1, 1980; however, the provisions of this section, as in effect on Oct. 16, 1980, shall continue in effect until March 31, 1981. During the period beginning on Oct. 1, 1980 and ending on March 31, 1981, the provisions of this section, as amended by Act Oct. 17, 1980, shall apply to veterans pursuing a program of vocational rehabilitation training under Chapter 31 of Title 38 [38 USCS §§ 3100 et seq.], in the same manner as former 38 USCS § 1504 applied to veterans pursuing a program of vocational rehabilitation training under such Chapter 31 on Sept. 30, 1980.

Effective date of amendments made by Title II, Part A, of Act Oct. 24, 1984. Act Oct. 24, 1984, P. L. 98-543, Title II, Part A, § 205, 98 Stat. 2740, provides: "The amendments made by this part [amending this section and 38 USCS §§ 3482, 3492, 3532, 3542, 3686, 3687, and 3698] shall take effect as of October 1, 1984.".

Effective date of Dec. 18, 1989 amendments. Act Dec. 18, 1989, P. L. 101-237, Title IV, § 402(b), 103 Stat. 2078, provides: "The amendment made by this section [amending the table in subsec. (b) of this section] shall take effect on January 1, 1990.".

Effective date of 1992 amendments. Act Oct. 29, 1992, P. L. 102-568, Title IV, § 405(c), 106 Stat. 4339, provides: "The amendments made by subsections (a) and (b) [amending subsec. (b) of this section] shall take effect on October 1, 1993.".

CODE OF FEDERAL REGULATIONS

Fiscal Service, Department of the Treasury—General regulations governing U. S. securities, 31 CFR Part 306.

Department of Veterans Affairs—Vocational rehabilitation and education, 38 CFR Part 21.

CROSS REFERENCES

This section is referred to in 38 USCS §§ 3104, 3106, 3112, 3680.

RESEARCH GUIDE

Am Jur:
77 Am Jur 2d, Veterans and Veterans' Laws § 72.

§ 3109. Entitlement to independent living services and assistance

In any case in which the Secretary has determined under section 3106(e) of this title that the achievement of a vocational goal by a veteran currently is not reasonably feasible, such veteran shall be entitled, in accordance with the provisions of section 3120 of this title, to a program of independent living services and assistance designed to enable such veteran to achieve maximum independence in daily living.
(Added Oct. 17, 1980, P. L. 96-466, Title I, § 101(a), 94 Stat. 2181; Oct. 28, 1986, P. L. 99-576, Title III, Part A, § 333(b)(5), 100 Stat. 3279; Dec. 18, 1989, P. L. 101-237, Title IV, § 423(b)(1)(A), 103 Stat. 2092; Aug. 6, 1991, P. L. 102-83, § 5(a), (c)(1), 105 Stat. 406; Oct. 9, 1996, P. L. 104-275, Title I, § 101(f)(2)(B), 110 Stat. 3325.)

HISTORY; ANCILLARY LAWS AND DIRECTIVES

Explanatory notes:
A prior § 3109 was redesignated by Act May 7, 1991, P. L. 102-40, Title IV, § 402(b)(1), 105 Stat. 238. For similar provisions, see 38 USCS § 5309.

Effective date of section:
Act Oct. 17, 1980, P. L. 96-466, Title VIII, § 802(a)(1), 94 Stat. 2217, provided that this section is effective on April 1, 1981.

Amendments:
1986. Act Oct. 28, 1986, inserted "currently".
1989. Act Dec. 18, 1989, substituted "Secretary" for "Administrator".
1991. Act Aug. 6, 1991, redesignated this section, formerly 38 USCS § 1509, as 38 USCS § 3109, and amended the references in this section to reflect the redesignations made by § 5(a) of such Act (see Table III preceding 38 USCS § 101).
1996. Act Oct. 9, 1996 (effective on enactment, as provided by § 101(j) of such Act, which appears as 38 USCS § 3101 note) substituted "3106(e)" for "3106(d)".

RESEARCH GUIDE

Am Jur:
77 Am Jur 2d, Veterans and Veterans' Laws § 72.

§ 3110. Leaves of absence

The Secretary shall prescribe such regulations as the Secretary determines necessary for granting leaves of absence to veterans pursuing rehabilitation programs under this chapter [38 USCS §§ 3100 et seq.]. During authorized leaves of absence, a veteran shall be considered to be pursuing such program.
(Added Oct. 17, 1980, P. L. 96-466, Title I, § 101(a), 94 Stat. 2181; Dec. 18,

1989, P. L. 101-237, Title IV, § 423(b)(1)(A), 103 Stat. 2092; Aug. 6, 1991, P. L. 102-83, § 5(a), 105 Stat. 406.)

HISTORY; ANCILLARY LAWS AND DIRECTIVES

Explanatory notes:
A prior § 3110 was redesignated by Act May 7, 1991, P. L. 102-40, Title IV, § 402(b)(1), 105 Stat. 238. For similar provisions, see 38 USCS § 5310.

Effective date of section:
Act Oct. 17, 1980, P. L. 96-466, Title VIII, § 802(a)(1), 94 Stat. 2217, provided that this section is effective on April 1, 1981.

Amendments:
1989. Act Dec. 18, 1989, substituted "Secretary" for "Administrator", wherever appearing.
1991. Act Aug. 6, 1991, redesignated this section, formerly 38 USCS § 1510, as 38 USCS § 3110.

RESEARCH GUIDE

Am Jur:
77 Am Jur 2d, Veterans and Veterans' Laws § 72.

§ 3111. Regulations to promote satisfactory conduct and cooperation

The Secretary shall prescribe such rules and regulations as the Secretary determines necessary to promote satisfactory conduct and cooperation on the part of veterans who are pursuing rehabilitation programs under this chapter [38 USCS §§ 3100 et seq.]. In any case in which the Secretary determines that a veteran has failed to maintain satisfactory conduct or cooperation, the Secretary may, after determining that all reasonable counseling efforts have been made and are not reasonably likely to be effective, discontinue services and assistance unless the Secretary determines that mitigating circumstances exist. In any case in which such services and assistance have been discontinued, the Secretary may reinstitute such services and assistance only if the Secretary determines that—

(1) the cause of the unsatisfactory conduct or cooperation of such veteran has been removed; and

(2) the rehabilitation program which such veteran proposes to pursue (whether the same or revised) is suitable to such veteran's abilities, aptitudes, and interests.

(Added Oct. 17, 1980, P. L. 96-466, Title I, § 101(a), 94 Stat. 2181; Dec. 18, 1989, P. L. 101-237, Title IV, § 423(b)(1)(A), 103 Stat. 2092; Aug. 6, 1991, P. L. 102-83, § 5(a), 105 Stat. 406.)

HISTORY; ANCILLARY LAWS AND DIRECTIVES

Explanatory notes:
A prior § 3111 was redesignated by Act May 7, 1991, P. L. 102-40, Title IV, § 402(b)(1), 105 Stat. 238. For similar provisions, see 38 USCS § 5311.

38 USCS § 3111

Effective date of section:
Act Oct. 17, 1980, P. L. 96-466, Title VIII, § 802(a)(1), 94 Stat. 2217, provided that this section is effective on April 1, 1981.

Amendments:
1989. Act Dec. 18, 1989, in the introductory matter, substituted "Secretary" for "Administrator", wherever appearing.
1991. Act Aug. 6, 1991, redesignated this section, formerly 38 USCS § 1511, as 38 USCS § 3111.

CODE OF FEDERAL REGULATIONS

Fiscal Service, Department of the Treasury—General regulations governing U. S. securities, 31 CFR Part 306.

RESEARCH GUIDE

Am Jur:
77 Am Jur 2d, Veterans and Veterans' Laws § 72.

INTERPRETIVE NOTES AND DECISIONS

Placement of appellant in interrupted status in vocational rehabilitation program was proper where appellant exhibited unsatisfactory conduct and cooperation and VA personnel fulfilled their obligations by notifying him, attempting to discuss situation with him, and by making reasonable efforts to provide him with counseling. McRae v Brown (1996) 9 Vet App 229, app dismd (1996, CA FC) 106 F3d 424, reported in full (1996, CA FC) 1996 US App LEXIS 34798 and cert den (1997, US) 137 L Ed 2d 1057, 117 S Ct 1855.

§ 3112. Revolving fund loans

The revolving fund established pursuant to part VII of Veterans Regulation Numbered 1(a) is continued in effect, and may be used by the Secretary, under regulations prescribed by the Secretary, for making advances, not in excess of twice the amount of the full-time institutional monthly subsistence allowance for a veteran with no dependents (as provided in section 3108(b) of this title) to veterans pursuing rehabilitation programs under this chapter [38 USCS §§ 3100 et seq.]. Such advances, and advances from such fund made before the effective date of the Veterans' Rehabilitation and Education Amendments of 1980, shall bear no interest and shall be repaid in such installments, as may be determined by the Secretary, by proper deductions from future payments of compensation, pension, subsistence allowance, educational assistance allowance, or retirement pay.
(Added Oct. 17, 1980, P. L. 96-466, Title I, § 101(a), 94 Stat. 2181; Dec. 18, 1989, P. L. 101-237, Title IV, § 423(b)(1)(A), 103 Stat. 2092; Aug. 6, 1991, P. L. 102-83, § 5(a), (c)(1), 105 Stat. 406.)

HISTORY; ANCILLARY LAWS AND DIRECTIVES

References in text:
"The revolving fund established pursuant to part VII of Veterans Regulation Numbered 1(a)", referred to in this section, is the vocational rehabilitation revolving fund established by para. 8 of part VII of Veterans Regulation Numbered 1(a) as added by Act March 24, 1943, ch 22, § 2, 57 Stat. 44, which was classified to former chapter 12A of title 38. The appropria-

tion for such fund made by Act July 12, 1943, ch 218, § 1, 57 Stat. 434, was reduced by Act June 24, 1954, ch 359, Title I, § 101, in part, 68 Stat. 293, and repealed by Act Sept. 2, 1958, P. L. 85-857, § 14(82), 72 Stat. 1272. Part VII of Veterans Regulation Numbered 1(a) was repealed by § 14(67) of Act Sept. 2, 1958, P. L. 85-857, effective Jan. 1, 1959.
"The effective date of the Veterans' Rehabilitation and Education Amendments of 1980", referred to in this section, is the effective date of Act Oct. 17, 1980, P. L. 96-466, 94 Stat. 2171. The effective date of such Act is provided for in § 802, which appears as notes to 38 USCS §§ 3100, 3202, 3224, 3452, 3681, 4101, and 5314.

Explanatory notes:
A prior § 3112 was redesignated by Act May 7, 1991, P. L. 102-40, Title IV, § 402(b)(1), 105 Stat. 238. For similar provisions, see 38 USCS § 5312.

Amendments:
1989. Dec. 18, 1989, substituted "Secretary" for "Administrator", wherever appearing.
1991. Act Aug. 6, 1991, redesignated this section, formerly 38 USCS § 1512, as 38 USCS § 3112, and amended the references in this section to reflect the redesignations made by § 5(a) of such Act (see Table III preceding 38 USCS § 101).

Other provisions:
Effective date of section; transition provision. Act Oct. 17, 1980, P. L. 96-466, Title VIII, § 802(a)(2), (4), 94 Stat. 2217, located at 38 USCS § 3100 note, provided that this section is effective on Oct. 1, 1980 and during the period beginning on Oct. 1, 1980, and ending on March 31, 1981, the provisions of this section shall apply to veterans pursuing a program of vocational rehabilitation training under Chapter 31 of Title 38 [38 USCS §§ 3100 et seq.], in the same manner as former 38 USCS § 1507 applied to veterans pursuing a program of vocational rehabilitation training under such Chapter 31 on Sept. 30, 1980.

CODE OF FEDERAL REGULATIONS
Department of Veterans Affairs—Adjudication, 38 CFR Part 3.

CROSS REFERENCES
This section is referred to in 38 USCS § 3104.

§ 3113. Vocational rehabilitation for hospitalized members of the Armed Forces and veterans

(a) Services and assistance may be provided under this chapter [38 USCS §§ 3100 et seq.] to a person described in subparagraphs (A)(ii) and (B) of section 3102(1) of this title who is hospitalized pending discharge from active military, naval, or air service. In such cases, no subsistence allowance shall be paid.

(b) Services and assistance may be provided under this chapter [38 USCS §§ 3100 et seq.] to a veteran who is receiving care in a Department of Veterans Affairs hospital, nursing home, or domiciliary facility or in any other hospital or medical facility.

38 USCS § 3113

(Added Oct. 17, 1980, P. L. 96-466, Title I, § 101(a), 94 Stat. 2181; Dec. 18, 1989, P. L. 101-237, Title IV, § 423(b)(1)(B), 103 Stat. 2092; Aug. 6, 1991, P. L. 102-83, § 5(a), (c)(1), 105 Stat. 406; Nov. 2, 1994, P. L. 103-446, Title XII, § 1201(d)(10), 108 Stat. 4684.)

HISTORY; ANCILLARY LAWS AND DIRECTIVES

Explanatory notes:
A prior § 3113 was redesignated by Act May 7, 1991, P. L. 102-40, Title IV, § 402(b)(1), 105 Stat. 238. For similar provisions, see 38 USCS § 5313.

Effective date of section:
Act Oct. 17, 1980, P. L. 96-466, Title VIII, § 802(a)(1), 94 Stat. 2217, provided that this section is effective on April 1, 1981.

Amendments:
1989. Act Dec. 18, 1989, in subsec. (b), substituted "Department of Veterans Affairs" for "Veterans' Administration".
1991. Act Aug. 6, 1991, redesignated this section, formerly 38 USCS § 1513, as 38 USCS § 3113, and amended the references in this section to reflect the redesignations made by § 5(a) of such Act (see Table III preceding 38 USCS § 101).
1994. Act Nov. 2, 1994, in subsec. (a), substituted "subparagraphs (A)(ii) and (B) of section 3102(1)" for "section 3102(1)(B) and (2)".

RESEARCH GUIDE

Am Jur:
77 Am Jur 2d, Veterans and Veterans' Laws § 72.

§ 3114. Vocational rehabilitation outside the United States

Under regulations which the Secretary shall prescribe, a vocational rehabilitation program under this chapter [38 USCS §§ 3100 et seq.] may be provided outside the United States if the Secretary determines that such training is (1) necessary in the particular case to provide the preparation needed to render a veteran employable and enable such veteran to obtain and retain suitable employment, and (2) in the best interest of such veteran and the Federal Government.

(Added Oct. 17, 1980, P. L. 96-466, Title I, § 101(a), 94 Stat. 2182; Dec. 18, 1989, P. L. 101-237, Title IV, § 423(b)(1)(A), 103 Stat. 2092; Aug. 6, 1991, P. L. 102-83, § 5(a), 105 Stat. 406.)

HISTORY; ANCILLARY LAWS AND DIRECTIVES

Explanatory notes:
A prior § 3114 was redesignated by Act May 7, 1991, P. L. 102-40, Title IV, § 402(b)(1), 105 Stat. 238. For similar provisions, see 38 USCS § 5314.

Effective date of section:
Act Oct. 17, 1980, P. L. 96-466, Title VIII, § 802(a)(1), 94 Stat. 2217, provided that this section is effective on April 1, 1981.

Amendments:
1989. Act Dec. 18, 1989, substituted "Secretary" for "Administrator", wherever appearing.
1991. Act Aug. 6, 1991, redesignated this section, formerly 38 USCS § 1514, as 38 USCS § 3114.

RESEARCH GUIDE
Am Jur:
77 Am Jur 2d, Veterans and Veterans' Laws § 72.

§ 3115. Rehabilitation resources

(a) Notwithstanding any other provision of law, for the purpose of providing services under this chapter [38 USCS §§ 3100 et seq.], the Secretary may—

(1) use the facilities of any Federal agency (including the Department of Veterans Affairs), of any State or local government agency receiving Federal financial assistance, or of any federally recognized Indian tribe, to provide training or work experience as part or all of a veteran's vocational rehabilitation program without pay or for nominal pay in any case in which the Secretary determines that such training or work experience is necessary to accomplish such veteran's rehabilitation;

(2) use the facilities, staff, and other resources of the Department of Veterans Affairs;

(3) employ such additional personnel and experts as the Secretary considers necessary; and

(4) use the facilities and services of any Federal, State, or other public agency, any agency maintained by joint Federal and State contributions, any federally recognized Indian tribe, any public or private institution or establishment, and any private individual.

(b)(1) While pursuing on-job training or work experience under subsection (a)(1) of this section at a Federal agency, a veteran shall be considered to be an employee of the United States for the purposes of the benefits of chapter 81 of title 5 [5 USCS §§ 8101 et seq.], but not for the purposes of laws administered by the Office of Personnel Management.

(2) Except as provided in chapter 17 of this title [38 USCS §§ 1701 et seq.], hospital care and medical services provided under this chapter [38 USCS §§ 3100 et seq.] shall be furnished in facilities over which the Secretary has direct jurisdiction.

(3) Use of the facilities of a State or local government agency under subsection (a)(1) of this section or use of facilities and services under subsection (a)(4) of this section, shall be procured through contract, agreement, or other cooperative arrangement.

(4) The Secretary shall prescribe regulations providing for the monitoring of training and work experiences provided under such subsection (a)(1) at State or local government agencies and otherwise ensuring that such training or work experience is in the best interest of the veteran and the Federal Government.

38 USCS § 3115

(c) For purposes of this section, the term "federally recognized Indian tribe" means any Indian tribe, band, nation, pueblo, or other organized group or community, including any Alaska Native village or regional corporation as defined in or established pursuant to the Alaska Native Claims Settlement Act, which is recognized as eligible for the special programs and services provided by the United States to Indians because of their status as Indians.

(Added Oct. 17, 1980, P. L. 96-466, Title I, § 101(a), 94 Stat. 2182; Nov. 18, 1988, P. L. 100-689, Title II, § 201, 102 Stat. 4175; Dec. 18, 1989, P. L. 101-237, Title IV, § 423(b)(1), 103 Stat. 2092; Aug. 6, 1991, P. L. 102-83, § 5(a), 105 Stat. 406; Nov. 2, 1994, P. L. 103-446, Title VI, § 602(a), 108 Stat. 4671.)

HISTORY; ANCILLARY LAWS AND DIRECTIVES

References in text:
The "Alaska Native Claims Settlement Act", referred to in this section, is Act Dec. 18, 1971, P. L. 92-203, 85 Stat. 688, which appears generally as 43 USCS §§ 1601 et seq. For full classification of this Act, consult USCS Tables volumes.

Explanatory notes:
A prior § 3115 was redesignated by Act May 7, 1991, P. L. 102-40, Title IV, § 402(b)(1), 105 Stat. 238. For similar provisions, see 38 USCS § 5315.

Effective date of section:
Act Oct. 17, 1980, P. L. 96-466, Title VIII, § 802(a)(1), 94 Stat. 2217, provided that this section is effective on April 1, 1981.

Amendments:
1988. Act Nov. 18, 1988, in subsec. (a)(1), inserted ", or of any State or local government agency receiving Federal financial assistance," after "Administration)"; and in subsec. (b), in para. (1), inserted "at a Federal agency", and substituted paras. (3) and (4) for former para. (3) which read: "Use of facilities and services under clause (4) of subsection (a) of this section, shall be procured through contract, agreement, or other cooperative arrangement.".

1989. Act Dec. 18, 1989, substituted "Secretary" for "Administrator", wherever appearing; and in subsec. (a), substituted "Department of Veterans Affairs" for "Veterans' Administration".

1991. Act Aug. 6, 1991, redesignated this section, formerly 38 USCS § 1515, as 38 USCS § 3115.

1994. Act Nov. 2, 1994, in subsec. (a), in para. (1), deleted "or" following "Veterans Affairs)" and inserted "or of any federally recognized Indian tribe,", and, in para. (4), inserted "any federally recognized Indian tribe,"; and added subsec. (c).

CODE OF FEDERAL REGULATIONS

Department of Veterans Affairs—General provisions, 38 CFR Part 1.

CROSS REFERENCES

This section is referred to in 38 USCS § 3108.

RESEARCH GUIDE

Am Jur:
77 Am Jur 2d, Veterans and Veterans' Laws §§ 63, 72.

§ 3116. Promotion of employment and training opportunities

(a) The Secretary shall actively promote the development and establishment of employment, training, and other related opportunities for (1) veterans who are participating or who have participated in a rehabilitation program under this chapter [38 USCS §§ 3100 et seq.], (2) veterans with service-connected disabilities, and (3) other veterans to whom the employment emphases set forth in chapter 42 of this title [38 USCS §§ 4211 et seq.] apply. The Secretary shall promote the development and establishment of such opportunities through Department of Veterans Affairs staff outreach efforts to employers and through Department of Veterans Affairs coordination with Federal, State, and local governmental agencies and appropriate nongovernmental organizations. In carrying out the provisions of this subsection with respect to veterans referred to in clause (3) of the first sentence of this subsection, the Secretary shall place particular emphasis on the needs of categories of such veterans on the basis of applicable rates of unemployment.

(b)(1) The Secretary, pursuant to regulations prescribed in accordance with paragraph (3) of this subsection, may make payments to employers for providing on-job training to veterans who have been rehabilitated to the point of employability in individual cases in which the Secretary determines that such payment is necessary to obtain needed on-job training or to begin employment. Such payments may not exceed the direct expenses incurred by such employers in providing such on-job training or employment opportunity.

(2) In any case in which a veteran described in paragraph (1) of this subsection participates in on-job training described in such paragraph that satisfies the criteria for payment of a training assistance allowance under section 3687 of this title, such veteran shall, to the extent that such veteran has remaining eligibility for and entitlement to such allowance, be paid such allowance.

(3) The Secretary shall prescribe regulations under this subsection in consultation with the Secretary of Labor and, in prescribing such regulations, shall take into consideration the provisions of title V of the Rehabilitation Act of 1973 (29 U.S.C. ch. 16, subch. V [29 USCS §§ 791 et seq.]) and section 4212 of this title, and regulations prescribed under such provisions.

(Added Oct. 17, 1980, P. L. 96-466, Title I, § 101(a), 94 Stat. 2182; Dec. 18, 1989, P. L. 101-237, Title IV, § 423(b)(1), 103 Stat. 2092; Aug. 6, 1991, P. L. 102-83, § 5(a), (c)(1), 105 Stat. 406.)

HISTORY; ANCILLARY LAWS AND DIRECTIVES

Explanatory notes:
A prior § 3116 was redesignated by Act May 7, 1991, P. L. 102-40, Title IV, § 402(b)(1), 105 Stat. 238. For similar provisions, see 38 USCS § 5316.

38 USCS § 3116

Effective date of section:
Act Oct. 17, 1980, P. L. 96-466, Title VIII, § 802(a)(2), 94 Stat. 2217, provided that this section is effective on Oct. 1, 1980.

Amendments:
1989. Act Dec. 18, 1989, substituted "Secretary" and "Department of Veterans Affairs" for "Administrator" and "Veterans' Administration", respectively, wherever appearing.

1991. Act Aug. 6, 1991, redesignated this section, formerly 38 USCS § 1516, as 38 USCS § 3116, and amended the references in this section to reflect the redesignations made by § 5(a) of such Act (see Table III preceding 38 USCS § 101).

Other provisions:
Coordination of benefits available to veterans for job training. Act Jan. 13, 1986, P. L. 99-238, Title II, § 202, 99 Stat. 1768; Aug. 6, 1991, P. L. 102-83, §§ 5(c)(2), 6(g), 105 Stat. 406, 408, provides:

"(a) In general. In carrying out section 1516(b) of title 38, United States Code [subsec. (b) of this section], the Secretary of Veterans Affairs shall take all feasible steps to establish and encourage, for veterans who are eligible to have payments made on their behalf under such section, the development of training opportunities through programs of job training consistent with the provisions of the Veterans' Job Training Act [29 USCS § 1721 note] (as redesignated by section 201(a)(1) of this Act) so as to utilize programs of job training established by employers pursuant to such Act [29 USCS § 1721 note].

"(b) Directive. In carrying out such Act [29 USCS § 1721 note], the Secretary of Veterans Affairs shall take all feasible steps to ensure that, in the cases of veterans who are eligible to have payments made on their behalf under both such Act [29 USCS § 1721 note] and section 1516(b) of title 38, United States Code [subsec. (b) of this section], the authority under such section is utilized, to the maximum extent feasible and consistent with the veteran's best interests, to make payments to employers on behalf of such veterans.".

RESEARCH GUIDE

Am Jur:
77 Am Jur 2d, Veterans and Veterans' Laws § 72.

§ 3117. Employment assistance

(a)(1) A veteran with a service-connected disability rated at 10 percent or more who has participated in a vocational rehabilitation program under this chapter [38 USCS §§ 3100 et seq.] or a similar program under the Rehabilitation Act of 1973 (29 U.S.C. 701 et seq.) and who the Secretary has determined to be employable shall be furnished assistance in obtaining employment consistent with such veteran's abilities, aptitudes, interests, and employment handicap, including assistance necessary to insure that such veteran receives the benefit of any applicable provisions of law or regulation providing for special consideration or emphasis or preference for such veteran in employment or training.

(2) Assistance provided under this subsection may include—
(A) direct placement of such veteran in employment;
(B) utilization of the services of disabled veterans outreach program specialists under section 4103A of this title; and
(C) utilization of the job development and placement services of (i) programs under the Rehabilitation Act of 1973 [29 USCS §§ 701 et seq.], (ii) the State employment service and the Veterans' Employment Service of the Department of Labor, (iii) the Office of Personnel Management, (iv) any other public or nonprofit organization having placement services available, and (v) any for-profit entity in a case in which the Secretary has determined that services necessary to provide such assistance are available from such entity and that comparably effective services are not available, or cannot be obtained cost-effectively, from the entities described in subclauses (i) through (iv) of this clause.

(b)(1) In any case in which a veteran has completed a vocational rehabilitation program for self-employment in a small business enterprise under this chapter [38 USCS §§ 3100 et seq.], the Secretary shall assist such veteran in securing, as appropriate, a loan under subchapter IV of chapter 37 of this title [38 USCS §§ 3741 et seq.] and shall cooperate with the Small Business Administration to assist such veteran to secure a loan for the purchase of equipment needed to establish such veteran's own business and to insure that such veteran receives the special consideration provided for in section 8 of the Small Business Act (15 U.S.C. 633(b)).

(2) In the case of a veteran described in clause (12) of section 3104(a) of this title who has trained under a State rehabilitation program with the objective of self-employment in a small business enterprise, the Secretary may, subject to the limitations and criteria provided for in such clause, provide such veteran with such supplementary equipment and initial stocks and supplies as are determined to be needed by such veteran if such supplementary equipment and initial stocks and supplies, or assistance in acquiring them, are not available through the State program or other sources.

(Added Oct. 17, 1980, P. L. 96-466, Title I, § 101(a), 94 Stat. 2183; Nov. 3, 1981, P. L. 97-72, Title III, § 303(k), 95 Stat. 1060; Nov. 18, 1988, P. L. 100-689, Title II, § 202(a), 102 Stat. 4175; Dec. 18, 1989, P. L. 101-237, Title IV, § 423(b)(1)(A), 103 Stat. 2092; June 13, 1991, P. L. 102-54, § 14(c)(4), 105 Stat. 285; Aug. 6, 1991, P. L. 102-83, § 5(a), (c)(1), 105 Stat. 406; Oct. 9, 1996, P. L. 104-275, Title I, § 101(h), 110 Stat. 3325.)

HISTORY; ANCILLARY LAWS AND DIRECTIVES

Explanatory notes:
A prior § 3117 was redesignated by Act May 7, 1991, P. L. 102-40, Title IV, § 402(b)(1), 105 Stat. 238. For similar provisions, see 38 USCS § 5317.

Effective date of section:
Act Oct. 17, 1980, P. L. 96-466, Title VIII, § 802(a)(1), 94 Stat. 2217, provided that this section is effective on April 1, 1981.

38 USCS § 3117

Amendments:
1981. Act Nov. 3, 1981 (effective 180 days after enactment, as provided by § 305 of such Act, which appears as 38 USCS § 3741 note), in subsec. (b)(1), inserted "shall assist such veteran in securing, as appropriate, a loan under subchapter IV of chapter 37 of this title and".

1988. Act Nov. 18, 1988 in subsec. (a)(2)(C), deleted "and" following "Management," and inserted ", and (v) any for-profit entity in a case in which the Administrator has determined that services necessary to provide such assistance are available from such entity and that comparably effective services are not available, or cannot be obtained cost-effectively, from the entities described in subclauses (i) through (iv) of this clause.".

1989. Act Dec. 18, 1989, substituted "Secretary" for "Administrator", wherever appearing.

1991. Act June 13, 1991, in subsec. (a), in para. (1), inserted "(29 U.S.C. 701 et seq.)" and, in para. (2)(C), deleted the second concluding period.

Act Aug. 6, 1991, redesignated this section, formerly 38 USCS § 1517, as 38 USCS § 3117, and amended the references in this section to reflect the redesignations made by § 5(a) of such Act (see Table III preceding 38 USCS § 101).

1996. Act Oct. 9, 1996 (effective on enactment, as provided by § 101(j) of such Act, which appears as 38 USCS § 3101 note), in subsec. (a)(1), inserted "rated at 10 percent or more".

Other provisions:
Authority of the Administrator to promulgate regulations. For the authority and effective date for the Administrator of Veterans' Affairs to promulgate regulations under 38 USCS §§ 3741 et seq., see § 305 of Act Nov. 3, 1981, which appears as 38 USCS § 3741 note.

CROSS REFERENCES
This section is referred to in 38 USCS § 3106.

RESEARCH GUIDE
Am Jur:
77 Am Jur 2d, Veterans and Veterans' Laws § 72.

§ 3118. Personnel training, development, and qualifications

(a) The Secretary shall provide a program of ongoing professional training and development for Department of Veterans Affairs counseling and rehabilitation personnel engaged in providing rehabilitation services under this chapter [38 USCS §§ 3100 et seq.]. The objective of such training shall be to insure that rehabilitation services for disabled veterans are provided in accordance with the most advanced knowledge, methods, and techniques available for the rehabilitation of handicapped persons. For this purpose, the Secretary may employ the services of consultants and may make grants to and contract with public or private agencies (including institutions of higher learning) to conduct such training and development.

(b) The Secretary shall coordinate with the Commissioner of the Rehabilitation Services Administration in the Department of Education and the Assistant Secretary for Veterans' Employment in the Department of Labor in planning and carrying out personnel training in areas of mutual programmatic concern.

(c) Notwithstanding any other provision of law, the Secretary shall establish such qualifications for personnel providing evaluation and rehabilitation services to veterans under this chapter [38 USCS §§ 3100 et seq.] and for employees performing the functions described in section 3106(f) of this title as the Secretary determines are necessary and appropriate to insure the quality of rehabilitation programs under this chapter. In establishing such qualifications, the Secretary shall take into account the qualifications established for comparable personnel under the Rehabilitation Act of 1973 (29 U.S.C. ch. 16) [29 USCS §§ 701 et seq.].

(Added Oct. 17, 1980, P. L. 96-466, Title I, § 101(a), 94 Stat. 2184; Dec. 18, 1989, P. L. 101-237, Title IV, § 423(b)(1), 103 Stat. 2092; Aug. 6, 1991, P. L. 102-83, § 5(a), (c)(1), 105 Stat. 406; Oct. 9, 1996, P. L. 104-275, Title I, § 101(f)(2)(C), 110 Stat. 3325.)

HISTORY; ANCILLARY LAWS AND DIRECTIVES

Explanatory notes:
A prior § 3118 was redesignated by Act May 7, 1991, P. L. 102-40, Title IV, § 402(b)(1), 105 Stat. 238. For similar provisions, see 38 USCS § 5318.

Effective date of section:
Act Oct. 17, 1980, P. L. 96-466, Title VIII, § 802(a)(2), 94 Stat. 2217, provided that this section is effective on Oct. 1, 1980.

Amendments:
1989. Act Dec. 18, 1989, substituted "Secretary" for "Administrator" wherever appearing; and in subsec. (a), substituted "Department of Veterans Affairs" for "Veterans' Administration".
1991. Act Aug. 6, 1991, redesignated this section, formerly 38 USCS § 1518, as 38 USCS § 3118, and amended the references in this section to reflect the redesignations made by § 5(a) of such Act (see Table III preceding 38 USCS § 101).
1996. Act Oct. 9, 1996 (effective on enactment, as provided by § 101(j) of such Act, which appears as 38 USCS § 3101 note), in subsec. (c), substituted "3106(f)" for "3106(e)".

RESEARCH GUIDE

Am Jur:
77 Am Jur 2d, Veterans and Veterans' Laws § 72.

§ 3119. Rehabilitation research and special projects

(a) The Secretary shall carry out an ongoing program of activities for the purpose of advancing the knowledge, methods, techniques, and resources available for use in rehabilitation programs for veterans. For this purpose, the Secretary shall conduct and provide support for the development or conduct, or both the development and conduct, of—

(1) studies and research concerning the psychological, educational, employment, social, vocational, industrial, and economic aspects of the rehabilitation of disabled veterans, including new methods of rehabilitation; and

(2) projects which are designed to increase the resources and potential for accomplishing the rehabilitation of disabled veterans.

(b) For the purpose specified in subsection (a) of this section, the Secretary is authorized to make grants to or contract with public or nonprofit agencies, including institutions of higher learning.

(c) The Secretary shall cooperate with the Commissioner of the Rehabilitation Services Administration and the Director of the Institute of Handicapped Research in the Department of Education, the Assistant Secretary for Veterans' Employment in the Department of Labor, and the Secretary of Health and Human Services regarding rehabilitation studies, research, and special projects of mutual programmatic concern.

(Added Oct. 17, 1980, P. L. 96-466, Title I, § 101(a), 94 Stat. 2184; Dec. 18, 1989, P. L. 101-237, Title IV, § 423(b)(1)(A), 103 Stat. 2092; Aug. 6, 1991, P. L. 102-83, § 5(a), 105 Stat. 406.)

HISTORY; ANCILLARY LAWS AND DIRECTIVES

Effective date of section:
Act Oct. 17, 1980, P. L. 96-466, Title VIII, § 802(a)(2), 94 Stat. 2217, provided that this section is effective on Oct. 1, 1980.

Amendments:
1989. Act Dec. 18, 1989, substituted "Secretary" for "Administrator", wherever appearing.
1991. Act Aug. 6, 1991, redesignated this section, formerly 38 USCS § 1519, as 38 USCS § 3119.

RESEARCH GUIDE

Am Jur:
77 Am Jur 2d, Veterans and Veterans' Laws § 72.

§ 3120. Program of independent living services and assistance

(a) The Secretary may, under contracts with entities described in subsection (f) of this section, or through facilities of the Veterans Health Administration, which possess a demonstrated capability to conduct programs of independent living services for severely handicapped persons, provide, under regulations which the Secretary shall prescribe, programs of independent living services and assistance under this chapter, in various geographic regions of the United States, to veterans described in subsection (b) of this section.

(b) A program of independent living services and assistance may be made available under this section only to a veteran who has a serious employment handicap resulting in substantial part from a service-connected disability described in section 3102(1)(A)(i) of this title and with respect to whom it is determined under section 3106(d) or (e) of this title that the achievement of a vocational goal currently is not reasonably feasible.

(c) The Secretary shall, to the maximum extent feasible, include among those veterans who are provided with programs of independent living services and assistance under this section substantial numbers of veterans described in subsection (b) of this section who are receiving long-term care in Department of Veterans Affairs hospitals and nursing homes and in nursing homes with which the Secretary contracts for the provision of care to veterans.

(d) A program of independent living services and assistance for a veteran shall consist of such services described in section 3104(a) and (b) of this title as the Secretary determines necessary to enable such veteran to achieve maximum independence in daily living. Such veteran shall have the same rights with respect to an individualized written plan of services and assistance as are afforded veterans under section 3107 of this title.

(e) Programs of independent living services and assistance shall be initiated for no more than five hundred veterans in each fiscal year, and the first priority in the provision of such programs shall be afforded to veterans for whom the reasonable feasibility of achieving a vocational goal is precluded solely as a result of a service-connected disability.

(f) Entities described in this subsection are (1) public or nonprofit agencies or organizations, and (2) for-profit entities in cases in which the Secretary determines that services comparable in effectiveness to services available from such an entity are not available, or cannot be obtained cost-effectively from, public or nonprofit agencies or through facilities of the Veterans Health Administration.

(Added Oct. 17, 1980, P. L. 96-466, Title I, § 101(a), 94 Stat. 2185; Oct. 28, 1986, P. L. 99-576, Title III, Part A, § 333(a), (b)(6), (c), 100 Stat. 3279; Nov. 18, 1988, P. L. 100-689, Title II, § 202(b), 102 Stat. 4176; Dec. 18, 1989, P. L. 101-237, Title IV, §§ 404, 423(b)(1), 103 Stat. 2080, 2092; Aug. 6, 1991, P. L. 102-83, § 5(a), (c)(1), 105 Stat. 406; Nov. 2, 1994, P. L. 103-446, Title XII, § 1201(b)(1), (d)(11), 108 Stat. 4682, 4684; Oct. 9, 1996, P. L. 104-275, Title I, § 101(f)(2)(D), (i), 110 Stat. 3325.)

HISTORY; ANCILLARY LAWS AND DIRECTIVES
Effective date of section:
Act Oct. 17, 1980, P. L. 96-466, Title VIII, § 802(a)(2), 94 Stat. 2217, provided that this section is effective on Oct. 1, 1980.

Amendments:
1986. Act Oct. 28, 1986, in the section heading, substituted "Program" for "Pilot program"; in subsec. (a), in para. (1), substituted "1989" for "1985", in para. (2), inserted "currently", in paras. (5) and (6), substituted "1989" for "1985"; and substituted subsec. (b) for one which read:

"(b) Not later than September 30, 1984, the Administrator shall submit to the Congress a report on the programs of independent living services and assistance provided for in subsection (a) of this section. Such report shall include—

"(1) the results of a study which the Administrator shall conduct of the accomplishments and cost-effectiveness of such programs, including the

38 USCS § 3120   VETERANS' BENEFITS

extent to which (A) such programs have met needs for comprehensive independent living services that would not otherwise have been met, (B) severely disabled veterans have achieved and maintained greater independence in daily living as a result of participation in the programs, and (C) costs of care in hospital, nursing home, and domiciliary facilities have been and may be avoided as the result of such programs; and

"(2) the Administrator's recommendations for any legislative changes with respect to the provision of independent living services and assistance to veterans for whom the achievement of a vocational goal is not feasible.".

1988. Act Nov. 18, 1988, in subsec. (a), in para. (1), substituted "entities described in paragraph (7) of this subsection" for "public or nonprofit private agencies or organizations", and added para. (7).

1989. Act Dec. 18, 1989, deleted subsec. (b) which read: "Not later than February 1, 1989, the Administrator shall submit to the Committees on Veterans' Affairs of the Senate and the House of Representatives statistical data regarding veterans' participation in the program conducted under subsection (a) of this section during fiscal years 1987 and 1988 and any recommendations of the Administrator for administrative or legislative action or both regarding the program.".

Such Act further, in subsec. (a), substituted "The" for "(1) During fiscal years 1982 through 1989, the", "subsection (f) of this section" for "paragraph (7) of this subsection", and "subsection (b) of this section" for "paragraph (2) of this subsection", deleted para. (5) which read: "Any contract for services initiated with respect to any veteran under this section before the end of fiscal year 1989 may be continued in effect after the end of such year for the purposes of providing services and assistance to such veteran in accordance with the provisions of this chapter", redesignated paras. (2)–(4), (6) and (7) as subsecs. (b)–(f), respectively; in subsec. (b), as redesignated, deleted "and who is selected pursuant to criteria provided for in regulations prescribed under paragraph (1) of this subsection", preceeding the concluding period; in subsec. (c), as redesignated, substituted "subsection (b) of this section" for "paragraph (2) of this subsection"; in subsec. (e), as redesignated, substituted "fiscal year" for "of the fiscal years 1982 through 1989"; and in subsec. (f), as redesignated, substituted "subsection", "(1)", and "(2)" for "paragraph", "(A)", and "(B)", respectively.

Such Act further, in subsec. (a), substituted "Secretary" for "Administrator" wherever appearing; in subsec. (c), as redesignated, substituted "Department of Veterans Affairs" for "Veterans' Administration" and "Secretary" for "Administrator", wherever appearing; and in subsecs. (d) and (f), as redesignated, substituted "Secretary" for "Administrator".

1991. Act Aug. 6, 1991, redesignated this section, formerly 38 USCS § 1520, as 38 USCS § 3120, and amended the references in this section to reflect the redesignations made by § 5(a) of such Act (see Table III preceding 38 USCS § 101).

1994. Act Nov. 2, 1994, in subsecs. (a) and (f), substituted "Veterans Health Administration" for "Department of Medicine and Surgery".

Such Act further, in subsec. (b), purported to substitute "section 3102(1)(A)(i)" for "section 3012(1)(A)"; although the latter phrase did not appear in the subsection, the substitution was made for "section 3102(1)(A)" in order to effectuate the intent of Congress.

1996. Act Oct. 9, 1996 (effective and applicable as provided by § 101(j) of such Act, which appears as 38 USCS § 3101 note), in subsec. (b), substituted "3106(d) or (e)" for "3106(d)".

Such Act further (effective as above) purported to amend subsec. (b) by substituting "serious employment handicap resulting in substantial part from a service-connected disability described in section 3102(1)(A)(i)" for "service-connected disability described in section 3102(1)(A)"; however, the substitution was made for "service-connected disability described in section 3102(1)(A)(i)" in order to effectuate the probable intent of Congress.

Other provisions:
Redesignation of Veterans Health Services and Research Administration; references to Department of Medicine and Surgery. Act May 7, 1991, P.L. 102-40, § 2, 105 Stat. 187, which appears as 38 USCS § 301 note, provides for the redesignation of the Veterans Health Services and Research Administration as the Veterans Health Administration. Such Act further provides that any reference to the Department of Medicine and Surgery of the Veterans' Administration shall be deemed to refer to the Veterans Health Administration.

CROSS REFERENCES
This section is referred to in 38 USCS § 3109.

RESEARCH GUIDE
Am Jur:
77 Am Jur 2d, Veterans and Veterans' Laws § 72.

§ 3121. Veterans' Advisory Committee on Rehabilitation

(a)(1) The Secretary shall appoint an advisory committee to be known as the Veterans' Advisory Committee on Rehabilitation (hereinafter in this section referred to as the "Committee").

(2) The members of the Committee shall be appointed by the Secretary from the general public and shall serve for terms to be determined by the Secretary not to exceed three years. Veterans with service-connected disabilities shall be appropriately represented in the membership of the Committee, and the Committee shall also include persons who have distinguished themselves in the public and private sectors in the fields of rehabilitation medicine, vocational guidance, vocational rehabilitation, and employment and training programs. The Secretary may designate one of the members of the Committee appointed under this paragraph to chair the Committee.

(3) The Committee shall also include as ex officio members the following: (A) one representative from the Veterans Health Administration and one from the Veterans Benefits Administration, (B) one representative from the Rehabilitation Services Administration of the Department of Education and one from the National Institute for Handicapped Research of the Department of Education, and (C) one representative of the Assistant Secretary of Labor for Veterans' Employment and Training of the Department of Labor.

(b) The Secretary shall, on a regular basis, consult with and seek the advice of the Committee with respect to the administration of veterans' rehabilitation programs under this title.

(c) The Committee shall submit to the Secretary an annual report on the rehabilitation programs and activities of the Department of Veterans Affairs and shall submit such other reports and recommendations to the Administrator as the Committee determines appropriate. The annual report shall include an assessment of the rehabilitation needs of veterans and a review of the programs and activities of the Department of Veterans Affairs designed to meet such needs. The Secretary shall submit with each annual report submitted to the Congress pursuant to section 529 of this title a copy of all reports and recommendations of the Committee submitted to the Secretary since the previous annual report of the Secretary was submitted to the Congress pursuant to such section.
(Added Oct. 17, 1980, P. L. 96-466, Title I, § 101(a), 94 Stat. 2186; Dec. 18, 1989, P. L. 101-237, Title IV, § 423(b)(1), 103 Stat. 2092; June 13, 1991, P. L. 102-54, § 14(c)(5), 105 Stat. 285; Aug. 6, 1991, P. L. 102-83, §§ 2(c)(3), 5(a), 105 Stat. 402, 406; Nov. 2, 1994, P. L. 103-446, Title XII, § 1201(b)(1), (i)(5), 108 Stat. 4682, 4688.)

HISTORY; ANCILLARY LAWS AND DIRECTIVES
Effective date of section:
Act Oct. 17, 1980, P. L. 96-466, Title VIII, § 802(a)(2), 94 Stat. 2217, provided that this section is effective on Oct. 1, 1980.

Amendments:
1989. Act Dec. 18, 1989, substituted "Secretary" and "Department of Veterans Affairs" for "Administrator" and "Veterans' Administration", respectively, wherever appearing.
1991. Act June 13, 1991, in subsec. (a)(3), inserted "and Training".
Act Aug. 6, 1991, redesignated this section, formerly 38 USCS § 1521, as 38 USCS § 3121; and, in subsec. (c), substituted "section 529" for "section 214".
1994. Act Nov. 2, 1994, in subsec. (a)(3), substituted "Veterans Health Administration" for "Department of Medicine and Surgery" and "Veterans Benefits Administration" for "Department of Veterans' Benefits".

Other provisions:
Termination of advisory committees, boards and councils, established after Jan. 5, 1973. Act Oct. 6, 1972, P. L. 92-463, §§ 3(2) and 14, 86 Stat. 770, 776 (effective 1/5/73, as provided by § 15 of such Act), which is classified as 5 USCS Appx, provides that advisory committees established after Jan. 5, 1973, are to terminate not later than the expiration of the two-year period beginning on the date of establishment unless, in the case of a board established by the President or an officer of the Federal Government, such board is renewed by appropriate action prior to the expiration of such two-year period, or in the case of a board established by the Congress, its duration is otherwise provided for by law.
Redesignation of Veterans Health Services and Research Administration; references to Department of Medicine and Surgery. Act May 7, 1991, P.L. 102-40, § 2, 105 Stat. 187, which appears as 38 USCS § 301

note, provides for the redesignation of the Veterans Health Services and Research Administration as the Veterans Health Administration. Such Act further provides that any reference to the Department of Medicine and Surgery of the Veterans' Administration shall be deemed to refer to the Veterans Health Administration.

CODE OF FEDERAL REGULATIONS

Fiscal Service, Department of the Treasury—General regulations governing U. S. securities, 31 CFR Part 306.

RESEARCH GUIDE

Am Jur:
77 Am Jur 2d, Veterans and Veterans' Laws § 72.

CHAPTER 32. POST-VIETNAM ERA VETERANS' EDUCATIONAL ASSISTANCE

SUBCHAPTER I. PURPOSE; DEFINITIONS

Section
3201. Purpose.
3202. Definitions.

SUBCHAPTER II. ELIGIBILITY; CONTRIBUTIONS; AND MATCHING FUND

3221. Eligibility.
3222. Contributions; matching fund.
3223. Refunds of contributions upon disenrollment.
3224. Death of participant.
3225. Discharge or release under conditions which would bar the use of benefits.

SUBCHAPTER III. ENTITLEMENT; DURATION

3231. Entitlement; loan eligibility.
3232. Duration; limitations.
3233. Apprenticeship or other on-job training.
3234. Tutorial assistance.

SUBCHAPTER IV. ADMINISTRATION

3241. Requirements.
[3242] [1642. Repealed]
3243. Deposits; reports.

HISTORY; ANCILLARY LAWS AND DIRECTIVES

Explanatory notes:
The bracketed section number "3242" was inserted to preserve numerical continuity following the section number redesignations made by Act Aug. 6, 1991, P. L. 102-83, § 5(a), 105 Stat. 406.
A prior Chapter 33, containing §§ 1601, 1610–1613, 1620–1626, 1631–1634, 1641–1645, 1651–1656, 1661–1669, was repealed by Act March 3, 1966, P. L. 89-358, § 4(a), 80 Stat. 23.

Amendments:
1976. Act Oct. 15, 1976, P. L. 94-502, Title IV, § 404, 90 Stat. 2393 (effective 1/1/77, as provided by § 406 of such Act), added the chapter analysis.
1982. Act Oct. 12, 1982, P. L. 97-295, § 4(36), 96 Stat. 1307, amended the analysis of this chapter, in item 1625, by inserting "the".
1986. Act Oct. 28, 1986, P. L. 99-576, Title III, Part A, § 310(b)(3), 100 Stat. 3272, amended the analysis of this chapter by adding item 1633.
1988. Act Nov. 18, 1988, P. L. 100-689, Title I, Part A, § 107(b)(2), 102 Stat. 4168, amended the analysis of this chapter by adding item 1634.

1991. Act March 22, 1991, P. L. 102-16, § 5(b), 105 Stat. 50, amended the analysis of this chapter by deleting item 1642, which read: "1642. Reporting requirements.".
Act Aug. 6, 1991, P. L. 102-83, § 5(b)(1), 105 Stat. 406, revised the analysis of this Chapter by amending the section numbers in accordance with the redesignations made by § 5(a) of such Act (see Table III preceding 38 USCS § 101).

Other provisions:
Application and construction of the Oct. 12, 1982 amendment of this chapter analysis. For provisions as to the application and construction of the Oct. 12, 1982 amendment of this chapter analysis, see § 5 of such Act, which appears as 10 USCS § 101 note.

SUBCHAPTER I. PURPOSE; DEFINITIONS

§ 3201. Purpose

It is the purpose of this chapter [38 USCS §§ 3201 et seq.] (1) to provide educational assistance to those men and women who enter the Armed Forces after December 31, 1976, and before July 1, 1985, (2) to assist young men and women in obtaining an education they might not otherwise be able to afford, and (3) to promote and assist the all volunteer military program of the United States by attracting qualified men and women to serve in the Armed Forces.
(Added Oct. 15, 1976, P. L. 94-502, Title IV, § 404, 90 Stat. 2393; Oct. 28, 1986, P. L. 99-576, Title III, Part A, § 309(a)(1), 100 Stat. 3270; Aug. 6, 1991, P. L. 102-83, § 5(a), 105 Stat. 406.)

HISTORY; ANCILLARY LAWS AND DIRECTIVES

Explanatory notes:
A prior § 3201 was redesignated by Act May 7, 1991, P. L. 102-40, Title IV, § 402(b)(1), 105 Stat. 238. For similar provisions, see 38 USCS § 5501.

Amendments:
1986. Act Oct. 28, 1986, in para. (1) inserted "and before July 1, 1985,".
1991. Act Aug. 6, 1991, redesignated this section, formerly 38 USCS § 1601, as 38 USCS § 3201.

Short title:
Act Oct. 15, 1976, P. L. 94-502, Title IV, § 401, 90 Stat. 2392, located at 38 USCS § 101 note, provided that Act Oct. 15, 1976, Title IV may be cited as the "Post-Vietnam Era Veterans' Educational Assistance Act of 1977".

Other provisions:
Effective date of Act Oct. 15, 1976, Title IV. Act Oct. 15, 1976 P. L. 94-502, Title IV, § 406, 90 Stat. 2397, provided: "The provisions of this title [enacting 38 USCS §§ 3201 et seq. and 3221 note; amending 31 USCS § 725s, and 38 USCS §§ 3452, 3461, 3462] shall become effective on January 1, 1977.".

38 USCS § 3201

VETERANS' BENEFITS

Termination of enrollments in Post-Vietnam era veteran's educational assistance program. Act Oct. 28, 1986, P. L. 99-576, Title III, Part A, § 309(c), (d), 100 Stat. 3270, provides:

"(c) Exception. Notwithstanding the amendments made by subsection (a) [amending this section and 38 USCS §§ 3202, 3221], any individual on active duty in the Armed Forces who was eligible on June 30, 1985, to enroll in the program established by chapter 32 of title 38, United States Code [38 USCS §§ 3201 et seq.], may enroll, before April 1, 1987, in such program.

"(d) Notice requirement. The Secretary of Defense, and the Secretary of Transportation with respect to the Coast Guard when it is not operating as a service in the Navy, shall carry out activities for the purpose of notifying, to the maximum extent feasible, individuals described in subsection (c) of the opportunity provided by such subsection.".

CODE OF FEDERAL REGULATIONS

Department of Veterans Affairs—Vocational rehabilitation and education, 38 CFR Part 21.

Department of Veterans Affairs—Loan guaranty and vocational rehabilitation and counseling programs, 48 CFR Part 871.

RESEARCH GUIDE

Am Jur:

77 Am Jur 2d, Veterans and Veterans' Laws §§ 32, 132, 134, 137, 141, 142, 144.

§ 3202. Definitions

For the purposes of this chapter [38 USCS §§ 3201 et seq.]—

(1)(A) The term "eligible veteran" means any veteran who is not eligible for educational assistance under chapter 34 of this title [38 USCS §§ 3451 et seq.] and who (i) entered military service on or after January 1, 1977, and before July 1, 1985, served on active duty for a period of more than 180 days commencing on or after January 1, 1977, and was discharged or released therefrom under conditions other than dishonorable, or (ii) entered military service on or after January 1, 1977, and before July 1, 1985, and was discharged or released from active duty after January 1, 1977, for a service-connected disability.

(B) The requirement of discharge or release, prescribed in subparagraph (A), shall be waived in the case of any participant who has completed his or her first obligated period of active duty (which began after December 31, 1976) or 6 years of active duty (which began after December 31, 1976), whichever period is less.

(C) For the purposes of subparagraphs (A) and (B), the term "active duty" does not include any period during which an individual (i) was assigned full time by the Armed Forces to a civilian institution for a course of education which was substantially the same as established courses offered to civilians, (ii) served as a cadet or midshipman at one of the service academies, or (iii) served under the provisions of section 511(d) of title 10 pursuant to an enlistment in the Army National Guard or the Air

National Guard, or as a Reserve for service in the Army Reserve, Naval Reserve, Air Force Reserve, Marine Corps Reserve, or Coast Guard Reserve.

(D)(i) The requirement of ineligibility for educational assistance under chapter 34 of this title [38 USCS §§ 3451 et seq.], prescribed in subparagraph (A), shall be waived in the case of a veteran described in division (ii) of this subparagraph who elects to receive benefits under this chapter [38 USCS §§ 3201 et seq.] instead of assistance under such chapter 34 [38 USCS §§ 3451 et seq.]. A veteran who makes such an election shall be ineligible for assistance under such chapter. Such an election is irrevocable.

(ii) A veteran referred to in division (i) of this subparagraph is a veteran who before January 1, 1977, performed military service described in subparagraph (C)(iii), is entitled under section 3452(a)(3)(C) of this title to have such service considered to be "active duty" for the purposes of chapter 34 of this title [38 USCS §§ 3451 et seq.], and is eligible for assistance under such chapter only by reason of having such service considered to be active duty.

(2) The term "program of education"—

(A) has the meaning given such term in section 3452 (b) of this title, and
(B) includes (i) a full-time program of apprenticeship or other on-job training approved as provided in clause (1) or (2), as appropriate, of section 3687(a) of this title, and (ii) in the case of an individual who is not serving on active duty, a cooperative program (as defined in section 3482(a)(2) of this title).

(3) The term "participant" is a person who is participating in the educational benefits program established under this chapter [38 USCS §§ 3201 et seq.].

(4) The term "educational institution" has the meaning given such term in section 3452(c) of this title.

(5) The term "training establishment" has the meaning given such term in section 3452(c) of this title.

(Added Oct. 15, 1976, P. L. 94-502, Title IV, § 404, 90 Stat. 2394; Oct. 17, 1980, P. L. 96-466, Title IV, § 401, 94 Stat. 2201; March 2, 1984, P. L. 98-223, Title II, § 203(a), 98 Stat. 41; Oct. 28, 1986, P. L. 99-576, Title III, Part A, §§ 309(a)(2), 310(a), 100 Stat. 3270, 3271; Nov. 18, 1988, P. L. 100-689, Title I, Part A, § 108(b)(1), 102 Stat. 4169; June 13, 1991, P. L. 102-54, § 14(c)(6), 105 Stat. 285; Aug. 6, 1991, P. L. 102-83, § 5(a), (c)(1), 105 Stat. 406.)

HISTORY; ANCILLARY LAWS AND DIRECTIVES

Explanatory notes:
A prior § 3202 was redesignated by Act May 7, 1991, P. L. 102-40, Title IV, § 402(b)(1), 105 Stat. 238. For similar provisions, see 38 USCS § 5502.

Effective date of section:
Act Oct. 15, 1976, P. L. 94-502, Title IV, § 406, 90 Stat. 2397, provided that this section is effective Jan. 1, 1977.

38 USCS § 3202

Amendments:

1980. Act Oct. 17, 1980, in para. (1)(A), inserted "who is not eligible for educational assistance under chapter 34 of this title and", and deleted "initially" following "(i)" and "(ii)".

1984. Act March 2, 1984, in para. (1), added subpara. (D).

1986. Act Oct. 28, 1986, in para. (1)(A), inserted "and before July 1, 1985," and substituted "January 1, 1977" for "such date" following "after"; substituted para. (2) for one which read: "The terms 'program of education' and 'educational institution' shall have the same meaning ascribed to them in sections 1652(b) and 1652(c), respectively, of this title."; and added paras. (4) and (5).

1988. Act Nov. 18, 1988 (effective 1/1/89, as provided by § 108(c) of such Act, which appears as 38 USCS § 3002 note), in para. (2)(B) inserted "(i)" and inserted ", and (ii) in the case of an individual who is not serving on active duty, a cooperative program (as defined in section 1682(a)(2) of this title)".

1991. Act June 13, 1991, in para. (1)(A), inserted a comma after "active duty after January 1, 1977".

Act Aug. 6, 1991, redesignated this section, formerly 38 USCS § 1602, as 38 USCS § 3202, and amended the references in this section to reflect the redesignations made by § 5(a) of such Act (see Table III preceding 38 USCS § 101).

Other provisions:

Effective date of amendments made by § 401 of Act Oct. 17, 1980. Act Oct. 17, 1980, P. L. 96-466, Title VIII, § 802(d)(1), 94 Stat. 2218, provided: "The amendments made by section 401 [amending this section] shall take effect as of January 1, 1977.".

Enrollment in program before April 1, 1987. Act Oct. 28, 1986, P. L. 99-576, Title III, Part A, § 309(c), (d), 100 Stat. 3270, which appears as 38 USCS § 3201 note, provided for continued eligibility for enrollment in the program established by 38 USCS §§ 3201 et seq. until April 1, 1987, of individuals on active duty in the Armed Forces who were eligible therefor on June 30, 1985, and required notice of such continued eligibility to affected individuals.

CODE OF FEDERAL REGULATIONS

Department of Veterans Affairs—United States Government life insurance, 38 CFR Part 6.

RESEARCH GUIDE

Law Review Articles:

Benefits for Conscientious Objectors. 19 Catholic Lawyer 62, Winter 1973.

Constitutional Law—Due Process—Conscientious Objectors Entitled to Same Veterans Educational Benefits Received By Regular Servicemen. 6 Creighton L Rev 393, 1972-73.

Constitutional Law—Equal Protection—Veteran's Educational Benefits for Conscientious Objectors. 8 Suffolk Univ L Rev 1239, Summer 1974.

Robison v Johnson (352 F Supp 848): Veterans' Educational Benefits for Conscientious Objectors. 121 Univ of Pa L Rev 1133, May 1973.

SUBCHAPTER II. ELIGIBILITY; CONTRIBUTIONS; AND MATCHING FUND

§ 3221. Eligibility

(a) Each person entering military service on or after January 1, 1977, and before July 1, 1985, shall have the right to enroll in the educational benefits program provided by this chapter [38 USCS §§ 3201 et seq.] (hereinafter in this chapter referred to as the "program" except where the text indicates otherwise) at any time during such person's service on active duty before July 1, 1985. When a person elects to enroll in the program, such person must participate for at least 12 consecutive months before disenrolling or suspending participation.

(b) The requirement for 12 consecutive months of participation required by subsection (a) of this section shall not apply when (1) the participant suspends participation or disenrolls from the program because of personal hardship as defined in regulations issued jointly by the Secretary and the Secretary of Defense, or (2) the participant is discharged or released from active duty.

(c) A participant shall be permitted to suspend participation or disenroll from the program at the end of any 12-consecutive-month period of participation. If participation is suspended, the participant shall be eligible to make additional contributions to the program under such terms and conditions as shall be prescribed by regulations issued jointly by the Secretary and the Secretary of Defense.

(d) If a participant disenrolls from the program, such participant forfeits any entitlement to benefits under the program except as provided in subsection (e) of this section. A participant who disenrolls from the program is eligible for a refund of such participant's contributions as provided in section 3223 of this title.

(e) A participant who has disenrolled may be permitted to reenroll in the program under such conditions as shall be prescribed jointly by the Secretary and the Secretary of Defense.

(f) An individual who serves in the Selected Reserve may not receive credit for such service under both the program established by this chapter [38 USCS §§ 3201 et seq.] and the program established by chapter 106 of title 10 [10 USCS §§ 2131 et seq.] but shall elect (in such form and manner as the Secretary of Veterans Affairs may prescribe) the program to which such service is to be credited.
(Added Oct. 15, 1976, P. L. 94-502, Title IV, § 404, 90 Stat. 2394; Oct. 28, 1986, P. L. 99-576, Title III, Part A, § 309(a)(3), 100 Stat. 3270; Dec. 18, 1989, P. L. 101-237, Title IV, §§ 410, 423(b)(1)(A), (4)(A), 103 Stat. 2092, 2093; Aug. 6, 1991, P. L. 102-83, § 5(a), (c)(1), 105 Stat. 406.)

HISTORY; ANCILLARY LAWS AND DIRECTIVES
Effective date of section:
Act Oct. 15, 1976, P. L. 94-502, Title IV, § 406, 90 Stat. 2397, provided that this section is effective Jan. 1, 1977.

Amendments:

1986. Act Oct. 28, 1986, in subsec. (a), inserted "and before July 1, 1985," after "January 1, 1977,", and "before July 1, 1985".

1989. Act Dec. 18, 1989, added subsec. (f).

Such Act further, in subsecs. (b), (c) and (e), substituted "Secretary" for "Administrator"; in subsec. (b), deleted "(hereinafter in this chapter referred to as the 'Secretary')" following "Defense"; and in subsecs. (c) and (d), inserted "of Defense".

1991. Act Aug. 6, 1991, redesignated this section, formerly 38 USCS § 1621, as 38 USCS § 3221, and amended the references in this section to reflect the redesignations made by § 5(a) of such Act (see Table III preceding 38 USCS § 101).

Other provisions:

Recommendation to Congress. Act Oct. 15, 1976, P. L. 94-502, Title IV, § 408, 90 Stat. 2397 (effective 1/1/77, as provided by § 406 of such Act), provided:

"(a)(1) No individual on active duty in the Armed Forces may initially enroll in the educational assistance program provided for in chapter 32 of title 38, United States Code [38 USCS §§ 3201 et seq.]. (as added by section 404 of this Act) after December 31, 1981, unless—

"(A) before June 1, 1981, the President submits to both Houses of Congress a written recommendation that such program continue to be open for new enrollments; and

"(B) before the close of the 60-day period after the day on which the President submits to Congress the recommendation described in subparagraph (A), neither the House of Representatives nor the Senate adopts, by an affirmative vote of a majority of those present and voting in that House, a resolution which in substance disapproves such recommendation.

"(2) For purposes of computing the 60-day period referred to in paragraph (1)(B), there shall be excluded—

"(A) the days on which either House is not in session because of an adjournment of more than 3 days to a day certain or an adjournment of the Congress sine die, and

"(B) any Saturday and Sunday, not excluded under the preceding subparagraph, when either House is not in session.

"The recommendation referred to in paragraph (1)(A) shall be delivered to both Houses of Congress on the same day and shall be delivered to the Clerk of the House of Representatives if the House is not in session and to the Secretary of the Senate if the Senate is not in session.

"(b) If new enrollments after December 31, 1981, in the educational assistance program provided for in such chapter 32 [38 USCS §§ 3201 et seq.] are authorized after the application of the provisions of subsection (a), then effective January 1, 1982, section 1622(b) [now section 3222(b)] of title 38, United States Code, is amended by striking out 'Veterans' Administration' and inserting in lieu thereof 'Department of Defense.'".

Suspension of right to enroll in Chapter 32 program. Act Oct. 19, 1984, P. L. 98-525, Title VII, § 704, 98 Stat. 2564, which formerly appeared as a note to this section, was repealed by Act Oct. 28, 1986, P. L. 99-576, Title III, Part A, § 309(b), 100 Stat. 3270.

Enrollment in program before April 1, 1987. Act Oct. 28, 1986, P. L. 99-576, Title III, Part A, § 309(c), (d), 100 Stat. 3270, which appears as 38 USCS § 3201 note, provided for continued eligibility for enrollment in the program established by 38 USCS §§ 3201 et seq. until April 1, 1987, of individuals on active duty in the Armed Forces who were eligible therefor on June 30, 1985, and required notice of such continued eligibility to affected individuals.

RESEARCH GUIDE

Am Jur:
77 Am Jur 2d, Veterans and Veterans' Laws § 134.

INTERPRETIVE NOTES AND DECISIONS

Individual who has not participated for 12 consecutive months because of hardship situation, but upon discharge has participated for 11 months, is eligible for Chapter 32 educational benefits. VA GCO 11-77.

§ 3222. Contributions; matching fund

(a) Except as provided in subsections (c) and (d) of this section, each person electing to participate in the program shall agree to have a monthly deduction made from such person's military pay. Such monthly deduction shall be in any amount not less than $25 nor more than $100 except that the amount must be divisible by 5. Any such amount contributed by the participant or contributed by the Secretary of Defense pursuant to subsection (c) of this section shall be deposited in a deposit fund account entitled the "Post-Vietnam Era Veterans Education Account" (hereinafter in this chapter [38 USCS §§ 3201 et seq.] referred to as the "fund") to be established in the Treasury of the United States. Contributions made by the participant shall be limited to a maximum of $2,700.

(b) Except as otherwise provided in this chapter [38 USCS §§ 3201 et seq.], each monthly contribution made by a participant under subsection (a) shall entitle the participant to matching funds from the Department of Veterans Affairs at the rate of $2 for each $1 contributed by the participant.

(c) The Secretary of Defense is authorized to contribute to the fund of any participant such contributions as the Secretary of Defense deems necessary or appropriate to encourage persons to enter or remain in the Armed Forces, including contributions in lieu of, or to reduce the amount of, monthly deductions under subsection (a) of this section. The Secretary of Defense is authorized to issue such rules and regulations as the Secretary of Defense deems necessary or appropriate to implement the provisions of this subsection.

(d) Subject to the maximum contribution prescribed by subsection (a) of this section, a participant shall be permitted, while serving on active duty, to make a lump-sum contribution to the fund. A lump-sum contribution to the fund by a participant shall be in addition to or in lieu of monthly deductions made from such participant's military pay and shall be considered, for the purposes of paragraph (2) of section 3231(a) of this title, to have been made by monthly deductions from such participant's military pay in the amount of $100 per month or in such lesser amount as may be specified by such participant pursuant to regulations issued jointly by the Secretary of Defense and the Secretary.

(e) Any amount transferred to the Secretary from the Secretary of a military department under an interagency agreement for the administration by the Department of Veterans Affairs of an educational assistance program established by the Secretary of Defense under chapter 107 of title 10 [10 USCS §§ 2141 et seq.] may be deposited into and disbursed from the fund for the purposes of such program.
(Added Oct. 15, 1976, P. L. 94-502, Title IV, § 404, 90 Stat. 2395; Oct. 17, 1980, P. L. 96-466, Title IV, § 406, 94 Stat. 2202; Oct. 14, 1982, P. L. 97-306, Title II, §§ 209, 210, 96 Stat. 1436; Nov. 21, 1983, P. L. 98-160, Title VII, § 702(6), 97 Stat. 1009; Dec. 18, 1989, P. L. 101-237, Title IV, § 423(b)(1), (4)(A), (B), (D), 103 Stat. 2092; Aug. 6, 1991, P. L. 102-83, § 5(a), (c)(1), 105 Stat. 406.)

HISTORY; ANCILLARY LAWS AND DIRECTIVES
Effective date of section:
Act Oct. 15, 1976, P. L. 94-502, Title IV, § 406, 90 Stat. 2397, provided that this section is effective Jan. 1, 1977.

Amendments:
1976. Act Oct. 15, 1976 (effective 1/1/82 and applicable as provided by § 408 of such Act, which appears as 38 USCS § 3221 note), in subsec. (b), substituted "Department of Defense" for "Veterans' Administration".
1980. Act Oct. 17, 1980 (effective 10/1/80, as provided by § 802(d)(2) of such Act, which appears as 38 USCS § 3224 note), in subsec. (a), substituted "Except as provided in subsections (c) and (d) of this section, each" for "Each", substituted "$25" for "$50", and substituted "$100" for "$75"; in subsec. (c), inserted ", including contributions in lieu of, or to reduce the amount of, monthly deductions under subsection (a) of this section"; and added subsec. (d).
1982. Act Oct. 14, 1982, in subsec. (d), substituted "$100" for "$75"; and added subsec. (e).
1983. Act Nov. 21, 1983, in subsec. (d), inserted "of this title".
1989. Act Dec. 18, 1989, in subsec. (a), inserted "of Defense"; in subsec. (b), substituted "Department of Veterans Affairs" for "Veterans' Administration"; in subsec. (c), inserted "of Defense" following "Secretary", wherever appearing; in subsec. (d), inserted "of Defense" following "Secretary", and substituted "Secretary" for "Administrator"; and in subsec. (e), inserted "of Defense" following "established by the Secretary", substituted "Secretary" for "Administrator", and substituted "Department of Veterans Affairs" for "Veterans' Administration".
1991. Act Aug. 6, 1991, redesignated this section, formerly 38 USCS § 1622, as 38 USCS § 3222, and amended the references in this section to reflect the redesignations made by § 5(a) of such Act (see Table III preceding 38 USCS § 101).

Other provisions:
Conditional 1976 amendment. Act Oct. 15, 1976, P. L. 94-502, Title IV, § 408(b), 90 Stat. 2398, located at 38 USCS § 3221 note, provided that subsec. (b) of this section, is amended by substituting "Department of Defense" for "Veterans' Administration", effective Jan. 1, 1982, if new

enrollments after Dec. 31, 1981, in the educational assistance program provided by this chapter are authorized after application of § 408(a) of such Act [38 USCS § 3221 note].

Payments made by government for certain enlistees and reenlistees. Act Sept. 8, 1980, P. L. 96-342, Title IX, § 903, 94 Stat. 1115, which appears as 10 USCS § 2141 note, provides that repayment contributions by those receiving assistance under this chapter (38 USCS §§ 3201 et seq.) shall be made by the Federal government.

Refunds for certain service academy graduates. Act Aug. 15, 1990, P. L. 101-366, Title II, § 207, 104 Stat. 442, provides:

"(a) In general. Upon receipt before January 1, 1992, of an application from an individual described in subsection (b)(3), the Secretary of Veterans Affairs shall—

"(1) not later than 60 days after receiving such application, refund to the individual concerned the amount, if any, of the individual's unused contributions to the VEAP Account;

"(2)(A) if the individual has received educational assistance under chapter 32 of title 38, United States Code [38 USCS §§ 3201 et seq.], for the pursuit of a program of education, pay to the individual (out of funds appropriated to the readjustment benefits account) a sum equal to the amount by which the amount of the educational assistance that the individual would have received under chapter 34 of such title [38 USCS §§ 3451 et seq.] for the pursuit of such program exceeds the amount of the educational assistance that the individual did receive under such chapter 32 for the pursuit of such program; or

"(B) if the individual has not received educational assistance under such chapter 32, pay to the individual (out of funds appropriated to the Department of Veterans Affairs Readjustment Benefits account) a sum equal to the amount of educational assistance that the individual would have received under chapter 34 of such title [38 USCS §§ 3451 et seq.] for the pursuit of a program of education if the individual had been entitled to assistance under such program during the period ending on December 31, 1989; and

"(3) refund to the Secretary of Defense the unused contributions by such Secretary to the VEAP Account on behalf of such individual.

"(b) Definitions. For purposes of this section—

"(1) the term "VEAP Account" means the Post-Vietnam Era Veterans Education Account established pursuant to section 1622(a) of title 38, United States Code [subsec. (a) of this section];

"(2) the term "active duty" has the same meaning given such term by section 101(21) of such title 38;

"(3) the term "individual described in subsection (b)(3)" means an individual who—

"(A) before January 1, 1977, commenced the third academic year as a cadet or midshipman at one of the service academies or the third academic year as a member of the Senior Reserve Officers' Training Corps in a program of educational assistance under section 2104 or 2107 of title 10, United States Code;

"(B) served on active duty for a period of more than 180 days pursuant to an appointment as a commissioned officer received upon graduation from one of the service academies or upon satisfactory completion of advanced training (as defined in section 2101 of such title 10) as a member of the Senior Reserve Officers' Training Corps;

"(C) after such period of active duty, was discharged or released therefrom under conditions other than dishonorable or continued to serve on active duty without a break in service; and

"(D) if enrolled under the program of educational assistance provided under chapter 32 of title 38, United States Code [38 USCS §§ 3201 et seq.], submits to the Secretary of Veterans Affairs, as part of the application made by the individual under subsection (a) in such form and manner as such Secretary shall prescribe by January 1, 1991, an irrevocable election to be disenrolled from such program at that time; and

"(4) the term "service academies" means the United States Military Academy, the United States Naval Academy, the United States Air Force Academy, and the United States Coast Guard Academy.".

CROSS REFERENCES

This section is referred to in 38 USCS §§ 3015, 3018B, 3035, 3223, 3243.

INTERPRETIVE NOTES AND DECISIONS

Service Academy graduates were entitled to educational assistance under § 207 of law entitled Refunds for Certain Service Academy Graduates (38 USCS § 3222 note) even though they previously received tuition benefits from Navy. Tallman v Brown (1997, CA FC) 105 F3d 613.

Service person who has completed obligated period of active duty or 6 years of active duty (whichever is less), which began after December 31, 1976, is still on active duty, is still making monthly contributions, but has made less than 12 monthly contributions, may nonetheless be entitled to Chapter 32 educational benefits before making 12 consecutive monthly contributions. VA GCO 11-77.

§ 3223. Refunds of contributions upon disenrollment

(a) Contributions made to the program by a participant may be refunded only after the participant has disenrolled from the program or as provided in section 3224 of this title.

(b) If a participant disenrolls from the program prior to discharge or release from active duty, such participant's contributions will be refunded on the date of the participant's discharge or release from active duty or within 60 days of receipt of notice by the Secretary of the participant's discharge or disenrollment, except that refunds may be made earlier in instances of hardship or other good reason as prescribed in regulations issued jointly by the Secretary and the Secretary of Defense.

(c) If a participant disenrolls from the program after discharge or release from active duty, the participant's contributions shall be refunded within 60 days of receipt of an application for a refund from the participant.

(d) In the event the participant (1) dies while on active duty, (2) dies after discharge or release from active duty, or (3) disenrolls or is disenrolled from the program without having utilized any entitlement, the participant may have accrued under the program, or, in the event the participant utilizes part of such participant's entitlement and disenrolls or is disenrolled from the program, the

READJUSTMENT BENEFITS 38 USCS § 3224

amount contributed by the Secretary of Defense under the authority of section 3222(c) of this title remaining in the fund shall be refunded to such Secretary.
(Added Oct. 15, 1976, P. L. 94-502, Title IV, § 404, 90 Stat. 2395; Nov. 21, 1983, P. L. 98-160, Title VII, § 702(7), 97 Stat. 1009; Dec. 18, 1989, P. L. 101-237, Title IV, § 423(b)(1)(A), (4)(A), (7), 103 Stat. 2092, 2093; Aug. 6, 1991, P. L. 102-83, § 5(a), (c)(1), 105 Stat. 406.)

HISTORY; ANCILLARY LAWS AND DIRECTIVES
Effective date of section:
Act Oct. 15, 1976, P. L. 94-502, Title IV, § 406, 90 Stat. 2397, provided that this section is effective Jan. 1, 1977.

Amendments:
1983. Act Nov. 21, 1983, in subsecs. (a) and (d), inserted "of this title".
1989. Act Dec. 18, 1989, in subsec. (b), substituted "Secretary" for "Administrator", and inserted "of Defense"; and in subsec. (d), inserted "of Defense" and substituted "such Secretary" for "the Secretary".
1991. Act Aug. 6, 1991, redesignated this section, formerly 38 USCS § 1623, as 38 USCS § 3223, and amended the references in this section to reflect the redesignations made by § 5(a) of such Act (see Table III preceding 38 USCS § 101).

CROSS REFERENCES
This section is referred to in 38 USCS §§ 3018A, 3018B, 3221.

§ 3224. Death of participant

In the event of a participant's death, the amount of such participant's unused contributions to the fund shall be paid to the living person or persons first listed below:
  (1) The beneficiary or beneficiaries designated by such participant under such participant's Servicemembers' Group Life Insurance policy.
  (2) The surviving spouse of the participant.
  (3) The surviving child or children of the participant, in equal shares.
  (4) The surviving parent or parents of the participant, in equal shares.

If there is no such person living, such amount shall be paid to such participant's estate.
(Added Oct. 15, 1976, P. L. 94-502, Title IV, § 404, 90 Stat. 2395; Oct. 17, 1980, P. L. 96-466, Title IV, § 402, 94 Stat. 2201; Aug. 6, 1991, P. L. 102-83, § 5(a), 105 Stat. 406; Oct. 9, 1996, P. L. 104-275, Title IV, § 405(c)(2), 110 Stat. 3340.)

HISTORY; ANCILLARY LAWS AND DIRECTIVES
Effective date of section:
Act Oct. 15, 1976, P. L. 94-502, Title IV, § 406, 90 Stat. 2397, provided that this section is effective Jan. 1, 1977.

Amendments:

1980. Act Oct. 17, 1980, substituted the text of this section for text which read:

"(a) If a participant dies, the amount of such participant's unused contributions to the fund shall be paid (1) to the beneficiary or beneficiaries designated by such participant under such participant's Servicemen's Group Life Insurance policy, or (2) to the participant's estate if no beneficiary has been designated under such policy or if the participant is not insured under the Servicemen's Group Life Insurance program.

"(b) If a participant dies after having been discharged or released from active duty and before using any or all of the contributions which the participant made to the fund, such unused contributions shall be paid as prescribed in subsection (a) of this section.".

1991. Act Aug. 6, 1991, redesignated this section, formerly 38 USCS § 1624, as 38 USCS § 3224.

1996. Act Oct. 9, 1996, in para. (1), substituted "Servicemembers'" for "Servicemen's".

Other provisions:
Effective date of amendments made by §§ 402–406 of Act Oct. 17, 1980.
Act Oct. 17, 1980, P. L. 96-466, Title VIII, § 802(d)(2), 94 Stat. 2218, provided: "The amendments made by sections 402 through 406 [amending 38 USCS §§ 3222, 3224, 3231, 3241] shall become effective on October 1, 1980.".

CROSS REFERENCES

This section is referred to in 38 USCS § 3223.

§ 3225. Discharge or release under conditions which would bar the use of benefits

If a participant in the program is discharged or released from active duty under dishonorable conditions, such participant is automatically disenrolled and any contributions made by such participant shall be refunded to such participant on the date of such participant's discharge or release from active duty or within 60 days from receipt of notice by the Secretary of such discharge or release, whichever is later.
(Added Oct. 15, 1976, P. L. 94-502, Title IV, § 404, 90 Stat. 2396; Dec. 18, 1989, P. L. 101-237, Title IV, § 423(b)(1)(A), 103 Stat. 2092; Aug. 6, 1991, P. L. 102-83, § 5(a), 105 Stat. 406.)

HISTORY; ANCILLARY LAWS AND DIRECTIVES
Effective date of section:
Act Oct. 15, 1976, P. L. 94-502, Title IV, § 406, 90 Stat. 2397, provided that this section is effective Jan. 1, 1977.

Amendments:
1989. Act Dec. 18, 1989, substituted "Secretary" for "Administrator".
1991. Act Aug. 6, 1991, redesignated this section, formerly 38 USCS § 1625, as 38 USCS § 3225.

SUBCHAPTER III. ENTITLEMENT; DURATION

§ 3231. Entitlement; loan eligibility

(a)(1) Subject to the provisions of section 3695 of this title limiting the aggregate period for which any person may receive assistance under two or more programs of educational or vocational assistance administered by the Department of Veterans Affairs, a participant shall be entitled to a maximum of 36 monthly benefit payments (or their equivalent in the event of part-time benefits).

(2) Except as provided in subsection (f) of this section, in paragraph (5)(E) of this subsection, and section 3233 of this title and subject to section 3241 of this title, amount of the monthly payment to which any eligible veteran is entitled shall be ascertained by (A) adding all contributions made to the fund by the eligible veteran, (B) multiplying the sum by 3, (C) adding all contributions made to the fund for such veteran by the Secretary of Defense, and (D) dividing the sum by the lesser of 36 or the number of months in which contributions were made by such veteran.

(3) Payment of benefits under this chapter [38 USCS §§ 3201 et seq.] may be made only for periods of time during which an eligible veteran is actually enrolled in and pursuing an approved program of education and, except as provided in paragraph (4), only after an eligible veteran has been discharged or released from active duty.

(4) Payment of benefits under this chapter [38 USCS §§ 3201 et seq.] may be made after a participant has completed his or her first obligated period of active duty (which began after December 31, 1976), or 6 years of active duty (which began after December 31, 1976), whichever period is less.

(5)(A) Notwithstanding any other provision of this chapter or chapter 36 of this title [38 USCS §§ 3201 et seq. or 3670 et seq.], any payment of an educational assistance allowance described in subparagraph (B) of this paragraph—

(i) shall not be charged against the entitlement of any eligible veteran under this chapter [38 USCS §§ 3201 et seq.]; and

(ii) shall not be counted toward the aggregate period for which section 3695 of this title limits an individual's receipt of assistance.

(B) The payment of an educational assistance allowance referred to in subparagraph (A) of this paragraph is any payment of a monthly benefit under this chapter to an eligible veteran for pursuit of a course or courses under this chapter [38 USCS §§ 3201 et seq.] if the Secretary finds that the eligible veteran—

(i) in the case of a person not serving on active duty, had to discontinue such course pursuit as a result of being ordered, in connection with the Persian Gulf War, to serve on active duty under section 672(a), (d), or (g), 673, 673b, or 688 of title 10 [10 USCS §§ 12301(a), (d), (g), 12302, 12304, 688] or

(ii) in the case of a person serving on active duty, had to discontinue such course pursuit as a result of being ordered, in connection with such War, to a new duty location or assignment or to perform an increased amount of work; and

(iii) failed to receive credit or training time toward completion of the individual's approved educational, professional, or vocational objective as a result of having to discontinue, as described in clause (i) or (ii) of this subparagraph, his or her course pursuit.

(C) The period for which, by reason of this subsection, an educational assistance allowance is not charged against entitlement or counted toward the applicable aggregate period under section 3695 of this title shall not exceed the portion of the period of enrollment in the course or courses for which the individual failed to receive credit or with respect to which the individual lost training time, as determined under subparagraph (B)(iii) of this paragraph.

(D) The amount in the fund for each eligible veteran who received a payment of an educational assistance allowance described in subparagraph (B) of this paragraph shall be restored to the amount that would have been in the fund for the veteran if the payment had not been made. For purposes of carrying out the previous sentence, the Secretary of Defense shall deposit into the fund, on behalf of each such veteran, an amount equal to the entire amount of the payment made to the veteran.

(E) In the case of a veteran who discontinues pursuit of a course or courses as described in subparagraph (B) of this paragraph, the formula for ascertaining the amount of the monthly payment to which the veteran is entitled in paragraph (2) of this subsection shall be implemented as if—

(i) the payment made to the fund by the Secretary of Defense under subparagraph (D) of this paragraph, and

(ii) any payment for a course or courses described in subparagraph (B) of this paragraph that was paid out of the fund,

had not been made or paid.

(b) Any enlisted member of the Armed Forces participating in the program shall be eligible to enroll in a course, courses, or program of education for the purpose of attaining a secondary school diploma (or an equivalency certificate), as authorized by section 3491(a) of this title, during the last six months of such member's first enlistment and at any time thereafter.

(c) When an eligible veteran is pursuing a program of education under this chapter [38 USCS §§ 3201 et seq.] by correspondence, such eligible veteran's entitlement shall be charged at the rate of 1 month's entitlement for each month of benefits paid to the eligible veteran (computed on the basis of the formula provided in subsection (a)(2) of this section).

(d)(1) Subject to the provisions of paragraph (2) of this subsection, the amount of the educational assistance benefits paid to an eligible veteran who is pursuing a program of education under this chapter [38 USCS §§ 3201 et seq.] while incarcerated in a Federal, State, or local penal institution for conviction of a felony may not exceed the lesser of (A) such amount as the

Secretary determines, in accordance with regulations which the Secretary shall prescribe, is necessary to cover the cost of established charges for tuition and fees required of similarly circumstanced nonveterans enrolled in the same program and the cost of necessary supplies, books, and equipment, or (B) the applicable monthly benefit payment otherwise prescribed in this section or section 3233 of this title. The amount of the educational assistance benefits payable to a veteran while so incarcerated shall be reduced to the extent that the tuition and fees of the veteran for any course are paid under any Federal program (other than a program administered by the Secretary) or under any State or local program.

(2) Paragraph (1) of this subsection shall not apply in the case of any veteran who is pursuing a program of education under this chapter while residing in a halfway house or participating in a work-release program in connection with such veteran's conviction of a felony.

(e)(1) Subject to subsection (a)(1) of this section, each individual who is pursuing a program of education consisting exclusively of flight training approved as meeting the requirements of section 3241(b) of this title shall be paid educational assistance under this chapter in the amount equal to 60 percent of the established charges for tuition and fees which similarly circumstanced nonveterans enrolled in the same flight course are required to pay.

(2) No payment may be paid under this chapter [38 USCS §§ 3201 et seq.] to an individual for any month during which such individual is pursuing a program of education consisting exclusively of flight training until the Secretary has received from that individual and the institution providing such training a certification of the flight training received by the individual during that month and the tuition and other fees charged for that training.

(3) The entitlement of an eligible veteran pursuing a program of education described in paragraph (1) of this subsection shall be charged at the rate of one month for each amount of educational assistance paid which is equal to the monthly benefit otherwise payable to such veteran (computed on the basis of the formula provided in subsection (a)(2) of this section).

(4) The number of solo flying hours for which an individual may be paid an educational assistance allowance under this subsection may not exceed the minimum number of solo flying hours required by the Federal Aviation Administration for the flight rating or certification which is the goal of the individual's flight training.

(Added Oct. 15, 1976, P. L. 94-502, Title IV, § 404, 90 Stat. 2396; Oct. 17, 1980, P. L. 96-466, Title IV, §§ 403, 404, 94 Stat. 2201; Aug. 13, 1981, P. L. 97-35, Title XX, §§ 2003(a)(1), 2005(a), 95 Stat. 782; Oct. 28, 1986, P. L. 99-576, Title III, Part A, § 310(b)(1), 100 Stat. 3271; Nov. 18, 1988, P. L. 100-689, Title I, Part A, § 108(b)(2), Part B, § 122, 102 Stat. 4170, 4174; Dec. 18, 1989, P. L. 101-237, Title IV, § 423(b)(1), (4)(A), 103 Stat. 2092; March 22, 1991, P. L. 102-16, § 7(b), 105 Stat. 51; Aug. 6, 1991, P. L. 102-83, § 5(a), (c)(1), 105 Stat. 406; Oct. 10, 1991, P. L. 102-127, § 2(b), 105 Stat. 619; Oct. 29, 1992, P. L. 102-568, Title III, § 310(c), 106 Stat. 4330; Oct. 9, 1996, P. L. 104-275, Title I, § 105(b), 110 Stat. 3327.)

38 USCS § 3231

HISTORY; ANCILLARY LAWS AND DIRECTIVES

Explanatory notes:
The bracketed reference "10 USCS §§ 12301(a), (d), (g), 12302, 12304, 688" has been inserted on authority of Act Oct. 5, 1994, P. L. 103-337, § 1662(e)(2), 108 Stat. 2992, which transferred 10 USCS §§ 672, 673, and 673b to 10 USCS §§ 12301, 12302, and 12304, respectively.

Effective date of section:
Act Oct. 15, 1976, P. L. 94-502, Title IV, § 406, 90 Stat. 2397, provided that this section is effective Jan. 1, 1977.

Amendments:
1980. Act Oct. 17, 1980 (effective 10/1/80, as provided by § 802(d)(2) of such Act, which appears as 38 USCS § 3224 note), substituted subsec. (a)(1) for one which read: "A participant shall be entitled to a maximum of 36 monthly benefit payments (or their equivalent in the event of part-time benefit payments)."; and substituted subsec. (b) for one which read: "Any enlisted member of the Armed Forces participating in the program shall be eligible to participate in the Predischarge Education Program (PREP), authorized by subchapter VI of chapter 34 of this title, during the last 6 months of such member's first enlistment.".

1981. Act Aug. 13, 1981, in subsec. (c), deleted "either" after pursuing" and deleted "or a program of flight training" after "correspondence"; and deleted subsec. (d) which read: "Eligible veterans participating in the program shall be eligible for education loans authorized by subchapter III of chapter 36 of this title in such amounts and on the same terms and conditions as provided in such subchapter, except that the term "eligible veteran" as used in such subchapter shall be deemed to include "eligible veteran" as defined in this chapter.". For the effective date and application of such amendments, see the Other provisions note to this section.

1986. Act Oct. 28, 1986, in subsec. (a)(2), substituted "Except as provided in section 1633 of this title and subject to section 1641 of this title, the" for "The".

1988. Act Nov. 18, 1988 added subsec. (e).
Such Act further (effective 1/1/89 as provided by § 108(c) of such Act, which appears as 38 USCS § 3002 note) added subsec. (d).

1989. Act Dec. 18, 1989, in subsec. (a), in para. (1), substituted "Department of Veterans Affairs" for "Veterans' Administration", and in para. (2), inserted "of Defense"; and in subsec. (e)(1), substituted "Secretary" for "Administrator", wherever, appearing.

1991. Act March 22, 1991 (effective 4/1/91 as provided by § 7(c) of such Act, which appears as a note to this section), in subsec. (a)(2), inserted "subsection (f) of this section and"; and added subsec. (f).
Act Aug. 6, 1991, redesignated this section, formerly 38 USCS § 1631, as 38 USCS § 3231, and amended the references in this section to reflect the redesignations made by § 5(a) of such Act (see Table III preceding 38 USCS § 101).
Act Oct. 10, 1991, in subsec. (a), in para. (2), inserted "in paragraph (5)(E) of this subsection and", and added para. (5).

1992. Act Oct. 29, 1992 (applicable to certain flight training received after 9/30/92, as provided by § 310(d) of such Act, which appears as 10 USCS

§ 16131 note), in subsec. (f), in para. (1), deleted "(other than tuition and fees charged for or attributable to solo flying hours)" following "for tuition and fees", and added para. (4).

1996. Act Oct. 9, 1996 deleted subsec. (d), which read:

"(d)(1) The amount of the monthly benefit payment to an individual pursuing a cooperative program under this chapter shall be 80 percent of the monthly benefit otherwise payable to such individual (computed on the basis of the formula provided in subsection (a)(2) of this section).

"(2) For each month that an individual is paid a monthly benefit payment for pursuit of a cooperative program under this chapter], the individual's entitlement under this chapter shall be charged at the rate 80 percent of a month.";

and redesignated subsecs. (e) and (f) as subsecs. (d) and (e), respectively.

Other provisions:

Effective date and application of amendments by §§ 2003 and 2005 of Act Aug. 13, 1981. Act Aug. 13, 1981, P. L. 97-35, Title XX, § 2006, 95 Stat. 783, provided:

"(a) Except as provided in subsection (b), the amendments made by sections 2003 and 2005 [amending this section among other things; for classification, consult USCS Tables volumes] shall take effect on October 1, 1981.

"(b) The amendments made by such sections shall not apply to any person receiving educational assistance under section [former] 1677 of title 38, United States Code, as such section was in effect on August 31, 1981, for the pursuit of a program of education (as defined in section 1652(b) of such title [now 38 USCS § 3452(b)]) in which such person was enrolled on that date, for as long as such person is continuously thereafter so enrolled and meets the requirements of eligibility for such assistance for the pursuit of such program under the provisions of chapters 34 and 36 of such title [38 USCS §§ 3451 et seq., 3670 et seq.], as in effect on that date.

Effective date of 1991 amendments. Act 105 Stat. 52, provides: "The amendments made by this section [amending this section and 38 USCS § 3241] shall take effect on April 1, 1991.".

CROSS REFERENCES

This section is referred to in 38 USCS § 3222.

§ 3232. Duration; limitations

(a)(1) Except as provided in paragraphs (2) and (3), and subject to paragraph (4), of this subsection, educational assistance benefits shall not be afforded an eligible veteran under this chapter [38 USCS §§ 3201 et seq.] more than 10 years after the date of such veteran's last discharge or release from active duty.

(2)(A) If any eligible veteran was prevented from initiating or completing such veteran's chosen program of education during the delimiting period determined under paragraph (1) of this subsection because of a physical or mental disability which was not the result of such veteran's own willful misconduct, such veteran shall, upon application made in accordance

38 USCS § 3232

with subparagraph (B) of this paragraph, be granted an extension of the applicable delimiting period for such length of time as the Secretary determines, from the evidence, that such veteran was so prevented from initiating or completing such program of education.

(B) An extension of the delimiting period applicable to an eligible veteran may be granted under subparagraph (A) of this paragraph by reason of the veteran's mental or physical disability only if the veteran submits an application for such extension to the Secretary within one year after (i) the last date of the delimiting period otherwise applicable to the veteran under paragraph (1) of this subsection, or (ii) the termination date of the period of the veteran's mental or physical disability, whichever is later.

(3) When an extension of the applicable delimiting period is granted an eligible veteran under paragraph (2) of this subsection, the delimiting period with respect to such veteran shall again begin to run on the first day after such veteran's recovery from such disability on which it is reasonably feasible, as determined in accordance with regulations prescribed by the Secretary, for such veteran to initiate or resume pursuit of a program of education with educational assistance under this chapter [38 USCS §§ 3201 et seq.].

(4) For purposes of paragraph (1) of this subsection, a veteran's last discharge or release from active duty shall not include any discharge or release from a period of active duty of less than 90 days of continuous service unless the individual involved is discharged or released for a service-connected disability, for a medical condition which preexisted such service and which the Secretary determines is not service connected, for hardship, or as a result of a reduction in force as described in section 3011(a)(1)(A)(ii)(III) of this title.

(b)(1) In the event that an eligible veteran has not utilized any or all of such veteran's entitlement by the end of the delimiting period applicable to the veteran under subsection (a) of this section and at the end of one year thereafter has not filed a claim for utilizing such entitlement, such eligible veteran is automatically disenrolled.

(2)(A) Any contributions which were made by a veteran disenrolled under paragraph (1) of this subsection and remain in the fund shall be refunded to the veteran after notice of disenrollment is transmitted to the veteran and the veteran applies for such refund.

(B) If no application for refund of contributions under subparagraph (A) of this paragraph is received from a disenrolled veteran within one year after the date the notice referred to in such subparagraph is transmitted to the veteran, it shall be presumed that the veteran's whereabouts is unknown and the funds shall be transferred to the Secretary for payments for entitlement earned under subchapter II of chapter 30 [38 USCS §§ 3011 et seq.].

(Added Oct. 15, 1976, P. L. 94-502, Title IV, § 404, 90 Stat. 2396; Sept. 13, 1982, P. L. 97-258, § 3(k)(2), 96 Stat. 1065; Nov. 21, 1983, P. L. 98-160, Title VII, § 702(8), 97 Stat. 1009; Oct. 28, 1986, P. L. 99-576, Title III, Part A,

§ 311, 100 Stat. 3272; Dec. 18, 1989, P. L. 101-237, Title IV, §§ 420(a)(2), 423(b)(1)(A), 103 Stat. 2087, 2092; March 22, 1991, P. L. 102-16, § 4, 105 Stat. 49; Aug. 6, 1991, P. L. 102-83, § 5(a), (c)(1), 105 Stat. 406; Oct. 9, 1996, P. L. 104-275, Title I, § 106(c)(1), 110 Stat. 3329.)

HISTORY; ANCILLARY LAWS AND DIRECTIVES
Effective date of section:
Act Oct. 15, 1976, P. L. 94-502, Title IV, § 406, 90 Stat. 2397, provided that this section is effective Jan. 1, 1977.

Amendments:
1982. Act Sept. 13, 1982 substituted "section 1322(a) of title 31" for "subsection (a) of section 725s of title 31"; and substituted "section 1322(a)" for "the last proviso of that subsection".
1983. Act Nov. 21, 1983, deleted a comma following "title 31", and substituted "such section" for "section 1322(a)".
1986. Act Oct. 28, 1986, substituted this section for one which read: "No educational assistance benefits shall be afforded an eligible veteran under this chapter beyond the date of 10 years after such veteran's last discharge or release from active duty. In the event an eligible veteran has not utilized any or all of such veteran's entitlement by the end of the 10-year period, such eligible veteran is automatically disenrolled and any contributions made by such veteran remaining in the fund shall be refunded to the veteran following notice to the veteran and an application by the veteran for such refund. If no application is received within 1 year from date of notice, it will be presumed for the purposes of section 1322(a) of title 31 that the individual's whereabouts is unknown and the funds shall be transferred as directed in such section.".
1989. Act Dec. 18, 1989, in subsec. (a), in para. (1), inserted ", and subject to paragraph (4),", and added para. (4).
Such Act further, in subsec. (a), in paras. (2) and (3), substituted "Secretary" for "Administrator", wherever appearing.
1991. Act March 22, 1991, in subsec. (b)(1), inserted "and at the end of one year thereafter has not filed a claim for utilizing such entitlement".
Act Aug. 6, 1991, redesignated this section, formerly 38 USCS § 1632, as 38 USCS § 3232, and amended the references in this section to reflect the redesignations made by § 5(a) of such Act (see Table III preceding 38 USCS § 101).
1996. Act Oct. 9, 1996, in subsec. (b)(2)(B), deleted ", for the purposes of section 1322(a) of title 31," following "presumed" and substituted "to the Secretary for payments for entitlement earned under subchapter II of chapter 30" for "as provided in such section".

RESEARCH GUIDE
Am Jur:
77 Am Jur 2d, Veterans and Veterans' Laws § 154.

§ 3233. Apprenticeship or other on-job training

(a) Except as provided in subsection (b) of this section, the amount of the

38 USCS § 3233   Veterans' Benefits

monthly benefit payment to an individual pursuing a full-time program of apprenticeship or other on-job training under this chapter [38 USCS §§ 3201 et seq.] is—

(1) for each of the first six months of the individual's pursuit of such program, 75 percent of the monthly benefit payment otherwise payable to such individual under this chapter [38 USCS §§ 3201 et seq.];

(2) for each of the second six months of the individual's pursuit of such program, 55 percent of such monthly benefit payment; and

(3) for each of the months following the first 12 months of the individual's pursuit of such program, 35 percent of such monthly benefit payment.

(b) In any month in which an individual pursuing a program of education consisting of a program of apprenticeship or other on-job training fails to complete 120 hours of training, the amount of the monthly benefit payment payable under this chapter [38 USCS §§ 3201 et seq.] to the individual shall be limited to the same proportion of the applicable rate determined under subsection (a) of this section as the number of hours worked during such month, rounded to the nearest eight hours, bears to 120 hours.

(c) For each month that an individual is paid a monthly benefit payment under this chapter [38 USCS §§ 3201 et seq.], the individual's entitlement under this chapter [38 USCS §§ 3201 et seq.] shall be charged at the rate of—

(1) 75 percent of a month in the case of payments made in accordance with subsection (a)(1) of this section;

(2) 55 percent of a month in the case of payments made in accordance with subsection (a)(2) of this section; and

(3) 35 percent of a month in the case of payments made in accordance with subsection (a)(3) of this section.

(d) For any month in which an individual fails to complete 120 hours of training, the entitlement otherwise chargeable under subsection (c) of this section shall be reduced in the same proportion as the monthly benefit payment payable is reduced under subsection (b) of this section.

(Added Oct. 28, 1986, P. L. 99-576, Title III, Part A, § 310(b)(2), 100 Stat. 3271; Dec. 18, 1989, P. L. 101-237, Title IV, § 423(a)(7), 103 Stat. 2091; Aug. 6, 1991, P. L. 102-83, § 5(a), 105 Stat. 406.)

HISTORY; ANCILLARY LAWS AND DIRECTIVES
Amendments:
1989. Act Dec. 18, 1989, added subsec. (d).
1991. Act Aug. 6, 1991, redesignated this section, formerly 38 USCS § 1633, as 38 USCS § 3233.

CROSS REFERENCES
This section is referred to in 38 USCS § 3231.

RESEARCH GUIDE
Am Jur:
77 Am Jur 2d, Veterans and Veterans' Laws § 144.

§ 3234. Tutorial assistance

(a) An individual entitled to benefits under this chapter [38 USCS §§ 3201 et seq.] shall also be entitled to the benefits provided an eligible veteran under section 3492 of this title, subject to the conditions applicable to an eligible veteran under such section. Any amount paid to an individual under this section shall be in addition to the amount of other benefits paid under this chapter [38 USCS §§ 3201 et seq.].

(b) An individual's period of entitlement to educational assistance under this chapter [38 USCS §§ 3201 et seq.] shall be charged only with respect to the amount of educational assistance paid to the individual under this section in excess of $600.

(c) An individual's period of entitlement to educational assistance under this chapter [38 USCS §§ 3201 et seq.] shall be charged at the rate of one month for each amount of assistance paid to the individual under this section in excess of $600 that is equal to the amount of monthly educational assistance the individual is otherwise eligible to receive for full-time pursuit of an institutional course under this chapter [38 USCS §§ 3201 et seq.].

(d) Payments of benefits under this section shall be made—

(1) in the case of the first $600 of such benefits paid to an individual, from funds appropriated, or otherwise available, to the Department of Veterans Affairs for the payment of readjustment benefits; and

(2) in the case of payments to an individual for such benefits in excess of $600, from the fund from contributions made to the fund by the veteran and by the Secretary of Defense in the same proportion as these contributions are used to pay other educational assistance to the individual under this chapter [38 USCS §§ 3201 et seq.].

(Added Nov. 18, 1988, P. L. 100-689, Title I, Part A, § 107(b)(1), 102 Stat. 4168; Dec. 18, 1989, P. L. 101-237, Title IV, § 423(b)(1)(B), 103 Stat. 2092; Aug. 6, 1991, P. L. 102-83, § 5(a), (c)(1), 105 Stat. 406.)

HISTORY; ANCILLARY LAWS AND DIRECTIVES
Amendments:

1989. Act Dec. 18, 1989, in subsec. (d)(1), substituted "Department of Veterans Affairs" for "Veterans' Administration".

1991. Act Aug. 6, 1991, redesignated this section, formerly 38 USCS § 1634, as 38 USCS § 3234, and amended the references in this section to reflect the redesignations made by § 5(a) of such Act (see Table III preceding 38 USCS § 101).

CROSS REFERENCES
This section is referred to in 38 USCS § 3680A.

RESEARCH GUIDE
Am Jur:

77 Am Jur 2d, Veterans and Veterans' Laws § 134.

SUBCHAPTER IV. ADMINISTRATION

§ 3241. Requirements

(a)(1) The provisions of sections 3470, 3471, 3474, 3483, and 3491(a)(1) of this title and the provisions of chapter 36 of this title [38 USCS §§ 3670 et seq.] (with the exception of section 3687) shall be applicable with respect to individuals who are pursuing programs of education while serving on active duty.

(2) The Secretary may, without regard to the application to this chapter [38 USCS §§ 3201 et seq.] of so much of the provisions of section 3471 of this title as prohibit the enrollment of an eligible veteran in a program of education in which the veteran is "already qualified", and pursuant to such regulations as the Secretary shall prescribe, approve the enrollment of such individual in refresher courses (including courses which will permit such individual to update knowledge and skills or be instructed in the technological advances which have occurred in the individual's field of employment during and since the period of such veteran's active military service), deficiency courses, or other preparatory or special education or training courses necessary to enable the individual to pursue an approved program of education.

(b) The Secretary may approve the pursuit of flight training (in addition to a course of flight training that may be approved under section 3680A(b) of this title) by an individual entitled to basic educational assistance under this chapter [38 USCS §§ 3201 et seq.] if—

(1) such training is generally accepted as necessary for the attainment of a recognized vocational objective in the field of aviation;

(2) the individual possesses a valid pilot's license and meets the medical requirements necessary for a commercial pilot's license; and

(3) the flight school courses meet Federal Aviation Administration standards for such courses and are approved by the Federal Aviation Administration and the State approving agency.

(c) The provisions of sections 3470, 3471, 3474, 3476, 3483, and 3491(a) (other than clause (1)) of this title and the provisions of chapter 36 of this title [38 USCS §§ 3670 et seq.] (with the exception of section 3687) shall be applicable with respect to individuals who are pursuing programs of education following discharge or release from active duty.

(Added Oct. 15, 1976, P. L. 94-502, Title IV, § 404, 90 Stat. 2397; Oct. 17, 1980, P. L. 96-466, Title IV, § 405, 94 Stat. 2202; Aug. 13, 1981, P. L. 97-35, Title XX, § 2003(a)(2), 95 Stat. 782; Oct. 28, 1986, P. L. 99-576, Title III, Part A, §§ 308(b), 310(c), 100 Stat. 3270, 3272; Nov. 18, 1988, P. L. 100-689, Title I, Part A, § 106(b), 102 Stat. 4167; Dec. 18, 1989, P. L. 101-237, Title IV, § 423(a)(5)(B), (b)(1)(A), 103 Stat. 2091, 2092; March 22, 1991, P. L. 102-16, §§ 2(b)(2), 7(a), 105 Stat. 49, 51; Aug. 6, 1991, P. L. 102-83, § 5(a), (c)(1), 105 Stat. 406; Oct. 29, 1992, P. L. 102-568, Title III, § 313(a)(5), 106 Stat. 4332; Nov. 2, 1994, P. L. 103-446, Title VI, § 601(b), Title XII, § 1201(d)(12), 108 Stat. 4670, 4684.)

HISTORY; ANCILLARY LAWS AND DIRECTIVES
Effective date of section:
Act Oct. 15, 1976, P. L. 94-502, Title IV, § 406, 90 Stat. 2397, provided that this section is effective Jan. 1, 1977.

Amendments:
1980. Act Oct. 17, 1980 (effective 10/1/80, as provided by § 802(d)(2) of such Act, which appears as 38 USCS § 3224 note), inserted "1663," and substituted "and 1691(a)(1)" for "1696, and 1698".

1981. Act Aug. 13, 1981 (effective as provided by § 2006 of such Act, which appears as 38 USCS § 3231 note), substituted this section for one which read: "The provisions of sections 1663, 1670, 1671, 1673, 1674, 1676, 1677, 1681(c), 1683, and 1691(a)(1) of this title and the provisions of chapter 36 of this title, with the exception of sections 1777, 1780(c), and 1787, shall be applicable to the program.".

1986. Act Oct. 28, 1986, designated existing matter as subsec. (a) and in such subsec. as so designated, inserted "1685" and substituted "section 1787) shall be applicable with respect to individuals who are pursuing programs of education while serving on active duty." for "sections 1777, 1780(c), and 1787) shall be applicable to the program."; and added subsec. (b).

1988. Act Nov. 18, 1988 (effective 8/15/89, as provided by § 106(d) of such Act, which appears as 38 USCS § 3034 note), in subsec. (a), designated the existing provisions as para. (1), and added para. (2); and, in subsec. (b), substituted "1691(a)(other than clause(1))" for "1691(a)(1)".

1989. Act Dec. 18, 1989, in subsec. (a)(2), substituted "employment during and since the period of such veteran's active military service)" for "employment)", and substituted "Secretary" for "Administrator", wherever appearing.

1991. Act March 22, 1991, in subsec. (a)(1), deleted "1663," following "sections".

Such Act further (effective 4/1/91 as provided by § 7(c) of such Act, which appears as 38 USCS § 3231 note) redesignated former subsec. (b) as subsec. (c); and added new subsec. (b).

Act Aug. 6, 1991, redesignated this section, formerly 38 USCS § 1641, as 38 USCS § 3241, and amended the references in this section to reflect the redesignations made by § 5(a) of such Act (see Table III preceding 38 USCS § 101).

1992. Act Oct. 29, 1992 (applicable as provided by § 313(b) of such Act, which appears as 10 USCS § 16136 note), in subsec. (a), in para. (1), deleted "3473," following "3471,"; in subsec. (b), in para. (1), substituted "3680A(b)" for "3473(b)"; and, in subsec. (c), deleted "3473," following "3471,".

1994. Act Nov. 2, 1994 (effective 10/1/94, as provided by § 601(d) of such Act, which appears as 38 USCS § 3034 note), in subsec. (b), deleted para. (2), which read: "This subsection shall not apply to a course of flight training that commences on or after October 1, 1994.", deleted the designation for para. (1), and redesignated subparas. (A), (B), and (C) as paras. (1), (2), and (3), respectively.

Such Act further, in subsec. (c), deleted "1663," preceding "3470".

CROSS REFERENCES
This section is referred to in 38 USCS § 3231, 3680A, 3688.

38 USCS § 3241

VETERANS' BENEFITS

RESEARCH GUIDE
Am Jur:
77 Am Jur 2d, Veterans and Veterans' Laws §§ 141, 142.

[§ 3242]. [§ 1642. Repealed]

HISTORY; ANCILLARY LAWS AND DIRECTIVES
The bracketed section number "3242" was inserted to preserve numerical continuity following the section number redesignations made by Act Aug. 6, 1991, P. L. 102-83, § 5(a), 105 Stat. 406.
This section (Act Oct. 15, 1976, P. L. 94-502, Title IV, § 404, 90 Stat. 2397; Oct. 12, 1982, P. L. 97-295, § 4(37) 96 Stat. 1307; Dec. 18, 1989, P. L. 101-237, Title IV, § 423(b)(1)(A), (4)(A), 103 Stat. 2092) was repealed by Act March 22, 1991, P. L. 102-16, § 5(a), 105 Stat. 50. This section provided for requirements for reporting to Congressional committees on veterans' affairs on implementation of the program provided for in this chapter.

§ 3243. Deposits; reports

Deductions made by the Department of Defense from the military pay of any participant shall be promptly transferred to the Secretary for deposit in the fund. The Secretary of Defense shall also submit to the Secretary a report each month showing the name, service number, and the amount of the deduction made from the military pay of each initial enrollee, any contribution made by the Secretary of Defense pursuant to section 3222(c) of this title, as well as any changes in each participant's enrollment and/or contribution. The report shall also include any additional information the Secretary and the Secretary of Defense deem necessary to administer this program. The Secretary shall maintain accounts showing contributions made to the fund by individual participants and by the Secretary of Defense as well as disbursements made from the fund in the form of benefits.
(Added Oct. 15, 1976, P. L. 94-502, Title IV, § 404, 90 Stat. 2397; Nov. 21, 1983, P. L. 98-160, Title VII, § 702(9), 97 Stat. 1009; Dec. 18, 1989, P. L. 101-237, Title IV, § 423(b)(1)(A), (4)(D) 103 Stat. 2092; Aug. 6, 1991, P. L. 102-83, § 5(a), (c)(1), 105 Stat. 406.)

HISTORY; ANCILLARY LAWS AND DIRECTIVES
Effective date of section:
Act Oct. 15, 1976, P. L. 94-502, Title IV, § 406, 90 Stat. 2397, provided that this section is effective Jan. 1, 1977.

Amendments:
1983. Act Nov. 21, 1983, inserted "of this title".
1989. Act Dec. 18, 1989, inserted "of Defense", following "Secretary", wherever appearing, and substituted "Secretary" for "Administrator", wherever appearing.

1991. Act Aug. 6, 1991, redesignated this section, formerly 38 USCS § 1643, as 38 USCS § 3243, and amended the references in this section to reflect the redesignations made by § 5(a) of such Act (see Table III preceding 38 USCS § 101).

CHAPTER 34. VETERANS' EDUCATIONAL ASSISTANCE

SUBCHAPTER I. PURPOSE—DEFINITIONS

Section
3451. Purpose.
3452. Definitions.

SUBCHAPTER II. ELIGIBILITY AND ENTITLEMENT

3461. Eligibility; entitlement; duration.
3462. Time limitations for completing a program of education.
[3463] [1663. Repealed]

SUBCHAPTER III. ENROLLMENT

3470. Selection of program.
3471. Applications; approval.
[3472] [1672. Repealed]
[3473. Repealed]
3474. Discontinuance for unsatisfactory conduct or progress.
[3475] [1675. Repealed]
3476. Education outside the United States.
[3477] [1677. Repealed]
[3478] [1678. Repealed]

SUBCHAPTER IV. PAYMENTS TO ELIGIBLE VETERANS; VETERAN-STUDENT SERVICES

3481. Educational assistance allowance.
3482. Computation of educational assistance allowances.
[3482A] [1682A. Repealed]
3483. Approval of courses.
3484. Apprenticeship or other on-job training; correspondence courses.
3485. Work-study allowance.
[3486] [1686. Repealed]
[3487] [1687. Repealed]

SUBCHAPTER V. SPECIAL ASSISTANCE FOR THE EDUCATIONALLY DISADVANTAGED

3490. Purpose.
3491. Elementary and secondary education and preparatory educational assistance.
3492. Tutorial assistance.
3493. Effect on educational entitlement.

[SUBCHAPTER VI. PREDISCHARGE EDUCATION PROGRAM]

[3495] [1695. Repealed]
[3496] [1696. Repealed]
[3497] [1697. Repealed]
[3498] [1698. Repealed]

HISTORY; ANCILLARY LAWS AND DIRECTIVES

Explanatory notes:
The bracketed section numbers "3463", "3472", "3475", "3477", "3478", "3482A", "3486", "3487", "3495", "3496", "3497", "3498" were inserted to preserve numerical continuity following the section number redesignations made by Act Aug. 6, 1991, P. L. 102-83, § 5(a), 105 Stat. 406.

A prior Chapter 33, containing §§ 1601, 1610–1613, 1620–1626, 1631–1634, 1641–1645, 1651–1656, 1661–1669, was repealed by Act March 3, 1966, P. L. 89-358, § 4(a), 80 Stat. 23.

Amendments:
1966. Act March 3, 1966, P. L. 89-358, § 2, 80 Stat. 12 (effective 3/3/66, as provided by § 12(a) of such Act), added this analysis.

1967. Act Aug. 31, 1967, P. L. 90-77, Title III, §§ 302(c), 304(b), 306(b)(1), 81 Stat. 185, 186, 188 (effective 10/1/67, as provided by § 405(a) of such Act), added items 1677 and 1678; and substituted items 1683–1687 for items 1683–1686 which read:

"1683. Measurement of courses.
"1684. Overcharges by educational institutions.
"1685. Approval of courses.
"1686. Discontinuance of allowances.".

1970. Act March 26, 1970, P. L. 91-219, Title II, § 204(b), 84 Stat. 81, deleted item 1687 which read: "Special training for the educationally disadvantaged."; and added subchapter V and VI headings and items 1690–1693, 1695–1697.

1972. Act Oct. 24, 1972, P. L. 92-540, Title IV, § 404(a), 86 Stat. 1090, deleted items 1672 and 1675 which read: "1672. Change of program." and "1675. Period of operation for approval."; substituted subchapter IV heading and items 1681–1685 for former subchapter IV heading and items 1681–1687 which read:

"SUBCHAPTER IV. PAYMENTS TO ELIGIBLE VETERANS
"1681. Educational assistance allowance.
"1682. Computation of educational assistance allowances.
"1683. Apprenticeship or other on-job training.
"1684. Measurement of courses.
"1685. Overcharges by educational institutions.
"1686. Approval of courses.
"1687. Discontinuance of allowances.";
and added item 1697A.

1974. Act Dec. 3, 1974, P. L. 93-508, Title III, § 302(b), 88 Stat. 1591 (effective 1/1/75, as provided by § 502 of such Act), added item 1686.

1976. Act Oct. 15, 1976, P. L. 94-502, Title II, § 210(4), 90 Stat. 2388 (effective 10/15/76, as provided by § 703(b) of such Act), redesignated item 1697A as item 1698.

1977. Act Nov. 23, 1977, P. L. 95-202, Title II, § 201(c)(1), 91 Stat. 1438 (effective 1/1/78, as provided by § 501 of such Act), added item 1682A.

1980. Act Oct. 17, 1980, P. L. 96-466, Title VI, § 601(a)(2), 94 Stat. 2208 (effective 10/1/80, as provided by § 802(f)(1) of such Act), deleted subchapter VI heading and items 1695–1698 which read:

38 USCS § 3451

"SUBCHAPTER VI. PREDISCHARGE EDUCATION PROGRAM
"1695. Purpose: definition.
"1696. Payment of educational assistance allowance.
"1697. Educational and vocational guidance.
"1698. Coordination with and participation by Department of Defense.".

1981. Act Aug. 13, 1981, P. L. 97-35, Title XX, § 2003(b)(3)(B), 95 Stat. 782 (effective as provided by § 2006 of such Act, which appears as 38 USCS § 1631 note], in the chapter analysis, deleted item 1677 which read "1677. Flight training."

1988. Act Nov. 18, 1988, P. L. 100-689, Title I, Part A, § 107(c)(2)(B), 102 Stat. 4169, amended the analysis of this chapter by substituting item 1692 for one which read "1692. Special supplementary assistance."

Act Nov. 18, 1988, P. L. 100-689, Title I, Part B, § 124(c)(1), 102 Stat. 4175, in the chapter analysis, deleted items 1682A and 1686 which read: "1682A. Accelerated payment of educational assistance allowances" and "1686. Education loans".

1989. Act Dec. 18, 1989, P. L. 101-237, Title IV, § 405(d)(4)(B), 103 Stat. 2082, effective 5/1/90 and applicable as provided by § 405(e) of such Act, which appears as 10 USCS § 2136 note, amended the analysis of this chapter by substituting item 1685 for one which read: "1685. Veteran-student services.".

1991. Act March 22, 1991, P. L. 102-16, § 2(b)(1)(B), 105 Stat. 49, amended the analysis of this chapter by deleting item 1663, which read: "1663. Educational and vocational counseling.".

Act Aug. 6, 1991, P. L. 102-83, § 5(b)(1), 105 Stat. 406, revised the analysis of this Chapter by amending the section numbers in accordance with the redesignations made by § 5(a) of such Act (see Table III preceding 38 USCS § 101).

1992. Act Oct. 29, 1992, P. L. 102-568, Title III, § 313(a)(3)(B), 106 Stat. 4332, applicable as provided by § 313(b) of such Act, which appears as 10 USCS § 2136 note, amended the analysis of this chapter by deleting item 3473, which read: "3473. Disapproval of enrollment in certain courses.".

SUBCHAPTER I. PURPOSE—DEFINITIONS

§ 3451. Purpose

The Congress of the United States hereby declares that the education program created by this chapter [38 USCS §§ 3451 et seq.] is for the purpose of (1) enhancing and making more attractive service in the Armed Forces of the United States, (2) extending the benefits of a higher education to qualified and deserving young persons who might not otherwise be able to afford such an education, (3) providing vocational readjustment and restoring lost educational opportunities to those service men and women whose careers have been interrupted or impeded by reason of active duty after January 31, 1955, and (4) aiding such persons in attaining the vocational and educational status which they might normally have aspired to and obtained had they not served their country.

READJUSTMENT BENEFITS   **38 USCS § 3451**

(Added March 3, 1966, P. L. 89-358, § 2, 80 Stat. 12; Aug. 6, 1991, P. L. 102-83, § 5(a), 105 Stat. 406.)

HISTORY; ANCILLARY LAWS AND DIRECTIVES

Explanatory notes:
Provisions similar to those contained in clauses (3) and (4) of this section were contained in former 38 USC § 1601(c), prior to repeal by Act March 3, 1966, P. L. 89-358, § 4(a), 80 Stat. 23.

Amendments:
1991. Act Aug. 6, 1991, redesignated this section, formerly 38 USCS § 1651, as 38 USCS § 3451.

Other provisions:
Savings provisions. Act March 3, 1966, P. L. 89-358, § 4(b), 80 Stat. 23, provided: "Nothing in this Act [adding 38 USCS §§ 3451 et seq., among other things; for full classification, consult USCS Tables volumes] or any amendment or repeal made by it, shall affect any right or liability (civil or criminal) which matured under chapter 33 of title 38 [former 38 USC §§ 1601 et seq.] before the date of enactment of this Act; and all offenses committed, and all penalties and forfeitures incurred, under any provision of law amended or repealed by this Act, may be punished or recovered, as the case may be, in the same manner and with the same effect as if such amendments or repeals had not been made.".

Effective date and application of Act March 3, 1966. Act March 3, 1966, P. L. 89-358, § 12(a), 80 Stat. 28, provided: "Except as otherwise specifically provided, the provisions of this Act [adding 38 USCS §§ 3451 et seq., among other things; for full classification of this Act, consult USCS Tables volumes] shall take effect on the date of its enactment, but no educational assistance allowance shall be payable under chapter 34 of title 38, United States Code, as added by section 2 of this Act [38 USCS §§ 3451 et seq.], for any period before June 1, 1966, nor for the month of June 1966, unless (1) the eligible veteran commenced the pursuit of the course of education on or after June 1, 1966, or (2) the pursuit of such course continued through June 30, 1966.".

CODE OF FEDERAL REGULATIONS

Department of Veterans Affairs—Vocational rehabilitation and education, 38 CFR Part 21.

RESEARCH GUIDE

Am Jur:
77 Am Jur 2d, Veterans and Veterans' Laws §§ 132, 134, 137, 140, 144.

Forms:
24A Am Jur Pl & Pr Forms (Rev), Veterans and Veterans' Laws, Form 21.

Annotations:
Who is "individual with handicaps" under Rehabilitation Act of 1973 (29 USCS §§ 701 et seq.). 97 ALR Fed 40.

Law Review Articles:
Benefits for Conscientious Objectors. 19 Catholic Lawyer 62, Winter 1973.

Constitutional Law—Due Process—Conscientious Objectors Entitled to Same Veterans Educational Benefits Received By Regular Servicemen. 6 Creighton L Rev 393, 1972-73.

Constitutional Law—Equal Protection—Veteran's Educational Benefits for Conscientious Objectors. 8 Suffolk Univ L Rev 1239, Summer 1974.

Robison v Johnson (352 F Supp 848): Veterans' Educational Benefits for Conscientious Objectors. 121 Univ of Pa L Rev 1133, May 1973.

Auto-Cite®: Cases and annotations referred to herein can be further researched through the Auto-Cite® computer-assisted research service. Use Auto-Cite to check citations for form, parallel references, prior and later history, and annotation references.

INTERPRETIVE NOTES AND DECISIONS

1. Generally
2. Constitutionality
3. Purpose
4. Applicability

1. Generally

State law, which excludes from state benefits honorably discharged conscientious objector who is eligible for federal educational benefits under provisions of 38 USCS §§ 1651 et seq., 1661 et seq. [now 38 USCS §§ 3451, et seq., 3461 et seq.], is invalid as state legislation, effect of which would be to frustrate congressional intention and to produce result diametrically opposed to those sought by federal law, and cannot stand, particularly in absence of showing of any present or future compelling state interest. Reynolds v Dukakis (1977, DC Mass) 441 F Supp 646.

2. Constitutionality

Statutory scheme restricting educational benefits under Veterans' Readjustment Benefits Act of 1966 (38 USCS §§ 1651-1697 [now 38 USCS §§ 3451-3497]) to veterans who served on active duty, thus denying benefits to conscientious objectors who performed required alternative civilian service, does not violate such conscientious objectors' First Amendment rights of free exercise of religion, since (1) withholding of educational benefits involved, at most, only incidental burden on free exercise of religion by conscientious objectors, (2) Act was enacted pursuant to Congress' powers under Article 1, § 8, of Constitution to advance neutral, secular governmental interests of enhancing military service and aiding readjustment to civilian life of military personnel who served on active duty, and (3) conscientious objectors who performed alternative civilian service were excluded not because of any legislative design to interfere with their free exercise of religion, but because to include them would not rationally promote Act's purposes-government's substantial interest in raising and supporting armies being of kind and weight clearly sufficient to sustain challenged legislation; although statutory scheme restricting educational benefits under Veterans' Readjustment Benefits Act of 1966 (38 USCS §§ 1651-1697 [now 38 USCS §§ 3451-3497]) to veterans who served on active duty, thus denying benefits to conscientious objectors who performed required alternative civilian service, would violate such conscientious objectors' Fifth Amendment due process rights, incorporating equal protection principles, if exclusion of such conscientious objectors was product of vindictive policy to punish them for adhering to their beliefs, nevertheless there is nothing to indicate that exclusion was product of such policy, and thus statutory scheme is not unconstitutional on such ground. Johnson v Robison (1974) 415 US 361, 39 L Ed 2d 389, 94 S Ct 1160 (criticized in Hall v United States Dep't Veterans' Affairs (1996, CA11 Fla) 85 F3d 532, 9 FLW Fed C 1171).

Legislation to make service in the armed forces more attractive by extending educational benefits to veterans is within Congress' power to raise and support armies under Article 1, § 8, of Constitution. Johnson v Robison (1974) 415 US 361, 39 L Ed 2d 389, 94 S Ct 1160 (criticized in Hall v United States Dep't Veterans' Affairs (1996, CA11 Fla) 85 F3d 532, 9 FLW Fed C 1171).

3. Purpose

Purpose of Veterans' Readjustment Benefits Act of 1966 (38 USCS §§ 1651-1697 [now 38 USCS §§ 3451-3497]) is not primarily to eliminate the educational gaps between persons who served their country and those who did not, but rather is to compensate for the disruption that military service causes to civilian lives; the aim of the Act is to assist those who served on active duty in the armed forces to readjust to civilian life. Johnson v Robison (1974) 415 US 361, 39 L Ed 2d 389, 94 S Ct 1160 (criticized in Hall v United States Dep't Veterans' Affairs (1996, CA11 Fla) 85 F3d 532, 9 FLW Fed C 1171).

4. Applicability

Commissioned Corps of Public Health Service was not within purview of Veterans' Readjustment Assistance Act of 1952 (38 USCS § 1651 et seq. [now 38 USCS § 3451 et seq.]), but members of Commissioned Corps of Public Health Service, detailed by proper authority for duty with Army, Navy, or Coast Guard, were members of such forces and, while on such detailed service, were within definition of "armed forces" under former 38 USC § 911; members of Commissioned Corps of Public Health Service in active service outside continental limits of United States or in Alaska in time of war who would otherwise be entitled to full military benefits on account of such service were not within purview of Veterans' Readjustment Assistance Act of 1952, unless such service was performed as member of, or on detail to, Army, Navy, Air Force, Marine Corps, or Coast Guard of United States. 1952 ADVA 919.

§ 3452. Definitions

For the purposes of this chapter [38 USCS §§ 3451 et seq.] and chapter 36 of this title [38 USCS §§ 3670 et seq.]—

(a)(1) The term "eligible veteran" means any veteran who—

(A) served on active duty for a period of more than 180 days, any part of which occurred after January 31, 1955, and before January 1, 1977, and was discharged or released therefrom under conditions other than dishonorable; or

(B) contracted with the Armed Forces and was enlisted in or assigned to a reserve component prior to January 1, 1977, and as a result of such enlistment or assignment served on active duty for a period of more than 180 days, any part of which commenced within 12 months after January 1, 1977, and was discharged or released from such active duty under conditions other than dishonorable; or

(C) was discharged or released from active duty, any part of which was performed after January 31, 1955, and before January 1, 1977, or following entrance into active service from an enlistment provided for under clause (B) of this paragraph, because of a service-connected disability.

(2) The requirement of discharge or release, prescribed in paragraph (1)(A) or (B), shall be waived in the case of any individual who served more than one hundred and eighty days in an active duty status for so long as such individual continues on active duty without a break therein.

(3) For purposes of paragraph (1)(A) and section 3461(a), the term "active duty" does not include any period during which an individual (A) was assigned full time by the Armed Forces to a civilian institution for a course of education which was substantially the same as established courses offered to civilians, (B) served as a cadet or midshipman at one of the service academies, or (C) served under the provisions of section 511(d) of title 10 [10 USCS § 12103(d)] pursuant to an enlistment in the Army National Guard or the Air National Guard or as a Reserve for service in the Army Reserve, Naval Reserve, Air Force Reserve, Marine Corps Reserve, or Coast Guard Reserve unless at some time subsequent to the completion of such period of active duty for training such individual served on active duty for a consecutive period of one year or more (not including any service as a cadet or midshipman at one of the service academies).

(b) The term "program of education" means any curriculum or any combination of unit courses or subjects pursued at an educational institution which is generally accepted as necessary to fulfill requirements for the attainment of a predetermined and identified educational, professional, or vocational objective. Such term also means any curriculum of unit courses or subjects pursued at an educational institution which fulfill requirements for the attainment of more than one predetermined and identified educational, professional, or vocational objective if all the objectives pursued are generally recognized as being reasonably related to a single career field. Such term also means any unit course or subject, or combination of courses or subjects, pursued by an eligible veteran at an educational institution, required by the Administrator of the Small Business Administration as a condition to obtaining financial assistance under the provisions of section 7(i)(1) of the Small Business Act (15 U.S.C. 636(i)(1)).

(c) The term "educational institution" means any public or private elementary school, secondary school, vocational school, correspondence school, business school, junior college, teachers' college, college, normal school, professional school, university, or scientific or technical institution, or other institution furnishing education for adults. Such term includes any entity that provides training required for completion of any State-approved alternative teacher certification program (as determined by the Secretary).

(d) The term "dependent" means—
  (1) a child of an eligible veteran;
  (2) a dependent parent of an eligible veteran; and
  (3) the spouse of an eligible veteran.

(e) The term "training establishment" means any establishment providing apprentice or other training on the job, including those under the supervision of a college or university or any State department of education, or any State apprenticeship agency, or any State board of vocational education, or any joint apprenticeship committee, or the Bureau of Apprenticeship and Training established pursuant to chapter 4C of title 29 [29 USCS §§ 50 et seq.] or any agency of the Federal Government authorized to supervise such training.

(f) The term "institution of higher learning" means a college, university, or similar institution, including a technical or business school, offering postsecondary level academic instruction that leads to an associate or higher degree if the school is empowered by the appropriate State education authority under State law to grant an associate or higher degree. When there is no State law to authorize the granting of a degree, the school may be recognized as an institution of higher learning if it is accredited for degree programs by a recognized accrediting agency. Such term shall also include a hospital offering educational programs at the postsecondary level without regard to whether the hospital grants a postsecondary degree. Such term shall also include an educational institution which is not located in a State, which offers a course leading to a standard college degree, or the equivalent, and which is recognized as such by the secretary of education (or comparable official) of the country or other jurisdiction in which the institution is located.

READJUSTMENT BENEFITS   38 USCS § 3452

(g) The term "standard college degree" means an associate or higher degree awarded by (1) an institution of higher learning that is accredited as a collegiate institution by a recognized regional or national accrediting agency; or (2) an institution of higher learning that is a "candidate" for accreditation as that term is used by the regional or national accrediting agencies; or (3) an institution of higher learning upon completion of a course which is accredited by an agency recognized to accredit specialized degree-level programs. For the purpose of this section, the accrediting agency must be one recognized by the Secretary of Education under the provisions of section 3675 of this title.

(Added March 3, 1966, P. L. 89-358, § 2, 80 Stat. 13; Aug. 31, 1967, P. L. 90-77, Title III, § 304(c), 81 Stat. 186; March 26, 1970, P. L. 91-219, Title II, § 201, 84 Stat. 78; Dec. 24, 1970, P. L. 91-584 § 10, 84 Stat. 1577; Dec. 3, 1974, P. L. 93-508, Title II, § 201, 88 Stat. 1581; Oct. 15, 1976, P. L. 94-502, Title II, §§ 202, 210(1), 211(1), Title IV, § 402, 90 Stat. 2385, 2388, 2392; Oct. 17, 1980, P. L. 96-466, Title III, Part A, § 307(a), Title VIII, § 801(a), 94 Stat. 2193, 2216; Oct. 12, 1982, P. L. 97-295, § 4(38), 96 Stat. 1307; Aug. 6, 1991, P. L. 102-83, § 5(a), (c)(1), 105 Stat. 406; Nov. 2, 1994, P. L. 103-446, Title VI, § 603(a), 108 Stat. 4671; Oct. 9, 1996, P. L. 104-275, Title I, § 102, 110 Stat. 3326.)

HISTORY; ANCILLARY LAWS AND DIRECTIVES

Explanatory notes:
The bracketed reference "10 USCS § 12103(d)" has been inserted in subsec. (a)(3) on authority of Act Oct. 4, 1994, P. L. 103-337, Div. A, Title XVI, § 1662(b)(2), 108 Stat. 2990, which redesignated 10 USCS § 511 as 10 USCS § 12103.

Provisions similar to those contained in subsecs. (a)–(d) were contained in former 38 USC §§ 1601(a)(2), (3), (5), (6), and 1611(a)(1), prior to repeal by Act March 3, 1966, P. L. 89-358, § 4(a), 80 Stat. 23.

Amendments:
1967. Act Aug. 31, 1967 (effective on the first day of the first calendar month which begins more than 10 days after enactment, as provided by § 405(a) of such Act, which appears as 38 USCS § 101 note), added subsec. (e).

1970. Act March 26, 1970, in subsec. (b), inserted "Such term also means any curriculum of unit courses or subjects pursued at an educational institution which fulfill requirements for the attainment of more than one predetermined and identified educational, professional, or vocational objective if all the objectives pursued are generally recognized as being reasonably related to a single career field."; and substituted new subsec. (c) for one which read: "The term 'educational institution' means any public or private secondary school, vocational school, correspondence school, business school, junior college, teachers' college, college, normal school, professional school, university, or scientific or technical institution, or any other institution if it furnishes education at the secondary school level or above.".

Act Dec. 24, 1970, in subsec. (a)(2), substituted "more than one hundred and eighty days" for "at least two years"; in subsec. (b), inserted "Such term also means any unit course or subject, or combination of courses or

38 USCS § 3452

subjects, pursued by an eligible veteran at an educational institution, required by the Administrator of the Small Business Administration as a condition to obtaining financial assistance under the provisions of 402(a) of the Economic Opportunity Act of 1964 (42 U.S.C. 2902(a)).''.

1974. Act Dec. 3, 1974, in subsec. (a)(3), inserted "unless at some time subsequent to the completion of such period of active duty for training such individual served on active duty for a consecutive period of one year or more (not including any service as a cadet or midshipman at one of the service academies)''.

1976. Act Oct. 15, 1976, § 402 (effective 1/1/77, as provided by § 406 of such Act, which appears as 38 USCS § 3201 note), in subsec. (a), substituted para. (1) for one which read: ''(1) The term 'eligible veteran' means any veteran who (A) served on active duty for a period of more than 180 days any part of which occurred after January 31, 1955, and who was discharged or released therefrom under conditions other than dishonorable or (B) was discharged or released from active duty after such date for a service-connected disability.'' and, in para. (2), inserted ''or (B)''.

Act Oct. 15, 1976, §§ 202, 210(1), 211(1) (effective 10/15/76, as provided by § 703(b) of such Act, which appears as 38 USCS § 3693 note), in subsec. (a)(2), substituted ''such individual'' for ''he''; in subsec. (d)(3), substituted ''spouse'' for ''wife''; in subsec. (e), deleted ''United States Code,'' following ''title 29,''; and added subsecs. (f) and (g).

1980. Act Oct. 17, 1980, § 801(a), in the introductory matter, inserted ''and chapter 36 of this title''; in subsecs. (e), (f) and (g), substituted ''The'' for ''For the purposes of this chapter and chapter 36 of this title, the''; and in subsec. (g), substituted ''Secretary'' for ''Commissioner''.

Act Oct. 17, 1980, § 307(a), in subsec. (f), inserted ''Such term shall also include an educational institution which is not located in a State, which offers a course leading to a standard college degree, or the equivalent, and which is recognized as such by the secretary of education (or comparable official) of the country or other jurisdiction in which the institution is located.''.

1982. Act Oct. 12, 1982, in subsec. (b), substituted ''section 7(i)(1) of the Small Business Act (15 U.S.C. 636(i)(1))'' for ''402(a) of the Economic Opportunity Act of 1964 (42 U.S.C. 2902(a))''.

1991. Act Aug. 6, 1991, redesignated this section, formerly 38 USCS § 1652, as 38 USCS § 3452, and amended the references in this section to reflect the redesignations made by § 5(a) of such Act (see Table III preceding 38 USCS § 101).

1994. Act Nov. 2, 1994, in subsec. (c), added the sentence beginning ''For the period ending . . .''.

1996. Act Oct. 9, 1996, in subsec. (c), substituted ''Such'' for ''For the period ending on September 30, 1996, such''.

Other provisions:

Effective date and application of section. Act March 3, 1966, P. L. 89-358, § 12(a), 80 Stat. 28, located at 38 USCS § 3451 note, provided that this section is effective on March 3, 1966, but no educational assistance allowance shall be payable under this chapter (38 USCS §§ 3451 et seq.) for any period before June 1, 1966, nor for the month of June 1966, unless (1) the eligible veteran commenced the pursuit of the course of education on or after June 1, 1966, or (2) the pursuit of such course continued through June 30, 1966.

Effective date of amendments made by Titles II and IV of Act Dec. 3, 1974. Act Dec. 3, 1974, P. L. 93-508, Title V, § 503, 88 Stat. 1601, provided: "Titles II and IV of this Act [amending this section, among other things; for full classification of these Titles, consult USCS Tables volumes] shall become effective on the date of their enactment.".

Effective date and application of amendments made by Title III of Act Oct. 17, 1980. Act Oct. 17, 1980, P. L. 96-466, Title VIII, § 802(c), 94 Stat. 2218, provided:

"(1) Except as provided in paragraph (2), the amendments made by title III [amending this section, among other things; for full classification of this title, consult USCS Tables volumes] shall become effective on October 1, 1980.

"(2) Paragraph (2) of section 1691(a) of title 38, United States Code, as added by section 311(2) [38 USCS § 3491(a)], shall not apply to any person receiving educational assistance under chapter 34 of title 38, United States Code [38 USCS §§ 3451 et seq.], on October 1, 1980, for the pursuit of a program of education, as defined in section 1652(b) of such title [subsec. (b) of this section], in which such person is enrolled on that date, for as long as such person continuously thereafter is so enrolled and meets the requirements of eligibility for such assistance for pursuit of such program.".

Effective date of amendments made by § 801 of Act Oct. 17, 1980. Act Oct. 17, 1980, P. L. 96-466, Title VIII, § 802(h), 94 Stat. 2219, provided: "Section 801 [amending this section and 38 USCS §§ 3501, 3675, 3681, 3690, 3698, 4101, 4213, 4214, and notes to 38 USCS §§ 106, 3473, 3474] shall become effective on October 1, 1980.".

Application and construction of Oct. 12, 1982 amendment. For provisions as to the application and construction of the Oct. 12, 1982 amendment of this section (see the Amendments note to this section), see § 5 of such Act, which appears as 10 USCS § 101 note.

CODE OF FEDERAL REGULATIONS

Department of Veterans Affairs—Vocational rehabilitation and education, 38 CFR Part 21.

CROSS REFERENCES

This section is referred to in 20 USCS § 1070d; 38 USCS §§ 1524, 3002, 3031, 3101, 3202, 3461, 3672, 3686, 3687.

RESEARCH GUIDE

Am Jur:
45B Am Jur 2d, Job Discrimination (1993) § 902.

Annotations:
Who is "individual with handicaps" under Rehabilitation Act of 1973 (29 USCS §§ 701 et seq.). 97 ALR Fed 40.

INTERPRETIVE NOTES AND DECISIONS

1. Generally
2. Eligible veteran

1. Generally

Legislative history of P. L. 94-502 indicated that

amendment of 38 USCS § 1652(f), (g) [now 38 USCS § 3452(f), (g)] by P. L. 94-502, constituted codification of long-standing practices and pre-existing regulations of Veterans' Administration [now Department of Veterans Affairs]; now and process of enactment of P. L. 94-502 did not operate to deprive veterans of due process of law [USCS Const, Amend 5]. Letellier v Cleland (1977, SD Iowa) 437 F Supp 936.

2. Eligible veteran
Individual's military service may be considered valid and honorable, for purposes of qualifying as eligible veteran under 38 USCS § 1652(a) [now 38 USCS § 3452(a)], notwithstanding service department has voided entire period of service while granting discharge under honorable conditions, where claimant had no statutory impediment to enlistment and was never convicted of felony. VA GCO 2-80.

SUBCHAPTER II. ELIGIBILITY AND ENTITLEMENT

§ 3461. Eligibility; entitlement; duration

Entitlement

(a) Except as provided in subsection (c) and in the second sentence of this subsection, each eligible veteran shall be entitled to educational assistance under this chapter [38 USCS §§ 3451 et seq.] or chapter 36 [38 USCS §§ 3670 et seq.] for a period of one and one-half months (or the equivalent thereof in part-time educational assistance) for each month or fraction thereof of the veteran's service on active duty after January 31, 1955. If an eligible veteran has served a period of 18 months or more on active duty after January 31, 1955, and has been released from such service under conditions that would satisfy the veteran's active duty obligation, the veteran shall be entitled to educational assistance under this chapter [38 USCS §§ 3451 et seq.] or chapter 36 [38 USCS §§ 3670 et seq.] for a period of 45 months (or the equivalent thereof in part-time educational assistance). In the case of any person serving on active duty on December 31, 1976, or a person whose eligibility is based on section 3452(a)(1)(B) of this chapter, the ending date for computing such person's entitlement shall be the date of such person's first discharge or release from active duty after December 31, 1976.

Entitlement Limitations

(b) Whenever the period of entitlement under this section of an eligible veteran who is enrolled in an educational institution regularly operated on the quarter or semester system ends during a quarter or semester, such period shall be extended to the termination of such unexpired quarter or semester. In educational institutions not operated on the quarter or semester system, whenever the period of eligibility ends after a major portion of the course is completed such period shall be extended to the end of the course or for twelve weeks, whichever is the lesser period.

(c) Except as provided in subsection (b) and in subchapter V of this chapter [38 USCS §§ 3490 et seq.], no eligible veteran shall receive educational assistance under this chapter in excess of 45 months.

(Added March 3, 1966, P. L. 89-858, § 2, 80 Stat. 13; Aug. 31, 1967, P. L. 90-77, Title III, § 306(b)(2), 81 Stat. 188; Oct. 23, 1968, P. L. 90-631, § 1(b), 82 Stat. 1331; March 26, 1970, P. L. 91-219, Title II, § 204(a)(1), 84 Stat. 79; Oct. 24, 1972, P. L. 92-540, Title IV, § 401(1), 86 Stat. 1089; Dec. 3, 1974,

READJUSTMENT BENEFITS   38 USCS § 3461

P. L. 93-508, Title II, § 202, 88 Stat. 1581; Oct. 15, 1976, P. L. 94-502, Title II, §§ 203, 211(2), Title IV, § 403(a), 90 Stat. 2386, 2388, 2393; Oct. 17, 1980, P. L. 96-466, Title VI, § 601(b), 94 Stat. 2208; Aug. 6, 1991, P. L. 102-83, § 5(a), (c)(1), 105 Stat. 406.)

HISTORY; ANCILLARY LAWS AND DIRECTIVES

Explanatory notes:
Provisions similar to those contained in subsecs. (a)–(c) of this section were contained in former 38 USC §§ 1610, 1611(a)(2), (3), (b), prior to repeal by Act March 3, 1966, P. L. 89-358, § 4(a), 80 Stat. 23.

Amendments:
1967. Act Aug. 31, 1967 (effective as provided by § 405(a) of such Act, which appears as 38 USCS § 101 note), in subsec. (b), introductory matter, inserted "and in section 1678 of this chapter".

1968. Act Oct. 23, 1968 (effective as provided by § 6(a) of such Act, which appears as 38 USCS § 3500 note), substituted new subsec. (a) for one which read: "Except as provided in subsection (b), each eligible veteran shall be entitled to educational assistance under this chapter for a period of one month (or to the equivalent thereof in part-time educational assistance) for each month or fraction thereof of his service on active duty after January 31, 1955."; deleted subsec. (b) which read:

"(b) Except as provided in subsection (c) and in section 1678 of this chapter, in no event shall an eligible veteran receive educational assistance under this chapter for a period which, when combined with education and training received under any or all of the laws listed below, will exceed thirty-six months—

 "(1) parts VII or VIII, Veterans Regulation Numbered 1(a), as amended;

 "(2) title II of the Veterans' Readjustment Assistance Act of 1952;

 "(3) the War Orphans' Educational Assistance Act of 1956;

 "(4) chapters 31, 33, and 35 of this title.";

redesignated subsec. (c) as subsec. (b), added a new subsec. (c), and deleted subsec. (d), which read: "If an eligible veteran is entitled to educational assistance under this chapter and also to vocational rehabilitation under chapter 31 of this title, he must, if he wants either, elect whether he will receive educational assistance or vocational rehabilitation. If an eligible veteran is entitled to educational assistance under this chapter and is not entitled to such vocational rehabilitation, but after beginning his program of education becomes entitled (as determined by the Administrator) to such vocational rehabilitation, he must, if he wants either, elect whether to continue to receive educational assistance or whether to receive such vocational rehabilitation. If he elects to receive vocational rehabilitation, the program of education under this chapter shall be utilized to the fullest extent practicable in determining the character and duration of vocational rehabilitation to be furnished him.".

1970. Act March 26, 1970, in subsec. (c), substituted "subchapters V and VI of this chapter" for "section 1678 of this title".

1972. Act Oct. 24, 1972, in subsec. (a), inserted "or chapter 36".

1974. Act Dec. 3, 1974 (effective 12/3/74, as provided by § 503 of such Act, which appears as 38 USCS § 3452 note), in subsec. (a), inserted "plus

38 USCS § 3461

an additional number of months, not exceeding nine, as may be utilized in pursuit of a program of education leading to a standard undergraduate college degree"; and in subsec. (c), substituted "subsections (a) and (b)" for "subsection (b)".

1976. Act Oct. 15, 1976, § 211(2) (effective 10/15/76, as provided by § 703(b) of such Act, which appears as 38 USCS § 3693 note), in subsec. (a), substituted "the veteran's" for "his" wherever appearing and substituted "the veteran" for "he".

Act Oct. 15, 1976 § 203 (effective 10/1/76, as provided by § 703(a) of such Act, which appears as 38 USCS § 3693 note), in subsec. (a), substituted "45 months (or the equivalent thereof in part-time educational assistance)." for "36 months (or the equivalent thereof in part-time educational assistance) plus an additional number of months, not exceeding nine, as may be utilized in pursuit of a program of education leading to a standard undergraduate college degree."; substituted new subsec. (c) for one which read: "Except as provided in subsections (a) and (b) and in subchapters V and VI of this chapter, no eligible veteran shall receive educational assistance under this chapter in excess of thirty-six months.".

Act Oct. 15, 1976, § 403(a) (effective 1/1/77, as provided by § 406 of such Act, which appears as 38 USCS § 3201), in subsec. (a), inserted "In the case of any person serving on active duty on December 31, 1976, or a person whose eligibility is based on section 1652(a)(1)(B) of this chapter, the ending date for computing such person's entitlement shall be the date of such person's first discharge or release from active duty after December 31, 1976.".

1980. Act Oct. 17, 1980 (effective 10/1/80, as provided by § 802(f)(1) of such Act, which appears as 38 USCS § 5314 note), in subsec. (c), substituted "subchapter V" for "subchapters V and VI".

1991. Act Aug. 6, 1991, redesignated this section, formerly 38 USCS § 1661, as 38 USCS § 3461, and amended the references in this section to reflect the redesignations made by § 5(a) of such Act (see Table III preceding 38 USCS § 101).

Other provisions:

Effective date and application of section. Act March 3, 1966, P. L. 89-358, § 12(a), 80 Stat. 28, located at 38 USCS § 3451 note, provided that this section is effective on March 3, 1966, but no educational assistance allowance shall be payable under this chapter (38 USCS §§ 3451 et seq.) for any period before June 1, 1966, nor for the month of June 1966, unless (1) the eligible veteran commenced the pursuit of the course of education on or after June 1, 1966, or (2) the pursuit of such course continued through June 30, 1966.

CROSS REFERENCES

This section is referred to in 38 USCS §§ 3452, 3462, 3482, 3493, 3698.

RESEARCH GUIDE

Am Jur:

77 Am Jur 2d, Veterans and Veterans' Laws §§ 134, 137.

Forms:

24A Am Jur Pl & Pr Forms (Rev), Veterans and Veterans' Laws, Form 21.

READJUSTMENT BENEFITS 38 USCS § 3462

Annotations:
Who is "individual with handicaps" under Rehabilitation Act of 1973 (29 USCS §§ 701 et seq.). 97 ALR Fed 40.

Effect on right to unemployment compensation benefits of receipt of subsistence allowance under Federal Servicemen's Readjustment Act. 21 ALR2d 1072.

INTERPRETIVE NOTES AND DECISIONS

1. Generally
2. Constitutionality
3. Computation of entitlement

1. Generally

Flight training school cannot recover from government difference between what veteran was paid in educational benefits under 38 USCS §§ 1651 et seq. [now 38 USCS §§ 3451 et seq.] and total cost of training, where Veterans' Administration [now Department of Veterans Affairs] mistakenly certified veteran for more months of entitlement than he was due and paid him based on actual entitlement after course was completed, since VA was without statutory authority to certify longer entitlement than veteran was due and had no power to pay larger amount in educational benefits. Augusta Aviation, Inc. v United States (1982, CA11 Ga) 671 F2d 445.

2. Constitutionality

In determining whether Fifth Amendment equal protection is denied by statutory scheme restricting educational benefits under Veterans' Readjustment Benefits Act of 1966 (38 USCS §§ 1651-1697 [38 USCS §§ 3451-3497]) to veterans who served on active duty, thus denying benefits to conscientious objectors who performed required alternative civilian service, statutory classification will not be subjected to strict scrutiny rather than traditional rational basis test, since (1) challenged classification does not violate right to free exercise of religion by conscientious objectors, and (2) class of conscientious objectors is not suspect class deserving special judicial protection—such class not possessing immutable characteristic determined solely by accident of birth, and not being saddled with such disabilities, or subject to such history of purposeful unequal treatment, or relegated to such position of political powerlessness as to command extraordinary protection from majoritarian political process. Johnson v Robison (1974) 415 US 361, 39 L Ed 2d 389, 94 S Ct 1160 (criticized in Hall v United States Dep't Veterans' Affairs (1996, CA11 Fla) 85 F3d 532, 9 FLW Fed C 1171).

3. Computation of entitlement

Veterans Administration [now Department of Veterans Affairs] policy under which extensions of delimiting date for educational benefits are denied based on veteran's inability to complete education due to alcoholism does not violate equal protection or due process rights, but does violate Rehabilitation Act (29 USCS § 794). Tinch v Walters (1983, ED Tenn) 573 F Supp 346, affd (1985, CA6 Tenn) 765 F2d 599.

Computation of period for which education allowance is to be granted under 38 USCS § 1661(a) [38 USCS § 3461(a)] must be based on "corresponding days" (from any given day of one calendar month to corresponding day of next), rather than actual calendar months. VA GCO 18-79.

Computation for multiple periods of noncontinuous service is to be accomplished by combining all includable periods of active duty and then dividing by 30, as opposed to giving credit for one month's service for each calendar month in which at least one day of active duty occurs. VA GCO 18-79.

§ 3462. Time limitations for completing a program of education

Delimiting Period for Completion

(a)(1) Subject to paragraph (4) of this subsection, no educational assistance shall be afforded an eligible veteran under this chapter [38 USCS §§ 3451 et seq.] beyond the date 10 years after the veteran's last discharge or release from active duty after January 31, 1955; except that, in the case of any eligible veteran who was prevented from initiating or completing such veteran's chosen program of education within such time period because of a physical or mental disability which was not the result of such veteran's own willful misconduct, such veteran shall, upon application made within one year after (A) the last date of the delimiting period otherwise applicable under this section, (B) the termination of the period of such mental or physical disability, or (C) October 1, 1980, whichever is the latest, be granted an extension of the applicable delimiting period for such length of time as the Secretary determines, from the evidence, that such veteran was so prevented from initiating or completing such program of education. When an extension of the applicable delimiting period is granted a veteran under the preceding sentence, the delimiting period with respect to such veteran will again begin running on the first day following such veteran's recovery from such disability on which it is reasonably feasible, as determined in accordance with regulations which the Secretary shall prescribe, for such veteran to initiate or resume pursuit of a program of education with educational assistance under this chapter [38 USCS §§ 3451 et seq.].

(2)(A) Notwithstanding the provisions of paragraph (1) of this subsection, any veteran shall be permitted to use any of such veteran's unused entitlement under section 3461 of this title for the purposes of eligibility for an education loan, pursuant to the provisions of subchapter III of chapter 36 of this title [38 USCS §§ 3698 et seq.], after the delimiting date otherwise applicable to such veteran under such paragraph (1), if such veteran was pursuing an approved program of education on a full-time basis at the time of the expiration of such veteran's eligibility.

(B) Notwithstanding any other provision of this chapter [38 USCS §§ 3451 et seq.] or chapter 36 of this title [38 USCS §§ 3670 et seq.], any veteran whose delimiting period is extended under subparagraph (A) of this paragraph may continue to use any unused loan entitlement under this paragraph as long as the veteran continues to be enrolled on a full-time basis in pursuit of the approved program of education in which such veteran was enrolled at the time of expiration of such veteran's eligibility (i) until such entitlement is exhausted, (ii) until the expiration of two years after November 23, 1977, or the date of the expiration of the delimiting date otherwise applicable to such veteran under paragraph (1) of this subsection, whichever is later, or (iii) until such veteran has completed the approved program of education in which such veteran was enrolled at the end of the delimiting period referred to in paragraph (1) of this subsection, whichever occurs first.

(3)(A) Subject to subparagraph (C) of this paragraph and notwithstanding the provisions of paragraph (1) of this subsection, an eligible veteran who served on active duty during the Vietnam era shall be permitted to use any of such veteran's unused entitlement under section 3461 of this title for the purpose of pursuing—

(i) a program of apprenticeship or other on-job training;
(ii) a course with an approved vocational objective; or
(iii) a program of secondary education, if the veteran does not have a secondary school diploma (or an equivalency certificate).

(B) Upon completion of a program or course pursued by virtue of eligibility provided by this paragraph, the Secretary shall provide the veteran with such employment counseling as may be necessary to assist the veteran in obtaining employment consistent with the veteran's abilities, aptitudes, and interests.

(C)(i) Educational assistance shall be provided a veteran for pursuit of a program or course described in clause (i) or (ii) of subparagraph (A) of this paragraph using eligibility provided by this paragraph unless the Secretary determines, based on an examination of the veteran's employment and training history, that the veteran is not in need of such a program or course in order to obtain a reasonably stable employment situation consistent with the veteran's abilities and aptitudes. Any such determination shall be made in accordance with regulations which the Secretary shall prescribe.

(ii) Educational assistance provided a veteran for pursuit of a program described in clause (iii) of subparagraph (A) of this paragraph using eligibility provided by this paragraph shall be provided at the rate determined under section 3491(b)(2) of this title.

(D) Educational assistance may not be provided by virtue of this paragraph after December 31, 1984.

(4) For purposes of paragraph (1) of this subsection, a veteran's last discharge or release from active duty shall not include any discharge or release from a period of active duty of less than 90 days of continuous service unless the individual involved is discharged or released for a service-connected disability, for a medical condition which preexisted such service and which the Secretary determines is not service connected, for hardship, or as a result of a reduction in force as described in section 3011(a)(1)(A)(ii)(III) of this title.

Correction of Discharge

(b) In the case of any eligible veteran who has been prevented, as determined by the Secretary, from completing a program of education under this chapter [38 USCS §§ 3451 et seq.] within the period prescribed by subsection (a), because the veteran had not met the nature of discharge requirements of this chapter [38 USCS §§ 3451 et seq.] before a change, correction, or modification of a discharge or dismissal made pursuant to section 1553 of title 10, the correction of the military records of the proper service department under section 1552 of title 10, or other corrective action by competent authority, then the 10-year delimiting period shall run from the date the veteran's discharge or dismissal was changed, corrected, or modified.

Savings clause

(c) In the case of any eligible veteran who was discharged or released from active duty before June 1, 1966 the 10-year delimiting period shall run from such date, if it is later than the date which otherwise would be applicable. In the case of any eligible veteran who was discharged or released from active duty before August 31, 1967, and who pursues a course of farm cooperative training, apprenticeship or other training on the job, the 10-year delimiting period shall run from August 31, 1967 if it is later than the date which would otherwise be applicable.

38 USCS § 3462
VETERANS' BENEFITS

(d) In the case of any veteran (1) who served on or after January 31, 1955, (2) who became eligible for educational assistance under the provisions of this chapter [38 USCS §§ 3451 et seq.] or chapter 36 of this title [38 USCS §§ 3670 et seq.], and (3) who, subsequent to the veteran's last discharge or release from active duty, was captured and held as a prisoner of war by a foreign government or power, there shall be excluded, in computing his 10-year period of eligibility for educational assistance, any period during which the veteran was so detained and any period immediately following the veteran's release from such detention during which the veteran was hospitalized at a military, civilian, or Department of Veterans Affairs medical facility.

(e) No educational assistance shall be afforded any eligible veteran under this chapter [38 USCS §§ 3451 et seq.] or chapter 36 of this title [38 USCS §§ 3670 et seq.] after December 31, 1989.

(Added March 3, 1966, P. L. 89-358, § 2, 80 Stat. 14; Aug. 31, 1967, P. L. 90-77, Title III, § 305, 81 Stat. 188; July 10, 1974, P. L. 93-337, § 1, 88 Stat. 292; Oct. 15, 1976, P. L. 94-502, Title II, § 211(3), Title IV, § 403(b), 90 Stat. 2388, 2393; Nov. 23, 1977, P. L. 95-202, Title II, § 203(a)(1), (b)(1), 91 Stat 1439; Oct. 17, 1980, P. L. 96-466, Title III, Part A, § 301, 94 Stat. 2191; Aug. 13, 1981, P. L. 97-35, Title XX, § 2003(b)(1), 95 Stat. 782; Nov. 3, 1981, P. L. 97-72, Title II, § 201(a), 95 Stat. 1054; Oct. 12, 1982, P. L. 97-295, § 4(39), 96 Stat. 1307; Oct. 14, 1982, P. L. 97-306, Title II, § 206(a), 96 Stat. 1435; Nov. 21, 1983, P. L. 98-160, Title VII, § 702(10), 97 Stat. 1009; Dec. 18, 1989, P. L. 101-237, Title IV, §§ 420(a)(3), 423(b)(1), 103 Stat. 2087, 2092; Aug. 6, 1991, P. L. 102-83, § 5(a), (c)(1), 105 Stat. 406.)

HISTORY; ANCILLARY LAWS AND DIRECTIVES

Explanatory notes:

Provisions similar to those contained in subsecs. (a) and (b) of this section were contained in former 38 USC §§ 1612(a), (c), 1613(a) prior to repeal by Act March 3, 1966, P. L. 89-358, § 4(a), 80 Stat. 23.

Amendments:

1967. Act Aug. 31, 1967 (effective as provided by § 405 of such Act, which appears as 38 USCS § 101 note), in subsec. (c), inserted "In the case of any eligible veteran who was discharged or released from active duty before the date of enactment of this sentence and who pursues a course of farm cooperative training, apprenticeship or other training on the job, or flight training within the provisions of section 1677 of this chapter, the eight-year delimiting period shall run from the date of enactment of this sentence, if it is later than the date which would otherwise be applicable.".

1974. Act July 10, 1974, in subsec. (a), substituted "10" for "eight"; in subsec. (b), substituted "10-year" for "8-year"; in subsec. (c), substituted "10-year" for "8-year" following "under this chapter, the" and substituted "10-year" for "eight-year" following "of this chapter, the"; and added subsec. (d).

1976. Act Oct. 15, 1976 (effective 10/15/76, as provided by § 703(b) of such Act, which appears as 38 USCS § 3693 note), in subsec. (a), substituted "the veteran's" for "his"; in subsec. (b), substituted "the

veteran's" and "the veteran" for "his" and "he", respectively; and in subsec. (d), substituted "the veteran's" and "the veteran" for "his" and "he", respectively wherever appearing.
Act Oct. 15, 1976 (effective 1/1/77, as provided by § 406 of such Act, which appears as 38 USCS § 3201 note), added subsec. (e).

1977. Act Nov. 23, 1977 (effective 5/31/1976 as provided by § 501 of such Act, which appears as 38 USCS § 101 note), redesignated subsec. (a) as subsec. (a)(1); in subsec. (a)(1), as so redesignated, inserted "; except that, in the case of any eligible veteran who was prevented from initiating or completing such veteran's chosen program of education within such time period because of a physical or mental disability which was not the result of such veteran's own willful misconduct, such veteran shall, upon application, be granted an extension of the applicable delimiting period for such length of time as the Administrator determines, from the evidence, that such veteran was prevented from initiating or completing such program of education,"; and added subsec. (a)(2).

1980. Act Oct. 17, 1980 (effective 10/1/80, as provided by § 802(c)(1) of such Act, which appears as 38 USCS § 3452 note), in subsec. (a)(1), inserted "made within one year after (A) the last date of the delimiting period otherwise applicable under this section, (B) the termination of the period of such mental or physical disability, or (C) the effective date of the Veterans' Rehabilitation and Education Amendments of 1980, whichever is the latest", inserted "so" preceding "prevented", and inserted "When an extension of the applicable delimiting period is granted a veteran under the preceding sentence, the delimiting period with respect to such veteran will again begin running on the first day following such veteran's recovery from such disability on which it is reasonably feasible, as determined in accordance with regulations which the Administrator shall prescribe, for such veteran to initiate or resume pursuit of a program of education with educational assistance under this chapter.".

1981. Act Aug. 13, 1981 (effective 10/1/1981, as provided by § 2006 of such Act, which appears as 38 USCS § 3231 note), in subsec. (c), deleted "or flight training within the provisions of section 1677 of this chapter," after "other training on the job,".

Act Nov. 3, 1981 (effective 1/1/82, as provided by § 201(b) of such Act), added subsec. (a)(3).

1982. Act Oct. 12, 1982, in subsec. (a)(2)(B), substituted "November 23, 1977," for "the date of enactment of this paragraph"; and, in subsec. (c), substituted "June 1, 1966" for "the date for which an educational assistance allowance is first payable under this chapter", and substituted "August 31, 1967" for "the date of enactment of this sentence", in two places.

Act Oct. 14, 1982 (effective 1/1/82 as provided by § 206(c) of such Act, which appears as a note to this section), in subsec. (a)(3), in subpara. (C)(i), substituted "shall" for "may" following "Educational assistance" and substituted "unless the Administrator determines, based on an examination of the veteran's employment and training history, that the veteran is not in need of such a program or course in order to obtain a reasonably stable employment situation consistent with the veteran's abilities and aptitudes." for "only if the veteran has been determined by the Administrator to be in need of such a program or course in order to achieve a suitable occupational or vocational objective."; and, in subpara (D), substituted "December 31, 1984" for "December 31, 1983".

1983. Act Nov. 21, 1983, in subsec. (a)(1)(C), substituted "October 1, 1980" for "the effective date of the Veterans' Rehabilitation and Education Amendments of 1980".

1989. Act Dec. 18, 1989, in subsec. (a), in para. (1), substituted "Subject to paragraph (4) of this subsection, no" for "No", and added para. (4).

Such Act further, in subsecs. (a) and (b), substituted "Secretary" for "Administrator", wherever appearing; and in subsec. (d), substituted "Department of Veterans Affairs" for "Veterans' Administration".

1991. Act Aug. 6, 1991, redesignated this section, formerly 38 USCS § 1662, as 38 USCS § 3462, and amended the references in this section to reflect the redesignations made by § 5(a) of such Act (see Table III preceding 38 USCS § 101).

Other provisions:

Effective date and application of section. Act March 3, 1966, P. L. 89-358, § 12(a), 80 Stat. 28, located at 38 USCS § 3451 note, provided that this section is effective on March 3, 1966, but no educational assistance allowance shall be payable under this chapter (38 USCS §§ 3451 et seq.) for any period before June 1, 1966, nor for the month of June 1966, unless (1) the eligible veteran commenced the pursuit of the course of education on or after June 1, 1966, or (2) the pursuit of such course continued through June 30, 1966.

Veterans' educational assistance; time extension. Act May 31, 1974, P. L. 93-293, § 1, 88 Stat. 176 provided: "Notwithstanding any other provision of law, the eight-year delimiting date for pursuit of educational programs under chapter 34 of title 38, United States Code [38 USCS §§ 3451 et seq.], for eligible veterans discharged or released from active duty between January 31, 1955, and September 1, 1966 (except for those veterans whose discharges are subject to the provisions of section 1662(b) of such chapter [now 38 USCS § 3462(b)], or who are pursuing courses of farm cooperative training, apprenticeship or other training on the job, or flight training under such chapter), shall run from July 1, 1966.".

Application and construction of the Oct. 12, 1982 amendment of this section. For provisions as to the application and construction of the Oct. 12, 1982 amendment of this section (see the Amendments note to this section), see § 5 of such Act, which appears as 10 USCS § 101 note.

Publication of regulations. Act Oct. 14, 1982, P. L. 97-306, Title II, § 206(b), 96 Stat. 1435, provides:

"(b)(1) Not later than 30 days after the date of the enactment of this Act [enacted Oct. 14, 1982], the Administrator of Veterans' Affairs shall publish in the Federal Register, for public review and comment for a period not to exceed 30 days, proposed regulations under section 1662(a)(3)(C)(i) of title 38, United States Code [subsec. (a)(3)(C)(i) of this section], as amended by subsection (a).

"(2) Not later than 90 days after the date of the enactment of this Act, the Administrator shall publish in the Federal Register final regulations under such section 1662(a)(3)(C)(i) [subsec. (a)(3)(C)(i) of this section].".

CROSS REFERENCES

This section is referred to in 38 USCS §§ 3512, 3698.

RESEARCH GUIDE

Am Jur:
77 Am Jur 2d, Veterans and Veterans' Laws §§ 132, 137.

Annotations:
Who is "individual with handicaps" under Rehabilitation Act of 1973 (29 USCS §§ 701 et seq.). 97 ALR Fed 40.

INTERPRETIVE NOTES AND DECISIONS

1. Generally
2. Effect of alcoholism on time limits

1. Generally

Extension of basic 10-year delimiting period for using G.I. Bill veterans' educational benefits is precluded for veteran, who has not pursued education during that period because of primary alcoholism, under provision of 38 USCS § 1662 [now 38 USCS § 3462] which precludes extensions because of veteran's own willful misconduct during that period, since it appears that Congress intended that Veterans' Administration [now Department of Veterans Affairs] apply same test for willful misconduct under § 1662 [now § 3462] that Veterans' Administration [now Department of Veterans Affairs] applies under other veterans' benefits statutes, where it must be assumed that Congress, at the time § 1662 [now § 3462] was enacted, was aware that Veterans' Administration [now Department of Veterans Affairs] regulation construing term willful misconduct included primary alcoholism as willful misconduct. Traynor v Turnage (1988) 485 US 535, 99 L Ed 2d 618, 108 S Ct 1372, 1 ADD 469, 2 AD Cas 214, 46 CCH EPD ¶ 37924 (superseded by statute on other grounds as stated in Larrabee v Derwinski (1992, CA2 Conn) 968 F2d 1497).

2. Effect of alcoholism on time limits

Regulation equating primary alcoholism with willful misconduct, for purposes of § 1662(a)(1) [now § 3462(a)(1)] extending educational assistance beyond 10 years where veteran was prevented from initiating or completing program within such period because of physical or mental disability which did not result from veteran's own willful misconduct, discriminates against otherwise qualified individual solely by reason of his handicap in violation of Rehabilitation Act (29 USCS § 794). Tinch v Walters (1985, CA6 Tenn) 765 F2d 599.

Veterans Administration [now Department of Veterans Affairs] refusal to extend delimiting date for use of education benefits for veteran claiming incapacity to timely use benefits due to alcoholism was not unreasonable, since Congress specifically considered issue at time it established delimiting date. Burns v Nimmo (1982, ND Iowa) 545 F Supp 544.

Veterans Administration [now Department of Veterans Affairs] policy under which extensions of delimiting date for educational benefits are denied based on veteran's inability to complete education due to alcoholism does not violate equal protection or due process rights, but does violate Rehabilitation Act (29 USCS § 794). Tinch v Walters (1983, ED Tenn) 573 F Supp 346, affd (1985, CA6 Tenn) 765 F2d 599.

Veterans Administration [now Department of Veterans Affairs] regulation (38 CFR § 3 301(c)(2)) precluding determination that primary alcoholism is disease which permits extension of time limits under 38 USCS § 1662(a)(1) [now 38 USCS § 3462(a)(1)] for utilizing educational benefits does not exceed statutory authority under 38 USCS § 210(c)(1) [now repealed] however, regulation violates 29 USCS § 794 prohibiting discrimination against handicapped persons in program receiving federal financial assistance. McKelvey v Walters (1984, DC Dist Col) 596 F Supp 1317, revd on other grounds (1986, App DC) 253 US App DC 126, 792 F2d 194, affd (1988) 485 US 535, 99 L Ed 2d 618, 108 S Ct 1372, 1 ADD 469, 2 AD Cas 214, 46 CCH EPD ¶ 37924 (superseded by statute on other grounds as stated in Larrabee v Derwinski (1992, CA2 Conn) 968 F2d 1497).

[§ 3463]. [§ 1663. Repealed]

HISTORY; ANCILLARY LAWS AND DIRECTIVES

The bracketed section number "3463" was inserted to preserve numerical continuity following the section number redesignations made by Act Aug. 6, 1991, P. L. 102-83, § 5(a), 105 Stat. 406.

This section (Act March 3, 1966, P. L. 89-358, § 2, 80 Stat. 15; Oct. 15, 1976, P. L. 94-502, Title II, § 211(4), 90 Stat. 2388; Nov. 23, 1977, P. L. 95-202, Title III, § 302(a), 91 Stat. 1440; Oct. 28, 1986, P. L. 99-576, Title

38 USCS § 3463

III, Part A, § 312, 100 Stat. 3273; Dec. 18, 1989, P. L. 101-237; Title IV, § 423(b)(1)(A), 103 Stat. 2092) was repealed by Act March 22, 1991, P. L. 102-16, § 2(b)(1)(A), 105 Stat. 49. This section provided for educational and vocational counseling for any eligible veteran.

SUBCHAPTER III. ENROLLMENT

§ 3470. Selection of program

Subject to the provisions of this chapter [38 USCS §§ 3451 et seq.], each eligible veteran may select a program of education to assist the veteran in attaining an educational, professional, or vocational objective at any educational institution (approved in accordance with chapter 36 of this title [38 USCS §§ 3670 et seq.]) selected by the veteran, which will accept and retain the veteran as a student or trainee in any field or branch of knowledge which such institution finds the veteran qualified to undertake or pursue.
(Added March 3, 1966, P.L. 89-358, § 2, 80 Stat. 15; Oct. 15, 1976, P.L. 94-502, Title II, § 211(5), 90 Stat. 2388; Aug. 6, 1991, P.L. 102-83, § 5(a), 105 Stat. 406.)

HISTORY; ANCILLARY LAWS AND DIRECTIVES

Explanatory notes:
Provisions similar to those contained in this section were contained in former 38 USC § 1620 prior to repeal by Act March 3, 1966, P.L. 89-358, § 4(a), 80 Stat. 23.

Amendments:
1976. Act Oct. 15, 1976 (effective 10/15/76, as provided by § 703(b) of such Act, which appears as 38 USCS § 3693 note), substituted "the veteran" for "him" wherever appearing.
1991. Act Aug. 6, 1991, redesignated this section, formerly 38 USCS § 1670, as 38 USCS § 3470.

Other provisions:
Effective date and application of section. Act March 3, 1966, P.L. 89-358, § 12(a), 80 Stat. 28, located at 38 USCS § 3451 note, provided that this section is effective on March 3, 1966, but no educational assistance allowance shall be payable under this chapter (38 USCS §§ 3451 et seq.) for any period before June 1, 1966, nor for the month of June 1966, unless (1) the eligible veteran commenced the pursuit of the course of education on or after June 1, 1966, or (2) the pursuit of such course continued through June 30, 1966.

CROSS REFERENCES
This section is referred to in 10 USCS § 16136; 38 USCS §§ 3034, 3241.

RESEARCH GUIDE
Am Jur:
77 Am Jur 2d, Veterans and Veterans' Laws §§ 132, 139, 140.

Forms:
24A Am Jur Pl & Pr Forms (Rev), Veterans and Veterans' Laws, Form 21.

INTERPRETIVE NOTES AND DECISIONS

Removal of veteran from position as contract representative at college was inappropriate even though veteran failed to notify Veterans' Administration [now Department of Veterans Affairs] through proper channels of change in educational program where veteran informally informed Veterans' Administration [now Department of Veterans Affairs] of changes in schedule and never attempted to defraud government. Joyce v United States (1986) 9 Cl Ct 440.

§ 3471. Applications; approval

Any eligible veteran, or any person on active duty (after consultation with the appropriate service education officer, who desires to initiate a program of education under this chapter [38 USCS §§ 3451 et seq.] shall submit an application to the Secretary which shall be in such form, and contain such information, as the Secretary shall prescribe. The Secretary shall approve such application unless the Secretary finds that (1) such veteran or person is not eligible for or entitled to the educational assistance for which application is made, (2) the veteran's or person's selected educational institution or training establishment fails to meet any requirement of this chapter or chapter 36 of this title [38 USCS §§ 3451 et seq. or 3670 et seq.], (3) the veteran's or person's enrollment in, or pursuit of, the program of education selected would violate any provision of this chapter or chapter 36 of this title [38 USCS §§ 3451 et seq. or 3670 et seq.], or (4) the veteran or person is already qualified, by reason of previous education or training, for the educational, professional, or vocational objective for which the program of education is offered. The Secretary shall notify the veteran or person of the approval or disapproval of the veteran's or person's application.
(Added March 3, 1966, P.L. 89-358, § 2, 80 Stat. 15; Oct. 24, 1972, P.L. 92-540, Title III, § 302, 86 Stat. 1080; Oct. 15, 1976, P.L. 94-502, Title II, § 211(6), 90 Stat. 2388; Oct. 17, 1980, P.L. 96-466, Title III, Part A, § 302, 94 Stat. 2192; Dec. 18, 1989, P.L. 101-237, Title IV, § 423(b)(1)(A), 103 Stat. 2092; Aug. 6, 1991, P.L. 102-83, § 5(a), 105 Stat. 406.)

HISTORY; ANCILLARY LAWS AND DIRECTIVES

Explanatory notes:
Provisions similar to those contained in this section were contained in former 38 USC § 1621 prior to repeal by Act March 3, 1966, P.L. 89-358, § 4(a), 80 Stat. 23.

Amendments:
1972. Act Oct. 24, 1972, substituted new section for one which read: "Any eligible veteran who desires to initiate a program of education under this chapter shall submit an application to the Administrator which shall be in such form, and contain such information, as the Administrator shall prescribe. The Administrator shall approve such application unless he finds that such veteran is not eligible for or entitled to the educational assistance applied for, or that his program of education fails to meet any of the requirements of this chapter, or that he is already qualified. The Administrator shall notify the eligible veteran of the approval or disapproval of his application.".

38 USCS § 3471

1976. Act Oct. 15, 1976 (effective 10/15/76, as provided by § 703(b) of such Act, which appears as 38 USCS § 3693 note), substituted "the Administrator" for "he" preceding "finds"; substituted "the veteran's or person's" for "his" wherever appearing; and substituted "the veteran or person" for "he".

1980. Act Oct. 17, 1980 (effective 10/1/80, as provided by § 802(c)(1) of such Act, which appears as 38 USCS § 3452 note), substituted "The Administrator shall approve such application unless the Administrator finds that (1) such veteran or person is not eligible for or entitled to the educational assistance for which application is made, (2) the veteran's or person's selected educational institution or training establishment fails to meet any requirement of this chapter or chapter 36 of this title, (3) the veteran's or person's enrollment in, or pursuit of, the program of education selected would violate any provision of this chapter or chapter 36 of this title, or (4) the veteran or person is already qualified, by reason of previous education or training, for the educational, professional, or vocational objective for which the program of education is offered." for "The Administrator shall approve such application unless the Administrator finds that such veteran or person is not eligible for or entitled to the educational assistance applied for, or the veteran's or person's program of education fails to meed any of the requirements of this chapter, or that the veteran or person is already qualified.".

1989. Act Dec. 18, 1989, substituted "Secretary" for "Administrator", wherever appearing.

1991. Act Aug. 6, 1991, redesignated this section, formerly 38 USCS § 1671, as 38 USCS § 3471.

Other provisions:

Effective date and application of section. Act March 3, 1966, P.L. 89-358, § 12(a), 80 Stat. 28, located at 38 USCS § 3451 note, provided that this section is effective on March 3, 1966, but no educational assistance allowance shall be payable under this chapter (38 USCS §§ 3451 et seq.) for any period before June 1, 1966, nor for the month of June 1966, unless (1) the eligible veteran commenced the pursuit of the course of education on or after June 1, 1966, or (2) the pursuit of such course continued through June 30, 1966.

CROSS REFERENCES

This section is referred to in 10 USCS § 16136; 38 USCS §§ 3034, 3241, 3482, 3491.

RESEARCH GUIDE

Federal Procedure L Ed:

33 Fed Proc L Ed, Veterans and Veterans' Affairs § 79:34.

Am Jur:

45B Am Jur 2d, Job Discrimination (1993) § 902.

77 Am Jur 2d, Veterans and Veterans' Laws §§ 132, 140, 141.

INTERPRETIVE NOTES AND DECISIONS

Action of administrator of Veterans' Administration [now Department of Veterans Affairs] in denying educational benefits to veteran who had received "blue" discharge, which signified separation from service under conditions neither honorable nor dishonorable, was not reviewable by Federal District Court. Longernecker v Higley (1955) 97 US App DC 144, 229 F2d 27.

[§ 3472]. [§ 1672. Repealed]

HISTORY; ANCILLARY LAWS AND DIRECTIVES

The bracketed section number "3472" was inserted to preserve numerical continuity following the section number redesignations made by Act Aug. 6, 1991, P.L. 102-83, § 5(a), 105 Stat. 406.

This section (Added Act March 3, 1966, P.L. 89-358, § 2, 80 Stat. 15) was repealed by Act Oct. 24, 1972, P.L. 92-540, Title IV, § 401(6), 86 Stat. 1090. It provided for a change of program. For similar provisions, see 38 USCS § 3691.

[§ 3473. Repealed]

HISTORY; ANCILLARY LAWS AND DIRECTIVES

This section (Added March 3, 1966, P. L. 89-358, § 2, 80 Stat. 16; Aug. 31, 1967, P. L. 90-77, Title III, §§ 302(a), 303(a), 81 Stat. 185; March 26, 1970, P. L. 91-219, Title II, § 202, 84 Stat. 78; Oct. 24, 1972, P. L. 92-540, Title IV, § 401(2), 86 Stat. 1090; Dec. 3, 1974, P. L. 93-508, Title II, § 203, 88 Stat. 1582; Oct. 15, 1976, P. L. 94-502, Title II, §§ 205, 211(7), 90 Stat. 2387, 2388; Nov. 23, 1977, P. L. 95-202, Title III, § 305(a)(2), 91 Stat. 1443; Oct. 17, 1980, P. L. 96-466, Title III, Part A, §§ 303-305, 94 Stat. 2192; Aug. 13, 1981, P. L. 97-35, Title XX, § 2003(b)(2), 95 Stat. 782; Oct. 12, 1982, P. L. 97-295, § 4(40), 96 Stat. 1308; Oct. 14, 1982, P. L. 97-306, Title II, Part B, §§ 202(a), 203(a), 96 Stat. 1433; Oct. 19, 1984, P. L. 98-525, Title VII, § 703(b), 98 Stat. 2564; Nov. 18, 1988, P. L. 100-689, Title I, Part A, § 111(a)(9), 102 Stat. 4172; Dec. 18, 1989, P. L. 101-237, Title IV, § 423(b)(1), 103 Stat. 2092; Aug. 6, 1991, P. L. 102-83, § 5(a), (c)(1), 105 Stat. 406) was repealed by Act Oct. 29, 1992, P. L. 102-568, Title III, § 313(a)(3)(A), 106 Stat. 4332, applicable as provided by § 313(b) of such Act, which appears as 10 USCS § 2136 note. Such section related to disapproval of enrollment in certain courses. For similar provisions, see 38 USCS § 3680A.

Other provisions:

Savings provision for repeal by Act Oct. 29, 1992. Act Oct. 29, 1992, P. L. 102-568, Title III, § 313(b), 106 Stat. 4333, which appears as 10 USCS § 16136 note, provides that the repeal of this section is not applicable to any person receiving educational assistance for pursuit of an independent study program in which the person was enrolled on Oct. 29, 1992, for as long as such person is continuously thereafter so enrolled and meets requirements of eligibility for such assistance.

§ 3474. Discontinuance for unsatisfactory conduct or progress

The Secretary shall discontinue the educational assistance allowance of an eligible veteran if, at any time, the Secretary finds that according to the regularly prescribed standards and practices of the educational institution, the veteran's attendance, conduct, or progress is unsatisfactory. The Secretary may renew the payment of the educational assistance allowance only if the Secretary finds that—

(1) the veteran will be resuming enrollment at the same educational institution in the same program of education and the educational institution has both approved such veteran's reenrollment and certified it to the Department of Veterans Affairs; or

(2) in the case of a proposed change of either educational institution or program of education by the veteran—

(A) the cause of the unsatisfactory attendance, conduct, or progress has been removed;

(B) the program proposed to be pursued is suitable to the veteran's aptitudes, interests, and abilities; and

(C) if a proposed change of program is involved, the change meets the requirements for approval under section 3691 of this title.

(Added March 3, 1966, P. L. 89-358, § 2, 80 Stat. 16; Oct. 15, 1976, P. L. 94-502, Title II, §§ 206, 211(8), 90 Stat. 2387, 2388; Nov. 23, 1977, P. L. 95-202, Title III, § 305(b)(1), 91 Stat. 1443; Oct. 17, 1980, P. L. 96-466, Title III, Part A, § 306, 94 Stat. 2193; Dec. 18, 1989, P. L. 101-237, Title IV, §§ 411(a), 412(b), 423(b)(1)(A), 103 Stat. 2084, 2085, 2092; Aug. 6, 1991, P. L. 102-83, § 5(a), (c)(1), 105 Stat. 406.)

HISTORY; ANCILLARY LAWS AND DIRECTIVES

Explanatory notes:

Provisions similar to those contained in the first sentence of this section were contained in former 38 USC §§ 1624 prior to repeal by Act March 3, 1966, P. L. 89-358, § 4(a), 80 Stat. 23.

Amendments:

1976. Act Oct. 15, 1976, § 211(8) (effective 10/15/76, as provided by § 703(b) of such Act, which appears as 38 USCS § 3693 note), in the preliminary matter, substituted "the veteran's" for "his" and substituted "the Administrator" for "he" following "only if"; in para. (2), substituted "the veteran's" for "his".

Act Oct. 15, 1976 § 206 (effective 12/1/76, as provided by § 703(c) of such Act, which appears as 38 USCS § 3693 note), in the preliminary matter, inserted "Unless the Administrator finds there are mitigating circumstances, progress will be considered unsatisfactory at any time the eligible veteran is not progressing at a rate that will permit such veteran to graduate within the approved length of the course based on the training time as certified to the Veterans' Administration.".

1977. Act Nov. 23, 1977 (effective as provided by § 501 of such Act, which appears as 38 USCS § 101 note), in the preliminary matter, inserted ", or within such other length of time (exceeding such approved length) as the Administrator determines to be reasonable in accordance with regulations".

1980. Act Oct. 17, 1980 (effective 10/1/80, as provided by § 802(c)(1) of such Act, which appears as 38 USCS § 3452 note), in the introductory matter, deleted "Unless the Administrator finds there are mitigating circumstances, progress will be considered unsatisfactory at any time the eligible veteran is not progressing at a rate that will permit such veteran to graduate within the approved length of the course based on the training time as certified to the Veterans' Administration, or within such other length of time (exceeding such approved length) as the Administrator determines to be reasonable in accordance with regulations." following "unsatisfactory.".

1989. Act Dec. 18, 1989, substituted paras. (1) and (2) for ones which read:

"(1) the cause of the unsatisfactory conduct or progress of the eligible veteran has been removed; and

"(2) the program which the eligible veteran now proposes to pursue (whether the same or revised) is suitable to the veteran's aptitudes, interests, and abilities.".

Such Act further, in the introductory matter, substituted "attendance, conduct," for "conduct" and "Secretary" for "Administrator", wherever appearing.

1991. Act Aug. 6, 1991, redesignated this section, formerly 38 USCS § 1674, as 38 USCS § 3474, and amended the references in this section to reflect the redesignations made by § 5(a) of such Act (see Table III preceding 38 USCS § 101).

Other provisions:

Effective date and application of section. Act March 3, 1966, P. L. 89-358, § 12(a), 80 Stat. 28, located at 38 USCS § 3451 note, provided that this section is effective on March 3, 1966, but no educational assistance allowance shall be payable under this chapter (38 USCS §§ 3451 et seq.) for any period before June 1, 1966, nor for the month of June 1966, unless (1) the eligible veteran commenced the pursuit of the course of education on or after June 1, 1966, or (2) the pursuit of such course continued through June 30, 1966.

Approval process study; authorization of appropriations; implementation of amendments to be suspended. Act Nov. 23, 1977, P. L. 95-202, Title III, § 305(b)(2)–(4), 91 Stat. 1443 (effective 11/23/77, as provided by § 501 of such Act); Oct. 17, 1980, P. L. 96-466, Title VIII, § 801(m)(2), 94 Stat. 2217 (effective 10/1/80, as provided by § 802(h) of such Act), provided:

"(2) The Administrator of Veterans' Affairs, in consultation with appropriate bodies, officials, persons, departments, and agencies, shall conduct a study to investigate (A) specific methods of improving the process by which postsecondary educational institutions and courses at such institutions are and continue to be approved for purposes of chapters 32, 34, 35, and 36 of title 38, United States Code [38 USCS §§ 3201 et seq., 3451 et seq., 3500 et seq., and 3670 et seq.]; and (B) in recognition of the importance of assuring that Federal assistance is made available to those eligible veterans and persons seriously pursuing and making satisfactory progress toward an educational or vocational objective under such chapters, the need for legislative or administrative action in regard to sections 1674 and 1724 of title 38, United States Code [now 38 USCS §§ 3474, 3524], and the regulations prescribed thereunder. A

38 USCS § 3474 VETERANS' BENEFITS

report of such study, together with such specific recommendations for administrative or legislative action as the Administrator deems appropriate, shall be submitted to the President and the Congress not later than September 30, 1979, except that the portion of the report of such study described in clause (B) of the preceding sentence shall be submitted not later than September 30, 1978.

"(3) For the purpose of carrying out paragraph (2) of this subsection, there are authorized to be appropriated $1,000,000.

"(4)(A) Until such time as the Administrator submits the report required under the second sentence of paragraph (2) of this subsection the Administrator shall suspend implementation of the amendments to sections 1674 and 1724 of title 38, United States Code [now this section and 38 USCS § 3524], made by sections 206 and 307, respectively, of Public Law 94-502, in the case of any accredited educational institution which submits to the Administrator its course catalog or bulletin and a certification that the policies and regulations described in clauses (6) and (7) of section 1776(b) [now 38 USCS § 3676(b)(6), (7)] are being enforced by such institution, unless the Administrator finds, pursuant to regulations which the Administrator shall prescribe, that such catalog or bulletin fails to state fully and clearly such policies and regulations.

"(B) The Administrator shall, where appropriate, bring to the attention of the Council on Postsecondary Accreditation and the appropriate accrediting and licensing bodies such catalogs, bulletins, and certifications submitted under subparagraph (A) of this paragraph which the Administrator believes may not be in compliance with the standards of such accrediting and licensing body.".

CROSS REFERENCES

This section is referred to in 10 USCS § 16136; 38 USCS §§ 3034, 3241.

RESEARCH GUIDE

Am Jur:
77 Am Jur 2d, Veterans and Veterans' Laws §§ 132, 145.

[§ 3475]. [§ 1675. Repealed]

HISTORY; ANCILLARY LAWS AND DIRECTIVES

The bracketed section number "3475" was inserted to preserve numerical continuity following the section number redesignations made by Act Aug. 6, 1991, P. L. 102-83, § 5(a), 105 Stat. 406.

This section (Added Act March 3, 1966, P. L. 89-358, § 2, 80 Stat. 16) was repealed by Act Oct. 24, 1972, P. L. 92-540, Title IV, § 401(6), 86 Stat. 1090. It provided for a period of operation for approval. For similar provisions, see 38 USCS § 3689.

§ 3476. Education outside the United States

An eligible veteran may not enroll in any course offered by an educational institution not located in a State unless that educational institution is an approved institution of higher learning and the course is approved by the Secretary. The Secretary may deny or discontinue educational assistance under this chapter [38 USCS §§ 3451 et seq.] in the case of any veteran enrolled in an institution of higher learning not located in a State if the Secretary determines that such enrollment is not in the best interest of the veteran or the Federal Government.

(Added March 3, 1966, P. L. 89-358, § 2, 80 Stat. 17; Oct. 15, 1976, P. L. 94-502, Title II, § 211(9), 90 Stat. 2389; Oct. 17, 1980, P. L. 96-466, Title III, Part A, § 307(b), 94 Stat. 2193; Dec. 18, 1989, P. L. 101-237, Title IV, § 423(b)(1)(A), 103 Stat. 2092; Aug. 6, 1991, P. L. 102-83, § 5(a), 105 Stat. 406; Nov. 2, 1994, P. L. 103-446, Title VI, § 604(a), 108 Stat. 4671.)

HISTORY; ANCILLARY LAWS AND DIRECTIVES

Explanatory notes:
Provisions similar to those contained in this section were contained in former 38 USC § 1620 (second and third sentences) prior to repeal by Act March 3, 1966, P. L. 89-358, § 4(a), 80 Stat. 23.

Amendments:
1976. Act Oct. 15, 1976 (effective 10/15/76, as provided by § 703(b) of such Act, which appears as 38 USCS § 3693 note), substituted "the Administrator's" for "his" and substituted "the Administrator" for "he" preceding "finds".

1980. Act Oct. 17, 1980 (effective 10/1/80, as provided by § 802(c)(1) of such Act, which appears as 38 USCS § 3452 note), substituted new section for one which read: "An eligible veteran may not pursue a program of education at an educational institution which is not located in a State, unless such program is pursued at an approved educational institution of higher learning. The Administrator in the Administrator's discretion may deny or discontinue the educational assistance under this chapter of any veteran in a foreign educational institution if the Administrator finds that such enrollment is not for the best interest of the veteran or the Government.".

1989. Act Dec. 18, 1989, substituted "Secretary" for "Administrator", wherever appearing.

1991. Act Aug. 6, 1991, redesignated this section, formerly 38 USCS § 1676, as 38 USCS § 3476.

1994. Act Nov. 2, 1994 (applicable with respect to courses approved on or after the date of enactment, as provided by § 604(b) of such Act, which appears as a note to this section), substituted the first sentence for one which read: "An eligible veteran may not enroll in any course at an educational institution not located in a State unless such course is pursued at an approved institution of higher learning and the course is approved by the Secretary.".

Other provisions:
Effective date and application of section. Act March 3, 1966, P. L. 89-358, § 12(a), 80 Stat. 28, located at 38 USCS § 3451 note, provided that this section is effective on March 3, 1966, but no educational assistance allowance shall be payable under this chapter (38 USCS §§ 3451 et seq.) for

38 USCS § 3476

any period before June 1, 1966, nor for the month of June 1966, unless (1) the eligible veteran commenced the pursuit of the course of education on or after June 1, 1966, or (2) the pursuit of such course continued through June 30, 1966.

Application of amendment made by Act Nov. 2, 1994. Act Nov. 2, 1994, P. L. 103-446, Title VI, § 604(b), 108 Stat. 4671, provides: "The amendment made by subsection (a) [amending this section] shall apply with respect to courses approved on or after the date of the enactment of this Act.".

CROSS REFERENCES

This section is referred to in 10 USCS § 16136; 38 USCS §§ 3034, 3241.

RESEARCH GUIDE

Am Jur:
77 Am Jur 2d, Veterans and Veterans' Laws §§ 132, 139.

[§ 3477]. [§ 1677. Repealed]

HISTORY; ANCILLARY LAWS AND DIRECTIVES

The bracketed section number "3477" was inserted to preserve numerical continuity following the section number redesignations made by Act Aug. 6, 1991, P. L. 102-83, § 5(a), 105 Stat. 406.

This section (Act Aug. 31, 1967, P. L. 90-77, Title III, § 302(b), 81 Stat. 185; Oct. 23, 1968, P. L. 90-631, § 5, 82 Stat. 1335; March 26, 1970, P. L. 91-219, Title I, § 102, Title II, § 203, 84 Stat. 76, 78; Oct. 24, 1972, P. L. 92-540, Title I, § 102(1), Title IV, § 401(3), 86 Stat. 1075, 1090; Dec. 3, 1974, P. L. 93-508, Title I, § 102(1), 88 Stat. 1579; Jan. 2, 1975, P. L. 93-602, Title II, § 203(a), 88 Stat. 1958; Nov. 23, 1977, P. L. 95-202, Title I, § 102(1), 91 Stat. 1433; Oct. 17, 1980, P. L. 96-466, Title II, Part A, § 201(1), Part B, § 211(1), Title VI, § 603(a), 94 Stat. 2187, 2189, 2209) was repealed by Act Aug. 13, 1981, P. L. 97-35, Title XX, § 2003(b)(3)(A), 95 Stat. 782, effective as provided by § 2006 of such Act, which appears as 38 USCS § 3231 note.

[§ 3478]. [§ 1678. Repealed]

HISTORY; ANCILLARY LAWS AND DIRECTIVES

The bracketed section number "3478" was inserted to preserve numerical continuity following the section number redesignations made by Act Aug. 6, 1991, P. L. 102-83, § 5(a), 105 Stat. 406.

This section (Added Act Aug. 31, 1967, P. L. 90-77, Title III, § 306(a), 81 Stat. 188) was repealed by Act March 26, 1970, P. L. 91-219, Title II, § 204(a)(2), 84 Stat. 79. It provided for special training for the educationally disadvantaged. For similar provisions, see 38 USCS §§ 3490 et seq.

READJUSTMENT BENEFITS   38 USCS § 3481

SUBCHAPTER IV. PAYMENTS TO ELIGIBLE VETERANS; VETERAN-STUDENT SERVICES

HISTORY; ANCILLARY LAWS AND DIRECTIVES

Amendments:
1972. Act Oct. 24, 1972, P. L. 92-540, Title IV, § 404(b), 86 Stat. 1091, inserted "; VETERAN-STUDENT SERVICES".

§ 3481. Educational assistance allowance

General

(a) The Secretary shall, in accordance with the applicable provisions of this section and chapter 36 of this title [38 USCS §§ 3670 et seq.], pay to each eligible veteran who is pursuing a program of education under this chapter [38 USCS §§ 3451 et seq.] an educational assistance allowance to meet, in part, the expenses of the veteran's subsistence, tuition, fees, supplies, books, equipment, and other educational costs.

Institutional Training

(b) The educational assistance allowance of an eligible veteran pursuing a program of education, other than a program exclusively by correspondence, at an educational institution shall be paid as provided in chapter 36 [38 USCS §§ 3670 et seq.] of this title.
(Added March 3, 1966, P. L. 89-358, § 2, 80 Stat. 17; March 26, 1970, P. L. 91-219, Title II, § 205, 84 Stat. 81; Dec. 24, 1970, P. L. 91-584, § 6, 84 Stat. 1576; Oct. 24, 1972, P. L. 92-540, Title II, § 202, 86 Stat. 1079; Oct. 15, 1976, P. L. 94-502, Title II §§ 210(2), 211(10), 90 Stat. 2388, 2389; Aug. 13, 1981, P. L. 97-35, Title XX, § 2003(b)(4), 95 Stat. 782; Dec. 18, 1989, P. L. 101-237, Title IV, § 423(b)(1)(A), 103 Stat. 2092; Aug. 6, 1991, P. L. 102-83, § 5(a), 105 Stat. 406.)

HISTORY; ANCILLARY LAWS AND DIRECTIVES

Explanatory notes:
Provisions similar to those contained in subsecs. (a), (b), (d), and (e) of this section were contained in former 38 USC § 1631 prior to repeal by Act March 3, 1966, P. L. 89-358, § 4(a), 80 Stat. 23.

Amendments:
1970. Act March 26, 1970, in subsec. (d), added the concluding matter.
Act Dec. 24, 1970, in subsec. (b)(2), inserted "(excluding programs of apprenticeship and programs of other on-job training authorized by section 1683 of this title)".
1972. Act Oct. 24, 1976, substituted new section for one which read:
"(a) The Administrator shall pay to each eligible veteran who is pursuing a program of education under this chapter an educational assistance allowance to meet, in part, the expenses of his subsistence, tuition, fees, supplies, books, equipment, and other educational costs.

"(b) The educational assistance allowance of an eligible veteran shall be paid, as provided in section 1682 of this title, only for the period of his enrollment as approved by the Administrator, but no allowance shall be paid—

"(1) to any veteran enrolled in a course which leads to a standard college degree for any period when such veteran is not pursuing his course in accordance with the regularly established policies and regulations of the educational institution and the requirements of this chapter, or of chapter 36;

"(2) to any veteran enrolled in a course which does not lead to a standard college degree (excluding programs of apprenticeship and programs of other on-job training authorized by section 1683 of this title) for any day of absence in excess of thirty days in a twelve-month period, not counting as absences weekends or legal holidays established by Federal or State law during which the institution is not regularly in session; or

"(3) to any veteran pursuing his program exclusively by correspondence for any period during which no lessons were serviced by the institution.

"(c) The Administrator may, pursuant to such regulations as he may prescribe, determine enrollment in, pursuit of, and attendance at, any program of education or course by an eligible veteran for any period for which he receives an educational assistance allowance under this chapter for pursuing such program or course.

"(d) No educational assistance allowance shall be paid to an eligible veteran enrolled in a course in an educational institution which does not lead to a standard college degree for any period until the Administrator shall have received—

"(1) from the eligible veteran a certification as to his actual attendance during such period or where the program is pursued by correspondence a certificate as to the number of lessons actually completed by the veteran and serviced by the institution; and

"(2) from the educational institution, a certification, or an endorsement on the veteran's certificate, that such veteran was enrolled in and pursuing a course of education during such period and, in the case of an institution furnishing education to a veteran exclusively by correspondence, a certificate, or an endorsement on the veteran's certificate, as to the number of lessons completed by the veteran and serviced by the institution.

"Notwithstanding the foregoing, the Administrator may pay an educational assistance allowance representing the initial payment of an enrollment period, not exceeding one full month, upon receipt of a certificate of enrollment.

"(e) Educational assistance allowances shall be paid as soon as practicable after the Administrator is assured of the veteran's enrollment in and pursuit of the program of education for the period for which such allowance is to be paid.".

1976. Act Oct. 15, 1976 (effective 10/15/76, as provided by § 703(b) of such Act, which appears as 38 USCS § 3693 note), in subsec. (a), substituted "chapter 36" for "section 1780" and substituted "the veteran's" for "his"; and in subsec. (b), substituted "chapter 36" for "section 1780".

1981. Act Aug. 13, 1981 (effective Oct. 1, 1981, as provided by § 2006 of such Act, which appears as 38 USCS § 3231 note), in subsec. (b), deleted "or a program of flight training" after "correspondence"; deleted subsec. (c) including the center heading preceding such subsection which read:

"Flight Training
"No educational assistance allowance for any month shall be paid to an eligible veteran who is pursuing a program of education consisting exclusively of flight training until the Administrator shall have received a certification from the eligible veteran and the institution as to actual flight training received by, and to cost thereof to, the veteran during that month.".
1989. Act Dec. 18, 1989, in subsec. (a), substituted "Secretary" for "Administrator".
1991. Act Aug. 6, 1991, redesignated this section, formerly 38 USCS § 1681, as 38 USCS § 3481.

Other provisions:
Effective date and application of section. Act March 3, 1966, P. L. 89-358, § 12(a), 80 Stat. 28, located at 38 USCS § 3451 note, provided that this section is effective on March 3, 1966, but no educational assistance allowance shall be payable under this chapter (38 USCS §§ 3451 et seq.) for any period before June 1, 1966, nor for the month of June 1966, unless (1) the eligible veteran commenced the pursuit of the course of education on or after June 1, 1966, or (2) the pursuit of such course continued through June 30, 1966.

CROSS REFERENCES
This section is referred to in 38 USCS § 3491.

RESEARCH GUIDE
Am Jur:
77 Am Jur 2d, Veterans and Veterans' Laws § 144.

Forms:
24A Am Jur Pl & Pr Forms (Rev), Veterans and Veterans' Laws, Form 21.

INTERPRETIVE NOTES AND DECISIONS

1. Generally
2. Constitutionality
3. Tests
4. Taxation
5. Miscellaneous

1. Generally
Portion of educational assistance allowance provided under 38 USCS §§ 3481 et seq. not expended for educational purposes, is includible in gross income under 12 USCS §§ 1701 et seq. for determining amount of federally-assisted rent payment. Ortiz v Department of Housing & Urban Dev. (1977, DC Puerto Rico) 448 F Supp 953.

Fact that state pays full tuition for incarcerated veterans to attend colleges or other schools does not affect their entitlement to benefits under 38 USCS § 3481. VA GCO 7-76.

2. Constitutionality
Evaluating propriety of suspension of veterans' educational assistance benefits requires considering private interest at stake, fairness and reliability of existing procedures preceding termination and public interest in avoiding administrative burdens that might result from required procedures; injunction against such termination and additional procedural requirements of 30 days advance written notice of termination, during which time veteran can explore and challenge basis for such termination and to seek in-person interview with Veterans' Administration [now Department of Veterans Affairs] representative that is informational rather than adversary in nature, are proper. Devine v Cleland (1980, CA9) 616 F2d 1080.

Eligible veterans possess constitutionally protected property interests in receipt of Veterans' Administration [now Department of Veterans Affairs] educational benefits. Mathes v Hornbarger (1987, CA7 Ind) 821 F2d 439.

3. Tests

Veterans' Administration [now Department of Veterans Affairs] may pay for administration of College Level Examination Program (CLEP) test to veterans eligible for GI Bill benefits where objective of examination is counseling of veteran for placement in proper educational program, but not for purpose of enabling veteran to obtain advance credit or degree. VA GCO 11-74.

4. Taxation

There is no rational basis to Revenue Rule (80-173) which treats Veterans Administration [now Department of Veterans Affairs] benefits received by flight trainees differently for tax purposes than those received by other veteran trainees. Baker v United States (1983, ND Ga) 575 F Supp 508, 84-1 USTC ¶ 9110, 53 AFTR 2d 84-660, affd (1984, CA11 Ga) 748 F2d 1465, 85-1 USTC ¶ 9101, 55 AFTR 2d 85-509, reh den, en banc (1985, CA11 Ga) 756 F2d 885 and acq.

5. Miscellaneous

Government is entitled to deduct amount paid veteran in form of subsistence payments in suit by veteran to recover back pay during period of unwarranted removal. Getzoff v United States (1953) 124 Ct Cl 232, 109 F Supp 712.

§ 3482. Computation of educational assistance allowances

(a)(1) Except as provided in subsection (b) [,] (c), or (g) of this section, or section 3687 of this title, while pursuing a program of education under this chapter [38 USCS §§ 3451 et seq.] of half-time or more, each eligible veteran shall be paid the monthly educational assistance allowance set forth in column II, III, IV, or V (whichever is applicable as determined by the veteran's dependency status) opposite the applicable type of program as shown in column I:

Column I Type of program	Column II No dependents	Column III One dependent	Column IV Two dependents	Column V More than two dependents The amount in column IV, plus the following for each dependent in excess of two:
Institutional training: Full-time	$376	$448	$510	$32
Three-quarter time	283	336	383	24
Half-time	188	224	255	17
Cooperative	304	355	404	23

(2) A "cooperative" program, other than a "farm cooperative" program, means a full-time program of education which consists of institutional courses and alternate phases of training in a business or industrial establishment with the training in the business or industrial establishment being strictly supplemental to the institutional portion.

(b) The educational assistance allowance of an individual pursuing a program of education—

READJUSTMENT BENEFITS   38 USCS § 3482

(1) while on active duty, or

(2) on less than a half-time basis,

shall be computed at the rate of (A) the established charges for tuition and fees which the institution requires similarly circumstanced nonveterans enrolled in the same program to pay, or (B) $376 per month for a full-time course, whichever is the lesser. An individual's entitlement shall be charged for institutional courses on the basis of the applicable monthly training time rate as determined under section 3688 of this title.

(c)(1) An eligible veteran who is enrolled in an educational institution for a "farm cooperative" program consisting of institutional agricultural courses prescheduled to fall within 44 weeks of any period of 12 consecutive months and who pursues such program on—
  (A) a full-time basis (a minimum of ten clock hours per week or four hundred and forty clock hours in such year pre-scheduled to provide not less than eighty clock hours in any three-month period),
  (B) a three-quarter-time basis (a minimum of 7 clock hours per week), or
  (C) a half-time basis (a minimum of 5 clock hours per week),

shall be eligible to receive an educational assistance allowance at the appropriate rate provided in the table in paragraph (2) of this subsection, if such eligible veteran is concurrently engaged in agricultural employment which is relevant to such institutional agricultural courses as determined under standards prescribed by the Secretary. In computing the foregoing clock hour requirements there shall be included the time involved in field trips and individual and group instruction sponsored and conducted by the educational institution through a duly authorized instructor of such institution in which the veteran is enrolled.

(2) The monthly educational assistance allowance of an eligible veteran pursuing a farm cooperative program under this chapter [38 USCS §§ 3451 et seq.] shall be paid as set forth in column II, III, IV, or V (whichever is applicable as determined by the veteran's dependency status) opposite the basis shown in column I:

Column I	Column II	Column III	Column IV	Column V
Basic	No dependents	More than two dependents	One dependent	Two dependents
				The amount in column IV, plus the following for each dependent in excess of two:
Full-time	$304	$355	$404	$23
Three-quarter time	228	266	303	18
Half-time	152	178	202	12

(d)(1) Notwithstanding the prohibition in section 3471 of this title prohibiting enrollment of an eligible veteran in a program of education in which suchveteran has "already qualified," a veteran shall be allowed up to six months of educational assistance (or the equivalent thereof in part-time assistance) for the pursuit of refresher training to permit such veteran to update such veteran's knowledge and skills and to be instructed in the technological advances which have occurred in such veteran's field of employment during and since the period of such veteran's active military service.

(2) A veteran pursuing refresher training under this subsection shall be paid an educational assistance allowance based upon the rate prescribed in the table in subsection (a)(1) or in subsection (c)(2) of this section, whichever is applicable.

(3) The educational assistance allowance paid under the authority of this subsection shall be charged against the period of entitlement the veteran has earned pursuant to section 3461(a) of this title.

(e) The educational assistance allowance of an eligible veteran pursuing an independent study program which leads to a standard college degree shall be computed at the rate provided in subsection (b) of this section. If the entire training is to be pursued by independent study, the amount of such veteran's entitlement to educational assistance under this chapter shall be charged in accordance with the rate at which the veteran is pursuing the independent study program but at not more than the rate at which such entitlement is charged for pursuit of such program on less than a half-time basis. In any case in which independent study is combined with resident training, the educational assistance allowance shall be paid at the applicable institutional rate based on the total training time determined by adding the number of semester hours (or the equivalent thereof) of resident training to the number of semester hours (or the equivalent thereof) of independent study that do not exceed the number of semester hours (or the equivalent thereof) required for the less than half-time institutional rate, as determined by the Secretary, for resident training. A veteran's entitlement shall be charged for a combination of independent study and resident training on the basis of the applicable monthly training time rate as determined under section 3688 of this title.

(f) The educational assistance allowance of an eligible veteran pursuing a course by open circuit television shall be computed in the same manner that such allowance is computed under subsection (e) of this section for an independent study program.

(g)(1) Subject to the provisions of paragraph (2) of this subsection, the amount of the educational assistance allowance paid to an eligible veteran who is pursuing a program of education under this chapter [38 USCS §§ 3451 et seq.] while incarcerated in a Federal, State, or local penal institution for conviction of a felony may not exceed such amount as the Secretary determines, in accordance with regulations which the Secretary shall prescribe, is necessary to cover the cost of established charges for tuition and fees required of similarly circumstanced nonveterans enrolled in the same program and to cover the cost of necessary supplies, books, and equipment, or the applicable monthly educational assistance allowance prescribed for a veteran with no dependents in subsection (a)(1) or (c)(2) of this section or section 3687(b)(1) of this title, whichever is the lesser. The amount of the educational assistance allowance payable to a veteran while so incarcerated shall be reduced to the extent that the tuition and fees of the veteran for any course are paid under any Federal program (other than a program administered by the Secretary) or under any State or local program.

(2) Paragraph (1) of this subsection shall not apply in the case of any veteran who is pursuing a program of education under this chapter [38 USCS §§ 3451 et seq.] while residing in a halfway house or participating in a work-release program in connection with such veteran's conviction of a felony.

(Added March 3, 1966, P. L. 89-358, § 2, 80 Stat. 18; Aug. 31, 1967, P. L. 90-77, Title III, §§ 301, 303(b), 81 Stat. 184, 185; Oct. 23, 1968, P. L. 90-631, § 3, 82 Stat. 1333; March 26, 1970, P. L. 91-219, Title I, § 103(a)–(d), Title II, § 204(a)(3), 84 Stat. 76, 79; Dec. 24, 1970, P. L. 91-584, § 9, 84 Stat. 1577; Oct. 24, 1972, P. L. 92-540, Title I, § 102(2)–(4), Title III, § 303, Title IV, § 401(4), (5), 86 Stat. 1075, 1081, 1090; Dec. 3, 1974, P. L. 93-508, Title I, § 102(2)–(4), Title II, § 204, 88 Stat. 1579, 1582; Jan. 2, 1975, P. L. 93-602, Title II, § 203(b), 88 Stat. 1958; Oct. 15, 1976, P. L. 94-502, Title II, §§ 201(1)–(3), 207, 90 Stat. 2384, 2387; Nov. 23, 1977, P. L. 95-202, Title I, § 102(2)–(4), 91 Stat. 1434; Oct. 17, 1980, P. L. 96-466, Title II, Part A, § 201(2)–(4), Part B, § 211(2)–(4), Title III, §§ 308–310, Title VI, § 602(a), 94 Stat. 2187, 2189, 2194, 2208; Aug. 13, 1981, P. L. 97-35, Title XX, § 2003(b)(5), 95 Stat. 782; Oct. 14, 1982, P. L. 97-306, Title II, §§ 204, 205(b), 96 Stat. 1434; Nov. 21, 1983, P. L. 98-160, Title VII, § 702(11), 97 Stat. 1009; Oct. 24, 1984, P. L. 98-543, Title II, Part A, § 202(1)–(3), 98 Stat. 2741; Dec. 18, 1989, P. L. 101-237, Title IV, § 423(b)(1)(A), 103 Stat. 2092; Aug. 6, 1991, P. L. 102-83, § 5(a), (c)(1), 105 Stat. 406; Oct. 9, 1996, P. L. 104-275, Title I, § 104(a), 110 Stat. 3327.)

HISTORY; ANCILLARY LAWS AND DIRECTIVES

Explanatory notes:
Provisions similar to those contained in subsecs. (a), (b)(2), (c)(1), (2) of this section were contained in former 38 USC §§ 1611(c), 1632(a), (b), (f), and (e) prior to repeal by Act March 3, 1966, P. L. 89-358, § 4(a), 80 Stat. 23.

The bracketed comma was inserted in subsec. (a)(1) to reflect the probable intent of Congress.

Amendments:
1967. Act Aug. 31, 1967 (effective 10/1/67, as provided by § 405(a) of such Act, which appears as 38 USCS § 101 note), in subsec. (a)(1), substituted "Except as provided in subsection (b), (c)(1), or (d) of this section, or section 1677 or 1683 of this title" for "Except as provided in subsection (b) or (c)(1)", substituted "column II, III, IV, or V" for "column II, III, or IV", and substituted new table for one which read:

38 USCS § 3482 VETERANS' BENEFITS

"Column I	Column II	Column III	Column IV
Type of program	No dependents	One dependent	Two or more dependents
Institutional:			
Full-time	$100	$125	$150
Three-quarter time	75	95	115
Half-time	50	65	75
Cooperative	80	100	120";

in subsec. (b), concluding matter, substituted "$130" for "$100"; and added subsec. (d).

1968. Act Oct. 23, 1968 (effective 12/1/68, as provided by § 6(a) of such Act, which appears as 38 USCS § 3500), in subsec. (a)(2), inserted ", other than a 'farm cooperative' program,"; substituted new subsec. (c)(2) for one which read: "In the case of any eligible veteran who is pursuing any program of education exclusively by correspondence, one-fourth of the elapsed time in following such program of education shall be charged against the veteran's period of entitlement."; and substituted new subsec. (d) for one which read: "An eligible veteran enrolled in an educational institution for a 'farm cooperative' program consisting of institutional agricultural courses for a minimum of 12 clock hours per week, shall be eligible to receive an educational assistance allowance at the appropriate rate provided in the table in subsection (a)(1) of this section opposite the word 'Cooperative' under Column I of such table, if such eligible veteran is concurrently engaged in agricultural employment which is relevant to such institutional agricultural courses as determined under standards prescribed by the Administrator.".

1970. Act March 26, 1970, § 103(a)–(d) (effective 2/1/70, as provided by § 301 of such Act, which appears as a note to this section), in subsec. (a)(1), substituted new table for one which read:

"Column I	Column II	Column III	Column IV	Column V
Type of program	No dependents	One dependent	Two dependents	More than two dependents
				The amount in column IV, plus the following for each dependent in excess of two:
Institutional:				
Full-time	$130	$155	$175	$10
Three-quarter time .	95	115	135	7
Half time	60	75	85	5
Cooperative	105	125	145	7";

in subsec. (b), concluding matter, and subsec. (c)(2), substituted "$175"

168

for "$130"; and, in subsec. (d)(2), substituted new table for one which read:

"Column I	Column II	Column III	Column IV	Column V
Basis	No dependents	One dependent	Two dependents	More than two dependents
				The amount in column IV, plus the following for each dependent in excess of two:
Full-time	$105	$125	$145	$7
Three-quarter time ...	75	90	105	5
Half-time	50	60	70	3"

Act March 26, 1970, § 204(a)(3), in subsec. (b), concluding matter, inserted "Notwithstanding provisions of section 1681 of this title, payment of the educational assistance allowance provided by this subsection may, and the educational assistance allowance provided by section 1696(b) shall, be made to an eligible veteran in an amount computed for the entire quarter, semester, or term during the month immediately following the month in which certification is received from the educational institution that the veteran has enrolled in and is pursuing a program at such institution.".

Act Dec. 24, 1970, in subsec. (c)(1), inserted "The term 'established charge' as used herein means the charge for the course or courses determined on the basis of the lowest extended time payment plan offered by the institution and approved by the appropriate State approving agency or the actual cost to the eligible veteran, whichever is the lesser.".

1972. Act Oct. 24, 1972, §§ 303, 401(4), (5), in subsec. (a)(1), substituted "or (c)" for "(c)(1), or (d)" and substituted "1787" for "1683"; in subsec. (b), concluding matter deleted "Notwithstanding provisions of section 1681 of this title, payment of the educational assistance allowance provided by this subsection may, and the educational assistance allowance provided by section 1696(b) shall, be made to an eligible veteran in an amount computed for the entire quarter, semester, or term during the month immediately following the month in which certification is received from the educational institution that the veteran has enrolled in and is pursuing a program at such institution." following "whichever is the lesser."; deleted subsec. (c) which read:

"(c)(1) The educational assistance allowance of an eligible veteran pursuing a program of education exclusively by correspondence shall be computed on the basis of the established charge which the institution requires nonveterans to pay for the course or courses pursued by the eligible veteran. The term 'established charge' as used herein means the charge for the course or courses determined on the basis of the lowest extended time payment plan offered by the institution and approved by the appropriate State approving agency or the actual cost to the eligible veteran, whichever is the lesser. Such allowance shall be paid quarterly on a pro rata basis for the lessons completed by the veteran and serviced by the institution, as certified by the institution.

38 USCS § 3482

"(2) The period of entitlement of any eligible veteran who is pursuing any program of education exclusively by correspondence shall be charged with one month for each $175 which is paid to the veteran as an educational assistance allowance for such course.";

redesignated subsec. (d) as subsec. (c); in subsec. (c)(1), as so redesignated; in subpara. (A), substituted "(a minimum of ten clock hours per week or four hundred and forty clock hours in such year prescheduled to provide not less than eighty clock hours in any three-month period)" for "(a minimum of 12 clock hours per week)", in subpara. (B), substituted "7" for "9", in subpara. (C), substituted "5" for "6", and in the concluding matter, inserted "In computing the foregoing clock hour requirements there shall be included the time involved in field trips and individual and group instruction sponsored and conducted by the educational institution through a duly authorized instructor of such institution in which the veteran is enrolled.".

Such Act further, in subsec. (a)(1), substituted new table for one which read:

"Column I	Column II	Column III	Column IV	Column V
Type of program	No dependents	One dependent	Two dependents	More than two dependents
				The amount in column IV, plus the following for each dependent in excess of two:
Institutional:				
Full-time	$175	$205	$230	$13
Three-quarter-time	128	152	177	10
Half-time	81	100	114	7
Cooperative	141	167	192	10";

in subsec. (b), concluding matter, substituted "$220" for "$175"; and in subsec. (c)(2), as redesignated by Act Oct. 24, 1972, § 303, substituted new table for one which read:

"Column I	Column II	Column III	Column IV	Column V
Basis	No dependents	One dependent	Two dependents	More than two dependents
				The amount in Column IV, plus the following for each dependent in excess of two:
Full-time	$141	$165	$190	$10

Three-quarter-time ...	101	119	138	7
Half-time	67	79	92	4'';

Section 601(a) of Act Oct. 24, 1972, which appears as a note to this section, provided that these amendments are generally effective Oct. 1, 1972.

1974. Act Dec. 3, 1974, § 102(2)–(4) (effective 9/1/74, as provided by § 501 of such Act, which appears as a note to this section), in subsec. (a)(1), substituted new table for one which read:

"Column I	Column II	Column III	Column IV	Column V
Type of program	No dependents	One dependent	Two dependents	More than two dependents
				The amount in column IV, plus the following for each dependent in excess of two:
Institutional				
Full-time	$220	$261	$298	$18
Three-quarter-time ...	165	196	224	14
Half-time	110	131	149	9
Cooperative	177	208	236	14'';

in subsec. (b), concluding matter, substituted "$260" for "$220"; and in subsec. (c)(2), substituted new table for one which read:

"Column I	Column II	Column III	Column IV	Column V
Basis	No dependents	One dependent	Two dependents	More than two dependents
				The amount in column IV, plus the following for each dependent in excess of two:
Full-time	$177	$208	$236	$14
Three-quarter-time ...	133	156	177	11
Half-time	89	104	118	7''.

Act Dec. 3, 1974, § 204 (effective 12/3/74, as provided by § 503 of such Act, which appears as 38 USCS § 3452 note), added subsec. (d).

1975. Act Jan. 2, 1975 (effective 1/1/75, as provided by § 206 of such Act, which appears as a note to this section), in subsec. (b), concluding matter, substituted "$270" for "$260".

1976. Act Oct. 15, 1976 (effective 10/1/76, as provided by § 703(a) of such Act, which appears as 38 USCS § 3693 note), in subsec. (a)(1), substituted new table for one which read:

38 USCS § 3482   Veterans' Benefits

"Column I	Column II	Column III	Column IV	Column V
Type of program	No dependents	One dependent	Two dependents	More than two dependents
				The amount in column IV, plus the following for each dependent in excess of two:
Institutional:				
Full-time	$270	$321	$366	$22
Three-quarter-time ...	203	240	275	17
Half-time	135	160	182	11
Cooperative	217	255	289	17";

in subsec. (b), concluding matter, substituted "$292" for "$270"; in subsec. (c)(2), substituted new table for one which read:

"Column I	Column II	Column III	Column IV	Column V
Basis	No dependents	One dependent	Two dependents	More than two dependents
				The amount in column IV, plus the following for each dependent in excess of two:
Full-time	$217	$255	$289	$17
Three-quarter-time ...	163	191	218	13
Half-time	109	128	145	9";

and added subsec. (e).

1977. Act Nov. 23, 1977, in subsec. (a)(1), substituted new table for one which read:

"Column I	Column II	Column III	Column IV	Column V
Type of program	No dependents	One dependent	Two dependents	More than two dependents
				The amount in column IV, plus the following for each dependent in excess of two:

READJUSTMENT BENEFITS 38 USCS § 3482

Institutional:				
Full-time	$292	$347	$396	$24
Three-quarter-time ...	219	260	297	18
Half-time	146	174	198	12
Cooperative	235	276	313	18'';

in subsec. (b), concluding matter, substituted "$311" for "$292"; and in subsec. (c)(2), substituted new table for one which read:

"Column I	Column II	Column III	Column IV	Column V
Basis	No dependents	One dependent	Two dependents	More than two dependents
				The amount in column IV, plus the following for each dependent in excess of two:
Full-time	$235	$276	$313	$18
Three-quarter-time ...	170	207	235	14
Half-time	118	138	157	9'';

Section 501 of Act Nov. 23, 1977, which appears as 38 USCS § 101 note, provided that these amendments are effective retroactively to Oct. 1, 1977.

1980. Act Oct. 17, 1980, § 201(2)–(4) (effective 10/1/80, as provided by § 802(b)(1) of such Act), in subsec. (a)(1), substituted new table for one which read:

"Column I	Column II	Column III	Column IV	Column V
Type of program	No dependents	One dependent	Two dependents	More than two dependents
				The amount in column IV, plus the following for each dependent in excess of two:
Institutional:				
Full time	$311	$ 70	$422	$26
Three-quarter time ...	233	277	317	19
Half-time	156	185	211	13
Cooperative	251	294	334	19'';

in subsec. (b), concluding matter, substituted "$327" for "$311"; and in subsec. (c)(2), substituted new table for one which read:

38 USCS § 3482   VETERANS' BENEFITS

"Column I	Column II	Column III	Column IV	Column V
Basis	No dependents	One dependent	Two dependents	More than two dependents
				The amount in column IV, plus the following for each dependent in excess of two:
Full-time	$251	$294	$334	$18
Three-quarter time ...	188	221	251	15
Half-time	126	147	167	10".

Act Oct. 17, 1980, § 211(2)–(4) (effective 1/1/81, as provided by § 802(b)(2) of such Act), in subsec. (a)(1), as amended by Act Oct. 17, 1980, § 201(2), substituted new table for one which read:

"Column I	Column II	Column III	Column IV	Column V
Basis	No dependents	One dependent	Two dependents	More than two dependents
				The amount in column IV, plus the following for each dependent in excess of two:
Institutional:				
Full-time	$327	$389	$443	$27
Three-quarter-time ...	245	292	332	20
Half-time	164	195	222	14
Cooperative	264	309	351	21";

in subsec. (b), as amended by Act Oct. 17, 1980, § 201(3), concluding matter, substituted "$342" for "$327"; and in subsec. (c)(2), as amended by Act Oct. 17, 1980, § 201(4), substituted new table for which read:

"Column I	Column II	Column III	Column IV	Column V
Basis	No dependents	One dependent	Two dependents	More than two dependents
				The amount in column IV, plus the following for each dependent in excess of two:

READJUSTMENT BENEFITS 38 USCS § 3482

Full-time	$264	$309	$351	$20
Three-quarter-time	198	232	263	15
Half-time	132	155	176	10".

Act Oct. 17, 1980, §§ 308–310, 602(a) (effective 10/1/80, as provided by § 802(c)(1), (f)(1) of such Act), in subsec. (b), concluding matter, inserted "An individual's entitlement shall be charged for institutional courses on the basis of the applicable monthly training time rate as determined under section 1788 of this title."; substituted new subsec. (e) for one which read: "The educational assistance allowance of an eligible veteran pursuing an independent study program which leads to a standard college degree shall be computed at the rate provided in subsection (b)(2) of this section. In those cases where independent study is combined with resident training and the resident training constitutes the major portion of such training, the maximum allowance may not exceed the full-time institutional allowance provided under subsection (a)(1) of this section."; and added subsecs. (f) and (g).

1981. Act Aug. 13, 1981 (effective as provided by § 2006 of such Act, which appears as 38 USCS § 3231 note), in subsec. (a)(1), introductory matter, deleted "1677 or" before "1787 of this title".

1982. Act Oct. 14, 1982, in subsec. (a)(1), substituted "(c), or (g)" for "or (c)"; in subsec. (e), substituted "the amount of such veteran's entitlement to educational assistance under this chapter shall be charged in accordance with the rate at which the veteran is pursuing the independent study program but at not more than the rate at which such entitlement is charged for pursuit of such program on less than a half-time basis" for "entitlement shall be charged at one-half of the full-time institutional rate"; and, in subsec. (g), in para. (1), added the sentence beginning "The amount of educational . . .", and in para. (2), inserted "not" following "shall", and deleted "if the Administrator determines that all the veteran's living expenses are being defrayed by a Federal, State, or local government".

1983. Act Nov. 21, 1983, in subsec. (c)(1)(C), added a concluding comma.

1984. Act Oct. 24, 1984 (effective 10/1/78, as provided by § 205 of such Act, which appears as 38 USCS § 3108 note), in subsec. (a)(1), substituted the table for one which read:

"Column I	Column II	Column III	Column IV	Column V
Type of program	No dependents	One dependent	Two dependents	More than two de pendents
				The amount in column IV, plus the following for each dependent in excess of two:
Institutional:				
Full-time	$342	$407	$464	$29
Three-quarter-time	257	305	348	22
Half-time	171	204	232	15
Cooperative	276	323	367	21".

175

38 USCS § 3482 VETERANS' BENEFITS

Such Act further, in subsec. (b), in the concluding matter, substituted "$376" for "$342"; and, in subsec. (c)(2), substituted the table for one which read:

"Column I	Column II	Column III	Column IV	Column V
Basis	No dependents	One dependent	Two dependents	More than two dependents
				The amount in column, IV plus the following for each dependent in excess of two:
Full-time	$276	$323	$367	$21
Three-quarter time	207	242	275	16
Half-time	138	162	184	11".

1989. Act Dec. 18, 1989, in subsecs. (c), (e) and (g), substituted "Secretary" for "Administrator", wherever appearing.

1991. Act Aug. 6, 1991, redesignated this section, formerly 38 USCS § 1682, as 38 USCS § 3482, and amended the references in this section to reflect the redesignations made by § 5(a) of such Act (see Table III preceding 38 USCS § 101).

1996. Act Oct. 9, 1996, in subsec. (f), deleted "in part" following "course".

Other provisions:

Effective date and application of section. Act March 3, 1966, P. L. 89-358, § 12(a), 80 Stat. 28, located at 38 USCS § 3451 note, provided that this section is effective on March 3, 1966, but no educational assistance allowance shall be payable under this chapter (38 USCS §§ 3451 et seq.) for any period before June 1, 1966, nor for the month of June 1966, unless (1) the eligible veteran commenced the pursuit of the course of education on or after June 1, 1966, or (2) the pursuit of such course continued through June 30, 1966.

Overpayment to veterans by Tangipahoa Parish School Board, Amite, Louisiana. Act Aug. 19, 1968, P. L. 90-493, § 5, 82 Stat. 809, provided that any veteran determined by the Administrator of Veterans' Affairs to have received overpayments of educational benefits under former chapter 33 of title 38, United States Code in connection with the institutional on-farm training program conducted by the Tangipahoa Parish School Board, Amite, Louisiana, would be relieved of all liability to the United States for the amount of such overpayment, remaining due on Aug. 19, 1968, by making application for relief within two years following Aug. 19, 1968.

Effective date of amendment made by Act March 26, 1970. Act March 26, 1970, P. L. 91-219, Title III, § 301, 84 Stat. 86, provides: "Title I of this Act [for full classification, consult USCS Tables volumes] takes effect February 1, 1970.".

Application of amendment made by Act Oct. 24, 1972. Act Oct. 24, 1972, P. L. 92-540, Title VI, § 601(a), 86 Stat. 1099, provides: "The rate increases provided in Title I of this Act [for full classification, consult USCS Tables volumes] and the rate increases provided by the provisions of section 1787, title 38, United States Code [38 USCS § 3687] (as added by section 316 of this Act) shall become effective October 1, 1972; except, for those veterans and eligible persons in training on the date of enactment, the effective date shall be the date of the commencement of the current enrollment period, but not earlier than September 1, 1972.".

Savings provisions. Act Oct. 24, 1972, p. 1. 92-540, Title VI, § 602(b), 86 Stat. 1099, which appears as 38 USCS § 3686 note, provided that notwithstanding the provisions of Act Oct. 24, 1972, § 602(a), any enrollment agreement entered into by an eligible veteran prior to Jan. 1, 1973, shall continue to be subject to the provisions of subsec. (c) of this section as it existed prior to repeal by Act Oct. 24, 1972, § 303.

Application of amendment made by Act Dec. 3, 1974. Act Dec. 3, 1974, P. l. 93-508, Title V, § 501, 88 Stat. 1601, provides: "Title I of this Act [for full classification, consult USCS Tables volumes] shall become effective on September 1, 1974.".

Application of amendment made by Act Jan. 2, 1975. Act Jan. 2, 1975, P. L. 93-602, Title II, § 206, 88 Stat. 1959, provides: "The provisions of this title [for full classification, consult USCS Table volumes]shall become effective on January 1, 1975.".

Application of subsec. (g)(1) of this section. Act Oct. 17, 1980, P. L. 96-466, Title VI, § 602(d), 94 Stat. 2209 (effective 10/1/80, as provided by § 802(f)(1) of such Act), provided: "The provisions of section 1682(g)(1) of title 38, United States Code, as added by subsection (a) [subsec. (g)(1) of this section], shall not apply to an apportionment made under section 3107(c) of such title [now 38 USCS § 5307(c)] before the date of the enactment of this Act.".

CROSS REFERENCES

This section is referred to in 10 USCS § 16136; 38 USCS §§ 3002, 3034, 3202, 3491, 3492, 3680.

RESEARCH GUIDE

Am Jur:
77 Am Jur 2d, Veterans and Veterans' Laws §§ 132, 144.

INTERPRETIVE NOTES AND DECISIONS

1. Generally
2. Constitutionality

1. Generally
Government may set off amounts already paid and to be paid against sums administrator of deceased serviceman has recovered from government under federal Tort Claims Act [28 USCS §§ 1346(b), 2671 et seq.]. Knecht v United States (1956, DC Pa) 144 F Supp 786, affd (1957, CA3 Pa) 242 F2d 929.

2. Constitutionality
1980 Amendments limiting education benefits of incarcerated veterans (38 USCS §§ 1682(g) and 1780(a)(6) [now 38 USCS §§ 3482(g) and former 3680(a)(6)] are constitutional. Jackson v Congress of United States (1983, SD NY) 558 F Supp 1288.

38 USCS § 1682(g) [now 38 USCS § 3482(g)] limiting benefits to incarcerated veteran to cost of tuition, fees, and supplies does not violate equal protection clause of Fifth Amendment to U. S. Constitution by denying incarcerated veterans subsistence benefits to which they would be entitled if they had not been incarcerated; nor does § 1682(g) [now § 3482(g)] constitute bill of attainder under Article I § 9 of Constitution. Greenwell v Walters (1984, MD Tenn) 596 F Supp 693.

[§ 3482A]. [§ 1682A. Repealed]

HISTORY; ANCILLARY LAWS AND DIRECTIVES

The bracketed section number "3482A" was inserted to preserve numerical continuity following the section number redesignations made by Act Aug. 6, 1991, P. L. 102-83, § 5(a), 105 Stat. 406.

This section (Act Nov. 23, 1977, P. L. 95-202, Title II, § 201(a), 91 Stat. 1436; Oct. 12, 1982, P. L. 97-295, § 4(41), 96 Stat. 1308) was repealed by Act Nov. 18, 1988, P. L. 100-689, Title I, Part B, § 124(a), 102 Stat. 4174. The section related to accelerated payment of educational assistance allowances.

§ 3483. Approval of courses

An eligible veteran shall receive the benefits of this chapter [38 USCS §§ 3451 et seq.] while enrolled in a course of education offered by an educational institution only if such course is approved in accordance with the provisions of subchapter I of chapter 36 of this title [38 USCS §§ 3670 et seq.].

(Added March 3, 1966, P. L. 89-358, § 2, 80 Stat. 19; Aug. 31, 1967, P. L. 90-77, Title III, § 304(a), 81 Stat. 186; Oct. 24, 1972, P. L. 92-540, Title IV, § 401(7) 86 Stat. 1090; Aug. 6, 1991, P. L. 102-83, § 5(a), 105 Stat. 406.)

HISTORY; ANCILLARY LAWS AND DIRECTIVES

Explanatory notes:
A former § 1683 (Added Act Aug. 31, 1967, P. L. 90-77, Title III, § 304(a), 81 Stat. 186; March 26, 1970, P. L. 91-219, Title I, § 103(e), 84 Stat. 77; Dec. 24, 1970, P. L. 91-584, § 7, 84 Stat. 1576) was repealed by Act Oct. 24, 1972, P. L. 92-540, Title IV, § 401(6), 86 Stat. 1090. It related to apprenticeship or other on-job training. For similar provisions, see 38 USCS § 3687.

Amendments:
1967. Act Aug. 31, 1967 (effective 10/1/67, as provided by § 405(a) of such Act), redesignated this section as § 1686, it formerly appeared as § 1685.

1972. Act Oct. 24, 1972, redesignated this section as § 1683; it formerly appeared as § 1686.

1991. Act Aug. 6, 1991, redesignated this section, formerly 38 USCS § 1683, as 38 USCS § 3483.

Other provisions:
Effective date and application of section. Act March 3, 1966, P. L. 89-358, § 12(a), 80 Stat. 28, located at 38 USCS § 3451 note, provided that this section is effective on March 3, 1966, but no educational assistance allowance shall be payable under this chapter (38 USCS §§ 3451 et seq.) for any period before June 1, 1966, nor for the month of June 1966, unless (1) the eligible veteran commenced the pursuit of the course of education on or after June 1, 1966, or (2) the pursuit of such course continued through June 30, 1966.

CROSS REFERENCES

This section is referred to in 10 USCS 16136; 38 USCS §§ 3034, 3241, 3670.

RESEARCH GUIDE
Am Jur:
77 Am Jur 2d, Veterans and Veterans' Laws §§ 132, 144.

§ 3484. Apprenticeship or other on-job training; correspondence courses

Any eligible veteran may pursue a program of apprenticeship or other on-job training or a program of education exclusively by correspondence and be paid an educational assistance allowance or training assistance allowance, as applicable, under the provisions of section 3687 or 3686 of this title.
(Added Oct. 24, 1972, P. L. 92-540, Title III, § 304, 86 Stat. 1081; Aug. 6, 1991, P. L. 102-83, § 5(a), (c)(1), 105 Stat. 406.)

HISTORY; ANCILLARY LAWS AND DIRECTIVES
Amendments:
1991. Act Aug. 6, 1991, redesignated this section, formerly 38 USCS § 1684, as 38 USCS § 3484, and amended the references in this section to reflect the redesignations made by § 5(a) of such Act (see Table III preceding 38 USCS § 101).

RESEARCH GUIDE
Am Jur:
77 Am Jur 2d, Veterans and Veterans' Laws § 144.

Forms:
24A Am Jur Pl & Pr Forms (Rev), Veterans and Veterans' Laws, Form 21.

§ 3485. Work-study allowance

(a)(1) Individuals utilized under the authority of subsection (b) of this section shall be paid an additional educational assistance allowance (hereafter referred to as "work-study allowance"). Such work-study allowance shall be paid in an amount equal to the applicable hourly minimum wage times the number of hours worked during the applicable period, in return for such individual's agreement to perform services, during or between periods of enrollment, aggregating not more than a number of hours equal to 25 times the number of weeks in the semester or other applicable enrollment period, required in connection with (A) the outreach services program under subchapter II of chapter 77 of this title [38 USCS §§ 7721 et seq.] as carried out under the supervision of a Department of Veterans Affairs employee, (B) the preparation and processing of necessary papers and other documents at educational institutions or regional offices or facilities of the Department of Veterans Affairs, (C) the provision of hospital and domiciliary care and medical treatment under chapter 17 of this Title [38 USCS §§ 1701 et seq.], (D) any other activity of the Department of Veterans Affairs as the Secretary shall determine appropriate, or (E) in the case of an individual who is receiving educational assistance under chapter 106 of title 10 [10 USCS §§ 2131 et seq.], activities relating to the administration of such chapter at

Department of Defense, Coast Guard, or National Guard facilities. An individual shall be paid in advance an amount equal to 40 percent of the total amount of the work-study allowance agreed to be paid under the agreement in return for the individual's agreement to perform the number of hours of work specified in the agreement (but not more than an amount equal to 50 times the applicable hourly minimum wage).

(2) For the purposes of paragraph (1) of this subsection and subsection (e) of this section, the term applicable hourly minimum wage means (A) the hourly minimum wage under section 6(a) of the Fair Labor Standards Act of 1938 (29 U.S.C. 206(a)), or (B) the hourly minimum wage under comparable law of the State in which the services are to be performed, if such wage is higher than the wage referred to in clause (A) and the Secretary has made a determination to pay such higher wage.

(b) Notwithstanding any other provision of law, the Secretary shall, subject to the provisions of subsection (e) of this section, utilize, in connection with the activities specified in subsection (a)(1) of this section, the services of individuals who are pursuing programs of rehabilitation, education, or training under chapter 30, 31, 32, or 34 of this title [38 USCS §§ 3001 et seq., 3100 et seq., 3201 et seq., or 3451 et seq.] or chapter 106 of title 10 [10 USCS §§ 2131 et seq.], at a rate equal to at least three-quarters of that required of a full-time student. In carrying out this section, the Secretary, wherever feasible, shall give priority to veterans with disabilities rated at 30 percent or more for purposes of chapter 11 of this title [38 USCS §§ 1101 et seq.]. In the event an individual ceases to be at least a three-quarter-time student before completing such agreement, the individual may, with the approval of the Secretary, be permitted to complete such agreement.

(c) The Secretary shall determine the number of individuals whose services the Department of Veterans Affairs can effectively utilize and the types of services that such individuals may be required to perform, on the basis of a survey, which the Secretary shall conduct annually, of each Department of Veterans Affairs' regional office in order to determine the numbers of individuals whose services can effectively be utilized during an enrollment period in each geographical area where Department of Veterans Affairs activities are conducted, and shall determine which individuals shall be offered agreements under this section in accordance with regulations which the Secretary shall prescribe, including as criteria (1) the need of the individual to augment the individual's educational assistance or subsistence allowance; (2) the availability to the individual of transportation to the place where the individual's services are to be performed; (3) the motivation of the individual; and (4) in the case of a disabled veteran pursuing a course of vocational rehabilitation under chapter 31 of this title [38 USCS §§ 3100 et seq.], the compatibility of the work assignment to the veteran's physical condition.

(d) While performing the services authorized by this section, individuals shall be deemed employees of the United States for the purposes of the benefits of chapter 81 of title 5 [5 USCS §§ 8101 et seq.] but not for the purposes of laws administered by the Office of Personnel Management.

(e)(1) Subject to paragraph (2) of this subsection, the Secretary may, notwithstanding any other provision of law, enter into an agreement with an individual under this section, or a modification of such an agreement, whereby the individual agrees to perform services of the kind described in clauses (A) through (E) of subsection (a)(1) of this section and agrees that the Secretary shall, in lieu of paying the work-study allowance payable for such services, as provided in subsection (a) of this section, deduct the amount of the allowance from the amount which the individual has been determined to be indebted to the United States by virtue of such individual's participation in a benefits program under this chapter [38 USCS §§ 3451 et seq.], chapter 30, 31, 32, 35, or 36 [38 USCS §§ 3001 et seq., 3100 et seq., 3201 et seq., 3500 et seq., or 3670 et seq.] (other than an education loan under subchapter III [38 USCS §§ 3698 et seq.]) of this title, or chapter 106 of title 10 [10 USCS §§ 2131 et seq.] (other than an indebtedness arising from a refund penalty imposed under section 2135 [10 USCS § 16135] of such title).

(2)(A) Subject to subparagraph (B) of this paragraph, the provisions of this section (other than those provisions which are determined by the Secretary to be inapplicable to an agreement under this subsection) shall apply to any agreement authorized under paragraph (1) of this subsection.

(B) For the purposes of this subsection, the Secretary may—

(i) waive, in whole or in part, the limitations in subsection (a) of this section concerning the number of hours and periods during which services can be performed by the individual and the provisions of subsection (b) of this section requiring the individual's pursuit of a program of rehabilitation, education, or training;

(ii) in accordance with such terms and conditions as may be specified in the agreement under this subsection, waive or defer charging interest and administrative costs pursuant to section 5315 of this title on the indebtedness to be satisfied by performance of the agreement; and

(iii) notwithstanding the indebtedness offset provisions of section 5314 of this title, waive or defer until the termination of an agreement under this subsection the deduction of all or any portion of the amount of indebtedness covered by the agreement from future payments to the individual as described in section 5314 of this title.

(3)(A) Subject to the provisions of subparagraphs (B) and (C) of this paragraph, an agreement authorized under this subsection shall terminate in accordance with the provisions of this section and the terms and conditions of the agreement which are consistent with this subsection.

(B) In no event shall an agreement under this subsection continue in force after the total amount of the individual's indebtedness described in paragraph (1) of this subsection has been recouped, waived, or otherwise liquidated.

(C) Notwithstanding the provisions of subparagraphs (A) and (B) of this paragraph, if the Secretary finds that an individual was without fault and was allowed to perform services described in the agreement after its termination, the Secretary shall, as reasonable compensation therefor, pay the individual at the applicable hourly minimum wage rate for such services as the Secretary determines were satisfactorily performed.

(4) The Secretary shall promulgate regulations to carry out this subsection.
(Added Oct. 24, 1972, P. L. 92-540, Title II, § 203, 86 Stat. 1079; Dec. 3, 1974, P. L. 93-508, Title II, § 205, 88 Stat. 1582; Oct. 15, 1976, P. L. 94-502, Title II, §§ 208, 211(11), 90 Stat. 2388; Nov. 23, 1977, P. L. 95-202, Title I, § 105, 91 Stat. 1435; Oct. 17, 1980, P. L. 96-466, Title VIII, § 801(b), 94 Stat. 2216; Oct. 12, 1982, P. L. 97-295, § 4(42), 96 Stat. 1308; Oct. 28, 1986, P. L. 99-576, Title III, Part A, § 308(c), 100 Stat. 3270; Dec. 18, 1989, P. L. 101-237, Title IV, §§ 405(a)–(d)(2), 4(A), 423(b)(1), 103 Stat. 2080, 2081, 2092; March 22, 1991, P. L. 102-16, §§ 6(a), (b)(1), (2), 10(a)(5), 105 Stat. 50, 51, 55; May 7, 1991, P. L. 102-40, Title IV, § 402(d)(1), 105 Stat. 239; Aug. 6, 1991, P. L. 102-83, §§ 2(c), 5(a), 105 Stat. 406; Oct. 29, 1992, P. L. 102-568, Title III, § 311, 106 Stat. 4330.)

HISTORY; ANCILLARY LAWS AND DIRECTIVES

Explanatory notes:
The bracketed reference "10 USCS § 16135" has been inserted on the authority of Act Oct. 5, 1994, P. L. 103-337, Div. A, Title XVI, § 1663(b)(2), 108 Stat. 3006, which redesignated 10 USCS § 2135 as 10 USCS § 16135.

Amendments:
1974. Act Dec. 3, 1974 (effective 12/3/74, as provided by § 503 of such Act, which appears as 38 USCS § 3452 note), in subsec. (a), substituted "Such work-study allowance shall be paid in the amount of $625 in return for such veteran-student's agreement to perform services, during or between periods of enrollment, aggregating two hundred and fifty hours" for "Such work-study allowance shall be paid in advance in the amount of $250 in return for such veteran-student's agreement to perform services, during or between periods of enrollment, aggregating one hundred hours", and substituted "An agreement may be entered into for the performance of services for periods of less than two hundred and fifty hours, in which case the amount of the work-study allowance to be paid shall bear the same ratio to the number of hours of work agreed to be performed as $625 bears to two hundred and fifty hours. In the case of any agreement providing for the performance of services for one hundred hours or more, the veteran student shall be paid $250 in advance, and in the case of any agreement for the performance of services for less than one hundred hours, the amount of the advance payment shall bear the same ratio to the number of hours of work agreed to be performed as $625 bears to two hundred and fifty hours." for "Advances of lesser amounts may be made in return for agreements to perform services for periods of less than one hundred hours, the amount of such advance to bear the same ratio to the number of hours of work agreed to be performed as $250 bears to one hundred hours."; and in subsec. (c), deleted "(not to exceed eight hundred man-years or their equivalent in man-hours during any fiscal year)" following "effectively utilize".

1976. Act Oct. 15, 1976 (effective 10/15/76, as provided by § 703(b) of such Act, which appears as 38 USCS § 3693 note), in subsec. (b), inserted "In the event the veteran ceases to be a full-time student before completing such agreement, the veteran may, with the approval of the Administrator, be permitted to complete such agreement."; and in subsec. (c), substituted "the Administrator" for "he" wherever appearing and substituted "the veteran's" for "his" preceding "educational assistance" and "services".

1977. Act Nov. 23, 1977 (effective 10/1/1977, as provided by § 501 of such Act, which appears as 38 USCS § 101 note), in subsec. (a), substituted "in an amount equal to either the amount of the hourly minimum wage in effect under section 6(a) of the Fair Labor Standards Act of 1938 times two hundred and fifty or $625, whichever is the higher," for "in the amount of $625", and substituted "An agreement may be entered into for the performance of services for periods of less than two hundred and fifty hours. The amount of the work-study allowance to be paid under any such agreement shall be determined by multiplying the number of hours of work performed by the veteran-student under such agreement times either the hourly minimum wage in effect under section 6(a) of the Fair Labor Standards Act of 1938 during the period the work is to be performed or $2.50, whichever is the higher. A veteran-student shall be paid in advance an amount equal to 40 per centum of the total amount of the work-study allowance agreed to be paid under the agreement in return for the veteran-student's agreement to perform the number of hours of work specified in the agreement." for "An agreement may be entered into for the performance of services for periods of less than two hundred and fifty hours, in which case the amount of the work-study allowance to be paid shall bear the same ratio to the number of hours of work agreed to be performed as $625 bears to two hundred and fifty hours. In the case of any agreement providing for the performance of services for one hundred hours or more, the veteran student shall be paid $250 in advance, and in the case of any agreement for the performance of services for less than one hundred hours, the amount of the advance payment shall bear the same ratio to the number of hours of work agreed to be performed as $625 bears to two hundred and fifty hours.".

1980. Act Oct. 17, 1980 (effective 10/1/80, as provided by § 802(h) of such Act, which appears as 38 USCS § 3452 note), in subsec. (d), substituted "Office of Personnel Management" for "Civil Service Commission".

1982. Act Oct. 12, 1982, in subsec. (a), inserted "(29 U.S.C. 206(a))"

1986. Act Oct. 28, 1986, in subsec. (b), substituted "rehabilitation, education, or training under chapter 30, 31, 32, or 34" for "education or training under chapters 31 and 34".

1989. Act Dec. 18, 1989, (effective 5/1/90 and applicable to services performed on or after that date, as provided by § 405(e) of such Act, which appears as 10 USCS § 16136 note), substituted the section heading for one which read: "§ 1685. Veteran-student services"; in subsec. (a), designated the existing provisions as para. (1), in para. (1), as redesignated, substituted "Such work-study allowance shall be paid in an amount equal to the applicable hourly minimum wage times the number of hours worked during the applicable period, in return for such individual's agreement to perform services, during or between periods of enrollment, aggregating not more than a number of hours equal to 25 times the number of weeks in the semester or other applicable enrollment period," for "Such work-study allowance shall be paid in an amount equal to either the amount of the hourly minimum wage in effect under section 6(a) of the Fair Labor Standards Act of 1938 (29 U.S.C. 206(a)) times two hundred and fifty or $625, whichever is the higher, in return for such veteran-student's agreement to perform services, during or between periods of enrollment, aggregating two hundred and fifty hours during a semester or other applicable enrollment period,'', deleted two sentences which read: "An agreement may be entered into the performance of services for periods of less than two hundred and fifty hours. The amount of the work-study allowance to be paid under any such agreement shall be determined by multiplying the number of hours of work performed by the veteran-student under such agreement times either the hourly minimum wage in effect under section 6(a) of the Fair Labor Standards Act of 1938 during the period the work is to be performed or $2.50, whichever is the higher." preceding "An individual", deleted "or" following "Title,", deleted the period following "appropriate" and inserted ", or (5) in the case of an individual who is receiving educational assistance under chapter 106 of title 10, activities relating to the administration of such chapter at Department of Defense facilities.", substituted "Individuals" for "Veteran-students", "individual's" for "veteran-student's", and "An individual" for "A veteran-student", and added para. (2); in subsec. (b), substituted "subsection (a)(1)" for "subsection (a)", "individuals who are pursuing programs of rehabilitation, education, or training under chapter 30, 31, 32, or 34 of this title or chapter 106 of title 10, at a rate equal to at least three-quarters of that required of a full-time student." for "of veteran-students who are pursuing full-time programs of rehabilitation, education, or training under chapters 30, 31, 32, or 34 of this title.", "an individual ceases to be at least a three-quarter-time student before completing such agreement, the individual" for "the veteran ceases to be a full-time student before completing such agreement, the veteran", and "percent" for "per centum"; in subsec. (c), substituted "individuals" for "veteran-students" in two places, substituted "individuals" for "veterans", in para. (1)–(3), substituted "individual" for "veteran" and "individual's" for "veteran's", wherever appearing; and in subsec. (d), substituted "individuals" for "veteran-students".

Such Act further, throughout the entire section, substituted "Secretary" for "Administrator", and "Department of Veterans Affairs" for "Veterans' Administration", wherever appearing.

1991. Act March 22, 1991, in subsec. (a), in para. (1), redesignated former cls. (1)–(5) as cls. (A)–(E), and in cl. (E) as redesignated, inserted ", Coast Guard, or National Guard", in para. (2), inserted "and subsection (e) of this section"; in subsec. (b), inserted ", subject to the provisions of subsection (e) of this section,"; and added subsec. (e).

Act May 7, 1991, amended the references in this section to reflect the redesignations made by §§ 401(a)(4) and 402(b) of such Act (see Table II preceding 38 USCS § 101).

Act Aug. 6, 1991, redesignated this section, formerly 38 USCS § 1685, as 38 USCS § 3485, and amended the references in this section to reflect the redesignations made by § 5(a) of such Act (see Table III preceding 38 USCS § 101).

1992. Act Oct. 29, 1992, in subsec. (a), in para. (1), substituted "40 percent" for "40 per centum", and inserted "(but not more than an amount equal to 50 times the applicable hourly minimum wage)".

Other provisions:
Application and construction of the Oct. 12, 1982 amendment of this section. For provisions as to the application and construction of the Oct. 12, 1982 amendment of this section, see § 5 of such Act, which appears as 10 USCS § 101 note.

CROSS REFERENCES
This section is referred to in 10 USCS § 16136; 38 USCS §§ 1712A, 3034, 3104, 3241, 3537, 5314, 5315, 7722.

RESEARCH GUIDE
Am Jur:
77 Am Jur 2d, Veterans and Veterans' Laws § 144.

INTERPRETIVE NOTES AND DECISIONS

1. Generally
2. Relationship with other laws
3. Employment activities

1. Generally
Work-study students must work for Veterans' Administration [now Department of Veterans Affairs], under direct supervision and control of Veterans' Administration [now Department of Veterans Affairs] employee, but may be assigned to assist in outreach services. VA GCO 18-75.

2. Relationship with other laws
Congress never intended that allowances paid to veterans under work-study program should be considered wages for purposes of Dual Compensation Act (5 USCS § 5532). VA GCO 3-75.

3. Employment activities
Work-study veteran-student may not be used to provide transportation to school for service-disabled veteran training under provisions of 38 USCS §§ 1500 et seq [now 38 USCS §§ 3100 et seq.]. VA GCO 12-76.

[§ 3486]. [§ 1686. Repealed]

HISTORY; ANCILLARY LAWS AND DIRECTIVES
The bracketed section number "3486" was inserted to preserve numerical continuity following the section number redesignations made by Act Aug. 6, 1991, P. L. 102-83, § 5(a), 105 Stat. 406.
This section (Act Dec. 3, 1974, P. L. 93-508, Title III, § 302(a), 88 Stat. 1591; Aug. 13, 1981, P. L. 97-35, Title XX, § 2005(b), 95 Stat. 783) was repealed by Act Nov. 18, 1988, P. L. 100-689, Title I, Part B, § 124(a), 102 Stat. 4174. The section related to education loans.

[§ 3487]. [§ 1687. Repealed]

HISTORY; ANCILLARY LAWS AND DIRECTIVES
The bracketed section number "3487" was inserted to preserve numerical continuity following the section number redesignations made by Act Aug. 6, 1991, P. L. 102-83, § 5(a), 105 Stat. 406.
This section (Added as § 1686 by Act March 3, 1966, P. L. 89-358, § 2, 80 Stat. 19; Aug. 31, 1967, P. L. 90-77, Title III, § 304(a), 81 Stat. 186) was repealed by Act Oct. 24, 1972, P. L. 92-540, Title IV, § 401(6), 86 Stat. 1090. This section related to discontinuance of educational assistance allowances by the Administrator. For similar provisions, see 38 USCS § 3690(b).

SUBCHAPTER V. SPECIAL ASSISTANCE FOR THE EDUCATIONALLY DISADVANTAGED

§ 3490. Purpose

It is the purpose of this subchapter [38 USCS §§ 3490 et seq.] (1) to encourage and assist veterans who have academic deficiencies to attain a high school education or its equivalent and to qualify for and pursue courses of higher education, (2) to assist eligible veterans to pursue postsecondary education through tutorial assistance where required, and (3) to encourage educational institutions to develop programs which provide special tutorial, remedial, preparatory, or other educational or supplementary assistance to such veterans. (Added March 26, 1970, P. L. 91-219, Title II, § 204(a)(4), 84 Stat. 79; Aug. 6, 1991, P. L. 102-83, § 5(a), 105 Stat. 406.)

HISTORY; ANCILLARY LAWS AND DIRECTIVES
Amendments:
1991. Act Aug. 6, 1991, redesignated this section, formerly 38 USCS § 1690, as 38 USCS § 3490.

RESEARCH GUIDE
Forms:
24A Am Jur Pl & Pr Forms (Rev), Veterans and Veterans' Laws, Form 21.

§ 3491. Elementary and secondary education and preparatory educational assistance

(a) In the case of any eligible veteran who—
   (1) has not received a secondary school diploma (or an equivalency certificate), or
   (2) is not on active duty and who, in order to pursue a program of education for which the veteran would otherwise be eligible, needs refresher courses, deficiency courses, or other preparatory or special educational assistance to qualify for admission to an appropriate educational institution,

the Secretary may, without regard to so much of the provisions of section 3471 of this title as prohibit the enrollment of an eligible veteran in a program of education in which the veteran is "already qualified", approve the enrollment of such veteran in an appropriate course or courses or other special educational assistance program.

(b)(1) The Secretary shall pay to an eligible veteran pursuing a course or courses or program pursuant to subsection (a)(2) of this section, an educational assistance allowance as provided in sections 3481 and 3482(a) or (b) of this title.

(2) The Secretary shall pay to an eligible veteran described in subsection (a)(1) of this section who is pursuing a course or courses or program under this subchapter [38 USCS §§ 3490 et seq.] for the purpose of attaining a secondary school diploma (or an equivalency certificate) an educational as-

sistance allowance (A) at the rate of established charges for tuition and fees required of similarly circumstanced nonveterans enrolled in the same course, courses, or program, or (B) at the institutional full-time rate provided in section 3482(a) of this title, whichever is the lesser.

(c) The provisions of section 3473(d)(1) of this title relating to the disapproval of enrollment in certain courses, shall be applicable to the enrollment of an eligible veteran who, while serving on active duty, enrolls in one or more courses under this subchapter [38 USCS §§ 3490 et seq.] for the purpose of attaining a secondary school diploma (or an equivalency certificate).
(Added March 26, 1970, P. L. 91-219, Title II, § 204(a)(4), 84 Stat. 79; Oct. 24, 1972, P. L. 92-540, Title III, § 305, 86 Stat. 1081; Oct. 15, 1976, P. L. 94-502, Title II, § 211(12), 90 Stat. 2389; Oct. 17, 1980, P. L. 96-466, Title III, Part A, § 311, 94 Stat. 2194; Oct. 12, 1982, P. L. 97-295, § 4(43), 96 Stat. 1308; Oct. 14, 1982, P. L. 97-306, Title II, § 203(b), 96 Stat. 1434; Dec. 18, 1989, P. L. 101-237, Title IV, § 423(b)(1)(A), 103 Stat. 2092; Aug. 6, 1991, P. L. 102-83, § 5(a), (c)(1), 105 Stat. 406.)

HISTORY; ANCILLARY LAWS AND DIRECTIVES

References in text:
"Section 3473(d)(1) of this title", referred to in this section, was repealed by Act Oct. 29, 1992, P. L. 102-568, Title III, § 313(a)(3)(A), 106 Stat. 4332.

Amendments:
1972. Act Oct. 24, 1972, substituted new subsec. (b) for one which read: "The Administrator shall pay to an eligible veteran pursuing a course or courses or program pursuant to subsection (a) of this section, an educational assistance allowance as provided in sections 1681 and 1682 (a) or (b) of this title; except that no enrollment in adult evening secondary school courses shall be approved in excess of half-time training as defined pursuant to section 1684 of this title.".
1976. Act Oct. 15, 1976 (effective 10/15/76, as provided by § 703(b) of such Act, which appears as 38 USCS § 3693 note), in subsec. (a), in para. (1), substituted "the veteran's" for "his", and in para. (2) and the concluding matter, substituted "the veteran" for "he".
1980. Act Oct. 17, 1980, in subsec. (a), in the preliminary matter, deleted "not on active duty" following "veteran", in para. (1), deleted "at the time of the veteran's discharge or release from active duty" preceding ", or", and in para. (2), inserted "is not on active duty and who,"; redesignated subsec. (b) as subsec. (b)(1); in subsec. (b)(1), as so redesignated, inserted "(2)"; added subsec. (b)(2); and added subsec. (c).
1982. Act Oct. 12, 1982, in subsec. (a), in the concluding matter, and in subsec. (b), inserted "of this title".
Act Oct. 14, 1982, in subsec. (c), substituted "section 1673(d)(1)" for "section 1673(d)".
1989. Act Dec. 18, 1989, in subsecs. (a) and (b), substituted "Secretary" for "Administrator", wherever appearing.
1991. Act Aug. 6, 1991, redesignated this section, formerly 38 USCS § 1691, as 38 USCS § 3491, and amended the references in this section to

reflect the redesignations made by § 5(a) of such Act (see Table III preceding 38 USCS § 101).

Other provisions:
Effective date and application of amendments made by Act Oct. 17, 1980. Act Oct. 17, 1980, P. L. 96-466, Title VIII, § 802(c), 94 Stat. 2218, which appears as 38 USCS § 3452 note, provided that the amendments made to this section by Act Oct. 17, 1980, are effective on Oct. 1, 1980; however, subsec. (a)(2) of this section, as added by Act Oct. 17, 1980, shall not apply to any person receiving educational assistance under chapter 34 of title 38 [38 USCS §§ 3451 et seq.] on Oct. 1, 1980, for the pursuit of a program of education, as defined in 38 USCS § 3452(b), in which such person is enrolled on that date, for as long as such person continuously thereafter is so enrolled and meets the requirements of eligibility for such assistance for pursuit of such program.

Application and construction of the Oct. 12, 1982 amendment of this section. For provisions as to the application and construction of the Oct. 12, 1982 amendment of this section, see § 5 of such Act, which appears as 10 USCS § 101 note.

CROSS REFERENCES

This section is referred to in 38 USCS §§ 3231, 3241, 3462, 3473, 3533, 3680.

§ 3492. Tutorial assistance

(a) In the case of any eligible veteran who—
  (1) is enrolled in and pursuing a postsecondary course of education on a half-time or more basis at an educational institution; and
  (2) has a deficiency in a subject required as a part of, or which is prerequisite to, or which is indispensable to the satisfactory pursuit of, an approved program of education,

the Secretary may approve individualized tutorial assistance for such veteran if such assistance is necessary for the veteran to complete such program successfully.

(b) The Secretary shall pay to an eligible veteran receiving tutorial assistance pursuant to subsection (a) of this section, in addition to the educational assistance allowance provided in section 3482 of this title, the cost of such tutorial assistance in an amount not to exceed $100 per month, for a maximum of twelve months, or until a maximum of $1,200 is utilized, upon certification by the educational institution that—
  (1) the individualized tutorial assistance is essential to correct a deficiency of the eligible veteran in a subject required as a part of, or which is prerequisite to, or which is indispensable to the satisfactory pursuit of, an approved program of education;
  (2) the tutor chosen to perform such assistance is qualified and is not the eligible veteran's parent, spouse, child (whether or not married or over eighteen years of age), brother, or sister; and
  (3) the charges for such assistance do not exceed the customary charges for such tutorial assistance.

READJUSTMENT BENEFITS 38 USCS § 3492

(Added March 26, 1970, P. L. 91-219, Title II, § 204(a)(4), 84 Stat. 80; Oct. 24, 1972, P. L. 92-540, Title III, § 306, 86 Stat. 1081; Dec. 3, 1974, P. L. 93-508, Title II, § 206, 88 Stat. 1583; Oct. 15, 1976, P. L. 94-502, Title II, § 209, 90 Stat. 2388; Nov. 23, 1977, P. L. 95-202, Title I, § 102(5), 91 Stat. 1434; Oct. 17, 1980, P. L. 96-466, Title II, Part A, § 201(5), Part B, § 211(5), Title III, Part A, § 312, 94 Stat. 2188, 2190, 2195; Oct. 24, 1984, P. L. 98-543, Title II, Part A, § 202(4), 98 Stat. 2742; Nov. 18, 1988, P. L. 100-689, Title I, Part A, § 107(c)(1), (2)(A), 102 Stat. 4169; Dec. 18, 1989, P. L. 101-237, Title IV, § 423(b)(1)(A), 103 Stat. 2092; Aug. 6, 1991, P. L. 102-83, § 5(a), (c)(1), 105 Stat. 406.)

HISTORY; ANCILLARY LAWS AND DIRECTIVES
Amendments:
1972. Act Oct. 24, 1972, in subsec. (a)(2), deleted "marked" preceding "deficiency"; in subsec. (b), in the introductory matter, inserted "," following "month" and inserted "or until a maximum of $450 is utilized," and in para. (1), deleted "marked" preceding "deficiency".
1974. Act Dec. 3, 1974 (effective 12/3/74, as provided by § 503 of such Act, which appears as 38 USCS § 3452 note), in subsec. (b), introductory matter, substituted "$60" for "$50", "twelve months" for "nine months", and "$720" for "$450".
1976. Act Oct. 15, 1976 (effective 10/1/76, as provided by § 703(a) of such Act, which appears as 38 USCS § 3693 note), in subsec. (b), introductory matter, substituted "$65" for "$60" and "$780" for "$720".
1977. Act Nov. 23, 1977 (effective 10/1/77, as provided by § 501 of such Act, which appears as 38 USCS § 101 note), in subsec. (b), introductory matter, substituted "$69" for "$65" and "$828" for "$780".
1980. Act Oct. 17, 1980, §§ 201(5), 312 (effective 10/1/80, as provided by § 802(b)(1), (c)(1) of such Act, which appear as 38 USCS §§ 3452, 3482 notes, respectively), in subsec. (b), in the preliminary matter, substituted "$72" and "$869" for "$69" and "$828", respectively, and in para. (2), inserted "and is not the eligible veteran's parent, spouse, child (whether or not married or over eighteen years of age), brother, or sister".
Act Oct. 17, 1980, § 211(5), (effective 1/1/81, as provided by § 802(b)(2) of such Act, which appears as 38 USCS § 3452 note), in subsec. (b), preliminary matter, as amended by Act Oct. 17, 1980, § 201(5), substituted "$76" and "$911" for "$72" and "$869", respectively.
1984. Act Oct. 24, 1984 (effective 10/1/78, as provided by § 205 of such Act, which appears as 38 USCS § 3108 note), in subsec. (b), in the introductory matter, substituted "$84" for "$76" and substituted "$1,008" for "$911".
1988. Act Nov. 18, 1988 substituted the section heading for one which read: "1692. Special supplementary assistance"; and, in subsec. (b), substituted "$100" for "$84" and "$1,200" for "$1,008".
1989. Act Dec. 18, 1989, in subsecs. (a) and (b), substituted "Secretary" for "Administrator".
1991. Act Aug. 6, 1991, redesignated this section, formerly 38 USCS § 1692, as 38 USCS § 3492, and amended the references in this section to reflect the redesignations made by § 5(a) of such Act (see Table III preceding 38 USCS § 101).

CROSS REFERENCES
This section is referred to in 38 USCS §§ 3019, 3234, 3533.

§ 3493. Effect on educational entitlement

The educational assistance allowance or cost of individualized tutorial assistance authorized by this subchapter [38 USCS §§ 3490 et seq.] shall be paid without charge to any period of entitlement the veteran may have earned pursuant to section 3461(a) of this title.
(Added March 26, 1970, P. L. 91-219, Title II, § 204(a)(4), 84 Stat. 80; Aug. 6, 1991, P. L. 102-83, § 5(a), (c)(1), 105 Stat. 406.)

HISTORY; ANCILLARY LAWS AND DIRECTIVES
Amendments:
1991. Act Aug. 6, 1991, redesignated this section, formerly 38 USCS § 1693, as 38 USCS § 3493, and amended the references in this section to reflect the redesignations made by § 5(a) of such Act (see Table III preceding 38 USCS § 101).

[VI. REPEALED]

[§§ 3495-3498]. [§ 1695-1698. Repealed]

HISTORY; ANCILLARY LAWS AND DIRECTIVES
The bracketed section numbers "3495-3498" were inserted to preserve numerical continuity following the section number redesignations made by Act Aug. 6, 1991, P. L. 102-83, § 5(a), 105 Stat. 406.
These sections (§ 1695—Added Act March 26, 1970, P. L. 91-219, Title II, § 204(a)(4), 84 Stat. 80; § 1696—Added Act March 26, 1970, P. L. 91-219, Title II, § 204(a)(4), 84 Stat. 80; Oct. 24, 1972, P. L. 92-540, Title I, § 102(5), Title III, § 307, 86 Stat. 1075, 1081; Dec. 3, 1974, P. L. 93-508, Title I, § 102(5), 88 Stat. 1580; Jan. 2, 1975, P. L. 93-602, Title II, § 203(c), 88 Stat. 1958; Oct. 15, 1976, P. L. 94-502, Title II, §§ 201(4), 210(5), 211(13), 90 Stat. 2385, 2388, 2389; Nov. 23, 1977, P. L. 95-202, Title I, § 102(6), 91 Stat. 1434; § 1697—Added Act March 26, 1970, P. L. 91-219, Title II, § 204(a)(4), 84 Stat. 81; and § 1698—Added Act Oct. 24, 1972, P. L. 92-540, Title III, § 308, 86 Stat. 1082; Oct. 15, 1976, P. L. 94-502, Title II, §§ 210(3), 211(4), 90 Stat. 2388, 2389; Nov. 23, 1977, P. L. 95-202, Title III, § 302(b), 91 Stat. 1441) were repealed by Act Oct. 17, 1980, P. L. 96-466, Title VI, § 601(a)(1), 94 Stat. 2208, effective Oct. 1, 1980, as provided by § 802(f)(1) of Act Oct. 17, 1980. Section 1695 related to purpose and definitions for the predischarge education program; § 1696 related to payment of educational assistance allowances; § 1697 related to educational and vocational guidance; and § 1698 related to coordination with and participation by Department of Defense.

CHAPTER 35. SURVIVORS' AND DEPENDENTS' EDUCATIONAL ASSISTANCE

SUBCHAPTER I. DEFINITIONS

Section
3500. Purpose.
3501. Definitions.

SUBCHAPTER II. ELIGIBILITY AND ENTITLEMENT

3510. Eligibility and entitlement generally.
3511. Duration of educational assistance.
3512. Periods of eligibility.
3513. Application.
3514. Processing of applications.

SUBCHAPTER III. PROGRAM OF EDUCATION

3520. Educational and vocational counseling.
3521. Approval of application.
[3522] [1722. Repealed]
3523. Disapproval of enrollment in certain courses.
3524. Discontinuance for unsatisfactory progress.
[3525] [1725. Repealed]
[3526] [1726. Repealed]

SUBCHAPTER IV. PAYMENTS TO ELIGIBLE PERSONS

3531. Educational assistance allowance.
3532. Computation of educational assistance allowance.
3533. Special assistance for the educationally disadvantaged.
3534. Apprenticeship or other on-job training; correspondence courses.
3535. Approval of courses.
3536. Specialized vocational training courses.
3537. Work-study allowance.
[3538] [1738. Repealed]

SUBCHAPTER V. SPECIAL RESTORATIVE TRAINING

3540. Purpose.
3541. Entitlement to special restorative training.
3542. Special training allowance.
3543. Special administrative provisions.

SUBCHAPTER VI. MISCELLANEOUS PROVISIONS

3561. Authority and duties of Secretary.
3562. Nonduplication of benefits.
3563. Notification of eligibility.
[3564] [1764. Repealed]

SUBCHAPTER VII. PHILIPPINE COMMONWEALTH ARMY AND PHILIPPINE SCOUTS

3565. Children of certain Philippine veterans.
3566. Definitions.

[3567] [1767. Repealed]
[3568] [1768. Repealed]

HISTORY; ANCILLARY LAWS AND DIRECTIVES

Explanatory notes:
The bracketed section numbers "3522", "3525", "3526", "3538", "3564", "3567", "3568" were inserted to preserve numerical continuity following the section number redesignations made by Act Aug. 6, 1991, P. L. 102-83, § 5(a), 105 Stat. 406.

Amendments:
1963. Act Sept. 23, 1963, P. L. 88-126, § 5, 77 Stat. 163, added Subchapter VII heading and items 1771–1778.

1966. Act March 3, 1966, P. L. 89-358, § 3(a)(10), 80 Stat. 21 (effective 3/3/66, as provided by § 12(a) of such Act), deleted item 1726 which read: "1726. Institutions listed by Attorney General."; deleted items 1763–1768 which read:

"1763. Control by agencies of the United States.
"1764. Conflicting interests.
"1765. Reports by institutions.
"1766. Overpayments to eligible persons.
"1767. Examination of records.
"1768. False or misleading statements.";
and deleted Subchapter VII heading and items 1771–1778 which read:
"SUBCHAPTER VII—STATE APPROVING AGENCIES
"1771. Designation.
"1772. Approval of courses.
"1773. Cooperation.
"1774. Reimbursement of expenses.
"1775. Approval of accredited courses.
"1776. Approval of nonaccredited courses.
"1777. Notice of approval of courses.
"1778. Disapproval of courses.".
Act Sept. 30, 1966, P. L. 89-613, § 2, 80 Stat. 862, added Subchapter VII heading and items 1765, 1766.

1968. Act Oct. 23, 1968, P. L. 90-631, § 2(a)(2), (h)(1), 82 Stat. 1332 (effective on the first day of the second calendar month which begins after Oct. 23, 1968, as provided by § 6(a) of such Act), in the chapter heading, inserted "AND WIDOWS'"; and added item 1700.

1970. Act March 26, 1970, P. L. 91-219, Title II, § 207(b), 84 Stat. 82, added item 1763.

1972. Act Oct. 24, 1972, P. L. 92-540, Title IV, § 405, 86 Stat. 1091, deleted item 1722 which read: "1722. Change of program."; deleted item 1725 which read: "1725. Period of operation for approval."; and substituted items 1733–1736 for items 1733–1737 which read:

"1733. Measurement of courses.
"1734. Overcharges by educational institutions.
"1735. Approval of courses.
"1736. Discontinuance of allowances.

"1737. Specialized vocational training courses.".

1974. Act Dec. 3, 1974, P. L. 93-508, Title III, § 303(b), 88 Stat. 1592 (effective 1/1/75, as provided by § 502 of such Act), added item 1737.

1976. Act Oct. 15, 1976, P. L. 94-502, Title III, § 309(a), 90 Stat. 2391 (effective 10/15/76, as provided by § 703(b) of such Act), substituted new chapter heading for one which read: "WAR ORPHANS' AND WIDOWS' EDUCATIONAL ASSISTANCE".

1977. Act Nov. 23, 1977, P. L. 95-202, Title II, § 201(c)(2), 91 Stat. 1438 (effective 1/1/78, as provided by § 501 of such Act), added item 1738.

1986. Act Oct. 28, 1986, P. L. 99-576, Title III, Part A, § 314(b)(3), 100 Stat. 3274, amended the analysis of this chapter by substituting items 1720 and 1721 for ones which read "1720. Development of educational plan" and "1721. Final approval of application".

1988. Act Nov. 18, 1988, P. L. 100-689, Title I, Part B, § 124(c)(2), 102 Stat. 4175, amended the analysis of this chapter by deleting items 1737 and 1738 which read: "1737. Education loans" and "1738. Accelerated payment of educational assistance allowances".

1989. Act Dec. 18, 1989, P. L. 101-237, Title IV, § 406(a)(2), 103 Stat. 2082, effective 5/1/90, as provided by § 406(b) of such Act, which appears as a note to 38 USCS § 3537, amended the analysis of this chapter by adding item 1737. Act Dec. 18, 1989, P. L. 101-237, title IV, § 423(b)(1)(A), 103 Stat. 2092, amended the analysis of this chapter by substituting item 1761 for one which read: "1761. Authority and duties of Administrator.".

1991. Act Aug. 6, 1991, P. L. 102-83, § 5(b)(1), 105 Stat. 406, revised the analysis of this Chapter by amending the section numbers in accordance with the redesignations made by § 5(a) of such Act (see Table III preceding 38 USCS § 101).

SUBCHAPTER I. DEFINITIONS

§ 3500. Purpose

The Congress hereby declares that the educational program established by this chapter [38 USCS §§ 3500 et seq.] is for the purpose of providing opportunities for education to children whose education would otherwise be impeded or interrupted by reason of the disability or death of a parent from a disease or injury incurred or aggravated in the Armed Forces after the beginning of the Spanish-American War, and for the purpose of aiding such children in attaining the educational status which they might normally have aspired to and obtained but for the disability or death of such parent. The Congress further declares that the educational program extended to the surviving spouses of veterans who died of service-connected disabilities and to spouses of veterans with a service-connected total disability permanent in nature is for the purpose of assisting them in preparing to support themselves and their families at a standard of living level which the veteran, but for the veteran's death or service disability, could have expected to provide for the veteran's family.

(Added Oct. 23, 1968, P. L. 90-631, § 2(a)(1), 82 Stat. 1331; Oct. 15, 1976, P. L. 94-502, Title III, § 310(1), 90 Stat. 2391; Aug. 6, 1991, P. L. 102-83, § 5(a), 105 Stat. 406.)

38 USCS § 3500

HISTORY; ANCILLARY LAWS AND DIRECTIVES

Effective date of section:
Act Oct. 23, 1968, P. L. 90-631, § 6(a), 82 Stat. 1335, provided that this section is effective on the first day of the second calendar month which begins after Oct. 23, 1968.

Amendments:
1976. Act Oct. 15, 1976 (effective 10/15/76, as provided by § 703(b) of such Act, which appears as 38 USCS § 3693 note), substituted "surviving spouses" for "widows", substituted "spouses" for "wives", and substituted "the veteran's" for "his" wherever appearing.
1991. Act Aug. 6, 1991, redesignated this section, formerly 38 USCS § 1700, as 38 USCS § 3500.

CODE OF FEDERAL REGULATIONS

Department of Veterans Affairs—Vocational rehabilitation and education, 38 CFR Part 21.

RESEARCH GUIDE

Am Jur:
77 Am Jur 2d, Veterans and Veterans' Laws §§ 132, 146.

INTERPRETIVE NOTES AND DECISIONS

Appellant was not entitled to retroactive chapter 35 educational assistance benefits that were established to assist offspring in obtaining education that they might have achieved but for disability or death of veteran parent, since appellant's education was not impeded or interrupted by VA's delay in granting service connection for appellant's father's death, as evidenced by his degree. Erspamer v Brown (1996) 9 Vet App 507.

§ 3501. Definitions

(a) For the purposes of this chapter [38 USCS §§ 3500 et seq.] and chapter 36 of this title [38 USCS §§ 3670 et seq.]—

(1) The term "eligible person" means—

(A) a child of a person who—

(i) died of a service-connected disability,

(ii) has a total disability permanent in nature resulting from a service-connected disability, or who dies while a disability so evaluated was in existence, or

(iii) at the time of application for benefits under this chapter [38 USCS §§ 3500 et seq.] is a member of the Armed Forces serving on active duty listed, pursuant to section 556 of title 37 and regulations issued thereunder, by the Secretary concerned in one or more of the following categories and has been so listed for a total of more than ninety days: (A) missing in action, (B) captured in line of duty by hostile force, or (C) forcibly detained or interned in line of duty by a foreign government or power,

(B) the surviving spouse of any person who died of a service-connected disability,

(C) the spouse of any member of the Armed Forces serving on active duty who, at the time of application for benefits under this chapter [38 USCS §§ 3500 et seq.] is listed, pursuant to section 556 of title 37 and regulations issued thereunder, by the Secretary concerned in one or more of the following categories and has been so listed for a total of more than ninety days: (i) missing in action (ii) captured in line of duty by a hostile force, or (iii) forcibly detained or interned in line of duty by a foreign government or power, or

(D) the spouse of any person who has a total disability permanent in nature resulting from a service-connected disability, or the surviving spouse of a veteran who died while a disability so evaluated was in existence,

arising out of active military, naval, or air service after the beginning of the Spanish-American War, but only if such service did not terminate under dishonorable conditions. The standards and criteria for determining whether or not a disability arising out of such service is service connected shall be those applicable under chapter 11 of this title [38 USCS §§ 1101 et seq.].

(2) The term "child" includes individuals who are married and individuals who are above the age of twenty-three years.

(3) The term "duty with the Armed Forces" as used in section 3512 of this title means (A) active duty, (B) active duty for training for a period of six or more consecutive months, or (C) active duty for training required by section 12103(d) of title 10.

(4) The term "guardian" includes a fiduciary legally appointed by a court of competent jurisdiction, or any other person who has been appointed by the Secretary under section 5502 of this title to receive payment of benefits for the use and benefit of the eligible person.

(5) The term "program of education" means any curriculum or any combination of unit courses or subjects pursued at an educational institution which is generally accepted as necessary to fulfill the requirements for the attainment of a predetermined and identified educational, professional, or vocational objective.

(6) The term "educational institution" means any public or private secondary school, vocational school, correspondence school, business school, junior college, teachers' college, college, normal school, professional school, university, or scientific or technical institution, or any other institution if it furnishes education at the secondary school level or above.

(7) The term "special restorative training" means training furnished under subchapter V of this chapter [38 USCS §§ 3540 et seq.].

(8) The term "total disability permanent in nature" means any disability rated total for the purposes of disability compensation which is based upon an impairment reasonably certain to continue throughout the life of the disabled person.

(9) The term "training establishment" means any establishment providing apprentice or other training on the job, including those under the supervision of a college or university or any State department of education, or any State apprenticeship agency, or any State board of vocational education, or any

joint apprenticeship committee, or the Bureau of Apprenticeship and Training established pursuant to the Act of August 16, 1937, popularly known as the "National Apprenticeship Act" (29 U.S.C. 50 et seq.), or any agency of the Federal Government authorized to supervise such training.

(10) The term "institution of higher learning" means a college, university, or similar institution, including a technical or business school, offering postsecondary level academic instruction that leads to an associate or higher degree if the school is empowered by the appropriate State education authority under State law to grant an associate or higher degree. When there is no State law to authorize the granting of a degree, the school may be recognized as an institution of higher learning if it is accredited for degree programs by a recognized accrediting agency. Such term shall also include a hospital offering educational programs at the postsecondary level without regard to whether the hospital grants a postsecondary degree. Such term shall also include an educational institution which is not located in a State, which offers a course leading to a standard college degree, or the equivalent, and which is recognized by the secretary of education (or comparable official) of the country or other jurisdiction in which the institution is located.

(11) The term "standard college degree means an associate or higher degree awarded by (A) an institution of higher learning that is accredited as a collegiate institution by a recognized regional or national accrediting agency; or (B) an institution of higher learning that is a "candidate" for accreditation as that term is used by the regional or national accrediting agencies; or (C) an institution of higher learning upon completion of a course which is accredited by an agency recognized to accredit specialized degree-level programs. For the purpose of this section, the accrediting agency must be one recognized by the Secretary of Education under the provisions of section 3675 of this title.

(b) If an eligible person has attained the person's majority and is under no known legal disability, all references in this chapter [38 USCS §§ 3500 et seq.] to "parent or guardian" shall refer to the eligible person.

(c) Any provision of this chapter [38 USCS §§ 3500 et seq.] which requires any action to be taken by or with respect to the parent or guardian of an eligible person who has not attained the person's majority, or who, having attained the person's majority, is under a legal disability, shall not apply when the Secretary determines that its application would not be in the best interest of the eligible person, would result in undue delay, or would not be administratively feasible. In such a case the Secretary, where necessary to protect the interest of the eligible person, may designate some other person (who may be the eligible person) as the person by or with respect to whom the action so required should be taken.

(d) No eligible person may be afforded educational assistance under this chapter [38 USCS §§ 3500 et seq.] unless such person was discharged or released after each period such person was on duty with the Armed Forces under conditions other than dishonorable, or while such person is on duty with the Armed Forces.
(Sept. 2, 1958, P. L. 85-857, § 1, 72 Stat. 1193; Sept. 8, 1959, P. L. 86-236,

§ 1, 73 Stat. 471; Sept. 14, 1960, P. L. 86-785, §§ 1-3, 74 Stat. 1023; July 7, 1964, P. L. 88-361, § 1, 78 Stat. 297; Sept. 30, 1965, P. L. 89-222, § 3, 79 Stat. 896; Nov. 8, 1965, P. L. 89-349, § 1, 79 Stat. 1313; March 3, 1966, P. L. 89-358, § 4(j), 80 Stat. 24; Oct. 23, 1968, P. L. 90-631, § 2(b), (c), 82 Stat. 1332; June 11, 1969, P. L. 91-24, § 9(a), 83 Stat. 34; Dec. 24, 1970, P. L. 91-584, § 1, 84 Stat. 1575; Oct. 24, 1972, P. L. 92-540, Title III, § 309, 86 Stat. 1083; May 31, 1974, P. L. 93-295, Title III, § 302, 88 Stat. 184; Oct. 15, 1976, P. L. 94-502, Title III, §§ 302, 310(2)-(5), 90 Stat. 2389, 2391; Oct. 17, 1980, P. L. 96-466, Title III, Part B, § 327(a), Title VIII, § 801(c), 94 Stat. 2197, 2216; Nov. 21, 1983, P. L. 98-160, Title VII, § 702(12), 97 Stat. 1009; Dec. 18, 1989, P. L. 101-237, Title IV, § 423(b)(1)(A), 103 Stat. 2092; May 7, 1991, P. L. 102-40, Title IV, § 402(d)(1), 105 Stat. 239; Aug. 6, 1991, P. L. 102-83, § 5(a), (c)(1), 105 Stat. 406; Feb. 10, 1996, P. L. 104-106, Div A, Title XV, § 1501(e)(2)(C), 110 Stat. 501.)

HISTORY; ANCILLARY LAWS AND DIRECTIVES

Explanatory notes:
A prior § 3501 was redesignated by Act May 7, 1991, P. L. 102-40, Title IV, § 402(b)(1), 105 Stat. 238. For similar provisions, see 38 USCS § 6101.

Amendments:
1959. Act Sept. 8, 1959, in subsecs. (a)(1) and (d), inserted "the Spanish-American War,".
1960. Act Sept. 14, 1960, in subsec. (a)(1), substituted "the Korean conflict, or the induction period" for "or the Korean conflict", inserted "arising out of service during the Spanish-American War, World War I, World War II, or the Korean conflict", and inserted "The standards and criteria for determining whether or not a disability arising out of service during the induction period is service-connected shall be those applicable under chapter 11 of this title, except that the disability must (A) be shown to have directly resulted from, and the causative factor therefor must be shown to have arisen out of, the performance of active military, naval, or air service (but not including service described under section 106 of this title), or (B) have resulted (i) directly from armed conflict or (ii) from an injury or disease received while engaged in extrahazardous service (including such service under conditions simulating war)."; added subsec. (a)(9); in subsec. (d), substituted "the Korean conflict, or the induction period" for "or the Korean conflict".
1964. Act July 7, 1964, in subsec. (a)(1), inserted "Such term also includes the child of a person who has a total disability permanent in nature resulting from a service-connected disability arising out of service as described in the first sentence hereof, or who died while a disability so evaluated was in existence."; added subsec. (a)(10); and in subsec. (d), substituted "disability or death" for "death" wherever appearing.
1965. Act Sept. 30, 1965, in subsec. (a)(1), substituted "The standards and criteria for determining whether or not a disability arising out of such service is service connected shall be those applicable under chapter 11 of this title." for "The standards and criteria for determining whether or not a disability arising out of service during the Spanish-American War, World War I, World War II, or the Korean conflict is service-connected shall be

those applicable under chapter 11 of this title. The standards and criteria for determining whether or not a disability arising out of service during the induction period is service-connected shall be those applicable under chapter 11 of this title, except that the disability must (A) be shown to have directly resulted from, and the causative factor therefor must be shown to have arisen out of, the performance of active military, naval, or air service (but not including service described under section 106 of this title), or (B) have resulted (i) directly from armed conflict or (ii) from an injury or disease received while engaged in extrahazardous service (including such service under conditions simulating war).''.

Act Nov. 8, 1965, in subsec. (a)(1), substituted

"The term 'eligible person' means a child of a person who—

"(A) died of a service-connected disability, or

"(B) has a total disability permanent in nature resulting from a service-connected disability, or who died while a disability so evaluated was in existence,

arising out of active military, naval, or air service after the beginning of the Spanish-American War and prior to the end of the induction period, but only if such service did not terminate under dishonorable conditions.''

for "The term 'eligible person' means a child of a person who died of a service-connected disability arising out of active military, naval, or air service during the Spanish-American War, World War I, World War II, the Korean conflict, or the induction period, but only if such service did not terminate under dishonorable conditions. Such term also includes the child of a person who has a total disability permanent in nature resulting from a service-connected disability arising out of service as described in the first sentence hereof, or who died while a disability so evaluated was in existence.''; in subsec. (a)(9), deleted "(A) the period beginning September 16, 1940, and ending December 6, 1941, and the period beginning January 1, 1947, and ending June 26, 1950, and (B)'' following "means''; in subsec. (d), substituted "after the beginning of the Spanish-American War and prior to the end of the induction period,'' for "during the Spanish-American War, World War I, World War II, the Korean conflict, or the induction period,''.

1966. Act March 3, 1966, in subsec. (a), in para. (1), in the concluding matter, deleted "and prior to the end of the induction period'' following "Spanish-American War'', in para. (3)(C), substituted "511(d) of title 10'' for "1013(c)(1) of title 50'', deleted paras. (8) and (9) which read:

"(8) The term 'State' includes the Canal Zone.

"(9) The term 'induction period' means the period beginning on February 1, 1955, and ending on the day before the first day thereafter on which individuals (other than individuals liable for induction by reason of a prior deferment) are no longer liable for induction for training and service into the Armed Forces under the Universal Military Training and Service Act.'',

redesignated para. (10) as para. (8); and, in subsec. (d), deleted "and prior to the end of the induction period'' following "Spanish-American War''.

1968. Act Oct. 23, 1968 (effective 12/1/68, as provided by § 6(a) of such Act, which appears as 38 USCS § 3500), in subsec. (a), substituted para. (1) for one which read:

"The term 'eligible person' means a child of a person who—
"(A) died of a service-connected disability, or
"(B) has a total disability permanent in nature resulting from a service-connected disability, or who died while a disability so evaluated was in existence,
arising out of active military, naval, or air service after the beginning of the Spanish-American War, but only if such service did not terminate under dishonorable conditions. The standards and criteria for determining whether or not a disability arising out of such service is service connected shall be those applicable under chapter 11 of this title.";
and substituted subsec. (d) for one which read: "The Congress hereby declares that the educational program established by this chapter is for the purpose of providing opportunities for education to children whose education would otherwise be impeded or interrupted by reason of the disability or death of a parent from a disease or injury incurred or aggravated in the Armed Forces after the beginning of the Spanish-American War, and for the purpose of aiding such children in attaining the education status which they might normally have aspired to and obtained but for the disability or death of such parent.".

1969. Act June 11, 1969, in subsec. (a)(2), substituted "twenty-three" for "twenty-one".

1970. Act Dec. 24, 1970, in subsec. (a)(1), in subpara. (A)(i), deleted "or" following "disability,", in subpara. (A)(ii), inserted "or" following "existence,", added subpara. (A)(iii), in subpara. (B), deleted "or" following "disability,", redesignated subpara. (C) as subpara. (D), and added new subpara. (C).

1972. Act Oct. 24, 1972, substituted new subsec. (a)(6) for one which read: "The term 'educational institution' means any public or private secondary school, vocational school, business school, junior college, teachers' college, college, normal school, professional school, university, or scientific or technical institution, or any other institution if it furnishes education at the secondary school level or above."; and added subsec. (a)(9).

1974. Act May 31, 1974 (effective 7/1/74, as provided by § 401 of such Act, which appears as 38 USCS § 1114 note), substituted new subsec. (a)(4) for one which read: "The term 'guardian' includes a fiduciary legally appointed by a court of competent jurisdiction, or any person who is determined by the Administrator in accordance with section 3202 of this title to be otherwise legally vested with the care of the eligible person.".

1976. Act Oct. 15, 1976 (effective 10/15/76, as provided by § 703(b) of such Act, which appears as 38 USCS § 3693 note), in subsec. (a)(1), in subpara. (B), substituted "surviving spouse" for "widow", in subpara. (C), substituted "spouse" for "wife", and in subpara. (D), substituted "spouse" and "surviving spouse" for "wife" and "widow", respectively; added, subsec. (a)(10), (11); in subsec. (b), substituted "the person's" for "his" and deleted "himself" following "the eligible person"; in subsec. (c), substituted "such person's" for "his" wherever appearing; and in subsec. (d), substituted "such person" for "he" wherever appearing.

1980. Act Oct. 17, 1980 (effective 10/1/80, as provided by § 802(c)(1), (h) of such Act, which appears as 38 USCS § 3452 note), in subsec. (a), in the preliminary matter, inserted "and chapter 36 of this title", in para. (9), substituted "The" for "For the purposes of this chapter and chapter 36 of this title, the", in para. (10), substituted "The" for "For the purposes of this chapter and chapter 36 of this title, the" and inserted "Such term shall also include an educational institution which is not located in a State, which offers a course leading to a standard college degree, or the equivalent, and which is recognized by the secretary of education (or comparable official) of the country or other jurisdiction in which the institution is located.", and in para. (11), substituted "The" for "For the purposes of this chapter and chapter 36 of this title, the", and substituted "Secretary" for "Commissioner".

1983. Act Nov. 21, 1983, in subsec. (a), in para. (1), in subpara. (A), in clause (iii), deleted ", United States Code," following "title 37", and inserted a comma following "thereunder", in subpara. (C), deleted ", United States Code," following "title 37", and, in para. (9), substituted "the Act of August 16, 1937, popularly known as the 'National Apprenticeship Act' (29 U.S.C. 50 et seq.)" for "chapter 4C of title 29".

1989. Act Dec. 18, 1989, in subsecs. (a)(4) and (c), substituted "Secretary" for "Administrator", wherever appearing.

1991. Act May 7, 1991, § 402(d)(1), amended the references in this section to reflect the redesignations made by §§ 401(a)(4) and 402(b) of such Act (see Table II preceding 38 USCS § 101).

Act Aug. 6, 1991, redesignated this section, formerly 38 USCS § 1701, as 38 USCS § 3501, and amended the references in this section to reflect the redesignations made by § 5(a) of such Act (see Table III preceding 38 USCS § 101).

1996. Act Feb. 10, 1996 (effective as if included in Act Oct. 5, 1995, P. L. 103-337, as enacted on Oct. 5, 1994, as provided by § 1501(f)(3) of Act Feb. 10, 1996, which appears as 10 USCS § 113 note), in subsec. (a)(3)(C), substituted "section 12103(d) of title 10" for "section 511(d) of title 10".

Other provisions:
Eligible person. Act Sept. 14, 1960, P. L. 86-785, § 5, 74 Stat. 1024; Oct. 15, 1962, P. L. 87-815, § 2(b), 76 Stat. 927, formerly classified as a note to this section, was repealed by Act June 11, 1969, P. L. 91-24, § 14(c), 83 Stat. 35, except as to any indebtedness which may be due the Government as the result of any benefits granted under § 5. This note contained a savings clause which granted five years of educational training to certain children of veterans dying of disabilities incurred subsequent to the Korean War.

Termination of eligibility periods. For termination of eligibility period for a wife or widow, or an eligible person eight years from Oct. 24, 1972, see note containing Act Oct. 24, 1972, § 604, located at 38 USCS § 3512.

CODE OF FEDERAL REGULATIONS

Department of Veterans Affairs—Department of Veterans Benefits, fiduciary activities, 38 CFR Part 13.

Department of Veterans Affairs—Vocational rehabilitation and education, 38 CFR Part 21.

CROSS REFERENCES

This section is referred to in 5 USCS § 5924; 38 USCS §§ 3511, 3512, 3540, 3563, 3565, 3686, 3687, 7721.

RESEARCH GUIDE

Am Jur:

77 Am Jur 2d, Veterans and Veterans' Laws § 146.

Law Review Articles:

Benefits for Conscientious Objectors. 19 Catholic Lawyer 62, Winter 1973.

Constitutional Law—Due Process—Conscientious Objectors Entitled to Same Veterans Educational Benefits Received By Regular Servicemen. 6 Creighton L Rev 393, 1972-73.

Constitutional Law—Equal Protection—Veteran's Educational Benefits for Conscientious Objectors. 8 Suffolk Univ L Rev 1239, Summer 1974.

Robison v Johnson (352 F Supp 848): Veterans' Educational Benefits for Conscientious Objectors. 121 Univ of Pa L Rev 1133, May 1973.

INTERPRETIVE NOTES AND DECISIONS

Veteran's daughter was entitled to DEA benefits since she met statute's definition of child, veteran's hearing disability was permanent and total, and was service-connected since, despite fact that part of rating was attributable to pre-existing, non-service-related condition, disability would not have been rated as total except for veteran's service-connected disability. Kimberlin v Brown (1993) 5 Vet App 174.

SUBCHAPTER II. ELIGIBILITY AND ENTITLEMENT

§ 3510. Eligibility and entitlement generally

Each eligible person shall, subject to the provisions of this chapter [38 USCS §§ 3500 et seq.], be entitled to receive educational assistance.

(Sept. 2, 1958, P. L. 85-857, § 1, 72 Stat. 1194; Aug. 6, 1991, P. L. 102-83, § 5(a), 105 Stat. 406.)

HISTORY; ANCILLARY LAWS AND DIRECTIVES

Amendments:

1991. Act Aug. 6, 1991, redesignated this section, formerly 38 USCS § 1710, as 38 USCS § 3510.

CODE OF FEDERAL REGULATIONS

Department of Veterans Affairs—Vocational rehabilitation and education, 38 CFR Part 21.

RESEARCH GUIDE

Am Jur:

77 Am Jur 2d, Veterans and Veterans' Laws § 146.

§ 3511. Duration of educational assistance

(a)(1) Each eligible person shall be entitled to educational assistance under this chapter [38 USCS §§ 3500 et seq.] for a period not in excess of 45 months (or to the equivalent thereof in part-time training).

(2)(A) Notwithstanding any other provision of this chapter [38 USCS §§ 3500 et seq.] or chapter 36 of this title [38 USCS §§ 3670 et seq.], any payment of an educational assistance allowance described in subparagraph (B) of this paragraph shall not—

    (i) be charged against the entitlement of any individual under this chapter [38 USCS §§ 3500 et seq.]; or

    (ii) be counted toward the aggregate period for which section 3695 of this title limits an individual's receipt of assistance.

(B) The payment of the educational assistance allowance referred to in subparagraph (A) of this paragraph is the payment of such an allowance to an individual for pursuit of a course or courses under this chapter if the Secretary finds that the individual—

    (i) had to discontinue such course pursuit as a result of being ordered, in connection with the Persian Gulf War, to serve on active duty under section 672(a), (d), or (g), 673, 673b, or 688 of title 10 [10 USCS §§ 12301(a), (d), (g), 12302, 12304, 688]; and

    (ii) failed to receive credit or training time toward completion of the individual's approved educational, professional, or vocational objective as a result of having to discontinue, as described in clause (i) of this subparagraph, his or her course pursuit.

(C) The period for which, by reason of this subsection, an educational assistance allowance is not charged against entitlement or counted toward the applicable aggregate period under section 3695 of this title shall not exceed the portion of the period of enrollment in the course or courses for which the individual failed to receive credit or with respect to which the individual lost training time, as determined under subparagraph (B)(ii) of this paragraph.

(b) If any eligible person pursuing a program of education, or of special restorative training, under this chapter [38 USCS §§ 3500 et seq.] ceases to be an "eligible person" because—

(1) the parent or spouse from whom eligibility is derived is found no longer to have a "total disability permanent in nature", as defined in section 3501(a)(8) of this title,

(2) the parent or spouse from whom eligibility is derived based upon the provisions of section 3501(a)(1)(A)(iii) or 3501(a)(1)(C) of this title is no longer listed in one of the categories specified therein, or

(3) the spouse, as an eligible person under section 3501(a)(1)(D) of this title, is divorced, without fault on such person's part, from the person upon whose disability such person's eligibility is based,

then such eligible person (if such person has sufficient remaining entitlement) may, nevertheless, be afforded educational assistance under this chapter [38 USCS §§ 3500 et seq.] until the end of the quarter or semester for which enrolled if the educational institution in which such person is enrolled is operated on a quarter or semester system, or if the educational institution is not so operated until the end of the course, or until 12 weeks have expired, whichever first occurs.

(Sept. 2, 1958, P. L. 85-857, § 1, 72 Stat. 1194; July 7, 1964, P. L. 88-361, § 2,

Readjustment Benefits **38 USCS § 3511**

78 Stat. 297; March 3, 1966, P. L. 89-358, § 4(k), 80 Stat. 24; Oct. 23, 1968, P. L. 90-631, §§ 1(c), 2(d), 82 Stat. 1331; June 11, 1969, P. L. 91-24, § 9(b), 83 Stat. 34; Dec. 24, 1970, P. L. 91-584, § 2, 84 Stat. 1575; Oct. 15, 1976, P. L. 94-502, Title III, §§ 303, 310(6), 90 Stat. 2390, 2391; Aug. 6, 1991, P. L. 102-83, § 5(a), (c)(1), 105 Stat. 406; Oct. 10, 1991, P. L. 102-127, § 2(c), 105 Stat. 620.)

HISTORY; ANCILLARY LAWS AND DIRECTIVES

Explanatory notes:
The bracketed reference "10 USCS §§ 12301(a), (d), (g), 12302, 12304, 688" has been inserted on authority of Act Oct. 5, 1994, P. L. 103-337, § 1662(e)(2), 108 Stat. 2992, which transferred 10 USCS §§ 672, 673, and 673b to 10 USCS §§ 12301, 12302, and 12304, respectively.

Amendments:
1964. Act July 7, 1964, added subsec. (d).
1966. Act March 3, 1966, in subsec. (b), substituted "34" for "33" and inserted "or under chapter 33 of this title as in effect before February 1, 1965".
1968. Act Oct. 23, 1968 (effective 12/1/68, as provided by § 6(a) of such Act, which appears as 38 USCS § 3500 note), deleted subsecs. (b)–(d) which read:
"(b) The period of entitlement of an eligible person under this chapter shall be reduced by a period equivalent to any period of education or training received by him under chapter 31 or 34 of this title or under chapter 33 of this title as in effect before February 1, 1965.
"(c) If an eligible person is entitled to educational assistance under this chapter and also to vocational rehabilitation under chapter 31 of this title, he must elect whether he will receive educational assistance or vocational rehabilitation. If an eligible person is entitled to educational assistance under this chapter and is not entitled to such vocational rehabilitation, but after beginning his program of education or special restorative training becomes entitled (as determined by the Administrator) to such vocational rehabilitation, he must elect whether to continue to receive educational assistance or whether to receive such vocational rehabilitation. If he elects to receive vocational rehabilitation, the program of education or special restorative training pursued under this chapter shall be utilized to the fullest extent practicable in determining the character and duration of vocational rehabilitation to be furnished him.
"(d) If any child pursuing a program of education, or of specialized restorative training, under this chapter ceases to be an 'eligible person' because the parent from whom eligibility is derived is found to no longer have a 'total disability permanent in nature', as defined in section 1701(a)(10) of this title, then such child (if he has sufficient remaining entitlement) may, nevertheless, be afforded educational assistance under this chapter until the end of a quarter or semester for which enrolled if the educational institution in which he is enrolled is operated on a quarter or semester system, or if the educational institution is not so operated until the end of the course, or until nine weeks have expired, whichever first occurs."; and added subsec. (b).

1969. Act June 11, 1969, in subsec. (b)(1), substituted "section 1701(a)(8)" for "section 1701(a)(10)".

1970. Act Dec. 24, 1970, in subsec. (b), in para. (1), deleted "or" following "title,", redesignated para. (2) as para. (3), added new para. (2), in para. (3), as so redesignated, substituted "1701(a)(1)(D)" for "1701(a)(1)(C)".

1976. Act Oct. 15, 1976, § 303 (effective 10/1/76, as provided by § 703(a) of such Act, which appears as 38 USCS § 3693 note), in subsec. (a), substituted "45" for "thirty-six"; and in subsec. (b), concluding matter, substituted "12" for "nine".

Such Act further (effective 10/15/76, as provided by § 703(b) of such Act, which appears as 38 USCS § 3693 note), in subsec. (b), in para. (3), substituted "the spouse" for "she" and substituted "such person's" for "her" wherever appearing, in the concluding matter, substituted "such person" for "he or she" wherever appearing.

1991. Act Aug. 6, 1991, redesignated this section, formerly 38 USCS § 1711, as 38 USCS § 3511, and amended the references in this section to reflect the redesignations made by § 5(a) of such Act (see Table III preceding 38 USCS § 101).

Act Oct. 10, 1991 redesignated subsec. (a) as subsec. (a)(1), and added para. (2).

CODE OF FEDERAL REGULATIONS

Department of Veterans Affairs—Vocational rehabilitation and education, 38 CFR Part 21.

CROSS REFERENCES

This section is referred to in 38 USCS §§ 3512, 3533, 3541.

RESEARCH GUIDE

Am Jur:

24 Am Jur 2d, Divorce and Separation § 908.

77 Am Jur 2d, Veterans and Veterans' Laws § 146.

§ 3512. Periods of eligibility

(a) The educational assistance to which an eligible person within the meaning of section 3501(a)(1)(A) of this title is entitled under section 3511 of this title or subchapter V of this chapter [38 USCS §§ 3540 et seq.] may be afforded the person during the period beginning on the person's eighteenth birthday, or on the successful completion of the person's secondary schooling, whichever first occurs, and ending on the person's twenty-sixth birthday, except that—

(1) if the person is above the age of compulsory school attendance under applicable State law, and the Secretary determines that the person's best interests will be served thereby, such period may begin before the person's eighteenth birthday;

(2) if the person has a mental or physical handicap, and the Secretary determines that the person's best interest will be served by pursuing a program of special restorative training or a specialized course of vocational

training approved under section 3536 of this title, such period may begin before the person's eighteenth birthday, but not before the person's fourteenth birthday;

(3) if the Secretary first finds that the parent from whom eligibility is derived has a service-connected total disability permanent in nature, or if the death of the parent from whom eligibility is derived occurs, after the eligible person's eighteenth birthday but before the person's twenty-sixth birthday, then (unless paragraph (4) applies) such period shall end 8 years after, whichever date last occurs: (A) the date on which the Secretary first finds that the parent from whom eligibility is derived has a service-connected total disability permanent in nature, or (B) the date of death of the parent from whom eligibility is derived;

(4) if the person serves on duty with the Armed Forces as an eligible person after the person's eighteenth birthday but before the person's twenty-sixth birthday, then such period shall end eight years after the person's first discharge or release from such duty with the Armed Forces (excluding from such eight years all periods during which the eligible person served on active duty before August 1, 1962, pursuant to (A) a call or order thereto issued to the person as a Reserve after July 30, 1961, or (B) an extension of an enlistment, appointment, or period of duty with the Armed Forces pursuant to section 2 of Public Law 87-117) [former 10 USCS § 263 note]; however, in no event shall such period be extended beyond the person's thirty-first birthday by reason of this paragraph;

(5) if the person becomes eligible by reason of the provisions of section 3501(a)(1)(A)(iii) of this title after the person's eighteenth birthday but before the person's twenty-sixth birthday, then (unless clause (4) of this subsection applies) such period shall end eight years after the date on which the person becomes eligible by reason of such provisions, but in no event shall such period be extended beyond the person's thirty-first birthday by reason of this clause; and

(6)(A) if such person is enrolled in an educational institution regularly operated on the quarter or semester system and such period ends during a quarter or semester, such period shall be extended to the end of the quarter or semester; or

(B) if such person is enrolled in an educational institution operated on other than a quarter or semester system and such period ends after a major portion of the course is completed, such period shall be extended to the end of the course, or until 12 weeks have expired, whichever first occurs.

(b)(1) No person made eligible by section 3501(a)(1)(B) or (D) of this title may be afforded educational assistance under this chapter [38 USCS §§ 3500 et seq.] beyond 10 years after whichever of the following last occurs:

(A) The date on which the Secretary first finds the spouse from whom eligibility is derived has a service-connected total disability permanent in nature.

(B) The date of death of the spouse from whom eligibility is derived who dies while a total disability evaluated as permanent in nature was in existence.

(C) The date on which the Secretary determines that the spouse from whom eligibility is derived died of a service-connected disability.

(2) Notwithstanding the provisions of paragraph (1) of this subsection, in the case of any eligible person (as defined in section 3501(a)(1)(B), (C), or (D) of this title) who was prevented from initiating or completing such person's chosen program of education within such period because of a physical or mental disability which was not the result of such person's own willful misconduct, such person shall, upon application made within one year after (A) the last date of the delimiting period otherwise applicable under this section, (B) the termination of the period of mental or physical disability, or (C) October 1, 1980, whichever is the latest, be granted an extension of the applicable delimiting period for such length of time as the Secretary determines, from the evidence, that such person was so prevented from initiating or completing such program of education. When an extension of the applicable delimiting period is granted under the exception in the preceding sentence, the delimiting period will again begin running on the first day following such eligible person's recovery from such disability on which it is reasonably feasible, as determined in accordance with regulations which the Secretary shall prescribe, for such eligible person to initiate or resume pursuit of a program of education with educational assistance under this chapter [38 USCS §§ 3500 et seq.].

(3)(A) Notwithstanding the provisions of paragraph (1) of this subsection, any eligible person (as defined in clause (B) or (D) of section 3501(a)(1) of this title) may, subject to the approval of the Secretary, be permitted to elect a date referred to in subparagraph (B) of this paragraph to commence receiving educational assistance benefits under this chapter. The date so elected shall be the beginning date of the delimiting period applicable to such person under this section.

(B) The date which an eligible person may elect under subparagraph (A) of this paragraph is any date during the period beginning on the date the person became an eligible person within the meaning of clause (B) or (D) of section 3501(a)(1) of this title and ending on the date determined under subparagraph (A), (B), or (C) of paragraph (1) of this subsection to be applicable to such person.

(c) Notwithstanding the provisions of subsection (a) of this section, an eligible person may be afforded educational assistance beyond the age limitation applicable to such person under such subsection if (1) such person suspends pursuit of such person's program of education after having enrolled in such program within the time period applicable to such person under such subsection, (2) such person is unable to complete such program after the period of suspension and before attaining the age limitation applicable to such person under such subsection, and (3) the Secretary finds that the suspension was due to conditions beyond the control of such person; but in no event shall educational assistance be afforded such person by reason of this subsection beyond the age limitation applicable to such person under subsection (a) of this section plus a period of time equal to the period such person was required to suspend the pursuit of such person's program, or beyond such person's thirty-first birthday, whichever is earlier.

(d) The term "first finds" as used in this section means the effective date of the rating or date of notification to the veteran from whom eligibility is derived establishing a service-connected total disability permanent in nature whichever is more advantageous to the eligible person.

(e) No person made eligible by section 3501(a)(1)(C) of this title may be afforded educational assistance under this chapter [38 USCS §§ 3501 et seq.] beyond 10 years after the date on which the spouse was listed by the Secretary concerned in one of the categories referred to in such section or December 24, 1970, whichever last occurs.

(f) Any eligible person (as defined in section 3501(a)(1)(B), (C), or (D) of this chapter) shall be entitled to an additional period of eligibility for an education loan under subchapter III of chapter 36 of this title [38 USCS §§ 3698 et seq.] beyond the maximum period provided for in this section pursuant to the same terms and conditions set forth with respect to an eligible veteran in section 3462(a)(2) of this title.

(g) Any entitlement used by any eligible person as a result of eligibility under the provisions of section 3501(a)(1)(A)(iii) or 3501(a)(1)(C) of this title shall be deducted from any entitlement to which such person may subsequently become entitled under the provisions of this chapter [38 USCS §§ 3500 et seq.].
(Sept. 2, 1958, P. L. 85-857, § 1, 72 Stat. 1194; Oct. 15, 1962, P. L. 87-815, § 2(a), 76 Stat. 926; Oct. 15, 1962, P. L. 87-819, § 2, 76 Stat. 935; July 7, 1964, P. L. 88-361, § 3, 78 Stat. 297; Aug. 31, 1967, P. L. 90-77, Title III, § 307(a), 81 Stat. 189; Oct. 23, 1968, P. L. 90-631, § 2(e), 82 Stat. 1333; March 26, 1970, P. L. 91-219, Title II, § 208, 84 Stat. 83; Dec. 24, 1970, P. L. 91-584, § 3, 84 Stat. 1575; Oct. 24, 1972, P. L. 92-540, Title IV, § 402(1), 86 Stat. 1090; July 10, 1974, P. L. 93-337, § 2, 88 Stat. 292; Oct. 15, 1976, P. L. 94-502, Title III, §§ 304, 310(7)–(9), 90 Stat. 2390, 2391; Nov. 23, 1977, P. L. 95-202, Title II, § 203(a)(2), (b)(2), 91 Stat. 1439, 1440; Oct. 17, 1980, P. L. 96-466, Title III, Part B, §§ 321, 322, 94 Stat. 2195; Oct. 17, 1981, P. L. 97-66, Title VI, § 605(a), 95 Stat. 1036; Oct. 12, 1982, P. L. 97-295, § 4(44), 96 Stat. 1308; Nov. 21, 1983, P. L. 98-160, Title VII, § 702(13), 97 Stat. 1009; Oct. 28, 1986, P. L. 99-576, Title III, Part A, § 313, 100 Stat. 3273; Dec. 18, 1989, P. L. 101-237, Title IV, § 423(b)(1)(A), 103 Stat. 2092; Aug. 6, 1991, P. L. 102-83, § 5(a), (c)(1), 105 Stat. 406.)

HISTORY; ANCILLARY LAWS AND DIRECTIVES
Amendments:
1962. Act Oct. 15, 1962, P. L. 87-815, in subsec. (a), deleted para. (3) which read:
"if he had not reached his twenty-third birthday on June 29, 1956, and—
"(A) he had reached his eighteenth birthday on such date; or
"(B) he serves on duty with the Armed Forces as an eligible person before his twenty-third birthday and on or after such date; or

38 USCS § 3512 VETERANS' BENEFITS

"(C) the death of the parent from whom eligibility was derived occurs after such date and after his eighteenth birthday but before his twenty-third birthday;

then such period shall end five years after such date, his first discharge or release after such date from duty with the Armed Forces if such duty began before his twenty-third birthday, or the death of such parent, whichever occurs last, except that in no event shall such period be extended beyond his thirty-first birthday by reason of this paragraph; and'',

redesignated para. (4) as para. (5); and added paras. (3) and (4).

Act Oct. 15, 1962, P. L. 87-819, added subsec. (c).

1964. Act July 7, 1964, substituted new subsec. (a)(3) for one which read: "if the death of the parent from whom eligibility is derived occurs after the eligible person's eighteenth birthday but before his twenty-third birthday, then (unless paragraph (4) applies) such period shall end five years after the death of such parent;"; and added subsec. (d).

1967. Act Aug. 31, 1967 (effective as provided by § 405(a) of such Act, which appears as 38 USCS § 101 note), in subsec. (a), in the introductory matter, and paras. (3) and (4), substituted "twenty-sixth birthday" for "twenty-third birthday".

1968. Act Oct. 23, 1968 (effective 12/1/68, as provided by § 6(a) of such Act, which appears as 38 USCS § 3500 note), in subsec. (a), introductory matter, inserted "(within the meaning of section 1701(a)(1)(A))"; and substituted new subsec. (b) for one which read: "No eligible person may be afforded educational assistance under this chapter unless he was discharged or released after each period he was on duty with the Armed Forces under conditions other than dishonorable, or while he is on duty with the Armed Forces.".

1970. Act March 26, 1970, in subsec. (a)(3), substituted "last occurs" for "first occurs"; and added subsec. (e).

Act Dec. 24, 1970, in subsec. (b), introductory matter, substituted "1701(a)(1)(B) or (D)" for "1701(a)(1)(B) or (C)"; and added subsecs. (f) and (g).

1972. Act Oct. 24, 1972, in subsec. (a)(2), substituted "1736" for "1737".

1974. Act July 10, 1974, in subsec. (b), introductory matter and subsec. (f), substituted "10" for "eight".

1976. Act Oct. 15, 1976 § 310(7)–(9) (effective 10/15/76, as provided by § 703(b) of such Act, which appears as 38 USCS § 3693 note), in subsec. (a), in the introductory matter, substituted "the person" for "him" and substituted "the person's" for "his" wherever appearing, in paras. (1) and (2), substituted "the person" for "he" and substituted "the person's" for "his" wherever appearing, in para. (3), substituted "the person's" for "his", and in para. (4), substituted "the person" for "he" preceding "serves", substituted "the person's" for "his" wherever appearing, and substituted "the person" for "him" preceding "as a Reserve"; in subsec. (c), substituted "such person" for "him" preceding "under" wherever appearing, substituted "such person" for "he" preceding "suspends", "is", and "was", and substituted "such person's" for "his" wherever appearing; in subsec. (e), as redesignated by Act Oct. 15, 1976, § 304, substituted "the" for "her" preceding "spouse"; and in subsec. (f), as redesignated by Act Oct. 15, 1976, § 304, substituted "such person" for "he".

Act Oct. 15, 1976, § 304 (effective 10/1/76, as provided by § 703(a) of such Act, which appears as 38 USCS § 3693 note), in subsec. (a), in paras. (3) and (4), substituted "8" for "five" wherever appearing, and substituted new para. (5) for one which read:

"(5)(A) if he is enrolled in an educational institution regularly operated on a quarter or semester system and such period ends during the last half of a quarter or semester, such period shall be extended to the end of the quarter or semester; or

"(B) if he is enrolled in an educational institution operated other than on a quarter or semester system and such periods ends during the last half of the course, such period shall be extended to the end of the course, or until nine weeks have expired, whichever first occurs.";

deleted subsec. (d) which read: "Notwithstanding the provisions of subsection (a) of this section, an eligible person may be afforded educational assistance beyond the age limitation applicable to him under such subsection by a period of time equivalent to any period of time which elapses between the eighteenth birthday of such eligible person or the date on which an application for benefits of this chapter is filed on behalf of such eligible person, whichever is later, and the date of final approval of such application by the Administrator; but in no event shall educational assistance under this chapter be afforded an eligible person beyond his thirty-first birthday by reason of this subsection."; and redesignated subsecs. (e)–(g) (as so designated prior to amendment by Act Nov. 23, 1977) as subsecs. (d)–(f), respectively.

1977. Act Nov. 23, 1977 (effective 5/31/76, as provided by § 501 of such Act, which appears as 38 USCS § 101 note), in subsec. (b), redesignated existing matter as para. (1), redesignated paras. (1) and (2) as subparas. (A) and (B), and added para. (2); redesignated subsec. (f) (as so designated after amendment by Act Oct. 15, 1976, § 304) as subsec. (g); and added new subsec. (f).

1980. Act Oct. 17, 1980 (effective 10/1/80, as provided by § 802(c)(1) of such Act, which appears as 38 USCS § 3452 note), in subsec. (a), in para. (4), deleted "and" following "paragraph;", redesignated para. (5) as para. (6), and added new para. (5); in subsec. (b)(2), inserted "made within one year after (A) the last date of the delimiting period otherwise applicable under this section, (B) the termination of the period of mental or physical disability, or (C) the effective date of the Veterans' Rehabilitation and Education Amendments of 1980, whichever is the latest", inserted "so" following "such person was" and inserted "When an extension of the applicable delimiting period is granted under the exception in the preceding sentence, the delimiting period will again begin running on the first day following such eligible person's recovery from such disability on which it is reasonably feasible, as determined in accordance with regulations which the Administrator shall prescribe, for such eligible person to initiate or resume pursuit of a program of education with educational assistance under this chapter.".

1981. Act Oct. 17, 1981 (effective on enactment on 10/17/81, as provided by § 701(b)(1) of such Act, which appears as 38 USCS § 1114 note), in subsec. (b)(1), in the introductory matter, inserted "of the following", in cl. (A), substituted "The date" for "the date", and a period for ", or", and substituted cls. (B) and (C) for former cl. (B), which read: "(B) the date of death of the spouse from whom eligibility is derived.".

1982. Act Oct. 12, 1982, in subsec. (a), in the introductory matter, inserted "of this title" following "1701(a)(1)(A)", and, in para. (3), inserted a colon preceding "(A)"; in subsec. (b), in para. (1), in the introductory matter, substituted "title" for "chapter", and in para. (2), substituted "title" for "chapter"; and, in subsec. (e), substituted "December 24, 1970" for "the date of enactment of this subsection".

1983. Act Nov. 21, 1983, in subsec. (b)(2), in cl. (C), substituted "October 1, 1980" for "the effective date of the Veterans Rehabilitation and Education Amendments of 1980".

1986. Act Oct. 28, 1986, added subsec. (b)(3).

1989. Act Dec. 18, 1989, in subsecs. (a)–(c), substituted "Secretary" for "Administrator", wherever appearing.

1991. Act Aug. 6, 1991, redesignated this section, formerly 38 USCS § 1712, as 38 USCS § 3512, and amended the references in this section to reflect the redesignations made by § 5(a) of such Act (see Table III preceding 38 USCS § 101).

Other provisions:

Children of Spanish-American War veterans. Act Sept. 8, 1959, P. L. 86-236, § 2, 73 Stat. 471; Oct. 15, 1962, P. L. 87-815, § 2(b), 76 Stat. 927, formerly classified as a note to this section, was repealed by Act June 11, 1969, P. L. 91-24, § 14(b), 83 Stat. 35, effective June 11, 1969, except as to any indebtedness which may be due the Government as the result of any benefits granted thereunder. Section 2 contained a savings clause which granted 5 years of educational training to certain children of Spanish-American War veterans.

Extension of period for completion of education. Act Oct. 4, 1961, P. L. 87-377, § 2, 75 Stat. 806, formerly classified as a note to this section, was repealed by Act June 11, 1969, P. L. 91-24, § 14(d), 83 Stat. 35, effective June 11, 1969, except as to any indebtedness which may be due the Government as the result of any benefits granted thereunder. Section 2 contained a savings clause which granted 5 years of education training to certain children in the Philippines.

Termination of eligibility periods. Act July 7, 1964, P. L. 88-361, § 5, 78 Stat. 298, provided: "In the case of any individual who is an 'eligible person' within the meaning of section 1701(a)(1) of title 38, United States Code [now 38 USCS § 3501(a)(1)], solely by virtue of the amendments made by this Act, and who is above the age of seventeen years and below the age of twenty-three years on the date of enactment of this Act, the period referred to in section 1712 of title 38, United States Code [this section], shall not end with respect to such individual until the expiration of the five-year period which begins on the date of enactment of this Act, excluding from such five-year period any period of time which may elapse between the date on which application for benefits of chapter 35, United States Code [38 USCS §§ 3500 et seq.], is filed on behalf of an eligible person and the date of final approval of such application by the Administrator of Veterans' Affairs; but in no event shall educational assistance under chapter 35, title 38, United States Code [38 USCS §§ 3500 et seq.], be afforded to any eligible person beyond his thirty-first birthday by reason of this section [this note].".

Act Nov. 8, 1965, P. L. 89-349, § 2, 79 Stat. 1313, provided: "In the case of any individual who is an 'eligible person' within the meaning of section 1701(a)(1) of title 38, United States Code [now 38 USCS § 3501(a)(1)], solely by virtue of the amendment made by this Act, and who is above the age of seventeen years and below the age of twenty-three years on the date of enactment of this Act, the period referred to in section 1712 [now section 3512] of title 38, United States Code [this section], shall not end with respect to such individual until the expiration of the five-year period which begins on the date of enactment of this Act.".

Act Aug. 31, 1967, P. L. 90-77, § 307(b), 81 Stat. 189, provided: "In the case of any eligible person (within the meaning of section 1701(a)(1) or 1765(a) of title 38, United States Code [now 38 USCS § 3501(a)(1) or 3565(a)]) who is made eligible for educational assistance under the provisions of chapter 35 of title 38, United States Code [38 USCS §§ 3500 et seq.], solely by virtue of the amendments made by subsection (a) of this section, and who on the effective date of this Act [see 38 USCS § 101 note] is below the age of twenty-six years, the period referred to in section 1712 of such title [this section] shall not end with respect to such person until the expiration of the five-year period which begins on the effective date of this Act, excluding from such five-year period any period of time which may elapse between the date on which application for benefits of such chapter 35 [38 USCS §§ 3500 et seq.] is filed on behalf of such person and the date of final approval of such application by the Administrator of Veterans' Affairs; but in no event shall educational assistance under such chapter 35 [38 USCS §§ 3500 et seq.] be afforded to any eligible person beyond his thirty-first birthday by reason of this section [this section and this note].".

Running of delimiting period. Act Oct. 23, 1968, P. L. 90-631, § 2(f), 82 Stat. 1333 (effective 12/1/68, as provided by § 6(a) of such Act); Oct. 17, 1981, P. L. 97-66, Title VI, § 605(b), 95 Stat. 1036 (effective on enactment on 10/17/81, as provided by § 701(b)(1) of such Act, which appears as 38 USCS § 1114 note), provides:

"(1) Except as provided in paragraph (2) of this subsection, in the case of any person who is an eligible person by reason of subparagraph (B) or (D) of section 1701(a)(1) of title 38, United States Code [now 38 USCS § 3501(a)(1)(B) or (D)], if the date of death or the date of the determination of service-connected total disability permanent in nature of the person from whom eligibility is derived occurred before December 1, 1968, the 10-year delimiting period referred to in section 1712(b)(1) of such title [subsec. (b)(1) of this section] shall run from such date.

"(2) If the death of the person from whom such eligibility is derived occurred before December 1, 1968, and the date on which the Administrator of Veterans' Affairs determines that such person died of a service-connected disability is later than December 1, 1968, the delimiting period referred to in section 1712(b)(1) of such title [subsec. (b)(1) of this section] shall run from the date on which the Administrator makes such determination.".

Termination of eligibility period for a wife, widow, or eligible person. Act Oct. 24, 1972, P. L. 92-540, Title VI, § 604, 86 Stat. 1099; July 10, 1974, P. L. 93-337, § 3, 88 Stat. 292, provided:

"(a) Notwithstanding the provisions of section 1712(b) of title 38, United States Code [subsec. (b) of this section], a wife or widow (1) eligible to

38 USCS § 3512 VETERANS' BENEFITS

pursue a program of education exclusively by correspondence by virtue of the provisions of section 1786 of such title (as added by section 316 of this Act) [now 38 USCS § 3686] or (2) entitled to receive the benefits of subsection (a) of section 1733 of this title (as added by Section 313 of this Act) [now 38 USCS § 3533(a)] shall have 10 years from the date of the enactment of this Act in which to complete such a program of education or receive such benefits.

"(b) Notwithstanding the provisions of section 1712(a) or 1712(b) of title 38, United States Code [subsecs. (a), (b) of this section], an eligible person, as defined in section 1701(a)(1) of such title [now 38 USCS § 3501(a)(1)], who is entitled to pursue a program of apprenticeship or other on-job training by virtue of the provisions of section 1787 of such title (as added by section 316 of this Act) [now 38 USCS § 3687] shall have 10 years from the date of the enactment of this Act in which to complete such a program of training, except that an eligible person defined in section 1701(a)(1)(A) of such title [now 38 USCS § 3501(a)(1)(A)] may not be afforded educational assistance beyond his thirty-first birthday.".

Application and construction of the Oct. 12, 1982 amendment of this section. For provisions as to the application and construction of the Oct. 12, 1982 amendment of this section, see § 5 of such Act, which appears as 10 USCS § 101 note.

CODE OF FEDERAL REGULATIONS

Department of Veterans Affairs—Vocational rehabilitation and education, 38 CFR Part 21.

CROSS REFERENCES

This section is referred to in 38 USCS §§ 3501, 3565.

RESEARCH GUIDE

Am Jur:
77 Am Jur 2d, Veterans and Veterans' Laws § 146.

§ 3513. Application

The parent or guardian of a person or the eligible person if such person has attained legal majority for whom educational assistance is sought under this chapter [38 USCS §§ 3500 et seq.] shall submit an application to the Secretary which shall be in such form and contain such information as the Secretary shall prescribe. If the Secretary finds that the person on whose behalf the application is submitted is an eligible person, the Secretary shall approve the application provisionally. The Secretary shall notify the parent or guardian or eligible person (if the person has attained legal majority) of the provisional approval or of the disapproval of the application.

(Sept. 2, 1958, P. L. 85-857, § 1, 72 Stat. 1195; Oct. 15, 1976, P. L. 94-502, Title III, § 305, 90 Stat. 2390; Dec. 18, 1989, P. L. 101-237, Title IV, § 423(b)(1)(A), 103 Stat. 2092; Aug. 6, 1991, P. L. 102-83, § 5(a), 105 Stat. 406.)

HISTORY; ANCILLARY LAWS AND DIRECTIVES
Amendments:
1976. Act Oct. 15, 1976 (effective 10/15/76, as provided by § 703(b) of such Act, which appears as 38 USCS § 3693 note), substituted new section for one which read: "The parent or guardian of a person for whom educational assistance is sought under this chapter shall submit an application to the Administrator which shall be in such form and contain such information as the Administrator shall prescribe. If the Administrator finds that the person on whose behalf the application is submitted is an eligible person, he shall approve the application provisionally. The Administrator shall notify the parent or guardian of his provisional approval, or of his disapproval of the application.".
1989. Dec. 18, 1989, substituted "Secretary" for "Administrator", wherever appearing.
1991. Act Aug. 6, 1991, redesignated this section, formerly 38 USCS § 1713, as 38 USCS § 3513.

CODE OF FEDERAL REGULATIONS
Department of Veterans Affairs—Vocational rehabilitation and education, 38 CFR Part 21.

RESEARCH GUIDE
Federal Procedure L Ed:
33 Fed Proc L Ed, Veterans and Veterans' Affairs § 79:37.

§ 3514. Processing of applications

(a) Further processing of an application for educational assistance and the award of such assistance shall be pursuant to the requirements of subchapters III and IV of this chapter [38 USCS §§ 3520 et seq., 3531 et seq.] unless the parent or guardian requests special restorative training for the eligible person, in which case the application will be processed under subchapter V of this chapter [38 USCS §§ 3540 et seq.].

(b) If the request for special restorative training is approved, educational assistance will be afforded pursuant to the terms of subchapter V of this chapter [38 USCS §§ 3540 et seq.]. If the request for special restorative training is disapproved, or if approved the restorative training is completed or discontinued, any educational assistance subsequently afforded will be in accordance with subchapters III and IV of this chapter [38 USCS §§ 3520 et seq., 3531 et seq.].
(Sept. 2, 1958, P. L. 85-857, § 1, 72 Stat. 1195; Aug. 6, 1991, P. L. 102-83, § 5(a), 105 Stat. 406.)

HISTORY; ANCILLARY LAWS AND DIRECTIVES
Amendments:
1991. Act Aug. 6, 1991, redesignated this section, formerly 38 USCS § 1714, as 38 USCS § 3514.

CODE OF FEDERAL REGULATIONS
Department of Veterans Affairs—Vocational rehabilitation and education, 38 CFR Part 21.

RESEARCH GUIDE

Am Jur:
77 Am Jur 2d, Veterans and Veterans' Laws § 146.

SUBCHAPTER III. PROGRAM OF EDUCATION

§ 3520. Educational and vocational counseling

The Secretary may, upon request, arrange for educational or vocational counseling for persons eligible for benefits under this chapter to assist such persons in selecting their educational, vocational, or professional objectives and in developing their programs of education.
(Sept. 2, 1958, P. L. 85-857, § 1, 72 Stat. 1195; Oct. 23, 1968, P. L. 90-631, § 2(g), 82 Stat. 1333; Dec. 24, 1970, P. L. 91-584, § 4, 84 Stat. 1576; Oct. 24, 1972, P. L. 92-540, Title III, § 310, 86 Stat. 1083; Oct. 15, 1976, P. L. 94-502, Title III, § 310(10), 90 Stat. 2391; Oct. 17, 1980, P. L. 96-466, Title III, Part B, § 323(a), 94 Stat. 2196; Oct. 12, 1982, P. L. 97-295, § 4(45), 96 Stat. 1308; Oct. 28, 1986, P. L. 99-576, Title III, Part A, § 314(a), 100 Stat. 3273; Dec. 18, 1989, P. L. 101-237, Title IV, § 423(b)(1)(A), 103 Stat. 2092; Aug. 6, 1991, P. L. 102-83, § 5(a), 105 Stat. 406.)

HISTORY; ANCILLARY LAWS AND DIRECTIVES
Amendments:
1968. Act Oct. 23, 1968 (effective 12/1/68, as provided by § 6(a) of such Act, which appears as 38 USCS § 3500 note), designated existing matter as subsec. (a); in subsec. (a), as so designated, inserted "for a person eligible within the meaning of section 1701(a)(1)(A)"; and added subsec. (b).
1970. Act Dec. 24, 1970, in subsec. (b), substituted "section 1701(a)(1)(B), (C), or (D)" for "section 1701(a)(1)(B) or (C)".
1972. Act Oct. 24, 1972, in subsec. (a), inserted "Such counseling shall not be required where the eligible person has been accepted for, or is pursuing, courses which lead to a standard college degree, at an approved institution.".
1976. Act Oct. 15, 1976 (effective 10/15/76, as provided by § 703(b) of such Act, which appears as 38 USCS § 3693 note), in subsec. (a), substituted "such person's" for "his" wherever appearing.
1980. Act Oct. 17, 1980 (effective 10/1/80, as provided by § 802(c)(1) of such Act, which appears as 38 USCS § 3452 note), in subsec. (a), substituted "may, upon request, arrange for" for "shall arrange for, and the eligible person shall take advantage of,", and deleted "Such counseling shall not be required where the eligible person has been accepted for, or is pursuing, courses which lead to a standard college degree, at an approved institution." following "person's program of education.".
1982. Act Oct. 12, 1982, in subsec. (a), inserted "of this title"; and, in subsec. (b), substituted "title" for "chapter".
1986. Act Oct. 28, 1986, substituted this section and catchline for ones which read:
"§ 1720: Development of educational plan

"(a) Upon provisional approval of an application for educational assistance for a person eligible within the meaning of section 1701(a)(1)(A) of this title, the Administrator may, upon request, arrange for educational or vocational counseling to assist the parent or guardian and the eligible person in selecting such person's educational, vocational, or professional objective and in developing such person's program of education. During, or after, such counseling, the parent or guardian shall prepare for the eligible person an educational plan which shall set forth the selected objective, the proposed program of education, a list of the educational institutions at which such program would be pursued, an estimate of the sum which would be required for tuition and fees in completion of such program, and such other information as the Administrator shall require. This educational plan shall be signed by the parent or guardian and shall become an integral part of the application for educational assistance under this chapter.

"(b) The Administrator may, on request, arrange for educational counseling for persons eligible for educational assistance under section 1701(a)(1)(B), (C), or (D) of this title.".

1989. Act Dec. 18, 1989, substituted "Secretary" for "Administrator".

1991. Act Aug. 6, 1991, redesignated this section, formerly 38 USCS § 1720, as 38 USCS § 3520.

Other provisions:

Application and construction of the Oct. 12, 1982 amendment of this section. For provisions as to the application and construction of the Oct. 12, 1982 amendment of this section, see § 5 of such Act, which appears as 10 USCS § 101 note.

CODE OF FEDERAL REGULATIONS

Department of Veterans Affairs—Vocational rehabilitation and education, 38 CFR Part 21.

CROSS REFERENCES

This section is referred to in 38 USCS § 3561.

§ 3521. Approval of application

The Secretary shall approve an application if the Secretary finds that—

(1) the proposed program of education constitutes a "program of education" as that term is defined in this chapter [38 USCS §§ 3500 et seq.];

(2) the eligible person is not already qualified, by reason of previous education or training, for the educational, professional, or vocational objective for which the program of education is offered;

(3) the eligible person's proposed educational institution or training establishment is in compliance with all the requirements of this chapter and chapter 36 of this title [38 USCS §§ 3500 et seq. and 3670 et seq.]; and

(4) it does not appear that the enrollment in or pursuit of such person's program of education would violate any provisions of this chapter or chapter 36 of this title [38 USCS §§ 3500 et seq. or 3670 et seq.].

(Sept. 2, 1958, P. L. 85-857, § 1, 72 Stat. 1196; Oct. 15, 1976, P. L. 94-502, Title III, § 310(11), 90 Stat. 2391; Oct. 17, 1980, P. L. 96-466, Title III, Part

B, § 324, 94 Stat. 2196; Oct. 28, 1986, P. L. 99-576, Title III, Part A, § 314(b)(1), (2), 100 Stat. 3273; Dec. 18, 1989, P. L. 101-237, Title IV, § 423(b)(1)(A), 103 Stat. 2092; Aug. 6, 1991, P. L. 102-83, § 5(a), 105 Stat. 406.)

HISTORY; ANCILLARY LAWS AND DIRECTIVES
Amendments:
1976. Act Oct. 15, 1976 (effective 10/15/76, as provided by § 703(b) of such Act, which appears as 38 USCS § 3693 note), substituted "the Administrator" for "he".
1980. Act Oct. 17, 1980 (effective 10/1/80, as provided by § 802(c)(1) of such Act, which appears as 38 USCS § 3452 note), substituted new section for one which read:
"The Administrator shall finally approve an application if the Administrator finds (1) that section 1720 of this title has been complied with, (2) that the proposed program of education constitutes a "program of education" as that term is defined in this chapter, (3) that the eligible person is not already qualified, by reason of previous education or training, for the educational, professional, or vocational objective for which the courses of the program of education are offered, and (4) that it does not appear that the pursuit of such program would violate any provision of this chapter.".
1986. Act Oct. 28, 1986, substituted the catchline of this section for one which read "Final approval of application"; in the introductory matter deleted "finally" following "shall", deleted para. (1) which read: "section 1720 of this title has been complied with;" and redesignated para. (2)–(5) as (1)–(4) respectively.
1989. Act Dec. 18, 1989, in the introductory matter, substituted "Secretary" for "Administrator", wherever appearing.
1991. Act Aug. 6, 1991, redesignated this section, formerly 38 USCS § 1721, as 38 USCS § 3521.

CODE OF FEDERAL REGULATIONS
Department of Veterans Affairs—Vocational rehabilitation and education, 38 CFR Part 21.

[§ 3522]. [§ 1722. Repealed]

HISTORY; ANCILLARY LAWS AND DIRECTIVES
The bracketed section number "3522" was inserted to preserve numerical continuity following the section number redesignations made by Act Aug. 6, 1991, P. L. 102-83, § 5(a), 105 Stat. 406.
This section (Act Sept. 2, 1958, P. L. 85-857, § 1, 72 Stat. 1196) was repealed by Act Oct. 24, 1972, P. L. 92-540, Title IV, § 402(2), 86 Stat. 1090. It provided for a change of program.

§ 3523. Disapproval of enrollment in certain courses

(a) The Secretary shall not approve the enrollment of an eligible person in—
　(1) any bartending course or personality development course;

(2) any sales or sales management course which does not provide specialized training within a specific vocational field;

(3) any type of course which the Secretary finds to be avocational or recreational in character (or the advertising for which the Secretary finds contains significant avocational or recreational themes) unless the eligible person submits justification showing that the course will be of bona fide use in the pursuit of the person's present or contemplated business or occupation; or

(4) any independent study program except an accredited independent study program (including open circuit television) leading to a standard college degree.

(b) The Secretary shall not approve the enrollment of an eligible person in any course of flight training other than one given by an educational institution of higher learning for credit toward a standard college degree the eligible person is seeking.

(c) The Secretary shall not approve the enrollment of an eligible person in any course to be pursued by radio.

(d) The Secretary shall not approve the enrollment of an eligible person in any course which is to be pursued as a part of such person's regular secondary school education (except as provided in section 3533 of this title), but this subsection shall not prevent the enrollment of an eligible person in a course not leading to a standard college degree if the Secretary finds that such person has ended such person's secondary school education (by completion or otherwise) and that such course is a specialized vocational course pursued for the purpose of qualifying in a bona fide vocational objective.

(e) An eligible person may not enroll in any course at an educational institution which is not located in a State or in the Republic of the Philippines, unless such course is pursued at an approved institution of higher learning and the course is approved by the Secretary. The Secretary, in the Secretary's discretion, may deny or discontinue educational assistance under this chapter [38 USCS §§ 3500 et seq.] in the case of any eligible person in such an institution if the Secretary determines that such enrollment is not in the best interest of the eligible person or the Federal Government.

(Sept. 2, 1958, P. L. 85-857, § 1, 72 Stat. 1196; Sept. 14, 1960, P. L. 86-785, § 4, 74 Stat. 1024; July 25, 1962, P. L. 87-546, 76 Stat. 216; March 26, 1970, P. L. 91-219, Title II, § 209, 84 Stat. 83; Oct. 24, 1972, P. L. 92-540, Title III, § 311, 86 Stat. 1083; Dec. 3, 1974, P. L. 93-508, Title II, § 207, 88 Stat. 1583; Oct. 15, 1976, P. L. 94-502, Title III, §§ 306, 310(12)–(14), 90 Stat. 2390, 2392; Oct. 17, 1980, P. L. 96-466, Title III, Part B, §§ 325, 326, 327(b), 94 Stat. 2196; Oct. 14, 1982, P. L. 97-306, Title II, § 202(b), 96 Stat. 1433; Dec. 18, 1989, P. L. 101-237, Title IV, § 423(b)(1)(A), (2), 103 Stat. 2092; Aug. 6, 1991, P. L. 102-83, § 5(a), (c)(1), 105 Stat. 406; Oct. 29, 1992, P. L. 102-568, Title III, § 313(a)(7), 106 Stat. 4333; Oct. 9, 1996, P. L. 104-275, Title I, § 104(b), 110 Stat. 3327.)

HISTORY; ANCILLARY LAWS AND DIRECTIVES
Amendments:
1960. Act Sept. 15, 1960, in subsec. (c), substituted "open circuit television (except as herein provided)" for "television" and inserted "The Administrator may approve the enrollment of an eligible person in a course, to be pursued in residence, leading to a standard college degree which includes, as an integral part thereof, subjects offered through the medium of open circuit televised instruction, if the major portion of the course requires conventional classroom or laboratory attendance.".

1962. Act July 25, 1962, in subsec. (c), inserted "Notwithstanding the first sentence of this subsection, enrollment in a foreign educational institution may be approved by the Administrator in the case of any eligible person, if (1) the subject to be taken by such person at such foreign educational institution are an integral part of and are fully creditable toward the satisfactory completion of an approved course in which such person is enrolled in an institution of higher learning (hereafter in this sentence referred to as his 'principal institution') which is located in a State or in the Republic of the Philippines, (2) the tuition and fees for attendance at such foreign educational institution are paid for by the principal institution, and (3) the principal institution agrees to assume the responsibility for submitting to the Veterans' Administration required enrollment certificates and monthly certifications of training as to attendance, conduct, and progress.".

1970. Act March 26, 1970, substituted subsec. (a) for one which read:
"(a)(1) The Administrator shall not approve the enrollment of an eligible person in any bartending course, dancing course, or personality development course.

"(2) The Administrator shall not approve the enrollment of an eligible person—

"(A) in any photography course or entertainment course; or

"(B) in any music course—instrumental or vocal—public speaking course, or course in sports or athletics such as horseback riding, swimming, fishing, skiing, golf, baseball, tennis, bowling, sports officiating, or other sport or athletic courses, except courses of applied music, physical education, or public speaking which are offered by institutions of higher learning for credit as an integral part of a program leading to an educational objective; or

"(C) in any other type of course which the Administrator finds to be avocational or recreational in character; unless the eligible person submits justification showing that the course will be of bona fide use in the pursuit of his present or contemplated business or occupation.".

1972. Act Oct. 24, 1972, substituted subsec. (c) for one which read: "The Administrator shall not approve the enrollment of an eligible person in any course of apprentice or other training on the job, any course of institutional on-farm training, any course to be pursued by correspondence, open circuit television (except as herein provided), or radio, or any course to be pursued at an educational institution not located in a State or in the Republic of the Philippines. The Administrator may approve the enrollment of an eligible person in a course, to be pursued in residence, leading to a standard college degree which includes, as an integral part thereof, subjects offered through the medium of open circuit televised instruction, if the major portion of the course requires conventional classroom or laboratory attendance.

Notwithstanding the first sentence of this subsection, enrollment in a foreign educational institution may be approved by the Administrator in the case of any eligible person, if (1) the subject to be taken by such person at such foreign educational institution are an integral part of and are fully creditable toward the satisfactory completion of an approved course in which such person is enrolled in an institution of higher learning (hereafter in this sentence referred to as his 'principal institution') which is located in a State or in the Republic of the Philippines, (2) the tuition and fees for attendance at such foreign educational institution are paid for by the principal institution, and (3) the principal institution agrees to assume the responsibility for submitting to the Veterans' Administration required enrollment certificates and monthly certifications of training as to attendance, conduct, and progress.''; and, in subsec. (d), inserted "(except as provided in section 1733 of this title)".

1974. Act Dec. 3, 1974 (effective 12/3/74, as provided by § 503 of such Act, which appears as 38 USCS § 3452 note), substituted new subsec. (a)(2) for one which read: "any sales or sales management course which does not provide specialized training within a specific vocational field, unless the eligible person or the institution offering such course submits justification showing that at least one-half of the persons completing such course over the preceding two-year period have been employed in the sales or sales management field; or"; in subsec. (a)(3), inserted "(or the advertising for which he finds contains significant avocational or recreational themes)"; in subsec. (c), deleted "any course of institutional on-farm training," following "an eligible person in"; and in subsec. (d), substituted "not leading to a standard college degree" for "to be pursued below the college level".

1976. Act Oct. 15, 1976 (effective 10/15/76, as provided by § 703(b) of such Act, which appears as 38 USCS § 3693 note), in subsec. (a), in para. (2), deleted "or" following "active duty);"; in para. (3), substituted "the Administrator" for "he" following "advertising for which", substituted "the person's for "his", and substituted "; or" for a period. and added para. (4); in subsec. (c), substituted "the Administrator's" for "his" and substituted "the Administrator" for "he" preceding "finds"; and, in subsec. (d), substituted "such person's" for "his" wherever appearing.

1980. Act Oct. 17, 1980 (effective 10/1/80, as provided by § 802(c)(1) of such Act, which appears as 38 USCS § 3452 note), in subsec. (a), redesignated existing matter as para. (1), redesignated paras. (1)–(4) as subparas. (A)–(D), respectively, substituted new para. (1)(B) for one, as so redesignated, which read: "(B) any sales or sales management course which does not provide specialized training within a specific vocational field, or in any other course with a vocational objective, unless the eligible person or the institution offering such course submits justification showing that at least one-half of the persons who completed such course over the preceding two-year period, and who are not unavailable for employment, have been employed in the occupational category for which the course was designed to provide training (but in computing the number of persons who completed such course over any such two-year period, there shall not be included the number of persons who completed such course with assistance under this title while serving on active duty);", and added para. (2); substituted new subsec. (c) for one which read: "(c) The Administrator shall not approve the enrollment of an eligible person in any course to be pursued by correspondence (except as provided in section 1786 of this title), open circuit television (except as herein provided), or a radio, or any course to be pursued at an educational institution not located in a State or in the Republic of the Philippines (except as herein provided). The Administrator may approve the enrollment of an eligible person in a course, to be pursued in residence, leading to a standard college degree which includes, as an integral part thereof, subjects offered through the medium of open circuit televised instruction, if the major portion of the course requires conventional classroom or laboratory attendance. The Administrator may approve the enrollment at an educational institution which is not located in a State or in the Republic of the Philippines if such program is pursued at an approved educational institution of higher learning. The Administrator in the Administrator's discretion may deny or discontinue the educational assistance under this chapter of any eligible person in a foreign educational institution if the Administrator finds that such enrollment is not in the best interest of the eligible person or the Government."; and added subsec. (e).

1982. Act Oct. 14, 1982 (effective 10/1/82 as provided by § 202(c) of such Act, which appears as 38 USCS § 3473 note), in subsec. (a), deleted "(1)" preceding "The", redesignated subpara. (A) as para. (1), added para. (2), deleted subpara. (B), which read: "any course with a vocational objective, unless the eligible person or the institution offering such course presents evidence satisfactory to the Administrator showing that at least one-half of the persons who completed such course over such period, and who are not unavailable for employment, attained employment for an average of ten hours a week in an occupational category for which the course was designed to provide training", redesignated former subparas. (C) and (D) as paras. (3) and (4) respectively, and deleted former para. (2), which read:

"(2)(A) For the purposes of clause (B) of paragraph (1) of this subsection, in computing the number of persons who discontinued or completed a course over any two-year period, there shall not be included in such number those persons who received assistance under this title for pursuing such course while serving on active duty.

"(B) The provisions of clause (B) of paragraph (1) of this subsection shall not apply in the case of a particular course offered by an educational institution in a particular year if the total number of eligible veterans (as defined in section 1652(a)(1) of this title) and eligible persons enrolled in the institution during the two-year period preceding such year did not exceed 35 percent of the total enrollment in such institution during such period and the course has met the requirements of such clause for any two-year period ending on or after the date of the enactment of this paragraph.

"(C) The Administrator may waive the requirements under clause (B) of paragraph (1) of this subsection if the Administrator determines, under regulations which the Administrator shall prescribe, that such requirements would work an undue administrative hardship on an educational institution because of the small proportion of eligible veterans (as defined in section 1652(a)(1) of this title) and eligible persons enrolled in such institution.".

1989. Act Dec. 18, 1989, in the entire section, substituted "Secretary" for "Administrator", wherever appearing; and in subsec. (e), substituted "Secretary's" for "Administrator's".

1991. Act Aug. 6, 1991, redesignated this section, formerly 38 USCS

§ 1723, as 38 USCS § 3523, and amended the references in this section to reflect the redesignations made by § 5(a) of such Act (see Table III preceding 38 USCS § 101).

1992. Act Oct. 29, 1992, in subsec. (a), in para. (4), substituted "an accredited independent study program leading to a standard college degree." for "one leading to a standard college degree.".

1996. Act Oct. 9, 1996, in subsec. (a)(4), inserted "(including open circuit television)"; and, in subsec. (c), substituted "radio." for "radio or by open circuit television, except that the Secretary may approve the enrollment of an eligible person in a course, to be pursued in residence, leading to a standard college degree which includes, as an integral part thereof, subjects offered through open circuit television.".

CODE OF FEDERAL REGULATIONS

Department of Veterans Affairs—Vocational rehabilitation and education, 38 CFR Part 21.

§ 3524. Discontinuance for unsatisfactory progress

The Secretary shall discontinue the educational assistance allowance on behalf of an eligible person if, at any time, the Secretary finds that according to the regularly prescribed standards and practices of the educational institution such person is attending, the person's attendance, conduct, or progress is unsatisfactory. The Secretary may renew the payment of the educational assistance allowance only if the Secretary finds that—

(1) the eligible person will be resuming enrollment at the same educational institution in the same program of education and the educational institution has both approved such eligible person's reenrollment and certified it to the Department of Veterans Affairs; or

(2) in the case of a proposed change of either educational institution or program of education by the eligible person—

(A) the cause of the unsatisfactory attendance, conduct, or progress has been removed;

(B) the program proposed to be pursued is suitable to the eligible person's aptitudes, interests, and abilities; and

(C) if a proposed change of program is involved, the change meets the requirements for approval under section 3691 of this title.

(Sept. 2, 1958, P. L. 85-857, § 1, 72 Stat. 1197; Oct. 15, 1976, P. L. 94-502, Title III, §§ 307, 310(15), 90 Stat. 2390, 2392; Nov. 23, 1977, P. L. 95-202, Title III, § 305(b)(1), 91 Stat. 1443; Oct. 17, 1980, P. L. 96-466, Title III, Part B, § 328, 94 Stat. 2197; Dec. 18, 1989, P. L. 101-237, Title IV, §§ 411(b), 412(b), 423(b)(1)(A), 103 Stat. 2084, 2085, 2092; Aug. 6, 1991, P. L. 102-83, § 5(a), (c)(1), 105 Stat. 406.)

HISTORY; ANCILLARY LAWS AND DIRECTIVES
Amendments:
1976. Act Oct. 15, 1976 (effective 10/15/76, as provided by § 703(b) of such Act, which appears as 38 USCS § 3693), in the introductory matter,

substituted "such person" for "he", "the person's" for "his" and "the Administrator" for "he" following "if"; and in para. (2), substituted "the person's" for "his".

Such Act further (effective 12/1/76, as provided by § 703(c) of such Act, which appears as 38 USCS § 3693 note), in the introductory matter, inserted "Unless the Administrator finds there are mitigating circumstances, progress will be considered unsatisfactory at any time an eligible person is not progressing at a rate that will permit such person to graduate within the approved length of the course based on the training time as certified to the Veterans' Administration.".

1977. Act Nov. 23, 1977 (effective 2/1/78, as provided by § 501 of such Act, which appears as 38 USCS § 101 note), in the introductory matter, inserted ", or within such other length of time (exceeding such approved length) as the Administrator determines to be reasonable in accordance with regulations".

1980. Act Oct. 17, 1980 (effective 10/1/80, as provided by § 802(c)(1) of such Act, which appears as 38 USCS § 3452 note), in the introductory matter, deleted "Unless the Administrator finds there are mitigating circumstances, progress will be considered unsatisfactory at any time an eligible person is not progressing at a rate that will permit such person to graduate within the approved length of the course based on the training time as certified to the Veterans' Administration, or within such other length of time (exceeding such approved length) as the Administrator determines to be reasonable in accordance with regulations." following "or progress is unsatisfactory.".

1989. Act Dec. 18, 1989, substituted paras. (1) and (2) for ones which read:
"(1) the cause of the unsatisfactory conduct or progress of the eligible person has been removed; and
"(2) the program which the eligible person now proposes to pursue (whether the same or revised) is suitable to the person's aptitudes, interests, and abilities.".

Such Act further, in the introductory matter, substituted "attendance, conduct," for "conduct", and "Secretary" for "Administrator", wherever appearing.

1991. Act Aug. 6, 1991, redesignated this section, formerly 38 USCS § 1724, as 38 USCS § 3524, and amended the references in this section to reflect the redesignations made by § 5(a) of such Act (see Table III preceding 38 USCS § 101).

Other provisions:

Approval process study; authorization of appropriations; implementation of amendments to be suspended. Act Nov. 23, 1977, P. L. 95-202, Title III, § 305(b)(2)–(4), 91 Stat. 1443 (effective 11/23/77, as provided by § 501 of such Act, which appears as 38 USCS § 101 note), provided:

"(2) The Administrator of Veterans' Affairs, in consultation with appropriate bodies, officials, persons, departments, and agencies, shall conduct a study to investigate (A) specific methods of improving the process by which postsecondary educational institutions and courses at such institutions are and continue to be approved for purposes of chapters 32, 34, 35, and 36 of title 38, United States Code [38 USCS §§ 3201, et seq., 3451 et seq., 3500 et seq., and 3670 et seq.]; and (B) in recognition of the importance of assuring that Federal assistance is made available to those eligible veterans and persons seriously pursuing and making satisfactory progress toward an educational or vocational objective under such chapters, the need for legislative or administrative action in regard to sections 1674 and 1724 of title 38, United States Code [now 38 USCS §§ 3474, 3524], and the regulations prescribed thereunder. A report of such study, together with such specific recommendations for administrative or legislative action as the Administrator deems appropriate, shall be submitted to the President and the Congress not later than September 30, 1979, except that the portion of the report of such study described in clause (B) of the preceding sentence shall be submitted not later than September 30, 1978.

"(3) For the purpose of carrying out paragraph (1) of this subsection, there are authorized to be appropriated $1,000,000.

"(4)(A) Until such time as the Administrator submits the report required under the second sentence of paragraph (2) of this subsection, the Administrator shall suspend implementation of the amendments to sections 1674 and 1724 of title 38, United States Code [now 38 USCS §§ 3474, 3524], made by sections 206 and 307; respectively, of Public Law 94-502, in the case of any accredited educational institution which submits to the Administrator its course catalog or bulletin and a certification that the policies and regulations described in clauses (6) and (7) of section 1776(b) [now 38 USCS § 3676(b)(6), (7)] are being enforced by such institution, unless the Administrator finds, pursuant to regulations which the Administrator shall prescribe, that such catalog or bulletin fails to state fully and clearly such policies and regulations.

"(B) The Administrator shall, where appropriate, bring to the attention of the Council on Postsecondary Accreditation and the appropriate accrediting and licensing bodies such catalogs, bulletins, and certifications submitted under subparagraph (A) of this paragraph which the Administrator believes may not be in compliance with the standards of such accrediting and licensing body.".

CODE OF FEDERAL REGULATIONS

Department of Veterans Affairs—Vocational rehabilitation and education, 38 CFR Part 21.

CROSS REFERENCES

This section is referred to in 5 USCS § 5569; 10 USCS § 2184.

INTERPRETIVE NOTES AND DECISIONS

Purpose of 38 USCS § 1724 [now 38 USCS § 3524] is to attempt to insure that enrolled veteran actually does something constructive while he is in school and attempts to insure that each veteran, instead of merely enjoying academic environment, makes definite progress toward educational goal. Francis v Cleland (1977, DC SD) 433 F Supp 605, revd on other grounds (1978) 435 US 213, 55 L Ed 2d 225, 98 S Ct 1024.

38 USCS § 3525]
VETERANS' BENEFITS

[§ 3525]. [§ 1725. Repealed]

HISTORY; ANCILLARY LAWS AND DIRECTIVES

The bracketed section number "3525" was inserted to preserve numerical continuity following the section number redesignations made by Act Aug. 6, 1991, P. L. 102-83, § 5(a), 105 Stat. 406.

This section (Act Sept. 2, 1958, P. L. 85-857, § 1, 72 Stat. 1197) was repealed by Act Oct. 24, 1972, P. L. 92-540, Title IV, § 402(2), 86 Stat. 1090. It provided for a period of operation for approval. For similar provisions, see 38 USCS § 3689.

[§ 3526]. [§ 1726. Repealed]

HISTORY; ANCILLARY LAWS AND DIRECTIVES

The bracketed section number "3526" was inserted to preserve numerical continuity following the section number redesignations made by Act Aug. 6, 1991, P. L. 102-83, § 5(a), 105 Stat. 406.

This section (Act Sept. 2, 1958, P. L. 85-857, § 1, 72 Stat. 1197) was repealed by Act March 3, 1966, P. L. 89-358, § 3(a)(3), 80 Stat. 20. It provided for listing of institutions by Attorney General.

SUBCHAPTER IV. PAYMENTS TO ELIGIBLE PERSONS

§ 3531. Educational assistance allowance

(a) The Secretary shall, in accordance with the provisions of chapter 36 of this title [38 USCS §§ 3670 et seq.], pay to the parent or guardian of each eligible person who is pursuing a program of education under this chapter [38 USCS §§ 3500 et seq.], and who applies therefor on behalf of such eligible person, an educational assistance allowance to meet, in part, the expenses of the eligible person's subsistence, tuition, fees, supplies, books, equipment, and other educational costs.

(b) The educational assistance allowance of an eligible person pursuing a program of education at an educational institution shall be paid as provided in chapter 36 of this title [38 USCS §§ 3670 et seq.].

(Sept. 2, 1958, P. L. 85-857, § 1, 72 Stat. 1197; March 3, 1966, P. L. 89-358, § 4(1), 80 Stat. 24; Oct. 24, 1972, P. L. 92-540, Title III, § 312, 86 Stat. 1083; Oct. 15, 1976, P. L. 94-502, Title III, §§ 309(c), 310(16), 90 Stat. 2391, 2392; Oct. 17, 1980, P. L. 96-466, Title III, Part B, § 329, 94 Stat. 2197; Dec. 18, 1989, P. L. 101-237, Title IV, § 423(b)(1)(A), 103 Stat. 2092; Aug. 6, 1991, P. L. 102-83, § 5(a), 105 Stat. 406.)

HISTORY; ANCILLARY LAWS AND DIRECTIVES
Amendments:

1966. Act March 3, 1966, substituted subsecs. (c), (d), and (e), for subsec. (c), which read:

"(c) No educational assistance allowance shall be paid on behalf of an eligible person for any period until the Administrator shall have received—

READJUSTMENT BENEFITS
38 USCS § 3531

"(1) from the eligible person (A) in the case of an eligible person enrolled in a course which leads to a standard college degree, a certification that he was actually enrolled in and pursuing the course as approved by the Administrator, or (B) in the case of an eligible person enrolled in a course which does not lead to a standard college degree, a certification as to actual attendance during such period; and

"(2) from the educational institution a certification, or an endorsement on the eligible person's certificate, that he was enrolled in and pursuing a course of education during such period.

Educational assistance allowances shall, insofar as practicable, be paid within twenty days after receipt by the Administrator of the certifications required by this subsection.".

1972. Act Oct. 24, 1972, in subsec. (a), inserted ", in accordance with the provisions of section 1780 of this title," deleted subsecs. (b), (c), and (e), which read:

"(b) The educational assistance allowance on behalf of an eligible person shall be paid, as provided in section 1732 of this title, only for the period of his enrollment as approved by the Administrator, but no allowance shall be paid—

"(1) on behalf of any person enrolled in a course which leads to a standard college degree for any period when such person is not pursuing his course in accordance with the regularly established policies and regulations of the educational institution and the requirements of this chapter; or

"(2) on behalf of any person enrolled in a course which does not lead to a standard college degree for any day of absence in excess of thirty days in a twelve-month period, not counting as absences weekends or legal holidays established by Federal or State law (or in the case of the Republic of the Philippines, Philippine law) during which the institution is not regularly in session.",

"(c) The Administrator may, pursuant to such regulations as he may prescribe, determine enrollment in, pursuit of, and attendance at, any program of education or course by an eligible person for any period for which an educational assistance allowance is paid on behalf of such eligible person under this chapter for pursuing such program or course."

"(e) Educational assistance allowances shall be paid as soon as practicable after the Administrator is assured of the eligible person's enrollment in and pursuit of the program of education for the period for which such allowance is to be paid."; and redesignated subsec. (d) as subsec. (b).

1976. Act Oct. 15, 1976 (effective 10/15/76, as provided by § 703(b) of such Act, which appears as 38 USCS § 3693 note), in subsec. (a), substituted "chapter 36" for "section 1780"; and in subsec. (b), in para. (1), substituted "the person's" for "his" and in para. (2), substituted "the person" for "he".

1980. Act Oct. 17, 1980 (effective 10/1/80, as provided by § 802(c)(1) of such Act, which appears as 38 USCS § 3452 note), substituted new subsec. (b) for one which read:

"(b) No educational assistance allowance shall be paid on behalf of an eligible person enrolled in a course in an educational institution which does not lead to a standard college degree for any period until the Administrator shall have received—

"(1) from the eligible person a certification as to the person's actual attendance during such period; and

"(2) from the educational institution, a certification, or an endorsement on the eligible person's certificate, that the person was enrolled in and pursuing a course of education during such period.".

1989. Act Dec. 18, 1989, in subsec. (a), substituted "Secretary" for "Administrator".

1991. Act Aug. 6, 1991, redesignated this section, formerly 38 USCS § 1731, as 38 USCS § 3531.

CODE OF FEDERAL REGULATIONS

Department of Veterans Affairs—Vocational rehabilitation and education, 38 CFR Part 21.

RESEARCH GUIDE

Am Jur:
77 Am Jur 2d, Veterans and Veterans' Laws § 146.

§ 3532. Computation of educational assistance allowance

(a)(1) The educational assistance allowance on behalf of an eligible person who is pursuing a program of education consisting of institutional courses shall be paid at the monthly rate of $404 for full-time, $304 for three-quarter-time, or $202 for half-time pursuit.

(2) The educational assistance allowance on behalf of an eligible person pursuing a program of education on less than a half-time basis shall be paid at the rate of (A) the established charges for tuition and fees that the educational institution involved requires similarly circumstanced nonveterans enrolled in the same program to pay, or (B) $404 per month for a full-time course, whichever is the lesser.

(b) The educational assistance allowance to be paid on behalf of an eligible person who is pursuing a full-time program of education which consists of institutional courses and alternate phases of training in a business or industrial establishment with the training in the business or industrial establishment being strictly supplemental to the institutional portion, shall be computed at the rate of $404 per month.

(c)(1) An eligible person who is enrolled in an educational institution for a "farm cooperative" program consisting of institutional agricultural courses prescheduled to fall within forty-four weeks of any period of twelve consecutive months and who pursues such program on—

(A) a full-time basis (a minimum of ten clock hours per week or four hundred and forty clock hours in such year prescheduled to provide not less than eighty clock hours in any three-month period),

(B) a three-quarter-time basis (a minimum of seven clock hours per week), or

(C) a half-time basis (a minimum of five clock hours per week),

shall be eligible to receive an educational assistance allowance at the appropriate rate provided in paragraph (2) of this subsection, if such eligible person is concurrently engaged in agricultural employment which is relevant to such institutional agricultural courses as determined under standards prescribed by the Secretary. In computing the foregoing clock hour requirements there shall be included the time involved in field trips and individual and group instruction sponsored and conducted by the educational institution through a duly authorized instructor of such institution in which the person is enrolled.

(2) The monthly educational assistance allowance to be paid on behalf of an eligible person pursuing a farm cooperative program under this chapter [38 USCS §§ 3500 et seq.] shall be $327 for full-time, $245 for three-quarter-time, and $163 for half-time pursuit.

(d) If a program of education is pursued by an eligible person at an institution located in the Republic of the Philippines, the educational assistance allowance computed for such person under this section shall be paid at the rate of $0.50 for each dollar.

(e) In the case of an eligible person who is pursuing a program of education under this chapter [38 USCS §§ 3500 et seq.] while incarcerated in a Federal, State, or local penal institution for conviction of a felony, the educational assistance allowance shall be paid in the same manner prescribed in section 3482(g) of this title for incarcerated veterans, except that the references therein to the monthly educational assistance allowance prescribed for a veteran with no dependents shall be deemed to refer to the applicable allowance payable to an eligible person under corresponding provisions of this chapter [38 USCS §§ 3500 et seq.] or chapter 36 of this title [38 USCS §§ 3670 et seq.], as determined by the Secretary.

(Sept. 2, 1958, P. L. 85-857, § 1, 72 Stat. 1198; Sept. 30, 1965, P. L. 89-222, § 1, 79 Stat. 896; March 26, 1970, P. L. 91-219, Title I, § 104(a), (b), Title II, § 210, 84 Stat. 77, 83; Oct. 24, 1972, P. L. 92-540, Title I, § 103(1)–(3), 86 Stat. 1075; Dec. 3, 1974, P. L. 93-508, Title I, § 103(1)–(3), Title II, § 208, 88 Stat. 1580, 1584; Jan. 2, 1975, P. L. 93-602, Title II, § 204(a), 88 Stat. 1958; Oct. 15, 1976, P. L. 94-502, Title III, §§ 301(1), 308, 90 Stat. 2389, 2390; Nov. 23, 1977, P. L. 95-202, Title I, § 103(1), 91 Stat. 1434; Oct. 17, 1980, P. L. 96-466, Title II, Part A, § 202(1), Part B, § 212(1), Title III, Part B, § 330, Title VI, § 602(b), 94 Stat. 2188, 2190, 2198, 2209; Oct. 24, 1984, P. L. 98-543, Title II, Part A, § 203(1), 98 Stat. 2742; Dec. 18, 1989, P. L. 101-237, Title IV, §§ 403(a)(1)–(7), 423(b)(1)(A), 103 Stat. 2078, 2079, 2092; March 22, 1991, P. L. 102-16, § 10(a)(6), 105 Stat. 56; Aug. 6, 1991, P. L. 102-83, § 5(a), (c)(1), 105 Stat. 406; Oct. 29, 1992, P. L. 102-568, Title III, § 316(b), 106 Stat. 4334; Nov. 2, 1994, P. L. 103-446, Title V, § 507(b), 108 Stat. 4664; Oct. 9, 1996, P. L. 104-275, Title I, § 105(c), 110 Stat. 3327.)

HISTORY; ANCILLARY LAWS AND DIRECTIVES
Amendments:
1965. Act Sept. 30, 1965 (effective as provided by § 4 of such Act, which appears as a note to this section), in subsec. (a), substituted "$130",

"$95", and "$60" for "$110", "$80", and "$50", respectively; and in subsec. (b), substituted "$105" for "$90".

1970. Act March 26, 1970, § 104(a), (b) (effective 2/1/70, as provided by § 301 of such Act, which appears as 38 USCS § 3482 note), substituted subsec. (a) for one which read: "The educational assistance allowance on behalf of an eligible person who is pursuing a program of education consisting of institutional courses shall be computed at the rate of (1) $130 per month if pursued on a full-time basis, (2) $95 per month if pursued on a three-quarters time basis, and (3) $60 per month if pursued on a half-time basis."; in subsec. (b), substituted "$141" for "$105".

Act March 26, 1970, § 210, substituted subsec. (c) for one which read: "No educational assistance allowance shall be paid on behalf of an eligible person for any period during which he is enrolled in and pursuing an institutional course on a less than half-time basis, or any course described in subsection (b), on a less than full-time basis.".

1972. Act Oct. 24, 1972 (effective as provided by § 601(a) of such Act, which appears as 38 USCS § 3482 note), in subsec. (a), substituted para. (1) for one which read: "The educational assistance allowance on behalf of an eligible person who is pursuing a program of education consisting of institutional courses shall be computed at the rate of (A) $175 per month if pursued on a full-time basis, (B) $128 per month if pursued on a three-quarter-time basis, and (C) $81 per month if pursued on a half-time basis." and, in para. (2), substituted "$220" for "$175"; and, in subsec. (b), substituted "$177" for "$141".

1974. Act Dec. 3, 1974, § 103(1)–(3) (effective 9/1/74, as provided by § 501 of such Act, which appears as 38 USCS § 3482 note), in subsec. (a), substituted para. (1) for one which read: "The educational assistance allowance on behalf of an eligible person who is pursuing a program of education consisting of institutional courses shall be computed at the rate of (A) $220 per month if pursued on a full-time basis, (B) $165 per month if pursued on a three-quarter-time basis, and (C) $110 per month if pursued on a half-time basis." and, in para. (2), substituted "prescribed in section 1682(b)(2) of this title for less-than-half-time pursuit of an institutional program by an eligible veteran." for "of (A) the established charges for tuition and fees which the institution requires other individuals enrolled in the same program to pay, or (B) $220 per month for a full-time course, whichever is the lesser."; and, in subsec. (b), substituted "$209" for "$177".

Act Dec. 3, 1974, § 208 (effective 12/3/74, as provided by § 503 of such Act, which appears as 38 USCS § 3452 note), redesignated subsec. (c) as subsec. (d); and added new subsec. (c).

1975. Act Jan. 2, 1975 (effective 1/1/75, as provided by § 206 of such Act, which appears as 38 USCS § 3482 note), in subsec. (b), substituted "$217" for "$209".

1976. Act Oct. 15, 1976 (effective 10/1/76, as provided by § 703(a) of such Act, which appears as 38 USCS § 3693 note), in subsec. (b), substituted "$235" for "$217"; added subsec. (c)(3).

1977. Act Nov. 23, 1977 (effective 10/1/77, as provided by § 501 of such Act, which appears as 38 USCS § 101 note), in subsec. (b), substituted "$251" for "$235".

1980. Act Oct. 17, 1980, §§ 202(1), 330, 602(b) (effective 10/1/80, as provided by § 802(b)(1), (c)(1), (f)(1) of such Act, which appear as 38 USCS §§ 3482, 3452, 5314 notes, respectively), in subsec. (b), substituted "$264" for "$251"; added subsec. (c)(4); and added subsec. (e).

Act Oct. 17, 1980, § 212(1) (effective 1/1/81, as provided by § 802(b)(2) of such Act, which appears as 38 USCS § 3482 note), in subsec. (b), as amended by § 202(1) of Act Oct. 17, 1980, substituted "$276" for "$264".

1984. Act Oct. 24, 1984 (effective 10/1/78, as provided by § 205 of such Act, which appears as 38 USCS § 3108 note), in subsec. (b), substituted "$304" for "$276".

1989. Act Dec. 18, 1989 (effective 1/1/90, as provided by § 403(c) of such Act, which appears as a note to this section), in subsec. (a), in para. (1), substituted "paid at the monthly rate of $404 for full-time, $304 for three-quarter-time, or $202 for half-time pursuit." for "computed at the rate prescribed in section 1682(a)(1) of this title for full-time, three-quarter-time, or half-time pursuit, as appropriate, of an institutional program by an eligible veteran with no dependents.", in para. (2), substituted "paid at the rate of (A) the established charges for tuition and fees that the educational institution involved requires similarly circumstanced nonveterans enrolled in the same program to pay, or (B) $404 per month for a full-time course, whichever is the lesser." for "computed at the rate prescribed in section 1682(b)(2) of this title for less-than-half-time pursuit of an institutional program by an eligible veteran."; in subsec. (b), substituted "$327" for "$304"; in subsec. (c), in para. (2), substituted "$327 for full-time, $245 for three-quarter-time, and $163 for half-time pursuit." for "computed at the rate prescribed in section 1682(c)(2) of this title for full-time, three-quarter-time, or half-time pursuit, as appropriate, of a farm cooperative program by an eligible veteran with no dependents."; substituted para. (3) for one which read: "The monthly educational assistance allowance to be paid on behalf of an eligible person pursuing an independent study program which leads to a standard college degree shall be computed at the rate prescribed in section 1682(e) of this title.", in para. (4), substituted "paragraph (3) of this subsection" for "section 1632(e) of this title"; and in subsec. (e), inserted ", except that the references therein to the monthly educational assistance allowance prescribed for a veteran with no dependents shall be deemed to refer to the applicable allowance payable to an eligible person under corresponding provisions of this chapter or chapter 36 of this title, as determined by the Secretary of Veterans Affairs".

Such Act further, in subsec. (c)(1), in the concluding matter, substituted "Secretary" for "Administrator".

1991. Act March 22, 1991, in subsecs. (c)(3) and (e), substituted "Secretary" for "Secretary of Veterans Affairs".

Act Aug. 6, 1991, redesignated this section, formerly 38 USCS § 1732, as 38 USCS § 3532, and amended the references in this section to reflect the redesignations made by § 5(a) of such Act (see Table III preceding 38 USCS § 101).

1992. Act Oct. 29, 1992 (applicable to enrollments in courses beginning on or after 7/1/93, as provided by § 316(c) of such Act, which appears as a note to this section), in subsec. (c), deleted paras. (3) and (4), which read:

"(3) The monthly educational assistance allowance to be paid on behalf of an eligible person pursuing an independent study program which leads to a standard college degree shall be computed at the rate provided in subsection (a)(2) of this section for less than half-time but more than quarter-time pursuit. If the entire training is to be pursued by independent study, the amount of the eligible person's entitlement to educational assistance under this chapter shall be charged in accordance with the rate at which such person is pursuing the independent study program but at not more than the rate at which such entitlement is charged for pursuit of such program on less than a half-time basis. In any case in which independent study is combined with resident training, the educational assistance allowance shall be paid at the applicable institutional rate based on the total training time determined by adding the number of semester hours (or the equivalent thereof) of resident training to the number of semester hours (or the equivalent thereof) of independent study that do not exceed the number of semester hours (or the equivalent thereof) required for the less than half-time, institutional rate, as determined by the Secretary, for resident training. An eligible person's entitlement shall be charged for a combination of independent study and resident training on the basis of the applicable monthly training time rate as determined under section 3688 of this title.

"(4) The monthly educational assistance allowance to be paid on behalf of an eligible person pursuing a course in part by open circuit television shall be computed in the same manner that such allowance is computed under paragraph (3) of this subsection for an independent study program.".

1994. Act Nov. 2, 1994 (applicable to payments made after 12/31/94, as provided by § 507(c) of such Act, which appears as 38 USCS § 107 note), in subsec. (d), substituted "the rate of" for "a rate in Phillipine pesos equivalent to".

1996. Act Oct. 9, 1996, in subsec. (b), substituted "$404" for "$327".

Other provisions:

Effective date of amendments made by §§ 1, 2 of Act Sept. 30, 1965. Act Sept. 30, 1965, P. L. 89-222, § 4, 79 Stat. 896, provided: "The amendments made by the first and second sections of this Act [amending this section and 38 USCS § 3542] shall take effect on the first day of the second calendar month following the date of enactment of this Act.".

Effective date of Dec. 18, 1989 amendments. Act Dec. 18, 1989, P. L. 101-237, Title IV, § 403(c), 103 Stat. 2080, provides: "The amendments made by this section [amending 38 USCS §§ 3532, 3533, 3534, 3542, 3687] shall take effect on January 1, 1990.".

Applicability of Oct. 29, 1992 amendments. Act Oct. 29, 1992, P. L. 102-568, Title III, § 316(c), 106 Stat. 4334, provides: "The amendments made by this section [amending 38 USCS §§ 3532(c) and 3688] apply to enrollments in courses beginning on or after July 1, 1993.".

CODE OF FEDERAL REGULATIONS

Department of Veterans Affairs—Vocational rehabilitation and education, 38 CFR Part 21.

CROSS REFERENCES

This section is referred to in 38 USCS §§ 3565, 3680.

RESEARCH GUIDE
Am Jur:
77 Am Jur 2d, Veterans and Veterans' Laws § 146.

§ 3533. Special assistance for the educationally disadvantaged

(a)(1) Any eligible person shall be entitled to the assistance provided an eligible veteran under section 3491(a) (if pursued in a State) of this title and be paid an educational assistance allowance therefor in the manner prescribed by section 3491(b) of this title, except that the corresponding rate provisions of this chapter [38 USCS §§ 3500 et seq.] shall apply, as determined by the Secretary, to such pursuit by an eligible person.

(2) Educational assistance under this chapter [38 USCS §§ 3500 et seq.] for the first five months of full-time pursuit of a program (or the equivalent thereof in part-time educational assistance) consisting of such course or courses shall be provided without charge to entitlement.

(b) Any eligible person shall, without charge to any entitlement such person may have under section 3511 of this title, be entitled to the benefits provided an eligible veteran under section 3492 of this title.

(Added Oct. 24, 1972, P. L. 92-540, Title III, § 313, 86 Stat. 1084; Oct. 15, 1976, P. L. 94-502, Title III, § 310(17), (18), 90 Stat. 2392; March 2, 1984, P. L. 98-223, Title II, § 203(b), 98 Stat. 41; Nov. 18, 1988, P. L. L 100-689, Title I, Part A, § 106(c), 102 Stat. 4167; Dec. 18, 1989, P. L. 101-237, Title IV, § 403(a)(8), 103 Stat. 2079; March 22, 1991, P. L. 102-16, § 10(a)(6), 105 Stat. 56; Aug. 6, 1991, P. L. 102-83, § 5(a), (c)(1), 105 Stat. 406.)

HISTORY; ANCILLARY LAWS AND DIRECTIVES

1976. Act Oct. 15, 1976 (effective 10/15/76, as provided by § 703(b) of such Act, which appears as 38 USCS § 3693 note), in subsec. (a), substituted "spouse or surviving spouse" for "wife or widow" and substituted "such spouse" for "she"; and in subsec. (b), substituted "such person" for "he".

1984. Act March 2, 1984, in subsec. (a), inserted "(with no dependents)" and deleted "and be paid an educational assistance allowance under the provisions of section 1732(a) of this title" following "of this title" the second time it appears.

1988. Act Nov. 18, 1988 (effective 8/15/89, as provided by § 106(d) of such Act, which appears as 38 USCS § 3034 note) substituted subsec. (a) for one which read: "Any eligible spouse or surviving spouse shall, without charge to any entitlement such spouse may have under section 1711 of this title, be entitled to the benefits provided an eligible veteran (with no dependents) under section 1691 (if pursued in a State) of this title".

1989. Act Dec. 18, 1989 (effective 1/1/90 as provided by § 403(c) of such Act, which appears as 38 USCS § 3532 note), in subsec. (a)(1), substituted "assistance provided an eligible veteran under section 1691(a) (if pursued in a State) of this title and be paid an educational assistance allowance therefor in the manner prescribed by section 1691(b) of this title, except that the corresponding rate provisions of this chapter shall apply, as determined by the Secretary of Veterans Affairs, to such pursuit by an eligible person.'' for ''benefits provided an eligible veteran (with no dependents) under section 1691 (if pursued in a State) of this title.''.

1991. Act March 22, 1991, in subsec. (a)(1), substituted ''Secretary'' for ''Secretary of Veterans Affairs''.

Act Aug. 6, 1991, redesignated this section, formerly 38 USCS § 1733, as 38 USCS § 3533, and amended the references in this section to reflect the redesignations made by § 5(a) of such Act (see Table III preceding 38 USCS § 101).

Other provisions:

Termination of eligibility. For termination of eligibility period for a wife or widow, or an eligible person 8 years from Oct. 24, 1972, see note containing Act Oct. 24, 1972, P. L. 92-540, Title VI, § 604, 86 Stat. 1099, located at 38 USCS § 3512.

CODE OF FEDERAL REGULATIONS

Department of Veterans Affairs—Vocational rehabilitation and education, 38 CFR Part 21.

CROSS REFERENCES

This section is referred to in 38 USCS § 3523, 3688.

RESEARCH GUIDE

Am Jur:

77 Am Jur 2d, Veterans and Veterans' Laws § 146.

§ 3534. Apprenticeship or other on-job training; correspondence courses

(a) Any eligible person shall be entitled to pursue, in a State, a program of apprenticeship or other on-job training and be paid a training assistance allowance as provided in section 3687 of this title.

(b) Any eligible spouse or surviving spouse shall be entitled to pursue a program of education exclusively by correspondence and be paid an educational assistance allowance as provided in section 3686 (other than subsection (a)(2)) of this title and the period of such spouse's entitlement shall be charged with one month for each $404 which is paid to the spouse as an educational assistance allowance for such course.

(Added Oct. 24, 1972, P. L. 92-540, Title III, § 313, 86 Stat. 1084; Oct. 15, 1976, P. L. 94-502, Title III, § 310(19), 90 Stat. 2392; Dec. 18, 1989, P. L. 101-237, Title IV, § 403(a)(9), 103 Stat. 2079; Aug. 6, 1991, P. L. 102-83, § 5(a), (c)(1), 105 Stat. 406.)

HISTORY; ANCILLARY LAWS AND DIRECTIVES

Amendments:

1976. Act Oct. 15, 1976 (effective 10/15/76, as provided by § 703(b) of such Act, which appears as 38 USCS § 3693 note), in subsec. (b), substituted ''spouse or surviving spouse'' for ''wife or widow''.

1989. Act Dec. 18, 1989 (effective 1/1/90, as provided by § 403(c) of such Act, which appears as 38 USCS § 3532 note), in subsec. (b), substituted "1786 (other than subsection (a)(2)) of this title and the period of such spouse's entitlement shall be charged with one month for each $404 which is paid to the spouse as an educational assistance allowance for such course" for "1786 of this title".

1991. Act Aug. 6, 1991, redesignated this section, formerly 38 USCS § 1734, as 38 USCS § 3534, and amended the references in this section to reflect the redesignations made by § 5(a) of such Act (see Table III preceding 38 USCS § 101).

CODE OF FEDERAL REGULATIONS

Department of Veterans Affairs—Vocational rehabilitation and education, 38 CFR Part 21.

RESEARCH GUIDE

Am Jur:
77 Am Jur 2d, Veterans and Veterans' Laws § 146.

§ 3535. Approval of courses

An eligible person shall receive the benefits of this chapter [38 USCS §§ 3500 et seq.] while enrolled in a course of education offered by an educational institution only if such course (1) is approved in accordance with the provisions of subchapter I of chapter 36 of this title [38 USCS §§ 3670 et seq.], or (2) is approved for the enrollment of the particular individual under the provisions of section 3536 of this title.
(Sept. 2, 1958, P. L. 85-857, § 1, 72 Stat. 1199; Sept. 23, 1963, P. L. 88-126, § 2, 77 Stat. 162; March 3, 1966, P. L. 89-358, § 4(n), 80 Stat. 25; Oct. 24, 1972, P. L. 92-540, Title IV, § 402(4), 86 Stat. 1090; Aug. 6, 1991, P. L. 102-83, § 5(a), (c)(1), 105 Stat. 406.)

HISTORY; ANCILLARY LAWS AND DIRECTIVES

Amendments:

1963. Act Sept. 23, 1963, in subsec. (a), substituted "Until the date for the expiration of all education and training under chapter 33 of this title, and" for "An", and inserted "or subchapter VII of this chapter"; in subsec. (b), inserted "or section 1778"; and deleted subsec. (c) which read: "After the date for the expiration of all education and training under chapter 33 of this title, the Administrator shall be responsible for the approval of any additional courses for the purposes of this chapter. In approving such a course, the criteria of sections 1653 and 1654 of this title shall be applicable to approvals under this subsection and the Administrator may utilize the services of State educational agencies in connection therewith.".

1966. Act March 3, 1966, substituted new section for one which read:

"(a) Until the date for the expiration of all education and training under chapter 33 of this title, and eligible person shall receive the benefits of this subchapter while enrolled in a course of education offered by an educational institution only if such course (1) is approved in accordance with the provisions of this section or subchapter VII of this chapter, or (2) is approved for the enrollment of the particular individual under the provisions of section 1737 of this title.

"(b) Any course offered by an educational institution (as defined in this chapter) shall be considered approved for the purposes of this chapter if it is approved under either section 1653 or section 1654 of this title before the date for the expiration of all education and training under chapter 33 of this title, and has not been disapproved under section 1656 or section 1778 of this title.".

1972. Act Oct. 24, 1972, substituted "1736" for "1737".

1991. Act Aug. 6, 1991, redesignated this section, formerly 38 USCS § 1735, as 38 USCS § 3535, and amended the references in this section to reflect the redesignations made by § 5(a) of such Act (see Table III preceding 38 USCS § 101).

CODE OF FEDERAL REGULATIONS
Department of Veterans Affairs—Vocational rehabilitation and education, 38 CFR Part 21.

RESEARCH GUIDE
Am Jur:
77 Am Jur 2d, Veterans and Veterans' Laws § 146.

§ 3536. Specialized vocational training courses

The Secretary may approve a specialized course of vocational training leading to a predetermined vocational objective for the enrollment of an eligible person under this subchapter [38 USCS §§ 3531 et seq.] if the Secretary finds that such course, either alone or when combined with other courses, constitutes a program of education which is suitable for that person and is required because of a mental or physical handicap.

(Sept. 2, 1958, P. L. 85-857, § 1, 72 Stat. 1199; Sept. 23, 1963, P. L. 88-126, § 4, 77 Stat. 162; Oct. 24, 1972, P. L. 92-540, Title IV, § 402(3), 86 Stat. 1090; Oct. 15, 1976, P. L. 94-502, Title III, § 310(20), 90 Stat. 2392; Dec. 18, 1989, P. L. 101-237, Title IV, § 423(b)(1)(A), 103 Stat. 2092; Aug. 6, 1991, P. L. 102-83, § 5(a), 105 Stat. 406.)

HISTORY; ANCILLARY LAWS AND DIRECTIVES
Amendments:

1963. Act Sept. 23, 1963, substituted "The" for "Notwithstanding the provisions of subsections (b) and (c) of section 1735 of this title, the".

1972. Act Oct. 24, 1972, redesignated this section as § 1736, it formerly appeared as § 1737.

1976. Act Oct. 15, 1976 (effective 10/15/76, as provided by § 703(b) of such Act, which appears as 38 USCS § 3693 note), substituted "the Administrator" for "he" preceding "finds".

1989. Act Dec. 18, 1989, substituted "Secretary" for "Administrator", wherever appearing.

1991. Act Aug. 6, 1991, redesignated this section, formerly 38 USCS § 1736, as 38 USCS § 3536.

CODE OF FEDERAL REGULATIONS
Department of Veterans Affairs—Vocational rehabilitation and education, 38 CFR Part 21.

CROSS REFERENCES
This section is referred to in 38 USCS §§ 3512, 3535, 3672.

RESEARCH GUIDE
Am Jur:
77 Am Jur 2d, Veterans and Veterans' Laws § 146.

§ 3537. Work-study allowance

(a) Subject to subsection (b) of this section, the Secretary shall utilize, in connection with the activities described in section 3485(a) of this title, the services of any eligible person who is pursuing, in a State, at least a three-quarter-time program of education (other than a course of special restorative training) and shall pay to such person an additional educational assistance allowance (hereafter in this section referred to as "work-study allowance") in return for such eligible person's agreement to perform such services. The amount of the work-study allowance shall be determined in accordance with section 3485(a) of this title.

(b) The Secretary's utilization of, and payment of a work-study allowance for, the services of an eligible person pursuant to subsection (a) of this section shall be subject to the same requirements, terms, and conditions as are set out in section 3485 of this title with regard to individuals pursuing at least three-quarter-time programs of education referred to in subsection (b) of such section.

(Dec. 18, 1989, P. L. 101-237, Title IV, § 406(a), 103 Stat. 2082; Aug. 6, 1991, P. L. 102-83, § 5(a), (c)(1), 105 Stat. 406.)

HISTORY; ANCILLARY LAWS AND DIRECTIVES

Explanatory notes:
A prior § 1737 (Act Dec. 3, 1974, P. L. 93-508, Title III, § 303(a), 88 Stat. 1591; Aug. 13, 1981, P. L. 97-35, Title XX, § 2005(c), 95 Stat. 783) was repealed by Act Nov. 18, 1988, P. L. 100-689, Title I, Part B, § 124(a), 102 Stat. 4174. It related to education loans.

Effective date of section:
Act Dec. 18, 1989, P. L. 101-237, Title IV, § 406(b), 103 Stat. 2082, provides: "The amendments made by this section [adding this section and amending the table of sections] shall take effect on May 1, 1990.".

Amendments:
1991. Act Aug. 6, 1991, redesignated this section, formerly 38 USCS § 1737, as 38 USCS § 3537.

CODE OF FEDERAL REGULATIONS
Department of Veterans Affairs—Vocational rehabilitation and education, 38 CFR Part 21.

RESEARCH GUIDE
Am Jur:
77 Am Jur 2d, Veterans and Veterans' Laws § 146.

[§ 3538]. [§ 1738. Repealed]

HISTORY; ANCILLARY LAWS AND DIRECTIVES
The bracketed section number "3538" was inserted to preserve numerical continuity following the section number redesignations made by Act Aug. 6, 1991, P. L. 102-83, § 5(a), 105 Stat. 406.

This section (Act Nov. 23, 1977, P. L. 95-202, Title II, § 201(b), 91 Stat. 1437) was repealed by Act Nov. 18, 1988, P. L. 100-689, Title I, Part B, § 124(a), 102 Stat. 4174. The section related to accelerated payment of educational assistance allowances.

SUBCHAPTER V. SPECIAL RESTORATIVE TRAINING

§ 3540. Purpose

The purpose of special restorative training is to overcome, or lessen, the effects of a manifest physical or mental disability which would handicap an eligible person (as defined in section 3501(a)(1)(A) of this title) in the pursuit of a program of education.
(Sept. 2, 1958, P.L. 85-857, § 1, 72 Stat. 1200; Oct. 17, 1980, P. L. 96-466, Title III, Part B, § 331, 94 Stat. 2198; Aug. 6, 1991, P. L. 102-83, § 5(a), (c)(1), 105 Stat. 406.)

HISTORY; ANCILLARY LAWS AND DIRECTIVES
Amendments:
1980. Act Oct. 17, 1980 (effective 10/1/80, as provided by § 802(c)(1) of such Act, which appears as 38 USCS § 3452 note), inserted "(as defined in section 1701(a)(1)(A) of this title)".
1991. Act Aug. 6, 1991, redesignated this section, formerly 38 USCS § 1740, as 38 USCS § 3540.

CODE OF FEDERAL REGULATIONS
Department of Veterans Affairs—Vocational rehabilitation and education, 38 CFR Part 21.

RESEARCH GUIDE
Am Jur:
77 Am Jur 2d, Veterans and Veterans' Laws § 146.

§ 3541. Entitlement to special restorative training

(a) The Secretary at the request of the parent or guardian of an eligible person is authorized—
　(1) to determine whether such person is in need of special restorative training; and

(2) where need is found to exist, to prescribe a course which is suitable to accomplish the purposes of this chapter [38 USCS §§ 3500 et seq.].

Such a course, at the discretion of the Secretary, may contain elements that would contribute toward an ultimate objective of a program of education.

(b) The total period of educational assistance under this subchapter [38 USCS §§ 3540 et seq.] and other subchapters of this chapter [38 USCS §§ 3500 et seq.] may not exceed the amount of entitlement as established in section 3511 of this title, except that the Secretary may extend such period in the case of any person if the Secretary finds that additional assistance is necessary to accomplish the purpose of special restorative training as stated in subsection (a) of this section.

(Sept. 2, 1958, P. L. 85-857, § 1, 72 Stat. 1200; July 7, 1964, P. L. 88-361, § 6, 78 Stat. 298; Oct. 15, 1976, P. L. 94-502, Title III, § 310(21), 90 Stat. 2392, Dec. 18, 1989, P. L. 101-237, Title IV, § 423(b)(1)(A), 103 Stat. 2092; Aug. 6, 1991, P. L. 102-83, § 5(a), (c)(1), 105 Stat. 406.)

HISTORY; ANCILLARY LAWS AND DIRECTIVES

Amendments:

1964. Act July 7, 1964, substituted new subsec. (b) for one which read: "In no event shall the total period of educational assistance under this subchapter and other subchapters of this chapter exceed the amount of entitlement as established in section 1711 of this title.".

1976. Act Oct. 15, 1976 (effective 10/15/76, as provided by § 703(b) of such Act, which appears as 38 USCS § 3693 note), in subsec. (b), substituted "the Administrator" for "he" preceding "finds".

1989. Act Dec. 18, 1989, in subsec. (a), in the introductory and concluding matter, and in subsec. (b), substituted "Secretary" for "Administrator", wherever appearing.

1991. Act Aug. 6, 1991, redesignated this section, formerly 38 USCS § 1741, as 38 USCS § 3541, and amended the references in this section to reflect the redesignations made by § 5(a) of such Act (see Table III preceding 38 USCS § 101).

Other provisions:

Effective date of amendment made by § 6 of Act July 7, 1964. Act Aug. 14, 1964, P. L. 88-433, § 2, 78 Stat. 442, provided: "The amendments made by section 6 of the Act of July 7, 1964 (Public Law 88-361, 78 Stat. 297) [amending this section], shall take effect as of January 1, 1964.".

CODE OF FEDERAL REGULATIONS

Department of Veterans Affairs—Vocational rehabilitation and education, 38 CFR Part 21.

RESEARCH GUIDE

Am Jur:
77 Am Jur 2d, Veterans and Veterans' Laws § 146.

§ 3542. Special training allowance

(a) While the eligible person is enrolled in and pursuing a full-time course of special restorative training, the parent or guardian shall be entitled to receive on behalf of such person a special training allowance computed at the basic rate of $404 per month. If the charges for tuition and fees applicable to any such course are more than $127 per calendar month, the basic monthly allowance may be increased by the amount that such charges exceed $127 a month, upon election by the parent or guardian of the eligible person to have such person's period of entitlement reduced by one day for each $13.46 that the special training allowance paid exceeds the basic monthly allowance.

(b) No payments of a special training allowance shall be made for the same period for which the payment of an educational assistance allowance is made or for any period during which the training is pursued on less than a full-time basis.

(c) Full-time training for the purpose of this section shall be determined by the Secretary with respect to the capacities of the individual trainee.
(Sept. 2, 1958, P. L. 85-857, § 1, 72 Stat. 1200; Sept. 30, 1965, P. L. 89-222, § 2, 79 Stat. 896; March 26, 1970, P. L. 91-219, Title I, § 104(c), 84 Stat. 78; Oct. 24, 1972, P. L. 92-540, Title I, § 103(4), 86 Stat. 1076; Dec. 3, 1974, P. L. 93-508, Title I, § 103(4), 88 Stat. 1580; Jan. 2, 1975, P. L. 93-602, Title II, § 204(b), 88 Stat. 1958; Oct. 15, 1976, P. L. 94-502, Title III, § 301(2), 90 Stat. 2389; Nov. 23, 1977, P. L. 95-202, Title I, § 103(2), 91 Stat. 1435; Oct. 17, 1980, P. L. 96-466, Title II, Part A, § 202(2), Part B, § 212(2), 94 Stat. 2188, 2190; Oct. 24, 1984, P. L. 98-543, Title II, Part A, § 203(2), 98 Stat. 2742; Dec. 18, 1989, P. L. 101-237, Title IV, §§ 403(a)(10), 423(b)(1)(A), 103 Stat. 2080, 2092; Aug. 6, 1991, P. L. 102-83, § 5(a), 105 Stat. 406.)

HISTORY; ANCILLARY LAWS AND DIRECTIVES
Amendments:
1965. Act Sept. 30, 1965 (effective as provided by § 4 of such Act, which appears as 38 USCS § 3532 note), in subsec. (a), substituted "$130", "$41", "$41", and "$4.25" for "$110", "$35", "$35", and "$3.60".
1970. Act March 26, 1970 (effective 2/1/70, as provided by § 301 of such Act, which appears as 38 USCS § 3482 note), substituted new subsec. (a) for one which read: "While the eligible person is enrolled in and pursuing a full-time course of special restorative training, the parent or guardian shall be entitled to receive on his behalf a special training allowance computed at the basic rate of $130 per month. If the charges for tuition and fees applicable to any such course are more than $41 per calendar month the basic monthly allowance may be increased by the amount that such charges exceed $41 a month, upon election by the parent or guardian of the eligible person to have such person's period of entitlement reduced by one day for each $4.25 that the special training allowance paid exceeds the basic monthly allowance.".
1972. Act Oct. 24, 1972 (effective 10/1/72, as provided by § 601(a) of such Act, which appears as 38 USCS § 3482 note), substituted new subsec. (a) for one which read: "While the eligible person is enrolled in and pursuing a full-time course of special restorative training, the parent or guardian shall be entitled to receive on his behalf a special training allowance computed at the basic rate of $175 per month. If the charges for tuition and fees ap-

plicable to any such course are more than $55 per calendar month the basic monthly allowance may be increased by the amount that such charges exceed $55 a month, upon election by the parent or guardian of the eligible person to have such person's period of entitlement reduced by one day for each $6.80 that the special training allowance paid exceeds the basic monthly allowance.".

1974. Act Dec. 3, 1974 (effective 9/1/74, as provided by § 501 of such Act, which appears as 38 USCS § 3482 note), substituted new subsec. (a) for one which read: "While the eligible person is enrolled in and pursuing a full-time course of special restorative training, the parent or guardian shall be entitled to receive on his behalf a special training allowance computed at the basic rate of $220 per month. If the charges for tuition and fees applicable to any such course are more that $69 per calendar month, the basic monthly allowance may be increased by the amount that such charges exceed $69 a month, upon election by the parent or guardian of the eligible person to have such person's period of entitlement reduced by one day for each $7.35 that the special training allowance paid exceeds the basic monthly allowance.".

1975. Act Jan. 2, 1975 (effective 1/1/75, as provided by § 206 of such Act, which appears as 38 USCS § 3482 note), substituted new subsec. (a) for one which read: "While the eligible person is enrolled in and pursuing a full-time course of special restorative training, the parent or guardian shall be entitled to receive on behalf of such person a special training allowance computed at the basic rate of $260 per month. If the charges for tuition and fees applicable to any such course are more than $82 per calendar month, the basic monthly allowance may be increased by the amount that such charges exceed $82 a month, upon election by the parent or guardian of the eligible person to have such person's period of entitlement reduced by one day for each $8.69 that the special training allowance paid exceeds the basic monthly allowance.".

1976. Act Oct. 15, 1976 (effective 10/1/76, as provided by § 703(a) of such Act, which appears as 38 USCS § 3693 note), substituted new subsec. (a) for one which read: "While the eligible person is enrolled in and pursuing a full-time course of special restorative training, the parent or guardian shall be entitled to receive on behalf of such person a special training allowance computed at the basic rate of $270 per month. If the charges for tuition and fees applicable to any such course are more than $85 per calendar month, the basic monthly allowance may be increased by the amount that such charges exceed $85 a month, upon election by the parent or guardian of the eligible person to have such person's period of entitlement reduced by one day for each $9.02 that the special training allowance paid exceeds the basic monthly allowance.".

1977. Act Nov. 23, 1977 (effective 10/1/1977, as provided by § 501 of such Act, which appears as 38 USCS § 101 note), in subsec. (a), substituted "$311", "$98", "$98", and "$10.40" for "$292", "$92", $92", and "$9.76", respectively.

1980. Act Oct. 17, 1980, § 202(2) (effective 10/1/80, as provided by § 802(b)(1) of such Act, which appears as 38 USCS § 3482 note), in subsec. (a), substituted "$327", "$103", "$103", and "$10.92" for "$311", "$98", "$98", and "$10.40", respectively.

Act Oct. 17, 1980, § 212(2) (effective 1/1/81, as provided by § 802(b)(2) of such Act, which appears as 38 USCS § 3482 note), in subsec. (a), as amended by § 202(2) of Act Oct. 17, 1980, substituted "$342", "$108", "$108", and "$11.44" for "$327", "$103", "$10.92", respectively.

1984. Act Oct. 24, 1984 (effective 10/1/78, as provided by § 205 of such Act, which appears as 38 USCS § 3108 note), in subsec. (a), substituted "$376" for "$342", "$119" for "$108" in both places it appears, and "$12.58" for "$11.44".

1989. Act Dec. 18, 1989 (effective 1/1/90, as provided by § 403(c) of such Act, which appears as 38 USCS § 3532 note), in subsec. (a), substituted "$404" and "$13.46" for "$376" and "$12.58", respectively, and substituted "$127" for "$119" in two places.

Such Act further, in subsec. (c), substituted "Secretary" for "Administrator".

1991. Act Aug. 6, 1991, redesignated this section, formerly 38 USCS § 1742, as 38 USCS § 3542.

CODE OF FEDERAL REGULATIONS

Department of Veterans Affairs—Vocational rehabilitation and education, 38 CFR Part 21.

CROSS REFERENCES

This section is referred to in 38 USCS § 3565.

RESEARCH GUIDE

Am Jur:
77 Am Jur 2d, Veterans and Veterans' Laws § 146.

§ 3543. Special administrative provisions

(a) In carrying out the Secretary's responsibilities under this chapter [38 USCS §§ 3500 et seq.] the Secretary may by agreement arrange with public or private educational institutions or others to provide training arrangements as may be suitable and necessary to accomplish the purposes of this subchapter [38 USCS §§ 3540 et seq.]. In any instance where the Secretary finds that a customary tuition charge is not applicable, the Secretary may agree on the fair and reasonable amounts which may be charged the parent or guardian for the training provided to an eligible person.

(b) The Secretary shall make such rules and regulations as the Secretary may deem necessary in order to promote good conduct on the part of the persons who are following courses of special restorative training and otherwise to carry out the purposes of this chapter [38 USCS §§ 3500 et seq.].

(Sept. 2, 1958, P. L. 85-857, § 1, 72 Stat. 1200; Oct. 15, 1976, P. L. 94-502, Title III, § 310(22), 90 Stat. 2392; Dec. 18, 1989, P. L. 101-237, Title IV, § 423(b)(1)(A), (2), 103 Stat. 2092; Aug. 6, 1991, P. L. 102-83, § 5(a), 105 Stat. 406.)

HISTORY; ANCILLARY LAWS AND DIRECTIVES
Amendments:
1976. Act Oct. 15, 1976 (effective 10/15/76, as provided by § 703(b) of such Act, which appears as 38 USCS § 3693 note), in subsec. (a),

substituted "the Administrator's" for "his" and substituted "the Administrator" for "he" preceding "may agree"; in subsec. (b), substituted "the Administrator" for "he" preceding "may deem".

1989. Act Dec. 18, 1989, in subsec. (a), substituted "Secretary's" for "Administrator's" and "Secretary" for "Administrator" wherever appearing; and in subsec. (b), substituted "Secretary" for "Administrator".

1991. Act Aug. 6, 1991, redesignated this section, formerly 38 USCS § 1743, as 38 USCS § 3543.

CODE OF FEDERAL REGULATIONS

Department of Veterans Affairs—Vocational rehabilitation and education, 38 CFR Part 21.

RESEARCH GUIDE

Am Jur:
77 Am Jur 2d, Veterans and Veterans' Laws § 146.

SUBCHAPTER VI. MISCELLANEOUS PROVISIONS

§ 3561. Authority and duties of Secretary

(a) The Secretary may provide the educational and vocational counseling authorized under section 3520 of this title, and may provide additional counseling if the Secretary deems it to be necessary to accomplish the purposes of this chapter [38 USCS §§ 3500 et seq.].

(b) Where any provision of this chapter [38 USCS §§ 3500 et seq.] authorizes or requires any function, power, or duty to be exercised by a State, or by any officer or agency thereof, such function, power, or duty shall, with respect to the Republic of the Philippines, be exercised by the Secretary.

(Sept. 2, 1958, P. L. 85-857, § 1, 72 Stat. 1200; March 3, 1966, P. L. 89-358, § 3(a)(1), 80 Stat. 19; Oct. 15, 1976, P. L. 94-502, Title III, § 310(23), 90 Stat. 2392; Oct. 17, 1980, P. L. 96-466, Title III, Part B, § 323(b), 94 Stat. 2196; Dec. 18, 1989, P. L. 101-237, Title IV, § 423(b)(1)(A), 103 Stat. 2092; Aug. 6, 1991, P. L. 102-83, § 5(a), (c)(1), 105 Stat. 406.)

HISTORY; ANCILLARY LAWS AND DIRECTIVES

Amendments:
1966. Act March 3, 1966 (effective 3/3/66, as provided by § 12(a) of such Act), substituted new section for one which read:

"(a) Payments under this chapter shall be subject to audit and review by the General Accounting Office, as provided by the Budget and Accounting Act of 1921, and the Budget and Accounting Procedures Act of 1950.

"(b) The Administrator may provide the educational and vocational counseling required under section 1720 of this title, and may provide or require additional counseling if he deems it to be necessary to accomplish the purposes of this chapter.

"(c) In carrying out his functions under this chapter, the Administrator may utilize the facilities and services of any other Federal department or agency.

Any such utilization shall be pursuant to proper agreement with the Federal department or agency concerned; and payment to cover the cost thereof shall be made either in advance or by way of reimbursement, as may be provided in such agreement.

"(d) Where any provision of this chapter authorizes or requires any function, power, or duty to be exercised by a State, or by any officer or agency thereof, such function, power, or duty shall, with respect to the Republic of the Philippines, be exercised by the Administrator.".

1976. Act Oct. 15, 1976 (effective 10/15/76, as provided by § 703(b) of such Act, which appears as 38 USCS § 3693 note), in subsec. (a), substituted "the Administrator" for "he" preceding "deems".

1980. Act Oct. 17, 1980 (effective 10/1/80, as provided by § 802(c)(1) of such Act, which appears as 38 USCS § 3452 note), in subsec. (a), substituted "authorized" for "required", and deleted "or require" preceding "additional counseling".

1989. Act Dec. 18, 1989, in the section catchline and throughout the section, substituted "Secretary" for "Administrator", wherever appearing.

1991. Act Aug. 6, 1991, redesignated this section, formerly 38 USCS § 1761, as 38 USCS § 3561, and amended the references in this section to reflect the redesignations made by § 5(a) of such Act (see Table III preceding 38 USCS § 101).

CODE OF FEDERAL REGULATIONS

Department of Veterans Affairs—Vocational rehabilitation and education, 38 CFR Part 21.

§ 3562. Nonduplication of benefits

The commencement of a program of education or special restorative training under this chapter [38 USCS §§ 3500 et seq.] shall be a bar (1) to subsequent payments of compensation, dependency and indemnity compensation, or pension based on the death of a parent to an eligible person over the age of eighteen by reason of pursuing a course in an educational institution, or (2) to increased rates, or additional amounts, of compensation, dependency and indemnity compensation, or pension because of such a person whether eligibility is based upon the death or upon the total permanent disability of the parent.
(Sept. 2, 1958, P. L. 85-857, § 1, 72 Stat. 1201; July 7, 1964, P. L. 88-361, § 4, 78 Stat. 298; March 3, 1966, P. L. 89-358, § 3(a)(2), 80 Stat. 20; Aug. 6, 1991, P. L. 102-83, § 5(a), 105 Stat. 406.)

HISTORY; ANCILLARY LAWS AND DIRECTIVES

Amendments:

1964. Act July 7, 1964, in subsec. (a), inserted "whether eligibility is based upon the death or upon the total permanent disability of the parent".

1966. Act March 3, 1966 (effective 3/3/66, as provided by § 12(a) of such Act, which appears as 38 USCS § 3693 note), deleted "(a)" preceding "The commencement" and deleted subsec. (b) which read: "(b) No educational assistance allowance or special training allowance shall be paid on behalf of any eligible person under this chapter for any period during which such person is enrolled in and pursuing a course of education or training paid for by the United States under any provision of law other than this chapter, where the payment of an allowance would constitute a duplication of benefits paid from the Federal Treasury to the eligible person or to his parent or guardian in his behalf.".

1991. Act Aug. 6, 1991, redesignated this section, formerly 38 USCS § 1762, as 38 USCS § 3562.

CODE OF FEDERAL REGULATIONS

Department of Veterans Affairs—Vocational rehabilitation and education, 38 CFR Part 21.

RESEARCH GUIDE

Am Jur:
77 Am Jur 2d, Veterans and Veterans' Laws § 146.

§ 3563. Notification of eligibility

The Secretary shall notify the parent or guardian of each eligible person defined in section 3501(a)(1)(A) of this title of the educational assistance available to such person under this chapter [38 USCS §§ 3500 et seq.]. Such notification shall be provided not later than the month in which such eligible person attains such person's thirteenth birthday or as soon thereafter as feasible.

(Added March 26, 1970, P. L. 91-219, Title II, § 207(a), 84 Stat. 82; Oct. 15, 1976, P. L. 94-502, Title III, § 310(24), 90 Stat. 2392; Oct. 12, 1982, P. L. 97-295, § 4(46), 96 Stat. 1308; Dec. 18, 1989, P. L. 101-237, Title IV, § 423(b)(1)(A), 103 Stat. 2092; Aug. 6, 1991, P. L. 102-83, § 5(a), (c)(1), 105 Stat. 406.)

HISTORY; ANCILLARY LAWS AND DIRECTIVES

Explanatory notes:
A prior § 1763 (Act Sept. 2, 1958, P. L. 85-857, § 1, 72 Stat. 1201) was repealed by Act March 3, 1966, P. L. 89-358, § 3(a)(3), 80 Stat. 20, effective March 3, 1966, as provided by § 12(a) of such Act. This section provided for control by agencies of the United States. For similar provisions, see 38 USCS § 3682.

Amendments:
1976. Act Oct. 15, 1976 (effective 10/15/76, as provided by § 703(b) of such Act, which appears as 38 USCS § 3693 note), substituted "such person's" for "his".

1982. Act Oct. 12, 1982 substituted "title" for "chapter".

1989. Act Dec. 18, 1989, substituted "Secretary" for "Administrator".

1991. Act Aug. 6, 1991, redesignated this section, formerly 38 USCS § 1763, as 38 USCS § 3563, and amended the references in this section to reflect the redesignations made by § 5(a) of such Act (see Table III preceding 38 USCS § 101).

Other provisions:
Application and construction of the Oct. 12, 1982 amendment of this section. For provisions as to the application and construction of the Oct.

38 USCS § 3563 Veterans' Benefits

12, 1982 amendment of this section, see § 5 of such Act, which appears as 10 USCS § 101 note.

CODE OF FEDERAL REGULATIONS
Department of Veterans Affairs—Vocational rehabilitation and education, 38 CFR Part 21.

RESEARCH GUIDE
Am Jur:
77 Am Jur 2d, Veterans and Veterans' Laws § 146.

[§ 3564]. [§ 1764. Repealed]

HISTORY; ANCILLARY LAWS AND DIRECTIVES
The bracketed section number "3564" was inserted to preserve numerical continuity following the section number redesignations made by Act Aug. 6, 1991, P. L. 102-83, § 5(a), 105 Stat. 406.

This section (Act Sept. 2, 1958, P. L. 85-857, § 1, 72 Stat. 1201) was repealed by Act March 3, 1966, P. L. 89-358, § 3(a)(3), 80 Stat. 20, effective March 3, 1966, as provided by § 12(a) of Act March 3, 1966. This section provided for dismissal for conflict of interest reasons. For similar provisions, see 38 USCS § 3683.

SUBCHAPTER VII. PHILIPPINE COMMONWEALTH ARMY AND PHILIPPINE SCOUTS

§ 3565. Children of certain Philippine veterans

Basic Eligibility

(a) The term "eligible person" as used in section 3501(a)(1) of this title includes the children of those Commonwealth Army veterans and "New" Philippine Scouts who meet the requirements of service-connected disability or death, based on service as defined in section 3566 of this title.

Administrative Provisions

(b) The provisions of this chapter [38 USCS §§ 3500 et seq.] and chapter 36 [38 USCS §§ 3670 et seq.] shall apply to the educational assistance for children of Commonwealth Army veterans and "New" Philippine Scouts, except that—

(1) educational assistance allowances authorized by section 3532 of this title and the special training allowance authorized by section 3542 of this title shall be paid the rate of $0.50 for each dollar, and

(2) any reference to a State approving agency shall be deemed to refer to the Secretary.

Delimiting Dates

(c) In the case of any individual who is an eligible person solely by virtue of

READJUSTMENT BENEFITS 38 USCS § 3565

subsection (a) of this section, and who is above the age of seventeen years and below the age of twenty-three years on September 30, 1966, the period referred to in section 3512 of this title shall not end until the expiration of the five-year period which begins on September 30, 1966.
(Added Sept. 30, 1966, P. L. 89-613, § 1, 80 Stat. 861; June 11, 1969, P. L. 91-24, § 9(c), 83 Stat. 34; Oct. 12, 1982, P. L. 97-295, § 4(47), 96 Stat. 1308; Dec. 18, 1989, P. L. 101-237, Title IV, § 423(b)(1)(A), 103 Stat. 2092; Aug. 6, 1991, P. L. 102-83, § 5(a), (c)(1), 105 Stat. 406; Nov. 2, 1994, P. L. 103-446, Title V, § 507(b), 108 Stat. 4664.)

HISTORY; ANCILLARY LAWS AND DIRECTIVES

Explanatory notes:
A prior § 1765 (Act Sept. 2, 1958, P. L. 85-857, § 1, 72 Stat. 1202) was repealed by Act March 3, 1966, P. L. 89-358, § 3(a)(3), 80 Stat. 20, effective March 3, 1966, as provided by § 12(a) of Act March 3, 1966. Act March 3, 1966, P. L. 89-358, § 12(b), 80 Stat. 28, provided that the provisions of former subsec. (b) of § 1765, in effect immediately before March 3, 1966, should remain in effect until May 31, 1966. This section provided for reports by institutions. For similar provisions, see 38 USCS § 3684.

Amendments:
1969. Act June 11, 1969, substituted new subsec. (c) for one which read: "In the case of any individual who is an 'eligible person' solely by virtue of subsection (a) of this section, and who is above the age of seventeen years and below the age of twenty-three years on the date of enactment of this section, the period referred to in section 1712 of this title shall not end until the expiration of the five-year period which begins on the date of enactment of such section.".
1982. Act Oct. 12, 1982, in subsec. (a), inserted "of this title" following "section 1766".
1989. Act Dec. 18, 1989, in subsec. (b)(2), substituted "Secretary" for "Administrator".
1991. Act Aug. 6, 1991, redesignated this section, formerly 38 USCS § 1765, as 38 USCS § 3565, and amended the references in this section to reflect the redesignations made by § 5(a) of such Act (see Table III preceding 38 USCS § 101).
1994. Act Nov. 2, 1994 (applicable to payments made after 12/31/94, as provided by § 507(c) of such Act, which appears as 38 USCS § 107 note), in subsec. (b)(1), substituted "the rate of" for "a rate in Phillipine pesos equivalent to".

Other provisions:
Application and construction of the Oct. 12, 1982 amendment of this section. For provisions as to the application and construction of the Oct. 12, 1982 amendment of this section, see § 5 of such Act, which appears as 10 USCS § 101 note.

CODE OF FEDERAL REGULATIONS

Department of Veterans Affairs—Vocational rehabilitation and education, 38 CFR Part 21.

RESEARCH GUIDE
Am Jur:
77 Am Jur 2d, Veterans and Veterans' Laws § 146.

§ 3566. Definitions

(a) The term "Commonwealth Army veterans" means persons who served before July 1, 1946, in the organized military forces of the Government of the Philippines, while such forces were in the service of the Armed Forces pursuant to the military order of the President dated July 26, 1941, including among such military forces organized guerrilla forces under commanders appointed, designated, or subsequently recognized by the Commander-in-Chief, Southwest Pacific Area, or other competent authority in the Army of the United States, and who were discharged or released from such service under conditions other than dishonorable.

(b) The term "'New' Philippine Scouts" means Philippine Scouts who served under section 14 of the Armed Forces Voluntary Recruitment Act of 1945, and who were discharged or released from such service under conditions other than dishonorable.
(Added Sept. 30, 1966, P. L. 89-613, § 1, 80 Stat. 861; Aug. 6, 1991, P. L. 102-83, § 5(a), 105 Stat. 406.)

HISTORY; ANCILLARY LAWS AND DIRECTIVES

References in text:
"Section 14 of the Armed Forces Voluntary Recruitment Act of 1945", referred to in subsec. (b), is Act Oct. 6, 1945, ch 393, § 14, 59 Stat. 543, which was formerly classified to 10 USC § 637, and omitted in the general revision of Title 10 by Act Aug. 10, 1956, ch 1041, 70A Stat. 1.

Explanatory notes:
A prior § 1766 (Act Sept. 2, 1958, P. L. 85-857, § 1, 72 Stat. 1202) was repealed by Act March 3, 1966, P. L. 89-358, § 3(a)(3), 80 Stat. 20, effective March 3, 1966, as provided by § 12(a) of Act March 3, 1966. This section related to overpayments of eligible persons. For similar provisions, see 38 USCS § 3685.

Amendments:
1991. Act Aug. 6, 1991, redesignated this section, formerly 38 USCS § 1766, as 38 USCS § 3566.

CROSS REFERENCES
This section is referred to in 38 USCS §§ 101, 3565.

RESEARCH GUIDE
Am Jur:
77 Am Jur 2d, Veterans and Veterans' Laws § 146.

[§§ 3567, 3568]. [§§ 1767, 1768. Repealed]

HISTORY; ANCILLARY LAWS AND DIRECTIVES

The bracketed section numbers "3567" and "3568" were inserted to preserve numerical continuity following the section number redesignations made by Act Aug. 6, 1991, P. L. 102-83, § 5(a), 105 Stat. 406.

These sections (§§ 1767, 1768—Act Sept. 2, 1958, P. L. 85-857, § 1, 72 Stat. 1202) were repealed by Act March 3, 1966, P. L. 89-358, § 3(a)(3), 80 Stat. 20, effective March 3, 1966, as provided by § 12(a) of Act March 3, 1966. They related to the examination of records and false or misleading statements.

CHAPTER 36. ADMINISTRATION OF EDUCATIONAL BENEFITS

SUBCHAPTER I. STATE APPROVING AGENCIES

Section
3670. Scope of approval.
3671. Designation.
3672. Approval of courses.
3673. Cooperation.
3674. Reimbursement of expenses.
3674A. Evaluations of agency performance; qualifications and performance of agency personnel.
3675. Approval of accredited courses.
3676. Approval of nonaccredited courses.
3677. Approval of training on the job.
3678. Notice of approval of courses.
3679. Disapproval of courses.

SUBCHAPTER II. MISCELLANEOUS PROVISIONS

3680. Payment of educational assistance or subsistence allowances.
3680A. Disapproval of enrollment in certain courses.
3681. Limitations on educational assistance.
3682. Control by agencies of the United States.
3683. Conflicting interests.
3684. Reports by veterans, eligible persons, and institutions; reporting fee.
3684A. Procedures relating to computer matching programs.
3685. Overpayments to eligible persons or veterans.
3686. Correspondence courses.
3687. Apprenticeship or other on-job training.
3688. Measurement of courses.
[3689. Repealed]
3690. Overcharges by educational institutions; discontinuance of allowances; examination of records; false or misleading statements.
3691. Change of program.
3692. Advisory committee.
3693. Compliance surveys.
3694. Use of other Federal agencies.
3695. Limitation on period of assistance under two or more programs.
3696. Limitation on certain advertising, sales, and enrollment practices.
3697. Funding of contract educational and vocational counseling.
3697A. Educational and vocational counseling.

SUBCHAPTER III. EDUCATION LOANS

3698. Eligibility for loans; amount and conditions of loans; interest rate on loans.
3699. Revolving fund; insurance.

HISTORY; ANCILLARY LAWS AND DIRECTIVES

1966. Act March 3, 1966, P. L. 89-358, § 3(a)(4), 80 Stat. 20 (effective 3/3/66, as provided by § 12(a) of such Act), substituted

"CHAPTER 36. ADMINISTRATION OF EDUCATIONAL BENEFITS

"SUBCHAPTER I. STATE APPROVING AGENCIES"

"1770. Scope of approval.
"1771. Designation.
"1772. Approval of courses.
"1773. Cooperation.
"1774. Reimbursement of expenses.
"1775. Approval of accredited courses.
"1776. Approval of nonaccredited courses.
"1777. Notice of approval of courses.
"1778. Disapproval of courses.

"SUBCHAPTER II. MISCELLANEOUS PROVISIONS

"1781. Nonduplication of benefits.
"1782. Control by agencies of the United States.
"1783. Conflicting interests.
"1784. Reports by institutions.
"1785. Overpayments to eligible persons or veterans.
"1786. Examination of records.
"1787. False or misleading statements.
"1788. Advisory committee.
"1789. Institutions listed by Attorney General.
"1790. Use of other Federal agencies.

"SUBCHAPTER I. STATE APPROVING AGENCIES"
for heading in Chapter 35 which read: "SUBCHAPTER VII. STATE APPROVING AGENCIES".

1967. Act Aug. 31, 1967, P. L. 90-77, Title III, §§ 304(e), 308(b), 81 Stat. 188 (effective on the first day of the first calendar month which begins more than 10 days after Aug. 31, 1967, as provided by § 405(a) of such Act), substituted items 1777-1779 for items 1777 and 1778 which read:

"1777. Notice of approval of courses.

"1778. Disapproval of courses."; and substituted new item 1784 for one which read: "1784. Reports by institutions.".

1968. Act Oct. 23, 1968, P. L. 90-631, § 1(d)(2), 82 Stat. 1331 (effective on the first day of the second calendar month which begins after Oct. 23, 1968, as provided by § 6(a) of such Act), added item 1791.

1970. Act March 26, 1970, P. L. 91-219, Title II, § 213(2), 84 Stat. 84, substituted item 1781 for one which read: "Nonduplication of benefits.".

1972. Act Oct. 24, 1972, P. L. 92-540, Title IV, § 406, 86 Stat. 1091, added item 1780 and substituted items 1786-1795 for items 1786-1791 which read:

"1786. Examination of records.
"1787. False or misleading statements.
"1788. Advisory committee.

"1789. Institutions listed by Attorney General.
"1790. Use of other Federal agencies.
"1791. Limitation on period of assistance under two or more programs.".
1974. Act Dec. 3, 1974, P. L. 93-508, Title II, § 212(b), 83 Stat. 1586 (effective 12/3/74, as provided by § 503 of such Act), added item 1796.
Act Dec. 3, 1974, P. L. 93-508, Title III, § 301(b), 88 Stat. 1591 (effective 1/1/75, as provided by § 502 of such Act), added subchapter III heading and items 1798 and 1799.
1976. Act Oct. 15, 1976, P. L. 94-502, Title V, § 511(2), 90 Stat. 2402 (effective 10/15/76, as provided by § 703(b) of such Act), substituted item 1793 for one which read: "Institutions listed by Attorney General.".
1980. Act Oct. 17, 1980, P. L. 96-466, Title III, Part C, § 343(b)(2), 94 Stat. 2199 (effective 10/1/80, as provided by § 802(c)(1) of such Act), substituted item 1784 for one which read: "Reports by institutions; reporting fee.".
1982. Act Oct. 12, 1982, P. L. 97-295, § 4(48), 96 Stat. 1308, amended the analysis of this chapter in the item relating to section 1780 by inserting "assistance".
1988. Act May 20, 1988, P. L. 100-323, § 13(b)(1)(B), 102 Stat. 573, effective on enactment as provided by § 16(a) of such Act, which appears as 38 USCS § 3104 note, amended the analysis of this chapter by adding item 1774A.
Act Nov. 18, 1988, P. L. 100-689, Title I, Part B, § 124(c)(3), 102 Stat. 4175, amended the analysis of this chapter by substituting "SUBCHAPTER III. EDUCATION LOANS" for "SUBCHAPTER III. EDUCATION LOANS TO ELIGIBLE VETERANS AND ELIGIBLE PERSONS".
Act Nov. 18, 1988, P. L. 100-687, Div B, Title XIII, § 1302(b), 102 Stat. 4128, amended the analysis of this chapter by adding item 1797.
1990. Act Aug. 15, 1990, P. L. 101-366, Title II, § 206(a), 104 Stat. 441, amended the analysis of this chapter by adding item 1784A.
1991. Act March 22, 1991, P. L. 102-16, § 2(b)(4), 105 Stat. 49, amended the analysis of this chapter by adding item 1797A.
Act Aug. 6, 1991, P. L. 102-83, § 5(b)(1), 105 Stat. 406, revised the analysis of this Chapter by amending the section numbers in accordance with the redesignations made by § 5(a) of such Act (see Table III preceding 38 USCS § 101).
1992. Act Oct. 29, 1992, P. L. 102-568, Title III, § 313(a)(8), 106 Stat. 4333, amended the analysis of this chapter by adding item 3680A.
1996. Act Oct. 9, 1996, P. L. 104-275, Title I, § 103(a)(1)(B), 110 Stat. 3326, amended the analysis of this chapter by deleting item 3689, which read: "3689. Period of operation for approval.".

Other provisions:
Application and construction of Oct. 12, 1982 amendment. For provisions as to the application and construction of the Oct. 12, 1982 amendment of this chapter analysis, see § 5 of such Act, which appears as 10 USCS § 101 note.

SUBCHAPTER I. STATE APPROVING AGENCIES

§ 3670. Scope of approval

(a) A course approved under and for the purposes of this chapter [38 USCS

§§ 3670 et seq.] shall be deemed approved for the purposes of chapters 34 and 35 of this title [38 USCS §§ 3451 et seq. and 3500 et seq.].

(b) Any course approved under chapter 33 of this title, prior to February 1, 1965, under subchapter VII of chapter 35 of this title, prior to March 3, 1966, and not disapproved under section 3483, section 3456 (as in effect prior to February 1, 1965), or section 3679 of this title, shall be deemed approved for the purposes of this chapter [38 USCS §§ 3670 et seq.].

(Added March 3, 1966, P. L. 89-358, § 3(a)(5), 80 Stat. 20; Oct. 24, 1972, P. L. 92-540, Title IV, § 403(1), 86 Stat. 1090; Oct. 12, 1982, P. L. 97-295, § 4(49), 96 Stat. 1308; Aug. 6, 1991, P. L. 102-83, § 5(a), (c)(1), 105 Stat. 406.)

HISTORY; ANCILLARY LAWS AND DIRECTIVES

References in text:
"Chapter 33 of this title, prior to February 1, 1965", referred to in subsec. (b), is Act Sept. 2, 1958, P. L. 85-857, § 1, 72 Stat. 1174, which was classified to 38 USC §§ 1601, 1610–1613, 1620–1626, 1631–1634, 1641–1645, 1651–1656, and 1661–1669, prior to repeal by Act March 3, 1966, P. L. 89-358, § 4(a), 80 Stat. 23, effective March 3, 1966, as provided by § 12(a) of Act March 3, 1966.

"Subchapter VII of chapter 35 of this title, prior to the March 3, 1966", referred to in subsec. (b), is Act Sept. 23, 1963, P. L. 88-126, § 1, 77 Stat. 158, which was classified to 38 USC §§ 1771-1778 in subchapter VII of chapter 35 and in effect, redesignated as §§ 1771–1778 in subchapter I of chapter 36 by Act March 3, 1966, P. L. 89-358, § 3(a)(4), 80 Stat. 20, effective March 3, 1966, as provided by § 12(a) of Act March 3, 1966.

Amendments:
1972. Act Oct. 24, 1972, in subsec. (b), substituted "1683" for "1686".

1982. Act Oct. 12, 1982, in subsec. (b), substituted "March 3, 1966" for "the date of enactment of this chapter"; and substituted "1779" for "1778".

1991. Act Aug. 6, 1991, redesignated this section, formerly 38 USCS § 1770, as 38 USCS § 3670, and amended the references in this section to reflect the redesignations made by § 5(a) of such Act (see Table III preceding 38 USCS § 101).

Other provisions:
Application and construction of the Oct. 12, 1982 amendment of this section. For provisions as to the application and construction of the Oct. 12, 1982 amendment of this section, see § 5 of such Act, which appears as 10 USCS § 101 note.

CODE OF FEDERAL REGULATIONS

Department of Veterans Affairs—Vocational rehabilitation and education, 38 CFR Part 21.

Department of Veterans Affairs—Loan guaranty and vocational rehabilitation and counseling programs, 48 CFR Part 871.

RESEARCH GUIDE
Am Jur:
77 Am Jur 2d, Veterans and Veterans' Laws §§ 61, 132, 144.

§ 3671. Designation

(a) Unless otherwise established by the law of the State concerned, the chief executive of each State is requested to create or designate a State department or agency as the "State approving agency" for such State for the purposes of this chapter and chapters 34 and 35 of this title [38 USCS §§ 3670 et seq., 3451 et seq., and 3500 et seq.].

(b)(1) If any State fails or declines to create or designate a State approving agency, or fails to enter into an agreement under section 3674(a), the provisions of this chapter [38 USCS §§ 3670 et seq.] which refer to the State approving agency shall, with respect to such State, be deemed to refer to the Secretary.

(2) In the case of courses subject to approval by the Secretary under section 3672 of this title, the provisions of this chapter [38 USCS §§ 3670 et seq.] which refer to a State approving agency shall be deemed to refer to the Secretary.

(Added Sept. 23, 1963, P. L. 88-126, § 1, 77 Stat. 158; March 3, 1966, P. L. 89-358, § 3(a)(6), 80 Stat. 20; Oct. 24, 1972, P. L. 92-540, Title IV, § 403(2), 86 Stat. 1090; Oct. 15, 1976, P. L. 94-502, Title V, § 513(a)(1), 90 Stat. 2402; May 20, 1988, P. L. 100-323, § 13(b)(4), 102 Stat. 573; Dec. 18, 1989, P. L. 101-237, Title IV, § 423(b)(1)(A), 103 Stat. 2092; Aug. 6, 1991, P. L. 102-83, § 5(a), (c)(1), 105 Stat. 406.)

HISTORY; ANCILLARY LAWS AND DIRECTIVES
Amendments:
1966. Act March 3, 1966 (effective 3/3/66, as provided by § 12(a) of such Act), in subsec. (a), substituted "chapters 34 and 35 of this title" for "this chapter after the date for the expiration of all education and training provided in chapter 33 of this title. Such agency may be the agency designated or created in accordance with section 1641 of this title".

1972. Act Oct. 24, 1972, in subsec. (a), inserted "this chapter and".

1976. Act Oct. 15, 1976 (effective 10/15/76, as provided by § 703(b) of such Act, which appears as 38 USCS § 3693 note), in subsec. (a), substituted "such" for "his".

1988. Act May 20, 1988 (effective on enactment as provided by § 16(a) of such Act, which appears as 38 USCS § 3104 note), in subsec. (b)(1), substituted "approving agency, or fails to enter into an agreement under section 1774(a)," for "approving agency,".

1989. Act Dec. 18. 1989, in subsec. (b), substituted "Secretary" for "Administrator", wherever appearing.

1991. Act Aug. 6, 1991, redesignated this section, formerly 38 USCS § 1771, as 38 USCS § 3671, and amended the references in this section to reflect the redesignations made by § 5(a) of such Act (see Table III preceding 38 USCS § 101).

CODE OF FEDERAL REGULATIONS

Department of Veterans Affairs—Vocational rehabilitation and education, 38 CFR Part 21.

Department of Veterans Affairs—Loan guaranty and vocational rehabilitation and counseling programs, 48 CFR Part 871.

§ 3672. Approval of courses

(a) An eligible person or veteran shall receive the benefits of this chapter and chapters 34 and 35 of this title [38 USCS §§ 3670 et seq., 3451 et seq., and 3500 et seq.] while enrolled in a course of education offered by an educational institution only if (1) such course is approved as provided in this chapter and chapters 34 and 35 of this title [38 USCS §§ 3670 et seq., 3451 et seq., and 3500 et seq.] by the State approving agency for the State where such educational institution is located, or by the Secretary, or (2) such course is approved (A) for the enrollment of the particular individual under the provisions of section 3536 of this title or (B) for special restorative training under subchapter V of chapter 35 of this title [38 USCS §§ 3540 et seq.]. Approval of courses by State approving agencies shall be in accordance with the provisions of this chapter and chapters 34 and 35 of this title [38 USCS §§ 3670 et seq., 3451 et seq., and 3500 et seq.] and such other regulations and policies as the State approving agency may adopt. Each State approving agency shall furnish the Secretary with a current list of educational institutions specifying courses which it has approved, and, in addition to such list, it shall furnish such other information to the Secretary as it and the Secretary may determine to be necessary to carry out the purposes of this chapter and chapters 34 and 35 of this title [38 USCS §§ 3670 et seq., 3451 et seq., and 3500 et seq.]. Each State approving agency shall notify the Secretary of the disapproval of any course previously approved and shall set forth the reasons for such disapproval.

(b) The Secretary shall be responsible for the approval of courses of education offered by any agency of the Federal Government authorized under other laws to supervise such education. The Secretary may approve any course in any other educational institution in accordance with the provisions of this chapter and chapters 34 and 35 of this title [38 USCS §§ 3670 et seq., 3451 et seq., and 3500 et seq.].

(c) In the case of programs of apprenticeship where—
  (1) the standards have been approved by the Secretary of Labor pursuant to section 2 of the Act of August 16, 1937 (popularly known as the "National Apprenticeship Act") (29 U.S.C. 50a), as a national apprenticeship program for operation in more than one State, and
  (2) the training establishment is a carrier directly engaged in interstate commerce which provides such training in more than one State,

the Secretary shall act as a "State approving agency" as such term is used in section 3687(a)(1) of this title and shall be responsible for the approval of all such programs.

(d) Pursuant to regulations prescribed by the Secretary in consultation with the

38 USCS § 3672   VETERANS' BENEFITS

Secretary of Labor, the Secretary shall actively promote the development of programs of training on the job (including programs of apprenticeship) for the purposes of sections 3677 and 3687 of this title and shall utilize the services of disabled veterans' outreach program specialists under section 4103A of this title to promote the development of such programs.

(e) A program of education exclusively by correspondence, and the correspondence portion of a combination correspondence-residence course leading to a vocational objective, that is offered by an educational institution (as defined in section 3452(c) of this title) may be approved only if (1) the educational institution is accredited by an entity recognized by the Secretary of Education, and (2) at least 50 percent of those pursuing such a program or course require six months or more to complete the program or course.

(Added Sept. 23, 1963, P. L. 88-126, § 1, 77 Stat. 158; March 3, 1966, P. L. 89-358, § 3(a)(7), (8), 80 Stat. 20; March 26, 1970, P. L. 91-219, Title II, § 211, 84 Stat. 83; Oct. 24, 1972, P. L. 92-540, Title IV, § 403(3)–(5), 86 Stat. 1090; Oct. 17, 1980, P. L. 96-466, Title V, § 502, 94 Stat. 2203;Oct. 12, 1982, P. L. 97-295, § 4(50), 96 Stat. 1308; Dec. 18, 1989, P. L. 101-237, Title IV, § 423(b)(1)(A), 103 Stat. 2092; Aug. 6, 1991, P. L. 102-83, § 5(a), (c)(1), 105 Stat. 406; Nov. 2, 1994, P. L. 103-446, Title VI, § 605(a)(1), 108 Stat. 4671.)

HISTORY; ANCILLARY LAWS AND DIRECTIVES
Amendments:

1966. Act March 3, 1966 (effective 3/3/66, as provided by § 12(a) of such Act), in subsec. (a), substituted "eligible person or veteran" for "eligible person", substituted "chapters 34 and 35" for "this chapter" following "benefits of", "provided in", "provisions of", and "purposes of", and substituted "under subchapter V of chapter 35 of this title" for "under subchapter V of this chapter"; in subsec. (b), substituted "chapters 34 and 35" for "this chapter".

Such Act further, purported to purported to substitute "chapters 34 and 35" for "this chapter" in the fourth sentence of subsec. (a) of this section. However, such amendment could not be executed because because such amendment had already been executed.

1970. Act March 26, 1970, added subsec. (c)

1972. Act Oct. 24, 1972, in subsec. (a), inserted "this chapter and" wherever appearing, and substituted "1736" for "1737"; in subsec. (b), inserted "this chapter and"; and in subsec. (c), concluding matter, substituted "1787(a)(1)" for "1683(a)(1)".

1980. Act Oct. 17, 1980 (effective 10/1/80, as provided by § 802(e) of such Act, which appears as 38 USCS § 4101 note), added subsec. (d).

1982. Act Oct. 12, 1982, in subsecs. (a) and (b), inserted "of this title" following "34 and 35" each place it appears; and, in subsec. (c)(1), substituted "section 2 of the Act of August 16, 1937 (popularly known as the 'National Apprenticeship Act') (29 U.S.C. 50a)," for "section 50a of title 29".

1989. Act Dec. 18, 1989, substituted "Secretary" for "Administrator", wherever appearing.

1991. Act Aug. 6, 1991, redesignated this section, formerly 38 USCS

§ 1772, as 38 USCS § 3672, and amended the references in this section to reflect the redesignations made by § 5(a) of such Act (see Table III preceding 38 USCS § 101).

1994. Act Nov. 2, 1994 (applicable to programs and courses commencing more than 90 days after the date of enactment, as provided by § 605(b) of such Act, which appears as a note to this section) added subsec. (e).

Other provisions:

Application and construction of the Oct. 12, 1982 amendment of this section. For provisions as to the application and construction of the Oct. 12, 1982 amendment of this section, see § 5 of such Act, which appears as 10 USCS § 101 note.

Application of amendments made by Act Nov. 2, 1994. Act Nov. 2, 1994, P. L. 103-446, Title VI, § 605(b), 108 Stat. 4672, provides: "The amendments made by subsection (a) [amending this section and 38 USCS §§ 3675, 3680, and 3686] shall apply with respect to programs of education exclusively by correspondence and to correspondence-residence courses commencing more than 90 days after the date of the enactment of this Act.".

CODE OF FEDERAL REGULATIONS

Department of Veterans Affairs—Vocational rehabilitation and education, 38 CFR Part 21.

Department of Veterans Affairs—Loan guaranty and vocational rehabilitation and counseling programs, 48 CFR Part 871.

CROSS REFERENCES

This section is referred to in 38 USCS § 3671, 3675.

INTERPRETIVE NOTES AND DECISIONS

Veteran was not entitled to educational benefits for real estate courses where school had not applied either to state's approving agency or directly to VA for approval of its real estate courses. Piotrowski v Brown (1996) 9 Vet App 215.

§ 3673. Cooperation

(a) The Secretary and each State approving agency shall take cognizance of the fact that definite duties, functions and responsibilities are conferred upon the Secretary and each State approving agency under the educational programs established under this chapter and chapters 34 and 35 of this title [38 USCS §§ 3670 et seq., 3451 et seq., and 3500 et seq.]. To assure that such programs are effectively and efficiently administered, the cooperation of the Secretary and the State approving agencies is essential. It is necessary to establish an exchange of information pertaining to activities of educational institutions, and particular attention should be given to the enforcement of approval standards, enforcement of enrollment restrictions, and fraudulent and other criminal activities on the part of persons connected with educational institutions in which eligible persons or veterans are enrolled under this chapter and chapters 34 and 35 of this title [38 USCS §§ 3670 et seq., 3451 et seq., and 3500 et seq.].

(b) The Secretary will furnish the State approving agencies with copies of such Department of Veterans Affairs informational material as may aid them in car-

38 USCS § 3673

rying out chapters 34 and 35 of this title [38 USCS §§ 3451 et seq. and 3500 et seq.].
(Added Sept. 23, 1963, P. L. 88-126, § 1, 77 Stat. 158; March 3, 1966, P. L. 89-358, § 3(a)(7), (11), 80 Stat. 20, 21; Oct. 24, 1972, P. L. 92-540, Title IV, § 403(6), 86 Stat. 1090; Oct. 12, 1982, P. L. 97-295, § 4(51) in part, 96 Stat. 1308; Dec. 18, 1989, P. L. 101-237, Title IV, § 423(b)(1), 103 Stat. 2092; Aug. 6, 1991, P. L. 102-83, § 5(a), 105 Stat. 406.)

HISTORY; ANCILLARY LAWS AND DIRECTIVES
Amendments:
1966. Act March 3, 1966 (effective 3/3/66, as provided by § 12(a) of such Act), in subsec. (a), substituted "chapters 34 and 35" for "this chapter" wherever appearing and substituted "eligible persons or veterans" for "eligible persons"; and in subsec. (b), substituted "chapters 34 and 35" for "this chapter".

1972. Act Oct. 24, 1972, in subsec. (a), inserted "this chapter and" wherever appearing.

1982. Act Oct. 12, 1982, in subsecs. (a) and (b), inserted "of this title" each place it appears.

1989. Act Dec. 18, 1989, substituted "Secretary" for "Administrator", wherever appearing; and in subsec. (b), substituted "Department of Veterans Affairs" for "Veterans' Administration".

1991, Act Aug. 6, 1991, redesignated this section, formerly 38 USCS § 1773, as 38 USCS § 3673.

Other provisions:
Application and construction of the Oct. 12, 1982 amendment of this section. For provisions as to the application and construction of the Oct. 12, 1982 amendment of this section, see § 5 of such Act, which appears as 10 USCS § 101 note.

CODE OF FEDERAL REGULATIONS
Department of Veterans Affairs—Vocational rehabilitation and education, 38 CFR Part 21.

Department of Veterans Affairs—Loan guaranty and vocational rehabilitation and counseling programs, 48 CFR Part 871.

§ 3674. Reimbursement of expenses

(a)(1) Subject to paragraphs (2) through (4) of this subsection, the Secretary is authorized to enter into contracts or agreements with State and local agencies to pay such State and local agencies for reasonable and necessary expenses of salary and travel incurred by employees of such agencies and an allowance for administrative expenses in accordance with the formula contained in subsection (b) of this section in (A) rendering necessary services in ascertaining the qualifications of educational institutions for furnishing courses of education to eligible persons or veterans under this chapter and chapters 30 through 35 of this title and chapter 106 of title 10 [38 USCS §§ 3001 et seq. through 3500 et seq. and 10 USCS §§ 2131 et seq.], and in the supervision of such educational institutions, and (B) furnishing, at the request of the Secretary, any other services in connection with such chapters. Each such contract or agreement shall be conditioned upon compliance with the standards and provisions of such chapters. The Secretary may also reimburse such agencies for work performed by their subcontractors where such work has a direct relationship to the requirements of such chapters, and has had the prior approval of the Secretary.

(2)(A) The Secretary shall, effective at the beginning of fiscal year 1988, make payments to State and local agencies, out of amounts available for the payment of readjustment benefits, for the reasonable and necessary expenses of salary and travel incurred by employees of such agencies in carrying out contracts or agreements entered into under this section, for expenses approved by the Secretary that are incurred in carrying out activities described in section 3674A(a)(4) of this title (except for administrative overhead expenses allocated to such activities), and for the allowance for administrative expenses described in subsection (b).

(B) The Secretary shall make such a payment to an agency within a reasonable time after the agency has submitted a report pursuant to paragraph (3)[(A)] of this subsection.

(C) Subject to paragraph (4) of this subsection, the amount of any such payment made to an agency for any period shall be equal to the amount of the reasonable and necessary expenses of salary and travel certified by such agency for such period in accordance with paragraph (3) of this subsection plus the allowance for administrative expenses described in subsection (b) and the amount of expenses approved by the Secretary that are incurred in carrying out activities described in section 3674A(a)(4) of this title for such period (except for administrative overhead expenses allocated to such activities).

(3) Each State and local agency with which a contract or agreement is entered into under this section shall submit to the Secretary on a monthly or quarterly basis, as determined by the agency, a report containing a certification of the reasonable and necessary expenses incurred for salary and travel by such agency under such contract or agreement for the period covered by the report. The report shall be submitted in the form and manner required by the Secretary.

(4) The total amount made available under this section for any fiscal year may not exceed $13,000,000. For any fiscal year in which the total amount that would be made available under this section would exceed $13,000,000 except for the provisions of this paragraph, the Secretary shall provide that each agency shall receive the same percentage of $13,000,000 as the agency would have received of the total amount that would have been made available without the limitation of this paragraph.

(b) The allowance for administrative expenses incurred pursuant to subsection (a) of this section shall be paid in accordance with the following formula:

38 USCS § 3674

VETERANS' BENEFITS

Total salary cost reimbursable under this section	Allowable for administrative expense
$5,000 or less	$693.
Over $5,000 but not exceeding $10,000	$1,247.
Over $10,000 but not exceeding $35,000	$1,247 for the first $10,000, plus $1,155 for each additional $5,000 or fraction thereof.
Over $35,000 but not exceeding $40,000	$7,548.
Over $40,000 but not exceeding $75,000	$7,548 for the first $40,000, plus $999 for each additional $5,000 or fraction thereof.
Over $75,000 but not exceeding $80,000	$14,969.
Over $80,000	$14,969 for the first $80,000, plus $872 for each additional $5,000 or fraction thereof.

(c) Each State and local agency with which the Secretary contracts or enters into an agreement under subsection (a) of this section shall report to the Secretary on September 30, 1978, and periodically, but not less often than annually, thereafter, as determined by the Secretary, on the activities in the preceding twelve months (or the period which has elapsed since the last report under this subsection was submitted) carried out under such contract or agreement. Each such report shall describe, in such detail as the Secretary shall prescribe, services performed and determinations made in connection with ascertaining the qualifications of educational institutions in connection with this chapter and chapters 32, 34, and 35 of this title [38 USCS §§ 3670 et seq., 3201 et seq., 3450 et seq., and 3500 et seq.] and in supervising such institutions.
(Added Sept. 23, 1963, P. L. 88-126, § 1, 77 Stat. 159; March 3, 1966, P. L. 89-358, § 3(a)(7), (8), (11), 80 Stat. 20, 21; Oct. 23, 1968, P. L. 90-631, § 4, 82 Stat. 1334; Oct. 24, 1972, P. L. 92-540, Title IV, §§ 403(7), 411, 86 Stat. 1090, 1092; Dec. 3, 1974, P. L. 93-508, Title II, § 210(1), 88 Stat. 1584; Oct. 15, 1976, P. L. 94-502, Title V, § 503, 90 Stat. 2399; Nov. 23, 1977, P. L. 95-202, Title III, § 303, 91 Stat. 1441; Oct. 17, 1980, P. L. 96-466, Title II, Part A, § 203(1), Part B, § 2130, 94 Stat. 2188, 2190; Oct. 12, 1982, P. L. 97-295, § 4(51) in part, 96 Stat. 1308; May 20, 1988, P. L. 100-323, § 13(a)(1), (b)(5), 102 Stat. 571, 573; Dec. 18, 1989, P. L. 101-237, Title IV, §§ 414, 423(b)(1)(A) 103 Stat. 2085, 2092; March 22, 1991, P. L. 102-16, § 10(a)(7), 105 Stat. 56; Aug. 6, 1991, P. L. 102-83, § 5(a), (c)(1), 105 Stat. 406; Nov. 2, 1994, P. L. 103-446, Title VI, § 606(a)(1), (b), 108 Stat. 4672.)

HISTORY; ANCILLARY LAWS AND DIRECTIVES

References in text:
"Section 3674A(a)(4) of this title", referred to in this section, was redesignated 38 USCS § 3674A(a)(3) by Act Nov. 2, 1994, P. L. 103-446, Title VI, § 606(c)(1)(b), 108 Stat. 4672.

Explanatory notes:
The subparagraph designator "(A)" in para. (a)(2)(A) has been enclosed in

READJUSTMENT BENEFITS   38 USCS § 3674

brackets to indicate the probable intent of Congress to delete such designator.

Amendments:
1966. Act March 3, 1966 (effective 3/3/66, as provided by § 12(a) of such Act), substituted "chapters 34 and 35" for "this chapter" wherever appearing; substituted "eligible persons or veterans" for "eligible persons"; and purported to substitute "eligible person or veteran" for "eligible person"; however, such amendment could not be executed because the words "eligible person" did not appear in the section.

1968. Act Oct. 23, 1968 (effective as provided by § 6(b) of such Act, which appears as a note to this section), designated existing matter as subsec. (a); in subsec. (a), as so designated, inserted "and an allowance for administrative expenses in accordance with the formula contained in subsection (b) of this section"; and added subsec. (b).

1972. Act Oct. 24, 1972, in subsec. (a), inserted "this chapter and"; and substituted new subsec. (b) for one which read:

"(b) The allowance for administrative expenses incurred pursuant to subsection (a) of this section shall be paid in accordance with the following formula:

"Total salary cost reimbursable under this section	Allowable for administrative expense
$5,000 or less	$250.
Over $5,000 but not exceeding $10,000	$450.
Over $10,000 but not exceeding $35,000	$450 for the first $10,000, plus $400 for each additional $5,000 or fraction thereof.
Over $35,000 but not exceeding $40,000	$2,625.
Over $40,000 but not exceeding $75,000	$2,625 for the first $40,000, plus $350 for each additional $5,000 or fraction thereof.
Over $75,000 but not exceeding $80,000	$5,225.
Over $80,000	$5,225 for the first $80,000, plus $300 for each additional $5,000 or fraction thereof.".

1974. Act Dec. 3, 1974 (effective 12/3/74, as provided by § 503 of such Act, which appears as 38 USCS § 3452 note), substituted new subsec. (b) for one which read:

"(b) The allowance for administrative expenses incurred pursuant to subsection (a) of this section shall be paid in accordance with the following formula:

38 USCS § 3674

"Total salary cost reimbursable under this section	Allowable for administrative expense
$5,000 or less	$500.
Over $5,000 but not exceeding $10,000	$900.
Over $10,000 but not exceeding $35,000	$900 for the first $10,000, plus $800 for each additional $5,000 or fraction thereof.
Over $35,000 but not exceeding $40,000	$5,250.
Over $40,000 but not exceeding $75,000	$5,250 for the first $40,000, plus $700 for each additional $5,000 or fraction thereof.
Over $75,000 but not exceeding $80,000	$10,450.
Over $80,000	$10,450 for the first $80,000, plus $600 for each additional $5,000 or fraction thereof.".

1976. Act Oct. 15, 1976 (effective 10/1/76, as provided by § 703(a) of such Act), in subsec. (a), inserted "The Administrator may also reimburse such agencies for work performed by their subcontractors where such work has a direct relationship to the requirements of chapter 32, 34, 35, or 36 of this title, and has had the prior approval of the Administrator."; and substituted new subsec. (b) for one which read:

"(b) The allowance for administrative expenses incurred pursuant to subsection (a) of this section shall be paid in accordance with the following formula:

"Total salary cost reimbursable under this section	Allowable for administrative expense
$5,000 or less	$550.
Over $5,000 but not exceeding $10,000	$1,000.
Over $10,000 but not exceeding $35,000	$1,000 for the first $10,000, plus $925 for each additional $5,000 or fraction thereof.
Over $35,000 but not exceeding $40,000	$6,050.
Over $40,000 but not exceeding $75,000	$6,050 for the first $40,000, plus $800 for each additional $5,000 or fraction thereof.
Over $75,000 but not exceeding $80,000	$12,000.
Over $80,000	$12,000 for the first $80,000, plus $700 for each additional $5,000 or fraction thereof.".

1977. Act Nov. 23, 1977 (effective 2/1/78, as provided by § 501 of such Act, which appears as 38 USCS § 101 note), substituted new subsec. (b) for one which read:

"(b) The allowance for administrative expenses incurred pursuant to subsection (a) of this section shall be paid in accordance with the following formula:

READJUSTMENT BENEFITS   38 USCS § 3674

"Total salary cost reimbursable under this section	Allowable for administrative expense
$5,000 or less	$600.
Over $5,000 but not exceeding $10,000	$1,080.
Over $10,000 but not exceeding $35,000	$1,080 for the first $10,000, plus $1,000 for each additional $5,000 or fraction thereof.
Over $35,000 but not exceeding $40,000	$6,535.
Over $40,000 but not exceeding $75,000	$6,535 for the first $40,000, plus $865 for each additional $5,000 or fraction thereof.
Over $75,000 but not exceeding $80,000	$12,960.
Over $80,000	$12,960 for the first $80,000, plus $755 for each additional $5,000 or fraction thereof.".

and added subsec. (c).

1980. Act Oct. 17, 1980, § 203(1) (effective 10/1/80, as provided by § 802(b)(1) of such Act, which appears as 38 USCS § 3482), substituted new subsec. (b) for one which read:

"(b) The allowance for administrative expenses incurred pursuant to subsection (a) of this section shall be paid in accordance with the following formula:

"Total salary cost reimbursable under this section	Allowable for administrative expense
$5,000 or less	$630.
Over $5,000 but not exceeding $10,000	$1,134.
Over $10,000 but not exceeding $35,000	$1,134 for the first $10,000, plus $1,050 for each additional $5,000 or fraction thereof.
Over $35,000 but not exceeding $40,000	$6,862.
Over $40,000 but not exceeding $75,000	$6,862 for the first $40,000, plus $908 for each additional $5,000 or fraction thereof.
Over $75,000 but not exceeding $80,000	$13,608.
Over $80,000	$13,608 for the first $80,000, plus $793 for each additional $5,000 or fraction thereof.".

Act Oct. 17, 1980, § 213(1) (effective 1/1/81, as provided by § 802(b)(2) of such Act, which appears as 38 USCS § 3482 note), substituted subsec. (b) for former subsec. (b), as amended by § 203(1) of Act Oct. 17, 1980, which read:

"(b) The allowance for administrative expenses incurred pursuant to subsection (a) of this section shall be paid in accordance with the following formula:

38 USCS § 3674 — VETERANS' BENEFITS

"Total salary cost reimbursable under this section	Allowable for administrative expense
$5,000 or less	$662.
Over $5,000 but not exceeding $10,000	$1,191.
Over $10,000 but not exceeding $35,000	$1,191 for the first $10,000, plus $1,103 for each additional $5,000 or fraction thereof.
Over $35,000 but not exceeding $40,000	$7,205.
Over $40,000 but not exceeding $75,000	$7,205 for the first $40,000, plus $953 for each additional $5,000 or fraction thereof.
Over $75,000 but not exceeding $80,000	$14,288.
Over $80,000	$14,288 for the first $80,000, plus $833 for each additional $5,000 or fraction thereof.".

1982. Act Oct. 12, 1982, in subsec. (a), inserted "of this title" following "34 and 35" each place it appears.

1988. Act May 20, 1988 (effective on enactment as provided by § 16(a), of such Act, except as provided by § 16(b)(1)(D), which appear as 38 USCS § 3104 note), in subsec. (a), designated the existing provisions as para. (1) and, in para. (1) as so designated, inserted "Subject to paragraphs (2) through (4) of this subsection,", substituted "the" for "The", "(A)" for "(1)", and "(B)" for "(2)", substituted "chapters 30 through 35 of this title and chapters 106 and 107 of title 10" for "chapters 34 and 35 of this title", substituted "such chapters" for "chapters 34 and 35 of this title" following "connection with" and "provisions of", and substituted "such chapters" for "chapter 32, 34, 35, or 36 of this title", and added paras. (2)–(4).

1989. Act Dec. 18, 1989, in subsec. (a)(2), in subpara. (A), substituted "section, for expenses approved by the Secretary that are incurred in carrying out activities described in section 1774A(a)(4) of this title (except for administrative overhead expenses allocated to such activities), and for" for "section and for", and in subpara. (C), inserted "and the amount of expenses approved by the Secretary that are incurred in carrying out activities described in section 1774A(a)(4) of this title for such period (except for administrative overhead expenses allocated to such activities)".

Such Act further, in subsecs. (a) and (c), substituted "Secretary" for "Administrator" wherever appearing.

1991. Act March 22, 1991, in subsec. (a)(1)(A), substituted "chapter 106" for "chapters 106 and 107".

Act Aug. 6, 1991, redesignated this section, formerly 38 USCS § 1774, as 38 USCS § 3674, and amended the references in this section to reflect the redesignations made by § 5(a) of such Act (see Table III preceding 38 USCS § 101).

1994. Act Nov. 2, 1994 (applicable with respect to services provided after 9/30/94, as provided by § 606(a)(2) of such Act, which appears as a note to this section), in subsec. (a)(4), substituted "$13,000,000" for "$12,000,000" wherever appearing.

Such Act further, in subsec. (a)(3), deleted the designation for subpara. (A), and deleted subpara. (B), which read:

"(B) The Secretary shall transmit a report to the Congress on a quarterly basis which summarizes—

"(i) the amounts for which certifications were made by State and local agencies in the reports submitted under subparagraph (A) of this paragraph with respect to the quarter for which the report is made; and

"(ii) the amounts of the payments made by the Secretary for such quarter with respect to such certifications and with respect to administrative expenses.".

Other provisions:
Application of amendments made by § 4 of Act Oct. 23, 1968. Act Oct. 23, 1968, P. L. 90-631, § 6(b), 82 Stat. 1335, provided: "The amendments made by section 4 of this Act [amending this section] shall apply with respect to contracts and agreements entered into under section 1774 of title 38, United States Code [this section], effective for periods beginning after June 30, 1968.".

Application and construction of the Oct. 12, 1982 amendment of this section. For provisions as to the application and construction of the Oct. 12, 1982 amendment of this section, see § 5 of such Act, which appears as 10 USCS § 101 note.

Payment to State or local agency; reimbursement. Act May 20, 1988, P. L. 100-323, § 13(a)(2), 102 Stat. 572, effective on enactment, as provided by § 16(a) of such Act, which appears as 38 USCS § 3104 note, provides: "If any payment is made to State or local approving agencies with respect to activities carried out under subchapter I of chapter 36 of title 38, United States Code [38 USCS §§ 3670 et seq.], for fiscal year 1988 before the date of the enactment of this Act and from an account other than the account used for payment of readjustment benefits, the account from which such payment was made shall be reimbursed from the account used for payment of readjustment benefits.".

Application of amendments made by Act Nov. 2, 1994. Act Nov. 2, 1994, P. L. 103-446, Title VI, § 606(a)(2), 108 Stat. 4672, provides: "The amendments made by subsection (a) [amending subsec. (a)(4) of this section] shall apply with respect to services provided under such section after September 30, 1994.".

CODE OF FEDERAL REGULATIONS

Department of Veterans Affairs—Vocational rehabilitation and education, 38 CFR Part 21.

Department of Veterans Affairs—Loan guaranty and vocational rehabilitation and counseling programs, 48 CFR Part 871.

CROSS REFERENCES

This section is referred to in 38 USCS §§ 3671, 3674A, 3683.

§ 3674A. Evaluations of agency performance; qualifications and performance of agency personnel

(a) The Secretary shall—
(1)(A) conduct, in conjunction with State approving agencies, an annual

evaluation of each State approving agency on the basis of standards developed by the Secretary in conjunction with the State approving agencies, and (B) provide each such agency an opportunity to comment on the evaluation;

(2) take into account the results of annual evaluations carried out under clause (1) when negotiating the terms and conditions of a contract or agreement under section 3674 of this title;

(3) cooperate with State approving agencies in developing and implementing a uniform national curriculum, to the extent practicable, for training new employees and for continuing the training of employees of such agencies, and sponsor, with the agencies, such training and continuation of training; and

(4) prescribe prototype qualification and performance standards, developed in conjunction with State approving agencies, for use by such agencies in the development of qualification and performance standards for State approving agency personnel carrying out approval responsibilities under a contract or agreement entered into under section 3674(a).

(b)(1) Each State approving agency carrying out a contract or agreement with the Secretary under section 3674(a) of this title after the 18-month period beginning on the date of the enactment of this section [May 20, 1988] shall—

(A) apply qualification and performance standards based on the standards developed under subsection (a)(4); and

(B) make available to any person, upon request, the criteria used to carry out its functions under a contract or agreement entered into under section 3674(a) of this title.

(2) In developing and applying standards described in subsection (a)(4), the State approving agency may take into consideration the State's merit system requirements and other local requirements and conditions.

(3) The Secretary shall provide assistance in developing such standards to a State approving agency that requests it.

(Added May 20, 1988, P. L. 100-323, § 13(b)(1)(A), 102 Stat. 572; Dec. 18, 1989, P. L. 101-237, Title IV, § 423(b)(1)(A), 103 Stat. 2092; Aug. 6, 1991, P. L. 102-83, § 5(a), (c)(1), 105 Stat. 406; Nov. 2, 1994, P. L. 103-446, Title VI, § 606(c), 108 Stat. 4672.)

HISTORY; ANCILLARY LAWS AND DIRECTIVES
Effective date of section:
Act May 20, 1987, P. L. 100-323, § 16(a), 102 Stat. 575, which appears as 38 USCS § 3104 note, provides that this section is effective on enactment.

Amendments:
1989. Act Dec. 18, 1989, in the entire section, substituted "Secretary" for "Administrator", wherever appearing.

1991. Act Aug. 6, 1991, redesignated this section, formerly 38 USCS § 1774, as 38 USCS § 3674, and amended the references in this section to reflect the redesignations made by § 5(a) of such Act (see Table III preceding 38 USCS § 101).

1994. Act Nov. 2, 1994, in subsec. (a), deleted para. (3), which read: "(3) supervise functionally the provision of course-approval services by State approving agencies under this subchapter;", and redesignated paras. (4) and (5) as paras. (3) and (4), respectively; and, in subsec. (b), substituted "subsection (a)(4)" for "subsection (a)(5) of this section" wherever appearing and inserted "of this title" following "section 3674(a)" wherever appearing.

Other provisions:
Implementation of section. Act May 20, 1988, P. L. 100-323, § 13(b)(2), 102 Stat. 573, effective on enactment, as provided by § 16(a) of such Act, which appears as 38 USCS § 3104 note, provides:
"For purposes of implementing the amendments made by paragraph (1)—
  "(A) the Administrator of Veterans' Affairs shall, within 120 days after the date of the enactment of this Act, publish prototype standards developed under section 1774A(a)(5) [now § 3674A(a)(5)] of title 38, United States Code, as added by paragraph (1);
  "(B) each State approving agency shall, within 1 year after the Administrator has published prototype standards under subparagraph (A), submit to the Administrator of Veterans' Affairs a copy of the standards to be implemented by such agency under section 1774A(b)(1)(A) [now § 3674A(b)(1)(A)] of such title; and
  "(C) the Administrator may, within 30 days after receiving such standards from an agency, provide comments to the agency, especially with regard to whether the State's standards are consistent with the prototype standards developed by the Administrator under section 1774A(a)(5) [now § 3674A(a)(5)] of such title.".

Nonapplicability of standards to person remaining in same position. Act May 20, 1988, P. L. 100-323, § 13(b)(3), 102 Stat. 573, effective on enactment as provided by § 16(a) of such Act, which appears as 38 USCS § 3104 note, provides: "None of the qualification standards implemented pursuant to the amendments made by paragraph (1) [note to this section] shall apply to any person employed by a State approving agency on the date of the enactment of this Act as long as such person remains in the position in which the person is employed on such date.".

CODE OF FEDERAL REGULATIONS

Department of Veterans Affairs—Vocational rehabilitation and education, 38 CFR Part 21.

Department of Veterans Affairs—Loan guaranty and vocational rehabilitation and counseling programs, 48 CFR Part 871.

CROSS REFERENCES
This section is referred to in 38 USCS §§ 3674, 3682.

§ 3675. Approval of accredited courses

(a)(1) A State approving agency may approve the courses offered by an educational institution when—

  (A) such courses have been accredited and approved by a nationally recognized accrediting agency or association;

(B) such courses are conducted under the Act of February 23, 1917 (20 U.S.C. 11 et seq.);

(C) such courses are accepted by the State department of education for credit for a teacher's certificate or a teacher's degree; or

(D) such courses are approved by the State as meeting the requirement of regulations prescribed by the Secretary of Health and Human Services under sections 1819(f)(2)(A)(i) and 1919(f)(2)(A)(i) of the Social Security Act (42 U.S.C. 1395i-3(f)(2)(A)(i) and 1396r(f)(2)(A)(i)).

(2)(A) For the purposes of this chapter [38 USCS §§ 3670 et seq.], the Secretary of Education shall publish a list of nationally recognized accrediting agencies and associations which that Secretary determines to be reliable authority as to the quality of training offered by an educational institution.

(B) Except as provided in section 3672(e) of this title, a State approving agency may utilize the accreditation of any accrediting association or agency listed pursuant to subparagraph (A) of this paragraph for approval of courses specifically accredited and approved by such accrediting association or agency.

(3)(A) An educational institution shall submit an application for approval of courses to the appropriate State approving agency. In making application for approval, the institution (other than an elementary school or secondary school) shall transmit to the State approving agency copies of its catalog or bulletin which must be certified as true and correct in content and policy by an authorized representative of the institution.

(B) Each catalog or bulletin transmitted by an institution under subparagraph (A) of this paragraph shall—

(i) state with specificity the requirements of the institution with respect to graduation;

(ii) include the information required under paragraphs (6) and (7) of section 3676(b) of this title; and

(iii) include any attendance standards of the institution, if the institution has and enforces such standards.

(b) As a condition of approval under this section, the State approving agency must find the following:

(1) The educational institution keeps adequate records, as prescribed by the State approving agency, to show the progress and grades of the eligible person or veteran and to show that satisfactory standards relating to progress and conduct are enforced.

(2) The educational institution maintains a written record of the previous education and training of the eligible person or veteran that clearly indicates that appropriate credit has been given by the educational institution for previous education and training, with the training period shortened proportionately.

(3) The educational institution and its approved courses meet the criteria of paragraphs (1), (2), and (3) of section 3676(c) of this title.

(Added Sept. 23, 1963, P. L. 88-126, § 1, 77 Stat. 159; March 3, 1966, P. L.

READJUSTMENT BENEFITS 38 USCS § 3675

89-358, § 3(a)(8), 80 Stat. 21; Oct. 15, 1976, P. L. 94-502, Title V, §§ 504, 513(a)(2), 90 Stat. 2399, 2402; Oct 17, 1980, P. L. 96-466, Title VIII, § 801(d), 94 Stat. 2216; Dec. 18, 1989, P. L. 101-237, Title IV, § 423(b)(1)(A), 103 Stat. 2092; Aug. 6, 1991, P. L. 102-83, § 5(a), (c)(1), 105 Stat. 406 Oct. 29, 1992, P. L. 102-568, Title III, § 312, 106 Stat. 4330; Nov. 2, 1994, P. L. 103-446, Title VI, § 605(a)(2)(A), 108 Stat. 4672; Oct. 9, 1996, P. L. 104-275, Title I, § 103(c), 110 Stat. 3326.)

HISTORY; ANCILLARY LAWS AND DIRECTIVES
Amendments:
1966. Act March 3, 1966 (effective 3/3/66, as provided by § 12(a) of such Act), in subsec. (b), substituted "eligible person or veteran" for "eligible person" wherever appearing.
1976. Act Oct. 15, 1976, § 513(a)(2) (effective 10/15/76, as provided by § 703(b) of such Act, which appears as 38 USCS § 3693 note), in subsec. (a), concluding matter, substituted "the Commissioner" for "he" preceding "determines".
Such Act further, in § 504 (effective 12/1/76, as provided by § 703(c) of such Act, which appears as 38 USCS § 3693 note), in subsec. (a), concluding matter, inserted "which must be certified as true and correct in content and policy by an authorized representative of the school. The catalog or bulletin must specifically state its progress requirements for graduation and must include as a minimum the information required by sections 1776(b)(6) and (7) of this title."; and in subsec. (b), inserted "and must include as a minimum (except for attendance) the requirements set forth in section 1776(c)(7) of this title".
1980. Act Oct. 17, 1980 (effective 10/1/80, as provided by § 802(h) of such Act, which appears as 38 USCS § 3452 note), in subsec. (a), substituted "Secretary" for "Commissioner" wherever appearing.
1989. Act Dec. 18, 1989, in subsec. (b), substituted "Secretary" for "Administrator".
1991. Act Aug. 6, 1991, redesignated this section, formerly 38 USCS § 1775, as 38 USCS § 3675, and amended the references in this section to reflect the redesignations made by § 5(a) of such Act (see Table III preceding 38 USCS § 101).
1992. Act Oct. 29, 1992, in subsec. (a), redesignated the existing provisions as para. (1) of such subsection, redesignated former paras. (1)-(3) as subparas. (A)-(C), respectively, and deleted the concluding matter which read: "For the purposes of this chapter the Secretary of Education shall publish a list of nationally recognized accrediting agencies and associations which the Secretary determines to be reliable authority as to the quality of training offered by an educational institution and the State approving agencies may, upon concurrence, utilize the accreditation of such accrediting associations or agencies for approval of the courses specifically accredited and approved by such accrediting association or agency. In making application for approval, the institution shall transmit to the State approving agency copies of its catalog or bulletin which must be certified as true and correct in content and policy by an authorized representative of the school. The catalog or bulletin must specifically state its progress requirements for graduation and must include as a minimum the information required by sections 3676(b)(6) and (7) of this title.".

Such Act further, in subsec. (a), in para. (1) as redesignated, in subpara. (B) as redesignated, substituted "the Act of February 23, 1917 (20 U.S.C. 11 et seq.);" for "sections 11-28 of title 20; or", in subpara. (C) as redesignated, substituted "; or" for a concluding period, and added subpara. (D), and added new paras. (2) and (3).

1994. Act Nov. 2, 1994 (applicable to programs and courses commencing more than 90 days after the date of enactment, as provided by § 605(b) of such Act, which appears as 38 USCS § 3672 note), in subsec. (a)(2)(B), substituted "Except as provided in section 3672(e) of this title, a State" for "A State".

1996. Act Oct. 9, 1996 substituted subsec. (b) for one which read: "(b) As a condition to approval under this section, the State approving agency must find that adequate records are kept by the educational institution to show the progress of each eligible person or veteran and must include as a minimum (except for attendance) the requirements set forth in section 3676(c)(7) of this title. The State approving agency must also find that the educational institution maintains a written record of the previous education and training of the eligible person or veteran and clearly indicates that appropriate credit has been given by the institution for previous education and training, with the training period shortened proportionately and the eligible person or veteran and the Secretary so notified.".

CODE OF FEDERAL REGULATIONS

Department of Veterans Affairs—Vocational rehabilitation and education, 38 CFR Part 21.

Department of Veterans Affairs—Loan guaranty and vocational rehabilitation and counseling programs, 48 CFR Part 871.

CROSS REFERENCES

This section is referred to in 38 USCS §§ 3452, 3501, 3676.

INTERPRETIVE NOTES AND DECISIONS

38 USCS § 1775 [now 38 USCS § 3675] does not apply to educational institutions which are candidates for accreditation until such time as they are fully accredited. VA GCO 14-76.

§ 3676. Approval of nonaccredited courses

(a) No course of education which has not been approved by a State approving agency pursuant to section 3675 of this title, which is offered by a public or private, profit or nonprofit, educational institution shall be approved for the purposes of this chapter [38 USCS §§ 3670 et seq.] unless the educational institution offering such course submits to the appropriate State approving agency a written application for approval of such course in accordance with the provisions of this chapter [38 USCS §§ 3670 et seq.].

(b) Such application shall be accompanied by not less than two copies of the current catalog or bulletin which is certified as true and correct in content and policy by an authorized owner or official and includes the following:

(1) Identifying data, such as volume number and date of publication;

(2) Names of the institution and its governing body, officials and faculty;

(3) A calendar of the institution showing legal holidays, beginning and ending date of each quarter, term, or semester, and other important dates;

(4) Institution policy and regulations on enrollment with respect to enrollment dates and specific entrance requirements for each course;

(5) Institution policy and regulations relative to leave, absences, class cuts, makeup work, tardiness and interruptions for unsatisfactory attendance;

(6) Institution policy and regulations relative to standards of progress required of the student by the institution (this policy will define the grading system of the institution, the minimum grades considered satisfactory, conditions for interruption for unsatisfactory grades or progress and a description of the probationary period, if any, allowed by the institution, and conditions of reentrance for those students dismissed for unsatisfactory progress. A statement will be made regarding progress records kept by the institution and furnished the student);

(7) Institution policy and regulations relating to student conduct and conditions for dismissal for unsatisfactory conduct;

(8) Detailed schedules of fees, charges for tuition, books, supplies, tools, student activities, laboratory fees, service charges, rentals, deposits, and all other charges;

(9) Policy and regulations of the institution relative to the refund of the unused portion of tuition, fees, and other charges in the event the student does not enter the course or withdraws or is discontinued therefrom;

(10) A description of the available space, facilities, and equipment;

(11) A course outline for each course for which approval is requested, showing subjects or units in the course, type of work or skill to be learned, and approximate time and clock hours to be spent on each subject or unit; and

(12) Policy and regulations of the institution relative to granting credit for previous educational training.

(c) The appropriate State approving agency may approve the application of such institution when the institution and its nonaccredited courses are found upon investigation to have met the following criteria:

(1) The courses, curriculum, and instruction are consistent in quality, content, and length with similar courses in public schools and other private schools in the State, with recognized accepted standards.

(2) There is in the institution adequate space, equipment, instructional material, and instructor personnel to provide training of good quality.

(3) Educational and experience qualifications of directors, administrators, and instructors are adequate.

(4) The institution maintains a written record of the previous education and training of the eligible person and clearly indicates that appropriate credit has been given by the institution for previous education and training, with the training period shortened proportionately and the eligible person and the Secretary so notified.

(5) A copy of the course outline, schedule of tuition, fees, and other charges, regulations pertaining to absence, grading policy, and rules of operation and conduct will be furnished the eligible person upon enrollment.

(6) Upon completion of training, the eligible person is given a certificate by the institution indicating the approved course and indicating that training was satisfactorily completed.

(7) Adequate records as prescribed by the State approving agency are kept to show attendance and progress or grades, and satisfactory standards relating to attendance, progress, and conduct are enforced.

(8) The institution complies with all local, city, county, municipal, State, and Federal regulations, such as fire codes, building and sanitation codes. The State approving agency may require such evidence of compliance as is deemed necessary.

(9) The institution is financially sound and capable of fulfilling its commitments for training.

(10) The institution does not utilize advertising of any type which is erroneous or misleading, either by actual statement, omission, or intimation. The institution shall not be deemed to have met this requirement until the State approving agency (A) has ascertained from the Federal Trade Commission whether the Commission has issued an order to the institution to cease and desist from any act or practice, and (B) has, if such an order has been issued, given due weight to that fact.

(11) The institution does not exceed its enrollment limitations as established by the State approving agency.

(12) The institution's administrators, directors, owners, and instructors are of good reputation and character.

(13) The institution has and maintains a policy for the refund of the unused portion of tuition, fees, and other charges in the event the eligible person fails to enter the course or withdraws or is discontinued therefrom at any time prior to completion and such policy must provide that the amount charged to the eligible person for tuition, fees, and other charges for a portion of the course shall not exceed the approximate pro rata portion of the total charges for tuition, fees, and other charges that the length of the completed portion of the course bears to its total length.

(14) Such additional criteria as may be deemed necessary by the State approving agency.

(d) The Secretary may waive, in whole or in part, the requirements of subsection (c)(13) of this section in the case of an educational institution which—

(1) is a college, university, or similar institution offering postsecondary level academic instruction that leads to an associate or higher degree,

(2) is operated by an agency of a State or of a unit of local government,

(3) is located within such State or, in the case of an institution operated by an agency of a unit of local government, within the boundaries of the area over which such unit has taxing jurisdiction, and

(4) is a candidate for accreditation by a regional accrediting association,

if the Secretary determines, pursuant to regulations which the Secretary shall prescribe, that such requirements would work an undue administrative hardship because the total amount of tuition, fees, and other charges at such institution is nominal.

(e) Notwithstanding any other provision of this title, a course of education shall not be approved under this section if it is to be pursued in whole or in part by independent study.
(Added Sept. 23, 1963, P. L. 88-126, § 1, 77 Stat. 159; March 3, 1966, P. L. 89-358, § 3(a)(9), 80 Stat. 21; Oct. 17, 1981, P. L. 97-66, Title VI, § 606, 95 Stat. 1037; Dec. 18, 1989, P. L. 101-237, Title IV, § 423(b)(1)(A), 103 Stat. 2092; Aug. 6, 1991, P. L. 102-83, § 5(a), (c)(1), 105 Stat. 406; Oct. 29, 1992, P. L. 102-568, Title III, § 313(a)(1), 106 Stat. 4331.)

HISTORY; ANCILLARY LAWS AND DIRECTIVES
Amendments:
1966. Act March 3, 1966 (effective 3/3/66, as provided by § 12(a) of such Act), in subsec. (a), deleted "1653 or" preceding "1775 of".
1981. Act Oct. 17, 1981 (effective 10/17/81, as provided by § 701(b)(1) of such Act, which appears as 38 USCS § 1114 note) added subsec. (d).
1989. Act Dec. 18, 1989, in subsec. (c)(4) and in subsec. (d), in the introductory and concluding matters, substituted "Secretary" for "Administrator", wherever appearing.
1991. Act Aug. 6, 1991, redesignated this section, formerly 38 USCS § 1776, as 38 USCS § 3676, and amended the references in this section to reflect the redesignations made by § 5(a) of such Act (see Table III preceding 38 USCS § 101).
1992. Act Oct. 29, 1992 added subsec. (e).

CODE OF FEDERAL REGULATIONS
Department of Veterans Affairs—Vocational rehabilitation and education, 38 CFR Part 21.
Department of Veterans Affairs—Loan guaranty and vocational rehabilitation and counseling programs, 48 CFR Part 871.

CROSS REFERENCES
This section is referred to in 38 USCS § 3675.

§ 3677. Approval of training on the job

(a) Any State approving agency may approve a program of training on the job (other than a program of apprenticeship) only when it finds that the job which is the objective of the training is one in which progression and appointment to the next higher classification are based upon skills learned through organized and supervised training on the job and not on such factors as length of service and normal turnover, and that the provisions of subsections (b) and (c) of this section are met.

(b) The training establishment offering training which is desired to be approved for the purposes of this chapter [38 USCS §§ 3670 et seq.] must submit to the appropriate State approving agency a written application for approval which, in addition to furnishing such information as is required by the State approving agency, contains a certification that—
    (1) the wages to be paid the eligible veteran or person (A) upon entrance into

training, are not less than wages paid nonveterans in the same training position and are at least 50 per centum of the wages paid for the job for which the veteran or person is to be trained, and (B) such wages will be increased in regular periodic increments until, not later than the last full month of the training period, they will be at least 85 per centum of the wages paid for the job for which such eligible veteran or person is being trained; and

(2) there is reasonable certainty that the job for which the eligible veteran or person is to be trained will be available to the veteran or person at the end of the training period.

(c) As a condition for approving a program of training on the job (other than a program of apprenticeship) the State approving agency must find upon investigation that the following criteria are met:

(1) The training content of the course is adequate to qualify the eligible veteran or person for appointment to the job for which the veteran or person is to be trained.

(2) The job customarily requires full-time training for a period of not less than six months and not more than two years.

(3) The length of the training period is not longer than that customarily required by the training establishments in the community to provide an eligible veteran or person with the required skills, arrange for the acquiring of job knowledge, technical information, and other facts which the eligible veteran or person will need to learn in order to become competent on the job for which the veteran or person is being trained.

(4) Provision is made for related instruction for the individual eligible veteran or person who may need it.

(5) There is in the training establishment adequate space, equipment, instructional material, and instructor personnel to provide satisfactory training on the job.

(6) Adequate records are kept to show the progress made by each eligible veteran or person toward such veteran's or person's job objective.

(7) No course of training will be considered bona fide if given to an eligible veteran or person who is already qualified by training and experience for the job.

(8) A signed copy of the training agreement for each eligible veteran or person, including the training program and wage scale as approved by the State approving agency, is provided to the veteran or person and to the Secretary and the State approving agency by the employer.

(9) That the course meets such other criteria as may be established by the State approving agency.

(Added Aug. 31, 1967, P. L. 90-77, Title III, § 304(d), 81 Stat. 186; March 26, 1970, P. L. 91-219, Title II, § 212, 84 Stat. 83; Oct. 24, 1972, P. L. 92-540, Title III, § 314, 86 Stat. 1084; Oct. 15, 1976, P. L. 94-502, Title V, § 513(a)(3), 90 Stat. 2402; Dec. 18, 1989, P. L. 101-237, Title IV, § 423(b)(1)(A), 103 Stat. 2092; Aug. 6, 1991, P. L. 102-83, § 5(a), 105 Stat. 406.)

HISTORY; ANCILLARY LAWS AND DIRECTIVES

Effective date of section:
Act Aug. 31, 1967, P. L. 90-77, Title IV, § 405(a), 81 Stat. 191, provided that this section is effective on the first day of the first calendar month which begins more than 10 days after Aug. 31, 1967.

Amendments:
1970. Act March 26, 1970, in subsec. (a), inserted "and supervised".
1972. Act Oct. 24, 1972, in subsec. (b), in paras. (1) and (2), inserted "or person" wherever appearing; and in subsec. (c), in paras. (1), (3), (4), (6), (7) and (8), inserted "or person" wherever appearing.
1976. Act Oct. 15, 1976 (effective 10/15/76, as provided by § 703(b) of such Act, which appears as 38 USCS § 3693 note), in subsec. (b), in para. (1), substituted "the veteran or person" for "he", in para. (2), substituted "the veteran or person" for "him"; and in subsec. (c), in paras. (1) and (3), substituted "the veteran or person" for "he", and in para. (6), substituted "such veteran's or person's" for "his".
1989. Act Dec. 18, 1989, in subsec. (c)(8), substituted "Secretary" for "Administrator".
1991. Act Aug. 6, 1991, redesignated this section, formerly 38 USCS § 1777, as 38 USCS § 3677.

CODE OF FEDERAL REGULATIONS

Department of Veterans Affairs—Vocational rehabilitation and education, 38 CFR Part 21.
Department of Veterans Affairs—Loan guaranty and vocational rehabilitation and counseling programs, 48 CFR Part 871.

CROSS REFERENCES

This section is referred to in 38 USCS §§ 3672, 3687.

INTERPRETIVE NOTES AND DECISIONS

1. Generally
2. Purpose

1. Generally
Contract between veteran and his employer, whereby veteran, accepted by employer for on-the-job training, agreed that for one year after employment's termination, he would not engage in employer's type of business within specified territory which covered practically entire state, in part of which territory employer was not at time doing business and merely anticipated conducting business in future, was contrary to purpose of Servicemen's Readjustment Act [former 38 USCS §§ 693 et seq.] and unenforceable. Orkin Exterminating Co. v Dewberry (1949) 204 Ga 794, 51 SE2d 669 (ovrld in part on other grounds by Barry v Stanco Communications Products, Inc. (1979) 243 Ga 68, 252 SE2d 491, 1979-1 CCH Trade Cases ¶ 62715).

2. Purpose
Predecessor to 38 USCS § 3677 was intended to furnish veterans on-the-job training in order to speedily provide for their employment in gainful occupation, to reduce problem of unemployment among returning veterans, and to assure veterans, provided with on-the-job training, of reasonable certainty of using that training in gainful occupation; law was not intended as mere dole to veterans. Orkin Exterminating Co. v Dewberry (1949) 204 Ga 794, 51 SE2d 669 (ovrld in part on other grounds by Barry v Stanco Communications Products, Inc. (1979) 243 Ga 68, 252 SE2d 491, 1979-1 CCH Trade Cases ¶ 62715).

§ 3678. Notice of approval of courses

The State approving agency, upon determining that an educational institution has complied with all the requirements of this chapter [38 USCS §§ 3670 et seq.], will issue a letter to such institution setting forth the courses which have been approved for the purposes of this chapter [38 USCS §§ 3670 et seq.], and will furnish an official copy of such letter and any subsequent amendments to the Secretary. The letter of approval shall be accompanied by a copy of the catalog or bulletin of the institution, as approved by the State approving agency, and shall contain the following information:

(1) date of letter and effective date of approval of courses;

(2) proper address and name of each educational institution;

(3) authority for approval and conditions of approval, referring specifically to the approved catalog or bulletin published by the educational institution;

(4) name of each course approved;

(5) where applicable, enrollment limitations such as maximum numbers authorized and student-teacher ratio;

(6) signature of responsible official of State approving agency; and

(7) such other fair and reasonable provisions as are considered necessary by the appropriate State approving agency.

(Added Sept. 23, 1963, P. L. 88-126, § 1, 77 Stat. 162; Aug. 31, 1967, P. L. 90-77, Title III, § 304(d), 81 Stat. 186; Dec. 18, 1989, P. L. 101-237, Title IV, § 423(b)(1)(A), 103 Stat. 2092; Aug. 6, 1991, P. L. 102-83, § 5(a), 105 Stat. 406.)

HISTORY; ANCILLARY LAWS AND DIRECTIVES

Amendments:

1967. Act Aug. 31, 1967 (effective 10/1/67, as provided by § 405(a) of such Act), redesignated this section as § 1778; it formerly appeared as § 1777.

1989. Act Dec. 18, 1989, in the introductory matter, substituted "Secretary" for "Administrator".

1991. Act Aug. 6, 1991, redesignated this section, formerly 38 USCS § 1778, as 38 USCS § 3678.

CODE OF FEDERAL REGULATIONS

Department of Veterans Affairs—Vocational rehabilitation and education, 38 CFR Part 21.

Department of Veterans Affairs—Loan guaranty and vocational rehabilitation and counseling programs, 48 CFR Part 871.

§ 3679. Disapproval of courses

(a) Any course approved for the purposes of this chapter [38 USCS §§ 3670 et seq.] which fails to meet any of the requirements of this chapter [38 USCS §§ 3670 et seq.] shall be immediately disapproved by the appropriate State approving agency. An educational institution which has its courses disapproved by a State approving agency will be notified of such disapproval by a certified or registered letter of notification and a return receipt secured.

(b) Each State approving agency shall notify the Secretary of each course which

it has disapproved under this section. The Secretary shall notify the State approving agency of the Secretary's disapproval of any educational institution under chapter 31 of this title [38 USCS §§ 3100 et seq.].
(Added Sept. 23, 1963, P. L. 88-126, § 1, 77 Stat. 162; Aug. 31, 1967, P. L. 90-77, Title III, § 304(d), 81 Stat. 186; Oct. 15, 1976, P. L. 94-502, Title V, § 513(a)(4), 90 Stat. 2402; Dec. 18, 1989, P. L. 101-237, Title IV, § 423(b)(1)(A), (2), 103 Stat. 2092; Aug. 6, 1991, P. L. 102-83, § 5(a), 105 Stat. 406.)

HISTORY; ANCILLARY LAWS AND DIRECTIVES
Amendments:
1967. Act Aug. 31, 1967 (effective 10/1/67, as provided by § 405(a) of such Act), redesignated this section as § 1779; it formerly appeared as § 1778.
1976. Act Oct. 15, 1976 (effective 10/15/76, as provided by § 703(b) of such Act), in subsec. (b), substituted "the Administrator's" for "his".
1989. Act Dec. 18, 1989, in subsec. (b), substituted "Secretary" for "Administrator", wherever appearing, and substituted "Secretary's" for "Administrator's".
1991. Act Aug. 6, 1991, redesignated this section, formerly 38 USCS § 1779, as 38 USCS § 3679.

CODE OF FEDERAL REGULATIONS
Department of Veterans Affairs—Vocational rehabilitation and education, 38 CFR Part 21.
Department of Veterans Affairs—Loan guaranty and vocational rehabilitation and counseling programs, 48 CFR Part 871.

CROSS REFERENCES
This section is referred to in 38 USCS § 3670.

SUBCHAPTER II. MISCELLANEOUS PROVISIONS

§ 3680. Payment of educational assistance or subsistence allowances

Period for Which Payment May Be Made
(a) Payment of educational assistance or subsistence allowances to eligible veterans or eligible persons pursuing a program of education or training, other than a program by correspondence, in an educational institution under chapter 31, 34, or 35 of this title [38 USCS §§ 3100 et seq., 3451 et seq., or 3500 et seq.] shall be paid as provided in this section and, as applicable, in section 3108, 3482, 3491 or 3532 of this title. Such payments shall be paid only for the period of such veterans' or persons' enrollment in, and pursuit of, such program, but no amount shall be paid—
    (1) to any eligible veteran or eligible person for any period when such veteran or person is not pursuing such veteran's or person's course in accor-

dance with the regularly established policies and regulations of the educational institution, with the provisions of such regulations as may be prescribed by the Secretary pursuant to subsection (g) of this section, and with the requirements of this chapter or of chapter 34 or 35 of this title [38 USCS §§ 3670 et seq., 3451 et seq., or 3500 et seq.], but payment may be made for an actual period of pursuit of one or more unit subjects pursued for a period of time shorter than the enrollment period at the educational institution;

(2) to any eligible veteran or person for auditing a course; or

(3) to any eligible veteran or person for a course for which the grade assigned is not used in computing the requirements for graduation including a course from which the student withdraws unless—

(A) the eligible veteran or person withdraws because he or she is ordered to active duty; or

(B) the Secretary finds there are mitigating circumstances, except that, in the first instance of withdrawal (without regard to withdrawals described in subclause (A) of this clause) by the eligible veteran or person from a course or courses with respect to which the veteran or person has been paid assistance under this title, mitigating circumstances shall be considered to exist with respect to courses totaling not more than six semester hours or the equivalent thereof.

Notwithstanding the foregoing, the Secretary may, subject to such regulations as the Secretary shall prescribe, continue to pay allowances to eligible veterans and eligible persons enrolled in courses set forth in clause (1) of this subsection—

(A) during periods when the schools are temporarily closed under an established policy based upon an Executive order of the President or due to an emergency situation;

(B) during periods between consecutive school terms where such veterans or persons transfer from one approved educational institution to another approved educational institution for the purpose of enrolling in and pursuing a similar course at the second institution if the period between such consecutive terms does not exceed 30 days; or

(C) during periods between a semester, term, or quarter where the educational institution certifies the enrollment of the eligible veteran or eligible person on an individual semester, term, or quarter basis if the interval between such periods does not exceed one full calendar month.

Correspondence Training Certifications

(b) No educational assistance allowance shall be paid to an eligible veteran or spouse or surviving spouse enrolled in and pursuing a program of education exclusively by correspondence until the Secretary shall have received—

(1) from the eligible veteran or spouse or surviving spouse a certificate as to the number of lessons actually completed by the veteran or spouse or surviving spouse and serviced by the educational institution; and

(2) from the training establishment a certification or an endorsement on the

veteran's or spouse's or surviving spouse's certificate, as to the number of lessons completed by the veteran or spouse or surviving spouse and serviced by the institution.

Apprenticeship and Other On-Job Training

(c) No training assistance allowance shall be paid to an eligible veteran or eligible person enrolled in and pursuing a program of apprenticeship or other on-job training until the Secretary shall have received—

(1) from such veteran or person a certification as to such veteran's or person's actual attendance during such period; and

(2) from the training establishment a certification, or an endorsement on the veteran's or person's certificate, that such veteran or person was enrolled in and pursuing a program of apprenticeship or other on-job training during such period.

Advance Payment of Initial Educational Assistance or Subsistance Allowance

(d)(1) The educational assistance or subsistence allowance advance payment provided for in this subsection is based upon a finding by the Congress that eligible veterans and eligible persons may need additional funds at the beginning of a school term to meet the expenses of books, travel, deposits, and payment for living quarters, the initial installment of tuition, and the other special expenses which are concentrated at the beginning of a school term.

(2) Subject to the provisions of this subsection, and under regulations which the Secretary shall prescribe, an eligible veteran or eligible person shall be paid an educational assistance allowance or subsistence allowance, as appropriate, advance payment. Such advance payment shall be made in an amount equivalent to the allowance for the month or fraction thereof in which pursuit of the program will commence, plus the allowance for the succeeding month. In the case of a person on active duty, who is pursuing a program of education, the advance payment shall be in a lump sum based upon the amount payable for the entire quarter, semester, or term, as applicable. In no event shall an advance payment be made under this subsection to a veteran or person intending to pursue a program of education on less than a half-time basis. An advance payment may not be made under this subsection to any veteran or person unless the veteran or person requests such payment and the Secretary finds that the educational institution at which such veteran or person is accepted or enrolled has agreed to, and can satisfactorily, carry out the provisions of paragraphs 4(B) and (C) and (5) of this subsection. The application for advance payment, to be made on a form prescribed by the Secretary, shall—

(A) in the case if an initial enrollment of a veteran or person in an educational institution, contain information showing that the veteran or person (i) is eligible for educational benefits, (ii) has been accepted by the institution, and (iii) has notified the institution of such veteran's or person's intention to attend that institution; and

(B) in the case of a re-enrollment of a veteran or person, contain information showing that the veteran or person (i) is eligible to continue such veteran's or person's program of education or training and (ii) intends to re-enroll in the same institution,

and, in either case, shall also state the number of semester or clock-hours to be pursued by such veteran or person.

(3) For purposes of the Secretary's determination whether any veteran or person is eligible for an advance payment under this section, the information submitted by the institution, the veteran or person, shall establish such veteran's or person's eligibility unless there is evidence in such veteran's or person's file in the processing office establishing that the veteran or person is not eligible for such advance payment.

(4) The advance payment authorized by paragraph (2) of this subsection shall, in the case of an eligible veteran or eligible person, be (A) drawn in favor of the veteran or person; (B) mailed to the educational institution listed on the application form for temporary care and delivery to the veteran or person by such institution; and (C) delivered to the veteran or person upon such veteran's or person's registration at such institution, but in no event shall such delivery be made earlier than thirty days before the program of education is to commence.

(5) Upon delivery of the advance payment pursuant to paragraph (4) of this subsection, the institution shall submit to the Secretary a certification of such delivery. If such delivery is not effected within thirty days after commencement of the program of education in question, such institution shall return such payment to the Secretary forthwith.

Recovery of Erroneous Payments

(e)(1) Subject to paragraph (2), if an eligible veteran or eligible person fails to enroll in or pursue a course for which an educational assistance or subsistence allowance advance payment is made, the amount of such payment and any amount of subsequent payments which, in whole or in part, are due to erroneous information required to be furnished under subsection (d)(2) of this section shall become an overpayment and shall constitute a liability of such veteran or person to the United States and may be recovered, unless waived pursuant to section 5302 of this title, from any benefit otherwise due such veteran or person under any law administered by the Department of Veterans Affairs or may be recovered in the same manner as any other debt due the United States.

(2) Paragraph (1) shall not apply to the recovery of an overpayment of an educational allowance or subsistence allowance advance payment to an eligible veteran or eligible person who fails to enroll in or pursue a course of education for which the payment is made if such failure is due to the death of the veteran or person.

Payments for Less Than Half-Time Training

(f) Payment of educational assistance allowance in the case of any eligible veteran or eligible person pursuing a program of education on less than a half-time basis shall be made in an amount computed for the entire quarter, semester, or term not later than the last day of the month immediately following the month in which certification is received from the educational institution that such veteran or person has enrolled in and is pursuing a program at such institution. Such lump sum payment shall be computed at the rate provided in section 3482(b) or 3532(a)(2) of this title, as applicable.

Determination of Enrollment, Pursuit, and Attendance

(g) The Secretary may, pursuant to regulations which the Secretary shall prescribe, determine and define enrollment in, pursuit of, and attendance at, any program of education or training or course by an eligible veteran or eligible person for any period for which the veteran or person receives an educational assistance or subsistence allowance under this chapter [38 USCS §§ 3670 et seq.] for pursuing such program or course. Subject to such reports and proof as the Secretary may require to show an eligible veteran's or eligible person's enrollment in and satisfactory pursuit of such person's program, the Secretary may withhold payment of benefits to such eligible veteran or eligible person until the required proof is received and the amount of the payment is appropriately adjusted. The Secretary may accept such veteran's or person's monthly certification of enrollment in and satisfactory pursuit of such veteran's or person's program as sufficient proof of the certified matters.

(Added Oct. 24, 1972, P. L. 92-540, Title II, § 201, 86 Stat. 1076; Dec. 28, 1973, P. L. 93-208, 87 Stat. 907; Dec. 3, 1974, P. L. 93-508, Title II, § 209, 88 Stat. 1584; Oct. 15, 1976, P. L. 94-502, Title V, §§ 505, 506, 513(a)(5)–(12), 90 Stat. 2400, 2402; Oct. 17, 1980, P. L. 96-466, Title III, Part C, §§ 341, 342, Title VI, §§ 601(c), (d), 602(c), 94 Stat. 2198, 2208; Aug. 13, 1981, P. L. 97-35, Title XX, § 2003(c), 95 Stat. 782; Oct. 12, 1982, P. L. 97-295, § 4(52), 96 Stat. 1308; Oct. 14, 1982, P. L. 97-306, Title II, § 205(c), 96 Stat. 1434; Oct. 28, 1986, P. L. 99-576, Title III, Part A, §§ 315(a)(1), 316, Title VII, § 701(59), 100 Stat. 3274, 3296; Nov. 18, 1988, P. L. 100-689, Title I, Part B, § 121(a), 102 Stat. 4173; Dec. 18, 1989, P. L. 101-237, Title IV, §§ 412(a), 415(a), 423(b)(1), (2), 103 Stat. 2085, 2086, 2092; May 7, 1991, P. L. 102-40, Title IV, § 402(d)(1), 105 Stat. 239; Aug. 6, 1991, P. L. 102-83, § 5(a), (c)(1), 105 Stat. 406; Oct. 10, 1991, P. L. 102-127, § 6(a), 105 Stat. 622; Oct. 29, 1992, P. L. 102-568, Title III, § 314, 106 Stat. 4333; Nov. 2, 1994, P. L. 103-446, Title VI, § 605(a)(2)(B), Title XII, § 1201(i)(6), 108 Stat. 4672, 4688.)

HISTORY; ANCILLARY LAWS AND DIRECTIVES

Amendments:

1973. Act Dec. 28, 1973, in subsec. (a), added the concluding matter.

1974. Act Dec. 3, 1974 (effective 12/3/74, as provided by § 503 of such Act, which appears as 38 USCS § 3452 note), in subsec. (a)(2), inserted "(or customary vacation periods connected therewith)".

1976. Act Oct. 15, 1976, § 505 (effective 12/1/76, as provided by § 703(c) of such Act), in subsec. (a), in para. (1), deleted "or" following "of this title;", in para. (2), substituted a semicolon for the concluding period, and added paras. (3)–(5).

38 USCS § 3680   Veterans' Benefits

Act Oct. 15, 1976, §§ 506, 513(a)(5), (6), (11), (12), (effective 10/15/76, as provided by § 703(b) of such Act), in subsec. (a), in para. (1), substituted "such veteran's or person's" for "his", and substituted "Notwithstanding the foregoing, the Administrator may, subject to such regulations as the Administrator shall prescribe, continue to pay allowances to eligible veterans and eligible persons enrolled in courses set forth in clause (1) or (2) of this subsection—" and paras. (A)–(C) for concluding matter which read: "Notwithstanding the foregoing, the Administrator may, subject to such regulations as he shall prescribe, continue to pay allowances to eligible veterans and eligible persons enrolled in courses set forth in clause (1) or (2) of this subsection during periods when the schools are temporarily closed under an established policy based upon an Executive order of the President or due to an emergency situation, and such periods shall not be counted as absences for the purposes of clause (2)."; in subsec. (b), in the introductory matter and paras. (1) and (2), substituted "spouse or surviving spouse" for "wife or widow" wherever appearing, and in para. (2), substituted "spouse's or surviving spouse's" for "wife's or widow's"; in subsec. (c)(1), substituted "such veteran's or person's" for "his"; in subsec. (d), in para. (2)(A), (B), substituted "such veteran's or person's" for "his", in para. (4), substituted "such veteran's or person's" for "his" wherever appearing and substituted "the veteran or person" for "he" preceding "is not", and in para. (5), substituted "such veteran's or person's" for "his"; in subsec. (f) (prior to redesignation as subsec. (e) by Act Oct. 15, 1976, § 513(a)(10)), substituted "such veteran or person" for "him"; and in subsec. (h) (prior to redesignation as subsec. (g) by Act Oct. 15, 1976, § 513(a)(10)), substituted "the Administrator" for "he", and substituted "the veteran or person" for "he".

Act Oct. 15, 1976, § 513(a)(7)–(10) (effective as provided by § 513(b) of such Act, which appears as a note to this section), in subsec. (d)(1), inserted "may"; in subsec. (d)(2), introductory matter, inserted "An advance payment may not be made under this subsection to any veteran or person unless the veteran or person requests such payment and the Administrator finds that the educational institution at which such veteran or person is accepted or enrolled has agreed to, and can satisfactorily, carry out the provisions of paragraphs 5(B) and (C) and (6) of this subsection."; deleted subsec. (e) and the heading thereto which read:

"Prepayment of Subsequent Educational Assistance or Subsistence Allowance

"(e) Except as provided in subsection (g) of this section, subsequent payments of educational assistance or subsistence allowance to an eligible veteran or eligible person shall be prepaid each month, subject to such reports and proof of enrollment in and satisfactory pursuit of such programs as the Administrator may require. The Administrator may withhold the final payment for a period of enrollment until such proof is received and the amount of the final payment appropriately adjusted."; redesignated subsecs. (f)–(h) as subsecs. (e)–(g), respectively; and in subsec. (g), as so redesignated, inserted "Subject to such reports and proof as the Administrator may require to show an eligible veteran's or eligible person's enrollment in and satisfactory pursuit of such person's program, the Administrator is authorized to withhold the final payment of benefits to such person until the required proof is received and the amount of the final payment is appropriately adjusted.".

1980. Act Oct. 17, 1980 (effective 10/1/80, as provided by § 802(c)(1), (f)(1) of such Act, which appear as 38 USCS §§ 3452, 5314 notes, respectively), in subsec. (a), in the preliminary matter, inserted "in, and pursuit of, such program", in para. (1), substituted "institution, with the provisions of such regulations as may be prescribed by the Administrator pursuant to subsection (g) of this section, and with the requirements of this chapter or of chapter 34 or 35 of this title, but payment may be made for an actual period of pursuit of one or more unit subjects pursued for a period of time shorter than the enrollment period at the educational institution" for "institution and the requirements of this chapter or of chapter 34 or 35 of this title", in para. (2), inserted "and periods (not to exceed five days in any twelve-month period) when the institution is not in session because of teacher conferences or teacher training sessions", in para. (4), deleted "or" following "circumstances;", in para. (5), substituted "; or" for ".", and added para. (6); in subsec. (d), in para. (2), preliminary matter, deleted "(other than under subchapter VI of chapter 34)" following "pursuing a program of education", and substituted "paragraphs 4(B) and (C) and (5)" for "paragraphs 5(B) and (C) and (6)", deleted para. (3) which read:

"(3) Subject to the provisions of this subsection, and under regulations which the Administrator shall prescribe, a person eligible for education or training under the provisions of subchapter VI of chapter 34 of this title shall be entitled to a lump-sum educational assistance allowance advance payment. Such advance payment shall in no event be made earlier than thirty days prior to the date on which pursuit of the person's program of education or training is to commence. The application for the advance payment, to be made on a form prescribed by the Administrator, shall, in addition to the information prescribed in paragraph (2)(A), specify—

"(A) that the program to be pursued has been approved;

"(B) the anticipated cost and the number of Carnegie, clock, or semester hours to be pursued; and

"(C) where the program to be pursued is other than a high school credit course, the need of the person to pursue the course or courses to be taken.";

redesignated paras. (4)–(6), as paras. (3)–(5), respectively, in para. (4), as so redesignated, substituted "paragraph (2)" for "paragraphs (2) and (3)", and in para. (5), as so redesignated, substituted "paragraph (4)" for "paragraph (5)"; in subsec. (e), deleted "and (3)" following "subsection (d)(2)"; in subsec. (f), deleted "(except as provided by subsection (d)(3) of this section)" following "half-time basis"; and in subsec. (g), inserted "and define".

1981. Act Aug. 13, 1981 (effective as provided by § 2006 of such Act, which appears as 38 USCS § 3231 note), in subsec. (a), introductory matter, deleted "or a program of flight training" after "correspondence".

1982. Act Oct. 12, 1982, in subsec. (a), in the introductory matter, substituted "1508" for "1504", in para. (5), substituted "than 6" for "the 6", and, in cls. (A)–(C), inserted "of this subsection" following "(2)", each place it appears.

Act Oct. 14, 1982, in subsec. (a), in the introductory matter, purported to substitute "section 1508" for "section 1504" which amendment was previously made by Act Oct. 12, 1982 (see the 1982 Amendments notes to this section); in para. (4), inserted "or" following the concluding semicolon, in para. (5), substituted a period for "; or" following "institution", and deleted para. (6), which read: "to any eligible veteran or person incarcerated in a Federal, State, or local prison or jail for any course (A) to the extent the tuition and fees of the veteran or person are paid under any Federal program (other than a program administered by the Administrator) or under any State or local program, or (B) for which there are no tuition and fees.".

1986. Act Oct. 28, 1986, in subsec. (a), in para. (1), inserted ", or a course that meets the requirements of section 1788(a)(7) of this title," and in para. (2) inserted "courses that meet the requirements of section 1788(a)(7) of this title and"; in subsec. (d)(2), substituted "person" for "serviceman" following "case of a"; and in subsec. (f), substituted "not later than the last day of" for "during".

1988. Act Nov. 18, 1988 (applicable as provided by § 121(b) of such Act, which appears as a note to this section), in subsec. (a)(4), inserted ", except that, in the first instance of withdrawal by an eligible veteran or person from a course or courses with respect to which such veteran or person has been paid assistance under this title, mitigating circumstances shall be considered to exist with respect to courses totaling not more than six semester hours or the equivalent thereof".

1989. Act Dec. 18, 1989, in subsec. (a), in para. (1), deleted "enrolled in a course which leads to a standard college degree, or a course that meets the requirements of section 1788(a)(7) of this title," following "eligible person", deleted para. (2) which read: "to any eligible veteran or eligible person enrolled in a course which does not lead to a standard college degree (excluding courses that meet the requirements of section 1788(a)(7) of this title and programs of apprenticeship and programs of other on-job training authorized by section 1787 of this title) for any day of absence in excess of thirty days in a twelve-month period, not counting as absences weekends or legal holidays (or customary vacation periods connected therewith) established by Federal or State law (or in the case of the Republic of the Philippines, Philippine law) during which the institution is not regularly in session and periods (not to exceed five days in any twelve-month period) when the institution is not in session because of teacher conferences or teacher training sessions;", redesignated paras. (3)–(5) as paras. (2)–(5), respectively, in the intervening matter, substituted "set forth in clause (1)" for "set forth in clause (1) or (2)", in subpara. (A), deleted ", and such periods shall not be counted as absences for the purposes of clause (2) of this subsection" following "situation", in subpara. (B), deleted ", but such periods shall be counted as absences for the purposes of clause (2) of this subsection" following "30 days", and in subpara. (C), deleted ", but such periods shall be counted as absences for the purposes of clause (2) of this subsection" following "month"; and in subsec. (g), substituted "the Secretary may withhold payment of benefits to such eligible veteran or eligible person until the required proof is received and the amount of the payment is appropriately adjusted. The Secretary may accept such veteran's or person's monthly certification of enrollment in and satisfactory pursuit of such veteran's or person's program as sufficient proof of the certified matters." for "the Administrator is authorized to withhold the final payment of benefits to such person until the required proof is received and the amount of the final payment is appropriately adjusted.".

Such Act further, substituted "Secretary" for "Administrator", "Secretary's" for "Administrator's", and "Department of Veterans Affairs" for "Veterans' Administration", wherever appearing, throughout the entire section.

1991. Act May 7, 1991, § 402(d)(1), amended the references in this section to reflect the redesignations made by §§ 401(a)(4) and 402(b) of such Act (see Table II preceding 38 USCS § 101).

Act Aug. 6, 1991, redesignated this section, formerly 38 USCS § 1780, as 38 USCS § 3680, and amended the references in this section to reflect the redesignations made by § 5(a) of such Act (see Table III preceding 38 USCS § 101).

Act Oct. 10, 1991 (effective 8/1/90 as provided by § 6(b) of such Act, which appears as a note to this section) substituted subsec. (a)(3) for one which read: "to any eligible veteran or person for a course for which the grade assigned is not used in computing the requirements for graduation including a course from which the student withdraws unless the Administrator finds there are mitigating circumstances, except that, in the first instance of withdrawal by an eligible veteran or person from a course or courses with respect to which such veteran or person has been paid assistance under this title, mitigating circumstances shall be considered to exist with respect to courses totaling not more than six semester hours or the equivalent thereof; or".

1992. Act Oct. 29, 1992, in subsec. (e), designated the existing provisions as para. (1), in such paragraph as so designated, substituted "Subject to paragraph (2), if" for "If" and deleted a comma following "eligible person", and added para. (2).

1994. Act Nov. 2, 1994 (applicable to programs and courses commencing more than 90 days after the date of enactment, as provided by § 605(b) of such Act, which appears as 38 USCS § 3672 note), in subsec. (a), in para. (2), inserted "or" following the concluding semicolon, in para. (3), substituted a period for "; or" following "equivalent thereof", deleted para. (4), which read: "(4) to any eligible veteran or person for pursuit of a program of education exclusively by correspondence as authorized under section 3686 of this title or for the pursuit of a correspondence portion of a combination correspondence-residence course leading to a vocational objective where the normal period of time required to complete such correspondence course or portion is less than 6 months. A certification as to the normal period of time required to complete the course must be made to the Secretary by the educational institution.", and, in subpara. (C) of the concluding paragraph, substituted "one full" for "1 full".

Other provisions:

Effective dates of provisions of this section. Act Oct. 24, 1972, P. L. 92-540, Title VI, § 603, 86 Stat. 1099, provided:

"(a) The prepayment provisions of subsection (e) of section 1780 of title 38, United States Code (as added by section 201 of this Act) [former subsec. (e) of this section], shall become effective on November 1, 1972.

"(b) The advance payment provisions of section 1780 of title 38, United States Code (as added by section 201 of this Act), shall become effective on August 1, 1973, or at such time prior thereto as the Administrator of Veterans' Affairs shall specify in a certification filed with the Committees on Veterans' Affairs of the Congress.".

Study of tuition assistance allowance program abuses. Act Dec. 3, 1974, P. L. 93-508, Title I, § 105, 88 Stat. 1581 (effective 9/1/74, as provided by § 501 of such Act), provided:

"(a) The Administrator shall carry out directly a thorough study and investigation of the administrative difficulties and opportunities or abuse that would be occasioned by enactment of some form of variable tuition assistance allowance program, with reference to such difficulties and abuses experienced by the Veterans' Administration after the end of World War II in carrying out the provisions of Veterans' Regulation Numbered 1(a), relating to the payment of tuition and related expenses for veterans of World War II pursuing a program of education or training under the Servicemen's Readjustment Act of 1944 [58 Stat. 284], and to any such difficulties and abuses presently being experienced by the Veterans' Administration in carrying out existing tuition assistance programs under title 38, United States Code, including chapter 31 [38 USCS §§ 3100 et seq.] vocational rehabilitation, correspondence courses, flight training and PREP, and of ways in which any such difficulties and abuses could be avoided or minimized through legislative or administrative action so as to ensure an expeditious, orderly, and effective implementation of any tuition assistance allowance program.

"(b) In carrying out the study and investigation required by subsection (a), the Administrator shall consult with and solicit the views and suggestions of interested veterans' organizations, educational groups and associations, persons receiving assistance under chapters 31, 34, 35 and 36 of title 38, United States Code [38 USCS §§ 3100 et seq., 3451 et seq., 3500 et seq., and 3670 et seq.], other Federal departments and agencies, and other interested parties.

"(c) The Administrator shall report to the Congress and the President not later than one year after the date of enactment of this Act on the results of the study and investigation carried out under this section, including any recommendations for legislative or administrative action.".

Application and effective date of amendments made by § 513(a)(7)-(10) of Act Oct. 15, 1976. Act Oct. 15, 1976, P. L. 94-502, Title V, § 513(b), 90 Stat. 2404, provided: "The amendments made by paragraphs (7), (8), (9), and (10) of subsection (a) shall take effect June 1, 1977, and shall apply with respect to educational assistance allowances and subsistence allowances paid under title 38, United States Code, for months after May 1977.

Payment of educational benefits to veterans and dependents when schools are temporarily closed to conserve energy. Ex. Or. No. 12020 of Nov. 8, 1977, 42 Fed. Reg. 58509, provided:

"SECTION 1. Whenever an educational institution submits evidence which satisfies the Administrator of Veterans' Affairs that energy consumption will be abnormally high during the winter months or that available energy supplies will be inadequate to meet the needs of the school, and that, in the interest of energy conservation, the institution plans to close between semesters or terms for a period not to exceed 45 days, the Administrator may continue to pay monthly educational assistance benefits to veterans and eligible persons enrolled in such schools. Such authority may be exercised only once during any 12-month period with respect to any educational institution.

"SEC. 2. The Administrator shall advise veterans and other eligible persons of the effect of accepting educational assistance benefits under the provisions of Section 1 of this Order [this note] on their period of entitlement.".

Application and construction of the Oct. 12, 1982 amendment of this section. For provisions as to the application and construction of the Oct. 12, 1982 amendment of this section, see § 5 of such Act, which appears as 10 USCS § 101 note.

Application of amendment made to subsec. (a)(4) by Act Nov. 18, 1988. Act Nov. 18, 1988, P. L. 100-689, Title I, Part B, § 121(b), 102 Stat. 4173, provides: "The amendment made by subsection (a) [amending subsec. (a)(4) of this section] shall apply so as to require that mitigating circumstances be considered to exist only with respect to withdrawals from a course or courses being pursued with assistance under title 38, United States Code, that occur on or after June 1, 1989.".

CROSS REFERENCES

This section is referred to in 38 USCS §§ 3034, 3108, 3684, 3698, 5113.

RESEARCH GUIDE

Am Jur:
77 Am Jur 2d, Veterans and Veterans' Laws §§ 132, 133, 139, 140, 142–144.

INTERPRETIVE NOTES AND DECISIONS

1. Generally
2. Recovery of overpayments, generally
3. —Erroneous payments
4. —Termination of course prior to completion

1. Generally

38 USCS § 1780 [now 38 USCS § 3680] provides United States right of recovery against veterans who received benefits and then failed to earn grades which count towards graduation; government may seek reimbursement of educational benefits, and recovery of overpayments does not violate due process where recipient is informed of overpayments and right to seek waiver, but fails to seek waiver within 2 year limitations. United States v Brandon (1986, CA4 NC) 781 F2d 1051.

2. Recovery of overpayments, generally

Veteran's Administration [now Department of Veterans Affairs] may recover, as overpayments, payments made to veteran who did not receive passing grades in courses for which he had received monthly advance educational assistance benefits. United States v Brandon (1986, CA4 NC) 781 F2d 1051.

Failure or dropping out of course is not equivalent to obtaining original educational aid through "erroneous information," under 38 USCS § 1780 [now 38 USCS § 3680] provision for recovery from veterans of payments based upon erroneous information furnished to Administrator [now Secretary], nor may recovery of educational assistance already paid be based upon prospective language of § 1780 [now 38 USCS § 3680] prohibiting payment for course from which student withdraws. United States v Brandon (1984, WD NC) 584 F Supp 803.

Section 1780 [now section 3680] was intended to allow United States to recover funds disbursed to veterans for classes when no academic credit was achieved, in absence of mitigating circumstances. United States v Garrahan (1985, ND Fla) 614 F Supp 152.

3. —Erroneous payments

Veteran is required to reimburse government for erroneous overpayment of educational benefits by Veterans Administration [now Department of Veterans Affairs] under 38 USCS § 1780(e) [now 38 USCS § 3680(e)] where he received payment for period during which he completed no courses because of illness but failed to avail himself of right granted by § 1780(3) [now § 3680(3)] to apply for waiver of indebtedness pursuant to § 3102 [now § 5302], since reimbursement requirement applies regardless of whether overpayment results from fault of veteran or not. United States v Kirby (1981, ND Ga) 522 F Supp 424.

38 USCS § 1780 [now 38 USCS § 3680] confers no authority on government to recover erroneous overpayments of educational assistance to veteran not paid as advances. United States v Steinberg (1982, DC Mass) 553 F Supp 184.

4. —Termination of course prior to completion

United States was entitled to recover overpayment of Veteran's Administration [now Department of Veterans Affairs] educational benefits where veteran terminates his course prior to its completion and receives non-punitive grades; termination related back to first day of school term resulting in overpayment for entire term. United States v Duchene (1985, SD Iowa) 624 F Supp 177.

§ 3680A. Disapproval of enrollment in certain courses

(a) The Secretary shall not approve the enrollment of an eligible veteran in—

(1) any bartending course or personality development course;

(2) any sales or sales management course which does not provide specialized training within a specific vocational field;

(3) any type of course which the Secretary finds to be avocational or recreational in character (or the advertising for which the Secretary finds contains significant avocational or recreational themes) unless the veteran submits justification showing that the course will be of bona fide use in the pursuit of the veteran's present or contemplated business or occupation; or

(4) any independent study program except an accredited independent study program (including open circuit television) leading to a standard college degree.

(b) Except to the extent otherwise specifically provided in this title or chapter 106 of title 10 [10 USCS §§ 2131 et seq.], the Secretary shall not approve the enrollment of an eligible veteran in any course of flight training other than one given by an educational institution of higher learning for credit toward a standard college degree the eligible veteran is seeking.

(c) The Secretary shall not approve the enrollment of an eligible veteran in any course to be pursued by radio.

(d)(1) Except as provided in paragraph (2) of this subsection, the Secretary shall not approve the enrollment of any eligible veteran, not already enrolled, in any course for any period during which the Secretary finds that more than 85 percent of the students enrolled in the course are having all or part of their tuition, fees, or other charges paid to or for them by the educational institution or by the Department of Veterans Affairs under this title or under chapter 106 of title 10 [10 USCS §§ 2131 et seq.]. The Secretary may waive the requirements of this subsection, in whole or in part, if the Secretary determines, pursuant to regulations which the Secretary shall prescribe, it to be in the interest of the eligible veteran and the Federal Government. The provisions of this subsection shall not apply to any course offered by an educational institution if the total number of veterans and persons receiving assistance under this chapter [38 USCS §§ 3670 et seq.] or chapter 30, 31, 32, or 35 of this title [38 USCS §§ 3001 et seq., 3100 et seq., 3201 et seq., or 3500 et seq.] or under chapter 106 of title 10 [10 USCS § 2131 et seq.] who are enrolled in such institution equals 35 percent or less, or such other percent as the Secretary prescribes in regulations, of the total student enrollment at such institution (computed separately for the main campus and any branch or extension of such institution), except that the Secretary may apply the provisions of this subsection with respect to any course in which the Secretary has reason to believe that the enrollment of such veterans and persons may be in excess of 85 percent of the total student enrollment in such course.

(2) Paragraph (1) of this subsection does not apply with respect to the enrollment of a veteran—

(A) in a course offered pursuant to section 3019, 3034(a)(3), 3234, or 3241(a)(2) of this title;

(B) in a farm cooperative training course; or

(C) in a course described in subsection (g).

(e) The Secretary may not approve the enrollment of an eligible veteran in a course not leading to a standard college degree offered by a proprietary profit or proprietary nonprofit educational institution if—

(1) the educational institution has been operating for less than two years;

(2) the course is offered at a branch of the educational institution and the branch has been operating for less than two years; or

(3) following either a change in ownership or a complete move outside its original general locality, the educational institution does not retain substantially the same faculty, student body, and courses as before the change in ownership or the move outside the general locality (as determined in accordance with regulations the Secretary shall prescribe) unless the educational institution following such change or move has been in operation for at least two years.

(f) The Secretary may not approve the enrollment of an eligible veteran in a course as a part of a program of education offered by an educational institution if the course is provided under contract by another educational institution or entity and—

(1) the Secretary would be barred under subsection (e) from approving the enrollment of an eligible veteran in the course of the educational institution or entity providing the course under contract; or

(2) the educational institution or entity providing the course under contract has not obtained approval for the course under this chapter [38 USCS §§ 3670 et seq.].

(g) Notwithstanding subsections (e) and (f)(1), the Secretary may approve the enrollment of an eligible veteran in a course approved under this chapter if the course is offered by an educational institution under contract with the Department of Defense or the Department of Transportation and is given on or immediately adjacent to a military base, Coast Guard station, National Guard facility, or facility of the Selected Reserve.

(Added Oct. 29, 1992, P. L. 102-568, Title III, § 313(a)(2), 106 Stat. 4331; Oct. 9, 1996, P. L. 104-275, Title I, §§ 103(a)(2), (b), 104(c), 110 Stat. 3326, 3327; Nov. 21, 1997, P. L. 105-114, Title IV, § 401(d), (e), 111 Stat. 2293.)

HISTORY; ANCILLARY LAWS AND DIRECTIVES

Amendments:

1996. Act Oct. 9, 1996, in subsec. (c), substituted "radio." for "radio or by open circuit television, except that the Secretary may approve the enrollment of an eligible veteran in a course, to be pursued in residence, leading to a standard college degree which includes, as an integral part thereof, subjects offered through open circuit television."; in subsec. (d)(2)(C), substituted "subsection (g)" for "section 3689(b)(6) of this title"; and added subsecs. (e)–(g).

1997. Act Nov. 21, 1997, in subsec. (a)(4), inserted "(including open circuit television)"; and, in subsec. (g), substituted "subsections (e) and (f)(1)" for "subsections (e) and (f)".

Other provisions:
Applicability of section. Act Oct. 29, 1992, P. L. 102-568, § 313(b), which appears as 10 USCS § 2136 note, provides that this section is not applicable to any person receiving educational assistance for pursuit of an independent study program in which the person was enrolled on Oct. 29, 1992, for as long as such person is continuously thereafter so enrolled and meets the requirements of eligibility for such assistance for the pursuit of such program under Title 10 or Title 38, USCS, in effect on that date.

CROSS REFERENCES

This section is referred to in 10 USCS § 16136; 38 USCS §§ 3034, 3241.

RESEARCH GUIDE

Am Jur:
77 Am Jur 2d, Veterans and Veterans' Laws §§ 140, 142.

INTERPRETIVE NOTES AND DECISIONS

1. Generally
2. Constitutionality
3. Closed-circuit television courses

1. Generally

Regulation by Administrator [now Secretary] requiring finding of "complete justification," means "convincing evidence"; hence, decision by Administrator that evidence submitted was not convincing was final and was not subject to review by court. Slocumb v Gray (1949) 86 US App DC 5, 179 F2d 31.

Benefits are to be paid to those veterans who were properly enrolled prior to first day school was put on notice that its employment justification was invalid. VA GCO 6-77.

2. Constitutionality

As to two requirements of federal statutory provisions governing veterans' educational assistance program (38 USCS §§ 1651 et seq. [now 38 USCS §§ 3451 et seq.])—both of which may be waived by Administrator of Veterans Administration [now Department of Veterans Affairs] —under which veterans' educational benefits are not available if course in which veteran enrolls is (1) course in which more than 85 percent of students are receiving veterans' educational benefits or financial assistance from any federal agency (38 USCS § 1673 [now 38 USCS § 3680A]) or (2) course which has been offered for less than two years (38 USCS § 1789 [now 38 USCS § 3689]), substantial constitutional questions are not raised as to claim that restrictions violate substantive due process by interfering with freedom of educational choice, or claim that restrictions violate procedural due process by not affording affected veterans hearing on question whether restrictions should be applied or waived; 38 USCS § 1673 [now 38 USCS § 3473] or 38 USCS § 1789 [now 38 USCS § 3689] do not violate principle of equal protection under due process clause of Fifth Amendment on ground that other federal educational assistance programs do not contain such course limitations, since (1) requirements are valid exercises on Congress' power, it not being irrational for Congress to conclude that restricting benefits to established courses that have attracted substantial number of students whose educations are not being subsidized by federal government would be useful in accomplishing objectives of preventing waste of benefits on educational programs of little value and of preventing charlatans from obtaining veterans' education money, and (2) such otherwise reasonable restrictions are not made irrational because of their absence from other federal financial assistance programs, in view of (a) restrictions having been imposed in direct response to problems experienced in administration of veterans' benefits programs, (b) there being no indication that identical abuses had not been encountered in other

READJUSTMENT BENEFITS 38 USCS § 3681

federal grant programs, and (c) there being no requirement under Constitution that Congress detect and correct abuses in administration of all related programs before acting to combat those experienced in one. Cleland v National College of Business (1978) 435 US 213, 55 L Ed 2d 225, 98 S Ct 1024.

Fact that federal statutory provisions under which veterans' benefits are not generally available if course in which veteran enrolls is one in which more than 85 percent of students are receiving educational benefits from Veterans Administration or any federal agency (38 USCS § 1673 [now 38 USCS § 3680A]), or if course is one which has been offered for less than two years (38 USCS § 1789 [now 38 USCS § 3689]) may deprive those veterans living in areas where there are no programs which satisfy such statutory requirements of opportunity to take full advantage of benefits made available to veterans is not sufficient basis for United States Supreme Court to exercise greater judicial oversight, since undisputed importance of education will not alone cause court to depart from usual standard for reviewing social and economic legislation for purposes of equal protection. Cleland v National College of Business (1978) 435 US 213, 55 L Ed 2d 225, 98 S Ct 1024.

Provisions of 38 USCS § 1673(d) [now 38 USCS § 3680A(d)] are not unconstitutional as being in violation of Fifth Amendment (USCS Constitution, Amendment 5), in that unequal application of provisions of such section are not totally lacking in rational justification or patently arbitrary, nor were veterans denied due process of law in the promulgation of 1976 amendment to 38 USCS § 1673 [now 38 USCS § 3680A]; interest of veteran in veteran's benefits is such interest as is entitled to constitutional protection, but where both procedural and substantive due process are provided, court will not void legislation simply because it is faulty legislation. Fielder v Cleland (1977, ED Mich) 433 F Supp 115, affd without op (1978, CA6 Mich) 577 F2d 740.

Provisions of 38 USCS § 1673(d) [now 38 USCS § 3680A(d)] are not unconstitutional as denying equal protection to veterans seeking to enter saturated classes, in which ratio of veterans to nonveterans exceeds 85-15 limitation, when compared with those veterans seeking to enroll in not-yet saturated courses, and those nonveteran, but government-funded students, who are not burdened by 85-15 limitation expressed in 38 USCS § 1673(d) [now 38 USCS § 3680A(d)]; legislative goal of allowing free market mechanism to prove worth of course offered, by requiring course to respond to general dictates of open market as well as to those with available federal moneys to spend, is valid, rational goal, and while 85-15 rule may be imperfect, it is not unconstitutional. Rolle v Cleland (1977, DC RI) 435 F Supp 260.

3. Closed-circuit television courses

38 USCS § 1673(c) [now 38 USCS § 3680A(c)] does not bar payment for courses pursued by open circuit television in connection with residential program, even if majority of subjects are being pursued by television, as long as payments per credit hour for television courses are less than payments received per residential credit hour. VA GCO 11-79.

§ 3681. Limitations on educational assistance

(a) No educational assistance allowance granted under chapter 30, 34, 35, or 36 of this title [38 USCS §§ 3001 et seq., 3451 et seq., 3500 et seq., or 3670 et seq.] or 106 or 107 of title 10 [10 USCS §§ 2131 et seq. or 2141 et seq.], or subsistence allowance granted under chapter 31 of this title [38 USCS §§ 3100 et seq.] shall be paid to any eligible person (1) who is on active duty and is pursuing a course of education which is being paid for by the Armed Forces (or by the Department of Health and Human Services in the case of the Public Health Service); or (2) who is attending a course of education or training paid for under chapter 41 of title 5 [5 USCS §§ 4101 et seq.].

(b) No person may receive benefits concurrently under two or more of the provisions of law listed below:

(1) Chapters 30, 31, 32, 34, 35, and 36 of this title [38 USCS §§ 3001 et seq., 3100 et seq., 3201 et seq., 3451 et seq., 3500 et seq., and 3670 et seq.].
(2) Chapters 106 and 107 of title 10 [10 USCS §§ 2131 et seq. and 2141 et seq.].
(3) Section 903 of the Department of Defense Authorization Act, 1981 (Public Law 96-342, 10 U.S.C. 2141 note).
(4) The Hostage Relief Act of 1980 (Public Law 96-449, 5 U.S.C. 5561 note).

(5) The Omnibus Diplomatic Security and Antiterrorism Act of 1986 (Public Law 99-399) [22 USCS §§ 4801 et seq.].
(Added March 3, 1966, P. L. 89-358, § 3(b), 80 Stat. 21; March 26, 1970, P. L. 91-219, Title II, § 213(1), 84 Stat. 83; Oct. 24, 1972, P. L. 92-540, Title IV, § 403(8), 86 Stat. 1090; Oct. 15, 1976, P. L. 94-502, Title V, § 513(a)(13), 90 Stat. 2403; Oct. 17, 1980, P. L. 96-466, Title I, § 102, Title VIII, § 801(e), 94 Stat. 2187, 2216; Oct. 12, 1982, P. L. 97-295, § 4(53), 96 Stat. 1309; March 2, 1984, P. L. 98-223, Title II, § 203(c)(1), 98 Stat. 41; Oct. 19, 1984, P. L. 98-525, Title VII, § 703(c), 98 Stat. 2564; Oct. 28, 1986, P. L. 99-576, Title III, Part A, §§ 317, 321(9), 100 Stat. 3275, 3278; Dec. 18, 1989, P. L. 101-237, Title IV, § 423(a)(8)(A), 103 Stat. 2092; Aug. 6, 1991, P. L. 102-83, § 5(a), 105 Stat. 406; Oct. 29, 1992, P. L. 102-568, Title III, § 315, 106 Stat. 4333.)

HISTORY; ANCILLARY LAWS AND DIRECTIVES

Explanatory notes:
Provisions similar to those contained in this section were contained in former 38 USC §§ 1632(h)(1), 1762 prior to repeal by Act March 3, 1966, P. L. 89-358, §§ 3(a)(2), 4(a), 80 Stat. 23.

Effective date of section:
Act March 3, 1966, P. L. 89-358, § 12(a), 80 Stat. 28, provided that this section is effective on March 3, 1966.

Amendments:
1970. Act March 26, 1970, substituted new catchline and section for ones which read:
"§ 1781. Nonduplication of benefits
"No educational assistance allowance or special training allowance shall be paid on behalf of any eligible person or veteran under chapter 34 or 35 of this title for any period during which such person or veteran is enrolled in and pursuing a program of education or course paid for by the United States under any provision of law other than such chapters, where the payment of an allowance would constitute a duplication of benefits paid from the Federal Treasury to the eligible person or veteran or to his parent or guardian in his behalf.".
1972. Act Oct. 24, 1972, substituted "granted under chapter 34, 35, or 36" for "or special training allowance granted under chapter 34 or 35".
1976. Act Oct. 15, 1976 (effective 10/15/76, as provided by § 703(b) of such Act, which appears as 38 USCS § 3693 note) substituted "such person" for "him".
1980. Act Oct. 17, 1980 (effective 10/1/80, as provided by § 802(a)(6), (h) of such Act, which appear as a note to this section and to 38 USCS § 3452, respectively), inserted ", or subsistence allowance granted under chapter 31," and substituted "Department of Health and Human Services" for "Department of Health, Education, and Welfare".
1982. Act Oct. 12, 1982 substituted "chapter 41 of title 5" for "the Government Employees' Training Act".
1984. Act March 2, 1984 designated the existing provisions as subsec. (a); and added subsec. (b).
Act Oct. 19, 1984, in subsec. (a), inserted "30," substituted "36 of this

title or 106 or 107 of title 10," for "36," and deleted a comma following "chapter 31"; and in subsec. (b)(1), inserted "30,".
1986. Act Oct. 28, 1986, in subsec. (b), in the introductory matter, deleted "for the pursuit of the same program of education" following "below", and in para. (2), substituted "Chapters 106 and 107" for "Chapter 107".
1989. Act Dec. 18, 1989, in subsec. (b), added para. (5).
1991. Act Aug. 6, 1991, redesignated this section, formerly 38 USCS § 1781, as 38 USCS § 3681.
1992. Act Oct. 29, 1992, in subsec. (a), deleted "and whose full salary is being paid to such person while so training" following "paid for under chapter 41 of title 5".

Other provisions:
Duplication of benefits. Act Oct. 15, 1968, P. L. 90-574, Title V, § 504, 82 Stat. 1012, formerly classified as a note to this section, was repealed by Act March 26, 1970, P. L. 91-219, Title II, § 215(a), 84 Stat. 85. It related to the duplication of benefits.
Effective date of amendments made by §§ 102, 103 of Act Oct. 17, 1980. Act Oct. 17, 1980, P. L. 96-466, Title VIII, § 802(a)(6), 94 Stat. 2218, provided: "The amendments made by sections 102 and 103 [amending this section and 38 USCS § 3695] shall become effective on October 1, 1980.".
Application and construction of the Oct. 12, 1982 amendment of this section. For provisions as to the application and construction of the Oct. 12, 1982 amendment of this section, see § 5 of such Act, which appears as 10 USCS § 101 note.

RESEARCH GUIDE

Am Jur:
77 Am Jur 2d, Veterans and Veterans' Laws § 144.

INTERPRETIVE NOTES AND DECISIONS

1. Generally
2. Apprenticeship and job training programs
3. Health profession programs

1. Generally
Service Academy graduates were entitled to educational assistance under § 207 of law entitled Refunds for Certain Service Academy Graduates (38 USCS § 3222 note) even though they previously received tuition benefits from Navy. Tallman v Brown (1997, CA FC) 105 F3d 613.

2. Apprenticeship and job training programs
38 USCS § 1781 [now 38 USCS § 3681] does not apply to programs of apprenticeship and other on-the-job training given by agency of United States where some or all of period on which benefits payments are based consist of related instruction for which government pays tuition. VA GCO 9-77.

3. Health profession programs
Participants in Health Professions Scholarship Program may be paid GI Bill educational assistance benefits while enrolled in such program in inactive status. VA GCO 10-74.

§ 3682. Control by agencies of the United States

Except as provided in section 3674A of this title, no department, agency, or officer of the United States, in carrying out this chapter [38 USCS §§ 3670 et seq.], shall exercise any supervision or control, whatsoever, over any State approving agency, or State educational agency, or any educational institution. Nothing in this section shall be deemed to prevent any department, agency, or

38 USCS § 3682   Veterans' Benefits

officer of the United States from exercising any supervision or control which such department, agency, or officer is authorized by law to exercise over any Federal educational institution or to prevent the furnishing of education under this chapter or chapter 34 or 35 of this title [38 USCS §§ 3670 et seq. or 3451 et seq. or 3500 et seq.] in any institution over which supervision or control is exercised by such other department, agency, or officer under authority of law. (Added March 3, 1966, P. L. 89-358, § 3(b), 80 Stat. 21; Oct. 24, 1972, P. L. 92-540, Title IV, § 403(9), 86 Stat. 1090; May 20, 1988, P. L. 100-323, § 13(b)(6), 102 Stat. 574; Aug. 6, 1991, P. L. 102-83, § 5(a), (c)(1), 105 Stat. 406.)

HISTORY; ANCILLARY LAWS AND DIRECTIVES

Explanatory notes:
Provisions similar to those contained in this section were contained in former 38 USC §§ 1663, 1763, prior to repeal by Act March 3, 1966, P. L. 89-358, § 4(a), 80 Stat. 23.

Effective date of section:
Act March 3, 1966, P. L. 89-358, § 12(a), 80 Stat. 28, provided that this section is effective on March 3, 1966.

Amendments:
1972. Act Oct. 24, 1972, inserted "this chapter or".

1988. Act May 20, 1988 (effective on enactment as provided by § 16(a) of such Act, which appears as 38 USCS § 3104 note) substituted "Except as provided in section 1774A, no" for "No".

1991. Act Aug. 6, 1991, redesignated this section, formerly 38 USCS § 1782, as 38 USCS § 3682, and amended the references in this section to reflect the redesignations made by § 5(a) of such Act (see Table III preceding 38 USCS § 101).

INTERPRETIVE NOTES AND DECISIONS

1. Generally
2. Regulations
3. Subpoenas

1. Generally

Statutory framework in 38 USCS § 1782 [now 38 USCS § 3682] for Veterans Administration [now Department of Veterans Affairs] supervision for approval of courses and mechanics of payment of educational assistance to students creates no substantive rights for students participating in such programs. Rivera Carbana v Cruz (1984, DC Puerto Rico) 588 F Supp 80.

Veterans Administration [now Department of Veterans Affairs] has authority to independently determine that courses or subjects approved by state approval agency which constitute veteran's program of education lead to professional, vocational or educational objective no benefits may be paid if such programs do not, unless they may properly form basis of different program of education and veteran meets all criteria for appropriate change of program. VA GCO 12-83.

2. Regulations

Veterans Administration [now Department of Veterans Affairs] regulations promulgated pursuant to 38 USCS § 1785 [now 38 USCS § 3685], requiring that school must notify agency within 30 days of student's change of status in order to avoid potential liability for overpayments made to ineligible students, do not violate prohibition found in 38 USCS § 1782 [now 38 USCS § 3682] against any agency of United States exercising any supervision or control over state educational institution. Colorado v Veterans Administration (1977, DC Colo) 430 F Supp 551, affd (1979, CA10 Colo) 602 F2d 926, cert den (1980) 444 US 1014, 62 L Ed 2d 643, 100 S Ct 663.

3. Subpoenas

Provision prohibiting agency or its officers from

exercising any administration or control over any educational or training institution does not preclude Administrator [now Secretary] from issuing subpoenas. General Trades School, Inc. v United States (1954, CA8 Mo) 212 F2d 656.

§ 3683. Conflicting interests

(a) Every officer or employee of the Department of Veterans Affairs who has, while such an officer or employee, owned any interest in, or received any wages, salary, dividends, profits, gratuities, or services from any educational institution operated for profit in which an eligible person or veteran was pursuing a program of education or course under this chapter or chapter 34 or 35 of this title [38 USCS §§ 3670 et seq. or 3451 et seq. or 3500 et seq.] shall be immediately dismissed from such officer's or employee's office or employment.

(b) If the Secretary finds that any person who is an officer or employee of a State approving agency has, while such person was such an officer or employee, owned any interest in, or received any wages, salary, dividends, profits, gratuities, or services from, an educational institution operated for profit in which an eligible person or veteran was pursuing a program of education or course under this chapter or chapter 34 or 35 of this title [38 USCS §§ 3670 et seq. or 3451 et seq. or 3500 et seq.], the Secretary shall discontinue making payments under section 3674 of this title to such State approving agency unless such agency shall, without delay, take such steps as may be necessary to terminate the employment of such person and such payments shall not be resumed while such person is an officer or employee of the State approving agency, or State department of veterans' affairs or State department of education.

(c) A State approving agency shall not approve any course offered by an educational institution operated for profit, and, if any such course has been approved, shall disapprove each such course, if it finds that any officer or employee of the Department of Veterans Affairs or the State approving agency owns an interest in, or receives any wages, salary, dividends, profits, gratuities, or services from, such institution.

(d) The Secretary may, after reasonable notice and public hearings, waive in writing the application of this section in the case of any officer or employee of the Department of Veterans Affairs or of a State approving agency, if the Secretary finds that no detriment will result to the United States or to eligible persons or veterans by reasons of such interest or connection of such officer or employee.

(Added March 3, 1966, P. L. 89-358, § 3(b), 80 Stat. 22; Oct. 24, 1972, P. L. 92-540, Title IV, § 403(10), 86 Stat. 1090; Oct. 15, 1976, P. L. 94-502, Title V, § 513(a)(14)–(16), 90 Stat. 2403; Oct. 12, 1982, P. L. 97-295, § 4(54), 96 Stat. 1309; Dec. 18, 1989, P. L. 101-237, Title IV, § 423(b)(1), 103 Stat. 2092; Aug. 6, 1991, P. L. 102-83, § 5(a), (c)(1), 105 Stat. 406.)

HISTORY; ANCILLARY LAWS AND DIRECTIVES

Explanatory notes:
Provisions similar to those contained in this section were contained in for-

38 USCS § 3683

mer 38 USC §§ 1664, 1764 prior to repeal by Act March 3, 1966, P. L. 89-358, §§ 3(a)(3), 4(a), 80 Stat. 23.

Effective date of section:
Act March 3, 1966, P. L. 89-358, § 12(a), 80 Stat. 28, provided that this section is effective on March 3, 1966.

Amendments:
1972. Act Oct. 24, 1972, in subsecs. (a) and (b), inserted "this chapter or".
1976. Act Oct. 15, 1976 (effective 10/15/76, as provided by § 703(b) of such Act, which appears as 38 USCS § 3693 note), in subsec. (a), substituted "such officer's or employee's" for "his"; in subsec. (b), substituted "such person" for "he" and substituted "the Administrator" for "he" preceding "shall discontinue"; and in subsec. (d), substituted "the Administrator" for "he" preceding "finds".
1982. Act Oct. 12, 1982, in subsec. (a), inserted "of this title".
1989. Act Dec. 18, 1989, in subsecs. (a), (c) and (d), substituted "Department of Veterans Affairs" for "Veterans' Administration"; and in subsecs. (b) and (d), substituted "Secretary" for "Administrator", wherever appearing.
1991. Act Aug. 6, 1991, redesignated this section, formerly 38 USCS § 1783, as 38 USCS § 3683, and amended the references in this section to reflect the redesignations made by § 5(a) of such Act (see Table III preceding 38 USCS § 101).

Other provisions:
Application and construction of the Oct. 12, 1982 amendment of this section. For provisions as to the application and construction of the Oct. 12, 1982 amendment of this section, see § 5 of such Act, which appears as 10 USCS § 101 note.

§ 3684. Reports by veterans, eligible persons, and institutions; reporting fee

(a)(1) Except as provided in paragraph (2) of this subsection, the veteran or eligible person and the educational institution offering a course in which such veteran or eligible person is enrolled under chapter 31, 34, [,] 35, or 36 of this title [38 USCS §§ 3100 et seq. 3451 et seq., 3500 et seq., or 3670 et seq.] shall, without delay, report to the Secretary, in the form prescribed by the Secretary, such enrollment and any interruption or termination of the education of each such veteran or eligible person. The date of such interruption or termination will be the last date of pursuit, or, in the case of correspondence training, the last date a lesson was serviced by a school.

(2)(A) In the case of a program of independent study pursued on less than a half-time basis in an educational institution, the Secretary may approve a delay by the educational institution in reporting the enrollment or reenrollment of an eligible veteran or eligible person until the end of the term, quarter, or semester if the educational institution requests the delay and the Secretary determines that it is not feasible for the educational institution to monitor interruption or termination of the veteran's or eligible person's pursuit of such program.

(B) An educational institution which, pursuant to subparagraph (A) of this paragraph, is delaying the reporting of the enrollment or reenrollment of a veteran shall provide the veteran with notice of the delay at the time that the veteran enrolls or reenrolls.

(3)(A) Subject to subparagraph (B) of this paragraph, an educational institution offering courses on a term, quarter, or semester basis may certify the enrollment of a veteran who is not on active duty, or of an eligible person, in such courses for more than one term, quarter, or semester at a time, but not for a period extending beyond the end of a school year (including the summer enrollment period).

(B) Subparagraph (A) of this paragraph shall not apply with respect to any term, quarter, or semester for which the veteran or eligible person is enrolled on a less than half-time basis and shall not be construed as restricting the Secretary from requiring that an educational institution, in reporting an enrollment for more than one term, quarter, or semester, specify the dates of any intervals within or between any such terms, quarters, or semesters.

(b) The Secretary, prior to making payment of a reporting fee to an educational institution, as provided for in subsection (c) of this section, shall require such institution to certify that it has exercised reasonable diligence in determining whether such institution or any course offered by such institution approved for the enrollment of veterans or eligible persons meets all of the applicable requirements of chapters 31, 34, 35, and 36 of this title [38 USCS §§ 3100 et seq., 3451 et seq., 3500 et seq., and 3670 et seq.] and that it will, without delay, report any failure to meet any such requirement to the Secretary.

(c) The Secretary may pay to any educational institution, or to any joint apprenticeship training committee acting as a training establishment, furnishing education or training under either this chapter or chapter 31, 34 or 35 of this title [38 USCS §§ 3670 et seq. or 3100 et seq., 3451 et seq., or 3500 et seq.] a reporting fee which will be in lieu of any other compensation or reimbursement for reports or certifications which such educational institution or joint apprenticeship training committee is required to submit to the Secretary by law or regulation. Such reporting fee shall be computed for each calendar year by multiplying $7 by the number of eligible veterans or eligible persons enrolled under this chapter or chapter 31, 34 or 35 of this title [38 USCS §§ 3670 et seq. or 3100 et seq., 3451 et seq., or 3500 et seq.] or $11 in the case of those eligible veterans and eligible persons whose educational assistance checks are directed in care of each institution for temporary custody and delivery and are delivered at the time of registration as provided under section 3680(d)(4) of this title, on October 31 of that year; except that the Secretary may, where it is established by such educational institution or joint apprenticeship training committee that eligible veteran plus eligible person enrollment on such date varies more than 15 percent from the peak eligible veteran enrollment plus eligible person enrollment in such educational institution or joint apprenticeship training committee during such calendar year, establish such other date as representative of the peak enrollment as may be justified for such educational institution or joint apprenticeship training committee. The reporting fee shall be paid to such educational institution or joint apprenticeship training committee as soon as feasible after the end of the calendar year for which it is applicable. No reporting fee payable to an educational institution under this subsection shall be subject to offset by the Secretary against any liability of such institution for any overpayment for which such institution may be administratively determined to be liable under section 3685 of this title unless such liability is not contested by such institution or has been upheld by a final decree of a court of appropriate jurisdiction.

(Added March 3, 1966, P. L. 89-358, § 3(b), 80 Stat. 22; Aug. 31, 1967, P. L. 90-77, Title III, § 308(a), 81 Stat. 189; Oct. 24, 1972, P. L. 92-540, Title III, § 315, 86 Stat. 1084; Dec. 3, 1974, P. L. 93-508, Title II, § 210(2), 88 Stat. 1585; Oct. 15, 1976, P. L. 94-502, Title V, §§ 507, 508, 513(a)(17), 90 Stat. 2400, 2403; Nov. 23, 1977, P. L. 95-202, Title III, § 304(a)(1), 91 Stat. 1442; Oct. 17, 1980, P. L. 96-466, Title III, Part C, § 343(a), (b)(1), Title VI, § 601(e), 94 Stat. 2198, 2208; Oct. 12, 1982, P. L. 97-295, § 4(55), 96 Stat. 1309; Oct. 28, 1986, P. L. 99-576, Title III, Part A, §§ 318, 319, 100 Stat. 3275; Dec. 18, 1989, P. L. 101-237, Title IV, §§ 416(a), 423(b)(1)(A), 103 Stat. 2086, 2092; Aug. 6, 1991, P. L. 102-83, § 5(a), (c)(1), 105 Stat. 406.)

HISTORY; ANCILLARY LAWS AND DIRECTIVES

Explanatory notes:
The comma in subsec. (a)(1) was enclosed in brackets to indicate the probable intention of Congress to delete such punctuation.

Provisions similar to those contained in this section were contained in former 38 USC §§ 1665(a), 1765(a) prior to repeal by Act March 3, 1966, P. L. 89-358, §§ 3(a)(3), 4(a), 80 Stat. 23.

Effective date of section:
Act March 3, 1966, P. L. 89-358, § 12(a), 80 Stat. 28, provided that this section is effective on March 3, 1966.

Amendments:
1967. Act Aug. 31, 1967 (effective 10/1/67, as provided by § 405(a) of such Act, which appears as 38 USCS § 101 note), in the section catchline, inserted "; reporting fee"; designated existing matter as subsec. (a); and added subsec. (b).

1972. Act Oct. 24, 1972, in subsecs. (a) and (b), substituted "34, 35, or 36" for "34 or 35"; in subsec. (b), inserted "or eligible persons", and substituted "or eligible persons enrolled under chapters 34, 35, and 36 of this title, or $4 in the case of those eligible veterans and eligible persons whose educational assistance checks are directed in care of each institution for temporary custody and delivery and are delivered at the time of registration as provided under section 1780(d)(5) of this title" for "enrolled under chapter 34 of this title, plus the number of eligible persons enrolled under chapter 35 of this title".

1974. Act Dec. 3, 1974 (effective 12/3/74, as provided by § 503 of such Act, which appears as 38 USCS § 3452 note), substituted new subsec. (b) for one which read: "The Administrator may pay to any educational institution furnishing education under either chapter 34, 35, or 36 of this title, a reporting fee which will be in lieu of any other compensation or reimbursement for reports or certifications which such educational institution is required to report to him by law or regulation. Such reporting fee shall be computed for each calendar year by multiplying $3 by the number of eligible veterans or eligible persons or eligible persons enrolled under chapters 34, 35, and 36 of this title, or $4 in the case of those eligible veterans and eligible persons whose educational assistance checks are directed in care of each institution for temporary custody and delivery and are delivered at the time of registration as provided under section 1780(d)(5) of this title, on October 31 of that year; except that the Administrator may, where it is established by the educational institution that eligible veteran plus eligible person enrollment on such date varies more than 15 per centum from the peak eligible veteran plus eligible person enrollment in such institution during such calendar year, establish such other date as representative of the peak enrollment as may be justified for that institution. The reporting fee shall be paid to the educational institution as soon as feasible after the end of the calendar year for which it is applicable.".

1976. Act Oct. 15, 1976, § 513(a)(17) (effective 10/15/76, as provided by § 703(b) of such Act, which appears as 38 USCS § 3693 note), in subsec. (a), substituted "the Administrator" for "him" following "by"; and in subsec. (b), substituted "the Administrator" for "him" following "to".

Act Oct. 15, 1976, § 507 (effective 12/1/76, as provided by § 703(c) of such Act, which appears as 38 USCS § 3693 note), in subsec. (a), inserted "The date of interruption or termination will be the last date of pursuit or, in the case of correspondence training, the last date a lesson was serviced by the school.".

Act Oct. 15, 1976, § 508 (effective 10/1/76, as provided by § 703(a) of such Act, which appears as 38 USCS § 3693 note), in subsec. (b), substituted "$5" and "$6" for "$3" and "$4", respectively.

1977. Act Nov. 23, 1977, § 304(a)(1)(A) (effective 10/1/77, as provided by § 501 of such Act, which appears as 38 USCS § 101 note), in subsec. (b), substituted "$7" and "$11" for "$5" and "$6", respectively.

Act Nov. 23, 1977, § 304(a)(1)(B) (effective 11/23/77, as provided by § 501 of such Act, which appears as 38 USCS § 101 note), in subsec. (b), inserted "No reporting fee payable to an educational institution under this subsection shall be subject to offset by the Administrator against any liability of such institution for any overpayment for which such institution may be administratively determined to be liable under section 1785 of this title unless such liability is not contested by such institution or has been upheld by a final decree of a court of appropriate jurisdiction.".

1980. Act Oct. 17, 1980 (effective 10/1/80, as provided by § 802(c)(1), (f)(1) of such Act, which appear as 38 USCS §§ 3452, 5314 notes, respectively), substituted new catchline for one which read: "Reports by institutions; reporting fee"; substituted new subsec. (a) for one which read: "(a) Educational institutions shall, without delay, report to the Administrator in the form prescribed by the Administrator, the enrollment, interruption, and termination of the education of each eligible person or veteran enrolled therein under chapter 34, 35, or 36. The date of interruption or termination will be the last date of pursuit or, in the case of correspondence training, the last date a lesson was serviced by the school."; redesignated

subsec. (b) as subsec. (c); added new subsec. (b); in subsec. (c), as so redesignated, substituted "1780(d)(4)" for "1780(d)(5)".
1982. Act Oct. 12, 1982, in subsec. (c), substituted "percent" for "per centum".
1986. Act Oct. 28, 1986, in subsec. (a), substituted "(a)(1) Except as provided in paragraph (2) of this subsection, the" for "(a) The", and added paras. (2) and (3).
1989. Act Dec. 18, 1989 (effective 1/1/90 as provided by § 416(b) of such Act, which appears as a note to this section), in subsec. (a)(1), substituted "chapter 31, 34" for "chapter 34"; in subsec. (b), substituted "chapters 31, 34" for "chapters 34"; and in subsec. (c), substituted "chapter 31, 34," for "chapter 34". Such act further, substituted "Secretary" for "Administrator", wherever appearing, in the entire section.
1991. Act Aug. 6, 1991, redesignated this section, formerly 38 USCS § 1784, as 38 USCS § 3684, and amended the references in this section to reflect the redesignations made by § 5(a) of such Act (see Table III preceding 38 USCS § 101).

Other provisions:
Application and construction of the Oct. 12, 1982 amendment of this section. For provisions as to the application and construction of the Oct. 12, 1982 amendment of this section, see § 5 of such Act, which appears as 10 USCS § 101 note.
Effective date of amendments made by Act Dec. 18, 1989. Act Dec. 18, 1989, P. L. 101-237, Title IV, § 416(b), 103 Stat. 2086, provides: "The amendments made by this section [amending this section] shall take effect on January 1, 1990.".

CROSS REFERENCES
This section is referred to in 38 USCS §§ 3685, 3698.

RESEARCH GUIDE
Am Jur:
77 Am Jur 2d, Veterans and Veterans' Laws § 139.

INTERPRETIVE NOTES AND DECISIONS

1. Generally
2. Reports, generally
3. —Fees

1. Generally
Requirement of "without delay" under 38 USCS § 1784(a) [now 38 USCS § 3684(a)] is met if, within 30 days from date of veteran's reduction or termination of training or reduction in course load, educational institution reports fact to administrator. VA GCO 2-77.

2. Reports, generally
38 USCS § 1784 [now 38 USCS § 3684] requirement that college keep track of any student it has certified to government as being eligible to receive educational benefits and report interruption or termination of education of such persons does not violate principle of academic freedom. United States v Reinhardt College (1983, ND Ga) 597 F Supp 522.

3. —Fees
Congress intended that allowance be paid to schools per month for each month in which required report or certification is furnished with respect to enrolled veteran, and for purposes of such allowance, there is no distinction based on correspondence versus resident courses. Central Technical Institute v United States (1960) 284 F2d 377.

§ 3684A. Procedures relating to computer matching program

(a)(1) Notwithstanding section 552a(p) of title 5 and subject to paragraph (2) of this subsection, the Secretary may suspend, terminate, reduce, or make a final denial of any financial assistance or payment under an educational assistance program provided for in chapter 30 or 32 of this title [38 USCS §§ 3001 et seq. or 3201 et seq.] or in chapter 106 of title 10 [10 USCS §§ 2131 et seq.] in the case of any individual, or take other adverse action against such individual, based on information produced by a matching program with the Department of Defense.

(2) The Secretary may not take any action referred to in paragraph (1) of this subsection until—

(A) the individual concerned has been provided a written notice containing a statement of the findings of the Secretary based on the matching program, a description of the proposed action, and notice of the individual's right to contest such findings within 10 days after the date of the notice; and

(B) the 10-day period referred to in subparagraph (A) of this paragraph has expired.

(3) In computing the 10-day period referred to in paragraph (2) of this subsection, Saturdays, Sundays, and Federal holidays shall be excluded.

(b) For the purposes of subsection (q) of section 552a of title 5, compliance with the provisions of subsection (a) of this section shall be considered compliance with the provisions of subsection (p) of such section 552a.

(c) For purposes of this section, the term "matching program" has the same meaning provided in section 552a(a)(8) of title 5.

(Added Aug. 15, 1990, P. L. 101-366, Title II, § 206(a), 104 Stat. 441; Aug. 6, 1991, P. L. 102-83, § 5(a), 105 Stat. 406.)

HISTORY; ANCILLARY LAWS AND DIRECTIVES
Amendments:
1991. Act Aug. 6, 1991, redesignated this section, formerly 38 USCS § 1784A, as 38 USCS § 3684A.

RESEARCH GUIDE
Am Jur:
77 Am Jur 2d, Veterans and Veterans' Laws § 144.

§ 3685. Overpayments to eligible persons or veterans

(a) Whenever the Secretary finds that an overpayment has been made to a veteran or eligible person, the amount of such overpayment shall constitute a liability of such veteran or eligible person to the United States.

(b) Whenever the Secretary finds that an overpayment has been made to a veteran or eligible person as the result of (1) the willful or negligent failure of an educational institution to report, as required under this chapter or chapter 34 or 35 of this title [38 USCS §§ 3670 et seq. or 3451 et seq. or 3500 et seq.], to

38 USCS § 3685   VETERANS' BENEFITS

the Department of Veterans Affairs excessive absences from a course, or discontinuance or interruption of a course by the veteran or eligible person, or (2) the willful or negligent false certification by an educational institution, the amount of such overpayment shall constitute a liability of the educational institution to the United States.

(c) Any overpayment referred to in subsection (a) or (b) of this section may be recovered, except as otherwise provided in the last sentence of section 3684(c) of this title, in the same manner as any other debt due the United States.

(d) Any overpayment referred to in subsection (a) or (b) of this section may be waived as to a veteran or eligible person as provided in section 5302 of this title. Waiver of any such overpayment as to a veteran or eligible person shall in no way release any educational institution from liability under subsection (b) of this section.

(e)(1) Any amount collected from a veteran or eligible person pursuant to this section shall be reimbursed to the educational institution which is liable pursuant to subsection (b) of this section to the extent that collection was made from the educational institution.

(2) Nothing in this section or any other provision of this title shall be construed as (A) precluding the imposition of any civil or criminal liability under this title or any other law, or (B) requiring any institution of higher learning to maintain daily attendance records for any course leading to a standard college degree.

(Added March 3, 1966, P. L. 89-358, § 3(b), 80 Stat. 22; Oct. 24, 1972, P. L. 92-540, Title IV, § 403(11), 86 Stat. 1090; Nov. 23, 1977, P. L. 95-202, Title III, § 304(a)(2), 91 Stat. 1442; Oct. 17, 1980, P. L. 96-466, Title III, Part C, § 344, 94 Stat. 2199; Dec. 18, 1989, P. L. 101-237, Title IV, § 423(b)(1), 103 Stat. 2092; May 7, 1991, P. L. 102-40, Title IV, § 402(d)(1), 105 Stat. 239; Aug. 6, 1991, P. L. 102-83, § 5(a), (c)(1), 105 Stat. 406.)

HISTORY; ANCILLARY LAWS AND DIRECTIVES

Explanatory notes:
Provisions similar to those contained in this section were contained in former 38 USC §§ 1666, 1766 prior to repeal by Act March 3, 1966, P. L. 89-358, §§ 3(a)(3), 4(a), 80 Stat. 23.

Effective date of section:
Act March 3, 1966, P. L. 89-358, § 12(a), 80 Stat. 28, provided that this section is effective on March 3, 1966.

Amendments:
1972. Act Oct. 24, 1972, inserted "this chapter or".
1977. Act Nov. 23, 1977 (effective 11/23/77, as provided by § 501 of such Act, which appears as 38 USCS § 101 note), inserted ", except as otherwise provided in section 1784(b) of this title," and inserted "Nothing in this section or any other provision of this title shall be construed as requiring any institution of higher learning to maintain daily attendance records for any course leading to a standard college degree.".
1980. Act Oct. 17, 1980 (effective 10/1/80, as provided by § 802(c)(1) of

such Act, which appears as 38 USCS § 3452 note), substituted new section for one which read: "Whenever the Administrator finds that an overpayment has been made to an eligible person or veteran as the result of (1) the willful or negligent failure of an educational institution to report, as required by this chapter or chapter 34 or 35 of this title and applicable regulations, to the Veterans' Administration excessive absences from a course, or discontinuance or interruption of a course by the eligible person or veteran, or (2) false certification by an educational institution, the amount of such overpayment shall constitute a liability of such institution, and may be recovered, except as otherwise provided in section 1784(b) of this title, in the same manner as any other debt due the United States. Any amount so collected shall be reimbursed if the overpayment is recovered from the eligible person or veteran. This section shall not preclude the imposition of any civil or criminal liability under this or any other law. Nothing in this section or any other provision of this title shall be construed as requiring any institution of higher learning to maintain daily attendance records for any course leading to a standard college degree.".

1989. Act Dec. 18, 1989, in subsecs. (a) and (b), substituted "Secretary" for "Administrator"; and in subsec. (b), substituted "Department of Veterans Affairs" for "Veterans' Administration".

1991. Act May 7, 1991, § 402(d)(1), amended the references in this section to reflect the redesignations made by §§ 401(a)(4) and 402(b) of such Act (see Table II preceding 38 USCS § 101).

Act Aug. 6, 1991, redesignated this section, formerly 38 USCS § 1785, as 38 USCS § 3685, and amended the references in this section to reflect the redesignations made by § 5(a) of such Act (see Table III preceding 38 USCS § 101).

CROSS REFERENCES
This section is referred to in 38 USCS § 3684.

RESEARCH GUIDE
Am Jur:
77 Am Jur 2d, Veterans and Veterans' Laws § 144.

Auto-Cite®: Cases and annotations referred to herein can be further researched through the Auto-Cite® computer-assisted research service. Use Auto-Cite to check citations for form, parallel references, prior and later history, and annotation references.

INTERPRETIVE NOTES AND DECISIONS

1. Generally
2. Constitutionality
3. Right to recovery of overpayments
4. Administrative procedure
5. Withholding of benefits from veterans
6. Offset of fees against liability of institution
7. Time limitations on recovery

1. Generally
Provision of 38 USCS § 1785 [now 38 USCS

§ 3685] allowing recoupment by United States of overpayments resulting from negligence of state educational institutions is not unconstitutional violation of doctrine of intergovernmental immunity. Colorado v Veterans Administration (1977, DC Colo) 430 F Supp 551, affd (1979, CA10 Colo) 602 F2d 926, cert den (1980) 444 US 1014, 62 L Ed 2d 643, 100 S Ct 663.

2. Constitutionality

Veterans Administration [now Department of Veterans Affairs] regulations promulgated pursuant to 38 USCS § 1785 [now 38 USCS § 3685], requiring that school must notify agency within 30 days of student's change of status in order to avoid potential liability for overpayments made to ineligible students, did not violate prohibition found in 38 USCS § 1782 [now 38 USCS § 3682] against any agency of United States exercising any supervision or control over state educational institution. Colorado v Veterans Administration (1977, DC Colo) 430 F Supp 551, affd (1979, CA10 Colo) 602 F2d 926, cert den (1980) 444 US 1014, 62 L Ed 2d 643, 100 S Ct 663.

3. Right to recovery of overpayments

Government may not recover erroneous overpayments of education allowance absent finding of institutional failure to report veteran's discontinuance of or false certification. United States v Steinberg (1982, DC Mass) 553 F Supp 184.

United States is entitled to recover overpayment of Veteran's Administration [now Department of Veterans Affairs] educational benefits where veteran terminates his course prior to its completion and receives non-punitive grades; termination relates back to first day of school term resulting in overpayment for entire term. United States v Duchene (1985, SD Iowa) 624 F Supp 177.

Veterans already enrolled in education or training institution upon determination that institution falsely certified maintenance of 85 to 15 percent ratio required under former 38 USC § 931 and thereby disenrolled pursuant to former 38 USC § 966, whose education and training allowances for periods prior to disenrollment had not yet been paid, were not subject to overpayments since prohibition in former § 931 extended only to veterans not already enrolled,

and former § 966 did not direct that disenrollment was retrospective in operation; institution was not liable under former § 976, respecting payments made subsequent to date of finding of failure to maintain proper ratio, since such payments to veterans did not constitute "overpayments. . . to a veteran" for purposes of former § 976, and no liability exists under first sentence of former § 978 since such section applied only where person to whom payment was to be made had submitted false or misleading claim. 1953 ADVA 934.

4. Administrative procedure

There is no clear indication within 38 USCS § 1785 [now 38 USCS § 3685] that adversary hearing with the use of record is required for recovery of overpayments and, therefore, hearing procedures of Administrative Procedure Act (5 USCS § 554) are not applicable. Colorado v Veterans Admin. (1979, CA10 Colo) 602 F2d 926, cert den (1980) 444 US 1014, 62 L Ed 2d 643, 100 S Ct 663.

5. Withholding of benefits from veterans

It is proper for Veterans' Administration [now Department of Veterans Affairs] to withhold benefits for overpayments from individuals who reentered was training, notwithstanding that full amount of overpayment had already been collected from educational institution, since congressional intent was to have veteran reimburse school. VA GCO 10-77.

6. Offset of fees against liability of institution

Veterans' Administration [now Department of Veterans Affairs] may offset reporting fees due institution against its liability for overpayment. VA GCO 8-79.

7. Time limitations on recovery

Cause of action under 28 USCS § 1785 by federal government to recover from college overpayments of veterans' benefits resulting from college's improper failure to properly report changes in status of students certified as eligible for benefits, as required by 38 USCS § 1784 [now 38 USCS § 3684], is contractual in nature, since colleges are paid fee for required reports, and suit is governed by 28 USCS § 2415(a) 6-year statute of limitations applicable to contract actions. United States v Reinhardt College (1983, ND Ga) 597 F Supp 522.

§ 3686. Correspondence courses

(a)(1) Each eligible veteran (as defined in section 3452(a)(1) and (2) of this title) and each eligible spouse or surviving spouse (as defined in section 3501(a)(1)(B), (C), or (D) of this title) who enters into an enrollment agreement to pursue a program of education exclusively by correspondence shall be paid an educational assistance allowance computed at the rate of 55 percent of the established charge which the institution requires nonveterans to pay for the course or courses pursued by the eligible veteran or spouse or surviving spouse. The term "established charge" as used herein means the charge for the course or courses determined on the basis of the lowest extended time payment plan offered by the institution and approved by the appropriate State approving agency or the actual cost to the veteran or spouse or surviving spouse, whichever is the lesser. Such allowance shall be paid quarterly on a pro rata basis for the lessons completed by the veteran or spouse or surviving spouse and serviced by the institution.

(2) The period of entitlement of any veteran or spouse or surviving spouse who is pursuing any program of education exclusively by correspondence shall be charged with one month for each $376 which is paid to the veteran or spouse or surviving spouse as an educational assistance allowance for such course.

(3) Notwithstanding any other provision of law unless enacted in express limitation of this paragraph, funds in the Department of Veterans Affairs readjustment benefits account shall be available for payments under paragraph (1) of this subsection for pursuit of a program of education exclusively by correspondence in which the veteran or spouse or surviving spouse enrolls after September 30, 1981.

(b) The enrollment agreement shall fully disclose the obligation of both the institution and the veteran or spouse or surviving spouse and shall prominently display the provisions for affirmance, termination, refunds, and the conditions under which payment of the allowance is made by the Secretary to the veteran or spouse or surviving spouse. A copy of the enrollment agreement shall be furnished to each such veteran or spouse or surviving spouse at the time such veteran or spouse or surviving spouse signs such agreement. No such agreement shall be effective unless such veteran or spouse or surviving spouse shall, after the expiration of ten days after the enrollment agreement is signed, have signed and submitted to the Secretary a written statement, with a signed copy to the institution, specifically affirming the enrollment agreement. In the event the veteran or spouse or surviving spouse at any time notifies the institution of such veteran's or spouse's intention not to affirm the agreement in accordance with the preceding sentence, the institution, without imposing any penalty or charging any fee shall promptly make a full refund of all amounts paid.

(c) In the event a veteran or spouse or surviving spouse elects to terminate his enrollment under an affirmed enrollment agreement, the institution may charge the veteran or spouse or surviving spouse a registration or similar fee not in excess of 10 percent of the tuition for the course, or $50, whichever is less. Where the veteran or spouse or surviving spouse elects to terminate the agreement after completion of one or more but less than 25 percent of the total number of lessons comprising the course, the institution may retain such registration or similar fee plus 25 percent of the tuition for the course. Where the veteran or spouse or surviving spouse elects to terminate the agreement after completion of 25 percent but less than 50 percent of the lessons comprising the course, the institution may retain the full registration or similar fee plus 50 percent of the course tuition. If 50 percent or more of the lessons are completed, no refund of tuition is required.

38 USCS § 3686

(Added Oct. 24, 1972, P. L. 92-540, Title III, § 316(1), 86 Stat. 1084; Dec. 3, 1974, P. L. 93-508, Title I, § 104(1), 88 Stat. 1580; Jan. 2, 1975, P. L. 93-602, Title II, § 205(a), 88 Stat. 1958; Oct. 15, 1976, P. L. 94-502, Title V, §§ 501(1), 513(a)(18), 90 Stat. 2398, 2403; Nov. 23, 1977, P. L. 95-202, Title I, § 104(1), 91 Stat. 1435; Oct. 17, 1980, P. L. 96-466, Title II, Part A, § 203(2), Part B, § 213(2), Title VI, § 604, 94 Stat. 2189, 2191, 2209; Aug. 13, 1981, P. L. 97-35, Title XX, § 2004(a), 95 Stat. 782; May 4, 1982, P. L. 97-174, § 5(a), 96 Stat. 75; Oct. 12, 1982, P. L. 97-295, § 4(56), 96 Stat. 1309; Oct. 24, 1984, P. L. 98-543, Title II, Part A, § 204(1), 98 Stat. 2742; Dec. 18, 1989, P. L. 101-237, Title IV, § 423(b)(1), 103 Stat. 2092; Aug. 6, 1991, P. L. 102-83, § 5(a), (c)(1), 105 Stat. 406; Nov. 2, 1994, P. L. 103-446, Title VI, § 605(a)(2)(C), 108 Stat. 4672.)

HISTORY; ANCILLARY LAWS AND DIRECTIVES

Effective date of section:

Act March 3, 1966, P. L. 89-358, § 12(a), 80 Stat. 28, provided that this section is effective on March 3, 1966.

Amendments:

1974. Act Dec. 3, 1974 (effective 9/1/74, as provided by § 501 of such Act, which appears as 38 USCS § 3482 note), in subsec. (a)(2), substituted "$260" for "$220".

1975. Act Jan. 2, 1975 (effective 1/1/75, as provided by § 206 of such Act, which appears as 38 USCS § 3482 note), in subsec. (a)(2), substituted "$270" for "$260".

1976. Act Oct. 15, 1976, § 513(a)(18) (effective 10/15/76, as provided by § 703(b) of such Act, which appears as 38 USCS § 3693 note), in subsecs. (a)–(c), purported to substitute "spouse or surviving spouse" for "wife and widow" wherever appearing; however "spouse or surviving spouse" was substituted for "wife or widow" wherever appearing in this section, as the probable intent of Congress; and in subsecs. (b) and (c), substituted "such veteran's or spouse's" for "his".

Act Oct. 15, 1976, § 501(1) (effective 10/1/76, as provided by § 703(a) of such Act, which appears as 38 USCS § 3693 note), in subsec. (a)(2), substituted "$292" for "$270".

1977. Act Nov. 23, 1977 (effective 10/1/77, as provided by § 501 of such Act, which appears as 38 USCS § 101 note), in subsec. (a)(2), substituted "$311" for "$292".

1980. Act Oct. 17, 1980, § 604 (effective as provided by § 802(f) of such Act, which appears as 38 USCS § 5314 note), in subsec. (a)(1), substituted "70 percent" for "90 per centum".

Such Act further, in § 203(2) (effective 10/1/80, as provided by § 802(b)(1) of such Act, which appears as 38 USCS § 3482 note), in subsec. (a)(2), substituted "$327" for "$311".

Such Act further, in § 213(2) (effective 1/1/81, as provided by § 802(b)(2) of such Act, which appears as 38 USCS § 3482 note), in subsec. (a)(2), as amended by § 203(2) of Act Oct. 17, 1980, substituted "$342" for "$327".

1981. Act Aug. 13, 1981 (effective as provided by § 2004(b) of such Act), in subsec. (a)(1), substituted "55 percent" for "70 percent".

1982. Act May 4, 1982 (effective 10/1/81, as provided by § 5(b) of such Act, which appears as a note to this section), added subsec. (a)(3). Act Oct. 12, 1982, in subsec. (c), substituted "percent" for "per centum" each place it appears.

1984. Act Oct. 24, 1984 (effective 10/1/78, as provided by § 205 of such Act, which appears as 38 USCS § 1508 note), in subsec. (a)(2), substituted "$376" for "$342".

1989. Act Dec. 18, 1989, in subsec. (a)(3), substituted "Department of Veterans Affairs" for "Veterans' Administration"; and in subsec. (b), substituted "Secretary" for "Administrator", wherever appearing.

1991. Act Aug. 6, 1991, redesignated this section, formerly 38 USCS § 1786, as 38 USCS § 3686, and amended the references in this section to reflect the redesignations made by § 5(a) of such Act (see Table III preceding 38 USCS § 101).

1994. Act Nov. 2, 1994 (applicable to programs and courses commencing more than 90 days after the date of enactment, as provided by § 605(b) of such Act, which appears as 38 USCS § 3672 note), in subsec. (c), deleted "(other than one subject to the provisions of section 3676 of this title)" preceding "may charge the veteran or spouse".

Other provisions:
Effective dates and savings provisions for amendments made to section by Act Oct. 24, 1972. Act Oct. 24, 1972, P. L. 92-540, Title VI, § 602, 86 Stat. 1099, provided:

"(a) The provisions of section 1786 of title 38, United States Code (as added by section 316 of this Act) [this section], which apply to programs of education exclusively by correspondence, shall, as to those wives and widows made eligible for such training by that section, become effective January 1, 1973, and, as to eligible veterans, shall apply only to those enrollment agreements which are entered into on or after January 1, 1973.

"(b) Notwithstanding the provisions of subsection (a) of this section, any enrollment agreement entered into by an eligible veteran prior to January 1, 1973, shall continue to be subject to the provisions of section 1682(c) of title 38, United States Code, prior to its repeal by section 303 of this Act [former 38 USCS § 1682(c)].".

Termination of eligibility period. For termination of the eligibility period for a wife, widow, or eligible person eight years from Oct. 24, 1972, see note containing Act Oct. 24, 1972, P. L. 92-540, Title VI, § 604, 86 Stat. 1099, located at 38 USCS § 1712.

Effective date and application of amendment made by § 604 of Act Oct. 17, 1980. Act Oct. 17, 1980, P. L. 96-466, Title VIII, § 802(f), 94 Stat. 2218, located at 38 USCS § 5314 note, provided that the amendment made to this section by § 604 of Act Oct. 17, 1980 is effective on Oct. 1, 1980, except that the amendment shall not apply to any person receiving educational assistance under chapter 34 or 35 of title 38 [38 USCS §§ 3451 et seq. or 3500 et seq.], on Sept. 1, 1980, for the pursuit of a program of education, as defined in 38 USCS § 3452(b), in which such person is enrolled on that date, for as long as such person continuously thereafter is so enrolled and meets the requirements of eligibility for such assistance for the pursuit of such program under the provisions of such chapter and chapter 36 of such title [38 USCS §§ 3670 et seq.] as in effect on that date.

Application of amendment by Act Aug. 13, 1981. Act Aug. 13, 1981, P. L. 97-35, Title XX, § 2004(b), 95 Stat. 782, provided: "The amendment made by subsection (a) [amending this section] shall not apply to correspondence lessons completed and submitted to the educational institution concerned before October 1, 1981.".

Application and construction of the Oct. 12, 1982 amendment of this section. Act Oct. 12, 1982, P. L. 97-174, § 5(b), 96 Stat. 75, provides: "The amendment made by subsection (a) of this section [amending this section] shall take effect as of October 1, 1981.".

CROSS REFERENCES
This section is referred to in 10 USCS § 16136; 38 USCS §§ 3034, 3484, 3534.

RESEARCH GUIDE
Am Jur:
77 Am Jur 2d, Veterans and Veterans' Laws § 144.

§ 3687. Apprenticeship or other on-job training

(a) An eligible veteran (as defined in section 3452(a)(1) of this title) or an eligible person (as defined in section 3501(a) of this title) shall be paid a training assistance allowance as prescribed by subsection (b) of this section while pursuing a full-time—

(1) program of apprenticeship approved by a State approving agency as meeting the standards of apprenticeship published by the Secretary of Labor pursuant to section 2 of the Act of August 16, 1937 (popularly known as the "National Apprenticeship Act") (29 U.S.C. 50a) or

(2) program of other on-job training approved under provisions of section 3677 of this title,

subject to the conditions and limitations of chapters 34 and 35 of this title [38 USCS §§ 3451 et seq. and 3500 et seq.] with respect to educational assistance.

(b)(1) The monthly training assistance allowance of an eligible veteran pursuing a program described under subsection (a) shall be as follows:

Column I	Column II	Column III	Column IV	Column V
Periods of training	No dependents	One dependent	Two dependents	More than two dependents
				The amount in column IV, plus the following for each dependent in excess of two:
First 6 months	$274	$307	$336	$14
Second 6 months	205	239	267	14
Third 6 months	136	171	198	14
Fourth and any succeeding 6-month periods	68	101	131	14

(2) The monthly training assistance allowance of an eligible person pursuing a program described under subsection (a) shall be $294 for the first six

months, $220 for the second six months, $146 for the third six months, and $73 for the fourth and any succeeding six-month periods of training.

(3) In any month in which an eligible veteran or person pursuing a program of apprenticeship or a program of other on-job training fails to complete one hundred and twenty hours of training in such month, the monthly training assistance allowance set forth in subsection (b)(1) or (2) of this section, as applicable, shall be reduced proportionately in the proportion that the number of hours worked bears to one hundred and twenty hours rounded off to the nearest eight hours.

(c) For the purpose of this chapter [38 USCS §§ 3670 et seq.], the terms "program of apprenticeship" and "program of other on-job training" shall have the same meaning as "program of education"; and the term "training assistance allowance" shall have the same meaning as "educational assistance allowance" as set forth in chapters 34 and 35 of this title [38 USCS §§ 3451 et seq. and 3500 et seq.].

(Added Oct. 24, 1972, P. L. 92-540, Title III, § 316(1), 86 Stat. 1085; Dec. 3, 1974, P. L. 93-508, Title I, § 104(2), (3), 88 Stat. 1580; Jan. 2, 1975, P. L. 93-602, Title II, § 205(b), 88 Stat. 1959; Oct. 15, 1976, P. L. 94-502, Title V, § 501(2), 90 Stat. 2398; Nov. 23, 1977, P. L. 95-202, Title I, § 104(2), 91 Stat. 1435; Oct. 17, 1980, P. L. 96-466, Title II, Part A, § 203(3), Part B, § 213(3), 94 Stat. 2189, 2191; Oct. 12, 1982, P. L. 97-295, § 4(57), 96 Stat. 1309; Oct. 24, 1984, P. L. 98-543, Title II, Part A, § 204(2), 98 Stat. 2742; Dec. 18, 1989, P. L. 101-237, Title IV, § 403(b), 103 Stat. 2080; Aug. 6, 1991, P. L. 102-83, § 5(a), (c)(1), 105 Stat. 406.)

HISTORY; ANCILLARY LAWS AND DIRECTIVES

Explanatory notes:

Provisions similar to those contained in this section were contained in former 38 USC § 1683 prior to repeal by Act Oct. 24, 1972, P. L. 92-540, Title IV, § 401(6), 86 Stat. 1090.

Amendments:

1974. Act Dec. 3, 1974 (effective 9/1/74, as provided by § 501 of such Act, which appears as 38 USCS § 3482 note), in subsec. (b)(1), substituted new table for one which read:

Column I	Column II	Column III	Column IV	Column V
Periods of training	No dependents	One dependent	Two dependents	More than two dependents
				The amount in column IV, plus the following for each dependent in excess of two:
First 6 months	$160	$179	$196	$8.

38 USCS § 3687

Second 6 months	120	139	156	8.
Third 6 months	80	99	116	8.
Fourth and any succeeding 6-month periods	40	59	76	8".;

and substituted new subsec. (b)(2) for one which read: "The monthly training assistance allowance of an eligible person pursuing a program described under subsection (a) shall be (A) $160 during the first six-month period, (B) $120 during the second six-month period, (C) $80 during the third six-month period, and (D) $40 during the fourth and any succeeding six-month period.".

1975. Act Jan. 2, 1975 (effective 1/1/75, as provided by § 206 of such Act, which appears as 38 USCS § 3482 note), in subsec. (b)(1), substituted new table for one which read:

"Column I	Column II	Column III	Column IV	Column V
Periods of training	No dependents	One dependent	Two dependents	More than two dependents
				The amount in column IV, plus the following for each dependent in excess of two:
First 6 months	$189	$212	$232	$9
Second 6 months	142	164	184	9
Third 6 months	95	117	137	9
Fourth and any succeeding 6-month periods ...	47	70	90	9".

1976. Act Oct. 15, 1976 (effective 10/1/76, as provided by § 703(a) of such Act, which appears as 38 USCS § 3693 note), in subsec. (b)(1), substituted new table for one which read:

"Column I	Column II	Column III	Column IV	Column V
Periods of training	No dependents	One dependent	Two dependents	More than two dependents
				The amount in column IV, plus the following for each dependent in excess of two:
First 6 months	$196	$220	$240	$10

READJUSTMENT BENEFITS — 38 USCS § 3687

Second 6 months	147	171	191	10
Third 6 months	98	122	142	10
Fourth and any succeeding 6-month periods	49	73	93	10".

1977. Act Nov. 23, 1977 (effective 10/1/77, as provided by § 501 of such Act, which appears as 38 USCS § 101 note), in subsec. (b)(1), substituted new table for one which read:

"Column I	Column II	Column III	Column IV	Column V
Periods training	No dependents	One dependent	Two dependents	More than two dependents
				The amount in column IV, plus the following for each dependent in excess of two:
First 6 months	$212	$238	$260	$11
Second 6 months	159	185	207	11
Third 6 months	106	132	154	11
Fourth and any succeeding 6-month periods	53	79	101	11".

1980. Act Oct. 17, 1980, § 203(3) (effective 10/1/80, as provided by § 802(b)(1) of such Act, which appears as 38 USCS § 3482 note), in subsec. (b)(1) substituted new table for one which read:

"Column I	Column II	Column III	Column IV	Column V
Periods of training	No dependents	One dependent	Two dependents	More than two dependents
				The amount in column IV, plus the following for each dependent in excess of two:
First 6 months	$226	$254	$277	$12
Second 6 months	169	197	221	12
Third 6 months	113	141	164	12
Fourth and any succeeding 6-month periods	56	84	108	12".

Act Oct. 17, 1980, § 213(3) (effective 1/1/81, as provided by § 802(b)(2) of such Act, which appears as 38 USCS § 3482 note), in subsec. (b)(1),

38 USCS § 3687 VETERANS' BENEFITS

substituted new table for table, as amended by § 203(3) of Act Oct. 17, 1980, which read:

"Column I	Column II	Column III	Column IV	Column V
Periods of training	No dependents	One dependent	Two dependents	More than two dependents
				The amount in column IV, plus the following for each dependent in excess of two:
First 6 months	$237	$267	$291	$13
Second 6 months	177	207	232	13
Third 6 months	119	148	172	13
Fourth and any succeeding 6-month periods	59	88	113	13".

1982. Act Oct. 12, 1982, in subsec. (a), in para. (1), substituted "section 2 of the Act of August 16, 1937 (popularly known as the 'National Apprenticeship Act') (29 U.S.C. 50a)" for "section 50a of title 29", and, in the concluding matter, inserted "of this title".

1984. Act Oct. 24, 1984 (effective 10/1/78, as provided by § 205 of such Act, which appears as 28 USCS § 1508 note), in subsec. (b)(1), substituted the table for one which read:

"Column I	Column II	Column III	Column IV	Column V
Periods of training	No dependents	One dependent	Two dependents	More than two dependents
				The amount in column IV, plus the following for each dependent in excess of two:
First 6 months	$249	$279	$305	$13
Second 6 months	186	217	243	13
Third 6 months	124	155	180	13
Fourth and any succeeding 6-month periods	62	92	119	13".

1989. Act Dec. 18, 1989 (effective 1/1/90, as provided by § 403(c) of such Act, which appears as 38 USCS § 3532 note), in subsec. (b)(2), substituted "$294 for the first six months, $220 for the second six months, $146 for the third six months, and $73 for the fourth and any succeeding six-month periods of training." for "computed at the rate prescribed in paragraph (1) of this subsection for an eligible veteran with no dependents pursuing such a course.".

1991. Act Aug. 6, 1991, redesignated this section, formerly 38 USCS § 1787, as 38 USCS § 3687, and amended the references in this section to reflect the redesignations made by § 5(a) of such Act (see Table III preceding 38 USCS § 101).

Other provisions:
Effective date and application of amendments made by Act Oct. 24, 1972. Act Oct. 24, 1972, P. L. 92-540, Title VI, § 601(a), 86 Stat. 1099, which appears as 38 USCS § 3102 note, provided that the rate increases provided by the provisions of this section, as amended by Act Oct. 24, 1972, shall become effective Oct. 1, 1972; except, for those veterans and eligible persons in training on Oct. 24, 1972, the effective date shall be the date of the commencement of the current enrollment period, but not earlier than Sept. 1, 1972.

Termination of eligibility. For termination of eligibility period for a wife, widow, or eligible person eight years from Oct. 24, 1972, see note containing Act Oct. 24, 1972, P. L. 92-540, Title VI, § 604, 86 Stat. 1099, located at 38 USCS § 3512.

Application and construction of the Oct. 12, 1982 amendment of this section. For provisions as to the application and construction of the Oct. 12, 1982 amendment of this section, see § 5 of such Act, which appears as 10 USCS § 101 note.

CROSS REFERENCES
This section is referred to in 10 USCS § 16136; 29 USCS 1721: 38 USCS §§ 3002, 3034, 3116, 3202, 3241, 3482, 3484, 3534, 3672, 4102A, 4103A.

RESEARCH GUIDE
Am Jur:
45A Am Jur 2d, Job Discrimination (1993) § 687.

§ 3688. Measurement of courses

(a) For the purposes of this chapter and chapters 34 and 35 of this title [38 USCS §§ 3670 et seq. and 3451 et seq. and 3500 et seq.]—

(1) an institutional trade or technical course offered on a clock-hour basis, not leading to a standard college degree involving shop practice as an integral part thereof, shall be considered a full-time course when a minimum of 22 hours per week of attendance (excluding supervised study) is required, with no more than 2½ hours of rest periods per week allowed;

(2) an institutional course offered on a clock-hour basis, not leading to a standard college degree in which theoretical or classroom instruction predominates shall be considered a full-time course when a minimum of 18 hours per week net of instruction (excluding supervised study but which may include customary intervals not to exceed 10 minutes between hours of instruction) is required;

(3) an academic high school course requiring sixteen units for a full course shall be considered a full-time course when (A) a minimum of four units per year is required for (B) an individual is pursuing a program of education leading to an accredited high school diploma at a rate which, if continued, would result in receipt of such a diploma in four ordinary school years. For

the purpose of subclause (A) of this clause, a unit is defined to be not less than one hundred and twenty sixty-minute hours or their equivalent of study in any subject in one academic year;

(4) an institutional undergraduate course offered by a college or university on a standard quarter- or semester-hour basis, other than a course pursued as part of a program of education beyond the baccalaureate level, shall be considered a full-time course when a minimum of fourteen semester hours per semester or the equivalent thereof (including such hours for which no credit is granted but which are required to be taken to correct an educational deficiency and which the educational institution considers to be quarter or semester hours for other administrative purposes), for which credit is granted toward a standard college degree, is required, except that where such college or university certifies, upon the request of the Secretary, that (A) full-time tuition is charged to all undergraduate students carrying a minimum of less than fourteen semester hours or the equivalent thereof, or (B) all undergraduate students carrying a minimum of less than fourteen such semester hours or the equivalent thereof, are considered to be pursuing a full-time course for other administrative purposes, then such an institutional undergraduate course offered by such college or university with such minimum number of such semester hours shall be considered a full-time course, but in the event such minimum number of semester hours is less than twelve semester hours or the equivalent thereof, then twelve semester hours or the equivalent thereof shall be considered a full-time course;

(5) a program of apprenticeship or a program of other on-job training shall be considered a full-time program when the eligible veteran or person is required to work the number of hours constituting the standard workweek of the training establishment, but a workweek of less than thirty hours shall not be considered to constitute full-time training unless a lesser number of hours has been established as the standard workweek for the particular establishment through bona fide collective bargaining;

(6) an institutional course offered as part of a program of education, not leading to a standard college degree under section 3034(a)(3), 3241(a)(2), or 3533(a) of this title shall be considered a full-time course on the basis of measurement criteria provided in clause (2), (3), or (4) of this subsection as determined by the educational institution; and

(7) an institutional course not leading to a standard college degree offered by an educational institution on a standard quarter- or semester-hour basis shall be measured as full time on the same basis as provided in paragraph (4) of this subsection, but if the educational institution offering the course is not an institution of higher learning, then in no event shall such course be considered full time when it requires less than the minimum weekly hours of attendance required for full time by paragraph (1) or (2) of this subsection, as appropriate.

(b) The Secretary shall define part-time training in the case of the types of courses referred to in subsection (a), and shall define full-time and part-time training in the case of all other types of courses pursued under this chapter, chapter 30, 32, or 35 of this title [38 USCS §§ 3001 et seq. or 3201 et seq. or 3500 et seq.], or chapter 106 of title 10 [10 USCS §§ 2131 et seq.].

(Added Oct. 24, 1972, P. L. 92-540, Title III, § 316(2), 86 Stat. 1086; Dec. 3, 1974, P. L. 93-508, Title II, § 211, 88 Stat. 1585; Oct. 15, 1976, P. L. 94-502, Title V, § 509(a), 90 Stat. 2400; Nov. 23, 1977, P. L. 95-202, Title III, § 304(a)(3), 91 Stat. 1442; Oct. 17, 1980, P. L. 96-466, Title III, Part C, § 345, Title VI, § 601(f), 94 Stat. 2199, 2208; Oct. 12, 1982, P. L. 97-295, § 4(58), 96 Stat. 1309; Oct. 28, 1986, P. L. 99-576, Title III, Part A, § 315(a)(2), (b), 100 Stat. 3274; May 20, 1988, P. L. 100-322, Title III, Part C, § 321(a), 102 Stat. 535; Dec. 18, 1989, P. L. 101-237, Title IV, §§ 413(a), 417, 423(b)(1)(A), 103 Stat. 2085, 2086, 2092; Aug. 6, 1991, P. L. 102-83, § 5(a), (c)(1), 105 Stat. 406; Oct. 29, 1992, P. L. 102-568, Title III, § 316(a), 106 Stat. 4333; Nov. 2, 1994, P. L. 103-446, Title VI, § 607, Title XII, § 1201(e)(12), 108 Stat. 4672, 4685.)

HISTORY; ANCILLARY LAWS AND DIRECTIVES

Explanatory notes:
Provisions similar to those contained in this section were contained in former 38 USC §§ 1684 and 1733, prior to their general revision by Act Oct. 24, 1972, P. L. 92-540, Title III, §§ 304, 311, 86 Stat. 1081, 1084.
A former § 1788 was redesignated as § 1792 by Act Oct. 24, 1972, P. L. 92-540, Title III, § 316(2), 86 Stat. 1086.

Amendments:
1974. Act Dec. 3, 1974 (effective 12/3/74, as provided by § 503 of such Act, which appears as 38 USCS § 3452 note), in subsec. (a), in paras. (1) and (2), substituted ", not leading to a standard college degree," for "below the college level", in para. (6), substituted "not leading to a standard college degree" for "below the college level", and added the concluding matter.
1976. Act Oct. 15, 1976 (effective 12/1/76, as provided by § 703(c) of such Act, which appears as 38 USCS § 3693 note), in subsec. (a)(1), substituted ", but if such course is approved pursuant to section 1775 of this title, then 27 hours per week of attendance, with no more than 2 ½ hours of rest period per week allowed and excluding supervised study, shall be considered full time;" for ";"; and in subsec. (a)(2), substituted ", but if such course is approved pursuant to section 1775 of this title, then 22 hours per week net of instruction (excluding supervised study), which may include customary intervals not to exceed ten minutes between hours of instruction, shall be considered full time;" for ";".
1977. Act Nov. 23, 1977 (effective 2/1/78, as provided by § 501 of such Act, which appears as 38 USCS § 101 note), in subsec. (a)(1), inserted "and not more than 5 hours of supervised study" and substituted "22" for "27"; and in subsec. (a)(2), inserted "and not more than 5 hours of supervised study" and substituted "18" for "22".
1980. Act Oct. 17, 1980 (effective 10/1/80, as provided by § 802(c)(1), (f)(1) of such Act, which appear as 38 USCS §§ 3452, 5314 notes, respectively), in subsec. (a), in para. (1), inserted "(a)(1)", in para. (2), inserted "(a)(1)", in para. (4), substituted "in residence on a standard" for "on a" and inserted "per semester", and in para. (6), deleted "or 1696(a)(2)" following "1691(a)(2)"; and added subsecs. (c) and (d).
1982. Act Oct. 12, 1982, in subsec. (a)(6), inserted "of this subsection".

1986. Act Oct. 28, 1986, in subsec. (a), in para. (5), deleted "and" following "bargaining;", in para. (6), substituted "; and" for the concluding period, and added para. (7); in subsec. (c) deleted "(4)" following "(a)"; and added subsec. (e).

1988. Act May 20, 1988 (applicable as provided by § 321(b) of such Act, which appears as a note to this section), in subsec. (a), in the concluding matter, in cl. (B), and in subsec. (c), inserted "(or two 50-minute periods)".

1989. Act Dec. 18, 1989, in subsec. (a), in the concluding matter, in cl. (C) and in subsec. (c), inserted "(or three 50-minute periods)".

Such Act further, substituted subsec. (e) for one which read:

"(e) For the purpose of determining whether a course—

"(1) which is offered by an institution of higher learning, and

"(2) for which such institution requires one or more unit courses or subjects for which credit is granted toward a standard college degree

will, during the semester (or quarter or other applicable portion of the academic year) when such unit course or subject is being pursued, be considered full time under clause (1) or (2) of subsection (a) of this section, each of the numbers of hours specified in such clause shall be deemed to be reduced, during such semester (or other portion of the academic year), by the percentage described in the following sentence and rounded as the Administrator may prescribe. Such percentage is the percentage that the number of semester hours (or the equivalent thereof) represented by such unit course or subject is of the number of semester hours (or the equivalent thereof) which, under clause (4) of such subsection, constitutes a full-time institutional undergraduate course at such institution.".

Such Act further, in subsecs. (a)(4) and (b), substituted "Secretary" for "Administrator".

1991. Act Aug. 6, 1991, redesignated this section, formerly 38 USCS § 1788, as 38 USCS § 3688, and amended the references in this section to reflect the redesignations made by § 5(a) of such Act (see Table III preceding 38 USCS § 101).

1992. Act Oct. 29, 1992 (applicable to enrollments in courses beginning on or after 7/1/93, as provided by § 316(c) of such Act, which appears as 38 USCS § 3532 note), in subsec. (a), in para. (1), substituted "22 hours per week of attendance (excluding supervised study) is required, with no more than 2^1/$_2$ hours of rest periods per week allowed" for "thirty hours per week of attendance is required with no more than two and one-half hours of rest periods and not more than 5 hours of supervised study per week allowed, but if such course is approved pursuant to section 3675(a)(1) of this title, then 22 hours per week of attendance, with no more than 2^1/$_2$ hours of rest period per week allowed and excluding supervised study, shall be considered full time", in para. (2), substituted "18 hours per week net of instruction (excluding supervised study but which may include customary intervals not to exceed 10 minutes between hours of instruction) is required" for "twenty-five hours per week net of instruction and not more than 5 hours of supervised study (which may include customary intervals not to exceed ten minutes between hours of instruction) is required, but if such course is approved pursuant to section 3675(a)(1) of this title, then 18 hours per week net of instruction (excluding supervised study), which may include customary intervals not to exceed ten minutes between hours of instruction, shall be considered full time", in para. (4), deleted "in residence" following "by a college or university" and inserted ", other than a course pursued as part of a program of education beyond the baccalaureate level,", in para. (6), substituted "3034(a)(3), 3241(a)(2) or 3533(a)" for "3491(a)(2)", and substituted para. (7) for former para. (7) and concluding matter which read:

"(7) an institutional course not leading to a standard college degree, offered by a fully accredited institution of higher learning in residence on a standard quarter- or semester-hour basis, shall be measured as full time on the same basis as provided in clause (4) of this subsection if (A) such course is approved pursuant to section 3675 of this title, and (B) a majority of the total credits required for the course is derived from unit courses or subjects offered by the institution as part of a course, so approved, leading to a standard college degree.

"Notwithstanding the provisions of clause (1) or (2) of this subsection, an educational institution offering courses not leading to a standard college degree may measure such courses on a quarter- or semester-hour basis (with full time measured on the same basis as provided by clause (4) of this subsection); but (A) the academic portions of such courses must require outside preparation and be measured on not less than one quarter or one semester hour for each fifty minutes net of instruction per week or quarter or semester; (B) the laboratory portions of such courses must be measured on not less than one quarter or one semester hour for each two hours (or two 50-minute periods) of attendance per week per quarter or semester; and (C) the shop portions of such courses must be measured on not less than one quarter or one semester hour for each three hours (or three 50-minute periods) of attendance per week per quarter or semester. In no event shall such course be considered a full-time course when less than twenty-two hours per week of attendance is required.".

Such Act further (applicable as above), in subsec. (b), substituted "30, 32," for "34"; and deleted subsecs. (c), (d) and (e), which read:

"(c) For the purposes of subsection (a) of this section, the term 'in residence on a standard quarter- or semester-hour basis' means a study at a site or campus of a college or university, or off-campus at an official resident center, requiring pursuit of regularly scheduled weekly class instruction at the rate of one standard class session per week throughout the quarter or semester for one quarter or one semester hour of credit. For the purposes of the preceding sentence, the term 'standard class session' means one hour (or fifty-minute period) of academic instruction, two hours (or two 50-minute periods) of laboratory instruction, or three hours (or three 50-minute periods) of workshop training.

"(d) Notwithstanding any other provision of this title, an institutional undergraduate course leading to a standard college degree offered by a college or university in residence shall be considered to be a full-time course if—

"(1) the educational institution offering such course considers such course to be a full-time course and treats such course as a full-time course for all purposes, including (A) payment of tuition and fees, (B) the awarding of academic credit for the purpose of meeting graduation requirements, and (C) the transfer of such credits to an undergraduate course meeting the criteria set forth in subsection (a)(4) of this section;

"(2) less than 50 percent of the persons enrolled in such course are receiving educational assistance under this title;

"(3) such course would qualify as a full-time course under subsection (a)(4) of this section, except that it does not meet the requirements of such subsection with respect to weekly class instruction; and

"(4) the course requires—

"(A) pursuit of standard class sessions for each credit at a rate not less frequent than every two weeks; and

"(B) monthly pursuit of a total number of standard class sessions equal to that number of standard class sessions which, during the same period of time, is required for a course qualifying as a full-time course under subsection (a)(4) of this section.

"(e)(1) For the purpose of measuring clock hours of attendance or net of instruction under clause (1) or (2), respectively, of subsection (a) of this section for a course—

"(A) which is offered by an institution of higher learning, and

"(B) for which the institution requires one or more unit courses or subjects for which credit is granted toward a standard college degree pursued in residence on a standard quarter- or semester-hour basis,

the number of credit hours (semester or quarter hours) represented by such unit courses or subjects shall, during the semester, quarter, or other applicable portion of the academic year when pursued, be converted to equivalent clock hours, determined as prescribed in paragraph (2) of this subsection. Such equivalent clock hours then shall be combined with actual weekly clock hours of training concurrently pursued, if any, to determine the total clock hours of enrollment.

"(2) For the purpose of determining the clock-hour equivalency described in paragraph (1) of this subsection, the total number of credit hours being pursued will be multiplied by the factor resulting from dividing the number of clock hours which constitute full time under clause (1) or (2) of subsection (a) of this section, as appropriate, by the number of semester hours (or the equivalent thereof) which, under clause (4) of such subsection, constitutes a full-time institutional undergraduate course at such institution.".

1994. Act Nov. 2, 1994, in subsec. (a)(6), inserted a comma following "3241(a)(2)"; and, in subsec. (b), substituted "this chapter," for "this chapter or" and inserted ", or chapter 106 of title 10".

Other provisions:

Application and construction of the Oct. 12, 1982 amendment of this section. For provisions as to the application and construction of the Oct. 12, 1982 amendment of this section, see § 5 of such Act, which appears as 10 USCS § 101 note.

Application of Act May 20, 1988 amendments. Act May 20, 1988, P. L. 100-322, Title III, Part C, § 321(b), 102 Stat. 535, provides: "The amendments made by subsection (a) [amending subsecs. (a) and (c) of this section] shall apply to any enrollment or reenrollment commencing on or after the date of enactment of this Act.".

CROSS REFERENCES

This section is referred to in 38 USCS §§ 3482, 3532, 3680.

RESEARCH GUIDE

Am Jur:
77 Am Jur 2d, Veterans and Veterans' Laws § 144.

INTERPRETIVE NOTES AND DECISIONS

Administrator of Veterans Administration [now Secretary of Veterans Affairs] correctly established regulations requiring veterans to be enrolled in course of study which scheduled at least 12 standard classroom sessions per week in order to qualify for full-time educational assistance benefits since Administrator [now Secretary] congressional parameters of full-time study, but rather explained what Congress meant by term "semester hour" in 38 USCS § 1788(a)(4) [now 38 USCS § 3688(a)(4)]. Wayne State University v Cleland (1978, CA6 Mich) 590 F2d 627.

Veteran's Administration [now Department of Veterans Affairs] had statutory authority to mandate twelve semester hour minimum for all undergraduate students who seek to obtain full-time benefits and to define "semester hour" as one hour (or 50 minutes) in classroom per week for standard semester. Merged Area X (Education) v Cleland (1979, CA8 Iowa) 604 F2d 1075; Evergreen State College v Cleland (1980, CA9 Wash) 621 F2d 1002.

[§ 3689. Repealed]

HISTORY; ANCILLARY LAWS AND DIRECTIVES

This section (Act Oct. 24, 1972, P. L. 92-540, Title III, § 316(2), 86 Stat. 1087; Oct. 15, 1976, P. L. 94-502, Title V, § 509(b), 90 Stat. 2401; Nov. 23, 1977, P. L. 95-202, Title III, § 305(a)(1), 91 Stat. 1442; Oct. 17, 1980, P. L. 96-466, Title VI, § 601(g), 94 Stat. 2208; Dec. 18, 1989, P. L. 101-237, Title IV, §§ 418, 423(b)(1)(A), 103 Stat. 2087, 2092; Aug. 6, 1991, P. L. 102-83, § 5(a), 105 Stat. 406) was repealed by Act Oct. 9, 1996, P. L. 104-275, Title I, § 103(a)(1)(A), 110 Stat. 3326. It provided for the period of operation required for approval of a course.

Explanatory notes:
Provisions similar to those of this section were contained in former 38 USC §§ 1675, 1725, prior to repeal by Act Oct. 24, 1972, P. L. 92-540, Title IV, §§ 401(6), 402(2), 86 Stat. 1090.

§ 3690. Overcharges by educational institutions; discontinuance of allowances; examination of records; false or misleading statements

Overcharges by Educational Institutions

(a) If the Secretary finds that an educational institution has—

(1) charged or received from any eligible veteran or eligible person pursuing a program of education under this chapter or chapter 34 or 35 of this title [38 USCS §§ 3670 et seq. or 3451 et seq. or 3500 et seq.] any amount for any course in excess of the charges for tuition and fees which such institution requires similarly circumstanced nonveterans not receiving assistance under such chapters who are enrolled in the same course to pay, or

(2) instituted, after October 24, 1972, a policy or practice with respect to the payment of tuition, fees, or other charges in the case of eligible veterans and the Secretary finds that the effect of such policy or practice substantially denies to veterans the benefits of the advance allowances under such section.

38 USCS § 3690　　　　　　　　　　　　　　　　　　　VETERANS' BENEFITS

the Secretary may disapprove such educational institution for the enrollment of any eligible veteran or eligible person not already enrolled therein under this chapter or chapter 31, 34, or 35 of this title [38 USCS §§ 3670 et seq. or 3101 et seq., 3451 et seq., or 3500 et seq.].

Discontinuance of Allowances

(b)(1) The Secretary may discontinue the educational assistance allowance of any eligible veteran or eligible person if the Secretary finds that the program of education or any course in which the veteran or person is enrolled fails to meet any of the requirements of this chapter or chapter 34 or 35 of this title [38 USCS §§ 3670 et seq. or 3451 et seq. or 3500 et seq.], or if the Secretary finds that the educational institution offering such program or course has violated any provision of this chapter or chapter 34 or 35 of this title [38 USCS §§ 3670 et seq. or 3451 et seq. or 3500 et seq.], or fails to meet any of the requirements of such chapters.

(2) Except as provided in paragraph (3) of this subsection, any action by the Secretary under paragraph (1) of this subsection to discontinue (including to suspend) assistance provided to any eligible veteran or eligible person under this chapter [38 USCS §§ 3670 et seq.] or chapter 31, 32, 34, or 35 of this title [38 USCS §§ 3101 et seq., 3201 et seq., 3451 et seq., or 3500 et seq.] shall be based upon evidence that the veteran or eligible person is not or was not entitled to such assistance. Whenever the Secretary so discontinues any such assistance, the Secretary shall concurrently provide written notice to such veteran or person of such discontinuance and that such veteran or person is entitled thereafter to a statement of the reasons for such action and an opportunity to be heard thereon.

(3)(A) The Secretary may suspend educational assistance to eligible veterans and eligible persons already enrolled, and may disapprove the enrollment or reenrollment of any eligible veteran or eligible person, in any course as to which the Secretary has evidence showing a substantial pattern of eligible veterans or eligible persons, or both, who are receiving such assistance by virtue of their enrollment in such course but who are not entitled to such assistance because (i) the course approval requirements of this chapter are not being met, or (ii) the educational institution offering such course has violated one or more of the recordkeeping or reporting requirements of this chapter [38 USCS §§ 3670 et seq.] or chapter 30, 32, 34, or 35 of this title [38 USCS §§ 3001 et seq., 3201 et seq., 3451 et seq., or 3500 et seq.].

(B) Action may be taken under subparagraph (A) of this paragraph only after—

　(i) the Secretary provides to the State approving agency concerned and the educational institution concerned written notice of any such failure to meet such approval requirements and any such violation of such recordkeeping or reporting requirements;

　(ii) such institution refuses to take corrective action or does not within 60 days after such notice (or within such longer period as the Secretary determines is reasonable and appropriate) take corrective action; and

(iii) the Secretary, not less than 30 days before taking action under such subparagraph, provides to each eligible veteran and eligible person already enrolled in such course written notice of the Secretary's intent to take such action (and the reasons therefor) unless such corrective action is taken within such 60 days (or within such longer period as the Secretary has determined is reasonable and appropriate), and of the date on which the Secretary intends to take action under such subparagraph.

Examination of Records

(c) Notwithstanding any other provision of law, the records and accounts of educational institutions pertaining to eligible veterans or eligible persons who received educational assistance under this chapter [38 USCS §§ 3670 et seq.] or chapter 31, 32, 34, or 35 of this title [38 USCS §§ 3100 et seq., 3201 et seq., 3451 et seq., or 3500 et seq.] as well as the records of other students which the Secretary determines necessary to ascertain institutional compliance with the requirements of such chapters, shall be available for examination by duly authorized representatives of the Government.

False or Misleading Statements

(d) Whenever the Secretary finds that an educational institution has willfully submitted a false or misleading claim, or that a veteran or person, with the complicity of an educational institution, has submitted such a claim, the Secretary shall make a complete report of the facts of the case to the appropriate State approving agency and, where deemed advisable, to the Attorney General of the United States for appropriate action.
(Added Oct. 24, 1972, P. L. 92-540, Title III, § 316(2), 86 Stat. 1088; Oct. 15, 1976, P. L. 94-502, Title V, §§ 510, 513(a)(19), 90 Stat. 2401, 2403; Nov. 23, 1977, P. L. 95-202, Title III, § 306, 91 Stat. 1445; Oct. 17, 1980, P. L. 96-466, Title VIII, § 801(f), 94 Stat. 2216; Oct. 12, 1982, P. L. 97-295, § 4(59), 96 Stat. 1309; Oct. 14, 1982, P. L. 97-306, Title II, § 207, 96 Stat. 1435; Dec. 18, 1989, P. L. 101-237, Title IV, § 423(a)(9), (b)(1)(A), (2), 103 Stat. 2092; Aug. 6, 1991, P. L. 102-83, § 5(a), 105 Stat. 406; Aug. 14, 1991, P. L. 102-86, Title V, § 506(b)(1), 105 Stat. 426.)

HISTORY; ANCILLARY LAWS AND DIRECTIVES

Explanatory notes:
Act Aug. 14, 1991, P. L. 102-86, Title V, § 506(b)(1), 105 Stat. 426 (effective Dec. 18, 1989 as provided by § 506(b) of such Act), amended the directory language of Act Dec. 18, 1989, P. L. 101-237, § 423(b)(2), 103 Stat. 2092, without affecting the text of this section.

Provisions similar to those contained in subsec. (a) of this section were contained in former 38 USCS §§ 1685 and 1734, prior to their general amendment by Act Oct. 24, 1972, P. L. 92-540, Title II, § 203, Title III, § 313, 86 Stat. 1079, 1084.

38 USCS § 3690 VETERANS' BENEFITS

Provisions similar to those contained in subsec. (b) of this section were contained in former 38 USCS §§ 1687, 1736 prior to their repeal by Act Oct. 24, 1972, P. L. 92-540, Title IV, §§ 401(6), 402(2), 86 Stat. 1090.

Provisions similar to those contained in subsec. (c) of this section were contained in former 38 USCS § 1786 prior to its general revision by Act Oct. 24, 1972, P. L. 92-540, Title III, § 316(1), 86 Stat. 1084.

Provisions similar to those contained in subsec. (d) of this section were contained in former 38 USCS § 1787 prior to its general revision by Act Oct. 24, 1972, P. L. 92-540, Title III, § 316(1), 86 Stat. 1084.

A former § 1790 was redesignated as § 1794 by Act Oct. 24, 1972, P. L. 92-540, Title III, § 316(2), 86 Stat. 1088.

Amendments:

1976. Act Oct. 15, 1976 (effective 10/15/76, as provided by § 703(b) of such Act, which appears as 38 USCS § 3693 note), in subsec. (a), concluding matter, substituted "the Administrator" for "he"; in subsec. (b), substituted "the Administrator" for "he" preceding "finds" wherever appearing; substituted new subsec. (c) for one which read: "The records and accounts of educational institutions pertaining to eligible veterans or eligible persons who received educational assistance under this chapter or chapter 31, 34, or 35 of this title shall be available for examination by duly authorized representatives of the Government."; and in subsec. (d), substituted "the Administrator" for "he" preceding "shall make".

1977. Act Nov. 23, 1977 (effective 11/23/77, as provided by § 501 of such Act, which appears as 38 USCS § 101 note), in subsec. (b), designated existing matter as para. (1), and added para. (2).

1980. Act Oct. 17, 1980 (effective 10/1/80, as provided by § 802(h) of such Act, which appears as 38 USCS § 3452 note), in subsec. (b)(2), substituted "for" for "therefor".

1982. Act Oct. 12, 1982, in subsec. (a), in para. (2), substituted "October 24, 1972" for "after the effective date of section 1780 of this title", and, in the concluding matter, deleted a comma following "35"; and, in subsec. (b)(1), inserted "of this title" preceding ", or fails".

Act Oct. 14, 1982, in subsec. (b), in para. (2), substituted "Except as provided in paragraph (3) of this subsection, any" for "Any", and added para. (3).

1989. Act Dec. 18, 1989, in subsec. (a)(2), deleted "and prepayment" following "the advance"; and in subsec. (b)(3), in subpara. (A), inserted "30,", in subpara. (B), substituted "(B)" for "(B)(i)", and redesignated items (I)–(III) as cls. (i)–(iii), respectively.

Such Act further, in subsec. (a), in the introductory matter, in para. (2) and in the concluding matter, substituted "Secretary" for "Administrator"; in subsec. (b), in paras. (1) and (2), substituted "Secretary" for "Administrator" wherever appearing, and in para. (3), in subpara. (A), in the introductory matter, substituted "Secretary" for "Administrator", wherever appearing, and in subpara. (B), in cls. (i)-(iii), as redesignated, substituted "Secretary" for "Administrator", wherever appearing, and in cl. (iii), as redesignated, substituted "Secretary's" for "Administrator's"; and in subsecs. (c) and (d), substituted "Secretary" for "Administrator", wherever appearing.

1991. Act Aug. 6, 1991, redesignated this section, formerly 38 USCS § 1790, as 38 USCS § 3690.

Other provisions:
Application and construction of the Oct. 12, 1982 amendment of this section. For provisions as to the application and construction of the Oct. 12, 1982 amendment of this section, see § 5 of such Act, which appears as 10 USCS § 101 note.

INTERPRETIVE NOTES AND DECISIONS

1. Generally
2. Notice to veteran

1. Generally

Owner of traffic educational institute was not entitled to enjoin officials of Veterans' Administration [now Department of Veterans Affairs] district office from making known to General Accounting Office that institute had been overpaid for tuition furnished veterans as disclosed by audit conducted by employes of General Accounting Office, since finding disclosed by audit was conclusive on all departments. Burkley v United States (1950, CA7 Ill) 185 F2d 267.

2. Notice to veteran

Notice of veteran's rights may not be given to him or her on date later than effective date of suspension, nor may effective date of suspension precede date notice is given to veteran. VA GCO 24-79.

§ 3691. Change of program

(a) Except as provided in subsections (b) and (c) of this section, each eligible veteran and eligible person may make not more than one change of program of education, but an eligible veteran or eligible person whose program has been interrupted or discontinued due to the veteran's or person's own misconduct, the veteran's or person's own neglect, the veteran's or person's own lack of application shall not be entitled to any such change.

(b) The Secretary, in accordance with procedures that the Secretary may establish, may approve a change other than a change under subsection (a) of this section (or an initial change in the case of a veteran or person not eligible to make a change under subsection (a)) in program if the Secretary finds that—

(1) the program of education which the eligible veteran or eligible person proposes to pursue is suitable to the veteran's or person's aptitudes, interests, and abilities; and

(2) in any instance where the eligible veteran or eligible person has interrupted, or failed to progress in, the veteran's or person's program due to the veteran's or person's own misconduct, the veteran's or person's own neglect, or the veteran's or person's own lack of application, there exists a reasonable likelihood with respect to the program which the eligible veteran or eligible person proposes to pursue that there will not be a recurrence of such an interruption or failure to progress.

(c) The Secretary may also approve additional changes in program if the Secretary finds such changes are necessitated by circumstances beyond the control of the eligible veteran or eligible person.

(d) For the purposes of this section, the term "change of program of education" shall not be deemed to include a change by a veteran or eligible person from the pursuit of one program to the pursuit of another program if—

(1) the veteran or eligible person has successfully completed the former program;

(2) the program leads to a vocational, educational, or professional objective in the same general field as the former program;

(3) the former program is a prerequisite to, or generally required for, pursuit of the subsequent program; or

(4) in the case of a change from the pursuit of a subsequent program to the pursuit of a former program, the veteran or eligible person resumes pursuit of the former program without loss of credit or standing in the former program.

(Added Oct. 24, 1972, P. L. 92-540, Title III, § 316(2), 86 Stat. 1089; Oct. 15, 1976, P. L. 94-502, Title V, § 513(a)(20), 90 Stat. 2403; Dec. 18, 1989, P. L. 101-237, Title IV, § 423(b)(1)(A), 103 Stat. 2092; Aug. 15, 1990, P. L. 101-366, Title II, § 208(a), 104 Stat. 443; Aug. 6, 1991, P. L. 102-83, § 5(a), 105 Stat. 406; Oct. 29, 1992, P. L. 102-568, Title III, § 317, 106 Stat. 4334.)

HISTORY; ANCILLARY LAWS AND DIRECTIVES

Explanatory notes:
Provisions similar to those contained in this section were contained in former 38 USC §§ 1672, 1722, prior to repeal by Act Oct. 24, 1972, P. L. 92-540, Title IV, §§ 401(6), 402(2), 86 Stat. 1090.

Amendments:
1976. Act Oct. 15, 1976 (effective 10/15/76, as provided by § 703(b) of such Act, which appears as 38 USCS § 3693 note), in subsec. (a), substituted "the veteran's or person's" for "his" wherever appearing; in subsec. (b), in the preliminary matter, substituted "the Administrator" for "he" and in paras. (1) and (2), substituted "the veteran's or person's" for "his" wherever appearing; and in subsec. (c), substituted "the Administrator" for "he".

1989. Act Dec. 18, 1989, in subsecs. (b) and (c), substituted "Secretary" for "Administrator", wherever appearing.

1990. Act Aug. 15, 1990 (effective 6/1/91 as provided by § 208(a) of such Act, which appears as a note to this section), in subsec. (b), in the introductory matter, substituted "The Secretary, in accordance with procedures that the Secretary may establish, may approve a change other than a change under subsection (a) of this section" for "The Secretary may approve one additional change".

1991. Act Aug. 6, 1991, redesignated this section, formerly 38 USCS § 1791, as 38 USCS § 3691.

1992. Act Oct. 29, 1992 substituted subsec. (d) for one which read: "(d) As used in this section the term 'change of program of education' shall not be deemed to include a change from the pursuit of one program to pursuit of another where the first program is prerequisite to, or generally required for, entrance into pursuit of the second.".

Other provisions:
Effective date of Act Aug. 15, 1990 amendment of subsec. (b). Act Aug. 15, 1990, P. L. 101-366, Title II, § 208(b), 104 Stat. 443, provides: "The amendment made by subsection (a) [amending subsec. (b) of this section] shall take effect on June 1, 1991.".

CROSS REFERENCES
This section is referred to in 38 USCS §§ 3474, 3524.

READJUSTMENT BENEFITS 38 USCS § 3692

RESEARCH GUIDE

Am Jur:
77 Am Jur 2d, Veterans and Veterans' Laws §§ 143, 145.

INTERPRETIVE NOTES AND DECISIONS

Request for third change of program to pursue computer programming course at another school did not constitute change of program under more liberal statute enacted during pendency of appeal because it was in same general field of study as previous programs, but amendment did not help appellant since it precluded effective date earlier than its effective date. DeSousa v Gober (1997) 10 Vet App 461.

§ 3692. Advisory committee

(a) There shall be a Veterans' Advisory Committee on Education formed by the Secretary which shall be composed of persons who are eminent in their respective fields of education, labor, and management and of representatives of institutions and establishments furnishing education to eligible veterans or persons enrolled under chapter 30, 32, or 35 of this title [38 USCS §§ 3001 et seq., 3201 et seq., or 3500 et seq.] and chapter 106 of title 10 [10 USCS §§ 2131 et seq.]. The committee shall also include veterans representative of World War II, the Korean conflict era, the post-Korean conflict era, the Vietnam era, the post-Vietnam era, and the Persian Gulf War. The Assistant Secretary of Education for Postsecondary Education (or such other comparable official of the Department of Education as the Secretary of Education may designate) and the Assistant Secretary of Labor for Veterans' Employment and Training shall be ex officio members of the advisory committee.

(b) The Secretary shall consult with and seek the advice of the committee from time to time with respect to the administration of this chapter [38 USCS §§ 3670 et seq], chapter [chapters] 30, 32, and 35 of this title [38 USCS §§ 3001 et seq., 3201 et seq., and 3500 et seq.], and chapter 106 of title 10 [10 USCS §§ 2131 et seq.]. The committee may make such reports and recommendations as it considers desirable to the Secretary and the Congress.

(c) The committee shall remain in existence until December 31, 2003.

(Added March 3, 1966, P. L. 89-358, § 3(b), 80 Stat. 23; Oct. 24, 1972, P. L. 92-540, Title III, § 316(2), (3), 86 Stat. 1089; Oct. 17, 1980, P. L. 96-466, Title III, Part C, § 346, 94 Stat. 2200; Oct. 28, 1986, P. L. 99-576, Title III, Part A, § 304, 100 Stat. 3269; Nov. 18, 1988, P. L. 100-689, Title I, Part B, § 122, 102 Stat. 4174; Dec. 18, 1989, P. L. 101-237, Title IV, § 423(b)(1)(A), 103 Stat. 2092; April 6, 1991, P. L. 102-25, Title III, Part C, § 338, 105 Stat. 91; June 13, 1991, P. L. 102-54, § 14(c)(7), 105 Stat. 285; Aug. 6, 1991, P. L. 102-83, § 5(a), 105 Stat. 406; Dec. 20, 1993, P. L. 103-210, § 2(d), 107 Stat. 2497; Nov. 2, 1994, P. L. 103-446, Title VI, § 608, 108 Stat. 4672.)

HISTORY; ANCILLARY LAWS AND DIRECTIVES

Explanatory notes:
The bracketed word "sections" has been inserted in subsec. (b) as the word probably intended by Congress.
Provisions similar to those contained in this section were contained in for-

mer 38 USC § 1662, prior to repeal by Act March 3, 1966, P. L. 89-358, § 4(a), 80 Stat. 23.

Amendments:

1972. Act Oct. 24, 1972, redesignated this section, which formerly appeared as § 1788, as § 1792; and inserted "The Committee shall also include veterans representative of World War II, the Korean conflict era, the post-Korean conflict era, and the Vietnam era.".

1980. Act Oct. 17, 1980 (effective 10/1/80, as provided by § 802(c)(1) of such Act, which appears as 38 USCS § 3452 note), substituted new section for one which read:

"There shall be an advisory committee formed by the Administrator which shall be composed of persons who are eminent in their respective fields of education, labor, and management, and of representatives of the various types of institutions and establishments furnishing vocational rehabilitation under chapter 31 of this title or education to eligible persons or veterans enrolled under chapter 34 or 35 of this title. The Committee shall also include veterans representative of World War II, the Korean conflict era, the post-Korean conflict era, and the Vietnam era. The Commissioner of Education and the Administrator, Manpower Administration, Department of Labor, shall be ex officio members of the advisory committee. The Administrator shall advise and consult with the committee from time to time with respect to the administration of this chapter and chapters 31, 34, and 35 of this title, and the committee may make such reports and recommendations as it deems desirable to the Administrator and to the Congress.".

1986. Act Oct. 28, 1986, in subsec. (a), substituted "a Veterans Advisory Committee on Education" for "an advisory committee", and inserted "30,"; and in subsec. (b), inserted "30,".

1988. Act Nov. 18, 1988, in subsec. (c), substituted "December 31, 1993" for "December 31, 1989".

1989. Act Dec. 18, 1989, in subsecs. (a) and (b), substituted "Secretary" for "Administrator", wherever appearing.

1991. Act April 6, 1991, in subsec. (a), substituted "the post-Vietnam era, and the Persian Gulf War" for "and the post-Vietnam era".

Act June 13, 1991, in subsec. (a), inserted "and Training".

Act Aug. 6, 1991, redesignated this section, formerly 38 USCS § 1792, as 38 USCS § 3692.

1993. Act Dec. 20, 1993, in subsec. (c), substituted "December 31, 1994" for "December 31, 1993".

1994. Act Nov. 2, 1994, in subsec. (a), deleted "34," preceding "or 35" and inserted "and chapter 106 of title 10"; in subsec. (b), substituted "this chapter, chapter 30, 32, and 35 of this title, and chapter 106 of title 10" for "this chapter and chapters 30, 32, 34, and 35 of this title"; and, in subsec. (c), substituted "December 31, 2003" for "December 31, 1994".

Other provisions:

Termination of advisory committees, boards and councils, in existence on Jan. 5, 1973. Act Oct. 6, 1972, P. L. 92-463, §§ 3(2) and 14, 86 Stat. 770, 776 (effective 1/5/73, as provided by § 15 of such Act), which is classified as 5 USCS Appx, provides that the advisory committees in existence on Jan. 5, 1973, are to terminate not later than the expiration of the two-year period following Jan. 5, 1973, unless, in the case of a board established by the President or an officer of the Federal Government, such board is renewed by appropriate action prior to the expiration of such two-year period, or in the case of a board established by the Congress, its duration is otherwise provided for by law.

Study of operation of post-Korean conflict programs of educational assistance. Act Oct. 24, 1972, P. L. 92-540, Title IV, § 413, 86 Stat. 1093, provided for a comparative study of the operation of the post-Korean conflict program of educational assistance with similar prior programs available to veterans of World War II and the Korean conflict, the results of such study and recommendations for improvement to be transmitted to the President and Congress within 6 months of Oct. 24, 1972.

Study of educational assistance programs for veterans, survivors, and dependents; submission to Congress and President by Sept. 30, 1979. Act Nov. 23, 1977, P. L. 95-202, Title III, § 304(b), 91 Stat. 1442, provided that the Administrator of Veterans' Affairs, in consultation with the Advisory Committee formed pursuant to this section, conduct a study respecting the operation of the programs of educational assistance carried out under 38 USCS §§ 3670 et seq. and 3451 et seq. and that a report concerning such study be submitted to the Congress not later than Sept. 30, 1979.

Commission to assess veterans' education policy. Act Oct. 28, 1986, P. L. 99-576, Title III, Part A, § 320, 100 Stat. 3275, as amended May 20, 1988, P. L. 100-323, § 14, 102 Stat. 574, effective on enactment as provided by § 16(a) of such Act, which appears as 38 USCS § 3104 note, provides:

"(a) Establishment and members. (1) There is established a Commission on Veterans' Education Policy (hereafter in this section referred to as the 'Commission').

"(2)(A) The Commission shall consist of 11 members, 10 of whom shall be appointed, not later than March 1, 1987, by the Administrator of Veterans' Affairs in consultation with the chairmen and the ranking minority members of the Committees on Veterans' Affairs of the Senate and of the House of Representatives (hereafter in this section referred to as 'the Committees'), and one of whom shall be the chairman of the Advisory Committee on Education established under section 1792 [now § 3692] of title 38, United States Code (as amended by section 304).

"(B) The members of the Commission—

"(i) shall be broadly representative of entities engaged in providing education and training and of veterans' service organizations; and

"(ii) shall be selected on the basis of their knowledge of and experience in education and training policy and the implementation of such policy with respect to programs of assistance administered by the Veterans' Administration.

"(3) The Administrator of Veterans' Affairs, the ex officio members of the Advisory Committee on Education referred to in paragraph (2)(A), the Assistant Secretary of Defense for Force Management and Personnel, and the chairmen and ranking minority members of the Committees (or, in the case of any such individual, a designee of any such individual) shall be ex officio, nonvoting members of the Commission.".

"(4)(A) The Administrator shall designate a member from among the voting members of the Commission to chair the Commission.

"(B) The chairman of the Commission, with the concurrence of the Commission, shall appoint an executive director, who shall be the chief executive officer of the Commission and shall perform such duties as are prescribed by the Commission.

"(C) The Administrator shall furnish the Commission with such professional, technical, and clerical staff and services and administrative support as the Commission determines necessary for the Commission to carry out the provisions of this section effectively.

"(b) First report. (1) Not later than 18 months after the date on which at least 8 members of the Commission have been appointed, the Commission shall submit a report on the Commission's findings and recommendations on the matters described in paragraph (2) of this subsection to the Administrator and the Committees.

"(2) The report required by paragraph (1) shall include the Commission's findings, views, and recommendations on the following matters:

"(A) The need for distinctions between certificate-granting courses and degree-granting courses.

"(B) The measurement of courses for the purposes of payment of educational assistance benefits.

"(C) The vocational value of courses offered through home study.

"(D) The role of innovative and nontraditional programs of education and the manner in which such programs should be treated for purposes of payment of educational assistance benefits by the Veterans' Administration, including courses that result in the achievement of continuing education units.

"(E) Such other matters relating to administration of chapters 30, 31, 32, 34, 35, and 36 of title 38, United States Code [38 USCS §§ 3001 et seq., 3100 et seq., 3201 et seq., 3451 et seq., 3500 et seq., and 3670 et seq.], by the Veterans' Administration as (i) the Commission considers appropriate or necessary, or (ii) are suggested by the Administrator or, concurrently, by the chairmen and ranking minority members of the Committees.

"(c) Interim and final reports. (1) Not later than 6 months after the date on which the report is submitted under subsection (b), the Administrator shall submit an interim report to the Committees. The interim report shall contain—

"(A) the Administrator's views on the desirability, feasibility, and cost of implementing each of the Commission's recommendations, and the actions taken or planned with respect to the implementation of such recommendations;

"(B)(i) the Administrator's views on any legislation or regulations proposed by the Commission,

(ii) the Administrator's views on the need for any alternative or additional legislation or regulations to implement the Commission's recommendations, (iii) the Administrator's recommendations for any such alternative or additional legislation, (iv) the proposed text of any regulations referred to in subclause (i) or (ii) which the Administrator considers necessary and the proposed text of any legislation referred to in such subclause which is recommended by the Administrator, and (v) a cost estimate for the implementation of any regulations and legislation referred to in such subclause; and

"(C) any other proposals that the Administrator considers appropriate in light of the Commission's report.

"(2) Not later than 90 days after the date on which the Administrator's interim report is submitted under paragraph (1), the Commission shall submit a report to the Administrator and the Committees containing the Commission's views on the Administrator's interim report.

"(3) Not later than two years after the date on which the Commission's report is submitted under subsection (b), the Administrator shall submit a final report to the Committees. The final report shall include the actions taken with respect to the recommendations of the Commission and any further recommendations the Administrator considers appropriate.

"(d) Termination. The Commission shall terminate 90 days after the date on which the Administrator submits the final report required by subsection (c)(3).".

CROSS REFERENCES
This section is referred to in 10 USCS § 16136; 38 USCS § 306.

RESEARCH GUIDE
Am Jur:
77 Am Jur 2d, Veterans and Veterans' Laws § 132.

§ 3693. Compliance surveys

(a) Except as provided in subsection (b) of this section, the Secretary shall conduct an annual compliance survey of each institution offering one or more courses approved for the enrollment of eligible veterans or persons if at least 300 veterans or persons are enrolled in such course or courses under provisions of this title or if any such course does not lead to a standard college degree. Such compliance survey shall be designed to ensure that the institution and approved courses are in compliance with all applicable provisions of chapters 30 through 36 of this title [38 USCS §§ 3001 et seq. through §§ 3670 et seq.]. The Secretary shall assign at least one education compliance specialist to work on compliance surveys in any year for each 40 compliance surveys required to be made under this section for such year.

(b) The Secretary may waive the requirement in subsection (a) of this section for an annual compliance survey with respect to an institution if the Secretary determines, based on the institution's demonstrated record of compliance with all the applicable provisions of chapters 30 through 36 of this title [38 USCS §§ 3001 et seq. through §§ 3670 et seq.], that the waiver would be appropriate and in the best interest of the United States Government.

(Added Oct. 15, 1976, P. L. 94-502, Title V, § 511(1), 90 Stat. 2401; May 20, 1988, P. L. 100-322, Title III, Part C, § 322, 102 Stat. 535; Dec. 18, 1989, P. L. 101-237, Title IV, § 423(b)(1)(A), 103 Stat. 2092; Aug. 6, 1991, P. L. 102-83, § 5(a), 105 Stat. 406.)

38 USCS § 3693

HISTORY; ANCILLARY LAWS AND DIRECTIVES

Effective date of section:

Act Oct. 15, 1976, P. L. 94-502, § 703(b), 90 Stat. 2406, provided that this section is effective on October 15, 1976

Amendments:

1988. Act May 20, 1988 substituted this section for one which read: "The Administrator shall conduct an annual compliance survey of each institution offering one or more courses approved for the enrollment of eligible veterans or persons where at least 300 veterans or persons are enrolled under provisions of this title or where the course does not lead to a standard college degree. Such compliance survey shall assure that the institution and approved courses are in compliance with all applicable provisions of chapters 31, 34, 35, and 36 of this title. The Administrator shall assign at least one education compliance specialist to work on compliance surveys in any year for each 40 compliance surveys required to be made under this section.".

1989. Act Dec. 18, 1989, in subsecs. (a) and (b), substituted "Secretary" for "Administrator", wherever appearing.

1991. Act Aug. 6, 1991, redesignated this section, formerly 38 USCS § 1793, as 38 USCS § 3693.

§ 3694. Use of other Federal agencies

In carrying out the Secretary's functions under this chapter or chapter 34 or 35 of this title [38 USCS §§ 3670 et seq. or 3451 et seq. or 3500 et seq.], the Secretary may utilize the facilities and services of any other Federal department or agency. Any such utilization shall be pursuant to proper agreement with the Federal department or agency concerned; and payment to cover the cost thereof shall be made either in advance or by way of reimbursement, as may be provided in such agreement.

(Added March 3, 1966, P. L. 89-358, § 3(b), 80 Stat. 23; Oct. 24, 1972, P. L. 92-540, Title III, § 316(2), 86 Stat. 1086; Oct. 15, 1976, P. L. 94-502, Title V, § 513(a)(21), 90 Stat. 2403; Dec. 18, 1989, P. L. 101-237, Title IV, § 423(b)(1)(A), (2), 103 Stat. 2092; Aug. 6, 1991, P. L. 102-83, § 5(a), 105 Stat. 406.)

HISTORY; ANCILLARY LAWS AND DIRECTIVES

Explanatory notes:

Provisions similar to those contained in this section were contained in former 38 USC §§ 1644, 1761(c), prior to repeal by Act March 3, 1966, P. L. 89-358, § 4(a), 80 Stat. 23.

Effective date of section:

Act March 3, 1966, P. L. 89-358, § 12(a), 80 Stat. 28, provided that this section is effective on March 3, 1966.

Amendments:

1972. Act Oct. 24, 1972, redesignated this section as § 1794; it formerly appeared as § 1790.

1976. Act Oct. 15, 1976 (effective 10/15/76, as provided by § 703(b) of such Act, which appears as 38 USCS § 3693 note), substituted "the Administrator's" for "his".

1989. Act Dec. 18, 1989, substituted "Secretary's" and "Secretary" for "Administrator's" and "Administrator", respectively.

1991. Act Aug. 6, 1991, redesignated this section, formerly 38 USCS § 1794, as 38 USCS § 3694.

CROSS REFERENCES
This section is referred to in 38 USCS § 3696.

§ 3695. Limitation on period of assistance under two or more programs

(a) The aggregate period for which any person may receive assistance under two or more of the provisions of law listed below may not exceed 48 months (or the part-time equivalent thereof):

(1) Parts VII or VIII, Veterans Regulation numbered 1(a), as amended.

(2) Title II of the Veterans' Readjustment Assistance Act of 1952.

(3) The War Orphans' Educational Assistance Act of 1956,

(4) Chapters 30, 32, 34, 35, and 36 of this title [38 USCS §§ 3001 et seq., 3201 et seq., 3451 et seq., 3500 et seq., and 3670 et seq.], and the former chapter 33.

(5) Chapters 106 and 107 of title 10 [10 USCS §§ 2131 et seq. and 2141 et seq.].

(6) Section 903 of the Department of Defense Authorization Act, 1981 (Public Law 96-342, 10 U.S.C. 2141 note).

(7) The Hostage Relief Act of 1980 (Public Law 96-449, 5 U.S.C. 5561 note).

(8) The Omnibus Diplomatic Security and Antiterrorism Act of 1986 (Public Law 99-399) [22 USCS §§ 4801 et seq.].

(b) No person may receive assistance under chapter 31 of this title [38 USCS §§ 3100 et seq.] in combination with assistance under any of the provisions of law cited in subsection (a) of this section in excess of 48 months (or the part-time equivalent thereof) unless the Secretary determines that additional months of benefits under chapter 31 of this title [38 USCS §§ 3100 et seq.] are necessary to accomplish the purposes of a rehabilitation program (as defined in section 3101(5) of this title) in the individual case.

(Added Oct. 23, 1968, P. L. 90-631, § 1(d)(1), 82 Stat. 1331; Oct. 24, 1972, P. L. 92-540, Title III, § 316(2), Title IV, § 403(13), 86 Stat. 1086, 1090; Oct. 17, 1980, P. L. 96-466, Title I, § 103, 94 Stat. 2187; March 2, 1984, P. L. 98-223, Title II, § 203(c)(2), 98 Stat. 41; Oct. 19, 1984, P. L. 98-525, Title VII, § 703(d), 98 Stat. 2564; Dec. 18, 1989, P. L. 101-237, Title IV, § 423(a)(8)(B), (b)(1)(A), 103 Stat. 2092; Aug. 6, 1991, P. L. 102-83, § 5(a), (c)(1), 105 Stat. 406.)

HISTORY; ANCILLARY LAWS AND DIRECTIVES

References in text:

"Parts VII or VIII, Veterans Regulation numbered 1(a)", referred to in para. (1), were added to Veterans Regulation numbered 1(a) in Chapter 12A of former Title 38 by Acts March 24, 1943, ch 22, § 2, 57 Stat. 43 and June 22, 1944, ch 268, Title II, § 400(b) 58 Stat. 287, and were repealed by Act Sept. 2, 1958, P. L. 85-857, § 14(67), 72 Stat. 1272.

"Title II of the Veterans' Readjustment Assistance Act of 1952", referred to in para. (2), was Act July 16, 1952, ch 875, Title II, 66 Stat. 663, as amended, which was generally classified to former 38 USC §§ 911 et seq. prior to repeal by Act Sept. 2, 1958, P. L. 85-857, § 14(101), 72 Stat. 1268. For similar provisions, see Chapter 34 (38 USCS §§ 3451 et seq.).

"The War Orphans' Educational Assistance Act of 1956", referred to in para. (3), was Act June 29, 1956, ch 476, 70 Stat. 441, as amended, which was generally classified to former 38 USC §§ 1031 et seq. prior to repeal by Act Sept. 2, 1958, P. L. 85-857, § 14(113), 72 Stat. 1274. For similar provisions, see Chapter 35 (38 USCS §§ 3500 et seq.).

"The former chapter 33", referred to in para. (4), was Act Sept. 2, 1958, P. L. 85-857, § 1, 72 Stat. 1174, as amended, which was classified to former 38 USC §§ 1601 et seq. prior to repeal by Act March 3, 1966, P. L. 89-858, 4(a), 80 Stat. 23.

Effective date of section:

Act Oct. 23, 1968, P. L. 90-631, § 6(a), 82 Stat. 1335, provided that this section is effective on the first day of the second calendar month which begins after Oct. 23, 1968.

Amendments:

1972. Act Oct. 24, 1972, redesignated this section, which formerly appeared as § 1791, as § 1795; and in para. (4), substituted "chapters 31, 34, 35, and 36" for "Chapters 31, 34, and 35".

1980. Act Oct. 13, 1980 (effective 10/1/80, as provided by § 802(a)(6) of such Act, which appears as 38 USCS § 3681 note), designated existing matter as subsec. (a); in subsec. (a), as so designated, substituted new para. (4) for one which read: "Chapters 31, 34, 35, and 36 of this title, and the former chapter 33", and in the concluding matter, deleted ", but this section shall not be deemed to limit the period for which assistance may be received under chapter 31 alone" following "thereof)"; and added subsec. (b).

1984. Act March 2, 1984 substituted subsec. (a) for one which read:

"(a) The aggregate period for which any person may receive assistance under two or more of the laws listed below—

"(1) parts VII or VIII, Veterans Regulation numbered 1(a), as amended;

"(2) title II of the Veterans' Readjustment Assistance Act of 1952;

"(3) the War Orphans' Educational Assistance Act of 1956;

"(4) chapters 32, 34, 35, and 36 of this title and the former chapter 33; may not exceed forty-eight months (or the part-time equivalent thereof).".

Such Act further, in subsec. (b), substituted "subsection (a)" for "clauses (1), (2), (3), and (4)" and "48" for "forty-eight"..

Act Oct. 19, 1984, in subsec. (a), in para. (4), inserted "30,", and in para. (5), substituted "Chapters 106 and 107" for "Chapter 107".

1989. Act Dec. 18, 1989, in subsec. (a), added para. (8); and in subsec. (b), substituted "Secretary" for "Administrator".

1991. Act Aug. 6, 1991, redesignated this section, formerly 38 USCS § 1795, as 38 USCS § 3695, and amended the references in this section to reflect the redesignations made by § 5(a) of such Act (see Table III preceding 38 USCS § 101).

CROSS REFERENCES

This section is referred to in 10 USCS § 16131; 38 USCS §§ 3013, 3231, 3511.

RESEARCH GUIDE

Am Jur:

77 Am Jur 2d, Veterans and Veterans' Laws § 137.

INTERPRETIVE NOTES AND DECISIONS

Limitation on entitlement under various programs for assistance to veterans, contained in 38 USCS § 1795 [now 38 USCS § 3695], is constitutional and recipients whose benefits are limited are not denied due process or equal protection of laws. Burke v United States (1973, CA9 Cal) 480 F2d 279, cert den (1973) 414 US 913, 38 L Ed 2d 152, 94 S Ct 258.

§ 3696. Limitation on certain advertising, sales, and enrollment practices

(a) The Secretary shall not approve the enrollment of an eligible veteran or eligible person in any course offered by an institution which utilizes advertising, sales, or enrollment practices of any type which are erroneous, deceptive, or misleading either by actual statement, omission, or intimation.

(b) To ensure compliance with this section, any institution offering courses approved for the enrollment of eligible persons or veterans shall maintain a complete record of all advertising, sales, or enrollment materials (and copies thereof) utilized by or on behalf of the institution during the preceding 12-month period. Such record shall be available for inspection by the State approving agency or the Secretary. Such materials shall include but are not limited to any direct mail pieces, brochures, printed literature used by sales persons, films, video tapes, and audio tapes disseminated through broadcast media, material disseminated through print media, tear sheets, leaflets, handbills, fliers, and any sales or recruitment manuals used to instruct sales personnel, agents, or representatives of such institution.

(c) The Secretary shall, pursuant to section 3694 of this title, enter into an agreement with the Federal Trade Commission to utilize, where appropriate, its services and facilities, consistent with its available resources, in carrying out investigations and making the Secretary's determinations under subsection (a) of this section. Such agreement shall provide that cases arising under subsection (a) of this section or any similar matters with respect to any of the requirements of this chapter or chapters 34 and 35 of this title [38 USCS §§ 3670 et seq. or 3451 et seq. or 3500 et seq.] shall be referred to the Federal Trade Commission which in its discretion will conduct an investigation and make preliminary findings. The findings and results of any such investigations shall

be referred to the Secretary who shall take appropriate action in such cases within ninety days after such referral.
(Added Dec. 3, 1974, P. L. 93-508, Title II, § 212(a), 88 Stat. 1585; Oct. 15, 1976, P. L. 94-502, Title V, §§ 512, 513(a)(22), 90 Stat. 2402, 2403; Oct. 24, 1984, P. L. 98-543, Title IV, § 401, 98 Stat. 2749; Dec. 18, 1989, P. L. 101-237, Title IV, § 423(b)(1)(A), (2), 103 Stat. 2092; Aug. 6, 1991, P. L. 102-83, § 5(a), (c)(1), 105 Stat. 406.)

HISTORY; ANCILLARY LAWS AND DIRECTIVES
Effective date of section:
Act Dec. 3, 1974, P. L. 93-508, Title V, § 503, 88 Stat. 1601, provided that this section is effective on Dec. 3, 1974.

Amendments:
1976. Act Oct. 15, 1976 (effective 12/1/76, as provided by § 703(c) of such Act, which appears as 38 USCS § 3693 note), redesignated subsecs. (b) and (c) as subsecs. (c) and (d), respectively; and added a new subsec. (b).

Such Act further (effective 10/15/76, as provided by § 703(b) of such Act, which appears as 38 USCS § 3693 note), in subsec. (c), as redesignated by Act Oct. 15, 1976, § 512, substituted "the Administrator's" for "his".

1984. Act Oct. 24, 1984 deleted subsec. (d), which read: "Not later than sixty days after the end of each fiscal year, the Administrator shall report to Congress on the nature and disposition of all cases arising under this section.".

1989. Act Dec. 18, 1989, in subsecs. (a)–(c), substituted "Secretary" for "Administrator", wherever appearing; and in subsec. (c), substituted "Secretary's" for "Administrator's".

1991. Act Aug. 6, 1991, redesignated this section, formerly 38 USCS § 1796, as 38 USCS § 3696, and amended the references in this section to reflect the redesignations made by § 5(a) of such Act (see Table III preceding 38 USCS § 101).

RESEARCH GUIDE
Am Jur:
77 Am Jur 2d, Veterans and Veterans' Laws § 139.

§ 3697. Funding of contract educational and vocational counseling

(a) Subject to subsection (b) of this section, educational or vocational counseling services obtained by the Department of Veterans Affairs by contract and provided to an individual under section 3697A of this title or to an individual applying for or receiving benefits under section 524 or chapter 30, 32, 34, or 35 of this title [38 USCS §§ 3001 et seq., 3201 et seq., 3451 et seq., or 3500 et seq.] or chapter 106 of Title 10 [10 USCS §§ 2131 et seq.], shall be paid for out of funds appropriated, or otherwise available, to the Department of Veterans Affairs for payment of readjustment benefits.

(b) Payments under this section shall not exceed $6,000,000 in any fiscal year.
(Added Nov. 18, 1988, P. L. 100-687, Div B, Title XIII, § 1302(a), 102 Stat. 4128; Dec. 18, 1989, P. L. 101-237, Title IV, § 423(b)(1)(B), 103 Stat. 2092;

READJUSTMENT BENEFITS 38 USCS § 3697A

March 22, 1991, P. L. 102-16, § 2(b)(3), 105 Stat. 49; Aug. 6, 1991, P. L. 102-83, § 5(a), (c)(1), 105 Stat. 406; Nov. 2, 1994, P. L. 103-446, Title VI, § 609(a), 108 Stat. 4673.)

HISTORY; ANCILLARY LAWS AND DIRECTIVES
Amendments:
1989. Act Dec. 18, 1989, in subsec. (a), substituted "Department of Veterans Affairs" for "Veterans' Administration", wherever appearing.
1991. Act March 22, 1991, in subsec. (a), inserted "under section 1797A of this title or to an individual".
Act Aug. 6, 1991, redesignated this section, formerly 38 USCS § 1797, as 38 USCS § 3697, and amended the references in this section to reflect the redesignations made by § 5(a) of such Act (see Table III preceding 38 USCS § 101).
1994. Act Nov. 2, 1994 (effective 10/1/94, as provided by § 609(b) of such Act, which appears as a note to this section), in subsec. (b), substituted "$6,000,000" for "$5,000,000".

Other provisions:
Effective date of amendment made by Act Nov. 2, 1994. Act Nov. 2, 1994, P. L. 103-446, Title VI, § 609(b), 108 Stat. 4673, provides: "The amendment made by subsection (a) [amending subsec. (b) of this section] shall take effect on October 1, 1994.".

RESEARCH GUIDE
Am Jur:
77 Am Jur 2d, Veterans and Veterans' Laws § 133.

§ 3697A. Educational and vocational counseling

(a) The Secretary shall make available to an individual described in subsection (b) of this section, upon such individual's request, counseling services, including such educational and vocational counseling and guidance, testing, and other assistance as the Secretary determines necessary to aid the individual in selecting—

(1) an educational or training objective and an educational institution or training establishment appropriate for the attainment of such objective; or

(2) an employment objective that would be likely to provide such individual with satisfactory employment opportunities in the light of the individual's personal circumstances.

(b) For the purposes of this section, the term "individual" means an individual who—

(1) is eligible for educational assistance under chapter 30, 31, or 32 of this title [38 USCS §§ 3001 et seq., 3100 et seq., or 3201 et seq.] or chapter 106 or 107 of title 10 [10 USCS §§ 2131 et seq. or 2141 et seq.];

(2) was discharged or released from active duty under conditions other than dishonorable if not more than one year has elapsed since the date of such last discharge or release from active duty; or

(3) is serving on active duty in any State with the Armed Forces and is within 180 days of the estimated date of such individual's discharge or release from active duty under conditions other than dishonorable, including those who are making a determination of whether to continue as members of the Armed Forces.

(c) In any case in which the Secretary has rated the individual as being incompetent, the counseling services described in subsection (a) of this section shall be required to be provided to the individual before the selection of a program of education or training.

(d) At such intervals as the Secretary determines necessary, the Secretary shall make available information concerning the need for general education and for trained personnel in the various crafts, trades, and professions. Facilities of other Federal agencies collecting such information shall be utilized to the extent the Secretary determines practicable.

(e) The Secretary shall take appropriate steps (including individual notification where feasible) to acquaint all individuals described in subsection (b) of this section with the availability and advantages of counseling services under this section.
(Added March 22, 1991, P. L. 102-16, § 2(a), 105 Stat. 48; Aug. 6, 1991, P. L. 102-83, § 5(a), 105 Stat. 406.)

HISTORY; ANCILLARY LAWS AND DIRECTIVES
Amendments:
1991. Act Aug. 6, 1991, redesignated this section, formerly 38 USCS § 1797A, as 38 USCS § 3697A.

CROSS REFERENCES
This section is referred to in 38 USCS § 3697.

RESEARCH GUIDE
Am Jur:
77 Am Jur 2d, Veterans and Veterans' Laws § 133.

SUBCHAPTER III. EDUCATION LOANS

§ 3698. Eligibility for loans; amount and conditions of loans; interest rate on loans

(a)(1) Subject to paragraph (2) of this subsection, each eligible veteran shall be entitled to a loan under this subchapter [38 USCS §§ 3698 et seq.] (if the program of education is pursued in a State) in an amount determined under, and subject to the conditions specified in, subsection (b)(1) of this section if the veteran satisfies the requirements set forth in subsection (c) of this section and the criteria established under subsection (g) of this section.

(2) Except in the case of a veteran to whom section 3462(a)(2) of this title is applicable, no loan may be made under this subchapter [38 USCS §§ 3698 et seq.] after September 30, 1981.

(b)(1) Subject to paragraph (3) of this subsection, the amount of the loan to which an eligible veteran shall be entitled under this subchapter [38 USCS §§ 3698 et seq.] for any academic year shall be equal to the amount needed by such veteran to pursue a program of education at the institution at which the veteran is enrolled, as determined under paragraph (2) of this subsection.

(2)(A) The amount needed by a veteran to pursue a program of education at an institution for any academic year shall be determined by subtracting (i) the total amount of financial resources (as defined in subparagraph (B) of this paragraph) available to the veteran which may be reasonably expected to be expended by such veteran for educational purposes in any year from (ii) the actual cost of attendance (as defined in subparagraph (C) of this paragraph) at the institution in which such veteran is enrolled.

(B) The term "total amount of financial resources" of any veteran for any year means the total of the following:

(i) The annual adjusted effective income of the veteran less Federal income tax paid or payable by such veteran with respect to such income.

(ii) The amount of cash assets of the veteran.

(iii) The amount of financial assistance received by the veteran under the provisions of title IV of the Higher Education Act of 1965 (20 U.S.C. 1070 et seq.).

(iv) Educational assistance received by the veteran under this title other than under this subchapter [38 USCS §§ 3698 et seq.].

(v) Financial assistance received by the veteran under any scholarship or grant program other than those specified in clauses (iii) and (iv).

(C) The term "actual cost of attendance" means, subject to such regulations as the Secretary may provide, the actual per-student charges for tuition, fees, room and board (or expenses related to reasonable commuting), books, and an allowance for such other expenses as the Secretary determines by regulation to be reasonably related to attendance at the institution at which the veteran is enrolled.

(3) The aggregate of the amounts any veteran may borrow under this subchapter [38 USCS §§ 3698 et seq.] may not exceed $376 multiplied by the number of months such veteran is entitled to receive educational assistance under section 3461 of this title, but not in excess of $2,500 in any one regular academic year.

(c) An eligible veteran shall be entitled to a loan under this subchapter [38 USCS §§ 3698 et seq.] if such veteran—

(1) is in attendance at an educational institution on at least a half-time basis and (A) is enrolled in a course leading to a standard college degree, or (B) is enrolled in a course, the completion of which requires six months or longer, leading to an identified and predetermined professional or vocational objective, except that the Secretary may waive the requirements of subclause (B) of this clause, in whole or in part, if the Secretary determines, pursuant to regulations which the Secretary shall prescribe, it to be in the interest of the eligible veteran and the Federal Government;

38 USCS § 3698 VETERANS' BENEFITS

(2) enters into an agreement with the Secretary meeting the requirements of subsection (d) of this section; and

(3) satisfies any criteria established under subsection (g) of this section.

No loan shall be made under this subchapter [38 USCS §§ 3698 et seq.] to an eligible veteran pursuing a program of correspondence, or apprenticeship or other on-job training.

(d) Any agreement between the Secretary and a veteran under this subchapter [38 USCS §§ 3698 et seq.]—

(1) shall include a note or other written obligation which provides for repayment to the Secretary of the principal amount of, and payment of interest on, the loan in installments (A) over a period beginning nine months after the date on which the borrower ceases to be at least a half-time student and ending ten years and nine months after such date; or (B) over such shorter period as the Secretary may have prescribed under subsection (g) of this section;

(2) shall include provision for acceleration of repayment of all or any part of the loan, without penalty, at the option of the borrower;

(3) shall provide that the loan shall bear interest, on the unpaid balance of the loan, at a rate prescribed by the Secretary, at the time the loan is contracted for which rate shall be comparable to the rate of interest charged students at such time on loans insured by the Secretary of Education, under part B of title IV of the Higher Education Act of 1965 [20 USCS §§ 1071 et seq.], but in no event shall the rate so prescribed by the Secretary exceed the rate charged students on such insured loans, and shall provide that no interest shall accrue prior to the beginning date of repayment; and

(4) shall provide that the loan shall be made without security and without endorsement.

(e)(1) Except as provided in paragraph (2) of this subsection, whenever the Secretary determines that a default has occurred on any loan made under this subchapter [38 USCS §§ 3698 et seq.], the Secretary shall declare an overpayment, and such overpayment shall be recovered from the veteran concerned in the same manner as any other debt due the United States.

(2) If a veteran who has received a loan under this section dies or becomes permanently and totally disabled, then the Secretary shall discharge the veteran's liability on such loan by repaying the amount owed on such loan.

(f) Payment of a loan made under this section shall be drawn in favor of the eligible veteran and mailed promptly to the educational institution in which such veteran is enrolled. Such institution shall deliver such payment to the eligible veteran as soon as practicable after receipt thereof. Upon delivery of such payment to the eligible veteran, such educational institution shall promptly submit to the Secretary a certification, on such form as the Secretary shall prescribe, of such delivery, and such delivery shall be deemed to be an advance payment under section 3680(d)(4) of this title for purposes of section 3684(b) of this title.

(g)(1) The Secretary shall conduct, on a continuing basis, a review of the default experience with respect to loans made under this section.

(2)(A) To ensure that loans are made under this section on the basis of financial need directly related to the costs of education, the Secretary may, by regulation, establish (i) criteria for eligibility for such loans, in addition to the criteria and requirements prescribed by subsections (c) and (d) of this section, in order to limit eligibility for such loans to eligible veterans attending educational institutions with relatively high rates of tuition and fees, and (ii) criteria under which the Secretary may prescribe a repayment period for certain types of loans made under this section that is shorter than the repayment period otherwise applicable under subsection (d)(1)(A) of this section. Criteria established by the Secretary under clause (i) of the preceding sentence may include a minimum amount of tuition and fees that an eligible veteran may pay in order to be eligible for such a loan (except that any such criterion shall not apply with respect to a loan for which the veteran is eligible as a result of an extension of the period of eligibility of such veteran for loans under this section provided for by section 3462(a)(2) of this title.

(B) In prescribing regulations under subparagraph (A) of this paragraph, the Secretary shall take into consideration information developed in the course of the review required by paragraph (1) of this subsection.

(C) Regulations may be prescribed under subparagraph (A) of this paragraph only after opportunity has been afforded for public comment thereon.

(Added Dec. 3, 1974, P. L. 93-508, Title III, § 301(a), 88 Stat. 1589; Oct. 15, 1976, P. L. 94-502, Title V, §§ 502(a), 513(a)(23), 90 Stat. 2399, 2403; Nov. 23, 1977, P. L. 95-202, Title I, § 104(3), Title II, § 202, 91 Stat. 1435, 1438; Oct. 18, 1978, P. L. 95-476, Title II, § 201, 92 Stat. 1502; Oct. 17, 1980, P. L. 96-466, Title II, Part A, § 203(4), Part B, § 213(4), Title VI, §§ 601(h), 603(b), Title VIII, § 801(g), 94 Stat. 2189, 2191, 2208, 2216; Aug. 13, 1981, P. L. 97-35, Title XX, § 2005(d), 95 Stat. 783; Oct. 12, 1982, P. L. 97-295, § 4(60), 96 Stat. 1309; Oct. 14, 1982, P. L. 97-306, Title II, § 208, 96 Stat. 1436; Oct. 24, 1984, P. L. 98-543, Title II, Part A, § 204(3), 98 Stat. 2742; Nov. 18, 1988, P. L. 100-689, Title I, Part B, § 124(b), 102 Stat. 4174; Dec. 18, 1989, P. L. 101-237, Title IV, § 423(b)(1)(A), 103 Stat. 2092; March 22, 1991, P. L. 102-16, § 5(a), 105 Stat. 50; Aug. 6, 1991, P. L. 102-83, § 5(a), (c)(1), 105 Stat. 406.)

HISTORY; ANCILLARY LAWS AND DIRECTIVES

References in text:
"Title IV of the Higher Education Act of 1965", referred to in this section, is Act Nov. 8, 1965, P. L. 89-329, Title IV, 79 Stat. 1232, as amended, which is generally classified to 20 USCS §§ 1070 et seq. For full classification of this Title, consult USCS Tables volumes.

Amendments:
1976. Act Oct. 15, 1976, (effective 10/15/76, as provided by § 703(b) of such Act, which appears as 38 USCS § 3693 note), in subsec. (b)(1), substituted "the veteran or person" for "he"; and in subsec. (e)(1), substituted "the Administrator" for "he" preceding "shall declare".

Such Act further (effective 10/1/76, as provided by § 703(a) of such Act, which appears as 38 USCS § 3693 note), in subsec. (b)(3), substituted "$292" and "$1,500" for "$270" and "$600", respectively; and substituted new subsec. (d)(3) for one which read: "shall provide that the loan shall bear interest, on the unpaid balance of the loan, at a rate prescribed by the Administrator, with the concurrence of the Secretary of the Treasury, but at a rate not less than a rate determined by the Secretary, taking into consideration the current average market yield on outstanding marketable obligations of the United States with remaining periods to maturity comparable to the maturity of loans made under this subchapter, except that no interest shall accrue prior to the beginning date of repayment; and".

1977. Act Nov. 23, 1977 (effective 10/1/77, as provided by § 501 of such Act, which appears as 38 USCS § 101 note), in subsec. (b)(3), substituted "$311" for "$292".

Such Act further (effective 1/1/78, as provided by § 501 of such Act, which appears as 38 USCS § 101 note), in subsec. (b)(3), substituted "$2,500" for "$1,500"; in subsec. (c), in para. (1), substituted ", except that the Administrator may waive the requirements of subclause (B) of this clause, in whole or in part, if the Administrator determines, pursuant to regulations which the Administrator shall prescribe, it to be in the interest of the eligible veteran and the Federal Government; and" for ";", deleted para. (2) which read: "has sought and is unable to obtain a loan, in the full amount needed by such veteran or person, as determined under subsection (b) of this section, under a student loan program insured pursuant to the provisions of part B of title IV of the Higher Education Act of 1965, as amended, or any successor authority; and", and redesignated para. (3) as para. (2); in subsec. (e)(3), inserted ", separately with respect to loans made under this section the repayment of which is accelerated under section 1682A of this title and loans made under this section the repayment of which is not so accelerated"; and added subsec. (f).

1978. Act Oct. 18, 1978 (effective 10/18/78, as provided by 205(a) of such Act, which appears as 38 USCS § 2303 note), in subsec. (a), inserted "and the criteria established under subsection (g) of this section"; in subsec. (c), in para. (1), deleted "and" following "Government;", in para. (2), substituted "; and" for ".", and added para. (3); in subsec. (d)(1), inserted "(A)" and inserted ", or (B) over such shorter period as the Administrator may have prescribed under subsection (g) of this section"; substituted new subsec. (e)(3) for one which read: "The Administrator shall submit to the Committees on Veterans' Affairs of the Senate and the House of Representatives, not later than one year after the date of enactment of the Vietnam Era Veterans' Readjustment Assistance Act of 1974 and annually thereafter, a separate report specifying the default experience and default rate at each educational institution along with a comparison of the collective default experience and default rate at all such institutions, separately with respect to loans made under this section the repayment of which is accelerated under section 1682A of this title and loans made under this section the repayment of which is not so accelerated."; in subsec. (f)(3), substituted "1701(a)(1)" for "1701(1)"; and added subsec. (g).

1980. Act Oct. 17, 1980, (effective 10/1/80, as provided by § 802(b)(1), (f)(1), (h) of such Act), in subsec. (b)(3), substituted "$327" for "$311"; in subsec. (d)(3), substituted "Secretary of Education" for "Commissioner of Education, Department of Health, Education and Welfare"; and in subsec. (f)(2), substituted "1780(d)(4)" for "1780(d)(5)".

Such Act further (effective 1/1/81, as provided by § 802(b)(2) of such Act), in subsec. (b)(3), as amended by § 203(4) of Act Oct. 17, 1980, substituted "$342" for "$327".

Such Act further (applicable as provided by § 802(f) of such Act, which appears as 38 USCS § 5314 note), in subsec. (c), concluding matter, substituted "or apprenticeship or other on-job training" for "flight, apprentice, or other on-job, or PREP training".

1981. Act Aug. 13, 1981 (effective as provided by § 2006 of such Act, which appears as 38 USCS § 3231 note), in subsec. (a), substituted "(1) Subject to paragraph (2) of this subsection, each" for "Each" and added para. (2).

1982. Act Oct. 12, 1982, in subsec. (b)(2)(B)(iii), substituted "(20 U.S.C. 1070 et seq.)" for ", as amended".

Such Act further, in subsec. (e), in para. (3), in the introductory matter, deleted "in maximum feasible detail" preceding the concluding hyphen, in subpara. (A), inserted "and" following "loans;", and substituted subpara. (B) for former subparas. (B) and (C), which read:

"(B) data regarding the default experience and default rate at each educational institution (i) with respect to loans made under this section in connection with accelerated payments under section 1682A of this title, and (ii) with respect to other loans made under this section; and

"(C) comparisons of the collective default experience and default rates with respect to such loans at all such institutions to the default experience and default rates with respect to such loans at each such institution.".

1984. Act Oct. 24, 1984 (effective 10/1/84, as provided by § 205 of such Act, which appears as 38 USCS § 3108 note), in subsec. (b)(3), substituted "$376" for "$342".

1988. Act Nov. 18, 1988, in subsec. (a)(1), deleted "and eligible person" following "eligible veteran", inserted "(if the program of education is pursued in a State)", and deleted "or person" following "the veteran"; in subsec. (b), in para. (1), deleted "or eligible person" following "an eligible veteran", deleted "or person" following "such veteran", and "the veteran", in para. (2), deleted "or person" following "veteran" wherever appearing, and in para. (3), deleted "or person" following "veteran" and deleted "or subchapter II of chapter 35, respectively," following "section 1661"; in subsec. (c), in the introductory and concluding matter, deleted "or person" following "veteran" wherever appearing; in subsec. (d), in the introductory matter, deleted "or person" following "a veteran"; in subsec. (e), in para. (1), deleted "or person" following "veteran", in para. (2), deleted "or person" and "or person's" following "veteran" and "veteran's", respectively, and substituted para. (3)(B) for one which read: "data regarding the default experience and default rate with respect to (i) loans made under this section in connection with accelerated payments under section 1682A of this title, and (ii) other loans made under this section."; in subsec. (f), deleted para. (1) which read:

"At the time of application by any eligible veteran for a loan under this section, such veteran shall assign to the benefit of the Veterans' Administration (for deposit in the Veterans' Administration Education Loan Fund established under section 1799 of this title) the amount of any accelerated payment to which such eligible veteran may become entitled from the

Administrator and any matching contribution by a State or local governmental unit pursuant to section 1682A(b)(8) of this title in connection with the school term for which such veteran has applied.", redesignated para. (2) as subsec. (f), and deleted para. (3) which read:

"For purposes of this subsection, the term 'eligible veteran' includes eligible person as such term is defined in section 1701(a)(1) of this title.";
and, in subsec. (g), in para. (2)(A), deleted "and eligible persons" and "or eligible person" following "eligible veterans" and "eligible veteran", respectively.

1989. Act Dec. 18, 1989, in the entire section, substituted "Secretary" for "Administrator", wherever appearing.

1991. Act March 22, 1991, in subsec. (e), deleted para. (3), which read:

"(3) The Secretary shall submit to the appropriate committees of the Congress not later than December 31 of each year a report on the current results of the continuing review required by subsection (g)(1) of this section to be made regarding the default experience with respect to loans made under this section and any steps being taken to reduce default rates on such loans. Such report shall include—

"(A) data regarding the cumulative default experience, and the default experience during the preceding fiscal year, with respect to such loans; and

"(B) data regarding the default experience and default rate with respect to loans made under this section.

"(C) comparisons of the collective default experience and default rates with respect to such loans at all such institutions to the default experience and default rates with respect to such loans at each such institution.".

Act Aug. 6, 1991, redesignated this section, formerly 38 USCS § 1798, as 38 USCS § 3698, and amended the references in this section to reflect the redesignations made by § 5(a) of such Act (see Table III preceding 38 USCS § 101).

Other provisions:

Effective date and exception for amendments made by Title III of Act Dec. 3, 1974. Act Dec. 3, 1974, P. L. 93-508, Title V, § 502, 88 Stat. 1601 provided: "Title III of this Act [enacting 38 USCS §§ 3486, 3537, 3698, 3699] shall become effective on January 1, 1975, except that eligible persons shall, upon application, be entitled (and all such persons shall be notified by the Administrator of Veterans' Affairs of such entitlement) to a loan under the new subchapter III of chapter 36 of title 38, United States Code, as added by section 301 of this Act [this section and 38 USCS § 3699], the terms of which take into account the full amount of the actual cost of attendance (as defined in section 1798(b)(2)(C) of such title [now 38 USCS § 3698(b)(2)(C)]) which such persons incurred for the academic year beginning on or about September 1, 1974.".

Application of amendments made by § 502(a) of Act Oct. 15, 1976. Act Oct. 15, 1976, P. L. 94-502, Title V, § 502(b), 90 Stat. 2399, provided: "The amendments made by subsection (a) [amending this section] shall be effective with respect to loans made under section 1798 of title 38, United States Code [this section], on and after Oct. 1, 1976.".

Effective date and application of amendment made by § 603(b) of Act Oct. 17, 1980. Act Oct. 17, 1980, P. L. 96-466, Title VIII, § 802(f), 94 Stat. 2218, located at 38 USCS § 5314 note, provided that the amendment made to this section by § 603(b) of Act Oct. 17, 1980, is effective on Oct. 1, 1980, except that it shall not apply to any person receiving educational assistance under chapter 34 or 35 of title 38 [38 USCS §§ 3451 et seq. or 3500 et seq.], on Sept. 1, 1980, for the pursuit of a program of education, as defined in 38 USCS § 1652(b) [now 38 USCS § 3452(b)], in which such person is enrolled on that date, for as long as such person continuously thereafter is so enrolled and meets the requirements of eligibility for such assistance for the pursuit of such program under the provisions of such chapter and chapter 36 of such title [38 USCS §§ 3670 et seq.] as in effect on that date.

Application and construction of the Oct. 12, 1982 amendment of this section. For provisions as to the application and construction of the Oct. 12, 1982 amendment of this section, see § 5 of such Act, which appears as 10 USCS § 101 note.

CROSS REFERENCES

This section is referred to in 38 USCS § 3699.

RESEARCH GUIDE

Am Jur:
77 Am Jur 2d, Veterans and Veterans' Laws § 132.

INTERPRETIVE NOTES AND DECISIONS

Mere fact that veteran is permanently and totally disabled at time he applies for loan does not affect propriety of grant; however, granting of loan to individual already permanently and totally disabled would not allow administrator [now Secretary] to subsequently write off loan on that basis. VA GCO 2-79.

§ 3699. Revolving fund; insurance

(a) There is hereby established in the Treasury of the United States a revolving fund to be known as the "Department of Veterans Affairs Education Loan Fund" (hereinafter in this section referred to as the "Fund").

(b) The Fund shall be available to the Secretary, without fiscal year limitation, for the making of loans under this subchapter [38 USCS §§ 3698 et seq.].

(c) There shall be deposited in the Fund (1) by transfer from current and future appropriations for readjustment benefits such amounts as may be necessary to establish and supplement the Fund in order to meet the requirements of the Fund, and (2) all collections of fees and principal and interest (including overpayments declared under section 3698(e) of this title) on loans made under this subchapter [38 USCS §§ 3698 et seq.].

(d) The Secretary shall determine annually whether there has developed in the Fund a surplus which, in the Secretary's adjustment, is more than necessary to meet the needs of the Fund, and such surplus, if any, shall be deemed to have been appropriated for readjustment benefits.

(e) A fee shall be collected from each veteran or person obtaining a loan made under this subchapter [38 USCS §§ 3698 et seq.] for the purpose of insuring

38 USCS § 3699

against defaults on loans made under this subchapter [38 USCS §§ 3698 et seq.]; and no loan shall be made under this subchapter [38 USCS §§ 3698 et seq.] until the fee payable with respect to such loan has been collected and remitted to the Secretary. The amount of the fee shall be established from time to time by the Secretary, but shall in no event exceed 3 percent of the total loan amount. The amount of the fee may be included in the loan to the veteran or person and paid from the proceeds thereof.

(Added Dec. 3, 1974, P. L. 93-508, Title III, § 301(a), 88 Stat. 1591; Oct. 15, 1976, P. L. 94-502, Title V, § 513(a)(24), 90 Stat. 2404; Oct. 12, 1982, P. L. 97-295, § 4(61) in part, 96 Stat. 1309; Dec. 18, 1989, P. L. 101-237, Title IV, § 423(b)(1), (2) 103 Stat. 2092; Aug. 6, 1991, P. L. 102-83, § 5(a), (c)(1), 105 Stat. 406.)

HISTORY; ANCILLARY LAWS AND DIRECTIVES

Amendments:

1976. Act Oct. 15, 1976 (effective 10/15/76, as provided by 703(b) of such Act, which appears as 38 USCS § 3693 note), in subsec. (d), substituted "the Administrator's" for "his".

1982. Act Oct. 12, 1982, in subsec. (e), substituted "percent" for "per centum".

1989. Act Dec. 18, 1989, in subsec. (a), substituted "Department of Veterans Affairs" for "Veterans' Administration"; in subsecs. (b), (d) and (e), substituted "Secretary" for "Administrator", wherever appearing; and in subsec. (d), substituted "Secretary's" for "Administrator's".

1991. Act Aug. 6, 1991, redesignated this section, formerly 38 USCS § 1799, as 38 USCS § 3699, and amended the references in this section to reflect the redesignations made by § 5(a) of such Act (see Table III preceding 38 USCS § 101).

Other provisions:

Effective date of section and exception. Act Dec. 3, 1974, P. L. 93-508, Title V, § 502, 88 Stat. 1601, located at 38 USCS § 3698 note, provided that this section is effective on Jan. 1, 1975, except that eligible persons shall, upon application, be entitled to a loan under 38 USCS §§ 3698, 3699, the terms of which take into account the full amount of the actual cost of attendance, as defined in 38 USCS § 3698(b)(2)(C), which such persons incurred for the academic year beginning on or about Sept. 1, 1974.

Application and construction of the Oct. 12, 1982 amendment of this section. For provisions as to the application and construction of the Oct. 12, 1982 amendment of this section, see § 5 of such Act, which appears as 10 USCS § 101 note.

CHAPTER 37. HOUSING AND SMALL BUSINESS LOANS

SUBCHAPTER I. GENERAL

Section
3701. Definitions.
3702. Basic entitlement.
3703. Basic provisions relating to loan guaranty and insurance.
3704. Restrictions on loans.
3705. Warranties.
3706. Escrow of deposits and downpayments.
3707. Adjustable rate mortgages.
3708. Authority to buy down interest rates: pilot program.

SUBCHAPTER II. LOANS

3710. Purchase or construction of homes.
3711. Direct loans to veterans.
3712. Loans to purchase manufactured homes and lots.
3713. Release from liability under guaranty.
3714. Assumptions; release from liability.
[3715] [1815. Transferred]
[3716] [1816. Transferred]
[3717] [1817. Transferred]
[3717A] [1817A. Transferred]
[3718] [1818. Repealed]
[3719] [1819. Transferred]

SUBCHAPTER III. ADMINISTRATIVE PROVISIONS

3720. Powers of Secretary.
3721. Incontestability.
[3722. Repealed]
3723. Direct loan revolving fund.
3724. Loan Guaranty Revolving Fund.
3725. Guaranty and Indemnity Fund.
3726. Withholding of payments, benefits, etc.
3727. Expenditures to correct or compensate for structural defects in mortgaged homes.
3728. Exemption from State anti-usury provisions.
3729. Loan fee.
3730. Use of attorneys in court.
3731. Appraisals.
3732. Procedure on default.
3733. Property management.
3734. Annual submission of information on the Loan Guaranty Revolving Fund and the Guaranty and Indemnity Fund.
3735. Housing assistance for homeless veterans.
3736. Reporting requirements.

SUBCHAPTER IV. SMALL BUSINESS LOANS

3741. Definitions.

3742. Small business loan program.
3743. Liability on loans.
3744. Approval of loans by the Secretary.
3745. Interest on loans.
3746. Maturity of loans.
3747. Eligible financial institutions.
3748. Preference for disabled veterans.
3749. Revolving fund.
3750. Incorporation of other provisions by the Secretary.
3751. Termination of program.

SUBCHAPTER V. NATIVE AMERICAN VETERAN HOUSING LOAN PILOT PROGRAM

3761. Pilot program.
3762. Direct housing loans to Native American veterans.
3763. Housing loan program account.
3764. Definitions.

HISTORY; ANCILLARY LAWS AND DIRECTIVES

Explanatory notes:
The bracketed section numbers "3715", "3716", "3717", "3717A", "3718", "3719", and "3722" were inserted to preserve numerical continuity following the section number redesignations made by Act Aug. 6, 1991, P. L. 102-83, § 5(a), 105 Stat. 406.

Amendments:
1960. Act July 14, 1960, P. L. 86-665, § 6(b), 74 Stat. 532, added item 1806.
Act July 14, 1960, P. L. 86-665, § 7(b), 74 Stat. 533 (effective 7/1/61, as provided by § 7(c) of such Act), substituted items 1824 and 1825 for item 1824 which read: "Waiver of discharge requirements for hospitalized persons.".
1966. Act March 3, 1966, P. L. 89-358, § 5(b), (f)(2), 80 Stat. 26 (effective 3/3/66, as provided by § 12(a) of such Act), added items 1818 and 1826.
1968. Act May 7, 1968, P. L. 90-301, § 5(b), 82 Stat. 116, added item 1827.
1970. Act Oct. 23, 1970, P. L. 91-506, § 7, 84 Stat. 1114, added item 1819.
1974. Act Dec. 31, 1974, P. L. 93-569, § 7(b), (c), 88 Stat. 1866 (effective 12/31/74, as provided by § 10 of such Act), substituted new chapter heading for one which read: "CHAPTER 37. HOME, FARM, AND BUSINESS LOANS"; and deleted items 1812–1814 and 1822 which read:
"1812. Purchase of farms and farm equipment.
"1813. Purchase of business property.
"1814. Loans to refinance delinquent indebtedness." and
"1822. Recovery of damages.".
1976. Act June 30, 1976, P. L. 94-324, § 2(b), 90 Stat. 720 (effective 10/1/76, as provided by § 9(b) of such Act), added item 1807.
1978. Act Oct. 18, 1978, P. L. 95-476, Title I, § 106(b), 92 Stat. 1500 (ef-

fective 10/1/78, as provided by § 108(a) of such Act), substituted new item 1818 for one which read: "Veterans who serve after January 31, 1955.".

1979. Act Nov. 28, 1979, P. L. 96-128, Title IV, § 401(b), 93 Stat. 987 (effective 11/28/79, as provided by § 601(b) of such Act), added item 1828.

1981. Nov. 3, 1981, P. L. 97-72, Title III, § 302(b)(1), (3), 95 Stat. 1959 (effective 180 days after enactment, as provided by § 305 of such Act, which appears as 42 USCS § 1841 note), amended the title of this chapter by substituting this title for one which read: "CHAPTER 37. HOME, CONDOMINIUM, AND MOBILE HOME LOANS", and amended the analysis of this chapter by adding subchapter IV and items 1841–1851.

1982. Sept. 8, 1982, P. L. 97-253, Title IV, § 406(a)(2), 96 Stat. 805, amended the analysis of this chapter by adding item 1829.

Act Oct. 14, 1982, P. L. 97-306, Title IV, § 406(c)(3), 96 Stat. 1445, amended the analysis of this chapter by substituting item for one which read: "1819. Loans to purchase mobile homes and mobile home lots.".

1984. July 18, 1984, P. L. 98-369, Division B, Title V, Part B, § 2512(b)(2), 98 Stat. 1120, amended the analysis of this chapter by adding item 1830.

1986. Act Oct. 28, 1986, P. L. 99-576, Title IV, Part A, §§ 407(b), 408(b), 100 Stat. 3283, amended the analysis of this chapter by adding items 1831 and 1832.

1987. Act Dec. 21, 1987, P. L. 100-198, § 10(a)(3), 101 Stat. 1323, amended the analysis of this chapter by adding item 1817A.

1988. Act May 20, 1988, P. L. 100-322, Title IV, Part B, § 415(e), 102 Stat. 552, amended the analysis of this chapter by substituting item 1803 for one which read: "1803. Basic provisions relating to loan guaranty and insurance.", deleting item 1807 which read: "1807. Service after July 25, 1947, and prior to June 27, 1950.", and substituting the items in subchapter II for ones which read:

"1810. Purchase or construction of homes.

"1811. Direct loans to veterans.

"[1812–1814. Repealed]

"1815. Insurance of loans.

"1816. Procedure on default.

"1817. Release from liability under guaranty.

"1817A. Assumptions; release from liability.

"1818. Service after January 31, 1955, and prior to August 5, 1964, or after May 7, 1975.

"1819. Loans to purchase manufactured homes and lots.".

Such Act further substituted item 1832 for one which read: "1832. Furnishing information to real estate professionals to facilitate the disposition of properties."; and added item 1833.

1989. Act Dec. 18, 1989, P. L. 101-237, Title III, § 302(a)(3)(B), (b)(2), 103 Stat. 2070, 2071, amended the analysis of this chapter by substituting items 1824 and 1825 for ones which read: "1824. Loan guaranty revolving fund." and "1825. Waiver of discharge requirements for hospitalized persons.", respectively, and by adding item 1834.

Act Dec. 18, 1989, P. L. 101-237, Title III, § 313(b)(1), 103 Stat. 2077, amended the analysis of this chapter by substituting "Secretary" for "Administrator" in items 1820, 1844 and 1850.

38 USCS § 3701 VETERANS' BENEFITS

1991. Act June 13, 1991, P. L. 102-54, § 9(b), 105 Stat. 273, amended the analysis of this chapter by adding item 1835.

Act Aug. 6, 1991, P. L. 102-83, § 5(b)(1), 105 Stat. 406, revised the analysis of this chapter by amending the section numbers in accordance with the redesignations made by § 5(a) of such Act (see Table III preceding 38 USCS § 101).

1992. Act Oct. 28, 1992, P. L. 102-547, §§ 3(a)(2), 8(c), 106 Stat. 3635, 3640, amended the analysis of this chapter by adding item 3707, the Subchapter V heading, and items 3761–3764.

1996. Act Feb. 10, 1996, P. L. 104-106, Div B, Title XXVIII, § 2822(b)(2), 110 Stat. 557, amended the analysis of this chapter by adding item 3708.

Act Feb. 13, 1996, P. L. 104-110, Title II, § 201(a)(2), 110 Stat. 770, amended the analysis of this chapter by adding item 3736.

SUBCHAPTER I. GENERAL

§ 3701. Definitions

(a) For the purpose of this chapter [38 USCS §§ 3701 et seq.], the term "housing loan" means a loan for any of the purposes specified by sections 3710(a) and 3712(a)(1) of this title.

(b) For the purposes of housing loans under this chapter [38 USCS §§ 3701 et seq.]—

(1) The term "World War II" (A) means the period beginning on September 16, 1940, and ending on July 25, 1947, and (B) includes, in the case of any veteran who enlisted or reenlisted in a Regular component of the Armed Forces after October 6, 1945, and before October 7, 1946, the period of the first such enlistment or reenlistment.

(2) The term "veteran" includes the surviving spouse of any veteran (including a person who died in the active military, naval, or air service) who died from a service-connected disability, but only if such surviving spouse is not eligible for benefits under this chapter [38 USCS §§ 3701 et seq.] on the basis of the spouse's own active duty. The active duty or service in the Selected Reserve of the deceased spouse shall be deemed to have been active duty or service in the Selected Reserve by such surviving spouse for the purposes of this chapter [38 USCS §§ 3701 et seq.].

(3) The term "veteran" also includes, for purposes of home loans, the spouse of any member of the Armed Forces serving on active duty who is listed, pursuant to section 556 of title 37, United States Code, and regulations issued thereunder, by the Secretary concerned in one or more of the following categories and has been so listed for a total of more than ninety days: (A) missing in action, (B) captured in line of duty by a hostile force, or (C) forcibly detained or interned in line of duty by a foreign government or power. The active duty of the member shall be deemed to have been active duty by such spouse for the purposes of this chapter [38 USCS §§ 3701 et seq.]. The loan eligibility of such spouse under this paragraph shall be limited to one loan guaranteed or made for the acquisition of a home, and

entitlement to such loan shall terminate automatically, if not used, upon receipt by such spouse of official notice that the member is no longer listed in one of the categories specified in the first sentence of this paragraph.

(4) The term "veteran" also includes an individual serving on active duty.

(5)(A) The term "veteran" also includes an individual who is not otherwise eligible for the benefits of this chapter [38 USCS §§ 3701 et seq.] and (i) who has completed a total service of at least 6 years in the Selected Reserve and, following the completion of such service, was discharged from service with an honorable discharge, was placed on the retired list, was transferred to the Standby Reserve or an element of the Ready Reserve other than the Selected Reserve after service in the Selected Reserve characterized by the Secretary concerned as honorable service, or continues serving in the Selected Reserve, or (ii) who was discharged or released from the Selected Reserve before completing 6 years of service because of a service-connected disability.

(B) The term "Selected Reserve" means the Selected Reserve of the Ready Reserve of any of the reserve components (including the Army National Guard of the United States and the Air National Guard of the United States) of the Armed Forces, as required to be maintained under section 10143(a) of title 10.

(c) Benefits shall not be afforded under this chapter [38 USCS §§ 3701 et seq.] to any individual on account of service as a commissioned officer of the National Oceanic and Atmospheric Administration (or predecessor entity), or of the Regular or Reserve Corps of the Public Health Service, unless such service would have qualified such individual for benefits under title III of the Servicemen's Readjustment Act of 1944.

(Sept. 2, 1958, P. L. 85-857, § 1, 72 Stat. 1203; Dec. 24, 1970, P. L. 91-584, § 5(a), 84 Stat. 1576; June 30, 1976, P. L. 94-324, § 7(1), (2), 90 Stat. 721; Nov. 3, 1981, P. L. 97-72, Title III, § 303(a), 95 Stat. 1059; Oct. 12, 1982, P. L. 97-295, § 4(62), 96 Stat. 1309; May 20, 1988, P. L. 100-322, Title IV, Part C, § 415(c)(1), 102 Stat. 550; Dec. 18, 1989, P. L. 101-237, Title III, § 313(a), 103 Stat. 2077; Aug. 6, 1991, P. L. 102-83, § 5(a), (c)(1), 105 Stat. 406; Oct. 28, 1992, P. L. 102-547, § 2(a)(1), 106 Stat. 3633; Nov. 2, 1994, P. L. 103-446, Title IX, § 901, 108 Stat. 4675; Feb. 10, 1996, P. L. 104-106, Div A, Title XV, § 1501(e)(2)(B), 110 Stat. 501.)

HISTORY; ANCILLARY LAWS AND DIRECTIVES

References in text:

"Title III of the Servicemen's Readjustment Act of 1944", referred to in this section, is title III of Act June 22, 1944, ch 268, 58 Stat. 284, as amended, which was classified to former 38 USCS §§ 693g-693i and repealed by Act Sept. 2, 1958, P. L. 85-857, § 14(87), 72 Stat. 1273, in the general revision of Title 38. For similar provisions see tables preceding 38 USCS § 101.

Amendments:

1970. Act Dec. 24, 1970, added subsec. (a)(3).

1976. Act June 30, 1976 (effective as provided by § 9 of such Act, which appears as a note to this section), in subsec. (a)(2), substituted "surviving spouse" for "widow" wherever appearing, substituted "the spouse's own" for "her own" and substituted "the spouse" for "her husband"; in subsec. (a)(3), substituted "spouse" for "wife" preceding "of any member", "for the purposes", "under this paragraph", and "of official notice", and substituted "the spouse" for "her husband" preceding "shall be deemed" and "is no longer listed".

1981. Act Nov. 3, 1981 (effective 180 days after enactment on Nov. 3, 1981, as provided by § 305 of such Act, which appears 38 USCS § 3741 note), redesignated former subsecs. (a) and (b) as subsecs. (b) and (c), and added subsec. (a), in subsec. (b), as redesignated, substituted "housing loans under this chapter—" for "this chapter—"; and, in subsec. (c) as redesignated, substituted "National Oceanic and Atmospheric Administration (or predecessor entity)" for "Coast and Geodetic Survey".

1982. Act Oct. 12, 1982, in subsec. (b)(3), substituted "member shall be deemed" for "spouse shall be deemed", and substituted "member is no longer listed" for "spouse is no longer listed".

1988. Act May 20, 1988, in subsec. (a)(1), substituted "1812(a)(1)" for "1819(a)(1)".

1989. Act Dec. 18, 1989, in subsec. (b), added para. (4).

1991. Act Aug. 6, 1991, redesignated this section, formerly 38 USCS § 1801, as 38 USCS § 3701, and amended the references in this section to reflect the redesignations made by § 5(a) of such Act (see Table III preceding 38 USCS § 101).

1992. Act Oct. 28, 1992, in subsec. (b), added para. (5).

1994. Act Nov. 2, 1994, in subsec. (b), in para. (2), substituted "deceased spouse shall" for "spouse shall" and inserted "or service in the Selected Reserve" in two places, and, in para. (5), inserted "(i)" and ", or (ii) who was discharged or released from the Selected Reserve before completing 6 years of service because of a service-connected disability".

1996. Act Feb. 10, 1996 (effective as if included in Act Oct. 5, 1995, P. L. 103-337, as enacted on Oct. 5, 1994, as provided by § 1501(f)(3) of Act Feb. 10, 1996, which appears as 10 USCS § 113 note), in subsec. (b)(5)(B), substituted "section 10143(a) of title 10" for "section 268(b) of title 10".

Other provisions:

Effective dates of Act June 30, 1976. Act June 30, 1976, P. L. 94-324, § 9, 90 Stat. 723, provided:

"(a) Except as provided in subsection (b), the provisions of this Act [enacting 38 USCS § 3707 and 12 USCS § 1709-1a, and amending 38 USCS §§ 3701, 3706, 3710, 3711, 3715–3720, 3723–3727] shall become effective on the date of enactment.

"(b) Sections 2 and 3 [enacting 38 USCS § 3707 and amending 38 USCS § 3711] shall become effective on October 1, 1976. Section 5 [amending 38 USCS § 3719] shall become effective on July 1, 1976.".

Authority of the Administrator to promulgate regulations. For the authority and effective date for the Administrator of Veterans's Affairs to promulgate regulations under 38 USCS §§ 3741 et seq., see § 305 of Act Nov. 3, 1981, which appears as 38 USCS § 3741 note.

Application and construction of the Oct. 12, 1982 amendment of this

section. For provisions as to the application and construction of the Oct. 12, 1982 amendment of this section, see § 5 of such Act, which appears as 10 USCS § 101 note.

Ban on lead water pipes, solder, and flux in VA and HUD insured or assisted property. For provisions as to the ban of lead water pipes, solder, and flux in VA and HUD insured or assisted property, see Act June 19, 1986, P. L. 99-339, Title I, § 109(c), 100 Stat. 652, which appears as 42 USCS § 300g-6 note.

CODE OF FEDERAL REGULATIONS
Department of Veterans Affairs—Loan guaranty, 38 CFR Part 36.

CROSS REFERENCES
This section is referred to in 38 USCS §§ 3702, 3729, 5302.

RESEARCH GUIDE
Federal Procedure L Ed:
4A Fed Proc L Ed, Banking and Financing §§ 8:1414, 1415, 1417, 1424, 1425.

Am Jur:
77 Am Jur 2d, Veterans and Veterans' Laws §§ 119–121, 123, 126–129, 173.

Law Review Articles:
Benefits for Conscientious Objectors. 19 Catholic Lawyer 62, Winter 1973.

INTERPRETIVE NOTES AND DECISIONS

1. Generally
2. Purpose
3. Surviving spouse

1. Generally
38 USCS §§ 1801 et seq. [now 38 USCS §§ 3701 et seq.] does not impose a legal duty upon the Veterans Administration [now Department of Veterans Affairs] to undertake loan servicing of guaranteed loans. Rank v Nimmo (1982, CA9 Cal) 677 F2d 692, cert den (1982) 459 US 907, 74 L Ed 2d 168, 103 S Ct 210.

2. Purpose
Policy of predecessor to 38 USCS §§ 3701 et seq. was to enable veterans to obtain loans and to obtain them with least risk of loss upon foreclosure, to both veteran and Veterans' Administration [now Department of Veterans Affairs] as guarantor of his indebtedness. United States v Shimer (1961) 367 US 374, 6 L Ed 2d 908, 81 S Ct 1554.

3. Surviving spouse
Unremarried widow of person who served in the military or naval forces of government allied with United States in World War II was not, by virtue of his service, eligible for benefits under former 38 USC § 694. 1950 ADVA 851.

Unremarried widow of veteran who died in action on July 13, 1950 was eligible for her own guaranty benefits under former 38 USC § 694 since veteran met basic requirements. 1951 ADVA 864.

Unremarried widow of eligible veteran, who died as result of service-connected injuries, was not entitled to benefits under § 500a of Servicemen's Readjustment Act of 1944 (38 USCS § 1801 [now 38 USCS § 3701]) since widow was eligible for such benefits by reason of her own military service. 1951 ADVA 880.

Acquisition of guaranteed loan by wife of serviceman missing in action under 38 USCS § 1801(a)(3) [now 38 USCS § 3701(a)(3)] did not bar use of any subsequent entitlement to which she became eligible as widow for such former serviceman. VA GCO 6-74.

§ 3702. Basic entitlement

(a)(1) The veterans described in paragraph (2) of this subsection are eligible for the housing loan benefits of this chapter [38 USCS §§ 3701 et seq.]. In the case of any veteran who served on active duty during two or more of the periods specified in paragraph (2), for which eligibility for the housing loan benefits under this chapter [38 USCS §§ 3701 et seq.] may be granted, entitlement derived from service during the most recent such period (A) shall cancel any unused entitlement derived from service during any earlier such period, and (B) shall be reduced by the amount by which entitlement from service during any earlier such period has been used to obtain a direct, guaranteed, or insured housing loan—

    (i) on real property which the veteran owns at the time of application; or

    (ii) as to which the Secretary has incurred actual liability or loss, unless in the event of loss or the incurrence and payment of such liability by the Secretary the resulting indebtedness of the veteran to the United States has been paid in full.

(2) The veterans referred to in the first sentence of paragraph (1) of this subsection are the following:

(A) Each veteran who served on active duty at any time during World War II, the Korean conflict, or the Vietnam era and whose total service was for 90 days or more.

(B) Each veteran who after September 15, 1940, was discharged or released from a period of active duty for a service-connected disability.

(C) Each veteran, other than a veteran described in clause (A) or (B) of this paragraph, who—

    (i) served after July 25, 1947, for a period of more than 180 days and was discharged or released therefrom under conditions other than dishonorable; or

    (ii) has served more than 180 days in active duty status and continues on active duty without a break therein.

(D) Each veteran who served on active duty for 90 days or more at any time during the Persian Gulf War, other than a veteran ineligible for benefits under this title by reason of section 5303A(b) of this title.

(E) For the period beginning on October 28, 1992, and ending on October 27, 1999, each veteran described in section 3701(b)(5) of this title.

(3) Any unused entitlement of World War II or Korean conflict veterans which expired under provisions of law in effect before October 23, 1970, is hereby restored and shall not expire until used.

(4) A veteran's entitlement under this chapter [38 USCS §§ 3701 et seq.] shall not be reduced by any entitlement used by the veteran's spouse which was based upon the provisions of paragraph (3) of section 3701(b) of this title.

(b) In computing the aggregate amount of guaranty or insurance housing loan entitlement available to a veteran under this chapter [38 USCS §§ 3701 et seq.], the Secretary may exclude the amount of guaranty or insurance housing loan

entitlement used for any guaranteed, insured, or direct loan under the following circumstances:
  (1)(A) The property which secured the loan has been disposed of by the veteran or has been destroyed by fire or other natural hazard; and
  (B) the loan has been repaid in full, or the Secretary has been released from liability as to the loan, or if the Secretary has suffered a loss on such loan, the loss has been paid in full.
  (2) A veteran-transferee has agreed to assume the outstanding balance on the loan and consented to the use of the veteran transferee's entitlement, to the extent that the entitlement of the veteran-transferor had been used originally, in place of the veteran-transferor's for the guaranteed, insured, or direct loan, and the veteran-transferee otherwise meets the requirements of this chapter [38 USCS §§ 3701 et seq.].
  (3)(A) The loan has been repaid in full; and
  (B) the loan for which the veteran seeks to use entitlement under this chapter [38 USCS §§ 3701 et seq.] is secured by the same property which secured the loan referred to in subparagraph (A) of this paragraph.
  (4) In a case not covered by paragraph (1) or (2)—
  (A) the loan has been repaid in full and, if the Secretary has suffered a loss on the loan, the loss has been paid in full; or
  (B) the Secretary has been released from liability as to the loan and, if the Secretary has suffered a loss on the loan, the loss has been paid in full.

The Secretary may, in any case involving circumstances the Secretary deems appropriate, waive one or more of the conditions prescribed in paragraph (1). The authority of the Secretary under this subsection to exclude an amount of guaranty or insurance housing loan entitlement previously used by a veteran may be exercised only once for that veteran under the authority of paragraph (4).

(c) An honorable discharge shall be deemed to be a certificate of eligibility to apply for a guaranteed loan. Any veteran who does not have a discharge certificate, or who received a discharge other than honorable, may apply to the Secretary for a certificate of eligibility. Upon making a loan guaranteed or insured under this chapter [38 USCS §§ 3701 et seq.], the lender shall forthwith transmit to the Secretary a report thereon in such detail as the Secretary may, from time to time, prescribe. Where the loan is guaranteed, the Secretary shall provide the lender with a loan guaranty certificate or other evidence of the guaranty. The Secretary shall also endorse on the veteran's discharge, or eligibility certificate, the amount and type of guaranty used, and the amount, if any, remaining. Nothing in this chapter [38 USCS §§ 3701 et seq.] shall preclude the assignment of any guaranteed loan or the security therefor.

(d) Housing loans will be automatically guaranteed under this chapter [38 USCS §§ 3701 et seq.] only if made (1) by any Federal land bank, national bank, State bank, private bank, building and loan association, insurance company, credit union, or mortgage and loan company, that is subject to examination and supervision by an agency of the United States or of any State,

38 USCS § 3702 VETERANS' BENEFITS

(2) by any State, or (3) by any lender approved by the Secretary pursuant to standards established by the Secretary. Any housing loan proposed to be made to a veteran pursuant to this chapter [38 USCS §§ 3701 et seq.] by any lender not of a class specified in the preceding sentence may be guaranteed by the Secretary if the Secretary finds that it is in accord otherwise with the provisions of this chapter [38 USCS §§ 3701 et seq.].

(e) The Secretary may at any time upon thirty days' notice require housing loans to be made by any lender or class of lenders to be submitted to the Secretary for prior approval. No guaranty or insurance liability shall exist with respect to any such loan unless evidence of guaranty or insurance is issued by the Secretary.

(f) Any housing loan at least 20 percent of which is guaranteed under this chapter [38 USCS §§ 3701 et seq.] may be made by any national bank or Federal savings and loan association, or by any bank, trust company, building and loan association, or insurance company, organized or authorized to do business in the District of Columbia. Any such loan may be so made without regard to the limitations and restrictions of any other law relating to—

(1) ratio of amount of loan to the value of the property;
(2) maturity of loan;
(3) requirement for mortgage or other security;
(4) dignity of lien; or
(5) percentage of assets which may be invested in real estate loans.

(Sept. 2, 1958, P. L. 85-857, § 1, 72 Stat. 1203; June 30, 1959, P. L. 86-73, § 1, 73 Stat. 156; July 6, 1961, P. L. 87-84, § 1(b), 75 Stat. 201; May 25, 1967, P. L. 90-19, § 25(1), 81 Stat. 28; Aug. 31, 1967, P. L. 90-77, Title IV, § 403(a), 81 Stat. 190; Oct. 23, 1970, P. L. 91-506, § 2(a), 84 Stat. 1108; Dec. 24, 1970, P. L. 91-584, § 5(b), 84 Stat. 1576; Dec. 31, 1974, P. L. 93-569, § 2(a), (b), 88 Stat. 1863; June 30, 1976, P. L. 94-324, § 7(3)–(5), 90 Stat. 721; Oct. 18, 1978, P. L. 95-476, Title I, § 102, 92 Stat. 1497; Nov. 3, 1981, P. L. 97-72, Title III, § 303(b), 95 Stat. 1060; Oct. 12, 1982, P. L. 97-295, § 4(61) in part, 96 Stat. 1309; March 2, 1984, P. L. 98-223, Title II, § 204, 98 Stat. 42; May 20, 1988, P. L. 100-322, Title IV, Part B, § 415(a)(1), (2), 102 Stat. 549; Dec. 18, 1989, P. L. 101-237, Title III, §§ 310, 313(b)(1), 103 Stat. 2075, 2077; April 6, 1991, P. L. 102-25, Title III, Part C, § 341, 105 Stat. 92; May 7, 1991, P. L. 102-40, Title IV, § 402(d)(1), 105 Stat. 239; Aug. 6, 1991, P. L. 102-83, § 5(a), (c)(1), 105 Stat. 406; Oct. 28, 1992, P. L. 102-547, § 2(a)(2), 106 Stat. 3633; Nov. 2, 1994, P. L. 103-446, Title IX, § 902, Title XII, § 1201(f)(4), 108 Stat. 4676, 4687.)

HISTORY; ANCILLARY LAWS AND DIRECTIVES
Amendments:
1959. Act June 30, 1959, in subsec. (d), deleted "or" preceding "(2)" and inserted ", or (3) by any Federal Housing Administration approved mortgagee designated by the Federal Housing Commissioner as a certified agent and which is acceptable to the Administrator".

1961. Act July 6, 1961, in subsec. (b), substituted new concluding matter for matter which read: "Entitlement restored under this subsection may be used at any time before February 1, 1965.".

1967. Act May 25, 1967, in subsec. (d), substituted "mortgagee approved by the Secretary of Housing and Urban Development and designated by him" for "Federal Housing Administration approved mortgagee designated by the Federal Housing Commissioner".

Act Aug. 31, 1967 (effective 10/1/67, as provided by § 405(a) of such Act, which appears as 38 USCS § 101 note), in subsec. (b), concluding matter, substituted "July 26, 1970" for "July 26, 1967".

1970. Act Oct. 23, 1970, in subsec. (b), deleted the concluding matter which read: "Entitlement restored under this subsection may be used by a World War II veteran at any time before July 26, 1970, and by a Korean conflict veteran at any time before February 1, 1975.".

Act Dec. 24, 1970, added subsec.(g).

1974. Act Dec. 31, 1974 (effective as provided by § 10 of such Act, which appears as a note to this section), substituted new subsec. (b) for one which read:

"(b) In computing the aggregate amount of guaranty or insurance entitlement available to a veteran under this chapter—

"(1) the Administrator may exclude the initial use of the veteran's entitlement for any loan with respect to which the security has been (A) taken (by condemnation or otherwise) by the United States or any State, or by any local government agency for public use, (B) destroyed by fire or other natural hazard, or (C) disposed of because of other compelling reasons devoid of fault on the part of the veteran; and

"(2) the Administrator shall exclude the amount of guaranty or insurance entitlement previously used for any guaranteed or insured home loan which has been repaid in full, and with respect to which the real property which served as security for the loan has been disposed of because the veteran, while on active duty, was transferred by the service department with which he was serving.";

and in subsec. (d), substituted "(3) by any lender approved by the Administrator pursuant to standards established by him." for "(3) by any mortgagee approved by the Secretary of Housing and Urban Development and designated by him as a certified agent and which is acceptable to the Administrator.".

1976. Act June 30, 1976 (effective 6/30/76, as provided by § 9(a) of such Act, which appears as 38 USCS § 3701 note), in subsec. (b), in para. (3), substituted "the veteran-transferee's" for "his" preceding "entitlement", and in the concluding matter, substituted "the Administrator" for "he"; in subsec. (c), substituted "The Administrator" for "He" preceding "shall"; in subsec. (d), substituted "the Administrator" for "him" following "standards established by", and substituted "the Administrator" for "he" preceding "finds"; in subsec. (e), substituted "the Administrator" for "him" following "submitted to"; and in subsec. (g), substituted "the veteran's spouse" for "his wife".

1978. Act Oct. 18, 1978 (effective as provided by § 108 of such Act, which appears as a note to this section), in subsec. (a), substituted "World War II, the Korean conflict, or the Vietnam era" for "World War II or the Korean conflict" wherever appearing, and substituted "In the case of any

38 USCS § 3702   VETERANS' BENEFITS

veteran who served on active duty during two or more of the periods specified in the preceding sentence, or in section 1818 of this title, for which eligibility for the benefits under this chapter may be granted, entitlement derived from service during the most recent such period (1) shall cancel any unused entitlement derived from service during any earlier such period, and (2) shall be reduced by the amount by which entitlement from service during any earlier such period has" for "Entitlement derived from service during the Korean conflict (1) shall cancel any unused entitlement derived from service during World War II, and (2) shall be reduced by the amount by which entitlement from service during World War II, has"; and in subsec. (b), redesignated para. (1) as para. (1)(A), redesignated para. (2) as para. (1)(B), redesignated para. (3) as para. (2), and in the concluding matter, substituted "clause (1) of the preceding sentence" for "clauses (1) and (2) above".

1981. Act Nov. 3, 1981 (effective 180 days after enactment on Nov. 3, 1981, as provided by § 305 of such Act, which appears as 38 USCS § 3741 note) in subsec. (a), inserted "housing loan" preceding "benefits", wherever appearing, and inserted "housing" following "insured"; in subsec. (b), inserted "housing loan", wherever appearing; in subsec. (d), substituted "Housing loans" for "Loans" and inserted "housing" following "Any"; and in subsecs. (e) and (f), inserted "housing".

1982. Act Oct. 12, 1982, in subsec. (f), substituted "percent" for "per centum".

1984. Act March 2, 1984, in subsec. (b)(2), substituted "a" for "an immediate" preceding "veteran-transferee has agreed".

1988. Act May 20, 1988, in subsec. (a), designated the existing provisions as para. (1), and in para. (1), as so designated, substituted the sentence beginning "The veterans described . . ." for one which read: "Each veteran who served on active duty at any time during World War II, the Korean conflict, or the Vietnam era and whose total service was for ninety days or more, or who was discharged or released from a period of active duty, any part of which occurred during World War II, the Korean conflict, or the Vietnam era for a service-connected disability, shall be eligible for the housing loan benefits of this chapter.", substituted "in paragraph (2)" for "in the preceding sentence, or in section 1818 of this title", redesignated paras. (1) and (2) as subparas. (A) and (B) respectively, redesignated subparas. (A) and (B) as cls. (i) and (ii) respectively, and added new paras. (2) and (3); and redesignated subsec. (g) as subsec. (a)(4), and in subsec. (a)(4), as so redesignated, substituted "1801(b)" for "1801(a)".

1989. Act Dec. 15, 1989, in subsec. (b), in para. (1)(B), deleted "or" following "full;", in para. (2), substituted "; or" for the concluding period, and added para. (3).

Such Act further, substituted "Secretary" for "Administrator", wherever appearing, in the entire section.

1991. Act April 6, 1991, in subsec. (a)(2), added subpara. (D).

Act May 7, 1991, § 402(d)(1), amended the references in this section to reflect the redesignations made by §§ 401(a)(4) and 402(b) of such Act (see Table II preceding 38 USCS § 101).

Act Aug. 6, 1991, redesignated this section, formerly 38 USCS § 1802, as 38 USCS § 3702, and amended the references in this section to reflect the redesignations made by § 5(a) of such Act (see Table III preceding 38 USCS § 101).

1992. Act Oct. 28, 1992, in subsec. (a)(2), added subpara. (E).

1994. Act Nov. 2, 1994, in subsec. (a)(2)(E), substituted "For the period beginning on October 28, 1992, and ending on October 27, 1999," for "For the 7-year period beginning on the date of enactment of this subparagraph,"; and, in subsec. (b), in the introductory matter, substituted "loan under the following circumstances:" for "loan, if—", in para. (1), substituted "The property" for "the property" and substituted a period for a semicolon following "paid in full", in para. (2), substituted "A veteran-transferee" for "a veteran-transferee" and substituted a period for "; or" following "this chapter", in para. (3)(A), substituted "The loan" for "the loan", added para. (4), and, in the concluding matter, substituted "paragraph (1)" for "clause (1) of the preceding sentence" and added the sentence beginning "The authority of the Secretary . . .".

Other provisions:

Effective dates of Act Dec. 31, 1974. Act Dec. 31, 1974, P. L. 93-569, § 10, 88 Stat. 1867, provided: "The provisions of this Act [amending this section and 38 USCS §§ 2102, 3703, 3704, 3710, 3711, 3715, 3718, and 3719, and 12 USCS § 1757; repealing 38 USCS §§ 3712, 3714, 3722] shall become effective on the date of enactment except that the amendments made by sections 2(a)(3) [probably amendment to subsec. (b)(3) of this section] and 2(b) [amending subsec. (d)(3) of this section] and sections 3(2) and 3(4) [amending 38 USCS § 3710] shall become effective ninety days after such date of enactment.".

Effective dates of Title I of Act Oct. 18, 1978. Act Oct. 18, 1978, P. L. 95-476, Title I, § 108, 92 Stat. 1502, provided that:

"(a) Except as provided in subsection (b) of this section, the amendments made by this title [amending this section and 38 USCS §§ 2102, 3703, 3710, 3711, 3718, and 3719] shall take effect on October 1, 1978.

"(b) The amendment made by clause (1) of section 104 of this title [amending 38 USCS § 3710(a)(6)] shall take effect on July 1, 1979, except with respect to the authority to prescribe regulations for the implementation of such amendment, which shall be effective on the date of the enactment of this Act.".

Authority of the Administrator to promulgate regulations. For the authority and effective date for the Administrator of Veterans's Affairs to promulgate regulations under 38 USCS §§ 3741 et seq., see § 305 of Act Nov. 3, 1981, which appears as 38 USCS § 3741 note.

Application and construction of the Oct. 12, 1982 amendment. For provisions as to the application and construction of the Oct. 12, 1982 amendment of this section, see § 5 of such Act, which appears as 10 USCS § 101 note.

Clarification of references. Act May 20, 1988, P. L. 100-322, Title IV, Part B, § 415(c)(7), 102 Stat. 552, provides: "Any reference, in effect on the date of the enactment of this Act, in any law, rule, or regulation to any of the sections, or parts thereof, which are redesignated or transferred by this section [amending generally 38 USCS §§ 3701 et seq.] shall be construed to refer to the section, or part thereof, as redesignated or transferred by this section [amending generally 38 USCS §§ 3701 et seq.].".

Technical nature of May 20, 1988 amendments. Act May 20, 1988,

38 USCS § 3702
VETERANS' BENEFITS

P. L. 100-322, Title IV, Part B, § 415(f), 102 Stat. 553, provides: "The status of any veteran with respect to benefits under chapter 37 of title 38, United States Code [38 USCS §§ 3701 et seq.], shall not be affected by the amendments made by, or other provisions of, this section [amending generally 38 USCS §§ 3701 et seq.].".

Repeal of provision relating to report concerning mortgage loans pursuant to Oct. 28, 1992 amendments. Act Oct. 28, 1992, P. L. 102-547, § 2(c), 106 Stat. 3634, which formerly appeared as a note to this section, was repealed by Act Feb. 13, 1996, P. L. 104-110, Title II, § 201(b), 110 Stat. 770. Such note related to an annual report to the Committees on Veterans' Affairs of the Senate and House of Representatives by the Secretary of Veterans Affairs dealing with veterans receiving mortgage loans guaranteed by the Secretary.

CODE OF FEDERAL REGULATIONS
Department of Veterans Affairs—Loan guaranty, 38 CFR Part 36.

CROSS REFERENCES
This section is referred to in 12 USCS § 1715z-13a; 38 USCS §§ 3703, 3710, 3712, 3714, 3731, 3744, 5102.

RESEARCH GUIDE
Federal Procedure L Ed:
4A Fed Proc L Ed, Banking and Financing §§ 8:1408, 1411.

Am Jur:
77 Am Jur 2d, Veterans and Veterans' Laws §§ 120, 121.

INTERPRETIVE NOTES AND DECISIONS

1. Generally
2. Purpose
3. Persons entitled to benefits
4. Lenders eligible for loan guaranty
5. Scope of guaranty
6. Use of benefits for ineligible person
7. False claim actions

1. Generally
Classification of veterans is entirely constitutional. Valley Nat'l Bank v Glover (1945) 62 Ariz 538, 159 P2d 292.

2. Purpose
Policy of Servicemen's Readjustment Act (predecessor to 38 USCS §§ 3701 et seq.) was to enable veterans to obtain loans and to obtain them with least risk of loss, to both veteran and Veterans Administration [now Department of Veterans Affairs], upon foreclosure. United States v Shimer (1961) 367 US 374, 6 L Ed 2d 908, 81 S Ct 1554.

Servicemen's Readjustment Act (predecessor to 38 USCS §§ 3701 et seq.) was designed in part to protect veterans from payment of excessive prices for purchase or construction of homes and from terms of payment not bearing proper relation to their present and anticipated income and expenses. Young v Hampton (1951) 36 Cal 2d 799, 228 P2d 1, 19 ALR2d 830.

3. Persons entitled to benefits
Period of service under former 38 USC § 694 did not include time lost by reason of unauthorized absence for which service person had forfeited pay. 1944 ADVA 613.

For purposes of Servicemen's Readjustment Act of 1944 (38 USCS §§ 1801 et seq. [now 38 USCS §§ 3701 et seq.]), honorable discharge of enlisted man to accept commission or of member of reserve to accept commission in regular establishment was sufficient to entitle such individual to certificate of eligibility for loan guaranties. 1946 ADVA 725.

Service person not entitled to separation under point or length of service system, but otherwise eligible to be completely separated from active service, was so separated for purposes of benefits administered by Veterans' Administration [now Department of Veterans Affairs] where department would have released him had he so requested at time he accepted commission or affected other change in status. 1947 ADVA 771.

Case of veteran discharged honorably from Canadian armed forces in 1942 to accept commission in American forces was similar to that of service person in Administrator's [now Secretary's] decision No. 725 who was discharged to accept commission or change in status prior to eligibility for discharge under point or length of service system; thus, Canadian service did not qualify as separate period of service for benefits purposes, and discharge under dishonorable conditions from United States armed forces barred benefits based upon Canadian services. 1948 ADVA 782.

Veteran who served less than 90 days during World War II and was discharged from active military or naval service for disability considered to have incurred in such service was entitled to benefits under former 38 USC § 694. 1951 ADVA 874.

Veteran who acquired loan guaranty entitlement for active duty in both World War II and Korean conflict was eligible to use his subsisting entitlement to loan assistance benefits for longest period of time afforded by his service in either conflict; such privilege applied not only where veteran had made no previous use of World War II entitlement, but also where Korean entitlement had either been reduced or saved from reduction on account of used World War II entitlement pursuant to 38 USCS § 1802 [now 38 USCS § 3702]. 1961 ADVA 978.

Veteran was not entitled to loan guaranty in amount of his full eligibility since VA's acceptance of deed in lieu of foreclosure from veteran's assignees extinguished portion veteran had originally received; veteran did not have property interest in restoration of his expended entitlement since there was no evidence that assignee-veteran ever agreed to substitute his entitlement for plaintiff's, and his right to redeem was transferred to assignees with interest in underlying property and exercised when they conveyed property to VA in lieu of foreclosure. Wells v Brown (1996) 9 Vet App 293, affd without op (1997, CA FC) 114 F3d 1207, reported in full (1997, CA FC) 1997 US App LEXIS 13412 and cert den (1998, US) 139 L Ed 2d 632, 118 S Ct 685.

4. Lenders eligible for loan guaranty

Lenders supervised and qualified under former 38 USC § 694 we not eligible for automatic insurance; however, lender who complied with applicable provisions and regulations was entitled as legal right to issuance of certificate of guaranty or insurance credit. 1945 ADVA 767.

Lending organization otherwise deemed qualified for loan guaranties under former 38 USC § 694 but which was not, by reason of Federal, state, territorial, or District of Columbia law, subject to examination and supervision by agency thereof, was not entitled to such loan guaranties without prior approval of Administrator [now Secretary] of Veterans Affairs. 1946 ADVA 692.

Lender that belongs to Federal Home Loan Bank is eligible for loan guaranties so long as it is subject to inspection and regulation as member of bank or pursuant to other Federal or state law. 1946 ADVA 708.

Mortgage loan company which qualified as affiliate of national bank or of other bank, so long as such other bank belonged to Federal Reserve System, was within class described by former 38 USC § 694, and was accordingly entitled to make loans which were automatically guaranteed. 1946 ADVA 709.

All federally-chartered credit unions qualify under 38 USCS § 1802 [now 38 USCS § 3702] to process loans for automatic guaranty; state-chartered credit unions may qualify if subject to both examination and supervision by state agency under 38 USCS § 1802(d)(1) [now 38 USCS § 3702(d)(1)], or if not subject to examination and supervision, under 38 USCS § 1802(d)(3) [now 38 USCS § 3702(d)(3)]. VA GCO 25-75.

5. Scope of guaranty

Expenses customarily connected with placing and initially servicing loan are includable as part of obligation upon which Administrator's [now Secretary's] guaranty of such loan is to be based. 1944 ADVA 591.

Value of interest owned by veteran and spouse in property to be encumbered is basis for extent of guaranty and is not to be limited to value of such interest owned by veteran exclusive of value particularly attributable to spouse's interest where such interest was acquired by virtue of relationship. 1945 ADVA 619.

6. Use of benefits for ineligible person

Veteran who bought real estate as tenant in common with other veteran, acquiring one-half undivided interest in property, was not entitled to apply unused balance of his benefits to cover his copurchaser's half of loan, where copurchaser had already used all but small amount of his guaranty privilege. Gowanda Co-op. Sav. & Loan Asso. v Gray (1950, CA2 NY) 183 F2d 367.

Agreement by veteran purchasing property under loan guaranty to hold property in trust for person ineligible for loan guaranty was invalid, even though supported by consideration. Glosser v Powers (1952) 209 Ga 149, 71 SE2d 230; Dunn v Dunn (1956, 2d Dept) 1 App Div 2d 888, 149 NYS2d 351.

Veteran's oral agreement to take title to house in his own name and to hold title in trust for relative who furnished money for obtaining and preserving property, thereby securing lower interest rate, longer term, and other advantages, was invalid to extent that agreement attempted to obtain benefits for relative to which only veterans were entitled, even though veteran lived in house with relative. Perkins v Hilton (1952) 329 Mass 291, 107 NE2d 822, 33 ALR2d 1281.

38 USCS § 3702, n 6   VETERANS' BENEFITS

Although remedy of constructive trust was not available to person ineligible for loan guaranty, who made agreement with eligible veteran for veteran to take title in his name and reconvey property after loan guaranty, equitable lien would be impressed upon property in favor of nonveteran, limited to money paid by him out of his own funds at closing and thereafter in reduction of principal of mortgage indebtedness, to extent to which moneys expended by him for permanent improvements enhanced value of property. Badami v Badami (1968, 2d Dept) 29 App Div 2d 645, 286 NYS2d 590.

Where in order to receive for his mother benefits which were his under "G. I. Bill of Rights" veteran used his mother's money to purchase house and made oral trust to convey to her later, agreement was illegal as fraud although veteran lived in house purchased, and in suit by veteran's trustee in bankruptcy mother was not allowed credit for payments made by her before veteran conveyed to her but was allowed credit for payments made after conveyance. Perkins v Hilton (1952) 329 Mass 291, 107 NE2d 822, 33 ALR2d 1281.

Where title to home was taken in name of veteran merely as means of financing purchase, and veteran did not occupy it for number of years, constructive trust in favor of veteran's stepfather, who, with his wife until her death occupied it, made payments on mortgage, and capital improvements, would not be imposed, but stepfather was entitled to lien for such expenditures. Towner v Berg (1958, 3d Dept) 5 App Div 2d 481, 172 NYS2d 258.

7. False claim actions

Gratuitous payment of 4 percent of amount of guaranty previously provided for provided adequate basis for false claim action against dealer who knew at time transaction was closed that veteran did not intend to occupy house bought pursuant to guaranteed loan. United States v De Witt (1959, CA5 Tex) 265 F2d 393, cert den (1959) 361 US 866, 4 L Ed 2d 105, 80 S Ct 121.

Dealer who completed transaction knowing that veteran did not intend to live in house purchased with guaranteed mortgage funds could be found guilty of making false claim against United States. United States v De Witt (1959, CA5 Tex) 265 F2d 393, cert den (1959) 361 US 866, 4 L Ed 2d 105, 80 S Ct 121.

"Non-supervised" lenders have no duty to verify accuracy of information supplied by veterans and real estate brokers before passing information on to Veterans Administration [now Department of Veterans Affairs] in application for loan guarantee under this act; consequently lender's knowledge of falsity of statements in application, such knowledge being necessary for liability under False Claims Act [31 USCS §§ 231 et seq.], cannot be established by mere failure to so verify. United States v Ekelman & Assoc., Inc. (1976, CA6 Mich) 532 F2d 545, 35 ALR Fed 794 (superseded by statute on other grounds as stated in United States v Macomb Contracting Corp. (1988, MD Tenn) 1988 US Dist LEXIS 17608) and (superseded by statute on other grounds as stated in United States v Murphy (1991, CA6 Tenn) 937 F2d 1032, 37 CCF ¶ 76123, 1991-1 CCH Trade Cases ¶ 69482).

Defendants charged with making false statements in application for home loan guaranty of eligible ex-service man were not entitled to dismissal on ground that charge did not set forth or allege commission of offense. United States v Oakland (1948, DC La) 81 F Supp 343.

Real estate broker, who represented both seller and buyer, was not guilty of filing false claim, where buyer alone signed certificate representing that consideration paid was not in excess of appraised value, if evidence failed to show that broker acted as attorney for parties; presence of seller at meetings where purchaser signed false certificate stating that price paid for property was not in excess of appraised value did not make him guilty of filing a false claim, if evidence failed to show he knew about requirement. United States v Mignon (1952, DC Pa) 103 F Supp 20.

§ 3703. Basic provisions relating to loan guaranty and insurance

(a)(1)(A) Any loan to a veteran eligible for benefits under this chapter [38 USCS §§ 3701 et seq.], if made for any of the purposes specified in section 3710 of this title and in compliance with the provisions of this chapter [38 USCS §§ 3701 et seq.], is automatically guaranteed by the United States in an amount not to exceed the lesser of—

    (i) (I) in the case of any loan of not more than $45,000, 50 percent of the loan;

    (II) in the case of any loan of more than $45,000, but not more than $56,250, $22,500;

    (III) except as provided in subclause (IV) of this clause, in the case of any loan of more than $56,250, the lesser of $36,000 or 40 percent of the loan; or

(IV) in the case of any loan of more than $144,000 for a purpose specified in clause (1), (2), (3), (6), or (8) of section 3710(a) of this title, the lesser of $50,750 or 25 percent of the loan; or''; and

(ii) the maximum amount of guaranty entitlement available to the veteran as specified in subparagraph (B) of this paragraph.

(B) The maximum amount of guaranty entitlement available to a veteran for purposes specified in section 3710 of this title shall be $36,000, or in the case of a loan described in subparagraph (A)(i)(IV) of this paragraph, $50,750, reduced by the amount of entitlement previously used by the veteran under this chapter [38 USCS §§ 3701 et seq.] and not restored as a result of the exclusion in section 3702(b) of this title.

(2)(A) Any housing loan which might be guaranteed under the provisions of this chapter [38 USCS §§ 3701 et seq.], when made or purchased by any financial institution subject to examination and supervision by an agency of the United States or of any State may, in lieu of such guaranty, be insured by the Secretary under an agreement whereby the Secretary will reimburse any such institution for losses incurred on such loan up to 15 per centum of the aggregate of loans so made or purchased by it.

(B) Loans insured under this section shall be made on such other terms, conditions, and restrictions as the Secretary may prescribe within the limitations set forth in this chapter [38 USCS §§ 3701 et seq.].

(b) The liability of the United States under any guaranty, within the limitations of this chapter [38 USCS §§ 3701 et seq.], shall decrease or increase pro rata with any decrease or increase of the amount of the unpaid portion of the obligation.

(c)(1) Loans guaranteed or insured under this chapter [38 USCS §§ 3701 et seq.] shall be payable upon such terms and conditions as may be agreed upon by the parties thereto, subject to the provisions of this chapter [38 USCS §§ 3701 et seq.] and regulations of the Secretary issued pursuant to this chapter [38 USCS §§ 3701 et seq.], and shall bear interest not in excess of such rate as the Secretary may from time to time find the loan market demands, except that in establishing the rate of interest that shall be applicable to such loans, the Secretary shall consult with the Secretary of Housing and Urban Development regarding the rate of interest applicable to home loans insured under section 203(b) of the National Housing Act (12 U.S.C. 1709(b)).

(2) The provisions of the Servicemen's Readjustment Act of 1944 which were in effect before April 1, 1958, with respect to the interest chargeable on loans made or guaranteed under such Act shall, notwithstanding the provisions of paragraph (1) of this subsection, continue to be applicable—

(A) to any loan made or guaranteed before April 1, 1958; and

(B) to any loan with respect to which a commitment to guarantee was entered into by the Secretary before April 1, 1958.

(3) This section shall not be construed to prohibit a veteran from paying to a lender any reasonable discount required by such lender, when the proceeds from the loan are to be used—

(A) to refinance indebtedness pursuant to clause (5), (8), or 9(b)(i) of section 3710(a) of this title or section 3712(a)(1)(F) of this title;

(B) to repair, alter, or improve a farm residence or other dwelling pursuant to clauses (4) and (7) of section 3710(a) of this title;

(C) to construct a dwelling or farm residence on land already owned or to be acquired by the veteran except where the land is directly or indirectly acquired from a builder or developer who has contracted to construct such dwelling for the veteran;

(D) to purchase a dwelling from a class of sellers which the Secretary determines are legally precluded under all circumstances from paying such a discount if the best interest of the veteran would be so served; or

(E) to refinance indebtedness and purchase a manufactured-home lot pursuant to section 3710(a)(9)(B)(ii) or 3712(a)(1)(G) of this title, but only with respect to that portion of the loan used to refinance such indebtedness.

(4)(A) In guaranteeing or insuring loans under this chapter [38 USCS §§ 3701 et seq.], the Secretary may elect whether to require that such loans bear interest at a rate that is—

(i) agreed upon by the veteran and the mortgagee; or

(ii) established under paragraph (1).

The Secretary may, from time to time, change the election under this subparagraph.

(B) Any veteran, under a loan described in subparagraph (A)(i), may pay reasonable discount points in connection with the loan. Except in the case of a loan for the purpose specified in section 3710(a)(8), 3710(b)(7), or 3712(a)(1)(F) of this title, discount points may not be financed as part of the principal amount of a loan guaranteed or insured under this chapter [38 USCS §§ 3701 et seq.].

(C) Not later than 10 days after an election under subparagraph (A), the Secretary shall transmit to the Committees on Veterans' Affairs of the Senate and House of Representatives a notification of the election, together with an explanation of the reasons therefor.

(d)(1) The maturity of any housing loan shall not be more than thirty years and thirty-two days.

(2)(A) Any loan for a term of more than five years shall be amortized in accordance with established procedure.

(B) The Secretary may guarantee loans with provisions for various rates of amortization corresponding to anticipated variations in family income. With respect to any loan guaranteed under this subparagraph—

(i) the initial principal amount of the loan may not exceed the reasonable value of the property as of the time the loan is made; and

(ii) the principal amount of the loan thereafter (including the amount of all interest to be deferred and added to principal) may not at any time be scheduled to exceed the projected value of the property.

(C) For the purposes of subparagraph (B) of this paragraph, the projected value of the property shall be calculated by the Secretary by increasing the reasonable value of the property as of the time the loan is made at a rate not in excess of 2.5 percent per year, but in no event may the projected value of the property for the purposes of such subparagraph exceed 115 percent of such reasonable value. A loan made for a purpose other than the acquisition of a single-family dwelling unit may not be guaranteed under such subparagraph.

(3) Any real estate housing loan (other than for repairs, alterations, or improvements) shall be secured by a first lien on the realty. In determining whether a loan for the purchase or construction of a home is so secured, the Secretary may disregard a superior lien created by a duly recorded covenant running with the realty in favor of a private entity to secure an obligation to such entity for the homeowner's share of the costs of the management, operation, or maintenance of property, services or programs within and for the benefit of the development or community in which the veteran's realty is located, if the Secretary determines that the interests of the veteran borrower and of the Government will not be prejudiced by the operation of such covenant. In respect to any such superior lien to be created after June 6, 1969, the Secretary's determination must have been made prior to the recordation of the covenant.

(e)(1) Except as provided in paragraph (2) of this subsection, an individual who pays a fee under section 3729 of this title, or who is exempted under section 3729(c)(1) of this title from paying such fee, with respect to a housing loan guaranteed or insured under this chapter that is closed after December 31, 1989, shall have no liability to the Secretary with respect to the loan for any loss resulting from any default of such individual except in the case of fraud, misrepresentation, or bad faith by such individual in obtaining the loan or in connection with the loan default.

(2) The exemption from liability provided by paragraph (1) of this subsection shall not apply to—

(A) an individual from whom a fee is collected (or who is exempted from such fee) under section 3729(b) of this title; or

(B) a loan made for any purpose specified in section 3712 of this title.

(f) The application for or obtaining of a loan made, insured, or guaranteed under this chapter [38 USCS §§ 3701 et seq.] shall not be subject to reporting requirements applicable to requests for, or receipts of, Federal contracts, grants, loans, loan guarantees, loan insurance, or cooperative agreements except to the extent that such requirements are provided for in, or by the Secretary pursuant to, this title.

(Sept. 2, 1958, P. L. 85-857, § 1, 72 Stat. 1205; June 30, 1959, P. L. 86-73, § 2, 73 Stat. 156; July 14, 1960, P. L. 86-665, § 1, 74 Stat. 531; July 6, 1961, P. L. 87-84, § 1(a), 75 Stat. 201; March 3, 1966, P. L. 89-358, § 5(d), 80 Stat. 26; Aug. 31, 1967, P. L. 90-77, Title IV, § 403(b), 81 Stat. 190; June 6, 1969, P. L. 91-22, § 4, 83 Stat. 32; Oct. 23, 1970, P. L. 91-506, § 2(b), (c), 84 Stat. 1108; July 26, 1973, P. L. 93-75, 87 Stat. 176; Dec. 31, 1974, P. L. 93-569, §§ 2(c), 8(1)–(5), 88 Stat. 1863, 1866; June 30, 1976, P. L. 94-324, § 7(6), (16),

38 USCS § 3703 VETERANS' BENEFITS

90 Stat. 721; Oct. 18, 1978, P. L. 95-476, Title I, § 103, 92 Stat. 1498; Oct. 7, 1980, P. L. 96-385, Title IV, § 401(c)(1), 94 Stat. 1533; Oct. 17, 1981, P. L. 97-66, Title V, § 501(a), 95 Stat. 1031; Nov. 3, 1981, P. L. 97-72, Title III, § 303(c), 95 Stat. 1060; Oct. 12, 1982, P. L. 97-295, § 4(61), (63), 96 Stat. 1309; Oct. 14, 1982, P. L. 97-306, Title IV, § 406(b), 96 Stat. 1444; March 2, 1984, P. L. 98-223, Title II, § 205(c), 98 Stat. 43; Dec. 21, 1987, P. L. 100-198, § 3(a)(1), 101 Stat. 1315; Feb. 29, 1988, P. L. 100-253, § 3(a), 102 Stat. 20; May 20, 1988, P. L. 100-322, Title IV, Part C, § 415(a)(3)(A)(iii), (B), (c)(2), (d)(1), 102 Stat. 550; Dec. 18, 1989, P. L. 101-237, Title III, §§ 304(a), 306(a), 313(b)(1), (6), 103 Stat. 2073, 2074, 2077; June 13, 1991, P. L. 102-54, §§ 4(b), 6, 105 Stat. 268; Aug. 6, 1991, P. L. 102-83, § 5(a), (c)(1), 105 Stat. 406; Oct. 28, 1992, P. L. 102-547, § 10(a), 106 Stat. 3643; Aug. 13, 1993, P. L. 103-78, § 6, 107 Stat. 769; Oct. 13, 1994, P. L. 103-353, § 7, 108 Stat. 3175; Feb. 13, 1996, P. L. 104-110, Title I, § 101(d), 110 Stat. 768.)

HISTORY; ANCILLARY LAWS AND DIRECTIVES

References in text:

The "Servicemen's Readjustment Act of 1944", referred to in subsec. (c)(2), is Act June 22, 1944, ch 268, 58 Stat. 284, as amended, which was generally classified to former 38 USC §§ 693–697g prior to repeal by Act Sept. 2, 1958, P. L. 85-857, § 14(87), 72 Stat. 1273, in the general revision of Title 38. For similar provisions, see tables preceding 38 USCS § 101.

Amendments:

1959. Act June 30, 1959, in subsec. (c)(1), deleted ", but the rate of interest so prescribed by the Administrator shall not exceed at any time the rate of interest (exclusive of premium charges for insurance, and service charges if any), established by the Federal Housing Commissioner under section 203(b)(5) of the National Housing Act, less one-half of 1 per centum per annum" following "loan market demands", and substituted "5¼ per centum per annum" for "4 ¾ per centum per annum".

1960. Act July 14, 1960, in subsec. (a), in para. (1), substituted "1962" for "1960" and substituted "fifteen years" for "thirteen years", and in para. (2), substituted "1962" for "1960" wherever appearing, and substituted "after such date" for "before July 26, 1961".

1961. Act July 6, 1961, substituted new subsec. (a) for one which read:

"(a)(1) Any loan made to a World War II veteran, if made before July 26, 1962 (or, in the case of a veteran described in section 1801(a)(1)(B) of this title, before the expiration of fifteen years after World War II is deemed to have ended with respect to him), or to a Korean conflict veteran, if made before February 1, 1965, for any of the purposes, and in compliance with the provisions, specified in this chapter, is automatically guaranteed by the United States in an amount not more than 60 per centum of the loan if the loan is made for any of the purposes specified in section 1810 of this title and not more than 50 per centum of the loan if the loan is for any of the purposes specified in section 1812, 1813, or 1814 of this title.

"(2) If a loan report or an application for loan guaranty relating to a loan under this chapter to a World War II veteran whose entitlement would otherwise expire on July 25, 1962, has been received by the Administrator before July 26, 1962, such loan may be guaranteed or insured under the provisions of this chapter after such date.".

1966. Act March 3, 1966 (effective 3/3/66, as provided by § 12(a) of such Act), in subsec. (c)(1), substituted "may from time to time find the loan market demands; except that such rate shall in no event exceed that in effect under the provisions of section 203(b)(5) of the National Housing Act." for ", with the approval of the Secretary of the Treasury, may from time to time find the loan market demands; except that such rate shall in no event exceed $5^{1}/_{4}$ per centum per annum.".

1967. Act Aug. 31, 1967 (effective 10/1/67, as provided by § 405(a) of such Act, which appears as 38 USCS § 101 note), in subsec. (a)(3)(A), in clauses (i) and (ii), substituted "July 25, 1970" for "July 25, 1967".

1969. Act June 6, 1969, substituted new subsec. (d)(3) for one which read: "Any real-estate loan (other than for repairs, alterations, or improvements) shall be secured by a first lien on the realty. Any non-real-estate loan (other than for working or other capital, merchandise, goodwill, and other intangible assets) shall be secured by personality to the extent legal and practicable.".

1970. Act Oct. 23, 1970, substituted new subsec. (a) for one which read:

"(a)(1) Any loan to a World War II or Korean conflict veteran, if made within the applicable period prescribed in paragraph (3) of this subsection for any of the purposes, and in compliance with the provisions, specified in this chapter is automatically guaranteed by the United States in an amount not more than 60 per centum of the loan if the loan is made for any of the purposes specified in section 1810 of this title and not more than 50 per centum of the loan if the loan is for any of the purposes specified in section 1812, 1813, or 1814 of this title.

"(2) If a loan report or an application for loan guaranty relating to a loan under this chapter is received by the Administrator before the date of the expiration of the veteran's entitlement, the loan may be guaranteed or insured under the provisions of this chapter after such date.

"(3)(A) A World War II veteran's entitlement to the benefits of this chapter will expire as follows:

"(i) ten years from the date of discharge or release from the last period of active duty of the veteran, any part of which occurred during World War II, plus an additional period equal to one year for each three months of active duty performed by the veteran during World War II, except that entitlement shall not continue in any case after July 25, 1970, nor shall entitlement expire in any case prior to July 25, 1962; or

"(ii) on July 25, 1970, for a veteran discharged or released for a service-connected disability from a period of active duty, any part of which occurred during World War II.

"(B) A Korean conflict veteran's entitlement to the benefits of this chapter will expire as follows:

"(i) ten years from the date of discharge or release from the last period of active duty of the veteran, any part of which occurred during the Korean conflict, plus an additional period equal to one year for each three months of active duty performed by the veteran during the Korean conflict, except that entitlement shall not

38 USCS § 3703   VETERANS' BENEFITS

continue in any case after January 31, 1975, nor shall entitlement expire in any case prior to January 31, 1965; or

"(ii) on January 31, 1975, for a veteran discharged or released for a service-connected disability from a period of active duty, any part of which occurred during the Korean conflict.";

in subsec. (b), substituted "1810, 1811, and 1819" for "1810 and 1811"; and in subsec. (d)(1), inserted "except as provided in section 1819 of this title".

1973. Act July 26, 1973, in subsec. (c)(1), substituted ", except that in establishing the rate of interest that shall be applicable to such loans, the Administrator shall consult with the Secretary of Housing and Urban Development regarding the rate of interest the Secretary considers necessary to meet the mortgage market for home loans insured under section 203(b) of the National Housing Act, and, to the maximum extent practicable, carry out a coordinated policy on interest rates on loans insured under such section 203(b) and on loans guaranteed or insured under this chapter." for "; except that such rate shall in no event exceed that in effect under the provisions of section 203(b)(5) of the National Housing Act.".

1974. Act Dec. 31, 1974 (effective 12/31/74, as provided by § 10 of such Act, which appears as 38 USCS § 3702 note), in subsec. (a)(1), deleted "and not more than 50 per centum of the loan if the loan is for any of the purposes specified in section 1812, 1813, or 1814 of this title" following "of this title"; in subsec. (b), deleted "Except as provided in sections 1810, 1811, and 1819 of this title, the aggregate amount guaranteed shall not be more than $2,000 in the case of non-real-estate loans, nor $4,000 in the case of real-estate loans, or a prorated portion thereof on loans of both types or combination thereof." preceding "The liability"; added subsec. (c)(3); substituted new subsec. (d)(1) for one which read: "The maturity of any non-real-estate loan shall not be more than ten years except as provided in section 1819 of this title. The maturity of any real-estate loan (other than a loan on farm realty) shall not be more than thirty years, and in the case of a loan on farm realty, shall not be more than forty years."; and in subsec. (d)(3), deleted "Any non-real-estate loan (other than for working or other capital, merchandise, goodwill, and other intangible assets) shall be secured by personalty to the extent legal and practicable." following "of the covenant.".

1976. Act June 30, 1976 (effective 6/30/76, as provided by § 9(a) of such Act, which appears as 38 USCS § 3701 note), in subsec. (d)(3), substituted "the Administrator" for "he" preceding "determines".

1978. Act Oct. 18, 1978 (effective 10/1/78, as provided by § 108(a) of such Act, which appears as 38 USCS § 3702 note), in subsec. (a)(1), substituted "veteran eligible for benefits under this chapter" for "World War II or Korean conflict veteran"; in subsec. (c)(1), inserted "In establishing rates of interest under this paragraph for one or more of the purposes described in clauses (4) and (7) of section 1810(a) of this title, the Administrator may establish a rate or rates higher than the rate specified for other purposes under such section, but any such rate may not exceed such rate as the Administrator may from time to time find the loan market demands for loans for such purposes."; and in subsec. (c)(3)(B), substituted "clauses (4) and (7) of section 1810(a) of this title" for "section 1810(a)(4)".

1980. Act Oct. 7, 1980 (effective 10/7/80, as provided by § 601(d) of such

Act, which appears as 38 USCS § 1114 note), in subsec. (c)(3)(A), substituted "clause (5) or (8) of section 1810(a) of this title or section 1819(a)(1)(F) of this title" for "section 1810(a)(5)".

1981. Act Oct. 17, 1981 (effective 10/17/81, as provided by § 701(b)(1) of such Act, which appears as 38 USCS § 1114 note), in subsec. (d)(2), designated existing provisions as subpara. (A) and added subparas. (B) and (C).

Act Nov. 3, 1981 (effective 180 days after enactment on Nov. 3, 1981, as provided by § 305 of such Act, which appears as 38 USCS § 3741 note), in subsec. (d), in paras. (1) and (3), inserted "housing".

1982. Act Oct. 12, 1982, in subsec. (a), in para. (1), substituted "percent" for "per centum", and in para. (2), substituted "before October 23, 1970" for "prior to the date of enactment of the Veterans' Housing Act of 1970"; in subsec. (c)(1), inserted "(12 U.S.C. 1709(b))"; and, in subsec. (d)(3), substituted "June 6, 1969" for "prior to the effective date of this amendment".

Act Oct. 14, 1982, in subsec. (c)(3), in the introductory matter, substituted "used—" for "used:", in subpara. (C), deleted "or" following "veteran;", in subpara. (D), substituted "; or" for the concluding period, and added subpara. (E).

1984. Act March 2, 1984, in subsec. (c)(3), in subpara. (A), substituted ", (8), or 9(B)(i)", and, in subpara. (E), inserted "1810(a)(9)(B)(ii) or".

1987. Act Dec. 21, 1987 (applicable as provided by § 3(d) of such Act, which appears as a note to this section), in subsec. (a), substituted para. (1) for one which read: "Any loan to a veteran eligible for benefits under this chapter, if made for any of the purposes, and in compliance with the provisions, specified in this chapter is automatically guaranteed by the United States in an amount not more than 60 percent of the loan if the loan is made for any of the purposes specified in section 1810 of this title.".

1988. Act Feb. 29, 1988 (applicable as provided by § 3(a) of such Act, which appears as a note to this section), substituted subsec. (a)(1) for one which read: "Any loan to a veteran eligible for benefits under this chapter, if made for any of the purposes specified in section 1810 of this title and in compliance with the provisions of this chapter, is automatically guaranteed by the United States in an amount not to exceed—

"(A) in the case of any loan of not more than $45,000, 50 percent of the loan; or

"(B) in the case of any loan of more than $45,000, 40 percent of the loan or $36,000, whichever is less, except that the amount of such guaranty for any such loan shall not be less than $22,500;

reduced by the amount of entitlement previously used by the veteran under this chapter and not restored as a result of the exclusion in section 1802(b) of this title.".

Act May 20, 1988 substituted the section catchline for one which read: "§ 1803. Basic provisions relating to loan guaranty"; in subsec. (a), in para. (1), in subpara. (A)(ii), inserted "as specified in subparagraph (B) of this paragraph", in subpara. (B), substituted "for purposes specified in section 1810 of this title" for "under section 1810 of this chapter", and deleted para. (2) which read: "Any unused entitlement of World War II or Korean conflict veterans which expired under provisions of law in effect before October 23, 1970 is hereby restored and shall not expire until used.".

38 USCS § 3703

Such Act further redesignated 38 USCS § 1815(a) and (b) as subsec. (a)(2)(A) and (B) of this section respectively; in subsec. (c)(3), in subpara. (A), substituted "section 1812" for "section 1819", and in subpara. (E), substituted "or 1812" for "or 1819".

1989. Act Dec. 18, 1989, added subsec. (e).

Such Act further (effective and applicable as provided by § 306(b) of such Act, which appears as a note to this section), in subsec. (a)(1), in subpara. (A)(i), in subcl. (I), deleted "or" following "loan;", substituted subcl. (II) for one which read: "in the case of any loan of more than $45,000, the lesser of $36,000 or 40 percent of the loan, except that the amount of such guaranty for any such loan shall not be less than $22,500; or", added subcls. (III) and (IV), and in subpara. (B), substituted "$36,000, or in the case of a loan described in subparagraph (A)(i)(IV) of this paragraph, $46,000," for "$36,000".

Such Act further, substituted "Secretary" and "Secretary's" for "Administrator" and "Administrator's", respectively, wherever appearing, in the entire section.

Such Act further, in subsec. (c)(1), inserted "of Housing and Urban Development" following "interest the Secretary".

1991. Act June 13, 1991, in subsec. (a)(1)(A)(i), in subcl. (III), inserted "except as provided in subclause (IV) of this clause," and deleted "but not more than $144,000," before "the lesser", and, in subcl. (IV), substituted "(6), or (8)" for "or (6)"; and added subsec. (f).

Act Aug. 6, 1991, redesignated this section, formerly 38 USCS § 1803, as 38 USCS § 3703, and amended the references in this section to reflect the redesignations made by § 5(a) of such Act (see Table III preceding 38 USCS § 101).

1992. Act Oct. 28, 1992, in subsec. (c), in para. (1), substituted "applicable to" for "the Secretary of Housing and Urban Development considers necessary to meet the mortgage market for", substituted the concluding period for ", and, to the maximum extent practicable, carry out a coordinated policy on interest rates on loans insured under such section 203(b) and on loans guaranteed or insured under this chapter [38 USCS §§ 3701 et seq.]. In establishing rates of interest under this paragraph for one or more of the purposes described in clauses (4) and (7) of section 3710(a) of this title, the Secretary may establish a rate or rates higher than the rate specified for other purposes under such section, but any such rate may not exceed such rate as the Secretary may from time to time find the loan market demands for loans for such purposes.", and added para. (4).

1993. Act Aug. 13, 1993, in subsec. (c)(4)(B), substituted "Except in the case of a loan for the purpose specified in section 3710(a)(8), 3710(b)(7), or 3712(a)(1)(F) of this title, discount" for "Discount".

1994. Act Oct. 13, 1994 (effective and applicable as provided by § 8 of such Act, which appears as 38 USCS § 4301 note), in subsec. (a)(1), in paras. (A)(i)(IV) and (B), substituted "$50,750" for "$46,000".

1996. Act Feb. 13, 1996, in subsec. (c)(4), deleted subpara. (D), which read: "This paragraph shall expire on December 31, 1995.".

Other provisions:

Expiration of loan benefit entitlement of certain World War II veterans. Act Aug. 31, 1967, P. L. 90-77, Title IV, § 403(c), 81 Stat. 190; Aug.

6, 1991, P. L. 102-83, § 5(c)(2), 105 Stat. 406, provided: "The World War II loan benefit entitlement of any veteran whose period of entitlement as computed under the provisions of section 3703(a)(3)(A) of title 38, United States Code, as amended by this section [subsec. (a)(3)(A) of this section], extended beyond July 25, 1967, shall not be deemed to expire earlier than ninety days after the effective date of this section.".

Section 405(a) of Act Aug. 31, 1967, provided that this note is effective on the first day of the first calendar month which begins more than 10 days after Aug. 31, 1967.

Authority of the Administrator to promulgate regulations. For the authority and effective date for the Administrator of Veterans's Affairs to promulgate regulations under 38 USCS §§ 3741 et seq., see § 305 of Act Nov. 3, 1981, which appears as 38 USCS § 3741 note.

Application and construction of Oct. 12, 1982 amendment. For provisions as to the application and construction of the Oct. 12, 1982 amendment of this section, see § 5 of such Act, which appears as 10 USCS § 101 note.

Application of § 3 of Act Dec. 21, 1987 amendments. Act Dec. 21, 1987, P. L. 100-198, § 3(d), 101 Stat. 1316, provides: "The amendments made by this section [amending subsec. (a)(1) of this section and 38 USCS §§ 3711(d)(2)(A) and 3719(c)(3), (4), and repealing 38 USCS §§ 1310(c)] shall apply to loans which are closed on or after February 1, 1988, except that they shall not apply to any loan for which a guaranty commitment is made on or before December 31, 1987.".

Effective date and application of Act Dec. 18, 1989 amendments of subsec. (a)(1). Act Dec. 18, 1989, P. L. 101-237, Title III, § 306(b), 103 Stat. 2074, provides: "The amendments made by subsection (a) [amending subsec. (a)(1) of this section] shall take effect on the date of the enactment of this Act and shall apply only with respect to loans closed after such date.".

Repeal of provision relating to report concerning mortgage loans. Act Oct. 28, 1992, P. L. 102-547, § 10(b), 106 Stat. 3643; Nov. 2, 1994, P. L. 103-446, Title XII, § 1202(d), 108 Stat. 4689, which formerly appeared as a note to this section, was repealed by Act Feb. 13, 1996, P. L. 104-110, Title II, § 201(b), 110 Stat. 770. Such note related to an annual report to the Committees on Veterans' Affairs of the Senate and House of Representatives by the Secretary of Veterans Affairs dealing with veterans receiving mortgage loans guaranteed by the Secretary.

CODE OF FEDERAL REGULATIONS

Department of Veterans Affairs—Loan guaranty, 38 CFR Part 36.

Department of Veterans Affairs—Government debarment and suspension (nonprocurement) and governmentwide requirements for drug-free workplace (grants), 38 CFR Part 44.

CROSS REFERENCES

This section is referred to in 12 USCS § 1715u; 38 USCS §§ 3710, 3712, 3732, 3762.

RESEARCH GUIDE

Federal Procedure L Ed:
4A Fed Proc L Ed, Banking and Financing §§ 8:1408, 1410, 1411.

38 USCS § 3703

Am Jur:
77 Am Jur 2d, Veterans and Veterans' Laws §§ 119, 121, 127.

INTERPRETIVE NOTES AND DECISIONS

1. Generally
2. Purpose
3. Relationship with state laws
4. Terms and conditions of loan
5. Grounds for denial of guaranty
6. Liability on default

1. Generally

Administrator [now Secretary] of Veterans Affairs, by simply guaranteeing loan, does not also warrant homeowner's house. Potnick v United States (1973, ND Miss) 356 F Supp 395.

2. Purpose

Congress intended guaranty provisions of Servicemen's Readjustment Act of 1944 (predecessor to 38 USCS §§ 3701 et seq.), 58 Stat 284, as amended, to operate as substantial equivalent of down payment in same amount by veteran on purchase price, in order to induce prospective mortgagee-creditors to provide 100 per cent financing for veteran's home. United States v Shimer (1961) 367 US 374, 6 L Ed 2d 908, 81 S Ct 1554.

3. Relationship with state laws

State law releasing veteran from liability to mortgagee when mortgagee fails to follow state procedures for securing deficiency judgment is inapplicable to prevent United States from recovering from veteran amounts paid under guaranty, where Veterans' Administration [now Department of Veterans Affairs] regulation provides that such payments shall constitute debt owing to United States by veteran; regulations providing that Administrator [now Secretary] may specify, in advance of foreclosure sale, minimum amount which shall be credited on mortgage debt, which gives foreclosing mortgagee who purchases property at foreclosure sale option of selling property to Veterans Administration [now Department] for specified amount, constitute valid exercise of rulemaking authority given to Administrator [now Secretary] and operate to displace state statute governing mortgagee's purchase at foreclosure sale. United States v Shimer (1961) 367 US 374, 6 L Ed 2d 908, 81 S Ct 1554.

Hail insurance premiums provided for by state statute were in fact taxes, but under applicable regulation did not preclude Administrator [now Secretary] of Veterans Affairs from approving application for loan guaranty despite provisions giving state first lien on property. 1945 ADVA 627.

VA's lending program does not preempt established, nondiscriminatory state law, where loan is considered to be first lien, since properties acquired under program remain subject to state power to tax. United States v Marion County (1993, MD Fla) 826 F Supp 1400, 7 FLW Fed D 110.

4. Terms and conditions of loan

Bank which accepts guaranty of its loan by Veterans Administration [now Department of Veterans Affairs] cannot urge invalidity of Administration's [now Department's] regulation, since 38 USCS § 1803 [now 38 USCS § 3703] makes terms and conditions of loan subject to such regulations. Mt. Vernon Co-op. Bank v Gleason (1966, DC Mass) 250 F Supp 952, affd (1966, CA1 Mass) 367 F2d 289.

Loan, for which ultimate maturity is more than 5 years from date veteran acquires property or becomes liable on indebtedness, is not eligible for guaranty under Servicemen's Readjustment Act of 1944 (38 USCS §§ 1801 et seq. [now 38 USCS §§ 3701 et seq.]) as amortized loan if language of note or other evidence of indebtedness requires repayment in installments which are not approximately equal throughout remaining life of loan, including ultimate maturity date thereof, or are not sufficient to pay entire amount of loan. 1945 ADVA 631.

5. Grounds for denial of guaranty

Application for loan guaranty is not to be denied because veteran provides security to lender consisting of property not subject of purchase with loan proceeds. 1945 ADVA 621.

Application for guaranty under provisions of Servicemen's Readjustment Act of 1944 (38 USCS §§ 1801 et seq. [now 38 USCS § 3701]), is not to be denied because indebtedness is not evidenced by instrument separate from that creating encumbrance; also, it is immaterial whether instrument submitted is negotiable since it is assignable, and assignability is sufficient to meet requirements of regulations with respect to exercising certain options when claim is made. 1945 ADVA 623.

6. Liability on default

Under Veterans Administration [now Department of Veterans Affairs] home loan guaranty program, agency is not obligated to take foreclosure-avoidance measures nor does such duty arise from statements promulgated through information circulars and booklets provided by agency to advise veterans and lenders of procedures. Rank v Nimmo (1982, CA9 Cal) 677 F2d 692, cert den (1982) 459 US 907, 74 L Ed 2d 168, 103 S Ct 210.

When default occurs, liability on guaranty or on insurance of loan made to eligible veteran and to one or more ineligible borrowers is determined as if obligation were several and amount thereof for which veteran assumed liability were only his proportionate part of entire debt, notwithstanding that in fact it is joint and several obligation as between debtors and creditors. 1947 ADVA 757.

§ 3704. Restrictions on loans

(a) No loan for the purchase or construction of residential property shall be financed through the assistance of this chapter [38 USCS §§ 3701 et seq.] unless the property meets or exceeds minimum requirements for planning, construction, and general acceptability prescribed by the Secretary; however, this subsection shall not apply to a loan for the purchase of residential property on which construction is fully completed more than one year before such loan is made.

(b) Subject to notice and opportunity for a hearing, the Secretary may refuse to appraise any dwelling or housing project owned, sponsored, or to be constructed by any person identified with housing previously sold to veterans under this chapter [38 USCS §§ 3701 et seq.] as to which substantial deficiencies have been discovered, or as to which there has been a failure or indicated inability to discharge contractual liabilities to veterans, or as to which it is ascertained that the type of contract of sale or the methods or practices pursued in relation to the marketing of such properties were unfair or unduly prejudicial to veteran purchasers. The Secretary may also refuse to appraise any dwelling or housing project owned, sponsored, or to be constructed by any person refused the benefits of participation under the National Housing Act pursuant to a determination of the Secretary of Housing and Urban Development.

(c)(1) Except as provided in paragraph (2) of this subsection, no loan for the purchase or construction of residential property shall be financed through the assistance of this chapter [38 USCS §§ 3701 et seq.] unless the veteran applicant, at the time that the veteran applies for the loan, and also at the time that the loan is closed, certifies in such form as the Secretary may require, that the veteran intends to occupy the property as the veteran's home. Except as provided in paragraph (2) of this subsection, no loan for the repair, alteration, or improvement of residential property shall be financed through the assistance of the provisions of this chapter [38 USCS §§ 3701 et seq.] unless the veteran applicant, at the time that the veteran applies to the lender for the loan, and also at the time that the loan is closed, certifies, in such form as may be required by the Secretary, that the veteran occupies the property as the veteran's home. Notwithstanding the foregoing provisions of this subsection, in the case of a loan automatically guaranteed under this chapter [38 USCS §§ 3701 et seq.], the veteran shall be required to make the certification only at the time the loan is closed. For the purposes of this chapter [38 USCS §§ 3701 et seq.] the requirement that the veteran recipient of a guaranteed or direct home loan must occupy or intend to occupy the property as the veteran's home means that the veteran as of the date of the veteran's certification actually lives in the property personally as the veteran's residence or actually intends upon completion of the loan and acquisition of the dwelling unit to move into the property personally within a reasonable time and to utilize such property as the veteran's residence.

Notwithstanding the foregoing requirements of this subsection, the provisions for certification by the veteran at the time the veteran applies for the loan and at the time the loan is closed shall be considered to be satisfied if the Secretary finds that (1) in the case of a loan for repair, alteration, or improvement the veteran in fact did occupy the property at such times, or (2) in the case of a loan for construction or purchase the veteran intended to occupy the property as the veteran's home at such times and the veteran did in fact so occupy it when, or within a reasonable time after, the loan was closed.

(2) In any case in which a veteran is in active duty status as a member of the Armed Forces and is unable to occupy a property because of such status, the occupancy requirements of—

(A) paragraph (1) of this subsection;

(B) paragraphs (1) through (5) and paragraph (7) of section 3710(a) of this title;

(C) section 3712(a)(5)(A)(i) of this title; and

(D) section 3712(e)(5) of this title;

shall be considered to be satisfied if the spouse of the veteran occupies the property as the spouse's home and the spouse makes the certification required by paragraph (1) of this subsection.

(d) Subject to notice and opportunity for a hearing, whenever the Secretary finds with respect to guaranteed or insured loans that any lender or holder has failed to maintain adequate loan accounting records, or to demonstrate proper ability to service loans adequately or to exercise proper credit judgment or has willfully or negligently engaged in practices otherwise detrimental to the interest of veterans or of the Government, the Secretary may refuse either temporarily or permanently to guarantee or insure any loans made by such lender or holder and may bar such lender or holder from acquiring loans guaranteed or insured under this chapter [38 USCS §§ 3701 et seq.]; however, the Secretary shall not refuse to pay a guaranty or insurance claim on loans theretofore entered into in good faith between a veteran and such lender. The Secretary may also refuse either temporarily or permanently to guarantee or insure any loans made by a lender or holder refused the benefits of participation under the National Housing Act pursuant to a determination of the Secretary of Housing and Urban Development.

(e) Any housing loan which is financed through the assistance of this chapter and to which section 3714 of this chapter applies shall include a provision that the loan is immediately due and payable upon transfer of the property securing such loan to any transferee unless the acceptability of the assumption of the loan is established pursuant to such section 3714.

(f) A loan for the purchase or construction of new residential property, the construction of which began after the energy efficiency standards under section 109 of the Cranston-Gonzalez National Affordable Housing Act (42 U.S.C. 12709), as amended by section 101(c) of the Energy Policy Act of 1992, take effect, may not be financed through the assistance of this chapter unless the new residential property is constructed in compliance with such standards.

(Sept. 2, 1958, P. L. 85-857, § 1, 72 Stat. 1206; June 30, 1959, P. L. 86-73, § 3, 73 Stat. 156; July 14, 1960, P. L. 86-665, § 5, 74 Stat. 532; Aug. 10, 1965, P. L. 89-117, Title II, § 217(b), 79 Stat. 473; May 25, 1967, P. L. 90-19, § 25(2), 81 Stat. 28; Oct. 23, 1970, P. L. 91-506, § 2(d), 84 Stat. 1108; Dec. 31, 1974, P. L. 93-569, § 2(d), (e), 88 Stat. 1863; June 30, 1976, P. L. 94-324, § 7(7), (8), 90 Stat. 721; Oct. 12, 1982, P. L. 97-295, § 4(64), 96 Stat. 1309; Dec. 21, 1987, P. L. 100-198, §§ 8(a)(1), 10(b); 101 Stat. 1319, 1323; May 20, 1988, P. L. 100-322, Title IV, Part B, § 415(c)(3), 102 Stat. 551; Dec. 18, 1989, P. L. 101-237, Title III, § 313(b)(1), 103 Stat. 2077; Aug. 6, 1991, P. L. 102-83, § 5(a), (c)(1), 105 Stat. 406; Oct. 24, 1992, P. L. 102-486, Title I, Subtitle A, § 101(c)(2), 106 Stat. 2787; Nov. 2, 1994, P. L. 103-446, Title IX, § 903, 108 Stat. 4676.)

HISTORY; ANCILLARY LAWS AND DIRECTIVES

References in text:
"The National Housing Act", referred to in subsecs. (b) and (d), is Act June 27, 1934, ch 847, 48 Stat. 1246, as amended, which is generally classified to 12 USCS §§ 1701 et seq. For full classification of this Act, consult USCS Tables volumes.

Amendments:
1959. Act June 30, 1959, in subsec. (b), inserted "The Administrator may also refuse to appraise any dwelling or housing project owned, sponsored, or to be constructed by any person refused the benefits of participation under the National Housing Act pursuant to a determination of the Federal Housing Commissioner under section 512 of that Act."; and in subsec. (d), inserted "The Administrator may also refuse either temporarily or permanently to guarantee or insure any loans made by a lender or holder refused the benefits of participation under the National Housing Act pursuant to a determination of the Federal Housing Commissioner under section 512 of that Act.".

1960. Act July 14, 1960, in subsec. (c), inserted "Notwithstanding the foregoing requirements of this subsection, the provisions for certification by the veteran at the time he applies for the loan and at the time the loan is closed shall be considered to be satisfied if the Administrator finds that (1) in the case of a loan for repair, alteration, or improvement the veteran in fact did occupy the property at such times, or (2) in the case of a loan for construction or purchase the veteran intended to occupy the property as his home at such times and he did in fact so occupy it when, or within a reasonable time after, the loan was closed.".

1965. Act Aug. 10, 1965, added subsec. (e).

1967. Act May 25, 1967, in subsecs. (b), (d) and (e), substituted "Secretary of Housing and Urban Development" for "Federal Housing Commissioner".

1970. Act Oct. 23, 1970, in subsec. (b), substituted "Subject to notice and opportunity for a hearing, the" for "The"; and in subsec. (d), substituted "Subject to notice and opportunity for a hearing, whenever" for "Whenever".

1974. Act Dec. 31, 1974 (effective 12/31/74, as provided by § 10 of such Act, which appears as 38 USCS § 3702 note), in subsec. (b), deleted "under section 512 of that Act" following "Urban Development"; in subsec. (c), inserted "Notwithstanding the foregoing provisions of this subsection, in the case of a loan automatically guaranteed under this chapter, the veteran shall be required to make the certification only at the time the loan is closed."; and in subsec. (d), deleted "under section 512 of that Act" following "Urban Development".

1976. Act June 30, 1976 (effective 6/30/76, as provided by § 9(a) of such Act, which appears as 38 USCS § 3701 note), in subsec. (c), substituted "the veteran" for "he" preceding "applies" wherever appearing and preceding "intends", "occupies", and "did in fact", and substituted "the veteran's" for "his" wherever appearing; and in subsec. (d), substituted "the Administrator" for "he" preceding "may refuse".

1982. Act Oct. 12, 1982, in subsec. (e), inserted "(12 U.S.C. 1749aa et seq.)", and substituted "August 10, 1965" for "the date of the enactment of the Housing and Urban Development Act of 1965".

1987. Act Dec. 21, 1987 (applicable as provided by § 8(c) of such Act, which appears as a note to this section), in subsec. (c), substituted "(1) Except as provided in paragraph (2) of this subsection, no" for "No", substituted "Except as provided in paragraph (2) of this subsection, no loan" for "No loan", and added para. (2).

Such Act further added subsec. (f).

1988. Act May 20, 1988, in subsec. (c)(2), in subparas. (C) and (D), substituted "section 1812" for "section 1819"; and in subsec. (f), substituted "section 1814" for "1817A" wherever appearing.

1989. Act Dec. 18, 1989, in subsec. (a), substituted "Secretary" for "Administrator"; and in subsecs. (b), (c)(1), and (d), substituted "Secretary" for "Administrator", wherever appearing.

1991. Act Aug. 6, 1991, redesignated this section, formerly 38 USCS § 1804, as 38 USCS § 3704, and amended the references in this section to reflect the redesignations made by § 5(a) of such Act (see Table III preceding 38 USCS § 101).

1992. Act Oct. 24, 1992, added subsec. (g).

1994. Act Nov. 2, 1994, deleted subsec. (e), which read: "(e) No loan for the purchase or construction of new residential property (other than property served by a water and sewerage system approved by the Secretary of Housing and Urban Development pursuant to title X of the National Housing Act (12 U.S.C. 1749aa et seq.)) shall be financed through the assistance of this chapter, except pursuant to a commitment made prior to August 10, 1965, if such property is not served by a public or adequate community water and sewerage system and is located in an area where the appropriate local officials certify that the establishment of such systems is economically feasible. For purposes of this subsection, the economic feasibility of establishing public or adequate community water and sewerage systems shall be determined without regard to whether such establishment is authorized by law or is subject to approval by one or more local governments or public bodies."; and redesignated subsecs. (f) and (g) as subsecs. (e) and (f), respectively.

Other provisions:

Application and construction of the Oct. 12, 1982 amendment of this section. For provisions as to the application and construction of the Oct.

12, 1982 amendment of this section, see § 5 of such Act, which appears as 10 USCS § 101 note.

Application of amendments made by Act Dec. 21, 1987. Act Dec. 21, 1987, P. L. 100-198, § 8(c), 101 Stat. 1320, provides: "The amendments made by this section [amending subsec. (c) of this section and 38 USCS §§ 3710(a) and 3719(a)(5) and (e)(5)] shall apply with respect to loans made more than 30 days after the date of the enactment of this Act.".

CODE OF FEDERAL REGULATIONS

Department of Veterans Affairs—Loan guaranty, 38 CFR Part 36.

CROSS REFERENCES

This section is referred to in 38 USCS §§ 3706, 3710, 3711, 3712, 3762.

RESEARCH GUIDE

Federal Procedure L Ed:
4A Fed Proc L Ed, Banking and Financing §§ 8:1409, 1415, 1429, 1433.

Am Jur:
77 Am Jur 2d, Veterans and Veterans' Laws §§ 119, 121.

INTERPRETIVE NOTES AND DECISIONS

Regulations issued by Administrator [now Secretary] within his authority have force and effect of law. Gowanda Co-op. Sav. & Loan Asso. v Gray (1950, CA2 NY) 183 F2d 367.

In implementing 38 USCS § 1804(d) [now 38 USCS § 3704(d)], VA Pamphlet 26-7, Department of Veterans' Benefits [now Department of Veterans Affairs] Circular and internal VA manuals do not require that Veterans' Administration [now Department] and private lenders must take all reasonable measures to avoid foreclosure. Rank v Cleland (1978, CD Cal) 460 F Supp 920, revd on other grounds (1982, CA9 Cal) 677 F2d 692, cert den (1982) 459 US 907, 74 L Ed 2d 168, 103 S Ct 210.

§ 3705. Warranties

(a) The Secretary shall require that in connection with any property upon which there is located a dwelling designed principally for not more than a four-family residence and which is appraised for guaranty or insurance before the beginning of construction, the seller or builder, and such other person as may be required by the Secretary to become warrantor, shall deliver to the purchaser or owner of such property a warranty that the dwelling is constructed in substantial conformity with the plans and specifications (including any amendments thereof, or changes and variations therein, which have been approved in writing by the Secretary) on which the Secretary based the Secretary's valuation of the dwelling. The Secretary shall deliver to the builder, seller, or other warrantor the Secretary's written approval (which shall be conclusive evidence of such appraisal) of any amendment of, or change or variation in, such plans and specifications which the Secretary deems to be a substantial amendment thereof, or change or variation therein, and shall file a copy of such written approval with such plans and specifications. Such warranty shall apply only with respect to such instances of substantial nonconformity to such approved plans and specifications (including any amendments thereof, or changes or variations therein, which have been approved in writing, as provided in this section, by the Secretary) as to which the purchaser or home owner has section, by the

Secretary) as to which the purchaser or home owner has given written notice to the warrantor within one year from the date of conveyance of title to, or initial occupancy of, the dwelling, whichever first occurs. Such warranty shall be in addition to, and not in derogation of, all other rights and privileges which such purchaser or owner may have under any other law or instrument. The provisions of this section shall apply to any such property covered by a mortgage insured or guaranteed by the Secretary on and after October 1, 1954, unless such mortgage is insured or guaranteed pursuant to a commitment therefor made before October 1, 1954.

(b) The Secretary shall permit copies of the plans and specifications (including written approvals of any amendments thereof, or changes or variations therein, as provided in this section) for dwellings in connection with which warranties are required by subsection (a) of this section to be made available in their appropriate local offices for inspection or for copying by any purchaser, home owner, or warrantor during such hours or periods of time as the Secretary may determine to be reasonable.

(Sept. 2, 1958, P. L. 85-857, § 1, 72 Stat. 1206; June 30, 1976, P. L. 94-324, § 7(9), 90 Stat. 721; Dec. 18, 1989, P. L. 101-237, Title III, § 313(b)(1), 103 Stat. 2077; June 13, 1991, P. L. 102-54, § 15(a)(1), 105 Stat. 288; Aug. 6, 1991, P. L. 102-83, § 5(a), 105 Stat. 406; Nov. 2, 1994, P. L. 103-446, Title XII, § 1202(a)(2), 108 Stat. 4689.)

HISTORY; ANCILLARY LAWS AND DIRECTIVES

Amendments:

1976. Act June 30, 1976 (effective 6/30/76, as provided by § 9(a) of such Act, which appears as 38 USCS § 3701 note), in subsec. (a), substituted "the Administrator's" for "his" wherever appearing.

1989. Act Dec. 18, 1989, substituted "Secretary" and "Secretary's" for "Administrator" and "Administrator's", respectively, wherever appearing, in the entire section.

1991. Act June 13, 1991, as amended by Act Nov. 2, 1994 (effective as of 6/13/91, and as if included in the enactment of Public Law 102-54, as provided by § 1202(a) of such Act), in subsec. (a), substituted "appraised" for "approved" and "appraisal)" for "approval)".

Act Aug. 6, 1991, redesignated this section, formerly 38 USCS § 1705, as 38 USCS § 3705.

1994. Act Nov. 2, 1994 amended the directory language of Act June 13, 1991, P. L. 102-54, without affecting the text of this section

Other provisions:

Effective date and application of amendments made by Act Nov. 2, 1994. Act Nov. 2, 1994, P. L. 103-446, Title XII, § 1202(a), 108 Stat. 4689, provides that the amendments made by such section [amending §§ 13(e) and 15(a)(1)(A) of Public Law, 102-54, which are classified to 15 USCS § 644 and this section, respectively] shall be effective as of June 13, 1991, and as if included in the enactment of Public Law 102-54.

RESEARCH GUIDE
Am Jur:
77 Am Jur 2d, Veterans and Veterans' Laws § 122.

INTERPRETIVE NOTES AND DECISIONS

Indictment charging that defendants for purpose of inducing Administrator to insure dwelling made false statement warranting that dwelling had been constructed "in substantial conformity with the plans and specifications therefor" was not invalid on ground of vagueness as to warranty. United States v Wender (1958, DC NY) 158 F Supp 496.

§ 3706. Escrow of deposits and downpayments

(a) Any deposit or downpayment made by an eligible veteran in connection with the purchase of proposed or newly constructed and previously unoccupied residential property in a project on which the Secretary has issued a Certificate of Reasonable Value, which purchase is to be financed with a loan guaranteed, insured, or made under the provisions of this chapter [38 USCS §§ 3701 et seq.], shall be deposited forthwith by the seller, or the agent of the seller, receiving such deposit or payment, in a trust account to safeguard such deposit or payment from the claims of creditors of the seller. The failure of the seller or the seller's agent to create such trust account and to maintain it until the deposit or payment has been disbursed for the benefit of the veteran purchaser at settlement or, if the transaction does not materialize, is otherwise disposed of in accordance with the terms of the contract, may constitute an unfair marketing practice within the meaning of section 3704(b) of this title.

(b) If an eligible veteran contracts for the construction of a property in a project on which the Secretary has issued a Certificate of Reasonable Value and such construction is to be financed with the assistance of a construction loan to be guaranteed, insured, or made under the provisions of this chapter [38 USCS §§ 3701 et seq.], it may be considered an unfair marketing practice under section 3704(b) of this title if any deposit or downpayment of the veteran is not maintained in a special trust account by the recipient until it is either (1) applied on behalf of the veteran to the cost of the land or to the cost of construction or (2), if the transaction does not materialize, is otherwise disposed of in accordance with the terms of the contract.

(Added July 14, 1960, P. L. 86-665, § 6(a), 74 Stat. 532; June 30, 1976, P. L. 94-324, § 7(10), 90 Stat. 721; Dec. 18, 1989, P. L. 101-237, Title III, § 313(b)(1), 103 Stat. 2077; Aug. 6, 1991, P. L. 102-83, § 5(a), (c)(1), 105 Stat. 406; Nov. 2, 1994, P. L. 103-446, Title XII, § 1201(e)(13), 108 Stat. 4685.)

HISTORY; ANCILLARY LAWS AND DIRECTIVES
Amendments:
1976. Act June 30, 1976 (effective 6/30/76, as provided by § 9(a) of such Act, which appears as 38 USCS § 3701 note), in subsec. (a), substituted "the seller's" for "his".

1989. Act Dec. 18, 1989, in subsecs. (a) and (b), substituted "Secretary" for "Administrator".

1991. Act Aug. 6, 1991, redesignated this section, formerly 38 USCS

§ 1806, as 38 USCS § 3706, and amended the references in this section to reflect the redesignations made by § 5(a) of such Act (see Table III preceding 38 USCS § 101).

1994. Act Nov. 2, 1994 purported to substitute "of this title" for "of this chapter" in the second and third places in which such phrase appeared; however, the amendment was executed in the second and fourth places in which the phrase appeared in order to effectuate the intent of Congress.

RESEARCH GUIDE
Am Jur:
77 Am Jur 2d, Veterans and Veterans' Laws § 121.

§ 3707. Adjustable rate mortgages

(a) The Secretary shall carry out a demonstration project under this section during fiscal years 1993, 1994, and 1995 for the purpose of guaranteeing loans in a manner similar to the manner in which the Secretary of Housing and Urban Development insures adjustable rate mortgages under section 251 of the National Housing Act [12 USCS § 1715z-16].

(b) Interest rate adjustment provisions of a mortgage guaranteed under this section shall—

(1) correspond to a specified national interest rate index approved by the Secretary, information on which is readily accessible to mortgagors from generally available published sources;

(2) be made by adjusting the monthly payment on an annual basis;

(3) be limited, with respect to any single annual interest rate adjustment, to a maximum increase or decrease of 1 percentage point; and

(4) be limited, over the term of the mortgage, to a maximum increase of 5 percentage points above the initial contract interest rate.

(c) The Secretary shall promulgate underwriting standards for loans guaranteed under this section, taking into account—

(1) the status of the interest rate index referred to in subsection (b)(1) and available at the time an underwriting decision is made, regardless of the actual initial rate offered by the lender;

(2) the maximum and likely amounts of increases in mortgage payments that the loans would require;

(3) the underwriting standards applicable to adjustable rate mortgages insured under title II of the National Housing Act; and

(4) such other factors as the Secretary finds appropriate.

(d) The Secretary shall require that the mortgagee make available to the mortgagor, at the time of loan application, a written explanation of the features of the adjustable rate mortgage, including a hypothetical payment schedule that displays the maximum potential increases in monthly payments to the mortgagor over the first five years of the mortgage term.

(Added Oct. 28, 1992, P. L. 102-547, § 3(a)(1), 106 Stat. 3634; Aug. 13, 1993, P. L. 103-78, § 7, 107 Stat. 769.)

Readjustment Benefits 38 USCS § 3708

HISTORY; ANCILLARY LAWS AND DIRECTIVES

References in text:
"Title II of the National Housing Act", referred to in this section, is Title II of Act June 27, 1934, ch 847, 48 Stat. 1247, which appears generally as 12 USCS § 1707 et seq. For full classification of such Title, consult USCS Tables volumes.

Explanatory notes:
A prior § [3707] 1807 (Act June 30, 1976, P. L. 94-324, § 2(a), 90 Stat. 720; Nov. 3, 1981, P. L. 97-72, Title III, § 303(d), 95 Stat. 1060) was repealed by Act May 20, 1988, P. L. 100-322, Title IV, Part B, § 415(a)(4), 102 Stat. 550. Such section provided for service after July 25, 1947, and prior to June 27, 1950. (The bracketed section number "3707" was inserted to preserve numerical continuity following general renumbering of Title 38, USCS, by Act Aug. 6, 1991, P. L. 102-83, § 5(a), 105 Stat. 406.)

Amendments:
1993. Act Aug. 13, 1993, in subsec. (b)(2), deleted "on the anniversary of the date on which the loan was closed" following "annual basis".

Other provisions:
Repeal of provision relating to report concerning mortgage loans. Act Oct. 28, 1992, P. L. 102-547, § 3(b), 106 Stat. 3635, which formerly appeared as a note to this section, was repealed by Act Feb. 13, 1996, P. L. 104-110, Title II, § 201(b), 110 Stat. 770. Such note related to a report to the Committees on Veterans' Affairs of the Senate and House of Representatives by the Secretary of Veterans Affairs dealing with veterans receiving mortgage loans guaranteed by the Secretary.

CODE OF FEDERAL REGULATIONS
Department of Veterans Affairs—Loan guaranty, 38 CFR Part 36.

RESEARCH GUIDE
Am Jur:
77 Am Jur 2d, Veterans and Veterans' Laws § 121.

§ 3708. Authority to buy down interest rates: pilot program

(a) In order to enable the purchase of housing in areas where the supply of suitable military housing is inadequate, the Secretary may conduct a pilot program under which the Secretary may make periodic or lump sum assistance payments on behalf of an eligible veteran for the purpose of buying down the interest rate on a loan to that veteran that is guaranteed under this chapter [38 USCS §§ 3701 et seq.] for a purpose described in paragraph (1), (6), or (10) of section 3710(a) of this title.

(b) An individual is an eligible veteran for the purposes of this section if—

(1) the individual is a veteran, as defined in section 3701(b)(4) of this title;

(2) the individual submits an application for a loan guaranteed under this chapter [38 USCS §§ 3701 et seq.] within one year of an assignment of the individual to duty at a military installation in the United States designated by the Secretary of Defense as a housing shortage area;

(3) at the time the loan referred to in subsection (a) is made, the individual is an enlisted member, warrant officer, or an officer (other than a warrant officer) at a pay grade of O-3 or below;

(4) the individual has not previously used any of the individual's entitlement to housing loan benefits under this chapter [38 USCS §§ 3701 et seq.]; and

(5) the individual receives comprehensive prepurchase counseling from the Secretary (or the designee of the Secretary) before making application for a loan guaranteed under this chapter [38 USCS §§ 3701 et seq.].

(c) Loans with respect to which the Secretary may exercise the buy down authority under subsection (a) shall—

(1) provide for a buy down period of not more than three years in duration;

(2) specify the maximum and likely amounts of increases in mortgage payments that the loans would require; and

(3) be subject to such other terms and conditions as the Secretary may prescribe by regulation.

(d) The Secretary shall promulgate underwriting standards for loans for which the interest rate assistance payments may be made under subsection (a). Such standards shall be based on the interest rate for the second year of the loan.

(e) The Secretary or lender shall provide comprehensive prepurchase counseling to eligible veterans explaining the features of interest rate buy downs under subsection (a), including a hypothetical payment schedule that displays the increases in monthly payments to the mortgagor over the first five years of the mortgage term. For the purposes of this subsection, the Secretary may assign personnel to military installations referred to in subsection (b)(2).

(f) There is authorized to be appropriated $3,000,000 annually to carry out this section.

(g) The Secretary may not guarantee a loan under this chapter [38 USCS §§ 3701 et seq.] after September 30, 1998, on which the Secretary is obligated to make payments under this section.

(Added Feb. 10, 1996, P. L. 104-106, Div B, Title XXVIII, Subtitle B, § 2822(b)(1), 110 Stat. 556.)

HISTORY; ANCILLARY LAWS AND DIRECTIVES

Other provisions:
Authority of Secretary of Defense. Act Feb. 10, 1996, P. L. 104-106, Div B, Title XXVIII, Subtitle B, § 2822(c), 110 Stat. 557, provides:

"(1) Reimbursement for buy down costs. The Secretary of Defense shall reimburse the Secretary of Veterans Affairs for amounts paid by the Secretary of Veterans Affairs to mortgagees under section 3708 of title 38, United States Code, as added by subsection (b).

"(2) Designation of housing shortage areas. For purposes of section 3708 of title 38, United States Code, the Secretary of Defense may designate as a housing shortage area a military installation in the United States at which the Secretary determines there is a shortage of suitable housing to meet the military family needs of members of the Armed Forces and the dependents of such members.

"(3) Report. Not later than March 30, 1998, the Secretary shall submit to Congress a report regarding the effectiveness of the authority provided in section 3708 of title 38, United States Code, in ensuring that members of the Armed Forces and their dependents have access to suitable housing. The report shall include the recommendations of the Secretary regarding whether the authority provided in this subsection should be extended beyond the date specified in paragraph (5).

"(4) Earmark. Of the amount provided in section 2405(a)(11)(B) [unclassified], $10,000,000 for fiscal year 1996 shall be available to carry out this subsection.

"(5) Sunset. This subsection shall not apply with respect to housing loans guaranteed after September 30, 1998, for which assistance payments are paid under section 3708 of title 38, United States Code.".

RESEARCH GUIDE
Am Jur:
77 Am Jur 2d, Veterans and Veterans' Laws § 121.

SUBCHAPTER II. LOANS

§ 3710. Purchase or construction of homes

(a) Except as provided in section 3704(c)(2) of this title, any loan to a veteran, if made pursuant to the provisions of this chapter [38 USCS §§ 3701 et seq.], is automatically guaranteed if such loan is for one or more of the following purposes:

(1) To purchase or construct a dwelling to be owned and occupied by the veteran as a home.

(2) To purchase a farm on which there is a farm residence to be owned and occupied by the veteran as the veteran's home.

(3) To construct on land owned by the veteran a farm residence to be occupied by the veteran as the veteran's home.

(4) To repair, alter, or improve a farm residence or other dwelling owned by the veteran and occupied by the veteran as the veteran's home.

(5) To refinance existing mortgage loans or other liens which are secured of record on a dwelling or farm residence owned and occupied by the veteran as the veteran's home.

(6) To purchase a one-family residential unit in a condominium housing development or project, if such development or project is approved by the Secretary under criteria which the Secretary shall prescribe in regulations.

(7) To improve a dwelling or farm residence owned by the veteran and occupied by the veteran as the veteran's home through energy efficiency improvements, as provided in subsection (d).

(8) To refinance in accordance with subsection (e) of this section an existing loan guaranteed, insured, or made under this chapter [38 USCS §§ 3701 et seq.].

(9)(A)(i) To purchase a manufactured home to be permanently affixed to a lot that is owned by the veteran.

(ii) To purchase a manufactured home and a lot to which the home will be permanently affixed.

(B)(i) To refinance, in accordance with the terms and conditions applicable under the provisions of subsection (e) of this section (other than paragraph (1)(E) of such subsection) to the guaranty of a loan for the purpose specified in clause (8) of this subsection, an existing loan guaranteed, insured, or made under this chapter [38 USCS §§ 3701 et seq.] that is secured by a manufactured home permanently affixed to a lot that is owned by the veteran.

(ii) To refinance, in accordance with section 3712(a)(5) of this title, an existing loan that was made for the purchase of, and that is secured by, a manufactured home that is permanently affixed to a lot and to purchase the lot to which the manufactured home is affixed.

(10) To purchase a dwelling to be owned and occupied by the veteran as a home and make energy efficiency improvements, as provided in subsection (d).

(11) To refinance in accordance with subsection (e) an existing loan guaranteed, insured, or made under this chapter [38 USCS §§ 3701 et seq.], and to improve the dwelling securing such loan through energy efficiency improvements, as provided in subsection (d).

If there is an indebtedness which is secured by a lien against land owned by the veteran, the proceeds of a loan guaranteed under this section or made under section 3711 of this title for construction of a dwelling or farm residence on such land may be used also to liquidate such lien, but only if the reasonable value of the land is equal to or greater than the amount of the lien.

(b) No loan may be guaranteed under this section or made under section 3711 of this title unless—

(1) the proceeds of such loan will be used to pay for the property purchased, constructed, or improved;

(2) the contemplated terms of payment required in any mortgage to be given in part payment of the purchase price or the construction cost bear a proper relation to the veteran's present and anticipated income and expenses;

(3) the veteran is a satisfactory credit risk, as determined in accordance with the credit underwriting standards established pursuant to subsection (g) of this section;

(4) the nature and condition of the property is such as to be suitable for dwelling purposes;

(5) except in the case of a loan described in clause (7) or (8) of this subsection, the loan to be paid by the veteran for such property or for the cost of construction, repairs, or alterations, does not exceed the reasonable value thereof as determined pursuant to section 3731 of this title; and,

(6) if the loan is for repair, alteration, or improvement of property, such repair, alteration, or improvement substantially protects or improves the basic livability or utility of such property;

(7) in the case of a loan (other than a loan made for a purpose specified in subsection (a)(8) of this section) that is made to refinance—

(A) a construction loan,

(B) an installment land sales contract, or

(C) a loan assumed by the veteran that provides for a lower interest rate than the loan being refinanced,

the amount of the loan to be guaranteed or made does not exceed the lesser of—

> (i) the reasonable value of the dwelling or farm residence securing the loan, as determined pursuant to section 3731 of this title; or
>
> (ii) the sum of the outstanding balance on the loan to be refinanced and the closing costs (including discounts) actually paid by the veteran, as specified by the Secretary in regulations; and

(8) in the case of a loan to refinance a loan (other than a loan or installment sales contract described in clause (7) of this subsection or a loan made for a purpose specified in subsection (a)(8) of this section), the amount of the loan to be guaranteed or made does not exceed 90 percent of the reasonable value of the dwelling or farm residence securing the loan, as determined pursuant to section 3731 of this title.

(c) [Repealed]

(d)(1) The Secretary shall carry out a program to demonstrate the feasibility of guaranteeing loans for the acquisition of an existing dwelling and the cost of making energy efficiency improvements to the dwelling or for energy efficiency improvements to a dwelling owned and occupied by a veteran. A loan may be guaranteed under this subsection only if it meets the requirements of this chapter [38 USCS §§ 3701 et seq.], except as those requirements are modified by this subsection.

(2) The cost of energy efficiency measures that may be financed by a loan guaranteed under this section may not exceed the greater of—

(A) the cost of the energy efficiency improvements, up to $3,000; or

(B) $6,000, if the increase in the monthly payment for principal and interest does not exceed the likely reduction in monthly utility costs resulting from the energy efficiency improvements.

(3) Notwithstanding the provisions of section 3703(a)(1)(A) of this title, any loan guaranteed under this subsection shall be guaranteed in an amount equal to the sum of—

(A) the guaranty that would be provided under those provisions for the dwelling without the energy efficiency improvements; and

(B) an amount that bears the same relation to the cost of the energy efficiency improvements as the guaranty referred to in subparagraph (A) bears to the amount of the loan minus the cost of such improvements.

(4) The amount of the veteran's entitlement, calculated in accordance with section 3703(a)(1)(B) of this title, shall not be affected by the amount of the guaranty referred to in paragraph (3)(B).

(5) The Secretary shall take appropriate actions to notify eligible veterans, participating lenders, and interested realtors of the availability of loan guarantees under this subsection and the procedures and requirements that apply to the obtaining of such guarantees.

(6) For the purposes of this subsection:

(A) The term "energy efficiency improvement" includes a solar heating system, a solar heating and cooling system, or a combined solar heating and cooling system, and the application of a residential energy conservation measure.

(B) The term "solar heating" has the meaning given such term in section 3(1) of the Solar Heating and Cooling Demonstration Act of 1974 (42 U.S.C. 5502(1)) and, in addition, includes a passive system based on conductive, convective, or radiant energy transfer.

(C) The terms "solar heating and cooling" and "combined solar heating and cooling" have the meaning given such terms in section 3(2) of the Solar Heating and Cooling Demonstration Act of 1974 (42 U.S.C. 5502(2)) and, in addition, include a passive system based on conductive, convective, or radiant energy transfer.

(D) The term "passive system" includes window and skylight glazing, thermal floors, walls, and roofs, movable insulation panels (when in conjunction with glazing), portions of a residential structure that serve as solar furnaces so as to add heat to the structure, double-pane window insulation, and such other energy-related components as are determined by the Secretary to enhance the natural transfer of energy for the purpose of heating or heating and cooling a residence.

(E) The term "residential energy conservation measure" means—

(i) caulking and weatherstripping of all exterior doors and windows;

(ii) furnace efficiency modifications limited to—

(I) replacement burners, boilers, or furnaces designed to reduce the firing rate or to achieve a reduction in the amount of fuel consumed as a result of increased combustion efficiency,

(II) devices for modifying flue openings which will increase the efficiency of the heating system, and

(III) electrical or mechanical furnace ignition systems which replace standing gas pilot lights;

(iii) clock thermostats;

(iv) ceiling, attic, wall, and floor insulation;

(v) water heater insulation;

(vi) storm windows and doors;

(vii) heat pumps; and

(viii) such other energy conservation measures as the Secretary may identify for the purposes of this subparagraph.

(e)(1) For a loan to be guaranteed for the purpose specified in subsection (a)(8) or for the purpose specified in subsection (a)(11) of this section—

(A) the interest rate of the loan must be less than the interest rate of the loan being refinanced or, in a case in which the loan is a fixed rate loan and the loan being refinanced is an adjustable rate loan, the loan bears interest at a rate that is agreed upon by the veteran and the mortgagee;

(B) the loan must be secured by the same dwelling or farm residence as was the loan being refinanced;

(C) the amount of the loan may not exceed—
   (i) an amount equal to the sum of the balance of the loan being refinanced and such closing costs (including any discount permitted pursuant to section 3703(c)(3)(A) of this title) as may be authorized by the Secretary (under regulations which the Secretary shall prescribe) to be included in the loan; or
   (ii) in the case of a loan for the purpose specified in subsection (a)(11), an amount equal to the sum of the amount referred to with respect to the loan under clause (i) and the amount specified under subsection (d)(2);
(D) notwithstanding section 3703(a)(1) of this title, the amount of the guaranty of the loan may not exceed the greater of (i) the original guaranty amount of the loan being refinanced, or (ii) 25 percent of the loan;
(E) the term of the loan may not exceed the original term of the loan being refinanced by more than 10 years; and
(F) the veteran must own the dwelling or farm residence securing the loan and—
   (i) must occupy such dwelling or residence as such veteran's home;
   (ii) must have previously occupied such dwelling or residence as such veteran's home and must certify, in such form as the Secretary shall require, that the veteran has previously so occupied such dwelling or residence; or
   (iii) in any case in which a veteran is in active duty status as a member of the Armed Forces and is unable to occupy such residence or dwelling as a home because of such status, the spouse of the veteran must occupy, or must have previously occupied, such dwelling or residence as such spouse's home and must certify such occupancy in such form as the Secretary shall require.
(2) A loan to a veteran may be guaranteed by the Secretary under this chapter [38 USCS §§ 3701 et seq.] for the purpose specified in clause (8) of subsection (a) of this section without regard to the amount of outstanding guaranty entitlement available for use by such veteran, and the amount of such veteran's guaranty entitlement shall not be charged as a result of any guaranty provided for such purpose. For purposes of section 3702(b) of this title, such loan shall be deemed to have been obtained with the guaranty entitlement used to obtain the loan being refinanced.
(3) If a veteran is deceased and if such veteran's surviving spouse was a co-obligor under an existing loan guaranteed, insured, or made under this chapter [38 USCS §§ 3701 et seq.], such surviving spouse shall, only for the purpose specified in subsection (a)(8) of this section, be deemed to be a veteran eligible for benefits under this chapter [38 USCS §§ 3701 et seq.].

(f)(1) For a loan to be guaranteed for the purpose specified in subclause (A)(ii) or (B)(ii) of subsection (a)(9) of this section, the purchase of (or the refinancing of a loan secured by) the manufactured home and the lot for that home shall be considered as one loan and must comply with such criteria as may be prescribed by the Secretary in regulations.

(2) A loan may not be guaranteed for the purposes of subsection (a)(9) of this section unless the manufactured home purchased, upon being permanently affixed to the lot, is considered to be real property under the laws of the State where the lot is located.

(g)(1) For the purposes of this subsection, the term "veteran", when used with respect to a loan guaranteed or to be guaranteed under this chapter [38 USCS §§ 3701 et seq.], includes the veteran's spouse if the spouse is jointly liable with the veteran under the loan.

(2) For the purpose of determining whether a veteran meets the standards referred to in subsection (b)(3) of this section and section 3712(e)(2) of this title, the Secretary shall prescribe regulations which establish—

(A) credit underwriting standards to be used in evaluating loans to be guaranteed under this chapter [38 USCS §§ 3701 et seq.]; and

(B) standards to be used by lenders in obtaining credit information and processing loans to be guaranteed under this chapter [38 USCS §§ 3701 et seq.].

(3) In the regulations prescribed under paragraph (2) of this subsection, the Secretary shall establish standards that include—

(A) debt-to-income ratios to apply in the case of the veteran applying for the loan;

(B) criteria for evaluating the reliability and stability of the income of the veteran applying for the loan; and

(C) procedures for ascertaining the monthly income required by the veteran to meet the anticipated loan payment terms.

If the procedures described in clause (C) of this paragraph include standards for evaluating residual income, the Secretary shall, in establishing such standards, give appropriate consideration to State statistics (in States as to which the Secretary determines that such statistics are reliable) pertinent to residual income and the cost of living in the State in question rather than in a larger region.

(4)(A) Any lender making a loan under this chapter [38 USCS §§ 3701 et seq.] shall certify, in such form as the Secretary shall prescribe, that the lender has complied with the credit information and loan processing standards established under paragraph (2)(B) of this subsection, and that, to the best of the lender's knowledge and belief, the loan meets the underwriting standards established under paragraph (2)(A) of this subsection.

(B) Any lender who knowingly and willfully makes a false certification under subparagraph (A) of this paragraph shall be liable to the United States Government for a civil penalty equal to two times the amount of the Secretary's loss on the loan involved or to another appropriate amount, not to exceed $10,000, whichever is greater. All determinations necessary to carry out this subparagraph shall be made by the Secretary.

(5) Pursuant to regulations prescribed to carry out this paragraph, the Secretary may, in extraordinary situations, waive the application of the credit underwriting standards established under paragraph (2) of this subsection

when the Secretary determines, considering the totality of circumstances, that the veteran is a satisfactory credit risk.
(Sept. 2, 1958, P. L. 85-857, § 1, 72 Stat. 1207; May 7, 1968, P. L. 90-301, §§ 1(a), 2(a), 82 Stat. 113; Oct. 23, 1970, P. L. 91-506, § 3, 84 Stat. 1108; Dec. 31, 1974, P. L. 93-569, § 3, 88 Stat. 1864; June 30, 1976, P. L. 94-324, § 7(11), 90 Stat. 721; Oct. 18, 1978, P. L. 95-476, Title I, §§ 104, 105(a), 92 Stat. 1498; Oct. 7, 1980, P. L. 96-385, Title IV, §§ 401(a), 402(a), 94 Stat. 1532; March 2, 1984, P. L. 98-223, Title II, § 205(a), 98 Stat. 42; Oct. 28, 1986, P. L. 99-576, Title IV, Part A, § 402(a), (b), 100 Stat. 3280; Dec. 21, 1987, P.L. 100-198, §§ 3(a)(2), 7(a), (c), 8(a)(2), 11 [(c)](b), 13, 101 Stat. 1315, 1318–1320, 1325; May 20, 1988, P. L. 100-322, Title IV, Part B, § 415(c)(4), 102 Stat. 551; Dec. 18, 1989, P. L. 101-237, Title III, §§ 309, 313(b)(1), 103 Stat. 2075, 2077; Aug. 6, 1991, P. L. 102-83, §§ 4(a)(2)(A)(iv), 5(a), (c)(1), 105 Stat. 403, 406; Oct. 28, 1992, P. L. 102-547, §§ 6(1), 9(a), (b), 106 Stat. 3636, 3641; Nov. 2, 1994, P. L. 103-446, Title IX, §§ 904(a), (b), 905, 108 Stat. 4676, 4677; Feb. 13, 1996, P. L. 104-110, Title I, § 101(e), 110 Stat. 768.)

HISTORY; ANCILLARY LAWS AND DIRECTIVES
Amendments:
1968. Act May 7, 1968, in subsec. (b), substituted new para. (5) for one which read: "the price paid or to be paid by the veteran for such property, or for the cost of construction, repairs, or alterations, does not exceed the reasonable value thereof as determined by the Administrator; and''; and added the concluding matter; and in subsec. (c), substituted "$12,500" for "$7,500".
1970. Act Oct. 23, 1970, added subsecs. (a)(5) and (d).
1974. Act Dec. 31, 1974, § 3(1), (3) (effective 12/31/74, as provided by § 10 of such Act, which appears as 38 USCS § 3702 note), in subsec. (a)(5), deleted "Nothing is this chapter shall preclude a veteran from paying to a lender any discount required by such lender in connection with such refinancing." following "as his home."; and in subsec. (c), substituted "$17,500" for "$12,500".
Act Dec. 31, 1974, § 3(2), (4) (effective 90 days after Dec. 31, 1974, as provided by § 10 of such Act, which appears as 38 USCS § 3702 note), added subsec. (a)(6) and deleted subsec. (d) which read: "(d) Nothing in this chapter shall be deemed to preclude the guaranty of a loan to an eligible veteran to purchase a one-family residential unit to be owned and occupied by him as a home in a condominium housing development or project as to which the Secretary of Housing and Urban Development has issued, under section 234 of the National Housing Act, as amended (12 U.S.C. 1715y), evidence of insurance on at least one loan for the purchase of a one-family unit. The Administrator shall guarantee loans to veterans on such residential units when such loans meet those requirements of this chapter which he shall, by regulation, determine to be applicable to such loans.".
1976. Act June 30, 1976 (effective 6/30/76, as provided by § 9(a) of such Act, which appears as 38 USCS § 3701 note), in subsec. (a), in para. (1), substituted "the veteran" for "him", in para. (2), substituted "the veteran" and "the veteran's" for "him" and "his", respectively, in paras. (3) and (4), substituted "the veteran" for "him" wherever appearing and

substituted "the veteran's" for "his", in para. (5), substituted "the veteran" and "the veteran's" for "him" and "his", respectively, and in para. (6), substituted "the Administrator" for "he" preceding "shall prescribe".

1978. Act Oct. 18, 1978, § 104(1) (effective 7/1/79, as provided by § 108(b) of such Act, which appears as 38 USCS § 3702 note), substituted new subsec. (a)(6) for one which read: "(6) To purchase a one-family residential unit in a new condominium housing development or project, or in a structure built and sold as a condominium, provided such development, project or structure is approved by the Administrator under such criteria as he shall prescribe.".

Act Oct. 18, 1978, §§ 104(2), (3), 105(a) (effective 10/1/78, as provided by § 108(a) of such Act, which appears as 38 USCS § 3702 note), added subsec. (a)(7); in subsec. (c), substituted "$25,000" for "$17,000"; and added subsec. (d).

1980. Act Oct. 7, 1980, § 401 (effective 10/7/80, as provided by § 601(d) of such Act, which appears as 38 USCS § 1114 note), added subsecs. (a)(8) and (e).

Act Oct. 7, 1980, § 402 (effective 10/1/80, as provided by § 601(b) of such Act, which appears as 38 USCS § 1114 note), in subsec. (c), substituted "$27,500" for "$25,000".

1984. Act March 2, 1984, in subsec. (a), added para. (9); and added subsec. (f).

1986. Act Oct. 28, 1986, in subsec. (b)(3), inserted ", as determined in accordance with the credit underwriting standards established pursuant to subsection (g) of this section", and added subsec. (g).

1987. Act Dec. 21, 1987 (applicable as provided by § 3(d) of such Act, which appears as 38 USCS § 3703 note) deleted subsec. (c), which read: "(c) The amount of guaranty entitlement available to a veteran under this section shall not be more than $27,500 less such entitlement as may have been used previously under this section and other sections of this chapter.".

Such Act further, in subsec. (b), in para. (5), substituted "pursuant to section 1831 of this title" for "by the Administrator", and deleted the concluding matter of subsec. (b), which read: "After the reasonable value of any property, construction, repairs, or alterations is determined under paragraph (5), the Administrator shall, as soon as possible thereafter, notify the veteran concerned of such determination.".

Such Act further (applicable as provided by § 7(d) of such Act, which appears as a note to this section), in subsec. (e)(1), in subpara. (B), deleted "and such dwelling or residence must be owned and occupied by the veteran as such veteran's home" following "refinanced", in subpara. (D), deleted "and" following the semicolon, in subpara. (E), substituted "by more than 10 years; and" for the concluding period, and added subpara. (F); and added subsec. (h).

Such Act further (applicable as provided by § 8(c) of such Act, which appears as 38 USCS § 1804 note), in subsec. (a), substituted "Except as provided in section 1804(c)(2) of this title, any" for "Any".

Such Act further, in subsec. (g)(3), added the concluding matter.

1988. Act May 20, 1988, in subsec. (a)(9)(B)(ii), substituted "section 1812(a)(5)" for "section 1819(a)(5)"; and in subsec. (g)(2), in the introductory matter, substituted "section 1812(e)(2)" for "section 1819(e)(2)".

1989. Act Dec. 18, 1989, in subsec. (b), in para. (5), inserted "except in the case of a loan described in clause (7) or (8) of this subsection,", and deleted "and," following "title;", in para. (6), substituted a semicolon for the concluding period, and added paras. (7) and (8); and repealed subsec. (h) which read: "The amount of a loan guaranteed for the purpose specified in subsection (a)(5) of this section may not exceed the amount equal to 90 percent of the appraised value of the dwelling or farm residence which will secure the loan, as determined by the Administrator.".

Such Act further, substituted "Secretary" and "Secretary's" for "Administrator" and "Administrator's", respectively, wherever appearing, in the entire section.

1991. Act Aug. 6, 1991, redesignated this section, formerly 38 USCS § 1810, as 38 USCS § 3710, amended the references in this section to reflect the redesignations made by § 5(a) of such Act (see Table III preceding 38 USCS § 101), and, in subsec. (e)(2), substituted "Secretary" for "Veterans' Administration".

1992. Act Oct. 28, 1992, in subsec. (a), substituted para. (7) for one which read: "To improve a dwelling or farm residence owned by the veteran and occupied by the veteran as the veteran's home through the installation of a solar heating system, a solar heating and cooling system, or a combined solar heating and cooling system or through the application of a residential energy conservation measure." and added para. (10); substituted subsec. (d) for one which read:

"(d) For the purposes of subsection (a)(7) of this section:

"(1) The term 'solar heating' has the meaning given such term in section 3(1) of the Solar Heating and Cooling Demonstration Act of 1974 (42 U.S.C. 5502(1)) and, in addition, includes a passive system based on conductive, convective, or radiant energy transfer.

"(2) The terms 'solar heating and cooling' and 'combined solar heating and cooling' have the meaning given such terms in section 3(2) of the Solar Heating and Cooling Demonstration Act of 1974 (42 U.S.C. 5502(2)) and, in addition, include a passive system based on conductive, convective, or radiant energy transfer.

"(3) The term 'passive system' includes window and skylight glazing, thermal floors, walls, and roofs, movable insulation panels (when in conjunction with glazing), portions of a residential structure that serve as solar furnaces so as to add heat to the structure, double-pane window insulation, and such other energy-related components as are determined by the Secretary to enhance the natural transfer of energy for the purpose of heating or heating and cooling a residence.

"(4) The term 'residential energy conservation measure' means—

"(A) caulking and weatherstripping of all exterior doors and windows;

"(B) furnace efficiency modifications limited to—

"(i) replacement burners, boilers, or furnaces designed to reduce the firing rate or to achieve a reduction in the amount of fuel consumed as a result of increased combustion efficiency,

"(ii) devices for modifying flue openings which will increase the efficiency of the heating system, and

"(iii) electrical or mechanical furnace ignition systems which replace standing gas pilot lights;

"(C) clock thermostats;

"(D) ceiling, attic, wall, and floor insulation;

"(E) water heater insulation;

"(F) storm windows and doors;

"(G) heat pumps; and

"(H) such other energy conservation measures as the Secretary may identify for the purposes of this clause.'';

and, in subsec. (e)(1), substituted subpara. (D) for one which read: "the amount of the guaranty of the loan may not exceed the original guaranty amount of the loan being refinanced;''.

1994. Act Nov. 2, 1994, in subsec. (a), added para. (11); and, in subsec. (e)(1), in the introductory matter, inserted "or for the purpose specified in subsection (a)(11)", in subpara. (A), inserted "or, in a case in which the loan is a fixed rate loan and the loan being refinanced is an adjustable rate loan, the loan bears interest at a rate that is agreed upon by the veteran and the mortgagee", and, in subpara. (C), substituted "may not exceed—

(i) an amount equal to the sum of the balance of the loan being refinanced and such closing costs (including any discount permitted pursuant to section 3703(c)(3)(A) of this title) as may be authorized by the Secretary (under regulations which the Secretary shall prescribe) to be included in the loan; or

(ii) in the case of a loan for the purpose specified in subsection (a)(11), an amount equal to the sum of the amount referred to with respect to the loan under clause (i) and the amount specified under subsection (d)(2);''

for "may not exceed an amount equal to the sum of the balance of the loan being refinanced and such closing costs (including any discount permitted pursuant to section 3703(c)(3)(A) of this title) as may be authorized by the Secretary, under regulations which the Secretary shall prescribe, to be included in such loan;''.

1996. Act Feb. 13, 1996, in subsec. (d), deleted para. (7), which read: "A loan may not be guaranteed under this subsection after December 31, 1995.''.

Other provisions:

Application of amendments made by § 7 of Act Dec. 21, 1987. Act Dec. 21, 1987, P. L. 100-198, § 7(d), 101 Stat. 1319, provides:

"(1) The amendments made by subsections (a) [amending subsec. (e) of this section] and (b) [amending 38 USCS § 3719(a)(4)(A) of this section shall apply to loans made more than 30 days after the date of the enactment of this Act.

"(2) The amendment made by subsection (c) of this section [adding subsec. (h) of this section] shall apply to loans for which commitments are made more than 60 days after the date of the enactment of this Act.''.

Repeal of provision relating to reports concerning mortgage loans. Act Oct. 28, 1992, P. L. 102-547, § 9(c), 106 Stat. 3642, which formerly appeared as a note to this section, was repealed by Act Feb. 13, 1996, P. L. 104-110, Title II, § 201(b), 110 Stat. 770. Such note related to an annual report to the Committees on Veterans' Affairs of the Senate and House of Representatives by the Secretary of Veterans Affairs dealing with veterans receiving mortgage loans guaranteed by the Secretary.

CODE OF FEDERAL REGULATIONS

Department of Veterans Affairs—Loan guaranty, 38 CFR Part 36.

CROSS REFERENCES

This section is referred to in 38 USCS §§ 3701, 3703, 3704, 3711–3714, 3732, 3733.

RESEARCH GUIDE

Federal Procedure L Ed:

4A Fed Proc L Ed, Banking and Financing §§ 8:1414, 1415, 1417, 1424, 1425.

Am Jur:

77 Am Jur 2d, Veterans and Veterans' Laws §§ 121, 123.

Annotations:

Validity and effect of side agreement affecting cost of property covered by veteran's loan under Servicemen's Readjustment Act. 19 ALR2d 836.

Construction of clause in building contract that structure will comply with regulations, plans, or standards of the Federal Housing Administration or the Veterans' Administration. 67 ALR2d 1017.

Auto-Cite®: Cases and annotations referred to herein can be further researched through the Auto-Cite® computer-assisted research service. Use Auto-Cite to check citations for form, parallel references, prior and later history, and annotation references.

INTERPRETIVE NOTES AND DECISIONS

1. Generally
2. Purpose
3. Agency authority, generally
4. Scope of guaranty
5. False statements and certificates
6. Contracts, generally
7. —Ancillary agreements
8. Miscellaneous

1. Generally

Loan association, which failed to give 30 days notice to Veterans' Administration [now Department of Veterans Affairs] after completion of loan, and also failed to furnish Veterans' Administration [now Department of Veterans Affairs] with statement setting forth full name of veteran, amount and terms of loan, and legal description and appraisal, did not have contract of guaranty with Veterans' Administration [now Department of Veterans Affairs]. Hartford Acci. & Indem. Co. v Schwartz (1946, DC NY) 89 F Supp 83.

Duty and burden rests upon veteran to procure fire insurance on residence undergoing construction under GI loan plan. Graddon v Knight (1950) 99 Cal App 2d 700, 222 P2d 329.

2. Purpose

Congress intended guaranty provisions of 38 USCS § 1810 [now 38 USCS § 3710] to operate as substantial equivalent of downpayments in same amount by veteran on purchase price of home, in order to induce 100 percent financing for veteran's home. United States v Shimer (1961) 367 US 374, 6 L Ed 2d 908, 81 S Ct 1554.

Provision of 38 USCS § 1810 [now 38 USCS § 3710] limiting loan to reasonable value of property was enacted to protect borrower from acquiring property at exorbitant price. Sattler v Van Natta (1953) 120 Cal App 2d 349, 260 P2d 982.

3. Agency authority, generally

Only property over which Veterans' Administration [now Department of Veterans Affairs] has right and interest to control price is that property on which purchaser will execute mortgage to secure loan, amount of which loan must be approved by Administration [now Department]. Hansel v De Salle (1959, La App, Orleans) 115 So 2d 867.

4. Scope of guaranty

Loan guaranty for purchase or construction includes any land purchased for construction of dwelling. Karrell v United States (1950, CA9 Cal) 181 F2d 981, cert den (1950) 340 US 891, 95 L Ed 646, 71 S Ct 206.

Where regulation of administrator [now Secretary] provided that maximum guarantee on joint obligation of veterans would be treated as though obligations were several, and two veterans borrowed $8,500 from plaintiff association to finance purchase of real estate as joint tenant, veteran who had only $250 left on his guaranty was entitled only to guaranty in that amount, and other veteran who had not used his guaranty was entitled only to guaranty of 50 percent of his share, to wit: $2,150. Gowanda Co-op. Sav. & Loan Asso. v Gray (1950, CA2 NY) 183 F2d 367.

5. False statements and certificates

Defendants were properly convicted under conspiracy statutes where it appeared that they joined in scheme to defraud United States government by misrepresenting price of home sold to veteran in order to obtain government guarantee of mortgage loan. Heald v United States (1949, CA10 Colo) 175 F2d 878, cert den (1949) 338 US 859, 94 L Ed 526, 70 S Ct 101 and cert den (1949) 338 US 859, 94 L Ed 526, 70 S Ct 102.

Where defendant was indicted for making false affidavit concerning amount of sale price of lot and house to veteran for purpose of securing GI loan, such indictment charged offense. Young v United States (1949, CA9 Cal) 178 F2d 78, cert den (1950) 339 US 913, 94 L Ed 1339, 70 S Ct 573.

Where defendant was convicted of making false reports to government in procurement of GI loans to six veterans, restitution to veterans as condition for suspension of sentence should be based on difference between fair appraisal value and amount actually charged veteran. Karrell v United States (1950, CA9 Cal) 181 F2d 981, cert den (1950) 340 US 891, 95 L Ed 646, 71 S Ct 206.

Defendant, who furnished funds for down payment by veterans in order that they might file application for loan, and upon completion of loan paid veterans stipulated amount out of proceeds, was liable for making of false affidavits and applications even though veterans voluntarily filed papers. Turner v United States (1953, CA9 Cal) 202 F2d 523.

6. Contracts, generally

So long as reasonable normal value of contract is determinable, contract between vendor and veteran contemplating that no deed shall be delivered to veteran conveying home or other property purchased until all or stated portion of purchase price shall have been paid by installments extending over period of years, not exceeding 20 years, such purchase contract is eligible for loan guaranties, upon general conditions that would be substantially applicable if transaction evidenced by contract were evidenced by deed, mortgage, and note secured by mortgage. 1945 ADVA 640.

Contract contrary to Servicemen's Readjustment Act violates basic public policy and is unenforceable. Rosenblum v Corodas (1953) 119 Cal App 2d 802, 260 P2d 151; Sattler v Van Natta (1953) 120 Cal App 2d 349, 260 P2d 982.

Written contract signed by contractor and sent to veteran certifying maximum complete cost supersedes all oral agreements and other verbal stipulations. Higby v Hooper (1950) 124 Mont 331, 221 P2d 1043.

7. —Ancillary agreements

Where contractor and veteran made "side" agreement providing for cost-plus contract, after Veterans' Administration [now Department of Veterans Affairs] and bank had approved fixed-fee contract, contractor could not enforce cost-plus contract. Young v Hampton (1951) 36 Cal 2d 799, 228 P2d 1, 19 ALR2d 830.

Where plaintiff arranged for GI loan and "builder's contract" with defendant was made calling for fixed construction cost to be paid contractor and on same day they by letter agreed to cost-plus contract, which was illegal, obligation of note and trust deed given to contract or on account thereof was reduced. Pitts v Highland Constr. Co. (1953) 115 Cal App 2d 206, 252 P2d 14.

Veteran's consideration, in form of promissory note for additional sum above appraisal value of house, was illegal and such note was unenforceable. Sattler v Van Natta (1953) 120 Cal App 2d 349, 260 P2d 982.

Vendor who was ignorant of violation of predecessor to 38 USCS § 3710 and acted in good faith was entitled to enforce promissory note and deed of trust securing note, representing difference between appraised value and purchase price, against veteran who was aware of violation at time note was executed. Lewis v Wainscott (1954) 124 Cal App 2d 345, 268 P2d 835.

Under predecessor to 38 USCS § 3710, side agreement increasing cost beyond appraisal value was invalid and unenforceable, regardless of fact that neither party to agreement was aware of illegality. Cole v Ames (1957, 2nd Dist) 155 Cal App 2d 8, 317 P2d 662.

Where Veterans' Administration [now Department of Veterans Affairs] consented to loan not in excess of $8,370 on certain house to be built for veteran but building expenses were $10,475 and veteran by oral contract agreed to pay balance of $2,271.50 directly to contractor, oral agreement was unenforceable. Bamber v Mayeux (1957) 232 La 42, 93 So 2d 687.

Side agreement covering well, pump, tank, and pipe located on lot purchased by veteran is valid where appraisal was done only on house and lot, and price of such additional property was not inflated. Voorhies v Hance (1955, La App 1st Cir) 79 So 2d 615.

Side agreement whereby veteran agreed to pay cost of street improvements was not invalid merely because not reflected in deed from seller to purchaser, where Veterans' Administration [now Department of Veterans Affairs] had appraised property as it was prior to improvements and had not been consulted about including such costs in purchase price, and there was no showing that Veterans' Administration [now Department of Veterans Affairs] would have refused to increase appraisal to include such cost if request to do so had been made. Hansel v De Salle (1959, La App, Orleans) 115 So 2d 867.

Contractor could not recover sum in excess of maximum amount recited in letter delivered to lender, which letter certified that complete cost of home would not exceed certain sum and formed basis on which loan was approved by loan company and guaranteed by government. Higby v Hooper (1950) 124 Mont 331, 221 P2d 1043.

Promissory note given by veteran for additional sum above appraisal value was based on illegal consideration and note was unenforceable. Veino v Bedell (1954) 99 NH 274, 109 A2d 555.

Reasonable value limitation of 38 USCS § 1810 [now 38 USCS § 3710] relates merely to conditions upon which government will guaranty loan to veteran in first instance, not to validity or effect of contract entered into between veteran and third persons, and side agreement in connection with veteran's housing loan is enforceable against parties to agreement. Bryant v Stablein (1947) 28 Wash 2d 739, 184 P2d 45.

Agreement between veteran and seller, to effect that purchase price of one property would be reduced to amount at which Veterans' Administration [now Department of Veterans Affairs] had appraised it, so that veteran could get guaranteed loan, in consideration for which veteran would also buy adjoining property, did not violate predecessor to 38 USCS § 3710. Ewing v Ford (1948) 31 Wash 2d 126, 195 P2d 650.

8. Miscellaneous

No congressional purpose in enacting loan legislation was impaired by upholding terms of individually negotiated Deed of Trust which departed from form usually employed by Veterans' Administration [now Department of Veterans Affairs] notwithstanding fact that effect under facts was to bar deficiency judgment by United States. United States v Stewart (1975, CA9 Wash) 523 F2d 1070.

§ 3711. Direct loans to veterans

(a) The Congress finds that housing credit for purposes specified in section 3710 or 3712 of this title is not and has not been generally available to veterans living in rural areas, or in small cities and towns not near large metropolitan areas. It is therefore the purpose of this section to provide housing credit for veterans living in such rural areas and such small cities and towns.

(b) Whenever the Secretary finds that private capital is not generally available in any rural area or small city or town for the financing of loans guaranteed for purposes specified in section 3710 or 3712 of this title, the Secretary shall designate such rural area or small city or town as a "housing credit shortage area". The Secretary shall, with respect to any such area, make, or enter into commitments to make, to any veteran eligible under this title, a loan for any or all of the purposes described in section 3710(a) or 3712 of this title (other than the refinancing of a loan under section 3710(a)(8) or 3712(a)(1)(F)).

(c) No loan may be made under this section to a veteran unless the veteran shows to the satisfaction of the Secretary that—

(1) the veteran is unable to obtain from a private lender in such housing credit shortage area, at an interest rate not in excess of the rate authorized for guaranteed home loans or manufactured home loans, as appropriate, a loan for such purpose for which the veteran is qualified under section 3710 or 3712 of this title, as appropriate; and

(2) the veteran is unable to obtain a loan for such purpose from the Secretary of Agriculture under title III of the Consolidated Farm and Rural

Development Act (7 U.S.C. 1921 et seq.) or title V of the Housing Act of 1949 (42 U.S.C. 1471 et seq.).

(d)(1) Loans made under this section shall bear interest at a rate determined by the Secretary, not to exceed the rate authorized for guaranteed home loans or manufactured home loans, as appropriate, and shall be subject to such requirements or limitations prescribed for loans guaranteed under this title as may be applicable.

(2)(A) Except for any loan made under this chapter [38 USCS §§ 3701 et seq.] for the purposes described in section 3712 of this title, the original principal amount of any loan made under this section shall not exceed an amount which bears the same ratio to $33,000 as the amount of guaranty to which the veteran is entitled under section 3710 of this title at the time the loan is made bears to $36,000; and the guaranty entitlement of any veteran who heretofore or hereafter has been granted a loan under this section shall be charged with an amount which bears the same ratio to $36,000 as the amount of the loan bears to $33,000.

(B) The original principal amount of any loan made under this section for the purposes described in section 3712 of this title shall not exceed the amount that bears the same ratio to $33,000 as the amount of guaranty to which the veteran is entitled under such section at the time the loan is made bears to $20,000. The amount of the guaranty entitlement for purposes specified in section 3710 of this title of any veteran who is granted a loan under this section, or who before October 18, 1978, was granted a loan under this section, shall be charged with the amount that bears the same ratio to $20,000 as the amount of the loan bears to $33,000.

(3) No veteran may obtain loans under this section aggregating more than $33,000.

(e) Loans made under this section shall be repaid in monthly installments, except that in the case of any such loan made for any of the purposes described in paragraphs (2), (3), or (4) of section 3710(a) of this title, the Secretary may provide that such loan shall be repaid in quarterly, semiannual, or annual installments.

(f) In connection with any loan under this section, the Secretary may make advances in cash to pay taxes and assessments on the real estate, to provide for repairs, alterations, and improvements, and to meet the incidental expenses of the transaction. The Secretary shall determine the expenses incident to origination of loans made under this section, which expenses, or a reasonable flat allowance in lieu thereof, shall be paid by the veteran in addition to the loan closing costs.

(g) The Secretary may sell, and shall offer for sale, to any person or entity approved for such purpose by the Secretary, any loan made under this section at a price which the Secretary determines to be reasonable under the conditions prevailing in the mortgage market when the agreement to sell the loan is made; and shall guarantee any loan thus sold subject to the same conditions, terms, and limitations which would be applicable were the loan guaranteed for purposes specified in section 3710 or 3712 of this title, as appropriate.

(h) The Secretary may exempt dwellings constructed through assistance provided by this section from the minimum land planning and subdivision requirements prescribed pursuant to subsection (a) of section 3704 of this title, and with respect to such dwellings may prescribe special minimum land planning and subdivision requirements which shall be in keeping with the general housing facilities in the locality but shall require that such dwellings meet minimum requirements of structural soundness and general acceptability.

(i) The Secretary is authorized, without regard to the provisions of subsections (a), (b), and (c) of this section, to make or enter into a commitment to make a loan to any veteran to assist the veteran in acquiring a specially adapted housing unit authorized under chapter 21 of this title [38 USCS §§ 2101 et seq.], if the veteran is determined to be eligible for the benefits of such chapter 21 [38 USCS §§ 2101 et seq.], and is eligible for loan guaranty benefits under this chapter [38 USCS §§ 3701 et seq.].

(j)(1) If any builder or sponsor proposes to construct one or more dwellings in a housing credit shortage area, or in any area for a veteran who is determined to be eligible for assistance in acquiring a specially adapted housing unit under chapter 21 of this title [38 §§ 2101 et seq.], the Secretary may enter into commitment with such builder or sponsor, under which funds available for loans under this section will be reserved for a period not in excess of three months, or such longer period as the Secretary may authorize to meet the needs in any particular case, for the purpose of making loans to veterans to purchase such dwellings. Such commitment may not be assigned or transferred except with the written approval of the Secretary. The Secretary shall not enter into any such commitment unless such builder or sponsor pays a nonrefundable commitment fee to the Secretary in an amount determined by the Secretary, not to exceed 2 percent of the funds reserved for such builder or sponsor.

(2) Whenever the Secretary finds that a dwelling with respect to which funds are being reserved under this subsection has been sold, or contracted to be sold, to a veteran eligible for a direct loan under this section, the Secretary shall enter into a commitment to make the veteran a loan for the purchase of such dwelling. With respect to any loan made to an eligible veteran under this subsection, the Secretary may make advances during the construction of the dwelling, up to a maximum in advances of (A) the cost of the land plus (B) 80 percent of the value of the construction in place.

(k) Without regard to any other provision of this chapter [38 USCS §§ 3701 et seq.], the Secretary may take or cause to be taken such action as in the Secretary's judgment may be necessary or appropriate for or in connection with the custody, management, protection, and realization or sale of investments under this section, may determine the Secretary's necessary expenses and expenditures, and the manner in which the same shall be incurred, allowed and paid, may make such rules, regulations, and orders as the Secretary may deem necessary or appropriate for carrying out the Secretary's functions under this section and section 3723 of this title and, except as otherwise expressly provided in this chapter [38 USCS §§ 3701 et seq.], may employ, utilize,

38 USCS § 3711

compensate, and, to the extent not inconsistent with the Secretary's basic responsibilities under this chapter [38 USCS §§ 3701 et seq.], delegate any of the Secretary's functions under this section and section 3723 of this title to such persons and such corporate or other agencies, including agencies of the United States, as the Secretary may designate.

(Sept. 2, 1958, P. L. 85-857, § 1, 72 Stat. 1208; July 14, 1960, P. L. 86-665, § 2, 74 Stat. 531; July 6, 1961, P. L. 87-84, § 2, 75 Stat. 201; Aug. 4, 1964, P. L. 88-402, 78 Stat. 380; March 3, 1966, P. L. 89-358, § 5(e), 80 Stat. 26; Aug. 31, 1967, P. L. 90-77, Title IV, § 404, 81 Stat. 190; May 7, 1968, P. L. 90-301, § 1(b), 82 Stat. 113; June 6, 1969, P. L. 91-22, § 3, 83 Stat. 32; Oct. 23, 1970, P. L. 91-506, § 4, 84 Stat. 1109; Aug. 5, 1971, P. L. 92-66, 85 Stat. 173; Dec. 31, 1974, P. L. 93-569, § 4, 88 Stat. 1864; June 30, 1976, P. L. 94-324, §§ 3, 7(12)–(15) 90 Stat. 720, 721; Oct. 18, 1978, P. L. 95-476, Title I, § 105(b), 92 Stat. 1499; Oct. 7, 1980, P. L. 96-385, Title IV, §§ 401(c)(2), 402(b), 94 Stat. 1533; Oct. 12, 1982, P. L. 97-295, § 4(65), 96 Stat. 1309; Oct. 14, 1982, P. L. 97-306, Title IV, § 406(c), 96 Stat. 1445; Dec. 21, 1987, P. L. 100-198, § 3(c), 101 Stat. 1316; May 20, 1988, P. L. 100-322, Title IV, Part B, § 415(c)(5), (d)(2), 102 Stat. 551, 552; Dec. 18, 1989, P. L. 101-237, Title III, § 313(b)(1), 103 Stat. 2077; Aug. 6, 1991, P. L. 102-83, § 5(a), (c)(1), 105 Stat. 406.)

HISTORY; ANCILLARY LAWS AND DIRECTIVES
Amendments:

1960. Act July 14, 1960, in subsec. (h), substituted "1962" for "1960".

1961. Act July 6, 1961, in subsec. (d), in paras. (2) and (3), substituted "$15,000" for "$13,500" wherever appearing; and substituted new subsec. (h) for one which read: "No loan may be made under this section after July 25, 1962, except pursuant to commitments issued by the Administrator before that date.".

1964. Act Aug. 4, 1964, substituted new subsec. (g) for one which read: "The Administrator may sell, and shall offer for sale, to any person or entity approved for such purpose by him, any loan made under this section at a price not less than par; that is, the unpaid balance plus accrued interest, and shall guarantee any loan thus sold subject to the same conditions, terms, and limitations which would be applicable were the loan guaranteed under section 1810 of this title.".

1966. Act March 3, 1966 (effective 3/3/66, as provided by § 12(a) of such Act), in subsec. (d), in paras. (2) and (3), substituted "$17,500" for "$15,000" wherever appearing.

1967. Act Aug. 31, 1967 (effective 10/1/67, as provided by § 405(a) of such Act, which appears as 38 USCS § 101 note), in subsec. (d), in para. (2), inserted "; except that the Administrator may increase the $17,500 limitations specified in this paragraph to an amount not to exceed $25,000 where he finds that cost levels so require", and in para. (3), inserted "; except that the Administrator may increase such aggregate amount to an amount not to exceed $25,000 where he finds that cost levels so require".

1968. Act May 7, 1968, in subsec. (d)(2), substituted "$12,500" for "$7,500" wherever appearing.

1969. Act June 6, 1969, in subsec. (d), in paras. (2) and (3), substituted "$21,000" for "$17,500" wherever appearing.

1970. Act Oct. 23, 1970, in subsecs. (a) and (b), substituted "1810 or 1819" for "1810"; in subsec. (b), substituted "He shall, with respect to any such area, make, or enter into commitments to make, to any veteran eligible under this title, a loan for any or all of the purposes described in section 1810(a) or 1819 of this title." for "He shall make, or enter into commitments to make, to any veteran eligible under this title, a loan for any or all of the purposes listed in section 1810(a) in such area."; in subsec. (c)(1), inserted "or mobile home loans, as appropriate" and substituted "1810 or 1819 of this title, as appropriate" for "1810 of this title"; in subsec. (d), in para. (1), inserted "or mobile home loans, as appropriate", in para. (2), substituted "(A) Except for any loan made under this chapter for the purposes described in section 1819 of this title, the" for "The", and added para. (2)(B); in subsec. (g), substituted "1810 or 1819 of this title, as appropriate" for "1810 of this title"; and substituted new subsecs. (h)–(j) for ones which read:

"(h) No loan may be made under this section to any veteran after the expiration of his entitlement pursuant to section 1803(a)(3) of this title except pursuant to a commitment issued by the Administrator before such entitlement expires.

"(i)(1) If any builder or sponsor purposes to construct one or more dwellings in a housing credit shortage area, the Administrator may enter into commitment with such builder or sponsor, under which funds available for loans under this section will be reserved for a period not in excess of three months, or such longer period as the Administrator may authorize to meet the needs in any particular case, for the purpose of making loans to veterans to purchase such dwellings. Such commitment may not be assigned or transferred except with the written approval of the Administrator. The Administrator shall not enter into any such commitment unless such builder or sponsor pays a nonrefundable commitment fee to the Administrator in an amount determined by the Administrator, not to exceed 2 per centum of the funds reserved for such builder or sponsor.

"(2) Whenever the Administrator finds that a dwelling with respect to which funds are being reserved under this subsection has been sold, or contracted to be sold, to a veteran eligible for a direct loan under this section, the Administrator shall enter into a commitment to make the veteran a loan for the purchase of such dwelling. With respect to any loan made to an eligible veteran under this subsection, the Administrator may make advances during the construction of the dwelling, up to a maximum in advances of (A) the cost of the land plus (B) 80 per centum of the value of the construction in place.

"(3) After the Administrator has entered into a commitment to make a veteran a loan under this subsection, he may refer the proposed loan to the Voluntary Home Mortgage Credit Committee, in order to afford a private lender the opportunity to acquire such loan subject to guaranty as provided in subsection (g) of this section. If, before the expiration of sixty days after the loan made to the veteran by the Administrator is fully disbursed, a private lender agrees to purchase such loan, all or any part of the commitment fee paid to the Administrator with respect to such loan may be paid to such private lender when such loan is so purchased. If a private lender has not purchased or agreed to purchase such loan before the expiration of sixty days after the loan made by the Administrator is fully disbursed, the commitment fee paid with respect to such loan shall become a part of the special deposit account referred to in subsection (c) of section 1823 of this title. If a loan is not made to a veteran for the purchase of a dwelling, the commitment fee paid with respect to such dwelling shall become a part of such special deposit account.

"(4) The Administrator may exempt dwellings constructed through assistance provided by this subsection from the minimum land planning and subdivision requirements prescribed pursuant to subsection (a) of section 1804 of this title, and with respect to such dwellings may prescribe special minimum land planning and subdivision requirements which shall be in keeping with the general housing facilities in the locality but shall require that such dwellings meet minimum requirements of structural soundness and general acceptability.

"(j)(1) The Administrator shall commence the processing of any application for a loan under this section upon the receipt of such application, and shall continue such processing notwithstanding the fact that the assistance of the Voluntary Home Mortgage Credit Committee has been requested by the Administrator for the purpose of ascertaining whether or not such loan can be placed with a private lender.

"(2) If the assistance of such Committee has been requested by the Administrator in connection with any such application, and the Administrator is not notified by such Committee within twenty working days after such assistance has been requested that it has been successful in enabling the applicant to place such loan with a private lender or expects to do so within ten additional working days, the Administrator shall proceed forthwith to complete any part of the processing of such application remaining unfinished, and to grant or deny the application in accordance with the provisions of this section.

"(3) As used in this subsection, the term 'working days' means calendar days exclusive of Saturdays, Sundays, and legal holidays.".

1971. Act Aug. 5, 1971, substituted new subsec. (g) for one which read: "The Administrator may sell, and shall offer for sale, to any person or entity approved for such purpose by him, any loan made under this section at a price which he determines to be reasonable but not less than 98 per centum of the unpaid principal balance, plus the full amount of accrued interest, except that if loans are offered to an investor in a package or block of two or more loans no sale shall be made at less than 98 per centum of the aggregate unpaid principal balance of the loans included in such package or block, plus the full amount of accrued interest; and the Administrator shall guarantee any loan thus sold subject to the same conditions, terms, and limitations which would be applicable were the loan guaranteed under section 1810 or 1819 of this title, as appropriate.".

1974. Act Dec. 31, 1974 (effective 12/31/74, as provided by § 10 of such Act, which appears as 38 USCS § 3702 note), in subsec. (d)(2)(A), substituted "$17,500" for "$12,500" wherever appearing.

1976. Act June 30, 1976 (effective 6/30/76, as provided by § 9(a) of such Act, which appears as 38 USCS § 3701 note), in subsec. (b), substituted "the Administrator" for "he" preceding "shall designate" and substituted "The Administrator" for "He" preceding "shall, with respect"; in subsec.

(c), in paras. (1) and (2), substituted "the veteran" for "he"; in subsec. (g), substituted "the Administrator" for "him" following "by" and substituted "the Administrator" for "he" preceding "determines"; and in subsec. (k), substituted "the Administrator's" for "his" wherever appearing and substituted "the Administrator" for "he" preceding "may deem" and "may designate".

Such Act further (effective 10/1/76, as provided by § 9(b) of such Act, which appears as 38 USCS § 3701 note), in subsec. (d), in para. (2)(A), substituted "$33,000" for "$21,000" and substituted "$33,000." for "$21,000; except that the Administrator may increase the $21,000 limitations specified in this paragraph to an amount not to exceed $25,000 where he finds that cost levels so require.", and in para. (3), substituted "$33,000." for "$21,000; except that the Administrator may increase such aggregate amount to an amount not to exceed $25,000 where he finds that cost levels require.".

1978. Act Oct. 18, 1978 (effective 10/1/78, as provided by § 108(a) of such Act, which appears as 38 USCS § 3702 note), in subsec. (d)(2), in subpara. (A), substituted "$25,000" for "$17,500" wherever appearing, and in subpara. (B), substituted "that bears the same ratio to $33,000 as the amount of guaranty to which the veteran is entitled under such section at the time the loan is made bears to $17,500. The amount of the guaranty entitlement under section 1810(c) of this title of any veteran who is granted a loan under this section, or who before the date of the enactment of the Veterans' Housing Benefits Act of 1978 was granted a loan under this section, shall be charged with the amount that bears the same ratio to $17,500 as the amount of the loan bears to $33,000." for "specified by the Administrator pursuant to subsection (d) of such section.".

1980. Act Oct. 7, 1980 (effective 10/7/80, as provided by § 601(d) of such Act, which appears as 38 USCS § 1114 note), in subsec. (b), inserted "(other than the refinancing of a loan under section 1810(a)(8) or 1819(a)(1)(F))".

Such Act further (effective 10/1/80, as provided by § 602(b) of such Act, which appears as 38 USCS § 1114 note), in subsec. (d)(2), in subpara. (A), substituted "$27,500" for "$25,000" wherever appearing, and in subpara. (B), substituted "$20,000" for "$17,500" wherever appearing.

1982. Act Oct. 12, 1982, in subsec. (c)(2), substituted "title III of the Consolidated Farm and Rural Development Act (7 U.S.C. 1921 et seq.) or title V of the Housing Act of 1949 (42 U.S.C. 1471 et seq.)" for "sections 1000–1029 of title 7 or under sections 1471–1483 of title 42"; in subsec. (d)(2)(B), substituted "October 18, 1978," for "the date of the enactment of the Veterans' Housing Benefits Act of 1978"; and, in subsec. (j), in paras. (1) and (2), substituted "percent" for "per centum".

Act Oct. 14, 1982, in subsecs. (c)(1) and (d)(1), substituted "manufactured home" for "mobile home".

1987. Act Dec. 21, 1987 (applicable as provided by § 3(d) of such Act, which appears as 38 USCS § 3703 note), in subsec. (d)(2)(A), substituted "$36,000" for "$27,500" in two places.

1988. Act May 20, 1988, in subsecs. (a) and (b), substituted "for purposes specified in section 1810 or" for "under section 1810 or" and "1812" for "1819" wherever appearing; in subsec. (c)(1), substituted "1812" for "1819"; in subsec. (d)(2), in subpara. (A), substituted "section 1812" for "section 1819", in subpara. (B), substituted "section 1812" for "section 1819", and "for purposes specified in section 1810" for "under section 1810(c)"; and in subsec. (g), substituted "for purposes specified in section 1810 or 1812" for "under section 1710 or 1819".

1989. Act Dec. 18, 1989, substituted "Secretary" and "Secretary's" for "Administrator" and "Administrator's", respectively, wherever appearing, in the entire section.

1991. Act Aug. 6, 1991, redesignated this section, formerly 38 USCS § 1811, as 38 USCS § 3711, and amended the references in this section to reflect the redesignations made by § 5(a) of such Act (see Table III preceding 38 USCS § 101).

Other provisions:
Application and construction of the Oct. 12, 1982 amendment of this section. For provisions as to the application and construction of the Oct. 12, 1982 amendment of this section, see § 5 of such Act, which appears as 10 USCS § 101 note.

CODE OF FEDERAL REGULATIONS
Department of Veterans Affairs—Loan guaranty, 38 CFR Part 36.

CROSS REFERENCES
This section is referred to in 38 USCS §§ 3710, 3712, 3723, 3725, 3729, 3732.

RESEARCH GUIDE
Federal Procedure L Ed:
4A Fed Proc L Ed, Banking and Financing § 8:1408.

Am Jur:
77 Am Jur 2d, Veterans and Veterans' Laws §§ 121, 127.

INTERPRETIVE NOTES AND DECISIONS

Direct loan may properly be made to veteran whose dwelling is not located in area designated as housing credit shortage area for purposes of financing remodeling of home where such remodeling is also being financed by specially adapted housing grant under 38 USCS § 802 [now 38 USCS § 2102]. VA GCO 3-76.

§ 3712. Loans to purchase manufactured homes and lots

(a)(1) Notwithstanding any other provision of this chapter [38 USCS §§ 3701 et seq.], any loan to a veteran eligible for the housing loan benefits of this chapter [38 USCS §§ 3701 et seq.], if made pursuant to the provisions of this section, may be guaranteed if such loan is for one of the following purposes:

(A) To purchase a lot on which to place a manufactured home already owned by the veteran.

(B) To purchase a single-wide manufactured home.

(C) To purchase a single-wide manufactured home and a lot on which to place such home.

(D) To purchase a double-wide manufactured home.

(E) To purchase a double-wide manufactured home and a lot on which to place such home.

(F) To refinance in accordance with paragraph (4) of this subsection an existing loan guaranteed, insured, or made under this section.

(G) To refinance in accordance with paragraph (5) of this subsection an existing loan that was made for the purchase of, and that is secured by, a manufactured home and to purchase a lot on which such manufactured home is or will be placed.

(2) A loan for any of the purposes described in paragraph (1) of this subsection (other than the refinancing under clause (F) of such paragraph of an existing loan) may include an amount determined by the Secretary to be appropriate to cover the cost of necessary preparation of a lot already owned or to be acquired by the veteran, including the costs of installing utility connections and sanitary facilities, of paving, and of constructing a suitable pad for the manufactured home.

(3) Any loan made for the purposes described in clause (C), (E), or (G) of paragraph (1) of this subsection shall be considered as part of one loan. The transaction may be evidenced by a single loan instrument or by separate loan instruments for (A) that portion of the loan which finances the purchase of the manufactured home, and (B) that portion of the loan which finances the purchase of the lot and the necessary preparation of such lot.

(4)(A) For a loan to be guaranteed for the purpose specified in clause (F) of paragraph (1) of this subsection—

(i) the interest rate of the loan must be less than the interest rate of the loan being refinanced;

(ii) the loan must be secured by the same manufactured home or manufactured-home lot, or manufactured home and manufactured-home lot, as was the loan being refinanced;

(iii) the amount of the loan may not exceed an amount equal to the sum of the balance of the loan being refinanced and such closing costs (including any discount permitted pursuant to section 3703(c)(3)(A) of this title) as may be authorized by the Secretary, under regulations which the Secretary shall prescribe, to be included in such loan;

(iv) notwithstanding section 3703(a)(1) of this title, the amount of the guaranty of the loan may not exceed the greater of (I) the original guaranty amount of the loan being refinanced, or (II) 25 percent of the loan;

(v) the term of the loan may not exceed the original term of the loan being refinanced;

(vi) the veteran must own the manufactured home, or the manufactured-home lot, or the manufactured home and the manufactured-home lot, securing the loan and—

(I) must occupy the home, a manufactured home on the lot, or the home and the lot, securing the loan;

(II) must have previously occupied the home, a manufactured home on the lot, or the home and the lot, securing the loan as the veteran's home and must certify, in such form as the Secretary shall require, that the veteran has previously so occupied the home (or such a home on the lot); or

(III) in any case in which a veteran is in active duty status as a member of the Armed Forces and is unable to occupy the home, a manufactured home on the lot, or the home and the lot, as a home because of such status, the spouse of the veteran must occupy, or must have previously occupied, the manufactured home on the lot, or the home and the lot, as such spouse's home and must certify such occupancy in such form as the Secretary shall require.

(B) A loan to a veteran may be guaranteed by the Secretary under this chapter [38 USCS §§ 3701 et seq.] for the purpose specified in clause (F) of paragraph (1) of this subsection without regard to the amount of outstanding guaranty entitlement available for use by such veteran, and the amount of such veteran's guaranty entitlement shall not be charged as a result of any guaranty provided for such purpose. For purposes of section 3702(b) of this title, such loan shall be deemed to have been obtained with the guaranty entitlement used to obtain the loan being refinanced.

(C) If a veteran is deceased and if such veteran's surviving spouse was a co-obligor under an existing loan previously guaranteed, insured, or made for purposes specified in this section, such surviving spouse shall, only for the purpose specified in clause (F) of paragraph (1) of this subsection, be deemed to be a veteran eligible for benefits under this chapter [38 USCS §§ 3701 et seq.].

(5)(A) For a loan to be guaranteed for the purpose specified in paragraph (1)(G) of this subsection or section 3710(a)(9)(B)(ii) of this title—

(i) the loan must be secured by the same manufactured home as was the loan being refinanced and such manufactured home must be owned and occupied by the veteran (except as provided in section 3704(c)(2) of this title) as such veteran's home; and

(ii) the amount of the loan may not exceed an amount equal to the sum of—

(I) the purchase price of the lot,

(II) the amount (if any) determined by the Secretary to be appropriate under paragraph (2) of this subsection to cover the cost of necessary preparation of such lot,

(III) the balance of the loan being refinanced, and

(IV) such closing costs (including any discount permitted pursuant to section 3703(c)(3)(E) of this title) as may be authorized by the Secretary, under regulations which the Secretary shall prescribe, to be included in such loan.

(B) When a loan is made to a veteran for the purpose specified in paragraph (1)(G) of this subsection or section 3710(a)(9)(B)(ii) of this title and the loan being refinanced was guaranteed, insured, or made under this section, the portion of the loan made for the purpose of refinancing such loan may be guaranteed by the Secretary under this chapter [38 USCS §§ 3701 et seq.] without regard to the amount of outstanding guaranty entitlement available for use by such veteran, and the amount of such veteran's guaranty entitlement shall not be charged as a result of any guaranty provided for such portion of such loan. For the purposes of section 3702(b) of this title, such portion of such loan shall be deemed to have been obtained with the guaranty entitlement used to obtain the loan being refinanced.

(b)(1) Use of entitlement for purposes specified in this section for the purchase of a manufactured home unit shall preclude the use of remaining entitlement for the purchase of an additional manufactured home unit until the unit which secured the loan has been disposed of by the veteran or has been destroyed by fire or other natural hazard.

(2) The Secretary shall restore entitlement to all housing loan benefits under this chapter [38 USCS §§ 3701 et seq.] for the veteran when the conditions prescribed in section 3702(b) of this title have been met.

(c)(1) Loans for any of the purposes authorized by subsection (a) of this section shall be submitted to the Secretary for approval prior to the closing of the loan, except that the Secretary may exempt any lender of a class listed in section 3702(d) of this title from compliance with such prior approval requirement if the Secretary determines that the experience of such lender or class of lenders in manufactured home financing warrants such exemption.

(2) Upon determining that a loan submitted for prior approval is eligible for guaranty for purposes specified in this section, the Secretary shall issue a commitment to guarantee such loan and shall thereafter guarantee the loan when made if such loan qualifies therefor in all respects.

(3)(A) The Secretary's guaranty may not exceed the lesser of (i) the lesser of $20,000 or 40 percent of the loan, or (ii) the maximum amount of the guaranty entitlement available to the veteran as specified in paragraph (4) of this subsection.

(B) A claim under the Secretary's guaranty shall, at the election of the holder of a loan, be made by the filing of an accounting with the Secretary—

(i) within a reasonable time after the receipt by such holder of an appraisal by the Secretary of the value of the security for the loan; or

(ii) after liquidation of the security for the loan.

(C) If the holder of a loan applies for payment of a claim under clause (i) of subparagraph (B) of this paragraph, the amount of such claim payable by the Secretary shall be the lesser of—

(i) the amount equal to the excess, if any, of the total indebtedness over the amount of the appraisal referred to in such clause; or

(ii) the amount equal to the guaranty under this section.

(D) If the holder of a loan files for payment of a claim under clause (ii) of subparagraph (B) of this paragraph, the amount of such claim payable by the Secretary shall be the lesser of—

(i) the amount equal to the excess, if any, of the total indebtedness over the greater of the value of the property securing the loan, as determined by the Secretary, or the amount of the liquidation or resale proceeds; or

(ii) the amount equal to the guaranty under this section.

(E) In any accounting filed pursuant to subparagraph (B)(ii) of this paragraph, the Secretary shall permit to be included therein accrued unpaid interest from the date of the first uncured default to such cutoff date as the Secretary may establish, and the Secretary shall allow the holder of the loan to charge against the liquidation or resale proceeds accrued interest from the cutoff date established to such further date as the Secretary may determine and such costs and expenses as the Secretary determines to be reasonable and proper.

(F) The liability of the United States under the guaranty provided for by this paragraph shall decrease or increase pro rata with any decrease or increase of the amount of the unpaid portion of the obligation.

(4) The maximum amount of guaranty entitlement available to a veteran for purposes specified in this section shall be $20,000 reduced by the amount of any such entitlement previously used by the veteran. Use of entitlement for purposes specified in section 3710 or 3711 of this title shall reduce entitlement available for use under this section to the same extent that entitlement available for purposes specified in such section 3710 is reduced below $20,000.

(5) The amount of any loan guaranteed for purposes specified in this section shall not exceed an amount equal to 95 percent of the purchase price of the property securing the loan.

(d)(1) The maturity of any loan guaranteed for purposes specified in this section shall not be more than—

(A) fifteen years and thirty-two days, in the case of a loan for the purchase of a lot;

(B) twenty years and thirty-two days, in the case of a loan for the purchase of—

(i) a single-wide manufactured home; or

(ii) a single-wide manufactured home and a lot;

(C) twenty-three years and thirty-two days, in the case of a loan for the purchase of a double-wide manufactured home; or

(D) twenty-five years and thirty-two days, in the case of a loan for the purchase of a double-wide manufactured home and a lot.

(2) Nothing in paragraph (1) of this subsection shall preclude the Secretary, under regulations which the Secretary shall prescribe, from consenting to necessary advances for the protection of the security or the holder's lien, to a reasonable extension of the term of such loan, or to a reasonable reamortization of such loan.

(e) No loan shall be guaranteed for purposes specified in this section unless—

(1) the loan is repayable in approximately equal monthly installments;

(2) the terms of repayment bear a proper relationship to the veteran's present and anticipated income and expenses, and the veteran is a satisfactory credit risk, as determined in accordance with the regulations prescribed under section 3710(g) of this title and taking into account the purpose of this

program to make available lower cost housing to low and lower income veterans, especially those who have been recently discharged or released from active military, naval, or air service, who may not have previously established credit ratings;

(3) the loan is secured by a first lien on the manufactured home purchased with the proceeds of the loan and on any lot acquired or improved with the proceeds of the loan;

(4) the amount of the loan to be paid by the veteran is not in excess of the amount determined to be reasonable, based upon—

    (A) with respect to any portion of the loan to purchase a new manufactured home, such cost factors as the Secretary considers proper to take into account;

    (B) with respect to any portion of the loan to purchase a used manufactured home, the reasonable value of the property, as determined by the Secretary;

    (C) with respect to any portion of the loan to purchase a lot, the reasonable value of such lot, as determined by the Secretary; and

    (D) with respect to any portion of the loan to cover the cost of necessary site preparation, an appropriate amount, as determined by the Secretary;

(5) the veteran certifies, in such form as the Secretary shall prescribe, that the veteran will personally occupy the property as the veteran's home; except that the requirement of this clause shall not apply (A) in the case of a guaranteed loan that is for the purpose described in paragraph (1)(F) of subsection (a), or (B) in the case described in section 3704(c)(2);

(6) the manufactured home is or will be placed on a site which meets specifications which the Secretary shall establish by regulation; and

(7) the interest rate to be charged on the loan does not exceed the permissible rate established by the Secretary.

(f) The Secretary shall establish such rate of interest for manufactured home loans and manufactured home lot loans as the Secretary's determines to be necessary in order to assure a reasonable supply of manufactured home loan financing for veterans for purposes specified in this section.

(g) The Secretary shall promulgate such regulations as the Secretary determines to be necessary or appropriate in order to fully implement the provisions of this section, and such regulations may specify which provisions in other sections of this chapter [38 USCS §§ 3701 et seq.] the Secretary determines should be applicable to loans guaranteed or made for purposes specified in this section. The Secretary shall have such powers and responsibilities in respect to matters arising under this section as the Secretary has in respect to loans made or guaranteed or under other sections of this chapter [38 USCS §§ 3701 et seq.].

(h)(1) No loan for the purchase of a manufactured home shall be guaranteed for purposes specified in this section unless the manufactured home and lot, if any, meet or exceed standards for planning, construction, and general acceptability as prescribed by the Secretary and no loan for the purchase of a lot on which to place a manufactured home owned by a veteran shall be guaranteed under this section unless the lot meets such standards prescribed for manufactured home lots. Such standards shall be designed to encourage the maintenance and development of sites for manufactured homes which will be attractive residential areas and which will be free from, and not substantially contribute to, adverse scenic or environmental conditions.

(2) Any manufactured housing unit properly displaying a certification of conformity to all applicable Federal manufactured home construction and safety standards pursuant to section 616 of the National Manufactured Housing Construction and Safety Standards Act of 1974 (42 U.S.C. 5415) shall be deemed to meet the standards required by paragraph (1).

(i) The Secretary shall require the manufacturer to become a warrantor of any new manufactured home which is approved for purchase with financing through the assistance of this chapter [38 USCS §§ 3701 et seq.] and to furnish to the purchaser a written warranty in such form as the Secretary shall require. Such warranty shall include (1) a specific statement that the manufactured home meets the standards prescribed by the Secretary pursuant to the provisions of subsection (h) of this section; and (2) a provision that the warrantor's liability to the purchaser or owner is limited under the warranty to instances of substantial nonconformity to such standards which become evident within one year from date of purchase and as to which the purchaser or owner gives written notice to the warrantor not later than ten days after the end of the warranty period. The warranty prescribed herein shall be in addition to, and not in derogation of, all other rights and privileges which such purchaser or owner may have under any other law or instrument and shall so provide in the warranty document.

(j) Subject to notice and opportunity for a hearing, the Secretary is authorized to deny guaranteed or direct loan financing in the case of—

(1) manufactured homes constructed by a manufacturer who fails or is unable to discharge the manufacturer's obligations under the warranty;

(2) manufactured homes which are determined by the Secretary not to conform to the standards provided for in subsection (h); or

(3) a manufacturer of manufactured homes who has engaged in procedures or practices determined by the Secretary to be unfair or prejudicial to veterans or the Government.

(k) Subject to notice and opportunity for a hearing, the Secretary may refuse to approve as acceptable any site in a manufactured home park or subdivision owned or operated by any person whose rental or sale methods, procedures, requirements, or practices are determined by the Secretary to be unfair or prejudicial to veterans renting or purchasing such sites. The Secretary may also refuse to guarantee or make direct loans for veterans to purchase manufactured homes offered for sale by any dealer if substantial deficiencies have been discovered in such homes, or if the Secretary determines that there has been a failure or indicated inability of the dealer to discharge contractual liabilities to veterans, or that the type of contract of sale or methods, procedures, or practices pursued by the dealer in the marketing of such properties have been unfair or prejudicial to veteran purchasers.

(l) The provisions of sections 3704(d) and 3721 of this title shall be fully applicable to lenders making guaranteed manufactured home loans and manufactured home lot loans and holders of such loans.
(Added Oct. 23, 1970, P. L. 91-506, § 5, 84 Stat. 1110; Dec. 31, 1974, P. L. 93-569, § 5, 88 Stat. 1864; June 30, 1976, P. L. 94-324, §§ 5, 7(20)–(23), 90 Stat. 720, 722; Oct. 18, 1978, P. L. 95-476, Title I, § 107, 92 Stat. 1500; Oct. 7, 1980, P. L. 96-385, Title IV, §§ 401(b), 402(c), 94 Stat. 1532; Oct. 17, 1981, P. L. 97-66, Title V, § 503, 95 Stat. 1032; Nov. 3, 1981, P. L. 97-72, Title III, § 303(h), (i), 95 Stat. 1060; Oct. 12, 1982, P. L. 97-295, § 4(66) in part, 96 Stat. 1810; Oct. 14, 1982, P. L. 97-306, Title IV, § 406(a), (c)(1), (2), 96 Stat. 1444, 1445; March 2, 1984, P. L. 98-223, Title II, § 205(b), 98 Stat. 43; Oct. 28, 1986, P. L. 99-576, Title 10, Part A, § 402(c)(2), 100 Stat. 3281; Dec. 21, 1987, P. L. 100-198, §§ 3(b), 7(b), 8(b), 101 Stat. 1315, 1319, 1320; Feb. 29, 1988, P. L. 100-253, § 3(b), 102 Stat. 20; May 20, 1988, P. L. 100-322, Title IV, Part B, § 415(b)(4), 102 Stat. 551; Dec. 18, 1989, P. L. 101-237, Title III, § 313(b)(1), (7) 103 Stat. 2077; Nov. 5, 1990, P. L. 101-508, Title VIII, Subtitle D, § 8031(a), 104 Stat. 1388-348; June 13, 1991, P. L. 102-54, § 14(c)(8), 105 Stat. 285; Aug. 6, 1991, P. L. 102-83, §§ 4(a)(2)(A)(v), 5(a), (c)(1), 105 Stat. 403, 406; Oct. 28, 1992, P. L. 102-547, § 6(2), 106 Stat. 3636; Nov. 2, 1994, P. L. 103-446, Title IX, § 906, Title XII, § 1201(e)(14), 108 Stat. 4677, 4685; Dec. 21, 1995, P. L. 104-66, Title I, Subtitle N, § 1141(b), 109 Stat. 726.)

HISTORY; ANCILLARY LAWS AND DIRECTIVES

Explanatory notes:
A prior § 1812 (Act Sept. 2, 1958, P. L. 85-857, § 1, 72 Stat. 1210) was repealed by Act Dec. 31, 1974, P. L. 93-569, § 7(a), 88 Stat. 1866. Such section provided for automatically guaranteed loans to a veteran for the purpose of purchasing farms and farm equipment.

Effective date of section:
Act Oct. 23, 1970, P. L. 91-506, § 8, 84 Stat. 1114, provided that this section is effective sixty days following Oct. 23, 1970.

Amendments:
1974. Act Dec. 31, 1974 (effective 12/31/74, as provided by § 10 of such Act, which appears as 38 USCS § 3701 note), in subsec. (a), inserted "or the mobile home lot loan guaranty benefit, or both," wherever appearing, and deleted "mobile home" following "this chapter until the"; in subsec. (b), designated existing matter as para. (1), redesignated clauses (1) and (2) as clauses (A) and (B), respectively, and added para. (2); in subsec. (c)(1), redesignated clauses (1) and (2) as clauses (A) and (B), respectively, and substituted "or for the purchase of a used mobile home which meets or exceeds minimum requirements for construction, design, and general acceptability prescribed by the Administrator, or the loan is for the purpose of purchasing a lot on which to place a mobile home previously purchased by the veteran, whether or not such mobile home was purchased with a loan guaranteed, insured or made by another Federal agency, and" for "or for the purchase of a used mobile home which is the security for a prior loan guaranteed or made under this section or for a loan guaranteed, insured or made by another Federal agency, and" in subsec. (d)(1), substituted "In

the case of any lot on which to place a mobile home, whether or not the mobile home was financed with assistance under this section, and in the case of necessary site preparation, the loan amount for such purposes may not exceed the reasonable value of such lot or an amount appropriate to cover the cost of necessary site preparation or both, as determined by the Administrator." for "In the case of any lot on which to place a mobile home financed through the assistance of this section and in the case of necessary site preparation, the loan amount shall not be increased by an amount in excess of the reasonable value of such lot or an amount appropriate to cover the cost of necessary site preparation or both, as determined by the Administrator."; in subsec. (d)(2), substituted subparas. (A)–(H) for subparas. (A)–(C) which read:

"(A) $10,000 for twelve years and thirty-two days in the case of a loan covering the purchase of a mobile home only, and such additional amount as is determined by the Administrator to be appropriate to cover the cost of necessary site preparation where the veteran owns the lot, or

"(B) $15,000 (but not to exceed $10,000 for the mobile home) for fifteen years and thirty-two days in the case of a loan covering the purchase of a mobile home and an undeveloped lot on which to place such home, and such additional amount as is determined by the Administrator to be appropriate to cover the cost of necessary site preparation, or

"(C) $17,500 (but not to exceed $10,000 for the mobile home) for fifteen years and thirty-two days in the case of a loan covering the purchase of a mobile home and a suitably developed lot on which to place such home.";

substituted new subsec. (e)(3) for one which read: "the loan is secured by a first lien on the mobile home and any lot acquired or improved with the proceeds of the loan;"; in subsec. (f), inserted "and mobile home lot loans"; in subsec. (i), inserted "and no loan for the purchase of a lot on which to place a mobile home owned by a veteran shall be guaranteed under this section unless the lot meets such standards prescribed for mobile home lots"; in subsec. (n), inserted "and mobile home lot loans"; and deleted subsec. (o) which read: "(o) No loans shall be guaranteed or made by the Administrator under the provisions of this section on and after July 1, 1975, except pursuant to commitments issued prior to such date.".

1976. Act June 30, 1976 (effective 6/30/76, as provided by § 9(a) of such Act, which appears as 38 USCS § 3701 note), in subsec. (c), in para. (1), substituted "the Administrator" for "he" preceding "determines", and in para. (3), substituted "the Administrator" for "he" preceding "shall allow", "may determine", and "determines"; in subsec. (d), in para. (1), substituted "the Administrator's" for "his", and in para. (3), substituted "the Administrator" for "he" preceding "shall prescribe"; in subsec. (e), in para. (4), substituted "subsection" for "subparagraph", and in para. (5), substituted "the veteran" for "he" following "that", and substituted "the veteran's" for "his"; in subsec. (f), substituted "the Administrator" for "he" preceding "determines"; in subsec. (h), substituted "the Administrator" for "he" preceding "determines to", "determines should", and "has"; in subsec. (k), substituted "the manufacturer's" for "his"; and in subsec. (l), substituted "the Administrator" for "he" preceding "determines".

Such Act further (effective 7/1/76, as provided by § 9(b) of such Act, which appears as 38 USCS § 3701 note), in subsec. (c)(3), substituted "50 percent" for "30 per centum".

1978. Act Oct. 18, 1978 (effective 10/1/78, as provided by § 108(a) of such Act, which appears as 38 USCS § 3702 note), substituted new subsecs. (a) and (b) for ones which read:

"(a) Notwithstanding any other provision of this chapter, any veteran eligible for loan guaranty benefits under this chapter who has maximum home loan guaranty entitlement available for use shall be eligible for the mobile home loan guaranty benefit or the mobile home lot loan guaranty benefit, or both, under this section. Use of the mobile home loan guaranty benefit or the mobile home lot loan guaranty benefit, or both, provided by this section shall preclude the use of any home loan guaranty entitlement under any other section of this chapter until the loan guaranteed under this section has been paid in full.

"(b)(1) Subject to the limitations in subsection (d) of this section, a loan to purchase a mobile home under this section may include (or be augmented by a separate loan for) (A) an amount to finance the acquisition of a lot on which to place such home, and (B) an additional amount to pay expenses reasonably necessary for the appropriate preparation of such a lot, including, but not limited to, the installation of utility connections, sanitary facilities and paving, and the construction of a suitable pad.

"(2) Subject to the limitations in subsection (d) of this section, a loan may be made to purchase a lot on which to place a mobile home if the veteran already has such a home. Such a loan may include an amount sufficient to pay expenses reasonably necessary for the appropriate preparation of such a lot, including, but not limited to, the installation of utility connections, sanitary facilities, and paving, and the construction of a suitable pad.";

in subsec. (c), substituted new para. (1) for one which read: "(1) Any loan to a veteran eligible under subsection (a) shall be guaranteed by the Administrator if (A) the loan is for the purpose of purchasing a new mobile home or for the purchase of a used mobile home which meets or exceeds minimum requirements for construction, design, and general acceptability prescribed by the Administrator, or the loan is for the purpose of purchasing a lot on which to place a mobile home previously purchased by the veteran, whether or not such mobile home was purchased with a loan guaranteed, insured or made by another Federal agency, and (B) the loan complies in all other respects with the requirements of this section. Loans for such purpose (including those which will also finance the acquisition of a lot or site preparation as authorized by subsection (b) of this section) shall be submitted to the Administrator for approval prior to loan closing except that the Administrator may exempt any lender of a class listed in section 1802(d) of this title from compliance with such prior approval requirement if the Administrator determines that the experience of such lender or class of lenders in mobile home financing warrants such exemption.", in para. (3), substituted "The Administrator's guaranty may not exceed the lesser of 50 per centum of the loan amount or the maximum loan guaranty entitlement available, not to exceed $17,500. Payment of a claim under such guaranty shall be made only after liquidation of the security for the loan

38 USCS § 3712　　　　　　　　　　　　　　　　Veterans' Benefits

and the filing of an accounting with the Administrator." for "The Administrator's guaranty shall not exceed 50 percent of the loan, including any amount for lot acquisition and site preparation, and payment of such guaranty shall be made only after liquidation of the security for the loan and the filing of an accounting with the Administrator.", and added para. (4); substituted new subsec. (d) for one which read:

"(d)(1) The Administrator shall establish a loan maximum for each type of loan authorized by this section. In the case of a new mobile home, the Administrator may establish a maximum loan amount based on the manufacturer's invoice cost to the dealer and such other cost factors as the Administrator considers proper to take into account. In the case of a used mobile home, the Administrator shall establish a maximum loan amount based on the Administrator's determination of the reasonable value of the property. In the case of any lot on which to place a mobile home, whether or not the mobile home was financed with assistance under this section, and in the case of necessary site preparation, the loan amount for such purposes may not exceed the reasonable value of such lot or an amount appropriate to cover the cost of necessary site preparation or both, as determined by the Administrator.

"(2) The maximum permissible loan amounts and the term for which the loans are made shall not exceed—

"(A) $12,500 for twelve years and thirty-two days in the case of a loan covering the purchase of a single-wide mobile home only and such additional amount as is determined by the Administrator to be appropriate to cover the cost of necessary site preparation where the veteran owns the lot, or

"(B) $20,000 for twenty years and thirty-two days in the case of a loan covering the purchase of a double-wide mobile home only and such additional amount as is determined by the Administrator to be appropriate to cover the cost of necessary site preparation where the veteran owns the lot, or

"(C) $20,000 (but not to exceed $12,500 for the mobile home) for fifteen years and thirty-two days in the case of a loan covering the purchase of a single-wide mobile home and an undeveloped lot on which to place such home, which includes such amount as is determined by the Administrator to be appropriate to cover the cost of necessary site preparation, or

"(D) $27,500 (but not to exceed $20,000 for the mobile home) for twenty years and thirty-two days in the case of a loan covering the purchase of a double-wide mobile home and an undeveloped lot on which to place such home, which includes such amount as is determined by the Administrator to be appropriate to cover the cost of necessary site preparation, or

"(E) $20,000 (but not to exceed $12,500 for the mobile home) for fifteen years and thirty-two days in the case of a loan covering the purchase of a single-wide mobile home and a suitably developed lot on which to place such home, or

"(F) $27,500 (but not to exceed $20,000 for the mobile home) for twenty years and thirty-two days in the case of a loan covering the purchase of a double-wide mobile home and a suitably developed lot on which to place such home, or

"(G) $7,500 for twelve years and thirty-two days in the case of a loan covering the purchase of only an undeveloped lot on which to place a mobile home owned by the veteran, which includes such amount as is determined by the Administrator to be appropriate to cover the cost of necessary site preparation, or

"(H) $7,500 for twelve years and thirty-two days in the case of a loan covering the purchase of a suitably developed lot on which to place a mobile home owned by the veteran.

"(3) Such limitations set forth in paragraph (2) of this subsection on the amount and term of any loan shall not be deemed to preclude the Administrator, under regulations which the Administrator shall prescribe, from consenting to necessary advances for the protection of the security or the holder's lien, or to a reasonable extension of the term or reamortization of such loan.";

in subsec. (e), substituted para. (4) for one which read: "(4) the amount of the loan, subject to the maximums established in subsection (d) of this section, is not in excess of the maximum amount prescribed by the Administrator;"; deleted subsec. (g) which read: "(g) Entitlement to the loan guaranty benefit used under this section shall be restored a single time for any veteran by the Administrator provided the first loan has been repaid in full."; redesignated subsecs. (h)–(n) as subsecs. (g)–(m), respectively; in subsec. (h), as so redesignated, designated existing matter as para. (1), in para. (1), as so designated, deleted "For the purpose of assuring compliance with such standards, the Administrator shall from time to time inspect the manufacturing process of mobile homes to be sold to veterans and conduct random onsite inspections of mobile homes purchased with assistance under this chapter." following "environmental conditions."; and added para. (2); in subsecs. (i) and (j), as so redesignated, substituted "subsection (h)" for "subsection (i)"; and in subsec. (l), as so redesignated, substituted "subsection (h)" for "subsection (i)" and substituted "subsection (i)" for "subsection (j)".

1980. Act Oct. 7, 1980, § 401(b) (effective 10/7/80, as provided by § 601(d) of such Act, which appears as 38 USCS § 1114 note), added subsec. (a)(1)(F) and (a)(4).

Such Act further (effective 10/1/80, as provided by § 601(b) of such Act, which appears as 38 USCS § 1114 note), in subsec. (c), in paras. (3) and (4), substituted "$20,000" for "$17,500" wherever appearing.

1981. Act Oct. 17, 1981 (effective on enactment on 10/17/81, as provided by § 701(b)(1) of such Act, which appears as 38 USCS § 1114 note), in subsec. (d), substituted para. (1) for one which read:

"(1) The maturity of any loan guaranteed under this section shall not be more than—

"(A) fifteen years and thirty-two days, in the case of a loan for the purchase of—

"(i) a lot;

"(ii) a single-wide mobile home; or

"(iii) a single-wide mobile home and a lot; or

"(B) twenty years and thirty-two days, in the case of a loan for the purchase of—

"(i) a double-wide mobile home; or

"(ii) a double-wide mobile home and a lot.".

Act Nov. 3, 1981 (effective 180 days after enactment on Nov. 3, 1981, as provided by § 305 of such Act, which appears as 38 USCS § 3741 note), in subsec. (a)(1), introductory matter, inserted "housing loan"; and in subsec. (b)(2), substituted "housing loan" for "loan guaranty".

1982. Act Oct. 12, 1982, in subsec. (l), substituted "October 23, 1970" for "the date of enactment of the Veterans' Housing Act of 1970".

Act Oct. 14, 1982 substituted this catchline for one which read: "§ 1819. Loans to purchase mobile homes and mobile home lots"; in subsec. (a), in para. (1), in subparas. (A)–(E), substituted "manufactured home" for "mobile home", and added subpara. (G), in para. (2), inserted "(other than the refinancing under clause (F) of such paragraph of an existing loan)", and substituted "manufactured home" for "mobile home", in para. (3), substituted "(C), (E), or (G)" for "(C) or (E)" and substituted "manufactured home" for "mobile home", in para. (4)(A)(ii), substituted "manufactured home" for "mobile home" and "manufactured-home" for "mobile-home", wherever appearing, and added para. (5); and in subsecs. (b)(1), (c)(1), (d)(1)(B)–(D), (e)(3), (4)(A), (B), (6), (f), (h)–(k), and (m), substituted "manufactured home" for "mobile home", wherever appearing.

1984. Act March 2, 1984, in subsec. (a)(5), in subpara. (A), in the introductory matter, and in subsec. (b), inserted "or section 1810(a)(9)(B)(ii) of this title".

1986. Act Oct. 28, 1986, in subsec. (e)(2), inserted "as determined in accordance with the regulations prescribed under section 1810(g) of this title and".

1987. Act Dec. 21, 1987 (applicable as provided by § 3(d) of such Act, which appears as 38 USCS § 3703 note), in subsec. (c), in para. (3), substituted the sentence beginning "The Administrator's guaranty . . ." for "The Administrator's guaranty may not exceed the lesser of 50 per centum of the loan amount or the maximum loan guaranty entitlement available, not to exceed $20,000.", and, in para. (4), substituted the sentence beginning "The amount of any loan . . ." for "The amount of guaranty entitlement available to a veteran under this section shall not be more than $20,000, less the amount of any such entitlement as may have been used under this section.".

Such Act further (applicable as provided by § 7(d)(1) of such Act, which appears as 38 USCS § 3710 note), in subsec. (a)(4)(A), in cl. (ii), deleted "and such manufactured home (or a manufactured home on such lot) must be owned and occupied by the veteran as such veteran's home" following "refinanced", in cl. (iv), deleted "and" following the semicolon, in cl. (v), substituted a semicolon for the concluding period, and added cl. (vi).

Such Act further (applicable as provided by § 8(c) of such Act, which appears as 38 USCS § 3704 note), in subsec. (a)(5)(A)(i), inserted "(except as provided in section 1804(c)(2) of this title)"; and in subsec. (e)(5), inserted "; except that the requirement of this clause shall not apply (A) in the case of a guaranteed loan that is for the purpose described in paragraph (1)(F) of subsection (a), or (B) in the case described in section 1804(c)(2)".

1988. Act Feb. 29, 1988 (applicable as provided by § 3(c) of such Act, which appears as 38 USCS § 3703 note), in subsec. (c), in para. (3), substituted the sentence, beginning "The Administrator's . . ." for one which read: "The Administrator's guaranty may not exceed 40 percent of the loan, or $20,000, whichever is less, reduced by the amount of entitlement previously used by the veteran under this chapter and not restored as a result of the exclusion in section 1802(b) of this title.", in para. (4), substituted the first sentence for one which read: "The amount of any loan guaranteed under this section shall not exceed an amount equal to 95 percent of the purchase price of the property securing such loan.", and added para. (5).

Act May 20, 1988 redesignated 38 USCS § 1819 as 38 USCS § 1812; and in subsecs. (a)(4)(C), (b)(1), (c)(2), (4), (d)(1), in the introductory matter, (e), in the introductory matter, (f), (g), and (h)(1), substituted "for purposes specified in this section" for "under this section"; and, in subsec. (c), in para. (3), inserted "as specified in paragraph (4) of this subsection", and in para. (4), substituted "for purposes specified in section 1810" for "under section 1810" and "for purposes specified in such section 1810" for "under such section 1810".

1989. Act Dec. 18, 1989, with the exception of subsec. (h)(2)(B), substituted "Secretary" for "Administrator", wherever appearing, and substituted "Secretary's" for "Administrator's", wherever appearing, in the entire section.

Such Act further, in subsec. (h)(2)(B), substituted "Secretary of Housing and Urban Development pursuant" for "Secretary pursuant", and substituted "Secretary of Veterans Affairs" for "Administrator", wherever appearing.

1990. Act Nov. 5, 1990 (applicable as provided by § 8031(b) of such Act, which appears as a note to this section), in subsec. (c), substituted para. (3) for one which read: "The Secretary's guaranty may not exceed the lesser of (A) the lesser of $20,000 or 40 percent of the loan, or (B) the maximum amount of guaranty entitlement available to the veteran as specified in paragraph (4) of this subsection. Payment of a claim under such guaranty shall be made only after liquidation of the security for the loan and the filing of an accounting with the Secretary. In any such accounting the Secretary shall permit to be included therein accrued unpaid interest from the date of the first uncured default to such cutoff date as the Secretary may establish, and the Secretary shall allow the holder of the loan to charge against the liquidation or resale proceeds, accrued interest from the cutoff date established, to such further date as the Secretary may determine and such costs and expenses as the Secretary determines to be reasonable and proper. The liability of the United States under the guaranty provided for by this section shall decrease or increase pro rata with any decrease or increase of the amount of the unpaid portion of the obligation.".

1991. Act June 13, 1991, in subsec. (c)(5), substituted "for purposes specified in this section" for "under this section"; and, in subsec. (1), deleted ", beginning 12 months following October 23, 1970," after "Congress shall".

Act Aug. 6, 1991, redesignated this section, formerly 38 USCS § 1812, as 38 USCS § 3712, amended the references in this section to reflect the redesignations made by § 5(a) of such Act (see Table III preceding 38 USCS § 101), and, in subsec. (a), in subparas. (4)(B) and (5)(B), substituted "Secretary" for "Veterans' Administration".

1992. Act Oct. 28, 1992, in subsec. (a)(4)(A), substituted cl. (iv) for one which read: "the amount of the guaranty of the loan may not exceed the original guaranty amount of the loan being refinanced;".

1994. Act Nov. 2, 1994, in subsec. (c)(3), in subpara. (D), inserted "of" following "subparagraph (B)", and, in subpara. (E), substituted "of this paragraph" for "of this subsection".

Such Act further, in subsec. (h), substituted para. (2) for one which read:

"(2)(A) For the purpose of assuring compliance with the standards prescribed under paragraph (1) of this subsection, the Secretary shall from time to time inspect the manufacturing process of manufacturers of manufactured homes sold to veterans utilizing assistance under this chapter. For the purpose stated in the preceding sentence and for the additional purpose of monitoring safety factors involved in the installation of manufactured homes purchased through the utilization of assistance under this chapter, the Secretary shall from time to time conduct random onsite inspections of manufactured homes purchased through the utilization of such assistance.

"(B) The Secretary of Veterans Affairs may, with the agreement of the Secretary of Housing and Urban Development, delegate to the Secretary of Housing and Urban Development the duty of the Secretary of Veterans Affairs under subparagraph (A) of this paragraph to inspect the manufacturing process of manufacturers of manufactured homes, but any such delegation shall be subject to an agreement that the Secretary of Housing and Urban Development, upon the request of the Secretary of Veterans Affairs, shall promptly provide the Secretary of Veterans Affairs with the complete results of any inspection made by the Secretary of Housing and Urban Development pursuant to such delegation. The Secretary of Veterans Affairs shall have the right to withdraw any delegation under the preceding sentence at any time and in whole or in part.".

Such Act further, in subsec. (j), substituted "in the case of—

(1) manufactured homes constructed by a manufacturer who fails or is unable to discharge the manufacturer's obligations under the warranty;

(2) manufactured homes which are determined by the Secretary not to conform to the standards provided for in subsection (h); or

(3) a manufacturer of manufactured homes who has engaged in procedures or practices determined by the Secretary to be unfair or prejudicial to veterans or the Government."

for "in the case of manufactured homes constructed by any manufacturer who refuses to permit the inspections provided for in subsection (h) of this section; or in the case of manufactured homes which are determined by the Secretary not to conform to the aforesaid standards; or where the manufacturer of manufactured homes fails or is unable to discharge the manufacturer's obligations under the warranty."

Such Act further, in subsec. (l), deleted "the results of inspections required by subsection (h) of this section," following "including" and "of this section," following "subsection (i)"; and, in subsec. (m), substituted "sections 3704(d) and 3721 of this title" for "section 3704(d) and section 3721 of this chapter".

1995. Act Dec. 21, 1995 repealed subsec. (l), which read: "The Secretary's annual report to Congress shall include a report on operations under this section, including experience with compliance with the warranty required by subsection (i) and the experience regarding defaults and foreclosures.''; and redesignated subsec. (m) as subsec. (l).

Other provisions:
Authority of the Administrator to promulgate regulations. For the authority and effective date for the Administrator of Veterans' Affairs to promulgate regulations under 38 USCS §§ 3741 et seq., see § 305 of Act Nov. 3, 1981, which appears as 38 USCS § 3741 note.
Application and construction of Oct. 12, 1982 amendment. For provisions as to the application and construction of the Oct. 12, 1982 amendment of this section, see § 5 of such Act, which appears as 10 USCS § 101 note.
Application of 1990 amendment of subsec. (c)(3). Act Nov. 5, 1990, P. L. 101-508, Title VIII, Subtitle D, § 8031(b), 104 Stat. 1388-348, provides: "The amendment made by this section [amending subsec. (c)(3) of this section] shall apply to claims filed with the Secretary of Veterans Affairs on or after the date of the enactment of this Act.''.

CODE OF FEDERAL REGULATIONS
Department of Veterans Affairs—Loan guaranty, 38 CFR Part 36.

CROSS REFERENCES
This section is referred to in 38 USCS §§ 3701, 3703, 3704, 3710, 3711, 3724, 3725, 3729, 3762.

RESEARCH GUIDE
Federal Procedure L Ed:
4A Fed Proc L Ed, Banking and Financing §§ 8:1426, 1434.

Am Jur:
77 Am Jur 2d, Veterans and Veterans' Laws § 121.

§ 3713. Release from liability under guaranty

(a) Whenever any veteran disposes of residential property securing a guaranteed, insured, or direct housing loan obtained by the veteran, the Secretary, upon application made by such veteran and by the transferee incident to such disposal, shall issue to such veteran in connection with such disposal a release relieving the veteran of all further liability to the Secretary on account of such loan (including liability for any loss resulting from any default of the transferee or any subsequent purchaser of such property) if the Secretary has determined, after such investigation as the Secretary may deem appropriate, that (1) the loan is current, and (2) the purchaser of such property from such veteran (A) is obligated by contract to purchase such property and to assume full liability for the repayment of the balance of the loan remaining unpaid, and has assumed by contract all of the obligations of the veteran under the terms of the instruments creating and securing the loan, and (B) qualifies from a credit standpoint, to the same extent as if the transferee were a veteran eligible for purposes specified in section 3710 of this title, for a guaranteed or insured or direct loan in an amount equal to the unpaid balance of the obligation for which the transferee has assumed liability.

(b) If any veteran disposes of residential property securing a guaranteed, insured, or direct housing loan obtained by the veteran under this chapter [38 USCS §§ 3701 et seq.] without receiving a release from liability with respect to such loan under subsection (a), and a default subsequently occurs which results in liability of the veteran to the Secretary on account of the loan, the Secretary may relieve the veteran of such liability if the Secretary determines, after such investigation as the Secretary deems appropriate, that the property was disposed of by the veteran in such a manner, and subject to such conditions, that the Secretary would have issued the veteran a release from liability under subsection (a) with respect to the loan if the veteran had made application therefor incident to such disposal. Failure of a transferee to assume by contract all of the liabilities of the original veteran-borrower shall bar such release of liability only in cases in which no acceptable transferee, either immediate or remote, is legally liable to the Secretary for the indebtedness of the original veteran-borrower arising from termination of the loan. The failure of a veteran to qualify for release from liability under this subsection does not preclude relief from being granted under section 5302(b) of this title, if the veteran is eligible for relief under that section.

(c) This section shall apply only to loans for which commitments are made before March 1, 1988.

(Sept. 2, 1958, P. L. 85-857, § 1, 72 Stat. 1212; June 30, 1972, P. L. 92-328, Title II, § 204, 86 Stat. 397; June 30, 1976, P. L. 94-324, § 7(18), (19), 90 Stat. 722; Nov. 3, 1981, P. L. 97-72, Title III, § 303(f), 95 Stat. 1060; Dec. 21, 1987, P. L. 100-198, § 10(a)(2), 101 Stat. 1323; May 20, 1988, P. L. 100-322, Title IV, Part C, § 415(b)(2), 102 Stat. 550; Dec. 18, 1989, P. L. 101-237, Title III, § 313(b)(1), 103 Stat. 2077; May 7, 1991, P. L. 102-40, Title IV, § 402(d)(1), 105 Stat. 239; Aug. 6, 1991, P. L. 102-83, § 5(a), (c)(1), 105 Stat. 406; Nov. 2, 1994, P. L. 103-446, Title XII, § 1201(e)(15), 108 Stat. 4686.)

HISTORY; ANCILLARY LAWS AND DIRECTIVES

Explanatory notes:
A prior § 1813 (Act Sept. 2, 1958, P. L. 85-857, § 1, 72 Stat. 1211) was repealed by Act Dec. 31, 1974, P. L. 93-569, § 7(a), 88 Stat. 1866. Such section provided for automatically guaranteed loans made to a veteran if made for the purpose of purchasing business property.

Amendments:
1972. Act June 30, 1972 (effective 6/30/72, as provided by § 301(c) of such Act, which appears as a note to this section), designated existing matter as subsec. (a); and added subsec. (b).
1976. Act June 30, 1976 (effective 6/30/76, as provided by § 9(a) of such Act, which appears as 38 USCS § 3701 note), in subsec. (a), substituted "the veteran" for "him" following "by" and "relieving", substituted "the Administrator" for "he" preceding "may deem", substituted "is obligated" for "has obligated himself", and substituted "the transferee" for "he" preceding "were" and "has assumed"; and in subsec. (b), substituted "the veteran" for "him" preceding "under this chapter", and substituted "the Administrator" for "he" preceding "determines" and "deems".

1981. Act Nov. 3, 1981 (effective 180 days after enactment on Nov. 3, 1981, as provided by § 305 of such Act, which appears as 38 USCS § 3741 note), in subsecs. (a) and (b), inserted "housing".
1987. Act Dec. 21, 1987 added subsec. (c).
1988. Act May 20, 1988 redesignated 38 USCS § 1817 as this section (38 USCS § 1813); and in subsec. (a), as so redesignated, substituted "for purposes specified in section 1810" for "under section 1810".
1989. Act Dec. 18, 1989, in subsecs. (a) and (b), substituted "Secretary" for "Administrator", wherever appearing.
1991. Act May 7, 1991, § 402(d)(1), amended the references in this section to reflect the redesignations made by §§ 401(a)(4) and 402(b) of such Act (see Table II preceding 38 USCS § 101).
Act Aug. 6, 1991, redesignated this section, formerly 38 USCS § 1813, as 38 USCS § 3713, and amended the references in this section to reflect the redesignations made by § 5(a) of such Act (see Table III preceding 38 USCS § 101).
1994. Act Nov. 2, 1994, in subsec. (b), substituted "section 5302(b) of this title, if the veteran is eligible for relief under that section" for "subsection 5302(b) of this title, if eligible thereunder".

Other provisions:
Authority of the Administrator to promulgate regulations. For the authority and effective date for the Administrator of Veterans' Affairs to promulgate regulations under 38 USCS §§ 3741 et seq., see § 305 of Act Nov. 3, 1981, which appears as 38 USCS § 3741 note.

CODE OF FEDERAL REGULATIONS
Department of Veterans Affairs—Loan guaranty, 38 CFR Part 36.

RESEARCH GUIDE
Federal Procedure L Ed:
4A Fed Proc L Ed, Banking and Financing § 8:1425.
Am Jur:
77 Am Jur 2d, Veterans and Veterans' Laws §§ 123, 127.

INTERPRETIVE NOTES AND DECISIONS

1. Generally
2. Release under particular circumstances
3. Miscellaneous

1. Generally
Only Veterans Administration [now Department of Veterans Affairs] has power to grant release from liability under guaranteed loan and absent such release from Veterans Administration [now Department], veteran-borrower remains under obligation to indemnify Veterans Administration [now Department] for amounts paid under guaranty. Davis v National Homes Acceptance Corp. (1981, ND Ala) 523 F Supp 477.

2. Release under particular circumstances
Veteran may be released from all personal liability resulting from VA guaranteed loan when property securing loan is transferred upon divorce to veteran's spouse who assumes total responsibility for loan, provided (1) divorce is final and absolute and no appeal will be taken, (2) entire estate has become vested in spouse, (3) loan is current, (4) Veterans Administration [now Department of Veterans Affairs] income and credit requirements can be met by spouse and (5) no property settlement exists which would make veteran liable as between parties. VA GCO 1-78.

Statute clearly requires Veterans' Administration [now Department of Veterans Affairs] to look at situation as it existed at time of transfer when deciding whether veteran would have been entitled to release had he applied for one incident to disposal of property subject to guarantee; hence decision that veteran was not entitled to waiver because transferee who assumed defaulted during first 12 months and was therefore not considered satisfactory risk was erroneous. Travelstead v Derwinski (1991) 1 Vet App 344, affd (1992, CA) 978 F2d 1244, 93 Daily Journal DAR 1163.

3. Miscellaneous

Board erred in failing to make determination on veteran's claim contesting legitimacy of asserted indebtedness, contending that Ro, as well as lender, failed to provide him with adequate notice of default and foreclosure sale. Carlson v Derwinski (1992) 2 Vet App 144.

Remand was required for BVA to readjudicate matter regarding retroactive release from liability by applying correct statutory standard to facts of case regarding creditworthiness of transferees to determine whether release from liability would have been granted had veteran applied for one at time of transfer of property to subsequent purchaser. Elkins v Derwinski (1992) 2 Vet App 422.

§ 3714. Assumptions; release from liability

(a)(1) Except as provided in subsection (f) of this section, if a veteran or any other person disposes of residential property securing a loan guaranteed, insured, or made under this chapter [38 USCS §§ 3701 et seq.] and the veteran or other person notifies the holder of the loan in writing before the property is disposed of, the veteran or other person, as the case may be, shall be relieved of all further liability to the Secretary with respect to the loan (including liability for any loss resulting from any default of the purchaser or any subsequent owner of the property) and the application for assumption shall be approved if the holder determines that—

(A) the loan is current; and

(B) the purchaser of the property from such veteran or other person—

(i) is obligated by contract to purchase such property and to assume full liability for the repayment of the balance of the loan remaining unpaid and has assumed by contract all of the obligations of the veteran under the terms of the instruments creating and securing the loan; and

(ii) qualifies from a credit standpoint, to the same extent as if the purchaser were a veteran eligible under section 3710 of this title, for a guaranteed or insured or direct loan in an amount equal to the unpaid balance of the obligation for which the purchaser is to assume liability.

(2) For the purposes of paragraph (1), paragraph (3), and paragraph (4)(C)(ii) of this subsection, the Secretary shall be considered to be the holder of the loan if the actual holder is not an approved lender described in section 3702.

(3) If the holder of the loan determines that the loan is not current or that the purchaser of the property does not meet the requirements of paragraph (1)(B) of this subsection, the holder shall—

(A) notify the transferor and the Secretary of such determination; and

(B) notify the transferor that the transferor may appeal the determination to the Secretary.

(4)(A) Upon the appeal of the transferor after a determination described in paragraph (3) is made, the Secretary shall, in a timely manner, review and make a determination (or a redetermination in any case in which the Secretary made the determination described in such paragraph) with respect to whether the loan is current and whether the purchaser of the property meets the requirements of paragraph (1)(B) of this subsection. The Secretary shall transmit, in writing, a notice of the nature of such determination to the transferor and the holder and shall inform them of the action that shall or may be taken under subparagraph (B) of this paragraph as a result of the determination of the Secretary.

(B)(i) If the Secretary determines under subparagraph (A) of this paragraph that the loan is current and that the purchaser meets the requirements of paragraph (1)(B) of this subsection, the holder shall approve the assumption of the loan, and the transferor shall be relieved of all liability to the Secretary with respect to such loan.

(ii) If the Secretary determines under subparagraph (A) of this paragraph that the purchaser does not meet the requirements of paragraph (1)(B) of this subsection, the Secretary may direct the holder to approve the assumption of the loan if—

(I) the Secretary determines that the transferor of the property is unable to make payments on the loan and has made reasonable efforts to find a buyer who meets the requirements of paragraph (1)(B) of this subsection and that, as a result, the proposed transfer is in the best interests of the Department and the transferor;

(II) the transferor has requested, within 15 days after receiving the notice referred to in subparagraph (A) of this paragraph, that the Secretary approve the assumption; and

(III) the transferor will, upon assumption of the loan by the purchaser, be secondarily liable on the loan.

(C) If— (i) the loan is not approved for assumption under subparagraph (B) of this paragraph or paragraph (1) of this subsection; or

(ii) no appeal is made by the transferor under subparagraph (A) of this paragraph within 30 days after the holder informs the transferor of its determination under paragraph (3) of this subsection,

the holder may demand immediate, full payment of the principal, and all interest earned thereon, of such loan if the transferor disposes of the property.

(b) If a person disposes of residential property described in subsection (a)(1) of this section and the person fails to notify the holder of the loan before the property is disposed of, the holder, upon learning of such action by the person, may demand immediate and full payment of the principal, interest, and all other amounts owing under the terms of the loan.

(c)(1) In any case in which the holder of a loan described in subsection (a)(1) of this section has knowledge of a person's disposing of residential property securing the loan, the holder shall notify the Secretary of such action.

(2) If the holder fails to notify the Secretary in such a case, the holder shall be liable to the Secretary for any damage sustained by the Secretary as a result of the holder's failure, as determined at the time the Secretary is required to make payments in accordance with any insurance or guaranty provided by the Secretary with respect to the loan concerned.

(d) The Secretary shall provide that the mortgage or deed of trust and any other instrument evidencing the loan entered into by a person with respect to a loan guaranteed, insured, or made under this chapter shall contain provisions, in such form as the Secretary shall specify, implementing the requirements of this section, and shall bear in conspicuous position in capital letters on the first page of the document in type at least 2 and ½ times larger than the regular type on such page the following: "This loan is not assumable without the approval of the Department of Veterans Affairs or its authorized agent.".

(e) The Secretary shall establish in regulations a reasonable amount as the maximum amount that a lender may charge for processing an application for a creditworthiness determination and assumption of a loan pursuant to this section. Such regulations shall establish requirements for the timely processing of applications for acceptance of assumptions.

(f)(1) This section shall apply—
    (A) in the case of loans other than loans to finance the purchase of real property described in section 3733(a)(1) of this title, only to loans for which commitments are made on or after March 1, 1988; and
    (B) in the case of loans to finance the purchase of such property, only to loans which are closed more than 45 days after the date of the enactment of the Veterans' Benefits and Programs Improvement Act of 1988 [enacted Nov. 18, 1988].

(2) This section shall not apply to a loan which the Secretary has sold without recourse.

(Added Dec. 21, 1987, P. L. 100-198, § 10(a)(1), 101 Stat. 1321; May 20, 1988, P. L. 100-322, Title IV, Part B, § 415(b)(2)(B), 102 Stat. 551; Nov. 18, 1988, P. L. 100-689, Title III, § 302, 102 Stat. 4176; Dec. 18, 1989, P. L. 101-237, Title III, § 313(b)(1), 103 Stat. 2077; Aug. 6, 1991, P. L. 102-83, §§ 4(a)(2)(B)(iv), (3), (4), 5(a), (c)(1), 105 Stat. 403, 404, 406.)

HISTORY; ANCILLARY LAWS AND DIRECTIVES

Explanatory notes:
A prior § 1814 (Act Sept. 2, 1958, P. L. 85-857, § 1, 72 Stat. 1211; July 14, 1960, P. L. 86-665, § 3, 74 Stat. 531; July 6, 1961, P. L. 87-84, § 1(c), 75 Stat. 201) was repealed by Act Dec. 31, 1974, P. L. 93-569, § 7(a), 88 Stat. 1866. Such section provided for automatically guaranteed loans made to a veteran if made for the purpose of refinancing delinquent indebtedness.

Amendments:
1988. Act May 20, 1988 redesignated 38 USCS § 1817A as 38 USCS § 1814.

Act Nov. 18, 1988, in subsec. (a)(1), in the introductory matter, substituted "Except as provided in subsection (f) of this section, if" for "If" and substituted "loan guaranteed, insured, or made" for "guaranteed, insured, or direct housing loan obtained by a veteran"; and substituted subsec. (f) for one which read: "This section shall apply only to loans for which commitments are made on or after March 1, 1988.".

1989. Act Dec. 18, 1989, substituted "Secretary" for "Administrator", wherever appearing, in the entire section.

1991. Act Aug. 6, 1991, redesignated this section, formerly 38 USCS § 1814, as 38 USCS § 3714, amended the references in this section to reflect the redesignations made by § 5(a) of such Act (see Table III preceding 38 USCS § 101), and, in subsec. (d), substituted "Department of Veterans Affairs" for "Veterans' Administration".

Such Act further, in subsec. (a)(4)(B)(ii)(I), substituted "Department" for "Veterans' Administration".

CODE OF FEDERAL REGULATIONS
Department of Veterans Affairs—Loan guaranty, 38 CFR Part 36.

CROSS REFERENCES
This section is referred to in 38 USCS §§ 3704, 3729.

RESEARCH GUIDE
Federal Procedure L Ed:
4A Fed Proc L Ed, Banking and Financing § 8:1425.

Am Jur:
77 Am Jur 2d, Veterans and Veterans' Laws § 123.

[§ 3715]. [§ 1815. Transferred]

HISTORY; ANCILLARY LAWS AND DIRECTIVES
The bracketed section number "3715" was inserted to preserve numerical continuity following the section number redesignations made by Act Aug. 6, 1991, P. L. 102-83, § 5(a), 105 Stat. 406.

This section (Act Sept. 2, 1958, P. L. 85-857, § 1, 72 Stat. 1212; Dec. 31, 1974, P. L. 93-569, § 8(5), 88 Stat. 1866; June 30, 1976, P. L. 94-324, § 7(16), 90 Stat. 721; Nov. 3, 1981, P. L. 97-72, Title III, § 303(e), 95 Stat. 1060) was amended and transferred to 38 USCS § 1803(a)(2) by Act May 20, 1988, P. L. 100-322, Title IV, Part C, § 415(a)(3)(A), 102 Stat. 500.

[§ 3716]. [§ 1816. Transferred]

HISTORY; ANCILLARY LAWS AND DIRECTIVES
The bracketed section number "3716" was inserted to preserve numerical continuity following the section number redesignations made by Act Aug. 6, 1991, P. L. 102-83, § 5(a), 105 Stat. 406.

This section (Act Sept. 2, 1958, P. L. 85-857, § 1, 72 Stat. 1212; Aug. 10, 1965, P. L. 89-117, Title I, § 107(f), 79 Stat. 460; June 30, 1976, P. L. 94-324, § 7(17), 90 Stat. 722.) was amended and subsecs. (a)-(c) were transferred to 38 USCS § 1832(a)-(c), respectively, and subsecs. (d)-(f) were transferred to 38 USCS § 1833(a)-(c), respectively, by Act May 20, 1988, P. L. 100-322, Title IV, Part B, § 415(b)(1), 102 Stat. 550.

[§ 3717]. [§ 1817. Transferred]

HISTORY; ANCILLARY LAWS AND DIRECTIVES
The bracketed section number "3717" was inserted to preserve numerical continuity following the section number redesignations made by Act Aug. 6, 1991, P. L. 102-83, § 5(a), 105 Stat. 406.

38 USCS § 3717]

This section (Act Sept. 2, 1958, P. L. 85-857, § 1, 72 Stat. 1212; June 30, 1972, P. L. 92-328, Title II, § 204, 86 Stat. 397; June 30, 1976, P. L. 94-324, § 7(18), (19), 90 Stat. 722.) was redesignated and transferred to 38 USCS § 1813 by Act May 20, 1988, P. L. 100-322, § 415(b)(2), 102 Stat. 551.

[§ 3717A]. [§ 1817A. Transferred]

HISTORY; ANCILLARY LAWS AND DIRECTIVES

The bracketed section number "3717A" was inserted to preserve numerical continuity following the section number redesignations made by Act Aug. 6, 1991, P. L. 102-83, § 5(a), 105 Stat. 406.

This section was redesignated and transferred to 38 USCS § 1814 by Act May 20, 1988, P. L. 100-322, Title IV, Part B, § 415(b)(2)(B), 102 Stat. 550.

[§ 3718]. [§ 1818. Repealed]

HISTORY; ANCILLARY LAWS AND DIRECTIVES

The bracketed section number "3718" was inserted to preserve numerical continuity following the section number redesignations made by Act Aug. 6, 1991, P. L. 102-83, § 5(a), 105 Stat. 406.

This section (Act March 3, 1966, P. L. 89-358, § 5(a), 80 Stat. 25; Oct. 23, 1970, P. L. 91-506, § 2(e), 84 Stat. 1108; Dec. 31, 1974, P. L. 93-569, § 8(6), (7), 88 Stat. 1866; June 30, 1976, P. L. 94-324, § 4, 90 Stat. 720; Oct. 18, 1978, P. L. 95-476, Title I, § 106(a), 92 Stat. 1499; Nov. 3, 1981, P. L. 97-72, Title III, § 303(g), 95 Stat. 1060; Oct. 12, 1982, P. L. 97-295, § 4(66) in part, 96 Stat. 1310) was repealed by Act May 20, 1988, P. L. 100-322, Title IV, Part B, § 415(b)(3), 102 Stat. 551. Such section provided for service after January 31, 1955, and prior to August 5, 1964, or after May 7, 1975.

[§ 3719]. [§ 1819. Transferred]

HISTORY; ANCILLARY LAWS AND DIRECTIVES

The bracketed section number "3719" was inserted to preserve numerical continuity following the section number redesignations made by Act Aug. 6, 1991, P. L. 102-83, § 5(a), 105 Stat. 406.

This section (Act Oct. 23, 1970, P. L. 91-506, § 5, 84 Stat. 1110; Dec. 31, 1974, P. L. 93-569, § 5, 88 Stat. 1864; June 30, 1976, P. L. 94-324, §§ 5, 7(20)-(23), 90 Stat. 720, 722; Oct. 18, 1978, P. L. 95-476, Title I, § 107, 92 Stat. 1500; Oct. 7, 1980, P. L. 96-385, Title IV, §§ 401(b), 402(c), 94 Stat. 1532.) was amended and transferred to 38 USCS § 1812 by Act May 20, 1988, P. L. 100-322, Title IV, Part B, § 415(b)(4), 102 Stat. 551.

SUBCHAPTER III. ADMINISTRATIVE PROVISIONS

§ 3720. Powers of Secretary

(a) Notwithstanding the provisions of any other law, with respect to matters arising by reason of this chapter [38 USCS §§ 3701 et seq.], the Secretary may—

(1) sue and be sued in the Secretary's official capacity in any court of competent jurisdiction, State or Federal, but nothing in this clause shall be construed as authorizing garnishment or attachment against the Secretary, the Department of Veterans Affairs, or any of its employees;

(2) subject to specific limitations in this chapter [38 USCS §§ 3701 et seq.], consent to the modification, with respect to rate of interest, time of payment of principal or interest or any portion thereof, security or other provisions of any note, contract, mortgage or other instrument securing a loan which has been guaranteed, insured, made or acquired under this chapter [38 USCS §§ 3701 et seq.];

(3) pay, or compromise, any claim on, or arising because of, any such guaranty or insurance;

(4) pay, compromise, waive or release any right, title, claim, lien or demand, however acquired, including any equity or any right of redemption;

(5) purchase at any sale, public or private, upon such terms and for such prices as the Secretary determines to be reasonable, and take title to, property, real, personal or mixed; and similarly sell, at public or private sale, exchange, assign, convey, or otherwise dispose of any such property; and

(6) complete, administer, operate, obtain and pay for insurance on, and maintain, renovate, repair, modernize, lease, or otherwise deal with any property acquired or held pursuant to this chapter [38 USCS §§ 3701 et seq.]. The acquisition of any such property shall not deprive any State or political subdivision thereof of its civil or criminal jurisdiction of, on, or over such property (including power to tax) or impair the rights under the State or local law of any persons on such property. Without regard to section 3302(b) of title 31 or any other provision of law not expressly in limitation of this paragraph, the Secretary may permit brokers utilized by the Secretary in connection with such properties to deduct from rental collections amounts covering authorized fees, costs, and expenses incurred in connection with the management, repair, sale, or lease of any such properties and remit the net balances to the Secretary.

(b) The powers granted by this section may be exercised by the Secretary without regard to any other provision of law not enacted expressly in limitation of this section, which otherwise would govern the expenditure of public-funds; however, section 3709 of the Revised Statutes (41 U.S.C. 5) shall apply to any contract for services or supplies on account of any property acquired pursuant to this section if the amount of such contract exceeds the amount prescribed in clause (1) of the first sentence of such section.

(c) The financial transactions of the Secretary incident to, or arising out of, the guaranty or insurance of loans pursuant to this chapter [38 USCS §§ 3701 et seq.], and the acquisition, management, and disposition of property, real, personal, or mixed, incident to such activities and pursuant to this section, shall be final and conclusive upon all officers of the Government.

(d) The right to redeem provided for by section 2410(c) of title 28 shall not arise in any case in which the subordinate lien or interest of the United States derives from a guaranteed or insured loan.

(e)(1) The Secretary is authorized from time to time, as the Secretary determines advisable, to set aside first mortgage loans, and installment sale contracts, owned and held by the Secretary under this chapter [38 USCS §§ 3701 et seq.] as the basis for the sale of participation certificates as herein provided. For this purpose the Secretary may enter into agreements, including trust agreements, with the Government National Mortgage Association, and any other Federal agency, under which the Association as fiduciary may sell certificates of participation based on principal and interest collections to be received by the Secretary and the Association or any other such agency on first mortgage loans and installment sale contracts comprising mortgage pools established by them. The agreement may provide for substitution or withdrawal of mortgage loans, or installment sale contracts, or for substitution of cash for mortgages in the pool. The agreement shall provide that the Governmental National Mortgage Association shall promptly pay to the Secretary the entire proceeds of any sale of certificates of participation to the extent such certificates are based on mortgages, including installment sale contracts, set aside by the Secretary and the Secretary shall periodically pay to the Association, as fiduciary, such funds as are required for payment of interest and principal due on outstanding certificates of participation to the extent of the pro rata amount allocated to the Secretary pursuant to the agreement. The agreement shall also provide that the Secretary shall retain ownership of mortgage loans and installment sale contracts set aside by the Secretary pursuant to the agreement unless transfer of ownership to the fiduciary is required in the event of default or probable default in the payment of participation certificates. The Secretary is authorized to purchase outstanding certificates of participation to the extent of the amount of the Secretary's commitment to the fiduciary on participations outstanding and to pay the Secretary's proper share of the costs and expenses incurred by the Government National Mortgage Association as fiduciary pursuant to the agreement.

(2) The Secretary shall proportionately allocate and deposit the entire proceeds received from the sale of participations into the funds established pursuant to sections 3723 and 3724 of this chapter, as determined on an estimated basis, and the amounts so deposited shall be available for the purposes of the funds. The Secretary may nevertheless make such allocations of that part of the proceeds of participation sales representing anticipated interest collections on mortgage loans, including installment sale contracts, on other than an estimated proportionate basis if determined necessary to assure payment of interest on advances theretofore made to the Secretary by the Secretary of the Treasury for direct loan purposes. The Secretary shall set aside and maintain necessary reserves in the funds established pursuant to sections 3723 and 3724 of this chapter to be used for meeting commitments pursuant to this subsection and, as the Secretary determines to be necessary, for meeting interest payments on advances by the Secretary of the Treasury for direct loan purposes.

(f) Whenever loss, destruction, or damage to any residential property securing loans guaranteed, insured, made, or acquired by the Secretary under this chapter [38 USCS §§ 3701 et seq.] occurs as the result of a major disaster as determined by the President under the Disaster Relief and Emergency Assistance Act (42 U.S.C. 5121 et seq.), the Secretary shall (1) provide counseling and such other service to the owner of such property as may be feasible and shall inform such owner concerning the disaster assistance available from other Federal agencies and from State or local agencies, and (2) pursuant to subsection (a)(2) of this section, extend on an individual case basis such forbearance or indulgence to such owner as the Secretary determines to be warranted by the facts of the case and the circumstances of such owner.

(g) The Secretary shall, at the request of the Secretary of Housing and Urban Development and without reimbursement, certify to such Secretary whether an applicant for assistance under any law administered by the Department of Housing and Urban Development is a veteran.

(h)(1) The Secretary may, upon such terms and conditions as the Secretary considers appropriate, issue or approve the issuance of, and guarantee the timely payment of principal and interest on, certificates or other securities evidencing an interest in a pool of mortgage loans made in connection with the sale of properties acquired under this chapter [38 USCS §§ 3701 et seq.].
(2) The Secretary may not under this subsection guarantee the payment of principal and interest on certificates or other securities issued or approved after December 31, 2002.

(Sept. 2, 1958, P. L. 85-857, § 1, 72 Stat. 1213; Oct. 17, 1963, P. L. 88-151, § 1, 77 Stat. 271; Sept. 2, 1964, P. L. 88-560, Title VII, § 701(e)(1), 78 Stat. 800; Oct. 4, 1966, P. L. 89-625, 80 Stat. 874; Nov. 6, 1966, P. L. 89-769, § 3(c), 80 Stat. 1316; Aug. 1, 1968, P. L. 90-448, Title VIII, § 807(h), 82 Stat. 545; Dec. 31, 1970, P. L. 91-606, Title II, § 233, 84 Stat. 1753; June 30, 1972, P. L. 92-328, Title II, § 205, 86 Stat. 397; May 22, 1974, P. L. 93-288, Title VII, [VI] § 702(l) [602(l)], 88 Stat. 164; June 30, 1976, P. L. 94-324, § 7(24)–(26), 90 Stat. 722; Oct. 3, 1977, P. L. 95-117, Title IV, § 403(a), 91 Stat. 1066; Oct. 12, 1982, P. L. 97-295, § 4(67), 96 Stat. 1310; Sept. 13, 1982, P. L. 97-258, § 3(k)(3), 96 Stat. 1065; Nov. 21, 1983, P. L. 98-160, Title VII, § 702(14), 97 Stat. 1009; Oct. 28, 1986, P. L. 99-576, Title IV, Part A, § 404, 100 Stat. 3281; Nov. 23, 1988, P. L. 100-707, Title I, § 109(n), 102 Stat. 4709; Dec. 18, 1989, P. L. 101-237, Title III, § 313(b)(1), (2), 103 Stat. 2077; June 13, 1991, P. L. 102-54, § 4(a), 105 Stat. 268; Aug. 6, 1991, P. L. 102-83, § 5(a), (c)(1), 105 Stat. 406; May 20, 1992, P. L. 102-291, § 5(a), 106 Stat. 179; Oct. 28, 1992, P. L. 102-547, § 4, 106 Stat. 3636; Oct. 5, 1994, P. L. 103-337, Div C, Title XXXIV, Subtitle B, § 3411(a)(1), (2), 108 Stat. 3100; Feb. 13, 1996, P. L. 104-110, Title I, § 101(f), 110 Stat. 768; Oct. 9, 1996, P. L. 104-275, Title II, Subtitle A, § 201, 110 Stat. 3330; Aug. 5, 1997, P. L. 105-33, Title VIII, Subtitle A, § 8011, 111 Stat. 664.)

HISTORY; ANCILLARY LAWS AND DIRECTIVES

References in text:
The "Disaster Relief and Emergency Assistance Act", referred to in this

38 USCS § 3720 VETERANS' BENEFITS

section, is Act May 22, 1974, P. L. 93-288, 88 Stat. 143, also known as the Robert T. Stafford Disaster Relief and Emergency Assistance Act, which appears generally as 42 USCS §§ 5121 et seq. For full classification of such Act, consult USCS Tables volumes.

Amendments:
1963. Act Oct. 17, 1963, in subsec. (a)(4), inserted "and the authority to waive or release claims may include partial or total waiver of payment by the veteran, or his spouse, following default and loss of the property where the Administrator determines that the default arose out of compelling reasons without fault on the part of the veteran or that collection of the indebtedness would otherwise work a severe hardship upon the veteran;".
1964. Act Sept. 2, 1964, added subsec. (e).
1966. Act Oct. 4, 1966, in subsec. (a)(6), inserted "Without regard to section 3617, Revised Statutes (31 U.S.C. 484), or any other provision of law not expressly in limitation of this paragraph, the Administrator may permit brokers utilized by him in connection with such properties to deduct from rental collections amounts covering authorized fees, costs, and expenses incurred in connection with the management, repair, sale, or lease of any such properties and remit the net balances to the Administrator.".

Act Nov. 6, 1966 (effective as provided by § 14 of such Act), added subsec. (f).

1968. Act Aug. 1, 1968 (effective as provided by § 808 of such Act, which appears as 12 USCS § 1716b note), in subsec. (e)(1), substituted "Government National" for "Federal National" wherever appearing.
1970. Act Dec. 31, 1970 (effective as of 4/1/70, as provided by § 304 of such Act), substituted subsec. (a)(2) for one which read: "(2) subject to specific limitations in this chapter, consent to the modification, with respect to rate of interest, time of payment of principal or interest or any portion thereof, security or other provisions of any note, contract, mortgage or other instrument securing a loan which has been guaranteed or insured under this chapter;" and substituted subsec. (f) for one which read: "(f) The Administrator is authorized to refinance any loan made, or acquired by the Veterans' Administration when he finds such refinancing necessary because of the loss, destruction, or damage to property securing such loan as the result of a major disaster as determined by the President pursuant to the Act entitled 'An Act to authorize Federal assistance to States and local governments in major disasters, and for other purposes', approved September 30, 1950, as amended (42 U.S.C. 1855-1855g). The interest rate on any loan refinanced under this subsection may be reduced to a rate not less than (i) a rate determined by the Secretary of the Treasury taking into consideration the current average market yield on outstanding marketable obligations of the United States with remaining periods to maturity comparable to the average maturity of such loan, adjusted to the nearest one-eighth of 1 per centum, less (ii) not to exceed 2 per centum per annum, and the term thereof may be extended for such period as will provide a maturity of not to exceed forty years; except that the Administrator may authorize a suspension in the payment of principal and interest charges on, and an additional extension in the maturity of, any such loan for a period not to exceed five years if he determines that such action is necessary to avoid severe financial hardship.".

1972. Act June 30, 1972 (effective 6/30/72, as provided by § 301(a) of such

Act, which appears as 38 USCS § 3713 note), in subsec. (a)(4), deleted "and the authority to waive or release claims may include partial or total waiver of payment by the veteran, or his spouse, following default and loss of the property where the Administrator determines that the default arose out of compelling reasons without fault on the part of the veteran or that collection of the indebtedness would otherwise work a severe hardship upon the veteran;" following "right of redemption;".

1974. Act May 22, 1974 (effective 4/1/74, as provided by § 605 of such Act which appears as 42 USCS § 5121 note), in subsec. (f), substituted "the Disaster Relief Act of 1974" for "the Disaster Assistance Act of 1970".

1976. Act June 30, 1976 (effective 6/30/76, as provided by § 9(a) of such Act, which appears as 38 USCS § 3701 note), in subsec. (a), in para. (1), substituted "the Administrator's" for "his", in para. (5), substituted "the Administrator" for "he", and in para. (6), substituted "the Administrator" for "him" following "by"; and in subsec. (e), in para. (1), substituted "the Administrator" for "he" preceding "determines" and "shall periodically", substituted "the Administrator" for "him" following "set aside by", and substituted "the Administrator's" for "his" wherever appearing and in para. (2), substituted "the Administrator" for "he" preceding "determines".

1977. Act Oct. 3, 1977 (effective as provided by § 403(b) of such Act, which appears as a note to this section), in subsec. (a)(1), inserted ", but nothing in this clause shall be construed as authorizing garnishment or attachment against the Administrator, the Veterans' Administration, or any of its employees".

1982. Act Sept. 13, 1982, in subsec. (a)(6), substituted "section 3302(b) of title 31" for "section 3617, Revised Statutes (31 U.S.C 484)".

Act Oct. 12, 1982, in subsec. (f), inserted "(42 U.S.C. 5121 et seq.)".

1983. Act Nov. 21, 1983, in subsec. (a)(6), deleted a comma following "title 31"; and, in subsec. (b), substituted "section 3709 of the Revised Statutes (41 U.S.C. 5)" for "section 5 of title 41".

1986. Act Oct. 28, 1986, in subsec. (b), substituted "the amount prescribed in clause (1) of the first sentence of such section" for "$1,000".

1988. Act Nov. 23, 1988, in subsec. (f), substituted "and Emergency Assistance Act" for "Act of 1974".

1989. Act Dec. 18, 1989, substituted "Secretary" for "Administrator", "Secretary's" for "Administrator's", and "Department of Veterans Affairs" for "Veterans' Administration", wherever appearing, in the section heading, and throughout the entire section.

1991. Act June 13, 1991 added subsec. (g).

Act Aug. 6, 1991, redesignated this section, formerly 38 USCS § 1820, as 38 USCS § 3720, and amended the references in this section to reflect the redesignations made by § 5(a) of such Act (see Table III preceding 38 USCS § 101).

1992. Act May 20, 1992, added subsec. (h).

Act Oct. 23, 1992, in subsec. (h), substituted "1995" for "1992".

1996. Act Feb. 13, 1996, in subsec. (h)(2), substituted "December 31, 1996" for "December 31, 1995".

Act Oct. 9, 1996, in subsec. (h)(2), substituted "December 31, 1997" for "December 31, 1996".

1997. Act Aug. 5, 1997, in subsec. (h)(2), substituted "December 31, 2002" for "December 31, 1997".

Redesignation:
Section 602(l) of Title VI of Act May 22, 1974, P. L. 93-288, which amended this section, was redesignated § 702(l) of Title VII of such Act by Act Oct. 5, 1994, P. L. 103-337, Div C, Title XXXIV, Subtitle B, § 3411(a)(1), (2), 108 Stat. 3100.

Other provisions:
Waiver of indebtedness; report to Congress. Act Oct. 17, 1963, P. L. 88-151, § 2, 77 Stat. 271, provided: "The Administrator of Veterans' Affairs shall submit to the Committee on Labor and Public Welfare of the Senate and the Committee on Veterans' Affairs of the House of Representatives, not later than December 31 of each year, a written report concerning each case in which a waiver of indebtedness has been made under the authority of the amendment made by the first section of this Act. Such report shall include, together with such other information as the Administrator deems appropriate, the name and address of each person with respect to which a waiver of indebtedness has been made and the total amount of such waiver.".

Administration of trusts by Federal National Mortgage Association. Act May 24, 1966, P. L. 89-429, § 6(a), 80 Stat. 167, located at 12 USCS § 1717 note, provided that provision for participation sales and administration of trusts by the Federal National Mortgage Association shall not be construed as a repeal or modification of the provisions of subsec. (e) of this section respecting the authority of the Administrator of Veterans' Affairs.

Application of Nov. 6, 1966 amendment. Act Nov. 6, 1966, P. L. 89-769, § 14, 80 Stat. 1321, provided that the amendment made to this section by Act Nov. 6, 1966, is applicable with respect to any major disaster occurring after Oct. 3, 1964.

Effective date of amendment made by § 403(a) of Act Oct. 3, 1977. Act Oct. 3, 1977, P. L. 95-117, Title IV, § 403(b), 91 Stat. 1066, provided: "The amendment made by subsection (a) of this section [amending this section] shall be effective on the date of enactment of this Act.".

Housing solar energy and weatherization study. Act Nov. 23, 1977, P. L. 95-202, Title III, § 311, 91 Stat. 1449 (effective on the first day of the first month beginning 60 days after 11/23/77, as provided by § 501 of such Act), provided: "In accordance with the national policy to conserve energy and promote the maximum utilization of solar energy, the Administrator of Veterans' Affairs, in consultation with the Secretary of Energy and the Secretary of Housing and Urban Development, shall conduct a study to determine the most effective specific methods of using the programs carried out under, or amending the provisions of, chapter 37 of title 38, United States Code [38 USCS §§ 3701 et seq.], in order to aid and encourage present and prospective veteran homeowners to install in their homes solar heating, solar heating and cooling, or combined solar heating and cooling, and to apply residential energy conservation measures. The report of such study shall include a description of plans for administrative action to carry out such national policy as well as such recommendations for legislative action as the Administrator deems appropriate, and shall be submitted to the President and the Congress not later than March 1, 1978.".

READJUSTMENT BENEFITS
38 USCS § 3720

Application and construction of Oct. 12, 1982 amendment. For provisions as to the application and construction of the Oct. 12, 1982 amendment of this section, see § 5 of such Act, which appears as 10 USCS § 101 note.
Property management. Act Dec. 21, 1987, P. L. 100-198, § 9, 101 Stat. 1320; Aug. 6, 1991, P. L. 102-83, § 6(i), 105 Stat. 408, provides:

"(a) Homeless program. (1) To assist homeless veterans and their families acquire shelter, the Secretary of Veterans Affairs may enter into agreements described in paragraph (2) of this subsection with—

"(A) nonprofit organizations, with preference being given to any organization named in, or approved by the Secretary of Veterans Affairs under, section 3402 [now section 5902] of title 38, United States Code; or

"(B) any State, as defined in section 101(20) of such title, or any political subdivision thereof.

"(2) To carry out paragraph (1) of this subsection, the Secretary of Veterans Affairs may enter into agreements to sell real property, and improvements thereon, acquired by the Secretary of Veterans Affairs as the result of a default on a loan made or guaranteed under chapter 37 of title 38, United States Code [38 USCS §§ 3701 et seq.]. Such sale shall be for such consideration as the Secretary of Veterans Affairs determines is in the best interests of homeless veterans and the Federal Government.

"(3) The Secretary of Veterans Affairs may enter into an agreement under paragraph (1) only if—

"(A) the Secretary of Veterans Affairs determines that such an action will not adversely affect the ability of the Department of Veterans Affairs—

"(i) to fulfill its statutory missions with respect to the Department of Veterans Affairs loan guaranty program and the short- and long-term solvency of the Loan Guaranty Revolving Fund under such chapter 37; or

"(ii) to carry out other functions and administer other programs authorized by law;

"(B) the entity to which the property is sold agrees to (i) utilize the property solely as a shelter primarily for homeless veterans and their families, (ii) comply with all zoning laws relating to the property, (iii) make no use of the property that is not compatible with the area where the property is located, and (iv) take such other actions as the Secretary of Veterans Affairs determines are necessary or appropriate in the best interests of homeless veterans and the Federal Government; and

"(C) the Secretary of Veterans Affairs determines that there is no significant likelihood of the property being sold for a price sufficient to reduce the liability of the Department of Veterans Affairs or the veteran who had defaulted on the loan guaranteed under such chapter 37.

"(4) Any agreement, deed, or other instrument executed by the Secretary of Veterans Affairs under this subsection shall be on such terms and conditions as the Secretary of Veterans Affairs determines to be appropriate and necessary to carry out the purpose of such agreement.

"(b) Job training program. (1) To assist veterans to obtain training pursuant to the Veterans' Job Training Act (29 U.S.C. 1721 note), the Secretary of Veterans Affairs may convey to persons described in paragraph (2) of this subsection real property and improvements described in subsection (a)(2) of this section for an amount not less than 75 percent of the fair market value of such real property and improvements.

"(2) The Secretary of Veterans Affairs may convey such property to persons who enter into an agreement with the Secretary of Veterans Affairs to—

"(A) use veterans in a program of job training under the Veterans' Job Training Act in the rehabilitation of residences on such real property; and

"(B) provide a priority to veterans in the sale of such rehabilitated residences.

"(3) The Secretary of Veterans Affairs may include appropriate enforcement provisions in any agreement described in paragraph (2), including provision for reasonable liquidated damages.

"(4) The Secretary of Veterans Affairs shall reduce the amount of any liability that a veteran has with respect to any property conveyed under this section by an amount equal to the reduction in the sale price of the property below the fair market value of the property.

"(c) Termination. The authority provided in subsections (a) and (b) shall terminate on October 1, 1990.

"(d) Report. The Administrator of Veterans' Affairs shall, by March 1, 1990, transmit to the Congress a report of the activities carried out, through December 31, 1989, under this section.".

CODE OF FEDERAL REGULATIONS
Department of Veterans Affairs—Loan guaranty, 38 CFR Part 36.

CROSS REFERENCES
This section is referred to in 28 USCS § 2410, 38 USCS §§ 3733, 5701.

RESEARCH GUIDE
Federal Procedure L Ed:
4A Fed Proc L Ed, Banking and Financing §§ 8:1414, 1415, 1417, 1424, 1425.
11 Fed Proc L Ed, Enforcement of Judgments § 31:81.

Am Jur:
6 Am Jur 2d, Attachment and Garnishment § 79.
47 Am Jur 2d, Judicial Sales § 335.
77 Am Jur 2d, Veterans and Veterans' Laws § 126.

Texts:
Hermann, Better Settlements Through Leverage.
Hornwood, Systematic Settlements.

Auto-Cite®: Cases and annotations referred to herein can be further researched through the Auto-Cite® computer-assisted research service. Use Auto-Cite to check citations for form, parallel references, prior and later history, and annotation references.

INTERPRETIVE NOTES AND DECISIONS

1. Generally
2. Governing law
3. Actions and remedies against government, generally
4. —Administrative relief
5. —Garnishment
6. —Interest
7. Right of recovery of government, generally
8. —Waiver of debt

1. Generally

Internal Veterans' Administration [now Department of Veterans Affairs] publications establishing policies, procedures and practices in connection with carrying out powers granted under 38 USCS § 1820 [now 38 USCS § 3720] are not judicially enforceable, since they are for use of agency employees only, have not been published in Federal Register, and are not adopted with procedural requirements for rulemaking. Gatter v Nimmo (1982, CA3 Pa) 672 F2d 343.

Statute stipulating that service of process may be had in certain matters upon Veterans' Administrator [now Secretary of Veterans Affairs] does not make valid service which is bad upon assistant, without proof that authority had been conferred upon said assistant to accept such service. Whipple v Fuller (1952, Sup) 109 NYS2d 62.

2. Governing law

Federal law, not state law, is applicable to questions of federal rights and liabilities involving vendee account loan program of the Veterans Administration [now Department of Veterans Affairs]. United States v Wells (1968, CA5 Fla) 403 F2d 596.

State law requirement that indemnor be notified of foreclosure proceedings as prerequisite to obtaining deficiency judgment against indemnor did not apply to VA regulations governing foreclosure of VA-financed property since indemnity is independent right arising under federal law, but due process requires that indemnor be given notice of foreclosure proceedings; however, absence of notice of foreclosure hearing in present case and failure to give more than 5 days notice of foreclosure sale was of no substantive significance since indemnor took no action before sale nor took post-sale action available to him. Boley v Brown (1993, CA4 NC) 10 F3d 218.

3. Actions and remedies against government, generally

Waiver of sovereign immunity of Veterans Administration [now Department of Veterans Affairs] is contained in sue and be sued provision of 38 USCS § 1820 [now 38 USCS § 3720]; agency may be held liable for damages for torts of its agents, whether authorized or not. Baker v F & F Inv. Co. (1973, CA7 Ill) 489 F2d 829.

4. —Administrative relief

The "sue and be sued" provision of 38 USCS § 1820 [now 38 USCS § 3720] does not entitle homeowners to seek in federal court discretionary administrative relief available under 38 USCS § 1827 [now 38 USCS § 3727]. Potnick v United States (1973, ND Miss) 356 F Supp 395.

5. —Garnishment

Prior to 1977 amendment expressly exempting Veteran's Administration [now Department of Veterans Affairs] from garnishments, doctrine of sovereign immunity precluded execution of garnishment against Veteran's Administration [now Department of Veterans Affairs] arising from state court judgment against Administration [now Department] employee; legislative history of 38 USCS § 1820 [now 38 USCS § 3720] indicates congressional intent that Administration [now Department] should not be subject to garnishments. May Dept. May Dep't Stores Co. v Smith (1978, CA8 Mo) 572 F2d 1275, cert den (1978) 439 US 837, 58 L Ed 2d 134, 99 S Ct 122.

Administrator [now Secretary] is under no obligation to answer garnishment upon employee's wages, and garnishment will be quashed, as under provisions of 38 USCS § 1820(a)(1) [now 38 USCS § 3720(a)(1)], Administrator [now Secretary] has only limited capacity to sue and be sued. De Paul Community Health Center, etc. v Campbell (1977, ED Mo) 445 F Supp 484.

6. —Interest

Sovereign immunity does not bar award of interest on sums recoverable from Veterans Administrator [now Secretary of Veterans Affairs] on home-loan mortgages which Veterans Administration [now Department of Veterans Affairs] has guaranteed. New York Guardian Mortgagee Corp. v Cleland (1979, SD NY) 473 F Supp 422.

7. Right of recovery of government, generally

Veterans Administration [now Department of Veterans Affairs] has right to seek indemnity from defaulting mortgage under 38 USCS § 1820(a)(6) [now 38 USCS § 3720(a)(6)], despite state statute barring deficiency judgments against principal debtors by creditors or guarantors, because nothing in § 1820(a)(6) [now 38 USCS § 3720(a)(6)] indicates intent by Congress to adopt state anti-deficiency laws as federal law. Jones v Turnage (1988, ND Cal) 699 F Supp 795, affd without op (1990, CA9 Cal) 914 F2d 1496, cert den (1991) 499 US 920, 113 L Ed 2d 243, 111 S Ct 1309.

Administrator [now Secretary] of Veterans Affairs has authority under 38 USCS § 1820(a)(1) [now 38 USCS § 3720(a)(6)] to sue in state court to recover possession of real property from assignee of individuals who purchased property on installment contract for sale of real estate, and under same provision, may be sued on counterclaim without necessity of cause being removed to Federal District Court. Administrator of Veterans' Affairs v Family Bible Study Church, Inc. (1982, Dist Ct) 114 Misc 2d 615, 452 NYS2d 150.

8. —Waiver of debt

No government official is authorized to forgive debt due United States, but recovery from benefits otherwise payable to veteran or other person is subject to whole or partial waiver in accordance with equitable considerations found in former 38 USC § 453; release, whole or partial waiver of claim for such indebtedness, and compromise of claim or suit are authorized under former 38 USC § 694 of Servicemen's Readjustment Act of 1944 (38 USCS §§ 1801 et seq.). 1949 ADVA 825.

Veterans' Administration [now Department of Veterans Affairs] is not authorized to grant general waiver of debt simply because of hardship and present inability of veteran to pay, and right to grant waiver where recovery of debt would be against equity and good conscience does not give Administration [now Department] power to grant general waiver permanently negating government's opportunity to recover without considering veteran's fault in creation of indebtedness and general equitable rules; Administration [now Department] is to consider whether whole or partial recovery would defeat purposes of veterans' benefits otherwise payable or would be against equity and good conscience. 1951 ADVA 887.

§ 3721. Incontestability

Any evidence of guaranty or insurance issued by the Secretary shall be conclusive evidence of the eligibility of the loan for guaranty or insurance under the provisions of this chapter [38 USCS §§ 3701 et seq.] and of the amount of such guaranty or insurance. Nothing in this section shall preclude the Secretary from establishing, as against the original lender, defenses based on fraud or material misrepresentation. The Secretary shall not, by reason of anything contained in this section, be barred from establishing, by regulations in force at the date of such issuance or disbursement, whichever is the earlier, partial defenses to the amount payable on the guaranty or insurance.

(Sept. 2, 1958, P. L. 85-857, § 1, 72 Stat. 1213; Dec. 18, 1989, P. L. 101-237, Title III, § 313(b)(1), 103 Stat. 2077; Aug. 6, 1991, P. L. 102-83, § 5(a), 105 Stat. 406.)

HISTORY; ANCILLARY LAWS AND DIRECTIVES

Amendments:

1989. Act Dec. 18, 1989, substituted "Secretary" for "Administrator", wherever appearing.

1991. Act Aug. 6, 1991, redesignated this section, formerly 38 USCS § 1821, as 38 USCS § 3721.

CROSS REFERENCES

This section is referred to in 38 USCS § 3712.

RESEARCH GUIDE

Federal Procedure L Ed:
4A Fed Proc L Ed, Banking and Financing § 8:1423.

Am Jur:
77 Am Jur 2d, Veterans and Veterans' Laws § 119.

INTERPRETIVE NOTES AND DECISIONS

1. Generally
2. Forgery

1. Generally

Regulation denying liability on the government's part on account of a loan guaranty in a case where any of the documents involved are forged in not inconsistent with 38 USCS § 1821 [now 38 USCS § 3721] and is valid. Mt. Vernon Cooperative Bank v Gleason (1966, CA1 Mass) 367 F2d 289.

2. Forgery

Assignee of mortgage guaranteed by Veterans' Administration [now Department of Veterans Affairs] cannot recover under guaranty if mortgagor's signature on critical documents was forged, notwithstanding provisions of 38 USCS § 1821 [now 38 USCS § 3721] making guaranty conclusive evidence of loan's eligibility for guaranty and of amount of guaranty. Carter v Crown Hosiery Mills, Inc. (1980, CA4 NC) 618 F2d 96, 22 BNA FEP Cas 1818, cert den (1980) 447 US 924, 65 L Ed 2d 1117, 100 S Ct 3017, 22 BNA FEP Cas 1832.

Veterans Administration [now Department of Veterans Affairs] is estopped from asserting defense of forgery against assignee of foreclosed mortgage where agency was aware of possibility that veteran's wife's signatures on note and mortgage were forgeries at time of sheriff's sale but never informed assignee. Home Sav. & Loan Ass'n v Nimmo (1982, CA10 Okla) 695 F2d 1251, vacated, remanded (1984) 467 US 1223, 81 L Ed 2d 870, 104 S Ct 2673, reh den (1984) 468 US 1224, 82 L Ed 2d 916, 105 S Ct 21.

[§ 3722. Repealed]

HISTORY; ANCILLARY LAWS AND DIRECTIVES

The bracketed section number "3722" was inserted to preserve numerical continuity following the section number redesignations made by Act Aug. 6, 1991, P. L. 102-83, § 5(a), 105 Stat. 406.

This section (Act Sept. 2, 1958, P. L. 85-857, § 1, 72 Stat. 1214; March 3, 1966, P. L. 89-358, § 5(c), 80 Stat. 26; Oct. 4, 1966, P. L. 89-623, § 1, 80 Stat. 873; May 7, 1968, P. L. 90-301, § 2(b), 82 Stat. 113) was repealed by Act Dec. 31, 1974, P. L. 93-569, § 7(a), 88 Stat. 1866, effective Dec. 31, 1974, as provided by § 10 of Act Dec. 31, 1974. This section provided for recovery of treble damages in cases where sales were made to veterans of property in excess of the approved appraised value.

§ 3723. Direct loan revolving fund

(a) For the purposes of section 3711 of this title, the revolving fund heretofore established by section 513 of the Servicemen's Readjustment Act of 1944 is continued in effect. For the purposes of further augmenting the revolving fund, the Secretary of the Treasury is authorized and directed to advance to the Secretary from time to time after December 31, 1958, and until June 30, 1961, such sums (not in excess of $150,000,000 in any one fiscal year, including prior advancements in fiscal year 1959) as the Secretary may request, except that the aggregate so advanced in any one quarter annual period shall not exceed the sum of $50,000,000, less that amount which has been returned to the revolving fund during the preceding quarter annual period from the sale of loans pursu-

38 USCS § 3723 VETERANS' BENEFITS

ant to section 3711(g) of this title. In addition to the sums authorized in this subsection the Secretary of the Treasury shall also advance to the Secretary such additional sums, not in excess of $100,000,000, as the Secretary may request, and the sums so advanced shall be made available without regard to any limitation contained in this subsection with respect to the amount which may be advanced in any one quarter annual period. The Secretary of the Treasury shall also advance to the Secretary from time to time such additional sums as the Secretary may request, not in excess of $100,000,000 to be immediately available, plus an additional amount not in excess of $400,000,000 after June 30, 1961, plus $200,000,000 after June 30, 1962, plus $150,000,000 after June 30, 1963, plus $15,000,000 after June 30, 1964, plus $100,000,000 after June 30, 1965, plus $100,000,000 after June 30, 1966. Any such authorized advance which is not requested by the Secretary in the fiscal year in which the advance may be made shall be made thereafter when requested by the Secretary, except that no such request or advance may be made after June 30, 1967. Such authorized advances are not subject to the quarter annual limitation in the second sentence of this subsection, but the amount authorized to be advanced in any fiscal year after June 30, 1962, shall be reduced only by the amount which has been returned to the revolving fund during the preceding fiscal year from the sale of loans pursuant to section 3711(g) of this title. In addition the Secretary of the Treasury is authorized and directed to make available to the Secretary for this purpose from time to time as the Secretary may request the amount of any funds which may have been deposited to the credit of miscellaneous receipts under this subsection or subsection (c) of this section.

(b) On advances to such revolving fund by the Secretary of the Treasury, less those amounts deposited in miscellaneous receipts under subsections (a) and (c) the Secretary shall pay semiannually to the Treasurer of the United States interest at the rate or rates determined by the Secretary of the Treasury, taking into consideration the current average rate on outstanding marketable obligations of the United States as of the last day of the month preceding the advance. The Secretary shall not be required to pay interest on transfers made pursuant to the Act of February 13, 1962 (76 Stat. 8), from the capital of the "direct loans to veterans and reserves revolving fund" to the "loan guaranty revolving fund" and adjustments shall be made for payments of interest on such transfers before February 29, 1964.

(c) In order to make advances to such revolving fund, as authorized by law to effectuate the purposes and functions authorized in section 3711 of this title, the Secretary of the Treasury may use, as a public debt transaction, the proceeds of the sale of any securities may be issued under chapter 31 of title 31 [31 USCS §§ 3101 et seq.], and the purposes for which securities may be issued under chapter 31 of title 31 [31 USCS §§ 3101 et seq.] include such purposes. Such sums, together with receipts under this section and section 3711 of this title; shall be deposited with the Treasurer of the United States, in a special deposit account, and shall be available, respectively, for disbursement for the purposes of section 3711 of this title. Except as otherwise provided in subsection (a) of this section, the Secretary shall from time to time cause to be deposited into the Treasury of the United States, to the credit of miscellaneous receipts, such of the funds in such account as in the Secretary's judgment are not needed for the purposes for which they were provided, including the proceeds of the sale of any loans.

(d)(1) The Secretary of the Treasury shall transfer from the direct loan revolving fund to the loan guaranty revolving fund established by section 3724(a) of this title such amounts as the Secretary determines are not needed in the direct loan revolving fund.

(2) Not later than 30 days after the date on which the Secretary of the Treasury makes a transfer under paragraph (1) of this subsection, the Secretary shall submit a notice of such transfer to the appropriate committees of the Congress.

(Sept. 2, 1958, P. L. 85-857, § 1, 72 Stat. 1214; June 30, 1959, P. L. 86-73, § 4, 73 Stat. 156; July 14, 1960, P. L. 86-665, § 4, 74 Stat. 532; July 6, 1961, P. L. 87-84, § 3, 75 Stat. 202; Feb. 29, 1964, P. L. 88-274, 78 Stat. 147; Sept. 2, 1964, P. L. 88-560, Title VII, § 701(e)(2), 78 Stat. 801; June 30, 1976, P. L. 94-324, §§ 6, 7(27), 90 Stat. 721; Oct. 12, 1982, P. L. 97-295, § 4(68), 96 Stat. 1310; Jan. 12, 1983, P. L. 97-452, § 2(e)(2), 96 Stat. 2479; Oct. 28, 1986, P. L. 99-576, Title IV, Part A, § 405, 100 Stat. 3281; Dec. 18, 1989, P. L. 101-237, Title III, § 313(b)(1), (8), (9), 103 Stat. 2077; Aug. 6, 1991, P. L. 102-83, § 5(a), (c)(1), 105 Stat. 406.)

HISTORY; ANCILLARY LAWS AND DIRECTIVES

References in text:
"Section 513 of the Servicemen's Readjustment Act of 1944", referred to in subsec. (a), is Act June 22, 1944, ch 268, Title V, § 503, as added April 20, 1950, ch 94, Title III, § 301(h), 64 Stat. 75, which was not classified to the Code. The entire Servicemen's Readjustment Act of 1944 was repealed by Act Sept. 2, 1958, P. L. 85-857, § 14(87), 72 Stat. 1273.

"Act of February 13, 1962 (76 Stat. 8)," referred to in subsec. (b), is Act Feb. 13, 1962, P. L. 87-404, 76 Stat. 8, which provided: "An additional amount of not to exceed $115,247,000 shall be available in the 'Loan guaranty revolving fund' for expenses for property acquisitions and other loan guaranty and insurance operations under chapter 37, title 38, United States Code [38 USCS §§ 1801 et seq.], except administrative expenses, as authorized by section 1824 of such title: Provided, That in addition to amounts heretofore made available, not to exceed $115,247,000 of the 'Direct loans to veterans and reserves revolving fund' shall be available, during the current fiscal year, for transfer to said 'Loan guaranty revolving fund' in such amounts as may be necessary to provide for the foregoing expenses.".

Amendments:
1959. Act June 30, 1959, in subsec. (a), inserted "In addition to the sums authorized in this subsection the Secretary of the Treasury shall also advance to the Administrator such additional sums, not in excess of $100,000,000, as the Administrator may request, and the sums so advanced shall be made available without regard to any limitation contained in this subsection with respect to the amount which may be advanced in any one quarter annual period.".

1960. Act July 14, 1960, in subsec. (a), substituted "1962" for "1960" wherever appearing; and in subsec. (c), substituted "1963" for "1961".

1961. Act July 6, 1961, in subsec. (a), substituted "June 30, 1961" for "June 30, 1962", inserted "The Secretary of the Treasury shall also advance to the Administrator from time to time such additional sums as the Administrator may request, not in excess of $100,000,000 to be immediately available, plus an additional amount not in excess of $400,000,000 after June 30, 1961, plus $200,000,000 after June 30, 1962, plus $150,000,000 after June 30, 1963, plus $150,000,000 after June 30, 1964, plus $100,000,000 after June 30, 1965, plus $100,000,000 after June 30, 1966. Any such authorized advance which is not requested by the Administrator in the fiscal year in which the advance may be made shall be made thereafter when requested by the Administrator, except that no such request or advance may be made after June 30, 1967. Such authorized advances are not subject to the quarter annual limitation in the second sentence of this subsection, but the amount authorized to be advanced in any fiscal year after June 30, 1962, shall be reduced only by the amount which has been returned to the revolving fund during the preceding fiscal year from the sale of loans pursuant to section 1811(g) of this title.", and deleted ", except that no sums may be made available after July 25, 1962" following "subsection (c) of this section"; and in subsec. (c), substituted "June 30, 1976" for "June 30, 1963".

1964. Act Feb. 29, 1964, in subsec. (b), inserted "The Administrator shall not be required to pay interest on transfers made pursuant to the Act of February 13, 1962 (76 Stat. 8), from the capital of the 'direct loans to veterans and reserves revolving fund' to the 'loan guaranty revolving fund' and adjustments shall be made for payments of interest on such transfers before the date of enactment of this sentence.".

Act Sept. 2, 1964, in subsec. (a), inserted ", and a reasonable reserve for meeting commitments pursuant to subsection 1820(e) of this title"; and in subsec. (c), inserted "and for the purposes of meeting commitments under subsection 1820(e) of this title".

1976. Act June 30, 1976 (effective 6/30/76, as provided by § 9(a) of such Act, which appears as 38 USCS § 3701 note), in subsec. (a), substituted "the Administrator" for "he" following "from time to time as", and deleted "After the last day on which the Administrator may make loans under section 1811 of this title, he shall cause to be deposited with the Treasurer of the United States, to the credit of miscellaneous receipts, that part of all sums in such revolving fund, and all amounts thereafter received, representing unexpended advances or the repayment or recovery of the principal of direct home loans, retaining, however, a reasonable reserve for making loans with respect to which he has entered into commitments with veterans before such last day, and a reasonable reserve for meeting commitments pursuant to subsection 1820(e) of this title." following "subsection (c) of this section"; and in subsec. (c), substituted "the Administrator's" for "his", and deleted ", and not later than June 30, 1976, he shall cause to be so deposited all sums in such account and all amounts received thereafter in repayment of outstanding obligations, or otherwise, except so much thereof as he may determine to be necessary for purposes of liquidation of loans made from the revolving fund and for the purposes of meeting commitments under section 1820(e) of this title" following "sale of any loans".

1982. Act Oct. 12, 1982, in subsec. (b), substituted "February 29, 1964" for "the date of enactment of this sentence".

1983. Act Jan. 12, 1983, in subsec. (c), substituted "chapter 31 of title 31" for "the Second Liberty Bond Act" wherever appearing.

1986. Act Oct. 28, 1986, added subsec. (d).

1989. Act Dec. 18, 1989, substituted "Secretary" for "Administrator", and "Secretary's" for "Administrator's", wherever appearing, in the section. Such Act further, in subsec. (a), inserted "of the Treasury" following "In addition the Secretary"; and in subsec. (d)(2), inserted "of the Treasury".

1991. Act Aug. 6, 1991, redesignated this section, formerly 38 USCS § 1823, as 38 USCS § 3723, and amended the references in this section to reflect the redesignations made by § 5(a) of such Act (see Table III preceding 38 USCS § 101).

Other provisions:

Revolving fund amount reduced. Act Sept. 6, 1966, P. L. 89-555, Title I, § 101, 80 Stat. 679, provided: "The amount authorized by section 1823(a) of title 38, United States Code [subsec. (a) of this section], to be advanced after June 30, 1966, by the Secretary of the Treasury to the Administrator, for the purposes of the 'Direct loan revolving fund' is hereby reduced by the amount of $100,000,000.".

Application and construction of the Oct. 12, 1982 amendment of this section. For provisions as to the application and construction of the Oct. 12, 1982 amendment of this section, see § 5 of such Act, which appears as 10 USCS § 101 note.

CROSS REFERENCES

This section is referred to in 38 USCS §§ 2106, 3711, 3720, 3727.

RESEARCH GUIDE

Am Jur:

77 Am Jur 2d, Veterans and Veterans' Laws § 119.

§ 3724. Loan guaranty revolving fund

(a) There is hereby established in the Treasury of the United States a revolving fund known as the Department of Veterans Affairs Loan Guaranty Revolving Fund (hereinafter called the Fund).

(b) The Fund shall be available to the Secretary when so provided in appropriation Acts and within such limitations as may be included in such Acts, without fiscal year limitation, for all housing loan guaranty and insurance operations under this chapter [38 USCS §§ 3701 et seq.], except administrative expenses and the operations carried out in connection with the Guaranty and Indemnity Fund established by section 3725 of this title. For purposes of this subsection, the term "administrative expenses" shall not include expenses incurred by the Secretary for appraisals performed after February 1, 1986, on a contractual basis in connection with the liquidation of housing loans guaranteed, insured, or made under this chapter [38 USCS §§ 3701 et seq.].

(c) There shall be deposited in the Fund (1) by transfer from current and future appropriations for readjustment benefits such amounts as may be necessary to supplement the Fund in order to meet the requirements of the Fund, (2) amounts received by the Secretary as fees collected under section 3729 of this title for loans closed before January 1, 1990, except that fees collected (A) for all loans made for any purpose specified in section 3712 of this title, or (B) under subsection (b) of such section 3729 for guaranteed or insured loans that are closed before January 1, 1990, and subsequently assumed shall also be deposited in the Fund, and (3) all amounts now held or hereafter received by the Secretary incident to housing loan guaranty and insurance operations under this chapter [38 USCS §§ 3701 et seq.] (other than operations for which the Guaranty and Indemnity Fund established under section 3725 of this title is available), including but not limited to all collections of principal and interest and the proceeds from the use of property held or the sale of property disposed of.

(d) The Secretary shall determine annually whether there has developed in such Fund a surplus which, in the Secretary's judgment, is more than necessary to meet the needs of the Fund, and such surplus, if any, shall immediately be transferred into the general fund receipts of the Treasury.

(e)(1) Notwithstanding subsection (b) of this section, the Fund shall be available to the Secretary, to such extent as is or in such amounts as are provided for in appropriation Acts and subject to paragraph (3) of this subsection, for—

    (A) contracts for the performance of such supplementary services described in paragraph (2) of this subsection for which the Secretary is otherwise authorized to contract; and

    (B) the acquisition of such supplementary equipment described in such paragraph,

(not including services or equipment for which the Fund is available under subsection (b) of this section), as the Secretary determines would assist in ensuring the long-term stability and solvency of the Fund.

(2) The supplementary services and equipment referred to in paragraph (1) of this subsection are services or equipment not performed or available during fiscal year 1988, or services in excess of the level of such services performed during fiscal year 1988, and may include, among other things, the services of—

    (A) appraisers to review appraisal reports and issue certificates of reasonable value;

    (B) loan-servicing companies and individuals to perform personal supplemental servicing of loans guaranteed, insured, or made under this chapter [38 USCS §§ 3701 et seq.];

    (C) accounting firms to conduct on-site audits of lenders making such loans and to review lender submissions regarding such loans;

    (D) real estate brokers to promote the sale of real property acquired by the Secretary as the result of a default on a loan guaranteed, insured, or made under this chapter [38 USCS §§ 3701 et seq.];

    (E) contractors to review loan documents in order to achieve compliance with Department of Veterans Affairs requirements under this chapter [38 USCS §§ 3701 et seq.] and to issue guaranty certifications;

(F) contractors to list for sale in local newspapers real property acquired by the Secretary as the result of a default on a loan guaranteed, insured, or made under this chapter [38 USCS §§ 3701 et seq.];

(G) contractors to prepare closing documents and review them after closing; and

(H) contractors to provide automated data processing equipment, supplies, services, and software for carrying out the program administered under this chapter [38 USCS §§ 3701 et seq.].

(3) The Secretary may not in any fiscal year obligate more than a total of $25,000,000 for services or equipment under this subsection and section 3725(e) of this title.

(Added July 14, 1960, P. L. 86-665, § 7(a), 74 Stat. 532; June 30, 1976, P. L. 94-324, § 7(28), 90 Stat. 722; Nov. 3, 1981, P. L. 97-72, Title III, § 303(j), 95 Stat. 1060; July 18, 1984, P. L. 98-369, Division B, Title V, Part B, § 2511(b), 98 Stat. 1117; May 23, 1986, P. L. 99-322, § 2(a), 100 Stat. 494; Nov. 18, 1988, P. L. 100-689, Title III, § 303, 102 Stat. 4177; Dec. 18, 1989, P. L. 101-237, Title III, §§ 302(a)(2), (3)(A), (C), 313(b)(1), (2), 103 Stat. 2070, 2077; Aug. 6, 1991, P. L. 102-83, § 5(a), (c)(1), 105 Stat. 406.)

HISTORY; ANCILLARY LAWS AND DIRECTIVES

Explanatory notes:
A prior § 1824 was redesignated as § 1825 by Act July 14, 1960, P. L. 86-665, § 7(a), 74 Stat. 532.

Amendments:
1976. Act June 30, 1976 (effective 6/30/76, as provided by § 9(a) of such Act, which appears as 38 USCS § 3701 note), in subsec. (d), substituted "the Administrator's" for "his".

1981. Act Nov. 3, 1981 (effective 180 days after enactment on Nov. 3, 1981, as provided by § 305 of such Act, which appears as 38 USCS § 3741 note), in subsecs. (b) and (c), inserted "housing".

1984. Act July 18, 1984 (effective as provided by § 2511(c)(2), which appears as 38 USCS § 3729 note), in subsec. (c), substituted "(2) amounts received by the Administrator as fees collected under section 1829 of this title, and (3)" for "and (2)".

1986. May 23, 1986, in subsec. (b), added the sentence beginning "For purposes of this subsection, ...".

1988. Act Nov. 18, 1988 added subsec. (e).

1989. Act Dec. 18, 1989, substituted the section heading for one which read: "§ 1824. Loan guaranty revolving fund"; in subsec. (b), inserted "and the operations carried out in connection with the Guaranty and Indemnity Fund established by section 1825 of this title"; in subsec. (c), in para. (2), inserted "for loans closed before January 1, 1990, except that fees collected (A) for all loans made for any purpose specified in section 1812 of this title, or (B) under subsection (b) of such section 1829 for guaranteed or insured loans that are closed before January 1, 1990, and subsequently assumed shall also be deposited in the Fund'', and in para. (3), inserted ''(other than operations for which the Guaranty and Indemnity Fund established under section 1825 of this title is available)''; and in subsec. (e)(3), inserted ''a total of'' and ''and section 1825(e) of this title''. Such Act further, substituted ''Secretary'' for ''Administrator'', ''Secretary's'' for ''Administrator's'', and ''Department of Veterans Affairs'' for ''Veterans' Administration'', wherever appearing, in the entire section.

1991. Act Aug. 6, 1991, redesignated this section, formerly 38 USCS § 1824, as 38 USCS § 3724, and amended the references in this section to reflect the redesignations made by § 5(a) of such Act (see Table III preceding 38 USCS § 101).

Other provisions:

Effective date of § 7 of Act July 14, 1960. Act July 14, 1960, P. L. 86-665, § 7(c), 74 Stat. 533, provided: "This section [redesignating 38 USCS § 1824 as § 1825; adding 38 USCS § 3724; amending 38 USCS prec. § 3701] shall become effective as of July 1, 1961.''.

Authority of the Administrator to promulgate regulations. For the authority and effective date for the Administrator of Veteran's Affairs to promulgate regulations under 38 USCS §§ 3741 et seq., see § 305 of Act Nov. 3, 1981, which appears as 38 USCS § 3741 note.

Application of amendment made by § 2511(b) of Act July 18, 1984. Act July 18, 1984, P. L. 98-369, Division B, Title V, Part B, § 2511(c), 98 Stat. 1117, which appears as 38 USCS § 3729 note, provides that the amendment made to subsec. (c) of this section by § 2511(b) of such Act shall apply with respect to loans closed on or after enactment on July 18, 1984.

Administrator's report to Committee on Veterans' Affairs; contents. Act July 18, 1984, P. L. 98-369, Division B, Title V, Part B, § 2512(e), 98 Stat. 1121, provided:

"(e)(1) Not later than December 1, 1986, the Administrator of Veterans' Affairs shall submit to the Committees on Veterans' Affairs of the Senate and House of Representatives a report on the administration and functioning of the loan guaranty program conducted by the Veterans' Administration under chapter 37 of title 38, United States Code [38 USCS §§ 3701 et seq.], and the status of such title [now 38 USCS § 3724(a)].

"(2) The report shall include—

"(A) a description of the actions taken by the Administrator during the period beginning on June 1, 1984, and ending on September 30, 1986, and the actions planned as of September 30, 1986 (together with a schedule for completing any actions planned), to maintain the effective functioning of that program and to ensure the solvency of the Fund, including actions with respect to the acquisition of properties following liquidation sales, the making of loans (known as 'vendee loans') to finance the sale of properties so acquired, the quality of property appraisals by the Veterans' Administration, and assessments of home-buyer credit worthiness;

"(B) the Administrator's evaluation of the effects of the amendments made by subsection (a) [amending 38 USCS § 3716] (relating to acquisition of properties after liquidation sales and to vendee loans), including the Administrator's evaluation of the effects of subsection

(d) of section 1816 of title 38, United States Code [now 38 USCS § 3716(d)] (as added by subsection (a)(2)) (relating to vendee loans), on the operation and effective functioning of such program; and

"(C) the recommendations of the Administrator regarding any need for administrative or legislative action with respect to such program, including the Administrator's recommendations as to whether or not subsection (c)(2) [38 USCS § 3716 note] (providing for the termination of provisions relating to the acquisition of properties and to vendee loans) should be amended.".

Use of saving. Act May 23, 1986, P. L. 99-322, § 2(b), 100 Stat. 494, provides: "Any saving in the General Operating Expenses Account of the Veterans' Administration that results from the implementation of the amendment made by subsection (a) [amending subsec. (b) of this section] shall be used by the Administrator of Veterans' Affairs for the purpose of administering the housing, compensation, pension, and education programs in title 38, United States Code, in a more timely manner.".

CROSS REFERENCES

This section is referred to in 38 USCS §§ 2106, 3720, 3723, 3725, 3727, 3733.

RESEARCH GUIDE

Am Jur:
77 Am Jur 2d, Veterans and Veterans' Laws § 119.

§ 3725. Guaranty and Indemnity Fund

(a) There is hereby established in the Treasury of the United States a revolving fund known as the Guaranty and Indemnity Fund.

(b) The Guaranty and Indemnity Fund shall be available to the Secretary for all operations carried out with respect to housing loans guaranteed or insured under this chapter [38 USCS §§ 3701 et seq.] that are closed after December 31, 1989, except for operations with respect to loans for any purpose specified in section 3712 of this title, for loans guaranteed under section 3711(g) of this title, and for administrative expenses. For purposes of this subsection, the term "administrative expenses" shall not include expenses incurred by the Secretary for appraisals performed after December 31, 1989, on a contractual basis in connection with the liquidation of housing loans guaranteed, insured, or made under this chapter [38 USCS §§ 3701 et seq.].

(c)(1) All fees collected under section 3729 of this title for loans with respect to which the Guaranty and Indemnity Fund is available shall be credited to such Fund.

(2) Except as provided in paragraph (3) of this subsection, there shall also be credited to the Guaranty and Indemnity Fund—

(A) for each loan (other than loans described in section 3729(a)(2)(D) of this title) closed during fiscal year 1990 with respect to which the Guaranty and Indemnity Fund is available, an amount equal to 0.375 percent of the original amount of such loan for each of the fiscal years 1991 and 1992;

(B) for each loan (other than loans described in section 3729(a)(2)(D) of this title) closed after fiscal year 1990 with respect to which the Guaranty and Indemnity Fund is available, an amount equal to 0.25 percent of the original amount of such loan for each of the three fiscal years beginning with the fiscal year in which such loan is closed;

(C) all collections of principal and interest and the proceeds from the use or sale of property which secured a loan with respect to which the Guaranty and Indemnity Fund is available;

(D) amounts required to be credited under subsections (a)(3) and (c)(2), including amounts credited pursuant to subsections (a)(4) and (c)(3), of section 3729 of this title;

(E) fees collected under section 3729(b) of this title with respect to guaranteed or insured loans that are closed after December 31, 1989, and subsequently assumed; and

(F) all income from the investments described in subsection (d) of this section.

(3) In the case of a loan described in clause (C) of section 3729(a)(2) of this title, there shall be credited to the Guaranty and Indemnity Fund, in lieu of any amount that would otherwise be credited for such a loan under subparagraph (A) or (B) of paragraph (2) of this subsection—

(A) for each loan closed during fiscal year 1990, an amount equal to 0.25 percent of the original amount of the loan for each of the fiscal years 1991 and 1992;

(B) for each loan closed after fiscal year 1990, an amount equal to 0.25 percent of the original amount of the loan for the fiscal year in which the loan is closed and for the following fiscal year.

(d)(1) The Secretary of the Treasury shall invest the portion of the Guaranty and Indemnity Fund that is not required to meet current payments made from such Fund, as determined by the Secretary of Veterans Affairs, in obligations of the United States or in obligations guaranteed as to principal and interest by the United States.

(2) In making investments under paragraph (1) of this subsection, the Secretary of the Treasury shall select obligations having maturities suitable to the needs of the Guaranty and Indemnity Fund, as determined by the Secretary of Veterans Affairs, and bearing interest at suitable rates, as determined by the Secretary of the Treasury, taking into consideration current market yields on outstanding marketable obligations of the United States of comparable maturities.

(e)(1) Notwithstanding subsection (b) of this section, the Guaranty and Indemnity Fund shall be available to the Secretary, to such extent as is, or in such amounts as are, provided for in appropriation Acts and subject to paragraph (2) of this subsection, for—

(A) contracts for the performance of supplementary services described in paragraph (2) of section 3724(e) of this title for which the Secretary is otherwise authorized to contract; and

(B) the acquisition of supplementary equipment described in such paragraph, (not including services or equipment for which the Guaranty and Indemnity Fund is available under subsection (b) of this section), as the Secretary determines would assist in ensuring the long-term stability and solvency of the Guaranty and Indemnity Fund.

(2) The Secretary may not in any fiscal year obligate more than a total of $25,000,000 for services or equipment under this subsection and section 3724(e) of this title.

(Sept. 2, 1958, P. L. 85-857, § 1, 72 Stat. 1215; July 14, 1960, P. L. 86-665, § 7(a), 74 Stat. 532; June 30, 1976, P. L. 94-324, § 7(29), 90 Stat. 722; Dec. 18, 1989, P. L. 101-237, Title III, § 302(a)(1), 103 Stat. 2069; June 13, 1991, P. L. 102-54, § 15(a)(2), 105 Stat. 289; Aug. 6, 1991, P. L. 102-83, § 5(a), (c)(1), 105 Stat. 406; Oct. 28, 1992, P. L. 102-547, § 2(b)(2), 106 Stat. 3634.)

HISTORY; ANCILLARY LAWS AND DIRECTIVES

References in text:
"Subsections (a)(3) and (a)(4) of section 3729 of this title", referred to in this section, were repealed by Act June 13, 1991, P. L. 102-54, § 15(a)(3), 105 Stat. 289.

Amendments:
1960. Act July 14, 1960 (effective 7/1/61, as provided by § 7(c) of such Act), redesignated this section as § 1825, it formerly appeared as § 1824.

1976. Act June 30, 1976 (effective 6/30/76, as provided by § 9(a) of such Act, which appears as 38 USCS § 3701 note), substituted "said person" for "he".

1989. Act Dec. 18, 1989, substituted the section heading and section for ones which read:

"§ 1825. Waiver of discharge requirements for hospitalized persons

"The benefits of this chapter may be afforded to any person who is hospitalized pending final discharge from active duty, if said person is qualified therefor in every respect except for discharge.".

1991. Act June 13, 1991, in subsec. (c), in para. (2), in the introductory matter, substituted "Except as provided in paragraph (3) of this subsection, there" for "There", and added para. (3).

Act Aug. 6, 1991, redesignated this section, formerly 38 USCS § 1825, as 38 USCS § 3725, and amended the references in this section to reflect the redesignations made by § 5(a) of such Act (see Table III preceding 38 USCS § 101).

1992. Act Oct. 28, 1992, in subsec. (c)(2), in subparas. (A) and (B), inserted "(other than loans described in section 3729(a)(2)(D) of this title)".

Other provisions:
Ratification. Act June 13, 1991, P. L. 102-54, § 15(b), 105 Stat. 289, provides:

"(1) Any action of the Secretary of Veterans Affairs or the Secretary of the Treasury—

"(A) that was taken during the period beginning on October 1, 1990, and ending on the date of the enactment of this Act; and

"(B) that would have been an action carried out under section

38 USCS § 3725 VETERANS' BENEFITS

1825(c)(3) of title 38, United States Code [this section], if the amendment made by paragraph (2) of subsection (a) of this section [amending subsec. (a) and adding subsec. (c)(2) of this section] had been made before October 1, 1990.
is hereby ratified.

"(2) Any failure to act by the Secretary of Veterans Affairs or the Secretary of the Treasury during such period under section 1829(a)(3) [now section 3729(a)(3)] of such title is hereby ratified.".

CROSS REFERENCES
This section is referred to in 38 USCS §§ 3724, 3729, 3734.

RESEARCH GUIDE
Am Jur:
77 Am Jur 2d, Veterans and Veterans' Laws § 119.

§ 3726. Withholding of payments, benefits, etc.

(a) No officer, employee, department, or agency of the United States shall set off against, or otherwise withhold from, any veteran or the surviving spouse of any veteran any payments (other than benefit payments under any law administered by the Department of Veterans Affairs) which such veteran or surviving spouse would otherwise be entitled to receive because of any liability to the Secretary allegedly arising out of any loan made to, assumed by, or guaranteed or insured on account of, such veteran or surviving spouse under this chapter [38 USCS §§ 3701 et seq.], unless the Secretary provides such veteran or surviving spouse with notice by certified mail with return receipt requested of the authority of the Secretary to waive the payment of indebtedness under section 5302(b) of this title.

(b) If the Secretary does not waive the entire amount of the liability, the Secretary shall then determine whether the veteran or surviving spouse should be released from liability under section 3713(b) of this title.

(c) If the Secretary determines that the veteran or surviving spouse should not be released from liability, the Secretary shall notify the veteran or surviving spouse of that determination and provide a notice of the procedure for appealing that determination, unless the Secretary has previously made such determination and notified the veteran or surviving spouse of the procedure for appealing the determination.

(Added March 3, 1966, P. L. 89-358, § 5(f)(1), 80 Stat. 26; June 30, 1976, P. L. 94-324, § 7(30), 90 Stat. 722; Oct. 17, 1981, P. L. 97-66, Title V, § 504, 95 Stat. 1033; Dec. 18, 1989, P. L. 101-237, Title III, § 313(b)(1), (2), 103 Stat. 2077; Aug. 6, 1991, P. L. 102-83, § 5(a), 105 Stat. 406; Aug. 5, 1997, P. L. 105-33, Title VIII, Subtitle C, § 8033(a), 111 Stat. 669.)

HISTORY; ANCILLARY LAWS AND DIRECTIVES
Effective date of section:
Act March 3, 1966, P. L. 89-358, § 12(a), 80 Stat. 28, provided that this section is effective on March 3, 1966.

Amendments:

1976. Act June 30, 1976 (effective 6/30/76, as provided by § 9(a) of such Act, which appears as 38 USCS § 3701 note), in subsec. (a), substituted "the Administrator" for "he" preceding "first"; and in subsec. (b), substituted "surviving spouse" for "widow" wherever appearing.

1981. Act Oct. 17, 1981 (effective 10/17/80, as provided by § 701(b)(3) of such Act, which appears as 38 USCS § 1114 note) deleted subsec. (a), which read: "The Administrator shall not, unless the Administrator first obtains the consent in writing of an individual, set off against, or otherwise withhold from, such individual any benefits payable to such individual under any law administered by the Veterans' Administration because of liability allegedly arising out of any loan made to, assumed by, or guaranteed or insured on account of, such individual under this chapter.", and deleted "(b)" preceding "No officer".

1989. Act Dec. 18, 1989, substituted "Secretary" and "Department of Veterans Affairs" for "Administrator" and "Veterans' Administration", respectively, wherever appearing.

1991. Act Aug. 6, 1991, redesignated this section, formerly 38 USCS § 1826, as 38 USCS § 3726.

1997. Act Aug. 5, 1997 (applicable as provided by § 8033(b) of such Act, which appears as a note to this section), designated the existing provisions as subsec. (a), and, in such subsection, substituted "unless the Secretary provides such veteran or surviving spouse with notice by certified mail with return receipt requested of the authority of the Secretary to waive the payment of indebtedness under section 5302(b) of this title." for "unless (1) there is first received the consent in writing of such veteran or surviving spouse, as the case may be, or (2) such liability and the amount thereof was determined by a court of competent jurisdiction in a proceeding to which such veteran or surviving spouse was a party."; and added subsecs. (b) and (c).

Other provisions:

Application of Aug. 5, 1997 amendments. Aug. 5, 1997, P. L. 105-33, Title VIII, Subtitle C, § 803(c), 111 Stat. 669, provides: "The amendments made by this section [amending 38 USCS §§ 3726 and 5302(b)] shall apply with respect to any indebtedness to the United States arising pursuant to chapter 37 of title 38, United States Code [38 USCS §§ 3701 et seq.], before, on, or after the date of enactment of this Act.".

RESEARCH GUIDE

Am Jur:
77 Am Jur 2d, Veterans and Veterans' Laws § 119.

§ 3727. Expenditures to correct or compensate for structural defects in mortgaged homes

(a) The Secretary is authorized, with respect to any property improved by a one-to-four-family dwelling inspected during construction by the Department of Veterans Affairs or the Federal Housing Administration which the Secretary finds to have structural defects seriously affecting the livability of the property, to make expenditures for (1) correcting such defects, (2) paying the claims of the owner of the property arising from such defects, or (3) acquiring title to the property; except that such authority of the Secretary shall exist only (A) if the owner requests assistance under this section not later than four years (or such shorter time as the Secretary may prescribe) after the mortgage loan was made, guaranteed, or insured, and (B) if the property is encumbered by a mortgage which is made, guaranteed, or insured under this chapter [38 USCS §§ 3701 et seq.] after the date of enactment of this section [enacted May 7, 1968].

(b) The Secretary shall by regulation prescribe the terms and conditions under which expenditures and payments may be made under the provisions of this section, and the Secretary's decisions regarding such expenditures or payments, and the terms and conditions under which the same are approved or disapproved, shall be final and conclusive, and shall not be subject to judicial review.

(c) The Secretary is authorized to make expenditures for the purposes of this section from the funds established pursuant to sections 3723 and 3724 of this title, as applicable.

(Added May 7, 1968, P. L 90-301, § 5(a), 82 Stat. 116; June 30, 1976, P. L. 94-324, § 7(31), 90 Stat. 722; Dec. 18, 1989, P. L. 101-237, Title III, § 313(b)(1), (2), 103 Stat. 2077; Aug. 6, 1991, P. L. 102-83, § 5(a), (c)(1), 105 Stat. 406.)

HISTORY; ANCILLARY LAWS AND DIRECTIVES
Amendments:
1976. Act June 30, 1976 (effective 6/30/76, as provided by § 9(a) of such Act, which appears as 38 USCS § 3701 note), in subsec. (a), substituted "the Administrator for "he" preceding "finds"; and in subsec. (b), substituted "the Administrator's" for "his".
1989. Act Dec. 18, 1989, substituted "Secretary" for "Administrator", "Secretary's" for "Administrator's", and "Department of Veterans Affairs" for "Veterans' Administration", wherever appearing, in the entire section.
1991. Act Aug. 6, 1991, redesignated this section, formerly 38 USCS § 1827, as 38 USCS § 3727, and amended the references in this section to reflect the redesignations made by § 5(a) of such Act (see Table III preceding 38 USCS § 101).

RESEARCH GUIDE
Am Jur:
35 Am Jur 2d, Federal Torts Claims Act § 46.
77 Am Jur 2d, Veterans and Veterans' Laws §§ 121, 126.

INTERPRETIVE NOTES AND DECISIONS

1. Generally
2. Purpose
3. Remedies

1. Generally
Plaintiff, in action against defendants and Veterans Administration [now Department of Veterans Affairs] alleging faulty workmanship done on home purchased from defendants and inspected by agency, did not state claim upon which relief could be granted since 38 USCS § 1827 [now 38 USCS § 3727] is not applicable to other than new construction and since language in 38 USCS § 1827(b) [now 38 USCS § 3727(b)] precludes judicial review. Stanley v Veterans Administration (1978, ED Pa) 454 F Supp 9.

2. Purpose

Fundamental purpose of 38 USCS § 1827 [now 38 USCS § 3727] is to authorize Administrator [now Secretary] to correct substantial defects in inspected home before foreclosure occurs and agency is faced with burden of recouping loss on ordinarily unmarketable structure; agency, by 38 USCS § 1827 [now 38 USCS § 3707], is given authority similar to that provided by § 518 of National Housing Act (12 USCS § 1715u) authorizing Administrator [now Secretary], in his discretion, to extend aid to distressed homeowners who discover defects in property purchased with Guaranteed Loan after relying on agency construction standards. Potnick v United States (1973, ND Miss) 356 F Supp 395.

3. Remedies

Sole remedy for houseowner complaining of structural defects in house purchased with Veterans' Administration [now Department of Veterans Affairs] Guaranteed Loan is to seek discretionary aid of Administrator's [now Secretary's] office under 38 USCS § 1827 [now 38 USCS § 3727] and he is not entitled to seek relief in federal court under "sue and be sued" provision of 38 USCS § 1820 [now 38 USCS § 3720]. Potnick v United States (1973, ND Miss) 356 F Supp 395.

§ 3728. Exemption from State anti-usury provisions.

If, under any law of the United States, loans and mortgages insured under title I or title II of the National Housing Act are exempt from the application of the provisions of any State constitution or law (1) limiting the rate or amount of interest, discount points, or other charges which may be charged, taken, received, or reserved by lenders, (2) restricting the manner of calculating such interest (including prohibition of the charging of interest on interest), or (3) requiring a minimum amortization of principal, then loans guaranteed or insured under this chapter [38 USCS §§ 3701 et seq.] are also exempt from the application of such provisions.
(Added Nov. 28, 1979, P. L. 96-128, Title IV, § 401(a), 93 Stat. 986; Oct. 17, 1981, P. L. 97-66, Title V, § 501(b), 95 Stat. 1032; Aug. 6, 1991, P. L. 102-83, § 5(a), 105 Stat. 406.)

HISTORY; ANCILLARY LAWS AND DIRECTIVES

References in text:
"The National Housing Act", referred to in this section, is Act June 27, 1934, ch 847, 48 Stat. 1246, as amended. Titles I and II of the Act are generally classified to 12 USCS §§ 1702 et seq. and 1707 et seq, respectively. For full classification of these Titles, consult USCS Tables volumes.

Effective date of section:
Act Nov. 28, 1979, P. L. 96-128, Title VI, § 601(b), 93 Stat. 988, provided that this section is effective on Nov. 28, 1979.

Amendments:
1981. Act Oct. 17, 1981 (effective on enactment on 10/17/81, as provided by § 701(b)(1) of such Act, which appears as 38 USCS § 1114 note), inserted "(1)" and "(2) restricting the manner of calculating such interest (including prohibition of the charging of interest on interest), or (3) requiring a minimum amortization of principal,".
1991. Act Aug. 6, 1991, redesignated this section, formerly 38 USCS § 1828, as 38 USCS § 3728.

RESEARCH GUIDE

Am Jur:
77 Am Jur 2d, Veterans and Veterans' Laws § 119.

INTERPRETIVE NOTES AND DECISIONS

1. Generally
2. Mobile home financing contracts

1. Generally

Arkansas constitutional amendment concerning maximum legal rate of interest did not override FHA/VA pre-emption provisions since it specifically stated that its provisions were not intended nor should they be deemed to supersede or otherwise invalidate any provisions of federal law applicable to loans or interest rates including loans secured by residential real property. Burris v First Financial Corp. (1991, CA8 Ark) 928 F2d 797, cert den (1991) 502 US 867, 116 L Ed 2d 155, 112 S Ct 195.

2. Mobile home financing contracts

State overrode federal pre-emption statutes (12 USCS § 1735f-7a, and 38 USCS § 1828 [now 38 USCS § 3728]), that allow exemption from state usury laws for mobile home financing contracts, when state amended its own usury limit on mobile home transactions even though state amendments did not refer to either of the federal usury pre-emption statutes nor to loans insured by the FHA and VA, since state which re-enacts or raises its usury limit on particular class of loans overrides FHA, and VA usury pre-emption statutes for that type of loan in absence of statement to the contrary. Doyle v Southern Guaranty Corp. (1986, CA11 Ga) 795 F2d 907.

Lender who complies with 12 USCS § 1735f-7 and 38 USCS § 1828 [now 38 USCS § 3728], federal statutes exempting lenders from state usury laws on mobile home retail installment contracts, need not also comply with Depository Institutions Deregulation and Monetary Control Act (12 USCS § 1735f-7a) in order to exempt itself from state usury limits, notwithstanding that DIDMCA encompasses federal mobile home loans and overlaps with federal state usury exemption statutes since dual coverage does not nullify preemptions as applied to mobile home loans. Doyle v Southern Guaranty Corp. (1986, CA11 Ga) 795 F2d 907.

Interest charged installment buyers of mobile homes through program for veterans was not usurious under 38 USCS § 1828 [now 38 USCS § 3728], where state constitutional limitation on interest rates cited by buyers specified that it did not "supersede or otherwise invalidate" interest rates under federal programs. Burris v First Financial Corp. (1990, ED Ark) 733 F Supp 1270, affd (1991, CA8 Ark) 928 F2d 797, cert den (1991) 502 US 867, 116 L Ed 2d 155, 112 S Ct 195.

§ 3729. Loan fee

(a)(1) Except as provided in subsection (c)(1) of this section, a fee shall be collected from each veteran obtaining a housing loan guaranteed, insured, or made under this chapter [38 USCS §§ 3701 et seq.], and from each person obtaining a loan under section 3733(a) of this title, and no such loan may be guaranteed, insured, or made under this chapter until the fee payable under this section has been remitted to the Secretary.

(2) Except as provided in paragraphs (4) and (5) of this of subsection, the amount of such fee shall be 1.25 percent of the total loan amount, except that—

(A) in the case of a loan made under section 3711 of this title or for any purpose specified in section 3712 (other than section 3712(a)(1)(F)) of this title, the amount of such fee shall be one percent of the total loan amount;

(B) in the case of a guaranteed or insured loan for a purchase (except for a purchase referred to in section 3712(a) of this title), or for construction, with respect to which the veteran has made a downpayment of 5 percent or more, but less than 10 percent, of the total purchase price or construction cost, the amount of such fee shall be 0.75 percent of the total loan amount;

(C) in the case of a guaranteed or insured loan for a purchase (except for a purchase referred to in section 3712(a) of this title), or for construction, with respect to which the veteran has made a downpayment of 10 percent or more of the total purchase price or construction cost, the amount of such fee shall be 0.50 percent of the total loan amount;

(D) in the case of a loan made to, or guaranteed or insured on behalf of, a veteran described in section 3701(b)(5) of this title under this chapter [38 USCS §§ 3701 et seq.], the amount of such fee shall be—

(i) two percent of the total loan amount;

(ii) in the case of a loan for any purpose specified in section 3712 of this title, one percent of such amount; or

(iii) in the case of a loan for a purchase (other than a purchase referred to in section 3712 of this title) or for construction with respect to which the veteran has made a downpayment of 5 percent or more of the total purchase price or construction cost—

(I) 1.50 percent of the total loan amount if such downpayment is less than 10 percent of such price or cost; or

(II) 1.25 percent of the total loan amount if such downpayment is 10 percent or more of such price or cost;

(E) in the case of a loan guaranteed under section 3710(a)(8), 3710(a)(9)(B)(i), 3710(a)(11), 3712(a)(1)(F), or 3762(h) of this title, the amount of such fee shall be 0.5 percent of the total loan amount; and

(F) in the case of a loan made under section 3733(a) of this title, the amount of such fee shall be 2.25 percent of the total loan amount.

(3) The amount of the fee to be collected under paragraph (1) of this subsection may be included in the loan and paid from the proceeds thereof.

(4) With respect to a loan closed after September 30, 1993, and before October 1, 2002, for which a fee is collected under paragraph (1), the amount of such fee, as computed under paragraph (2), shall be increased by 0.75 percent of the total loan amount other than in the case of a loan described in subparagraph (A), (D)(ii), (E), or (F) of paragraph (2).

(5)(A) Except as provided in subparagraph (B) of this paragraph, notwithstanding paragraphs (2) and (4) of this subsection, after a veteran has obtained an initial loan pursuant to section 3710 of this title, the amount of such fee with respect to any additional loan obtained under this chapter by such veteran shall be 3 percent of the total loan amount.

(B) Subparagraph (A) of this paragraph does not apply with respect to (i) a loan obtained by a veteran with a downpayment described in paragraph (2)(B), (2)(C), or (2)(D)(iii) of this subsection, and (ii) loans described in paragraph (2)(E) of this subsection.

(C) This paragraph applies with respect to a loan closed after September 30, 1993, and before October 1, 2002.

(b) Except as provided in subsection (c) of this section, a fee shall be collected from a person assuming a loan to which section 3714 of this title applies. The amount of the fee shall be equal to 0.50 percent of the balance of the loan on the date of the transfer of the property.

(c)(1) A fee may not be collected under this section from a veteran who is receiving compensation (or who but for the receipt of retirement pay would be entitled to receive compensation) or from a surviving spouse of any veteran (including a person who died in the active military, naval, or air service) who died from a service-connected disability.

(2) There shall be credited to the Guaranty and Indemnity Fund (in addition to the amount required to be credited to such Fund under clause (A) or (B) of paragraph (2) of section 3725(c) of this title or paragraph (3) of that section), on behalf of a veteran or surviving spouse described in paragraph (1) of this subsection, an amount equal to the fee that, except for paragraph (1) of this subsection, would be collected from such veteran or surviving spouse.

(3) Credits to the Guaranty and Indemnity Fund under paragraph (2) of this subsection with respect to loans guaranteed, insured, or made under this chapter that are closed during fiscal year 1990 shall be made in October 1990.

(Added Sept. 8, 1982, P. L. 97-253, Title IV, § 406(a)(1), 96 Stat. 805; July 18, 1984, P. L. 98-369, Division B, Title V, Part B, § 2511(a), 98 Stat. 1117; Dec. 21, 1987, P. L. 100-198, §§ 2, 10(c), 101 Stat. 1315, 1823; Dec. 22, 1987, P. L. 100-203, Title VII, § 7002, 101 Stat. 1330-279; May 20, 1988, P. L. 100-322, Title IV, Part B, § 415(c)(6), 102 Stat. 551; Dec. 18, 1989, P. L. 101-237, Title III, §§ 303(a), 313(b)(1), (2), 103 Stat. 2071, 2077; Dec. 19, 1989, P. L. 101-239, Title V, § 5001, 103 Stat. 2136; Nov. 5, 1990, P. L. 101-508, Title VIII, Subtitle D, § 8032, 104 Stat. 1388-348; June 13, 1991, P. L. 102-54, § 15(a)(3), (4), 105 Stat. 289; Aug. 6, 1991, P. L. 102-83, § 5(a), (c)(1), 105 Stat. 406; Oct. 28, 1992, P. L. 102-547, §§ 2(b)(1), 5, 106 Stat. 3633, 3636; Aug. 10, 1993, P. L. 103-66, Title XII, § 12007, 107 Stat. 414; Nov. 2, 1994, P. L. 103-446, Title IX, § 904(c), 108 Stat. 4677; Oct. 9, 1996, P. L. 104-275, Title II, Subtitle A, § 202(b), 110 Stat. 3330; Aug. 5, 1997, P. L. 105-33, Title VIII, Subtitle A, § 8012, Subtitle C, § 8032, 111 Stat. 664, 669.)

HISTORY; ANCILLARY LAWS AND DIRECTIVES
Amendments:
1984. Act July 18, 1984 (effective as provided by § 2511(c) of such Act, which appears as a note to this section), in subsec. (a), inserted "and from each person obtaining a loan from the Administrator to finance the purchase of real property from the Administrator," and deleted "one-half of" preceding "one percent" and "to the veteran" following "in the loan"; deleted subsec. (c) which read: "Fees collected under this section shall be deposited into the Treasury of the United States as miscellaneous receipts."; redesignated subsec. (d) as subsec. (c) and in subsec. (c), as redesignated, substituted "September 30, 1987" for "September 30, 1985".

1987. Act Dec. 21, 1987, in subsec. (b), substituted "of any veteran (including a person who died in the active military, naval, or air service) who died from a service-connected disability" for "described in section 1801(b)(2) of this title"; and, in subsec. (c), substituted "1989" for "1987"; and added subsec. (d).

Act Dec. 22, 1987, in subsec. (c), purported to substitute "1989" for "1987", but such amendment could not be executed because Act Dec. 21, 1987 had already made the same amendment.

1988. Act May 20, 1988, is subsec. (d), substituted "section 1814" for "section 1817A".

1989. Act Dec. 18, 1989 (effective 1/1/90 as provided by § 303(b) of such Act, which appears as a note to this section), substituted this section for one which read:

"(a) Except as provided in subsection (b) of this section, a fee shall be collected from each veteran obtaining a housing loan guaranteed, made, or insured under this chapter, and from each person obtaining a loan from the Administrator to finance the purchase of real property from the Administrator, and no such loan may be guaranteed, made, or insured under this chapter until the fee payable with respect to such loan has been remitted to the Administrator. The amount of the fee shall be one percent of the total loan amount. The amount of the fee may be included in the loan and paid from the proceeds thereof.

"(b) A fee may not be collected under this section from a veteran who is receiving compensation (or who but for the receipt of retirement pay would be entitled to receive compensation) or from a surviving spouse of any veteran (including a person who died in the active military, naval, or air service) who died from a service-connected disability.

"(c) A fee may not be collected under this section with respect to any loan closed after September 30, 1989.

"(d) Except as provided in subsection (b) of this section, a fee shall be collected from a person assuming a loan to which section 1814 of this chapter applies. The amount of the fee shall be equal to one-half of one percent of the balance of such loan on the date of the transfer of the property.".

Such Act further purported to amend subsec. (a) by substituting "Secretary" for "Administrator" wherever appearing; however, because of a prior amendment, this amendment could not be executed.

Act Dec. 19, 1989 purported to amend subsec. (c) by substituting "September 30, 1990" for "September 30, 1989"; however, because of a prior amendment, this amendment could not be executed.

1990. Act Nov. 5, 1990, in subsec. (a)(2), substituted "Except as provided in paragraph (6) of this subsection, the amount" for "The amount", and, added para. (6).

1991. Act June 13, 1991, in subsec. (a), deleted paras. (3) and (4), which read:

"(3) Except as provided in paragraph (4) of this subsection, there shall be credited to the Guaranty and Indemnity Fund (in addition to the amount required to be credited to such Fund under section 1825(c)(2)(A) or (B) of this title), on behalf of a veteran who has made a downpayment described in paragraph (2)(C) of this subsection, an amount equal to 0.25 percent of the total loan amount for the fiscal year in which the loan is closed and for the following fiscal year.

"(4) Credits to the Guaranty and Indemnity Fund under paragraph (3) of this subsection with respect to loans guaranteed or insured under this chapter that are closed during fiscal year 1990 shall be made in October 1990 and October 1991.",

and redesignated para. (5) as para. (3); and, in subsec. (c)(2), substituted "clause (A) or (B) of paragraph (2) of section 1825(c) of this title or paragraph (3) of that section" for "section 1825(c)(2) (A) or (B) of this title and subsection (a)(3) of this section".

Act Aug. 6, 1991, redesignated this section, formerly 38 USCS § 1829, as 38 USCS § 3729, and amended the references in this section to reflect the redesignations made by § 5(a) of such Act (see Table III preceding 38 USCS § 101).

1992. Act Oct. 28, 1992, in subsec. (a)(2), in subpara. (A), inserted "(other than section 3712(a)(1)(F))", in subpara. (B), deleted "and" following the concluding semicolon, in subpara. (C), substituted a semicolon for the concluding period, and added subparas. (D) and (E).

1993. Act Aug. 10, 1993, in subsec. (a), in para. (2), in the introductory matter, substituted "paragraphs (4) and (5)" for "paragraph (6)", added new paras. (4) and (5), and deleted para. (6), which read: "(6) With respect to each loan closed during the period beginning on November 1, 1990, and ending on September 30, 1991, each amount specified in paragraph (2) of this subsection shall be increased by 0.625 percent of the total loan amount.".

1994. Act Nov. 2, 1994, in subsec. (a)(2)(E), inserted "3710(a)(11),".

1996. Act Oct. 9, 1996, in subsec. (a)(2)(E), substituted "3712(a)(1)(F), or 3762(h)" for "or 3712(a)(1)(F)".

1997. Act Aug. 5, 1997, in subsec. (a), in para. (2), in subpara. (A), deleted "or 3733(a)" following "3711", in subpara. (D)(iii)(II), deleted "and" after the concluding semicolon, in subpara. (E), substituted "; and" for a concluding period, and added subsec. (F), in para. (4), substituted "October 1, 2002" for "October 1, 1998" and substituted "(E), or (F)" for "or (E)" and, in para. (5)(C), substituted "October 1, 2002" for "October 1, 1998".

Other provisions:
Application of section. Act Sept. 8, 1982, P. L. 97-253, Title IV, § 406(b), 96 Stat. 805; Aug. 6, 1991, P. L. 102-83, § 5(c)(2), 105 Stat. 406, provides: "Section 3729 of title 38, United States Code, as added by subsection (a), shall apply only to loans closed after September 30, 1982.".

Application of amendments made by § 2511 of Act July 18, 1984. Act July 18, 1984, P. L. 98-369, Division B, Title V, Part B, § 2511(c), 98 Stat. 1117, provided:

"(1) The amendments made by subsection (a)(1) [amending subsec. (a) of this section] shall apply with respect to loans closed after the end of the 30-day period beginning on the date of the enactment of this Act.

"(2) The amendments made by subsections (a)(2) and (b) [deleting subsec. (c) of this section and amending 42 USCS § 3724(c)] shall apply with respect to loans closed on or after the date of the enactment of this Act.

"(3) The amendment made by subsection (a)(3) [redesignating subsec. (d) of this section as subsec. (c) and amending it] shall take effect on the date of the enactment of this Act.".

Home loan origination fee. Act Oct. 28, 1986, P. L. 99-576, Title IV, Part A, § 409, 100 Stat. 3283, provides: "It is the sense of the Congress that the Veterans' Administration loan origination fee should not be increased above its present level of one percent of the amount of the loan guaranteed.".

Interim extension of collection of fees. Act Oct. 16, 1987, P. L. 100-136, § 1(b), 101 Stat. 813; provides: "Notwithstanding subsection (c) of section

1829 of such title [subsec. (c) of this section], fees may be collected under such section with respect to loans closed through November 15, 1987.".

Extension of Department of Veterans Affairs home-loan fee. Act Oct. 6, 1989, P. L. 101-110, § 2, 103 Stat. 682 (effective Oct. 1, 1989, as provided by § 3(a) of such Act, which appears as 38 USCS § 8133 note), provides: "Notwithstanding the provisions of subsection (c) of section 1829 of title 38, United States Code [this section], fees may be collected under such section with respect to loans closed before December 1, 1989.".

Effective date of Dec. 18, 1989 amendments. Act Dec. 18, 1989, P. L. 101-237, Title III, § 303(b), 103 Stat. 2073, provides: "The amendments made by this section [amending this section] shall take effect on January 1, 1990.".

Fee collection through 1989. Act Dec. 18, 1989, P. L. 101-237, Title III, § 303(c), 103 Stat. 2073, (effective 1/1/90 as provided by § 303(b) of such Act, which appears as a note to this section), provides: "Notwithstanding any other provision of law, the Secretary of Veterans Affairs shall collect fees under section 1829 of title 38, United States Code, through December 31, 1989.".

Ratification. For provisions as to ratification of actions taken by the Secretary of Veterans Affairs in carrying out provisions of this section, see § 604 of Act Dec. 18, 1989, P. L. 101-237, Title VI, 103 Stat. 2097, which appears as 38 USCS § 1720B note.

CODE OF FEDERAL REGULATIONS

Department of Veterans Affairs—Loan guaranty, 38 CFR Part 36.

CROSS REFERENCES

This section is referred to in 38 USCS §§ 3703, 3724, 3725, 3733–3735.

RESEARCH GUIDE

Am Jur:
77 Am Jur 2d, Veterans and Veterans' Laws §§ 126, 127.

§ 3730. Use of attorneys in court

(a) Within 180 days after the date of the enactment of this section [enacted July 18, 1984], the Secretary shall take appropriate steps to authorize attorneys employed by the Department of Veterans Affairs to exercise the right of the United States to bring suit in court to foreclose a loan made or acquired by the Secretary under this chapter [38 USCS §§ 3701 et seq.] and to recover possession of any property acquired by the Secretary under this chapter [38 USCS §§ 3701 et seq.]. The Secretary may acquire the services of attorneys, other than those who are employees of the Department of Veterans Affairs, to exercise that right. The activities of attorneys in bringing suit under this section shall be subject to the direction and supervision of the Attorney General and to such terms and conditions as the Attorney General may prescribe.

(b) Nothing in this section derogates from the authority of the Attorney General under sections 516 and 519 of title 28 to direct and supervise all litigation to which the United States or an agency or officer of the United States is a party.

38 USCS § 3730
VETERANS' BENEFITS

(Added July 18, 1984, P. L. 98-369, Division B, Title V, Part B, § 2512(b)(1), 98 Stat. 1120; Oct. 28, 1986, P. L. 99-576, Title 10, Part A, § 406, 100 Stat. 3282; Dec. 18, 1989, P. L. 101-237, Title III, § 313(b)(1), (2), 103 Stat. 2077; Aug. 6, 1991, P. L. 102-83, § 5(a), 105 Stat. 406.)

HISTORY; ANCILLARY LAWS AND DIRECTIVES
Effective date of section:
Act July 18, 1984, P. L. 98-369, Division B, Title V, Part B, § 2512(c)(3), 98 Stat. 1120, which appears as a note to this section, provided that this section take effect on July 18, 1984.

Amendments:
1986. Act Oct. 28, 1986, in subsec. (a), substituted "The" for "With the concurrence of the Attorney General of the United States, the".

1989. Act Dec. 18, 1989, in subsec. (a), substituted "Secretary" and "Department of Veterans Affairs" for "Administrator" and "Veterans' Administration", wherever appearing.

1991. Act Aug. 6, 1991, redesignated this section, formerly 38 USCS § 1830, as 38 USCS § 3730.

Other provisions:
Effective date of section as added by § 2512(b) of Act July 18, 1984. Act July 18, 1984, P. L. 98-369, Division B, Title V, Part B, § 2512(c)(3), 98 Stat. 1120, provided:

"The amendments made by subsection (b) [adding this section and amending 38 USCS prec § 3701] shall take effect on the date of the enactment of this Act.".

RESEARCH GUIDE
Federal Procedure L Ed:
33 Fed Proc L Ed, Veterans and Veterans' Affairs § 79:15.

Am Jur:
77 Am Jur 2d, Veterans and Veterans' Laws § 126.

§ 3731. Appraisals

(a) The Secretary shall—

(1) subject to subsection (b)(2) and in consultation with appropriate representatives of institutions which are regularly engaged in making housing loans, prescribe uniform qualifications for appraisers, including the successful completion of a written test, submission of a sample appraisal, certification of an appropriate number of years of experience as an appraiser, and submission of recommendations from other appraisers:

(2) use such qualifications in determining whether to approve an appraiser to make appraisals of the reasonable value of any property, construction, repairs, or alterations for the purposes of this chapter [38 USCS §§ 3701 et seq.]; and

(3) in consultation with local representatives of institutions described in clause (1) of this subsection, develop and maintain lists of appraisers who

are approved under clause (2) of this subsection to make appraisals for the purposes of this chapter [38 USCS §§ 3701 et seq.].

(b)(1) The Secretary shall select appraisers from a list required by subsection (a)(3) of this section on a rotating basis to make appraisals for the purposes of this chapter [38 USCS §§ 3701 et seq.].

(2) If uniform qualifications become applicable for appraisers who perform appraisals for or in connection with the Federal Government, the qualifications required by subsection (a)(1) of this section may be more stringent than such uniform qualifications, but the Secretary may use no written test in determining the qualifications of appraisers other than the test prescribed to implement such uniform qualifications.

(c) Except as provided in subsection (f) of this section, the appraiser shall forward an appraisal report to the Secretary for review. Upon receipt of such report, the Secretary shall determine the reasonable value of the property, construction, repairs, or alterations for purposes of this chapter [38 USCS §§ 3701 et seq.], and notify the veteran of such determination. Upon request, the Secretary shall furnish a copy of the appraisal made of property for the purposes of this chapter [38 USCS §§ 3701 et seq.] to the lender proposing to make the loan which is to be secured by such property and is to be guaranteed under this chapter [38 USCS §§ 3701 et seq.].

(d) If a lender (other than a lender authorized under subsection (f) of this section to determine reasonable value—

(1) has proposed to make a loan to be guaranteed under this chapter [38 USCS §§ 3701 et seq.],

(2) has been furnished a certificate of reasonable value of any property or of any construction, repairs, or alterations of property which is to be the security for such loan, and

(3) within a reasonable period prescribed by the Secretary, has furnished to the Secretary an additional appraisal of the reasonable value of such property, construction, repairs, or alterations which was made by an appraiser selected by the lender from the list required by subsection (a)(3) of this section,

the Secretary shall consider both the initial appraisal and the additional appraisal and shall, if appropriate, issue a revised certificate of reasonable value of such property, construction, repairs, or alterations.

(e)(1) In no case may a veteran be required to pay all or any portion of the cost of the additional appraisal described in subsection (d)(3) of this section.

(2) If a veteran, within a reasonable period prescribed by the Secretary, has furnished to the Secretary an additional appraisal of the reasonable value of such property, construction, repairs, or alterations which was made by an appraiser selected by the veteran from the list required by subsection (a)(3) of this section, the Secretary shall consider such appraisal, along with other appraisals furnished to the Secretary, and shall, if appropriate, issue a revised certificate of reasonable value of such property, construction, repairs, or alterations.

38 USCS § 3731

(f)(1) Subject to the provisions of paragraphs (2) and (3) of this subsection, the Secretary may, in accordance with standards and procedures established in regulations prescribed by the Secretary, authorize a lender to determine the reasonable value of property for the purposes of this chapter [38 USCS §§ 3701 et seq.] if the lender is authorized to make loans which are automatically guaranteed under section 3702(d) of this title. In such a case, the appraiser selected by the Secretary pursuant to subsection (b) of this section shall submit the appraisal report directly to the lender for review, and the lender shall, as soon as possible thereafter, furnish a copy of the appraisal to the veteran who is applying for the loan concerned and to the Secretary.

(2) In exercising the authority provided in paragraph (1) of this subsection, the Secretary shall assign a sufficient number of personnel to carry out an appraisal-review system to monitor, on at least a random-sampling basis, the making of appraisals by appraisers and the effectiveness and the efficiency of the determination of reasonable value of property by lenders.

(3) [Deleted]

(4) Not later than April 30 of each year following a year in which the Secretary authorizes lenders to determine reasonable value of property under this subsection, the Secretary shall submit to the Committees on Veterans' Affairs of the Senate and the House of Representatives a report relating to the exercise of that authority during the year in which the authority was exercised.

(5) A report submitted pursuant to paragraph (4) of this subsection shall include, for the period covered by each report—

(A) the number and value of loans made by lenders exercising the authority of this subsection;

(B) the number and value of such loans reviewed by the appraisal-review monitors referred to in paragraph (2) of this subsection;

(C) the number and value of loans made under this subsection of which the Secretary received notification of default;

(D) the amount of guaranty paid by the Secretary to such lenders by reason of defaults on loans as to which reasonable value was determined under this subsection; and

(E) such recommendations as the Secretary considers appropriate to improve the exercise of the authority provided for in this subsection and to protect the interests of the United States.

(Added Oct. 28, 1986, P. L. 99-576, Title IV, Part A, § 407(a), 100 Stat. 3282; Dec. 21, 1987, P. L. 100-198, § 11(a), (b), 101 Stat. 1324; Dec. 18, 1989, P. L. 101-237, Title III, § 313(b)(1), 103 Stat. 2077; June 13, 1991, P. L. 102-54, § 3(b), (c), 105 Stat. 267; Aug. 6, 1991, P. L. 102-83, § 5(a), (c)(1), 105 Stat. 406; Oct. 28, 1992, P. L. 102-547, § 7, 106 Stat. 3636; Feb. 13, 1996, P. L. 104-110, Title I, § 101(g), 110 Stat. 768.)

HISTORY; ANCILLARY LAWS AND DIRECTIVES

Amendments:

1987. Act Dec. 21, 1987, in subsec. (a)(1), inserted "subject to subsection (b)(2) and" and ", including the successful completion of a written test, submission of a sample appraisal, certification of an appropriate number of years of experience as an appraiser, and submission of recommendations from other appraisers"; in subsec. (b), designated the existing provisions as para. (1) and added para. (2); in subsec. (c), substituted "Except as provided in subsection (f) of this section, the appraiser shall forward an appraisal report to the Administrator for review. Upon receipt of such report, the Administrator shall determine the reasonable value of the property, construction, repairs, or alterations for purposes of this chapter, and notify the veteran of such determination. Upon request, the Administrator shall" for "The Administrator shall, upon request,"; in subsec. (d), inserted "(other than a lender authorized under subsection (f) of this section to determine reasonable value)"; and added subsec. (f).

1989. Act Dec. 18, 1989, substituted "Secretary" for "Administrator", wherever appearing, in the entire section.

1991. Act June 13, 1991, in subsec. (f), in para. (3), substituted "December 31, 1992" for "October 1, 1990", and added paras. (4) and (5).

Act Aug. 6, 1991, redesignated this section, formerly 38 USCS § 1831, as 38 USCS § 3731, and amended the references in this section to reflect the redesignations made by § 5(a) of such Act (see Table III preceding 38 USCS § 101).

1992. Act Oct. 28, 1992, in subsec. (f)(3), substituted "1995" for "1992".

1996. Act Feb. 13, 1996, in subsec. (f), deleted para. (3), which read: "The authority provided in this subsection shall terminate on December 31, 1995.".

CROSS REFERENCES

This section is referred to in 38 USCS § 3710, 3762.

RESEARCH GUIDE

Am Jur:
77 Am Jur 2d, Veterans and Veterans' Laws §§ 119, 126.

§ 3732. Procedure on default

(a)(1) In the event of default in the payment of any loan guaranteed under this chapter [38 USCS §§ 3701 et seq.], the holder of the obligation shall notify the Secretary of such default. Upon receipt of such notice, the Secretary may, subject to subsection (c) of this section, pay to such holder the guaranty not in excess of the pro rata portion of the amount originally guaranteed. Except as provided in section 3703(e) of this title, if the Secretary makes such a payment, the Secretary shall be subrogated to the rights of the holder of the obligation to the extent of the amount paid on the guaranty.

(2) Before suit or foreclosure the holder of the obligation shall notify the Secretary of the default, and within thirty days thereafter the Secretary may, at the Secretary's option, pay the holder of the obligation the unpaid balance of the obligation plus accrued interest and receive an assignment of the loan

and security. Nothing in this section shall preclude any forbearance for the benefit of the veteran as may be agreed upon by the parties to the loan and approved by the Secretary.

(3) The Secretary may establish the date, not later than the date of judgment and decree of foreclosure or sale, upon which accrual of interest or charges shall cease.

(4)(A) Upon receiving a notice pursuant to paragraph (1) of this subsection, the Secretary shall—

    (i) provide the veteran with information and, to the extent feasible, counseling regarding—

        (I) alternatives to foreclosure, as appropriate in light of the veteran's particular circumstances, including possible methods of curing the default, conveyance of the property to the Secretary by means of a deed in lieu of foreclosure, and the actions authorized by paragraph (2) of this subsection; and

        (II) what the Department of Veterans Affairs' and the veteran's liabilities would be with respect to the loan in the event of foreclosure; and

    (ii) advise the veteran regarding the availability of such counseling;

except with respect to loans made by a lender which the Secretary has determined has a demonstrated record of consistently providing timely and accurate information to veterans with respect to such matters.

(B) The Secretary shall, to the extent of the availability of appropriations, ensure that sufficient personnel are available to administer subparagraph (A) of this paragraph effectively and efficiently.

(5) In the event of default in the payment of any loan guaranteed or insured under this chapter [38 USCS §§ 3701 et seq.] in which a partial payment has been tendered by the veteran concerned and refused by the holder, the holder of the obligation shall notify the Secretary as soon as such payment has been refused. The Secretary may require that any such notification include a statement of the circumstances of the default, the amount tendered, the amount of the indebtedness on the date of the tender, and the reasons for the holder's refusal.

(b) With respect to any loan made under section 3711 which has not been sold as provided in subsection (g) of such section, if the Secretary finds, after there has been a default in the payment of any installment of principal or interest owing on such loan, that the default was due to the fact that the veteran who is obligated under the loan has become unemployed as the result of the closing (in whole or in part) of a Federal installation, the Secretary shall (1) extend the time for curing the default to such time as the Secretary determines is necessary and desirable to enable such veteran to complete payments on such loan, including an extension of time beyond the stated maturity thereof, or (2) modify the terms of such loan for the purpose of changing the amortization provisions thereof by recasting, over the remaining term of the loan, or over such longer period as the Secretary may determine, the total unpaid amount then due with the modification to become effective currently or upon the termination of an agreed-upon extension of the period for curing the default.

(c)(1) For purposes of this subsection—
  (A) The term "defaulted loan" means a loan that is guaranteed under this chapter [38 USCS §§ 3701 et seq.], that was made for a purpose described in section 3710(a) of this title, and that is in default.
  (B) The term "liquidation sale" means a judicial sale or other disposition of real property to liquidate a defaulted loan that is secured by such property.
  (C) The term "net value", with respect to real property, means the amount equal to (i) the fair market value of the property, minus (ii) the total of the amounts which the Secretary estimates the Secretary would incur (if the Secretary were to acquire and dispose of the property) for property taxes, assessments, liens, property maintenance, property improvement, administration, resale (including losses sustained on the resale of the property), and other costs resulting from the acquisition and disposition of the property, excluding any amount attributed to the cost to the Government of borrowing funds.
  (D) Except as provided in subparagraph (D) of paragraph (10) of this subsection, the term "total indebtedness", with respect to a defaulted loan, means the amount equal to the total of (i) the unpaid principal of the loan, (ii) the interest on the loan as of the date applicable under paragraph (10) of this subsection, and (iii) such reasonably necessary and proper charges (as specified in the loan instrument and permitted by regulations prescribed by the Secretary to implement this subsection) associated with liquidation of the loan, including advances for taxes, insurance, and maintenance or repair of the real property securing the loan.
(2)(A) Except as provided in subparagraph (B) of this paragraph, this subsection applies to any case in which the holder of a defaulted loan undertakes to liquidate the loan by means of a liquidation sale.
  (B) This subsection does not apply to a case in which the Secretary proceeds under subsection (a)(2) of this section.
(3)(A) Before carrying out a liquidation sale of real property securing a defaulted loan, the holder of the loan shall notify the Secretary of the proposed sale. Such notice shall be provided in accordance with regulations prescribed by the Secretary to implement this subsection.
  (B) After receiving a notice described in subparagraph (A) of this paragraph, the Secretary shall determine the net value of the property securing the loan and the amount of the total indebtedness under the loan and shall notify the holder of the loan of the determination of such net value.
(4) A case referred to in paragraphs (5), (6), and (7) of this subsection as being described in this paragraph is a case in which the net value of the property securing a defaulted loan exceeds the amount of the total indebtedness under the loan minus the amount guaranteed under this chapter [38 USCS §§ 3701 et seq.].
(5) In a case described in paragraph (4) of this subsection, if the holder of the defaulted loan acquires the property securing the loan at a liquidation

sale for an amount that does not exceed the lesser of the net value of the property or the total indebtedness under the loan—

    (A) the holder shall have the option to convey the property to the United States in return for payment by the Secretary of an amount equal to the lesser of such net value or total indebtedness; and

    (B) the liability of the United States under the loan guaranty under this chapter [18 USCS §§ 3701 et seq.] shall be limited to the amount of such total indebtedness minus the net value of the property.

(6) in a case described in paragraph (4) of this subsection, if the holder of the defaulted loan does not acquire the property securing the loan at the liquidation sale, the liability of the United States under the loan guaranty under this chapter [38 USCS §§ 3701 et seq.] shall be limited to the amount equal to (A) the amount of such total indebtedness, minus (B) the amount realized by the holder incident to the sale or the net value of the property, whichever is greater.

(7) In a case described in paragraph (4) of this subsection, if the holder of the defaulted loan acquires the property securing the loan at the liquidation sale for an amount that exceeds the lesser of the total indebtedness under the loan or the net value and—

    (A)(i) the amount was the minimum amount for which, under applicable State law, the property was permitted to be sold at the liquidation sale, the holder shall have the option to convey the property to the United States in return for payment by the Secretary of an amount equal to the lesser of the amount for which the holder acquired the property or the total indebtedness under the loan; or

    (ii) there was no minimum amount for which the property had to be sold at the liquidation sale under applicable State law, the holder shall have the option to convey the property to the United States in return for payment by the Secretary of an amount equal to the lesser of such net value or total indebtedness; and

    (B) the liability of the United States under the loan guaranty under this chapter [38 USCS §§ 3701 et seq.] is as provided in paragraph (6) of this subsection.

(8) If the net value of the property securing a defaulted loan is not greater than the amount of the total indebtedness under the loan minus the amount guaranteed under this chapter [38 USCS §§ 3701 et seq.]—

    (A) the Secretary may not accept conveyance of the property from the holder of the loan; and

    (B) the liability of the United States under the loan guaranty shall be limited to the amount of the total indebtedness under the loan minus the amount realized by the holder of the loan incident to the sale at a liquidation sale of the property.

(9) In no event may the liability of the United States under a guaranteed loan exceed the amount guaranteed with respect to that loan under section 3703(b) of this title. All determinations under this subsection of net value and total indebtedness shall be made by the Secretary.

(10)(A) Except as provided in subparagraphs (B) and (C) of this paragraph, the date referred to in paragraph (1)(D)(ii) of this subsection shall be the date of the liquidation sale of the property securing the loan or such earlier date following the expiration of a reasonable period of time for such sale to occur as the Secretary may specify pursuant to regulations prescribed by the Secretary to implement this subsection).

(B)(i) Subject to division (ii) of this subparagraph, in any case in which there is a substantial delay in such sale caused by the holder of the loan exercising forebearance at the request of the Secretary, the date referred to in paragraph (1)(D)(ii) of this subsection shall be such date, on or after the date on which forebearance was requested and prior to the date of such sale, as the Secretary specifies pursuant to regulations which the Secretary shall prescribe to implement this paragraph.

(ii) The Secretary may specify a date under subdivision (i) of this subparagraph only if, based on the use of a date so specified for the purposes of such paragraph (1)(D)(ii), the Secretary is authorized, under paragraph (5)(A) or (7)(A) of this subsection, to accept conveyance of the property.

(C) In any case in which there is an excessive delay in such liquidation sale caused—

(i) by the Department of Veterans Affairs (including any delay caused by its failure to provide bidding instructions in a timely fashion); or

(ii) by a voluntary case commenced under title 11, United States Code (relating to bankruptcy);

the date referred to in paragraph (1)(D)(ii) of this subsection shall be a date, earlier than the date of such liquidation sale, which the Secretary specifies pursuant to regulations which the Secretary shall prescribe to implement this paragraph.

(D) For the purpose of determining the liability of the United States under a loan guaranty under clause (B) of paragraphs (5), [(6)], (7), and (8) of this subsection, the amount of the total indebtedness with respect to such loan guaranty shall include, in any case in which there was an excessive delay caused by the Department of Veterans of Affairs in the liquidation sale of the property securing such loan, any interest which had accrued as of the date of such sale and which would not be included, except for this subparagraph, in the calculation of such total indebtedness as a result of the specification of an earlier date under subparagraph (C)(i) of this paragraph.

(11) This subsection shall apply to loans closed before October 1, 2002.

(Sept. 2, 1958, P. L. 85-857, § 1, 72 Stat. 1212; Aug. 10, 1965, P. L. 89-117, Title I, § 107(f), 79 Stat. 460; June 30, 1976, P. L. 94-324, § 7(17), 90 Stat. 722; July 18, 1984, P. L. 98-369, Division B, Title V, Part B, § 2512(a), 98 Stat. 1117; Dec. 21, 1987, P. L. 100-198, §§ 4(a), 5(a), 101 Stat. 1316, 1317; May 20, 1988, P. L. 100-322, Title IV, Part B, § 415(b)(1), (5)(A), (B), 102 Stat. 550, 551; Dec. 18, 1989, P. L. 101-237, Title III, §§ 304(b), 307, 308(a), (b)(1), 313(b)(1), (2), 103 Stat. 2073–2075, 2077; June 13, 1991, P. L. 102-54,

38 USCS § 3732

VETERANS' BENEFITS

§§ 1, 3(a), 14(g)(1), 105 Stat. 267, 288; Aug. 6, 1991, P. L. 102-83, § 5(a), (c)(1), 105 Stat. 406; Aug. 10, 1993, P. L. 103-66, Title XII, § 12006(a), 107 Stat. 414; Nov. 2, 1994, P. L. 103-446, Title IX, § 907, 108 Stat. 4677; Aug. 5, 1997, P. L. 105-33, Title VIII, Subtitle A, § 8013, 111 Stat. 664.)

HISTORY; ANCILLARY LAWS AND DIRECTIVES

Explanatory notes:

The paragraph designator "(6)", in para. (10)(D), has been enclosed in brackets to indicate the probable intent of Congress to refer to the entire of paragraph (6).

Amendments:

1965. Act Aug. 10, 1965, designated existing matter as subsec. (a); and added subsec. (b).

1976. Act June 30, 1976 (effective 6/30/76, as provided by § 9(a) of such Act, which appears as 38 USCS § 3701 note), in subsec. (a), substituted "the Administrator's" for "his"; and in subsec. (b), substituted "the Administrator" for "he" preceding "shall", "determines" and "may determine".

1984. Act July 18, 1984 (effective 10/1/84, as provided in § 2612(c)(1) of such Act, which appears as a note to this section), designated the provisions of subsec. (a) as paras. (1), (2), and (3), in para. (1), as redesignated, substituted "Administrator of such default. Upon receipt of such notice, the Administrator may, subject to subsection (c) of this section," for "Administrator who shall thereupon", and "guaranteed. If the Administrator makes such a payment, the Administrator shall" for "guaranteed, and shall"; and added subsecs. (c) and (d).

1987. Act Dec. 21, 1987 (effective 3/1/88, as provided by § 4(b) of such Act, which appears as a note to this section) added subsec. (a)(4).

Such Act further (applicable as provided by § 5(c) of such Act, which appears as a note to this section), in subsec. (c), in para. (1), in subpara. (D), substituted "Except as provided in subparagraph (D) of paragraph (10) of this subsection, the" for "The", in cl. (ii), substituted "applicable under (10) of this subsection, and" for "of the liquidation sale of the property securing the loan (or such earlier date following the expiration of a reasonable period of time for such sale to occur as the Administrator may specify pursuant to regulations prescribed by the Administrator to implement this subsection), and", in cl. (iii), substituted "regulations prescribed by the Administrator to implement this subsection" for "such regulations", and added paras. (10) and (11).

1988. Act May 20, 1988, as amended by § 14(g)(1) of Act June 13, 1991, P. L. 102-54, substituted the section catchline for one which read: "1832. Furnishing information to real estate professionals to facilitate the disposition of properties"; redesignated former subsecs. (a) and (b) as subsec. (d), paras. (1) and (2), respectively and further redesignated such subsec. (d) as 38 USCS § 1833(d); redesignated 38 USCS § 1816(a)–(c) as subsecs. (a)–(c) of this section; and in subsec. (a)(4)(A)(i)(I), as redesignated, substituted "paragraph (2) of this subsection" for "section 1816(a)(2) of this title"; and in subsec. (c)(10), in subpara. (A), as redesignated, inserted "(or such earlier date following the expiration of a reasonable period of time for such sale to occur as the Administrator may specify pursuant to regulations prescribed by the Administrator to implement this subsection)'', and in subpara. (B)(ii), inserted "(5)(A)".

1989. Act Dec. 18, 1989, in subsec. (a), in para. (1), substituted "Except as provided in section 1803(e) of this title, if" for "If", and added para. (5); and in subsec. (c)(1)(C)(ii), inserted ", excluding any amount attributed to the cost to the Government of borrowing funds".

Such Act further (effective 10/1/89 as provided by § 308(b)(2) of such Act, which appears as a note to this section), in subsec. (c)(11), substituted "October 1, 1991" for "October 1, 1989".

Such Act further, substituted "Secretary" for "Administrator", "Secretary's" for "Administrator's", "Department of Veterans Affairs" for "Veterans' Administration", and "Department of Veterans Affairs' " for "Veterans' Administration's", wherever appearing, in the entire section.

1991. Act June 13, 1991, in subsec. (a)(4), deleted subpara. (C), which read: "The authority to carry out this paragraph shall terminate on March 1, 1991."; and in subsec. (c)(11), substituted "December 31, 1992" for "October 1, 1991".

Such Act further amended the directory language of § 415(b)(5)(C) of Act May 20, 1988, P. L. 100-322, without affecting the text of this section.

Act Aug. 6, 1991, redesignated this section, formerly 38 USCS § 1832, as 38 USCS § 3732, and amended the references in this section to reflect the redesignations made by § 5(a) of such Act (see Table III preceding 38 USCS § 101).

1993. Act Aug. 10, 1993 (effective Oct. 1, 1993, as provided by § 12006(b) of such Act, which appears as a note to this section), in subsec. (c), in para. (1)(C), substituted "resale (including losses sustained on the resale of the property)," for "resale,", and, in para. (11), substituted "shall apply to loans closed before October 1, 1998." for "shall cease to have effect on December 31, 1992.".

1994. Act Nov. 2, 1994, in subsec. (c)(6), deleted "either" following "defaulted loan", substituted "sale, the" for "sale or acquires the property at such sale for an amount that exceeds the lesser of the net value of the property or the total indebtedness under the loan—

(A) the Secretary may not accept conveyance of the property except as provided in paragraph (7) of this subsection; and

(B) the",

and substituted "(A)" and "(B)" for "(i)" and "(ii)", respectively.

Such Act further, in subsec. (c)(7), in the introductory matter, deleted "that was the minimum amount for which, under applicable State law, the property was permitted to be sold at the liquidation sale" following "net value and", in subpara. (A), designated the existing language as cl. (i), in cl. (i) as so designated, substituted "the amount was the minimum amount for which, under applicable State law, the property was permitted to be sold at the liquidation sale, the holder shall have the option to convey the property to the United States in return for payment by the Secretary of an amount equal to" for "the Secretary may accept conveyance of the property to the United States for a price not exceeding" and substituted "or" for "and" following the concluding semicolon, and added cl. (ii), and, in subpara. (B), substituted "paragraph (6)" for "paragraph (6)(B)".

38 USCS § 3732   VETERANS' BENEFITS

1997. Act Aug. 5, 1997, in subsec. (c)(11), substituted "October 1, 2002" for "October 1, 1998".

Other provisions:

Application of amendments made by § 2512(a) of Act July 18, 1984, Act July 18, 1984, P. L. 98-369, Division B, Title V, Part B, § 2512(c)(1), (2), 98 Stat. 1120; Dec. 31, 1987, P. L. 100-198, § 5(b), 101 Stat. 1317, provides:

"(1) The amendments made by subsection (a) [amending this section] shall take effect on October 1, 1984.".

Interim extension of formula for acquiring property. Act Oct. 16, 1987, P. L. 100-136, § 1(a), 101 Stat. 813, provides: "Notwithstanding section 2512(c) of the Deficit Reduction Act of 1984 (Public Law 98-369 [amending this section]), the provisions of section 1816(c) of title 38, United States Code [now subsec. (c) of this section; see the 1988 Amendment note to this section], shall continue in effect through November 15, 1987.".

Application of 1987 amendment made to subsec. (a). Act Dec. 21, 1987, P. L. 100-198, § 4(b), 101 Stat. 1316, provides: "The amendment made by subsection (a) [amending subsec. (a) of this section] shall take effect on March 1, 1988.".

Application of 1987 amendments made to subsec. (c). Act Dec. 21, 1987, P. L. 100-198, § 5(c), 101 Stat. 1317, provides: "The amendments made by subsection (a) [amending subsec. (c) of this section] shall apply to defaults which occur more than 60 days after the date of the enactment of this Act.".

Rule for construction of duplicate provisions. Act Dec. 22, 1987, P. L. 100-203, Title VII, § 7004(b), 101 Stat. 1330-280, provides: "In applying the provisions of this title [this note, amending this section and 38 USCS § 1829(c)] and the provisions of the Veterans' Home Loan Program Improvements and Property Rehabilitation Act of 1987 [38 USCS § 101 note; for full classification, consult USCS Tables volumes] which make the same amendments as the provisions of this title—

"(1) the identical provisions of title 38, United States Code, amended by the provisions of this title [this note, amending this section and 38 USCS § 3729(c)] and the provisions of such Act [38 USCS § 101 note; for full classification, consult USCS Tables volumes] shall be treated as having been amended only once; and

"(2) in executing to title 38, United States Code, the amendments made by this title [this note, amending this section and 38 USCS § 3729(c)] and by such Act [38 USCS § 101 note; for full classification, consult USCS Tables volumes], such amendments shall be executed so as to appear only once in the law.".

Effective date of Act Dec. 18, 1989 amendment of subsec. (c)(11). Act Dec. 18, 1989, P. L. 101-237, Title III, § 308(b)(2), 103 Stat. 2075, provides: "The amendment made by paragraph (1) [amending subsec. (c)(11) of this section] shall take effect as of October 1, 1989.".

Definition of "net value" for purposes of subsec. (c)(4)–(10). Act Oct. 6, 1992, P. L. 102-389, Title I, 106 Stat. 1574, provides: "Notwithstanding the provisions of 38 U.S.C. 3732(c)(1)(C) and (c)(11) or any other law, with respect to any loan guaranteed for any purpose specified in 38 U.S.C. 3710 which was closed before October 1, 1993, the term 'net value' for purposes of paragraphs (4) through (10) of 38 U.S.C. 3732[(c)] shall mean 'the amount equal to (i) the fair market value of the property, minus (ii) the total of the amounts which the Secretary estimates the Secretary would incur (if the Secretary were to acquire and dispose of the property) for property taxes, assessments, liens, property maintenance, property improvement, administration, resale (including losses sustained on the resale of the property), and other costs resulting from the acquisition and disposition of the property, excluding any amount attributed to the cost of the Government of borrowing funds'.''.

CODE OF FEDERAL REGULATIONS
Department of Veterans Affairs—Loan guaranty, 38 CFR Part 36.

RESEARCH GUIDE
Federal Procedure L Ed:
4A Fed Proc L Ed, Banking and Financing §§ 8:1414–1417, 1424.

Am Jur:
77 Am Jur 2d, Veterans and Veterans' Laws §§ 127, 128.

Auto-Cite®: Cases and annotations referred to herein can be further researched through the Auto-Cite® computer-assisted research service. Use Auto-Cite to check citations for form, parallel references, prior and later history, and annotation references.

INTERPRETIVE NOTES AND DECISIONS

1. Generally
2. Rights of government on default, generally
3. —Indemnification
4. —Subrogation
5. —Setoff against benefits
6. Determination of amount guaranteed
7. Recovery of interest on indebtedness
8. Notice of default and foreclosure to veteran
9. Miscellaneous

1. Generally
Regulations adopted by Veterans' Administrator [now Secretary of Veterans Affairs], which provided that in case of guaranteed mortgage Veterans' Administrator [now Secretary of Veterans Affairs] could specify in advance of foreclosure sale minimum amount which must be credited on mortgage debt, giving foreclosing mortgagee who purchases property at foreclosure sale for specified minimum or lower price option of selling property to agency for specified minimum, were valid exercise of statutory rule-making authority given to Administrator by § 504 of the Servicemen's Readjustment Act of 1944 58 Stat 284, 293, as amended, and were reasonable accommodation of twin statutory purposes of (1) making federal guaranty substantial equivalent of down payment, and (2) protecting both agency and veteran from unnecessary loss on foreclosure sale. United States v Shimer (1961) 367 US 374, 6 L Ed 2d 908, 81 S Ct 1554.

2. Rights of government on default, generally
Veterans' Administration [now Department of Veterans Affairs] was not entitled to reduce indebtedness to plaintiff mortgage lender by larger amount mistakenly bid by plaintiff at first foreclosure sale which was later voided for mistake, instead of by smaller amount successfully bid by plaintiff at later valid sale, where (1) mistake resulted in part from failure of agency to comply with its own established procedures, upon which plaintiff relied; (2) agency derived benefits from second sale; and (3) agency suffered no harm or prejudice through correction of initial error. Mortgage Assocs. v Cleland (1981, CA7 Ill) 653 F2d 1144.

Foreclosure of guaranteed mortgage and sale of mortgaged property under execution did not bar action by United States to recover from veteran amounts which government was required to pay to lender. United States v Henderson (1953, DC Iowa) 121 F Supp 343.

In asserting debt against veteran who had sold property to third party who then defaulted on assumed home loan, Board was required to make determination on validity of asserted debt and question of validity of asserted debt, when challenged, was issue that must be determined by Board in deciding on waiver-of-indebtedness application. Schaper v Derwinski (1991) 1 Vet App 430, app dismd (1994, Vet App) 1994 US Vet App LEXIS 199.

3. —Indemnification

Servicemen's Readjustment Act of 1944 (predecessor to 38 USCS §§ 3701 et seq.), as amended, gave direct right of indemnity, independent of subrogation rights, to Veterans' Administration [now Department of Veterans Affairs] against veteran, upon proper payment by Veterans' Administration [now Department of Veterans Affairs] of its obligations as guarantor of mortgage loan of veteran. United States v Shimer (1961) 367 US 374, 6 L Ed 2d 908, 81 S Ct 1554.

Amount owing by veteran to United States was fixed by trustee sale of mortgaged property, and fact that it maintained loss by later selling property was immaterial. McKnight v United States (1958, CA9 Cal) 259 F2d 540.

Although VA had no subrogation rights against veterans who defaulted on their VA-guaranteed home loans because lenders failed to secure deficiency judgments under state law to preserve rights against veterans to which VA could later be subrogated, VA had independent contractual right of indemnity against veterans for amount of guarantee paid to lenders since indemnification right is governed entirely by federal law and unaffected by state deficiency judgment requirements. Dixon v United States (1995, CA10 Okla) 68 F3d 1253, CCH Bankr L Rptr ¶ 76679, cert den (1996) 517 US 1167, 134 L Ed 2d 665, 116 S Ct 1566.

Notwithstanding state laws limiting creditor's proceeds to amount received in foreclosure sale and notwithstanding that mortgagee could not obtain collectible personal judgment against veteran, United States was entitled to indemnification from veteran for amounts paid pursuant to guaranty of such veteran's debt. 1945 ADVA 625.

Veteran was liable to indemnify Administrator for loan guaranty proceeds for which Administrator [now Secretary] is liable to third party purchaser of loan. 1951 ADVA 886.

4. —Subrogation

Administration [now Department] may enforce deficiency judgments against veterans for loan guaranty payments made to mortgage lenders following nonjudicial foreclosure of Minnesota real estate pursuant to rights to indemnity and subrogation under 38 USCS § 1832 [now 38 USCS § 3732] when the Administration [now Department] has made a good faith effort to provide reasonable personal notice to the veteran prior to the foreclosure sale. Vail v Derwinski (1991, CA8 Minn) 946 F2d 589, reh, en banc, den (1992, CA8 Minn) 956 F2d 812, summary judgment den, remanded (1994, DC Minn) 841 F Supp 909, affd (1994, CA8 Minn) 39 F3d 208, cert den (1995) 515 US 1102, 132 L Ed 2d 254, 115 S Ct 2245.

Upon payment by Veterans' Administration [now Department] of claim under guaranty, Government was at once subrogated to right of holder of obligation but only to extent of guaranty paid, and such right of subrogation was inferior to rights of holder of obligation until holder had been paid in full. 1946 ADVA 691.

5. —Setoff against benefits

Amounts paid pursuant to loan guaranty and not recouped from property pledged were recoverable from veteran's pension or insurance payments, unless Administrator [now Secretary] in his discretion determined that veteran was not at fault and that such recovery would defeat purposes of such benefits otherwise payable or would be inequitable; however, benefits payable to veteran's widow or dependents from pension or from any insurance payable to beneficiary after death are not subject to recovery. 1944 ADVA 607.

Administrator [now Secretary] was entitled to offset benefits otherwise payable to unremarried widow of serviceman killed in action in World War II and her minor children against proceeds paid on loan guaranteed under Servicemen's Readjustment Act of 1944 (38 USCS §§ 1801 et seq. [now 38 USCS §§ 3701 et seq.]), but benefits payable to minor children in their own right were not subject to offset for amounts paid on guaranty. 1953 ADVA 925.

Agency's withholding benefits to collect debt incurred by it when purchaser from veteran defaulted did not violate equity and good conscience where veteran had failed to secure release from liability upon selling home. Branham v Derwinski (1990) 1 Vet App 93.

6. Determination of amount guaranteed

Absent irregularity or fraud material to rights of Government, method of computing amount payable under loan guaranty certificate issued pursuant to Servicemen's Readjustment Act of 1944 (38 USCS §§ 1801 et seq. [now 38 USCS §§ 3701 et seq.]) was same whether claim was made before or after foreclosure sale of encumbered property securing guaranteed loan, and was equal to amount due as percentage of loan guaranty reduced by proceeds of foreclosure sale. 1946 ADVA 690.

7. Recovery of interest on indebtedness

Obligor on loan guaranteed or insured under Servicemen's Readjustment Act of 1944 (38 USCS §§ 1801 et seq. [now 38 USCS §§ 3701 et seq.]) was liable to Administrator [now Secretary] for payment of interest on indebtedness resulting from payment

READJUSTMENT BENEFITS

38 USCS § 3733

of guaranty or insurance claim, and liability included interest which accrued against obligor after payment of claim as well as interest which accrued on original guaranteed debt and which therefore constituted part of amount paid on claim. 1949 ADVA 825.

Holder of insured loan in default was entitled to deduct amount equal to interest on unpaid indebtedness for period between cut-off date and date of receipt of payments from or on behalf of debtor received subsequent to cut-off date and before payment of insurance claim upon such loan. 1950 ADVA 839.

Agency's obligation to acquire property held by lender who held defaulted loan was purely statutory, not contractual one entitling lender to seek interest under Prompt Payment Act (31 USCS §§ 3901-3907). New York Guardian Mortg. Corp. v United States (1990, CA) 916 F2d 1558.

8. Notice of default and foreclosure to veteran

Veterans' challenge to Veterans Administration's exercise of indemnity rights after foreclosure on property based on veterans' failure to pay VA mortgages is dismissed, where VA followed state nonjudicial foreclosure procedure, and provided veterans with general notice that mortgage was in default and that foreclosure was possible, without providing specific notice of time and place of foreclosure because VA notices and regulations are sufficient to satisfy due process rights of veterans. Vail v Brown (1994, DC Minn) 841 F Supp 909, affd (1994, CA8 Minn) 39 F3d 208, cert den (1995) 515 US 1102, 132 L Ed 2d 254, 115 S Ct 2245.

Veteran's loan guarantee indebtedness was valid, notwithstanding veteran's claim that he did not receive notice of transferee's default and subsequent foreclosure, since record demonstrated that VA followed appropriate guidelines to notify appellant of default and impending foreclosure; letter was addressed to appellant's correct address and was not returned undelivered and contained requisite information. East v Brown (1995) 8 Vet App 34.

9. Miscellaneous

In suit by homeowner of guaranteed home loan against Veterans Administration [now Department] and private lender for relief against foreclosure of home loan, under former 38 USCS § 1816, when veteran borrower is in default on his guaranteed home loan, agency could refund to lender unpaid balance of obligation and receive assignment of loan and security thus putting agency in position to grant forbearance to borrower; refusal by VA to take such action in case at bar did not constitute abuse of discretion. Rank v Nimmo (1982, CA9 Cal) 677 F2d 692, cert den (1982) 459 US 907, 74 L Ed 2d 168, 103 S Ct 210.

Mortgagor had no right of action in federal court against Veterans Administration [now Department of Veterans Affairs] to enforce duties relative to insured home mortgage; thus, action brought by mortgagors to defend against foreclosure actions brought against them and their residences for being in default on mortgage must be dismissed where mortgagors alleged agency failed to monitor properly lenders' servicing of their mortgage loans prior to foreclosure and failed to provide supplemental servicing of loans by offering mortgagors opportunity to refund and assign their mortgages to agency, thus avoiding foreclosure following default. First Family Mortg. Corp. v Earnest (1988, CA6 Ohio) 851 F2d 843.

Indebtedness of veteran arising from default upon loan guaranteed by United States was subject to bankruptcy, assuming proper procedure was followed, and withholding of other benefits due veteran by Veterans' Administration [now Department of Veterans Affairs] to satisfy such claim was in effect legal set off prohibited by bankruptcy laws. 1950 ADVA 850-A.

§ 3733. Property management

(a)(1) Of the number of purchases made during any fiscal year of real property acquired by the Secretary as the result of a default on a loan guaranteed under this chapter [38 USCS §§ 3701 et seq.] for a purpose described in section 3710(a) of this title, not more than 65 percent, nor less than 50 percent, of such purchases may be financed by a loan made by the Secretary. The maximum percentage stated in the preceding sentence may be increased to 80 percent for any fiscal year if the Secretary determines that such an increase is necessary in order to maintain the effective functioning of the loan guaranty program.

(2) After September 30, 1990, the percentage limitations described in paragraph (1) of this subsection shall have no effect.

(3) The Secretary may, beginning on October 1, 1990, sell any note evidencing a loan referred to in paragraph (1)—

    (A) with recourse; or

(B) without recourse, but only if the amount received is equal to an amount which is not less than the unpaid balance of such loan.

(4)(A) Except as provided in subparagraph (B) of this paragraph, the amount of a loan made by the Secretary to finance the purchase of real property from the Secretary described in paragraph (1) of this subsection may not exceed an amount equal to 95 percent of the purchase price of such real property.

(B)(i) The Secretary may waive the provisions of subparagraph (A) of this paragraph in the case of any loan described in paragraph (5) of this subsection.

(ii) A loan described in subparagraph (A) of this paragraph may, to the extent the Secretary determines to be necessary in order to market competitively the property involved, exceed 95 percent of the purchase price.

(5) The Secretary may include, as part of a loan to finance a purchase of real property from the Secretary described in paragraph (1) of this subsection, an amount to be used only for the purpose of rehabilitating such property. Such amount may not exceed the amount necessary to rehabilitate the property to a habitable state, and payments shall be made available periodically as such rehabilitation is completed.

(6) The Secretary shall make a loan to finance the sale of real property described in paragraph (1) of this subsection at an interest rate that is lower than the prevailing mortgage market interest rate in areas where, and to the extent, the Secretary determines, in light of prevailing conditions in the real estate market involved, that such lower interest rate is necessary in order to market the property competitively and is in the interest of the long-term stability and solvency of the Department of Veterans Affairs Loan Guaranty Revolving Fund established by section 3724(a) of this title.

(b) The Secretary may not make a loan to finance a purchase of property acquired by the Secretary as a result of a default on a loan guaranteed under this chapter unless the purchaser meets the credit underwriting standards established under section 3710(g)(2)(A) of this title.

(c)(1) The Secretary shall identify and compile information on common factors which the Secretary finds contribute to foreclosures on loans guaranteed under this chapter [38 USCS §§ 3701 et seq.].

(2) The Secretary shall include a summary of the information compiled, and the Secretary's findings, under paragraph (1) of this subsection in the annual report submitted to the Congress under section 529 of this title. As part of such summary and findings, the Secretary shall provide a separate analysis of the factors which contribute to foreclosures of loans which have been assumed.

(d)(1) The Secretary shall furnish to real estate brokers and other real estate sales professionals information on the availability of real property for disposition under this chapter and the procedures used by the Department of Veterans Affairs to dispose of such property.

(2) For the purpose of facilitating the most expeditious sale, at the highest

possible price, of real property acquired by the Secretary as the result of a default on a loan guaranteed, insured, or made under this chapter, the Secretary shall list all such property with real estate brokers under such arrangements as the Secretary determines to be most appropriate and cost effective.

(e) Notwithstanding any other provision of law, the amount received from the sale of any note evidencing a loan secured by real property described in subsection (a)(1) of this section, and the amount received from the sale of securities under section 3720(h) of this title, shall be credited, without any reduction and for the fiscal year in which the amount is received, as offsetting collections of—

(1) the revolving fund for which a fee under section 3729 of this title was collected (or was exempted from being collected) at the time of the original guaranty of the loan that was secured by the same property; or

(2) in any case in which there was no requirement of (or exemption from) a fee at the time of the original guaranty of the loan that was secured by the same property, the Loan Guaranty Revolving Fund; and

the total so credited to any revolving fund for a fiscal year shall offset outlays attributed to such revolving fund during such fiscal year.

(Sept. 2, 1958, P. L. 85-857, § 1, 72 Stat. 1212; July 18, 1984, P. L. 98-369, Div. B, Title V, § 2512(a)(2), 98 Stat. 1117; Oct. 28, 1986, P. L. 99-576, Title IV, Part A, § 408(a), 100 Stat. 3283; Oct. 16, 1987, P. L. 100-136, § 2, 101 Stat. 813; Dec. 21, 1987, P. L. 100-198, § 14, 101 Stat. 1325; Dec. 22, 1987, P. L. 100-203, Title VII, §§ 7001, 7003(a), 101 Stat. 1330-278, 1330-279; Feb. 29, 1988, P. L. 100-253, § 2, 102 Stat. 20; May 20, 1988, P. L. 100-322, Title IV, Part B, § 415(b)(1)(D), (5)(C), 102 Stat. 550, 551; Nov. 18, 1988, P. L. 100-689, Title III, § 301, 102 Stat. 4176; Dec. 18, 1989, P. L. 101-237, Title III, §§ 305(a), 313(b)(1), 103 Stat. 2073, 2077; Dec. 19, 1989, P. L. 101-239, Title V, §§ 5002, 5003(a), 103 Stat. 2136; June 13, 1991, P. L. 102-54, §§ 2, 14(g)(1), 15(a)(5), 105 Stat. 267, 288, 289; Aug. 6, 1991, P. L. 102-83, §§ 2(c)(3), 5(a), (c)(1), 105 Stat. 402, 406; May 20, 1992, P. L. 102-291, § 5(b), 106 Stat. 180.)

HISTORY; ANCILLARY LAWS AND DIRECTIVES

Amendments:

1984. Act July 18, 1984 (effective 10/1/1984, as provided by § 2512(c) of such Act, which appears as 38 USCS § 3732 note), added subsec. (d).

1986. Act Oct. 28, 1986, added subsecs. (e) and (f).

1987. Act Oct. 16, 1987 substituted subsec. (d)(3) for one which read: "Notes securing such loans may be sold with recourse only to the extent that the Administrator determines that selling such notes with recourse is necessary in order to maintain the effective functioning of the loan guaranty program under this chapter.".

Act Dec. 21, 1987 (effective 10/1/87, as provided by § 6(a)(2) of such Act), in subsec. (d)(1), substituted "not more than 65 percent, nor less than 50 percent," for "not more than 75 percent, nor less than 60 percent,".

Such Act further (applicable as provided by § 6(b)(2) of such Act, which appears as a note to this section), in subsec. (d), added paras. (4)–(6).

Act Dec. 22, 1987, purported to amend subsec. (d)(1) of § 1816 by substituting "not more than 65 percent, nor less than 50 percent," for "not more than 75 percent nor less than 60 percent,". However, such amendment could not be executed as it was already effected by Act Dec. 21, 1987, P. L. 100-198.

Such Act further amended subsec. (d) of § 1816, by redesignating para. (3) as para. (2)(C), in para. (2)(C) as so redesignated, in the introductory matter, substituted "Beginning on October 1, 1989, the Administrator may sell any note evidencing" for "The Administrator may sell any note securing", redesignated cls. (A) and (B) as cls. (i) and (ii), respectively, and added a new para. (3).

Such Act further (effective on 10/1/87 as provided by § 7003(b) of such Act, which appears as a note to this section), in subsec. (d)(1) of § 1816, substituted "not more than 65 percent, nor less than 50 percent," for "not more than 75 percent, nor less than 60 percent,".

1988. Act Feb. 29, 1988, in subsec. (d)(4), in subpara. (B), designated existing provisions as cl. (i), and added cl. (ii).

Act May 20, 1988 inserted the section catchline; redesignated 38 USCS § 1816(d)–(f) as subsecs. (a)–(c) of this section; and redesignated 38 USCS § 1832(d) as subsec. (d) of this section.

Act Nov. 18, 1988, in subsec. (a), added para. (7).

1989. Act Dec. 18, 1989, in para. (a)(6), substituted "December 31" for "October 1".

Such Act further (applicable as provided by § 305(b)(2) of such Act, which appears as a note to this section), added subsec. (e).

Such Act further, substituted "Secretary" for "Administrator", and "Department of Veterans Affairs" for "Veterans' Administration", wherever appearing, in the entire section.

Act Dec. 19, 1989, in subsec. (a)(3), in the introductory matter of subparas. (A), (B), and (C), substituted "October 1, 1990" for "October 1, 1989".

Section 5003(a) of such Act (applicable as provided by § 5003(b) of such Act, which appears as a note to this section) purported to add a subsec. (e), but such amendment was not executed because such subsec. (e) was identical to that added by Act Dec. 18, 1989.

1991. Act June 13, 1991, in subsec. (a), substituted paras. (2) and (3) for ones which read:

"(2) In carrying out paragraph (1) of this subsection, the Secretary, to the maximum extent consistent with that paragraph and with maintaining the effective functioning of the loan guaranty program under this chapter shall minimize the number of loans made by the Secretary to finance purchases of real property from the Secretary described in that paragraph.

"(3)(A) Before October 1, 1990, notes evidencing such loans may be sold with or without recourse as determined by the Secretary, with respect to specific proposed sales of such notes, to be in the best interest of the effective functioning of the loan guaranty program under this chapter, taking into consideration the comparative cost-effectiveness of each type of sale. In comparing the cost-effectiveness of conducting a proposed sale of such notes with recourse or without recourse, the Secretary shall, based on available estimates regarding likely market conditions and other pertinent factors as of the time of the sale, determine and consider—

"(i) the average amount by which the selling price for such notes sold with recourse would exceed the selling price for such notes if sold without recourse; and

"(ii) the total cost of selling such notes with recourse, including—

"(I) any estimated discount or premium;

"(II) the projected cost, based on Department of Veterans Affairs experience with the sale of notes evidencing vendee loans with recourse and the quality of the loans evidenced by the notes to be sold, of repurchasing defaulted notes;

"(III) the total servicing cost with respect to repurchased notes, including the costs of taxes and insurance, collecting monthly payments, servicing delinquent accounts, and terminating insoluble loans;

"(IV) the costs of managing and disposing of properties acquired as the result of defaults on such notes;

"(V) the loss or gain on resale of such properties; and

"(VI) any other cost determined appropriate by the Secretary.

"(B) Not later than 60 days after making any sale described in subparagraph (A) of this paragraph occurring before October 1, 1990, the Secretary shall submit to the Committees on Veterans' Affairs of the Senate and the House of Representatives a report describing—

"(i) the application of the provisions of such subparagraph, and each of the determinations required thereunder, in the case of such sale;

"(ii) the results of the sale in comparison to the anticipated results; and

"(iii) actions taken by the Secretary to facilitate the marketing of the notes involved.

"(C) Beginning on October 1, 1990, the Secretary may sell any note evidencing such a loan—

"(i) with recourse; or

"(ii) without recourse but only if the amount received is equal to an amount which is not less than the unpaid balance of such loan.".

Such Act further, in subsec. (a), deleted para. (6), which read: "This subsection shall cease to have effect on December 31, 1990.", and redesignated para. (7) as new para. (6).

Such Act further, amended the directory language of Act May 20, 1988, P. L. 100-322, § 415(b)(5)(C).

Such Act Act further, purported to delete a subsec. (e) added by § 5003(a) of Act Dec. 19, 1989; however, the amendment was not executed since the addition of such subsec. (e) had not been executed. See the 1989 Amendment notes.

Act Aug. 6, 1991, redesignated this section, formerly 38 USCS § 1833, as 38 USCS § 3733, amended the references in this section to reflect the redesignations made by § 5(a) of such Act (see Table III preceding 38 USCS § 101); and, in subsec. (c), in para. (2), substituted "section 529" for "section 214".

1992. Act May 20, 1992, in subsec. (e), in the introductory matter, inserted ", and the amount received from the sale of securities under section 3720(h) of this title,".

Other provisions:

Application of subsec. (d)(4)–(6). Act Dec. 21, 1987, P. L. 100-198, § 6(b)(2), 101 Stat. 1318, provides: "The amendment made by this subsection [adding subsec. (d)(4)–(6) of this section] shall apply to loans made more than 30 days after the date of the enactment of this Act.".

Report to Congress. Act Dec. 21, 1987, P. L. 100-198, § 6(c), 101 Stat. 1319, provides: "The Administrator of Veterans' Affairs shall, by March 1, 1990, transmit to the Congress a report of the activities carried out, through December 31, 1989, under paragraphs (4) and (5) of section 1816(d) of title 38, United States Code [now subsec. (d) of this section; see the 1988 Amendments note to this section], as added by subsection (b) of this section.".

Effective date of Act Dec. 22, 1987 amendment of subsec. (d)(1). Act Dec. 22, 1987, P. L. 100-203, Title VII, § 7003(b), 101 Stat. 1330-279, provides: "The amendment made by subsection (a) [amending subsec. (d)(1) of this section] shall take effect as of October 1, 1987.".

Rule for construction of duplicate provisions. Act Dec. 22, 1987, P. L. 100-203, Title VII, § 7004(b), 101 Stat. 1330-280, provides: "In applying the provisions of this title [this note, amending this section and 38 USCS § 3729(c)] and the provisions of the Veterans' Home Loan Program Improvements and Property Rehabilitation Act of 1987 [38 USCS § 101 note; for full classification, consult USCS Tables volumes] which make the same amendments as the provisions of this title—

"(1) the identical provisions of title 38, United States Code, amended by the provisions of this title [this note, amending this section and 38 USCS § 3729(c)] and the provisions of such Act [38 USCS § 101 note; for full classification, consult USCS Tables volumes] shall be treated as having been amended only once; and

"(2) in executing to title 38, United States Code, the amendments made by this title [this note, amending this section and 38 USCS § 3729(c)] and by such Act [38 USCS § 101 note; for full classification, consult USCS Tables volumes], such amendments shall be executed so as to appear only once in the law.".

Contingent amendment of subsec. (a)(3) by Act Dec. 18, 1989. Act Dec. 18, 1989, P. L. 101-237, § 305(b)(1), 103 Stat. 2074, provides:

"If, before the date and time of the enactment of this Act, no provision of law has been enacted amending section 1833 [now § 3733] of title 38, United States Code, by adding a new subsection (e) with a text substantively identical to the text of the new subsection (e) added to such section 1833 [now § 3733] by subsection (a)(3) of this section, the provisions of subsection (a)(1) of this section amending subsection (a)(3) of such section 1833 [now § 3733] shall not take effect.".

Subsection (a)(1) of § 305 of the Act provides:

"in subsection (a)(3) [of 38 USCS § 3733]—

"Section 1833 [now § 3733] is amended—

"(A) in subparagraph (A), by striking out 'Before October 1, 1990,' and inserting in lieu thereof 'Subject to subparagraph (C) of this paragraph,';

"(B) in subparagraph (B), by striking out 'occurring before October 1, 1990'; and

"(C) in subparagraph (C), by striking out 'October 1, 1990,'' and inserting in lieu thereof "October 1, 1989,' ".

Application of subsec. (e) as added by Act Dec. 18, 1989. Act Dec. 18, 1989, P. L. 101-237, Title III, § 305(b)(2), 103 Stat. 2074, provides: "Subsection (e) of section 1833 [now § 3733] of such title 38, as added by subsection (a)(3), shall apply with respect to amounts referred to in such subsection (e) received after September 30, 1989.".

Application of subsec. (e) as added by Act Dec. 19, 1989. Act Dec. 19, 1989, P. L. 101-239, Title V, § 5003(b), 103 Stat. 2137, provides: "Subsection (e) of section 1833 [now § 3733] of title 38, United States Code, as added by subsection (a), shall apply with respect to amounts referred to in such subsection (e) received on or after October 1, 1989.". [Subsec. (a) of Act Dec. 19, 1989, P. L. 101-239, Title V, § 5003, 103 Stat. 2137, was not executed, since it made the same amendment as that made by Act Dec. 18, 1989, P. L. 101-237, Title III, § 305(a)(3), 103 Stat. 2074. (See the 1989 Amendment notes to this section.)]

CROSS REFERENCES

This section is referred to in 38 USCS §§ 3714, 3729, 3735.

RESEARCH GUIDE

Am Jur:
77 Am Jur 2d, Veterans and Veterans' Laws § 127.

§ 3734. Annual submission of information on the Loan Guaranty Revolving Fund and the Guaranty and Indemnity Fund

(a) In the documents providing detailed information on the budget for the Department of Veterans Affairs that the Secretary submits to the Congress in conjunction with the President's budget submission for each fiscal year pursuant to section 1105 of title 31, United States Code, the Secretary shall include—

(1) a description of the operations of the Loan Guaranty Revolving Fund and the Guaranty and Indemnity Fund during the fiscal year preceding the fiscal year in which such budget is submitted; and

(2) the needs of such funds, if any, for appropriations in—

(A) the fiscal year in which the budget is submitted; and

(B) the fiscal year for which the budget is submitted.

(b) The matters submitted under subsection (a) of this section shall include, with respect to each fund referred to in subsection (a), the following:

(1) Information and financial data on the operations of the fund during the fiscal year before the fiscal year in which such matters are submitted and estimated financial data and related information on the operation of the fund for—

(A) the fiscal year of the submission; and

(B) the fiscal year following the fiscal year of the submission.

(2) Estimates of the amount of revenues derived by the fund in the fiscal

year preceding the fiscal year of the submission, in the fiscal year of the submission, and in the fiscal year following the fiscal year of the submission from each of the following sources:

 (A) Fees collected under section 3729(a) of this title for each category of loan guaranteed, insured, or made under this chapter or collected under section 3729(b) of this title for assumed loans.

 (B) Federal Government contributions made under clauses (A) and (B) of section 3725(c)(2) of this title.

 (C) Federal Government payments under subsections (a)(3) and (c)(2) of section 3729 of this title.

 (D) Investment income.

 (E) Sales of foreclosed properties.

 (F) Loan asset sales.

 (G) Each additional source of revenue.

(3) Information, for each fiscal year referred to in paragraph (2) of this subsection, regarding the types of dispositions made and anticipated to be made of defaults on loans guaranteed, insured, or made under this chapter, including the cost to the fund, and the numbers, of such types of dispositions.

(Added Dec. 18, 1989, P. L. 101-237, Title III, § 302(b)(1), 103 Stat. 2070; Aug. 6, 1991, P. L. 102-83, § 5(a), (c)(1), 105 Stat. 406.)

HISTORY; ANCILLARY LAWS AND DIRECTIVES

References in text:

"Subsection (a)(3) of section 3729 of this title", referred to in this section, was repealed by Act June 13, 1991, P. L. 102-54, § 15(a)(3), 105 Stat. 289.

Amendments:

1991. Act Aug. 6, 1991, redesignated this section, formerly 38 USCS § 1833, as 38 USCS § 3733, and amended the references in this section to reflect the redesignations made by § 5(a) of such Act (see Table III preceding 38 USCS § 101).

RESEARCH GUIDE

Am Jur:

77 Am Jur 2d, Veterans and Veterans' Laws § 126.

§ 3735. Housing assistance for homeless veterans

(a)(1) To assist homeless veterans and their families in acquiring shelter, the Secretary may enter into agreements described in paragraph (2) with—

 (A) nonprofit organizations, with preference being given to any organization named in, or approved by the Secretary under, section 5902 of this title; or

 (B) any State or any political subdivision thereof.

(2) To carry out paragraph (1), the Secretary may enter into agreements to sell, lease, lease with an option to purchase, or donate real property, and

improvements thereon, acquired by the Secretary as the result of a default on a loan made, insured, or guaranteed under this chapter [38 USCS §§ 3701 et seq.]. Such sale or lease or donation shall be for such consideration as the Secretary determines is in the best interests of homeless veterans and the Federal Government.

(3) The Secretary may enter into an agreement under paragraph (1) of this subsection only if—

  (A) the Secretary determines that such an action will not adversely affect the ability of the Department—

    (i) to fulfill its statutory missions with respect to the Department loan guaranty program and the short- and long-term solvency of the Loan Guaranty Revolving Fund and the Guaranty and Indemnity Fund under this chapter [38 USCS §§ 3701 et seq.]; or

    (ii) to carry out other functions and administer other programs authorized by law;

  (B) the entity to which the property is sold, leased, or donated agrees to—

    (i) utilize the property solely as a shelter primarily for homeless veterans and their families,

    (ii) comply with all zoning laws relating to the property,

    (iii) make no use of the property that is not compatible with the area where the property is located, and

    (iv) take such other actions as the Secretary determines are necessary or appropriate in the best interests of homeless veterans and the Federal Government; and

  (C) the Secretary determines that there is no significant likelihood of the property being sold for a price sufficient to reduce the liability of the Department or the veteran who defaulted on the loan.

(4) The term of any lease under this subsection may not exceed three years.

(5) An approved entity that leases a property from the Secretary under this section shall be responsible for the payment of any taxes, utilities, liability insurance, and other maintenance charges or similar charges that apply to the property.

(6) Any agreement, deed, or other instrument executed by the Secretary under this subsection shall be on such terms and conditions as the Secretary determines to be appropriate and necessary to carry out the purpose of such agreement.

(b)(1) Subject to paragraphs (2) and (3), the Secretary may make loans to organizations described in paragraph (1)(A) of subsection (a) to finance the purchase of property by such organizations under such subsection.

(2) In making a loan under this subsection, the Secretary–

  (A) shall establish credit standards to be used for this purpose;

  (B) may, pursuant to section 3733(a)(6) of this title, provide that the loan will bear interest at a rate below the rate that prevails for similar loans in the market in which the loan is made; and

  (C) may waive the collection of a fee under section 3729 of this title in any case in which the Secretary determines that such a waiver would be appropriate.

(c) The Secretary may not enter into agreements under subsection (a) after December 31, 1999.

(Added June 13, 1991, P. L. 102-54, § 9(a), 105 Stat. 272; Aug. 6, 1991, P. L. 102-83, § 5(a), (c)(1), 105 Stat. 406; Nov. 10, 1992, P. L. 102-590, §§ 8, 9, 106 Stat. 5140; Nov. 2, 1994, P. L. 103-446, Title XII, § 1201(d)(13), 108 Stat. 4684; Feb. 13, 1996, P. L. 104-110, Title I, § 101(h), 110 Stat. 768; Nov. 21, 1997, P. L. 105-144, Title II, § 203(a), 111 Stat. 2288.)

HISTORY; ANCILLARY LAWS AND DIRECTIVES

Amendments:

1991. Act Aug. 6, 1991, redesignated this section, formerly 38 USCS § 1835, as 38 USCS § 3735, and amended the references in this section to reflect the redesignations made by § 5(a) of such Act (see Table III preceding 38 USCS § 101).

1992. Act Nov. 10, 1992, in subsec. (a), in para. (2), inserted ", lease, lease with an option to purchase, or donate" and "or lease or donation", in para. (3)(B), in the introductory matter, inserted ", leased, or donated", redesignated para. (4) as para. (6) and added new paras. (4) and (5); redesignated subsec. (b) as subsec. (c); added a new subsec. (b); and, in subsec. (c) as redesignated, substituted "December 31, 1995" for "September 30, 1993".

1994. Act Nov. 2, 1994, in subsec. (a)(1)(A), substituted "section 5902" for "section 3402".

1996. Act Feb. 13, 1996, in subsec. (c), substituted "December 31, 1997" for "December 31, 1995".

1997. Act Nov. 21, 1997, in subsec. (c), substituted "December 31, 1999" for "December 31, 1997".

RESEARCH GUIDE

Am Jur:

77 Am Jur 2d, Veterans and Veterans' Laws § 127.

§ 3736. Reporting requirements

The annual report required by section 529 of this title shall include a discussion of the activities under this chapter [38 USCS §§ 3701 et seq.]. Beginning with the report submitted at the close of fiscal year 1996, and every second year thereafter, this discussion shall include information regarding the following:

(1) Loans made to veterans whose only qualifying service was in the Selected Reserve.

(2) Interest rates and discount points which were negotiated between the lender and the veteran pursuant to section 3703(c)(4)(A)(i) of this title.

(3) The determination of reasonable value by lenders pursuant to section 3731(f) of this title.

(4) Loans that include funds for energy efficiency improvements pursuant to section 3710(a)(10) of this title.

(5) Direct loans to Native American veterans made pursuant to subchapter V of this chapter [38 USCS §§ 3761 et seq.].

(Added Feb. 13, 1996, P. L. 104-110, Title II, § 201(a)(1), 110 Stat. 770.)

RESEARCH GUIDE
Am Jur:
77 Am Jur 2d, Veterans and Veterans' Laws § 126.

SUBCHAPTER IV. SMALL BUSINESS LOANS

§ 3741. Definitions

For the purposes of this subchapter [38 USCS §§ 3741 et seq.]—

(1) The term "disabled veteran" means (A) a veteran who is entitled to compensation under laws administered by the Secretary for a disability rated at 30 percent or more, or (B) a veteran whose discharge or release from active duty was for a disability incurred or aggravated in line of duty.

(2) The term "veteran of the Vietnam era" means a person (A) who served on active duty for a period of more than 180 days, any part of which occurred during the Vietnam era, and who was discharged or released therefrom with other than a dishonorable discharge, or (B) who was discharged or released from active duty for a service-connected disability if any part of such active duty was performed during the Vietnam era.
(Added Act Nov. 3, 1981, P. L. 97-72, Title III, § 302(a), 95 Stat. 1955; Oct. 28, 1986, P. L. 99-576, Title VII, § 702(9), 100 Stat. 3302; Aug. 6, 1991, P. L. 102-83, §§ 4(a)(1), 5(a), 105 Stat. 403, 406.)

HISTORY; ANCILLARY LAWS AND DIRECTIVES
Effective date of section:
Act Nov. 3, 1981, P. L. 97-72, Title III, § 305, 95 Stat. 1060, which appears as an Other provisions note to this section, provides that this section is effective 180 days after enactment.

Amendments:
1986. Act Oct. 28, 1986, in para. (1), substituted "percent" for "per centum"; and in para. (2) substituted "180 days" for "one hundred and eighty days".
1991. Act Aug. 6, 1991, redesignated this section, formerly 38 USCS § 1841, as 38 USCS § 3741.
Such Act further, in para. (1), substituted "administered by the Secretary" for "administered by the Veterans' Administration".

Short title:
Act Nov. 3, 1981, P. L. 97-72, Title III, § 301, 95 Stat. 1055, provided that this title [which appears generally as 38 USCS §§ 3741 et seq.; for full classification of such Title, consult USCS Tables volumes] may be cited as the Veterans' Small Business Loan Act of 1981".

Other provisions:
Authorization of appropriations for establishment of program. Act Nov. 3, 1981, P. L. 97-72, Title III, § 304, 95 Stat. 1060, provided: "There is authorized to be appropriated a total of $750,000 for fiscal years 1982

38 USCS § 3741 VETERANS' BENEFITS

through 1986 for use by the Administrator of Veterans' Affairs for expenses incidental to the establishment of the small business loan program authorized by subchapter IV of chapter 37 of title 38, United States Code (as added by section 302) [38 USCS §§ 3741 et seq.].".

Effective date of amendments made by Act Nov. 3, 1981; effective date of Administrator's authority to promulgate regulations. Act Nov. 3, 1981, P. L. 97-72, Title III, § 305, 95 Stat. 1060, provided: "The amendments made by this title [adding 38 USCS §§ 3741 et seq., generally; for full classification of such Title, consult USCS Tables volumes] shall take effect at the end of the one-hundred-and-eighty-day period beginning on the date of the enactment of this Act, except that the authority of the Administrator of Veterans' Affairs to promulgate regulations under subchapter IV of chapter 37 of title 38, United States Code (as added by section 302) [38 USCS §§ 3741 et seq.], shall take effect on such date of enactment.".

RESEARCH GUIDE

Federal Procedure L Ed:
4A Fed Proc L Ed, Banking and Financing §§ 8:1414, 1415, 1417, 1424, 1425.

Am Jur:
77 Am Jur 2d, Veterans and Veterans' Laws § 125.

§ 3742. Small business loan program

(a)(1) Subject to subsection (b) of this section, the Secretary may provide financial assistance to veterans' small business concerns for the purpose of (A) financing plant construction, conversion, or expansion (including the acquisition of land), (B) financing the acquisition of equipment, facilities, machinery, supplies, or materials, or (C) supplying such concerns with working capital.

(2) Subject to paragraph (3)(A) of this subsection, financial assistance under this section may be provided in the form of (A) loan guaranties, or (B) direct loans.

(3) The Secretary shall specify in regulations the criteria to be met for a business concern to qualify as a veterans' small business concern for the purposes of this subchapter [38 USCS §§ 3741 et seq.]. Such regulations shall include requirements—

(A) that at least 51 percent of a business concern must be owned by individuals who are veterans of the Vietnam era or disabled veterans in order for such concern to qualify for a loan guaranty and that at least 51 percent of a business concern must be owned by disabled veterans in order for such concern to qualify for a direct loan; and

(B) that the management and daily business operations of the concern must be directed by one or more of the veterans whose ownership interest is part of the majority ownership for the purposes of meeting the requirement in clause (A) of this paragraph.

(b) The availability of financial assistance under subsection (a) of this section is subject to the following limitations:

(1) The Secretary may not make a direct loan under this section unless the veterans' small business concern applying for the loan shows to the satisfaction of the Secretary that the concern is unable to obtain a loan guaranteed by the Department under this section or made or guaranteed by the Small Business Administration.

(2) The Secretary may not guarantee a loan under this section if the loan bears a rate of interest in excess of the maximum rate of interest prescribed under section 3745 of this title.

(3) The Secretary may not make or guarantee a loan under this section for an amount in excess of $200,000.

(4) The original liability of the Secretary on any loan guaranteed under this section may not exceed 90 percent of the amount of the loan, and such liability shall decrease or increase pro rata with any decrease or increase of the amount of the unpaid portion of the loan, but such liability may not exceed the amount of the original guaranty.

(c) Each loan made or guaranteed under this subchapter [38 USCS §§ 3741 et seq.] shall be of such sound value, taking into account the creditworthiness of the veterans' small business concern (and the individual owners) applying for such loan, or so secured as reasonably to assure payment.

(d)(1) Except as provided in paragraph (2) of this subsection, the Secretary may not make or guarantee a loan under this subchapter [38 USCS §§ 3741 et seq.] to a veterans' small business concern in which an ownership interest is held by a veteran who also has an ownership interest in another small business concern if such ownership interest was considered in qualifying that other concern for an outstanding loan made or guaranteed under this subchapter [38 USCS §§ 3741 et seq.] or the Small Business Act (15 U.S.C. 631 et seq.).

(2) Paragraph (1) of this subsection shall not apply if 51 percent or more of the business concern seeking a direct or guaranteed loan under this subchapter [38 USCS §§ 3741 et seq.] is owned by veterans of the Vietnam era or disabled veterans without including the ownership interest of the veteran whose ownership interest in another small business concern was previously considered in qualifying that other concern for an outstanding guaranteed or direct business loan under this subchapter [38 USCS §§ 3741 et seq.] or the Small Business Act (15 U.S.C. 631 et seq.).

(e)(1) In order to protect the interest of the United States, upon application by a veterans' small business concern which is the recipient of a loan guaranteed under this subchapter [38 USCS §§ 3741 et seq.], the Secretary (subject to the provisions of this subsection) may undertake the veterans' small business concern's obligation to make payments under such loan or, if the loan was a direct loan made by the Secretary, may suspend such obligation. While such payments are being made by the Secretary pursuant to the undertaking of such obligation or while such obligation is suspended, no such payment with respect to the loan may be required from the concern.

(2) The Secretary may undertake or suspend a veterans' small business concern's obligation under this subsection only if—

(A) such undertaking or suspension of the obligation is, in the judgment of the Secretary, necessary to protect the interest of the United States;

(B) with the undertaking or suspension of the obligation, the small business concern would, in the judgment of the Secretary, become or remain a viable small business entity; and

(C) the small business concern executes an agreement in writing satisfactory to the Secretary as provided by paragraph (4) of this subsection.

(3) The period of time for which the Secretary undertakes or suspends the obligation on a loan under this subsection may not exceed five years. The Secretary may extend the maturity of any loan on which the Secretary undertakes or suspends the obligation under this subsection for a corresponding period of time.

(4)(A) Before the Secretary may undertake or suspend a veterans' small business concern's obligation under this subsection, the Secretary shall require the small business concern to execute an agreement to repay the aggregate amount of the payments which were required under the loan during the period for which the obligation was undertaken or suspended—

(i) by periodic payments not less in amount or less frequently falling due than those which were due under the loan during such period,

(ii) pursuant to a repayment schedule agreed upon by the Secretary and the small business concern, or

(iii) by a combination of the method of payments described in clauses (i) and (ii) of this subparagraph.

(B) In addition to requiring the small business concern to execute the agreement described in subparagraph (A) of this paragraph, the Secretary shall, before the undertaking or suspension of the obligation, take such action and require the small business concern to take such action as the Secretary considers appropriate in the circumstances, including the provision of such security as the Secretary considers necessary or appropriate, to assure that the rights and interests of the United States and any lender will be safeguarded adequately during and after the period in which such obligation is so undertaken or suspended.

(Added Act Nov. 3, 1981, P. L. 97-72, Title III, § 302(a), 95 Stat. 1955; Oct. 28, 1986, P. L. 99-576, Title VII, § 702(10), 100 Stat. 3302; Dec. 18, 1989, P. L. 101-237, Title III, § 313(b)(1), 103 Stat. 2077; Aug. 6, 1991, P. L. 102-83, §§ 4(a)(3), (4), 5(a), (c)(1), 105 Stat. 404, 406.)

HISTORY; ANCILLARY LAWS AND DIRECTIVES

References in text:

"The Small Business Act", referred to in this section, is Act July 18, 1958, P. L. 85-536, 72 Stat. 384, which appears generally as 15 USCS §§ 631 et seq. For full classification of such Act, consult USCS Tables volumes.

Effective date of section:

Act Nov. 3, 1981, P. L. 97-72, Title III, § 305, 95 Stat. 1060, which appears as 38 USCS § 3741 note, provided that this section is effective 180 days after enactment on Nov. 3, 1981.

Amendments:
1986. Act Oct. 28, 1986, substituted "percent" for "per centum" wherever appearing.
1989. Act Dec. 18, 1989, substituted "Secretary" for "Administrator", wherever appearing, in the entire section.
1991. Act Aug. 6, 1991, redesignated this section, formerly 38 USCS § 1842, as 38 USCS § 3742, and amended the references in this section to reflect the redesignations made by § 5(a) of such Act (see Table III preceding 38 USCS § 101).
Such Act further, in subsec. (b)(1), substituted "Department" for "Veterans' Administration".

Other provisions:
Authority of the Secretary to promulgate regulations. For the authority and effective date for the Secretary of Veterans' Affairs to promulgate regulations under 38 USCS §§ 3741 et seq., see § 305 of Act Nov. 3, 1981, which appears as 38 USCS § 3741 note.

RESEARCH GUIDE
Am Jur:
77 Am Jur 2d, Veterans and Veterans' Laws § 125.

§ 3743. Liability on loans

Each individual who has an ownership interest in a veterans' small business concern that is provided a direct loan under this subchapter [38 USCS §§ 3741 et seq.], or that obtains a loan guaranteed under this subchapter [38 USCS §§ 3741 et seq.], shall execute a note or other document evidencing the direct or guaranteed business loan, and such individuals shall be jointly and severally liable to the United States for the amount of such direct loan or, in the case of a guaranteed loan, for any amount paid by the Secretary on account of such loan.
(Added Act Nov. 3, 1981, P. L. 97-72, Title III, § 302(a), 95 Stat. 1957; Dec. 18, 1989, P. L. 101-237, Title III, § 313(b)(1), 103 Stat. 2077; Aug. 6, 1991, P. L. 102-83, § 5(a), 105 Stat. 406.)

HISTORY; ANCILLARY LAWS AND DIRECTIVES
Effective date of section:
Act Nov. 3, 1981, P. L. 97-72, Title III, § 305, 95 Stat. 1060, which appears as 38 USCS § 3741 note, provided that this section is effective 180 days after enactment on Nov. 3, 1981.

Amendments:
1989. Act Dec. 18, 1989, substituted "Secretary" for "Administrator".
1991. Act Aug. 6, 1991, redesignated this section, formerly 38 USCS § 1843, as 38 USCS § 3743.

Other provisions:
Authority of the Secretary to promulgate regulations. For the authority and effective date for the Secretary of Veterans's Affairs to promulgate regulations under 38 USCS §§ 3741 et seq., see § 305 of Act Nov. 3, 1981, which appears as 38 USCS § 3741 note.

RESEARCH GUIDE
Am Jur:
77 Am Jur 2d, Veterans and Veterans' Laws § 125.

§ 3744. Approval of loans by the Secretary

(a) Except as provided in subsection (b) of this section, a loan may not be guaranteed under this subchapter [38 USCS §§ 3741 et seq.] unless, before the closing of the loan, it is submitted to the Secretary for approval and the Secretary grants approval.

(b) The Secretary may exempt any lender of a class of lenders listed in section 3702(d) of this title from the prior approval requirement in subsection (a) of this section if the Secretary determines that the experience of such lender or class of lenders warrants such exemption.

(c) The Secretary may at any time upon thirty days' notice require loans to be made by any lender or class of lenders under this subchapter [38 USCS §§ 3741 et seq.] to be submitted to the Secretary for prior approval. No guaranty shall exist with respect to any such loan unless evidence of the guaranty is issued by the Secretary.

(Added Act Nov. 3, 1981, P. L. 97-72, Title III, § 302(a), 95 Stat. 1057; Dec. 18, 1989, P. L. 101-237, Title III, § 313(b)(1), 103 Stat. 2077; Aug. 6, 1991, P. L. 102-83, § 5(a), (c)(1), 105 Stat. 406.)

HISTORY; ANCILLARY LAWS AND DIRECTIVES
Effective date of section:
Act Nov. 3, 1981, P. L. 97-72, Title III, § 305, 95 Stat. 1060, which appears as 38 USCS § 3741 note, provided that this section is effective 180 days after enactment on Nov. 3, 1981.

Amendments:
1989. Act Dec. 18, 1989, in the section heading and throughout the section, substituted "Secretary" for "Administrator", wherever appearing.
1991. Act Aug. 6, 1991, redesignated this section, formerly 38 USCS § 1844, as 38 USCS § 3744, and amended the references in this section to reflect the redesignations made by § 5(a) of such Act (see Table III preceding 38 USCS § 101).

Other provisions:
Authority of the Secretary to promulgate regulations. For the authority and effective date for the Secretary of Veterans's Affairs to promulgate regulations under 38 USCS §§ 3741 et seq., see § 305 of Act Nov. 3, 1981, which appears as 38 USCS § 3741 note.

RESEARCH GUIDE
Am Jur:
77 Am Jur 2d, Veterans and Veterans' Laws § 125.

§ 3745. Interest on loans

(a) Loans guaranteed under this subchapter [38 USCS §§ 3741 et seq.] shall

READJUSTMENT BENEFITS
38 USCS § 3746

bear interest not in excess of such rate as the Secretary may from time to time find the loan market demands. In establishing the rate of interest that shall be applicable to such loans, the Secretary shall consult with the Administrator of the Small Business Administration.

(b) The rate of interest on any direct loan made by the Secretary under this subchapter [38 USCS §§ 3741 et seq.] may not exceed the maximum rate in effect under subsection (a) of this section at the time the direct loan is made.
(Added Act Nov. 3, 1981, P. L. 97-72, Title III, § 302(a), 95 Stat. 1058; Dec. 18, 1989, P. L. 101-237, Title III, § 313(b)(1), 103 Stat. 2077; Aug. 6, 1991, P. L. 102-83, § 5(a), 105 Stat. 406; Nov. 2, 1994, P. L. 103-446, Title XII, § 1201(a)(3), 108 Stat. 4682.)

HISTORY; ANCILLARY LAWS AND DIRECTIVES

Effective date of section:
Act Nov. 3, 1981, P. L. 97-72, Title III, § 305, 95 Stat. 1060, which appears as 38 USCS § 3741 note, provided that this section is effective 180 days after enactment on Nov. 3, 1981.

Amendments:
1989. Act Dec. 18, 1989, substituted "Secretary" for "Administrator", wherever appearing, other than the third place "Administrator" appeared.
1991. Act Aug. 6, 1991, redesignated this section, formerly 38 USCS § 1845, as 38 USCS § 3745; in subsec. (a), substituted "Secretary" for "Administrator".
1994. Act Nov. 2, 1994, in subsec. (a), substituted "Administrator" for "Secretary" following "consult with the".

Other provisions:
Authority of the Secretary to promulgate regulations. For the authority and effective date for the Secretary of Veterans' Affairs to promulgate regulations under 38 USCS §§ 3741 et seq., see § 305 of Act Nov. 3, 1981, which appears as 38 USCS § 3741 note.

CROSS REFERENCES
This section is referred to in 38 USCS § 3742.

RESEARCH GUIDE
Am Jur:
77 Am Jur 2d, Veterans and Veterans' Laws § 125.

§ 3746. Maturity of loans

The maturity of a loan made or guaranteed under this subchapter [38 USCS §§ 3741 et seq.] that is used in whole or in part for the construction, conversion, or expansion of facilities or for acquisition of real property may not exceed twenty years plus such additional reasonable time as the Secretary may determine, at the time the loan is made, is required to complete the construction, acquisition, or expansion of such facilities. The maturity of any other loan made or guaranteed under this subchapter [38 USCS §§ 3741 et seq.] may not exceed ten years.

38 USCS § 3746

(Added Act Nov. 3, 1981, P. L. 97-72, Title III, § 302(a), 95 Stat. 1958; Dec. 18, 1989, P. L. 101-237, Title III, § 313(b)(1), 103 Stat. 2077; Aug. 6, 1991, P. L. 102-83, § 5(a), 105 Stat. 406.)

HISTORY; ANCILLARY LAWS AND DIRECTIVES
Effective date of section:
Act Nov. 3, 1981, P. L. 97-72, Title III, § 305, 95 Stat. 1060, which appears as 38 USCS § 3741 note, provided that this section is effective 180 days after enactment on Nov. 3, 1981.

Amendments:
1989. Act Dec. 18, 1989, substituted "Secretary" for "Administrator".
1991. Act Aug. 6, 1991, redesignated this section, formerly 38 USCS § 1846, as 38 USCS § 3746.

Other provisions:
Authority of the Secretary to promulgate regulations. For the authority and effective date for the Secretary of Veterans's Affairs to promulgate regulations under 38 USCS §§ 3741 et seq., see § 305 of Act Nov. 3, 1981, which appears as 38 USCS § 3741 note.

RESEARCH GUIDE
Am Jur:
77 Am Jur 2d, Veterans and Veterans' Laws § 125.

§ 3747. Eligible financial institutions

The Secretary may not guarantee under this subchapter [38 USCS §§ 3741 et seq.] a loan made by an entity not subject to examination and supervision by an agency of the United States or of a State.
(Added Act Nov. 3, 1981, P. L. 97-72, Title III, § 302(a), 95 Stat. 1958; Dec. 18, 1989, P. L. 101-237, Title III, § 313(b)(1), 103 Stat. 2077; Aug. 6, 1991, P. L. 102-83, § 5(a), 105 Stat. 406.)

HISTORY; ANCILLARY LAWS AND DIRECTIVES
Effective date of section:
Act Nov. 3, 1981, P. L. 97-72, Title III, § 305, 95 Stat. 1060, which appears as 38 USCS § 3741 note, provided that this section is effective 180 days after enactment on Nov. 3, 1981.

Amendments:
1989. Act Dec. 18, 1989, substituted "Secretary" for "Administrator".
1991. Act Aug. 6, 1991, redesignated this section, formerly 38 USCS § 1847, as 38 USCS § 3747.

Other provisions:
Authority of the Secretary to promulgate regulations. For the authority and effective date for the Secretary of Veterans' Affairs to promulgate regulations under 38 USCS §§ 3741 et seq., see § 305 of Act Nov. 3, 1981, which appears as 38 USCS § 3741 note.

READJUSTMENT BENEFITS   38 USCS § 3749

RESEARCH GUIDE
Am Jur:
77 Am Jur 2d, Veterans and Veterans' Laws § 125.

§ 3748. Preference for disabled veterans

In the extension of financial assistance under this subchapter [38 USCS §§ 3741 et seq.], the Secretary shall give preference, first, to veterans' small business concerns in which disabled veterans who have successfully completed a vocational rehabilitation program for self-employment in a small business enterprise under chapter 31 of this title [38 USCS §§ 3100 et seq.] have a significant ownership interest, and, second, to veterans' small business concerns in which other disabled veterans have a significant ownership interest.
(Added Act Nov. 3, 1981, P. L. 97-72, Title III, § 302(a), 95 Stat. 1958; Dec. 18, 1989, P. L. 101-237, Title III, § 313(b)(1), 103 Stat. 2077; Aug. 6, 1991, P. L. 102-83, § 5(a), 105 Stat. 406.)

HISTORY; ANCILLARY LAWS AND DIRECTIVES
Effective date of section:
Act Nov. 3, 1981, P. L. 97-72, Title III, § 305, 95 Stat. 1060, which appears as 38 USCS § 3741 note, provided that this section is effective 180 days after enactment on Nov. 3, 1981.

Amendments:
1989. Act Dec. 18, 1989, substituted "Secretary" for "Administrator".
1991. Act Aug. 6, 1991, redesignated this section, formerly 38 USCS § 1848, as 38 USCS § 3748.

Other provisions:
Authority of the Secretary to promulgate regulations. For the authority and effective date for the Secretary of Veterans's Affairs to promulgate regulations under 38 USCS §§ 3741 et seq., see § 305 of Act Nov. 3, 1981, which appears as 38 USCS § 3741 note.

RESEARCH GUIDE
Am Jur:
77 Am Jur 2d, Veterans and Veterans' Laws § 125.

§ 3749. Revolving fund

(a) There is established in the Treasury a revolving fund to be known as the "Department of Veterans Affairs Small Business Loan Revolving Fund" (hereinafter in this section referred to as the "fund").

(b) Amounts in the fund shall be available to the Secretary without fiscal year limitation for all loan guaranty and direct loan operations under this subchapter [38 USCS §§ 3741 et seq.] other than administrative expenses and may not be used for any other purpose.

(c)(1) There is authorized to be appropriated to the fund a total of $25,000,000.
   (2) There shall be deposited into the fund all amounts received by the Sec-

38 USCS § 3749 VETERANS' BENEFITS

retary derived from loan operations under this subchapter [38 USCS §§ 3741 et seq.], including all collection of principal and interest and the proceeds from the use of property held or of property sold.

(d) The Secretary shall determine annually whether there has developed in the fund a surplus which, in the Secretary's judgment, is more than necessary to meet the needs of the fund. Any such surplus shall immediately be transferred into the general fund of the Treasury.

(e) Not later than two years after the termination of the authority of the Secretary to make new commitments for financial assistance under this subchapter [38 USCS §§ 3741 et seq.], the Secretary shall transfer into the general fund of the Treasury all amounts in the fund except those that the Secretary determines may be required for the liquidation of obligations under this subchapter [38 USCS §§ 3741 et seq.]. All amounts received thereafter derived from loan operations under this subchapter [38 USCS §§ 3741 et seq.], except so much thereof as the Secretary may determine to be necessary for liquidating outstanding obligations under this subchapter [38 USCS §§ 3741 et seq.], shall also be so deposited.

(Added Act Nov. 3, 1981, P. L. 97-72, Title III, § 302(a), 95 Stat. 1958; Oct. 28, 1986, P. L. 99-576, Title VII, § 702(11), 100 Stat. 3302; Dec. 18, 1989, P. L. 101-237, Title III, § 313(b)(1), 103 Stat. 2077; Aug. 6, 1991, P. L. 102-83, §§ 4(a)(2)(B)(v), 5(a), 105 Stat. 403, 406.)

HISTORY; ANCILLARY LAWS AND DIRECTIVES
Effective date of section:
Act Nov. 3, 1981, P. L. 97-72, Title III, § 305, 95 Stat. 1060, which appears as 38 USCS § 3741 note, provided that this section is effective 180 days after enactment on Nov. 3, 1981.

Amendments:
1986. Act Oct. 28, 1986, in subsec. (c)(1), substituted "There" for "Effective for fiscal year 1982 and fiscal years thereafter, there".

1989. Act Dec. 18, 1989, substituted "Secretary" for "Administrator", and "Secretary's" for "Administrator's", wherever appearing, in the entire section.

1991. Act Aug. 6, 1991, redesignated this section, formerly 38 USCS § 1849, as 38 USCS § 3749; and, in subsec. (a), substituted "Department of Veterans Affairs" for "Veterans' Administration".

Other provisions:
Authority of the Secretary to promulgate regulations. For the authority and effective date for the Secretary of Veterans' Affairs to promulgate regulations under 38 USCS §§ 3741 et seq., see § 305 of Act Nov. 3, 1981, which appears as 38 USCS § 3741 note.

RESEARCH GUIDE
Am Jur:
77 Am Jur 2d, Veterans and Veterans' Laws § 125.

§ 3750. Incorporation of other provisions by the Secretary

The Secretary may provide that the provisions of sections of other subchapters

of this chapter [38 USCS §§ 3701 et seq.] that are not otherwise applicable to loans made or guaranteed under this subchapter [38 USCS §§ 3741 et seq.] shall be applicable to loans made or guaranteed under this subchapter [38 USCS §§ 3741 et seq.]. The Secretary shall exercise authority under the preceding sentence by regulations prescribed after publication in the Federal Register and a period of not less than thirty days for public comment.
(Added Act Nov. 3, 1981, P. L. 97-72, Title III, § 302(a), 95 Stat. 1959; Dec. 18, 1989, P. L. 101-237, Title III, § 313(b)(1), 103 Stat. 2077; Aug. 6, 1991, P. L. 102-83, § 5(a), 105 Stat. 406.)

HISTORY; ANCILLARY LAWS AND DIRECTIVES
Effective date of section:
Act Nov. 3, 1981, P. L. 97-72, Title III, § 305, 95 Stat. 1060, which appears as 38 USCS § 3741 note, provided that this section is effective 180 days after enactment on Nov. 3, 1981.

Amendments:
1989. Act Dec. 18, 1989, in the section heading and throughout the entire section, substituted "Secretary" for "Administrator", wherever appearing.
1991. Act Aug. 6, 1991, redesignated this section, formerly 38 USCS § 1850, as 38 USCS § 3750.

Other provisions:
Authority of the Secretary to promulgate regulations. For the authority and effective date for the Secretary of Veterans' Affairs to promulgate regulations under 38 USCS §§ 3741 et seq., see § 305 of Act Nov. 3, 1981, which appears as 38 USCS § 3741 note.

§ 3751. Termination of program

The Secretary may not make commitments for financial assistance under this subchapter [38 USCS §§ 3741 et seq.] after September 30, 1986.
(Added Act Nov. 3, 1981, P. L. 97-72, Title III, § 302(a), 95 Stat. 1959; Dec. 18, 1989, P. L. 101-237, Title III, § 313(b)(1), 103 Stat. 2077; Aug. 6, 1991, P. L. 102-83, § 5(a), 105 Stat. 406.)

HISTORY; ANCILLARY LAWS AND DIRECTIVES
Effective date of section:
Act Nov. 3, 1981, P. L. 97-72, Title III, § 305, 95 Stat. 1060, which appears as 38 USCS § 3741 note, provided that this section is effective 180 days after enactment on Nov. 3, 1981.

Amendments:
1989. Act Dec. 18, 1989, substituted "Secretary" for "Administrator".
1991. Act Aug. 6, 1991, redesignated this section, formerly 38 USCS § 1851, as 38 USCS § 3751.

Other provisions:
Authority of the Secretary to promulgate regulations. For the authority and effective date for the Secretary of Veterans's Affairs to promulgate regulations under 38 USCS §§ 3741 et seq., see § 305 of Act Nov. 3, 1981, which appears as 38 USCS § 3741 note.

RESEARCH GUIDE

Am Jur:
77 Am Jur 2d, Veterans and Veterans' Laws § 125.

SUBCHAPTER V. NATIVE AMERICAN VETERAN HOUSING LOAN PILOT PROGRAM

§ 3761. Pilot program

(a) The Secretary shall establish and implement a pilot program under which the Secretary may make direct housing loans to Native American veterans. The purpose of such loans is to permit such veterans to purchase, construct, or improve dwellings on trust land. The Secretary shall establish and implement the pilot program in accordance with the provisions of this subchapter [38 USCS §§ 3761 et seq.].

(b) In carrying out the pilot program under this subchapter [38 USCS §§ 3761 et seq.], the Secretary shall, to the extent practicable, make direct housing loans to Native American veterans who are located in a variety of geographic areas and in areas experiencing a variety of economic circumstances.

(c) No loans may be made under this subchapter [38 USCS §§ 3761 et seq.] after December 31, 2001.
(Added Oct. 28, 1992, P. L. 102-547, § 8(a), 106 Stat. 3636; Nov. 21, 1997, P. L. 105-114, Title II, § 201(a), 111 Stat. 2282.)

HISTORY; ANCILLARY LAWS AND DIRECTIVES

Amendments:
1997. Act Nov. 21, 1997, in subsec. (c), substituted "December 31, 2001" for "September 30, 1997".

Other provisions:
Consultation with Advisory Committee on Native-American Veterans. Act Oct. 28, 1992, P. L. 102-547, § 8(b), 106 Stat. 3640, provides: "In carrying out the direct housing loan pilot program authorized under subchapter V of chapter 37 of title 38, United States Code [38 USCS §§ 3761 et seq.] (as added by subsection (a)), the Secretary of Veterans Affairs shall consider the views and recommendations, if any, of the Advisory Committee on Native-American Veterans established under section 19032 of the Veterans' Health-Care Amendments of 1986 (title XIX of Public Law 99-272; 100 Stat. 388 [38 USCS § 527 note]).".

Repeal of provision relating to annual reports. Act Oct. 28, 1992, P. L. 102-547, § 8(d), 106 Stat. 3640, which formerly appeared as a note to this section, was repealed by Act Feb. 13, 1996, P. L. 104-110, Title II, § 201(b), 110 Stat. 770. Such note related to an annual report to the Committees on Veterans' Affairs of the Senate and House of Representatives by the Secretary of Veterans Affairs dealing with implementation of a Native American veterans direct housing loan pilot program.

Authorization of appropriations. Act Oct. 28, 1992, P. L. 102-547, § 8(e), 106 Stat. 3640, provides: "New direct loan obligations for Native American veteran housing loans under subchapter V of chapter 37 of title 38, United States Code [38 USCS §§ 3761 et seq.] (as added by subsection (a)), may be incurred only to the extent that appropriations of budget authority to cover the anticipated cost, as defined in section 502 of the Congressional Budget Act of 1974 [2 USCS § 661a], for such loans are made in advance. There is authorized to be appropriated for such purpose $5,000,000 for fiscal year 1993, which amount shall remain available without fiscal year limitation.".

RESEARCH GUIDE

Am Jur:
77 Am Jur 2d, Veterans and Veterans' Laws § 121.

§ 3762. Direct housing loans to Native American veterans

(a) The Secretary may make a direct housing loan to a Native American veteran if—

(1) the Secretary has entered into a memorandum of understanding with respect to such loans with the tribal organization that has jurisdiction over the veteran; and

(2) the memorandum is in effect when the loan is made.

(b)(1) Subject to paragraph (2), the Secretary shall ensure that each memorandum of understanding that the Secretary enters into with a tribal organization shall provide for the following:

(A) That each Native American veteran who is under the jurisdiction of the tribal organization and to whom the Secretary makes a direct loan under this subchapter [38 USCS §§ 3761 et seq.]—

(i) holds, possesses, or purchases using the proceeds of the loan a meaningful interest in a lot or dwelling (or both) that is located on trust land; and

(ii) will purchase, construct, or improve (as the case may be) a dwelling on the lot using the proceeds of the loan.

(B) That each such Native American veteran will convey to the Secretary by an appropriate instrument the interest referred to in subparagraph (A) as security for a direct housing loan under this subchapter [38 USCS §§ 3761 et seq.].

(C) That the tribal organization and each such Native American veteran will permit the Secretary to enter upon the trust land of that organization or veteran for the purposes of carrying out such actions as the Secretary determines are necessary—

(i) to evaluate the advisability of the loan; and

(ii) to monitor any purchase, construction, or improvements carried out using the proceeds of the loan.

(D) That the tribal organization has established standards and procedures that apply to the foreclosure of the interest conveyed by a Native American veteran pursuant to subparagraph (B), including—

(i) procedures for foreclosing the interest; and

(ii) procedures for the resale of the lot or the dwelling (or both) purchased, constructed, or improved using the proceeds of the loan.

(E) That the tribal organization agrees to such other terms and conditions with respect to the making of direct loans to Native American veterans under the jurisdiction of the tribal organization as the Secretary may require in order to ensure that the pilot program established under this subchapter [38 USCS §§ 3761 et seq.] is implemented in a responsible and prudent manner.

(2) The Secretary may not enter into a memorandum of understanding with a tribal organization under this subsection unless the Secretary determines that the memorandum provides for such standards and procedures as are necessary for the reasonable protection of the financial interests of the United States.

(c)(1)(A) Except as provided in subparagraph (B), the principal amount of any direct housing loan made to a Native American under this section may not exceed $80,000.

(B) The Secretary may make loans exceeding the amount specified in subparagraph (A) in a geographic area if the Secretary determines that housing costs in the area are significantly higher than average housing costs nationwide. The amount of such increase shall be the amount that the Secretary determines is necessary in order to carry out the pilot program under this subchapter [38 USCS §§ 3761 et seq.] in a manner that demonstrates the advisability of making direct housing loans to Native American veterans who are located in a variety of geographic areas and in geographic areas experiencing a variety of economic conditions.

(2) Loans made under this section shall bear interest at a rate determined by the Secretary, which rate may not exceed the appropriate rate authorized for guaranteed loans under section 3703(c)(1) or section 3712(f) of this title, and shall be subject to such requirements or limitations prescribed for loans guaranteed under this title as the Secretary may prescribe.

(3) Notwithstanding section 3704(a) of this title, the Secretary shall establish minimum requirements for planning, construction, improvement, and general acceptability relating to any direct loan made under this section.

(d)(1) The Secretary shall establish credit underwriting standards to be used in evaluating loans made under this subchapter [38 USCS §§ 3761 et seq.]. In establishing such standards, the Secretary shall take into account the purpose of this program to make available housing to Native American veterans living on trust lands.

(2) The Secretary shall determine the reasonable value of the interest in property that will serve as security for a loan made under this section and shall establish procedures for appraisals upon which the Secretary may base such determinations. The procedures shall incorporate generally the relevant requirements of section 3731 of this title, unless the Secretary determines that such requirements are impracticable to implement in a geographic area, on particular trust lands, or under circumstances specified by the Secretary.

(e) Loans made under this section shall be repaid in monthly installments.

(f) In connection with any loan under this section, the Secretary may make advances in cash to provide for repairs, alterations, and improvements and to meet incidental expenses of the loan transaction. The Secretary shall determine the amount of any expenses incident to the origination of loans made under this section, which expenses, or a reasonable flat allowance in lieu thereof, shall be paid by the veteran in addition to the loan closing costs.

(g) Without regard to any provision of this chapter (other than a provision of this section), the Secretary may—

(1) take any action that the Secretary determines to be necessary with respect to the custody, management, protection, and realization or sale of investments under this section;

(2) determine any necessary expenses and expenditures and the manner in which such expenses and expenditures shall be incurred, allowed, and paid;

(3) make such rules, regulations, and orders as the Secretary considers necessary for carrying out the Secretary's functions under this section; and

(4) in a manner consistent with the provisions of this chapter [38 USCS §§ 3701 et seq.] and with the Secretary's functions under this subchapter [38 USCS §§ 3761 et seq.], employ, utilize, and compensate any persons, organizations, or departments or agencies (including departments and agencies of the United States) designated by the Secretary to carry out such functions.

(h)(1) The Secretary may make direct loans to Native American veterans in order to enable such veterans to refinance existing loans made under this section.

(2)(A) The Secretary may not make a loan under this subsection unless the loan meets the requirements set forth in subparagraphs (B), (C), and (E) of paragraph (1) of section 3710(e) of this title.

(B) The Secretary may not make a loan under this subsection unless the loan will bear an interest rate at least one percentage point less than the interest rate borne by the loan being refinanced.

(C) Paragraphs (2) and (3) of such section 3710(e) shall apply to any loan made under this subsection, except that for the purposes of this subsection the reference to subsection (a)(8) of section 3710 of this title in such paragraphs (2) and (3) shall be deemed to be a reference to this subsection.

(i)(1) The Secretary shall, in consultation with tribal organizations (including the National Congress of American Indians and the National American Indian Housing Council), carry out an outreach program to inform and educate Native American veterans of the pilot program provided for under this subchapter [38 USCS §§ 3761 et seq.] and the availability of direct housing loans for Native American veterans who live on trust lands.

(2) Activities under the outreach program shall include the following:

(A) Attending conferences and conventions conducted by the National Congress of American Indians in order to work with the National Congress in providing information and training to tribal organizations and

Native American veterans regarding the availability of housing benefits under the pilot program and in assisting such organizations and veterans in participating in the pilot program.

(B) Attending conferences and conventions conducted by the National American Indian Housing Council in order to work with the Housing Council in providing information and training to tribal organizations and tribal housing entities regarding the availability of such benefits.

(C) Attending conferences and conventions conducted by the Department of Hawaiian Homelands in order to work with the Department of Hawaiian Homelands in providing information and training to tribal housing entities in Hawaii regarding the availability of such benefits.

(D) Producing and disseminating information to tribal governments, tribal veterans service organizations, and tribal organizations regarding the availability of such benefits.

(E) Assisting tribal organizations and Native American veterans in participating in the pilot program.

(F) Outstationing loan guarantee specialists in tribal facilities on a part-time basis if requested by the tribal government.

(j) Not later than February 1 of each year through 2002, the Secretary shall transmit to the Committees on Veterans' Affairs of the Senate and House of Representatives a report relating to the implementation of the pilot program under this subchapter during the fiscal year preceding the date of the report. Each such report shall include the following:

(1) The Secretary's exercise during such fiscal year of the authority provided under subsection (c)(1)(B) to make loans exceeding the maximum loan amount.

(2) The appraisals performed for the Secretary during such fiscal year under the authority of subsection (d)(2), including a description of—

(A) the manner in which such appraisals were performed;

(B) the qualifications of the appraisers who performed such appraisals; and

(C) the actions taken by the Secretary with respect to such appraisals to protect the interests of veterans and the United States.

(3) The outreach activities undertaken under subsection (i) during such fiscal year, including—

(A) a description of such activities on a region-by-region basis; and

(B) an assessment of the effectiveness of such activities in encouraging the participation of Native American veterans in the pilot program.

(4) The pool of Native American veterans who are eligible for participation in the pilot program, including—

(A) a description and analysis of the pool, including income demographics;

(B) a description and assessment of the impediments, if any, to full participation in the pilot program of the Native American veterans in the pool; and

READJUSTMENT BENEFITS 38 USCS § 3764

(C) the impact of low-cost housing programs operated by the Department of Housing and Urban Development and other Federal or State agencies on the demand for direct loans under this section.

(5) The Secretary's recommendations, if any, for additional legislation regarding the pilot program.

(Added Oct. 28, 1992, P. L. 102-547, § 8(a), 106 Stat. 3637; Oct. 9, 1996, P. L. 104-275, Title II, Subtitle A, § 202(a), 110 Stat. 3330; Nov. 21, 1997, P. L. 105-114, Title II, § 201(b), (c), 111 Stat. 2282.)

HISTORY; ANCILLARY LAWS AND DIRECTIVES

Amendments:

1996. Act Oct. 9, 1996 redesignated subsec. (h) as subsec. (i); and added new subsec. (h).

1997. Act Nov. 21, 1997, in subsec. (i), designated the existing provisions as para. (1), in para. (1) as so designated, inserted ", in consultation with tribal organizations (including the National Congress of American Indians and the National American Indian Housing Council),", deleted "tribal organizations and" following "inform and educate", and added para. (2); and added subsec. (j).

§ 3763. Housing loan program account

(a) There is hereby established in the Treasury of the United States an account known as the "Native American Veteran Housing Loan Program Account" (hereafter in this subchapter [38 USCS §§ 3761 et seq.] referred to as the "Account").

(b) The Account shall be available to the Secretary to carry out all operations relating to the making of direct housing loans to Native American veterans under this subchapter [38 USCS §§ 3761 et seq.], including any administrative expenses relating to the making of such loans. Amounts in the Account shall be available without fiscal year limitation.

(Added Oct. 28, 1992, P. L. 102-547, § 8(a), 106 Stat. 3639.)

§ 3764. Definitions

For the purposes of this subchapter [38 USCS §§ 3761 et seq.]—

(1) The term "trust land" means any land that—

(A) is held in trust by the United States for Native Americans;

(B) is subject to restrictions on alienation imposed by the United States on Indian lands (including native Hawaiian homelands);

(C) is owned by a Regional Corporation or a Village Corporation, as such terms are defined in section 3(g) and 3(j) of the Alaska Native Claims Settlement Act, respectively (43 U.S.C. 1602(g), (j)); or

(D) is on any island in the Pacific Ocean if such land is, by cultural tradition, communally-owned land, as determined by the Secretary.

(2) The term "Native American veteran" means any veteran who is a Native American.

(3) The term "Native American" means—
(A) an Indian, as defined in section 4(d) of the Indian Self-Determination and Education Assistance Act (25 U.S.C. 450b(d));
(B) a native Hawaiian, as that term is defined in section 201(a)(7) of the Hawaiian Homes Commission Act, 1920 (Public Law 67-34; 42 Stat. 108);
(C) an Alaska Native, within the meaning provided for the term "Native" in section 3(b) of the Alaska Native Claims Settlement Act (43 U.S.C. 1602(b)); and
(D) a Pacific Islander, within the meaning of the Native American Programs Act of 1974 (42 U.S.C. 2991 et seq.).
(4) The term "tribal organization" shall have the meaning given such term in section 4(l) of the Indian Self-Determination and Education Assistance Act (25 U.S.C. 450b(l)) and shall include the Department of Hawaiian Homelands, in the case of native Hawaiians, and such other organizations as the Secretary may prescribe.
(Added Oct. 28, 1992, P. L. 102-547, § 8(a), 106 Stat. 3639.)

HISTORY; ANCILLARY LAWS AND DIRECTIVES

References in text:
"Section 201(a)(7) of the Hawaiian Homes Commission Act, 1920 (Public Law 67-34; 42 Stat. 108)", referred to in this section, is Act July 9, 1921, ch 42, Title II, § 201, 42 Stat. 108, as amended, which was formerly classified as 48 USCS § 692. Such section was omitted from the Code as obsolete.

RESEARCH GUIDE

Am Jur:
77 Am Jur 2d, Veterans and Veterans' Laws § 121.

CHAPTER 39. AUTOMOBILES AND ADAPTIVE EQUIPMENT FOR CERTAIN DISABLED VETERANS AND MEMBERS OF THE ARMED FORCES

Section
3901. Definitions.
3902. Assistance for providing automobile and adaptive equipment.
3903. Limitations on assistance; special training courses.
3904. Research and development.
[3905] [1905. Omitted]

HISTORY; ANCILLARY LAWS AND DIRECTIVES

Explanatory notes:
The bracketed section number "3905" was inserted to preserve numerical continuity following the section number redesignations made by Act Aug. 6, 1991, P. L. 102-83, § 5(a), 105 Stat. 406.

Amendments:
1971. Act Jan. 11, 1971, P. L. 91-666, § 2(a), 84 Stat. 1999, substituted new chapter heading and items 1901–1903 for former chapter heading and items 1901–1905 which read:
"CHAPTER 39. AUTOMOBILES FOR DISABLED VETERANS
"Sec.
"1901. Veterans eligible for assistance.
"1902. Limitation on types of assistance furnished and veterans otherwise entitled.
"1903. Limitation on amounts paid by United States.
"1904. Prohibition against duplication of benefits.
"1905. Applications.".
1974. Act Dec. 22, 1974, P. L. 93-538, §§ 4(c), 5(b), 88 Stat. 1737 (effective on the first day of the second calendar month following Dec. 22, 1974, as provided by § 6 of such Act), substituted item 1903 for one which read: "1903. Limitations on assistance."; and added item 1904.
1976. Act Oct. 21, 1976, P. L. 94-581, Title II, § 205(b)(1), 90 Stat. 2858 (effective 10/21/76, as provided by § 211 of such Act), substituted new item 1904 for one which read: "Research and development; coordination with other Federal programs.".
1991. Act Aug. 6, 1991, P. L. 102-83, § 5(b)(1), 105 Stat. 406, revised the analysis of this Chapter by amending the section numbers in accordance with the redesignations made by § 5(a) of such Act (see Table III preceding 38 USCS § 101).

§ 3901. Definitions

For purposes of this chapter [38 USCS §§ 3901 et seq.]

(1) The term "eligible person" means—
    (A) any veteran entitled to compensation under chapter 11 of this title [38 USCS §§ 1101 et seq.] for any of the disabilities described in subclause (i),

(ii), or (iii) below, if the disability is the result of any injury incurred or disease contracted in or aggravated by active military, naval, or air service:
  (i) The loss or permanent loss of use of one or both feet;
  (ii) The loss or permanent loss of use of one or both hands;
  (iii) The permanent impairment of vision of both eyes of the following status: central visual acuity of 20/200 or less in the better eye, with corrective glasses, or central visual acuity of more than 20/200 if there is a field defect in which the peripheral field has contracted to such an extent that the widest diameter of visual field subtends an angular distance no greater than twenty degrees in the better eye; or
(B) any member of the Armed Forces serving on active duty who is suffering from any disability described in subclause (i), (ii), or (iii) of clause (A) of this paragraph if such disability is the result of an injury incurred or disease contracted in or aggravated by active military, naval, or air service.

(2) The term "adaptive equipment" includes, but is not limited to, power steering, power brakes, power window lifts, power seats, and special equipment necessary to assist the eligible person into and out of the automobile or other conveyance. Such term also includes (A) air-conditioning equipment when such equipment is necessary to the health and safety of the veteran and to the safety of others, regardless of whether the automobile or other conveyance is to be operated by the eligible person or is to be operated for such person by another person; and (B) any modification of the size of the interior space of the automobile or other conveyance if needed because of the physical condition of such person in order for such person to enter or operate the vehicle.
(Added Jan. 11, 1971, P. L. 91-666, § 2(a), 84 Stat. 1999; Dec. 22, 1974, P. L. 93-538, § 2, 88 Stat. 1736; Sept. 30, 1976, P. L. 94-433, Title III, § 303, 90 Stat. 1377; Oct. 3, 1977, P. L. 95-116, § 1(a), 91 Stat. 1062; Aug. 6, 1991, P. L. 102-83, § 5(a), 105 Stat. 406.)

HISTORY; ANCILLARY LAWS AND DIRECTIVES
Amendments:
1974. Act Dec. 22, 1974 (effective as provided by § 6 of such Act, which appears as a note to this section), in para. (1), in subpara. (A), introductory matter, substituted "World War II or thereafter:" for "World War II or the Korean conflict; or if the disability is the result of an injury incurred or disease contracted in or aggravated by active military, naval, or air service performed after January 31, 1955, and the injury was incurred or the disease was contracted in line of duty as a direct result of the performance of military duty:", in subpara. (B), substituted "World War II or thereafter." for "World War II, the Korean conflict, or the Vietnam era; or if such disability is the result of an injury incurred or disease contracted in or aggravated by any other active military, naval, or air service performed after January 31, 1955, and the injury was incurred or the disease was contracted in line of duty as a direct result of the performance of military duty."; and substituted new para. (2) for one which read: "(2) The term 'World War II' includes, in the case of any eligible person, any period of continuous service performed by him after December 31, 1946, and before July 26, 1947, if such period began before January 1, 1947.".

1976. Act Sept. 30, 1976 (effective 10/1/76, as provided by § 406 of such Act, which appears as 38 USCS § 1101 note), in (1), in subpara. (A), introductory matter, substituted "on or after September 16, 1940" for "during World War II or thereafter", and in subpara. (B), substituted "on or after September 16, 1940" for "during World War II or thereafter".

1977. Act Oct. 3, 1977 (effective 10/1/77, as provided by § 1(b) of such Act, which appears as a note to this section), in para. (1), in subpara. (A), introductory matter, deleted "on or after September 16, 1940" following "or air service", and in subpara. (B), deleted "on or after September 16, 1940" following "or air service".

1991. Act Aug. 6, 1991, redesignated this section, formerly 38 USCS § 1901, as 38 USCS § 3901.

Short title:
Act Jan. 11, 1971, P. L. 91-666, § 1, 84 Stat. 1998, provided: "This Act [38 USCS §§ 3901 et seq.] may be cited as the 'Disabled Veterans' and Servicemen's Automobile Assistance Act of 1970'.".

Other provisions:
Effective dates of Act Dec. 22, 1974. Act Dec. 22, 1974, P. L. 93-538, § 6, 88 Stat. 1737, provided: "The provisions of this Act [adding 38 USCS § 101 note, 38 USCS § 3904; amending 38 USCS §§ 3901, 3902, 3903] shall become effective on the first day of the second calendar month following the date of enactment [enacted Dec. 22, 1974], except that clause (3) of section 3 [amending 38 USCS § 3902(c)(2)] shall take effect on January 11, 1971.".

Effective date of Act Oct. 3, 1977. Act Oct. 3, 1977, P. L. 95-116, § 1(b), 91 Stat. 1062, provided: "The amendment made by subsection (a) of this section [amending this section] shall become effective October 1, 1977.".

RESEARCH GUIDE

Am Jur:
77 Am Jur 2d, Veterans and Veterans' Laws §§ 5, 78.

INTERPRETIVE NOTES AND DECISIONS

1. Eligible persons
2. Adaptive equipment

1. Eligible persons

Veteran was entitled to automobile under former 38 USC § 252 where injury initially occurred in service prior to World War II, but ultimate condition required amputation occurred or culminated after beginning of such war. 1947 ADVA 743.

Loss of use of extremities, resulting from treatment of service-connected hemorrhoids which were incurred in active service during World War II, was a result of disability incurred during World War II for purposes of former 38 USC § 252, and veteran was entitled to be furnished automobile under such provision. 1947 ADVA 744.

Persons whose service consisted of service in organized military forces of Commonwealth of Philippines who were ordered into service of United States Armed Forces pursuant to military order of President of United States dated July 26, 1941 were not entitled to automobiles or other conveyances under applicable benefits laws, even though such persons were entitled to compensation, under laws administered by Veterans' Administration [now Department], for loss or loss of use of one or both legs, at or above ankle, incurred in services in World War II. 1947 ADVA 749.

National guardsman injured during period of encampment for authorized instruction, that is, during period of training duty as distinguished from active military service, under circumstances which otherwise entitled him to benefits, was not entitled to automobile or other conveyance under provisions of former 38 USC § 252a, notwithstanding his disability met physical criteria for entitlement under such section. 1952 ADVA 915.

Veteran, blind in one eye when he entered service

and thereafter suffering service incurred or aggravated disability to his other eye, was entitled to assistance in securing conveyance, if no deduction was to be made for disability which existed when he entered service in determining compensation evaluation for his bilateral visual acuity; visual disability which existed at time of entering service was not to be deducted from valuation of bilateral visual acuity if bilateral vision amounted to total disability. 1952 ADVA 903.

2. Adaptive equipment

Tool bar lister, planting attachment, row cultivator, and two-way mounted plow were includible in purchase price of tractor to be paid by Administrator [now Secretary] pursuant to former 38 USC § 252. 1947 ADVA 734.

§ 3902. Assistance for providing automobile and adaptive equipment

(a) The Secretary, under regulations which the Secretary shall prescribe, shall provide or assist in providing an automobile or other conveyance to each eligible person by paying the total purchase price of the automobile or other conveyance (including all State, local, and other taxes) or $8,000, whichever is the lesser, to the seller from whom the eligible person is purchasing under a sales agreement between the seller and the eligible person.

(b)(1) The Secretary, under regulations which the Secretary shall prescribe, shall provide each eligible person the adaptive equipment deemed necessary to insure that the eligible person will be able to operate the automobile or other conveyance in a manner consistent with such person's own safety and the safety of others and so as to satisfy the applicable standards of licensure established by the State of such person's residency or other proper licensing authority.

(2) In the case of any veteran (other than a person eligible for assistance under paragraph (1) of this subsection) who is entitled to compensation for ankylosis of one or both knees, or one or both hips, the Secretary, under the terms and conditions set forth in subsections (a), (c), and (d) of section 3903 of this title and under regulations which the Secretary shall prescribe, shall provide such adaptive equipment to overcome the disability resulting from such ankylosis as (A) is necessary to meet the applicable standards of licensure established by the State of such veteran's residency or other proper licensing authority for the operation of such veteran's automobile or other conveyance by such veteran, and (B) is determined to be necessary by the Under Secretary for Health for the safe operation of such automobile or other conveyance by such veteran.

(c) In accordance with regulations which the Secretary shall prescribe, the Secretary shall (1) repair, replace, or reinstall adaptive equipment deemed necessary for the operation of an automobile or other conveyance acquired in accordance with the provisions of this chapter [38 USCS §§ 3901 et seq.], and (2) provide, repair, replace, or reinstall such adaptive equipment for any automobile or other conveyance which an eligible person may previously or subsequently have acquired.

(d) If an eligible person cannot qualify to operate an automobile or other conveyance, the Secretary shall provide or assist in providing an automobile or other conveyance to such person, as provided in subsection (a) of this section,

if the automobile or other conveyance is to be operated for the eligible person by another person.
(Added Jan. 11, 1971, P. L. 91-666, § 2(a), 84 Stat. 1999; Dec. 22, 1974, P. L. 93-538, § 3, 88 Stat. 1736; Oct. 18, 1978, P. L. 95-479, Title III, § 304, 92 Stat. 1565; Oct. 17, 1981, P. L. 97-66, Title III, §§ 301, 302, 303 in part, 95 Stat. 1030; Oct. 24, 1984, P. L. 98-543, Title III, § 305(a), 98 Stat. 2748; May 20, 1988, P. L. 100-322, Title III, Part A, § 302, 102 Stat. 534; Aug. 6, 1991, P. L. 102-83, §§ 4(b)(1), (2)(E), 5(a), (c)(1), 105 Stat. 404, 405, 406; Oct. 9, 1992, P. L. 102-405, Title III, § 302(c)(1), 106 Stat. 1984; June 9, 1998, P. L. 105-178, Title VIII, Subtitle B, § 8205(a), 112 Stat. 494.)

HISTORY; ANCILLARY LAWS AND DIRECTIVES
Amendments:
1974. Act Dec. 22, 1974 (effective 2/1/75, as provided by § 6 of such Act, which appears as 38 USCS § 3901 note), in subsec. (a), inserted "(including all State, local, and other taxes)" and substituted "$3,300," for "$2,800,".
Such Act further (effective 1/11/71, as provided by § 6 of such Act), in subsec. (c), inserted "previously or".
1978. Act Oct. 18, 1978 (effective 10/1/78, as provided by § 401(a) of such Act, which appears as 38 USCS § 1114 note), in subsec. (a), substituted "$3,800" for "$3,300".
1981. Act Oct. 17, 1981 (effective 10/1/81, as provided by § 701(a) of such Act, which appears as 38 USCS § 1114 note), in subsec. (a), substituted "the Administrator" for "he" and "$4,400" for "$3,800"; in subsec. (b), designated existing provisions as para. (1), in para. (1) as so designated, substituted "the Administrator" for "he" and "such person's" for "his" wherever appearing, and added para. (2); and in subsec. (c), substituted "the Administrator" for "he" following "which".
1984. Act Oct. 24, 1984 (effective 1/1/85, as provided by § 305(c)(1) of such Act, which appears as 38 USCS § 3903 note), in subsec. (a), substituted "$5,000" for "$4,400".
1988. Act May 20, 1988 (effective $/1/1988, as provided by § 304, which appears as 38 USCS § 2102 note), substituted subsec. (a) for one which read: "The Administrator, under regulations which the Administrator shall prescribe, shall provide or assist in providing an automobile or other conveyance to each eligible person by paying the total purchase price of the automobile or other conveyance (including all State, local, and other taxes) or $5,000, whichever is the lesser, to the seller from whom the eligible person is purchasing under a sales agreement between the seller and the eligible person.".
1991. Act Aug. 6, 1991, redesignated this section, formerly 38 USCS § 1902, as 38 USCS § 3902, and amended the references in this section to reflect the redesignations made by § 5(a) of such Act (see Table III preceding 38 USCS § 101).
Such Act further substituted "Secretary" for "Administrator" wherever appearing.
1992. Act Oct. 9, 1992, in subsec. (b)(2), substituted "Under Secretary for Health" for "Chief Medical Director".

38 USCS § 3902

1998. Act June 9, 1998 (applicable with respect to assistance furnished on or after 10/1/98, as provided by § 8205(b) of such Act, which appears as a note to this section), in subsec. (a), substituted "$8,000" for "$5,500".

Other provisions:

Application of June 9, 1998 amendment. Act June 9, 1998, P. L. 105-178, Title VIII, Subtitle B, § 8205(b), 112 Stat. 494, provides: "The amendment made by subsection (a) [amending subsec. (a) of this section] shall apply with respect to assistance furnished under section 3902 of such title on or after October 1, 1998.".

CROSS REFERENCES

This section is referred to in 38 USCS § 3903.

RESEARCH GUIDE

Am Jur:

77 Am Jur 2d, Veterans and Veterans' Laws § 78.

§ 3903. Limitations on assistance; special training courses

(a) No eligible person shall be entitled to receive more than one automobile or other conveyance under the provisions of this chapter [38 USCS §§ 3901 et seq.], and no payment shall be made under this chapter [38 USCS §§ 3901 et seq.] for the repair, maintenance, or replacement of an automobile or other conveyance.

(b) Except as provided in subsection (d) of section 3902 of this title, no eligible person shall be provided an automobile or other conveyance under this chapter [38 USCS §§ 3901 et seq.] until it is established to the satisfaction of the Secretary, in accordance with regulations the Secretary shall prescribe, that the eligible person will be able to operate the automobile or other conveyance in a manner consistent with such person's own safety and the safety of others and will satisfy the applicable standards of licensure to operate the automobile or other conveyance established by the State of such person's residency or other proper licensing authority.

(c)(1) An eligible person shall not be entitled to adaptive equipment under this chapter [38 USCS §§ 3901 et seq.] for more than two automobiles or other conveyances at any one time or (except as provided in paragraph (2) of this subsection) during any four-year period.

(2) In a case in which the four-year limitation in paragraph (1) of this subsection precludes an eligible person from being entitled to adaptive equipment under this chapter [38 USCS §§ 3901 et seq.], if the Secretary determines that, due to circumstances beyond the control of such person, one of the automobiles or other conveyances for which adaptive equipment was provided to such person during the applicable four-year period is no longer available for the use of such person, the Secretary may provide adaptive equipment to such person for an additional automobile or other conveyance during such period. Provision of adaptive equipment under this paragraph is within the discretion of the Secretary. Any action to provide adaptive equipment under this paragraph shall be made pursuant to regulations which the Secretary shall prescribe.

(d) Adaptive equipment shall not be provided under this chapter [38 USCS §§ 3901 et seq.] unless it conforms to minimum standards of safety and quality prescribed by the Secretary.

(e)(1) The Secretary shall provide, directly or by contract, for the conduct of special driver training courses at every hospital and, where appropriate, at regional offices and other medical facilities, of the Department to instruct such eligible person to operate the type of automobile or other conveyance such person wishes to obtain with assistance under this chapter [38 USCS §§ 3901 et seq.], and may make such courses available to any veteran, eligible for care under chapter 17 of this title [38 USCS §§ 1701 et seq.] or member of the Armed Forces, who is determined by the Secretary to need the special training provided in such courses even though such veteran or member is not eligible for the assistance provided under this chapter [38 USCS §§ 3901 et seq.].

(2) The Secretary is authorized to obtain insurance on automobiles and other conveyances (not owned by the Government) used in conducting the special driver training courses provided under this subsection and to obtain, at Government expense, personal liability and property damage insurance for all persons taking such courses without regard to whether such persons are taking the course on an in-patient or out-patient basis.

(3) Notwithstanding any other provision of law, the Secretary may obtain, by purchase, lease, gift, or otherwise, any automobile, motor vehicle, or other conveyance deemed necessary to carry out the purposes of this subsection, and may sell, assign, transfer, or convey any such automobile, vehicle, or conveyance to which the Department obtains title for such price and upon such terms as the Secretary deems appropriate; and any proceeds received from any such disposition shall be credited to the applicable Department appropriation.

(Added Jan. 11, 1971, P. L. 91-666, § 2(a), 84 Stat. 2000; Dec. 22, 1974, P. L. 93-538, § 4(a), (b), 88 Stat. 1736; Oct. 21, 1976, P. L. 94-581, Title I, § 108, 90 Stat. 2847; Oct. 17, 1981, P. L. 97-66, Title III, § 303 in part, 95 Stat. 1030; Oct. 24, 1984, P. L. 98-543, Title III, § 305(b), 98 Stat. 2748; Aug. 6, 1991, P. L. 102-83, §§ 4(a)(3), (4), (b)(1), (2)(E), 5(a), (c), (1), 105 Stat. 404–406.)

HISTORY; ANCILLARY LAWS AND DIRECTIVES
Amendments:
1974. Act Dec. 22, 1974 (effective 2/1/75, as provided by § 6 of such Act, which appears as 38 USCS § 3901 note), in the catchline, inserted "; special training courses"; and added subsec. (e).

1976. Act Oct. 21, 1976 (effective 10/21/76, as provided by § 211 of such Act, which appears as 38 USCS § 111), in subsec. (e), in para. (1), deleted "or member of the Armed Forces" following "any veteran" and inserted "or member of the Armed Forces" following "title", and added para. (3).

1981. Act Oct. 17, 1981 (effective 10/1/81, as provided by § 701(a) of such Act, which appears as 38 USCS § 1114 note), in subsec. (b), substituted "the Administrator" for "he" preceding "shall prescribe" and substituted "such person's" for "his", wherever appearing.

1984. Act Oct. 24, 1984 (effective 1/1/85, as provided by § 305(c)(1) of such Act, which appears as a note to this section), substituted subsec. (c) for one which read: "An eligible person shall not be entitled to adaptive equipment under this chapter for more than one automobile or other conveyance at any one time.".

1991. Act Aug. 6, 1991, redesignated this section, formerly 38 USCS § 1903, as 38 USCS § 3903, and amended the references in this section to reflect the redesignations made by § 5(a) of such Act (see Table III preceding 38 USCS § 101).

Such Act further substituted "Department" for "Veterans' Administration" wherever appearing, and substituted "Secretary" for "Administrator" wherever appearing.

Other provisions:
Effective date and application of amendments made by § 305 of Act Oct. 24, 1984 and application. Act Oct. 24, 1984, P. L. 98-543, Title III, § 305(c), 98 Stat. 2748, provides:

"(c)(1) The amendments made by this section [amending this section and 42 USCS § 3902] shall take effect on January 1, 1985.

"(2) In the case of a person who during the four-year period ending on December 31, 1984, was provided adaptive equipment under chapter 39 of title 38, United States Code [38 USCS §§ 3902 et seq.], for an automobile or other conveyance and who has such automobile or other conveyance available for use on the date of the enactment of this Act, the first four-year period applicable to such person under subsection (c) of section 1903 of such title [subsec. (c) of this section] (as amended by subsection (a)) shall begin on the most recent date before January 1, 1985, on which such person was provided such equipment.".

CROSS REFERENCES
This section is referred to in 38 USCS §§ 3902, 3904.

RESEARCH GUIDE
Am Jur:
77 Am Jur 2d, Veterans and Veterans' Laws § 78.

§ 3904. Research and development

(a) In carrying out medical and prosthetic research under section 7303 of this title, the Secretary, through the Under Secretary for Health, shall provide for special emphasis on the research and development of adaptive equipment and adapted conveyances (including vans) meeting standards of safety and quality prescribed under subsection (d) of section 3903, including support for the production and distribution of devices and conveyances so developed.

(b) In carrying out subsection (a) of this section, the Secretary, through the Under Secretary for Health, shall consult and cooperate with the Secretary of Health and Human Services and the Secretary of Education, in connection with programs carried out under section 204(b)(2) of the Rehabilitation Act of 1973 (29 U.S.C. 762(b)(2)) (relating to the establishment and support of Rehabilitation Engineering Research Centers).

READJUSTMENT BENEFITS   **38 USCS § 3904**

(Added Dec. 22, 1974, P. L. 93-538, § 5(a), 88 Stat. 1737; Oct. 21, 1976, P. L. 94-581, Title II, § 205(b)(2), (3), 90 Stat. 2859; Nov. 6, 1978, P. L. 95-602, Title I, § 122(f), 92 Stat. 2987; Oct. 12, 1982, P. L. 97-295, § 4(69), 96 Stat. 1310; May 7, 1991, P. L. 102-40, Title IV, § 403(b)(1), 105 Stat. 239; Aug. 6, 1991, P. L. 102-83, §§ 4(b)(1), (2)(E), 5(a), (c)(1), 105 Stat. 404, 405, 406; Oct. 9, 1992, P. L. 102-405, Title III, § 302(c)(1), 106 Stat. 1984.)

HISTORY; ANCILLARY LAWS AND DIRECTIVES

References in text:
"Section 204(b)(2) of the Rehabilitation Act of 1973", referred to in this section, is subsec. (b)(2) of Act Sept. 26, 1973, P. L. 93-112, § 204, which appeared as 29 USCS § 762(b)(2), prior to replacement with a new subsec. (b)(2) by Act Oct. 29, 1992, P. L. 102-569, Title II, § 205(b)(2), 106 Stat. 4403. For similar provisions, see 29 USCS § 762(b)(3).

Explanatory notes:
A prior § 1904 (Act Sept. 2, 1958, P. L. 85-857, § 1, 72 Stat. 1216) was omitted in the general amendment of this Chapter by Act Jan. 11, 1971, P. L. 91-66, § 2(a), 84 Stat. 1998. The section related to prohibitions against duplication of benefits.

Effective date of section:
Act Dec. 22, 1974, P. L. 93-538, § 6, 88 Stat. 1737, provided that this section is effective on the first day of the second calendar month following Dec. 22, 1974.

Amendments:
1976. Act Oct. 21, 1976 (effective 10/21/76, as provided by § 211 of such Act, which appears as 38 USCS § 111 note), substituted new catchline for one which read: "Research and development; coordination with other Federal programs"; and in subsec. (a), substituted "medical and prosthetic research" for "prosthetic and orthopedic appliance research under section 216 and medical research".
1978. Act Nov. 6, 1978, in subsec. (b), substituted "and section 204(b)(2)" for "section 202(b)(2)" and deleted ", and section 405 of such Act (relating to the Secretarial responsibilities for planning, analysis, promoting utilization of scientific advances, and information clearinghouse activities)" following "Research Centers)".
1982. Act Oct. 12, 1982, in subsec. (b), substituted "Health and Human Services and the Secretary of Education" for "Health, Education, and Welfare and the Commissioner of the Rehabilitation Services Administration, Department of Health, Education, and Welfare", and substituted "section 204(b)(2) of the Rehabilitation Act of 1973 (29 U.S.C. 762(b)(2))" for "section 3(b) of the Rehabilitation Act of 1973 (Public Law 93-112; 87 Stat. 357) (relating to the development and support, and the stimulation of the development and utilization, including production and distribution of new and existing devices, of innovative methods of applying advanced medical technology, scientific achievement, and psychological and social knowledge to solve rehabilitation problems), and section 204(b)(2) of such Act".
1991. Act May 7, 1991, in subsec. (a), substituted "section 7303" for "section 4101".

38 USCS § 3904

Act Aug. 6, 1991, redesignated this section, formerly 38 USCS § 1904, as 38 USCS § 3904, and amended the references in this section to reflect the redesignations made by § 5(a) of such Act (see Table III preceding 38 USCS § 101).

Such Act further substituted "Secretary" for "Administrator" wherever appearing.

1992. Act Oct. 9, 1992 substituted "Under Secretary for Health" for "Chief Medical Director" wherever appearing.

Other provisions:

Application and construction of the Oct. 12, 1982 amendment of this section. For provisions as to the application and construction of the Oct. 12, 1982 amendment of this section (see the Amendments note to this section), see § 5 of such Act, which appears as 10 USCS § 101 note.

RESEARCH GUIDE

Am Jur:
77 Am Jur 2d, Veterans and Veterans' Laws § 78.

[§ 3905]. [1905. Omitted]

HISTORY; ANCILLARY LAWS AND DIRECTIVES

The bracketed section number "3905" was inserted to preserve numerical continuity following the section number redesignations made by Act Aug. 6, 1991, P. L. 102-83, § 5(a), 105 Stat. 406.

This section (Act Sept. 2, 1958, P. L. 85-857, § 1, 72 Stat. 1216; Aug. 31, 1967, P. L. 90-77, Title II, § 204(b), 81 Stat. 184) was omitted by Act Jan. 11, 1971, P. L. 91-666, § 2(a), 84 Stat. 1998, which amended Chapter 39 in its entirety. It related to applications.

CHAPTER 41. JOB COUNSELING, TRAINING, AND PLACEMENT SERVICE FOR VETERANS

Section
4100. Findings.
4101. Definitions.
4102. Purpose
4102A. Assistant Secretary of Labor for Veterans' Employment and Training; Regional Administrators.
4103. Directors and Assistant Directors for Veterans' Employment and Training.
4103A. Disabled veterans' outreach program.
4104. Local veterans' employment representatives.
4104A. Performance of disabled veterans' outreach program specialists and local veterans' employment representatives.
4105. Cooperation of Federal agencies.
4106. Estimate of funds for administration; authorization of appropriations.
4107. Administrative controls; annual report.
4108. Cooperation and coordination.
4109. National Veterans' Employment and Training Services Institute.
4110. Advisory Committee on Veterans Employment and Training.
4110A. Special unemployment study.
[4111—4120. Repealed]
[4121—4124. Repealed]
[4131—4134. Transferred]
[4141, 4142. Transferred]
[4151, 4152. Repealed]
[4161—4168. Transferred]

HISTORY; ANCILLARY LAWS AND DIRECTIVES

Explanatory notes:
This chapter, as enacted by Act Sept. 2, 1958, P. L. 85-857, § 1, 72 Stat. 1216, contained two subchapters. The subchapter I heading, which read: "Subchapter I. Unemployment Compensation" and preceded former § 2001, and the subchapter II heading, which read: "Subchapter II— Employment Service for Veterans" and preceded former § 2010, were repealed by Act Sept. 19, 1962, P. L. 87-675, § 1(d), 76 Stat. 559.

Amendments:
1962. Act Sept. 19, 1962, P. L. 87-675, § 1(b), 76 Stat. 558, substituted the analysis, including items 2001–2005 for one which read:

"SUBCHAPTER I. UNEMPLOYMENT COMPENSATION
"Sec.
"2001. Compensation for veterans under State agreements.
"2002. Unemployment compensation in absence of State agreements.
"2003. Payments to States.
"2004. Information.
"2005. Penalties.

38 USCS § 4100
VETERANS' BENEFITS

"2006. Regulations.
"2007. Definitions.
"2008. Nonduplication of benefits.
"2009. Terminations.
"SUBCHAPTER II. EMPLOYMENT SERVICE FOR VETERANS
"2010. Purpose.
"2011. Assignment of veterans' employment representative.
"2012. Employees of local offices.
"2013. Cooperation of Federal agencies.
"2014. Estimate of funds for administration.".

1966. Act March 3, 1966, P. L. 89-358, § 6(a), 80 Stat. 27 (effective 3/3/66, as provided by § 12(a) of such Act), substituted the chapter heading for one which read: "CHAPTER 41. UNEMPLOYMENT BENEFITS FOR VETERANS".

1972. Act Oct. 24, 1972, P. L. 92-540, Title V, § 502(a), 86 Stat. 1094 (effective 90 days after 10/24/72, as provided by § 601(b) of such Act), substituted the chapter heading and analysis for ones which read:
"CHAPTER 41. JOB COUNSELING AND EMPLOYMENT PLACEMENT SERVICE FOR VETERANS
"Sec.
"2001. Purpose.
"2002. Assignment of veterans' employment representative.
"2003. Employees of local offices.
"2004. Cooperation of Federal agencies.
"2005. Estimate of funds for administration.".

1976. Act Oct. 15, 1976, P. L. 94-502, Title VI, § 601(b)(2), 90 Stat. 2404 (effective 12/1/76, as provided by § 703(c) of such Act), added item 2002A.

1980. Act Oct. 17, 1980, P. L. 96-466, Title V, §§ 504(a)(1), 506(b), 94 Stat. 2203, 2205 (effective 10/1/80, as provided by § 802(e) of such Act), in item 2002A, deleted "Deputy" preceding "Assistant Secretary"; and added item 2003A.

1982. Act Oct. 14, 1982, P. L. 97-306, Title III, §§ 301(b)(1), 304(a)(2), 308(b), 96 Stat. 1437, 1438, 1441 amended the analysis of this chapter by adding the item relating to section 2000, by substituting the item relating to section 2003 for one which read: "2003. Assignment of veterans' employment representative.", and by adding the items relating to sections 2009 and 2010.

1988. Act May 20, 1988, P. L. 100-323, §§ 2(e)(3)(B), 3(c), 15(c)(3)(B), 102 Stat. 559, 562, 574, effective on enactment as provided by § 16(a) of such Act, which appears as 38 USCS § 3104 note, amended the analysis of this chapter by adding item 1774A and by substituting items 2002A, 2003, and 2004 for ones which read: "2002A. Assistant Secretary of Labor for Veterans' Employment.", "2003. Assignment of veterans' employment representative.", and "2004. Employees of local offices.".

Act May 20, 1988, P. L. 100-323, §§ 4(b), 6(b)(2)(B), 8(b), 9(b), 102 Stat. 563, 564, 566, effective on the 60th day after enactment, as provided by § 16(b)(2) of such Act, which appears as 38 USCS § 3104 note, amended the analysis of this chapter by adding items 2004A and 2010A, and by substituting items 2008 and 2009 for ones which read: "2008. Cooperation

and coordination with the Veterans' Administration." and "2009. National veterans' employment and training programs.".
1991. Act March 22, 1991, P. L. 102-16, § 8(b), 105 Stat. 53, amended the analysis of this chapter by substituting item 2010 for one which read: "2010. Secretary of Labor's Committee on Veterans' Employment.".
Act Aug. 6, 1991, P. L. 102-83, § 5(b)(1), 105 Stat. 406, revised the analysis of this Chapter by amending the section numbers in accordance with the redesignations made by § 5(a) of such Act (see Table III preceding 38 USCS § 101).

§ 4100. Findings

The Congress makes the following findings:

(1) As long as unemployment and underemployment continue as serious problems among disabled veterans and Vietnam-era veterans, alleviating unemployment and underemployment among such veterans is a national responsibility.

(2) Because of the special nature of employment and training needs of such veterans and the national responsibility to meet those needs, policies and programs to increase opportunities for such veterans to obtain employment, job training, counseling, and job placement services and assistance in securing advancement in employment should be effectively and vigorously implemented by the Secretary of Labor and such implementation should be accomplished through the Assistant Secretary of Labor for Veterans' Employment and Training.
(Added Oct. 14, 1982, P. L. 97-306, Title III, § 301(a), 96 Stat. 1436; May 20, 1988, P. L. 100-323, § 15(b)(1), 102 Stat. 574; Aug. 6, 1991, P. L. 102-83, § 5(a), 105 Stat. 406.)

HISTORY; ANCILLARY LAWS AND DIRECTIVES
Amendments:
1988. Act May 20, 1988 (effective on enactment as provided by § 16(a) of such Act, which appears as 38 USCS § 3104 note), in para. (2), inserted "and Training".
1991. Act Aug. 6, 1991, redesignated this section, formerly 38 USCS § 2000, as 38 USCS § 4100.

Other provisions:
Pilot program to furnish employment and training information and services to members of the Armed Forces separating from the Armed Forces. Act Dec. 18, 1989, P. L. 101-237, Title IV, § 408, 103 Stat. 2083; Dec. 21, 1995, P. L. 104-66, Title I, Subtitle J, § 1101, 109 Stat. 722, provides:
"(a) Requirement for program. During the three-year period beginning on January 1, 1990, the Secretary of Labor (hereafter in this section referred to as the 'Secretary'), in conjunction with the Secretary of Veterans Affairs and the Secretary of Defense, shall conduct a pilot program to furnish employment and training information and services to members of the Armed Forces within 180 days before such members are separated from the Armed Forces.

"(b) Areas to be covered by the program. The Secretary shall conduct the pilot program in at least five, but not more than ten, geographically dispersed States in which the Secretary determines that employment and training services to eligible veterans will not be unduly limited by the provision of such services to members of the Armed Forces under the pilot program.

"(c) Utilization of specific personnel. The Secretary shall utilize disabled veterans' outreach program specialists or local veterans' employment representatives to the maximum extent feasible to furnish employment and training information and services under the pilot program.

CODE OF FEDERAL REGULATIONS

Employment and Training Administration, Department of Labor—Administration provisions governing the Job Service System, 20 CFR Part 658.

RESEARCH GUIDE

Am Jur:
53 Am Jur 2d, Military, and Civil Defense § 44.
77 Am Jur 2d, Veterans and Veterans' Laws §§ 106, 109.

§ 4101. Definitions

For the purposes of this chapter [38 USCS §§ 4101 et seq.]—

(1) The term "special disabled veteran" has the same meaning provided in section 4211(1) of this title.

(2) The term "veteran of the Vietnam era" has the same meaning provided in section 4211(2) of this title.

(3) The term "disabled veteran" has the same meaning provided in section 4211(3) of this title.

(4) The term "eligible veteran" has the same meaning provided in section 4211(4) of this title.

(5) The term "eligible person" means—

(A) the spouse of any person who died of a service-connected disability,

(B) the spouse of any member of the Armed Forces serving on active duty who, at the time of application for assistance under this chapter [38 USCS §§ 4101 et seq.], is listed, pursuant to section 556 of title 37 and regulations issued thereunder, by the Secretary concerned in one or more of the following categories and has been so listed for a total of more than ninety days: (i) missing in action, (ii) captured in line of duty by a hostile force, or (iii) forcibly detained or interned in line of duty by a foreign government or power, or

(C) the spouse of any person who has a total disability permanent in nature resulting from a service-connected disability or the spouse of a veteran who died while a disability so evaluated was in existence.

(6) The term "State" means each of the several States of the United States, the District of Columbia, and the Commonwealth of Puerto Rico, and may include,

to the extent determined necessary and feasible, Guam, American Samoa, the Virgin Islands, the Commonwealth of the Northern Marianas Islands, and the Trust Territory of the Pacific Islands.

(7) The term "local employment service office" means a service delivery point which has an intrinsic management structure and at which employment services are offered in accordance with the Wagner-Peyser Act.

(8) The term "Secretary" means the Secretary of Labor.
(Sept. 2, 1958, P. L. 85-857, § 1, 72 Stat. 1221; Sept. 19, 1962, P. L. 87-675, § 1(a), 76 Stat. 558; Oct. 24, 1972, P. L. 92-540, Title V, § 502(a), 86 Stat. 1094; Dec. 3, 1974, P. L. 93-508, Title IV, § 401(a), 88 Stat. 1592; Oct. 17, 1980, P. L. 96-466, Title V, § 503, Title VIII, § 801(h), 94 Stat. 2203, 2216; May 20, 1988, P. L. 100-323, §§ 3(b), 15(a)(1), 102 Stat. 562, 574; Aug. 6, 1991, P. L. 102-83, § 5(a), (c)(1), 105 Stat. 406.)

HISTORY; ANCILLARY LAWS AND DIRECTIVES

References in text:
"The Wagner-Peyser Act", referred to in this section, is Act June 6, 1933, ch 49, 48 Stat. 113, which appears generally as 29 USCS §§ 49 et seq. For full classification of such Act, consult USCS Tables volumes.

Explanatory notes:
A prior § 4101 (Act Sept. 2, 1958, P. L. 85-857, § 1, 72 Stat. 1243; Nov. 7, 1966, P. L. 89-785, Title I, § 101, 80 Stat. 1368; Aug. 2, 1973, P. L. 93-82, Title II, § 201, 87 Stat. 187; Oct. 21, 1976, P. L. 94-581, Title II, §§ 205(a), 209(a)(1), (3), 210(c)(1), 90 Stat. 2857, 2860, 2863; Aug. 26, 1980, P. L. 96-330, Title I, Part A, § 105(a), Title III, § 302, Title IV, § 408, 94 Stat. 1036, 1048, 1053; Oct. 12, 1982, P. L. 97-295, § 4(80), 96 Stat. 1311; Oct. 19, 1984, P. L. 98-528, Title I, § 104, 98 Stat. 2689; Dec. 3, 1985, P. L. 99-166, Title II, § 202, 99 Stat. 950; May 20, 1988, P. L. 100-322, Title I, Part D, § 135, 102 Stat. 507; Nov. 18, 1988, P. L. 100-687, Div B, Title XV, § 1506(a), 102 Stat. 4135) was repealed by Act May 7, 1991, P. L. 102-40, Title IV, § 401(a)(3), 105 Stat. 210. Such section provided for the functions of the Department of Medicine and Surgery.
A prior § 2001 (Act Sept. 2, 1958, P. L. 85-857, § 1, 72 Stat. 1217), contained in Subchapter I of Chapter 41, was repealed by Act Sept. 19, 1962, P. L. 87-675, § 1(a), 76 Stat. 558. It related to compensation for veterans under state agreements.

Amendments:
1962. Act Sept. 19, 1962, redesignated this section as § 2001; it formerly appeared as § 2010 in Subchapter II of Chapter 41.
1966. Act March 3, 1966 (effective 3/3/66, as provided by § 12(a) of such Act), inserted "or of service after January 31, 1955"
1972. Act Oct. 24, 1972 (effective 90 days after enactment as provided by § 601(b) of such Act, which appears as a note to this section), substituted new catchline and section for ones which read:
"§ 2001. Purpose
"The Congress declares as its intent and purpose that there shall be an effective job counseling and employment placement service for veterans of

any war or of service after January 31, 1955, and that, to this end, policies shall be promulgated and administered, so as to provide for them the maximum of job opportunity in the field of gainful employment.".

1974. Act Dec. 3, 1974 (effective 12/3/74, as provided by § 503 of such Act, which appears as 38 USCS § 3452 note), redesignated para. (2) as para. (3); and added new para. (2).

1980. Act Oct. 17, 1980, § 503 (effective 10/1/1980 as provided by § 802(e) of such Act, which appears as a note to this section), substituted new para. (1) for one which read: "(1) The term 'eligible veteran' means a person who served in the active military, naval, or air service and who was discharged or released therefrom with other than a dishonorable discharge."; redesignated paras. (2) and (3) as paras. (5) and (6), respectively; and added new paras. (2), (3), and (4).

Act Oct. 17, 1980, § 801(h) (effective 10/1/80, as provided by § 802(h) of such Act, which appears as 38 USCS § 3452 note), in para. (5), as redesignated by § 503 of Act Oct. 17, 1980, in the introductory matter, substituted "The" for "the"; and in para. (6), as redesignated by § 503 of Act Oct. 17, 1980, inserted "the Commonwealth of the Northern Marianas Islands,".

1988. Act May 20, 1988 (effective on enactment as provided by § 16(a) of such Act, which appears as 38 USCS § 3104 note) added paras. (7) and (8).

1991. Act Aug. 6, 1991, redesignated this section, formerly 38 USCS § 2001, as 38 USCS § 4101, and amended the references in this section to reflect the redesignations made by § 5(a) of such Act (see Table III preceding 38 USCS § 101).

Other provisions:

Savings provisions. Act Sept. 19, 1962, P. L. 87-675, § 1(e), 76 Stat. 559, provided: "Claims for benefits under sections 2001 through 2009 of chapter 41 of title 38, United States Code [former 38 USC §§ 2001–2009], for any benefit week beginning before January 31, 1960, which claims are pending on the date these sections are repealed [repealed Sept. 19, 1962], shall be adjudicated in the same manner and with the same effect as if the sections had not been repealed. For the purpose of administering the program with respect to such claims, all functions, powers, and duties conferred upon the Secretary of Labor by sections 2001 through 2009 are continued in effect, and all rules and regulations established by the Secretary of Labor pursuant to these sections, and in effect when the sections are repealed, shall remain in full force and effect until modified or suspended.".

Effective date of amendments made by Title V of Act Oct. 24, 1972. Act Oct. 24, 1972, P. L. 92-540, Title VI, § 601(b), 86 Stat. 1099, provided: "The provisions of title V of this Act [enacting 38 USCS §§ 4106–4108, 4211–4213, 50 USCS Appx. § 591; amending this section and 38 USCS §§ 4102–4105, 4007, 50 USCS Appx. § 511] shall become effective 90 days after the date of enactment of this Act.".

Employment assistance and services for veterans ineligible for assistance under this chapter. Act Oct. 17, 1980, P. L. 96-466, Title V, § 512, 94 Stat. 2207 (effective 10/1/80, as provided by § 802(e) of such Act), provided: "The Secretary of Labor shall assure that any veteran who is made ineligible for employment assistance under chapter 41 of title 38, United States Code [38 USCS §§ 4101 et seq.], by virtue of the amendments made by section 503(1) of this Act shall be provided with the employment assistance and services made available under the provisions of the Act entitled 'An Act to provide for the establishment of a national employment system and for cooperation with the States in the promotion of such system, and for other purposes', approved June 6, 1933 (commonly referred to as the 'Wagner-Peyser Act'), (29 U.S.C. 49-49k), the Comprehensive Employment and Training Act (29 U.S.C. et seq.) [29 USCS §§ 801 et seq., generally; for full classification, consult USCS Tables volumes], and other applicable provisions of law.''.

Termination of Trust Territory of the Pacific Islands. For termination of Trust Territory of the Pacific Islands, see note preceding 48 USCS §§ 1681.

Effective date of amendments made by Title V of Act Oct. 17, 1980. Act Oct. 17, 1980, P. L. 96-466, Title VIII, § 802(e), 94 Stat. 2218, provided: "The amendments made by title V and the provisions of sections 512 and 513 [amending this section, among other things; for full classification, consult USCS Tables volumes] shall become effective on October 1, 1980.''.

CODE OF FEDERAL REGULATIONS

Employment and Training Administration, Department of Labor—Administration provisions governing the Job Service System, 20 CFR Part 658.

RESEARCH GUIDE

Am Jur:
53 Am Jur 2d, Military, and Civil Defense § 44.
77 Am Jur 2d, Veterans and Veterans' Laws § 106.

Annotations:
Availability, under 28 USCS § 1442(a)(1), to one who is not an "officer of the United States or any agency thereof" of right to remove state action to federal court. 64 ALR Fed 146.

Law Review Articles:
Benefits for Conscientious Objectors. 19 Catholic Lawyer 62, Winter 1973.

§ 4102. Purpose

The Congress declares as its intent and purpose that there shall be an effective (1) job and job training counseling service program, (2) employment placement service program, and (3) job training placement service program for eligible veterans and eligible persons and that, to this end policies and regulations shall be promulgated and administered by an Assistant Secretary of Labor for Veterans' Employment and Training, established by section 4102A of this title, through a Veterans' Employment and Training Service within the Department of Labor, so as to provide such veterans and persons the maximum of employment and training opportunities, with priority given to the needs of disabled veterans and veterans of the Vietnam era through existing programs, coordination and merger of programs and implementation of new programs.

(Sept. 2, 1958, P. L. 85-857, § 1, 72 Stat. 1221; Sept. 19, 1962, P. L. 87-675, § 1(a), 76 Stat. 558; March 3, 1966, P. L. 89-358, § 6(c), 80 Stat. 27; Oct. 24, 1972, P. L. 92-540, Title V, § 502(a), 86 Stat. 1094; Dec. 3, 1974, P. L. 93-

508, Title IV, § 401(b), 88 Stat. 1592; Oct. 15, 1976, P. L. 94-502, Title VI, § 601(a), 90 Stat. 2404; Oct. 17, 1980, P. L. 96-466, Title V, § 504(a)(2), 94 Stat. 2203; Oct. 14, 1982, P. L. 97-306, Title III, § 302, 96 Stat. 1437; Nov. 21, 1983, P. L. 98-160, Title VII, § 702(15) in part, 97 Stat. 1010; May 20, 1988, P. L. 100-323, § 15(b)(1), (d), 102 Stat. 574; Aug. 6, 1991, P. L. 102-83, § 5(a), (c)(1), 105 Stat. 406.)

HISTORY; ANCILLARY LAWS AND DIRECTIVES

Explanatory notes:
A prior § 4102 (Act Sept. 2, 1958, P. L. 85-857, § 1, 72 Stat. 1243; Nov. 7, 1966, P. L. 89-785, Title I, § 102, 80 Stat. 1368; Oct. 21, 1976, P. L. 94-581, Title I, § 110(1), 90 Stat. 2848) was repealed by Act May 7, 1991, P. L. 102-40, Title IV, § 401(a)(3), 105 Stat. 210. Such section provided for the divisions of the Department of Medicine and Surgery.

Provisions similar to those contained in this section were contained in former 38 USCS § 2001 prior to the general amendment of this chapter by Act Oct. 24, 1972, P. L. 92-540, Title V, § 502, 86 Stat. 1094.

A prior § 2002 (Act Sept. 2, 1958, P. L. 85-857, § 1, 72 Stat. 1217), contained in Subchapter I of Chapter 41, was repealed by Act Sept. 19, 1962, P. L. 87-675, § 1(a), 76 Stat. 558. It related to unemployment compensation in absence of state agreements.

Amendments:
1962. Act Sept. 19, 1962, redesignated this section as § 2002; it formerly appeared as § 2011 in Subchapter II of Chapter 41.

1966. Act March 3, 1966 (effective 3/3/66, as provided by § 12(a) of such Act), in the introductory matter, inserted "or of service after January 31, 1955"; in para. (1), inserted "or of service after January 31, 1955," wherever appearing; para. (4), inserted "or of service after January 31, 1955," wherever appearing; and in para. (5), inserted "or of service after January 31, 1955".

1972. Act Oct. 24, 1972 (effective 90 days after 10/24/72, as provided by § 601(b) of such Act, which appears as 38 USCS § 4101 note), substituted new catchline and section for ones which read:

"§ 2002. Assignment of veterans' employment representative

"The Secretary of Labor shall assign to each of the States a veterans' employment representative, who shall be a veteran of any war or of service after January 31, 1955, who at the time of appointment shall have been a bona fide resident of the State for at least two years, and who shall be appointed in accordance with the civil-service laws, and whose compensation shall be fixed in accordance with the Classification Act of 1949. Each such veterans' employment representative shall be attached to the staff of the public employment service in the State to which he has been assigned. He shall be administratively responsible to the Secretary of Labor, for the execution of the Secretary's veterans' placement policies through the public employment service in the State. In cooperation with the public employment service staff in the State, he shall—

"(1) be functionally responsible for the supervision of the registration of veterans of any war or of service after January 31, 1955, in local employment offices for suitable types of employment and for placement of veterans of any war or of service after January 31, 1955, in employment;

"(2) assist in securing and maintaining current information as to the various types of available employment in public works and private industry or business;

"(3) promote the interests of employers in employing veterans of any war or of service after January 31, 1955;

"(4) maintain regular contact with employers and veterans' organizations with a view of keeping employers advised of veterans of any war or of service after January 31, 1955, available for employment and veterans of any war or of service after January 31, 1955, advised of opportunities for employment; and

"(5) assist in every possible way in improving working conditions and the advancement of employment of veterans of any war or of service after January 31, 1955.".

1974. Act Dec. 3, 1974 (effective 12/3/74, as provided by § 503 of such Act, which appears as 38 USCS § 3452 note), inserted "and eligible persons" and "and persons".

1976. Act Oct. 15, 1976 (effective 12/1/76, as provided by § 703(c) of such Act, which appears as 38 USCS § 3693 note), inserted "by a Deputy Assistant Secretary of Labor for Veterans' Employment, established by section 2002A of this title,".

1980. Act Oct. 17, 1980 (effective 10/1/80, as provided by § 802(e) of such Act, which appears as 38 USCS § 4101 note), deleted "Deputy" preceding "Assistant Secretary".

1982. Act Oct. 14, 1982 inserted "and regulations" and inserted ", with priority given to the needs of disabled veterans and veterans of the Vietnam era".

1983. Act Nov. 21, 1983, substituted "an" for "a" following "administered by".

1988. Act May 20, 1988 (effective on enactment as provided by § 16(a) of such Act, which appears as 38 USCS § 3104 note) inserted "and Training" in two places.

1991. Act Aug. 6, 1991, redesignated this section, formerly 38 USCS § 2002, as 38 USCS § 4102, and amended the references in this section to reflect the redesignations made by § 5(a) of such Act (see Table III preceding 38 USCS § 101).

Other provisions:

Veterans' employment provisions. Act Dec. 31, 1974, P. L. 93-567, Title I, § 104, 88 Stat. 1848; Oct. 1, 1976, P. L. 94-444, § 12(a), 90 Stat. 1483; Oct. 15, 1976, P. L. 94-502, Title VI, § 601(c), 90 Stat. 2404, formerly classified as a note to this section, was repealed by Act Oct. 27, 1978, P. L. 95-524, § 7, 92 Stat. 2021. Section 104 authorized the Secretary of Labor to provide for an outreach and public information program for veterans utilizing, to the maximum extent, the Departments of Labor and Health, Education, and Welfare and the Veterans' Administration.

CODE OF FEDERAL REGULATIONS

Employment and Training Administration, Department of Labor—Administration provisions governing the Job Service System, 20 CFR Part 658.

38 USCS § 4102

CROSS REFERENCES

This section is referred to in 42 USCS § 1101.

§ 4102A. Assistant Secretary of Labor for Veterans' Employment and Training; Regional Administrators

(a)(1) There is established within the Department of Labor an Assistant Secretary of Labor for Veterans' Employment and Training appointed by the President by and with the advice and consent of the Senate, who shall be the principal advisor to the Secretary with respect to the formulation and implementation of all departmental policies and procedures to carry out (A) the purposes of this chapter, chapter 42, and chapter 43 of this title [38 USCS §§ 4100 et seq., 4211 et seq., and [4321] 2021 et seq.], and (B) all other Department of Labor employment, unemployment, and training programs to the extent they affect veterans. The employees of the Department of Labor administering chapter 43 of this title [38 USCS §§ [4321] 2021 et seq.] shall be administratively and functionally responsible to the Assistant Secretary of Labor for Veterans' Employment and Training.

(2) There shall be within the Department of Labor a Deputy Assistant Secretary of Labor for Veterans' Employment and Training. The Deputy Assistant Secretary shall perform such functions as the Assistant Secretary of Labor for Veterans' Employment and Training prescribes. The Deputy Assistant Secretary shall be a veteran.

(b) The Secretary shall—

(1) except as expressly provided otherwise, carry out all provisions of this chapter and chapter 43 of this title [38 USCS §§ 4100 et seq., §§ [4321] 2021 et seq.] through the Assistant Secretary of Labor for Veterans' Employment and Training and administer through such Assistant Secretary all programs under the jurisdiction of the Secretary for the provision of employment and training services designed to meet the needs of disabled veterans, veterans of the Vietnam era, and all other eligible veterans and eligible persons;

(2) in order to make maximum use of available resources in meeting such needs, encourage all such programs and all grantees under such programs to enter into cooperative arrangements with private industry and business concerns (including small business concerns), educational institutions, trade associations, and labor unions;

(3) ensure that maximum effectiveness and efficiency are achieved in providing services and assistance to eligible veterans under all such programs by coordinating and consulting with the Secretary of Veterans Affairs with respect to (A) programs conducted under other provisions of this title, with particular emphasis on coordination of such programs with readjustment counseling activities carried out under section 1712A of this title, apprenticeship or other on-the-job training programs carried out under section 3687 of this title, and rehabilitation and training activities carried out under chapter 31 of this title [38 USCS §§ 3100 et seq.], and (B) the Veterans' Job Training Act (29 U.S.C. 1721 note);

(4) ensure that job placement activities are carried out in coordination and cooperation with appropriate State public employment service officials;

(5) subject to subsection (c)(2) of this section, make available for use in each State, directly or by grant or contract, such funds as may be necessary (A) to support (i) disabled veterans' outreach program specialists appointed under section 4103A(a)(1) of this title, and (ii) local veterans' employment representatives assigned under section 4104(b) of this title, and (B) to support the reasonable expenses of such specialists and representatives for training, travel, supplies, and fringe benefits, including travel expenses and per diem for attendance at the National Veterans' Employment and Training Services Institute established under section 4109 of this title;

(6) monitor and supervise on a continuing basis the distribution and use of funds provided for use in the States under paragraph (5) of this subsection; and

(7) monitor the appointment of disabled veterans' outreach specialists and the assignment of local veterans' employment representatives in order to ensure compliance with the provisions of sections 4103A(a)(1) and 4104(a)(4), respectively, of this title.

(c)(1) The distribution and use of funds under subsection (b)(5) of this section in order to carry out sections 4103A(a) and 4104(a) of this title shall be subject to the continuing supervision and monitoring of the Secretary and shall not be governed by the provisions of any other law, or any regulations prescribed thereunder, that are inconsistent with this section or section 4103A or 4104 of this title.

(2) In determining the terms and conditions of a grant or contract under which funds are made available in a State in order to carry out section 4103A or 4104 of this title, the Secretary shall take into account (A) the results of the evaluations, carried out pursuant to section 4103(c)(15) of this title, of the performance of local employment offices in the State, and (B) the monitoring carried out under this section.

(3) Each grant or contract by which funds are made available in a State shall contain a provision requiring the recipient of the funds to comply with the provisions of this chapter [38 USCS §§ 4100 et seq.].

(d) The Assistant Secretary of Labor for Veterans' Employment and Training shall promote and monitor participation of qualified veterans and eligible persons in employment and training opportunities under the Job Training Partnership Act and other federally funded employment and training programs.

(e)(1) The Secretary shall assign to each region for which the Secretary operates a regional office a representative of the Veterans' Employment and Training Service to serve as the Regional Administrator for Veterans' Employment and Training in such region. Each Regional Administrator appointed after the date of the enactment of the Veterans' Benefits Improvements Act of 1996 [enacted Oct. 9, 1996] shall be a veteran.

(2) Each such Regional Administrator shall be responsible for—

(A) ensuring the promotion, operation, and implementation of all veterans' employment and training programs and services within the region;

38 USCS § 4102A

(B) monitoring compliance with section 4212 of this title with respect to veterans' employment under Federal contracts within the region;

(C) protecting and advancing veterans' reemployment rights within the region; and

(D) coordinating, monitoring, and providing technical assistance on veterans' employment and training programs with respect to all entities receiving funds under grants from or contracts with the Department of Labor within the region.

(Added Oct. 15, 1976, P. L. 94-502, Title VI, § 601(b)(1), 90 Stat. 2404; Oct. 17, 1980, P. L. 96-466, Title V, § 504(a)(3), (4), 94 Stat. 2203; Oct. 14, 1982, P. L. 97-306, Title III, § 303, 96 Stat. 1437; Nov. 21, 1983, P. L. 98-160, Title VII, § 702(15) in part, 97 Stat. 1010; May 20, 1988, P. L. 100-323, §§ 2(a), (e)(3)(A), 15(a)(2), (b)(1), 102 Stat. 556, 559, 574; Dec. 18, 1989, P. L. 101-237, Title IV, § 423(b)(8)(A), 103 Stat. 2093; Aug. 6, 1991, P. L. 102-83, §§ 4(b)(1), (2)(E), 5(a), (c)(1), 105 Stat. 404, 405, 406; Nov. 2, 1994, P. L. 103-446, Title VII, § 701(a), Title XII, § 1201(a)(4), 108 Stat. 4674, 4682; Oct. 9, 1996, P. L. 104-275, Title III, Subtitle A, § 301, 110 Stat. 3332.)

HISTORY; ANCILLARY LAWS AND DIRECTIVES

References in text:

The "Job Training Partnership Act", referred to in this section, is Act Oct. 13, 1982, P. L. 97-300, 96 Stat. 1322, which appears generally as 29 USCS §§ 1501 et seq. For full classification of such Act, consult USCS Tables volumes.

Effective date of section:

Act Oct. 15, 1976, P. L. 94-502, Title VII, § 703(c), 90 Stat. 2406, provided that this section is effective on December 1, 1976.

Amendments:

1980. Act Oct. 17, 1980 (effective 10/1/80, as provided by § 802(e) of such Act, which appears as 38 USCS § 4101 note), in the catchline, deleted "Deputy" preceding "Assistant Secretary"; and in the section, deleted "Deputy" preceding "Assistant Secretary".

1982. Act Oct. 14, 1982 added the sentence beginning "The employees of the Department . . .".

1983. Act Nov. 21, 1983, substituted "an" for "a" following "Labor".

1988. Act May 20, 1988 (effective on enactment as provided by § 16(a) of such Act, except as provided by § 16(b)(1)(A) of such Act, which appears as 38 USCS § 3104 note) substituted the section heading for one which read: "§ 2002A. Assistant Secretary of Labor for Veterans' Employment"; designated the existing provisions as subsec. (a), in subsec. (a) as so designated, inserted "and Training" in two places and substituted "Secretary" for "Secretary of Labor"; and added subsecs. (b)–(e).

1989. Act Dec. 18, 1989, in subsec. (b)(3), substituted "Secretary of Veterans Affairs" for "Administrator".

1991. Act Aug. 6, 1991, redesignated this section, formerly 38 USCS § 2000A, as 38 USCS § 4102A, amended the references in this section to reflect the redesignations made by § 5(a) of such Act (see Table III preceding 38 USCS § 101), and substituted "Secretary" for "Administrator" wherever appearing.

1994. Act Nov. 2, 1994, in subsec. (a), designated the existing provisions as para. (1), in para. (1) as so designated, substituted "(A)" and "(B)" for "(1)" and "(2)", respectively, and added para. (2).

Such Act further, in subsec. (e), substituted "Regional Administrator" for "Regional Secretary" wherever appearing.

1996. Act Oct. 9, 1996, in subsec. (e)(1), added the sentence beginning "Each Regional Administrator appointed . . .".

Other provisions:
Transition provisions. Act Oct. 17, 1980, P. L. 96-466, Title V, § 504(b), (c), 94 Stat. 2203 (effective 10/1/80, as provided by § 802(e) of such Act), provided:

"(b) Any reference in any law, regulation, directive, or other document to the Deputy Assistant Secretary of Labor for Veterans' Employment shall be deemed to be a reference to the Assistant Secretary of Labor for Veterans' Employment.

"(c) Notwithstanding any other provision of law, the position of Deputy Assistant Secretary of Labor for Veterans' Employment, as constituted on the day before the date of the enactment of this section, shall remain in existence until a person has been appointed to and has qualified for the position of Assistant Secretary of Labor for Veterans' Employment (established by the amendments made by subsection (a) [amending 38 USCS prec. § 4101 and 38 USCS §§ 4102 and 4102A]).".

CODE OF FEDERAL REGULATIONS

Employment and Training Administration, Department of Labor—Administration provisions governing the Job Service System, 20 CFR Part 658.

CROSS REFERENCES

Assistant Secretaries of Labor, generally 29 USCS § 553.
Administration by Assistant Secretary for Veterans' Employment and Training of employment programs for veterans under Job Training Partnership Act 29 USCS § 1721.
This section is referred to in 38 USCS §§ 4102, 4103A, 4104, 4106, 4107.

RESEARCH GUIDE

Am Jur:
77 Am Jur 2d, Veterans and Veterans' Laws §§ 106, 109.

§ 4103. Directors and Assistant Directors for Veterans' Employment and Training

(a) The Secretary shall assign to each State a representative of the Veterans' Employment Service to serve as the Director for Veterans' Employment and Training, and shall assign full-time Federal clerical or other support personnel to each such Director. The Secretary shall also assign to each State one Assistant Director for Veterans' Employment and Training per each 250,000 veterans and eligible persons of the State veterans population and such additional Assistant Directors for Veterans' Employment and Training as the Secretary shall determine, based on the data collected pursuant to section 4107 of this title, to be necessary to assist the Director for Veterans' Employment and Training to carry out effectively in that State the purposes of this chapter [38 USCS §§ 4100 et seq.]. Full-time Federal clerical or other support personnel assigned to Directors for Veterans' Employment and Training shall be appointed in accordance with the provisions of title 5 governing appointments in the competitive service and shall be paid in accordance with the provisions of chapter 51 and subchapter III of chapter 53 of title 5 [5 USCS §§ 5101 et seq. and 5331 et seq.].

(b)(1)(A) Each Director for Veterans' Employment and Training and Assistant Director for Veterans' Employment and Training (i) shall, except as provided in subparagraph (B) of this paragraph, be a qualified veteran who at the time of appointment has been a bona fide resident of the State for at least two years, and (ii) shall be appointed in accordance with the provisions of title 5 governing appointments in the competitive service and shall be paid in accordance with the provisions of chapter 51 and subchapter III of chapter 53 of title 5 [5 USCS §§ 5101 et seq. and 5331 et seq.].

(B) If, in appointing a Director or Assistant Director for any State under this section, the Secretary determines that there is no qualified veteran available who meets the residency requirement in subparagraph (A)(i), the Secretary may appoint as such Director or Assistant Director any qualified veteran.

(2) Each Director for Veterans' Employment and Training and Assistant Director for Veterans' Employment and Training shall be attached to the public employment service system of the State to which they are assigned. They shall be administratively responsible to the Secretary for the execution of the veterans' and eligible persons' counseling and placement policies of the Secretary through the public employment service system and in cooperation with other employment and training programs administered by the Secretary, by grantees of Federal or federally funded employment and training programs in the State, or directly by the State.

(c) In cooperation with the staff of the public employment service system and the staffs of each such other program in the State, the Director for Veterans' Employment and Training and Assistant Directors for Veterans' Employment and Training shall—

(1)(A) functionally supervise the provision of services to eligible veterans and eligible persons by such system and such program and their staffs, and (B) be functionally responsible for the supervision of the registration of eligible veterans and eligible persons in local employment offices for suitable types of employment and training and for counseling and placement of eligible veterans and eligible persons in employment and job training programs, including the program conducted under the Veterans' Job Training Act (Public Law 98-77; 29 U.S.C. 1721 note);

(2) engage of job development and job advancement activities for eligible

veterans and eligible persons, including maximum coordination with appropriate officials of the Department of Veterans Affairs in that agency's carrying out of its responsibilities under subchapter II of chapter 77 of this title [38 USCS §§ 7721 et seq.] and in the conduct of job affairs, job marts, and other special programs to match eligible veterans and eligible persons with appropriate job and job training opportunities and otherwise to promote the employment of eligible veterans and eligible persons;

(3) assist in securing and maintaining current information as to the various types of available employment and training opportunities, including maximum use of electronic data processing and telecommunications systems and the matching of an eligible veteran's or an eligible person's particular qualifications with an available job or on-job training or apprenticeship opportunity which is commensurate with those qualifications;

(4) promote the interest of employers and labor unions in employing eligible veterans and eligible persons and in conducting on-job training and apprenticeship programs for such veterans and persons;

(5) maintain regular contact with employers, labor unions, training programs and veterans' organizations with a view to keeping them advised of eligible veterans and eligible persons available for employment and training and to keeping eligible veterans and eligible persons advised of opportunities for employment and training;

(6) promote and facilitate the participation of veterans in Federal and federally funded employment and training programs and directly monitor the implementation and operation of such programs to ensure that eligible veterans, veterans of the Vietnam era, disabled veterans, and eligible persons receive such priority or other special consideration in the provision of services as is required by law or regulation;

(7) assist in every possible way in improving working conditions and the advancement of employment of eligible veterans and eligible persons;

(8) supervise the listing of jobs and subsequent referrals of qualified veterans as required by section 4212 of this title;

(9) be responsible for ensuring that complaints of discrimination filed under such section are resolved in a timely fashion;

(10) working closely with appropriate Department of Veterans Affairs personnel engaged in providing counseling or rehabilitation services under chapter 31 of this title [38 USCS §§ 3101 et seq.], cooperate with employers to identify disabled veterans who have completed or are participating in a vocational rehabilitation training program under such chapter and who are in need of employment;

(11) cooperate with the staff of programs operated under section 1712A of this title in identifying and assisting veterans who have readjustment problems and who may need employment placement assistance or vocational training assistance;

(12) when requested by a Federal or State agency or a private employer, assist such agency or employer in identifying and acquiring prosthetic and sensory aids and devices which tend to enhance the employability of disabled veterans;

(13) monitor the implementation of Federal laws requiring veterans preference in employment and job advancement opportunities within the Federal Government and report to the Office of Personnel Management or other appropriate agency, for enforcement or other remedial action, any evidence of failure to provide such preference or to provide priority or other special consideration in the provision of services to veterans as is required by law or regulation;

(14) monitor, through disabled veterans' outreach program specialists and local veterans' employment representatives, the listing of vacant positions with State employment agencies by Federal agencies, and report to the Office of Personnel Management or other appropriate agency, for enforcement or other remedial action, any evidence of failure to provide priority or other special consideration in the provision of services to veterans as is required by law or regulation; and

(15)(A) not less frequently than annually, conduct, subject to subclause (B) of this clause, an evaluation at each local employment office of the services provided to eligible veterans and eligible persons and make recommendations for corrective action as appropriate; and

(B) carry out such evaluations in the following order of priority: (I) offices that demonstrated less than satisfactory performance during either of the two previous program years, (II) offices with the largest number of veterans registered during the previous program year, and (III) other offices as resources permit.

(Sept. 2, 1958, P. L. 85-857, § 1, 72 Stat. 1221; Sept. 19, 1962, P. L. 87-675, § 1(a), 76 Stat. 558; March 3, 1966, P. L. 89-358, § 6(c)(1), 80 Stat. 27; Oct. 24, 1972, P. L. 92-540, Title V, § 502(a), 86 Stat. 1094; Dec. 3, 1974, P. L. 93-508, Title IV, § 401(c), 88 Stat. 1592; Oct. 15, 1976, P. L. 94-502, Title VI, §§ 602, 606(1), 90 Stat. 2404, 2405; Oct. 17, 1980, P. L. 96-466, Title V, § 505, Title VIII, § 801(i), 94 Stat. 2204, 2216; Oct. 12, 1982, P. L. 97-295, § 4(70), 96 Stat. 1310; Oct. 14, 1982, P. L. 97-306, Title III, § 304(a)(1), (b), (c), 96 Stat. 1437; May 20, 1988, P. L. 100-323, §§ 5, 7(a), 15(a)(2), (c)(1), (3)(A), 102 Stat. 564, 574; Dec. 18, 1989, P. L. 101-237, Title IV, § 423(b)(8)(B), 103 Stat. 2093; Aug. 6, 1991, P. L. 102-83, § 5(a), (c)(1), 105 Stat. 406; Nov. 2, 1994, P. L. 103-446, Title XII, § 1201(d)(14), 108 Stat. 4684; Oct. 9, 1996, P. L. 104-275, Title III, Subtitle A, § 302, 110 Stat. 3332.)

HISTORY; ANCILLARY LAWS AND DIRECTIVES

References in text:

The "provisions of title 5 governing appointment in the competitive service", referred to in this section, appear generally as 5 USCS §§ 2101 et seq.

Explanatory notes:

A prior § 4103 (Act Sept. 2, 1958, P. L. 85-857, § 1, 72 Stat. 1243; July 1, 1960, P. L. 86-568, Title I, Part B, § 114(a)-(e), 74 Stat. 300; Aug. 6, 1962, P. L. 87-574, § 5, 76 Stat. 309; Oct. 11, 1962, P. L. 87-793, Part II, Title IV, § 801, 76 Stat. 859; May 8, 1963, P. L. 88-18, 77 Stat. 15; Aug. 14, 1964, P. L. 88-426, Title I, § 117(a), 78 Stat. 409; Nov. 7, 1966, P. L. 89-

785, Title I, § 103(a), (b), 80 Stat. 1368; Aug. 2, 1973, P. L. 93-82, Title II, § 202, 87 Stat. 188; Oct. 21, 1976, P. L. 94-581, Title I, § 110(2), Title II 205(d), 209(c)(1), 210(c)(2), 90 Stat. 2848, 2859, 2861, 2863; Aug. 26, 1980, P. L. 96-330, Title I, Part A, § 105(b), Title III, § 303, 94 Stat. 1036, 1050; Nov. 18, 1988, P. L. 100-687, Div B, Title XV, § 1506(b)(1), 102 Stat. 4136) was repealed by Act May 7, 1991, P. L. 102-40, Title IV, § 401(a)(3), 105 Stat. 210. Such section provided for the Office of the Chief Medical Director.

Provisions similar to those contained in this section were contained in former 38 USCS § 2002 prior to the general amendment of this chapter by Act Oct. 24, 1972, P. L. 92-540, Title V, § 502, 86 Stat. 1094.

A prior § 2003 (Act Sept. 2, 1958, P. L. 85-857, § 1, 72 Stat. 1218), contained in Subchapter I of Chapter 41, was repealed by Act Sept. 19, 1962, P. L. 87-675, § 1(a), 76 Stat. 558. It related to payments to States.

Amendments:

1962. Act Sept. 19, 1962, redesignated this section as § 2003; it formerly appeared as § 2012 in Subchapter II of Chapter 41.

1966. Act March 3, 1966 (effective 3/3/66, as provided by § 12(a) of such Act), inserted "or of service after January 31, 1955"

1972. Act Oct. 24, 1972 (effective 90 days after 10/24/72, as provided by § 601(b) of such Act, which appears as 38 USCS § 4101 note), substituted this section for one which read:

"§ 2003. Employees of local offices

"Where deemed necessary by the Secretary of Labor, there shall be assigned by the administrative head of the employment service in the State one or more employees, preferably veterans of any war or of service after January 31, 1955, of the staffs of local employment service offices, whose services shall be primarily devoted to discharging the duties prescribed for the veterans' employment representative.".

1974. Act Dec. 3, 1974 (effective 12/3/74, as provided by § 503 of such Act, which appears as 38 USCS § 3452 note), in the introductory matter, substituted "250,000 veterans and eligible persons" for "250,000 veterans" and substituted "veterans' and eligible persons' " for "veterans' "; in paras. (1) and (2), inserted "and eligible persons" wherever appearing; in para. (3), inserted "or an eligible person's"; in para. (4), inserted "and eligible persons" and "and persons"; and in paras. (5) and (6), inserted "and eligible persons" wherever appearing.

1976. Act Oct. 15, 1976 (effective 12/1/76, as provided by § 703(c) of such Act, which appears as 38 USCS § 3693 note), in the introductory matter, substituted "the Secretary" for "he" preceding "shall determine", inserted "or by prime sponsors under the Comprehensive Employment and Training Act", and substituted "such representative's" for "his"; in para. (5), deleted "and" following "employment and training;"; redesignated para. (6) as para. (7); and added new para. (6).

1980. Act Oct. 17, 1980 (effective 10/1/80, as provided by § 802(e), (h) of such Act), in the introductory matter, inserted "(and shall assign full-time clerical support to each such representative)", deleted ", United States Code," following "provisions of title 5", inserted "system" following "public employment service" wherever appearing, and substituted "employment" for "manpower" preceding "and training programs"; and in para. (6), inserted ", disabled veterans, and veterans of the Vietnam era".

1982. Act Oct. 12, 1982, in the introductory matter, substituted "chapter 51 and" for "chapter 51 of".

Such Act further substituted the catchline for one which read: "§ 2003. Assignment of veterans' employment representative"; and substituted subsecs. (a), (b), and the provisions of subsec. (c) preceding para. (1) for provisions which read: "The Secretary of Labor shall assign to each State a representative of the Veterans' Employment Service to serve as the veterans' employment representative (and shall assign full-time clerical support to each such representative), and shall further assign to each State one assistant veterans' employment representative per each 250,000 veterans and eligible persons of the State veterans population, and such additional assistant veterans' employment representatives as the Secretary shall determine, based on the data collected pursuant to section 2007 of this title, to be necessary to assist the veterans' employment representative to carry out effectively in that State the purposes of this chapter. Each veterans' employment representative and assistant veterans' employment representative shall be an eligible veteran who at the time of appointment shall have been a bona fide resident of the State for at least two years and who shall be appointed in accordance with the provisions of title 5 governing appointments in the competitive service, and shall be paid in accordance with the provisions of chapter 51 and subchapter III of chapter 53 of such title relating to classification and general schedule pay rates. Each such veterans' employment representative and assistant veterans' employment representative shall be attached to the staff of the public employment service system in the State to which they have been assigned. They shall be administratively responsible to the Secretary of Labor for the execution of the Secretary's veterans' and eligible persons' counseling and placement policies through the public employment service and in cooperation with employment and training programs administered by the Secretary or by prime sponsors under the Comprehensive Employment and Training Act in the State. In cooperation with the public employment service system staff and the staffs of each such other program in the State, the veterans' employment representative and such representative's assistants shall—";
and, in subsec. (c), substituted para. (6) for one which read: "promote the participation of veterans in Comprehensive Employment and Training Act programs and monitor the implementation and operation of Comprehensive Employment and Training Act programs to assure that eligible veterans, disabled veterans, and veterans of the Vietnam era receive special consideration when required; and", in para. (7), substituted a semicolon for the concluding period, and added paras. (8)–(12).

1988. Act May 20, 1988 (effective on enactment as provided by § 16(a) of such Act, which appears as 38 USCS § 3104 note) substituted the section heading for one which read: "§ 2003. State and Assistant State Directors for Veterans' Employment"; in subsec. (a), substituted "Secretary" for "Secretary of Labor" preceding "shall assign", deleted "State" preceding "Director" and inserted "and Training" wherever appearing: in subsec. (b)(1), deleted "State" preceding "Director" and inserted "and Training" wherever appearing, designated the existing provisions as subpara. (A), in subpara. (A) as so designated, redesignated cls. (A) and (B) as cls. (i) and (ii) and, in cl. (i) as redesignated, substituted ", except as provided in subparagraph (B) of this paragraph, be a qualified veteran" for "be an eligible veteran", and added subpara. (B), and in para. (2), inserted "and Training" and deleted "State" preceding "Director" wherever appearing; and, in subsec. (c), in the introductory matter, deleted "State" and inserted "and Training" wherever appearing.

Such Act further (effective on the 60th day after enactment, as provided by § 16(b)(2) of such Act, which appears as 38 USCS § 1504 note), in subsec. (c), in para. (1), inserted "(A) functionally supervise the provision of services to eligible veterans and eligible persons by such system and such program and their staffs, and (B)" after "(1)" and ", including the program conducted under the Veterans' Job Training Act (Public Law 98-77; 29 U.S.C. 1721 note)", in para. (2), inserted "and otherwise to promote the employment of eligible veterans and eligible persons", in para. (11), deleted "and" following "assistance;", in para. (12), substituted a semicolon for a concluding period, and added paras. (13)–(15).

1989. Act Dec. 18, 1989, in subsec. (c), in paras. (2) and (10), substituted "Department of Veterans Affairs" for "Veterans' Administration".

1991. Act Aug. 6, 1991, redesignated this section, formerly 38 USCS § 2003, as 38 USCS § 4103, and amended the references in this section to reflect the redesignations made by § 5(a) of such Act (see Table III preceding 38 USCS § 101).

1994. Act Nov. 2, 1994, in subsec. (c)(2), substituted "subchapter II of chapter 77" for "subchapter IV of chapter 3".

1996. Act Oct. 9, 1996, in subsec. (a), substituted "full-time Federal clerical or other support personnel" for "full-time Federal clerical support" and substituted "Full-time Federal clerical or other support personnel" for "Full-time Federal clerical support personnel".

Other provisions:
Application and construction of Oct. 12, 1982 amendment. For provisions as to the application and construction of the Oct. 12, 1982 amendment of this section, see § 5 of such Act, which appears as 10 USCS § 101 note.

CODE OF FEDERAL REGULATIONS

Employment and Training Administration, Department of Labor—Administration provisions governing the Job Service System, 20 CFR Part 658.

CROSS REFERENCES

This section is referred to in 38 USCS §§ 4102A, 4103A; 42 USCS § 1712A.

RESEARCH GUIDE

Am Jur:
77 Am Jur 2d, Veterans and Veterans' Laws § 109.

§ 4103A. Disabled veterans' outreach program

(a)(1) The amount of funds made available for use in a State under section 4102A(b)(5)(A)(i) of this title shall be sufficient to support the appointment of one disabled veterans' outreach program specialist for each 6,900 veterans residing in such State who are either veterans of the Vietnam era, veterans who first entered on active duty as a member of the Armed Forces after May 7, 1975, or disabled veterans. Each such specialist shall be a qualified veteran. Preference shall be given in the appointment of such specialists to qualified disabled veterans of the Vietnam era. If the Secretary finds that a qualified disabled veteran of the Vietnam era is not available for any such appointment, preference for such appointment shall be given to other qualified disabled veterans. If the Secretary finds that no qualified disabled veteran is available for such appointment, such appointment may be given to any qualified veteran. Each such specialist shall be compensated at rates comparable to those paid other professionals performing essentially similar duties in the State government of the State concerned.

(2) Specialists appointed pursuant to this subsection shall be in addition to and shall not supplant employees assigned to local employment service offices pursuant to section 4104 of this title.

(b)(1) Pursuant to regulations prescribed by the Secretary of Labor, disabled veterans' outreach program specialists shall be assigned only those duties directly related to meeting the employment needs of eligible veterans, with priority for the provision of services in the following order:

(A) Services to special disabled veterans.

(B) Services to other disabled veterans.

(C) Services to other eligible veterans in accordance with priorities determined by the Secretary taking into account applicable rates of unemployment and the employment emphases set forth in chapter 42 of this title [38 USCS §§ 4211 et seq.].

In the provision of services in accordance with this paragraph, maximum emphasis in meeting the employment needs of veterans shall be placed on assisting economically or educationally disadvantaged veterans.

(2) Not more than three-fourths of the disabled veterans' outreach program specialists in each State shall be stationed at local employment service offices in such State. The Secretary, after consulting the Secretary of Veterans Affairs and the Director for Veterans' Employment and Training assigned to a State under section 4103 of this title, may waive the limitation in the preceding sentence for that State so long as the percentage of all disabled veterans' outreach program specialists that are stationed at local employment service offices in all States does not exceed 80 percent. Specialists not so stationed shall be stationed at centers established by the Department of Veterans Affairs to provide a program of readjustment counseling pursuant to section 1712A of this title, veterans assistance offices established by the Department of Veterans Affairs pursuant to section 7723 of this title, and such other sites as may be determined to be appropriate in accordance with regulations prescribed by the Secretary after consultation with the Secretary of Veterans Affairs.

(c) Each disabled veterans' outreach program specialist shall carry out the following functions for the purpose of providing services to eligible veterans in accordance with the priorities set forth in subsection (b) of this section:

(1) Development of job and job training opportunities for such veterans through contacts with employers, especially small- and medium-size private sector employers.

(2) Pursuant to regulations prescribed by the Secretary after consultation with

the Secretary of Veterans Affairs, promotion and development of apprenticeship and other on-job training positions pursuant to section 3787 of this title.

(3) The carrying out of outreach activities to locate such veterans through contacts with local veterans organizations, the Department of Veterans Affairs, the State employment service agency and local employment service offices, and community-based organizations.

(4) Provision of appropriate assistance to community-based groups and organizations and appropriate grantees under other Federal and federally funded employment and training programs (including part C of title IV of the Job Training Partnership Act (29 U.S.C. 1501 et seq.)) in providing services to such veterans.

(5) Provision of appropriate assistance to local employment service office employees with responsibility for veterans in carrying out their responsibilities pursuant to this chapter [38 USCS §§ 4100 et seq.].

(6) Consultation and coordination with other appropriate representatives of Federal, State, and local programs (including the program conducted under the Veterans' Job Training Act (Public Law 98-77; 29 U.S.C. 1721 note)) for the purpose of developing maximum linkages to promote employment opportunities for and provide maximum employment assistance to such veterans.

(7) The carrying out of such other duties as will promote the development of entry-level and career job opportunities for such veterans.

(8) Development of outreach programs in cooperation with appropriate Department of Veterans Affairs personnel engaged in providing counseling or rehabilitation services under chapter 31 of this title [38 USCS §§ 3101 et seq.], with educational institutions, and with employers in order to ensure maximum assistance to disabled veterans who have completed or are participating in a vocational rehabilitation program under such chapter.

(9) Provision of vocational guidance or vocational counseling services, or both, to veterans with respect to veterans' selection of and changes in vocations and veterans' vocational adjustment.

(10) Provision of services as a case manager under section 14(b)(1)(A) of the Veterans' Job Training Act (Public Law 98-77; 29 U.S.C. 1721 note).
(Added Oct. 17, 1980, P. L. 96-466, Title V, § 506(a), 94 Stat. 2204; Oct. 14, 1982, P. L. 97-306, Title III, § 305, 96 Stat. 1439; May 20, 1988, P. L. 100-323, §§ 2(e)(1), 7(b), 15(c)(1), 102 Stat. 559, 565, 574; Dec. 18, 1989, P. L. 101-237, Title IV, § 423(b)(8), 103 Stat. 2093; Aug. 6, 1991, P. L. 102-83, §§ 2(c)(4), 5(a), (c)(1), 105 Stat. 402, 406; Oct. 29, 1992, P. L. 102-568, Title V, §§ 501, 503, 106 Stat. 4340; Nov. 2, 1994, P. L. 103-446, Title VII, § 701(b), 108 Stat. 4674.)

HISTORY; ANCILLARY LAWS AND DIRECTIVES
Effective date of section:
Act Oct. 17, 1980, P. L. 96-466, Title VIII, § 802(e), 94 Stat. 2218, provided that this section is effective on Oct. 1, 1980.

38 USCS § 4103A

Amendments:

1982. Act Oct. 14, 1982, in subsec. (a), in para. (1), inserted '', acting through the Assistant Secretary for Veterans' Employment,'' and substituted ''available for use in'' for ''available to'', in para. (2), substituted ''provided for use in'' for ''provided to'', in para. (3), inserted '', acting through the Assistant Secretary of Labor for Veterans' Employment,'' and substituted ''available for use in'' for ''available to'', and added para. (5); in subsec. (b)(2), inserted the sentence beginning ''The Secretary, after consulting . . .'' and substituted ''section 612A'' for ''section 621A''; in subsec. (c), in para. (4), substituted ''appropriate grantees under other Federal and federally funded employment and training programs'' for ''prime sponsors under the Comprehensive Employment and Training Act'', and added para. (8); deleted subsec. (d), which read: ''Persons serving as staff in the disabled veterans outreach program conducted under title III of the Comprehensive Employment and Training Act on the date of enactment of this section shall be appointed as disabled veterans' outreach program specialists in the State in which such individual is so serving, unless the Secretary for good cause shown determines that such individual is not qualified for such appointment.''; redesignated former subsec. (e) as subsec. (d); and in subsec. (d) as redesignated, added the sentence beginning ''The Secretary shall monitor . . .''

1988. Act May 20, 1988 (effective on enactment as provided by § 16(a) of such Act and applicable for all of fiscal year 1988 and subsequent fiscal years, as provided by § 16(b)(1) of such Act, which appears as 38 USCS § 3104 note), in subsec. (a), deleted para. (1), which read: ''The Secretary of Labor, acting through the Assistant Secretary for Veterans' Employment, shall make available for use in each State, directly or by grant or contract, such funds as may be necessary to support a disabled veterans' outreach program designated to meet the employment needs of veterans, especially disabled veterans of the Vietnam era.'', redesignated former para. (2) as para. (1), in para. (1) as redesignated, substituted the sentence beginning ''The amount of funds . . .'' for ''Funds provided for use in a State under this subsection shall be sufficient to support the appointment of one disabled veterans' outreach program specialist for each 5,300 veterans of the Vietnam era and disabled veterans residing in such State.'' and inserted ''qualified'' before ''veteran'' in two places and before ''disabled'' in three places, and deleted paras. (3) and (5), which read:

''(3) The Secretary, acting through the Assistant Secretary of Labor for Veterans' Employment, shall also make available for use in the States such funds, in addition to those made available to carry out paragraphs (1) and (2) of this subsection, as may be necessary to support the reasonable expenses of such specialists for training, travel, supplies, and fringe benefits.

''(5) The distribution and use of funds provided for use in States under this section shall be subject to the continuing supervision and monitoring of the Assistant Secretary for Veterans' Employment and shall not be governed by the provisions of any other law, or any regulations prescribed thereunder, that are inconsistent with this section.''.

Such Act further (effective and applicable as above), in subsec. (a), redesignated former para. (4) as para. (2) and, in para. (2) as redesignated, deleted ''paragraph (2) of'' preceding ''this subsection''.

Such Act further (effective on enactment as provided by § 16(a) of such Act, which appears as 38 USCS § 3104 note), in subsec. (b)(2), deleted "State" preceding "Director" and inserted "and Training"; and deleted subsec. (d), which read: "The Secretary of Labor shall administer the program provided for by this section through the Assistant Secretary of Labor for Veterans' Employment. The Secretary shall monitor the appointment of disabled veterans' outreach program specialists to ensure compliance with the provisions of subsection (a)(2) of this section with respect to the employment of such specialists.".

Such Act further (effective on the 60th day after enactment, as provided by § 16(b)(2) of such Act, which appears as 38 USCS § 3104 note), in subsec. (c), in para. (4), inserted "(including part C of title IV of the Job Training Partnership Act (29 U.S.C. 1501 et seq.))", in para. (6), inserted "(including the program conducted under the Veterans' Job Training Act (Public Law 98-77; 29 U.S.C. 1721 note))" and added paras. (9) and (10).

1989. Act Dec. 18, 1989, in subsecs. (b)(2) and (c)(2), substituted "Secretary of Veterans Affairs" for "Administrator", wherever appearing; and in subsec. (b)(2) and subsec. (c), in paras. (3) and (8), substituted "Department of Veterans Affairs" for "Veterans' Administration".

1991. Act Aug. 6, 1991, redesignated this section, formerly 38 USCS § 2003A, as 38 USCS § 4103A, amended the references in this section to reflect the redesignations made by § 5(a) of such Act (see Table III preceding 38 USCS § 101); and, in subsec. (b), in para. (2), substituted "section 7723" for "section 242".

1992. Act Oct. 29, 1992, in subsec. (a), in para. (1), substituted "specialist for each 6,900 veterans residing in such State who are either veterans of the Vietnam era, veterans who first entered on active duty as a member of the Armed Forces after May 7, 1975, or disabled veterans." for "specialist for each 5,300 veterans of the Vietnam era and disabled veterans residing in such State."; and, in subsec. (b), in para. (1), substituted subpara. (A) for one which read: "(A) Services to disabled veterans of the Vietnam era who are participating in or have completed a program of vocational rehabilitation under chapter 31 of this title.".

1994. Act Nov. 2, 1994, in subsec. (a)(1), substituted "rates comparable to those paid other professionals performing essentially similar duties" for "a rate not less than the rate prescribed for an entry level professional".

CODE OF FEDERAL REGULATIONS

Employment and Training Administration, Department of Labor—Administration provisions governing the Job Service System, 20 CFR Part 658.

CROSS REFERENCES

Employment programs for disabled veterans under Job Training Partnership Act 29 USCS § 1721.

This section is referred to in 29 USCS § 1721; 38 USCS §§ 3117, 3672, 4102A, 4104A, 4106, 4107.

RESEARCH GUIDE

Am Jur:
77 Am Jur 2d, Veterans and Veterans' Laws § 110.

INTERPRETIVE NOTES AND DECISIONS

If two qualified, disabled veterans apply for DVOP (disabled veteran outreach program) job, and one is Vietnam-era veteran, but other is not, 38 USCS § 4103A plainly affords Vietnam-era veteran priority in hiring. Appeal of New Hampshire Dep't of Empl. Sec. (1996) 140 NH 703, 672 A2d 697, 11 BNA IER Cas 1140.

§ 4104. Local veterans' employment representatives

(a)(1) Beginning with fiscal year 1988, the total of the amount of funds made available for use in the States under section 4102A(b)(5)(A)(ii) of this title shall be sufficient to support the appointment of 1,600 full-time local veterans' employment representatives and the States' administrative expenses associated with the appointment of that number of such representatives and shall be allocated to the several States so that each State receives funding sufficient to support—

   (A) the number of such representatives who were assigned in such State on January 1, 1987, for which funds were provided under this chapter, plus one additional such representative;

   (B) the percentage of the 1,600 such representatives for which funding is not provided under clause (A) of this paragraph which is equal to the average of (i) the percentage of all veterans residing in the United States who reside in such State, (ii) the percentage of the total of all eligible veterans and eligible persons registered for assistance with local employment service offices in the United States who are registered for assistance with local employment service offices in such State, and (iii) the percentage of all full-service local employment service offices in the United States which are located in such State; and

   (C) the State's administrative expenses associated with the appointment of the number of such representatives for which funding is allocated to the State under clauses (A) and (B) of this paragraph.

(2)(A) The local veterans' employment representatives allocated to a State pursuant to paragraph (1) of this subsection shall be assigned by the administrative head of the employment service in the State, after consultation with the Director for Veterans' Employment and Training for the State, so that as nearly as practical (i) one full-time representative is assigned to each local employment service office at which at least 1,100 eligible veterans and eligible persons are registered for assistance, (ii) one additional full-time representative is assigned to each local employment service office for each 1,500 eligible veterans and eligible persons above 1,100 who are registered at such office for assistance, and (iii) one half-time representative is assigned to each local employment service office at which at least 350 but less than 1,100 eligible veterans and eligible persons are registered for assistance.

   (B) In the case of a service delivery point (other than a local employment service office described in subparagraph (A) of this paragraph) at which employment services are offered under the Wagner-Peyser Act, the head of such service delivery point shall be responsible for ensuring compliance with the provisions of this title providing for priority services for veterans and priority referral of veterans to Federal contractors.

(3) For the purposes of this subsection, an individual shall be considered to be registered for assistance with a local employment service office during a program year if the individual—
   (A) registered, or renewed such individual's registration, for assistance with the office during that program year; or
   (B) so registered or renewed such individual's registration during a previous program year and, in accordance with regulations which the Secretary shall prescribe, is counted as still being registered for administrative purposes.
(4) In the appointment of local veterans' employment representatives on or after July 1, 1988, preference shall be given to qualified eligible veterans or eligible persons. Preference shall be accorded first to qualified service-connected disabled veterans; then, if no such disabled veteran is available, to qualified eligible veterans; and, if no such eligible veteran is available, then to qualified eligible persons.

(b) Local veterans' employment representatives shall—
   (1) functionally supervise the providing of services to eligible veterans and eligible persons by the local employment service staff;
   (2) maintain regular contact with community leaders, employers, labor unions, training programs, and veterans' organizations for the purpose of (A) keeping them advised of eligible veterans and eligible persons available for employment and training, and (B) keeping eligible veterans and eligible persons advised of opportunities for employment and training;
   (3) provide directly, or facilitate the provision of, labor exchange services by local employment service staff to eligible veterans and eligible persons, including intake and assessment, counseling, testing, job-search assistance, and referral and placement;
   (4) encourage employers and labor unions to employ eligible veterans and eligible persons and conduct on-the-job training and apprenticeship programs for such veterans and persons;
   (5) promote and monitor the participation of veterans in federally funded employment and training programs, monitor the listing of vacant positions with State employment agencies by Federal agencies, and report to the Director for Veterans' Employment and Training for the State concerned any evidence of failure to provide priority or other special consideration in the provision of services to veterans as is required by law or regulation;
   (6) monitor the listing of jobs and subsequent referrals of qualified veterans as required by section 4212 of this title;
   (7) work closely with appropriate Department of Veterans Affairs personnel engaged in providing counseling or rehabilitation services under chapter 31 of this title [38 USCS §§ 3100 et seq.], and cooperate with employers in identifying disabled veterans who have completed or are participating in a vocational rehabilitation training program under such chapter and who are in need of employment;
   (8) refer eligible veterans and eligible persons to training, supportive services, and educational opportunities, as appropriate;

(9) assist, through automated data processing, in securing and maintaining current information regarding available employment and training opportunities;

(10) cooperate with the staff of programs operated under section 1712A of this title in identifying and assisting veterans who have readjustment problems and who may need services available at the local employment service office;

(11) when requested by a Federal or State agency, a private employer, or a service-connected disabled veteran, assist such agency, employer, or veteran in identifying and acquiring prosthetic and sensory aids and devices needed to enhance the employability of disabled veterans; and

(12) facilitate the provision of guidance or counseling services, or both, to veterans who, pursuant to section 5(b)(3) of the Veterans' Job Training Act (29 U.S.C. 1721 note), are certified as eligible for participation under such Act.

(c) Each local veterans' employment representative shall be administratively responsible to the manager of the local employment service office and shall provide reports, not less frequently than quarterly, to the manager of such office and to the Director for Veterans' Employment and Training for the State regarding compliance with Federal law and regulations with respect to special services and priorities for eligible veterans and eligible persons.

(Sept. 2, 1958, P. L. 85-857, § 1, 72 Stat. 1221; Sept. 19, 1962, P. L. 87-675, § 1(a), 76 Stat. 558; March 3, 1966, P. L. 89-358, § 6(c)(1), 80 Stat. 27; Oct. 24, 1972, P. L. 92-540, Title V, § 502(a), 86 Stat. 1095; Oct. 15, 1976, P. L. 94-502, Title VI, § 606(2), 90 Stat. 2405; May 20, 1988, P. L. 100-323, § 3(a), 102 Stat. 562; Dec. 18, 1989, P. L. 101-237, Title IV, § 423(b)(8)(B), 103 Stat. 2093; March 22, 1991, P. L. 102-16, § 10(a)(8), 105 Stat. 56; Aug. 6, 1991, P. L. 102-83, § 5(a), (c)(1), 105 Stat. 406.)

HISTORY; ANCILLARY LAWS AND DIRECTIVES

References in text:

"The Wagner-Peyser Act", referred to in this section, is Act June 6, 1933, ch 49, 48 Stat. 113, which appears generally as 29 USCS §§ 49 et seq. For full classification of such Act, consult USCS Tables volumes.

Explanatory notes:

A prior § 4104 (Act Sept. 2, 1958, P. L. 85-857, § 1, 72 Stat. 1244; Nov. 7, 1966, P. L. 89-785, Title I, § 104, 80 Stat. 1369; Oct. 22, 1975, P. L. 94-123, § 5(a), 89 Stat. 675; Oct. 21, 1976, P. L. 94-581, Title I, § 110(3), Title II, §§ 209(a)(1), (2), 210(c)(3), 90 Stat. 2848, 2860, 2863; Dec. 20, 1979, P. L. 96-151, Title III, § 302(a), 93 Stat. 1096; Nov. 21, 1983, P. L. 98-160, Title II, § 201, 97 Stat. 1000; Oct. 19, 1984, P. L. 98-528, Title I, § 108, 98 Stat. 2690; May 20, 1988, P. L. 100-322, Title II, Part B, § 211(a), 102 Stat. 513; Aug. 15, 1990, P. L. 101-366, Title I, § 102(a), 104 Stat. 430) was repealed by Act May 7, 1991, P. L. 102-40, Title IV, § 401(a)(3), 105 Stat. 210. Such section provided for the appointment of additional personnel.

Provisions similar to those contained in this section were contained in for-

mer 38 USCS § 2003 prior to the general amendment of this chapter by Act Oct. 24, 1972, P. L. 92-540, Title V, § 502, 86 Stat. 1094.

A prior § 2004 (Act Sept. 2, 1958, P. L. 85-857, § 1, 72 Stat. 1219), contained in Subchapter I of Chapter 41, was repealed by Act Sept. 19, 1962, P. L. 87-675, § 1(a), 76 Stat. 558. It related to information.

Amendments:
1962. Act Sept. 19, 1962, redesignated this section as § 2004; it formerly appeared as § 2013 in Subchapter II of Chapter 41.
1966. Act March 3, 1966 (effective 3/3/66, as provided by § 12(a) of such Act), inserted "or of service after January 31, 1955".
1972. Act Oct. 24, 1972 (effective 90 days after 10/24/72, as provided by § 601(b) of such Act, which appears as 38 USCS § 4101 note), substituted this section for one which read:

"§ 2004. Cooperation of Federal agencies

"All Federal agencies shall furnish the Secretary such records, statistics, or information as may be deemed necessary or appropriate in administering the provisions of this chapter, and shall otherwise cooperate with the Secretary in providing continuous employment opportunities for veterans of any war, or of service after January 31, 1955.".
1976. Act Oct. 15, 1976 (effective 12/1/76, as provided by § 703(c) of such Act, which appears as 38 USCS § 3693 note), inserted "or eligible persons", and substituted "such representative's" for "his".
1988. Act May 20, 1988 (effective on enactment as provided by § 16(a) of such Act, and applicable as provided by § 16(b)(1) of such Act, which appears as 38 USCS § 3104 note) substituted this section for one which read:

"§ 2004. Employees of local offices

"Except as may be determined by the Secretary of Labor based on a demonstrated lack of need for such services, there shall be assigned by the administrative head of the employment service in each State one or more employees, preferably eligible veterans or eligible persons, on the staffs of local employment services offices, whose services shall be fully devoted to discharging the duties prescribed for the veterans' employment representative and such representative's assistants.".
1989. Act Dec. 18, 1989, in subsec. (b)(7), substituted "Department of Veterans Affairs" for "Veterans' Administration".
1991. Act March 22, 1991, in subsec. (a), in para. (1), in the introductory matter, substituted "appointment" for "assignment" in two places, in subpara. (C), substituted "appointment" for "assignment", and, in para. (4), substituted "appointment" for "assigning"; and deleted subsec. (d), which read: "(d) Local veterans' employment representatives shall be assigned, in accordance with this section, by the administrative head of the employment service in each State after consultation with the Director for Veterans' Employment and Training.".

Act Aug. 6, 1991, redesignated this section, formerly 38 USCS § 2004, as 38 USCS § 4104, and amended the references in this section to reflect the redesignations made by § 5(a) of such Act (see Table III preceding 38 USCS § 101).

Other provisions:
Pilot program to integrate and streamline functions of local veterans'

38 USCS § 4104

employment representatives. Act Oct. 9, 1996, P. L. 104-275, Title III, Subtitle A, § 303, 110 Stat. 3332, provides:

"(a) Authority to conduct pilot program. In order to assess the effects on the timeliness and quality of services to veterans resulting from re-focusing the staff resources of local veterans' employment representatives, the Secretary of Labor may conduct a pilot program under which the primary responsibilities of local veterans' employment representatives will be case management and the provision and facilitation of direct employment and training services to veterans.

"(b) Authorities under Chapter 41. To implement the pilot program, the Secretary of Labor may suspend or limit application of those provisions of chapter 41 of title 38, United States Code [38 USCS §§ 4101 et seq.] (other than sections 4104(b)(1) and (c)) that pertain to the Local Veterans' Employment Representative Program in States designated by the Secretary under subsection (d), except that the Secretary may use the authority of such chapter, as the Secretary may determine, in conjunction with the authority of this section, to carry out the pilot program. The Secretary may collect such data as the Secretary considers necessary for assessment of the pilot program. The Secretary shall measure and evaluate on a continuing basis the effectiveness of the pilot program in achieving its stated goals in general, and in achieving such goals in relation to their cost, their effect on related programs, and their structure and mechanisms for delivery of services.

"(c) Targeted veterans. Within the pilot program, eligible veterans who are among groups most in need of intensive services, including disabled veterans, economically disadvantaged veterans, and veterans separated within the previous four years from active military, naval, or air service shall be given priority for service by local veterans' employment representatives. Priority for the provision of service shall be given first to disabled veterans and then to the other categories of veterans most in need of intensive services in accordance with priorities determined by the Secretary of Labor in consultation with appropriate State labor authorities.

"(d) States designated. The pilot program shall be limited to not more than five States to be designated by the Secretary of Labor.

"(e) Reports to Congress. (1) Not later than one year after the date of the enactment of this Act, the Secretary of Labor shall submit to the Committees on Veterans' Affairs of the Senate and the House of Representatives an interim report describing in detail the development and implementation of the pilot program on a State by State basis.

"(2) Not later than 120 days after the expiration of this section under subsection (h), the Secretary of Labor shall submit to the Committees on Veterans' Affairs of the Senate and the House of Representatives a final report evaluating the results of the pilot program and make recommendations based on the evaluation, which may include legislative recommendations.

"(f) Definitions. For the purposes of this section:

"(1) The term 'veteran' has the meaning given such term by section 101(2) of title 38, United States Code.

"(2) The term 'disabled veteran' has the meaning given such term by section 4211(3) of such title.

"(3) The term 'active military, naval, or air service' has the meaning given such term by section 101(24) of such title.

READJUSTMENT BENEFITS 38 USCS § 4104A

"(g) Allocation of funds. Any amount otherwise available for fiscal year 1997, 1998, or 1999 to carry out section 4102A(b)(5) of title 38, United States Code, with respect to a State designated by the Secretary of Labor pursuant to subsection (d) shall be available to carry out the pilot program during that fiscal year with respect to that State.

"(h) Expiration date. The authority to carry out the pilot program under this section shall expire on October 1, 1999.".

CODE OF FEDERAL REGULATIONS

Employment and Training Administration, Department of Labor—Administration provisions governing the Job Service System, 20 CFR Part 658.

CROSS REFERENCES

This section is referred to in 5 USCS § 5948; 38 USCS §§ 4102A, 4103A, 4104A, 4106, 4107.

RESEARCH GUIDE

Am Jur:
77 Am Jur 2d, Veterans and Veterans' Laws § 111.

§ 4104A. Performance of disabled veterans' outreach program specialists and local veterans' employment representatives

(a)(1) Subject to paragraph (2) of this subsection, each State employment agency shall develop and apply standards for the performance of disabled veterans' outreach program specialists appointed under section 4103A(a) of this title and local veterans' employment representatives assigned under section 4104(b) of this title.

(2)(A) Such standards shall be consistent with the duties and functions specified in section 4103A(b) of this title with respect to such specialists and section 4104(b)(1) through (12) of this title with respect to such representatives.

  (B) In developing such standards, the State employment agency—

    (i) shall take into account (I) the prototype developed under paragraph (3) of this subsection, and (II) the comments submitted under clause (ii) of this subparagraph by the Director for Veterans' Employment and Training for the State;

    (ii) shall submit to such Director proposed standards for comment;

    (iii) may take into account the State's personnel merit system requirements and other local circumstances and requirements; and

    (iv) may request the assistance of such Director.

  (C) Such standards shall include as one of the measures of the performance of such a specialist the extent to which the specialist, in serving as a case manager under section 14(b)(1)(A) of the Veterans' Job Training Act (29 U.S.C. 1721 note), facilitates rates of successful completion of training by veterans participating in programs of job training under the Act.

  (3)(A) The Secretary, after consultation with State employment agencies or

38 USCS § 4104A

their representatives, or both, shall provide to such agencies a prototype of performance standards for use by such agencies in the development of performance standards under subsection (a)(1) of this section.

(B) Each Director for Veterans' Employment and Training—

(i) shall, upon the request of the State employment agency under paragraph (2)(B)(iv) of this subsection, provide appropriate assistance in the development of performance standards,

(ii) may, within 30 days after receiving proposed standards under paragraph (2)(B)(ii) of this subsection, provide comments on the proposed standards, particularly regarding the consistency of the proposed standards with such prototype.

(b)(1) Directors for Veterans' Employment and Training and Assistant Directors for Veterans' Employment and Training shall regularly monitor the performance of the specialists and representatives referred to in subsection (a)(1) of this section through the application of the standards required to be prescribed by subsection (a)(1).

(2) A Director for Veterans' Employment and Training for a State may submit to the head of the employment service in the State recommendations and comments in connection with each annual performance rating of such specialists and representatives in the State.

(Added May 20, 1988, P. L. 100-323, § 4(a)(1), 102 Stat. 562; Aug. 6, 1991, P. L. 102-83, § 5(a), (c)(1), 105 Stat. 406.)

HISTORY; ANCILLARY LAWS AND DIRECTIVES

Effective date of section:

Act May 20, 1988, P. L. 100-323, § 16(b)(2), 102 Stat. 575, which appears as 38 USCS § 3104 note, provides that this section is effective on the 60th day after enactment.

Amendments:

1991. Act Aug. 6, 1991, redesignated this section, formerly 38 USCS § 2004A, as 38 USCS § 4104A, and amended the references in this section to reflect the redesignations made by § 5(a) of such Act (see Table III preceding 38 USCS § 101).

Other provisions:

Performance standards. Act May 20, 1988, P. L. 100-323, § 4(a)(2), 102 Stat. 563, effective on the 60th day after enactment, as provided by § 16(b)(2) of such Act, which appears as 38 USCS § 3104 note, provides: "Each State employment agency (A) shall develop and promulgate standards under section 2004A [now § 4104A] of title 38, United States Code, as added by paragraph (1) of this subsection, as soon as feasible, and in doing so (B) shall submit proposed standards to the Director for Veterans' Employment and Training for the State not later than 12 months after the date on which the Secretary provides the agency with prototype standards under subsection (a)(3)(A) of such section, and (C) shall adopt final standards not later than 90 days after submitting the proposed standards to the Director for Veterans' Employment and Training for comment under subsection (a)(3)(B)(ii) of such section.''.

CODE OF FEDERAL REGULATIONS

Employment and Training Administration, Department of Labor—Administration provisions governing the Job Service System, 20 CFR Part 658.

RESEARCH GUIDE

Am Jur:
77 Am Jur 2d, Veterans and Veterans' Laws §§ 110, 111.

§ 4105. Cooperation of Federal agencies

(a) All Federal agencies shall furnish the Secretary such records, statistics, or information as the Secretary may deem necessary or appropriate in administering the provisions of this chapter [38 USCS §§ 4100 et seq.], and shall otherwise cooperate with the Secretary in providing continuous employment and training opportunities for eligible veterans and eligible persons.

(b) For the purpose of assisting the Secretary and the Secretary of Veterans Affairs in identifying employers with potential job training opportunities under the Veterans' Job Training Act (Public Law 98-77; 29 U.S.C. 1721 note) and otherwise in order to carry out this chapter [38 USCS §§ 4100 et seq.], the Secretary of Defense shall provide, not more than 30 days after the date of the enactment of this subsection [enacted May 20, 1988], the Secretary and the Secretary of Veterans Affairs with any list maintained by the Secretary of Defense of employers participating in the National Committee for Employer Support of the Guard and Reserve and shall provide, on the 15th day of each month thereafter, updated information regarding the list.

(Sept. 2, 1958, P. L. 85-857, § 1, 72 Stat. 1222; Sept. 19, 1962, P. L. 87-675, § 1(a), (c), 76 Stat. 558; Oct. 24, 1972, P. L. 92-540, Title V, § 502(a), 86 Stat. 1095; Dec. 3, 1974, P. L. 93-508, Title IV, § 401(d), 88 Stat. 1592; Oct. 15, 1976, P. L. 94-502, Title VI, § 606(3), 90 Stat. 2405; May 20, 1988, P. L. 100-323, §§ 6(a), 15(a)(2), 102 Stat. 564, 574; Dec. 18, 1989, P. L. 101-237, Title IV, § 423(b)(8)(A), 103 Stat. 209; Aug. 6, 1991, P. L. 102-83, § 5(a), 105 Stat. 406.)

HISTORY; ANCILLARY LAWS AND DIRECTIVES

Explanatory notes:
A prior § 4105 (Act Sept. 2, 1958, P. L. 85-857, § 1, 72 Stat. 1244; Aug. 6, 1962, P. L. 87-574, § 4(1), 76 Stat. 308; Nov. 7, 1966, P. L. 89-785, Title I, § 105, 80 Stat. 1369; Oct. 22, 1975, P. L. 94-123, § 5(b), 89 Stat. 675; Oct. 21, 1976, P. L. 94-581, Title I, § 110(4), Title II, §§ 205(e), 209(a)(1), (2), (4), (c)(2), 90 Stat. 2848, 2859, 2860, 2861; Nov. 23, 1977, P. L. 95-201, § 4(a)(1), 91 Stat. 1430; Dec. 20, 1979, P. L. 96-151, Title III, § 302(b), 93 Stat. 1096; Oct. 12, 1982, P. L. 97-295, § 4(81), 96 Stat. 1311; Nov. 21, 1983, P. L. 98-160, Title II, § 202, 97 Stat. 1000) was repealed by Act May 7, 1991, P. L. 102-40, Title IV, § 401(a)(3), 105 Stat. 210. Such section provided for the qualifications of appointees.

Provisions similar to those contained in this section were contained in former 38 USCS § 2004 prior to the general amendment of this chapter by Act Oct. 24, 1972, P. L. 92-540, Title V, § 502, 86 Stat. 1094.

A prior § 2005 (Act Sept. 2, 1958, P. L. 85-857, § 1, 72 Stat. 1219), contained in Subchapter I of Chapter 41, was repealed by Act Sept. 19, 1962, P. L. 87-675, § 1(a), 76 Stat. 558. It related to penalties.

Amendments:

1962. Act Sept. 19, 1962, redesignated this section, which formerly appeared as § 2014 in Subchapter II of Chapter 41,as § 2005 and substituted "chapter" for "subchapter".

1972. Act Oct. 24, 1972 (effective 90 days after 10/24/72, as provided by § 601(b) of such Act, which appears as 38 USCS § 4101 note), substituted new catchline and section for ones which read:

"§ 2005. Estimate of funds for administration

"The Secretary shall estimate the funds necessary for the proper and efficient administration of this chapter; such estimated sums shall include the annual amounts necessary for salaries, rents, printing and binding, travel and communications. Sums thus estimated shall be included as a special item in the annual budget of the Bureau of Employment Security. Any funds appropriated pursuant to this special item as contained in the budget of the Bureau of Employment Security shall not be available for any purpose other than that for which they were appropriated, except with the approval of the Secretary.".

1974. Act Dec. 3, 1974 (effective 12/3/74, as provided by § 503 of such Act, which appears as 38 USCS § 3452 note), inserted "and eligible persons".

1976. Act Oct. 15, 1976 (effective 12/1/76, as provided by § 703(c) of such Act, which appears as 38 USCS § 3693 note), substituted "the Secretary" for "he" preceding "may deem".

1988. Act May 20, 1988 (effective on enactment as provided by § 16(a) of such Act, which appears as 38 USCS § 3104 note) substituted "Secretary" for "Secretary of Labor" preceding "such records".

Such Act further (effective on the 60th day after enactment, as provided by § 16(b)(2) of such Act, which appears as 38 USCS § 3104 note) designated the existing provisions as subsec. (a); and added subsec. (b).

1989. Act Dec. 18, 1989, in subsec. (b), substituted "Secretary of Veterans Affairs" for "Administrator" wherever appearing.

1991. Act Aug. 6, 1991, redesignated this section, formerly 38 USCS § 2005, as 38 USCS § 4105.

CODE OF FEDERAL REGULATIONS

Employment and Training Administration, Department of Labor—Administration provisions governing the Job Service System, 20 CFR Part 658.

RESEARCH GUIDE

Am Jur:

37 Am Jur 2d, Fraud and Deceit § 11.

77 Am Jur 2d, Veterans and Veterans' Laws § 106.

Annotations:

Availability, under 28 USCS § 1442(a)(1), to one who is not an "officer of the United States or any agency thereof" of right to remove state action to federal court. 64 ALR Fed 146.

§ 4106. Estimate of funds for administration; authorization of appropriations

(a) The Secretary shall estimate the funds necessary for the proper and efficient administration of this chapter [38 USCS §§ 4100 et seq.] and chapters 42 and 43 of this title [38 USCS §§ 4211 et seq. and [4321] 2021 et seq.]. Such estimated sums shall include the annual amounts necessary for salaries, rents, printing and binding, travel, and communications. Sums thus estimated shall be included as a special item in the annual budget for the Department of Labor. Estimated funds necessary for proper counseling, placement, and training services to eligible veterans and eligible persons provided by the various State public employment service agencies shall each be separately identified in the budgets of those agencies as approved by the Department of Labor. Funds estimated pursuant to the first sentence of this subsection shall include amounts necessary in all of the States for the purposes specified in paragraph (5) of section 4102A(b) of this title and to fund the National Veterans' Employment and Training Services Institute under section 4109 of this title and shall be approved by the Secretary only if the level of funding proposed is in compliance with such sections. Each budget submission with respect to such funds shall include separate listings of the amount for the National Veterans' Employment and Training Services Institute and of the proposed numbers, by State, of disabled veterans' outreach program specialists appointed under section 4103A of this title and local veterans' employment representatives assigned under section 4104 of this title, together with information demonstrating the compliance of such budget submission with the funding requirements specified in the preceding sentence.

(b) There are authorized to be appropriated such sums as may be necessary for the proper and efficient administration of this chapter [38 USCS §§ 4100 et seq.].

(c) In the event that the regular appropriations Act making appropriations for administrative expenses for the Department of Labor with respect to any fiscal year does not specify an amount for the purposes specified in subsection (b) of this section for that fiscal year, then of the amounts appropriated in such Act there shall be available only for the purposes specified in subsection (b) of this section such amount as was set forth in the budget estimate submitted pursuant to subsection (a) of this section.

(d) Any funds made available pursuant to subsections (b) and (c) of this section shall not be available for any purpose other than those specified in such subsections.

(Added Oct. 24, 1972, P. L. 92-540, Title V, § 502(a), 86 Stat. 1096; Dec. 3, 1974, P. L. 93-508, Title IV, § 401(e), 88 Stat. 1592; Oct. 15, 1976, P. L. 94-502, Title VI, § 603, 90 Stat. 2404; Oct. 14, 1982, P. L. 97-306, Title III, § 306, 96 Stat. 1440; May 20, 1988, P. L. 100-323, §§ 2(b), (c), (e)(2), 15(a)(2), 102 Stat. 558, 559, 574; Aug. 6, 1991, P. L. 102-83, § 5(a), (c)(1), 105 Stat. 406.)

38 USCS § 4106   VETERANS' BENEFITS

HISTORY; ANCILLARY LAWS AND DIRECTIVES

Explanatory notes:
A prior § 4106 (Act Sept. 2, 1958, P. L. 85-857, § 1, 72 Stat. 1245; Nov. 7, 1966, P. L. 89-785, Title I, § 106, 80 Stat. 1369; Oct. 22, 1975, P. L. 94-123, § 5(c), 89 Stat. 675; Oct. 21, 1976, P. L. 94-581, Title I, § 110(5), title II, § 209(a)(1), (b)(1), 90 Stat. 2848, 2860, 2861; Dec. 20, 1979, P. L. 96-151, Title III, § 303, 93 Stat. 1096; Nov. 21, 1983, P. L. 98-160, Title II, § 203(a), 97 Stat. 1000; Oct. 28, 1986, P. L. 99-576, Title VII, § 701(86), 100 Stat. 3298; May 20, 1988, P. L. 100-322, Title II, Part C, § 221, 102 Stat. 531; Dec. 18, 1989, P. L. 101-237, Title II, § 203, 103 Stat. 2067) was repealed by Act May 7, 1991, P. L. 102-40, Title IV, § 401(a)(3), 105 Stat. 210. Such section provided for period of appointments, and promotions.

Provisions similar to those contained in this section were contained in former 38 USCS § 2005 prior to the general amendment of this chapter by Act Oct. 24, 1972, P. L. 92-540, Title V, § 502, 86 Stat. 1094.

A prior § 2006 (Act Sept. 2, 1958, P. L. 85-857, § 1, 72 Stat. 1219), contained in Subchapter I of Chapter 41, was repealed by Act Sept. 19, 1962, P. L. 87-675, § 1(a), 76 Stat. 558. It related to regulations.

Effective date of section:
Act Oct. 24, 1972, P. L. 92-540, Title VI, § 601(b), 86 Stat. 1099, provided that this section is effective 90 days after Oct. 24, 1972.

Amendments:
1974. Act Dec. 3, 1974 (effective 12/3/74, as provided by § 503 of such Act, which appears as 38 USCS § 3452 note), in subsec. (a), substituted "eligible veterans and eligible persons" for "veterans".

1976. Act Oct. 15, 1976 (effective 12/1/76, as provided by § 703(c) of such Act, which appears as 38 USCS § 3693 note), in subsec. (a), inserted "each".

1982. Act Oct. 14, 1982, in subsec. (a), inserted "and chapters 42 and 43 of this title" and added the sentences beginning "Funds estimated . . . .", "Each budget submission. . . ." and "The Secretary shall carry. . . ."; and, in subsec. (d), inserted ", upon the recommendation of the Assistant Secretary of Labor for Veterans' Employment,".

1988. Act May 20, 1988 (effective on enactment as provided by § 16(a) of such Act, which appears as 38 USCS § 3104 note), in subsec. (a), substituted "in all of the States for the purposes specified in paragraph (5) of section 2002A(b) of this title and to fund the National Veterans' Employment and Training Services Institute under section 2009" for "to fund the disabled veterans' outreach program under section 2003A", substituted "such sections" for "such section", and substituted the sentence beginning "Each budget submission . . . ." for "Each budget submission with respect to such funds shall include a separate listing of the proposed number, by State, for disabled veterans outreach program specialists appointed under such section. The Secretary shall carry out this subsection through the Assistant Secretary for Veterans' Employment"; and, in subsec. (d), deleted ", except with the approval of the Secretary of Labor, upon the recommendation of the Assistant Secretary of Labor for Veterans' Employment, based on a demonstrated lack of need for such funds for such purposes." following "subsections".

Such Act further (effective on enactment as provided by § 16(a) of such

Act, which appears as 38 USCS § 3104 note) in subsec. (a), substituted "Secretary" for "Secretary of Labor" in two places.

1991. Act Aug. 6, 1991, redesignated this section, formerly 38 USCS § 2006, as 38 USCS § 4106, and amended the references in this section to reflect the redesignations made by § 5(a) of such Act (see Table III preceding 38 USCS § 101).

CODE OF FEDERAL REGULATIONS

Employment and Training Administration, Department of Labor—Administration provisions governing the Job Service System, 20 CFR Part 658.

CROSS REFERENCES

This section is referred to in 38 USCS § 4107.

RESEARCH GUIDE

Am Jur:
77 Am Jur 2d, Veterans and Veterans' Laws § 106.

Annotations:
Availability, under 28 USCS § 1442(a)(1), to one who is not an "officer of the United States or any agency thereof" of right to remove state action to federal court. 64 ALR Fed 146.

§ 4107. Administrative controls; annual report

(a) The Secretary shall establish administrative controls for the following purposes:

(1) To insure that each eligible veteran, especially veterans of the Vietnam era and disabled veterans and each eligible person, who requests assistance under this chapter [38 USCS §§ 4100 et seq.] shall promptly be placed in a satisfactory job or job training opportunity or receive some other specific form of assistance designed to enhance such veteran's and eligible person's employment prospects substantially, such as individual job development or employment counseling services.

(2) To determine whether or not the employment agencies in each State have committed the necessary staff to insure that the provisions of this chapter [38 USCS §§ 4100 et seq.], are carried out; and to arrange for necessary corrective action where staff resources have been determined by the Secretary to be inadequate.

(b) The Secretary shall establish definitive performance standards for determining compliance by the State public employment service agencies with the provisions of this chapter [38 USCS §§ 4100 et seq.] and chapter 42 of this title [38 USCS §§ 4211 et seq.]. A full report as to the extent and reasons for any noncompliance by any such State agency during any fiscal year, together with the agency's plan for corrective action during the succeeding year, shall be included in the annual report of the Secretary required by subsection (c) of this section.

(c) Not later than February 1 of each year, the Secretary shall report to the Committees on Veterans' Affairs of the Senate and the House of Representatives on the success during the preceding program year of the Department of Labor and its affiliated State employment service agencies in carrying out the provisions of this chapter and programs for the provision of employment and training services to meet the needs of eligible veterans and eligible persons. The report shall include—

(1) specification, by State and by age group, of the numbers of eligible veterans, veterans of the Vietnam era, disabled veterans, special disabled veterans, and eligible persons who registered for assistance with the public employment service system and, for each of such categories, the numbers referred to and placed in permanent and other jobs, the numbers referred to and placed in jobs and job training programs supported by the Federal Government, the number counseled, and the number who received some, and the number who received no, reportable service;

(2) a comparison of the job placement rate for each of the categories of veterans and persons described in clause (1) of this subsection with the job placement rate for nonveterans of the same age groups registered for assistance with the public employment system in each State;

(3) any determination made by the Secretary during the preceding fiscal year under section 4106 of this title or subsection (a)(2) of this section and a statement of the reasons for such determination;

(4) a report on activities carried out during the preceding program year under sections 4103A and 4104 of this title; and

(5) a report on the operation during the preceding program year of programs for the provision of employment and training services designed to meet the needs of eligible veterans and eligible persons, including an evaluation of the effectiveness of such programs during such program year in meeting the requirements of section 4102A(b) of this title, the efficiency with which services were provided through such programs during such year, and such recommendations for further legislative action (including the need for any changes in the formulas governing the appointment of disabled veterans' outreach program specialists under section 4103A(a)(2) of this title and the assignment of local veterans' employment representatives under section 4104(b) of this title and the allocation of funds for the support of such specialists and representatives) relating to veterans' employment and training as the Secretary considers appropriate.

(Added Oct. 24, 1972, P.L. 92-540, Title V, § 502(a), 86 Stat. 1096; Dec. 3, 1974, P. L. 93-508, Title IV, § 401(f), 88 Stat. 1592; Oct. 15, 1976, P. L. 94-502, Title VI, § 604, 90 Stat. 2404; Nov. 23, 1977, P. L. 95-202, Title III, § 309(b), 91 Stat. 1446; Oct. 17, 1980, P. L. 96-466, Title V, § 507, 94 Stat. 2205; Oct. 14, 1982, P. L. 97-306, Title III, § 307, 96 Stat. 1440; May 20, 1988, P. L. 100-323, §§ 2(d), 15(a)(2), 102 Stat. 558, 574; Aug. 6, 1991, P. L. 102-83, § 5(a), (c)(1), 105 Stat. 406.)

HISTORY; ANCILLARY LAWS AND DIRECTIVES

Explanatory notes:
A prior § 4107 (Act Sept. 2, 1958, P. L. 85-857, § 1, 72 Stat. 1245; July 1,

READJUSTMENT BENEFITS 38 USCS § 4107

1960, P. L. 86-568, Title I, Part B, § 114(f), 74 Stat. 301; Oct. 11, 1962, P. L. 87-793, Part II, Title IV, § 802, 76 Stat. 860; Aug. 14, 1964, P. L. 88-426, Title I, § 118, 78 Stat. 410; Oct. 29, 1965, P. L. 89-301, § 7, 79 Stat. 1117; July 18, 1966, P. L. 89-504, Title I, § 105, 80 Stat. 291; Nov. 7, 1966, P. L. 89-785, Title I, § 107(a), 80 Stat. 1370; Dec. 16, 1967, P. L. 90-206, Title II, § 208, 81 Stat. 631; Oct. 22, 1970, P. L. 91-496, § 2(a), 84 Stat. 1092; Aug. 2, 1973, P. L. 93-82, Title II, § 203, 87 Stat. 188; Oct. 22, 1975, P. L. 94-123, §§ 2(b), 5(d), 89 Stat. 669, 675; Oct. 21, 1976, P. L. 94-581, Title I, § 110(6), Title II, §§ 209(a)(1), (2), (b)(2), (c)(3), 210(c)(4), 90 Stat. 2848, 2860, 2861, 2863; Nov. 23, 1977, P. L. 95-201, § 5(a)(1), (2), 91 Stat. 1432; June 13, 1979, P. L. 96-22, Title V, § 504, 93 Stat. 65; Aug. 26, 1980, P. L. 96-330, Title I, Part A, § 105(c), Part B, §§ 111, 112, 94 Stat. 1036; Oct. 7, 1980, P. L. 96-385, Title V, § 508(a), 94 Stat. 1538; Sept. 8, 1982, P. L. 97-251, § 2(a)-(c), 96 Stat. 711; Oct. 12, 1982, P. L. 97-295, § 4(82), 96 Stat. 1311; Nov. 21, 1983, P. L. 98-160, Title II, § 204, 97 Stat. 1001; Oct. 19, 1984, P. L. 98-528, Title I, §§ 101(b), 109, 98 Stat. 2688, 2691; Oct. 28, 1986, P. L. 99-576, Title VII, § 701(87), 100 Stat. 3299; May 20, 1988, P. L. 100-322, Title II, Part B, §§ 21(b), 213, 214(a), (b), 217, 102 Stat. 514, 516, 530; Nov. 18, 1988, P. L. 100-687, Div B, Title XV, § 1506(b)(2), 102 Stat. 4136; Dec. 18, 1989, P. L. 101-237, Title II, §§ 204, 205(a), 103 Stat. 2067; Aug. 15, 1990, P. L. 101-366, Title I, §§ 101(c), 102(c), 103, 104 Stat. 430, 436, 437) was repealed by Act May 7, 1991, P. L. 102-40, Title IV, § 401(a)(3), 105 Stat. 210. Such section provided for grades and pay scales.

A prior § 2007 (Act Sept. 2, 1958, P. L. 85-857, § 1, 72 Stat. 1220; June 25, 1959, P. L. 86-70, § 29(b), 73 Stat. 148; July 12, 1960, P. L. 86-624, § 25(c), 74 Stat. 418), contained in Subchapter I of Chapter 41, was repealed by Act Sept. 19, 1962, P. L. 87-675, § 1(a), 76 Stat. 558. It contained definitions of Korean conflict veterans, unemployment compensation, and State.

Effective date of section:
Act Oct. 24, 1972, P. L. 92-540, Title VI, § 601(b), 86 Stat. 1099, provided that this section is effective 90 days after Oct. 24, 1972.

Amendments:
1974. Act Dec. 3, 1974 (effective 12/3/74, as provided by § 503 of such Act, which appears as 38 USCS § 3452 note), in subsec. (a)(1), inserted "and each eligible person"; redesignated subsec. (b) as subsec. (c); added new subsec. (b); and in subsec. (c), as so redesignated, substituted "other eligible veterans, and eligible persons" for "and other eligible veterans".

1976. Act Oct. 15, 1976 (effective 12/1/76, as provided by § 703(c) of such Act, which appears as 38 USCS § 3693 note), in subsec. (a)(1), substituted "such veteran's and eligible person's" for "his"; and in subsec. (c), inserted "and public service employment" and substituted ", 2006, or 2007(a)" for "or 2006".

1977. Act Nov. 23, 1977 (effective 11/23/77, as provided by § 501 of such Act, which appears as 38 USCS § 101 note), in subsec. (c), purported to substitute "2004" for "2001"; however, such amendment could not be executed as "2001" did not appear in the text of subsec. (c).

1980. Act Oct. 17, 1980 (effective 10/1/80, as provided by § 802(e) of such Act, which appears as 38 USCS § 4101 note), in subsec. (a)(1), substituted "veterans of the Vietnam era and disabled veterans" for "those veterans who have been recently discharged or released from active duty"; and in subsec. (c), substituted "The report shall include, by State, specification of the numbers of eligible veterans, veterans of the Vietnam era, disabled veterans, special disabled veterans, and eligible persons who registered for assistance with the public employment service system and, of each of such categories, the number referred to jobs, the number placed in permanent jobs as defined by the Secretary, the number referred to and the number placed in employment and job training programs supported by the Federal Government, the number counseled, and the number who received some reportable service." for "The report shall include, by State, the number of recently discharged or released eligible veterans, veterans with service-connected disabilities, other eligible veterans, and eligible persons who requested assistance through the public employment service and, of these, the number placed in suitable employment or job training opportunities or who were otherwise assisted, with separate reference to occupational training and public service employment under appropriate Federal law.".

1982. Act Oct. 14, 1982, in subsec. (c), added "The report shall also include a report on activities carried out under section 2003A of this title.".

1988. Act May 20, 1988 (effective on enactment as provided by § 16(a) of such Act, which appears as 38 USCS § 3104 note) in subsec. (a), in the introductory matter and in para. (2), and in subsec. (b), substituted "Secretary" for "Secretary of Labor" wherever appearing; and substituted subsec. (c) for one which read: "The Secretary of Labor shall report annually to the Congress on the success of the Department of Labor and its affiliated State employment service agencies in carrying out the provisions of this chapter. The report shall include, by State, specification of the numbers of eligible veterans, veterans of the Vietnam era, disabled veterans, special disabled veterans, and eligible persons who registered for assistance with the public employment service system and, of each of such categories, the number referred to jobs, the number placed in permanent jobs as defined by the Secretary, the number referred to and the number placed in employment and job training programs supported by the Federal Government, the number counseled, and the number who received some reportable service.".

1991. Act Aug. 6, 1991, redesignated this section, formerly 38 USCS § 2007, as 38 USCS § 4107, and amended the references in this section to reflect the redesignations made by § 5(a) of such Act (see Table III preceding 38 USCS § 101).

Other provisions:

Requirement for Bureau of Labor Statistics to publish certain unemployment information annually. Act Oct. 17, 1980, P. L. 96-466, Title V, § 513, 94 Stat. 2207 (effective 10/1/80, as provided by § 802(e) of such Act), provided:

"(a) When the Commissioner of the Bureau of Labor Statistics publishes annual labor-market statistics relating specifically to veterans who served in the Armed Forces during the Vietnam era, the Commissioner shall also publish separate labor-market statistics on the same subject matter which apply only to veterans who served in the Vietnam theatre of operations. When the Commissioner of the Bureau of Labor Statistics publishes labor-market statistics which relate specifically to veterans who served in the Armed Forces during the Vietnam era in addition to those statistics published on an annual basis to which the preceding sentence applies, the Commissioner shall also, if feasible, publish separate labor-market statistics on the same subject matter which apply only to veterans who served in the Vietnam theatre of operations.

"(b) For the purposes of this section, veterans who during the Vietnam era served in Vietnam, in air missions over Vietnam, or in naval missions in the waters adjacent to Vietnam shall be considered to be veterans who served in the Vietnam theatre of operations.".

CODE OF FEDERAL REGULATIONS

Employment and Training Administration, Department of Labor—Administration provisions governing the Job Service System, 20 CFR Part 658.

CROSS REFERENCES

This section is referred to in 38 USCS §§ 4103, 4212.

RESEARCH GUIDE

Am Jur:
77 Am Jur 2d, Veterans and Veterans' Laws § 106.

§ 4108. Cooperation and coordination

(a) In carrying out the Secretary's responsibilities under this chapter [38 USCS §§ 4100 et seq.], the Secretary shall from time to time consult with the Secretary of Veterans Affairs and keep the Secretary of Veterans Affairs fully advised of activities carried out and all data gathered pursuant to this chapter to insure maximum cooperation and coordination between the Department of Labor and the Department of Veterans Affairs.

(b) The Secretary of Veterans Affairs shall provide to appropriate employment service offices and Department of Labor offices, as designated by the Secretary, on a monthly or more frequent basis, the name and address of each employer located in the areas served by such offices that offer a program of job training which has been approved by the Secretary of Veterans Affairs under section 7 of the Veterans' Job Training Act (29 U.S.C. 1721 note).

(Added Oct. 24, 1972, P. L. 92-540, Title V, § 502(a), 86 Stat. 1097; Oct. 15, 1976, P. L. 94-502, Title VI, § 606(4), 90 Stat. 2405; May 20, 1988, P. L. 100-323, §§ 6(b)(1), (2)(A), 15(a)(2), 102 Stat. 564, 574; Dec. 18, 1989, P. L. 101-237, Title IV, § 423(b)(8), 103 Stat. 2093; Aug. 6, 1991, P. L. 102-83, § 5(a), 105 Stat. 406.)

HISTORY; ANCILLARY LAWS AND DIRECTIVES

Explanatory notes:
A prior § 4108 (Act Sept. 2, 1958, P. L. 85-857, § 1, 72 Stat. 1246; July 1, 1960, P. L. 86-568, Title I, Part B, § 114(g), 74 Stat. 301; Aug. 6, 1962, P. L. 87-574, § 3, 76 Stat. 308; Oct. 11, 1962, P. L. 87-793, Part II, Title IV, § 803(a), 76 Stat. 860; Aug. 2, 1973, P. L. 93-82, Title II, § 204(a), 87 Stat. 190; Oct. 22, 1975, P. L. 94-123, § 5(e), 89 Stat. 675; Oct. 21, 1976, P. L. 94-581, Title I, § 110(7), Title II, §§ 205(f), 209(a)(1), (2), (c)(4), 210(c)(5), 90 Stat. 2849, 2859, 2860, 2862, 2864; June 13, 1979, P. L. 96-22, Title

38 USCS § 4108

V, § 501, 93 Stat. 64; Aug. 26, 1980, P. L. 96-330, Title I, Part B, § 113(a), 94 Stat. 1038; Oct. 12, 1982, P. L. 97-295, § 4(83), 96 Stat. 1312; Dec. 18, 1989, P. L. 101-237, Title II, § 206(a), 103 Stat. 2067) was repealed by Act May 7, 1991, P. L. 102-40, Title IV, § 401(a)(3), 105 Stat. 210. Such section provided for personnel administration.

A prior § 2008 (Act Sept. 2, 1958, P. L. 85-857, § 1, 72 Stat. 1220), contained in Subchapter I of Chapter 41, was repealed by Act Sept. 19, 1962, P. L. 87-675, § 1(a), 76 Stat. 558. It related to nonduplication of benefits.

Effective date of section:
Act Oct. 24, 1972, P. L. 92-540, Title VI, § 601(b), 86 Stat. 1099, provided that this section is effective 90 days after Oct. 24, 1972.

Amendments:
1976. Act Oct. 15, 1976 (effective 12/1/76, as provided by § 703(c) of such Act, which appears as 38 USCS § 3693 note), substituted "the Secretary's" for "his" and substituted "the Administrator" for "him" following "keep".

1988. Act May 20, 1988 (effective on enactment as provided by § 16(a) of such Act, which appears as 38 USCS § 3104 note), substituted "Secretary" for "Secretary of Labor".

Such Act further (effective on the 60th day after enactment, as provided by § 16(b)(2) of such Act, which appears as 38 USCS § 1504 note) substituted the section heading for one which read: "§ 2008. Cooperation and coordination with the Veterans' Administration"; designated the existing provisions as subsec. (a); and added subsec. (b).

1989. Act Dec. 18, 1989, in subsec. (a), substituted "Department of Veterans Affairs" for "Veterans' Administration"; and in subsecs. (a) and (b), substituted "Secretary of Veterans Affairs" for "Administrator", wherever appearing.

1991. Act Aug. 6, 1991, redesignated this section, formerly 38 USCS § 2008, as 38 USCS § 4108.

CODE OF FEDERAL REGULATIONS

Employment and Training Administration, Department of Labor—Administration provisions governing the Job Service System, 20 CFR Part 658.

RESEARCH GUIDE

Am Jur:
77 Am Jur 2d, Veterans and Veterans' Laws § 106.

Annotations:
Availability, under 28 USCS § 1442(a)(1), to one who is not an "officer of the United States or any agency thereof" of right to remove state action to federal court. 64 ALR Fed 146.

§ 4109. National Veterans' Employment and Training Services Institute

(a) In order to provide for such training as the Secretary considers necessary and appropriate for the efficient and effective provision of employment, job-training, counseling, placement, job-search, and related services to veterans, the Secretary shall establish and make available such funds as may be necessary to operate a National Veterans' Employment and Training Services Institute for the training of disabled veterans' outreach program specialists, local veterans' employment representatives, Directors for Veterans' Employment and Training, and Assistant Directors for Veterans' Employment and Training, Regional Administrators for Veterans' Employment and Training, and such other personnel involved in the provision of employment, job-training, counseling, placement, or related services to veterans as the Secretary considers appropriate, including travel expenses and per diem for attendance at the Institute.

(b) In implementing this section, the Secretary shall, as the Secretary considers appropriate, provide, out of program funds designated for the Institute, training for Veterans' Employment and Training Service personnel, including travel expenses and per diem to attend the Institute.
(Added Oct. 14, 1982, P. L. 97-306, Title III, § 308(a) in part, 96 Stat. 1440; May 20, 1988, P. L. 100-323, § 8(a), 102 Stat. 566; Aug. 6, 1991, P. L. 102-83, § 5(a), 105 Stat. 406.)

HISTORY; ANCILLARY LAWS AND DIRECTIVES
Explanatory notes:
A prior § 4109 (Act Sept. 2, 1958, P. L. 85-857, § 1, 72 Stat. 1246; Aug. 2, 1973, P. L. 93-82, Title II, § 205, 87 Stat. 192; Aug. 26, 1980, P. L. 96-330, Title I, Part B, § 114, 94 Stat. 1039; Oct. 7, 1980, P. L. 96-385, Title V, § 508(b), 94 Stat. 1538; Nov. 3, 1981, P. L. 97-72, Title IV, § 402(a), 95 Stat. 1062; Oct. 12, 1982, P. L. 97-295, § 4(84), 96 Stat. 1312; April 7, 1986, P. L. 99-272, Title XV, Subtitle B, § 15204(b), 100 Stat. 335; Oct. 21, 1986, P. L. 99-509, Title VII, § 7003(a), 100 Stat. 1949) was repealed by Act May 7, 1991, P. L. 102-40, Title IV, § 401(a)(3), 105 Stat. 210. Such section provided for retirement rights.
A prior § 2009 (Act Sept. 2, 1958, P. L. 85-857, § 1, 72 Stat. 1221), contained in former Subchapter I of Chapter 41, was repealed by Act Sept. 19, 1962, P. L. 87-675, § 1(a), 76 Stat. 558. It related to terminations.

Amendments:
1988. Act May 20, 1988 (effective on the 60th day after enactment, as provided by § 16(b)(2) of such Act, which appears as 38 USCS § 3104 note) substituted this heading and section for ones which read:
"§ 2009. National veterans' employment and training programs
"(a) The Secretary of Labor shall—
 "(1) administer through the Assistant Secretary of Labor for Veterans' Employment all national programs under the jurisdiction of the Secretary for the provision of employment and training services designed to meet the needs of disabled veterans and veterans of the Vietnam era;
 "(2) in order to make maximum use of available resources, encourage all such national programs and all grantees under such programs to enter into cooperative arrangements with private industry and business concerns (including small business concerns), educational institutions, trade associations, and labor unions;
 "(3) ensure that maximum effectiveness and efficiency are achieved in

providing services and assistance to such veterans under all such national programs by coordinating and consulting with the Administrator with respect to programs conducted under other provisions of this title, with particular emphasis on coordination of such national programs with readjustment counseling activities carried out under section 612A of this title, apprenticeship or other on-job training programs carried out under section 1787 of this title, and rehabilitation and training activities carried out under chapter 31 of this title, and

"(4) ensure that job placement activities are carried out in coordination and cooperation with appropriate State public employment service officials.

"(b) Not later than February 1 of each year, the Secretary of Labor shall submit to the Committees on Veterans' Affairs of the House of Representatives and the Senate a report on the operation during the preceding fiscal year of national programs for the provisions of employment and training services designed to meet the needs of veterans described in subsection (a) of this section. Each such report shall include an evaluation of the effectiveness of such programs during such fiscal year in meeting the goals established in such subsection, the efficiency with which services were provided under such programs during such year, and such recommendation for further legislative action relating to veterans' employment as the Secretary considers appropriate.".

1991. Act Aug. 6, 1991, redesignated this section, formerly 38 USCS § 2009, as 38 USCS § 4109.

CROSS REFERENCES

This section is referred to in 38 USCS §§ 4102A, 4106.

RESEARCH GUIDE

Am Jur:

77 Am Jur 2d, Veterans and Veterans' Laws § 113.

§ 4110. Advisory Committee on Veterans Employment and Training

(a)(1) There is hereby established within the Department of Labor an advisory committee to be known as the Advisory Committee on Veterans Employment and Training.

(2) The advisory committee shall—

(A) assess the employment and training needs of veterans;

(B) determine the extent to which the programs and activities of the Department of Labor are meeting such needs; and

(C) carry out such other activities that are necessary to make the reports and recommendations referred to in subsection (f) of this section.

(b) The Secretary of Labor shall, on a regular basis, consult with and seek the advice of the advisory committee with respect to the matters referred to in subsection (a)(2) of this section.

(c)(1) The Secretary of Labor shall appoint at least 12, but no more than 18, individuals to serve as members of the advisory committee consisting of—

(A) representatives nominated by veterans' organizations that have a national employment program; and

(B) not more than 6 individuals who are recognized authorities in the fields of business, employment, training, rehabilitation, or labor and who are not employees of the Department of Labor.

(2) A vacancy in the advisory committee shall be filled in the manner in which the original appointment was made.

(d) The following, or their representatives, shall be ex officio, nonvoting members of the advisory committee:

(1) The Secretary of Veterans Affairs.

(2) The Secretary of Defense.

(3) The Secretary of Health and Human Services.

(4) The Secretary of Education.

(5) The Director of the Office of Personnel Management.

(6) The Assistant Secretary of Labor for Veterans Employment and Training.

(7) The Assistant Secretary of Labor for Employment and Training.

(8) The Chairman of the Equal Employment Opportunity Commission.

(9) The Administrator of the Small Business Administration.

(10) The Postmaster General.

(11) The Director of the United States Employment Service.

(12) Representatives of—

(A) other Federal departments and agencies requesting a representative on the advisory committee; and

(B) nationally based organizations with a significant involvement in veterans employment and training programs, as determined necessary and appropriate by the Secretary of Labor.

(e)(1) The advisory committee shall meet at least quarterly.

(2) The Secretary of Labor shall appoint the chairman of the advisory committee who shall serve in that position for no more than 2 consecutive years.

(3)(A) Members of the advisory committee shall serve without compensation.

(B) Members of the advisory committee shall be allowed reasonable and necessary travel expenses, including per diem in lieu of subsistence, at rates authorized for persons serving intermittently in the Government service in accordance with the provisions of subchapter I of chapter 57 of title 5 [5 USCS §§ 5701 et seq.] while away from their homes or regular places of business in the performance of the responsibilities of the advisory committee.

(4) The Secretary of Labor shall provide staff and administrative support to the advisory committee through the Veterans Employment and Training Service.

(f)(1) Not later than July 1 of each year, the advisory committee shall submit to the Secretary of Labor a report on the employment and training needs of veterans. Each such report shall contain—

(A) an assessment of the employment and training needs of veterans;

(B) an evaluation of the extent to which the programs and activities of the Department of Labor are meeting such needs; and

(C) any recommendations for legislation, administrative action, and other action that the advisory committee considers appropriate.

(2) In addition to the annual reports made under paragraph (1), the advisory committee may make recommendations to the Secretary of Labor with respect to the employment and training needs of veterans at such times and in such manner as the advisory committee determines appropriate.

(g) Within 60 days after receiving each annual report referred to in subsection (f)(1), the Secretary of Labor shall transmit to Congress a copy of the report together with any comments concerning the report that the Secretary considers appropriate.

(h) The advisory committee shall continue until terminated by law.

(Added Oct. 14, 1982, P. L. 97-306, Title III, § 308(a) in part, 96 Stat. 1440; May 20, 1988, P. L. 100-323, §§ 10, 15(a)(2), (3), 102 Stat. 566, 574; Dec. 18, 1989, P. L. 101-237, Title IV, § 423(b)(8)(A) 103 Stat. 2092; March 22, 1991, P. L. 102-16, § 8(a), 105 Stat. 52; Aug. 6, 1991, P. L. 102-83, §§ 4(b)(1), (2)(E), 5(a), 105 Stat. 404, 405, 406; Oct. 29, 1992, P. L. 102-568, Title V, § 504, 106 Stat. 4340; Nov. 2, 1994, P. L. 103-446, Title XII, § 1201(a)(5), (g)(3), (i)(7), 108 Stat. 4682, 4687, 4688.)

HISTORY; ANCILLARY LAWS AND DIRECTIVES

Explanatory notes:
A prior section 4110 (Act Sept. 2, 1958, P. L. 85-857, § 1, 72 Stat. 1246; Dec. 17, 1963, P. L. 88-207, 77 Stat. 402; Nov. 21, 1983, P. L. 98-160, Title II, § 205, 97 Stat. 1001; Oct. 28, 1986, P. L. 99-576, Title VII, § 701(88), 100 Stat. 3299) was repealed by Act May 7, 1991, P. L. 102-40, Title IV, § 401(a)(3), 105 Stat. 210. Such section provided for disciplinary boards.

A prior section 2010 contained in Subchapter II of former Chapter 41 was transferred to 38 USCS § 2001 by Act Sept. 19, 1962, P. L. 87-675, § 1(a), 76 Stat. 558.

Amendments:
1988. Act May 20, 1988 (effective on enactment as provided by § 16(a) of such Act, which appears as 38 USCS § 3104 note), in subsec. (b), in the introductory matter, substituted "Notwithstanding section 2002A(b) of this title, the" for "The" and "Secretary" for "Secretary of Labor" and inserted "and Training".

Such Act further (effective on the 60th day after enactment, as provided by § 16(b)(2) of such Act, which appears as 38 USCS § 3104 note), in subsec. (b)(1), redesignated subparas. (D), (E), and (F) as subparas. (E), (F), and (G), respectively, added a new subpara. (D), in subparas. (F) and (G) as redesignated, deleted "and" following the concluding semicolon, and added subparas. (H) and (I).

1989. Act Dec. 18, 1989, in subsec. (b)(1)(A), substituted "Secretary of Veterans Affairs" for "Administrator".

1991. Act March 22, 1991 substituted this heading and section for ones which read:

"§ 2010. Secretary of Labor's Committee on Veterans' Employment

"(a) There is established within the Department of Labor an advisory committee to be known as the 'Secretary's Committee on Veterans' Employment'. The committee shall meet at least quarterly for the purpose of bringing to the attention of the Secretary problems and issues relating to veterans' employment.

"(b) Notwithstanding section 2002A(b) of this title, the committee shall be chaired by the Secretary. The Assistant Secretary of Labor for Veterans' Employment and Training shall serve as vice chairman of the committee. The committee shall include—

"(1) representatives of—

"(A) the Secretary of Veterans Affairs;

"(B) the Secretary of Defense;

"(C) the Secretary of Health and Human Services;

"(D) the Secretary of Education;

"(E) the Director of the Office of Personnel Management;

"(F) the Chairman of the Equal Employment Opportunity Commission;

"(G) the Administrator of the Small Business Administration;

"(H) the Postmaster General; and

"(I) any other agency of the Federal Government which has had its request to have a representative on the committee approved by the Secretary; and

"(2) a representative of each of the chartered veterans' organizations having a national employment program.

(c) Members of the committee shall serve without compensation or other reimbursement for their service on the committee.".

Act Aug. 6, 1991, redesignated this section, formerly 38 USCS § 2010, as 38 USCS § 4110, and substituted "Secretary" for "Administrator" wherever appearing.

1992. Act Oct. 29, 1992, in subsec. (c), in para. (1), in subpara. (A), deleted "are chartered by Federal law and" following "veterans' organizations that".

1994. Act Nov. 2, 1994, in subsec (c)(1), substituted "shall appoint" for "shall, within 90 days after the date of the enactment of this section, appoint"; in subsec. (d)(9), substituted "Administrator of the Small Business Administration" for "Secretary of the Small Business Administration"; and, in subsec. (e)(3)(B), deleted ", United States Code," following "title 5" and substituted "the advisory committee" for "the Board".

Other provisions:

Termination of advisory committees, boards and councils, established after Jan. 5, 1973. Act Oct. 6, 1972, P. L. 92-463, §§ 3(2) and 14, 86 Stat. 770, 776 (effective 1/5/73, as provided by § 15 of such Act), which is classified as 5 USCS Appx, provides that advisory committees established after Jan. 5, 1973, are to terminate not later than the expiration of the two-year period beginning on the date of establishment unless, in the case of a board established by the President or an officer of the Federal Government, such board is renewed by appropriate action prior to the expiration of such two-year period, or in the case of a board established by the Congress, its duration is otherwise provided for by law.

RESEARCH GUIDE

Am Jur:
77 Am Jur 2d, Veterans and Veterans' Laws § 112.

Annotations:
Availability, under 28 USCS § 1442(a)(1), to one who is not an "officer of the United States or any agency thereof" of right to remove state action to federal court. 64 ALR Fed 146.

Existence of pendent jurisdiction of federal court over state claim when joined with claim arising under laws, treaties, or Constitution of United States. 75 ALR Fed 600.

INTERPRETIVE NOTES AND DECISIONS

VA doctor's claims under Title 38 and Administrative Procedure Act (APA) (5 USCS §§ 701 et seq.) are dismissed, because (1) 38 USCS §§ 7421 et seq. are not applicable since case was filed before new regulations implementing those sections were promulgated, (2) judicial review of actions taken pursuant to 38 USCS § 4110 is available only under APA, and (3) doctor did not exhaust available administrative remedies to create final agency action. Gregor v Derwinski (1996, WD NY) 911 F Supp 643, 75 BNA FEP Cas 797 (criticized in Natale v Town of Darien (1998, DC Conn) 1998 US Dist LEXIS 2356).

§ 4110A. Special unemployment study

(a)(1) The Secretary, through the Bureau of Labor Statistics, shall conduct a study every two years of unemployment among each of the following categories of veterans:

(A) Special disabled veterans.

(B) Veterans of the Vietnam era who served in the Vietnam theater of operations during the Vietnam era.

(C) Veterans who served on active duty during the Vietnam era who did not serve in the Vietnam theater of operations.

(D) Veterans who served on active duty after the Vietnam era.

(E) Veterans discharged or released from active duty within four years of the applicable study.

(2) Within each of the categories of veterans specified in paragraph (1), the Secretary shall include a separate category for women who are veterans.

(3) The Secretary shall promptly submit to Congress a report on the results of each study under paragraph (1).

(b) The first study under this section shall be completed not later than 180 days after the date of the enactment of this section [enacted May 20, 1988].

(Added May 20, 1988, P. L. 100-323, § 9(a), 102 Stat. 566; Aug. 6, 1991, P. L. 102-83, § 5(a), 105 Stat. 406; Nov. 2, 1994, P. L. 103-446, Title VII, § 701(c), 108 Stat. 4674.)

READJUSTMENT BENEFITS   38 USCS § 4111

HISTORY; ANCILLARY LAWS AND DIRECTIVES
Effective date of section:
Act May 20, 1988, P. L. 100-323, § 16(b)(2), 102 Stat. 575, which appears as 38 USCS § 3104 note, provides that this section is effective on the 60th day after enactment.

Amendments:
1991. Act Aug. 6, 1991, redesignated this section, formerly 38 USCS § 2010A, as 38 USCS § 4110A.

1994. Act Nov. 2, 1994, substituted subsec. (a) for one which read:
"(a) The Secretary, through the Bureau of Labor Statistics, shall conduct, on a biennial basis, studies of unemployment among special disabled veterans and among veterans who served in the Vietnam Theater of Operations during the Vietnam era and promptly report to the Congress on the results of such studies.".

RESEARCH GUIDE
Am Jur:
77 Am Jur 2d, Veterans and Veterans' Laws § 106.

[§§ 4111–4119. Repealed]

HISTORY; ANCILLARY LAWS AND DIRECTIVES
These sections (Section 4111–Act Sept. 2, 1958, P. L. 85-857, § 1, 72 Stat. 1247; Oct. 11, 1962, P. L. 87-793, Part II, Title IV, § 804, 76 Stat. 861; Nov. 7, 1966, P. L. 89-785, Title I, § 108, 80 Stat. 1370; Nov. 21, 1983, P. L. 98-160, Title II, § 206, 97 Stat. 1001; § 4112–Act Sept. 2, 1958, P. L. 85-857, § 1, 72 Stat. 1247; Nov. 7, 1966, P. L. 89-785, Title I, § 109(a), 80 Stat. 1370; Aug. 2, 1973, P. L. 93-82, Title II, § 205(b), 87 Stat. 192; Oct. 21, 1976, P. L. 94-581, Title I, § 110(8), Title II, §§ 209(b)(3), 210(c)(6), 90 Stat. 2849, 2861, 2864; Dec. 20, 1979, P. L. 96-151, Title III, § 305, 93 Stat. 1096; Aug. 26, 1980, P. L. 96-303, Title I, Part B, § 115, 94 Stat. 1039; March 2, 1984, P. L. 98-223, Title II, § 209, 98 Stat. 44; May 20, 1988, P. L. 100-322, Title II, Part C, § 224, 102 Stat. 532; § 4113–Act Sept. 2, 1958, P. L. 85-857, § 1, 72 Stat. 1247; Nov. 7, 1966, P. L. 89-785, Title I, § 110, 80 Stat. 1371; Oct. 21, 1976, P. L. 94-581, Title I, § 110(9), Title II, § 209(a)(5), (c)(5), 90 Stat. 2849, 2860, 2862; § 4114–Act Sept. 2, 1958, P. L. 85-857, § 1, 72 Stat. 1247; Aug. 6, 1962, P. L. 87-574, § 4(2), 76 Stat. 309; Nov. 7, 1966, P. L. 89-785, Title I, § 111(a)-(c), 80 Stat. 1371; Oct. 22, 1970, P. L. 91-496, §§ 1, 3, 84 Stat. 1092; Aug. 2, 1973, P. L. 93-82, Title II, § 206, 87 Stat. 192; Oct. 21, 1976, P. L. 94-581, Title I, §§ 109, 110(10), Title II, §§ 205(g), 209(a)(6), (c)(6), 210(c)(7), 90 Stat. 2848, 2849, 2859, 2860, 2862, 2864; Nov. 23, 1977, P. L. 95-201, § 4(a)(2), 91 Stat. 1430; Aug. 26, 1980, P. L. 96-330, Title I, Part B, § 116(b), 94 Stat. 1039; Oct. 12, 1982, P. L. 97-295, § 4(85), 96 Stat. 1312; Dec. 3, 1985, P. L. 99-166, Title II, § 203, 99 Stat. 950; Oct. 28, 1986, P. L. 99-576, Title II, Part B, § 214, 100 Stat. 3258; May 20, 1988, P. L. 100-322, Title II, Part C, § 223, 102 Stat. 531; Nov. 18, 1988, P. L. 100-687, Div B, Title XV, § 1503(a)(2), 102 Stat. 4133; Aug. 15, 1990, P. L. 101-366, Title II, § 203, 104 Stat. 439; § 4115–Act Sept. 2, 1958, P. L. 85-857, § 1, 72 Stat. 1248; § 4116–Act Oct. 31, 1965, P. L. 89-311, § 6(a), 79

38 USCS § 4111   VETERANS' BENEFITS

Stat. 1156; July 18, 1966, P. L. 89-506, § 5(b), 80 Stat. 307; Aug. 2, 1973, P. L. 93-82, Title II, § 207, 87 Stat. 193; Oct. 21, 1976, P. L. 94-581, Title I, § 110(11), Title II, §§ 209(a)(7), 210(c)(8), 90 Stat. 2849, 2861, 2864; May 20, 1988, P. L. 100-322, Title II, Part A, § 203(a)(1), 102 Stat. 509; § 4117–Act Nov. 7, 1966, P. L. 89-785, Title I, § 112(a), 80 Stat. 1371; Aug. 2, 1973, P. L. 93-82, Title II, § 208, 87 Stat. 194; Oct. 21, 1976, P. L. 94-581, Titles I, § 110(12), Title II, § 209(a)(1), (8), 90 Stat. 2849, 2860, 2861; § 4118–Act Oct. 22, 1975, P. L. 94-123, § 2(d)(l), 89 Stat. 670; Nov. 23, 1977, P. L. 95-201, § 3(a), 91 Stat. 1429; Aug. 26, 1980, P. L. 96-330, Title I, Part A, §§ 102(a)(1), (b)-(d), 103(a), 104(a), Title II, § 202, 94 Stat. 1030, 1031, 1034, 1035, 1047; Oct. 12, 1982, P. L. 97-295, § 4(86), 96 Stat. 1312; Sept. 13, 1982, P. L. 97-258, § 3(k)(6), 96 Stat. 1065; Oct. 28, 1986, P. L. 99-576, Title II, Part D, § 231(a), 100 Stat. 3263; Jan. 8, 1988, P. L. 100-238, Title I, § 126, 101 Stat. 1757; § 4119–Act Aug. 26, 1980, P. L. 96-330, Title I, Part B, § 116(a)(1), 94 Stat. 1039) were repealed by Act May 7, 1991, P. L. 102-40, Title IV, § 401(a)(3), 105 Stat. 210. Section 4111 provided for appointment of additional employees; § 4112 provided for a special medical advisory group and other advisory bodies; § 4113 provided for travel expenses of employees; § 4114 provided for temporary full-time, part-time, and without compensation appointments, and residencies or internships; § 4115 provided for the promulgation of regulations necessary to the administration of the Department of Medicine and Surgery; § 4116 provided for the defense of certain malpractice and negligence suits; § 4117 provided for contracts for scarce medical specialist services; § 4118 provided for special pay for physicians and dentists; § 4119 provided for the relationship between this subchapter [former 38 USCS §§ 4101 et seq.] and other provisions of law.

[§ 4120. Transferred]

HISTORY; ANCILLARY LAWS AND DIRECTIVES

This section (Act May 20, 1988, P. L. 100-322, Title II, Part B, § 212(a)(1), 102 Stat. 514), as in effect on the day before the date of enactment of Act May 7, 1991, P. L. 102-40, was redesignated 38 USCS § 7458 by § 401(c)(4) of such Act.

[§ 4121. Repealed]

HISTORY; ANCILLARY LAWS AND DIRECTIVES

This section (Act Oct. 24, 1972, P. L. 92-541, § 3(a), 86 Stat. 1107; Oct. 21, 1976, P. L. 94-581, Title II, § 210(c)(9), 90 Stat. 2864; Oct. 28, 1986, P. L. 99-576, Title II, Part B, § 212(a), (b), 100 Stat. 3257) was repealed by Act May 7, 1991, P. L. 102-40, Title IV, § 401(a)(3), 105 Stat. 210. Such section provided for the designation of Regional Medical Education Centers.

[§ 4122. Repealed]

HISTORY; ANCILLARY LAWS AND DIRECTIVES

This section (Act Oct. 24, 1972, P. L. 92-541, § 3(a), 86 Stat. 1107; Oct.

21, 1976, P. L. 94-581, Title II, §§ 209(c)(7), 210(c)(10), 90 Stat. 2862, 2864) was repealed by Act May 7, 1991, P. L. 102-40, Title IV, § 401(a)(3), 105 Stat. 210. Such section provided for supervision and staffing of Regional Medical Education Centers.

[§ 4123. Repealed]

HISTORY; ANCILLARY LAWS AND DIRECTIVES

This section (Act Oct. 24, 1972, P. L. 92-541, § 3(a), 86 Stat. 1107; Oct. 21, 1976, P. L. 94-581, Title I, § 113, 90 Stat. 2852; Oct. 28, 1986, P. L. 99-576, Title II, Part B, § 212(c), 100 Stat. 3257) was repealed by Act May 7, 1991, P. L. 102-40, Title IV, § 401(a)(3), 105 Stat. 210. Such section provided for the eligibility of personnel for training in Regional Medical Education Centers.

[§ 4124. Repealed]

HISTORY; ANCILLARY LAWS AND DIRECTIVES

This section (Act Oct. 24, 1972, P. L. 92-541, § 3(a), 86 Stat. 1108) was repealed by Act May 7, 1991, P. L. 102-40, Title IV, § 401(a)(3), 105 Stat. 210. Such section provided for consultation of the Chief Medical Director with the Special Medical Advisory Group established pursuant to former 38 USCS 4112(a).

[§ 4131. Transferred]

HISTORY; ANCILLARY LAWS AND DIRECTIVES

This section (Act Oct. 21, 1976, P. L. 94-581, Title I, § 111(a)(1), 90 Stat. 2849) was transferred by Act May 7, 1991, P. L. 102-40, Title IV, § 401(a)(4)(A), 105 Stat. 221, and appears as 38 USCS § 7331.

[§ 4132. Transferred]

HISTORY; ANCILLARY LAWS AND DIRECTIVES

This section (Act Oct. 21, 1976, P. L. 94-581, Title I, § 111(a)(1), 90 Stat. 2849; May 20, 1988, P. L. 100-322, Title I, Part C, § 121, 102 Stat. 502) was transferred by Act May 7, 1991, P. L. 102-40, Title IV, § 401(a)(4)(A), 105 Stat. 221, and appears as 38 USCS § 7332.

[§ 4133. Transferred]

HISTORY; ANCILLARY LAWS AND DIRECTIVES

This section (Act Oct. 21, 1976, P. L. 94-581, Title I, § 111(a)(1), 90 Stat. 2850; May 20, 1988, P. L. 100-322, Title I, Part C, § 122(a), 102 Stat. 503) was transferred by Act May 7, 1991, P. L. 102-40, Title IV, § 401(a)(4)(A), 105 Stat. 221, and appears as 38 USCS § 7333.

[§ 4134. Transferred]

HISTORY; ANCILLARY LAWS AND DIRECTIVES

This section (Act Oct. 21, 1976, P. L. 94-581, Title I, § 111(a)(1), 90 Stat. 2851; Oct. 12, 1982, P. L. 97-295, § 4(87), 96 Stat. 1312; May 20, 1988, P. L. 100-322, Title I, Part C, § 122(a), 102 Stat. 504) was transferred by Act May 7, 1991, P. L. 102-40, Title IV, § 401(a)(4)(A), 105 Stat. 221, and appears as 38 USCS § 7334.

[§ 4141. Transferred]

HISTORY; ANCILLARY LAWS AND DIRECTIVES

This section (Act Aug. 15, 1990, P. L. 101-366, Title I, § 102(b), 104 Stat. 431; May 7, 1991, P. L. 102-40, Title III, § 301(b), (c), 105 Stat. 208) was transferred by Act May 7, 1991, P. L. 102-40, Title IV, § 401(c)(1)(A), 105 Stat. 238, and appears as 38 USCS § 7451.

A prior § 4141 (Act Aug. 26, 1980, P. L. 96-330, Title II, § 201(a)(1), 94 Stat. 1041) was repealed by Act May 20, 1988, P. L. 100-322, Title II, Part B, § 216(a), 102 Stat. 517. Such section provided for establishment of a Veterans' Administration Health Professional Scholarship Program.

[§ 4142. Transferred]

HISTORY; ANCILLARY LAWS AND DIRECTIVES

This section (Act Aug. 15, 1990, P. L. 101-366, Title I, § 102(b), 104 Stat. 435; May 7, 1990, P. L. 102-40, Title III, § 301(d), 105 Stat. 208) was transferred by Act May 7, 1991, P. L. 102-40, Title IV, § 401(c)(1)(A), 105 Stat. 238, and appears as 38 USCS § 7452.

A prior § 4142 (Act Aug. 26, 1980, P. L. 96-330, Title II, § 201(a)(1), 94 Stat. 1041; Sept. 8, 1982, P. L. 97-251, § 3(a), 96 Stat. 713; Dec. 21, 1982, P. L. 97-375, Title II, § 216, 96 Stat. 1827; Sept. 13, 1982, P. L. 97-258, § 3(k)(7), 96 Stat. 1065; Nov. 21, 1983, P. L. 98-160, Title VII, § 702(18), 97 Stat. 1010; Oct. 28, 1986, P. L. 99-576, Title II, Part B, § 213, 100 Stat. 3257) was repealed by Act May 20, 1988, P. L. 100-322, Title II, Part B, § 216(a), 102 Stat. 517. Such section provided for eligibility for and applications for the health professional scholarship program and for written contracts.

[§ 4151. Repealed]

HISTORY; ANCILLARY LAWS AND DIRECTIVES

This section (Act Dec. 3, 1985, P. L. 99-166, Title II, § 204(a)(1), 99 Stat. 950) was repealed by Act May 7, 1991, P. L. 102-40, Title IV, § 401(a)(2)(A), 105 Stat. 210. Such section provided for a quality-assurance program.

[§ 4152. Repealed]

HISTORY; ANCILLARY LAWS AND DIRECTIVES

This section (Act Dec. 3, 1985, P. L. 99-166, Title II, § 204(a)(1), 99 Stat.

951) was repealed by Act May 7, 1991, P. L. 102-40, Title IV, § 401(a)(2)(A), 105 Stat. 210. Such section provided for quality-assurance reports.

[§§ 4161–4168. Transferred]

HISTORY; ANCILLARY LAWS AND DIRECTIVES
These sections (Act May 20, 1988, P. L. 100-322, Title II, Part A, § 204(a), 102 Stat. 510) were transferred by Act May 7, 1991, P. L. 102-40, Title IV, § 401(a)(4)(B), 105 Stat. 221, and appear as 38 USCS §§ 7361 et seq.

CHAPTER 42. EMPLOYMENT AND TRAINING OF VETERANS

Section
[4201-4210. Transferred]
4211. Definitions.
4212. Veterans' employment emphasis under Federal contracts.
4213. Eligibility requirements for veterans under Federal employment and training programs.
4214. Employment within the Federal Government.

HISTORY; ANCILLARY LAWS AND DIRECTIVES
Amendments:
1972. Act Oct. 24, 1972, P. L. 92-540, Title V, § 503(a), 86 Stat. 1097 (effective 90 days after 10/24/72, as provided by § 601(b) of such Act) added this chapter analysis.
1974. Act Dec. 3, 1974, P. L. 93-508, Title IV, § 403(b), 88 Stat. 1594 (effective 12/3/74, as provided by § 503 of such Act), added item 2014.
1980. Act Oct. 17, 1980, P. L. 96-466, Title VIII, § 801(k)(2)(B), 94 Stat. 2217 (effective 10/1/80, as provided by § 802(h) of such Act), substituted item 2013 for one which read: "2013. Eligibility requirements for veterans under certain Federal manpower training programs.".
1991. Act March 22, 1991, P. L. 102-16, § 9(c)(1), 105 Stat. 55, applicable as provided by § 9(d) of such Act, which appears as 38 USCS § 2014 note, amended the title heading of this chapter by deleting "DISABLED AND VIETNAM ERA" preceding "VETERANS".
Act Aug. 6, 1991, P. L. 102-83, § 5(b)(1), 105 Stat. 406, revised the analysis of this Chapter by amending the section numbers in accordance with the redesignations made by § 5(a) of such Act (see Table III preceding 38 USCS § 101).

[§§ 4201—4210. Transferred]

HISTORY; ANCILLARY LAWS AND DIRECTIVES
These sections (§ 4201—Act Sept. 2, 1958, P. L. 85-857, § 1, 72 Stat. 1248; § 4202—Act Sept. 2, 1958, P. L. 85-857, § 1, 72 Stat. 1248; July 28, 1959, P. L. 86-109, § 1, 73 Stat. 258; Oct. 21, 1976, P. L. 94-581, Title II, § 201(d), 90 Stat. 2864; Oct. 12, 1982, P. L. 97-295, § 4(88), 96 Stat. 1312; Oct. 28, 1986, P. L. 99-576, Title VII, § 702(13), 100 Stat. 3302; § 4203—Act Sept. 2, 1958, P. L. 85-857, § 1, 72 Stat. 1249; § 4204—Act Sept. 2, 1958, P. L. 85-857, § 1, 72 Stat. 1250; June 6, 1972, P. L. 92-310, Title II, Part 1, § 209, 86 Stat. 204; Oct. 28, 1986, P. L. 99-576, Title VII, § 702(14), 100 Stat. 3302; § 4205—Act Sept. 2, 1958, P. L. 85-857, § 1, 72 Stat. 1250; May 20, 1988, P. L. 100-322, Title IV, Part B, § 414(a)(1), 102 Stat. 549; § 4206—Act Sept. 2, 1958, P. L. 85-857, § 1, 72 Stat. 1250; Sept. 13, 1982, P. L. 97-258, § 3(k)(8), 96 Stat. 1065; May 20, 1988, P. L. 100-322, Title IV, Part B, § 414(a)(2), 102 Stat. 549; § 4207—Act Sept. 2, 1958, P. L. 85-857, § 1, 72 Stat. 1250; Jan. 2, 1975, P. L. 93-604, Title VII, § 704, 88 Stat. 1964; Oct. 12, 1982, P. L. 97-295, § 4(89), 96 Stat. 1312; Jan. 12, 1983, P. L. 97-452, § 2(e)(3), 96 Stat. 2479; § 4208—Act Sept. 2,

1958, P. L. 85-857, § 1, 72 Stat. 1250; Oct. 12, 1982, P. L. 97-295, § 4(90), 96 Stat. 1312; § 4209—Act May 20, 1988, P. L. 100-322, Title IV, Part B, § 412(a), 102 Stat. 547; § 4210—Act May 20, 1988, P. L. 100-322, Title IV, Part B, § 414(b)(1), 102 Stat. 549) were transferred by Act May 7, 1991, P. L. 102-40, Title IV, § 402(b)(1), 105 Stat. 238, and appear as 38 USCS §§ 7801 et seq.

§ 4211. Definitions

As used in this chapter [38 USCS §§ 4211 et seq.]—

(1) The term "special disabled veteran" means—
   (A) a veteran who is entitled to compensation (or who but for the receipt of military retired pay would be entitled to compensation) under laws administered by the Secretary for a disability (i) rated at 30 percent or more, or (ii) rated at 10 or 20 percent in the case of a veteran who has been determined under section 3106 of this title to have a serious employment handicap; or
   (B) a person who was discharged or released from active duty because of service-connected disability.

(2) The term "veteran of the Vietnam era" means an eligible veteran any part of whose active military, naval, or air service was during the Vietnam era.

(3) The term "disabled veteran" means (A) a veteran who is entitled to compensation (or who but for the receipt of military retired pay would be entitled to compensation) under laws administered by the Secretary, or (B) a person who was discharged or released from active duty because of a service-connected disability.

(4) The term "eligible veteran" means a person who—
   (A) served on active duty for a period of more than 180 days and was discharged or released therefrom with other than a dishonorable discharge;
   (B) was discharged or released from active duty because of a service-connected disability; or
   (C) as a member of a reserve component under an order to active duty pursuant to section 12301(a), (d), or (g), 12302, or 12304 of title 10, served on active duty during a period of war or in a campaign or expedition for which a campaign badge is authorized and was discharged or released from such duty with other than a dishonorable discharge.

(5) The term "department or agency" means any agency of the Federal Government or the District of Columbia, including any Executive agency as defined in section 105 of title 5 and the United States Postal Service and the Postal Rate Commission, and the term "department, agency, or instrumentality in the executive branch" includes the United States Postal Service and the Postal Rate Commission.

(Added Oct. 24, 1972, P. L. 92-540, Title V, § 503(a), 86 Stat. 1097; Oct. 15, 1976, P. L. 94-502, Title VI, § 607(1), 90 Stat. 2405; Oct. 17, 1980, P. L. 96-466, Title V, § 508, 94 Stat. 2206; Oct. 14, 1982, P. L. 97-306, Title III, § 309, 96 Stat. 1441; March 2, 1984, P. L. 98-223, Title II, § 206, 98 Stat. 43; Dec.

18, 1989, P. L. 101-237, Title IV, § 407(a)(2), 103 Stat. 2082; March 22, 1991, P. L. 102-16, § 1, 105 Stat. 48; June 13, 1991, P. L. 102-54, § 14(c)(9), 105 Stat. 285; Aug. 6, 1991, P. L. 102-83, §§ 4(a)(1), 5(a), (c)(1), 105 Stat. 403, 406; Oct. 10, 1991, P. L. 102-127, § 5, 105 Stat. 622; Oct. 29, 1992, P. L. 102-568, Title V, § 502, 106 Stat. 4340; Feb. 10, 1996, P. L. 104-106, Div A, Title XV, § 1501(e)(2)(D), 110 Stat. 501.)

HISTORY; ANCILLARY LAWS AND DIRECTIVES

Explanatory notes:
A prior § 2011, contained in Subchapter II of former Chapter 41, was transferred to 38 USCS § 2002 by Act Sept. 19, 1962, P. L. 87-675, § 1(a), 76 Stat. 558.

Effective date of section:
Act Oct. 24, 1972, P. L. 92-540, Title VI, § 601(b), 86 Stat. 1099, provided that this section is effective 90 days after Oct. 24, 1972.

Amendments:
1976. Act Oct. 15, 1976 (effective 12/1/76, as provided by § 703(c) of such Act, which appears as 38 USCS § 3693 note), in para. (2), substituted "the person's" for "his".

1980. Act Oct. 17, 1980 (effective 10/1/80, as provided by § 802(e) of such Act, which appears as 38 USCS § 4101 note), substituted new section for one which read:

"As used in this chapter—

"(1) The term 'disabled veteran' means a person entitled to disability compensation under laws administered by the Veterans' Administration for a disability rated at 30 per centum or more, or a person whose discharge or release from active duty was for a disability incurred or aggravated in line of duty.

"(2) The term 'veteran of the Vietnam era' means a person (A) who (i) served on active duty for a period of more than 180 days, any part of which occurred during the Vietnam era, and was discharged or released therefrom with other than a dishonorable discharge, or (ii) was discharged or released from active duty for a service-connected disability if any part of such active duty was performed during the Vietnam era, and (B) who was so discharged or released within the 48 months preceding the person's application for employment covered under this chapter.

"(3) The term 'department and agency' means any department or agency of the Federal Government or any federally owned corporation.".

1982. Act Oct. 14, 1982, in paras. (1) and (3), inserted "(or who but for the receipt of military retired pay would be entitled to compensation)"; and, in para. (5), inserted "and the United States Postal Service and the Postal Rate Commission, and the term 'department, agency, or instrumentality in the executive branch' includes the United States Postal Service and the Postal Rate Commission".

1984. Act March 2, 1984 substituted para. (1) for one which read: "The term 'special disabled veteran' means (A) a veteran who is entitled to compensation (or who but for the receipt of military retired pay would be entitled to compensation) under laws administered by the Veterans' Administration for a disability rated at 30 percent or more, or (B) a person who was discharged or released from active duty because of a service-connected disability.''.

1989. Act Dec. 18, 1989 (effective 1/1/90 as provided by § 407(c) of such Act, which appears as a note to this section), in para. (2)(B), inserted "except for purposes of section 2014 of this title".

1991. Act March 22, 1991, in para. (2)(B), substituted "1994" for "1991". Act June 13, 1991, in para. (2)(B), inserted a comma before "except for". Act Aug. 6, 1991, redesignated this section, formerly 38 USCS § 2011, as 38 USCS § 4211, and amended the references in this section to reflect the redesignations made by § 5(a) of such Act (see Table III preceding 38 USCS § 101).

Such Act further, in paras. (1)(A) and (3), substituted "administered by the Secretary" for "administered by the Veterans' Administration".

Act Oct. 10, 1991 substituted para. (4) for one which read: "The term 'eligible veteran' means a person who (A) served on active duty for a period of more than 180 days and was discharged or released therefrom with other than a dishonorable discharge, or (B) was discharged or released from active duty because of a service-connected disability.''.

1992. Act Oct. 29, 1992, in para. (2), substituted "The term" for "(A) Subject to subparagraph (B) of this paragraph, the term", and deleted subpara. (B), which read: "(B) No veteran may be considered to be a veteran of the Vietnam era under this paragraph after December 31, 1994, except for purposes of section 4214 of this title.''.

1996. Act Feb. 10, 1996 (effective as if included in Act Oct. 5, 1995, P. L. 103-337, as enacted on Oct. 5, 1994, as provided by § 1501(f)(3) of Act Feb. 10, 1996, which appears as 10 USCS § 113 note), in para. (4)(C), substituted "section 12301(a), (d), or (g), 12302, or 12304 of title 10" for "section 672 (a), (d), or (g), 673, or 673b of title 10".

Other provisions:
Effective date of Dec. 18, 1989 amendments. Act Dec. 18, 1989, P. L. 101-237, Title IV, § 407(c), 103 Stat. 2083, provides: "The amendments made by this section [amending subsec. (a)(2) of this section and 38 USCS § 4214] shall take effect on January 1, 1990.''.

CODE OF FEDERAL REGULATIONS

Office of Federal Contract Compliance Programs, Equal Employment Opportunity; Department of Labor—Affirmative action obligations of contractors and subcontractors for disabled veterans of the Vietnam era, 41 CFR Part 60-250.

CROSS REFERENCES

This section is referred to in 15 USCS § 1022a: 38 USCS §§ 4101, 4214; 42 USCS § 6706.

RESEARCH GUIDE

Federal Procedure L Ed:
21 Fed Proc L Ed, Job Discrimination § 50:549.

Am Jur:
45A Am Jur 2d, Job Discrimination (1993) §§ 178, 672, 801.
45B Am Jur 2d, Job Discrimination (1993) § 1224.
77 Am Jur 2d, Veterans and Veterans' Laws §§ 101, 102.

§ 4212. Veterans' employment emphasis under Federal contracts

(a) Any contract in the amount of $10,000 or more entered into by any department or agency for the procurement of personal property and nonpersonal services (including construction) for the United States, shall contain a provision requiring that the party contracting with the United States shall take affirmative action to employ and advance in employment qualified special disabled veterans and veterans of the Vietnam era. The provisions of this section shall apply to any subcontract entered into by a prime contractor in carrying out any contract for the procurement of personal property and non-personal services (including construction) for the United States. In addition to requiring affirmative action to employ such veterans under such contracts and subcontracts and in order to promote the implementation of such requirement, the President shall implement the provisions of this section by promulgating regulations which shall require that (1) each such contractor undertake in such contract to list immediately with the appropriate local employment service office all of its employment openings except that the contractor may exclude openings for executive and top management positions, positions which are to be filled from within the contractor's organization, and positions lasting three days or less, and (2) each such local office shall give such veterans priority in referral to such employment openings.

(b) If any special disabled veteran or veteran of the Vietnam era believes any contractor of the United States has failed to comply or refuses to comply with the provisions of the contractor's contract relating to the employment of veterans, the veteran may file a complaint with the Secretary of Labor, who shall promptly investigate such complaint and take appropriate action in accordance with the terms of the contract and applicable laws and regulations.

(c) The Secretary of Labor shall include as part of the annual report required by section 4107(c) of this title the number of complaints filed pursuant to subsection (b) of this section, the actions taken thereon and the resolutions thereof. Such report shall also include the number of contractors listing suitable employment openings, the nature, types, and number of positions listed and the number of veterans receiving priority pursuant to subsection (a)(2) of this section.

(d)(1) Each contractor to whom subsection (a) of this section applies shall, in accordance with regulations which the Secretary of Labor shall prescribe, report at least annually to the Secretary of Labor on—

(A) the number of employees in the work force of such contractor, by job category and hiring location, who are veterans of the Vietnam era or special disabled veterans; and

(B) the total number of new employees hired by the contractor during the period covered by the report and the number of such employees who are veterans of the Vietnam era or special disabled veterans.

(2) The Secretary of Labor shall ensure that the administration of the reporting requirement under paragraph (1) of this subsection is coordinated with respect to any requirement for the contractor to make any other report to the Secretary of Labor.

(Added Oct. 24, 1972, P. L. 92-540, Title V, § 503(a), 86 Stat. 1097; Dec. 3, 1974, P. L. 93-508, Title IV, § 402, 88 Stat. 1593; Oct. 15, 1976, P. L. 94-502, Title VI, §§ 605, 607(2), 90 Stat. 2405; Oct. 26, 1978, P. L. 95-520, § 6(a), 92 Stat. 1821; Oct. 17, 1980, P. L. 96-466, Title V, § 509, Title VIII, § 801(j), 94 Stat. 2206, 2217; Oct. 14, 1982, P. L. 97-306, Title III, § 310(a), 96 Stat. 1442; Aug. 6, 1991, P. L. 102-83, § 4(b)(8), 5(a), (c)(1), 105 Stat. 405, 406; Nov. 2, 1994, P. L. 103-446, Title VII, § 702(a), 108 Stat. 4674.)

HISTORY; ANCILLARY LAWS AND DIRECTIVES

Explanatory notes:
A prior § 2012, contained in Subchapter II of former Chapter 41, was transferred to 38 USCS § 2003 by Act Sept. 19, 1962, P. L. 87-675, § 1(a), 76 Stat. 558.

Effective date of section:
Act Oct. 24, 1972, P. L. 92-540, Title VI, § 601(b), 86 Stat. 1099, provided that this section is effective 90 days after Oct. 24, 1972.

Amendments:
1974. Act Dec. 3, 1974 (effective 12/3/74, as provided by § 503 of such Act, which appears as 38 USCS § 3452 note), in subsec. (a), inserted "in the amount of $10,000 or more", deleted ", in employing persons to carry out such contract," following "a provision requiring that", substituted "take affirmative action to employ and advance in employment" for "give special emphasis to the employment of", and substituted "In addition to requiring affirmative action to employ such veterans under such contracts and subcontracts and in order to promote the implementation of such requirement, the" for "The"; and in subsec. (b), substituted "the employment of" for "giving special emphasis in employment to".

1976. Act Oct. 15, 1976 (effective 12/1/76, as provided by § 703(c) of such Act, which appears as 38 USCS § 3693 note), in subsec. (b), substituted "the contractor's" for "his"; and added subsec. (c).

1978. Act Oct. 26, 1978, in subsec. (b), inserted ", or if any veteran who is entitled to disability compensation under the laws administered by the Veterans' Administration believes that any such contractor has discriminated against such veteran because such veteran is a handicapped individual within the meaning of section 7(6) of the Rehabilitation Act of 1973 (29 U.S.C. 706(6))".

1980. Act Oct. 17, 1980 (effective 10/1/80, as provided by § 802(e), (h) of such Act), in subsec. (a), inserted "special", and substituted "which" for "within 60 days after the date of enactment of this section, which regulations"; and substituted new subsec. (b) for one which read: "(b) If any disabled veteran or veteran of the Vietnam era believes any contractor has failed or refuses to comply with the provisions of the contractor's contract with the United States, relating to the employment of veterans, or if any veteran who is entitled to disability compensation under the laws administered by the Veterans' Administration believes that any such contractor has discriminated against such veteran because such veteran is a handicapped individual within the meaning of section 7(6) of the Rehabilitation Act of 1973 (29 U.S.C. 706(6)), such veteran may file a complaint with the Veterans' Employment Service of the Department of Labor. Such complaint shall be promptly referred to the Secretary who shall promptly investigate such complaint and shall take such action thereon as the facts and circumstances warrant consistent with the terms of such contract and the laws and regulations applicable thereto.''.

1982. Act Oct. 14, 1982 added subsec. (d).

1991. Act Aug. 6, 1991, redesignated this section, formerly 38 USCS § 2012, as 38 USCS § 4212, amended the references in this section to reflect the redesignations made by § 5(a) of such Act (see Table III preceding 38 USCS § 101), and, in subsecs. (c) and (d), substituted "Secretary of Labor" for "Secretary" wherever appearing.

1994. Act Nov. 2, 1994, in subsec. (a), substituted "all of its employment openings except that the contractor may exclude openings for executive and top management positions, positions which are to be filled from within the contractor's organization, and positions lasting three days or less," for "all of its suitable employment openings,''.

Other provisions:

Employment of veterans by federal agencies and government contractors and subcontractors. Ex. Or. No. 11701 of Jan. 24, 1973, 38 Fed. Reg. 2675, provided:

On June 16, 1971, I issued Executive Order No. 11598 to facilitate the employment of returning veterans by requiring Federal agencies and Federal contractors and their subcontractors to list employment openings with the employment service systems. Section 503 of the Vietnam Era Veterans' Readjustment Assistance Act of 1972 (Public Law 92-540; 86 Stat. 1097) added a new section 2012 [now section 4212] to Title 38 of the United States Code which, in effect, provides statutory authority to extend the program developed under that order with respect to Government contractors and their subcontractors.

NOW, THEREFORE, by virtue of the authority vested in me by section 301 of Title 3 of the United States Code and as President of the United States, it is hereby ordered as follows:

Section 1. The Secretary of Labor shall issue rules and regulations requiring each department and agency of the executive branch of the Federal Government to list suitable employment openings with the appropriate office of the State Employment Service or the United States Employment Service. This section shall not be construed as requiring the employment of individuals referred by such office or as superseding any requirements of the Civil Service Laws. Rules, regulations, and orders to implement this section shall be developed in consultation with the Civil Service Commission.

Sec. 2. The Secretary of Labor is hereby designated and empowered to exercise, without the approval, ratification, or other action of the President, the authority of the President under Section 2012 [now section 4212] of Title 38 of the United States Code.

Sec. 3. The Secretary of Labor shall gather information on the effectiveness of the program established under this order and Section 2012 [now section 4212] of Title 38 of the United States Code and of the extent to which the employment service system is fulfilling the employment needs of veterans. The Secretary of Labor shall, from time to time, report to the President concerning his evaluation of the effectiveness of this order along with his recommendations for further action which the Secretary believes to be appropriate.

Sec. 4. Appropriate departments and agencies shall, in consultation with the Secretary of Labor, issue such amendments or additions to procurement rules and regulations as may be necessary to carry out the purposes of this order and Section 2012 [now section 4212] of Title 38 of the United States Code. Except as otherwise provided by law, all executive departments and agencies are directed to cooperate with the Secretary of Labor, to furnish the Secretary of Labor with such information and assistance as he may require in the performance of his functions under this order, and to comply with rules, regulations, and orders of the Secretary.

Sec. 5. Executive Order No. 11598 of June 16, 1971, is hereby superseded.

Secretary to prescribe regulations. Act Oct. 14, 1982, P. L. 97-306, Title III, § 310(b), 96 Stat. 1442, provides: "Within 90 days after the date of the enactment of this Act, the Secretary of Labor shall prescribe regulations under subsection (d) of section 2012 of Title 38, United States Code [subsec. (d) of this section], as added by the amendment made by subsection (a).".

CODE OF FEDERAL REGULATIONS

Office of Federal Contract Compliance Programs, Equal Employment Opportunity; Department of Labor—Rules of practice for administrative proceedings to enforce equal opportunity under Executive Order 11246, 41 CFR Part 60-30.

Office of Federal Contract Compliance Programs, Equal Employment Opportunity; Department of Labor—Affirmative action obligations of contractors and subcontractors for disabled veterans of the Vietnam era, 41 CFR Part 60-250.

CROSS REFERENCES

This section is referred to in 29 USCS § 1755; 38 USCS §§ 3116, 4102A, 4103, 4104.

RESEARCH GUIDE

Federal Procedure L Ed:

21 Fed Proc L Ed, Job Discrimination §§ 50:549, 550, 553, 555.

Am Jur:

45A Am Jur 2d, Job Discrimination (1993) §§ 23, 101, 177, 178, 619, 672, 801.

45B Am Jur 2d, Job Discrimination (1993) §§ 1224, 1606, 1610, 1620, 1901, 1943, 2018, 2123.

77 Am Jur 2d, Veterans and Veterans' Laws §§ 102, 107.

Annotations:

Availability of private right of action under § 503 of Rehabilitation Act of 1973 (29 USCS § 793), providing that certain federal contracts must contain provision requiring affirmative action to employ qualified handicapped individuals. 60 ALR Fed 329.

Employee's inability to work particular hours due to disability as grounds for termination or refusal of employment, notwithstanding federal statute or regulation requiring employer to make reasonable accommodation of disability. 116 ALR Fed 485.

Law Review Articles:

Choper. The Constitutionality of Affirmative Action: Views from the Supreme Court. 70 Kentucky L J 1, 1981-82.

INTERPRETIVE NOTES AND DECISIONS

1. Generally
2. Application
3. Complaints
4. Private right of action
5. Judicial review
6. Miscellaneous

1. Generally

While there is no obligation to make unreasonable efforts to accommodate handicapped employees under 38 USCS § 2012 [now 38 USCS § 4212], more than "evenhanded approach" is required; to determine whether federal contractor has violated 38 USCS § 2012 [now 38 USCS § 4212] consideration should be given whether handicapped individual is qualified to perform job in question despite existence of handicap and, if not, whether employee could with reasonable employer accommodation perform that job or some other job for same employer, whether requirements stated in official job description match those actually required to perform job, size of contractor, number of employees in job category which handicapped individual seeks to enter, and whether contractor's overall work-force is expanding or shrinking in numbers. OFCCP Policy Directive 80-34, Sep. 30, 1980.

Discrimination in employment practices against handicapped veterans includes discrimination in hiring, upgrading, demotion or transfer, recruitment or recruitment advertising, layoff or termination, rates of pay or other forms of compensation, and selection for training, including apprenticeships. OFCCP Order No. 720a1, April 5, 1982.

2. Application

For purposes of federal contract compliance laws, University of North Carolina system is single state agency and non-contracting campuses therefore must submit to compliance reviews regardless of whether they are direct participants in any federal contract. Board of Governors of University of North Carolina v United States Dep't of Labor (1990, CA4 NC) 917 F2d 812, 1 AD Cas 1704, 54 BNA FEP Cas 136, 135 BNA LRRM 2760, 36 CCF ¶ 75959, 55 CCH EPD ¶ 40370, cert den (1991) 500 US 916, 114 L Ed 2d 100, 111 S Ct 2013, 55 BNA FEP Cas 1104, 56 CCH EPD ¶ 40801.

Where 11 of 16 campuses in state university system had received federal contracts, campuses that did not enter contracts with federal government were nonetheless subject to affirmative action requirements of 29 USCS § 793 and Vietnam Era Veterans Readjustment Assistance Act of 1974 (38 USCS § 4212), since university system was single state agency of which non-contracting campuses were merely constituent parts. Board of Governors of University of North Carolina v United States Dep't of Labor (1990, CA4 NC) 917 F2d 812, 1 AD Cas 1704, 54 BNA FEP Cas 136, 135 BNA LRRM 2760, 36 CCF ¶ 75959, 55 CCH EPD ¶ 40370, cert den (1991) 500 US 916, 114 L Ed 2d 100, 111 S Ct 2013, 55 BNA FEP Cas 1104, 56 CCH EPD ¶ 40801.

Department of Labor's order canceling future government contracting with all University of North Carolina constituent institutions for failure of some institutions to comply with regulations implementing employment laws was not erroneous; both 29 USCS § 793(a) and 38 USCS § 2012 [now 38 USCS § 4212], requiring affirmative action to employ handicapped and Vietnam veterans, apply to "parties contracting" with U.S., and for purposes of such laws the University of North Carolina system constitutes a single, unified state agency, and campuses which have not entered contracts with the federal government must, nontheless, submit to compliance review. Board of Governors of University of North Carolina v United States Dep't of Labor (1990, CA4 NC) 917 F2d 812, 1 AD Cas 1704, 54 BNA FEP Cas 136, 135 BNA LRRM 2760, 36 CCF ¶ 75959, 55 CCH EPD ¶ 40370, cert den (1991) 500 US 916, 114 L Ed 2d 100, 111 S Ct 2013, 55 BNA FEP Cas 1104, 56 CCH EPD ¶ 40801.

Secretary of Labor does not have jurisdiction under 38 USCS § 2012 [now 38 USCS § 4212] to hear complaint that state division of employment security does not comply with provisions of Vietnam Era Veterans Readjustment Assistance Act (§§ 2011 et seq. [now §§ 4211 et seq.]), since agreements between state agency and Department of Labor constitute grants rather than contracts within meaning of § 2012 [now § 4212]. Hammond v Donovan (1982, WD Mo) 538 F Supp 1106, 113 BNA LRRM 3599, 30 CCF ¶ 70266, 30 CCH EPD ¶ 33012.

Complaints must be filed with Office of Federal

Contract Compliance Programs within 180 days of date of alleged violation unless time for filing is extended for good cause shown; date of filing is date complaint is first received in writing by office, and request for complaint form of verbal notice of intent to file complaint is not sufficient is establish filing date; filing or processing of grievance under collective bargaining agreement does not extend filing period; date of alleged violation is date complainant knew or reasonably should have known of alleged discriminatory act or violation. OFCCP Order No. 630a5, March 10, 1983.

3. Complaints

Where veteran's complaint alleged that his employer violated § 2012 [now 4212] by refusing to rehire him after he had voluntarily quit, allegation that employer tried to intimidate him from taking his complaint to Department of Labor was irrelevant to determination whether denial of complaint was abuse of discretion, since alleged intimidation came after refusal to rehire. Clementson v Donovan (1985, DC Hawaii) 608 F Supp 152, 121 BNA LRRM 3118, 36 CCH EPD ¶ 35061, 102 CCH LC ¶ 11429, affd (1986, CA9 Hawaii) 806 F2d 1402, 124 BNA LRRM 2422, 33 CCF ¶ 74923, 42 CCH EPD ¶ 36792.

4. Private right of action

Under 38 USCS § 2012 [now 38 USCS § 4212], Vietnam veteran did not have private right of action against private government contractor for failing to comply with hiring provisions of § 2012 [now § 4212], since review of legislative intent indicates Congress intended that enforcement and supervision of affirmative action hiring policy of § 2012 [now § 4212] is left to Department of Labor to which veteran could forward a complaint. Barron v Nightingale Roofing, Inc. (1988, CA1 Me) 842 F2d 20, 127 BNA LRRM 2996, 34 CCF ¶ 75462, 46 CCH EPD ¶ 37895.

Vietnam Era Veterans' Readjustment Assistance Act does not expressly provide for private actions; veterans who believe themselves to be victims of discrimination may complain to labor secretary, who enforces act administratively. Harris v Adams (1989, CA6 Mich) 873 F2d 929, 1 AD Cas 1475, 49 BNA FEP Cas 1304, 131 BNA LRRM 2405, 50 CCH EPD ¶ 38973.

Scope of 38 USCS § 2012 [now 38 USCS § 4212], as it existed prior to amendment of December 3, 1974, was limited to assuring listing of job openings with state employment agencies and to preference of certain veterans in referrals by those agencies, and it imposed no duties and created no rights with respect to employer's decision to hire or not to hire; thus, disabled veteran could not maintain action under 38 USCS § 2012 [now 38 USCS § 4212], as it read prior to amendment by act December 3, 1974, against prospective employer for failure to be hired due to service-connected disability. Wood v Diamond State Tel. Co. (1977, DC Del) 440 F Supp 1003, 18 BNA FEP Cas 647, 16 CCH EPD ¶ 8154.

There is no private right of action for violation of 38 USCS § 2012 [now 38 USCS § 4212]. Butler v McDonnell-Douglas Saudi Arabia Corp. (1981, SD Ohio) 93 FRD 384, 110 BNA LRRM 2048.

There is no private right of action under 38 USCS § 2012 [now 38 USCS § 4212], nor may state claim be maintained under third-party beneficiary theory. Stephens v Roadway Express Co. (1982, ND Ga) 37 BNA FEP Cas 1104, 119 BNA LRRM 2312, 29 CCH EPD ¶ 32941, 95 CCH LC ¶ 13893.

38 USCS § 2012 [now 38 USCS § 4212] establishes no private cause of action and provides no authority for aggrieved veterans to file suit in federal court, but is designed to provide remedy, through Department of Labor, against contractors who discriminate against such veterans or that fail to comply with affirmative action provision embodied therein. De Leon Cruz v Loubriel (1982, DC Puerto Rico) 539 F Supp 250.

University employee's claims against employer must be denied summarily, to extent they are based on noncompliance with university's conciliation agreement settling its alleged violations of 38 USCS § 4212, because (1) evidence that he served in military only until July 1964 leaves him outside definition of "Vietnam era veteran," and (2) § 4212 does not provide vehicle to assert violation of agreement, and neither do 42 USCS §§ 1983 or 1985. Brace v Ohio State Univ. (1994, SD Ohio) 866 F Supp 1069.

38 USCS § 4212 does not create private right of action for veterans alleging employment discrimination. Stefanovic v University of Tennessee (1996, ED Tenn) 935 F.Supp. 944, remanded on other grounds (1998, CA6 Tenn) 1998 US App LEXIS 1905.

Vietnam War veteran not hired to work as laborer on federal highway construction project has Vietnam Era Veterans Readjustment Assistance Act claim denied summarily, where it appears from language of statute that Congress intended persons protected under this statute to file complaint with Labor Secretary, because there is no private right of action under 38 USCS § 4212. Ledbetter v Koss Constr. Co. (1997, DC Kan) 981 F Supp 1394.

Complaint alleging violation of 38 USCS § 4212 is dismissed with prejudice, where veteran was terminated for alleged poor job performance on March 1, 1994 and claims he was discriminated against on basis of veteran status, even if such discrimination could be shown, because Congress chose not to create private right of action by which veterans may sue employers. Phillips v Merchants Ins. Group (1998, ND NY) 990 F Supp 99.

5. Judicial review

In absence of abandonment of statutory responsiblity, Secretary of Labor's decision to forego enforcement action under § 2012 [now § 4212] against federal contractor who failed to rehire disabled Vietnam Veteran who had resigned his position and then reapplied for same position was immune from judicial review since enforcement decision is within agency discretion. Clementson v Brock (1986, CA9 Hawaii) 806 F2d 1402, 124 BNA LRRM 2422, 33 CCF ¶ 74923, 42 CCH EPD ¶ 36792.

Record before court in veteran's suit seeking review of adverse determination by Department of Labor on his complaint asserting that employer violated § 2012 [now § 4212] was sufficient to support summary judgment notwithstanding that administrative record was not before court, where written complaints, agency's summary of evidence, and agency's recommended findings and reasons therefor were before court. Clementson v Donovan (1985, DC Hawaii) 608 F Supp 152, 121 BNA LRRM 3118, 36 CCH EPD ¶ 35061, 102 CCH LC ¶ 11429, affd (1986, CA9 Hawaii) 806 F2d 1402, 124 BNA LRRM 2422, 33 CCF ¶ 74923, 42 CCH EPD ¶ 36792.

Review of Secretary of Labor's decision to forego further legal action on disabled Vietnam era veteran's complaint alleging that his employer's failure to rehire him after he voluntarily quit his position violated employer's affirmative action obligation under § 2012 [now § 4212] is not de novo; such decision is to be reviewed under limited standard of abuse of discretion. Clementson v Donovan (1985, DC Hawaii) 608 F Supp 152, 36 CCH EPD ¶ 35061, 121 BNA LRRM 3118, 102 CCH LC ¶ 11429, affd (1986, CA9 Hawaii) 806 F2d 1402, 124 BNA LRRM 2422, 33 CCF ¶ 74923, 42 CCH EPD ¶ 36792.

Decision of Office of Federal Contract Compliance Program that employer had not violated its affirmative action obligation under § 2012 [now § 4212] did not fall within category of agency actions which, under 5 USCS § 701(a), are actions committed to agency discretion by law and not subject to judicial review. Clementson v Donovan (1985, DC Hawaii) 608 F Supp 152, 121 BNA LRRM 3118, 36 CCH EPD ¶ 35061, 102 CCH LC ¶ 11429, affd (1986, CA9 Hawaii) 806 F2d 1402, 124 BNA LRRM 2422, 33 CCF ¶ 74923, 42 CCH EPD ¶ 36792.

Disappointed applicant's court challenge to his disqualification from preapprenticeship training program on basis of low test score was dismissed, where federal agency concluded there was insufficient evidence that federal contractor violated Vietnam Era Veterans' Readjustment Assistance Act, because agency's decision to forego enforcement action under § 2012 [now § 4212] is immune from judicial review. Harris v McLaughlin (1989, ND Ohio) 732 F Supp 780, 133 BNA LRRM 2978.

6. Miscellaneous

Department of Labor's decision adverse to disabled Vietnam era veteran who claimed that his employer's failure to rehire him after he voluntarily quit violated § 2012 [now § 4212] was not arbitrary and capricious on ground of failure to consider whether employer had duty to transfer veteran to another job, where tenor of veteran's complaint was employer's refusal to rehire him for his old position, nor was failure to consider whether his service-induced ulcer made him tense and contributed to his turbulent relationship with his supervisor which in turn led to his quit or discharge arbitrary, where claim was not raised before agency and chain of causation was entirely too attenuated to require judicial relief. Clementson v Donovan (1985, DC Hawaii) 608 F Supp 152, 36 CCH EPD ¶ 35061, 121 BNA LRRM 3118, 102 CCH LC ¶ 11429, affd (1986, CA9 Hawaii) 806 F2d 1402, 124 BNA LRRM 2422, 33 CCF ¶ 74923, 42 CCH EPD ¶ 36792.

Where only evidence before Office of Federal Contract Compliance showed that reason for veteran's quit or discharge was personality dispute with supervisor, fact that employer did not have valid affirmative action program in place was not grounds for setting aside summary judgment in favor of employer in veteran's action for review of adverse Department of Labor decision on his complaint alleging that employer violated § 2012 [now § 4212] by failing to rehire him after he quit. Clementson v Donovan (1985, DC Hawaii) 608 F Supp 152, 36 CCH EPD ¶ 35061, 121 BNA LRRM 3118, 102 CCH LC ¶ 11429, affd (1986, CA9 Hawaii) 806 F2d 1402, 124 BNA LRRM 2422, 33 CCF ¶ 74923, 42 CCH EPD ¶ 36792.

§ 4213. Eligibility requirements for veterans under Federal employment and training programs

Any (1) amounts received as pay or allowances by any person while serving on active duty, (2) period of time during which such person served on such active duty, and (3) amounts received under chapters 11, 13, 30, 31, 35, and 36 of this title [38 USCS §§ 1101 et seq., 1301 et seq., 3100 et seq., 3500 et seq., and 3670 et seq.] by an eligible veteran, any amounts received by an eligible person under chapters 13 and 35 of such title [38 USCS §§ 1301 et seq. and

3500 et seq.], and any amounts received by an eligible person under chapter 106 of title 10 [10 USCS §§ 2131 et seq.], shall be disregarded in determining eligibility under any public service employment program, any emergency employment program, any job training program assisted under the Economic Opportunity Act of 1964, any employment or training program assisted under the Job Training Partnership Act (29 U.S.C. 1501 et seq.), or any other employment or training (or related) program financed in whole or in part with Federal funds.
(Added Oct. 24, 1972, P. L. 92-540, Title V, § 503(a), 86 Stat. 1098; Oct. 17, 1980, P. L. 96-466, Title VIII, § 801(k)(1), (2)(A), 94 Stat. 2217; June 13, 1991, P. L. 102-54, § 14(c)(10), 105 Stat. 285; Aug. 6, 1991, P. L. 102-83, § 5(a), 105 Stat. 406; Nov. 2, 1994, P. L. 103-446, Title VII, § 702(b), 108 Stat. 4675.)

HISTORY; ANCILLARY LAWS AND DIRECTIVES

References in text:
"The Economic Opportunity Act of 1964", referred to in this section, is Act Aug. 20, 1964, P. L. 88-452, 78 Stat. 508, as amended, which is generally classified to 42 USCS §§ 2701 et seq. For full classification of this Act, consult USCS Tables volumes.

Explanatory notes:
A prior § 2013, contained in Subchapter II of former Chapter 41, was transferred to 38 USCS § 2004 [now 38 USCS § 4104] by Act Sept. 19, 1962, P. L. 87-675, § 1(a), 76 Stat. 558.

Effective date of section:
Act Oct. 24, 1972, P. L. 92-540, Title VI, § 601(b), 86 Stat. 1099, provided that this section is effective 90 days after Oct. 24, 1972.

Amendments:
1980. Act Oct. 17, 1980 (effective 10/1/80, as provided by § 802(h) of such Act, which appears as 38 USCS § 3452 note), substituted new catchline for one which read: "§ 2013. Eligibility requirements for veterans under certain Federal manpower training programs"; substituted "an eligible veteran" for "a veteran (as defined in section 101(2) of this title) who served on active duty for a period of more than 180 days or was discharged or released from active duty for a service-connected disability"; and substituted "any employment or training program assisted under the Comprehensive Employment and Training Act, or any other employment or" for "any manpower training program assisted under the Manpower Development and Training Act of 1962, or any other manpower".
1991. Act June 13, 1991 substituted "the Job Training Partnership Act (29 U.S.C. 1501 et seq.)" for "the Comprehensive Employment and Training Act".
Act Aug. 6, 1991, redesignated this section, formerly 38 USCS § 2013, as 38 USCS § 4213.
1994. Act Nov. 2, 1994 substituted "chapters 11, 13, 30, 31, 35, and 36 of this title by an eligible veteran," for "chapters 11, 13, 31, 34, 35, and 36 of this title by an eligible veteran and" and "eligibility under" for "the needs or qualifications of participants in"; and inserted "and any amounts received by an eligible person under chapter 106 of title 10,".

RESEARCH GUIDE

Am Jur:
45A Am Jur 2d, Job Discrimination (1993) §§ 178, 672, 801.
45B Am Jur 2d, Job Discrimination (1993) § 1224.
77 Am Jur 2d, Veterans and Veterans' Laws § 114.

INTERPRETIVE NOTES AND DECISIONS

38 USCS § 2013 [now 38 USCS § 4213] requires state agency to disregard employee's period of military service and to carry forward period of his pre-enlistment employment in determining his qualifications for trade readjustment allowance benefits under Trade Act of 1974 (19 USCS §§ 2271 et seq.) Hulet v Review Bd. of Indiana Employment Sec. Div. (1980, Ind App) 412 NE2d 289, 105 BNA LRRM 3377.

§ 4214. Employment within the Federal Government

(a)(1) The United States has an obligation to assist veterans of the Armed Forces in readjusting to civilian life since veterans, by virtue of their military service, have lost opportunities to pursue education and training oriented toward civilian careers. The Federal Government is also continuously concerned with building an effective work force, and veterans constitute a major recruiting source. It is, therefore, the policy of the United States and the purpose of this section to promote the maximum of employment and job advancement opportunities within the Federal Government for disabled veterans and certain veterans of the Vietnam era and of the post-Vietnam era who are qualified for such employment and advancement.

(2) For the purposes of this section, the term "agency" means a department, agency, or instrumentality in the executive branch.

(b)(1) To further the policy stated in subsection (a) of this section, veterans referred to in paragraph (2) of this subsection shall be eligible, in accordance with regulations which the Office of Personnel Management shall prescribe, for veterans readjustment appointments, and for subsequent career-conditional appointments, under the terms and conditions specified in Executive Order Numbered 11521 (March 26, 1970) [5 USCS § 3302 note], except that—

(A) such an appointment may be made up to and including the level GS-11 or its equivalent;

(B) a veteran shall be eligible for such an appointment without regard to the number of years of education completed by such veteran;

(C) a veteran who is entitled to disability compensation under the laws administered by the Department of Veterans Affairs or whose discharge or release from active duty was for a disability incurred or aggravated in line of duty shall be given a preference for such an appointment over other veterans;

(D) a veteran receiving such an appointment shall—

(i) in the case of a veteran with less than 15 years of education, receive training or education; and

(ii) upon successful completion of the prescribed probationary period, acquire a competitive status; and

(E) a veteran given an appointment under the authority of this subsection whose employment under the appointment is terminated within one year after the date of such appointment shall have the same right to appeal that termination to the Merit Systems Protection Board as a career or career-conditional employee has during the first year of employment.

(2) This subsection applies to—

(A) a veteran of the Vietnam era; and

(B) veterans who first became a member of the Armed Forces or first entered on active duty as a member of the Armed Forces after May 7, 1975, and were discharged or released from active duty under conditions other than dishonorable.

(3)(A) Except as provided in subparagraph (C) of this paragraph, a veteran of the Vietnam era may receive an appointment under this section only during the period ending—

(i) 10 years after the date of the veteran's last discharge or release from active duty; or

(ii) December 31, 1995, whichever is later.

(B) Except as provided in subparagraph (C) of this paragraph, a veteran described in paragraph (2)(B) of this subsection may receive such an appointment only within the 10-year period following the later of—

(i) the date of the veteran's last discharge or release from active duty; or

(ii) December 31, 1989.

(C) The limitations of subparagraphs (A) and (B) of this paragraph shall not apply to a veteran who has a service-connected disability rated at 30 percent or more.

(D) For purposes of clause (i) of subparagraphs (A) and (B) of this paragraph, the last discharge or release from active duty shall not include any discharge or release from active duty of less than ninety days of continuous service unless the individual involved is discharged or released for a service-connected disability, for a medical condition which preexisted such service and which the Secretary determines is not service connected, for hardship, or as a result of a reduction in force described in section 3011(a)(1)(A)(ii)(III) of this title or of an involuntary separation described in section 3018A(a)(1).

(c) Each agency shall include in its affirmative action plan for the hiring, placement, and advancement of handicapped individuals in such agency as required by section 501(b) of the Rehabilitation Act of 1973 (29 U.S.C. 791(b)) a separate specification of plans (in accordance with regulations which the Office of Personnel Management shall prescribe in consultation with the Secretary, the Secretary of Labor, and the Secretary of Health and Human Services, consistent with the purposes, provisions, and priorities of such Act) to promote and carry out such affirmative action with respect to disabled veterans in order to achieve the purpose of this section.

(d) The Office of Personnel Management shall be responsible for the review and evaluation of the implementation of this section and the activities of each agency to carry out the purpose and provisions of this section. The Office shall periodically obtain (on at least an annual basis) information on the implementation of this section by each agency and on the activities of each agency to carry out the purpose and provisions of this section. The information obtained shall include specification of the use and extent of appointments made by each agency under subsection (b) of this section and the results of the plans required under subsection (c) of this section.

(e)(1) The Office of Personnel Management shall submit to the Congress annually a report on activities carried out under this section. Each such report shall include the following information with respect to each agency:

(A) The number of appointments made under subsection (b) of this section since the last such report and the grade levels in which such appointments were made.

(B) The number of individuals receiving appointments under such subsection whose appointments were converted to career or career-conditional appointments, or whose employment under such an appointment has terminated, since the last such report, together with a complete listing of categories of causes of appointment terminations and the number of such individuals whose employment has terminated falling into each such category.

(C) The number of such terminations since the last such report that were initiated by the agency involved and the number of such terminations since the last such report that were initiated by the individual involved.

(D) A description of the education and training programs in which individuals appointed under such subsection are participating at the time of such report.

(2) Information shown for an agency under clauses (A) through (D) of paragraph (1) of this subsection—

(A) shall be shown for all veterans; and

(B) shall be shown separately (i) for veterans of the Vietnam era who are entitled to disability compensation under the laws administered by the Secretary whose discharge or release from active duty was for a disability incurred or aggravated in line of duty, and (ii) for other veterans.

(f) Notwithstanding section 4211 of this title, the terms "veteran" and "disabled veteran" as used in subsection (a) of this section shall have the meaning provided for under generally applicable civil service law and regulations.

(g) To further the policy stated in subsection (a) of this section, the Secretary may give preference to qualified special disabled veterans and qualified veterans of the Vietnam era for employment in the Department as veterans' benefits counselors and veterans' claims examiners and in positions to provide the outreach services required under section 7722 of this title, to serve as veterans' representatives at certain educational institutions as provided in section 7724 of this title, or to provide readjustment counseling under section 1712A of this title to veterans of the Vietnam era.

READJUSTMENT BENEFITS   **38 USCS § 4214**

(Added Dec. 3, 1974, P. L. 93-508, Title IV, § 403(a), 88 Stat. 1593; Nov. 23, 1977, P. L. 95-202, Title III, § 308, 91 Stat. 1445; Oct. 26, 1978, P. L. 95-520, § 6(b), 92 Stat. 1821; Oct. 17, 1980, P. L. 96-466, Title V, § 510, Title VIII, § 801(l), 94 Stat. 2207, 2217; Nov. 3, 1981, P. L. 97-72, Title II, § 202(a), 95 Stat. 1054; Oct. 12, 1982, P. L. 97-295, § 4(95)(A) in part, 96 Stat. 1313; Oct. 24, 1984, P. L. 98-543, Title II, Part B, § 211, 98 Stat. 2743; Oct. 28, 1986, P. L. 95-576, Title III, Part A, § 332, 100 Stat. 3279; Dec. 18, 1989, P. L. 101-237, Title IV, § 407(a)(1), (b), 103 Stat. 2082; March 22, 1991, P. L. 102-16, § 9(a), (b), 105 Stat. 54; Aug. 6, 1991, P. L. 102-83, §§ 2(c)5, 4(a)(1), (3), (4), (b)(1), (2)(E), 5(a), (c)(1), 105 Stat. 402-406; Oct. 10, 1991, P. L. 102-127, § 4, 105 Stat. 622; Oct. 29, 1992, P. L. 102-568, Title V, § 505, 106 Stat. 4340.)

HISTORY; ANCILLARY LAWS AND DIRECTIVES

References in text:
The "civil service law", referred to in subsec. (f) generally appears as 5 USCS §§ 1101 et seq. and 3301 et seq.

Explanatory notes:
A prior § 2014, contained in Subchapter II of former Chapter 41, was transferred to 38 USCS § 2005 by Act Sept. 19, 1962, P. L. 87-675, § 1(a), 76 Stat. 558.

Effective date of section:
Act Dec. 3, 1974, P. L. 93-508, Title V, § 503, 88 Stat. 1601, provided that this section is effective on Dec. 3, 1974.

Amendments:
1977. Act Nov. 23, 1977 (effective 11/23/77, as provided by § 501 of such Act, which appears as 38 USCS § 101 note), in subsec. (b), inserted "The Chairman of the Civil Service Commission shall submit to the President and the Congress, not later than six months after the date of enactment of the GI Bill Improvement Act of 1977, a report on the need for the continuation after June 30, 1978, of the authority for veterans readjustment appointments contained in this subsection.".
1978. Act Oct. 26, 1978, substituted new subsec. (b) for one which read: "(b) To further this policy, veterans of the Vietnam era shall be eligible, in accordance with regulations which the Civil Service Commission shall prescribe, for veterans readjustment appointments up to and including the level GS-5, as specified in subchapter II of chapter 51 of title 5, and subsequent career-conditional appointments, under the terms and conditions specified in Executive Order Numbered 11521 (March 26, 1970), except that in applying the one-year period of eligibility specified in section 2(a) of such order to a veteran or disabled veteran who enrolls, within one year following separation from the Armed Forces or following release from hospitalization or treatment immediately following separation from the Armed Forces, in a program of education (as defined in section 1652 of this title) on more than a half-time basis (as defined in section 1788 of this title), the time spent in such program of education (including customary periods of vacation and permissible absences) shall not be counted. The eligibility of such a veteran for a readjustment appointment shall continue for not less than six months after such veteran first ceases to be enrolled

therein on more than a half-time basis. No veterans readjustment appointment may be made under authority of this subsection after June 30, 1978. The Chairman of the Civil Service Commission shall submit to the President and the Congress, not later than six months after the date of enactment of the GI Bill Improvement Act of 1977, a report on the need for the continuation after June 30, 1978, of the authority for veterans readjustment appointments contained in this subsection.''; in subsec. (d), substituted ''of this section'' for ''thereof'' following ''subsection (c)'', inserted ''Each report under the preceding sentence shall include in the specification of the use and extent of appointments made under subsection (b) of this section the following information (shown for all veterans and separately for veterans described in subsection (b)(1)(C) of this section and other veterans);'', and added paras. (1)–(4); and in subsec. (f), inserted ''subsection (a) of''.

1980. Act Oct. 17, 1980 (effective 10/1/80, as provided by § 802(e), (h) of such Act), in subsec. (b), in the introductory matter, substituted ''Office of Personnel Management'' for ''Civil Service Commission'', deleted para. (2) which read: ''(2) In this subsection, the term 'veteran of the Vietnam era' has the meaning given such term in section 2011(2)(A) of this title,'', and redesignated para. (3) as para. (2); in subsec. (c), substituted ''the Rehabilitation Act of 1973 (29 U.S.C. 791(b))'' for ''Public Law 93-112 (87 Stat. 391)'' and substituted ''Office of Personnel Management'' for ''Civil Service Commission''; in subsec. (d), introductory matter, substituted ''Office of Personnel Management'' for ''Civil Service Commission'' and substituted ''Office'' for ''Commission''; in subsec. (e), substituted ''Office of Personnel Management'' for ''Civil Service Commission'', substituted ''Office'' for ''Commission'' and substituted ''the Rehabilitation Act of 1973 (29 U.S.C. 791(d))'' for ''such Public Law 93-112''; and added subsec. (g).

1981. Act Nov. 3, 1981 (effective 10/1/81, as provided by § 207(3) of such Act, which appears as a note to this section), in subsec. (b)(2), substituted ''1984'' for ''1981''.

1982. Act Oct. 12, 1982, in subsec. (c), substituted ''Health and Human Services'' for ''Health, Education, and Welfare''.

1984. Act Oct. 24, 1984, in subsec. (a), designated the existing provisions as para. (1), and added para. (2); in subsec. (b), in para. (1), in subpara. (A), substituted ''GS-9'' for ''GS-7'', in subpara. (B), deleted ''and'' following the concluding semicolon, in subpara. (C), substituted ''; and'' for a concluding period, and added subpara. (D), in para. (2), substituted ''September 30, 1986'' for ''September 30, 1984''; in subsec. (c), substituted ''agency'' for ''department, agency, and instrumentality in the executive branch'' and substituted ''such agency'' for ''such department, agency, or instrumentality''; and substituted subsec. (d) and (e) for ones which read:

''(d) The Office of Personnel Management shall be responsible for the review and evaluation of the implementation of this section and the activities of each such department, agency, and instrumentality to carry out the purpose and provisions of this section. The Office shall periodically obtain and publish (on at least a semiannual basis) reports on such implementation and activities from each such department, agency, and instrumentality, including specification of the use and extent of appointments made under subsection (b) of this section and the results of the plans required under

READJUSTMENT BENEFITS
38 USCS § 4214

subsection (c) of this section. Each report under the preceding sentence shall include in the specification of the use and extent of appointments made under subsection (b) of this section the following information (shown for all veterans and separately for veterans described in subsection (b)(1)(C) of this section and other veterans):

"(1) The number of appointments made under such subsection since the last such report and the grade levels in which such appointments were made.

"(2) The number of individuals receiving appointments under such subsection whose appointments were converted to career conditional appointments, or whose employment under such an appointment has terminated, since the last such report, together with a complete listing of categories of causes of appointment terminations and the number of such individuals whose employment has terminated falling into each such category.

"(3) the number of such terminations since the last such report that were initiated by the department, agency, or instrumentality involved and the number of such terminations since the last such report that were initiated by the individual involved.

"(4) A description of the education and training programs in which individuals appointed under such subsection are participating at the time of such report.

"(e) The Office of Personnel Management shall submit to the Congress annually a report on activities carried out under this section, except that, with respect to subsection (c) of this section, the Office may include a report of such activities separately in the report required to be submitted by section 501(d) of the Rehabilitation Act of 1973 (29 U.S.C 791(d)), regarding the employment of handicapped individuals by each department, agency, and instrumentality.".

1986. Act Oct. 28, 1986, in subsec. (b)(2), substituted "December 31, 1989" for "September 30, 1986".

1989. Act Dec. 18, 1989 (effective 1/1/90 as provided by § 407(c) of such Act, which appears as 38 USCS § 4211 note), in subsec. (a)(1), substituted "certain veterans of the Vietnam era and veterans of the post-Vietnam era who are qualified for such employment and advancement" for "qualified disabled veterans and veterans of the Vietnam era", in subsec. (b), in para. (1), in the introductory matter, substituted "veterans referred to in paragraph (2) of this subsection" for "veterans of the Vietnam era", in subpara. (A), inserted "or in the case of a veteran referred to in paragraph (2)(A) of this subsection, the level of GS-11 or its equivalent", substituted subpara. (B) for one which read: "a veteran of the Vietnam era shall be eligible for such an appointment without any time limitations with respect to eligibility for such an appointment", in subpara. (C), inserted "referred to in paragraph (2) of this subsection" and deleted "and" following "veteran;", in subpara. (D), substituted "; and" for the concluding period, added subparas. (E) and (F), redesignated para. (2) as para. (4), in para. (4), as redesignated, substituted "1993" for "1989", and added paras. (2) and (3).

1991. Act March 22, 1991 (applicable as provided by § 9(d) of such Act, which appears as a note to this section), in subsec. (a)(1), substituted "The United States has an obligation to assist veterans of the Armed Forces in readjusting to civilian life since veterans, by virtue of their military service, have lost opportunities to pursue education and training oriented toward civilian careers. The Federal Government is also continuously concerned with building an effective work force, and veterans constitute a major recruiting source. It is, therefore, the policy of the United States" for "It is the policy of the United States" and substituted "disabled veterans and certain veterans of the Vietnam era and of the post-Vietnam era who are qualified for such employment and advancement." for "certain veterans of the Vietnam era and veterans of the post-Vietnam era who are qualified for such employment and advancement."; in subsec. (b)(1), in subpara. (A), substituted "up to and including the level GS-11 or its equivalent;" for "up to and including the level GS-9 or its equivalent or in the case of a veteran referred to in paragraph (2)(A) of this subsection, the level of GS-11 or its equivalent"; and substituted subparas. (B)–(D) for former subparas. (B) and (C), which read:

"(B) a veteran referred to in paragraph (2) of this subsection shall be eligible for such an appointment during (i) the four-year period beginning on the date of the veteran's last discharge or release from active duty, or (ii) the two-year period beginning on the date of the enactment of the Veterans Education and Employment Amendments of 1989, whichever ends later;

"(C) a veteran of the Vietnam era referred to in paragraph (2) of this subsection who is entitled to disability compensation under the laws administered by the Veterans' Administration or whose discharge or release from active duty was for a disability incurred or aggravated in line of duty shall be eligible for such an appointment without regard to the number of years of education completed by such veteran;".

Such Act further (applicable as above), in subsec. (b)(1), redesignated former subpara. (D) as subpara. (E), in such subpara. (E), substituted a period for "; and", and deleted subparas. (E) and (F), which read:

"(E) the requirement of an educational or training program for a veteran receiving such an appointment shall not apply if the veteran has 15 years or more of education; and

"(F) in the case of a veteran who is not a disabled veteran, the veteran may not have completed more than 16 years of education at the time of the veteran's appointment.".

Such Act further (applicable as above), in subsec. (b), in para. (2), substituted subpara. (B) for one which read: "(B) a veteran who served on active duty after the Vietnam era.", substituted para. (3) for one which read "(3) For purposes of paragraph (1)(B)(i) of this subsection, the last discharge or release from a period of active duty shall not include any discharge or release from a period of active duty of less than 90 days of continuous service unless the individual involved is discharged or released for a service-connected disability, for a medical condition which preexisted such service and which the Secretary determines is not service connected, for hardship, or as a result of a reduction in force as described in section 1411(a)(1)(A)(ii)(III) of this title.", and deleted para. (4) which read (4) No veterans readjustment appointment may be made under authority of this subsection after December 31, 1993.".

Act Aug. 6, 1991, redesignated this section, formerly 38 USCS § 2014, as 38 USCS § 4214, amended the references in this section to reflect the redesignations made by § 5(a) of such Act (see Table III preceding 38 USCS § 101), and, in subsec. (g), substituted "section 7722" for "section 241" and "section 7724" for "section 243".

Such Act further substituted "administered by the Secretary" for "administered by the Veterans' Administration" wherever appearing, substituted "Department" for "Veterans' Administration" wherever appearing, and substituted "Secretary" for "Administrator" wherever appearing.

Act Oct. 10, 1991, in subsec. (b)(2)(A), substituted cl. (i) for one which read: "has a service-connected disability".

1992. Act Oct. 29, 1992, in subsec. (b), in para. (2), substituted subpara. (A) for one which read:

"(A) a veteran of the Vietnam era who—

"(i) is entitled to disability compensation under the laws administered by the Secretary or whose discharge or release from active duty was for a disability incurred or aggravated in line of duty; or

"(ii) during such era, served on active duty in the Armed Forces in a campaign or expedition for which a campaign badge has been authorized; and"

and, in para. (3), in subpara. (A)(ii), substituted "December 31, 1995" for "December 31, 1993" and, in subpara. (B)(ii), substituted "December 31" for "December 18".

Other provisions:

Information to be included in reports. Act Oct. 13, 1978, P. L. 95-454, Title III, § 307(b)(2), 92 Stat. 1147 (effective 90 days after 10/13/78, as provided by § 907 of that Act); amended Act Aug. 6, 1991, P. L. 102-83, § 5(c)(2), 105 Stat. 406, provided: "the Director of the Office of Personnel Management shall include in the reports required by section 4214(d) of title 38, United States Code [subsec. (d) of this section], the same type of information regarding the use of the authority provided in section 3112 of title 5, United States Code, (as added by paragraph (1) of this subsection), as it required by such section 2014 [this section] with respect to the use of the authority to make veterans readjustment appointments.".

Application and construction of the Oct. 12, 1982 amendment of this section. For provisions as to the application and construction of this Oct. 12, 1982 amendment of the section, see § 5 of such Act, which appears as 10 USCS § 101 note.

Application of Act March 22, 1991 amendments. Act March 22, 1991, P. L. 102-16, § 9(d), 105 Stat. 55; Aug. 14, 1991, P. L. 102-86, Title V, § 506(c), 105 Stat. 426 (effective March 22, 1991, as provided by such section); Oct. 13, 1994, P. L. 103-353, § 6(a), 108 Stat. 3174 (effective as if included in P. L. 102-16, as provided by § 6(b) of the 1994 Act), provides: "The amendments made by this section [amending chapter 42 heading, item preceding 38 USCS § 101, and 38 USCS § 4214] shall apply only to appointments made after the date of the enactment of this Act.".

CODE OF FEDERAL REGULATIONS

Office of Personnel Management—Veterans readjustment appointments, 5 CFR Part 307.

38 USCS § 4214

VETERANS' BENEFITS

RESEARCH GUIDE

Am Jur:

45A Am Jur 2d, Job Discrimination (1993) §§ 178, 672, 801.

45B Am Jur 2d, Job Discrimination (1993) § 1224.

77 Am Jur 2d, Veterans and Veterans' Laws §§ 101, 107.

Forms:

16 Fed Procedural Forms L Ed, Veterans and Veterans' Laws § 68:42.

INTERPRETIVE NOTES AND DECISIONS

1. Generally
2. Appointment
3. Promotion
4. Removal
5. Private right of action

1. Generally

Office of Personnel Management has authority to regulate veterans readjustment appointments, which are subject to OPM investigation, and appointees must meet suitability standards; in order to render this authority meaningful and to enforce suitability standards, OPM must be able to direct action, including directing employee's removal, when violation is found. Logan v Office of Personnel Management (9/30/88, MSPB) Docket No. AT07548710221-1, 38 MSPR 615.

2. Appointment

Arbitrator's award that agency violated 38 USCS § 2014 by failing to select one of grievants who were disabled Viet Nam veterans was erroneous since statute does not require selection of disabled veterans for positions for which they are as qualified as other candidates. AFGE, Local 12 & Dept. of Labor (1991) 38 FLRA No. 126.

3. Promotion

Navy electrician's handicap discrimination claim must fail, even though he was passed over for promotion to WG-10 twice and could not get shipboard experience due to 10 period disability of his left knee, because evidence showed that lack of shipboard experience did not preclude WG-10 promotion, and that training, experience, and monetary awards, rather than Navy's lack of "affirmative action" to promote employees with disabilities, were factors that led to electrician's nonpromotion. Blizzard v Dalton (1995, ED Va) 905 F Supp 331, 13 ADD 999, 67 CCH EPD ¶ 43879.

Although 38 USCS § 4214(a)(1) declares that promotion of employment and job advancement opportunities of certain veterans is policy of United States, such is not sufficient basis on which to find waiver of sovereign immunity; thus, statute does not create private right of action for any alleged failure to adhere to such policy. Cook v Helfer (1996, DC Mass) 153 BNA LRRM 2155, 69 CCH EPD ¶ 44488, 133 CCH LC ¶ 11806.

4. Removal

Board lacked jurisdiction of removal appeal of temporary employees who thought their appointments were Veterans Readjustment Act appointments pursuant to provision for VRA appointee to receive protected position within competitive service of federal employment after two years' service, since SF-50 forms with which they were hired plainly stated that positions were temporary and they must have known they were receiving fewer benefits—notably health care—than employees in competitive service. Anderson v Merit Sys. Protection Bd. (1993, CA FC) 12 F3d 1069, 145 BNA LRRM 2008, cert den (1994) 512 US 1204, 129 L Ed 2d 809, 114 S Ct 2673, 146 BNA LRRM 2640.

Removal of employee who understated his level of education, thereby qualifying for appointment under Veterans Readjustment Assistance Act of 1974 (38 USCS § 2014 [now 38 USCS § 4214]), was not warranted where removal action was not commenced for period of 2 years subsequent to employee notifying agency that he had more education than permitted by VRA, and further where agency converted employee to competitive position and later promoted him within competitive service, such that employee had completed his probationary period and had been performing satisfactorily in competitive service for 2 years when agency removed him. Perry v Veterans Administration (1/9/87 MSPB) Docket No. SE07528510263, 32 MSPR 81.

Veteran, appointed under Veterans' Administration Programs Extension Act of 1978 (92 Stat. 1820), who was discharged as result of veteran's failure to disclose prior arrest and conviction for carrying concealed weapon, convictions for driving with expired vehicle license, and court martial, after completion of more than one year of employment and promotion to employee entitled to procedural protections, including administrative review of removal under 5 USCS §§ 7511 et seq; appointment obtained through fraud or misrepresentation is not nullity which is voidable at option of agency. Devine v Sutermeister (1983, CA) 724 F2d 1558, 116 BNA LRRM 2495 (superseded by statute on other grounds as stated in Bloomer v HHS (1992, CA) 966 F2d 1436, 92 Daily Journal DAR 8073).

5. Private right of action

Since 38 USCS § 4214 does not waive federal government's sovereign immunity, federal employee cannot maintain action for money damages against federal employer thereunder; further, there is no private right of action under 38 USCS § 4214. Antol v Perry (1996, CA3 Pa) 82 F3d 1291, 16 ADD 653, 5 AD Cas 769, 70 BNA FEP Cas 993.

Act's express requirement that federal agency include affirmative action plan for disabled veterans in its Rehabilitation Act affirmative action plan does not purport to waive sovereign immunity or to create express cause of action, hence veteran cannot maintain action for money damages against agency under Act. Antol v Perry (1996, CA3 Pa) 82 F3d 1291, 16 ADD 653, 5 AD Cas 769, 70 BNA FEP Cas 993.

Contractual employment relationship with U.S. was not established by plaintiff, who received veterans' readjustment appointment to excepted civil service position with U.S. Customs Service, since employment was based on appointment under statutory authority of 38 USCS § 2014 [now 38 USCS § 4214] and 5 USCS §§ 3301 and 3302; thus, plaintiff could not maintain suit in Claims Court regarding unlawful removal from employment under claim sounding in contract. Fahy v United States (1988) 14 Cl Ct 470, affd without op (1988, CA) 864 F2d 148, cert den (1989) 491 US 909, 105 L Ed 2d 705, 109 S Ct 3197.

Neither 38 USCS § 4214 nor 5 USCS § 2108 contains express waiver of sovereign immunity; thus, neither provides express or implied cause of action against federal employer. Taydus v Cisneros (1995, DC Mass) 150 BNA LRRM 2859, magistrate's recommendation (1995, DC Mass) 33 FR Serv 3d 1188, accepted (1995, DC Mass) 1995 US Dist LEXIS 14648 and ops combined at (1995, DC Mass) 902 F Supp 288.

Vietnam veteran denied promotion by Navy to position of WG-10 Electrician states cause of action under 38 USCS § 4214(c), where he alleges Navy discriminated on basis of his handicap, because § 4214(c), by incorporating 29 USCS § 791(b), establishes private right of action. Blizzard v Dalton (1995, ED Va) 876 F Supp 95, 8 ADD 695, 4 AD Cas 514, 148 BNA LRRM 2909 (criticized in Madden v Runyon (1995, ED Pa) 899 F Supp 217, 12 ADD 106, 4 AD Cas 1544) and judgment entered (1995, ED Va) 905 F Supp 331, 13 ADD 999, 67 CCH EPD ¶ 43879.

UNITED STATES CODE SERVICE
Lawyers Edition

★★★★★★★★★

Issued in

April 2013

CUMULATIVE SUPPLEMENT

By The Publisher's Editorial Staff

38 USCS
Veterans' Benefits
§§ 3001–4300

(Supplementing the 1998 Main Volume)

LexisNexis®

LexisNexis, the knowledge burst logo, and Michie are trademarks, *lexisnexis.com* is a service mark, and *Shepard's* is a registered trademark of Reed Elsevier Properties Inc., used under license. Matthew Bender is a registered trademark of Matthew Bender Properties Inc.

Copyright© 2013 by Matthew Bender & Company, a member of the LexisNexis Group. All rights reserved.

Copyright is not claimed in any works of the United States Government. Permission to copy material exceeding fair use, 17 USCS § 107, may be licensed for a fee of $1 per page per copy from the Copyright Clearance Center, 222 Rosewood Drive, Danvers, MA, 01923, telephone (978) 750-8400.

www.lexisnexis.com

Editorial Offices
701 East Water Street, Charlottesville, VA 22902
(800) 446-3410

For information about United States Code Service, call 1-800-446-3410 (8 a.m. – 5 p.m. EST), and ask for the USCS Hotline, or contact:
Derrick Wilborn, J.D., *Derrick.Wilborn@lexisnexis.com*
Lily Evans, J.D., *Elizabeth.Evans@lexisnexis.com*

ISBN 978-0-327-10277-9

5638226

Library of Congress Catalog Card Number 72-76254

(Pub.46902)

This supplement covers legislation through the Second Session of the 112th Congress. Consult the latest Cumulative Later Case and Statutory Service and the USCS Advance Service for later public laws.

Cases noted in this issue are included through:

183 L Ed 2d 574
132 S Ct 2566
567 US __
697 F3d 678
864 F Supp 2d 1370
283 FRD 302

106 Fed Cl 142
26 Vet App 1
115 MSPR 71
480 BR 392
71 MJ 566
104 USPQ2d 1393

This volume also includes casenotes based on decisions from the following federal agencies:

Boards of Contract Appeals
Bureau of Alcohol, Tobacco, Firearms, and Explosives
Commodity Futures Trading Commission
Department of Agriculture
Department of Defense
Department of Energy
Department of Labor
Department of the Interior
Fed. Mine Safety & Health Rev. Comm.
Federal Communications Commission
Federal Energy Regulatory Commission
Federal Labor Relations Authority
Federal Maritime Commission
Federal Reserve Board
Federal Trade Commission
Food & Drug Administration

Foreign Claims Settlement Comm.
General Services Administration
Internal Revenue Service
Merit Systems Protection Board
Nat. Oceanic & Atmospheric Admin.
Nat. Transportation Safety Board
National Labor Relations Board
Nuclear Regulatory Commission
Occupational Safety & Health Rev. Comm.
Office of Personnel Management
Patent and Trademark Office
Pension & Welfare Benefits Admin.
Pension Benefits Guaranty Corp.
Securities & Exchange Commission
Surface Transportation Board
U.S. Customs & Border Protection
U.S. Postal Service

Research Guide materials cited in this supplement include:

Administrative Law
Adoption Law and Practice
Antitrust Counseling and
    Litigation Techniques
Antitrust Laws and Trade
    Regulation (2nd ed.)
Banking Law
Bender's Federal Practice Forms
Benedict on Admiralty
Business Crime
Chisum on Patents
Civil Rights Actions
Cohen's Handbk. of Fed. Indian Law
Collier Bankruptcy Practice Guide
Collier on Bankruptcy (16th ed.)
Collier Forms Manual (3d ed. rev.)
Computer Law
Criminal Constitutional Law

Criminal Defense Techniques
Debtor-Creditor Law
Energy Law & Transactions
Environmental Law Practice Guide
Federal Criminal Trials
Fed. Income Taxation of Corporations
    Filing Consolidated Returns
Federal Income Taxation
    of Retirement Plans
Federal Rules of Evidence Manual
Fed. Habeas Corpus Practice & Proc.
Frumer & Friedman, Products Liability
Gilson, Trademark Protection
    and Practice
Goods in Transit
Government Contracts: Law,
    Administration & Procedure
Immigration Law and Procedure

Jayson & Longstreth, Handling
    Federal Tort Claims
Kintner, Federal Antitrust Law
L Ed 2d
Labor and Employment Law
Larson on Employment Discrimination
Liability of Corporate Officers
    and Directors
Milgrim on Licensing
Milgrim on Trade Secrets
Moore's Federal Practice (3d ed.)
National Labor Relations Act:
    Law and Practice
Nimmer on Copyright
Rabkin & Johnson, Current Legal Forms
Rabkin & Johnson, Federal Income,
    Gift and Estate Taxation

Rapp, Education Law
Regulation of Investment Companies
Rhoades & Langer, U.S. International
    Taxation & Tax Treaties
Securities Law Techniques
Tax Controversies: Audits,
    Investigations, Trials
The Law of Advertising
Treatise on Environmental Law
Weinstein's Federal Evidence (2d ed.)
ALR 6th
ALR Fed 2d
Am Jur 2d
Am Jur Proof of Facts 3d
Am Jur Trials

TITLES OF UNITED STATES CODE

* 1. General Provisions
  2. The Congress
* 3. The President
* 4. Flag and Seal, Seat of Government and the States
* 5. Government Organization and Employees; Appendix
  6. Domestic Security
  7. Agriculture
  8. Aliens and Nationality
* 9. Arbitration
* 10. Armed Forces
* 11. Bankruptcy
  12. Banks and Banking
* 13. Census
* 14. Coast Guard
  15. Commerce and Trade
  16. Conservation
* 17. Copyrights
* 18. Crimes and Criminal Procedure; Appendix
  19. Customs Duties
  20. Education
  21. Food and Drugs
  22. Foreign Relations and Intercourse
* 23. Highways
  24. Hospitals and Asylums
  25. Indians
  26. Internal Revenue Code
  27. Intoxicating Liquors
* 28. Judiciary and Judicial Procedure; Appendix
  29. Labor
  30. Mineral Lands and Mining
* 31. Money and Finance
* 32. National Guard
  33. Navigation and Navigable Waters
† 34. [Navy]
* 35. Patents
* 36. Patriotic and National Observances, Ceremonies, and Organizations
* 37. Pay and Allowances of the Uniformed Services
* 38. Veterans' Benefits
* 39. Postal Service
* 40. Public Buildings, Property, and Works
* 41. Public Contracts
  42. The Public Health and Welfare
  43. Public Lands
* 44. Public Printing and Documents
  45. Railroads
* 46. Shipping
  47. Telegraphs, Telephones, and Radiotelegraphs
  48. Territories and Insular Possessions
* 49. Transportation
  50. War and National Defense; Appendix
* 51. National and Commercial Space Programs

* This title has been enacted as positive law. However, any Appendix to the title has not been enacted as law.
† This title has been superseded by the enactment of Title 10 as positive law.
Titles of the United States Code which have been enacted into positive law are legal evidence of the general and permanent laws, while nonpositive law titles only establish prima facie the laws of the United States (1 USCS § 204(a)).

TITLES OF UNITED STATES CODE

1. General Provisions	28. Judiciary and Judicial Procedure; Appendix
2. The Congress	29. Labor
3. The President	30. Mineral Lands and Mining
4. Flag and Seal, Seat of Government, and the States	31. Money and Finance
5. Government Organization and Employees; Appendix	32. National Guard
6. Domestic Security	33. Navigation and Navigable Waters
7. Agriculture	[34. Repealed]
8. Aliens and Nationality	35. Patents
9. Arbitration	36. Patriotic and National Observances, Ceremonies, and Organizations
10. Armed Forces	37. Pay and Allowances of the Uniformed Services
[11. Bankruptcy]	38. Veterans' Benefits
12. Banks and Banking	39. Postal Service
13. Census	40. Public Buildings, Property, and Works
14. Coast Guard	41. Public Contracts
15. Commerce and Trade	42. The Public Health and Welfare
16. Conservation	43. Public Lands
17. Copyrights	44. Public Printing and Documents
18. Crimes and Criminal Procedure; Appendix	45. Railroads
19. Customs Duties	46. Shipping
20. Education	47. Telephone, Telegraphs, and Radiotelegraphs
21. Food and Drugs	48. Territories and Insular Possessions
22. Foreign Relations and Intercourse	49. Transportation
23. Highways	50. War and National Defense; Appendix
24. Hospitals and Asylums	51. National and Commercial Space Programs
25. Indians	
26. Internal Revenue Code	
27. Intoxicating Liquors	

This title has been enacted as positive law. However, any Appendix to this title has not been enacted as law.
† This title has been eliminated by the enactment of Title 10 as positive law.
Title 34 of the United States Code formerly have been set forth but has not been positive law and is legal evidence of the general and permanent laws while compilative law title only establishes prima facie evidence of the United States (1 USC§§4, 204(a)).

ABBREVIATIONS

Reporters, Texts, Etc.

A	Atlantic Reporter
A2d	Atlantic Reporter, Second Series
ACMR	Army Court of Military Review
AD	Appellate Division Reports (NY)
AD2d	Appellate Division Reports, Second Series (NY)
AD Cas	BNA Americans with Disabilities Cases
ADD	Americans With Disabilities Decisions
AdL2d	Pike and Fischer Administrative Law, Second Series
ADVA	Administrator's Decisions, Veterans' Administration
AFCMR	Air Force Court of Military Review
AFTR	American Federal Tax Reports
AFTR2d	American Federal Tax Reports, Second Series
AGBCA	Department of Agriculture Board of Contract Appeals
Agric Dec	Agriculture Decisions
ALAB	NRC Atomic Safety and Licensing Appeal Board
ALR	American Law Reports
ALR2d	American Law Reports, Second Series
ALR3d	American Law Reports, Third Series
ALR4th	American Law Reports, Fourth Series
ALR5th	American Law Reports, Fifth Series
ALR6th	American Law Reports, Sixth Series
ALR Fed	American Law Reports, Federal
ALR Fed 2d	American Law Reports, Federal, Second Series
Am Bankr NS	American Bankruptcy, New Series
AMC	American Maritime Cases
Am Disab	Americans With Disabilities: Practice and Compliance Manual
Am Jur 2d	American Jurisprudence, Second Edition
Am Jur Legal Forms 2d	American Jurisprudence Legal Forms, Second Edition
Am Jur Pl & Pr Forms (Rev ed)	American Jurisprudence Pleading and Practice Forms, Revised Edition
Am Jur Proof of Facts	American Jurisprudence Proof of Facts
Am Jur Proof of Facts 2d	American Jurisprudence Proof of Facts, Second Series
Am Jur Proof of Facts 3d	American Jurisprudence Proof of Facts, Third Series
Am Jur Trials	American Jurisprudence Trials
Am Law Prod Liab 3d	American Law of Products Liability, Third Edition
App DC	United States Court of Appeals for the District of Columbia
Appx	Appendix
ASBCA	Armed Services Board of Contract Appeals
ATF Qtrly Bull	Quarterly Bulletin, Alcohol, Tobacco and Firearms Bureau, U.S. Dept. Treas.
ATR Rul	Ruling of Alcohol, Tobacco and Firearms Bureau, U.S. Dept. Treas.
BAMSL	Bankruptcy Reporter of the Bar Association of Metropolitan St. Louis
BCA	Board of Contract Appeals
BCD	Bankruptcy Court Decisions
Bd App	Patent & Trademark Office Board of Appeals
Bd Imm App	Board of Immigration Appeals
Bd Pat Inter	Board of Patent Appeals and Interferences
BIA	Board of Immigration Appeals
Bkr L Ed	Bankruptcy Service, Lawyers Edition
BLR	BRBS Black Lung Reporter
BNA EBC	Employee Benefits Cases
BNA FEP Cas	Fair Employment Practices Cases
BNA IER Cas	Individual Employment Rights Cases
BNA Intl Trade Rep	International Trade Reporter
BNA LRRM	Labor Relations Reference Manual
BNA OSHC	Occupational Safety and Health Cases
BNA WH Cas	Wage and Hour Cases
BR	Bankruptcy Reporter
BRBS	Benefits Review Board Service

ABBREVIATIONS

BTA	Board of Tax Appeals
BTA Mem	Board of Tax Appeals Memorandum Decisions
CA	United States Court of Appeals
CAB Adv Dig	Civil Aeronautics Board Advance Digest
CAD	Customs Appeals Decisions
Cal Rptr	California Reporter
CB	Cumulative Bulletin of the Internal Revenue Service
CBC	Clark Boardman Callaghan or Collier Bankruptcy Cases
CBCA	Civilian Board of Contract Appeals
CBD	Customs Bulletin and Decisions, Customs Service, Department of the Treasury
CCF	CCH Contract Cases Federal
CCG	Consumer Credit Guide
CCH Bankr L Rptr	Bankruptcy Law Reporter
CCH BCA Dec	Board of Contract Appeals Decisions
CCH CCG	Consumer Credit Guide
CCH Comm Fut L Rep	Commodity Futures Law Reporter
CCH EEOC Dec	Decisions of the Equal Employment Opportunity Commission
CCH EPD	Employment Practice Decisions
CCH Fed Secur L Rep	Federal Securities Law Reporter
CCH FERC	Federal Energy Regulatory Commission Reports
CCH LC	Labor Cases
CCH NLRB	National Labor Relations Board Decisions
CCH OSHD	Occupational Safety and Health Decisions
CCH SEC Doc	CCH Securities Exchange Commission Docket
CCH TCM	Tax Court Memorandum Decisions
CCH Trade Cas	Trade Cases
CCH Trade Reg Rep	Trade Regulation Reports
CCH Unemployment Ins Rep	Unemployment Insurance Reporter
CCPA	Court of Customs and Patent Appeals
CD	Customs Decisions
CDOS	California Daily Opinion Service
CFR	Code of Federal Regulations
CFTC	Commodity Futures Trading Commission
CGCMR	Coast Guard Court of Military Review
CGLB	Coast Guard Law Bulletin
CIT	Court of International Trade
CLI	Commission Licensing Issuance
CMA	Court of Military Appeals
CMR	Court-Martial Reports
COGSA	Carriage of Goods by Sea Act
Colo J C A R	Colorado Journal, Colorado Appellate Reports
Comm Fut L Rep	Commodity Futures Law Reporter
Comp Gen	Decisions of the U.S. Comptroller General
Comp Gen Unpub Dec	Unpublished decisions of the U.S. Comptroller General
Comr Pat	Commissioner of Patents and Trademarks
Copy L Rep	CCH Copyright Law Reporter
CPD	Customs Penalty Decisions
CPSC Advisory Op No	Consumer Product Safety Commission Advisory Opinion Number
CRD	Customs Rules Decisions
CR L	Criminal Law Reporter
CSD	Customs Service Decisions
Ct Cl	Court of Claims
Cust Bull	Customs Bulletin and Decisions, US Department of Treasury
Cust Ct	Customs Court
Cust & Pat App (Cust)	U.S. Court of Customs and Patent Appeals (Customs)
Cust & Pat App (Pat)	U.S. Court of Customs and Patent Appeals (Patents)
Daily Journal DAR	California Daily Journal Daily Appellate Reports
DC	United States District Court
DCAB	Department of Commerce Contract Appeals Board
DCO	Department of Commerce Orders
Dist Col App	District of Columbia Court of Appeals
DOA	Department of Agriculture
DOC	Department of Commerce

ABBREVIATIONS

DOE	Department of Energy
DOHA	Department of Defense Office of Hearings and Appeals
DOT CAB	Department of Transportation Contract Appeals Board
DPRM	Denial of Petition for Rulemaking, NRC Decision
EBC	Employee Benefits Cases
EBCA	Department of Energy Board of Contract Appeals
ECAB	Employees' Compensation Appeals Board, U.S. Department of Labor
EEOC DEC	Equal Employment Opportunity Commission Decisions
ELR	Environmental Law Reporter
Em Ct App	Emergency Court of Appeals
EMP COORD	Employment Coordinator
ENG BCA	Corps of Engineers Board of Contract Appeals
EPD	Employment Practices Decisions
ERA	Economic Regulatory Administration
Envt Rep Cas	Environmental Reporter Cases
ERISA Op Letters	Employee Retirement Income Security Act Opinion Letters
Ex Or	Executive Order
F	Federal Reporter
F2d	Federal Reporter, Second Series
F3d	Federal Reporter, Third Series
F Cas	Federal Cases
FCC	Federal Communications Commission
FCC2d	Federal Communications Commission Reports, Second Series
FCSC	Foreign Claims Settlement Commission
FCSC 1981 Ann Rpt	FCSC Annual Report for 1981
FCSC Dec & Anno (1968)	FCSC Decisions and Annotations, 1968 edition
FDA	Food and Drug Administration
FDA Dec	Food and Drug Administration Decisions
FEA	Federal Energy Administration
Fed Appx	Federal Appendix
Fed Cl	Court of Federal Claims Reporter
Fed Evid Rep	Federal Rules of Evidence Service
Fed Proc L Ed	Federal Procedure, Lawyers Edition
Fed Procedural Forms, L Ed	Federal Procedure Forms, Lawyers Edition
Fed Reg	Federal Register
Fed Rules Evid Serv	Federal Rules of Evidence Service
FEP Case	Fair Employment Practice Cases (BNA)
FEPC	Fair Employment Practice Cases
FERC	Federal Energy Regulatory Commission Reports
Fed Secur L Rep	Federal Securities Law Reporter
FHLBB	Federal Home Loan Bank Board
FLRA	Federal Labor Relations Authority
FLRA GCO	Federal Labor Relations Authority, General Counsel Opinions
FLRC	Federal Labor Relations Council
FLW Fed	Florida Law Weekly Federal
FMC	Federal Maritime Commission
FMSHRC	Federal Mine Safety and Health Review Commission
FOIA	Freedom of Information Act
FPC	Federal Power Commission
FR	Federal Register
FRB	Federal Reserve Bulletin
FRCP	Federal Rules of Civil Procedure
FRCrP	Federal Rules of Criminal Procedure
FRD	Federal Rules Decisions
FRE	Federal Rules of Evidence
FRS	Federal Reserve System
FR Serv	Federal Rules Service
FR Serv 2d	Federal Rules Service, Second Series
FR Serv 3d	Federal Rules Service, Third Series
FSIP	Federal Service Impasses Panel
F Supp	Federal Supplement
F Supp 2d	Federal Supplement, Second Series
FTC	Federal Trade Commission
GAO	Government Accountability Office

ABBREVIATIONS

GSBCA	General Services Administration Board of Contract Appeals
HEW	Department of Health, Education and Welfare
HHS	Department of Health and Human Services
HUD	Department of Housing and Urban Development
HUD BCA	Department of Housing and Urban Development Board of Contract Appeals
IBCA	Interior Department Board of Contract Appeals
IBIA	Interior Board of Indian Appeals (Dept. of the Interior)
IBLA	Interior Board of Land Appeals (Dept. of Interior)
ICC	Interstate Commerce Commission
ID	Decisions of the Department of the Interior
I & N Dec	Immigration and Naturalization Service Decisions
ILS	Immigration Law Service
INS	Immigration and Naturalization Service
IRB	Internal Revenue Bulletin
IRS	Internal Revenue Service
ITRD	Internal Trade Reporter Decisions
JAG	Judge Advocate General
Jud Pan Mult Lit	Rulings of the Judicial Panel on Multidistrict Litigation
LBCA	Department of Labor Board of Contract Appeals
LC	Labor Cases
LD	Land Decisions
L Ed	Lawyers Edition U.S. Supreme Court Reports
L Ed 2d	Lawyers Edition U.S. Supreme Court Reports, Second Series
LRRM	Labor Relations Reference Manual
MA	Maritime Administration
MCC	Motor Carrier Cases (decided by ICC)
Media L R	Media Law Reporter
Mich	Michigan Reports
Mich App	Michigan Appeals Reports
Misc	Miscellaneous Reports (NY)
Misc 2d	Miscellaneous Reports, Second Series (NY)
MJ	Military Justice Reporter
MMLR	Medicare and Medicaid Law Reporter
MSB	Maritime Subsidy Board
MSPB	Merit Systems Protection Board
MSPR	United States Merit Systems Protection Board Reporter
Mun Ct App Dist Col	Municipal Court of Appeals for District of Columbia
NASA BCA	National Aeronautics and Space Administration Board of Contract Appeals
NCMR	Navy Court of Military Review
NE	North Eastern Reporter
NE2d	North Eastern Reporter, Second Series
NITA	The National Institute for Trial Advocacy
NLRB	Decisions and Orders of the National Labor Relations Board
NLRB Advice Mem Case No	National Labor Relations Board Advice Memorandum Case Number
NMCMR	U.S. Navy-Marine Corps Court of Military Review
NOAA	National Oceanic and Atmospheric Administration
NRC	Nuclear Regulatory Commission
NTSB	National Transportation Safety Board
NW	North Western Reporter
NW2d	North Western Reporter, Second Series
NY	New York Reports
NY2d	New York Reports, Second Series
NYS	New York Supplement
NYS2d	New York Supplement, Second Series
nt	note
nts	notes
OAG	Opinions of the Attorney General
OCSLA	Outer Continental Shelf Lands Act
OFCCP	Office of Federal Contract Compliance Programs
OHA	Office of Hearings and Appeals
Op Atty Gen	Opinions of Attorney General
Op Comp Gen	Opinions of Comptroller General
OPM	Office of Personnel Management

Abbreviations

ORW	Ocean Resources and Wildlife Reporter
OSAHRC	Occupational Safety and Health Review Commission (Official Reports)
OSHRC	Occupational Safety and Health Review Commission
P	Pacific Reporter
P. L.	Public Law
P2d	Pacific Reporter, Second Series
PBGC Op No	Pension Benefit Guaranty Corporation Opinion Number
PRD	Protest Review Decisions
prec	preceding
Proc	Proclamation
PSBCA	Postal Service Board of Contract Appeals
PS Docket	Postal Service Docket
PTE	Prohibited Transaction Exemption Decisions of the Office of Pension and Welfare Benefit Programs, Department of Labor
PUR3d	Public Utilities Reports, Third Series
PUR4th	Public Utilities Reports, Fourth Series
RD	Reappraisement Decision, U. S. Customs Court
RESPA	Real Estate Settlement Procedures Act
Rev Proc	Revenue Procedure
Rev Rul	Revenue Ruling
RIA	Research Institute of America
RIA Benefits Coord	RIA Benefits Coordinator
RIA Corp Capital Trans Coord	RIA Corporate Capital Transaction Coordinator
RIA Employee Ben Comp Coord	RIA Employee Benefits Compliance Coordinator
RIA Employment Coord	RIA Employee Coordinator
RIA Employ Discrim Coord	RIA Employment Discrimination Coordinator
RIA Estate Plan & Tax Coord	RIA Estate Planning & Taxation Coordinator
RIA Exec Comp & Tax Coord	RIA Executive Compensation & Taxation Coordinator
RIA Fed Tax Coord 2d	RIA Federal Tax Coordinator 2d
RIA Partnership & S Corp Coord	RIA Partnership & S Corporation Coordinator
RIA Pension Coord	RIA Pension Coordinator
RIA Real Estate Coord	RIA Real Estate Coordinator
RIA Tax Action Coord	RIA Tax Action Coordinator
RIA TC Memo	Tax Court Memorandum Decisions
RICO Bus Disp Guide	RICO Business Disputes Guide
RRRA	Regional Rail Reorganization Act
R.S.	Revised Statutes
RUSCC	Rules of United States Claims Court
S Ct.	United States Supreme Court Reporter
SE	South Eastern Reporter
SE2d	South Eastern Reporter, Second Series
SEC	Securities and Exchange Commission Reports
So	Southern Reporter
So 2d	Southern Reporter, Second Series
Soc Sec LP	Social Security Law and Practice
Soc Sec Rep Serv	Social Security Reporter Service
Soc Sec & Unemployment Ins Rep	Social Security and Unemployment Insurance Reporter
Sp Ct RRRA	Special Court, Regional Rail Reorganization Act
SSA	Social Security Administration
SSR	Social Security Rulings
Stat	Statutes at Large
STB	Surface Transportation Board
SW	South Western Reporter
SW2d	South Western Reporter, Second Series
TC	United States Tax Court Reports
TCM	Tax Court Memorandum
T Ct	United States Tax Court
TD	Treasury Decisions
TD ATF	Treasury Decisions concerning matters of Alco- hol, Tobacco and Firearms Bureau
TIAS	Treaties and International Agreements Series
TMT & App Bd	Trademark Trial and Appeal Board
TNT	Tax Notes Today
UCCRS	Uniform Commercial Code Reporting Service
UCCRS2d	Uniform Commercial Code Reporting Service, Second Series

Abbreviations

US	United States Reports
USC	United States Code
USCMA	United States Court of Military Appeals
USCS	United States Code Service
USEPA GCO	United States Environmental Protection Agency, General Counsel Opinions
USEPA RCO	United States Environmental Protection Agency, Regional Counsel Opinions
USEPA NPDES	United States Environmental Protection Agency, National Pollutant Discharge Elimination System
USLW	United States Law Week
USPQ	United States Patents Quarterly
USSG	United States Sentencing Guidelines
UST	United States Treaties and Other International Agreements
USTC	United States Tax Cases
VA CAB	Veterans Administration Contract Appeals Board
VA GCO	Veterans Administration, General Counsel Opinions
Vet Apps	Court of Veterans Appeals Reporter
Vet App R	Rules of Veterans Appeals
WAB	Wage Appeals Board Decision, Dept. of Labor
WGL	Warren Gorham Lamont
WGL Employee Ben Comp Coord	WGL Employee Benefits Compliance Coordinator
WGL Employment Coord	WGL Employee Coordinator
WGL Employ Discrim Coord	WGL Employment Discrimination Coordinator
WH Cases	Wage and Hour Cases
WH2d	Wage and Hour Cases, Second Series
WH Op Letter	Wage and Hour Opinion Letter

Legal Periodicals

ABA J	American Bar Association Journal
ABIJ	American Bankruptcy Institute Journal
Admin LJ Am U	Administrative Law Journal of American University
Admin L Rev	Administrative Law Review
Advoc (Boise)	Advocate (Boise, Id.)
AF L Rev	Air Force Law Review
AIPLA QJ	AIPLA Quarterly Journal
Ak Bar Rag	Alaska Bar Rag
Akron L Rev	Akron Law Review
Akron Tax J	Akron Tax Journal
Ala Law	Alabama Lawyer
Ala L Rev	Alabama Law Review
Alaska L Rev	Alaska Law Review
Alb L Envtl Outlook	Albany Law Environmental Outlook
Alb LJ Sci & Tech	Albany Law Journal of Science and Technology
Alb L Rev	Albany Law Review
Am Bankr Inst L Rev	American Bankruptcy Institute Law Review
Am Bankr LJ	American Bankruptcy Law Journal
Am B Found Res J	American Bar Foundation Research Journal
Am Bus LJ	American Business Law Journal
Am Crim L Rev	American Criminal Law Review
Am Indian L Rev	American Indian Law Review
Am J Comp L	American Journal of Comparative Law
Am J Crim L	American Journal of Criminal Law
Am J Fam L	American Journal of Family Law
Am J Int'l L	American Journal of International Law
Am J L and Med	American Journal of Law and Medicine
Am J Legal Hist	American Journal of Legal History
Am J Tax Pol'y	American Journal of Tax Policy
Am J Trial Advoc	American Journal of Trial Advocacy
Am L Rev	American Law Review
Am U Int'l L Rev	American University International Law Review
Am U J Gender & L	American University Journal of Gender & the Law
Am UJ Gender Soc Pol'y & L	American University Journal of Gender, Social Policy & the Law
Am U J Int'l L & Pol'y	American University Journal of International Law and Policy
Am UL Rev	American University Law Review

Abbreviations

Abbreviation	Full Name
Am U Modern Am	The Modern American
Animal L	Animal Law
Ann Health L	Annals of Health Law
Antitrust Bull	Antitrust Bulletin
Antitrust LJ	Antitrust Law Journal
Arb J	Arbitration Journal
Ariz Atty	Arizona Attorney
Ariz J Int'l & Comp L	Arizona Journal of International and Comparative Law
Ariz L Rev	Arizona Law Review
Ariz St LJ	Arizona State Law Journal
Ark L Rev	Arkansas Law Review
Army Law	Army Lawyer
Bank Dev J	Bankruptcy Developments Journal
Banking LJ	Banking Law Journal
Barry L Rev	Barry Law Review
Baylor L Rev	Baylor Law Review
BBJ	Boston Bar Journal
BC Envtl Aff L Rev	Boston College Environmental Affairs Law Review
BC Ind & Com LR	Boston College Industrial and Commercial Law Review
BC Int'l & Comp L Rev	Boston College International and Comparative Law Review
BC L Rev	Boston College Law Review
BC Third World LJ	Boston College Third World Law Journal
Behav Sci & L	Behavior Sciences & the Law
Benefits LJ	Benefits Law Journal
Berkeley Bus LJ	Berkeley Business Law Journal
Berk J Afr-Am L & Pol'y	Berkeley Journal of African-American Law & Policy
Berkeley J Emp & Lab L	Berkeley Journal of Employment and Labor Law
Berkeley J Int'l L	Berkeley Journal of International Law
Berkeley Tech LJ	Berkeley Technology Law Journal
Brook L Rev	Brooklyn Law Review
Brooklyn J Int'l L	Brooklyn Journal of International Law
Buff Intell Prop LJ	Buffalo Intellectual Property Law Journal
Buff L Rev	Buffalo Law Review
Buff Pub Interest LJ	Buffalo Public Interest Law Journal
BU Int'l LJ	Boston University International Law Journal
BU J Sci & Tech L	Boston University Journal of Science and Technology Law
BU L Rev	Boston University Law Review
BU Pub Int LJ	Boston University Public Interest Law Journal
Bus Law	Business Lawyer
BYU Educ & LJ	Brigham Young University Education and Law Journal
BYU J Pub L	Brigham Young University Journal of Public Law
BYU L Rev	Brigham Young University Law Review
Cal Bankr J	California Bankruptcy Journal
Cal Intl Prac	California International Practitioner
Cal Law	California Lawyer
Cal L Rev	California Law Review
Cal Real Prop J	California Real Property Journal
Cal St BJ	California State Bar Journal
Cal W Int'l LJ	California Western International Law Journal
Cal W L Rev	California Western Law Review
Campbell L Rev	Campbell Law Review
Cap Def J	Capital Defense Journal
Cap U L Rev	Capital University Law Review
Cardozo Arts & Ent LJ	Cardozo Arts and Entertainment Law Journal
Cardozo J Int'l & Comp L	Cardozo Journal of International and Comparative Law
Cardozo JL & Gender	Cardozo Journal of Law & Gender
Cardozo L Rev	Cardozo Law Review
Cardozo Pub L Pol'y & Ethics J	Cardozo Public Law, Policy & Ethics Journal
Case W Res	Case Western Reserve Law Review
Case W Res J Int'l L	Case Western Reserve Journal of International Law
Case W Res L Rev	Case Western Reserve Law Review
Cath Law	The Catholic Lawyer
Cath UL Rev	Catholic University Law Review
Champion	The Champion
Chap L Rev	Chapman Law Review

Abbreviations

Abbreviation	Full Name
Chi B Rec	Chicago Bar Record
Chi J Int'l L	Chicago Journal of International Law
Chi-Kent L Rev	Chicago-Kent Law Review
Children's Legal Rts J	Children's Legal Rights Journal
Clearinghouse Rev	Clearinghouse Review
Clev St L Rev	Cleveland State Law Review
Colo J Int'l Envtl L & Pol'y	Colorado Journal of Environmental Law and Policy
Colo Law	Colorado Lawyer
Colum Bus L Rev	Columbia Business Law Review
Colum Human Rights L Rev	Columbia Human Rights Law Review
Colum J Envtl L	Columbia Journal of Environmental Law
Colum J Eur L	Columbia Journal of European Law
Colum J Gender & L	Columbia Journal of Gender and Law
Colum JL & Arts	Columbia Journal of Law & the Arts
Colum JL & Soc Probs	Columbia Journal of Law and Social Problems
Colum J Transnat'l L	Columbia Journal of Transnational Law
Colum L Rev	Columbia Law Review
Colum Sci & Tech L Rev	Columbia Science and Technology Law Review
Colum-VLA JL & Arts	Columbia-VLA Journal of Law and the Arts
Com LJ	Commercial Law Journal
Comm & L	Communications and the Law
Comm L & Pol'y	Communications Law & Policy
CommLaw Conspectus	CommLaw Conspectus: Journal of Communications Law and Policy
Comp Lab L & Pol'y J	Comparative Labor Law and Policy Journal
Comp Lab LJ	Comparative Labor Law Journal
Comp L Rev & Tech J	Computer Law Review and Technology Journal
Computer Internet Law	Computer & Internet Lawyer
Computer Law	Computer Lawyer
Computer LJ	Computer Law Journal
Conn BJ	Connecticut Bar Journal
Conn Ins LJ	Connecticut Insurance Law Journal
Conn J Int'l L	Connecticut Journal of International Law
Conn L Rev	Connecticut Law Review
Conn Pub Int LJ	Connecticut Public Interest Law Journal
Const Commentary	Constitutional Commentary
Copyright L Symp	Copyright Law Symposium
Copyright World	Copyright World
Cornell Int'l LJ	Cornell International Law Journal
Cornell J L & Pub Pol'y	Cornell Journal of Law and Public Policy
Cornell L Rev	Cornell Law Review
Corp L Rev	Corporation Law Review
Corp Prac Comment	Corporate Practice Commentator
Court Review	Court Review
Creighton L Rev	Creighton Law Review
Crim Def	Criminal Defense
Crim L Bull	Criminal Law Bulletin
Crim LQ	Criminal Law Quarterly
Cumb L Rev	Cumberland Law Review
Cum-Sam L Rev	Cumberland-Samford Law Review
Dayton L Rev	University of Dayton Law Review
DCL J Int'l L & Prac	Journal of International Law and Practice
DC L Rev	University of the District of Columbia Law Review
Def Couns J	Defense Counsel Journal
Del J Corp L	Delaware Journal of Corporate Law
Del L Rev	Delaware Law Review
Denver LJ	Denver Law Journal
Denv J Int'l L & Pol'y	Denver Journal of International Law and Policy
Denv UL Rev	Denver University Law Review
DePaul Bus & Com LJ	DePaul Business and Commercial Law Journal
DePaul Bus LJ	DePaul Business Law Journal
DePaul J Health Care L	DePaul Journal of Health Care Law
DePaul J Sports L Contemp Probs	DePaul Journal of Sports Law & Contemporary Problems
DePaul-LCA J Art & Ent L	DePaul-LCA Journal of Art and Entertainment Law
DePaul L Rev	DePaul Law Review

ABBREVIATIONS

Det CL Rev	Detroit College of Law Review
Dick J Int'l L	Dickinson Journal of International Law
Dick L Rev	Dickinson Law Review
Drake J Agric L	Drake Journal of Agricultural Law
Drake L Rev	Drake Law Review
Duke Env L & Pol'y F	Duke Environmental Law & Policy Forum
Duke J Comp & Int'l L	Duke Journal of Comparative and International Law
Duke L & Tech Rev	Duke Law & Technology Review
Duke LJ	Duke Law Journal
Duq BLJ	Duquesne Business Law Journal
Duq L Rev	Duquesne Law Review
Ecology LQ	Ecology Law Quarterly
Elder LJ	Elder Law Journal
E Min L Inst	Eastern Mineral Law Institute
Emory Int'l L Rev	Emory International Law Review
Emory LJ	Emory Law Journal
Empl Rel LJ	Employee Relations Law Journal
Empl Rts & Employ Pol'y J	Employee Rights and Employment Policy Journal
Energy LJ	Energy Law Journal
Ent L Rev	Entertainment Law Review
Envtl Claims J	Environmental Claims Journal
Envtl L	Environmental Law
Est Plan	Estate Planning
Fam Adv	Family Advocate
Fam LQ	Family Law Quarterly
FCLR	Federal Courts Law Review
Fed BJ	Federal Bar Journal
Fed B News & J	Federal Bar News and Journal
Fed Cir BJ	Federal Circuit Bar Journal
Fed Comm LJ	Federal Communications Law Journal
Fed Cts L Rev	Federal Courts Law Review
Fed Law	Federal Lawyer
Fed L Rev	Federal Law Review
Fed Sent R	Federal Sentencing Reporter
Fed'n Def & Corp Couns Q	Federation of Defense & Corporate Counsel Quarterly
Fed'n Ins Couns Q	Federation of Insurance Counsel Quarterly
First Amend L Rev	First Amendment Law Review
Fla Bar J	Florida Bar Journal
Fla J Int'l L	Florida Journal of International Law
Fla L Rev	University of Florida Law Review
Fla St UL Rev	Florida State University Law Review
Fla Tax Rev	Florida Tax Review
Fl Coastal LJ	Florida Coastal Law Journal
Food Drug Cosm LJ	Food Drug and Cosmetic Law Journal
Food Drug Cosm & Med Device L Dig	Food, Drug, Cosmetic and Medical Device Law Digest
Food Drug LJ	Food and Drug Law Journal
Fordham Intell Prop Media & Ent LJ	Fordham Intellectual Property, Media & Entertainment Law Journal
Fordham Int'l LJ	Fordham International Law Journal
Fordham J Corp & Fin L	Fordham Journal of Corporate & Financial Law
Fordham L Rev	Fordham Law Review
Fordham Urb LJ	Fordham Urban Law Journal
Ga BJ	Georgia Bar Journal
Ga J Int'l & Comp L	Georgia Journal of International and Comparative Law
Ga L Rev	Georgia Law Review
Ga St UL Rev	Georgia State University Law Review
Geo Immigr LJ	Georgetown Immigration Law Journal
Geo Int'l Envtl L Rev	Georgetown International Environmental Law Review
Geo J Gender & L	Georgetown Journal of Gender and the Law
Geo J Int'l L	Georgetown Journal of International Law
Geo JL & Pub Pol'y	Georgetown Journal of Law & Public Policy
Geo J Legal Ethics	Georgetown Journal of Legal Ethics
Geo J Poverty Law & Pol'y	Georgetown Journal on Poverty Law & Policy
Geo LJ	Georgetown Law Journal

Abbreviations

Geo Mason L Rev	George Mason Law Review
Geo Mason U Civ Rts LJ	George Mason University Civil Rights Law Journal
Geo Wash Int'l L Rev	George Washington International Law Review
Geo Wash L Rev	George Washington Law Review
Golden Gate U L Rev	Golden Gate University Law Review
Gonz L Rev	Gonzaga Law Review
Green Bag 2d	Green Bag, Second Series
GW J Int'l L & Econ	George Washington Journal of International Law & Economics
Hamline J Pub L & Pol'y	Hamline Journal of Law and Public Policy
Hamline L Rev	Hamline Law Review
Harv BlackLetter J	Harvard BlackLetter Journal
Harv CR-CL L Rev	Harvard Civil Rights and Civil Liberties Law Review
Harv Envtl L Rev	Harvard Environmental Law Review
Harv Hum Rts J	Harvard Human Rights Journal
Harv Int'l LJ	Harvard International Law Journal
Harv J L & Gender	Harvard Journal of Law & Gender
Harv JL & Pub Pol'y	Harvard Journal of Law and Public Policy
Harv J Law & Tec	Harvard Journal of Law and Technology
Harv J on Legis	Harvard Journal on Legislation
Harv Latino L Rev	Harvard Latino Law Review
Harv L Rev	Harvard Law Review
Hastings Bus LJ	Hastings Business Law Journal
Hastings Comm & Ent LJ	Hastings Communications and Entertainment Law Journal
Hastings Const LQ	Hastings Constitutional Law Quarterly
Hastings Int'l & Comp L Rev	Hastings International and Comparative Law Review
Hastings LJ	Hastings Law Journal
Hastings W-NW J Envtl L & Pol'y	Hastings West-Northwest Journal of Environmental Law and Policy
Health Matrix	Health Matrix: Journal of Law Medicine
Hofstra Lab & Emp LJ	Hofstra Labor and Employment Law Journal
Hofstra Lab LJ	Hofstra Labor Law Journal
Hofstra L Rev	Hofstra Law Review
Hous Bus & Tax LJ	Houston Business and Tax Law Journal
Hous J Int'l L	Houston Journal of International Law
Hous L Rev	Houston Law Review
How LJ	Howard Law Journal
Idaho L Rev	Idaho Law Review
IDEA	IDEA: The Journal of Law and Technology
IFLR	International Financial Law Review
Ill BJ	Illinois Bar Journal
ILSA J Int'l & Comp L	ILSA Journal of International & Comparative Law
ILSA J Int'l L	ILSA Journal of International Law
Immigr Brief	Immigration Briefings
Ind Health L Rev	Indiana Health Law Review
Ind Int'l & Comp L Rev	Indiana International and Comparative Law Review
Ind J Global Leg Stud	Indiana Journal of Global Legal Studies
Ind LJ	Indiana Law Journal
Ind L Rev	Indiana Law Review
Indus Rel LJ	Industrial Relations Law Journal
Ins Counsel J	Insurance Counsel Journal
Inst on Sec Reg	Institute on Securities Regulation (Practicing Law Institute)
Int'l & Comp LQ	International and Comparative Law Quarterly
Int'l Company & Com L Rev	International Company and Commercial Law Review
Int'l Law	International Lawyer
Int'l Legal Persp	International Legal Perspectives
Iowa J Corp L	The Journal of Corporation Law
Iowa L Rev	Iowa Law Review
ISJLP	I/S: Journal of Law and Policy for the Information Society
Issues L & Med	Issues in Law and Medicine
J Am Acad Matrimonial Law	Journal of the American Academy of Matrimonial Lawyers
J Agr Tax & L	Journal of Agricultural Taxation & Law
J Air L & Com	Journal of Air Law and Commerce
J App Prac & Proc	Journal of Appellate Practice and Process
J Arts Mgmt & Law	Journal of Arts Management and Law

ABBREVIATIONS

J Bankr L & Prac	Journal of Bankruptcy Law and Practice
J Bus L	Journal of Business Law
J Contemp Health L & Pol'y	Journal of Contemporary Health Law & Policy
J Contemp L	Journal of Contemporary Law
J Copyright Soc'y USA	Journal of the Copyright Society of the USA
J Corp Tax'n	Journal of Corporate Taxation
J Crim L & Criminology	Journal of Criminal Law & Criminology
J Crim LC & PS	Journal of Criminal Law, Criminology, and Police Science
JC & UL	Journal of College and University Law
J Disp Resol	Journal of Dispute Resolution
J Envtl L & Litig	Journal of Environmental Law and Litigation
J Envtl Mgmt	Journal of Environmental Management
J Fam L	Journal of Family Law
J Gender Race & Just.	Journal of Gender, Race and Justice
J Health & Biomed Law	Journal of Health & Biomedical L
J Health & Hosp L	Journal of Health and Hospital Law
J Health L	Journal of Health Law
J High Tech L	Journal of High Technology Law
JICL	Journal of International & Comparative Law
J Intell Prop L	Journal of Intellectual Property Law
J Internet L	Journal of Internet Law
J Juv L	Journal of Juvenile Law
J Kan BA	Journal of the Kansas Bar Association
JL & Com	Journal of Law and Commerce
JL & Econ	Journal of Law & Economics
J L & Educ	Journal of Law & Education
J L & Politics	Journal of Law and Politics
JL & Pol'y	Journal of Law and Policy
J Land Use & Envtl L	Journal of Land Use and Environmental Law
J Law & Pub Pol'y	Florida Journal of Law and Public Policy
J Legal Aspects of Sport	Journal of Legal Aspects of Sport
J Legal Med	Journal of Legal Medicine
J Legal Prof	Journal of the Legal Profession
J Legal Stud	Journal of Legal Studies
J Legis	Journal of Legislation
J Fam Stud	Journal of Law and Family Studies
JL Med & Ethics	Journal of Law, Medicine and Ethics
J Soc'y	Journal of Law in Society
J Mar L & Com	Journal of Maritime Law and Commerce
Marshall J Computer & Info Law	John Marshall Journal of Computer and Information Law
J Marshall L Rev	John Marshall Law Review
J Mo B	Journal of the Missouri Bar
J NAALJ	Journal of the National Association of Administrative Law Judges
J Nat Resources & Envtl L	Journal of Natural Resources and Environmental Law
J NY State Bar Assoc.	Journal (New York State Bar Association)
J Online L	Journal of Online Law
J Pat & Trademark Off Soc'y	Journal of Patent and Trademark Office Society
J Psych & L	Journal of Psychiatry & Law
J Real Est Tax'n	Journal of Real Estate Taxation
J Small & Emerging Bus. L.	Journal of Small & Emerging Business Law
J St Taxn	Journal of State Taxation
J Tax'n	Journal of Taxation
J Tax'n Invest	Journal of Taxation of Investments
J Tech L & Pol'y	Journal of Technology Law & Policy
J Transnat'l L & Pol'y	Florida State University Journal of Transnational Law & Policy
J Transp L Logist & Pol'y	Journal of Transportation Law, Logistics and Policy
Judges' Journal	The Judges' Journal
Jurimetrics J	Jurimetrics Journal
Kan JL & Pub Pol'y	Kansas Journal of Law & Public Policy
Ky LJ	Kentucky Law Journal
La BJ	Louisiana Bar Journal
Lab LJ	Labor Law Journal
Lab Law.	Labor Lawyer
La L Rev	Louisiana Law Review

xvii

ABBREVIATIONS

Land & Water L Rev	Land and Water Law Review
L & Philosophy	Law and Philosophy
Law & Bus Rev Am	Law & Business Review of the Americas
Law & Contemp Probs	Law and Contemporary Problems
Law & Hist Rev	Law and History Review
Law & Hum Behav	Law and Human Behavior
Law & Ineq J	Law and Inequality Journal of Theory and Practice
Law & Pol'y Int'l Bus	Law and Policy in International Business
Law & Sex	Law and Sexuality A Review of Lesbian and Gay Legal Issues
Law & Soc Inquiry	Law and Social Inquiry
Law & Soc'y Rev	Law and Society Review
Law Libr J	Law Library Journal
Law Med & Health Care	Law, Medicine & Health Care
Law Sea Inst Proc	Law of the Sea Institute Proceedings
Lawyers J	Lawyers Journal
Legal Ref Serv Q	Legal Reference Services Quarterly
Lewis & Clark L Rev	Lewis & Clark Law Review
Lincoln L Rev	Lincoln Law Review
Litig	Litigation
Loy Intell Prop & High Tech J	Loyola Intellectual Property & High Technology Journal
Loy J Pub Int L	Loyola Journal of Public Interest Law
Loy LA Ent LJ	Loyola of Los Angeles Entertainment Law Journal
Loy LA Int'l & Comp LJ	Loyola of Los Angeles International and Comparative Law Journal
Loy LA Int'l & Comp L Rev	Loyola of Los Angeles International & Comparative Law Review
Loy LA Rev	Loyola of Los Angeles Law Review
Loy L Rev	Loyola Law Review
Loy Mar LJ	Loyola Maritime Law Journal
Loy U Chi LJ	Loyola University Chicago Law Journal
L Rev MSU-DCL	Law Review of Michigan State University - Detroit College of Law
Maine BJ	Maine Bar Journal
Marq L Rev	Marquette Law Review
Marq Sports LJ	Marquette Sports Law Journal
Marq Sports L Rev	Marquette Sports Law Review
Mass L Rev	Massachusetts Law Review
Mass LQ	Massachusetts Law Quarterly
McGeorge L Rev	McGeorge Law Review
Md BJ	Maryland Bar Journal
Md Int'l L & Trade	Maryland Journal of International Law and Trade
Md L Rev	Maryland Law Review
Me BJ	Maine Bar Journal
Media L & Pol'y	Media Law and Policy
Med Trial Tech Q	Medical Trial Technique Quarterly
Me L Rev	Maine Law Review
Mem St UL Rev	Memphis State University Law review
Mercer L Rev	Mercer Law Review
MI Bar Jnl	Michigan Bar Journal
Mich J Int'l L	Michigan Journal of International Law
Mich J Race & L	Michigan Journal of Race & Law
Mich L Rev	Michigan Law Review
Mich St J Med & Law	Michigan State University Journal of Medicine and Law
Mich St L Rev	Michigan State Law Review
Mich Telecomm Tech L Rev	Michigan Telecommunications and Technology Law Review
Mich YB Int'l Legal Stud	Michigan Yearbook of International Legal Studies
Mil L Rev	Military Law Review
Minn Intell Prop Rev	Minnesota Intellectual Property Review
Minn J Global Trade	Minnesota Journal of Global Trade
Minn JL Sci & Tech	Minnesota Journal of Law, Science & Technology
Minn L Rev	Minnesota Law Review
Miss C L Rev	Mississippi College Law Review
Miss LJ	Mississippi Law Journal
Mod L Rev	Modern Law Review
Mo Envtl L & Pol'y Rev	Missouri Environmental Law and Policy Review
Mo L Rev	Missouri Law Review

xviii

ABBREVIATIONS

Mont L Rev	Montana Law Review
MSU-DCL J Int'l L	Michigan State University-DCL Journal of International Law
Mun Fin J	Municipal Finance Journal
NAFTA L & Bus Rev Am	NAFTA: Law & Business Review of the Americas
Nat'l Black LJ	National Black Law Journal
Nat'l J Crim Def	National Journal of Criminal Defense
N Atl Reg Bus L Rev	North Atlantic Regional Business Law Review
Nat Resources & Envt	Natural Resources and Environment
Nat Resources J	Natural Resources Journal
Navy L Rev	Naval Law Review
NC Cent LJ	North Carolina Central Law Journal
NC J Int'l L & Com Reg	North Carolina Journal of International Law and Commercial Regulation
NC L Rev	North Carolina Law Review
ND L Rev	North Dakota Law Review
Neb L Rev	Nebraska Law Review
NE J on Crim & Civ Con	New England Journal on Criminal and Civil Confinement
New Eng L Rev	New England Law Review
New LJ	New Law Journal
Nev LJ	Nevada Law Journal
NH BJ	New Hampshire Bar Journal
N Ill U L Rev	Northern Illinois University Law Review
NJ Law	New Jersey Lawyer
N Ky L Rev	Northern Kentucky Law Review
NM L Rev	New Mexico Law Review
Notre Dame Law	Notre Dame Lawyer
Notre Dame L Rev	Notre Dame Law Review
Nova L Rev	Nova Law Review
Nw J Int'l L & Bus	Northwestern Journal of International Law and Business
Nw U L Rev	Northwestern University Law Review
NY Int'l L Rev	New York International Law Review
NY LF	New York Law Forum
NYL Sch J Hum Rts	New York Law School Journal of Human Rights
NYL Sch J Int'l & Comp L	New York Law School Journal of International and Comparative Law
NYL Sch L Rev	New York Law School Law Review
NY St BJ	New York State Bar Journal
NYU Ann Surv Am L	New York University Annual Survey of American Law
NYU Conf on Lab	NYU Conference on Labor
NYU Envtl LJ	New York University Environmental Law Journal
NYU J Int'l L & Pol	New York University Journal of International Law and Politics
NYU J L & Bus	New York University Journal of Law & Business
NYU J Legis & Pub Pol'y	New York University School of Law Journal of Legislation and Public Policy
NYU L Rev	New York University Law Review
NYU Rev L & Soc Change	New York University Review of Law and Social Change
Ohio NU L Rev	Ohio Northern University Law Review
Ohio St J Crim L	Ohio State Journal of Criminal Law
Ohio St J on Disp Resol	Ohio State Journal on Dispute Resolution
Ohio St LJ	Ohio State Law Journal
Oil & Gas Tax Q	Oil and Gas Tax Quarterly
Okla City UL Rev	Oklahoma City University Law Review
Okla L Rev	Oklahoma Law Review
Or L Rev	Oregon Law Review
Pa BAQ	Pennsylvania Bar Association Quarterly
Pace Envtl L Rev	Pace Environmental Law Review
Pace Int'l L Rev	Pace International Law Review
Pace L Rev	Pace Law Review
Pac LJ	Pacific Law Journal
Pac Rim L & Pol'y	Pacific Rim Law & Policy Journal
Pat World	Patent World
Penn St L Rev	Pennsylvania State Law Review
Pepp L Rev	Pepperdine Law Review
Pierce L Rev	Pierce Law Review
Prac Law	Practical Lawyer
Prac Litig	Practical Litigator

ABBREVIATIONS

Prac Real Est Law	Practical Real Estate Lawyer
Prac Tax Law	Practical Tax Lawyer
Priv Inv Abroad	Private Investments Abroad
Pub Cont LJ	Public Contract Law Journal
Pub Land and Resources L Reg	Public Land and Resources Law Register
Pub Land L Rev	Public Land Law Review
Public Law	Public Law
Quinnipiac L Rev	Quinnipiac Law Review•ridgeport Law Review
Real Est LJ	Real Estate Law Journal
Real Prop Prob & Tr J	Real Property, Probate and Trust Journal
Regent J Int'l L	Regent Journal of International Law
Regent UL Rev	Regent University Law Review
Res Gestae	Res Gestae
Rev Jur UPR	Revista Juridica Universidad de Puerto Rico
Rev Litig	Review of Litigation
Rev Tax Indiv	Review of Taxation of Individuals
RI Bar Jnl	Rhode Island Bar Journal
Rich J L & Tech	Richmond Journal of Law & Technology
Rocky Mt Min L Inst	Rocky Mountain Mineral Law Institute
Roger Williams U L Rev	Roger Williams University Law Review
RRGC	University of Maryland Law Journal of Race, Religion, Gender & Class
Rut Cam LJ	Rutgers-Camden Law Journal
Rutgers Computer & Tech LJ	Rutgers Computer and Technology Law Journal
Rutgers J Law & Relig	Rutgers Journal of Law and Religion
Rutgers LJ	Rutgers Law Journal
Rutgers L Rec	Rutgers Law Record
Rutgers L Rev	Rutgers Law Review
Rutgers Race & L Rev	Rutgers Race and the Law Review
San Diego L Rev	San Diego Law Review
SJ Agric L Rev	San Joaquin Agricultural Law Review
Santa Clara Computer & High Tech LJ	Santa Clara Computer and High Technology Law Journal
Santa Clara Law	Santa Clara Lawyer
Santa Clara L Rev	Santa Clara Law Review
S Cal Interdis LJ	Southern California Interdisciplinary Law Journal
S Cal L Rev	Southern California Law Review
S Carolina Lawyer	South Carolina Lawyer
Sch L Bull	School Law Bulletin
SCHOLAR	Scholar: St. Mary's Law Review on Minority Issues
SC L Rev	South Carolina Law Review
S Ct Econ Rev	Supreme Court Economic Review
SD L Rev	South Dakota Law Review
Seattle Univ L R	Seattle University Law Review
Sec Reg LJ	Securities Regulation Law Journal
Sedona Conf J	The Sedona Conference Journal
Seton Hall Const LJ	Seton Hall Constitutional Law Journal
Seton Hall J Sports L	Seton Hall Journal of Sports Law
Seton Hall L Rev	Seton Hall Law Review
Seton Hall Legis J	Seton Hall Legislative Journal
S Ill U LJ	Southern Illinois University Law Journal
SMU L Rev	SMU (Southern Methodist) Law Review
Sports Law J	Sports Lawyers Journal
Stan Envtl LJ	Stanford Environmental Law Journal
Stan JCR & CL	Stanford Journal of Civil Rights and Civil Liberties
Stan J Int'l L	Stanford Journal of International Law
Stan JL Bus & Fin	Stanford Journal of Law, Business & Finance
Stan L Rev	Stanford Law Review
Stetson L Rev	Stetson Law Review
S Tex L Rev	South Texas Law Review
St John's L Rev	St John's Law Review
St John's JL Comm	St John's Journal of Legal Commentary
St Louis U LJ	Saint Louis University Law Journal
St Louis U Pub L Rev	St. Louis University Public Law Review
St Mary's LJ	St Mary's Law Journal

Abbreviations

St Thomas L Rev	St Thomas Law Review
Suffolk J Trial & App Adv	Suffolk Journal of Trial and Appellate Advocacy
Suffolk Transnat'l LJ	Suffolk Transnational Law Journal
Suffolk U L Rev	Suffolk University Law Review
SU L Rev	Southern University Law Review
Sup Ct Rev	Supreme Court Review
Sw JL & Trade Am	Southwestern Journal of Law and Trade in the Americas
Sw LJ	Southwestern Law Journal
Sw U L Rev	Southwestern University Law Review
Syracuse J Int'l L & Com	Syracuse Journal of International Law and Commerce
Syracuse L Rev	Syracuse Law Review
Taxes	CCH Taxes—The Tax Magazine
Tax L Rev	Tax Law Review
Temp Envtl L & Tech J	Temple Environmental Law and Technology Journal
Temp L Rev	Temple Law Review
Temp Pol & Civ Rts L Rev	Temple Political and Civil Rights Law Review
Tenn BJ	Tennessee Bar Journal
Tenn L Rev	Tennessee Law Review
Tex BJ	Texas Bar Journal
Tex F on CL & CR	Texas Forum on Civil Liberties & Civil Rights
Tex Hisp JL & Pol'y	Texas Hispanic Journal of Law and Policy
Tex Intell Prop LJ	Texas Intellectual Property Law Journal
Tex Int'l LJ	Texas International Law Journal
Tex J Women & L	Texas Journal of Women and the Law
Tex L Rev	Texas Law Review
Tex Rev Ent & Sports L	Texas Review of Entertainment & Sports Law
Tex Rev Law & Pol	Texas Review of Law and Politics
Tex Tech J Tex Admin L	Texas Tech Journal of Texas Administrative Law
Tex Tech L Rev	Texas Tech Law Review
Tex Wesleyan L Rev	Texas Wesleyan Law Review
Theoretical Inq L	Theoretical Inquiries in Law
The Record	Record of the Association of Bar of the City of New York
T Jefferson L Rev	Thomas Jefferson Law Review
T Marshall L Rev	Thurgood Marshall Law Review
TM Cooley L Rev	Thomas M Cooley Law Review
Tort & Ins LJ	Tort and Insurance Law Journal
Touro L Rev	Touro Law Review
Trademark Rep	Trademark Reporter
Trademark World	Trademark World
Transnat'l L & Contemp Probs	Transnational Law & Contemporary Problems
Transnat'l Law	Transnational Lawyer
Transp LJ	Transportation Law Journal
Trial	Trial
Trial Law Guide	Trial Lawyer Guide
Tul Envtl LJ	Tulane Environmental Law Journal
Tul Eur & Civ LF	The Tulane European & Civil Law Forum
Tul J Int'l & Comp L	Tulane Journal of International and Comparative Law
Tul L Rev	Tulane Law Review
Tul Mar LJ	Tulane Maritime Law Journal
Tulsa J Comp & Int'l L	Tulsa Journal of Comparative and International Law
Tulsa LJ	Tulsa Law Journal
U Ark Little Rock L Rev	University of Arkansas Little Rock Law Review
U Balt Intell Prop LJ	University of Baltimore Intellectual Property Law Journal
U Balt J Envtl L	University of Baltimore Journal of Environmental Law
U Balt L Rev	University of Baltimore Law Review
UCC LJ	Uniform Commercial Code Law Journal
UC Davis Bus LJ	Business Law Journal, University of California, Davis
UC Davis J Juv L & Pol'y	UC Davis Journal of Juvenile Law & Policy
UC Davis L Rev	UC Davis Law Review
U Chi L Rev	University of Chicago Law Review
U Chi Legal F	University of Chicago Legal Forum
U Cin L Rev	University of Cincinnati Law Review
UCLA Alaska L Rev	UCLA Alaska Law Review
UCLA Ent L Rev	UCLA Entertainment Law Review
UCLA J Envtl L & Pol'y	UCLA Journal of Environmental Law and Policy

ABBREVIATIONS

Abbreviation	Full Name
UCLA JL & Tech	UCLA Journal of Law & Technology
UCLA L Rev	UCLA Law Review
UCLA Pac Basin LJ	UCLA Pacific Basin Law Journal
UCLA Women's LJ	UCLA Women's Law Journal
U Colo L Rev	University of Colorado Law Review
U Dayton L Rev	University of Dayton Law Review
U Det J Urb L	University of Detroit Journal of Urban Law
U Det Mercy L Rev	University of Detroit Mercy Law Review
U Fla JL & Pub Pol'y	University of Florida Journal of Law and Public Policy
U Haw L Rev	University of Hawaii Law Review
U Ill JL Tech & Pol'y	University of Illinois Journal of Law, Technology and Policy
U Ill LF	University of Illinois Law Forum
U Ill L Rev	University of Illinois Law Review
U Kan L Rev	University of Kansas Law Review
U Mem L Rev	University of Memphis Law Review
U Miami Bus L Rev	University of Miami Business Law Review
U Miami Inter-Am L Rev	University of Miami Inter-American Law Review
U Miami L Rev	University of Miami Law Review
U Mich JL Reform	University of Michigan Journal of Law Reform
UMKC L Rev	University of Missouri at Kansas City Law Review
U of Louisville J of Fam L	University of Louisville Journal of Family Law
U Pa J Const L	University of Pennsylvania Journal of Constitutional Law
U Pa J Int'l Econ L	University of Pennsylvania Journal of International Economic Law
U Pa J Lab & Emp L	University of Pennsylvania Journal of Labor and Employment Law
U Pa L Rev	University of Pennsylvania Law Review
U Pitt L Rev	University of Pittsburgh Law Review
U Puget Sound L Rev	University of Puget Sound Law Review
Urb Law	The Urban Lawyer
U Rich L Rev	University of Richmond Law Review
USAFA J Leg Stud	United States Air Force Academy Journal of Legal Studies
USF L Rev	University of San Francisco Law Review
Utah L Rev	Utah Law Review
UTLJ	University of Toronto Law Journal
U Tol L Rev	University of Toledo Law Review
U West LA L Rev	University of West Los Angeles Law Review
Va Envtl LJ	Virginia Environmental Law Journal
Va J Int'l L	Virginia Journal of International Law
Va JL & Tech	Virginia Journal of Law and Technology
Va J Soc Pol'y & L	Virginia Journal of Social Policy and the Law
Va J Sports & L	Virginia Journal of Sports and the Law
Va L Rev	Virginia Law Review
Val UL Rev	Valparaiso University Law Review
Va Tax Rev	Virginia Tax Review
Vand J Ent & Tech L	Vanderbilt Journal of Entertainment & Technology Law
Vand J Transnat'l L	Vanderbilt Journal of Transnational Law
Vand L Rev	Vanderbilt Law Review
Va Sports & Ent LJ	Virginia Sports & Entertainment Law Journal
Vill Envtl LJ	Villanova Environmental Law Journal
Vill L Rev	Villanova Law Review
Vill Sports & Ent LJ	Villanova Sports and Entertainment Law Journal
Vt L Rev	Vermont Law Review
Wake Forest Intell Prop LJ	Wake Forest Intellectual Property Law Journal
Wake Forest L Rev	Wake Forest Law Review
Wash & Lee J Civ Rts & Soc Just	Washington & Lee Journal of Civil Rights & Social Justice
Wash & Lee L Rev	Washington and Lee Law Review
Washburn LJ	Washburn Law Journal
Wash L Rev	Washington Law Review
Wash St B News	Washington State Bar News
Wash U Global Stud L Rev	Washington University Global Studies Law Review
Wash U JL & Pol'y	Washington University Journal of Law & Policy
Wash U J Urb & Contemp L	Washington University Journal of Urban and Contemporary Law
Wash U LQ	Washington University Law Quarterly
Wayne L Rev	Wayne Law Review

Abbreviations

Abbreviation	Full Name
Westchester BJ	Westchester Bar Journal
Whittier L Rev	Whittier Law Review
Whittier J Child & Fam Advoc	Whittier Journal of Child and Family Advocacy
Widener J Pub L	Widener Journal of Public Law
Widener L Rev	Widener Law Review
Widener L Symp J	Widener Law Symposium Journal
Willamette J Int'l L & Dispute Res	Willamette Journal of International Law and Dispute Resolution
Willamette L Rev	Willamette Law Review
Wis B Bull	Wisconsin Bar Bulletin
Wis Int'l LJ	Wisconsin International Law Journal
Wis Law	Wisconsin Lawyer
Wis L Rev	Wisconsin Law Review
Wis Women's LJ	Wisconsin Women's Law Journal
Wm & Mary Bill of Rts J	William and Mary Bill of Rights Journal
Wm & Mary J Envtl L	William and Mary Journal of Environmental Law
Wm & Mary J of Women & L	William and Mary Journal of Women and the Law
Wm & Mary L Rev	William and Mary Law Review
Wm Mitchell L Rev	William Mitchell Law Review
Women's Rts L Rep	Women's Rights Law Reporter
W New Eng L Rev	Western New England Law Review
W St U L Rev	Western State University Law Review
W Va L Rev	West Virginia Law Review
Yale HR & Dev LJ	Yale Human Rights and Development Law Journal
Yale J Int'l L	Yale Journal of International Law
Yale JL & Feminism	Yale Journal of Law & Feminism
Yale JL & Human	Yale Journal of Law and the Humanities
Yale JL & Tech	Yale Journal of Law and Technology
Yale J on Reg	Yale Journal on Regulation
Yale L & Pol'y Rev	Yale Law and Policy Review
Yale LJ	Yale Law Journal
Yearbook of Int'l Law	Yearbook of International Law

SHEPARD'S® Citations Service. For further research of authorities referenced here, use SHEPARD'S to be sure your case or statute is still good law and to find additional authorities that support your position. SHEPARD'S is available exclusively from LexisNexis®.

TITLE 38. VETERANS' BENEFITS

TABLE OF CONTENTS

Chapter		Beginning Section
20.	Benefits for Homeless Veterans	2001
63.	Outreach Activities	6301
75.	Visual Impairment and Orientation and Mobility Professionals Educational Assistance Program	7501
79.	Information Security Education Assistance Program	7901

THE CODE OF THE LAWS

OF THE

UNITED STATES OF AMERICA

TITLE 38 — VETERANS' BENEFITS

PART III. READJUSTMENT AND RELATED BENEFITS

Chapter   Sec.
33. Post-9/11 Educational Assistance 3301

HISTORY; ANCILLARY LAWS AND DIRECTIVES

Amendments:
2008. Act June 30, 2008, P. L. 110-252, Title V, § 5003(a)(2), 122 Stat. 2375, amended the analysis of this Part by adding item 33.

CHAPTER 30. ALL-VOLUNTEER FORCE EDUCATIONAL ASSISTANCE PROGRAM

SUBCHAPTER II. BASIC EDUCATIONAL ASSISTANCE

3014A.   Accelerated payment of basic educational assistance for education leading to employment in high technology occupation in high technology industry.
3020.   Authority to transfer unused education benefits to family members for career service members.

SUBCHAPTER IV. TIME LIMITATION FOR USE OF ELIGIBILITY AND ENTITLEMENT; GENERAL AND ADMINISTRATIVE PROVISIONS

[3036.   Repealed]

HISTORY; ANCILLARY LAWS AND DIRECTIVES

Amendments:
2001. Act Dec. 27, 2001, P. L. 107-103, Title I, § 104(a)(2), 115 Stat. 981, amended the analysis of this chapter by adding item 3014A.
Act Dec. 28, 2001, P. L. 107-107, Div A, Title VI, Subtitle E, § 654(a)(2), 115 Stat. 1156, amended the analysis of this chapter by adding item 3020.
2002. Act Dec. 6, 2002, P. L. 107-330, Title III, § 308(b)(2)(B), 116 Stat. 2827, amended the analysis of this chapter by substituting item 3014A for one which read "3014A. Accelerated payment of basic educational assistance for education leading to employment in high technology industry.".
2008. Act June 30, 2008, P. L. 110-252, Title V, § 5006(e)(1), 122 Stat. 2386, amended the analysis of this chapter by substituting item 3020 for one which read "3020. Transfer of entitlement to basic educational assistance: members of the Armed Forces with critical military skills.".
2010. Act Oct. 13, 2010, P. L. 111-275, Title X, § 1001(f), 124 Stat. 2896, amended the analysis of this chapter by substituting item 3020 for one which read: "3020. Authority to transfer unused education benefits to family members of career service members.".
2012. Act Aug. 6, 2012, P. L. 112-154, Title IV, § 402(b)(2), 126 Stat. 1190, amended the analysis of this chapter by deleting item 3036, which read: "3036. Reporting requirement.".

38 USCS § 3001

SUBCHAPTER I. PURPOSES; DEFINITIONS

§ 3001. Purposes

CODE OF FEDERAL REGULATIONS

Department of Veterans Affairs—Adjudication, 38 CFR 3.1 et seq.
Department of Veterans Affairs—Vocational rehabilitation and education, 38 CFR 21.1 et seq.
Department of Veterans Affairs—Loan guaranty and vocational rehabilitation and counseling programs, 48 CFR 871.100 et seq.

RESEARCH GUIDE

Am Jur:
77 Am Jur 2d, Veterans and Veterans' Laws §§ 124, 125, 130, 132, 135.

§ 3002. Definitions

For the purposes of this chapter [38 USCS §§ 3001 et seq.]—
  (1), (2) [Unchanged]
  (3) The term "program of education"—
    (A) has the meaning given such term in section 3452(b) of this title [38 USCS § 3452(b)];
    (B) includes—
      (i) a preparatory course for a test that is required or used for admission to an institution of higher education; and
      (ii) a preparatory course for a test that is required or used for admission to a graduate school;
    (C) in the case of an individual who is not serving on active duty, includes (i) a full-time program of apprenticeship or of other on-job training approved as provided in clause (1) or (2), as appropriate, of section 3687(a) of this title [38 USCS § 3687(a)], and (ii) a cooperative program (as defined in section 3482(a)(2) of this title [38 USCS § 3482(a)(2)]).
  (4) [Unchanged]
  (5) The term "Secretary of Defense" means the Secretary of Defense, except that it means the Secretary of Homeland Security with respect to the Coast Guard when it is not operating as a service in the Navy.
  (6) The term "active duty" does not include any period during which an individual (A) was assigned full time by the Armed Forces to a civilian institution for a course of education which was substantially the same as established courses offered to civilians, (B) served as a cadet or midshipman at one of the service academies, or (C) served under the provisions of section 12103(d) of title 10 [10 USCS § 12103(d)] pursuant to an enlistment in the Army National Guard or the Air National Guard, or as a Reserve for service in the Army Reserve, Navy Reserve, Air Force Reserve, Marine Corps Reserve, or Coast Guard Reserve.
  (7), (8) [Unchanged]
(As amended Nov. 30, 1999, P. L. 106-117, Title VII, Subtitle A, § 701, 113 Stat. 1582; Nov. 25, 2002, P. L. 107-296, Title XVII, § 1704(d), 116 Stat. 2315; Jan. 6, 2006, P. L. 109-163, Div A, Title V, Subtitle B, § 515(e)(2), 119 Stat. 3236.)

HISTORY; ANCILLARY LAWS AND DIRECTIVES

Amendments:
1999. Act Nov. 30, 1999, in para. (3), in subpara. (A), substituted the concluding semicolon for '', and'', redesignated subpara. (B) as subpara. (C), and added new subpara. (B).
2002. Act Nov. 25, 2002 (effective on 3/1/2003 pursuant to § 1704(g) of such Act, which appears as 10 USCS § 101 note), in para. (5), substituted "of Homeland Security" for "of Transportation".
2006. Act Jan. 6, 2006, in para. (6)(C), substituted "Navy Reserve" for "Naval Reserve".

CODE OF FEDERAL REGULATIONS

Department of Veterans Affairs—Vocational rehabilitation and education, 38 CFR 21.1 et seq.

RESEARCH GUIDE

Am Jur:
77 Am Jur 2d, Veterans and Veterans' Laws § 126.

SUBCHAPTER II. BASIC EDUCATIONAL ASSISTANCE

§ 3011. Basic educational assistance entitlement for service on active duty

(a) Except as provided in subsection (c) of this section, each individual—
  (1) who—

READJUSTMENT BENEFITS   38 USCS § 3011

(A) after June 30, 1985, first becomes a member of the Armed Forces or first enters on active duty as a member of the Armed Forces and—
   (i) who (I) in the case of an individual whose obligated period of active duty is three years or more, serves at least three years of continuous active duty in the Armed Forces, or (II) in the case of an individual whose obligated period of active duty is less than three years, serves at least two years of continuous active duty in the Armed Forces; or
   (ii) who serves in the Armed Forces and is discharged or released from active duty (I) for a service-connected disability, by reason of a sole survivorship discharge (as that term is defined in section 1174(i) of title 10), for a medical condition which preexisted such service on active duty and which the Secretary determines is not service connected, for hardship, or for a physical or mental condition that was not characterized as a disability and did not result from the individual's own willful misconduct but did interfere with the individual's performance of duty, as determined by the Secretary of each military department in accordance with regulations prescribed by the Secretary of Defense or by the Secretary of Homeland Security with respect to the Coast Guard when it is not operating as a service in the Navy; (II) for the convenience of the Government, if, in the case of an individual with an obligated period of service of two years, the individual completes not less than 20 months of continuous active duty under that period of obligated service, or, in the case of an individual with an obligated period of service of at least three years, the individual completes not less than 30 months of continuous active duty under that period of obligated service; or (III) involuntarily for the convenience of the Government as a result of a reduction in force, as determined by the Secretary of the military department concerned in accordance with regulations prescribed by the Secretary of Defense or by the Secretary of Homeland Security with respect to the Coast Guard when it is not operating as a service in the Navy;
(B) as of December 31, 1989, is eligible for educational assistance benefits under chapter 34 of this title [38 USCS §§ 3451 et seq.] and was on active duty at any time during the period beginning on October 19, 1984, and ending on July 1, 1985, continued on active duty without a break in service and—
   (i) [Unchanged]
   (ii) after June 30, 1985, is discharged or released from active duty (I) for a service-connected disability, by reason of a sole survivorship discharge (as that term is defined in section 1174(i) of title 10), for a medical condition which preexisted such service on active duty and which the Secretary determines is not service connected, for hardship, or for a physical or mental condition that was not characterized as a disability, as described in subparagraph (A)(ii)(I) of this paragraph; (II) for the convenience of the Government, if the individual completed not less than 30 months of continuous active duty after that date; or (III) involuntarily for the convenience of the Government as a result of a reduction in force, as determined by the Secretary of the military department concerned in accordance with regulations prescribed by the Secretary of Defense or by the Secretary of Homeland Security with respect to the Coast Guard when it is not operating as a service in the Navy; or
(C) as of December 31, 1989, was eligible for educational assistance benefits under chapter 34 of this title [38 USCS §§ 3451 et seq.] and—
   (i) was not on active duty on October 19, 1984;
   (ii) reenlists or reenters on a period of active duty after October 19, 1984; and
   (iii) on or after July 1, 1985, either—
      (I) serves at least three years of continuous active duty in the Armed Forces; or
      (II) is discharged or released from active duty (aa) for a service-connected disability, by reason of a sole survivorship discharge (as that term is defined in section 1174(i) of title 10), for a medical condition which preexisted such service on active duty and which the Secretary determines is not service connected, for hardship, or for a physical or mental condition that was not characterized as a disability, as described in subparagraph (A)(ii)(I) of this paragraph, (bb) for the convenience of the Government, if the individual completed not less than 30 months of continuous active duty after that date, or (cc) involuntarily for the convenience of the Government as a result of a reduction in force, as determined by the Secretary of the military department concerned in accordance with regulations prescribed by the Secretary of Defense or by the Secretary of Homeland Security with respect to the Coast Guard when it is not operating as a service in the Navy;
(2) who completes the requirements of a secondary school diploma (or equivalency certificate), or successfully completes (or otherwise receives academic credit for) the equivalent of 12 semester hours in a program of education leading to a standard college degree, before applying for benefits under this section; and

38 USCS § 3011

(3) [Unchanged]

is entitled to basic educational assistance under this chapter [38 USCS §§ 3001 et seq.].

(b)(1) Except as provided in paragraph (2), the basic pay of any individual described in subsection (a)(1)(A) of this section who does not make an election under subsection (c)(1) of this section shall be reduced by $100 for each of the first 12 months that such individual is entitled to such pay.

(2) In the case of an individual covered by paragraph (1) who is a member of the Selected Reserve, the Secretary of Defense shall collect from the individual an amount equal to $1,200 not later than one year after completion by the individual of the two years of service on active duty providing the basis for such entitlement. The Secretary of Defense may collect such amount through reductions in basic pay in accordance with paragraph (1) or through such other method as the Secretary of Defense considers appropriate.

(3) Any amount by which the basic pay of an individual is reduced under this subsection shall revert to the Treasury and shall not, for purposes of any Federal law, be considered to have been received by or to be within the control of such individual.

(c)(1), (2) [Unchanged]

(3) An individual who after December 31, 1976, receives a commission as an officer in the Armed Forces upon completion of a program of educational assistance under section 2107 of title 10 [10 USCS § 2107] is not eligible for educational assistance under this section if the individual enters on active duty—

(A) [Unchanged]

(B) after September 30, 1996, and while participating in such program received more than $3,400 for each year of such participation.

(d)(1) For purposes of this chapter [38 USCS §§ 3001 et seq.], any period of service described in paragraphs (2) and (3) of this subsection shall not be considered a part of an obligated period of active duty on which an individual's entitlement to assistance under this section is based.

(2), (3) [Unchanged]

(e)(1) Any individual eligible for educational assistance under this section who does not make an election under subsection (c)(1) may contribute amounts for purposes of receiving an increased amount of basic educational assistance as provided for under section 3015(g) of this title [38 USCS § 3015(g)]. Such contributions shall be in addition to any reductions in the basic pay of such individual under subsection (b).

(2) An individual covered by paragraph (1) may make the contributions authorized by that paragraph at any time while on active duty, but not more frequently than monthly.

(3) The total amount of the contributions made by an individual under paragraph (1) may not exceed $600. Such contributions shall be made in multiples of $20.

(4) Contributions under this subsection shall be made to the Secretary of the military department concerned. That Secretary shall deposit any amounts received as contributions under this subsection into the Treasury as miscellaneous receipts.

(f)(1) For the purposes of this chapter [38 USCS §§ 3001 et seq.], a member referred to in paragraph (2) or (3) of this subsection who serves the periods of active duty referred to in that paragraph shall be deemed to have served a continuous period of active duty the length of which is the aggregate length of the periods of active duty referred to in that paragraph.

(2) [Unchanged]

(3) This subsection applies to a member who after a period of continuous active duty as an enlisted member or warrant officer, and following successful completion of officer training school, is discharged in order to accept, without a break in service, a commission as an officer in the Armed Forces for a period of active duty.

(g) [Unchanged]

(h)(1) [Unchanged]

(2) This subsection applies to a member who—

(A) during the obligated period of active duty on which entitlement to assistance under this section is based, commences pursuit of a course of education—

(i), (ii) [Unchanged]

(B), (C) [Unchanged]

(i) The Secretary concerned shall inform any member of the Armed Forces who has not completed that member's obligated period of active duty (as described in subsection (a)(1)(A)) and who indicates the intent to be discharged or released from such duty for the convenience of the Government of the minimum active duty requirements for entitlement to educational assistance benefits under this chapter [42 USCS §§ 3001 et seq.]. Such information shall be provided to the member in a timely manner.

(As amended Nov. 11, 1998, P. L. 105-368, Title II, Subtitle A, §§ 203(a), 207(a), 112 Stat. 3326,

READJUSTMENT BENEFITS   38 USCS § 3011

3328; Nov. 30, 1999, P. L. 106-117, Title VII, Subtitle A, §§ 702(a), 704, 113 Stat. 1583, 1584; Nov. 1, 2000, P. L. 106-419, Title I, Subtitle A, §§ 102(a)(1), 103(a), 105(a)(1), 114 Stat. 1824, 1825, 1828; June 5, 2001, P. L. 107-14, § 7(a)(1), (c)(1), 115 Stat. 31, 32; Dec. 27, 2001, P. L. 107-103, Title I, §§ 105(a), 106(a), 115 Stat. 982, 983; Nov. 25, 2002, P. L. 107-296, Title XVII, § 1704(d), 116 Stat. 2315; Dec. 6, 2002, P. L. 107-330, Title III, § 308(a), 116 Stat. 2827; Dec. 10, 2004, P. L. 108-454, Title I, § 109(a), 118 Stat. 3604; Dec. 21, 2006, P. L. 109-444, § 8(b)(2), 120 Stat. 3313; Dec. 22, 2006, P. L. 109-461, Title X, § 1004(b)(2), 120 Stat. 3466; Aug. 29, 2008, P. L. 110-317, § 6(c)(1), 122 Stat. 3529.)

HISTORY; ANCILLARY LAWS AND DIRECTIVES

Explanatory notes:
Section 8(b)(2) of Act Dec. 21, 2006, P. L. 109-444, amended this section; however, pursuant to § 1006(b) of Act Dec. 22, 2006, P. L. 109-461, which appears as 38 USCS § 101 note, as of the enactment of Act Dec. 22, 2006, P. L. 109-461, Act Dec. 21, 2006, P. L. 109-444 and the amendments made by such Act were deemed for all purposes not to have taken effect and such § 8(b)(2) ceased to be in effect.

Amendments:
1998. Act Nov. 11, 1998 (effective on 10/1/98, as provided by § 203(b) of such Act, which appears as a note to this section), in subsec. (a)(2), substituted "successfully completed (or otherwise received academic credit for)" for "successfully completed" in two places.

Such Act further (effective 120 days after enactment, as provided by § 207(d)(1) of such Act, which appears as a note to this section) added subsec. (i).

1999. Act Nov. 30, 1999 (effective and applicable as provided by § 702(c) of such Act, which appears as a note to this section), in subsec. (f), in para. (1), substituted "paragraph (2) or (3)" for "paragraph (2)", and added para. (3).

Such Act further, in subsec. (i), deleted "Federal" before "Government".

2000. Act Nov. 1, 2000, in subsec. (a), in para. (1)(A), substituted cl. (i) for one which read: "(i) who (I) serves, as the individual's initial obligated period of active duty, at least three years of continuous active duty in the Armed Forces, or (II) in the case of an individual whose initial period of active duty is less than three years, serves at least two years of continuous active duty in the Armed Forces; or", in cl. (ii), substituted "if, in the case of an individual with an obligated period of service of two years, the individual completes not less than 20 months of continuous active duty under that period of obligated service, or, in the case of an individual with an obligated period of service of at least three years, the individual completes not less than 30 months of continuous active duty under that period of obligated service" for "in the case of an individual who completed not less than 20 months of continuous active duty, if the initial obligated period of active duty of the individual was less than three years, or in the case of an individual who completed not less than 30 months of continuous active duty if the initial obligated period of active duty of the individual was at least three years", and substituted para. (2) for one which read:

"(2) who, except as provided in subsection (e) of this section, completed the requirements of a secondary school diploma (or equivalency certificate) not later than—

"(A) the original ending date of the individual's initial obligated period of active duty in the case of an individual described in clause (1)(A) of this subsection, regardless of whether the individual is discharged or released from active duty on such date; or

"(B) December 31, 1989, in the case of an individual described in clause (1)(B) of this subsection;

except that (i) an individual described in clause (1)(B) of this subsection may meet the requirement of this clause by having successfully completed (or otherwise received academic credit for) the equivalent of 12 semester hours in a program of education leading to a standard college degree, and (ii) an individual described in clause (1)(A) of this subsection may meet such requirement by having successfully completed (or otherwise received academic credit for) the equivalent of such 12 semester hours before the end of the individual's initial obligated period of active duty; and";

in subsec. (d)(1), substituted "obligated period of active duty on which an individual's entitlement to assistance under this section is based" for "individual's initial obligated period of active duty"; deleted subsec. (e), which read: "(e) For the purposes of subsection (a)(2) of this section, an individual who was on active duty on August 2, 1990, and who completes the requirements of a secondary school diploma (or equivalency certificate) before October 28, 1994, shall be considered to have completed such requirements within the individual's initial obligated period of active duty."; in subsec. (h)(2)(A), in the introductory matter, substituted "during the obligated period of active duty on which entitlement to assistance under this section is based," for "during an initial period of active duty,"; and, in subsec. (i), deleted "initial" preceding "obligated".

Such Act further (effective 5/1/2001, as provided by § 105(c) of such Act, which appears as a note to this section), added subsec. (e).

2001. Act June 5, 2001 (effective as if enacted on 11/1/2000, immediately after enactment of Act Nov. 1, 2000, P. L. 106-419, as provided by § 7(a)(2) of the 2001 Act, which appears as a note to this section), in subsec. (a)(1)(A)(i), substituted "(I) in the case of an individual whose obligated period of active duty is three years or more, serves at least three years of continuous

5

active duty in the Armed Forces, or (II) in the case of an individual whose obligated period of active duty is less than three years, serves" for "serves an obligated period of active duty of".
Such Act further (effective as if included in the enactment of § 105 of Act Nov. 1, 2000, P. L. 106-419, as provided by § 7(c)(4) of the 2001 Act, which appears as a note to this section), in subsec. (e), in para. (2), inserted ", but not more frequently than monthly", in para. (3), substituted "$20" for "$4" and, in para. (4), substituted "Secretary of the military department concerned. That" for "Secretary. The", and deleted "by the Secretary" following "received".
Act Dec. 27, 2001, in subsec. (a)(1), in subpara. (A)(ii), deleted "or" following the concluding semicolon, in subpara. (B)(ii), added "or" following the semicolon, and added subpara. (C).
Such Act further (applicable as provided by § 106(b) of such Act, which appears as a note to this section), in subsec. (c)(3)(B), substituted "$3,400" for "$2,000".
2002. Act Nov. 25, 2002 (effective on 3/1/2003 pursuant to § 1704(g) of such Act, which appears as 10 USCS § 101 note), in subsec. (a)(1), in subparas. (A)(ii)(I), (B)(ii)(III), and (C)(ii-i)(II)(cc), substituted "of Homeland Security" for "of Transportation".
Such Act further (effective as above), as amended by Act Dec. 22, 2006 (effective 11/25/2002, as provided by § 1004(b) of Act Dec. 22, 2006, which appears as 38 USCS § 101 note), in subsec. (a)(1)(A)(ii)(III), substituted "of Homeland Security" for "of Transportation".
Act Dec. 6, 2002, in subsec. (a)(1)(C)(ii), deleted "on or" following "duty".
2004. Act Dec. 10, 2004, in subsec. (b), substituted "(1) Except as provided in paragraph (2), the basic pay" for "The basic pay", designated the former second sentence as para. (3) and, in such paragraph as so designated, substituted "this subsection" for "this chapter", and inserted para. (2).
2006. Act Dec. 22, 2006 amended the directory language of Act Nov. 25, 2002, without affecting the text of this section.
2008. Act Aug. 29, 2008 (applicable with respect to any sole survivorship discharge granted after 9/11/2001, as provided by § 10(a) of such Act, which appears as 5 USCS § 2108 note), in subsec. (a)(1), in subparas. (A)(ii), (B)(ii), and (C)(iii)(II), inserted "by reason of a sole survivorship discharge (as that term is defined in section 1174(i) of title 10),".

Other provisions:
Effective date of amendments made by § 203(a) of Act Nov. 11, 1998. Act Nov. 11, 1998, P. L. 105-368, Title II, Subtitle A, § 203(b), 112 Stat. 3326, provides: "The amendments made by subsection (a) [amending 38 USCS §§ 3011(a)(2), 3012(a)(2), 3018(b)(4)(ii), 3018A(a)(2), 3018B(a)(1)(B), (a)(2)(B), and 3018C(a)(3)] shall take effect on October 1, 1998.".
Effective date of amendments made by § 207(a), (b) of Act Nov. 11, 1998. Act Nov. 11, 1998, P. L. 105-368, Title II, Subtitle A, § 207(d)(1), 112 Stat. 3328, provides: "The amendments made by subsections (a) and (b) [adding 38 USCS §§ 3011(i) and 3012(g)] shall take effect 120 days after the date of the enactment of this Act.".
Effective date of amendment made by § 702(a) of Act Nov. 30, 1999. Act Nov. 30, 1999, P. L. 106-117, Title VII, Subtitle A, § 702(c), 113 Stat. 1583, provides: "The amendments made by subsection (a) [amending subsec. (f) of this section] shall take effect on the date of the enactment of this Act and apply with respect to an individual first appointed as a commissioned officer on or after July 1, 1985.".
Effective date of amendments made by § 105 of Act Nov. 1, 2000. Act Nov. 1, 2000, P. L. 106-419, Title I, Subtitle A, § 105(c), 114 Stat. 1829, provides: "The amendments made by this section [adding 38 USCS §§ 3011(e) and 3012(f), and amending 38 USCS § 3015] shall take effect on May 1, 2001.".
Contributions under 38 USCS § 3011(e) or 3012(f), as added effective May 1, 2001; transitional provisions. Act Nov. 1, 2000, P. L. 106-419, Title I, Subtitle A, § 105(d), 114 Stat. 1830, provides:
"(1) During the period beginning on May 1, 2001, and ending on July 31, 2001, an individual described in paragraph (2) may make contributions under section 3011(e) or 3012(f) of title 38, United States Code (as added by subsection (a)), whichever is applicable to that individual, without regard to paragraph (2) of that section and otherwise in the same manner as an individual eligible for educational assistance under chapter 30 of such title [38 USCS §§ 3001 et seq.] who is on active duty.
"(2) Paragraph (1) applies in the case of an individual who—
"(A) is discharged or released from active duty during the period beginning on the date of the enactment of this Act and ending on April 30, 2001; and
"(B) is eligible for educational assistance under chapter 30 of title 38, United States Code [38 USCS §§ 3001 et seq.].".
Effective date of amendment made by § 7(a)(1) of Act June 5, 2001. Act June 5, 2001, P. L. 107-14, § 7(a)(2), 115 Stat. 31, provides: "The amendment made by paragraph (1) [amending subsec. (a)(1)(A)(i) of this section] shall take effect as if enacted on November 1, 2000, immediately after the enactment of the Veterans Benefits and Health Care Improvement Act of 2000 (Public Law 106-419) [enacted Nov. 1, 2000].".
Effective date of amendments made by § 7(c) of Act June 5, 2001. Act June 5, 2001, P. L. 107-14, § 7(c)(4), 115 Stat. 33, provides: "The amendments made by this subsection [amending 38 USCS §§ 3011(e), 3012(f), and 3015(g)] shall take effect as if included in the enactment of section 105 of the Veterans Benefits and Health Care Improvement Act of 2000 (Public Law 106-419; 114 Stat. 1828) [enacted Nov. 1, 2000].".

READJUSTMENT BENEFITS   38 USCS § 3012

Application of amendments made by § 106(a) of Act Dec. 27, 2001. Act Dec. 27, 2001, P. L. 107-103, Title I, § 106(b), 115 Stat. 983, provides: "The amendments made by subsection (a) [amending 38 USCS §§ 3011(c)(3)(B) and 3012(d)(3)(B)] shall apply with respect to educational assistance allowances paid under chapter 30 of title 38, United States Code, for months beginning after the date of the enactment of this Act.".

CODE OF FEDERAL REGULATIONS
Department of Veterans Affairs—Adjudication, 38 CFR 3.1 et seq.
Department of Veterans Affairs—Vocational rehabilitation and education, 38 CFR 21.1 et seq.
Department of Veterans Affairs—Loan guaranty and vocational rehabilitation and counseling programs, 48 CFR 871.100 et seq.

RESEARCH GUIDE
Am Jur:
77 Am Jur 2d, Veterans and Veterans' Laws §§ 126–128.

INTERPRETIVE NOTES AND DECISIONS

2. Under particular circumstances

Although veteran was eligible for educational-assistance benefits under 38 USCS § 3452(a), when those benefits were terminated for all veterans, he was disqualified from conversion into eligibility for benefits under 38 USCS ch. 30 by 38 USCS § 3011(c)(2) and 38 CFR § 21.7044(c) because he did not meet exception set forth under § 21.7044(d) where he was commissioned upon graduating from military academy after December 1976 and before completing military service needed to establish such entitlement. Burton v Nicholson (2005) 19 Vet App 249, 2005 US App Vet Claims LEXIS 517.

Clause "while participating in such program" in 38 USCS § 3011(c)(3) refers only to program of educational assistance pursuant to 10 USCS § 2107; where veteran received financial assistance pursuant to 10 USCS § 2107 for his last three years in college, later denial of educational assistance under 38 USCS § 3011(c)(3) was proper because his participation in Naval Reserve Officer Training Corps as College Program Basic student during his first year was not relevant to his eligibility for assistance under 38 USCS § 3011. Rosenberg v Mansfield (2007) 22 Vet App 1, 2007 US App Vet Claims LEXIS 1841.

§ 3012. Basic educational assistance entitlement for service in the Selected Reserve

(a) Except as provided in subsection (d) of this section, each individual—
  (1) who—
    (A) after June 30, 1985, first becomes a member of the Armed Forces or first enters on active duty as a member of the Armed Forces—
      (i) serves an obligated period of active duty of at least two years of continuous active duty in the Armed Forces, subject to subsection (b) of this section, characterized by the Secretary concerned as honorable service; and
      (ii) subject to subsection (b) of this section and beginning within one year after completion of the service on active duty described in subclause (i) of this clause, serves at least four years of continuous duty in the Selected Reserve during which the individual participates satisfactorily in training as required by the Secretary concerned;
    (B) as of December 31, 1989, is eligible for educational assistance under chapter 34 of this title [38 USCS §§ 3451 et seq.] and was on active duty at any time during the period beginning on October 19, 1984, and ending on July 1, 1985, continued on active duty without a break in service and—
      (i) [Unchanged]
      (ii) after June 30, 1985, subject to subsection (b) of this section and beginning within one year after completion of such two years of service, serves at least four continuous years in the Selected Reserve during which the individual participates satisfactorily in training as prescribed by the Secretary concerned; or
    (C) as of December 31, 1989, was eligible for educational assistance under chapter 34 of this title [38 USCS §§ 3451 et seq.] and—
      (i) was not on active duty on October 19, 1984;
      (ii) reenlists or reenters on a period of active duty after October 19, 1984; and
      (iii) on or after July 1, 1985—
        (I) serves at least two years of continuous active duty in the Armed Forces, subject to subsection (b) of this section, characterized by the Secretary concerned as honorable service; and
        (II) subject to subsection (b) of this section and beginning within one year after completion of such two years of service, serves at least four continuous years in the Selected Reserve during which the individual participates satisfactorily in training as prescribed by the Secretary concerned;
  (2) who completes the requirements of a secondary school diploma (or equivalency certificate), or successfully completes (or otherwise receives academic credit for) the equivalent of 12

38 USCS § 3012

semester hours in a program of education leading to a standard college degree, before applying for benefits under this section; and

(3) [Unchanged]

is entitled to basic educational assistance under this chapter [38 USCS §§ 3001 et seq.]

(b)(1)(A) The requirement of two years of service under clauses (1)(A)(i) and (1)(B)(i) of subsection (a) of this section is not applicable to an individual who is discharged or released, during such two years, from active duty in the Armed Forces (i) for a service-connected disability, (ii) for a medical condition which preexisted such service on active duty and which the Secretary determines is not service connected, (iii) for hardship, (iv) in the case of an individual discharged or released after 20 months of such service, for the convenience of the Government, (v) involuntarily for the convenience of the Government as a result of a reduction in force, as determined by the Secretary of the military department concerned in accordance with regulations prescribed by the Secretary of Defense or by the Secretary of Homeland Security with respect to the Coast Guard when it is not operating as a service in the Navy, (vi) for a physical or mental condition that was not characterized as a disability, as described in section 3011(a)(1)(A)(ii)(I) of this title [38 USCS § 3011(a)(1)(A)(ii)(I)], or (vii) by reason of a sole survivorship discharge (as that term is defined in section 1174(i) of title 10).

(B) The requirement of four years of service under clauses (1)(A)(ii) and (1)(B)(ii) of subsection (a) of this section is not applicable to an individual—

(i) who, during the two years of service described in clauses (1)(A)(i) and (1)(B)(i) of subsection (a) of this section, was discharged or released from active duty in the Armed Forces for a service-connected disability, by reason of a sole survivorship discharge (as that term is defined in section 1174(i) of title 10), for a medical condition which preexisted such service on active duty and which the Secretary determines is not service connected, or for a physical or mental condition not characterized as a disability, as described in section 3011(a)(1)(A)(ii)(I) of this title [38 USCS § 3011(a)(1)(A)(ii)(I)], if the individual was obligated, at the beginning of such two years of service, to serve such four years of service;

(ii) who, during the four years of service described in clauses (1)(A)(ii) and (1)(B)(ii) of subsection (a) of this section, is discharged or released from service in the Selected Reserve (I) for a service-connected disability, (II) for a medical condition which preexisted the individual's becoming a member of the Selected Reserve and which the Secretary determines is not service connected, (III) for hardship, (IV) in the case of an individual discharged or released after 30 months of such service, for the convenience of the Government, (V) involuntarily for the convenience of the Government as a result of a reduction in force, as determined by the Secretary of the military department concerned in accordance with regulations prescribed by the Secretary of Defense or by the Secretary of Homeland Security with respect to the Coast Guard when it is not operating as a service in the Navy, (VI) for a physical or mental condition not characterized as a disability, as described in section 3011(a)(1)(A)(ii)(I) of this title [38 USCS § 3011 (a)(1)(A)(ii)(I)], or (VII) by reason of a sole survivorship discharge (as that term is defined in section 1174(i) of title 10); or

(iii) [Unchanged]

(2) [Unchanged]

(c)(1) Except as provided in paragraph (2), the basic pay of any individual described in subsection (a)(1)(a) of this section who does not make an election under subsection (d)(1) of this section shall be reduced by $100 for each of the first 12 months that such individual is entitled to such pay.

(2) In the case of an individual covered by paragraph (1) who is a member of the Selected Reserve, the Secretary of Defense shall collect from the individual an amount equal to $1,200 not later than one year after completion by the individual of the two years of service on active duty providing the basis for such entitlement. The Secretary of Defense may collect such amount through reductions in basic pay in accordance with paragraph (1) or through such other method as the Secretary of Defense considers appropriate.

(3) Any amount by which the basic pay of an individual is reduced under this subsection shall revert to the Treasury and shall not, for purposes of any Federal law, be considered to have been received by or to be within the control of such individual.

(d)(1), (2) [Unchanged]

(3) An individual who after December 31, 1976, receives a commission as an officer in the Armed Forces upon completion of a program of educational assistance under section 2107 of title 10 [10 USCS § 2107] is not eligible for educational assistance under this section if the individual enters on active duty—

(A) [Unchanged]

READJUSTMENT BENEFITS   38 USCS § 3012

(B) after September 30, 1996, and while participating in such program received more than $3,400 for each year of such participation.

(e)(1) An individual described in subclause (I) or (III) of subsection (b)(1)(B)(ii) of this section may elect entitlement to basic educational assistance under section 3011 of this title [38 USCS § 3011], based on an obligated period of active duty of two years, in lieu of entitlement to assistance under this section.

(2) [Unchanged]

(f)(1) Any individual eligible for educational assistance under this section who does not make an election under subsection (d)(1) may contribute amounts for purposes of receiving an increased amount of basic educational assistance as provided for under section 3015(g) of this title [38 USCS § 3015(g)]. Such contributions shall be in addition to any reductions in the basic pay of such individual under subsection (c).

(2) An individual covered by paragraph (1) may make the contributions authorized by that paragraph at any time while on active duty, but not more frequently than monthly.

(3) The total amount of the contributions made by an individual under paragraph (1) may not exceed $600. Such contributions shall be made in multiples of $20.

(4) Contributions under this subsection shall be made to the Secretary of the military department concerned. That Secretary shall deposit any amounts received as contributions under this subsection into the Treasury as miscellaneous receipts.

(g)(1) The Secretary concerned shall inform any member of the Armed Forces who has not completed that member's initial service (as described in paragraph (2)) and who indicates the intent to be discharged or released from such service for the convenience of the Government of the minimum service requirements for entitlement to educational assistance benefits under this chapter [38 USCS §§ 3001 et seq.]. Such information shall be provided to the member in a timely manner.

(2) The initial service referred to in paragraph (1) is the initial obligated period of active duty (described in subparagraph (A)(i) or (B)(i) of subsection (a)(1)) or the period of service in the Selected Reserve (described in subparagraph (A)(ii) or (B)(ii) of subsection (a)(1)).

(As amended Nov. 11, 1998, P. L. 105-368, Title II, Subtitle A, §§ 203(a), 207(b), 112 Stat. 3326, 3328; Nov. 30, 1999, P. L. 106-117, Title VII, Subtitle A, § 704, 113 Stat. 1584; Nov. 1, 2000, P. L. 106-419, Title I, Subtitle A, §§ 102(b), 103(b), 105(a)(2), Title IV, § 404(a)(6), 114 Stat. 1824, 1826, 1829, 1865; June 5, 2001, P. L. 107-14, § 7(c)(2), 115 Stat. 32; Dec. 27, 2001, P. L. 107-103, Title I, §§ 105(b), 106(a), 115 Stat. 982, 983; Nov. 25, 2002, P. L. 107-296, Title XVII, § 1704(d), 116 Stat. 2315; Dec. 10, 2004, P. L. 108-454, Title I, § 109(b), 118 Stat. 3604; June 15, 2006, P. L. 109-233, Title V, § 503(3), 120 Stat. 416; Aug. 29, 2008, P. L. 110-317, § 6(c)(2), 122 Stat. 3529.)

HISTORY; ANCILLARY LAWS AND DIRECTIVES

Amendments:

1998. Act Nov. 11, 1998 (effective on 10/1/98, as provided by § 203(b) of such Act, which appears as 38 USCS § 3011 note), in subsec. (a)(2), substituted "successfully completed (or otherwise received academic credit for)" for "successfully completed" in two places.

Such Act further (effective 120 days after enactment, as provided by § 207(d)(1) of such Act, which appears as 38 USCS § 3011 note) added subsec. (g).

1999. Act Nov. 30, 1999, in subsec. (g)(1), deleted "Federal" before "Government".

2000. Act Nov. 1, 2000, in subsec. (a), in para. (1)(A)(i), substituted "an obligated period of active duty of at least two years of continuous active duty in the Armed Forces" for ", as the individual's initial obligated period of active duty, at least two years of continuous active duty in the Armed Forces", and substituted para. (2) for one which read: "(2) who, except as provided in subsection (f) of this section, before completion of the service described in clause (1) of this subsection, has completed the requirements of a secondary school diploma (or an equivalency certificate), except that (i) an individual described in clause (1)(B) of this subsection may meet the requirement of this clause by having successfully completed (or otherwise received academic credit for) the equivalent of 12 semester hours in a program of education leading to a standard college degree, and (ii) an individual described in clause (1)(A) of this subsection may meet such requirement by having successfully completed (or otherwise received academic credit for) the equivalent of such 12 semester hours before the end of the individual's initial obligated period of active duty; and"; in subsec. (e)(1), deleted "initial" preceding "obligated"; deleted subsec. (f), which read: "(f) For the purposes of subsection (a)(2) of this section, an individual who was on active duty on August 2, 1990, and who completes the requirements of a secondary school diploma (or equivalency certificate) before October 28, 1994, shall be considered to have completed such requirements within the individual's initial obligated period of active duty."; and, in subsec. (g)(2), substituted "subparagraph" for "subparagraphs" in two places.

Such Act further (effective 5/1/2001, as provided by § 105(c) of such Act, which appears as 28 USCS § 3011 note), added subsec. (f).

38 USCS § 3012
VETERANS' BENEFITS

2001. Act June 5, 2001 (effective as if included in the enactment of § 105 of Act Nov. 1, 2000, P. L. 106-419, as provided by § 7(c)(4) of the 2001 Act, which appears as 38 USCS § 3011 note), in subsec. (f), in para. (2), inserted ", but not more frequently than monthly", in para. (3), substituted "$20" for "$4" and, in para. (4), substituted "Secretary of the military department concerned. That" for "Secretary. The", and deleted "by the Secretary" following "received".

Act Dec. 27, 2001, in subsec. (a)(1), in subpara. (A)(ii), deleted "or" following the concluding semicolon, in subpara. (B)(ii), added "or" following the semicolon, and added subpara. (C).

Such Act further (applicable as provided by § 106(b) of such Act, which appears as 38 USCS § 3011 note), in subsec. (d)(3)(B), substituted "$3,400" for "$2,000".

2002. Act Nov. 25, 2002 (effective on 3/1/2003 pursuant to § 1704(g) of such Act, which appears as 10 USCS § 101 note), in subsec. (b)(1), in subparas. (A)(v) and (B)(ii)(V), substituted "of Homeland Security" for "of Transportation".

2004. Act Dec. 10, 2004, in subsec. (c), substituted "(1) Except as provided in paragraph (2), the basic pay" for "The basic pay", designated the former second sentence as para. (3), and, in such paragraph as so designated, substituted "this subsection" for "this chapter", and inserted para. (2).

2006. Act June 15, 2006, in subsec. (a)(1)(C)(ii), deleted "on or" following "duty".

2008. Act Aug. 29, 2008 (applicable with respect to any sole survivorship discharge granted after 9/11/2001, as provided by § 10(a) of such Act, which appears as 5 USCS § 2108 note), in subsec. (b)(1), substituted ", (vi)" for ", or (vi)", and inserted ", or (vii) by reason of a sole survivorship discharge (as that term is defined in section 1174(i) of title 10)", in subpara. (B), in cl. (i), inserted "by reason of a sole survivorship discharge (as that term is defined in section 1174(i) of title 10),", and, in cl. (ii), substituted ", (VI)" for ", or (VI)".

Such Act further (applicable as above), in subsec. (b)(1)(B)(ii), inserted ", or (VII) by reason of a sole survivorship discharge (as that term is defined in section 1174(i) of title 10)". Although such Act purported to insert the matter preceding the concluding period in cl. (ii) of subsec. (b)(1)(B), the amendment was executed preceding the concluding semicolon in order to effectuate the probable intent of Congress.

CODE OF FEDERAL REGULATIONS
Department of Veterans Affairs—Adjudication, 38 CFR 3.1 et seq.
Department of Veterans Affairs—Vocational rehabilitation and education, 38 CFR 21.1 et seq.

RESEARCH GUIDE
Am Jur:
77 Am Jur 2d, Veterans and Veterans' Laws § 126.

§ 3013. Duration of basic educational assistance
(a)(1) [Unchanged]

(2) Subject to section 3695 of this title [38 USCS § 3695] and subsection (d) of this section, in the case of an individual described in section 3011(a)(1)(A)(ii)(I) or (III) of this title [38 USCS § 3011(a)(1)(A)(ii)(I) or (III)] who is not also described in section 3011(a)(1)(A)(i) of this title [38 USCS § 3011(a)(1)(A)(i)] or an individual described in section 3011(a)(1)(A)(ii)(I) or (III) of this title [38 USCS § 3011(a)(1)(A)(ii)(I) or (III)] who is not also described in section 3011(a)(1)(B)(i) of this title [38 USCS § 3011(a)(1)(B)(i)], the individual is entitled to one month of educational assistance benefits under this chapter [38 USCS §§ 3001 et seq.] for each month of continuous active duty served by such individual after June 30, 1985, as part of the obligated period of active duty on which such entitlement is based in the case of an individual described in section 3011(a)(1)(B)(ii)(I) or (III) of this title [38 USCS § 3011(a)(1)(B)(ii)(I) or (III)], or in the case of an individual described in section 3011(a)(1)(B)(ii)(I) or (III) of this title [38 USCS § 3011(a)(1)(B)(ii)(I) or (III)], after June 30, 1985.

(b) Subject to section 3695 of this title [38 USCS § 3695] and subsection (d) of this section, each individual entitled to basic educational assistance under section 3012 of this title [38 USCS § 3012] is entitled to (1) one month of educational assistance benefits under this chapter [38 USCS §§ 3001 et seq.] for each month of continuous active duty served by such individual after June 30, 1985, as part of the obligated period of active duty on which such entitlement is based in the case of an individual described in section 3012(a)(1)(A) of this title [38 USCS § 3012(a)(1)(A)], or in the case of an individual described in section 3012(a)(1)(B) of this title [38 USCS § 3012(a)(1)(B)], after June 30, 1985, and (2) one month of educational assistance benefits under this chapter [38 USCS §§ 3001 et seq.] for each four months served by such individual in the Selected Reserve "after the applicable date specified in clause (1) of this subsection (other than any month in which the individual served on active duty).

(c)–(e) [Unchanged]

(f)(1) [Unchanged]

(2) Subject to paragraph (3), the payment of the educational assistance allowance referred to in paragraph (1) is the payment of such an allowance to an individual for pursuit of a course or courses under this chapter if the Secretary finds that the individual—

(A) in the case of a person not serving on active duty, had to discontinue such course pursuit as a result of being ordered to serve on active duty under section 688, 12301(a), 12301(d), 12301(g), 12302, or 12304 of title 10 [10 USCS § 688, 12301(a), 12301(d), 12301(g), 12302, or 12304]; or

(B) in the case of a person serving on active duty, had to discontinue such course pursuit as a result of being ordered to a new duty location or assignment or to perform an increased amount of work; and

(C) [Unchanged]

(3) [Unchanged]

(As amended Nov. 1, 2000, P. L. 106-419, Title I, Subtitle A, § 103(c), 114 Stat. 1826; Dec. 27, 2001, P. L. 107-103, § 103(a), (d), 115 Stat. 979.)

HISTORY; ANCILLARY LAWS AND DIRECTIVES

Amendments:

2000. Act Nov. 1, 2000, in subsecs. (a)(2) and (b)(1), substituted "obligated period of active duty on which such entitlement is based" for "individual's initial obligated period of active duty".

2001. Act Dec. 27, 2001 (effective as of 9/11/2001, as provided by § 103(e) of such Act, which appears as a note to this section), in subsec. (f)(2), in subpara. (A), substituted "to serve on active duty under section 688, 12301(a), 12301(d), 12301(g), 12302, or 12304 of title 10;" for ", in connection with the Persian Gulf War, to serve on active duty under section 672(a), (d), or (g), 673, 673b, or 688 of title 10;", and, in subpara. (B), deleted ", in connection with such War," following "ordered".

Other provisions:

Effective date of Dec. 27, 2001 amendments. Act Dec. 27, 2001, P. L. 107-103, § 103(e), 115 Stat. 980, provides: "The amendments made by this section [amending 38 USCS §§ 3013, 3103, 3105, 3231, 3511, and 3512] shall take effect as of September 11, 2001.".

CODE OF FEDERAL REGULATIONS

Department of Veterans Affairs—Vocational rehabilitation and education, 38 CFR 21.1 et seq.

RESEARCH GUIDE

Am Jur:

77 Am Jur 2d, Veterans and Veterans' Laws § 129.

INTERPRETIVE NOTES AND DECISIONS

There is no indication in 38 USCS § 3015 that amount of educational assistance allowance that is actually paid is determinative of duration of veteran's education-benefits entitlement under 38 USCS § 3013, and decision of Board of Veterans' Appeals that veteran is not entitled to payment of educational assistance allowance for any period of time after 36 months of education-benefits eligibility had expired is affirmed. Breeden v West (2000) 13 Vet App 398, 2000 US App Vet Claims LEXIS 206.

§ 3014. Payment of basic educational assistance

(a) The Secretary shall pay to each individual entitled to basic educational assistance who is pursuing an approved program of education a basic educational assistance allowance to help meet, in part, the expenses of such individual's subsistence, tuition, fees, supplies, books, equipment, and other educational costs.

(b)(1) In the case of an individual entitled to basic educational assistance who is pursuing education or training described in subsection (a) or (c) of section 2007 of title 10 [10 USCS § 2007], the Secretary shall, at the election of the individual, pay the individual a basic educational assistance allowance to meet all or a portion of the charges of the educational institution for the education or training that are not paid by the Secretary of the military department concerned under such subsection.

(2)(A) The amount of the basic educational assistance allowance payable to an individual under this subsection for a month shall be the amount of the basic educational assistance allowance to which the individual would be entitled for the month under section 3015 of this title [38 USCS § 3015].

(B) The maximum number of months for which an individual may be paid a basic educational assistance allowance under paragraph (1) is 36.

(C) The number of months of entitlement charged under this chapter [38 USCS §§ 3001 et seq.] in the case of an individual who has been paid a basic educational assistance allowance under this subsection shall be equal to the number (including any fraction) determined by dividing the total amount of such educational assistance allowance paid the individual by the full-time monthly institutional rate of educational assistance which such individual would otherwise be paid under subsection (a)(1), (b)(1), (c)(1), (d)(1), or (e)(1) of section 3015 of this title [38 USCS § 3015], as the case may be.

38 USCS § 3014
VETERANS' BENEFITS

(As amended Oct. 30, 2000, P. L. 106-398, § 1, 114 Stat. 1654; June 5, 2001, P. L. 107-14, § 7(b)(1), 115 Stat. 31.)

HISTORY; ANCILLARY LAWS AND DIRECTIVES

Explanatory notes:
The amendments made by § 1 of Act Oct. 30, 2000, P. L. 106-398, are based on § 1602(b)(2) of Subtitle A of Title XVI of Division A of H.R. 5408 (114 Stat. 1654A-359), as introduced on Oct. 6, 2000, which was enacted into law by such § 1.

Amendments:
2000. Act Oct. 30, 2000, designated the existing provisions as subsec. (a), and added subsec. (b).

2001. Act June 5, 2001 (effective as if enacted on 11/1/2000, immediately after the enactment of Act Nov. 1, 2000, P. L. 106-419, as provided by § 7(b)(3) of the 2001 Act, which appears as a note to this section), in subsec. (b)(2), in subpara. (A), deleted "(without regard to subsection (g) of that section) were payment made under that section instead of under this subsection" following "title", and added subpara. (C).

Other provisions:
Effective date of amendments made by § 7(b)(1) and (2) of Act June 5, 2001. Act June 5, 2001, P. L. 107-14, § 7(b)(3), 115 Stat. 31, provides: "The amendments made by this subsection [amending 38 USCS §§ 3014(b)(2), 3015(a), (b), and (h), and 3032(b)] shall take effect as if enacted on November 1, 2000, immediately after the enactment of the Veterans Benefits and Health Care Improvement Act of 2000 (Public Law 106-419) [enacted Nov. 1, 2000]."

CODE OF FEDERAL REGULATIONS
Department of Veterans Affairs—Vocational rehabilitation and education, 38 CFR 21.1 et seq.

RESEARCH GUIDE
Am Jur:
77 Am Jur 2d, Veterans and Veterans' Laws § 135.

§ 3014A. Accelerated payment of basic educational assistance for education leading to employment in high technology occupation in high technology industry

(a) An individual described in subsection (b) who is entitled to basic educational assistance under this subchapter may elect to receive an accelerated payment of the basic educational assistance allowance otherwise payable to the individual under section 3015 of this title [38 USCS § 3015].

(b) An individual described in this subsection is an individual who is—

(1) enrolled in an approved program of education that leads to employment in a high technology occupation in a high technology industry (as determined pursuant to regulations prescribed by the Secretary); and

(2) charged tuition and fees for the program of education that, when divided by the number of months (and fractions thereof) in the enrollment period, exceeds the amount equal to 200 percent of the monthly rate of basic educational assistance allowance otherwise payable to the individual under section 3015 of this title [38 USCS § 3015].

(c)(1) The amount of the accelerated payment of basic educational assistance made to an individual making an election under subsection (a) for a program of education shall be the lesser of—

(A) the amount equal to 60 percent of the established charges for the program of education; or

(B) the aggregate amount of basic educational assistance to which the individual remains entitled under this chapter at the time of the payment.

(2) In this subsection, the term "established charges", in the case of a program of education, means the actual charges (as determined pursuant to regulations prescribed by the Secretary) for tuition and fees which similarly circumstanced nonveterans enrolled in the program of education would be required to pay. Established charges shall be determined on the following basis:

(A) In the case of an individual enrolled in a program of education offered on a term, quarter, or semester basis, the tuition and fees charged the individual for the term, quarter, or semester.

(B) In the case of an individual enrolled in a program of education not offered on a term, quarter, or semester basis, the tuition and fees charged the individual for the entire program of education.

(3) The educational institution providing the program of education for which an accelerated payment of basic educational assistance allowance is elected by an individual under subsection (a) shall certify to the Secretary the amount of the established charges for the program of education.

(d) An accelerated payment of basic educational assistance made to an individual under this section for a program of education shall be made not later than the last day of the month immediately following the month in which the Secretary receives a certification from the educational institution regarding—
  (1) the individual's enrollment in and pursuit of the program of education; and
  (2) the amount of the established charges for the program of education.
(e)(1) Except as provided in paragraph (2), for each accelerated payment of basic educational assistance made to an individual under this section, the individual's entitlement to basic educational assistance under this chapter shall be charged the number of months (and any fraction thereof) determined by dividing the amount of the accelerated payment by the full-time monthly rate of basic educational assistance allowance otherwise payable to the individual under section 3015 of this title [38 USCS § 3015] as of the beginning date of the enrollment period for the program of education for which the accelerated payment is made.
(2) If the monthly rate of basic educational assistance allowance otherwise payable to an individual under section 3015 of this title [38 USCS § 3015] increases during the enrollment period of a program of education for which an accelerated payment of basic educational assistance is made under this section, the charge to the individual's entitlement to basic educational assistance under this chapter shall be determined by prorating the entitlement chargeable, in the matter provided for under paragraph (1), for the periods covered by the initial rate and increased rate, respectively, in accordance with regulations prescribed by the Secretary.
(f) The Secretary may not make an accelerated payment under this section for a program of education to an individual who has received an advance payment under section 3680(d) of this title [38 USCS § 3680(d)] for the same enrollment period.
(g) The Secretary shall prescribe regulations to carry out this section. The regulations shall include requirements, conditions, and methods for the request, issuance, delivery, certification of receipt and use, and recovery of overpayment of an accelerated payment under this section.
(Added Dec. 27, 2001, P. L. 107-103, Title I, § 104(a)(1), 115 Stat. 980; Dec. 6, 2002, P. L. 107-330, Title III, § 308(b)(1), (2)(A), 116 Stat. 2827.)

HISTORY; ANCILLARY LAWS AND DIRECTIVES

Effective date of section:
This section became effective on October 1, 2002, pursuant to § 104(c) of Act Dec. 27, 2001, P. L. 107-103, which appears as a note to this section.

Amendments:
2002. Act Dec. 6, 2002, substituted the section heading for one which read: "§ 3014A. Accelerated payment of basic educational assistance for education leading to employment in high technology industry"; and, in subsec. (b)(1), substituted "employment in a high technology occupation in a high technology industry " for "employment in a high technology industry".

Other provisions:
Effective date and applicability of Dec. 27, 2001 amendments. Act Dec. 27, 2001, P. L. 107-103, Title I, § 104(c), 115 Stat. 982, provides: "The amendments made by this section [adding this section and amending 38 USCS § 3680(g) and the chapter analysis preceding 38 USCS § 3001] shall take effect October 1, 2002, and shall apply with respect to enrollments in courses or programs of education or training beginning on or after that date.".

§ 3015. Amount of basic educational assistance

(a) The amount of payment of educational assistance under this chapter [38 USCS §§ 3001 et seq.] is subject to section 3032 of this title [38 USCS § 3032]. Except as otherwise provided in this section, in the case of an individual entitled to an educational assistance allowance under this chapter [38 USCS §§ 3001 et seq.] whose obligated period of active duty on which such entitlement is based is three years, a basic educational assistance allowance under this subchapter [38 USCS §§ 3011 et seq.] shall be paid—
  (1) for an approved program of education pursued on a full-time basis, at the monthly rate of—
    (A) for months occurring during the period beginning on August 1, 2008, and ending on the last day of fiscal year 2009, $1,321; and
    (B) for months occurring during a subsequent fiscal year, the amount for months occurring during the previous fiscal year increased under subsection (h); or
    (C) [Deleted]
    (D) [Redesignated]
  (2) [Unchanged]
(b) In the case of an individual entitled to an educational assistance allowance under section 3011 or 3018 of this title [38 USCS § 3011 or 3018] whose obligated period of active duty on which such entitlement is based is two years, a basic educational assistance allowance under this chapter

38 USCS § 3015

[38 USCS §§ 3001 et seq.] shall (except as provided in the succeeding subsections of this section) be paid—

(1) for an approved program of education pursued on a full-time basis, at the monthly rate of—

(A) for months occurring during the period beginning on August 1, 2008, and ending on the last day of fiscal year 2009, $1,073; and

(B) for months occurring during a subsequent fiscal year, the amount for months occurring during the previous fiscal year increased under subsection (h); or

(C) [Deleted]

(D) [Redesignated]

(2) [Unchanged]

(c)(1) [Unchanged]

(2) Paragraph (1) of this subsection applies to an individual entitled to an educational assistance allowance under section 3011 of this title [38 USCS § 3011]—

(A) whose obligated period of active duty on which such entitlement is based is less than three years;

(B) who, beginning on the date of the commencement of such obligated period of active duty, serves a continuous period of active duty of not less than three years; and

(C) [Unchanged]

(d)(1) In the case of an individual who has a skill or specialty designated by the Secretary concerned as a skill or specialty in which there is a critical shortage of personnel or for which it is difficult to recruit, the Secretary concerned, pursuant to regulations to be prescribed by the Secretary of Defense, may, at the time the individual first becomes a member of the Armed Forces, increase the rate of the basic educational assistance allowance applicable to such individual to such rate in excess of the rate prescribed under subsections (a), (b), and (c) of this section as the Secretary of Defense considers appropriate, but the amount of any such increase may not exceed $950 per month.

(2) In the case of an individual who after October 7, 1997, receives an enlistment bonus under section 308a or 308f of title 37 [37 USCS § 308a or 308f], receipt of that bonus does not affect the eligibility of that individual for an increase under paragraph (1) in the rate of the basic educational assistance allowance applicable to that individual, and the Secretary concerned may provide such an increase for that individual (and enter into an agreement with that individual that the United States agrees to make payments pursuant to such an increase) without regard to any provision of law (enacted before, on, or after the date of the enactment of this paragraph [enacted Oct. 17, 1998]) that limits the authority to make such payments.

(e), (f) [Unchanged]

(g) In the case of an individual who has made contributions authorized by section 3011(e) or 3012(f) of this title [38 USCS § 3011(e) or 3012(f)], effective as of the first day of the enrollment period following receipt of such contributions from such individual by the Secretary concerned, the monthly amount of basic educational assistance allowance applicable to such individual under subsection (a), (b), or (c) shall be the monthly rate otherwise provided for under the applicable subsection increased by—

(1) an amount equal to $5 for each $20 contributed by such individual under section 3011(e) or 3012(f) of this title [38 USCS § 3011(e) or 3012(f)], as the case may be, for an approved program of education pursued on a full-time basis; or

(2) an appropriately reduced amount based on the amount so contributed, as determined under regulations which the Secretary shall prescribe, for an approved program of education pursued on less than a full-time basis

(h)(1) With respect to any fiscal year, the Secretary shall provide a percentage increase in the rates payable under subsections (a)(1) and (b)(1) equal to the percentage by which—

(A) the average cost of undergraduate tuition in the United States, as determined by the National Center for Education Statistics, for the last academic year preceding the beginning of the fiscal year for which the increase is made, exceeds

(B) the average cost of undergraduate tuition in the United States, as so determined, for the academic year preceding the academic year described in subparagraph (A).

(2) Any increase under paragraph (1) in a rate with respect to a fiscal year after fiscal year 2004 and before fiscal year 2014 shall be rounded down to the next lower whole dollar amount. Any such increase with respect to a fiscal year after fiscal year 2013 shall be rounded to the nearest whole dollar amount.

(As amended Oct. 17, 1998, P. L. 105-261, Div A, Title V, Subtitle G, § 565(a), Title VI, Subtitle E, § 656, 112 Stat. 2029, 2053; Oct. 30, 2000, P. L. 106-398, § 1, 114 Stat. 1654; Nov. 1, 2000, P. L. 106-419, Title I, Subtitle A, §§ 101(a), 103(d), 105(b), 114 Stat. 1824, 1826, 1829; June 5, 2001, P. L. 107-14, § 7(b)(2)(A), (c)(3), 115 Stat. 31, 32; Dec. 27, 2001, P. L. 107-103, Title I,

READJUSTMENT BENEFITS 38 USCS § 3015

§ 101(a), 115 Stat. 977; Dec. 16, 2003, P. L. 108-183, Title III, § 304(a), 117 Stat. 2659; June 30, 2008, P. L. 110-252, Title V, § 5004(a)–(c), 122 Stat. 2379.)

HISTORY; ANCILLARY LAWS AND DIRECTIVES

Explanatory notes:
The amendments made by § 1 of Act Oct. 30, 2000, P. L. 106-398, are based on § 1602(b)(3) of Subtitle A of Title XVI of Division A of H.R. 5408 (114 Stat. 1654A-359), as introduced on Oct. 6, 2000, which was enacted into law by such § 1.

Amendments:
Act Oct. 17, 1998 (effective and applicable as provided by § 565(b) of such Act, which appears as a note to this section), in subsec. (d), inserted ", at the time the individual first becomes a member of the Armed Forces,'' and substituted "$950 per month'' for "$400 per month, in the case of an individual who first became a member of the Armed Forces before November 29, 1989, or $700 per month, in the case of an individual who first became a member of the Armed Forces on or after that date''.

Such Act further, in subsec. (d), designated the existing provisions as para. (1) and added para. (2).

2000. Act Oct. 30, 2000, in subsecs. (a)(1) and (b)(1), deleted "subsection (g)" following "under"; redesignated subsec. (g) as subsec. (h); and inserted new subsec. (g).

Act Nov. 1, 2000, in subsec. (a), in the introductory matter, inserted "in the case of an individual entitled to an educational assistance allowance under this chapter whose obligated period of active duty on which such entitlement is based is three years,''; in subsec. (b), in the introductory matter, substituted "whose obligated period of active duty on which such entitlement is based is two years,'' for "and whose initial obligated period of active duty is two years,''; and, in subsec. (c)(2), substituted subparas. (A) and (B) for ones which read:

"(A) whose initial obligated period of active duty is less than three years;

"(B) who, beginning on the date of the commencement of the person's initial obligated period of such duty, serves a continuous period of active duty of not less than three years; and''.

Such Act further (effective and applicable as provided by § 101(b) of such Act, which appears as a note to this section), in subsec. (a)(1), substituted "$650'' for "$528''; and, in subsec. (b)(1), substituted "$528'' for "$429''.

Such Act further (effective 5/1/2001, as provided by § 105(c) of such Act, which appears as 28 USCS § 3011 note) purported to amend subsecs. (a)(1) and (b)(1) by substituting "subsection (h)'' for "subsection (g)''; however, these amendments could not be executed because "subsection (g)'' did not appear in such subsections.

Such Act further (effective 5/1/2001, as provided by § 105(c) of such Act, which appears as 28 USCS § 3011 note), redesignated subsec. (g) as subsec. (h); and inserted new subsec. (g).

2001. Act June 5, 2001 (effective as if enacted on 11/1/2000, immediately after enactment of Act Nov. 1, 2000, P. L. 106-419, as provided by § 7(b)(3) of the 2001 Act, which appears as 38 USCS § 3014 note), in subsecs. (a)(1) and (b)(1), inserted "subsection (h)''; and deleted subsec. (h), as redesignated by Act Nov. 1, 2000, which read:

"(h) In the case of an individual who has been paid a basic educational assistance allowance under section 3014(b) of this title, the rate of the basic educational assistance allowance applicable to the individual under this section shall be the rate otherwise applicable to the individual under this section reduced by an amount equal to—

"(1) the aggregate amount of such allowances paid the individual under such section 3014(b); divided by

"(2) 36.''.

Such Act further (effective as if included in the enactment of § 105 of Act Nov. 1, 2000, P. L. 106-419, as provided by § 7(c)(4) of the 2001 Act, which appears as 38 USCS § 3011 note), in subsec. (g), in the introductory matter, inserted "effective as of the first day of the enrollment period following receipt of such contributions from such individual by the Secretary concerned,'', and in para. (1), substituted "$5'' for "$1'', substituted "$20'' for "$4'', and inserted "of this title''.

Act Dec. 27, 2001, in subsec. (a), substituted para. (1) for one which read: "(1) at the monthly rate of $650 (as increased from time to time under subsection (h)) for an approved program of education pursued on a full-time basis; or''; and, in subsec. (b), substituted para. (1) for one which read: "(1) at the monthly rate of $528 (as increased from time to time under subsection (h)) for an approved program of education pursued on a full-time basis; or''.

2003. Act Dec. 16, 2003, in subsec. (h), designated the existing provisions as para. (1) and, in such paragraph, in the introductory matter, deleted "(rounded to the nearest dollar)'' following "increase'', redesignated former paras. (1) and (2) as subparas. (A) and (B), respectively, and, in subpara. (B) as redesignated, substituted "subparagraph (A)'' for "paragraph (1)'', and added new para. (2).

2008. Act June 30, 2008 (effective on 8/1/2008, as provided by § 5004(d)(1) of such Act, which appears as a note to this section), in subsec. (a)(1), substituted a new subpara. (A) for subparas. (A)–(C) which read:

"(A) for months beginning on or after January 1, 2002, $800;

"(B) for months occurring during fiscal year 2003, $900;
"(C) for months occurring during fiscal year 2004, $985; and",
and redesignated subpara. (D) as subpara. (B); in subsec. (b)(1), substituted a new subpara. (A) for subparas. (A)–(C) which read:
"(A) for months beginning on or after January 1, 2002, $650;
"(B) for months occurring during fiscal year 2003, $732;
"(C) for months occurring during fiscal year 2004, $800; and",
and redesignated subpara. (D) as subpara. (B); and, in subsec. (h)(1), substituted subparas. (A) and (B) for ones which read:
"(A) the Consumer Price Index (all items, United States city average) for the 12-month period ending on the June 30 preceding the beginning of the fiscal year for which the increase is made, exceeds
"(B) such Consumer Price Index for the 12-month period preceding the 12-month period described in subparagraph (A).".

Other provisions:
Effective date and application of amendment made by § 565(a) of Act Oct. 17, 1998. Act Oct. 17, 1998, P. L. 105-261, Div A, Title V, Subtitle G, § 565(b), 112 Stat. 2029, provides: "The amendments made by subsection (a) [amending subsec. (d) of this section] shall take effect on October 1, 1998, and shall apply with respect to individuals who first become members of the Armed Forces on or after that date.".
Effective date and application of amendment made by § 101 of Act Nov. 1, 2000. Act Nov. 1, 2000, P. L. 106-419, Title I, Subtitle A, § 101(b), 114 Stat. 1824, provides: "The amendments made by subsection (a) shall take effect on November 1, 2000, and shall apply with respect to educational assistance allowances paid under chapter 30 of title 38, United States Code, for months after October 2000.".
No CPI adjustment for fiscal years 2003 and 2004. Act Dec. 27, 2001, P. L. 107-103, Title I, § 101(b), 115 Stat. 978, provides: "No adjustment in rates of educational assistance shall be made under section 3015(h) of title 38, United States Code, for fiscal years 2003 and 2004.".
Effective date of June 30, 2008 amendments; no cost-of-living adjustment for fiscal year 2009. Act June 30, 2008, P. L. 110-252, Title V, § 5004(d), 122 Stat. 2379, provides:
"(1) In general. The amendments made by this section [amending subsecs. (a)(1), (b)(1), and (h)(1) of this section] shall take effect on August 1, 2008.
"(2) No cost-of-living adjustment for fiscal year 2009. The adjustment required by subsection (h) of section 3015 of title 38, United States Code (as amended by this section), in rates of basic educational assistance payable under subsections (a) and (b) of such section (as so amended) shall not be made for fiscal year 2009.".

CODE OF FEDERAL REGULATIONS
Department of Veterans Affairs—Vocational rehabilitation and education, 38 CFR 21.1 et seq.

RESEARCH GUIDE
Am Jur:
77 Am Jur 2d, Veterans and Veterans' Laws § 135.

INTERPRETIVE NOTES AND DECISIONS

There is no indication in 38 USCS § 3015 that amount of educational assistance allowance that is actually paid is determinative of duration of veteran's education-benefits entitlement under 38 USCS § 3013, and decision of Board of Veterans' Appeals that veteran is not entitled to payment of educational assistance allowance for any period of time after 36 months of education-benefits eligibility had expired is affirmed. Breeden v West (2000) 13 Vet App 398, 2000 US App Vet Claims LEXIS 206.

§ 3016. Inservice enrollment in a program of education

CODE OF FEDERAL REGULATIONS
Department of Veterans Affairs—Vocational rehabilitation and education, 38 CFR 21.1 et seq.

§ 3017. Death benefit
(a)(1) In the event of the service-connected death of any individual—
　(A) who—
　　(i) [Unchanged]
　　(ii) is on active duty in the Armed Forces and but for clause (1)(A)(i) or clause (2) of section 3011(a) [38 USCS § 3011(a)] or clause (1)(A)(i) or (ii) or clause (2) of section 3012(a) of this title [38 USCS § 3012(a)] would be eligible for such basic educational assistance; and
　(B) [Unchanged]
the Secretary shall make a payment, subject to paragraph (2)(B) of this subsection, in the amount described in subsection (b) of this section to the person or persons described in paragraph (2)(A) of this subsection.

(2) [Unchanged]
(b) The amount of any payment made under this section shall be equal to—
  (1) the total of—
    (A) the amount reduced from the individual's basic pay under section 3011(b), 3012(c), 3018(c), 3018A(b), 3018B(b), 3018C(b), or 3018C(e) of this title [38 USCS § 3011(b), 3012(c), 3018(c), 3018A(b), 3018B(b), 3018C(b), or 3018C(e)];
    (B) the amount reduced from the individual's retired pay under section 3018C(e) of this title [38 USCS § 3018C(e)];
    (C) the amount collected from the individual by the Secretary under section 3018B(b), 3018C(b), or 3018C(e) of this title [38 USCS § 3018B(b), 3018C(b), or 3018C(e)]; and
    (D) the amount of any contributions made by the individual under section 3011(e) or 3012(f) of this title [38 USCS § 3011(e) or 3012(f)], less
  (2) [Unchanged]
(c) [Unchanged]
(As amended Nov. 1, 2000, P. L. 106-419, Title I, Subtitle A, § 102(a)(2), 114 Stat. 1824; June 5, 2001, P. L. 107-14, § 7(d)(1), 115 Stat. 33; June 15, 2006, P. L. 109-233, Title V, § 503(4), 120 Stat. 416.)

HISTORY; ANCILLARY LAWS AND DIRECTIVES

Amendments:
2000. Act Nov. 1, 2000, in subsec. (a)(1)(A)(ii), substituted "clause (2)" for "clause (2)(A)" preceding "of section 3011(a)".
2001. Act June 5, 2001 (effective as of 5/1/2001, as provided by § 7(d)(2) of such Act, which appears as a note to this section), in subsec. (b), substituted para. (1) for one which read: "(1) the amount reduced from the individual's pay under section 3011(b), 3012(c), or 3018(c) of this title, less".
2006. Act June 15, 2006, in subsec. (b)(1)(D), substituted "3011(e)" for "3011(c)".

Other provisions:
Effective date of June 5, 2001 amendment. Act June 5, 2001, P. L. 107-14, § 7(d)(2), 115 Stat. 33, provides: "The amendment made by paragraph (1) [amending subsec. (b)(1) of this section] shall take effect as of May 1, 2001.".

§ 3018. Opportunity for certain active-duty personnel to withdraw election not to enroll

(a) [Unchanged]
(b) An individual described in clauses (1) through (3) of subsection (a) of this section who made an election under section 3011(c)(1) or 3012(d)(1) of this title [38 USCS § 3011(c)(1) or 3012(d)(1)] and who—
  (1), (2) [Unchanged]
  (3)(A) [Unchanged]
    (B) before completing such obligated period of service, is discharged or released from active duty for (i) a service-connected disability, (ii) a medical condition which preexisted such service and which the Secretary determines is not service connected, (iii) hardship, or (iv) a physical or mental condition that was not characterized as a disability and did not result from the individual's own willful misconduct but did interfere with the individual's performance of duty, as determined by the Secretary of each military department in accordance with regulations prescribed by the Secretary of Defense (or by the Secretary of Homeland Security with respect to the Coast Guard when it is not operating as a service of the Navy); or
    (C) [Unchanged]
  (4) before applying for benefits under this section—
    (A) completes the requirements of a secondary school diploma (or equivalency certificate); or
    (B) successfully completes (or otherwise receives academic credit for) the equivalent of 12 semester hours in a program of education leading to a standard college degree; and
  (5) [Unchanged]
is entitled to basic educational assistance under this chapter [38 USCS §§ 3001 et seq.].
(c), (d) [Unchanged]
(As amended Nov. 11, 1998, P. L. 105-368, Title II, Subtitle A, § 203(a), 112 Stat. 3326; Nov. 1, 2000, P. L. 106-419, Title I, Subtitle A, § 102(c), 114 Stat. 1825; Nov. 25, 2002, P. L. 107-296, Title XVII, § 1704(d), 116 Stat. 2315.)

HISTORY; ANCILLARY LAWS AND DIRECTIVES

Amendments:
1998. Act Nov. 11, 1998 (effective on 10/1/98, as provided by § 203(b) of such Act, which ap-

pears as 38 USCS § 3011 note), in subsec. (b)(4)(ii), substituted "successfully completed (or otherwise received academic credit for)" for "successfully completed".

2000. Act Nov. 1, 2000, in subsec. (b), substituted para. (4) for one which read: "(4) before completing such obligated period of service (i) has completed the requirements of a secondary school diploma (or an equivalency certificate), or (ii) has successfully completed (or otherwise received academic credit for) the equivalent of 12 semester hours in a program of education leading to a standard college degree; and".

2002. Act Nov. 25, 2002 (effective on 3/1/2003 pursuant to § 1704(g) of such Act, which appears as 10 USCS § 101 note), in subsec. (b)(3)(B)(iv), substituted "of Homeland Security" for "of Transportation".

RESEARCH GUIDE

Am Jur:
77 Am Jur 2d, Veterans and Veterans' Laws § 126.

§ 3018A. Opportunity for certain active-duty personnel to enroll before being involuntarily separated from service

(a) Notwithstanding any other provision of law, an individual who—
  (1) [Unchanged]
  (2) before applying for benefits under this section, has completed the requirements of a secondary school diploma (or equivalency certificate) or has successfully completed (or otherwise received academic credit for) the equivalent of 12 semester hours in a program of education leading to a standard college degree;
  (3) in the case of any individual who has made an election under section 3011(c)(1) or 3012(d)(1) of this title [38 USCS § 3011(c)(1) or 3012(d)(1)], withdraws such election before such separation pursuant to procedures which the Secretary of each military department shall provide in accordance with regulations prescribed by the Secretary of Defense for the purpose of carrying out this section or which the Secretary of Homeland Security shall provide for such purpose with respect to the Coast Guard when it is not operating as a service in the Navy;
  (4) in the case of any person enrolled in the educational benefits program provided by chapter 32 of this title [38 USCS §§ 3201 et seq.] makes an irrevocable election, pursuant to procedures referred to in paragraph (3), before such separation to receive benefits under this section in lieu of benefits under such chapter 32 [38 USCS §§ 3201 et seq.]; and
  (5) before such separation elects to receive assistance under this section pursuant to procedures referred to in paragraph (3),
is entitled to basic educational assistance under this chapter [38 USCS §§ 3001 et seq.].
(b) The basic pay of an individual described in subsection (a) shall be reduced by $1,200.
(c) A withdrawal referred to in subsection (a)(3) is irrevocable.
(d)(1) Except as provided in paragraph (3), an individual who is enrolled in the educational benefits program provided by chapter 32 of this title [38 USCS §§ 3201 et seq.] and who makes the election described in subsection (a)(4) shall be disenrolled from such chapter 32 program as of the date of such election.
  (2) [Unchanged]
  (3) Any contribution made by the Secretary of Defense to the Post-Vietnam Era Veterans Education Account pursuant to subsection (c) of section 3222 of this title [38 USCS § 3222] on behalf of any individual referred to in paragraph (1) shall remain in such Account to make payments of benefits to such individual under section 3015(f) of this title [38 USCS § 3015(f)].
(As amended Nov. 11, 1998, P. L. 105-368, Title II, Subtitle A, § 203(a), 112 Stat. 3326; Nov. 25, 2002, P. L. 107-296, Title XVII, § 1704(d), 116 Stat. 2315; June 15, 2006, P. L. 109-233, Title V, § 503(5), 120 Stat. 416.)

HISTORY; ANCILLARY LAWS AND DIRECTIVES

Amendments:
1998. Act Nov. 11, 1998 (effective on 10/1/98, as provided by § 203(b) of such Act, which appears as 38 USCS § 3011 note), in subsec. (a)(2), substituted "successfully completed (or otherwise received academic credit for)" for "successfully completed".
2002. Act Nov. 25, 2002 (effective on 3/1/2003 pursuant to § 1704(g) of such Act, which appears as 10 USCS § 101 note), in subsec. (a)(3), substituted "of Homeland Security" for "of Transportation".
2006. Act June 15, 2006, in subsec. (a), in paras. (4) and (5), deleted "of this subsection" following "paragraph (3)"; in subsec. (b), deleted "of this section" following "subsection (a)"; in subsec. (c), deleted "of this section" following "subsection (a)(3)"; in subsec. (d), in para. (1), deleted "of this subsection" following "paragraph (3)" and deleted "of this subsection" following "subsection (a)(4)", and, in para. (3), deleted "of this subsection" following "paragraph (1)" and substituted "of this title" for "of this chapter".

READJUSTMENT BENEFITS

38 USCS § 3018C

RESEARCH GUIDE

Am Jur:
77 Am Jur 2d, Veterans and Veterans' Laws § 126.

§ 3018B. Opportunity for certain persons to enroll

(a) Notwithstanding any other provision of law—
  (1) the Secretary of Defense shall, subject to the availability of appropriations, allow an individual who—
    (A) [Unchanged]
    (B) before applying for benefits under this section, has completed the requirements of a secondary school diploma (or equivalency certificate) or has successfully completed (or otherwise received academic credit for) the equivalent of 12 semester hours in a program of education leading to a standard college degree;
    (C) in the case of any individual who has made an election under section 3011(c)(1) or 3012(d)(1) of this title [38 USCS § 3011(c)(1) or 3012(d)(1)], withdraws such election before such separation pursuant to procedures which the Secretary of each military department shall provide in accordance with regulations prescribed by the Secretary of Defense for the purpose of carrying out this section or which the Secretary of Homeland Security shall provide for such purpose with respect to the Coast Guard when it is not operating as service in the Navy;
    (D), (E) [Unchanged]
  (2) the Secretary, in consultation with the Secretary of Defense, shall, subject to the availability of appropriations, allow an individual who—
    (A) [Unchanged]
    (B) before applying for benefits under this section, has completed the requirements of a secondary school diploma (or equivalency certificate) or has successfully completed (or otherwise received academic credit for) the equivalent of 12 semester hours in a program of education leading to a standard college degree;
    (C) in the case of any individual who has made an election under section 3011(c)(1) or 3012(d)(1) of this title [38 USCS § 3011(c)(1) or 3012(d)(1)], withdraws such election before making an election under this paragraph pursuant to procedures which the Secretary shall provide, in consultation with the Secretary of Defense and the Secretary of Homeland Security with respect to the Coast Guard when it is not operating as service in the Navy, which shall be similar to the regulations prescribed under paragraph (1)(C) of this subsection;
    (D) [Unchanged]
    (E) before October 23, 1993, elects to receive assistance under this section pursuant to procedures referred to in subparagraph (C) of this paragraph,
to elect to become entitled to basic education assistance under this chapter [38 USCS §§ 3001 et seq.].
(b)–(d) [Unchanged]
(As amended Nov. 11, 1998, P. L. 105-368, Title II, Subtitle A, § 203(a), Title X, § 1005(b)(6), 112 Stat. 3326, 3365; Nov. 25, 2002, P. L. 107-296, Title XVII, § 1704(d), 116 Stat. 2315.)

HISTORY; ANCILLARY LAWS AND DIRECTIVES

Amendments:
1998. Act Nov. 11, 1998 (effective on 10/1/98, as provided by § 203(b) of such Act, which appears as 38 USCS § 3011 note), in subsec. (a), in paras. (1)(B) and (2)(B), substituted "successfully completed (or otherwise received academic credit for)" for "successfully completed".
Such Act further, in subsec. (a)(2)(E), substituted "before October 23, 1993," for "before the one-year period beginning on the date of enactment of this section,".
2002. Act Nov. 25, 2002 (effective on 3/1/2003 pursuant to § 1704(g) of such Act, which appears as 10 USCS § 101 note), in subsec. (a), in paras. (1)(C) and (2)(C), substituted "of Homeland Security" for "of Transportation".

RESEARCH GUIDE

Am Jur:
77 Am Jur 2d, Veterans and Veterans' Laws § 126.

§ 3018C. Opportunity for certain VEAP participants to enroll

(a) Notwithstanding any other provision of law, an individual who—
  (1), (2) [Unchanged]
  (3) before applying for benefits under this section, has completed the requirements of a secondary school diploma (or equivalency certificate) or has successfully completed (or otherwise

received academic credit for) the equivalent of 12 semester hours in a program of education leading to a standard college degree;

(4) [Unchanged]

(5) during the one-year period beginning on October 9, 1996, makes an irrevocable election to receive benefits under this section in lieu of benefits under chapter 32 of this title [38 USCS §§ 3201 et seq.], pursuant to procedures which the Secretary of each military department shall provide in accordance with regulations prescribed by the Secretary of Defense for the purpose of carrying out this section or which the Secretary of Homeland Security shall provide for such purpose with respect to the Coast Guard when it is not operating as a service in the Navy;

may elect to become entitled to basic educational assistance under this chapter [38 USCS §§ 3001 et seq.].

(b) With respect to an individual who makes an election under subsection (a) to become entitled to basic education assistance under this chapter [38 USCS §§ 3001 et seq.]—

(1), (2) [Unchanged]

(c), (d) [Unchanged]

(e)(1) A qualified individual (described in paragraph (2)) may make an irrevocable election under this subsection, during the one-year period beginning on the date of the enactment of this subsection [enacted Nov. 1, 2000], to become entitled to basic educational assistance under this chapter [38 USCS §§ 3001 et seq.]. Such an election shall be made in the same manner as elections made under subsection (a)(5).

(2) A qualified individual referred to in paragraph (1) is an individual who meets each of the following requirements:

(A) The individual was a participant in the educational benefits program under chapter 32 of this title [38 USCS §§ 3201 et seq.] on or before October 9, 1996.

(B) The individual has continuously served on active duty since October 9, 1996 (excluding the periods referred to in section 3202(1)(C) of this title [38 USCS § 3202(1)(C)]), through at least April 1, 2000.

(C) The individual meets the requirements of subsection (a)(3).

(D) The individual, when discharged or released from active duty, is discharged or released therefrom with an honorable discharge.

(3)(A) Subject to the succeeding provisions of this paragraph, with respect to a qualified individual who makes an election under paragraph (1) to become entitled to basic education assistance under this chapter [38 USCS §§ 3001 et seq.]—

(i) the basic pay of the qualified individual shall be reduced (in a manner determined by the Secretary concerned) until the total amount by which such basic pay is reduced is $2,700; and

(ii) to the extent that basic pay is not so reduced before the qualified individual's discharge or release from active duty as specified in subsection (a)(4), at the election of the qualified individual—

(I) the Secretary concerned shall collect from the qualified individual; or

(II) the Secretary concerned shall reduce the retired or retainer pay of the qualified individual by,

an amount equal to the difference between $2,700 and the total amount of reductions under clause (i), which shall be paid into the Treasury of the United States as miscellaneous receipts.

(B)(i) The Secretary concerned shall provide for an 18-month period, beginning on the date the qualified individual makes an election under paragraph (1), for the qualified individual to pay that Secretary the amount due under subparagraph (A).

(ii) Nothing in clause (i) shall be construed as modifying the period of eligibility for and entitlement to basic education assistance under this chapter [38 USCS §§ 3001 et seq.] applicable under section 3031 of this title [38 USCS § 3031].

(C) The provisions of subsection (c) shall apply to qualified individuals making elections under this subsection in the same manner as they applied to individuals making elections under subsection (a)(5).

(4) With respect to qualified individuals referred to in paragraph (3)(A)(ii), no amount of educational assistance allowance under this chapter [38 USCS §§ 3001 et seq.] shall be paid to the qualified individual until the earlier of the date on which—

(A) the Secretary concerned collects the applicable amount under subclause (I) of such paragraph; or

(B) the retired or retainer pay of the qualified individual is first reduced under subclause (II) of such paragraph.

(5) The Secretary, in conjunction with the Secretary of Defense, shall provide for notice to

participants in the educational benefits program under chapter 32 of this title [38 USCS §§ 3201 et seq.] of the opportunity under this subsection to elect to become entitled to basic educational assistance under this chapter [38 USCS §§ 3001 et seq.].

(As amended Nov. 11, 1998, P. L. 105-368, Title II, Subtitle A, § 203(a), 112 Stat. 3326; Oct. 30, 2000, P. L. 106-398, § 1, 114 Stat. 1654; Nov. 1, 2000, P. L. 106-419, Title I, Subtitle A, § 104(a)–(c)(1), 114 Stat. 1827; June 5, 2001, P. L. 107-14, § 7(e)(1), 115 Stat. 33; Nov. 25, 2002, P. L. 107-296, Title XVII, § 1704(d), 116 Stat. 2315; Dec. 6, 2002, P. L. 107-330, Title III, § 308(g)(9), 116 Stat. 2829.)

HISTORY; ANCILLARY LAWS AND DIRECTIVES

Explanatory notes:
Section 1 of Act Oct. 30, 2000, P. L. 106-398, enacted into law § 1601 of H.R. 5408 (114 Stat. 1654A-357), as introduced on Oct. 6, 2000, which amended this section. However, pursuant to § 104(c)(1) of Act Nov. 1, 2000, P. L. 106-419, as of the enactment of Act Nov. 1, 2000, P. L. 106-419, the amendments made by § 1601 of H.R. 5408 shall be deemed for all purposes not to have taken effect and such § 1601 shall cease to be in effect.

Amendments:
1998. Act Nov. 11, 1998 (effective on 10/1/98, as provided by § 203(b) of such Act, which appears as 38 USCS § 2011 note), in subsec. (a)(3), substituted "successfully completed (or otherwise received academic credit for)" for "successfully completed".
2000. Act Nov. 1, 2000, in subsec. (b), in the introductory matter, substituted "subsection (a) or (e)" for "subsection (a)"; and added subsec. (e).
2001. Act June 5, 2001, in subsec. (b), in the introductory matter, deleted "or (e)" following "subsection (a)".
2002. Act Nov. 25, 2002 (effective on 3/1/2003 pursuant to § 1704(g) of such Act, which appears as 10 USCS § 101 note), in subsec. (a)(5), substituted "of Homeland Security" for "of Transportation".
Act Dec. 6, 2002, in subsec. (e)(2)(B), deleted a comma after "April".

Other provisions:
Treatment of certain amounts collected under subsec. (b) between Nov. 1, 2000 and June 5, 2001. Act June 5, 2001, P. L. 107-14, § 7(e)(2), 115 Stat. 33, provides: "Any amount collected under section 3018C(b) of title 38, United States Code (whether by reduction in basic pay under paragraph (1) of that section, collection under paragraph (2) of that section, or both), with respect to an individual who enrolled in basic educational assistance under section 3018C(e) of that title, during the period beginning on November 1, 2000, and ending on the date of the enactment of this Act, shall be treated as an amount collected with respect to the individual under section 3018C(e)(3)(A) of that title (whether as a reduction in basic pay under clause (i) of that section, a collection under clause (ii) of that section, or both) for basic educational assistance under section 3018C of that title.".

RESEARCH GUIDE
Am Jur:
77 Am Jur 2d, Veterans and Veterans' Laws § 126.

§ 3019. Tutorial assistance

RESEARCH GUIDE
Am Jur:
77 Am Jur 2d, Veterans and Veterans' Laws § 126.

§ 3020. Authority to transfer unused education benefits to family members for career service members

(a) In general. Subject to the provisions of this section, the Secretary of Defense may authorize the Secretary concerned, to promote recruitment and retention of members of the Armed Forces, to permit an individual described in subsection (b) who is entitled to basic educational assistance under this subchapter to elect to transfer to one or more of the dependents specified in subsection (c) the unused portion of entitlement to such assistance, subject to the limitation under subsection (d).

(b) Eligible individuals. An individual referred to in subsection (a) is any member of the Armed Forces—
(1) who, while serving on active duty or as a member of the Selected Reserve at the time of the approval by the Secretary concerned of the member's request to transfer entitlement to basic educational assistance under this section, has completed six years of service in the Armed Forces and enters into an agreement to serve at least four more years as a member of the Armed Forces; or
(2) as determined in regulations pursuant to subsection (k).

(c) Eligible dependents. An individual approved to transfer an entitlement to basic educational assistance under this section may transfer the individual's entitlement as follows:
  (1) To the individual's spouse.
  (2) To one or more of the individual's children.
  (3) To a combination of the individuals referred to in paragraphs (1) and (2).
(d) Limitation on months of transfer. (1) An individual approved to transfer an entitlement to basic educational assistance under this section may transfer any unused entitlement to one or more of the dependents specified in subsection (c).
  (2) The total number of months of entitlement transferred by an individual under this section may not exceed 36 months. The Secretary of Defense may prescribe regulations that would limit the months of entitlement that may be transferred under this section to no less than 18 months.
(e) Designation of transferee. An individual transferring an entitlement to basic educational assistance under this section shall—
  (1) designate the dependent or dependents to whom such entitlement is being transferred;
  (2) designate the number of months of such entitlement to be transferred to each such dependent; and
  (3) specify the period for which the transfer shall be effective for each dependent designated under paragraph (1).
(f) Time for transfer; revocation and modification. (1) Subject to the time limitation for use of entitlement under section 3031 of this title [38 USCS § 3031], an individual approved to transfer entitlement to basic educational assistance under this section may transfer such entitlement at any time after the approval of the individual's request to transfer such entitlement only while the individual is a member of the Armed Forces when the transfer is executed.
  (2)(A) An individual transferring entitlement under this section may modify or revoke at any time the transfer of any unused portion of the entitlement so transferred as long as the individual is serving on active duty or as a member of the Selected Reserve.
    (B) The modification or revocation of the transfer of entitlement under this paragraph shall be made by the submittal of written notice of the action to both the Secretary concerned and the Secretary of Veterans Affairs.
  (3) Entitlement transferred under this section may not be treated as marital property, or the asset of a marital estate, subject to division in a divorce or other civil proceeding.
(g) Commencement of use. A dependent to whom entitlement to basic educational assistance is transferred under this section may not commence the use of the transferred entitlement until—
  (1) in the case of entitlement transferred to a spouse, the completion by the individual making the transfer of six years of service in the Armed Forces; or
  (2) in the case of entitlement transferred to a child, both—
    (A) the completion by the individual making the transfer of 10 years of service in the Armed Forces; and
    (B) either—
      (i) the completion by the child of the requirements of a secondary school diploma (or equivalency certificate); or
      (ii) the attainment by the child of 18 years of age.
(h) Additional administrative matters. (1) The use of any entitlement to basic educational assistance transferred under this section shall be charged against the entitlement of the individual making the transfer at the rate of one month for each month of transferred entitlement that is used.
  (2) Except as provided under subsection (e)(2) and subject to paragraphs (5) and (6), a dependent to whom entitlement is transferred under this section is entitled to basic educational assistance under this subchapter [38 USCS §§ 3011 et seq.] in the same manner as the individual from whom the entitlement was transferred.
  (3)(A) Subject to subparagraph (B), the monthly rate of educational assistance payable to a dependent to whom entitlement is transferred under this section shall be the monthly amount payable under sections 3015 and 3022 of this title [38 USCS §§ 3015 and 3022] to the individual making the transfer.
    (B) The monthly rate of assistance payable to a dependent under subparagraph (A) shall be subject to the provisions of section 3032 of this title [38 USCS § 3032], except that the provisions of subsection (a)(1) of that section shall not apply even if the individual making the transfer to the dependent under this section is on active duty during all or any part of enrollment period of the dependent in which such entitlement is used.
  (4) The death of an individual transferring an entitlement under this section shall not affect the use of the entitlement by the dependent to whom the entitlement is transferred.

(5) Notwithstanding section 3031 of this title [38 USCS § 3031], a child to whom entitlement is transferred under this section may use the benefit without regard to the 10-year delimiting date, but may not use any entitlement so transferred after attaining the age of 26 years.

(6) The administrative provisions of this chapter [38 USCS §§ 3001 et seq.] (including the provisions set forth in section 3034(a)(1) of this title [38 USCS § 3034(a)(1)]) shall apply to the use of entitlement transferred under this section, except that the dependent to whom the entitlement is transferred shall be treated as the eligible veteran for purposes of such provisions.

(7) The purposes for which a dependent to whom entitlement is transferred under this section may use such entitlement shall include the pursuit and completion of the requirements of a secondary school diploma (or equivalency certificate).

(i) Overpayment. (1) In the event of an overpayment of basic educational assistance with respect to a dependent to whom entitlement is transferred under this section, the dependent and the individual making the transfer shall be jointly and severally liable to the United States for the amount of the overpayment for purposes of section 3685 of this title [38 USCS § 3685].

(2) Except as provided in paragraph (3), if an individual transferring entitlement under this section fails to complete the service agreed to by the individual under subsection (b)(3) in accordance with the terms of the agreement of the individual under that subsection, the amount of any transferred entitlement under this section that is used by a dependent of the individual as of the date of such failure shall be treated as an overpayment of basic educational assistance under paragraph (1).

(3) Paragraph (2) shall not apply in the case of an individual who fails to complete service agreed to by the individual—

(A) by reason of the death of the individual; or

(B) for a reason referred to in section 3011(a)(1)(A)(ii)(I) of this title [38 USCS § 3011(a)(1)(A)(ii)(I)].

(j) Approvals of transfer subject to availability of appropriations. The Secretary concerned may approve transfers of entitlement to basic educational assistance under this section in a fiscal year only to the extent that appropriations for military personnel are available in that fiscal year for purposes of making deposits in the Department of Defense Education Benefits Fund under section 2006 of title 10 [10 USCS § 2006] in that fiscal year to cover the present value of future benefits payable from the Fund for the Department of Defense portion of payments of basic educational assistance attributable to increased usage of benefits as a result of such transfers of entitlement in that fiscal year.

(k) Regulations. The Secretary of Defense, in coordination with the Secretary of Veterans Affairs, shall prescribe regulations for purposes of this section. Such regulations shall specify—

(1) the manner of authorizing the military departments to offer transfer of entitlements under this section;

(2) the eligibility criteria in accordance with subsection (b);

(3) the limitations on the amount of entitlement eligible to be transferred; and

(4) the manner and effect of an election to modify or revoke a transfer of entitlement under subsection (f)(2).

(l) Secretary concerned defined. Notwithstanding section 101(25) of this title [38 USCS § 101(25)], in this section, the term "Secretary concerned" means—

(1) the Secretary of the Army with respect to matters concerning the Army;

(2) the Secretary of the Navy with respect to matters concerning the Navy or the Marine Corps;

(3) the Secretary of the Air Force with respect to matters concerning the Air Force; and

(4) the Secretary of Defense with respect to matters concerning the Coast Guard, or the Secretary of Homeland Security when it is not operating as a service in the Navy.

(Added Dec. 28, 2001, P. L. 107-107, Div A, Title VI, Subtitle E, § 654(a)(1), 115 Stat. 1153; Nov. 25, 2002, P. L. 107-296, Title XVII, § 1704(d), 116 Stat. 2315; Dec. 2, 2002, P. L. 107-314, Div A, Title VI, Subtitle E, § 643(a), 116 Stat. 2577; June 30, 2008, P. L. 110-252, Title V, § 5006(a), 122 Stat. 2380; Dec. 31, 2011, P. L. 112-81, Div A, Title X, Subtitle G, § 1063(b), 125 Stat. 1586.)

HISTORY; ANCILLARY LAWS AND DIRECTIVES

Explanatory notes:

A prior § 3020 was redesignated 38 USCS § 5120 by Act May 7, 1991, P. L. 102-40, Title IV, § 402(b)(1), 105 Stat. 238.

Amendments:

2002. Act Nov. 25, 2002 (effective on 3/1/2003 pursuant to § 1704(g) of such Act, which appears as 10 USCS § 101 note), in subsec. (m)(4), substituted "of Homeland Security" for "of Transportation".

Act Dec. 2, 2002 (effective as if included in the enactment of this section by Act Dec. 28, 2001,

P. L. 107-107, as provided by § 643(c)(1) of the 2002 Act, which appears as a note to this section), in subsec. (h), in para. (2), substituted "paragraphs (5) and (6)" for "paragraphs (4) and (5)" and deleted "and at the same rate" following "manner", redesignated paras. (3)-(6) as paras. (4)-(7), respectively, and inserted new para. (3).

2008. Act June 30, 2008, substituted the section heading for one which read: "§ 3020. Transfer of entitlement to basic educational assistance: members of the Armed Forces with critical military skills"; substituted subsecs. (a) and (b) for one which read:

"(a) In general. Subject to the provisions of this section, each Secretary concerned may, for the purpose of enhancing recruitment and retention of members of the Armed Forces with critical military skills and at such Secretary's sole discretion, permit an individual described in subsection (b) who is entitled to basic educational assistance under this subchapter to elect to transfer to one or more of the dependents specified in subsection (c) a portion of such individual's entitlement to such assistance, subject to the limitation under subsection (d).

"(b) Eligible individuals. An individual referred to in subsection (a) is any member of the Armed Forces who, at the time of the approval by the Secretary concerned of the member's request to transfer entitlement to basic educational assistance under this section—

"(1) has completed six years of service in the Armed Forces;
"(2) either—
"(A) has a critical military skill designated by the Secretary concerned for purposes of this section; or
"(B) is in a military specialty designated by the Secretary concerned for purposes of this section as requiring critical military skills; and
"(3) enters into an agreement to serve at least four more years as a member of the Armed Forces.";

substituted subsec. (d) for one which read: "(d) Limitation on months of transfer. The total number of months of entitlement transferred by an individual under this section may not exceed 18 months."; in subsec. (f), in para. (1), substituted "only while" for "without regard to whether", in para. (2), inserted "as long as the individual is serving on active duty or as a member of the Selected Reserve", and added para. (3); in subsec. (h)(5), inserted "may use the benefit without regard to the 10-year delimiting date, but"; and substituted subsec. (k) for one which read: "(k) Regulations. The Secretary of Defense shall prescribe regulations for purposes of this section. Such regulations shall specify the manner and effect of an election to modify or revoke a transfer of entitlement under subsection (f)(2) and shall specify the manner of the applicability of the administrative provisions referred to in subsection (h)(5) to a dependent to whom entitlement is transferred under this section.".

2011. Act Dec. 31, 2011, deleted subsec. (l), which read:

"(l) Annual report. (1) Not later than January 31 each year (beginning in 2003), the Secretary of Defense shall submit to the Committees on Armed Services and the Committees on Veterans' Affairs of the Senate and House of Representatives a report on the transfers of entitlement to basic educational assistance under this section that were approved by each Secretary concerned during the preceding fiscal year.

"(2) Each report shall set forth—
"(A) the number of transfers of entitlement under this section that were approved by such Secretary during the preceding fiscal year; or
"(B) if no transfers of entitlement under this section were approved by such Secretary during that fiscal year, a justification for such Secretary's decision not to approve any such transfers of entitlement during that fiscal year.";

and redesignated subsec. (m) as subsec. (l).

Other provisions:

Plan for implementation. Act Dec. 28, 2001, P. L. 107-107, Div A, Title VI, Subtitle E, § 654(c), 115 Stat. 1157, provides: "Not later than June 30, 2002, the Secretary of Defense shall submit to Congress a report describing the manner in which the Secretaries of the military departments and the Secretary of Transportation propose to exercise the authority granted by section 3020 of title 38, United States Code, as added by subsection (a). The report shall include the regulations prescribed under subsection (k) of that section for purposes of the exercise of the authority.".

Effective date of Dec. 2, 2002 amendments. Act Dec. 2, 2002, P. L. 107-314, Div A, Title VI, Subtitle E, § 643(c)(1), 116 Stat. 2578, provides: "The amendments made by subsection (a) [amending subsec. (h) of this section] shall take effect as if included in the enactment of section 3020 of title 38, United States Code, by section 654(a)(1) of the National Defense Authorization Act for Fiscal Year 2002 (Public Law 107-107; 115 Stat. 1153).".

SUBCHAPTER III. SUPPLEMENTAL EDUCATIONAL ASSISTANCE

§ 3021. Supplemental educational assistance for additional service

CODE OF FEDERAL REGULATIONS

Department of Veterans Affairs—Adjudication, 38 CFR 3.1 et seq.
Department of Veterans Affairs—Vocational rehabilitation and education, 38 CFR 21.1 et seq.

READJUSTMENT BENEFITS
38 USCS § 3031

Department of Veterans Affairs—Loan guaranty and vocational rehabilitation and counseling programs, 48 CFR 871.100 et seq.

§ 3022. Amount of supplemental educational assistance

CODE OF FEDERAL REGULATIONS
Department of Veterans Affairs—Vocational rehabilitation and education, 38 CFR 21.1 et seq.

RESEARCH GUIDE
Am Jur:
77 Am Jur 2d, Veterans and Veterans' Laws § 135.

§ 3023. Payment of supplemental educational assistance under this subchapter

CODE OF FEDERAL REGULATIONS
Department of Veterans Affairs—Vocational rehabilitation and education, 38 CFR 21.1 et seq.

RESEARCH GUIDE
Am Jur:
77 Am Jur 2d, Veterans and Veterans' Laws § 135.

SUBCHAPTER IV. TIME LIMITATION FOR USE OF ELIGIBILITY AND ENTITLEMENT; GENERAL AND ADMINISTRATIVE PROVISIONS

§ 3031. Time limitation for use of eligibility and entitlement

(a) Except as provided in subsections (b) through (g), and subject to subsection (h), of this section, the period during which an individual entitled to educational assistance under this chapter [38 USCS §§ 3001 et seq.] may use such individual's entitlement expires at the end of the 10-year period beginning on the date of such individual's last discharge or release from active duty, except that such 10-year period shall begin—

(1) in the case of an individual who becomes entitled to such assistance under clause (A) or (B) of section 3012(a)(1) of this title [38 USCS § 3012(a)(1)], on the later of the date of such individual's last discharge or release from active duty or the date on which the four-year requirement described in clause (A)(ii) or (B)(ii), respectively, of such section 3012(a)(1) is met;

(2) in the case of an individual who becomes entitled to such assistance under section 3011(a)(1)(B) [38 USCS § 3011(a)(1)(B)], on the later of the date of such individual's last discharge or release from active duty or January 1, 1990; and

(3) in the case of an individual who becomes entitled to such assistance under section 3011(a)(1)(C) or 3012(a)(1)(C) of this title [38 USCS § 3011(a)(1)(C) or 3012(a)(1)(C)], on December 27, 2001.

(b), (c) [Unchanged]

(d)(1) In the case of an individual eligible for educational assistance under this chapter who is prevented from pursuing the individual's chosen program of education before the expiration of the 10-year period for the use of entitlement under this chapter otherwise applicable under this section because of a physical or mental disability which is not the result of the individual's own willful misconduct, such 10-year period—

(A) shall not run during the period the individual is so prevented from pursuing such program; and

(B) shall again begin running on the first day after the individual's recovery from such disability on which it is reasonably feasible, as determined under regulations prescribed by the Secretary, for the individual to initiate or resume pursuit of a program of education with educational assistance under this chapter.

(2)(A) Subject to subparagraph (B), in the case of an individual eligible for educational assistance under this chapter who is prevented from pursuing the individual's chosen program of education before the expiration of the 10-year period for the use of entitlement under this chapter otherwise applicable under this section by reason of acting as the primary provider of personal care services for a veteran or member of the Armed Forces under section 1720G(a) of this title [38 USCS § 1720G(a)], such 10-year period—

(i) shall not run during the period the individual is so prevented from pursuing such program; and

(ii) shall again begin running on the first day after the date of the recovery of the veteran or member from the injury, or the date on which the individual ceases to be the primary provider of personal care services for the veteran or member, whichever is earlier, on which it is reasonably feasible, as so determined, for the individual to initiate or resume

25

pursuit of a program of education with educational assistance under this chapter [38 USCS §§ 3001 et seq.].

(B) Subparagraph (A) shall not apply with respect to the period of an individual as a primary provider of personal care services if the period concludes with the revocation of the individual's designation as such a primary provider under section 1720G(a)(7)(D) of this title [38 USCS § 1720G(a)(7)(D)].

(e)(1) Except as provided in paragraph (2) of this subsection, in the case of an individual described in section 3011(a)(1)(B), 3011(a)(1)(C), 3012(a)(1)(B), or 3012(a)(1)(C) of this title [38 USCS § 3011(a)(1)(B), 3011(a)(1)(C), 3012(a)(1)(B), or 3012(a)(1)(C)] who is entitled to basic educational assistance under this chapter, the 10-year period prescribed in subsection (a) of this section shall be reduced by an amount of time equal to the amount of time that such individual was not serving on active duty during the period beginning on January 1, 1977, and ending on June 30, 1985.

(2) [Unchanged]

(f) [Unchanged]

(g) In the case of an individual described in section 3011(f)(3) of this title [38 USCS § 3011(f)(3)], the period during which that individual may use the individual's entitlement to educational assistance allowance expires on the last day of the 10-year period beginning on the date of the enactment of the Veterans Millennium Health Care and Benefits Act [enacted Nov. 30, 1999] if that date is later than the date that would otherwise be applicable to that individual under this section.

(h) For purposes of subsection (a) of this section, an individual's last discharge or release from active duty shall not include any discharge or release from a period of active duty of less than 90 days of continuous service unless the individual involved is discharged or released for a service-connected disability, for a medical condition which preexisted such service and which the Secretary determines is not service connected, for hardship, or as a result of a reduction in force as described in section 3011(a)(1)(A)(ii)(III) of this title [38 USCS § 3011(a)(1)(A)(ii)(III)].

(As amended Nov. 30, 1999, P. L. 106-117, Title VII, Subtitle A, § 702(b), 113 Stat. 1583; Dec. 27, 2001, P. L. 107-103, Title I, § 105(c), 115 Stat. 983; Dec. 6, 2002, P. L. 107-330, Title III, § 308(g)(10), 116 Stat. 2829; Jan. 4, 2011, P. L. 111-377, Title II, § 201(a), 124 Stat. 4122.)

HISTORY; ANCILLARY LAWS AND DIRECTIVES

Amendments:

1999. Act Nov. 30, 1999, in subsec. (a), in the introductory matter, substituted "through (g)" for "through (e)" and substituted "subsection (h)" for "subsection (g)"; redesignated subsec. (g) as subsec. (h); and added new subsec. (g).

2001. Act Dec. 27, 2001, in subsec. (a), in para. (1), deleted "and" following the concluding semicolon, in para. (2), substituted "; and" for a concluding period, and added para. (3); and, in subsec. (e)(1), substituted "section 3011(a)(1)(B), 3011(a)(1)(C), 3012(a)(1)(B), or 3012(a)(1)(C)" for "section 3011(a)(1)(B) or 3012(a)(1)(B)".

2002. Act Dec. 6, 2002, in subsec. (a)(3), substituted "December 27, 2001" for "the date of the enactment of this paragraph".

2011. Act Jan. 4, 2011 (effective on 8/1/2011, and applicable to preventions and suspension of pursuit of programs of education that commence on or after that date, as provided by § 201(d) of such Act, which appears as a note to this section), substituted subsec. (d) for one which read:

"(d) In the case of an individual eligible for educational assistance under this chapter—

"(1) who was prevented from pursuing such individual's chosen program of education before the expiration of the 10-year period for use of entitlement under this chapter otherwise applicable under this section because of a physical or mental disability which was not the result of the individual's own willful misconduct, and

"(2) who applies for an extension of such 10-year period within one year after (A) the last day of such period, or (B) the last day on which such individual was so prevented from pursuing such program, whichever is later,

such 10-year period shall not run with respect to such individual during the period of time that such individual was so prevented from pursuing such program and such 10-year period will again begin running on the first day following such individual's recovery from such disability on which it is reasonably feasible, as determined under regulations which the Secretary shall prescribe, for such individual to initiate or resume pursuit of a program of education with educational assistance under this chapter.".

Other provisions:

Delimiting period; individual ineligible by reason of secondary school diploma requirement. Act Nov. 1, 2000, P. L. 106-419, Title I, Subtitle A, § 102(e), 114 Stat. 1825, provides:

"(1) In the case of an individual described in paragraph (2), with respect to the time limitation under section 3031 of title 38, United States Code, for use of eligibility and entitlement of basic educational assistance under chapter 30 of such title, the 10-year period applicable under such section shall begin on the later of—

"(A) the date of the enactment of this Act; or
"(B) the date of the individual's last discharge or release from active duty.
"(2) An individual referred to in paragraph (1) is an individual who—
"(A) before the date of the enactment of this Act, was not eligible for such basic educational assistance by reason of the requirement of a secondary school diploma (or equivalency certificate) as a condition of eligibility for such assistance as in effect on the date preceding the date of the enactment of this Act; and
"(B) becomes entitled to basic educational assistance under section 3011(a)(2), 3012(a)(2), or 3018(b)(4) of title 38, United States Code, by reason of the amendments made by this section [amending 10 USCS § 16132 and 38 USCS §§ 3011, 3012, 3017, and 3018].".

Delimiting period; individual ineligible by reason of initial obligated period of active duty requirement. Act Nov. 1, 2000, P. L. 106-419, Title I, Subtitle A, § 103(e), 114 Stat. 1826, provides:
"(1) In the case of an individual described in paragraph (2), with respect to the time limitation under section 3031 of title 38, United States Code, for use of eligibility and entitlement of basic educational assistance under chapter 30 of such title, the 10-year period applicable under such section shall begin on the later of—
"(A) the date of the enactment of this Act; or
"(B) the date of the individual's last discharge or release from active duty.
"(2) An individual referred to in paragraph (1) is an individual who—
"(A) before the date of the enactment of this Act, was not eligible for basic educational assistance under chapter 30 of such title [38 USCS §§ 3001 et seq.] by reason of the requirement of an initial obligated period of active duty as condition of eligibility for such assistance as in effect on the date preceding the date of the enactment of this Act; and
"(B) on or after such date becomes eligible for such assistance by reason of the amendments made by this section [amending 38 USCS §§ 3011, 3012, 3013, and 3105].".

Effective date and applicability of Jan. 4, 2011 amendments. Act Jan. 4, 2011, P. L. 111-377, Title II, § 201(d), 124 Stat. 4124, provides: "The amendments made by this section [amending 38 USCS §§ 3031(d), 3319(h)(5), and 3512(c)] shall take effect on August 1, 2011, and shall apply with respect to preventions and suspension of pursuit of programs of education that commence on or after that date.".

CODE OF FEDERAL REGULATIONS

Department of Veterans Affairs—Vocational rehabilitation and education, 38 CFR 21.1 et seq.
Department of Veterans Affairs—Loan guaranty and vocational rehabilitation and counseling programs, 48 CFR 871.100 et seq.

RESEARCH GUIDE

Am Jur:
77 Am Jur 2d, Veterans and Veterans' Laws § 129.

§ 3032. Limitations on educational assistance for certain individuals

(a) [Unchanged]
(b) The amount of the educational assistance allowance payable to an individual described in subsection (a) of this section is the least of the following: (1) the amount of the educational assistance allowance otherwise payable to such individual under this chapter [38 USCS §§ 3001 et seq.], (2) the established charges for tuition and fees that the educational institution involved requires similarly circumstanced nonveterans enrolled in the same program to pay, or (3) the amount of the charges of the educational institution elected by the individual under section 3014(b)(1) of this title [38 USCS § 3014(b)(1)].
(c)–(e) [Unchanged]
(f)(1) Subject to paragraph (3), the amount of educational assistance payable under this chapter for a licensing or certification test described in section 3452(b) of this title [38 USCS § 3452(b)] is the lesser of $2,000 or the fee charged for the test.
(2) The number of months of entitlement charged in the case of any individual for such licensing or certification test is equal to the number (including any fraction) determined by dividing the total amount of educational assistance paid such individual for such test by the full-time monthly institutional rate of educational assistance which, except for paragraph (1), such individual would otherwise be paid under subsection (a)(1), (b)(1), (d), or (e)(1) of section 3015 of this title [38 USCS § 3015], as the case may be.
(3) In no event shall payment of educational assistance under this subsection for such a test exceed the amount of the individual's available entitlement under this chapter [38 USCS §§ 3001 et seq.].
(g)(1) Subject to paragraph (3), the amount of educational assistance payable under this chapter for a national test for admission or national test providing an opportunity for course credit at institutions of higher learning described in section 3452(b) of this title [38 USCS § 3452(b)] is the amount of the fee charged for the test.

(2) The number of months of entitlement charged in the case of any individual for a test described in paragraph (1) is equal to the number (including any fraction) determined by dividing the total amount of educational assistance paid such individual for such test by the full-time monthly institutional rate of educational assistance, except for paragraph (1), such individual would otherwise be paid under subsection (a)(1), (b)(1), (d), or (e)(1) of section 3015 of this title [38 USCS § 3015], as the case may be.

(3) In no event shall payment of educational assistance under this subsection for a test described in paragraph (1) exceed the amount of the individual's available entitlement under this chapter [38 USCS §§ 3001 et seq.].

(As amended Nov. 1, 2000, P. L. 106-419, Title I, Subtitle C, § 122(b)(1), 114 Stat. 1833; June 5, 2001, P. L. 107-14, § 7(b)(2)(B), 115 Stat. 32; Dec. 10, 2004, P. L. 108-454, Title I, § 106(b)(1), 118 Stat. 3602.)

HISTORY; ANCILLARY LAWS AND DIRECTIVES

Amendments:

2000. Act Nov. 1, 2000 (effective 3/1/01 and applicable with respect to licensing and certification tests approved on or after such date, as provided by § 122(d) of such Act, which appears as a note to this section) added subsec. (f).

2001. Act June 5, 2001 (effective as if enacted on 11/1/2000, immediately after enactment of Act Nov. 1, 2000, P. L. 106-419, as provided by § 7(b)(3) of the 2001 Act, which appears as 38 USCS § 3014 note), in subsec. (b), substituted "the least of the following:" for "the lesser of", deleted "or" preceding "(2)", and inserted ", or (3) the amount of the charges of the educational institution elected by the individual under section 3014(b)(1) of this title".

2004. Act Dec. 10, 2004, added subsec. (g).

Other provisions:

Effective date and application of amendments made by § 122 of Act Nov. 1, 2000. Act Nov. 1, 2000, P. L. 106-419, Title I, Subtitle C, § 122(d), provides: "The amendments made by this section [amending 38 USCS §§ 3452(b), 3501(a)(5), and the chapter analysis preceding 38 USCS § 3670, and adding 38 USCS § 3032(f), 3232(c), 3482(h), 3532(f), and 3689], shall take effect on March 1, 2001, and shall apply with respect to licensing and certification tests approved by the Secretary of Veterans Affairs on or after such date.".

Increase in benefit for individuals pursuing apprenticeship or on-job training; Montgomery GI Bill. Act Dec. 10, 2004, P. L. 108-454, Title I, § 103(a), 118 Stat. 3600, provides:

"For months beginning on or after October 1, 2005, and before January 1, 2008, subsection (c)(1) of section 3032 of title 38, United States Code, shall be applied as if—

"(1) the reference to '75 percent' in subparagraph (A) were a reference to '85 percent';

"(2) the reference to '55 percent' in subparagraph (B) were a reference to '65 percent'; and

"(3) the reference to '35 percent' in subparagraph (C) were a reference to '45 percent'.".

RESEARCH GUIDE

Am Jur:

77 Am Jur 2d, Veterans and Veterans' Laws § 135.

§ 3033. Bar to duplication of educational assistance benefits

(a)(1) An individual entitled to educational assistance under a program established by this chapter [38 USCS §§ 3001 et seq.] who is also eligible for educational assistance under a program under chapter 31, 32, 33, or 35 of this title [38 USCS §§ 3100 et seq., 3201 et seq., 3301 et seq., or 3500 et seq.], under chapter 106 or 107 of title 10 [10 USCS §§ 2131 et seq. or 2151 et seq.], or under the Hostage Relief Act of 1980 (Public Law 96-449; 5 U.S.C. 5561 note) may not receive assistance under two or more of such programs concurrently but shall elect (in such form and manner as the Secretary may prescribe) under which program to receive educational assistance.

(2) [Unchanged]

(b) [Unchanged]

(c) An individual who serves in the Selected Reserve may not receive credit for such service under two or more of the programs established by this chapter [38 USCS §§ 3001 et seq.], chapter 33 of this title [38 USCS §§ 3301 et seq.], and chapters 1606 and 1607 of title 10 [10 USCS §§ 16131 et seq. and 16161 et seq.] but shall elect (in such form and manner as the Secretary may prescribe) the program to which such service is to be credited.

(As amended June 30, 2008, P. L. 110-252, Title V, § 5003(b)(1)(A), 122 Stat. 2375.)

HISTORY; ANCILLARY LAWS AND DIRECTIVES

Amendments:

2008. Act June 30, 2008 (effective on 8/1/2009, as provided by § 5003(d) of such Act, which appears as 10 USCS § 16163 note), in subsec. (a)(1), inserted "33,"; and, in subsec. (c), substituted "two or more of the programs established by this chapter, chapter 33 of this title,

READJUSTMENT BENEFITS   38 USCS § 3034

and chapters 1606 and 1607 of title 10" for "both the program established by this chapter and the program established by chapter 106 of title 10".

RESEARCH GUIDE
Am Jur:
77 Am Jur 2d, Veterans and Veterans' Laws § 135.

§ 3034. Program administration
(a)–(c) [Unchanged]
(d) The Secretary may approve the pursuit of flight training (in addition to a course of flight training that may be approved under section 3680A(b) of this title [38 USCS § 3680A(b)]) by an individual entitled to basic educational assistance under this chapter [38 USCS §§ 3001 et seq.] if—
  (1) [Unchanged]
  (2) the individual possesses a valid private pilot certificate and meets, on the day the individual begins a course of flight training, the medical requirements necessary for a commercial pilot certificate; and
  (3) the flight school courses are approved by the Federal Aviation Administration and are offered by a certified pilot school that possesses a valid Federal Aviation Administration pilot school certificate.
(e)(1) In the case of a member of the Armed Forces who participates in basic educational assistance under this chapter [38 USCS §§ 3001 et seq.], the Secretary shall furnish the information described in paragraph (2) to each such member. The Secretary shall furnish such information as soon as practicable after the basic pay of the member has been reduced by $1,200 in accordance with section 3011(b) or 3012(c) of this title [38 USCS § 3011(b) or 3012(c)] and at such additional times as the Secretary determines appropriate.
  (2) The information referred to in paragraph (1) is information with respect to the benefits, limitations, procedures, eligibility requirements (including time-in-service requirements), and other important aspects of the basic educational assistance program under this chapter, including application forms for such basic educational assistance under section 5102 of this title [38 USCS § 5102].
  (3) The Secretary shall furnish the forms described in paragraph (2) and other educational materials to educational institutions, training establishments, and military education personnel, as the Secretary determines appropriate.
  (4) The Secretary shall use amounts appropriated for readjustment benefits to carry out this subsection and section 5102 of this title [38 USCS § 5102] with respect to application forms under that section for basic educational assistance under this chapter [38 USCS §§ 3001 et seq.].
(As amended Nov. 11, 1998, P. L. 105-368, Title II, Subtitle A, §§ 204(a), 206(a), 112 Stat. 3327; Jan. 4, 2011, P. L. 111-377, Title II, § 203(a)(2)(A), 124 Stat. 4125.)

HISTORY; ANCILLARY LAWS AND DIRECTIVES
Amendments:
1998. Act Nov. 11, 1998 (applicable as provided by § 204(c) of such Act, which appears as 10 USCS § 16136 note), in subsec. (d)(2), substituted "pilot certificate" for "pilot's license" in two places, and inserted ", on the day the individual begins a course of flight training,".
Such Act further (effective 180 days after enactment, as provided by § 206(b) of such Act, which appears as a note to this section) added subsec. (e).
2011. Act Jan. 4, 2011 (effective on 8/1/2011, as provided by § 203(e) of such Act, which appears as a note to this section), in subsec. (d), substituted para. (3) for one which read: "(3) the flight school courses meet Federal Aviation Administration standards for such courses and are approved by the Federal Aviation Administration and the State approving agency.".

Other provisions:
Effective date of Nov. 11, 1998 amendment adding subsec. (e). Act Nov. 11, 1998, P. L. 105-368, Title II, Subtitle A, § 206(b), 112 Stat. 3328, provides: "The amendment made by this section [adding subsec. (e) of this section] shall take effect 180 days after the date of the enactment of this Act.".
Effective date of Jan. 4, 2011 amendments. Act Jan. 4, 2011, P. L. 111-377, Title II, § 203(e), 124 Stat. 4126, provides: "The amendments made by this section [amending 38 USCS §§ 3034, 3671, 3672, 3673, 3675, 3679, and 3689] shall take effect on August 1, 2011.".

RESEARCH GUIDE
Am Jur:
77 Am Jur 2d, Veterans and Veterans' Laws §§ 132, 133.

38 USCS § 3034

VETERANS' BENEFITS

INTERPRETIVE NOTES AND DECISIONS

Conclusion by Board of Veterans' Appeals that, while claimant pointed to paralegal program, he had not shown that he took any course in furtherance of gaining paralegal certificate, was not clearly erroneous; critically, certificates he submitted did not demonstrate that he enrolled in courses as part of approved program of study, such as paralegal program. Celano v Peake (2009) 22 Vet App 341, 2009 US App Vet Claims LEXIS 12.

§ 3035. Allocation of administration and of program costs

(a) [Unchanged]

(b)(1) Except to the extent provided in paragraphs (2), (3), and (4), payments for entitlement earned under subchapter II of this chapter [38 USCS §§ 3011 et seq.] shall be made from funds appropriated to, or otherwise available to, the Department of Veterans Affairs for the payment of readjustment benefits and from transfers from the Post-Vietnam Era Veterans Education Account pursuant to section 3232(b)(2)(B) of this title [38 USCS § 3232(b)(2)(B)].

(2) Payments for entitlements earned under subchapter II of this chapter [38 USCS §§ 3011 et seq.] that is established under section 3015(d) of this title [38 USCS § 3015(d)] at a rate in excess of the rate prescribed under subsection (a) or (b) of section 3015 of this title [38 USCS § 3015] shall, to the extent of that excess, be made from the Department of Defense Education Benefits Fund established under section 2006 of title 10 [10 USCS § 2006] or from appropriations made to the Department of Homeland Security, as appropriate.

(3) [Unchanged]

(4) Payments attributable to the increased usage of benefits as a result of transfers of entitlement to basic educational assistance under section 3020 of this title [38 USCS § 3020] shall be made from the Department of Defense Education Benefits Fund established under section 2006 of title 10 [10 USCS § 2006] or from appropriations made to the Department of Transportation, as appropriate.

(c) Payments for educational assistance provided under subchapter III of this chapter [38 USCS §§ 3021 et seq.] shall be made from the Department of Defense Education Benefits Fund established under section 2006 of title 10 [10 USCS § 2006] or from appropriations made to the Department of Homeland Security, as appropriate.

(d) Funds for the payment by the Secretary of benefits under this chapter [38 USCS §§ 3001 et seq.] that are to be paid from the Department of Defense Education Benefits Fund shall be transferred to the Department of Veterans Affairs from such Fund as necessary and in accordance with agreements entered into under section 2006 of title 10 [10 USCS § 2006] by the Secretary, the Secretary of Defense, and the Secretary of the Treasury. Funds for the payment by the Secretary of benefits under this chapter [38 USCS §§ 3001 et seq.] that are to be paid from appropriations made to the Department of Homeland Security shall be transferred to the Department of Veterans Affairs as necessary. The Secretary and the Secretary of Homeland Security shall enter into an agreement for the manner in which such transfers are to be made.

(e) Payments for tutorial assistance benefits under section 3019 of this title [38 USCS § 3019] shall be made—

(1) [Unchanged]

(2) in the case of payments to an individual for such benefits in excess of $600, from—

(A), (B) [Unchanged]

(C) funds appropriated to the Department of Homeland Security,

in the same proportion as the Fund described in subclause (B) of this clause and the funds described in subclause (A) or (C) of this clause are used to pay the educational assistance allowance to the individual under this chapter [38 USCS §§ 3001 et seq.].

(As amended Nov. 25, 2002, P. L. 107-296, Title XVII, § 1704(d), 116 Stat. 2315; Dec. 2, 2002, P. L. 107-314, Div A, Title VI, Subtitle E, § 643(b), 116 Stat. 2577; Dec. 6, 2002, P. L. 107-330, Title III, § 308(c)(1), 116 Stat. 2827.)

HISTORY; ANCILLARY LAWS AND DIRECTIVES

Amendments:

2002. Act Nov. 25, 2002 (effective on 3/1/2003 pursuant to § 1704(g) of such Act, which appears as 10 USCS § 101 note), in subsecs. (b)(2), (c), (d), and (e)(2)(C), substituted "of Homeland Security" for "of Transportation" wherever appearing.

Act Dec. 2, 2002 (effective as if the amendment was made by § 654 of Act Dec. 28, 2001, P. L. 107-107, as provided by § 643(c)(2) of the 2002 Act, which appears as a note to this section), in subsec. (b), in para. (1), substituted "paragraphs (2), (3), and (4)" for "paragraphs (2) and (3) of this subsection", and added para. (4).

Act Dec. 6, 2002 (effective as if included in the enactment of Act Dec. 28, 2001, P. L. 107-107, as provided by § 308(c)(2) of Act Dec. 6, 2002, which appears as a note to this section) purported to make the same amendments as Act Dec. 2, 2002; however, in order to effectuate the probable intent of Congress, these amendments were not executed.

READJUSTMENT BENEFITS   38 USCS § 3101

Other provisions:
Effective date of Dec. 2, 2002 amendments. Act Dec. 2, 2002, P. L. 107-314, Div A, Title VI, Subtitle E, § 643(c)(2), 116 Stat. 2578, provides: "The amendments made by subsection (b) [amending subsec. (b) of this section] shall take effect as if made by section 654 of the National Defense Authorization Act for Fiscal Year 2002 (Public Law 107-107; 115 Stat. 1153).".

Effective date of Dec. 6, 2002 amendments. Act Dec. 6, 2002, P. L. 107-330, Title III, § 308(c)(2), 116 Stat. 2824, provides: "The amendments made by this subsection [amending subsec. (b) of this section] shall take effect as if included in the enactment of the National Defense Authorization Act for Fiscal Year 2002 [enacted Dec. 28, 2001] (Public Law 107-107), to which such amendments relate.".

RESEARCH GUIDE
Am Jur:
77 Am Jur 2d, Veterans and Veterans' Laws § 124.

[§ 3036. Repealed]

HISTORY; ANCILLARY LAWS AND DIRECTIVES
This section (Act Oct. 19, 1984, P. L. 98-525, Title VII, § 702(a)(1) in part, 98 Stat. 2563; Dec. 18, 1989, P. L. 101-237, Title IV, §§ 423(b)(1)(A), (b)(4)(D), 103 Stat. 2092; Aug. 6, 1991, P. L. 102-83, § 5(a), 105 Stat. 406; Nov. 11, 1998, P. L. 105-368, Title II, Subtitle A, § 207(c), 112 Stat. 3328; Nov. 1, 2000, P. L. 106-419, Title IV, § 403(c)(4), 114 Stat. 1864; Dec. 21, 2006, P. L. 109-444, § 4(b), 120 Stat. 3308; Dec. 22, 2006, P. L. 109-461, Title III, § 305(b), 120 Stat. 3428) was repealed by Act Aug. 6, 2012, P. L. 112-154, Title IV, § 402(b)(1), 126 Stat. 1190. It contained reporting requirements relating to the all-volunteer force educational assistance program.

CHAPTER 31. TRAINING AND REHABILITATION FOR VETERANS WITH SERVICE-CONNECTED DISABILITIES

Section
3122.   Longitudinal study of vocational rehabilitation programs.

HISTORY; ANCILLARY LAWS AND DIRECTIVES
Amendments:
2008. Act Oct. 10, 2008, P. L. 110-389, Title III, Subtitle C, § 334(b), 122 Stat. 4173, amended the analysis of this chapter by adding item 3122.

§ 3100. Purposes

CODE OF FEDERAL REGULATIONS
Department of Veterans Affairs—Vocational rehabilitation and education, 38 CFR 21.1 et seq.
Department of Veterans Affairs—Loan guaranty and vocational rehabilitation and counseling programs, 48 CFR 871.100 et seq.

RESEARCH GUIDE
Am Jur:
77 Am Jur 2d, Veterans and Veterans' Laws § 68.

Labor and Employment:
10 Larson on Employment Discrimination, ch 173, Veterans' Preference Laws § 173.01.

§ 3101. Definitions

RESEARCH GUIDE
Am Jur:
24A Am Jur 2d, Divorce and Separation § 919.
77 Am Jur 2d, Veterans and Veterans' Laws § 130.

Intellectual Property:
1 Nimmer on Copyright (Matthew Bender), ch 6A, Community Property § 6A.03.

Commercial Law:
1A Debtor-Creditor Law (Matthew Bender), ch 9, Garnishment and Exemptions § 9.08.
3 Debtor-Creditor Law (Matthew Bender), ch 27, Enforcements of Money Judgments: Objectives and Restrictions § 27.03.
3 Debtor-Creditor Law (Matthew Bender), ch 31, Income Garnishment § 31.03.

§ 3102. Basic entitlement

(a) In general. A person shall be entitled to a rehabilitation program under the terms and conditions of this chapter [38 USCS §§ 3100 et seq.] if—

(1) the person—

(A) is—

(i) a veteran who has a service-connected disability rated at 20 percent or more which was incurred or aggravated in service on or after September 16, 1940; or

(ii) hospitalized or receiving outpatient medical care, services, or treatment for a service-connected disability pending discharge from the active military, naval, or air service, and the Secretary determines that—

(I) the hospital (or other medical facility) providing the hospitalization, care, services, or treatment is doing so under contract or agreement with the Secretary concerned, or is under the jurisdiction of the Secretary of Veterans Affairs or the Secretary concerned; and

(II) the person is suffering from a disability which will likely be compensable at a rate of 20 percent or more under chapter 11 of this title [38 USCS §§ 1101 et seq.]; and

(B) is determined by the Secretary to be in need of rehabilitation because of an employment handicap; or

(2) the person is a veteran who—

(A) has a service-connected disability rated at 10 percent which was incurred or aggravated in service on or after September 16, 1940; and

(B) is determined by the Secretary to be in need of rehabilitation because of a serious employment handicap.

(b) Additional rehabilitation programs for persons who have exhausted rights to unemployment benefits under State law. (1) Except as provided in paragraph (4), a person who has completed a rehabilitation program under this chapter [38 USCS §§ 3100 et seq.] shall be entitled to an additional rehabilitation program under the terms and conditions of this chapter [38 USCS §§ 3100 et seq.] if—

(A) the person is described by paragraph (1) or (2) of subsection (a); and

(B) the person—

(i) has exhausted all rights to regular compensation under the State law or under Federal law with respect to a benefit year;

(ii) has no rights to regular compensation with respect to a week under such State or Federal law; and

(iii) is not receiving compensation with respect to such week under the unemployment compensation law of Canada; and

(C) begins such additional rehabilitation program within six months of the date of such exhaustion.

(2) For purposes of paragraph (1)(B)(i), a person shall be considered to have exhausted such person's rights to regular compensation under a State law when—

(A) no payments of regular compensation can be made under such law because such person has received all regular compensation available to such person based on employment or wages during such person's base period; or

(B) such person's rights to such compensation have been terminated by reason of the expiration of the benefit year with respect to which such rights existed.

(3) In this subsection, the terms "compensation", "regular compensation", "benefit year", "State", "State law", and "week" have the respective meanings given such terms under section 205 of the Federal-State Extended Unemployment Compensation Act of 1970 (26 U.S.C. 3304 note).

(4) No person shall be entitled to an additional rehabilitation program under paragraph (1) from whom the Secretary receives an application therefor after March 31, 2014.

(As amended Nov. 21, 2011, P. L. 112-56, Title II, Subtitle C, § 233(a)(1), 125 Stat. 719.)

HISTORY; ANCILLARY LAWS AND DIRECTIVES

Amendments:

2011. Act Nov. 21, 2011 (effective on 6/1/2012 and applicable to rehabilitation programs beginning after such date, as provided by § 233(c) of such Act, which appears as a note to this section), designated the existing provisions as subsec. (a), inserted the subsection heading; and added subsec. (b).

Other provisions:

Effective date and application of Nov. 21, 2011 amendments. Act Nov. 21, 2011, P. L. 112-56, Title II, Subtitle C, § 233(c), 125 Stat. 720, provides: "The amendments made by subsections (a) and (b) [amending 38 USCS §§ 3102, 3103, and 3105] shall take effect on June 1, 2012, and shall apply with respect to rehabilitation programs beginning after such date.".

RESEARCH GUIDE

Am Jur:
77 Am Jur 2d, Veterans and Veterans' Laws § 68.

INTERPRETIVE NOTES AND DECISIONS

2. Requirement that disability be service-connected

Where veteran was denied entitlement to vocational rehabilitation benefits, court vacated Board of Veterans' Appeals' denial after it vacated Board's decision refusing to reopen veteran's claim of service-connected psychiatric disorder because issues were inextricably linked, and issue of entitlement to vocational rehabilitation benefits was dependent upon whether Board reopened and granted veteran's claim of service-connected psychiatric disorder. Hunt v Nicholson (2006) 20 Vet App 519, 2006 US App Vet Claims LEXIS 1351.

§ 3103. Periods of eligibility

(a) Except as provided in subsection (b), (c), (d), or (e) of this section, a rehabilitation program may not be afforded to a veteran under this chapter [38 USCS §§ 3100 et seq.] after the end of the twelve-year period beginning on the date of such veteran's discharge or release from active military, naval, or air service.

(b)–(d) [Unchanged]

(e)(1) The limitation in subsection (a) shall not apply to a rehabilitation program described in paragraph (2).

(2) A rehabilitation program described in this paragraph is a rehabilitation program pursued by a veteran under section 3102(b) of this title [38 USCS § 3102(b)].

(f) In any case in which the Secretary has determined that a veteran was prevented from participating in a vocational rehabilitation program under this chapter [38 USCS §§ 3100 et seq.] within the period of eligibility otherwise prescribed in this section as a result of being ordered to serve on active duty under section 688, 12301(a), 12301(d), 12301(g), 12302, or 12304 of title 10 [10 USCS § 688, 12301(a), 12301(d), 12301(g), 12302, or 12304], such period of eligibility shall not run for the period of such active duty service plus four months.

(As amended Dec. 27, 2001, P. L. 107-103, Title I, § 103(c)(2), 115 Stat. 979; Dec. 6, 2002, P. L. 107-330, Title III, § 308(h), 116 Stat. 2829; Nov. 21, 2011, P. L. 112-56, Title II, Subtitle C, § 233(b), 125 Stat. 720.)

HISTORY; ANCILLARY LAWS AND DIRECTIVES

Amendments:

2001. Act Dec. 27, 2001 (effective as of 9/11/2001, as provided by § 103(e) of such Act, which appears as 38 USCS § 3013 note), as amended by Act Dec. 6, 2002 (effective as of 12/27/2001 and as if included in Act Dec. 27, 2001 as originally enacted, as provided by § 308(h) of the 2002 Act, which appears as a note to this section), added subsec. (e).

2002. Act Dec. 6, 2002 (effective as of 12/27/2001 and as if included in Act Dec. 27, 2001 as originally enacted, as provided by § 308(h) of such Act, which appears as a note to this section) made technical corrections which did not affect the text of this section.

2011. Act Nov. 21, 2011 (effective on 6/1/2012 and applicable to rehabilitation programs beginning after such date, as provided by § 233(c) of such Act, which appears as 38 USCS § 3102 note), in subsec. (a), substituted "in subsection (b), (c), (d), or (e)" for "in subsection (b), (c), or (d)"; redesignated subsec. (e) as subsec. (f); and inserted new subsec. (e).

Other provisions:

Effective date of Dec. 6, 2002 amendment. Act Dec. 6, 2002, P. L. 107-330, Title III, § 308(h), 116 Stat. 2829, provided that the amendment made by such section to § 103(c)(2) of Act Dec. 27, 2001 (adding subsec. (e) of this section) is effective as of December 27, 2001, and as if included in 2001 act as originally enacted.

RESEARCH GUIDE

Am Jur:
77 Am Jur 2d, Veterans and Veterans' Laws § 68.

Criminal Law and Practice:
3 Criminal Defense Techniques (Matthew Bender), ch 61, Defense of Servicemembers § 61.09.

§ 3104. Scope of services and assistance

HISTORY; ANCILLARY LAWS AND DIRECTIVES

Other provisions:

Blind rehabilitation outpatient specialists. Act Dec. 22, 2006, P. L. 109-461, Title II, § 207, 120 Stat. 3412, provides:

38 USCS § 3104

"(a) Findings. Congress makes the following findings:

"(1) There are approximately 135,000 blind veterans throughout the United States, including approximately 35,000 who are enrolled with the Department of Veterans Affairs. An aging veteran population and injuries incurred in Operation Iraqi Freedom and Operation Enduring Freedom are increasing the number of blind veterans.

"(2) Since 1996, when the Department of Veterans Affairs hired its first 14 blind rehabilitation outpatient specialists (referred to in this section as 'Specialists'), Specialists have been a critical part of the continuum of care for blind and visually impaired veterans.

"(3) The Department of Veterans Affairs operates 10 residential blind rehabilitation centers that are considered among the best in the world. These centers have had long waiting lists, with as many as 1,500 blind veterans waiting for openings in 2004.

"(4) Specialists provide—

"(A) critically needed services to veterans who are unable to attend residential centers or are waiting to enter a residential center program;

"(B) a range of services for blind veterans, including training with living skills, mobility, and adaptation of manual skills; and

"(C) pre-admission screening and follow-up care for blind rehabilitation centers.

"(5) There are not enough Specialist positions to meet the increased numbers and needs of blind veterans.

"(b) Establishment of additional specialist positions. Not later than 30 months after the date of the enactment of this Act, the Secretary of Veterans Affairs shall establish an additional Specialist position at not fewer than 35 additional facilities of the Department of Veterans Affairs.

"(c) Selection of facilities. In identifying the most appropriate facilities to receive a Specialist position under this section, the Secretary shall—

"(1) give priority to facilities with large numbers of enrolled legally blind veterans;

"(2) ensure that each facility does not have such a position; and

"(3) ensure that each facility is in need of the services of a Specialist.

"(d) Coordination. The Secretary shall coordinate the provision of blind rehabilitation services for veterans with services for the care of the visually impaired offered by State and local agencies, especially to the extent to which such State and local agencies can provide necessary services to blind veterans in settings located closer to the residences of such veterans at similar quality and cost to the veteran.

"(e) Authorization of appropriations. There are authorized to be appropriated for the Department of Veterans Affairs to carry out this section $3,500,000 for each of fiscal years 2007 through 2012.".

CODE OF FEDERAL REGULATIONS
Department of Veterans Affairs—Medical, 38 CFR 17.30 et seq.

RESEARCH GUIDE
Am Jur:
77 Am Jur 2d, Veterans and Veterans' Laws §§ 68, 69, 76.

§ 3105. Duration of rehabilitation programs

(a) [Unchanged]

(b)(1) Except as provided in paragraph (2) and in subsection (c) of this section, the period of a vocational rehabilitation program for a veteran under this chapter [38 USCS §§ 3100 et seq.] following a determination of the current reasonable feasibility of achieving a vocational goal may not exceed forty-eight months, except that the counseling and placement and postplacement services described in section 3104(a)(2) and (5) of this title [38 USCS § 3104(a)(2) and (5)] may be provided for an additional period not to exceed eighteen months in any case in which the Secretary determines the provision of such counseling and services to be necessary to accomplish the purposes of a rehabilitation program in the individual case.

(2) The period of a vocational rehabilitation program pursued by a veteran under section 3102(b) of this title [38 USCS § 3102(b)] following a determination of the current reasonable feasibility of achieving a vocational goal may not exceed 12 months.

(c) [Unchanged]

(d)(1) Except as provided in paragraph (2), the period of a program of independent living services and assistance for a veteran under this chapter [38 USCS §§ 3100 et seq.] (following a determination by the Secretary that such veteran's disability or disabilities are so severe that the achievement of a vocational goal currently is not reasonably feasible) may not exceed twenty-four months.

(2)(A) The period of a program of independent living services and assistance for a veteran under this chapter [38 USCS §§ 3100 et seq.] may exceed twenty-four months as follows:

(i) If the Secretary determines that a longer period is necessary and likely to result in a substantial increase in the veteran's level of independence in daily living.

READJUSTMENT BENEFITS   38 USCS § 3108

(ii) If the veteran served on active duty during the Post-9/11 Global Operations period and has a severe disability (as determined by the Secretary for purposes of this clause) incurred or aggravated in such service.

(B) In this paragraph, the term "Post-9/11 Global Operations period" means the period of the Persian Gulf War beginning on September 11, 2001, and ending on the date thereafter prescribed by Presidential proclamation or by law.

(e)(1) Notwithstanding any other provision of this chapter or chapter 36 of this title [38 USCS §§ 3100 et seq. or §§ 3670 et seq.], any payment of a subsistence allowance and other assistance described in paragraph (2) shall not—

(A) be charged against any entitlement of any veteran under this chapter [38 USCS §§ 3100 et seq.]; or

(B) be counted toward the aggregate period for which section 3695 of this title [38 USCS § 3695] limits an individual's receipt of allowance or assistance.

(2) The payment of the subsistence allowance and other assistance referred to in paragraph (1) is the payment of such an allowance or assistance for the period described in paragraph (3) to a veteran for participation in a vocational rehabilitation program under this chapter if the Secretary finds that the veteran had to suspend or discontinue participation in such vocational rehabilitation program as a result of being ordered to serve on active duty under section 688, 12301(a), 12301(d), 12301(g), 12302, or 12304 of title 10 [10 USCS § 688, 12301(a), 12301(d), 12301(g), 12302, or 12304].

(3) The period for which, by reason of this subsection, a subsistence allowance and other assistance is not charged against entitlement or counted toward the applicable aggregate period under section 3695 of this title [38 USCS § 3695] shall be the period of participation in the vocational rehabilitation program for which the veteran failed to receive credit or with respect to which the veteran lost training time, as determined by the Secretary.

(As amended Dec. 27, 2001, P. L. 107-103, Title I, § 103(c)(1), 115 Stat. 979; Oct. 10, 2008, P. L. 110-389, Title III, Subtitle C, § 331, 122 Stat. 4170; Nov. 21, 2011, P. L. 112-56, Title II, Subtitle C, § 223(a)(2), 125 Stat. 720.)

HISTORY; ANCILLARY LAWS AND DIRECTIVES

Amendments:

2001. Act Dec. 27, 2001 (effective as of 9/11/2001, as provided by § 103(e) of such Act, which appears as 38 USCS § 3013 note), added subsec. (e).

2008. Act Oct. 10, 2008, in subsec. (d), substituted "(1) Except as provided in paragraph (2), the period of a program" for "Unless the Secretary determines that a longer period is necessary and likely to result in a substantial increase in a veteran's level of independence in daily living, the period of a program", and added para. (2).

2011. Act Nov. 21, 2011 (effective on 6/1/2012 and applicable to rehabilitation programs beginning after such date, as provided by § 233(c) of such Act, which appears as 38 USCS § 3102 note), in subsec. (b), designated the existing provisions as para. (1), inserted "in paragraph (2) and", and added para. (2).

RESEARCH GUIDE

Am Jur:

24 Am Jur 2d, Divorce and Separation § 508.

77 Am Jur 2d, Veterans and Veterans' Laws § 68.

§ 3106. Initial and extended evaluations; determinations regarding serious employment handicap

RESEARCH GUIDE

Am Jur:

77 Am Jur 2d, Veterans and Veterans' Laws § 68.

§ 3107. Individualized vocational rehabilitation plan

CODE OF FEDERAL REGULATIONS

Department of Veterans Affairs—Vocational rehabilitation and education, 38 CFR 21.1 et seq.

RESEARCH GUIDE

Am Jur:

77 Am Jur 2d, Veterans and Veterans' Laws § 68.

24A Am Jur 2d, Divorce and Separation § 919.

§ 3108. Allowances

(a)(1) [Unchanged]

(2)(A) In any case in which the Secretary determines, at the conclusion of such veteran's pursuit of a vocational rehabilitation program under this chapter [38 USCS §§ 3100 et seq.], that such veteran has been rehabilitated to the point of employability, such veteran shall be paid a subsistence allowance, as prescribed in this section for full-time training for the type of program that the veteran was pursuing, for two months while satisfactorily following a program of employment services provided under section 3104(a)(5) of this title [38 USCS § 3104(a)(5)].

(B) **[Caution: This subparagraph takes effect 1 year after enactment of Act Aug. 6, 2012, P. L. 112-154, as provided by § 701(g) of such Act, which appears as 38 USCS § 2109 note.]** In any case in which the Secretary determines that a veteran described in subparagraph (A) has been displaced as the result of a natural or other disaster while being paid a subsistence allowance under that subparagraph, as determined by the Secretary, the Secretary may extend the payment of a subsistence allowance under such subparagraph for up to an additional two months while the veteran is satisfactorily following a program of employment services described in such subparagraph.

(3) [Unchanged]

(b)(1)–(3) [Unchanged]

(4) A veteran entitled to a subsistence allowance under this chapter and educational assistance under chapter 33 of this title [38 USCS §§ 3301 et seq.] may elect to receive payment from the Secretary in lieu of an amount otherwise determined by the Secretary under this subsection in an amount equal to the applicable monthly amount of basic allowance for housing payable under section 403 of title 37 for a member with dependents in pay grade E-5 residing in the military housing area that encompasses all or the majority portion of the ZIP code area in which is located the institution providing rehabilitation program concerned.

(c)–(f) [Unchanged]

(g)(1) Notwithstanding any other provision of this title and subject to the provisions of paragraph (2) of this subsection, no subsistence allowance may be paid under this section in the case of any veteran who is pursuing a rehabilitation program under this chapter [38 USCS §§ 3100 et seq.] while incarcerated in a Federal, State, local, or other penal institution or correctional facility for conviction of a felony.

(2) [Unchanged]

(h), (i) [Unchanged]

(As amended Dec. 22, 2006, P. L. 109-461, Title X, § 1002(b); 120 Stat. 3465; Jan. 4, 2011, P. L. 111-377, Title II, § 205(a), 124 Stat. 4126; Aug. 6, 2012, P. L. 112-154, Title VII, § 701(b), 126 Stat. 1203.)

HISTORY; ANCILLARY LAWS AND DIRECTIVES

Amendments:

2006. Act Dec. 22, 2006, in subsec. (g)(1), substituted "local, or other penal institution or correctional facility" for "or local penal institution".

2011. Act Jan. 4, 2011 (effective 8/1/2011, as provided by § 205(b) of such Act, which appears as a note to this section), added subsec. (b)(4).

2012. Act Aug. 6, 2012 (effective 8/6/2013, as provided by § 701(g) of such Act, which appears as 38 USCS § 2109 note), in subsec. (a)(2), designated the existing provisions as subpara. (A), and added subpara. (B).

Other provisions:

Effective date of Jan. 4, 2011 amendment. Act Jan. 4, 2011, P. L. 111-377, Title II, § 205(b), 124 Stat. 4126, provides: "The amendment made by this section [adding subsec. (b)(4) of this section] shall take effect on August 1, 2011.".

CODE OF FEDERAL REGULATIONS

Department of Veterans Affairs—Vocational rehabilitation and education, 38 CFR 21.1 et seq.

RESEARCH GUIDE

Am Jur:

77 Am Jur 2d, Veterans and Veterans' Laws § 68.

§ 3109. Entitlement to independent living services and assistance

RESEARCH GUIDE

Am Jur:

77 Am Jur 2d, Veterans and Veterans' Laws § 68.

§ 3110. Leaves of absence

RESEARCH GUIDE

Am Jur:

77 Am Jur 2d, Veterans and Veterans' Laws § 68.

§ 3111. Regulations to promote satisfactory conduct and cooperation

RESEARCH GUIDE

Am Jur:
77 Am Jur 2d, Veterans and Veterans' Laws § 68.

§ 3113. Vocational rehabilitation for hospitalized members of the Armed Forces and veterans

RESEARCH GUIDE

Am Jur:
77 Am Jur 2d, Veterans and Veterans' Laws § 68.

§ 3114. Vocational rehabilitation outside the United States

RESEARCH GUIDE

Am Jur:
77 Am Jur 2d, Veterans and Veterans' Laws § 68.

§ 3115. Rehabilitation resources

RESEARCH GUIDE

Am Jur:
77 Am Jur 2d, Veterans and Veterans' Laws § 68.

§ 3116. Promotion of employment and training opportunities

(a) [Unchanged]
(b)(1) The Secretary, pursuant to regulations prescribed in accordance with paragraph (3) of this subsection, may make payments to employers for providing on-job training to veterans in individual cases in which the Secretary determines that such payment is necessary to obtain needed on-job training or to begin employment. Such payments may not exceed the direct expenses incurred by such employers in providing such on-job training or employment opportunity.

(2), (3) [Unchanged]

(As amended Nov. 21, 2011, P. L. 112-56, Title II, Subtitle C, § 232, 125 Stat. 719.)

HISTORY; ANCILLARY LAWS AND DIRECTIVES

Amendments:
2011. Act Nov. 21, 2011, in subsec. (b)(1), deleted "who have been rehabilitated to the point of employability" following "veterans".

CODE OF FEDERAL REGULATIONS
Department of Veterans Affairs—Medical, 38 CFR 17.30 et seq.

RESEARCH GUIDE

Am Jur:
77 Am Jur 2d, Veterans and Veterans' Laws § 68.

§ 3117. Employment assistance

(a)(1) [Unchanged]
  (2) Assistance provided under this subsection may include—
    (A) [Unchanged]
    (B) utilization of employment, training, and placement services under chapter 41 of this title [38 USCS §§ 4100 et seq.]; and
    (C) [Unchanged]
(b)(1) In any case in which a veteran has completed a vocational rehabilitation program for self-employment in a small business enterprise under this chapter [38 USCS §§ 3100 et seq.], the Secretary shall assist such veteran in securing, as appropriate, a loan under subchapter IV of chapter 37 of this title [38 USCS §§ 3741 et seq.] and shall cooperate with the Small Business Administration to assist such veteran to secure a loan for the purchase of equipment needed to establish such veteran's own business and to insure that such veteran receives the special consideration provided for in section 4(b)(1) of the Small Business Act (15 U.S.C. 633(b)(1)).
  (2) [Unchanged]

(As amended Nov. 7, 2002, P. L. 107-288, § 4(e)(2), 116 Stat. 2044; June 15, 2006, P. L. 109-233, Title V, § 503(6), 120 Stat. 416.)

38 USCS § 3117

HISTORY; ANCILLARY LAWS AND DIRECTIVES

Amendments:

2002. Act Nov. 7, 2002, in subsec. (a)(2), substituted subpara. (B) for one which read: "(B) utilization of the services of disabled veterans outreach program specialists under section 4103A of this title; and".

2006. Act June 15, 2006, in subsec. (b)(1), substituted "section 4(b)(1)" for "section 8" and substituted "633(b)(1)" for "633(b)".

RESEARCH GUIDE

Am Jur:

77 Am Jur 2d, Veterans and Veterans' Laws § 68.

§ 3118. Personnel training, development, and qualifications

RESEARCH GUIDE

Am Jur:

77 Am Jur 2d, Veterans and Veterans' Laws § 68.

§ 3119. Rehabilitation research and special projects

RESEARCH GUIDE

Am Jur:

77 Am Jur 2d, Veterans and Veterans' Laws § 68.

§ 3120. Program of independent living services and assistance

(a)–(d) [Unchanged]

(e)(1) Programs of independent living services and assistance shall be initiated for no more than 2,700 veterans in each fiscal year, and the first priority in the provision of such programs shall be afforded to veterans for whom the reasonable feasibility of achieving a vocational goal is precluded solely as a result of a service-connected disability.

(2) [**Caution: This paragraph takes effect 1 year after enactment of Act Aug. 6, 2012, P. L. 112-154, as provided by § 701(g) of such Act, which appears as 38 USCS § 2109 note.**] The limitation in paragraph (1) shall not apply in any case in which the Secretary determines that a veteran described in subsection (b) has been displaced as the result of, or has otherwise been adversely affected in the areas covered by, a natural or other disaster, as determined by the Secretary.

(f) [Unchanged]

(As amended Dec. 27, 2001, P. L. 107-103, Title V, § 508(a), 115 Stat. 997; Oct. 10, 2008, P. L. 110-389, Title III, Subtitle C, § 332, 122 Stat. 4170; Oct. 13, 2010, P. L. 111-275, Title VIII, § 801(a), 124 Stat. 2888; Aug. 6, 2012, P. L. 112-154, Title VII, § 701(c), 126 Stat. 1203.)

HISTORY; ANCILLARY LAWS AND DIRECTIVES

Amendments:

2001. Act Dec. 27, 2001 (effective as of 9/30/2001, as provided by § 508(b) of such Act, which appears as a note to this section), in subsec. (e), substituted "2,500" for "five hundred".

2008. Act Oct. 10, 2008, purported to amend subsec. (e) by substituting "2600 veterans" for "2500 veterans"; however the substitution has been made for "2,500 veterans" in order to effectuate the probable intent of Congress.

2010. Act Oct. 13, 2010 (applicable to fiscal years beginning after the date of enactment, as provided by § 801(b) of such Act, which appears as a note to this section), in subsec. (e), substituted "2,700" for "2600".

2012. Act Aug. 6, 2012 (effective 8/6/2013 as provided by § 701(g) of such Act, which appears as 38 USCS § 2109 note), in subsec. (e), designated the existing provisions as para. (1), and added para. (2).

Other provisions:

Effective date of Dec. 27, 2001 amendment. Act Dec. 27, 2001, P. L. 107-103, Title V, § 507(b), 115 Stat. 997, provides: "The amendment made by subsection (a) [amending subsec. (e) of this section] shall take effect as of September 30, 2001.".

Application of Oct. 13, 2010 amendment. Act Oct. 13, 2010, P. L. 111-275, Title VIII, § 801(b), 124 Stat. 2888, provides: "The amendment made by subsection (a) [amending subsec. (e) of this section] shall apply with respect to fiscal years beginning after the date of the enactment of this Act.".

RESEARCH GUIDE

Am Jur:

77 Am Jur 2d, Veterans and Veterans' Laws § 68.

READJUSTMENT BENEFITS 38 USCS § 3201

§ 3121. Veterans' Advisory Committee on Rehabilitation

RESEARCH GUIDE
Am Jur:
77 Am Jur 2d, Veterans and Veterans' Laws § 68.

§ 3122. Longitudinal study of vocational rehabilitation programs
(a) **Study required.** (1) Subject to the availability of appropriated funds, the Secretary shall conduct a longitudinal study of a statistically valid sample of each of the groups of individuals described in paragraph (2). The Secretary shall study each such group over a period of at least 20 years.
  (2) The groups of individuals described in this paragraph are the following:
    (A) Individuals who begin participating in a vocational rehabilitation program under this chapter during fiscal year 2010.
    (B) Individuals who begin participating in such a program during fiscal year 2012.
    (C) Individuals who begin participating in such a program during fiscal year 2014.
(b) **Annual reports.** By not later than July 1 of each year covered by the study required under subsection (a), the Secretary shall submit to the Committees on Veterans' Affairs of the Senate and House of Representatives a report on the study during the preceding year.
(c) **Contents of report.** The Secretary shall include in the report required under subsection (b) any data the Secretary determines is necessary to determine the long-term outcomes of the individuals participating in the vocational rehabilitation programs under this chapter [38 USCS §§ 3100 et seq.]. The Secretary may add data elements from time to time as necessary. In addition, each such report shall contain the following information:
  (1) The number of individuals participating in vocational rehabilitation programs under this chapter [38 USCS §§ 3100 et seq.] who suspended participation in such a program during the year covered by the report.
  (2) The average number of months such individuals served on active duty.
  (3) The distribution of disability ratings of such individuals.
  (4) The types of other benefits administered by the Secretary received by such individuals.
  (5) The types of social security benefits received by such individuals.
  (6) Any unemployment benefits received by such individuals.
  (7) The average number of months such individuals were employed during the year covered by the report.
  (8) The average annual starting and ending salaries of such individuals who were employed during the year covered by the report.
  (9) The number of such individuals enrolled in an institution of higher learning, as that term is defined in section 3452(f) of this title [38 USCS § 3452(f)].
  (10) The average number of academic credit hours, degrees, and certificates obtained by such individuals during the year covered by the report.
  (11) The average number of visits such individuals made to Department medical facilities during the year covered by the report.
  (12) The average number of visits such individuals made to non-Department medical facilities during the year covered by the report.
  (13) The average annual income of such individuals.
  (14) The average total household income of such individuals for the year covered by the report.
  (15) The percentage of such individuals who own their principal residences.
  (16) The average number of dependents of each such veteran.
(Added Oct. 10, 2008, P. L. 110-389, Title III, Subtitle C, § 334(a), 122 Stat. 4172.)

CHAPTER 32. POST-VIETNAM ERA VETERANS' EDUCATIONAL ASSISTANCE

SUBCHAPTER I. PURPOSE; DEFINITIONS

§ 3201. Purpose

CODE OF FEDERAL REGULATIONS
Department of Veterans Affairs—Vocational rehabilitation and education, 38 CFR 21.1 et seq.
Department of Veterans Affairs—Loan guaranty and vocational rehabilitation and counseling programs, 48 CFR 871.100 et seq.

§ 3202. Definitions

For the purposes of this chapter [38 USCS §§ 3201 et seq.]—

(1)(A), (B) [Unchanged]

(C) For the purposes of subparagraphs (A) and (B), the term "active duty" does not include any period during which an individual (i) was assigned full time by the Armed Forces to a civilian institution for a course of education which was substantially the same as established courses offered to civilians, (ii) served as a cadet or midshipman at one of the service academies, or (iii) served under the provisions of section 511(d) of title 10 [10 USCS § 511(d)] pursuant to an enlistment in the Army National Guard or the Air National Guard, or as a Reserve for service in the Army Reserve, Navy Reserve, Air Force Reserve, Marine Corps Reserve, or Coast Guard Reserve.

(D) [Unchanged]

(2)–(5) [Unchanged]

(As amended Jan. 6, 2006, P. L. 109-163, Div A, Title V, Subtitle B, § 515(e)(3), 119 Stat. 3236.)

HISTORY; ANCILLARY LAWS AND DIRECTIVES

Amendments:
2006. Act Jan. 6, 2006, in para. (1)(C)(iii), substituted "Navy Reserve" for "Naval Reserve".

CODE OF FEDERAL REGULATIONS
Department of Veterans Affairs—Adjudication, 38 CFR 3.1 et seq.

SUBCHAPTER II. ELIGIBILITY; CONTRIBUTIONS; AND MATCHING FUND

§ 3221. Eligibility

CODE OF FEDERAL REGULATIONS
Department of Veterans Affairs—Vocational rehabilitation and education, 38 CFR 21.1 et seq.
Department of Veterans Affairs—Loan guaranty and vocational rehabilitation and counseling programs, 48 CFR 871.100 et seq.

SUBCHAPTER III. ENTITLEMENT; DURATION

§ 3231. Entitlement; loan eligibility

(a)(1) [Unchanged]

(2) Except as provided in subsection (e) of this section, in paragraph (5)(E) of this subsection, and section 3233 of this title [38 USCS § 3233] and subject to section 3241 of this title [38 USCS § 3241], amount of the monthly payment to which any eligible veteran is entitled shall be ascertained by (A) adding all contributions made to the fund by the eligible veteran, (B) multiplying the sum by 3, (C) adding all contributions made to the fund for such veteran by the Secretary of Defense, and (D) dividing the sum by the lesser of 36 or the number of months in which contributions were made by such veteran.

(3), (4) [Unchanged]

(5)(A) [Unchanged]

(B) The payment of an educational assistance allowance referred to in subparagraph (A) of this paragraph is any payment of a monthly benefit under this chapter to an eligible veteran for pursuit of a course or courses under this chapter [38 USCS §§ 3201 et seq.] if the Secretary finds that the eligible veteran—

(i) in the case of a person not serving on active duty, had to discontinue such course pursuit as a result of being ordered, in connection with the Persian Gulf War to serve on active duty under section 688, 12301(a), 12301(d), 12301(g), 12302, or 12304 of title 10 [10 USCS § 688, 12301(a), 12301(d), 12301(g), 12302, or 12304]; or

(ii) in the case of a person serving on active duty, had to discontinue such course pursuit as a result of being ordered to a new duty location or assignment or to perform an increased amount of work; and

(iii) [Unchanged]

(C)–(E) [Unchanged]

(b), (c) [Unchanged]

(d)(1) Subject to the provisions of paragraph (2) of this subsection, the amount of the educational assistance benefits paid to an eligible veteran who is pursuing a program of education under this chapter [38 USCS §§ 3201 et seq.] while incarcerated in a Federal, State, local, or other penal institution or correctional facility for conviction of a felony may not exceed the lesser of (A) such amount as the Secretary determines, in accordance with regulations which the Secretary shall prescribe, is necessary to cover the cost of established charges for tuition and

READJUSTMENT BENEFITS 38 USCS § 3233

fees required of similarly circumstanced nonveterans enrolled in the same program and the cost of necessary supplies, books, and equipment, or (B) the applicable monthly benefit payment otherwise prescribed in this section or section 3233 of this title [38 USCS § 3233]. The amount of the educational assistance benefits payable to a veteran while so incarcerated shall be reduced to the extent that the tuition and fees of the veteran for any course are paid under any Federal program (other than a program administered by the Secretary) or under any State or local program.

(2) [Unchanged]

(e) [Unchanged]

(As amended Nov. 11, 1998, P. L. 105-368, Title X, § 1005(b)(7), 112 Stat. 3365; Dec. 27, 2001, P. L. 107-103, Title I, § 103(a), (d), 115 Stat. 979; Dec. 22, 2006, P. L. 109-461, Title X, § 1002(c), 120 Stat. 3465.)

HISTORY; ANCILLARY LAWS AND DIRECTIVES

Amendments:

1998. Act Nov. 11, 1998, in subsec. (a)(2), substituted "subsection (e)" for "subsection (f)".

2001. Act Dec. 27, 2001 (effective as of 9/11/2001, as provided by § 103(e) of such Act, which appears as 38 USCS § 3013 note), in subsec. (a)(5)(B), in cl. (i), substituted "to serve on active duty under section 688, 12301(a), 12301(d), 12301(g), 12302, or 12304 of title 10;" for ", in connection with the Persian Gulf War, to serve on active duty under section 672(a), (d), or (g), 673, 673b, or 688 of title 10;", and, in cl. (ii), deleted ", in connection with such War," following "ordered".

2006. Act Dec. 22, 2006, in subsec. (d)(1), substituted "local, or other penal institution or correctional facility" for "or local penal institution".

CODE OF FEDERAL REGULATIONS

Department of Veterans Affairs—Vocational rehabilitation and education, 38 CFR 21.1 et seq.
Department of Veterans Affairs—Loan guaranty and vocational rehabilitation and counseling programs, 48 CFR 871.100 et seq.

§ 3232. Duration; limitations

(a), (b) [Unchanged]

(c)(1) Subject to paragraph (3), the amount of educational assistance payable under this chapter [38 USCS §§ 3201 et seq.] for a licensing or certification test described in section 3452(b) of this title [38 USCS § 3452(b)] is the lesser of $2,000 or the fee charged for the test.

(2) The number of months of entitlement charged in the case of any individual for such licensing or certification test is equal to the number (including any fraction) determined by dividing the total amount paid to such individual for such test by the full-time monthly institutional rate of the educational assistance allowance which, except for paragraph (1), such individual would otherwise be paid under this chapter [38 USCS §§ 3201 et seq.].

(3) In no event shall payment of educational assistance under this subsection for such a test exceed the amount of the individual's available entitlement under this chapter [38 USCS §§ 3201 et seq.].

(d)(1) Subject to paragraph (3), the amount of educational assistance payable under this chapter for a national test for admission or national test providing an opportunity for course credit at institutions of higher learning described in section 3452(b) of this title [38 USCS § 3452(b)] is the amount of the fee charged for the test.

(2) The number of months of entitlement charged in the case of any individual for a test described in paragraph (1) is equal to the number (including any fraction) determined by dividing the total amount of educational assistance paid such individual for such test by the full-time monthly institutional rate of educational assistance, except for paragraph (1), such individual would otherwise be paid under this chapter [38 USCS §§ 3201 et seq.].

(3) In no event shall payment of educational assistance under this subsection for a test described in paragraph (1) exceed the amount of the individual's available entitlement under this chapter [38 USCS §§ 3201 et seq.].

(As amended Nov. 1, 2000, P. L. 106-419, Title I, Subtitle C, § 122(b)(2), 114 Stat. 1834; Dec. 10, 2004, P. L. 108-454, Title I, § 106(b)(2), 118 Stat. 3603.)

HISTORY; ANCILLARY LAWS AND DIRECTIVES

Amendments:

2000. Act Nov. 1, 2000 (effective 3/1/01 and applicable with respect to licensing and certification tests approved on or after such date, as provided by § 122(d) of such Act, which appears as 38 USCS § 3032 note) added subsec. (c).

2004. Act Dec. 10, 2004, added subsec. (d).

§ 3233. Apprenticeship or other on-job training

HISTORY; ANCILLARY LAWS AND DIRECTIVES

Other provisions:

Increase in benefit for individuals pursuing apprenticeship or on-job training; post-

38 USCS § 3233

Vietnam Era veterans' educational assistance. Act Dec. 10, 2004, P. L. 108-454, Title I, § 103(b), 118 Stat. 3600, provides:

"For months beginning on or after October 1, 2005, and before January 1, 2008, subsection (a) of section 3233 of title 38, United States Code, shall be applied as if—
  "(1) the reference to '75 percent' in paragraph (1) were a reference to '85 percent';
  "(2) the reference to '55 percent' in paragraph (2) were a reference to '65 percent'; and
  "(3) the reference to '35 percent' in paragraph (3) were a reference to '45 percent'."

SUBCHAPTER IV. ADMINISTRATION

§ 3241. Requirements

(a) [Unchanged]
(b) The Secretary may approve the pursuit of flight training (in addition to a course of flight training that may be approved under section 3680A(b) of this title [38 USCS § 3680A(b)]) by an individual entitled to basic educational assistance under this chapter [38 USCS §§ 3201 et seq.] if—
  (1) [Unchanged]
  (2) the individual possesses a valid pilot certificate and meets, on the day the individual begins a course of flight training, the medical requirements necessary for a commercial pilot certificate; and
  (3) [Unchanged]
(c) [Unchanged]
(As amended Nov. 11, 1998, P. L. 105-368, Title II, Subtitle A, § 204(a), 112 Stat. 3327.)

HISTORY; ANCILLARY LAWS AND DIRECTIVES

Amendments:
1998. Act Nov. 11, 1998 (applicable as provided by § 204(c) of such Act, which appears as 10 USCS § 16136 note), in subsec. (b)(2), substituted "pilot certificate" for "pilot's license" in two places, and inserted ", on the day the individual begins a course of flight training,".

CODE OF FEDERAL REGULATIONS

Department of Veterans Affairs—Vocational rehabilitation and education, 38 CFR 21.1 et seq.
Department of Veterans Affairs—Loan guaranty and vocational rehabilitation and counseling programs, 48 CFR 871.100 et seq.

RESEARCH GUIDE

Am Jur:
77 Am Jur 2d, Veterans and Veterans' Laws §§ 132, 133.

CHAPTER 33. POST-9/11 EDUCATIONAL ASSISTANCE

Section

SUBCHAPTER I. DEFINITIONS
3301. Definitions.

SUBCHAPTER II. EDUCATIONAL ASSISTANCE
3311. Educational assistance for service in the Armed Forces commencing on or after September 11, 2001: entitlement.
3312. Educational assistance: duration.
3313. Educational assistance: amount; payment.
3314. Tutorial assistance.
3315. Licensure and certification tests.
3315A. National tests.
3316. Supplemental educational assistance: members with critical skills or specialty; members serving additional service.
3317. Public-private contributions for additional educational assistance.
3318. Additional assistance: relocation or travel assistance for individual relocating or traveling significant distance for pursuit of a program of education.
3319. Authority to transfer unused education benefits to family members.

READJUSTMENT BENEFITS 38 USCS § 3301

SUBCHAPTER III. ADMINISTRATIVE PROVISIONS

3321. Time limitation for use of and eligibility for entitlement.
3322. Bar to duplication of educational assistance benefits.
3323. Administration.
3324. Allocation of administration and costs.
3325. Reporting requirement.

HISTORY; ANCILLARY LAWS AND DIRECTIVES

Amendments:

2008. Act June 30, 2008, P. L. 110-252, Title V, § 5003(a)(1), 122 Stat. 2358, added the chapter analysis.

2011. Act Jan. 4, 2011, P. L. 111-377, Title I, § 108(a)(2), 124 Stat. 4119, amended the analysis of this chapter by adding item 3315A.

2012. Act Aug. 6, 2012, P. L. 112-154, Title IV, § 402(a)(2), 126 Stat. 1189, amended the analysis of this chapter by adding item 3325.

SUBCHAPTER I. DEFINITIONS

§ 3301. Definitions

In this chapter [38 USCS §§ 3301 et seq.]:

(1) The term "active duty" has the meanings as follows (subject to the limitations specified in sections 3002(6) and 3311(b) [38 USCS §§ 3002(6) and 3311(b)]):

(A) In the case of members of the regular components of the Armed Forces, the meaning given such term in section 101(21)(A) [38 USCS § 101(21)(A)].

(B) In the case of members of the reserve components of the Armed Forces, service on active duty under a call or order to active duty under section 688, 12301(a), 12301(d), 12301(g), 12302, or 12304 of title 10 or section 712 of title 14.

(C) In the case of a member of the Army National Guard of the United States or Air National Guard of the United States, in addition to service described in subparagraph (B), full-time service—

(i) in the National Guard of a State for the purpose of organizing, administering, recruiting, instructing, or training the National Guard; or

(ii) in the National Guard under section 502(f) of title 32 when authorized by the President or the Secretary of Defense for the purpose of responding to a national emergency declared by the President and supported by Federal funds.

(2) The term "entry level and skill training" means the following:

(A) In the case of members of the Army, Basic Combat Training and Advanced Individual Training or One Station Unit Training.

(B) In the case of members of the Navy, Recruit Training (or Boot Camp) and Skill Training (or so-called "A" School).

(C) In the case of members of the Air Force, Basic Military Training and Technical Training.

(D) In the case of members of the Marine Corps, Recruit Training and Marine Corps Training (or School of Infantry Training).

(E) In the case of members of the Coast Guard, Basic Training and Skill Training (or so-called "A" School).

(3) The term "program of education" has the meaning given such term in section 3002 [38 USCS § 3002], except to the extent otherwise provided in section 3313 [38 USCS § 3313].

(4) The term "Secretary of Defense" means the Secretary of Defense, except that the term means the Secretary of Homeland Security with respect to the Coast Guard when it is not operating as a service in the Navy.

(Added June 30, 2008, P. L. 110-252, Title V, § 5003(a)(1), 122 Stat. 2359; Jan. 4, 2011, P. L. 111-377, Title I, § 101(a), 124 Stat. 4107; Jan. 2, 2013, P. L. 112-239, Div A, Title VI, Subtitle I, § 681(c), 126 Stat. 1795.)

HISTORY; ANCILLARY LAWS AND DIRECTIVES

Effective date of section:

This section took effect on August 1, 2009, pursuant to § 5003(d) of Act June 30, 2008, P. L. 110-252, which appears as 10 USCS § 16163 note.

Amendments:

2011. Act Jan. 4, 2011 (effective 8/1/2009, as if included in the enactment of this chapter, and as provided by § 101(d)(1) of such Act, which appears as a note to this section), in para. (1), added subpara. (C).

Such Act further (effective on enactment, as provided by § 101(d)(2) of such Act, which appears as a note to this section), in para. (2)(A), inserted "or One Station Unit Training".

Such Act further (effective on the date of enactment and applicable to individuals entering service on or after such date, as provided by § 101(d)(3) of such Act, which appears as a note to this section), in para. (2)(E), inserted "and Skill Training (or so-called 'A' School)".

2013. Act Jan. 2, 2013 (applicable as provided by § 681(d) of such Act, which appears as 10 USCS § 101 note), in para. (1)(B), inserted "or section 712 of title 14".

Other provisions:
Post-9/11 Veterans Educational Assistance Act; findings. Act June 30, 2008, P. L. 110-252, Title V, § 5002, 122 Stat. 2357, provides:
"Congress makes the following findings:

"(1) On September 11, 2001, terrorists attacked the United States, and the brave members of the Armed Forces of the United States were called to the defense of the Nation.

"(2) Service on active duty in the Armed Forces has been especially arduous for the members of the Armed Forces since September 11, 2001.

"(3) The United States has a proud history of offering educational assistance to millions of veterans, as demonstrated by the many 'G.I. Bills' enacted since World War II. Educational assistance for veterans helps reduce the costs of war, assist veterans in readjusting to civilian life after wartime service, and boost the United States economy, and has a positive effect on recruitment for the Armed Forces.

"(4) The current educational assistance program for veterans is outmoded and designed for peacetime service in the Armed Forces.

"(5) The people of the United States greatly value military service and recognize the difficult challenges involved in readjusting to civilian life after wartime service in the Armed Forces.

"(6) It is in the national interest for the United States to provide veterans who serve on active duty in the Armed Forces after September 11, 2001, with enhanced educational assistance benefits that are worthy of such service and are commensurate with the educational assistance benefits provided by a grateful Nation to veterans of World War II.".

Applicability to individuals under Montgomery GI Bill Program. Act June 30, 2008, P. L. 110-252, Title V, § 5003(c), 122 Stat. 2375 (effective on 8/1/2009, as provided by § 5003(d) of such Act, which appears as 10 USCS § 16163 note), provides:

"(1) Individuals eligible to elect participation in post-9/11 educational assistance. An individual may elect to receive educational assistance under chapter 33 of title 38, United States Code [38 USCS §§ 3301 et seq.] (as added by subsection (a)), if such individual—

"(A) as of August 1, 2009—

"(i) is entitled to basic educational assistance under chapter 30 of title 38, United States Code [38 USCS §§ 3001 et seq.], and has used, but retains unused, entitlement under that chapter;

"(ii) is entitled to educational assistance under chapter 107, 1606, or 1607 of title 10, United States Code [10 USCS §§ 2151 et seq., 16131 et seq., or 16161 et seq.], and has used, but retains unused, entitlement under the applicable chapter;

"(iii) is entitled to basic educational assistance under chapter 30 of title 38, United States Code [38 USCS §§ 3001 et seq.], but has not used any entitlement under that chapter;

"(iv) is entitled to educational assistance under chapter 107, 1606, or 1607 of title 10, United States Code [10 USCS §§ 2151 et seq., 16131 et seq., or 16161 et seq.], but has not used any entitlement under such chapter;

"(v) is a member of the Armed Forces who is eligible for receipt of basic educational assistance under chapter 30 of title 38, United States Code [38 USCS §§ 3001 et seq.], and is making contributions toward such assistance under section 3011(b) or 3012(c) of such title [38 USCS § 3011(b) or 3012(c)]; or

"(vi) is a member of the Armed Forces who is not entitled to basic educational assistance under chapter 30 of title 38, United States Code [38 USCS §§ 3001 et seq.], by reason of an election under section 3011(c)(1) or 3012(d)(1) of such title [38 USCS § 3011(c)(1) or 3012(d)(1)]; and

"(B) as of the date of the individual's election under this paragraph, meets the requirements for entitlement to educational assistance under chapter 33 of title 38, United States Code [38 USCS §§ 3301 et seq.] (as so added).

"(2) Cessation of contributions toward GI bill. Effective as of the first month beginning on or after the date of an election under paragraph (1) of an individual described by subparagraph (A)(v) of that paragraph, the obligation of the individual to make contributions under section 3011(b) or 3012(c) of title 38, United States Code, as applicable, shall cease, and the requirements of such section shall be deemed to be no longer applicable to the individual.

"(3) Revocation of remaining transferred entitlement. (A) Election to revoke. If, on the date an individual described in subparagraph (A)(i) or (A)(iii) of paragraph (1) makes an election under that paragraph, a transfer of the entitlement of the individual to basic educational assistance under section 3020 of title 38, United States Code, is in effect and a number of months of the entitlement so transferred remain unutilized, the individual may elect to revoke all or a portion of the entitlement so transferred that remains unutilized.

"(B) Availability of revoked entitlement. Any entitlement revoked by an individual under this paragraph shall no longer be available to the dependent to whom transferred, but shall be available to the individual instead for educational assistance under chapter 33 of title 38, United States Code [38 USCS §§ 3301 et seq.] (as so added), in accordance with the provisions of this subsection.

"(C) Availability of unrevoked entitlement. Any entitlement described in subparagraph (A) that is not revoked by an individual in accordance with that subparagraph shall remain available to the dependent or dependents concerned in accordance with the current transfer of such entitlement under section 3020 of title 38, United States Code.

"(4) Post-9/11 educational assistance. (A) In general. Subject to subparagraph (B) and except as provided in paragraph (5), an individual making an election under paragraph (1) shall be entitled to educational assistance under chapter 33 of title 38, United States Code [38 USCS §§ 3301 et seq.] (as so added), in accordance with the provisions of such chapter, instead of basic educational assistance under chapter 30 of title 38, United States Code [38 USCS §§ 3001 et seq.], or educational assistance under chapter 107, 1606, or 1607 of title 10, United States Code [10 USCS §§ 2151 et seq., 16131 et seq., or 16161 et seq.], as applicable.

"(B) Limitation on entitlement for certain individuals. In the case of an individual making an election under paragraph (1) who is described by subparagraph (A)(i) of that paragraph, the number of months of entitlement of the individual to educational assistance under chapter 33 of title 38, United States Code [38 USCS §§ 3301 et seq.] (as so added), shall be the number of months equal to—

"(i) the number of months of unused entitlement of the individual under chapter 30 of title 38, United States Code [38 USCS § 3001 et seq.], as of the date of the election, plus

"(ii) the number of months, if any, of entitlement revoked by the individual under paragraph (3)(A).

"(5) Continuing entitlement to educational assistance not available under 9/11 assistance program. (A) In general. In the event educational assistance to which an individual making an election under paragraph (1) would be entitled under chapter 30 of title 38, United States Code [38 USCS §§ 3001 et seq.], or chapter 107, 1606, or 1607 of title 10, United States Code [10 USCS §§ 2151 et seq., 16131 et seq., or 16161 et seq.], as applicable, is not authorized to be available to the individual under the provisions of chapter 33 of title 38, United States Code [38 USCS §§ 3301 et seq.] (as so added), the individual shall remain entitled to such educational assistance in accordance with the provisions of the applicable chapter.

"(B) Charge for use of entitlement. The utilization by an individual of entitlement under subparagraph (A) shall be chargeable against the entitlement of the individual to educational assistance under chapter 33 of title 38, United States Code [38 USCS §§ 3301 et seq.] (as so added), at the rate of one month of entitlement under such chapter 33 for each month of entitlement utilized by the individual under subparagraph (A) (as determined as if such entitlement were utilized under the provisions of chapter 30 of title 38, United States Code [38 USCS §§ 3001 et seq.], or chapter 107, 1606, or 1607 of title 10, United States Code [10 USCS §§ 2151 et seq., 16131 et seq., or 16161 et seq.], as applicable).

"(6) Additional post-9/11 assistance for members having made contributions toward GI bill. (A) Additional assistance. In the case of an individual making an election under paragraph (1) who is described by clause (i), (iii), or (v) of subparagraph (A) of that paragraph, the amount of educational assistance payable to the individual under chapter 33 of title 38, United States Code [38 USCS §§ 3301 et seq.] (as so added), as a monthly stipend payable under paragraph (1)(B) of section 3313(c) of such title [38 USCS § 3313(c)], or under paragraphs (2) through (7) of that section (as applicable), shall be the amount otherwise payable as a monthly stipend under the applicable paragraph increased by the amount equal to—

"(i) the total amount of contributions toward basic educational assistance made by the individual under section 3011(b) or 3012(c) of title 38, United States Code, as of the date of the election, multiplied by

"(ii) the fraction—

"(I) the numerator of which is—

"(aa) the number of months of entitlement to basic educational assistance under chapter 30 of title 38, United States Code [38 USCS §§ 3001 et seq.], remaining to the individual at the time of the election; plus

"(bb) the number of months, if any, of entitlement under such chapter 30 revoked by the individual under paragraph (3)(A); and

"(II) the denominator of which is 36 months.

"(B) Months of remaining entitlement for certain individuals. In the case of an individual covered by subparagraph (A) who is described by paragraph (1)(A)(v), the number of months of entitlement to basic educational assistance remaining to the individual for purposes of subparagraph (A)(ii)(I)(aa) shall be 36 months.

"(C) Timing of payment. The amount payable with respect to an individual under subparagraph (A) shall be paid to the individual together with the last payment of the monthly stipend payable to the individual under paragraph (1)(B) of section 3313(c) of title 38, United States Code [38 USCS § 3313(c)] (as so added), or under paragraphs (2) through (7) of that section (as applicable), before the exhaustion of the individual's entitlement to educational assistance under chapter 33 of such title [38 USCS §§ 3301 et seq.] (as so added).

"(7) Continuing entitlement to additional assistance for critical skills or speciality and additional service. An individual making an election under paragraph (1)(A) who, at the time of the election, is entitled to increased educational assistance under section 3015(d) of title 38, United States Code, or section 16131(i) of title 10, United States Code, or supplemental educational assistance under subchapter III of chapter 30 of title 38, United States Code [38 USCS §§ 3021 et seq.], shall remain entitled to such increased educational assistance or supplemental educational assistance in the utilization of entitlement to educational assistance under chapter 33 of title 38, United States Code [38 USCS §§ 3301 et seq.] (as so added), in an amount equal to the quarter, semester, or term, as applicable, equivalent of the monthly amount of such increased educational assistance or supplemental educational assistance payable with respect to the individual at the time of the election.

"(8) Irrevocability of elections. An election under paragraph (1) or (3)(A) is irrevocable.".

Effective date of Jan. 4, 2011 amendments. Act Jan. 4, 2011, P. L. 111-377, Title I, § 101(d)(1)–(3), 124 Stat. 4108, provides:

"(1) Service in National Guard as active duty. The amendment made by subsection (a)(1) [adding para. (1)(C) of this section] shall take effect on August 1, 2009, as if included in the enactment of chapter 33 of title 38, United States Code [38 USCS §§ 3301 et seq.], pursuant to the Post-9/11 Veterans Educational Assistance Act of 2008 (title V of Public Law 110-252). However, no benefits otherwise payable by reason of such amendment for the period beginning on August 1, 2009, and ending on September 30, 2011, may be paid before October 1, 2011.

"(2) One Station Unit Training. The amendment made by subsection (a)(2) [amending para. (2)(A) of this section] shall take effect on the date of the enactment of this Act.

"(3) Entry level and skill training for the Coast Guard. The amendment made by subsection (a)(3) [amending para. (2)(E) of this section] shall take effect on the date of the enactment of this Act, and shall apply with respect to individuals entering service on or after that date.".

Establishing principles of excellence for educational institutions serving service members, veterans, spouses, and other family members. Ex. Or. No. 13607 of April 27, 2012, 77 Fed. Reg. 25861, provides:

"By the authority vested in me as President by the Constitution and the laws of the United States of America, and in order to ensure that Federal military and veterans educational benefits programs are providing service members, veterans, spouses, and other family members with the information, support, and protections they deserve, it is hereby ordered as follows:

"Section 1. Policy. The original GI Bill, approved just weeks after D-Day, educated nearly 8 million Americans and helped transform this Nation. We owe the same obligations to this generation of service men and women as was afforded that previous one. This is the promise of the Post-9/11 Veterans Educational Assistance Act of 2008 (title V, Public Law 110-252) (Post-9/11 GI Bill) and the continued provision of educational benefits in the Department of Defense's Tuition Assistance Program (10 U.S.C. 2007): to provide our service members, veterans, spouses, and other family members the opportunity to pursue a high-quality education and gain the skills and training they need to fill the jobs of tomorrow.

"Since the Post-9/11 GI Bill became law, there have been reports of aggressive and deceptive targeting of service members, veterans, and their families by some educational institutions. For example, some institutions have recruited veterans with serious brain injuries and emotional vulnerabilities without providing academic support and counseling; encouraged service members and veterans to take out costly institutional loans rather than encouraging them to apply for Federal student loans first; engaged in misleading recruiting practices on military installations; and failed to disclose meaningful information that allows potential students to determine whether the institution has a good record of graduating service members, veterans, and their families and positioning them for success in the workforce.

"To ensure our service members, veterans, spouses, and other family members have the information they need to make informed decisions concerning their well-earned Federal military and veterans educational benefits, I am directing my Administration to develop Principles of Excellence to strengthen oversight, enforcement, and accountability within these benefits programs.

"Sec. 2. Principles of Excellence for Educational Institutions Serving Service Members, Veterans, Spouses, and Other Family Members. The Departments of Defense, Veterans Affairs, and Education shall establish Principles of Excellence (Principles) to apply to educational institutions receiving funding from Federal military and veterans educational benefits programs, including benefits programs provided by the Post-9/11 GI Bill and the Tuition Assistance Program. The Principles should ensure that these educational institutions provide meaningful information to service members, veterans, spouses, and other family members about the financial cost and quality of educational institutions to assist those prospective students in making choices about how to use their Federal educational benefits; prevent abusive and deceptive recruiting practices that target the recipients of Federal military and veterans educational benefits; and ensure that educational institutions provide high-quality academic and student support services to active-duty service members, reservists, members of the National Guard, veterans, and military families.

"To the extent permitted by law, the Principles, implemented pursuant to section 3 of this order, should require educational institutions receiving funding pursuant to Federal military and veterans educational benefits to:

"(a) prior to enrollment, provide prospective students who are eligible to receive Federal military and veterans educational benefits with a personalized and standardized form, as developed in a manner set forth by the Secretary of Education, working with the Secretaries of Defense and Veterans Affairs, to help those prospective students understand the total cost of the educational program, including tuition and fees; the amount of that cost that will be covered by Federal educational benefits; the type and amount of financial aid they may qualify for; their estimated student loan debt upon graduation; information about student outcomes; and other information to facilitate comparison of aid packages offered by different educational institutions;

"(b) inform students who are eligible to receive Federal military and veterans educational benefits of the availability of Federal financial aid and have in place policies to alert those students of their potential eligibility for that aid before packaging or arranging private student loans or alternative financing programs;

"(c) end fraudulent and unduly aggressive recruiting techniques on and off military installations, as well as misrepresentation, payment of incentive compensation, and failure to meet State authorization requirements, consistent with the regulations issued by the Department of Education (34 C.F.R. 668.71-668.75, 668.14, and 600.9);

"(d) obtain the approval of the institution's accrediting agency for new course or program offerings before enrolling students in such courses or programs, provided that such approval is appropriate under the substantive change requirements of the accrediting agency;

"(e) allow service members and reservists to be readmitted to a program if they are temporarily unable to attend class or have to suspend their studies due to service requirements, and take additional steps to accommodate short absences due to service obligations, provided that satisfactory academic progress is being made by the service members and reservists prior to suspending their studies;

"(f) agree to an institutional refund policy that is aligned with the refund of unearned student aid rules applicable to Federal student aid provided through the Department of Education under Title IV of the Higher Education Act of 1965 [20 USCS §§ 1070 et seq.], as required under section 484B of that Act [20 USCS § 1091b] when students withdraw prior to course completion;

"(g) provide educational plans for all individuals using Federal military and veterans educational benefits that detail how they will fulfill all the requirements necessary to graduate and the expected timeline of completion; and

"(h) designate a point of contact for academic and financial advising (including access to disability counseling) to assist service member and veteran students and their families with the successful completion of their studies and with their job searches.

"Sec. 3. Implementation of the Principles of Excellence.

"(a) The Departments of Defense and Veterans Affairs shall reflect the Principles described in section 2 of this order in new agreements with educational institutions, to the extent practicable and permitted by law, concerning participation in the Yellow Ribbon Program for veterans under the Post-9/11 GI Bill or the Tuition Assistance Program for active duty service members. The Department of Veterans Affairs shall also notify all institutions participating in the Post-9/11 GI Bill program that they are strongly encouraged to comply with the Principles and shall post on the Department's website those that do.

"(b) The Secretaries of Defense, Veterans Affairs, and Education, in consultation with the Director of the Bureau of Consumer Financial Protection (CFPB) and the Attorney General, shall take immediate action to implement this order, and, within 90 days from the date of this order, report to the President their progress on implementation, including promptly revising regulations, Department of Defense Instructions, guidance documents, Memoranda of Understanding, and other policies governing programs authorized or funded by the Post-9/11 GI Bill and the Tuition Assistance Program to implement the Principles, to the extent permitted by law.

"(c) The Secretaries of Defense, Veterans Affairs, and Education shall develop a comprehensive strategy for developing service member and veteran student outcome measures that are comparable, to the maximum extent practicable, across Federal military and veterans educational benefit programs, including, but not limited to, the Post-9/11 GI Bill and the Tuition Assistance Program. To the extent practicable, the student outcome measures should rely on existing administrative data to minimize the reporting burden on institutions participating in these benefit programs. The student outcome measures should permit comparisons across Federal educational programs and across institutions and types of institutions. The Secretary of Education, in consultation with the Secretaries of Defense and Veterans Affairs, shall also collect from educational institutions, as part of the Integrated Postsecondary Education Data System and other data collection systems, information on the amount of funding received pursuant to the Post-9/11 GI Bill and the Tuition Assistance Program. The Secretary of Education shall make this information publicly available on the College Navigator Website.

"(d) The Secretary of Veterans Affairs, in consultation with the Secretaries of Defense and Education, shall provide to prospective military and veteran students, prior to using their benefits, streamlined tools to compare educational institutions using key measures of affordability and value through the Department of Veterans Affairs' eBenefits portal. The eBenefits portal shall be updated to facilitate access to school performance information, consumer protection information, and key Federal financial aid documents. The Secretaries of Defense and Veterans Affairs shall also ensure that service members and veterans have access to that information through educational counseling offered by those Departments.

"Sec. 4. Strengthening Enforcement and Compliance Mechanisms. Service members, veterans, spouses, and other family members should have access to a strong enforcement system through which to file complaints when institutions fail to follow the Principles. Within 90 days of the date of this order, the Secretaries of Defense and Veterans Affairs, in consultation with the Secretary of Education and the Director of the CFPB, as well as with the Attorney General, as appropriate, shall submit to the President a plan to strengthen enforcement and compliance mechanisms. The plan shall include proposals to:

"(a) create a centralized complaint system for students receiving Federal military and veterans educational benefits to register complaints that can be tracked and responded to by the Departments of Defense, Veterans Affairs, Justice, and Education, the CFPB, and other relevant agencies;

"(b) institute uniform procedures for receiving and processing complaints across the State Approving Agencies (SAAs) that work with the Department of Veterans Affairs to review participating institutions, provide a coordinated mechanism across SAAs to alert the Department of Veterans Affairs to any complaints that have been registered at the State level, and create procedures for sharing information about complaints with the appropriate State officials, accrediting agency representatives, and the Secretary of Education;

"(c) institute uniform procedures for referring potential matters for civil or criminal enforcement to the Department of Justice and other relevant agencies;

"(d) establish procedures for targeted risk-based program reviews of institutions to ensure compliance with the Principles;

"(e) establish new uniform rules and strengthen existing procedures for access to military installations by educational institutions. These new rules should ensure, at a minimum, that only those institutions that enter into a memorandum of agreement pursuant to section 3(a) of this order are permitted entry onto a Federal military installation for the purposes of recruitment. The Department of Defense shall include specific steps for instructing installation commanders on commercial solicitation rules and the requirement of the Principles outlined in section 2(c) of this order; and

"(f) take all appropriate steps to ensure that websites and programs are not deceptively and fraudulently marketing educational services and benefits to program beneficiaries, including initiating a process to protect the term "GI Bill" and other military or veterans-related terms as trademarks, as appropriate.

"Sec. 5. General Provisions. (a) This order shall be implemented consistent with applicable law and subject to the availability of appropriations.

"(b) Nothing in this order shall be construed to impair or otherwise affect:

"(i) the authority granted by law to an executive department, agency, or the head thereof; or

"(ii) the functions of the Director of the Office of Management and Budget relating to budgetary, administrative, or legislative proposals.

"(c) This order is not intended to, and does not, create any right or benefit, substantive or procedural, enforceable at law or in equity by any party against the United States, its departments, agencies, or entities, its officers, employees, or agents, or any other person.".

CODE OF FEDERAL REGULATIONS

Office of the Secretary of Defense—Post-9/11 GI Bill, 32 CFR 65.1 et seq.

RESEARCH GUIDE

Annotations:

Civil Liability of Psychiatrist Arising out of Patient's Violent Conduct Resulting in Injury to or Death of Patient or Third Party Allegedly Caused in Whole or Part by Mental Disorder. 80 ALR6th 469.

SUBCHAPTER II. EDUCATIONAL ASSISTANCE

§ 3311. Educational assistance for service in the Armed Forces commencing on or after September 11, 2001: entitlement

(a) Entitlement. Subject to subsections (d) and (e), each individual described in subsection (b) is entitled to educational assistance under this chapter [38 USCS §§ 3301 et seq.].

(b) Covered individuals. An individual described in this subsection is any individual as follows:

(1) An individual who—

(A) commencing on or after September 11, 2001, serves an aggregate of at least 36 months on active duty in the Armed Forces (including service on active duty in entry level and skill training); and

(B) after completion of service described in subparagraph (A)—

(i) continues on active duty; or

READJUSTMENT BENEFITS 38 USCS § 3311

(ii) is discharged or released from active duty as described in subsection (c).
(2) An individual who—
   (A) commencing on or after September 11, 2001, serves at least 30 continuous days on active duty in the Armed Forces; and
   (B) after completion of service described in subparagraph (A), is discharged or released from active duty in the Armed Forces for a service-connected disability.
(3) An individual who—
   (A) commencing on or after September 11, 2001, serves an aggregate of at least 30 months, but less than 36 months, on active duty in the Armed Forces (including service on active duty in entry level and skill training); and
   (B) after completion of service described in subparagraph (A)—
      (i) continues on active duty for an aggregate of less than 36 months; or
      (ii) before completion of service on active duty of an aggregate of 36 months, is discharged or released from active duty as described in subsection (c).
(4) An individual who—
   (A) commencing on or after September 11, 2001, serves an aggregate of at least 24 months, but less than 30 months, on active duty in the Armed Forces (including service on active duty in entry level and skill training); and
   (B) after completion of service described in subparagraph (A)—
      (i) continues on active duty for an aggregate of less than 30 months; or
      (ii) before completion of service on active duty of an aggregate of 30 months, is discharged or released from active duty as described in subsection (c).
(5) An individual who—
   (A) commencing on or after September 11, 2001, serves an aggregate of at least 18 months, but less than 24 months, on active duty in the Armed Forces (excluding service on active duty in entry level and skill training); and
   (B) after completion of service described in subparagraph (A)—
      (i) continues on active duty for an aggregate of less than 24 months; or
      (ii) before completion of service on active duty of an aggregate of 24 months, is discharged or released from active duty as described in subsection (c).
(6) An individual who—
   (A) commencing on or after September 11, 2001, serves an aggregate of at least 12 months, but less than 18 months, on active duty in the Armed Forces (excluding service on active duty in entry level and skill training); and
   (B) after completion of service described in subparagraph (A)—
      (i) continues on active duty for an aggregate of less than 18 months; or
      (ii) before completion of service on active duty of an aggregate of 18 months, is discharged or released from active duty as described in subsection (c).
(7) An individual who—
   (A) commencing on or after September 11, 2001, serves an aggregate of at least 6 months, but less than 12 months, on active duty in the Armed Forces (excluding service on active duty in entry level and skill training); and
   (B) after completion of service described in subparagraph (A)—
      (i) continues on active duty for an aggregate of less than 12 months; or
      (ii) before completion of service on active duty of an aggregate of 12 months, is discharged or released from active duty as described in subsection (c).
(8) An individual who—
   (A) commencing on or after September 11, 2001, serves an aggregate of at least 90 days, but less than 6 months, on active duty in the Armed Forces (excluding service on active duty in entry level and skill training); and
   (B) after completion of service described in subparagraph (A)—
      (i) continues on active duty for an aggregate of less than 6 months; or
      (ii) before completion of service on active duty of an aggregate of 6 months, is discharged or released from active duty as described in subsection (c).
(9) An individual who is the child of a person who, on or after September 11, 2001, dies in line of duty while serving on active duty as a member of the Armed Forces.

(c) Covered discharges and releases. A discharge or release from active duty of an individual described in this subsection is a discharge or release as follows:
(1) A discharge from active duty in the Armed Forces with an honorable discharge.
(2) A release after service on active duty in the Armed Forces characterized by the Secretary

38 USCS § 3311 VETERANS' BENEFITS

concerned as honorable service and placement on the retired list, transfer to the Fleet Reserve or Fleet Marine Corps Reserve, or placement on the temporary disability retired list.

(3) A release from active duty in the Armed Forces for further service in a reserve component of the Armed Forces after service on active duty characterized by the Secretary concerned as honorable service.

(4) A discharge or release from active duty in the Armed Forces after service on active duty in the Armed Forces characterized by the Secretary concerned as honorable service for—

   (A) a medical condition which preexisted the service of the individual as described in the applicable paragraph of subsection (b) and which the Secretary determines is not service-connected;

   (B) hardship; or

   (C) a physical or mental condition that was not characterized as a disability and did not result from the individual's own willful misconduct but did interfere with the individual's performance of duty, as determined by the Secretary concerned in accordance with regulations prescribed by the Secretary of Defense.

(d) Prohibition on treatment of certain service as period of active duty. The following periods of service shall not be considered a part of the period of active duty on which an individual's entitlement to educational assistance under this chapter [38 USCS §§ 3301 et seq.] is based:

(1) A period of service on active duty of an officer pursuant to an agreement under section 2107(b) of title 10 [10 USCS § 2107(b)].

(2) A period of service on active duty of an officer pursuant to an agreement under section 4348, 6959, or 9348 of title 10 [10 USCS § 4348, 6959, or 9348] or section 182 of title 14 [14 USCS § 182].

(3) A period of service that is terminated because of a defective enlistment and induction based on—

   (A) the individual's being a minor for purposes of service in the Armed Forces;

   (B) an erroneous enlistment or induction; or

   (C) a defective enlistment agreement.

(e) Treatment of individuals entitled under multiple provisions. In the event an individual entitled to educational assistance under this chapter [38 USCS §§ 3301 et seq.] is entitled by reason of both paragraphs (4) and (5) of subsection (b), the individual shall be treated as being entitled to educational assistance under this chapter [38 USCS §§ 3301 et seq.] by reason of paragraph (5) of subsection (b).

(f) Marine Gunnery Sergeant John David Fry Scholarship. (1) In general. Educational assistance payable by reason of paragraph (9) of subsection (b) shall be known as the "Marine Gunnery Sergeant John David Fry scholarship".

(2) Definition of child. For purposes of that paragraph, the term "child" includes a married individual or an individual who is above the age of twenty-three years.

(Added June 30, 2008, P. L. 110-252, Title V, § 5003(a)(1), 122 Stat. 2359; June 24, 2009, P. L. 111-32, Title X, § 1002(a), 123 Stat. 1889; Jan. 4, 2011, P. L. 111-377, Title I, § 101(b), (c), 124 Stat. 4107.)

HISTORY; ANCILLARY LAWS AND DIRECTIVES

Effective date of section:

This section took effect on August 1, 2009, pursuant to § 5003(d) of Act June 30, 2008, P. L. 110-252, which appears as 10 USCS § 16163 note.

Amendments:

2009. Act June 24, 2009 (effective 8/1/2009 and applicable as provided by § 1002(d) of such Act, which appears as a note to this section), added subsecs. (b)(9) and (f).

2011. Act Jan. 4, 2011 (effective on the date of enactment and applicable to discharges and releases from the Armed Forces that occur on or after that date, as provided by § 101(d)(4) of such Act, which appears as a note to this section), in subsec. (c)(4), in the introductory matter, inserted "after service on active duty in the Armed Forces characterized by the Secretary concerned as honorable service".

Such Act further (effective on the date of enactment, and applicable to individuals entering into agreements on service in the Coast Guard on or after that date, as provided by § 101(d)(5) of such Act, which appears as a note to this section), in subsec. (d)(2), inserted "or section 182 of title 14".

Other provisions:

Effective date and applicability of June 24, 2009 amendments. Act June 24, 2009, P. L. 111-32, Title X, § 1002(d), 123 Stat. 1890, provides:

"(1) Effective date. The amendments made by this section [amending 38 USCS §§ 3311, 3313, and 3321] shall take effect on August 1, 2009.

READJUSTMENT BENEFITS 38 USCS § 3313

"(2) Applicability. The Secretary of Veterans Affairs shall begin making payments to individuals entitled to educational assistance by reason of paragraph (9) of section 3311(b) of title 38, United States Code, as added by subsection (a), by not later than August 1, 2010. In the case of an individual entitled to educational assistance by reason of such paragraph for the period beginning on August 1, 2009, and ending on July 31, 2010, the Secretary shall make retroactive payments to such individual for such period by not later than August 1, 2010.".

Effective date and applicability of Jan. 4, 2011 amendments. Act Jan. 4, 2011, P. L. 111-377, Title I, § 101(d)(4), (5), 124 Stat. 4108, provides:

"(4) Honorable service requirement. The amendment made by subsection (b) [amending subsec. (c)(4) of this section] shall take effect on the date of the enactment of this Act, and shall apply with respect to discharges and releases from the Armed Forces that occur on or after that date.

"(5) Service in connection with attendance at Coast Guard Academy. The amendment made by subsection (c) [amending subsec. (d)(2) of this section] shall take effect on the date of the enactment of this Act, and shall apply with respect to individuals entering into agreements on service in the Coast Guard on or after that date.".

CODE OF FEDERAL REGULATIONS

Office of the Secretary of Defense—Post-9/11 GI Bill, 32 CFR 65.1 et seq.

§ 3312. Educational assistance: duration

(a) In general. Subject to section 3695 [38 USCS § 3695] and except as provided in subsections (b) and (c), an individual entitled to educational assistance under this chapter [38 USCS §§ 3301 et seq.] is entitled to a number of months of educational assistance under section 3313 [38 USCS § 3313] equal to 36 months.

(b) Continuing receipt. The receipt of educational assistance under section 3313 [38 USCS § 3313] by an individual entitled to educational assistance under this chapter [38 USCS §§ 3301 et seq.] is subject to the provisions of section 3321(b)(2) [38 USCS § 3321(b)(2)].

(c) Discontinuation of education for active duty. (1) In general. Any payment of educational assistance described in paragraph (2) shall not—

    (A) be charged against any entitlement to educational assistance of the individual concerned under this chapter [38 USCS §§ 3301 et seq.]; or

    (B) be counted against the aggregate period for which section 3695 [38 USCS § 3695] limits the individual's receipt of educational assistance under this chapter [38 USCS §§ 3301 et seq.].

(2) Description of payment of educational assistance. Subject to paragraph (3), the payment of educational assistance described in this paragraph is the payment of such assistance to an individual for pursuit of a course or courses under this chapter [38 USCS §§ 3301 et seq.] if the Secretary finds that the individual—

    (A)(i) in the case of an individual not serving on active duty, had to discontinue such course pursuit as a result of being called or ordered to serve on active duty under section 688, 12301(a), 12301(d), 12301(g), 12302, or 12304 of title 10 [10 USCS § 688, 12301(a), 12301(d), 12301(g), 12302, or 12304]; or

    (ii) in the case of an individual serving on active duty, had to discontinue such course pursuit as a result of being ordered to a new duty location or assignment or to perform an increased amount of work; and

    (B) failed to receive credit or lost training time toward completion of the individual's approved education, professional, or vocational objective as a result of having to discontinue, as described in subparagraph (A), the individual's course pursuit.

(3) Period for which payment not charged. The period for which, by reason of this subsection, educational assistance is not charged against entitlement or counted toward the applicable aggregate period under section 3695 of this title [38 USCS § 3695] shall not exceed the portion of the period of enrollment in the course or courses from which the individual failed to receive credit or with respect to which the individual lost training time, as determined under paragraph (2)(B).

(Added June 30, 2008, P. L. 110-252, Title V, § 5003(a)(1), 122 Stat. 2362.)

HISTORY; ANCILLARY LAWS AND DIRECTIVES

Effective date of section:

This section took effect on August 1, 2009, pursuant to § 5003(d) of Act June 30, 2008, P. L. 110-252, which appears as 10 USCS § 16163 note.

§ 3313. Educational assistance: amount; payment

(a) Payment. The Secretary shall pay to each individual entitled to educational assistance under this chapter [38 USCS §§ 3301 et seq.] who is pursuing an approved program of education (other than a program covered by subsections (e) and (f)) the amounts specified in subsection (c) to meet

38 USCS § 3313

VETERANS' BENEFITS

the expenses of such individual's subsistence, tuition, fees, and other educational costs for pursuit of such program of education.

(b) Approved programs of education. A program of education is an approved program of education for purposes of this chapter [38 USCS §§ 3301 et seq.] if the program of education is approved for purposes of chapter 30 [38 USCS §§ 3001 et seq.] (including approval by the State approving agency concerned).

(c) Programs of education leading to a degree pursued at institutions of higher learning on more than half-time basis. The amounts payable under this subsection for pursuit of an approved program of education leading to a degree at an institution of higher learning (as that term is defined in section 3452(f) [38 USCS § 3452(f)]) are amounts as follows:

  (1) In the case of an individual entitled to educational assistance under this chapter [38 USCS §§ 3301 et seq.] by reason of paragraph (1), (2), or (9) of section 3311(b) [38 USCS § 3311(b)], amounts as follows:

    (A) An amount equal to the following:

      (i) In the case of a program of education pursued at a public institution of higher learning, the actual net cost for in-State tuition and fees assessed by the institution for the program of education after the application of—

        (I) any waiver of, or reduction in, tuition and fees; and

        (II) any scholarship, or other Federal, State, institutional, or employer-based aid or assistance (other than loans and any funds provided under section 401(b) of the Higher Education Act of 1965 (20 U.S.C. 1070a)) that is provided directly to the institution and specifically designated for the sole purpose of defraying tuition and fees.

      (ii) In the case of a program of education pursued at a non-public or foreign institution of higher learning, the lesser of—

        (I) the actual net cost for tuition and fees assessed by the institution for the program of education after the application of—

          (aa) any waiver of, or reduction in, tuition and fees; and

          (bb) any scholarship, or other Federal, State, institutional, or employer-based aid or assistance (other than loans and any funds provided under section 401(b) of the Higher Education Act of 1965 [20 USCS § 1070a(b)]) that is provided directly to the institution and specifically designated for the sole purpose of defraying tuition and fees; or

        (II) the amount equal to—

          (aa) for the academic year beginning on August 1, 2011, $17,500; or

          (bb) for an academic year beginning on any subsequent August 1, the amount for the previous academic year beginning on August 1 under this subclause, as increased by the percentage increase equal to the most recent percentage increase determined under section 3015(h) [38 USCS § 3015(h)].

    (B) A monthly stipend in an amount as follows:

      (i) Except as provided in clauses (ii) and (iii), for each month an individual pursues a program of education on more than a half-time basis, a monthly housing stipend equal to the product of—

        (I) the monthly amount of the basic allowance for housing payable under section 403 of title 37 [37 USCS § 403] for a member with dependents in pay grade E-5 residing in the military housing area that encompasses all or the majority portion of the ZIP code area in which is located the institution of higher learning at which the individual is enrolled, multiplied by

        (II) the lesser of—

          (aa) 1.0; or

          (bb) the number of course hours borne by the individual in pursuit of the program of education, divided by the minimum number of course hours required for full-time pursuit of the program of education, rounded to the nearest multiple of 10.

      (ii) In the case of an individual pursuing a program of education at a foreign institution of higher learning on more than a half-time basis, for each month the individual pursues the program of education, a monthly housing stipend equal to the product of—

        (I) the national average of the monthly amount of the basic allowance for housing payable under section 403 of title 37 [37 USCS § 403] for a member with dependents in pay grade E-5, multiplied by

        (II) the lesser of—

          (aa) 1.0; or

          (bb) the number of course hours borne by the individual in pursuit of the program of education, divided by the minimum number of course hours required for full-time pursuit of the program of education, rounded to the nearest multiple of 10.

(iii) In the case of an individual pursuing a program of education solely through distance learning on more than a half-time basis, a monthly housing stipend equal to 50 percent of the amount payable under clause (ii) if the individual were otherwise entitled to a monthly housing stipend under that clause for pursuit of the program of education.

(iv) For the first month of each quarter, semester, or term, as applicable, of the program of education pursued by the individual, a lump sum amount for books, supplies, equipment, and other educational costs with respect to such quarter, semester, or term in the amount equal to—

(I) $1,000, multiplied by

(II) the fraction which is the portion of a complete academic year under the program of education that such quarter, semester, or term constitutes.

(2) In the case of an individual entitled to educational assistance under this chapter [38 USCS §§ 3301 et seq.] by reason of section 3311(b)(3) [38 USCS § 3311(b)(3)], amounts equal to 90 percent of the amounts that would be payable to the individual under paragraph (1) for the program of education if the individual were entitled to amounts for the program of education under paragraph (1) rather than this paragraph.

(3) In the case of an individual entitled to educational assistance under this chapter [38 USCS §§ 3301 et seq.] by reason of section 3311(b)(4) [38 USCS § 3311(b)(4)], amounts equal to 80 percent of the amounts that would be payable to the individual under paragraph (1) for the program of education if the individual were entitled to amounts for the program of education under paragraph (1) rather than this paragraph.

(4) In the case of an individual entitled to educational assistance under this chapter [38 USCS §§ 3301 et seq.] by reason of section 3311(b)(5) [38 USCS § 3311(b)(5)], amounts equal to 70 percent of the amounts that would be payable to the individual under paragraph (1) for the program of education if the individual were entitled to amounts for the program of education under paragraph (1) rather than this paragraph.

(5) In the case of an individual entitled to educational assistance under this chapter [38 USCS §§ 3301 et seq.] by reason of section 3311(b)(6) [38 USCS § 3311(b)(6)], amounts equal to 60 percent of the amounts that would be payable to the individual under paragraph (1) for the program of education if the individual were entitled to amounts for the program of education under paragraph (1) rather than this paragraph.

(6) In the case of an individual entitled to educational assistance under this chapter [38 USCS §§ 3301 et seq.] by reason of section 3311(b)(7) [38 USCS § 3311(b)(7)], amounts equal to 50 percent of the amounts that would be payable to the individual under paragraph (1) for the program of education if the individual were entitled to amounts for the program of education under paragraph (1) rather than this paragraph.

(7) In the case of an individual entitled to educational assistance under this chapter [38 USCS §§ 3301 et seq.] by reason of section 3311(b)(8) [38 USCS § 3311(b)(8)], amounts equal to 40 percent of the amounts that would be payable to the individual under paragraph (1) for the program of education if the individual were entitled to amounts for the program of education under paragraph (1) rather than this paragraph.

(d) Frequency of payment. (1) Quarter, semester, or term payments. Payment of the amounts payable under subsection (c)(1)(A), and of similar amounts payable under paragraphs (2) through (7) of subsection (c), for pursuit of a program of education shall be made for the entire quarter, semester, or term, as applicable, of the program of education.

(2) Monthly payments. Payment of the amount payable under subsection (c)(1)(B), and of similar amounts payable under paragraphs (2) through (7) of subsection (c), for pursuit of a program of education shall be made on a monthly basis.

(3) Regulations. The Secretary shall prescribe in regulations methods for determining the number of months (including fractions thereof) of entitlement of an individual to educational assistance under this chapter [38 USCS §§ 3301 et seq.] that are chargeable under this chapter for an advance payment of amounts under paragraphs (1) and (2) for pursuit of a program of education on a quarter, semester, term, or other basis.

(e) Programs of education leading to a degree pursued on active duty on more than half-time basis. (1) In general. Educational assistance is payable under this chapter [38 USCS §§ 3301 et seq.] for pursuit of an approved program of education leading to a degree while on active duty.

(2) Amount of assistance. The amounts of educational assistance payable under this chapter [38 USCS §§ 3301 et seq.] to an individual pursuing a program of education leading to a degree while on active duty are as follows:

(A) Subject to subparagraph (C), an amount equal to the lesser of—

(i) in the case of a program of education pursued at a public institution of higher learning, the actual net cost for in-State tuition and fees assessed by the institution for the program of education after the application of—

(I) any waiver of, or reduction in, tuition and fees; and
(II) any scholarship, or other Federal, State, institutional, or employer-based aid or assistance (other than loans and any funds provided under section 401(b) of the Higher Education Act of 1965 (20 U.S.C. 1070a)) that is provided directly to the institution and specifically designated for the sole purpose of defraying tuition and fees;
(ii) in the case of a program of education pursued at a non-public or foreign institution of higher learning, the lesser of—
(I) the actual net cost for tuition and fees assessed by the institution for the program of education after the application of—
(aa) any waiver of, or reduction in, tuition and fees; and
(bb) any scholarship, or other Federal, State, institutional, or employer-based aid or assistance (other than loans and any funds provided under section 401(b) of the Higher Education Act of 1965 [20 USCS § 1070a(b)]) that is provided directly to the institution and specifically designated for the sole purpose of defraying tuition and fees; or
(II) the amount equal to—
(aa) for the academic year beginning on August 1, 2011, $17,500; or
(bb) for an academic year beginning on any subsequent August 1, the amount for the previous academic year beginning on August 1 under this subclause, as increased by the percentage increase equal to the most recent percentage increase determined under section 3015(h) [38 USCS § 3015(h)]; or
(iii) the amount of the charges of the educational institution as elected by the individual in the manner specified in section 3014(b)(1) [38 USCS § 3014(b)(1)]. [.]
(B) Subject to subparagraph (C), for the first month of each quarter, semester, or term, as applicable, of the program of education pursued by the individual, a lump sum amount for books, supplies, equipment, and other educational costs with respect to such quarter, semester, or term in the amount equal to—
(i) $1,000, multiplied by
(ii) the fraction of a complete academic year under the program of education that such quarter, semester, or term constitutes.
(C) In the case of an individual entitled to educational assistance by reason of paragraphs (3) through (8) of section 3311(b) [38 USCS § 3311(b)], the amounts payable to the individual pursuant to subparagraphs (A)(i), (A)(ii), and (B) shall be the amounts otherwise determined pursuant to such subparagraphs multiplied by the same percentage applicable to the monthly amounts payable to the individual under paragraphs (2) through (7) of subsection (c).
(3) Quarter, semester, or term payments. Payment of the amount payable under paragraph (2) for pursuit of a program of education shall be made for the entire quarter, semester, or term, as applicable, of the program of education.
(4) Monthly payments. For each month (as determined pursuant to the methods prescribed under subsection (d)(3)) for which amounts are paid an individual under this subsection, the entitlement of the individual to educational assistance under this chapter [38 USCS §§ 3301 et seq.] shall be charged at the rate of one month for each such month.

(f) Programs of education pursued on half-time basis or less. (1) In general. Educational assistance is payable under this chapter [38 USCS §§ 3301 et seq.] for pursuit of an approved program of education on half-time basis or less whether a program of education pursued on active duty, a program of education leading to a degree, or a program of education other than a program of education leading to a degree.
(2) Amount of assistance. The educational assistance payable under this chapter [38 USCS §§ 3301 et seq.] to an individual pursuing a program of education covered by this subsection on half-time basis or less is the amounts as follows:
(A) The amount equal to the lesser of—
(i) the actual net cost for in-State tuition and fees assessed by the institution of higher learning for the program of education after the application of—
(I) any waiver of, or reduction in, tuition and fees; and
(II) any scholarship, or other Federal, State, institutional, or employer-based aid or assistance (other than loans and any funds provided under section 401(b) of the Higher Education Act of 1965 (20 U.S.C. 1070a)) that is provided directly to the institution and specifically designated for the sole purpose of defraying tuition and fees; or
(ii) the maximum amount that would be payable to the individual for the program of education under paragraph (1)(A) of subsection (c), or under the provisions of paragraphs

(2) through (7) of subsection (c) applicable to the individual, for the program of education if the individual were entitled to amounts for the program of education under subsection (c) rather than this subsection.

(B) A stipend in an amount equal to the amount of the appropriately reduced amount of the lump sum amount for books, supplies, equipment, and other educational costs otherwise payable to the individual under subsection (c).

(3) Quarter, term, or semester payments. Payment of the amounts payable to an individual under paragraph (2) for pursuit of a program of education on half-time basis or less shall be made for the entire quarter, semester, or term, as applicable, of the program of education.

(4) Monthly payments. For each month (as determined pursuant to the methods prescribed under subsection (d)(3)) for which amounts are paid an individual under this subsection, the entitlement of the individual to educational assistance under this chapter [38 USCS §§ 3301 et seq.] shall be charged at a percentage of a month equal to—

(A) the number of course hours borne by the individual in pursuit of the program of education involved, divided by

(B) the number of course hours for full-time pursuit of such program of education.

(g) Programs of education other than programs of education leading to a degree. (1) In general. Educational assistance is payable under this chapter for pursuit of an approved program of education other than a program of education leading to a degree at an institution other than an institution of higher learning (as that term is defined in section 3452(f) [38 USCS § 3452(f)]).

(2) Pursuit on half-time basis or less. The payment of educational assistance under this chapter for pursuit of a program of education otherwise described in paragraph (1) on a half-time basis or less is governed by subsection (f).

(3) Amount of assistance. The amounts of educational assistance payable under this chapter to an individual entitled to educational assistance under this chapter who is pursuing an approved program of education covered by this subsection are as follows:

(A) In the case of an individual enrolled in a program of education (other than a program described in subparagraphs (B) through (D)) in pursuit of a certificate or other non-college degree, the following:

(i) Subject to clause (iv), an amount equal to the lesser of—

(I) the actual net cost for in-State tuition and fees assessed by the institution concerned for the program of education after the application of—

(aa) any waiver of, or reduction in, tuition and fees; and

(bb) any scholarship, or other Federal, State, institutional, or employer-based aid or assistance (other than loans and any funds provided under section 401(b) of the Higher Education Act of 1965 (20 U.S.C. 1070a)) that is provided directly to the institution and specifically designated for the sole purpose of defraying tuition and fees; or

(II) the amount equal to—

(aa) for the academic year beginning on August 1, 2011, $17,500; or

(bb) for an academic year beginning on any subsequent August 1, the amount for the previous academic year beginning on August 1 under this subclause, as increased by the percentage increase equal to the most recent percentage increase determined under section 3015(h) [38 USCS § 3015(h)].

(ii) Except in the case of an individual pursuing a program of education on a half-time or less basis and subject to clause (iv), a monthly housing stipend equal to the product—

(I) of—

(aa) in the case of an individual pursuing resident training, the monthly amount of the basic allowance for housing payable under section 403 of title 37 for a member with dependents in pay grade E-5 residing in the military housing area that encompasses all or the majority portion of the ZIP code area in which is located the institution at which the individual is enrolled; or

(bb) in the case of an individual pursuing a program of education through distance learning, a monthly amount equal to 50 percent of the amount payable under item (aa), multiplied by

(II) the lesser of—

(aa) 1.0; or

(bb) the number of course hours borne by the individual in pursuit of the program of education involved, divided by the minimum number of course hours required for full-time pursuit of such program of education, rounded to the nearest multiple of 10.

(iii) Subject to clause (iv), a monthly stipend in an amount equal to $83 for each month (or pro rata amount for a partial month) of training pursued for books supplies, equipment, and other educational costs.

(iv) In the case of an individual entitled to educational assistance by reason of paragraphs (3) through (8) of section 3311(b) [38 USCS § 3311(b)], the amounts payable pursuant to clauses (i), (ii), and (iii) shall be the amounts otherwise determined pursuant to such clauses multiplied by the same percentage applicable to the monthly amounts payable to the individual under paragraphs (2) through (7) of subsection (c).

(B) In the case of an individual pursuing a full-time program of apprenticeship or other on-job training, amounts as follows:

(i) Subject to clauses (iii) and (iv), for each month the individual pursues the program of education, a monthly housing stipend equal to—

(I) during the first six-month period of the program, the monthly amount of the basic allowance for housing payable under section 403 of title 37 for a member with dependents in pay grade E-5 residing in the military housing area that encompasses all or the majority portion of the ZIP code area in which is located the employer at which the individual pursues such program;

(II) during the second six-month period of the program, 80 percent of the monthly amount of the basic allowance for housing payable as described in subclause (I);

(III) during the third six-month period of the program, 60 percent of the monthly amount of the basic allowance for housing payable as described in subclause (I);

(IV) during the fourth six-month period of such program, 40 percent of the monthly amount of the basic allowance for housing payable as described in subclause (I); and

(V) during any month after the first 24 months of such program, 20 percent of the monthly amount of the basic allowance for housing payable as described in subclause (I).

(ii) Subject to clauses (iii) and (iv), a monthly stipend in an amount equal to $83 for each month (or pro rata amount for each partial month) of training pursued for books supplies, equipment, and other educational costs.

(iii) In the case of an individual entitled to educational assistance by reason of paragraphs (3) through (8) of sections 3311(b) [38 USCS § 3311(b)], the amounts payable pursuant to clauses (i) and (ii) shall be the amounts otherwise determined pursuant to such clauses multiplied by the same percentage applicable to the monthly amounts payable to the individual under paragraphs (2) through (7) of subsection (c).

(iv) In any month in which an individual pursuing a program of education consisting of a program of apprenticeship or other on-job training fails to complete 120 hours of training, the amount of monthly educational assistance allowance payable under clauses (i) and (iii) to the individual shall be limited to the same proportion of the applicable rate determined under this subparagraph as the number of hours worked during such month, rounded to the nearest eight hours, bears to 120 hours.

(C) In the case of an individual enrolled in a program of education consisting of flight training (regardless of the institution providing such program of education), an amount equal to—

(i) the lesser of—

(I) the actual net cost for in-State tuition and fees assessed by the institution concerned for the program of education after the application of—

(aa) any waiver of, or reduction in, tuition and fees; and

(bb) any scholarship, or other Federal, State, institutional, or employer-based aid or assistance (other than loans and any funds provided under section 401(b) of the Higher Education Act of 1965 [20 USCS § 1070a(b)]) that is provided directly to the institution and specifically designated for the sole purpose of defraying tuition and fees; or

(II) the amount equal to—

(aa) for the academic year beginning on August 1, 2011, $10,000; or

(bb) for an academic year beginning on any subsequent August 1, the amount for the previous academic year beginning on August 1 under this subclause, as increased by the percentage increase equal to the most recent percentage increase determined under section 3015(h) [38 USCS § 3015(h)], multiplied by—

(ii) either—

(I) in the case of an individual entitled to educational assistance by reason of paragraphs (1), (2), or (9) of section 3311(b) [38 USCS § 3311(b)], 100 percent; or

(II) in the case of an individual entitled to educational assistance by reason of paragraphs (3) through (8) of section 3311(b) [38 USCS § 3311(b)], the same percentage as would otherwise apply to the monthly amounts payable to the individual under paragraphs (2) through (7) of subsection (c).

(D) In the case of an individual enrolled in a program of education that is pursued

exclusively by correspondence (regardless of the institution providing such program of education), an amount equal to—
   (i) the lesser of—
      (I) the actual net cost for tuition and fees assessed by the institution concerned for the program of education after the application of—
         (aa) any waiver of, or reduction in, tuition and fees; and
         (bb) any scholarship, or other Federal, State, institutional, or employer-based aid or assistance (other than loans and any funds provided under section 401(b) of the Higher Education Act of 1965 [20 USCS § 1070a(b)]) that is provided directly to the institution and specifically designated for the sole purpose of defraying tuition and fees.
      (II) the amount equal to—
         (aa) for the academic year beginning on August 1, 2011, $8,500; or
         (bb) for an academic year beginning on any subsequent August 1, the amount for the previous academic year beginning on August 1 under this subclause, as increased by the percentage increase equal to the most recent percentage increase determined under section 3015(h) [38 USCS § 3015(h)], multiplied by—
   (ii) either—
      (I) in the case of an individual entitled to educational assistance by reason of paragraphs (1), (2), or (9) of section 3311(b) [38 USCS § 3311(b)], 100 percent; or
      (II) in the case of an individual entitled to educational assistance by reason of paragraphs (3) through (8) of section 3311(b) [38 USCS § 3311(b)], the same percentage as would otherwise apply to the monthly amounts payable to the individual under paragraphs (2) through (7) of subsection (c).

(4) Frequency of payment. (A) Quarter, semester, or term payments. Payment of the amounts payable under paragraph (3)(A)(i) for pursuit of a program of education shall be made for the entire quarter, semester, or term, as applicable, of the program of education.

(B) Monthly payments. Payment of the amounts payable under paragraphs (3)(A)(ii) and (3)(B)(i) for pursuit of a program of education shall be made on a monthly basis.

(C) Lump sum payments. (i) Payment for the amount payable under paragraphs (3)(A)(iii) and (3)(B)(ii) shall be paid to the individual for the first month of each quarter, semester, or term, as applicable, of the program education pursued by the individual.

   (ii) Payment of the amount payable under paragraph (3)(C) for pursuit of a program of education shall be made upon receipt of certification for training completed by the individual and serviced by the training facility.

(D) Quarterly payments. Payment of the amounts payable under paragraph (3)(D) for pursuit of a program of education shall be made quarterly on a pro rata basis for the lessons completed by the individual and serviced by the institution.

(5) Charge against entitlement for certificate and other non-college degree programs. (A) In general. In the case of amounts paid under paragraph (3)(A)(i) for pursuit of a program of education, the charge against entitlement to educational assistance under this chapter of the individual for whom such payment is made shall be one month for each of—
   (i) the amount so paid, divided by
   (ii) subject to subparagraph (B), the amount equal to one-twelfth of the amount applicable in the academic year in which the payment is made under paragraph (3)(A)(i)(II).

(B) Pro rata adjustment based on certain eligibility. If the amount otherwise payable with respect to an individual under paragraph (3)(A)(i) is subject to a percentage adjustment under paragraph (3)(A)(iv), the amount applicable with respect to the individual under subparagraph (A)(ii) shall be the amount otherwise determined pursuant to such subparagraph subject to a percentage adjustment equal to the percentage adjustment applicable with respect to the individual under paragraph (3)(A)(iv).

(h) Payment of established charges to educational institutions. Amounts payable under subsections (c)(1)(A) (and of similar amounts payable under paragraphs (2) through (7) of subsection (c)), (e)(2), and (f)(2)(A), and under subparagraphs (A)(i), (C), and (D) of subsection (g)(3), shall be paid directly to the educational institution concerned.

(i) Determination of housing stipend payments for academic years. Any monthly housing stipend payable under this section during the academic year beginning on August 1 of a calendar year shall be determined utilizing rates for basic allowances for housing payable under section 403 of title 37 in effect as of January 1 of such calendar year.

(Added June 30, 2008, P. L. 110-252, Title V, § 5003(a)(1), 122 Stat. 2363; June 24, 2009, P. L. 111-32, Title X, § 1002(b), 123 Stat. 1889; Oct. 13, 2010, P. L. 111-275, Title X, § 1001(g)(1)–(3), 124 Stat. 2896; Jan. 4, 2011, P. L. 111-377, Title I, §§ 102(a), (b), 103(a), (b), 104(a), (b), 105(a)–(c), 106(a), 112(a), 124 Stat. 4108, 4110, 4112, 4117, 4121.)

38 USCS § 3313

HISTORY; ANCILLARY LAWS AND DIRECTIVES

Explanatory notes:

A period has been enclosed in brackets in subsec. (e)(2)(A)(iii) to indicate the probable intent of Congress to delete it.

Effective date of section:

This section took effect on August 1, 2009, pursuant to § 5003(d) of Act June 30, 2008, P. L. 110-252, which appears as 10 USCS § 16163 note.

Amendments:

2009. Act June 24, 2009 (effective 8/1/2009, as provided by § 1002(d)(1) of such Act, which appears as 38 USCS § 3313 note), in subsec. (c)(1), in the introductory matter, substituted "paragraph (1), (2), or (9) of section 3311(b)" for "section 3311(b)(1) or 3311(b)(2)".

2010. Act Oct. 13, 2010, in subsec. (c)(1), substituted "higher learning" for "higher education" wherever appearing; in subsec. (d)(3), inserted "under" after "assistance"; and in subsec. (e)(2)(B), added the concluding period.

2011. Act Jan. 4, 2011 (effective 8/1/2011, as provided by § 106(b) of such Act, which appears as a note to this section), added subsec. (i).

Such Act further, purported to amend the section by substituting "higher learning" for "higher education" wherever appearing; however, because of prior amendments, such amendment could not be executed.

Such Act further, in subsec. (e)(2)(B), added the concluding period.

Such Act further (effective 60 days after enactment, and as provided by § 103(c) of such Act, which appears as a note to this section), in subsec. (e), substituted the subsection heading for one which read: "Programs of education pursued on active duty."; in para. (1), inserted "leading to a degree", and substituted para. (2) for one which read:

"(2) Amount of assistance. The amount of educational assistance payable under this chapter to an individual pursuing a program of education while on active duty is the lesser of—

"(A) the established charges which similarly circumstanced nonveterans enrolled in the program of education involved would be required to pay; or

"(B) the amount of the charges of the educational institution as elected by the individual in the manner specified in section 3014(b)(1).[.]".

Such Act further (effective 8/1/2011, and as provided by § 102(c) of such Act, which appears as a note to this section), in subsec. (c), substituted the subsection heading for one which read: "Amount of educational assistance.", in the introductory matter, inserted "leading to a degree at an institution of higher learning (as that term is defined in section 3452(f))", and in para. (1), substituted subpara. (A) for one which read: "(A) An amount equal to the established charges for the program of education, except that the amount payable under this subparagraph may not exceed the maximum amount of established charges regularly charged in-State students for full-time pursuit of approved programs of education for undergraduates by the public institution of higher learning offering approved programs of education for undergraduates in the State in which the individual is enrolled that has the highest rate of regularly-charged established charges for such programs of education among all public institutions of higher learning in such State offering such programs of education.", and in subpara. (B), redesignated cl. (ii) as cl. (iv), and substituted cls. (i)–(iii) for former cl. (i), which read: "(i) For each month the individual pursues the program of education (other than, in the case of assistance under this section only, a program of education offered through distance learning), a monthly housing stipend amount equal to the monthly amount of the basic allowance for housing payable under section 403 of title 37 for a member with dependents in pay grade E-5 residing in the military housing area that encompasses all or the majority portion of the ZIP code area in which is located the institution of higher learning at which the individual is enrolled.".

Such Act further (effective 8/1/2011, and applicable to amounts payable for educational assistance for pursuit of programs of education on or after that date, as provided by § 104(c) of such Act, which appears as a note to this section), in subsec. (f), in para. (1), inserted "whether a program of education pursued on active duty, a program of education leading to a degree, or a program of education other than a program of education leading to a degree", and in para. (2), in the introductory matter, inserted "covered by this subsection", and in subpara. (A), substituted cl. (i) for one which read: "(i) the established charges which similarly circumstanced nonveterans enrolled in the program of education involved would be required to pay; or".

Such Act further (effective 10/1/2011, and applicable to amounts payable for educational assistance for pursuit of programs of education on or after that date, as provided by § 105(d) of such Act, which appears as a note to this section), in subsec. (b), deleted "is offered by an institution of higher learning (as that term is defined in section 3452(f)) and" before "is approved"; deleted subsec. (h), which read:

"(h) Established charges defined. (1) In general. In this section, the term 'established charges', in the case of a program of education, means the actual charges (as determined pursuant to regulations prescribed by the Secretary) for tuition and fees which similarly circumstanced nonveterans enrolled in the program of education would be required to pay.

"(2) Basis of determination. Established charges shall be determined for purposes of this subsection on the following basis:

"(A) In the case of an individual enrolled in a program of education offered on a term, quarter, or semester basis, the tuition and fees charged the individual for the term, quarter, or semester.

"(B) In the case of an individual enrolled in a program of education not offered on a term, quarter, or semester basis, the tuition and fees charged the individual for the entire program of education.";

redesignated subsec. (g) as subsec. (h); inserted new subsec. (g); and in subsec. (h) as redesignated, inserted ", and under subparagraphs (A)(i), (C), and (D) of subsection (g)(3),".

Other provisions:

Effective date and applicability of amendments made by § 102 of Act Jan. 4, 2011. Act Jan. 4, 2011, P. L. 111-377, Title I, § 102(c), 124 Stat. 4110, provides:

"(1) In general. Except as provided in paragraph (2), the amendments made by this section [amending subsec. (c) of this section] shall take effect on August 1, 2011, and shall apply with respect to amounts payable for educational assistance for pursuit of programs of education on or after that date.

"(2) Stipend for distance learning on more than half-time basis. Clause (iii) of section 3313(c)(1)(B) of title 38, United States Code (as added by subsection (b)(2) of this section), shall take effect on October 1, 2011, and shall apply with respect to amounts payable for educational assistance for pursuit of programs of education as covered by such clause on or after that date.".

Effective date and applicability of amendments made by § 103 of Act Jan. 4, 2011. Act Jan. 4, 2011, P. L. 111-377, Title I, § 103(c), 124 Stat. 4112, provides:

"(1) In general. Except as provided in paragraph (2), the amendments made by this section [amending subsec. (e) of this section] shall take effect on the date that is 60 days after the date of the enactment of this Act, and shall apply with respect to amounts payable for educational assistance for pursuit of programs of education on or after such effective date.

"(2) Lump sum for books and other educational costs. Subparagraph (B) of section 3313(e)(2) of title 38, United States Code (as added by subsection (a)(2)(E) of this section), shall take effect on October 1, 2011, and shall apply with respect to amounts payable for educational assistance for pursuit of programs of education on or after that date.".

Effective date and applicability of amendments made by § 104 of Act Jan. 4, 2011. Act Jan. 4, 2011, P. L. 111-377, Title I, § 104(c), 124 Stat. 4112, provides: "The amendments made by this section [amending subsec. (f) of this section] shall take effect on August 1, 2011, and shall apply with respect to amounts payable for educational assistance for pursuit of programs of education on or after that date.".

Effective date and applicability of amendments made by § 105 of Act Jan. 4, 2011. Act Jan. 4, 2011, P. L. 111-377, Title I, § 105(d), 124 Stat. 4117, provides: "The amendments made by this section [amending this section] shall take effect on October 1, 2011, and shall apply with respect to amounts payable for educational assistance for pursuit of programs of education on or after that date.".

Effective date of amendments made by § 106 of Act Jan. 4, 2011. Act Jan. 4, 2011, P. L. 111-377, Title I, § 106(b), 124 Stat. 4118, provides: "The amendment made by subsection (a) [adding subsec. (i) of this section] shall take effect on August 1, 2011.".

Preservation of higher rates for tuition and fees for programs of education at non-public institutions of higher learning pursued by individuals enrolled in such programs prior to change in maximum amount. Act Aug. 3, 2011, P. L. 112-26, § 2, 125 Stat. 268, provides:

"(a) In general. Notwithstanding paragraph (1)(A)(ii) of section 3313(c) of title 38, United States Code (as amended by the Post-9/11 Veterans Educational Assistance Improvements Act of 2010 (Public Law 111-377)), the amount payable under that paragraph (or as appropriately adjusted under paragraphs (2) through (7) of that section) for tuition and fees for pursuit by an individual described in subsection (b) of an approved program of education at a non-public institution of higher learning during the period beginning on August 1, 2011, and ending on July 31, 2014, shall be the greater of—

"(1) $17,500; or

"(2) the established charges payable for the program of education determined using the table of the Department of Veterans Affairs entitled 'Post-9/11 GI Bill 2010–2011 Tuition and Fee In-State Maximums', published October 27, 2010 (75 Fed. Reg. 66193), as if that table applied to the pursuit of the program of education by that individual during that period.

"(b) Covered individuals. An individual described in this subsection is an individual entitled to educational assistance under chapter 33 of title 38, United States Code [38 USCS §§ 3301 et seq.], who, since January 4, 2011, has been enrolled in the same non-public institution of higher learning in a State in which—

"(1) the maximum amount of tuition per credit in the 2010–2011 academic year, as determined pursuant to the table referred to in subsection (a)(2), exceeded $700; and

"(2) the combined amount of tuition and fees for full-time attendance in the program of education in such academic year exceeded $17,500.

"(c) Definitions. In this section:

"(1) The term 'approved program of education' has the meaning given that term in section 3313(b) of title 38, United States Code.

"(2) The term 'established charges', with respect to a program of education, means the actual charges (as determined pursuant to regulations prescribed by the Secretary of Veterans

38 USCS § 3313   VETERANS' BENEFITS

Affairs on the basis of a full academic year) for tuition and fees which similarly circumstanced nonveterans enrolled in the program of education would be required to pay.

"(3) The term 'institution of higher learning' has the meaning given that term in section 3452(f) of title 38, United States Code.".

§ 3314. Tutorial assistance

(a) In general. Subject to subsection (b), an individual entitled to educational assistance under this chapter [38 USCS §§ 3301 et seq.] shall also be entitled to benefits provided an eligible veteran under section 3492 [38 USCS § 3492].

(b) Conditions. (1) In general. The provision of benefits under subsection (a) shall be subject to the conditions applicable to an eligible veteran under section 3492 [38 USCS § 3492].

(2) Certification. In addition to the conditions specified in paragraph (1), benefits may not be provided to an individual under subsection (a) unless the professor or other individual teaching, leading, or giving the course for which such benefits are provided certifies that—

    (A) such benefits are essential to correct a deficiency of the individual in such course; and

    (B) such course is required as a part of, or is prerequisite or indispensable to the satisfactory pursuit of, an approved program of education.

(c) Amount. (1) In general. The amount of benefits described in subsection (a) that are payable under this section may not exceed $100 per month, for a maximum of 12 months, or until a maximum of $1,200 is utilized.

(2) As additional assistance. The amount provided an individual under this subsection is in addition to the amounts of educational assistance paid the individual under section 3313 [38 USCS § 3313].

(d) No charge against entitlement. Any benefits provided an individual under subsection (a) are in addition to any other educational assistance benefits provided the individual under this chapter [38 USCS §§ 3301 et seq.].

(Added June 30, 2008, P. L. 110-252, Title V, § 5003(a)(1), 122 Stat. 2366.)

HISTORY; ANCILLARY LAWS AND DIRECTIVES

Effective date of section:

This section took effect on August 1, 2009, pursuant to § 5003(d) of Act June 30, 2008, P. L. 110-252, which appears as 10 USCS § 16163 note.

§ 3315. Licensure and certification tests

(a) In general. An individual entitled to educational assistance under this chapter [38 USCS §§ 3301 et seq.] shall also be entitled to payment for licensing or certification tests described in section 3452(b) [38 USCS § 3452(b)].

(b) Limitation on amount. The amount payable under subsection (a) for a licensing or certification test may not exceed the lesser of—

    (1) $2,000;

    (2) the fee charged for the test; or

    (3) the amount of entitlement available to the individual under this chapter at the time of payment for the test under this section.

(c) Charge against entitlement. The charge against an individual's entitlement under this chapter for payment for a licensing or certification test shall be determined at the rate of one month (rounded to the nearest whole month) for each amount paid that equals—

    (1) for the academic year beginning on August 1, 2011, $1,460; or

    (2) for an academic year beginning on any subsequent August 1, the amount for the previous academic year beginning on August 1 under this subsection, as increased by the percentage increase equal to the most recent percentage increase determined under section 3015(h) [38 USCS § 3015(h)].

(Added June 30, 2008, P. L. 110-252, Title V, § 5003(a)(1), 122 Stat. 2367; Jan. 4, 2011, P. L. 111-377, Title I, § 107(a), (b), 124 Stat. 4118.)

HISTORY; ANCILLARY LAWS AND DIRECTIVES

Effective date of section:

This section took effect on August 1, 2009, pursuant to § 5003(d) of Act June 30, 2008, P. L. 110-252, which appears as 10 USCS § 16163 note.

Amendments:

2011. Act Jan. 4, 2011 (effective on 8/1/2011, and applicable to licensure and certification tests taken on or after that date, as provided by § 107(c) of such Act, which appears as a note to this section), in subsec. (a), substituted "licensing or certification tests" for "one licensing or certification test"; in subsec. (b), in para. (1), deleted "or" following the concluding semicolon, in para. (2), substituted "; or" for a concluding period, and added para. (3); and substituted subsec. (c) for one which read: "(c) No charge against entitlement. Any amount paid an

READJUSTMENT BENEFITS   38 USCS § 3316

individual under subsection (a) is in addition to any other educational assistance benefits provided the individual under this chapter.''.

Other provisions:
Effective date and applicability of Jan. 4, 2011 amendments. Act Jan. 4, 2011, P. L. 111-377, Title I, § 107(c), 124 Stat. 4118, provides: "The amendments made by this section [amending this section] shall take effect on August 1, 2011, and shall apply with respect to licensure and certification tests taken on or after that date.''.

§ 3315A. National tests
(a) In general. An individual entitled to educational assistance under this chapter [38 USCS §§ 3301 et seq.] shall also be entitled to educational assistance for the following:

(1) A national test for admission to an institution of higher learning as described in the last sentence of section 3452(b) [38 USCS § 3452(b)].

(2) A national test providing an opportunity for course credit at an institution of higher learning as so described.

(b) Amount. The amount of educational assistance payable under this chapter [38 USCS §§ 3301 et seq.] for a test described in subsection (a) is the lesser of—

(1) the fee charged for the test; or

(2) the amount of entitlement available to the individual under this chapter [38 USCS §§ 3301 et seq.] at the time of payment for the test under this section.

(c) Charge against entitlement. The number of months of entitlement charged an individual under this chapter [38 USCS §§ 3301 et seq.] for a test described in subsection (a) shall be determined at the rate of one month (rounded to the nearest whole month) for each amount paid that equals—

(1) for the academic year beginning on August 1, 2011, $1,460; or

(2) for an academic year beginning on any subsequent August 1, the amount for the previous academic year beginning on August 1 under this subsection, as increased by the percentage increase equal to the most recent percentage increase determined under section 3015(h) [38 USCS § 3015(h)].

(Added Jan. 4, 2011, P. L. 111-377, Title I, § 108(a)(1), 124 Stat. 4118.)

HISTORY; ANCILLARY LAWS AND DIRECTIVES
Effective date of section:
This section took effect on Aug. 1, 2011, as provided by § 108(b) of Act Jan. 4, 2011, P. L. 111-377, which appears as a note to this section.

Other provisions:
Effective date and applicability of section. Act Jan. 4, 2011, P. L. 111-377, Title I, § 108(b), 124 Stat. 4118, provides: "The amendments made by this section [adding this section and amending the chapter analysis preceding 38 USCS § 3301] shall take effect on August 1, 2011, and shall apply with respect to national tests taken on or after that date.''.

§ 3316. Supplemental educational assistance: members with critical skills or specialty; members serving additional service
(a) Increased assistance for members with critical skills or specialty. (1) In general. In the case of an individual who has a skill or specialty designated by the Secretary concerned as a skill or specialty in which there is a critical shortage of personnel or for which it is difficult to recruit or, in the case of critical units, retain personnel, the Secretary concerned may increase the monthly amount of educational assistance otherwise payable to the individual under paragraph (1)(B) of section 3313(c) [38 USCS § 3313(c)], or under paragraphs (2) through (7) of such section (as applicable).

(2) Maximum amount of increase in assistance. The amount of the increase in educational assistance authorized by paragraph (1) may not exceed the amount equal to the monthly amount of increased basic educational assistance providable under section 3015(d)(1) [38 USCS § 3015(d)(1)] at the time of the increase under paragraph (1).

(b) Supplemental assistance for additional service. (1) In general. The Secretary concerned may provide for the payment to an individual entitled to educational assistance under this chapter [38 USCS §§ 3301 et seq.] of supplemental educational assistance for additional service authorized by subchapter III of chapter 30 [38 USCS §§ 3021 et seq.]. The amount so payable shall be payable as an increase in the monthly amount of educational assistance otherwise payable to the individual under paragraph (1)(B) of section 3313(c) [38 USCS § 3313(c)], or under paragraphs (2) through (7) of such section (as applicable).

(2) Eligibility. Eligibility for supplemental educational assistance under this subsection shall be determined in accordance with the provisions of subchapter III of chapter 30 [38 USCS §§ 3021 et seq.], except that any reference in such provisions to eligibility for basic educational assistance under a provision of subchapter II of chapter 30 [38 USCS §§ 3011 et seq.] shall be

treated as a reference to eligibility for educational assistance under the appropriate provision of this chapter [38 USCS §§ 3301 et seq.].

(3) Amount. The amount of supplemental educational assistance payable under this subsection shall be the amount equal to the monthly amount of supplemental educational assistance payable under section 3022 [38 USCS § 3022].

(c) **Continuation of increased educational assistance.** (1) In general. An individual who made an election to receive educational assistance under this chapter pursuant to section 5003(c)(1)(A) of the Post-9/11 Veterans Educational Assistance Act of 2008 (38 U.S.C. 3301 note) and who, at the time of the election, was entitled to increased educational assistance under section 3015(d) [38 USCS § 3015(d)] or section 16131(i) of title 10 shall remain entitled to increased educational assistance in the utilization of the individual's entitlement to educational assistance under this chapter [33 USCS §§ 3301 et seq.].

(2) Rate. The monthly rate of increased educational assistance payable to an individual under paragraph (1) shall be—

(A) the rate of educational assistance otherwise payable to the individual under section 3015(d) [38 USCS § 3015(d)] or section 16131(i) of title 10, as the case may be, had the individual not made the election described in paragraph (1), multiplied by

(B) the lesser of—

(i) 1.0; or

(ii) the number of course hours borne by the individual in pursuit of the program of education involved divided by the minimum number of course hours required for full-time pursuit of the program of education, rounded to the nearest multiple of 10.

(3) Frequency of payment. Payment of the amounts payable under paragraph (1) during pursuit of a program of education shall be made on a monthly basis.

(d) **Funding.** Payments for increased educational assistance under this section shall be made from the Department of Defense Education Benefits Fund under section 2006 of title 10 or from appropriations available to the Department of Homeland Security for that purpose, as applicable.

(e) **Regulations.** The Secretaries concerned shall administer this section in accordance with such regulations as the Secretary of Defense shall prescribe.

(Added June 30, 2008, P. L. 110-252, Title V, § 5003(a)(1), 122 Stat. 2367; Oct. 13, 2010, P. L. 111-275, Title X, § 1001(g)(4), (5), 124 Stat. 2896; Jan. 4, 2011, P. L. 111-377, Title I, § 109(a), (b)(1), 124 Stat. 4119.)

HISTORY; ANCILLARY LAWS AND DIRECTIVES

Effective date of section:
This section took effect on August 1, 2009, pursuant to § 5003(d) of Act June 30, 2008, P. L. 110-252, which appears as 10 USCS § 16163 note.

Amendments:
2010. Act Oct. 13, 2010, in subsec. (b), in para. (2), substituted "supplemental" for "supplement", and in para. (3), substituted "assistance payable under section" for "payable under section".

2011. Act Jan. 4, 2011 (effective on 8/1/2011, as provided by § 109(c) of such Act, which appears as 10 USCS § 2006 note), redesignated subsec. (c) as subsec. (e); and inserted new subsecs. (c) and (d).

§ 3317. Public-private contributions for additional educational assistance

(a) **Establishment of program.** In instances where the educational assistance provided pursuant to section 3313(c)(1)(A) [38 USCS § 3313(c)(1)(A)] does not cover the full cost of established charges (as specified in section 3313 [38 USCS § 3313]), the Secretary shall carry out a program under which colleges and universities can, voluntarily, enter into an agreement with the Secretary to cover a portion of those established charges not otherwise covered under section 3313(c)(1)(A) [38 USCS § 3313(c)(1)(A)], which contributions shall be matched by equivalent contributions toward such costs by the Secretary. The program shall only apply to covered individuals described in paragraphs (1) and (2) of section 3311(b) [38 USCS § 3311(b)].

(b) **Designation of program.** The program under this section shall be known as the "Yellow Ribbon G.I. Education Enhancement Program".

(c) **Agreements.** The Secretary shall enter into an agreement with each college or university seeking to participate in the program under this section. Each agreement shall specify the following:

(1) The manner (whether by direct grant, scholarship, or otherwise) of the contributions to be made by the college or university concerned.

(2) The maximum amount of the contribution to be made by the college or university concerned with respect to any particular individual in any given academic year.

(3) The maximum number of individuals for whom the college or university concerned will make contributions in any given academic year.

(4) Such other matters as the Secretary and the college or university concerned jointly consider appropriate.

(d) Matching contributions. (1) In general. In instances where the educational assistance provided an individual under section 3313(c)(1)(A) [38 USCS § 3313(c)(1)(A)] does not cover the full cost of tuition and mandatory fees at a college or university, the Secretary shall provide up to 50 percent of the remaining costs for tuition and mandatory fees if the college or university voluntarily enters into an agreement with the Secretary to match an equal percentage of any of the remaining costs for such tuition and fees.

(2) Use of appropriated funds. Amounts available to the Secretary under section 3324(b) [38 USCS § 3324(b)] for payment of the costs of this chapter [38 USCS §§ 3301 et seq.] shall be available to the Secretary for purposes of paragraph (1).

(e) Outreach. The Secretary shall make available on the Internet website of the Department available to the public a current list of the colleges and universities participating in the program under this section. The list shall specify, for each college or university so listed, appropriate information on the agreement between the Secretary and such college or university under subsection (c).
(Added June 30, 2008, P. L. 110-252, Title V, § 5003(a)(1), 122 Stat. 2368.)

HISTORY; ANCILLARY LAWS AND DIRECTIVES
Effective date of section:
This section took effect on August 1, 2009, pursuant to § 5003(d) of Act June 30, 2008, P. L. 110-252, which appears as 10 USCS § 16163 note.

Other provisions:
Pat Tillman Veterans' Scholarship Initiative. Act Oct. 13, 2010, P. L. 111-275, Title I, § 107, 124 Stat. 2872, provides:
"(a) Availability of scholarship information. By not later than June 1, 2011, the Secretary of Veterans Affairs shall include on the Internet website of the Department of Veterans Affairs a list of organizations that provide scholarships to veterans and their survivors and, for each such organization, a link to the Internet website of the organization.
"(b) Maintenance of scholarship information. The Secretary of Veterans Affairs shall make reasonable efforts to notify schools and other appropriate entities of the opportunity to be included on the Internet website of the Department of Veterans Affairs pursuant to subsection (a).".

§ 3318. Additional assistance: relocation or travel assistance for individual relocating or traveling significant distance for pursuit of a program of education

(a) Additional assistance. Each individual described in subsection (b) shall be paid additional assistance under this section in the amount of $500.

(b) Covered individuals. An individual described in this subsection is any individual entitled to educational assistance under this chapter [38 USCS §§ 3301 et seq.]—
　(1) who resides in a county (or similar entity utilized by the Bureau of the Census) with less than seven persons per square mile, according to the most recent decennial Census; and
　(2) who—
　　(A) physically relocates a distance of at least 500 miles in order to pursue a program of education for which the individual utilizes educational assistance under this chapter [38 USCS §§ 3301 et seq.]; or
　　(B) travels by air to physically attend an institution of higher learning for pursuit of such a program of education because the individual cannot travel to such institution by automobile or other established form of transportation due to an absence of road or other infrastructure.

(c) Proof of residence. For purposes of subsection (b)(1), an individual may demonstrate the individual's place of residence utilizing any of the following:
　(1) DD Form 214, Certification of Release or Discharge from Active Duty.
　(2) The most recent Federal income tax return.
　(3) Such other evidence as the Secretary shall prescribe for purposes of this section.

(d) Single payment of assistance. An individual is entitled to only one payment of additional assistance under this section.

(e) No charge against entitlement. Any amount paid an individual under this section is in addition to any other educational assistance benefits provided the individual under this chapter [38 USCS §§ 3301 et seq.].
(Added June 30, 2008, P. L. 110-252, Title V, § 5003(a)(1), 122 Stat. 2369; Oct. 13, 2010, P. L. 111-275, Title X, § 1001(g)(6), 124 Stat. 2896.)

HISTORY; ANCILLARY LAWS AND DIRECTIVES
Effective date of section:
This section took effect on August 1, 2009, pursuant to § 5003(d) of Act June 30, 2008, P. L. 110-252, which appears as 10 USCS § 16163 note.

38 USCS § 3318

Amendments:
2010. Act Oct. 13, 2010, in subsec. (b)(2)(B), substituted "higher learning" for "higher education".

§ 3319. Authority to transfer unused education benefits to family members
(a) In general. (1) Subject to the provisions of this section, the Secretary concerned may permit an individual described in subsection (b) who is entitled to educational assistance under this chapter [38 USCS §§ 3301 et seq.] to elect to transfer to one or more of the dependents specified in subsection (c) a portion of such individual's entitlement to such assistance, subject to the limitation under subsection (d).
(2) The purpose of the authority in paragraph (1) is to promote recruitment and retention in the uniformed services. The Secretary concerned may exercise the authority for that purpose when authorized by the Secretary of Defense in the national security interests of the United States.
(b) Eligible individuals. An individual referred to in subsection (a) is any member of the uniformed services who, at the time of the approval of the individual's request to transfer entitlement to educational assistance under this section, has completed at least—
   (1) six years of service in the armed forces and enters into an agreement to serve at least four more years as a member of the uniformed services; or
   (2) the years of service as determined in regulations pursuant to subsection (j).
(c) Eligible dependents. An individual approved to transfer an entitlement to educational assistance under this section may transfer the individual's entitlement as follows:
   (1) To the individual's spouse.
   (2) To one or more of the individual's children.
   (3) To a combination of the individuals referred to in paragraphs (1) and (2).
(d) Limitation on months of transfer. The total number of months of entitlement transferred by a individual under this section may not exceed 36 months. The Secretary of Defense may prescribe regulations that would limit the months of entitlement that may be transferred under this section to no less than 18 months.
(e) Designation of transferee. An individual transferring an entitlement to educational assistance under this section shall—
   (1) designate the dependent or dependents to whom such entitlement is being transferred;
   (2) designate the number of months of such entitlement to be transferred to each such dependent; and
   (3) specify the period for which the transfer shall be effective for each dependent designated under paragraph (1).
(f) Time for transfer; revocation and modification. (1) Time for transfer. Subject to the time limitation for use of entitlement under section 3321 [38 USCS § 3321] an individual approved to transfer entitlement to educational assistance under this section may transfer such entitlement only while serving as a member of the armed forces when the transfer is executed.
   (2) Modification or revocation. (A) In general. An individual transferring entitlement under this section may modify or revoke at any time the transfer of any unused portion of the entitlement so transferred.
      (B) Notice. The modification or revocation of the transfer of entitlement under this paragraph shall be made by the submittal of written notice of the action to both the Secretary concerned and the Secretary of Veterans Affairs.
   (3) Prohibition on treatment of transferred entitlement as marital property. Entitlement transferred under this section may not be treated as marital property, or the asset of a marital estate, subject to division in a divorce or other civil proceeding.
(g) Commencement of use. A dependent to whom entitlement to educational assistance is transferred under this section may not commence the use of the transferred entitlement until—
   (1) in the case of entitlement transferred to a spouse, the completion by the individual making the transfer of at least—
      (A) six years of service in the armed forces; or
      (B) the years of service as determined in regulations pursuant to subsection (j); or
   (2) in the case of entitlement transferred to a child, both—
      (A) the completion by the individual making the transfer of at least—
         (i) ten years of service in the armed forces; or
         (ii) the years of service as determined in regulations pursuant to subsection (j); and
      (B) either—
         (i) the completion by the child of the requirements of a secondary school diploma (or equivalency certificate); or
         (ii) the attainment by the child of 18 years of age.

(h) **Additional administrative matters.** (1) Use. The use of any entitlement to educational assistance transferred under this section shall be charged against the entitlement of the individual making the transfer at the rate of one month for each month of transferred entitlement that is used.

(2) Nature of transferred entitlement. Except as provided under subsection (e)(2) and subject to paragraphs (5) and (6)—

(A) in the case of entitlement transferred to a spouse under this section, the spouse is entitled to educational assistance under this chapter [38 USCS §§ 3301 et seq.] in the same manner as the individual from whom the entitlement was transferred; or

(B) in the case of entitlement transferred to a child under this section, the child is entitled to educational assistance under this chapter [38 USCS §§ 3301 et seq.] in the same manner as the individual from whom the entitlement was transferred as if the individual were not on active duty.

(3) Rate of payment. The monthly rate of educational assistance payable to a dependent to whom entitlement referred to in paragraph (2) is transferred under this section shall be payable—

(A) in the case of a spouse, at the same rate as such entitlement would otherwise be payable under this chapter [38 USCS §§ 3301 et seq.] to the individual making the transfer; or

(B) in the case of a child, at the same rate as such entitlement would otherwise be payable under this chapter [38 USCS §§ 3301 et seq.] to the individual making the transfer as if the individual were not on active duty.

(4) Death of transferor. The death of an individual transferring an entitlement under this section shall not affect the use of the entitlement by the dependent to whom the entitlement is transferred.

(5) Limitation on age of use by child transferees. (A) In general. A child to whom entitlement is transferred under this section may use the benefits transferred without regard to the 15-year delimiting date specified in section 3321 [38 USCS § 3321], but may not, except as provided in subparagraph (B), use any benefits so transferred after attaining the age of 26 years.

(B) Primary caregivers of seriously injured members of the Armed Forces and veterans. (i) In general. Subject to clause (ii), in the case of a child who, before attaining the age of 26 years, is prevented from pursuing a chosen program of education by reason of acting as the primary provider of personal care services for a veteran or member of the Armed Forces under section 1720G(a) [38 USCS § 1720G(a)], the child may use the benefits beginning on the date specified in clause (iii) for a period whose length is specified in clause (iv).

(ii) Inapplicability for revocation. Clause (i) shall not apply with respect to the period of an individual as a primary provider of personal care services if the period concludes with the revocation of the individual's designation as such a primary provider under section 1720G(a)(7)(D) [38 USCS § 1720G(a)(7)(D)].

(iii) Date for commencement of use. The date specified in this clause for the beginning of the use of benefits by a child under clause (i) is the later of—

(I) the date on which the child ceases acting as the primary provider of personal care services for the veteran or member concerned as described in clause (i);

(II) the date on which it is reasonably feasible, as determined under regulations prescribed by the Secretary, for the child to initiate or resume the use of benefits; or

(III) the date on which the child attains the age of 26 years.

(iv) Length of use. The length of the period specified in this clause for the use of benefits by a child under clause (i) is the length equal to the length of the period that—

(I) begins on the date on which the child begins acting as the primary provider of personal care services for the veteran or member concerned as described in clause (i); and

(II) ends on the later of—

(aa) the date on which the child ceases acting as the primary provider of personal care services for the veteran or member as described in clause (i); or

(bb) the date on which it is reasonably feasible, as so determined, for the child to initiate or resume the use of benefits.

(6) Scope of use by transferees. The purposes for which a dependent to whom entitlement is transferred under this section may use such entitlement shall include the pursuit and completion of the requirements of a secondary school diploma (or equivalency certificate).

(7) Additional administrative provisions. The administrative provisions of this chapter [38 USCS §§ 3301 et seq.] shall apply to the use of entitlement transferred under this section, except that the dependent to whom the entitlement is transferred shall be treated as the eligible individual for purposes of such provisions.

(i) Overpayment. (1) Joint and several liability. In the event of an overpayment of educational assistance with respect to a dependent to whom entitlement is transferred under this section, the dependent and the individual making the transfer shall be jointly and severally liable to the United States for the amount of the overpayment for purposes of section 3685 [38 USCS § 3685].

(2) Failure to complete service agreement. (A) In general. Except as provided in subparagraph (B), if an individual transferring entitlement under this section fails to complete the service agreed to by the individual under subsection (b)(1) in accordance with the terms of the agreement of the individual under that subsection, the amount of any transferred entitlement under this section that is used by a dependent of the individual as of the date of such failure shall be treated as an overpayment of educational assistance under paragraph (1).

(B) Exception. Subparagraph (A) shall not apply in the case of an individual who fails to complete service agreed to by the individual—

    (i) by reason of the death of the individual; or

    (ii) for a reason referred to in section 3311(c)(4).

(j) Regulations. (1) The Secretary of Defense, in coordination with the Secretary of Veterans Affairs, shall prescribe regulations for purposes of this section.

(2) Such regulations shall specify—

(A) the manner of authorizing the transfer of entitlements under this section;

(B) the eligibility criteria in accordance with subsection (b); and

(C) the manner and effect of an election to modify or revoke a transfer of entitlement under subsection (f)(2).

(k) [Deleted]

(Added June 30, 2008, P. L. 110-252, Title V, § 5003(a)(1), 122 Stat. 2369; Oct. 13, 2010, P. L. 111-275, Title X, § 1001(g)(7), 124 Stat. 2896; Jan. 4, 2011, P. L. 111-377, Title I, §§ 110(a), (b), 112(b), Title II, § 201(b), 124 Stat. 4120, 4122, 4123.)

HISTORY; ANCILLARY LAWS AND DIRECTIVES

Effective date of section:
This section took effect on August 1, 2009, pursuant to § 5003(d) of Act June 30, 2008, P. L. 110-252, which appears as 10 USCS § 16163 note.

Amendments:
2010. Act Oct. 13, 2010, in subsec. (b)(2), substituted "subsection (j)" for "section (k)".

2011. Act Jan. 4, 2011, purported to amend subsec. (b)(2) by substituting "subsection (j)" for "subsection (k)"; however, because of prior amendments, this amendment could not be executed.

Such Act further (effective on 8/1/2011, as provided by § 110(c) of such Act, which appears as a note to this section), in subsec. (a), substituted "(1) Subject to the provisions of this section, the Secretary concerned my permit" for "Subject to the provisions of this section, the Secretary of Defense may authorize the Secretary concerned, to promote recruitment and retention of members of the Armed Forces, to permit", and added para. (2); in subsec. (b), substituted "uniformed services" for "Armed Forces" in the introductory matter and para. (1); and deleted subsec. (k), which read:

"(k) Secretary concerned defined. Notwithstanding section 101(25), in this section, the term 'Secretary concerned' means—

    "(1) the Secretary of the Army with respect to matters concerning the Army;

    "(2) the Secretary of the Navy with respect to matters concerning the Navy or the Marine Corps;

    "(3) the Secretary of the Air Force with respect to matters concerning the Air Force; and

    "(4) the Secretary of Defense with respect to matters concerning the Coast Guard, or the Secretary of Homeland Security when it is not operating as a service in the Navy.".

Such Act further (effective on 8/1/2011, and applicable to preventions and suspension of pursuit of programs of education that commence on or after that date, as provided by § 201(d) of such Act, which appears as 38 USCS § 3031 note), in subsec. (h), substituted para. (5) for one which read: "Limitation on age of use by child transferees. A child to whom entitlement is transferred under this section may use the benefit without regard to the 15-year delimiting date, but may not use any entitlement so transferred after attaining the age of 26 years.".

Other provisions:
Effective date of Jan. 4, 2011 amendments. Act Jan. 4, 2011, P. L. 111-377, Title I, § 110(c), 124 Stat. 4120, provides: "The amendments made by this section [amending this section] shall take effect on August 1, 2011.".

SUBCHAPTER III. ADMINISTRATIVE PROVISIONS

§ 3321. Time limitation for use of and eligibility for entitlement

(a) In general. Except as provided in this section, the period during which an individual entitled to educational assistance under this chapter [38 USCS §§ 3301 et seq.] may use such individual's entitlement expires at the end of the 15-year period beginning on the date of such individual's last discharge or release from active duty.

(b) Exceptions. (1) Applicability of section 3031 [38 USCS § 3031] to running of period. Subsections (b), (c), and (d) of section 3031 [38 USCS § 3031] shall apply with respect to the running of the 15-year period described in subsection (a) of this section in the same manner as such subsections apply under section 3031 [38 USCS § 3031] with respect to the running of the 10-year period described in section 3031(a) [38 USCS § 3031(a)].

(2) Applicability of section 3031 to termination. Section 3031(f) [38 USCS § 3031(f)] shall apply with respect to the termination of an individual's entitlement to educational assistance under this chapter [38 USCS §§ 3301 et seq.] in the same manner as such section applies to the termination of an individual's entitlement to educational assistance under chapter 30 [38 USCS §§ 3001 et seq.], except that, in the administration of such section for purposes of this chapter [38 USCS §§ 3301 et seq.], the reference to section 3013 [38 USCS § 3013] shall be deemed to be a reference to section 3312 of this title [38 USCS § 3312].

(3) Determination of last discharge or release. For purposes of subsection (a), an individual's last discharge or release from active duty shall not include any discharge or release from a period of active duty of less than 90 days of continuous service, unless the individual is discharged or released as described in section 3311(b)(2) [38 USCS § 3311(b)(2)].

(4) Applicability to children of deceased members. The period during which an individual entitled to educational assistance by reason of section 3311(b)(9) [38 USCS § 3311(b)(9)] may use such individual's entitlement expires at the end of the 15-year period beginning on the date of such individual's eighteenth birthday.

(Added June 30, 2008, P. L. 110-252, Title V, § 5003(a)(1), 122 Stat. 2373; June 24, 2009, P. L. 111-32, Title X, § 1002(c), 123 Stat. 1889; Oct. 13, 2010, P. L. 111-275, Title X, § 1001(g)(8), 124 Stat. 2896.)

HISTORY; ANCILLARY LAWS AND DIRECTIVES

Effective date of section:
This section took effect on August 1, 2009, pursuant to § 5003(d) of Act June 30, 2008, P. L. 110-252, which appears as 10 USCS § 16163 note.

Amendments:
2009. Act June 24, 2009 (effective 8/1/2009, as provided by § 1002(d)(1) of such Act, which appears as 38 USCS § 3311 note), added subsec. (b)(4).
2010. Act Oct. 13, 2010, in subsec. (b)(2), substituted "section 3312 of this title" for "3312".

CODE OF FEDERAL REGULATIONS
Office of the Secretary of Defense—Post-9/11 GI Bill, 32 CFR 65.1 et seq.

§ 3322. Bar to duplication of educational assistance benefits

(a) In general. An individual entitled to educational assistance under this chapter [38 USCS §§ 3301 et seq.] who is also eligible for educational assistance under chapter 30, 31, 32, or 35 of this title [38 USCS §§ 3001 et seq., 3101 et seq., 3201 et seq., or 3500 et seq.], chapter 107, 1606, or 1607 or section 510 of title 10 [10 USCS §§ 2151 et seq., 16131 et seq., 16161 et seq., or 510], or the provisions of the Hostage Relief Act of 1980 (Public Law 96-449; 5 U.S.C. 5561 note) may not receive assistance under two or more such programs concurrently, but shall elect (in such form and manner as the Secretary may prescribe) under which chapter or provisions to receive educational assistance.

(b) Inapplicability of service treated under educational loan repayment programs. A period of service counted for purposes of repayment of an education loan under chapter 109 of title 10 [10 USCS §§ 2171 et seq.] may not be counted as a period of service for entitlement to educational assistance under this chapter [38 USCS §§ 3301 et seq.].

(c) Service in Selected Reserve. An individual who serves in the Selected Reserve may receive credit for such service under only one of this chapter [38 USCS §§ 3301 et seq.], chapter 30 of this title [38 USCS §§ 3001 et seq.], and chapters 1606 and 1607 of title 10 [10 USCS §§ 16131 et seq. and 16161 et seq.], and shall elect (in such form and manner as the Secretary may prescribe) under which chapter such service is to be credited.

(d) Additional coordination matters. In the case of an individual entitled to educational assistance under chapter 30, 31, 32, or 35 of this title [38 USCS §§ 3001 et seq., 3101 et seq., 3201 et seq., or 3500 et seq.], chapter 107, 1606, or 1607 of title 10 [10 USCS §§ 2151 et seq., 16131 et seq., or 16161 et seq.], or the provisions of the Hostage Relief Act of 1980 [5 USCS § 5561 note], or making contributions toward entitlement to educational assistance under chapter 30 of this title [38 USCS §§ 3001 et seq.], as of August 1, 2009, coordination of entitlement to educational assistance under this chapter [38 USCS §§ 3301 et seq.], on the one hand, and such chapters or provisions, on the other, shall be governed by the provisions of section 5003(c) of the Post-9/11 Veterans Educational Assistance Act of 2008 [38 USCS § 3301 note].

(e) Bar to concurrent receipt of transferred education benefits and Marine Gunnery Sergeant John David Fry Scholarship Assistance. An individual entitled to educational assistance under both sections 3311(b)(9) and 3319 [38 USCS §§ 3311(b)(9) and 3319] may not receive assistance under both provisions concurrently, but shall elect (in such form and manner as the Secretary may prescribe) under which provision to receive educational assistance.

(f) Bar to receipt of compensation and pension and Marine Gunnery Sergeant John David Fry Scholarship Assistance. The commencement of a program of education under section 3311(b)(9) [38 USCS § 3311(b)(9)] shall be a bar to the following:

(1) Subsequent payments of dependency and indemnity compensation or pension based on the death of a parent to an eligible person over the age of 18 years by reason of pursuing a course in an educational institution.

(2) Increased rates, or additional amounts, of compensation, dependency and indemnity compensation, or pension because of such a person, whether eligibility is based upon the death of the parent.

(g) Bar to concurrent receipt of transferred education benefits. A spouse or child who is entitled to educational assistance under this chapter [38 USCS §§ 3301 et seq.] based on a transfer of entitlement from more than one individual under section 3319 [38 USCS § 3319] may not receive assistance based on transfers from more than one such individual concurrently, but shall elect (in such form and manner as the Secretary may prescribe) under which source to utilize such assistance at any one time.

(h) Bar to duplication of eligibility based on a single event or period of service. (1) Active-duty service. An individual with qualifying service in the Armed Forces that establishes eligibility on the part of such individual for educational assistance under this chapter [38 USCS §§ 3301 et seq.], chapter 30 or 32 of this title [38 USCS §§ 3001 et seq. and 3201 et seq.], and chapter 1606 or 1607 of title 10, shall elect (in such form and manner as the Secretary may prescribe) under which authority such service is to be credited.

(2) Eligibility for educational assistance based on parent's service. A child of a member of the Armed Forces who, on or after September 11, 2001, dies in the line of duty while serving on active duty, who is eligible for educational assistance under either section 3311(b)(9) or chapter 35 of this title [38 USCS § 3311(b)(9) or §§ 3500 et seq.] based on the parent's death may not receive such assistance under both this chapter and chapter 35 of this title [38 USCS §§ 3301 et seq. and 3500 et seq.], but shall elect (in such form and manner as the Secretary may prescribe) under which chapter to receive such assistance.

(Added June 30, 2008, P. L. 110-252, Title V, § 5003(a)(1), 122 Stat. 2373; Jan. 4, 2011, P. L. 111-377, Title I, § 111(a)–(d), Title II, § 202(a), 124 Stat. 4120, 4124.)

HISTORY; ANCILLARY LAWS AND DIRECTIVES

Effective date of section:
This section took effect on August 1, 2009, pursuant to § 5003(d) of Act June 30, 2008, P. L. 110-252, which appears as 10 USCS § 16163 note.

Amendments:
2011. Act Jan. 4, 2011 (effective on 8/1/2011, as provided by § 111(e) of such Act, which appears as a note to this section), added subsecs. (e)–(h).

Such Act further (effective on 8/1/2011, as provided by § 202(c) of such Act, which appears as a note to this section), in subsec. (a), inserted "or section 510".

Other provisions:
Effective date of amendments made by § 111 of Act Jan. 4, 2011. Act Jan. 4, 2011, P. L. 111-377, Title I, § 111(e), 124 Stat. 4121, provides: "The amendments made by this section [adding subsecs. (e)–(h) of this section] shall take effect on August 1, 2011.".

Effective date of amendments made by § 202 of Act Jan. 4, 2011. Act Jan. 4, 2011, P. L. 111-377, Title II, § 202(c), 124 Stat. 4124, provides: "The amendments made by this section [amending 38 USCS §§ 3322(a) and 3681(b)(2)] shall take effect on August 1, 2011.".

§ 3323. Administration

(a) In general. (1) In general. Except as otherwise provided in this chapter [38 USCS §§ 3301 et seq.], the provisions specified in sections 3034(a)(1) and 3680(c) [38 USCS §§ 3034(a)(1) and 3680(c)] shall apply to the provision of educational assistance under this chapter [38 USCS §§ 3301 et seq.].

(2) Special rule. In applying the provisions referred to in paragraph (1) to an individual entitled to educational assistance under this chapter [38 USCS §§ 3301 et seq.] for purposes of this section, the reference in such provisions to the term "eligible veteran" shall be deemed to refer to an individual entitled to educational assistance under this chapter [38 USCS §§ 3301 et seq.].

(3) Rule for applying section 3474. In applying section 3474 [38 USCS § 3474] to an individual entitled to educational assistance under this chapter [38 USCS §§ 3301 et seq.] for purposes of this section, the reference in such section 3474 to the term "educational assistance allowance" shall be deemed to refer to educational assistance payable under section 3313 [38 USCS § 3313].

(4) Rule for applying section 3482. In applying section 3482(g) [38 USCS § 3482(g)] to an individual entitled to educational assistance under this chapter [38 USCS §§ 3301 et seq.] for purposes of this section—

(A) the first reference to the term "educational assistance allowance" in such section 3482(g) [38 USCS § 3482(g)] shall be deemed to refer to educational assistance payable under section 3313 [38 USCS § 3313]; and

(B) the first sentence of paragraph (1) of such section 3482(g) [38 USCS § 3482(g)] shall be applied as if such sentence ended with "equipment".

(b) Information on benefits. (1) Timing for providing. The Secretary shall provide the information described in paragraph (2) to each member of the Armed Forces at such times as the Secretary and the Secretary of Defense shall jointly prescribe in regulations.

(2) Description of information. The information described in this paragraph is information on benefits, limitations, procedures, eligibility requirements (including time-in-service requirements), and other important aspects of educational assistance under this chapter [38 USCS §§ 3301 et seq.], including application forms for such assistance under section 5102 [38 USCS § 5102].

(3) To whom provided. The Secretary of Veterans Affairs shall furnish the information and forms described in paragraph (2), and other educational materials on educational assistance under this chapter [38 USCS §§ 3301 et seq.], to educational institutions, training establishments, military education personnel, and such other persons and entities as the Secretary considers appropriate.

(c) Regulations. (1) In general. The Secretary shall prescribe regulations for the administration of this chapter [38 USCS §§ 3301 et seq.].

(2) Uniformity. Any regulations prescribed by the Secretary of Defense for purposes of this chapter [38 USCS §§ 3301 et seq.] shall apply uniformly across the Armed Forces.

(Added June 30, 2008, P. L. 110-252, Title V, § 5003(a)(1), 122 Stat. 2374; Jan. 4, 2011, P. L. 111-377, Title I, § 112(c), 124 Stat. 4122.)

HISTORY; ANCILLARY LAWS AND DIRECTIVES

Effective date of section:
This section took effect on August 1, 2009, pursuant to § 5003(d) of Act June 30, 2008, P. L. 110-252, which appears as 10 USCS § 16163 note.

Amendments:
2011. Act Jan. 4, 2011, in subsec. (a)(1), substituted "sections 3034(a)(1) and 3680(c)" for "section 3034(a)(1)".

§ 3324. Allocation of administration and costs

(a) Administration. Except as otherwise provided in this chapter [38 USCS §§ 3301 et seq.], the Secretary shall administer the provision of educational assistance under this chapter [38 USCS §§ 3301 et seq.].

(b) Costs. Payments for entitlement to educational assistance earned under this chapter [38 USCS §§ 3301 et seq.] shall be made from funds appropriated to, or otherwise made available to, the Department for the payment of readjustment benefits.

(Added June 30, 2008, P. L. 110-252, Title V, § 5003(a)(1), 122 Stat. 2375.)

HISTORY; ANCILLARY LAWS AND DIRECTIVES

Effective date of section:
This section took effect on August 1, 2009, pursuant to § 5003(d) of Act June 30, 2008, P. L. 110-252, which appears as 10 USCS § 16163 note.

§ 3325. Reporting requirement

(a) In general. For each academic year—

(1) the Secretary of Defense shall submit to Congress a report on the operation of the program provided for in this chapter; and

(2) the Secretary shall submit to Congress a report on the operation of the program provided for in this chapter [38 USCS §§ 3301 et seq.] and the program provided for under chapter 35 of this title [38 USCS §§ 3500 et seq.].

(b) Contents of Secretary of Defense reports. The Secretary of Defense shall include in each report submitted under this section—

(1) information—
(A) indicating the extent to which the benefit levels provided under this chapter [38 USCS §§ 3301 et seq.] are adequate to achieve the purposes of inducing individuals to enter and remain in the Armed Forces and of providing an adequate level of financial assistance to help meet the cost of pursuing a program of education;
(B) indicating whether it is necessary for the purposes of maintaining adequate levels of well-qualified active-duty personnel in the Armed Forces to continue to offer the opportunity for educational assistance under this chapter [38 USCS §§ 3301 et seq.] to individuals who have not yet entered active-duty service; and
(C) describing the efforts under section 3323(b) of this title [38 USCS § 3323(b)] to inform members of the Armed Forces of the active duty service requirements for entitlement to educational assistance under this chapter [38 USCS §§ 3301 et seq.] and the results from such efforts; and
(2) such recommendations for administrative and legislative changes regarding the provision of educational assistance to members of the Armed Forces and veterans, and their dependents, as the Secretary of Defense considers appropriate.
(c) **Contents of Secretary of Veterans Affairs reports.** The Secretary shall include in each report submitted under this section—
(1) information concerning the level of utilization of educational assistance and of expenditures under this chapter [38 USCS §§ 3301 et seq.] and under chapter 35 of this title [38 USCS §§ 3500 et seq.];
(2) appropriate student outcome measures, such as the number of credit hours, certificates, degrees, and other qualifications earned by beneficiaries under this chapter [38 USCS §§ 3301 et seq.] and chapter 35 of this title [38 USCS §§ 3500 et seq.] during the academic year covered by the report; and
(3) such recommendations for administrative and legislative changes regarding the provision of educational assistance to members of the Armed Forces and veterans, and their dependents, as the Secretary considers appropriate.
(d) **Termination.** No report shall be required under this section after January 1, 2021.
(Added Aug. 6, 2012, P. L. 112-154, Title IV, § 402(a)(1), 126 Stat. 1188.)

HISTORY; ANCILLARY LAWS AND DIRECTIVES

Other provisions:
Deadline for submittal of first report. Act Aug. 6, 2012, P. L. 112-154, Title IV, § 402(a)(3), 126 Stat. 1189, provides: "The first reports required under section 3325 of title 38, United States Code, as added by paragraph (1), shall be submitted by not later than November 1, 2013.".

CHAPTER 34. VETERANS' EDUCATIONAL ASSISTANCE

SUBCHAPTER I. PURPOSE—DEFINITIONS

§ 3451. Purpose

CODE OF FEDERAL REGULATIONS

Department of Veterans Affairs—Nondiscrimination in federally-assisted programs of the Department of Veterans Affairs-effectuation of Title VI of the Civil Rights Act of 1964, 38 CFR 18.1 et seq.
Department of Veterans Affairs—Delegation of responsibility in connection with Title VI, Civil Rights Act of 1964, 38 CFR 18a.1 et seq.
Department of Veterans Affairs—Practice and procedure under Title VI of the Civil Rights Act of 1964 and Part 18 of this chapter, 38 CFR 18b.1 et seq.
Department of Veterans Affairs—Vocational rehabilitation and education, 38 CFR 21.1 et seq.
Department of Veterans Affairs—Loan guaranty and vocational rehabilitation and counseling programs, 48 CFR 871.100 et seq.

RESEARCH GUIDE

Am Jur:
77 Am Jur 2d, Veterans and Veterans' Laws §§ 124, 135.

Other Treatises:
1 Rapp, Education Law (Matthew Bender), ch 5, Funding, Support and Finances of Education § 5.08.

§ 3452. Definitions

For the purposes of this chapter [38 USCS §§ 3451 et seq.] and chapter 36 of this title [38 USCS §§ 3670 et seq.]—

Readjustment Benefits 38 USCS § 3452

(a)(1) The term "eligible veteran" means any veteran who—
 (A) served on active duty for a period of more than 180 days, any part of which occurred after January 31, 1955, and before January 1, 1977, and was discharged or released therefrom under conditions other than dishonorable;
 (B) [Unchanged]
 (C) was discharged or released from active duty, any part of which was performed after January 31, 1955, and before January 1, 1977, or following entrance into active service from an enlistment provided for under subparagraph (B), because of a service-connected disability.

(2) The requirement of discharge or release, prescribed in subparagraph (A) or (B) of paragraph (1), shall be waived in the case of any individual who served more than 180 days in an active duty status for so long as such individual continues on active duty without a break therein.

(3) For purposes of paragraph (1)(A) and section 3461(a) [38 USCS § 3461(a)], the term "active duty" does not include any period during which an individual (A) was assigned full time by the Armed Forces to a civilian institution for a course of education which was substantially the same as established courses offered to civilians, (B) served as a cadet or midshipman at one of the service academies, or (C) served under the provisions of section 12103(d) of title 10 [10 USCS § 12103(d)] pursuant to an enlistment in the Army National Guard or the Air National Guard or as a Reserve for service in the Army Reserve, Navy Reserve, Air Force Reserve, Marine Corps Reserve, or Coast Guard Reserve unless at some time subsequent to the completion of such period of active duty for training such individual served on active duty for a consecutive period of one year or more (not including any service as a cadet or midshipman at one of the service academies).

(b) The term "program of education" means any curriculum or any combination of unit courses or subjects pursued at an educational institution which is generally accepted as necessary to fulfill requirements for the attainment of a predetermined and identified educational, professional, or vocational objective. Such term also means any curriculum of unit courses or subjects pursued at an educational institution which fulfill requirements for the attainment of more than one predetermined and identified educational, professional, or vocational objective if all the objectives pursued are generally recognized as being reasonably related to a single career field. Such term also means any unit course or subject, or combination of courses or subjects, pursued by an eligible veteran at an educational institution, required by the Administrator of the Small Business Administration as a condition to obtaining financial assistance under the provisions of section 7(i)(1) of the Small Business Act (15 U.S.C. 636(i)(1)). Such term also includes licensing or certification tests, the successful completion of which demonstrates an individual's possession of the knowledge or skill required to enter into, maintain, or advance in employment in a predetermined and identified vocation or profession, provided such tests and the licensing or credentialing organizations or entities that offer such tests are approved by the Secretary in accordance with section 3689 of this title [38 USCS § 3689]. Such term also includes any course, or combination of courses, offered by a qualified provider of entrepreneurship courses. Such term also includes national tests for admission to institutions of higher learning or graduate schools (such as the Scholastic Aptitude Test (SAT), Law School Admission Test (LSAT), Graduate Record Exam (GRE), and Graduate Management Admission Test (GMAT)) and national tests providing an opportunity for course credit at institutions of higher learning (such as the Advanced Placement (AP) exam and College-Level Examination Program (CLEP)).

(c) The term "educational institution" means any public or private elementary school, secondary school, vocational school, correspondence school, business school, junior college, teachers' college, college, normal school, professional school, university, or scientific or technical institution, or other institution furnishing education for adults. Such term includes any entity that provides training required for completion of any State-approved alternative teacher certification program (as determined by the Secretary). Such term also includes any private entity (that meets such requirements as the Secretary may establish) that offers, either directly or under an agreement with another entity (that meets such requirements), a course or courses to fulfill requirements for the attainment of a license or certificate generally recognized as necessary to obtain, maintain, or advance in employment in a profession or vocation in a high technology occupation (as determined by the Secretary). Such term also includes any qualified provider of entrepreneurship courses.

(d) [Unchanged]

(e) The term "training establishment" means any of the following:
 (1) An establishment providing apprentice or other on-job training, including those under the supervision of a college or university or any State department of education.
 (2) An establishment providing self-employment on-job training consisting of full-time training for a period of less than six months that is needed or accepted for purposes of obtaining licensure to engage in a self-employment occupation or required for ownership and operation of a franchise that is the objective of the training.

(3) A State board of vocational education.
(4) A Federal or State apprenticeship registration agency.
(5) The sponsor of a program of apprenticeship.
(6) An agency of the Federal Government authorized to supervise such training.

(f), (g) [Unchanged]

(h) The term "qualified provider of entrepreneurship courses" means any small business development center described in section 21 of the Small Business Act (15 U.S.C. 648), insofar as such center offers, sponsors, or cosponsors an entrepreneurship course, as that term is defined in section 3675(c)(2) [38 USCS § 3675(c)(2)].

(As amended Nov. 1, 2000, P. L. 106-419, Title I, Subtitle C, § 122(a), 114 Stat. 1833; June 5, 2001, P. L. 107-14, § 8(a)(4), 115 Stat. 34; Dec. 27, 2001, P. L. 107-103, Title I, § 110(a), 115 Stat. 986; Dec. 16, 2003, P. L. 108-183, Title III, §§ 301(a), 305(c)–(e), 117 Stat. 2658, 2660; Dec. 10, 2004, P. L. 108-454, Title I, §§ 106(a), 110(a), 118 Stat. 3602, 3605; Jan. 6, 2006, P. L. 109-163, Div A, Title V, Subtitle B, § 515(e)(4), 119 Stat. 3236; Jan. 2, 2013, P. L. 112-239, Div A, Title XVI, Subtitle D, Part IX, § 1699(c)(2), 126 Stat. 2092.)

HISTORY; ANCILLARY LAWS AND DIRECTIVES

Amendments:

2000. Act Nov. 1, 2000 (effective 3/1/01 and applicable with respect to licensing and certification tests approved on or after such date, as provided by § 122(d) of such Act, which appears as 38 USCS § 3032 note), in subsec. (b), added the sentence beginning "Such term also includes licensing or . . . .".

2001. Act June 5, 2001, in subsec. (a), in para. (1), in subpara. (A), deleted "or" following the concluding semicolon and, in subpara. (C), substituted "subparagraph (B)" for "clause (B) of this paragraph", in para. (2), substituted "subparagraph (A) or (B) of paragraph (1)" for "paragraph (1)(A) or (B)" and substituted "180 days" for "one hundred and eighty days" and, in para. (3), substituted "section 12103(d) of title 10" for "section 511(d) of title 10"; and, in subsec. (e), substituted "the Act of August 16, 1937, popularly known as the 'National Apprenticeship Act' (29 U.S.C. 50 et seq.)," for "chapter 4C of title 29,".

Act Dec. 27, 2001 (applicable as provided by § 110(b) of such Act, which appears as a note to this section), in subsec. (c), added the sentence beginning "Such term also includes . . . .".

2003. Act Dec. 16, 2003 (applicable as provided by § 305(f) of such Act, which appears as a note to this section), in subsec. (b), added the sentence beginning "Such term also includes any course . . . ."; in subsec. (c), added the sentence beginning "Such term also includes any qualified provider . . . ."; and added subsec. (h).

Such Act further (effective six months after enactment and applicable to self-employment on-job training approved and pursued on or after that date, as provided by § 301(b) of such Act, which appears as a note to this section), in subsec. (e), substituted "means any of the following:" and paras. (1)–(6) for "means any establishment providing apprentice or other training on the job, including those under the supervision of a college or university or any State department of education, or any State apprenticeship agency, or any State board of vocational education, or any joint apprenticeship committee, or the Bureau of Apprenticeship and Training established pursuant to the Act of August 16, 1937, popularly known as the 'National Apprenticeship Act' (29 U.S.C. 50 et seq.), or any agency of the Federal Government authorized to supervise such training.".

2004. Act Dec. 10, 2004, in subsec. (b), added the sentence beginning "Such term also includes national tests . . . ."; and, in subsec. (e), substituted para. (5) for one which read: "(5) A joint apprenticeship committee established pursuant to the Act of August 16, 1937, popularly known as the 'National Apprenticeship Act' (29 U.S.C. 50 et seq.).".

2006. Act Jan. 6, 2006, in subsec. (a)(3)(C), substituted "Navy Reserve" for "Naval Reserve".

2013. Act Jan. 2, 2013, substituted subsec. (h) for one which read:

"(h) The term 'qualified provider of entrepreneurship courses' means any of the following entities insofar as such entity offers, sponsors, or cosponsors an entrepreneurship course (as defined in section 3675(c)(2) of this title):

"(1) Any small business development center described in section 21 of the Small Business Act (15 U.S.C. 648).

"(2) The National Veterans Business Development Corporation (established under section 33 of the Small Business Act (15 U.S.C. 657c)).".

Other provisions:

Application of Dec. 27, 2001 amendments. Act Dec. 27, 2001, P. L. 107-103, Title I, § 110(b), 115 Stat. 986, provides: "The amendments made by subsection (a) [amending 38 USCS §§ 3452(c) and 3501(a)(6)] shall apply to enrollments in courses beginning on or after the date of the enactment of this Act.".

Effective date and applicability of amendment made by § 301(a) of Act Dec. 16, 2003. Act Dec. 16, 2003, P. L. 108-183, Title III, § 301(b), 117 Stat. 2658, provides: "The amendment made by subsection (a) [amending subsec. (e) of this section] shall take effect on the date that is six months after the date of the enactment of this Act and shall apply to self-employment on-job training approved and pursued on or after that date.".

READJUSTMENT BENEFITS
38 USCS § 3462

Applicability of amendments made by § 305 of Act Dec. 16, 2003. Act Dec. 16, 2003, P. L. 108-183, Title III, § 305(f), 117 Stat. 2661, provides: "The amendments made by this section [amending 38 USCS §§ 3452, 3471, and 3675] shall apply to courses approved by State approving agencies after the date of the enactment of this Act.".

CODE OF FEDERAL REGULATIONS

Office of Postsecondary Education, Department of Education—Talent search, 34 CFR 643.1 et seq.
Office of Postsecondary Education, Department of Education—Educational opportunity centers, 34 CFR 644.1 et seq.
Office of Postsecondary Education, Department of Education—Upward Bound program, 34 CFR 645.1 et seq.
Department of Veterans Affairs—Adjudication, 38 CFR 3.1 et seq.

INTERPRETIVE NOTES AND DECISIONS

2. Eligible veteran

Although veteran was eligible for educational-assistance benefits under 38 USCS § 3452(a), when those benefits were terminated for all veterans, he was disqualified from conversion into eligibility for benefits under 38 USCS ch. 30 by 38 USCS § 3011(c)(2) and 38 CFR § 21.7044(c) because he did not meet exception set forth under § 21.7044(d) where he was commissioned upon graduating from military academy after December 1976 and before completing military service needed to establish such entitlement. Burton v Nicholson (2005) 19 Vet App 249, 2005 US App Vet Claims LEXIS 517.

SUBCHAPTER II. ELIGIBILITY AND ENTITLEMENT

§ 3461. Eligibility; entitlement; duration

(a) Entitlement. Except as provided in subsection (c) and in the second sentence of this subsection, each eligible veteran shall be entitled to educational assistance under this chapter [38 USCS §§ 3451 et seq.] or chapter 36 [38 USCS §§ 3670 et seq.] for a period of one and one-half months (or the equivalent thereof in part-time educational assistance) for each month or fraction thereof of the veteran's service on active duty after January 31, 1955. If an eligible veteran has served a period of 18 months or more on active duty after January 31, 1955, and has been released from such service under conditions that would satisfy the veteran's active duty obligation, the veteran shall be entitled to educational assistance under this chapter [38 USCS §§ 3451 et seq.] or chapter 36 [38 USCS §§ 3670 et seq.] for a period of 45 months (or the equivalent thereof in part-time educational assistance). In the case of any person serving on active duty on December 31, 1976, or a person whose eligibility is based on section 3452(a)(1)(B) of this chapter, the ending date for computing such person's entitlement shall be the date of such person's first discharge or release from active duty after December 31, 1976.

(b) Entitlement limitations. Whenever the period of entitlement under this section of an eligible veteran who is enrolled in an educational institution regularly operated on the quarter or semester system ends during a quarter or semester, such period shall be extended to the termination of such unexpired quarter or semester. In educational institutions not operated on the quarter or semester system, whenever the period of eligibility ends after a major portion of the course is completed such period shall be extended to the end of the course or for twelve weeks, whichever is the lesser period.

(c) Duration of entitlement. Except as provided in subsection (b) and in subchapter V of this chapter [38 USCS §§ 3490 et seq.], no eligible veteran shall receive educational assistance under this chapter in excess of 45 months.

(As amended June 15, 2006, P. L. 109-233, Title V, § 503(8)(A), (B), 120 Stat. 416.)

HISTORY; ANCILLARY LAWS AND DIRECTIVES

Amendments:

2006. Act June 15, 2006, in subsecs. (a) and (b), inserted the subsection headings, which headings formerly appeared as centered headings preceding such subsections; and, in subsec. (c), inserted the subsection heading "Duration of Entitlement.".

CODE OF FEDERAL REGULATIONS

Department of Veterans Affairs—Nondiscrimination in federally-assisted programs of the Department of Veterans Affairs-effectuation of Title VI of the Civil Rights Act of 1964, 38 CFR 18.1 et seq.
Department of Veterans Affairs—Delegation of responsibility in connection with Title VI, Civil Rights Act of 1964, 38 CFR 18a.1 et seq.
Department of Veterans Affairs—Practice and procedure under Title VI of the Civil Rights Act of 1964 and Part 18 of this chapter, 38 CFR 18b.1 et seq.
Department of Veterans Affairs—Vocational rehabilitation and education, 38 CFR 21.1 et seq.
Department of Veterans Affairs—Loan guaranty and vocational rehabilitation and counseling programs, 48 CFR 871.100 et seq.

§ 3462. Time limitations for completing a program of education

(a) Delimiting period for completion. (1) [Unchanged]

38 USCS § 3462 — VETERANS' BENEFITS

(2), (3) [Deleted]

(4) [Unchanged]

(b) Correction of discharge. In the case of any eligible veteran who has been prevented, as determined by the Secretary, from completing a program of education under this chapter [38 USCS §§ 3451 et seq.] within the period prescribed by subsection (a), because the veteran had not met the nature of discharge requirements of this chapter [38 USCS §§ 3451 et seq.] before a change, correction, or modification of a discharge or dismissal made pursuant to section 1553 of title 10, the correction of the military records of the proper service department under section 1552 of title 10, or other corrective action by competent authority, then the 10-year delimiting period shall run from the date the veteran's discharge or dismissal was changed, corrected, or modified.

(c) Savings clause. In the case of any eligible veteran who was discharged or released from active duty before June 1, 1966 the 10-year delimiting period shall run from such date, if it is later than the date which otherwise would be applicable. In the case of any eligible veteran who was discharged or released from active duty before August 31, 1967, and who pursues a course of farm cooperative training, apprenticeship or other training on the job, the 10-year delimiting period shall run from August 31, 1967 if it is later than the date which would otherwise be applicable.

(d) Prisoners of war. In the case of any veteran (1) who served on or after January 31, 1955, (2) who became eligible for educational assistance under the provisions of this chapter [38 USCS §§ 3451 et seq.] or chapter 36 of this title [38 USCS §§ 3670 et seq.], and (3) who, subsequent to the veteran's last discharge or release from active duty, was captured and held as a prisoner of war by a foreign government or power, there shall be excluded, in computing his 10-year period of eligibility for educational assistance, any period during which the veteran was so detained and any period immediately following the veteran's release from such detention during which the veteran was hospitalized at a military, civilian, or Department of Veterans Affairs medical facility.

(e) Termination of assistance. No educational assistance shall be afforded any eligible veteran under this chapter [38 USCS §§ 3451 et seq.] or chapter 36 of this title [38 USCS §§ 3670 et seq.] after December 31, 1989.

(As amended June 5, 2001, P. L. 107-14, § 8(a)(5), 115 Stat. 34; Dec. 16, 2003, P. L. 108-183, Title III, § 306(d), 117 Stat. 2661; June 15, 2006, P. L. 109-233, Title V, § 503(8)(A), (C), 120 Stat. 416.)

HISTORY; ANCILLARY LAWS AND DIRECTIVES

Amendments:

2001. Act June 5, 2001, in subsec. (a), deleted para. (3), which read:

"(3)(A) Subject to subparagraph (C) of this paragraph and notwithstanding the provisions of paragraph (1) of this subsection, an eligible veteran who served on active duty during the Vietnam era shall be permitted to use any of such veteran's unused entitlement under section 3461 of this title for the purpose of pursuing—

"(i) a program of apprenticeship or other on-job training;

"(ii) a course with an approved vocational objective; or

"(iii) a program of secondary education, if the veteran does not have a secondary school diploma (or an equivalency certificate).

"(B) Upon completion of a program or course pursued by virtue of eligibility provided by this paragraph, the Secretary shall provide the veteran with such employment counseling as may be necessary to assist the veteran in obtaining employment consistent with the veteran's abilities, aptitudes, and interests.

"(C)(i) Educational assistance shall be provided a veteran for pursuit of a program or course described in clause (i) or (ii) of subparagraph (A) of this paragraph using eligibility provided by this paragraph unless the Secretary determines, based on an examination of the veteran's employment and training history, that the veteran is not in need of such a program or course in order to obtain a reasonably stable employment situation consistent with the veteran's abilities and aptitudes. Any such determination shall be made in accordance with regulations which the Secretary shall prescribe.

"(ii) Educational assistance provided a veteran for pursuit of a program described in clause (iii) of subparagraph (A) of this paragraph using eligibility provided by this paragraph shall be provided at the rate determined under section 3491(b)(2) of this title.

"(D) Educational assistance may not be provided by virtue of this paragraph after December 31, 1984.".

2003. Act Dec. 16, 2003 (effective on enactment, as provided by § 306(h)(1) of such Act, which appears as a note to this section), in subsec. (a), deleted para. (2), which read:

"(2)(A) Notwithstanding the provisions of paragraph (1) of this subsection, any veteran shall be permitted to use any of such veteran's unused entitlement under section 3461 of this title for the purposes of eligibility for an education loan, pursuant to the provisions of subchapter III of chapter 36 of this title, after the delimiting date otherwise applicable to such veteran under such paragraph (1), if such veteran was pursuing an approved program of education on a full-time basis at the time of the expiration of such veteran's eligibility.

"(B) Notwithstanding any other provision of this chapter or chapter 36 of this title, any veteran whose delimiting period is extended under subparagraph (A) of this paragraph may continue to use any unused loan entitlement under this paragraph as long as the veteran continues to be enrolled on a full-time basis in pursuit of the approved program of education in which such veteran was enrolled at the time of expiration of such veteran's eligibility (i) until such entitlement is exhausted, (ii) until the expiration of two years after November 23, 1977, or the date of the expiration of the delimiting date otherwise applicable to such veteran under paragraph (1) of this subsection, whichever is later, or (iii) until such veteran has completed the approved program of education in which such veteran was enrolled at the end of the delimiting period referred to in paragraph (1) of this subsection, whichever occurs first.''.

2006. Act June 15, 2006, in subsecs. (a)–(c), inserted the subsection headings, which headings formerly appeared as centered headings preceding such subsections; and, in subsecs. (d) and (e), inserted the subsection headings.

Other provisions:
Effective date of Dec. 16, 2003 amendment. Act Dec. 16, 2003, P. L. 108-183, Title III, § 306(h)(1), 117 Stat. 2661, provides: "The amendments made by subsection (d) [deleting subsec. (a)(2) of this section] shall take effect on the date of the enactment of this Act.''.

RESEARCH GUIDE
Am Jur:
77 Am Jur 2d, Veterans and Veterans' Laws § 124.

SUBCHAPTER III. ENROLLMENT

§ 3470. Selection of program

CODE OF FEDERAL REGULATIONS
Department of Veterans Affairs—Nondiscrimination in federally-assisted programs of the Department of Veterans Affairs-effectuation of Title VI of the Civil Rights Act of 1964, 38 CFR 18.1 et seq.
Department of Veterans Affairs—Delegation of responsibility in connection with Title VI, Civil Rights Act of 1964, 38 CFR 18a.1 et seq.
Department of Veterans Affairs—Practice and procedure under Title VI of the Civil Rights Act of 1964 and Part 18 of this chapter, 38 CFR 18b.1 et seq.
Department of Veterans Affairs—Vocational rehabilitation and education, 38 CFR 21.1 et seq.
Department of Veterans Affairs—Loan guaranty and vocational rehabilitation and counseling programs, 48 CFR 871.100 et seq.

RESEARCH GUIDE
Am Jur:
77 Am Jur 2d, Veterans and Veterans' Laws § 130.

§ 3471. Applications; approval

Any eligible veteran, or any person on active duty (after consultation with the appropriate service education officer, who desires to initiate a program of education under this chapter [38 USCS §§ 3451 et seq.] shall submit an application to the Secretary which shall be in such form, and contain such information, as the Secretary shall prescribe. The Secretary shall approve such application unless the Secretary finds that (1) such veteran or person is not eligible for or entitled to the educational assistance for which application is made, (2) the veteran's or person's selected educational institution or training establishment fails to meet any requirement of this chapter or chapter 36 of this title [38 USCS §§ 3451 et seq. or 3670 et seq.], (3) the veteran's or person's enrollment in, or pursuit of, the program of education selected would violate any provision of this chapter or chapter 36 of this title [38 USCS §§ 3451 et seq. or 3670 et seq.], or (4) the veteran or person is already qualified, by reason of previous education or training, for the educational, professional, or vocational objective for which the program of education is offered. The Secretary shall not treat a person as already qualified for the objective of a program of education offered by a qualified provider of entrepreneurship courses solely because such person is the owner or operator of a business. The Secretary shall notify the veteran or person of the approval or disapproval of the veteran's or person's application.

(As amended Dec. 16, 2003, P. L. 108-183, Title III, § 305(b), 117 Stat. 2660.)

HISTORY; ANCILLARY LAWS AND DIRECTIVES
Amendments:
2003. Act Dec. 16, 2003 (applicable as provided by § 305(f) of such Act, which appears as 38 USCS § 3452 note), inserted the sentence beginning "The Secretary shall not treat . . . .".

38 USCS § 3471

RESEARCH GUIDE
Am Jur:
77 Am Jur 2d, Veterans and Veterans' Laws §§ 131, 132.

§ 3474. Discontinuance for unsatisfactory conduct or progress

RESEARCH GUIDE
Am Jur:
77 Am Jur 2d, Veterans and Veterans' Laws § 136.

§ 3476. Education outside the United States

RESEARCH GUIDE
Am Jur:
77 Am Jur 2d, Veterans and Veterans' Laws § 130.

SUBCHAPTER IV. PAYMENTS TO ELIGIBLE VETERANS; VETERAN-STUDENT SERVICES

§ 3481. Educational assistance allowance

(a) General. The Secretary shall, in accordance with the applicable provisions of this section and chapter 36 of this title [38 USCS §§ 3670 et seq.], pay to each eligible veteran who is pursuing a program of education under this chapter [38 USCS §§ 3451 et seq.] an educational assistance allowance to meet, in part, the expenses of the veteran's subsistence, tuition, fees, supplies, books, equipment, and other educational costs.

(b) Institutional training. The educational assistance allowance of an eligible veteran pursuing a program of education, other than a program exclusively by correspondence, at an educational institution shall be paid as provided in chapter 36 of this title [38 USCS §§ 3670 et seq.].

(As amended June 15, 2006, P. L. 109-233, Title V, § 503(8)(A), 120 Stat. 416.)

HISTORY; ANCILLARY LAWS AND DIRECTIVES

Amendments:
2006. Act June 15, 2006, in subsecs. (a) and (b), inserted the subsection headings, which headings formerly appeared as centered headings preceding such subsections.

CODE OF FEDERAL REGULATIONS

Department of Veterans Affairs—Nondiscrimination in federally-assisted programs of the Department of Veterans Affairs-effectuation of Title VI of the Civil Rights Act of 1964, 38 CFR 18.1 et seq.
Department of Veterans Affairs—Delegation of responsibility in connection with Title VI, Civil Rights Act of 1964, 38 CFR 18a.1 et seq.
Department of Veterans Affairs—Practice and procedure under Title VI of the Civil Rights Act of 1964 and Part 18 of this chapter, 38 CFR 18b.1 et seq.
Department of Veterans Affairs—Vocational rehabilitation and education, 38 CFR 21.1 et seq.
Department of Veterans Affairs—Loan guaranty and vocational rehabilitation and counseling programs, 48 CFR 871.100 et seq.

RESEARCH GUIDE
Am Jur:
77 Am Jur 2d, Veterans and Veterans' Laws § 135.

§ 3482. Computation of educational assistance allowances

(a)–(f) [Unchanged]

(g)(1) Subject to the provisions of paragraph (2) of this subsection, the amount of the educational assistance allowance paid to an eligible veteran who is pursuing a program of education under this chapter [38 USCS §§ 3451 et seq.] while incarcerated in a Federal, State, local, or other penal institution or correctional facility for conviction of a felony may not exceed such amount as the Secretary determines, in accordance with regulations which the Secretary shall prescribe, is necessary to cover the cost of established charges for tuition and fees required of similarly circumstanced nonveterans enrolled in the same program and to cover the cost of necessary supplies, books, and equipment, or the applicable monthly educational assistance allowance prescribed for a veteran with no dependents in subsection (a)(1) or (c)(2) of this section or section 3687(b)(1) of this title [38 USCS § 3687(b)(1)], whichever is the lesser. The amount of the educational assistance allowance payable to a veteran while so incarcerated shall be reduced to the extent that the tuition and fees of the veteran for any course are paid under any Federal program (other than a program administered by the Secretary) or under any State or local program.

(2) [Unchanged]

(h)(1) Subject to paragraph (3), the amount of educational assistance payable under this chapter [38 USCS §§ 3451 et seq.] for a licensing or certification test described in section 3452(b) of this title [38 USCS § 3452(b)] is the lesser of $2,000 or the fee charged for the test.

(2) The number of months of entitlement charged in the case of any individual for such licensing or certification test is equal to the number (including any fraction) determined by dividing the total amount paid to such individual for such test by the full-time monthly institutional rate of the educational assistance allowance which, except for paragraph (1), such individual would otherwise be paid under this chapter [38 USCS §§ 3451 et seq.].

(3) In no event shall payment of educational assistance under this subsection for such a test exceed the amount of the individual's available entitlement under this chapter [38 USCS §§ 3451 et seq.].

(As amended Nov. 1, 2000, P. L. 106-419, Title I, Subtitle C, § 122(b)(3), 114 Stat. 1834; Dec. 22, 2006, P. L. 109-461, Title X, § 1002(d), 120 Stat. 3465.)

HISTORY; ANCILLARY LAWS AND DIRECTIVES

Amendments:
2000. Act Nov. 1, 2000 (effective 3/1/01 and applicable with respect to licensing and certification tests approved on or after such date, as provided by § 122(d) of such Act, which appears as a note to this section) added subsec. (h).
2006. Act Dec. 22, 2006, in subsec. (g)(1), substituted "local, or other penal institution or correctional facility" for "or local penal institution".

§ 3485. Work-study allowance

(a)(1) Individuals utilized under the authority of subsection (b) shall be paid an additional educational assistance allowance (hereinafter in this section referred to as "work-study allowance"). Such allowance shall be paid in return for an individual's entering into an agreement described in paragraph (3).

(2) Such work-study allowance shall be paid in an amount equal to the product of—

(A) the applicable hourly minimum wage; and

(B) the number of hours worked during the applicable period.

(3) An agreement described in this paragraph is an agreement of an individual to perform services, during or between periods of enrollment, aggregating not more than a number of hours equal to 25 times the number of weeks in the semester or other applicable enrollment period, required in connection with a qualifying work-study activity.

(4) For the purposes of this section, the term "qualifying work-study activity" means any of the following:

(A) The outreach services program under chapter 63 of this title [38 USCS §§ 6301 et seq.] as carried out under the supervision of a Department employee or, during the period preceding June 30, 2013, outreach services to servicemembers and veterans furnished by employees of a State approving agency.

(B) The preparation and processing of necessary papers and other documents at educational institutions or regional offices or facilities of the Department.

(C) The provision of hospital and domiciliary care and medical treatment under chapter 17 of this title [38 USCS §§ 1701 et seq.], including, during the period preceding June 30, 2013, the provision of such care to veterans in a State home for which payment is made under section 1741 of this title [38 USCS § 1741].

(D) Any other activity of the Department as the Secretary determines appropriate.

(E) In the case of an individual who is receiving educational assistance under chapter 1606 or 1607 of title 10 [10 USCS §§ 16131 et seq. or 16161 et seq.], an activity relating to the administration of that chapter at Department of Defense, Coast Guard, or National Guard facilities.

(F) During the period preceding June 30, 2013, an activity relating to the administration of a national cemetery or a State veterans' cemetery.

(G) Any activity of a State veterans agency related to providing assistance to veterans in obtaining any benefit under the laws administered by the Secretary or the laws of the State.

(H) A position working in a Center of Excellence for Veteran Student Success, as established pursuant to part T of title VIII of the Higher Education Act of 1965 (20 U.S.C. 1161t et seq.).

(I) A position working in a cooperative program carried out jointly by the Department and an institution of higher learning.

(J) Any other veterans-related position in an institution of higher learning.

(5) An individual may elect, in a manner prescribed by the Secretary, to be paid in advance an amount equal to 40 percent of the total amount of the work-study allowance agreed to be paid under the agreement in return for the individual's agreement to perform the number of hours

38 USCS § 3485 VETERANS' BENEFITS

of work specified in the agreement (but not more than an amount equal to 50 times the applicable hourly minimum wage).

(6) For the purposes of this subsection and subsection (e), the term "applicable hourly minimum wages" means—

(A) the hourly minimum wage under section 6(a) of the Fair Labor Standards Act of 1938 (29 U.S.C. 206(a)); or

(B) the hourly minimum wage under comparable law of the State in which the services are to be performed, if such wage is higher than the wage referred to in subparagraph (A) and the Secretary has made a determination to pay such higher wage.

(b) Notwithstanding any other provision of law, the Secretary shall, subject to the provisions of subsection (e) of this section, utilize, in connection with the activities specified in subsection (a)(1) of this section, the services of individuals who are pursuing programs of rehabilitation, education, or training under chapter 30, 31, 32, 33, or 34 of this title [38 USCS §§ 3001 et seq., 3100 et seq., 3201 et seq., 3301 et seq., or 3451 et seq.] or chapter 1606 or 1607 of title 10 [10 USCS §§ 16131 et seq. or 16161 et seq.], at a rate equal to at least three-quarters of that required of a full-time student. In carrying out this section, the Secretary, wherever feasible, shall give priority to veterans with disabilities rated at 30 percent or more for purposes of chapter 11 of this title [38 USCS §§ 1101 et seq.]. In the event an individual ceases to be at least a three-quarter-time student before completing such agreement, the individual may, with the approval of the Secretary, be permitted to complete such agreement.

(c), (d) [Unchanged]

(e)(1) Subject to paragraph (2) of this subsection, the Secretary may, notwithstanding any other provision of law, enter into an agreement with an individual under this section, or a modification of such an agreement, whereby the individual agrees to perform a qualifying work-study activity described in subsection (a)(4) and agrees that the Secretary shall, in lieu of paying the work-study allowance payable for such services, as provided in subsection (a) of this section, deduct the amount of the allowance from the amount which the individual has been determined to be indebted to the United States by virtue of such individual's participation in a benefits program under this chapter, chapter 30, 31, 32, 33, 35, or 36 of this title [38 USCS §§ 3451 et seq., 3001 et seq., 3100 et seq., 3201 et seq., 3500 et seq., or 3670 et seq.], or chapter 1606 or 1607 of title 10 [10 USCS §§ 16131 et seq. or 16161 et seq.] (other than an indebtedness arising from a refund penalty imposed under section 2135 [10 USCS § 16135] of such title).

(2)–(4) [Unchanged]

(As amended Nov. 11, 1998, P. L. 105-368, Title II, Subtitle A, § 202(a), 112 Stat. 3326; June 5, 2001, P. L. 107-14, § 8(a)(16), 115 Stat. 35; Dec. 27, 2001, P. L. 107-103, Title I, § 107(a), 115 Stat. 983; Dec. 6, 2002, P. L. 107-330, Title III, § 308(g)(11), 116 Stat. 2829; Dec. 16, 2003, P. L. 108-183, Title III, § 306(f)(1), 117 Stat. 2661; June 15, 2006, P. L. 109-233, Title IV, § 402(e)(1), 120 Stat. 411; Dec. 21, 2006, P. L. 109-444, § 2(g), 120 Stat. 3305; Dec. 22, 2006, P. L. 109-461, Title III, §§ 304, 307, 120 Stat. 3428, 3429; Dec. 26, 2007, P. L. 110-157, Title III, § 302, 121 Stat. 1836; June 30, 2008, P. L. 110-252, Title V, § 5003(b)(2)(A)(i), 122 Stat. 2375; Oct. 13, 2010, P. L. 111-275, Title I, § 101(a), (b), 124 Stat. 2866.)

HISTORY; ANCILLARY LAWS AND DIRECTIVES

Explanatory notes:
Section 2(g) of Act Dec. 21, 2006, P. L. 109-444, amended this section; however, pursuant to § 1006(b) of Act Dec. 22, 2006, P. L. 109-461, which appears as 38 USCS § 101 note, as of the enactment of Act Dec. 22, 2006, P. L. 109-461, Act Dec. 21, 2006, P. L. 109-444 and the amendments made by such Act were deemed for all purposes not to have taken effect and such § 2(g) ceased to be in effect.

Amendments:
1998. Act Nov. 11, 1998 (applicable with respect to agreements entered into under this section on or after 1/1/99, as provided by § 202(b) of such Act, which appears as a note to this section), in subsec. (a)(1), substituted "An individual may elect, in a manner prescribed by the Secretary, to be paid in advance" for "An individual shall be paid in advance".

2001. Act June 5, 2001, in subsec. (a)(1), substituted "hereinafter" for "hereafter".

Act Dec. 27, 2001 (applicable as provided by § 107(b) of such Act, which appears as a note to this section), substituted subsec. (a) for one which read:

"(a)(1) Individuals utilized under the authority of subsection (b) of this section shall be paid an additional educational assistance allowance (hereinafter referred to as 'work-study allowance'). Such work-study allowance shall be paid in an amount equal to the applicable hourly minimum wage times the number of hours worked during the applicable period, in return for such individual's agreement to perform services, during or between periods of enrollment, aggregating not more than a number of hours equal to 25 times the number of weeks in the semester or other applicable enrollment period, required in connection with (A) the outreach services program under subchapter II of chapter 77 of this title as carried out under the supervision of a Department of Veterans Affairs employee, (B) the preparation and processing of necessary papers and other documents at educational institutions or regional offices or facilities of the Department of Veterans Affairs, (C) the provision of hospital and domiciliary care and medical treatment under chapter 17 of this Title, (D) any other activity of the Department of Veterans Affairs as the Secretary shall determine appropriate, or (E) in the case of an individual who is receiving educational assistance under chapter 106 of title 10, activities relating to the administration of such chapter at Department of Defense, Coast Guard, or National Guard facilities. An individual may elect, in a manner prescribed by the Secretary, to be paid in advance an amount equal to 40 percent of the total amount of the work-study allowance agreed to be paid under the agreement in return for the individual's agreement to perform the number of hours of work specified in the agreement (but not more than an amount equal to 50 times the applicable hourly minimum wage).

"(2) For the purposes of paragraph (1) of this subsection and subsection (e) of this section, the term applicable hourly minimum wage means (A) the hourly minimum wage under section 6(a) of the Fair Labor Standards Act of 1938 (29 U.S.C. 206(a)), or (B) the hourly minimum wage under comparable law of the State in which the services are to be performed, if such wage is higher than the wage referred to in clause (A) and the Secretary has made a determination to pay such higher wage.".

2002. Act Dec. 6, 2002, in subsec. (a)(4), in subparas. (A), (C), and (F), substituted "the period preceding December 27, 2006" for "the five-year period beginning on the date of the enactment of the Veterans Education and Benefits Expansion Act of 2001".

2003. Act Dec. 16, 2003 (effective 90 days after enactment, as provided by § 306(h)(2) of such Act, which appears as a note to this section), in subsec. (e)(1), deleted "(other than an education loan under subchapter III)" following "or 36".

2006. Act June 15, 2006, in subsec. (a)(4)(A), substituted "chapter 63" for "subchapter II of chapter 77".

Act Dec. 22, 2006, in subsec. (a)(4), in subparas. (A) and (C), substituted "June 30, 2007" for "December 27, 2006", in subpara. (E), inserted "or 1607", and, in subpara. (F), substituted "June 30, 2007" for "December 27, 2006"; in subsec. (b), substituted "chapter 1606 or 1607" for "chapter 106"; and, in subsec. (e)(1), substituted "a qualifying work-study activity described in subsection (a)(4)" for "services of the kind described in clauses (A) through (E) of subsection (a)(1) of this section", and substituted "chapter 1606 or 1607" for "chapter 106'".

2007. Act Dec. 26, 2007, in subsec. (a)(4)(A), (C), and (F), substituted "June 30, 2010" for "June 30, 2007".

2008. Act June 30, 2008 (effective on 8/1/2009, as provided by § 5003(d) of such Act, which appears as 10 USCS § 16163 note), in subsecs. (b) and (c)(1), inserted "33,".

2010. Act Oct. 13, 2010, in subsec. (a)(4), in subpars. (A), (C), and (F), substituted "June 30, 2013" for "June 30, 2010".

Such Act further (effective on 10/1/2011, as provided by § 101(c) of such Act, which appears as a note to this section), in subsec. (a), added subparas. (G)–(J).

Other provisions:
Application of Nov. 11, 1998 amendment. Act Nov. 11, 1998, P. L. 105-368, Title II, Subtitle A, § 202(b), 112 Stat. 3326, provides: "The amendment made by subsection (a) [amending subsec. (a)(1) of this section] shall apply with respect to agreements entered into under section 3485 of title 38, United States Code, on or after January 1, 1999.".

Application of Dec. 27, 2001 amendment. Act Dec. 27, 2001, P. L. 107-103, Title I, § 107(b), 115 Stat. 984, provides: "The amendment made by this section [amending subsec. (a) of this section] shall apply with respect to agreements entered into under section 3485 of title 38, United States Code, on or after the date of the enactment of this Act.".

Effective date of Dec. 16, 2003 amendments. Act Dec. 16, 2003, P. L. 108-183, Title III, § 306(h)(2), 117 Stat. 2661, provides: "The amendments made by subsections (e), (f), and (g) [repealing 38 USCS §§ 3698 and 3699, and amending 38 USCS §§ 3485(e)(1), 3512, and the chapter analysis preceding § 3670] shall take effect 90 days after the date of the enactment of this Act.".

Effective date of amendments made by § 101(b) of Act Oct. 13, 2010. Act Oct. 13, 2010, P. L. 111-275, Title I, § 101(c), 124 Stat. 2866, provides: "The amendment made by subsection (b) [adding subsec. (a)(4)(G)–(J)] shall take effect on October 1, 2011.".

RESEARCH GUIDE

Am Jur:
77 Am Jur 2d, Veterans and Veterans' Laws § 135.

SUBCHAPTER V. SPECIAL ASSISTANCE FOR THE EDUCATIONALLY DISADVANTAGED

§ 3490. Purpose

CODE OF FEDERAL REGULATIONS

Department of Veterans Affairs—Nondiscrimination in federally-assisted programs of the Department of Veterans Affairs-effectuation of Title VI of the Civil Rights Act of 1964, 38 CFR 18.1 et seq.

38 USCS § 3490

Department of Veterans Affairs—Delegation of responsibility in connection with Title VI, Civil Rights Act of 1964, 38 CFR 18a.1 et seq.
Department of Veterans Affairs—Practice and procedure under Title VI of the Civil Rights Act of 1964 and Part 18 of this chapter, 38 CFR 18b.1 et seq.
Department of Veterans Affairs—Vocational rehabilitation and education, 38 CFR 21.1 et seq.
Department of Veterans Affairs—Loan guaranty and vocational rehabilitation and counseling programs, 48 CFR 871.100 et seq.

CHAPTER 35. SURVIVORS' AND DEPENDENTS' EDUCATIONAL ASSISTANCE

SUBCHAPTER VI. MISCELLANEOUS PROVISIONS

3564. Annual adjustment of amounts of educational assistance.

HISTORY; ANCILLARY LAWS AND DIRECTIVES

Amendments:
2000. Act Nov. 1, 2000, P. L. 106-419, Title I, Subtitle B, § 111(f)(1)(B), 114 Stat. 1831, amended the analysis of this chapter by adding item 3564.

SUBCHAPTER I. DEFINITIONS

§ 3500. Purpose

CODE OF FEDERAL REGULATIONS

Department of Veterans Affairs—Nondiscrimination in federally-assisted programs of the Department of Veterans Affairs-effectuation of Title VI of the Civil Rights Act of 1964, 38 CFR 18.1 et seq.
Department of Veterans Affairs—Delegation of responsibility in connection with Title VI, Civil Rights Act of 1964, 38 CFR 18a.1 et seq.
Department of Veterans Affairs—Practice and procedure under Title VI of the Civil Rights Act of 1964 and Part 18 of this chapter, 38 CFR 18b.1 et seq.
Department of Veterans Affairs—Vocational rehabilitation and education, 38 CFR 21.1 et seq.
Department of Veterans Affairs—Loan guaranty and vocational rehabilitation and counseling programs, 48 CFR 871.100 et seq.

RESEARCH GUIDE

Am Jur:
77 Am Jur 2d, Veterans and Veterans' Laws § 137.

INTERPRETIVE NOTES AND DECISIONS

Because benefits were based on status of child as eligible person through each disabled veteran parent, and absent aggregation restrictions, under 2003 version of 38 USCS § 3511(a)(1), appellant student with two disabled parents could receive educational benefits not to exceed 45 months from status of each parent; 38 USCS § 3500 did not prohibit child, being but one person, from nevertheless becoming eligible by reason of service-connected permanent and total disability or death of either or both parents. Osman v Peake (2008) 22 Vet App 252, 2008 US App Vet Claims LEXIS 1063.

§ 3501. Definitions

(a) For the purposes of this chapter [38 USCS §§ 3500 et seq.] and chapter 36 of this title [38 USCS §§ 3670 et seq.]—
   (1) The term "eligible person" means any of the following:
      (A) A child of a person who, as a result of qualifying service—
         (i) died of a service-connected disability; or
         (ii) has a total disability permanent in nature resulting from a service-connected disability, or who dies while a disability so evaluated was in existence.
         (iii) [Deleted]
      (B) The surviving spouse of any person who died of a service-connected disability sustained during a period of qualifying service.
      (C) The spouse or child of any member of the Armed Forces serving on active duty who, at the time of application for benefits under this chapter [38 USCS §§ 3500 et seq.] is listed, pursuant to section 556 of title 37 [37 USCS § 556] and regulations issued thereunder, by the Secretary concerned in one or more of the following categories and has been so listed for a total of more than ninety days: (i) missing in action (ii) captured in line of duty by a hostile force, or (iii) forcibly detained or interned in line of duty by a foreign government or power.
      (D) (i) The spouse of any person who has a total disability permanent in nature resulting

READJUSTMENT BENEFITS   38 USCS § 3501

from a service-connected disability sustained during a period of qualifying service, or (ii) the surviving spouse of a veteran who died while a disability so evaluated was in existence.

(E) The spouse or child of a person who—

(i) at the time of the Secretary's determination under clause (ii), is a member of the Armed Forces who is hospitalized or receiving outpatient medical care, services, or treatment;

(ii) the Secretary determines has a total disability permanent in nature incurred or aggravated in the line of duty in the active military, naval, or air service; and

(iii) is likely to be discharged or released from such service for such disability.

(2)–(4) [Unchanged]

(5) The term "program of education" means any curriculum or any combination of unit courses or subjects pursued at an educational institution which is generally accepted as necessary to fulfill the requirements for the attainment of a predetermined and identified educational, professional, or vocational objective. Such term also includes any preparatory course described in section 3002(3)(B) of this title [38 USCS § 3002(3)(B)]. Such term also includes licensing or certification tests, the successful completion of which demonstrates an individual's possession of the knowledge or skill required to enter into, maintain, or advance in employment in a predetermined and identified vocation or profession, provided such tests and the licensing or credentialing organizations or entities that offer such tests are approved by the Secretary in accordance with section 3689 of this title [38 USCS § 3689]. Such term also includes national tests for admission to institutions of higher learning or graduate schools (such as the Scholastic Aptitude Test (SAT), Law School Admission Test (LSAT), Graduate Record Exam (GRE), and Graduate Management Admission Test (GMAT)) and national tests providing an opportunity for course credit at institutions of higher learning (such as the Advanced Placement (AP) exam and College-Level Examination Program (CLEP)).

(6) The term "educational institution" means any public or private secondary school, vocational school, correspondence school, business school, junior college, teachers' college, college, normal school, professional school, university, or scientific or technical institution, or any other institution if it furnishes education at the secondary school level or above. Such term also includes any private entity (that meets such requirements as the Secretary may establish) that offers, either directly or under an agreement with another entity (that meets such requirements), a course or courses to fulfill requirements for the attainment of a license or certificate generally recognized as necessary to obtain, maintain, or advance in employment in a profession or vocation in a high technology occupation (as determined by the Secretary).

(7)–(11) [Unchanged]

(12) The term "qualifying service" means service in the active military, naval, or air service after the beginning of the Spanish-American War that did not terminate under dishonorable conditions.

(b)–(d) [Unchanged]

(As amended Nov. 1, 2000, P. L. 106-419, Title I, Subtitle B, § 114(a), Subtitle C, § 122(a), 114 Stat. 1833; Dec. 27, 2001, P. L. 107-103, Title I, §§ 108(a), 110(a), 115 Stat. 985, 986; Dec. 10, 2004, P. L. 108-454, Title I, § 106(a), 118 Stat. 3602; Dec. 21, 2006, P. L. 109-444, § 3(a), (b)(1), 120 Stat. 3305; Dec. 22, 2006, P. L. 109-461, Title III, § 301(a), (b)(1), 120 Stat. 3425.)

HISTORY; ANCILLARY LAWS AND DIRECTIVES

Explanatory notes:

Section 3(a), (b)(1) of Act Dec. 21, 2006, P. L. 109-444, amended this section; however, pursuant to § 1006(b) of Act Dec. 22, 2006, P. L. 109-461, which appears as 38 USCS § 101 note, as of the enactment of Act Dec. 22, 2006, P. L. 109-461, Act Dec. 21, 2006, P. L. 109-444 and the amendments made by such Act were deemed for all purposes not to have taken effect and such § 3(a), (b)(1) ceased to be in effect.

Amendments:

2000. Act Nov. 1, 2000, in subsec. (a)(5), added the sentence beginning "Such term also includes any . . .".

Section 122(a) of such Act (effective 3/1/01 and applicable with respect to licensing and certification tests approved on or after such date, as provided by § 122(d) of such Act, which appears as 38 USCS § 3032 note), in subsec. (a)(5), added the sentence beginning "Such term also includes licensing or . . .".

2001. Act Dec. 27, 2001, in subsec. (a)(1)(D), inserted "(i)" and "(ii)".

Such Act further (applicable as provided by § 110(b) of such Act, which appears as 38 USCS § 3452 note), in subsec. (a)(6), added the sentence beginning "Such term also includes . . .".

2004. Act Dec. 10, 2004, in subsec. (a)(5), added the sentence beginning "Such term also includes national tests . . .".

2006. Act Dec. 22, 2006 (applicable with respect to a payment of educational assistance for a course of education pursued after enactment, as provided by § 301(d) of such Act, which appears as a note to this section), in subsec. (a), in para. (1), in the introductory matter, substituted "means any of the following:" for "means—", in subpara. (A), in the introductory matter, substituted "A" for "a", and inserted ", as a result of qualifying service", in cl. (i), substituted "; or" for a concluding comma, in cl. (ii), substituted the concluding period for ", or", and deleted cl. (iii) which read: "(iii) at the time of application for benefits under this chapter is a member of the Armed Forces serving on active duty listed, pursuant to section 556 of title 37 and regulations issued thereunder, by the Secretary concerned in one or more of the following categories and has been so listed for a total of more than ninety days: (A) missing in action, (B) captured in line of duty by hostile force, or (C) forcibly detained or interned in line of duty by a foreign government or power,", in subpara. (B), substituted "The" for "the", and substituted "sustained during a period of qualifying service." for a concluding comma, in subpara. (C), substituted "The" for "the", inserted "or child", and substituted a concluding period for ", or", in subpara. (D), in cl. (i), substituted "The" for "the", inserted "sustained during a period of qualifying service", and substituted the concluding period for a concluding comma, and added subpara. (E), deleted the concluding matter which read: "arising out of active military, naval, or air service after the beginning of the Spanish-American War, but only if such service did not terminate under dishonorable conditions. The standards and criteria for determining whether or not a disability arising out of such service is service connected shall be those applicable under chapter 11 of this title.", and added para. (12).

Other provisions:
Repeal of application provisions of Dec. 21, 2006 amendments. Act Dec. 21, 2006, P. L. 109-444, § 3(d), 120 Stat. 3307, appeared as a note to this section; however, pursuant to § 1006(b) of Act Dec. 22, 2006, P. L. 109-461, which appears as 38 USCS § 101 note, as of the enactment of Act Dec. 22, 2006, P. L. 109-461, Act Dec. 21, 2006, P. L. 109-444 and the amendments made by such Act were deemed for all purposes not to have taken effect and such § 3(d) ceased to be in effect.
Application of Dec. 22, 2006 amendments. Act Dec. 22, 2006, P. L. 109-461, Title III, § 301(d), 120 Stat. 3427, provides: "The amendments made by this section [amending 38 USCS §§ 3501, 3511, 3512, 3540, 3563, 3686, 5113] shall apply with respect to a payment of educational assistance for a course of education pursued after the date of the enactment of this Act.".

CROSS REFERENCES
Sentencing Guidelines for the United States Courts, 18 USCS Appx § 2B1.1.

RESEARCH GUIDE
Am Jur:
77 Am Jur 2d, Veterans and Veterans' Laws § 137.

INTERPRETIVE NOTES AND DECISIONS

Appellant was not entitled to dependents' educational assistance under 38 USCS § 3501 where veteran died in 1988, service connection for veteran's cause of death was retroactively granted as result of change in law in 1994, and appellant completed college education in 1992. Pfau v West (1999) 12 Vet App 515, 1999 US App Vet Claims LEXIS 824.

Plain meaning of language of 38 USCS § 5113(b) is that if Secretary of Veterans Affairs awards service connection for cause of veteran's death and surviving spouse files application for dependents' educational assistance (DEA) benefits pursuant to 38 USCS § 3501 within one year after issuance of decision awarding service connection, DEA application may be considered as having been filed on surviving spouse's eligibility date; based on use of word "may" in 38 USCS § 5113(b)(1), plain language of statute dictates that decision as to whether award of retroactive dependents' educational assistance benefits pursuant to 38 USCS § 3501 should be made is expressly committed to discretion of Secretary of Veterans Affairs, who may consider individual's application as having been filed on eligibility date of individual if that eligibility date is more than one year before date of initial rating decision, and any action by Secretary in applying this provision or refusing to apply this provision may be reviewed to determine, pursuant to 38 USCS § 7261(a)(3)(A), whether such action was arbitrary and capricious, abuse of his discretion, or otherwise not in accordance with law. Friedsam v Nicholson (2006) 19 Vet App 555, 2006 US App Vet Claims LEXIS 301.

Because benefits were based on status of child as eligible person, as defined in 38 USCS § 3501(a)(1)(A)(i)–(ii), through each disabled veteran parent, and absent aggregation restrictions, under 2003 version of 38 USCS § 3511(a)(1), appellant student with two disabled parents could receive educational benefits not to exceed 45 months from status of each parent. Osman v Peake (2008) 22 Vet App 252, 2008 US App Vet Claims LEXIS 1063.

Board of Veterans' Appeals erred in denying veteran's wife Dependents' Education Assistance benefits under 38 USCS § 3512, on basis that she married veteran more than 10 years after he was deemed permanently and totally disabled, because 10-year period began on date wife became eligible under 38 USCS § 3501(a)(1)(D)(i), which was date she married veteran. Cypert v Peake (2008) 22 Vet App 307, 2008 US App Vet Claims LEXIS 1554.

READJUSTMENT BENEFITS 38 USCS § 3511

SUBCHAPTER II. ELIGIBILITY AND ENTITLEMENT

§ 3510. Eligibility and entitlement generally

CODE OF FEDERAL REGULATIONS

Department of Veterans Affairs—Nondiscrimination in federally-assisted programs of the Department of Veterans Affairs-effectuation of Title VI of the Civil Rights Act of 1964, 38 CFR 18.1 et seq.
Department of Veterans Affairs—Delegation of responsibility in connection with Title VI, Civil Rights Act of 1964, 38 CFR 18a.1 et seq.
Department of Veterans Affairs—Practice and procedure under Title VI of the Civil Rights Act of 1964 and Part 18 of this chapter, 38 CFR 18b.1 et seq.
Department of Veterans Affairs—Vocational rehabilitation and education, 38 CFR 21.1 et seq.
Department of Veterans Affairs—Loan guaranty and vocational rehabilitation and counseling programs, 48 CFR 871.100 et seq.

RESEARCH GUIDE

Am Jur:
77 Am Jur 2d, Veterans and Veterans' Laws § 137.

§ 3511. Duration of educational assistance

(a)(1) Each eligible person, whether made eligible by one or more of the provisions of section 3501(a)(1) of this title [38 USCS § 3501(a)(1)], shall be entitled to educational assistance under this chapter [38 USCS §§ 3500 et seq.] for an aggregate period not in excess of 45 months (or to the equivalent thereof in part-time training).

(2)(A) [Unchanged]

(B) The payment of the educational assistance allowance referred to in subparagraph (A) of this paragraph is the payment of such an allowance to an individual for pursuit of a course or courses under this chapter if the Secretary finds that the individual—

(i) had to discontinue such course pursuit as a result of being ordered to serve on active duty under section 688, 12301(a), 12301(d), 12301(g), 12302, or 12304 of title 10 [10 USCS § 688, 12301(a), 12301(d), 12301(g), 12302, or 12304] or of being involuntarily ordered to full-time National Guard duty under section 502(f) of title 32 [32 USCS § 502(f)]; and

(ii) [Unchanged]

(C) [Unchanged]

(b) If any eligible person pursuing a program of education, or of special restorative training, under this chapter [38 USCS §§ 3500 et seq.] ceases to be an "eligible person" because—

(1) [Unchanged]

(2) the parent or spouse from whom eligibility is derived based upon section 3501(a)(1)(C) of this title [38 USCS § 3501(a)(1)(A)(iii) or 3501(a)(1)(C)] is no longer listed in one of the categories specified therein,

(3) the spouse, as an eligible person under subparagraph (D) or (E) of section 3501(a)(1) of this title [38 USCS § 3501(a)(1)], is divorced, without fault on such person's part, from the person upon whose disability such person's eligibility is based, or

(4) the parent or spouse from whom such eligibility is derived based upon subparagraph (E) of section 3501(a)(1) of this title [38 USCS § 3501(a)(1)] no longer meets a requirement under clause (i), (ii), or (iii) of that subparagraph,

then such eligible person (if such person has sufficient remaining entitlement) may, nevertheless, be afforded educational assistance under this chapter [38 USCS §§ 3500 et seq.] until the end of the quarter or semester for which enrolled if the educational institution in which such person is enrolled is operated on a quarter or semester system, or if the educational institution is not so operated until the end of the course, or until 12 weeks have expired, whichever first occurs.

(c) [Deleted]

(As amended Dec. 27, 2001, P. L. 107-103, Title I, §§ 103(a), 108(b)(1), (c)(1), 115 Stat. 979, 985; June 15, 2006, P. L. 109-233, Title V, § 503(7), 120 Stat. 416; Dec. 21, 2006, P. L. 109-444, § 3(b)(2), 120 Stat. 3306; Dec. 22, 2006, P. L. 109-461, Title III, §§ 301(b)(2), 302(a), 120 Stat. 3425, 3428.)

HISTORY; ANCILLARY LAWS AND DIRECTIVES

Explanatory notes:
Section 3(b)(2) of Act Dec. 21, 2006, P. L. 109-444, amended this section; however, pursuant to § 1006(b) of Act Dec. 22, 2006, P. L. 109-461, which appears as 38 USCS § 101 note, as of the enactment of Act Dec. 22, 2006, P. L. 109-461, Act Dec. 21, 2006, P. L. 109-444 and the amendments made by such Act were deemed for all purposes not to have taken effect and such § 3(b)(2) ceased to be in effect.

Amendments:

2001. Act Dec. 27, 2001 (effective as of 9/11/2001, as provided by § 103(e) of such Act, which appears as 38 USCS § 3013 note), in subsec. (a)(2)(B)(i), substituted "to serve on active duty under section 688, 12301(a), 12301(d), 12301(g), 12302, or 12304 of title 10;" for ", in connection with the Persian Gulf War, to serve on active duty under section 672(a), (d), or (g), 673, 673b, or 688 of title 10;".

Such Act further added subsec. (c).

Such Act further (applicable as provided by § 108(c)(4) of such Act, which appears as a note to this section), in subsec. (a)(1), added the sentence beginning "In no event . . .".

2006. Act June 15, 2006, in subsec. (a)(1), inserted "sections".

Act Dec. 22, 2006 (applicable with respect to a payment of educational assistance for a course of education pursued after enactment, as provided by § 301(d) of such Act, which appears as 38 USCS § 3501 note), in subsec. (a)(1), substituted "Each eligible person, whether made eligible by one or more of the provisions of section 3501(a)(1) of this title," for "Each eligible person", substituted "an aggregate period" for "a period", and deleted the sentence "In no event may the aggregate educational assistance afforded to a spouse made eligible under both sections 3501(a)(1)(D)(i) and 3501(a)(1)(D)(ii) of this title exceed 45 months." following "training."; in subsec. (b), in para. (2), substituted "section" for "the provisions of section 3501(a)(1)(A)(iii) or", and deleted "or" following the concluding comma, in para. (3), substituted "subparagraph (D) or (E) of section 3501(a)(1)" for "section 3501(a)(1)(D)", and added "or" following the concluding comma, and added para. (4); and deleted subsec. (c) which read: "(c) Any entitlement used by an eligible person as a result of eligibility under section 3501(a)(1)(A)(iii), 3501(a)(1)(C), or 3501(a)(1)(D)(i) of this title shall be deducted from any entitlement to which such person may subsequently be entitled under this chapter.".

Such Act further (applicable with respect to a payment of educational assistance allowance made after 9/11/2001, as provided by § 302(b) of such Act, which appears as a note to this section), in subsec. (a)(2)(B)(i), inserted "or of being involuntarily ordered to full-time National Guard duty under section 502(f) of title 32".

Other provisions:

Application of amendments made by § 108(c) of Act Dec. 27, 2001. Act Dec. 27, 2001, P. L. 107-103, Title I, § 108(c)(4), provides: "The amendments made by this subsection [amending 38 USCS §§ 3511(a)(1) and 3512(b)] shall apply with respect to any determination (whether administrative or judicial) of the eligibility of a spouse or surviving spouse for educational assistance under chapter 35 of title 38, United States Code [38 USCS §§ 3500 et seq.], made on or after the date of the enactment of this Act, whether pursuant to an original claim for such assistance or pursuant to a reapplication or attempt to reopen or readjudicate a claim for such assistance.".

Application of amendments made by § 302(a) of Act Dec. 22, 2006. Act Dec. 22, 2006, P. L. 109-461, Title III, § 302(b), 120 Stat. 3428, provides: "The amendment made by subsection (a) [amending subsec. (a)(2)(B)(i) of this section] shall apply with respect to a payment of educational assistance allowance made after September 11, 2001.".

CODE OF FEDERAL REGULATIONS

Department of Veterans Affairs—Vocational rehabilitation and education, 38 CFR 21.1 et seq.

RESEARCH GUIDE

Am Jur:

77 Am Jur 2d, Veterans and Veterans' Laws § 137.

INTERPRETIVE NOTES AND DECISIONS

Because benefits were based on status of child as eligible person through each disabled veteran parent, and absent aggregation restrictions, under 2003 version of 38 USCS § 3511(a)(1), appellant student with two disabled parents could receive educational benefits not to exceed 45 months from status of each parent. Osman v Peake (2008) 22 Vet App 252, 2008 US App Vet Claims LEXIS 1063.

§ 3512. Periods of eligibility

(a) The educational assistance to which an eligible person whose eligibility is based on the death or disability of a parent or on a parent being listed in one of the categories referred to in section 3501(a)(1)(C) of this title [38 USCS § 3501(a)(1)(C)] is entitled under section 3511 of this title [38 USCS § 3511] or subchapter V of this chapter [38 USCS §§ 3540 et seq.] may be afforded the person during the period beginning on the person's eighteenth birthday, or on the successful completion of the person's secondary schooling, whichever first occurs, and ending on the person's twenty-sixth birthday, except that—

(1), (2) [Unchanged]

(3) if the Secretary first finds that the parent from whom eligibility is derived has a service-connected total disability permanent in nature, or if the death of the parent from whom eligibility is derived occurs, after the eligible person's eighteenth birthday but before the person's twenty-sixth birthday, then (unless paragraph (4) or (5) applies) such period shall end 8 years

after the date that is elected by that person to be the beginning date of entitlement under section 3511 of this title [38 USCS § 3511] or subchapter V of this chapter [38 USCS §§ 3540 et seq.] if—

(A) the Secretary approves that beginning date;

(B) the eligible person elects that beginning date by not later than the end of the 60-day period beginning on the date on which the Secretary provides written notice to that person of that person's opportunity to make such election, such notice including a statement of the deadline for the election imposed under this subparagraph; and

(C) that beginning date—

(i) in the case of a person whose eligibility is based on a parent who has a service-connected total disability permanent in nature, is the date determined pursuant to subsection (d), or any date between the two dates described in subsection (d); and

(ii) in the case of a person whose eligibility is based on the death of a parent, is between—

(I) the date of the parent's death; and

(II) the date of the Secretary's decision that the death was service-connected;

(4) if the person otherwise eligible under paragraph (3) fails to elect a beginning date of entitlement in accordance with that paragraph, the beginning date of the person's entitlement shall be the date of the Secretary's decision that the parent has a service-connected total disability permanent in nature, or that the parent's death was service-connected, whichever is applicable;

(5) if the person serves on duty with the Armed Forces as an eligible person after the person's eighteenth birthday but before the person's twenty-sixth birthday, then such period shall end eight years after the person's first discharge or release from such duty with the Armed Forces (excluding from such eight years all periods during which the eligible person served on active duty before August 1, 1962, pursuant to (A) a call or order thereto issued to the person as a Reserve after July 30, 1961, or (B) an extension of an enlistment, appointment, or period of duty with the Armed Forces pursuant to section 2 of Public Law 87-117) [former 10 USCS § 263 note]; however, in no event shall such period be extended beyond the person's thirty-first birthday by reason of this paragraph;

(6) if the person becomes eligible by reason of a parent being listed in one of the categories referred to in section 3501(a)(1)(C) of this title [38 USCS § 3501(a)(1)(C)] after the person's eighteenth birthday but before the person's twenty-sixth birthday, then (unless paragraph (5) applies) such period shall end eight years after the date on which the person becomes eligible by reason of such provisions, but in no event shall such period be extended beyond the person's thirty-first birthday by reason of this paragraph;

(7)(A) if such person is enrolled in an educational institution regularly operated on the quarter or semester system and such period ends during a quarter or semester, such period shall be extended to the end of the quarter or semester; or

(B) if such person is enrolled in an educational institution operated on other than a quarter or semester system and such period ends after a major portion of the course is completed, such period shall be extended to the end of the course, or until 12 weeks have expired, whichever first occurs; and

(8) if the person is pursuing a preparatory course described in section 3002(3)(B) of this title [38 USCS § 3002(3)(B)], such period may begin on the date that is the first day of such course pursuit, notwithstanding that such date may be before the person's eighteenth birthday, except that in no case may such person be afforded educational assistance under this chapter [38 USCS §§ 3500 et seq.] for pursuit of secondary schooling unless such course pursuit would otherwise be authorized under this subsection.

(b)(1)(A) Except as provided in subparagraph (B), (C), or (D), a person made eligible by subparagraph (B) or (D) of section 3501(a)(1) of this title [38 USCS § 3501(a)(1)] or a person made eligible by the disability of a spouse under section 3501(a)(1)(E) of this title [38 USCS § 3501(a)(1)(E)] may be afforded educational assistance under this chapter during the 10-year period beginning on the date (as determined by the Secretary) the person becomes an eligible person within the meaning of section 3501(a)(1)(B), 3501(a)(1)(D)(i), 3501(a)(1)(D)(ii), or 3501(a)(1)(E) of this title [38 USCS § 3501(a)(1)(B), 3501(a)(1)(D)(i), 3501(a)(1)(D)(ii), or 3501(a)(1)(E)]. In the case of a surviving spouse made eligible by clause (ii) of section 3501(a)(1)(D) of this title [38 USCS § 3501(a)(1)(D)], the 10-year period may not be reduced by any earlier period during which the person was eligible for educational assistance under this chapter as a spouse made eligible by clause (i) of that section.

(B) Notwithstanding subparagraph (A), an eligible person referred to in that subparagraph may, subject to the Secretary's approval, elect a later beginning date for the 10-year period than would otherwise be applicable to the person under that subparagraph. The beginning date so elected may be any date between the beginning date determined for the person under subparagraph (A) and whichever of the following dates applies:

38 USCS § 3512

(i) The date on which the Secretary notifies the veteran from whom eligibility is derived that the veteran has a service-connected total disability permanent in nature.

(ii) The date on which the Secretary determines that the veteran from whom eligibility is derived died of a service-connected disability.

(iii) The date on which the Secretary notifies the member of the Armed Forces from whom eligibility is derived that the member has a total disability permanent in nature incurred or aggravated in the line of duty in the active military, naval, or air service.

(C) Notwithstanding subparagraph (A), an eligible person referred to in that subparagraph who is made eligible under section 3501(a)(1)(B) of this title [38 USCS § 3501(a)(1)(B)] by reason of the death of a person on active duty may be afforded educational assistance under this chapter during the 20-year period beginning on the date (as determined by the Secretary) such person becomes an eligible person within the meaning of such section.

(D) Notwithstanding subparagraph (A), an eligible person referred to in that subparagraph who is made eligible under section 3501(a)(1)(D)(i) of this title [38 USCS § 3501(a)(1)(D)(i)] by reason of a service-connected disability that was determined to be a total disability permanent in nature not later than three years after discharge from service may be afforded educational assistance under this chapter during the 20-year period beginning on the date the disability was so determined to be a total disability permanent in nature, but only if the eligible person remains the spouse of the disabled person throughout the period.

(2) Notwithstanding the provisions of paragraph (1) of this subsection, in the case of any eligible person (as defined in section 3501(a)(1)(B), (C), (D), or (E) of this title [38 USCS § 3501(a)(1)(B), (C), (D), or (E)]) whose eligibility is based on the death or disability of a spouse or on a spouse being listed in one of the categories referred to in section 3501(a)(1)(C) of this title [38 USCS § 3501(a)(1)(C)] who was prevented from initiating or completing such person's chosen program of education within such period because of a physical or mental disability which was not the result of such person's own willful misconduct, such person shall, upon application made within one year after (A) the last date of the delimiting period otherwise applicable under this section, (B) the termination of the period of mental or physical disability, or (C) October 1, 1980, whichever is the latest, be granted an extension of the applicable delimiting period for such length of time as the Secretary determines, from the evidence, that such person was so prevented from initiating or completing such program of education. When an extension of the applicable delimiting period is granted under the exception in the preceding sentence, the delimiting period will again begin running on the first day following such eligible person's recovery from such disability on which it is reasonably feasible, as determined in accordance with regulations which the Secretary shall prescribe, for such eligible person to initiate or resume pursuit of a program of education with educational assistance under this chapter [38 USCS §§ 3500 et seq.].

(3) [Deleted]

(c)(1) Notwithstanding subsection (a) and subject to paragraph (2), an eligible person may be afforded educational assistance beyond the age limitation applicable to the person under such subsection if—

(A) the person suspends pursuit of such person's program of education after having enrolled in such program within the time period applicable to such person under such subsection;

(B) the person is unable to complete such program after the period of suspension and before attaining the age limitation applicable to the person under such subsection; and

(C) the Secretary finds that the suspension was due to either of the following:

(i) The actions of the person as the primary provider of personal care services for a veteran or member of the Armed Forces under section 1720G(a) of this title [38 USCS § 1720G(a)].

(ii) Conditions otherwise beyond the control of the person.

(2) Paragraph (1) shall not apply with respect to the period of an individual as a primary provider of personal care services if the period concludes with the revocation of the individual's designation as such a primary provider under section 1720G(a)(7)(D) of this title [38 USCS § 1720G(a)(7)(D)].

(3) Educational assistance may not be afforded a person under paragraph (1) after the earlier of—

(A) the age limitation applicable to the person under subsection (a), plus a period of time equal to the period the person was required to suspend pursuit of the person's program of education as described in paragraph (1); or

(B) the date of the person's thirty-first birthday.

(d) The term "first finds" as used in this section means the effective date of the rating or date of notification to the person from whom eligibility is derived establishing a service-connected total disability permanent in nature whichever is more advantageous to the eligible person.

(e) No person made eligible by section 3501(a)(1)(C) of this title [38 USCS § 3501(a)(1)(C)] based on a spouse being listed in one of the categories referred to in section 3501(a)(1)(C) of this title [38 USCS § 3501(a)(1)(C)] may be afforded educational assistance under this chapter [38 USCS §§ 3501 et seq.] beyond 10 years after the date on which the spouse was so listed.

(f), (g) [Deleted]

(h) Notwithstanding any other provision of this section, if an eligible person, during the delimiting period otherwise applicable to such person under this section, serves on active duty pursuant to an order to active duty issued under section 688, 12301(a), 12301(d), 12301(g), 12302, or 12304 of title 10 [10 USCS § 688, 12301(a), 12301(d), 12301(g), 12302, or 12304], or is involuntarily ordered to full-time National Guard duty under section 502(f) of title 32 [32 USCS § 502(f)], such person shall be granted an extension of such delimiting period for the length of time equal to the period of such active duty plus four months.

(As amended Nov. 1, 2000, P. L. 106-419, Title I, Subtitle B, §§ 112, 114(b), 114 Stat. 1831, 1833; June 5, 2001, P. L. 107-14, §§ 7(f)(1), 8(a)(6), 115 Stat. 33, 34; Dec. 27, 2001, P. L. 107-103, Title I, §§ 103(b), 108(b)(2), (c)(2), (3), 115 Stat. 979, 985; Dec. 6, 2002, P. L. 107-330, Title III, § 308(e)(1), 116 Stat. 2828; Dec. 16, 2003, P. L. 108-183, Title III, §§ 303(a), 306(f)(2), 117 Stat. 2659, 2661; Dec. 10, 2004, P. L. 108-454, Title I, § 105, 118 Stat. 3601; Dec. 21, 2006, P. L. 109-444, § 3(b)(3), 120 Stat. 3306; Dec. 22, 2006, P. L. 109-461, Title III, § 301(b)(3), 120 Stat. 3426; Oct. 10, 2008, P. L. 110-389, Title III, Subtitle B, § 321, 122 Stat. 4168; Oct. 13, 2010, P. L. 111-275, Title X, § 1001(h), 124 Stat. 2896; Jan. 4, 2011, P. L. 111-377, Title II, § 201(c), 124 Stat. 4124.)

HISTORY; ANCILLARY LAWS AND DIRECTIVES

Explanatory notes:
Section 3(b)(3) of Act Dec. 21, 2006, P. L. 109-444, amended this section; however, pursuant to § 1006(b) of Act Dec. 22, 2006, P. L. 109-461, which appears as 38 USCS § 101 note, as of the enactment of Act Dec. 22, 2006, P. L. 109-461, Act Dec. 21, 2006, P. L. 109-444 and the amendments made by such Act were deemed for all purposes not to have taken effect and such § 3(b)(3) ceased to be in effect.

Amendments:
2000. Act Nov. 1, 2000, in subsec. (a), in para. (3), substituted "8 years after the date that is elected by that person to be the beginning date of entitlement under section 3511 of this title or subchapter V of this chapter if—" and subparas. (A)–(C) for "8 years after, whichever date last occurs: (A) the date on which the Secretary first finds that the parent from whom eligibility is derived has a service-connected total disability permanent in nature, or (B) the date of death of the parent from whom eligibility is derived;", in para. (5), deleted "and" following the concluding semicolon, in para. (6), substituted "; and" for a concluding period, and added para. (7).

2001. Act June 5, 2001 (effective as if enacted on 11/1/2000, immediately after enactment of Act Nov. 1, 2000, as provided by § 7(f)(2) of the 2001 Act, in subsec. (a)(3), substituted subpara. (B) for one which read: "(B) the eligible person makes that election after the person's eighteenth birthday but before the person's twenty-sixth birthday; and", and, in subpara. (C)(i), substituted "the date determined pursuant to" for "between the dates described in".

Such Act further, in subsec. (a)(5), substituted "paragraph (4)" for "clause (4) of this subsection".

Such Act further purported to amend subsec. (b)(2) by substituting "willful" for "willfull"; however, this amendment could not be executed because the word "willfull" did not appear in such subsection.

Act Dec. 27, 2001 (applicable as provided by § 108(c)(4) of such Act, which appears as 38 USCS § 3511 note), in subsec. (b), substituted para. (1) for one which read:

"(1) No person made eligible by section 3501(a)(1)(B) or (D) of this title may be afforded educational assistance under this chapter beyond 10 years after whichever of the following last occurs:

"(A) The date on which the Secretary first finds the spouse from whom eligibility is derived has a service-connected total disability permanent in nature.

"(B) The date of death of the spouse from whom eligibility is derived who dies while a total disability evaluated as permanent in nature was in existence.

"(C) The date on which the Secretary determines that the spouse from whom eligibility is derived died of a service-connected disability.",

and deleted para. (3), which read:

"(3)(A) Notwithstanding the provisions of paragraph (1) of this subsection, any eligible person (as defined in clause (B) or (D) of section 3501(a)(1) of this title) may, subject to the approval of the Secretary, be permitted to elect a date referred to in subparagraph (B) of this paragraph to commence receiving educational assistance benefits under this chapter. The date so elected shall be the beginning date of the delimiting period applicable to such person under this section.

"(B) The date which an eligible person may elect under subparagraph (A) of this paragraph is any date during the period beginning on the date the person became an

38 USCS § 3512   VETERANS' BENEFITS

eligible person within the meaning of clause (B) or (D) of section 3501(a)(1) of this title and ending on the date determined under subparagraph (A), (B), or (C) of paragraph (1) of this subsection to be applicable to such person.''.

Such Act further deleted subsec. (g), which read: ''(g) Any entitlement used by any eligible person as a result of eligibility under the provisions of section 3501(a)(1)(A)(iii) or 3501(a)(1)(C) of this title shall be deducted from any entitlement to which such person may subsequently become entitled under the provisions of this chapter.''.

Such Act further (effective as of 9/11/2001, as provided by § 103(e) of such Act, which appears as 38 USCS § 3013 note), added subsec. (h).

2002. Act Dec. 6, 2002 (effective 11/1/2000, as provided by § 308(e)(2) of such Act, which appears as a note to this section), in subsec. (a), in para. (3), substituted ''paragraph (4) or (5)'' for ''paragraph (4)'', in subpara. (C)(i), substituted ''subsection (d), or any date between the two dates described in subsection (d)'' for ''subsection (d)'', redesignated paras. (4)–(7) as paras. (5)–(8), respectively, inserted new para. (4), and, in para. (6) as redesignated, substituted ''paragraph (5)'' for ''paragraph (4)''.

2003. Act Dec. 16, 2003 (effective as of 9/11/2001, as provided by § 303(b) of such act, which appears as a note to this section), in subsec. (h), inserted ''or is involuntarily ordered to full-time National Guard duty under section 502(f) of title 32,''.

Such Act further (effective 90 days after enactment, as provided by § 306(h)(2) of such Act, which appears as 38 USCS § 3485 note), deleted subsec. (f), which read: ''(f) Any eligible person (as defined in section 3501(a)(1)(B), (C), or (D) of this chapter) shall be entitled to an additional period of eligibility for an education loan under subchapter III of chapter 36 of this title beyond the maximum period provided for in this section pursuant to the same terms and conditions set forth with respect to an eligible veteran in section 3462(a)(2) of this title.''.

2004. Act Dec. 10, 2004, in subsec. (b)(1), in subpara. (A), substituted ''in subparagraph (B) or (C)'' for ''in subparagraph (B)'', and added subpara. (C).

2006. Act Dec. 21, 2006 (applicable with respect to a payment of educational assistance for a course of education pursued after enactment, as provided by § 301(d) of such Act, which appears as 38 USCS § 3501 note), in subsec. (a), in the introductory matter, substituted ''an eligible person whose eligibility is based on the death or disability of a parent or on a parent being listed in one of the categories referred to in section 3501(a)(1)(C) of this title'' for ''an eligible person within the meaning of section 3501(a)(1)(A) of this title'', and, in para. (6), substituted ''a parent being listed in one of the categories referred to in section 3501(a)(1)(C)'' for ''the provisions of section 3501(a)(1)(A)(iii)''; in subsec. (b), in para. (1), in subpara. (A), inserted ''or a person made eligible by the disability of a spouse made eligible by 3501(a)(1)(E) of this title'', and substituted ''3501(a)(1)(D)(ii), or 3501(a)(1)(E) of this title'' for ''or 3501(a)(1)(D)(ii) of this title'', and, in subpara. (B), added cl. (iii), in para. (2), substituted ''(D), or (E) of this title'' for ''or (D) of this title'', and inserted ''whose eligibility is based on the death or disability of a spouse or on a spouse being listed in one of the categories referred to in section 3501(a)(1)(C) of this title''; in subsec. (d), substituted ''person'' for ''veteran'' following ''notification to the''; and, in subsec. (e), inserted ''based on a spouse being listed in one of the categories referred to in section 3501(a)(1)(C) of this title'', inserted ''so'', and deleted ''by the Secretary concerned in one of the categories referred to in such section or December 24, 1970, whichever last occurs'' preceding the concluding period.

2008. Act Oct. 10, 2008, in subsec. (b)(1), in subpara. (A), substituted ''subparagraph (B), (C), or (D)'' for ''subparagraph (B) or (C)'', and added subpara. (D).

2010. Act Oct. 13, 2010, in subsec. (a)(6), substituted ''this paragraph'' for ''this clause''.

2011. Act Jan. 4, 2011 (effective on 8/1/2011, and applicable to preventions and suspension of pursuit of programs of education that commence on or after that date, as provided by § 201(d) of such Act, which appears as 38 USCS § 3031 note), substituted subsec. (c) for one which read: ''(c) Notwithstanding the provisions of subsection (a) of this section, an eligible person may be afforded educational assistance beyond the age limitation applicable to such person under such subsection if (1) such person suspends pursuit of such person's program of education after having enrolled in such program within the time period applicable to such person under such subsection, (2) such person is unable to complete such program after the period of suspension and before attaining the age limitation applicable to such person under such subsection, and (3) the Secretary finds that the suspension was due to conditions beyond the control of such person; but in no event shall educational assistance be afforded such person by reason of this subsection beyond the age limitation applicable to such person under subsection (a) of this section plus a period of time equal to the period such person was required to suspend the pursuit of such person's program, or beyond such person's thirty-first birthday, whichever is earlier.''.

Other provisions:

Effective date of amendments made by § 7(f)(1) of Act June 5, 2001. Act June 5, 2001, P. L. 107-14, § 7(f)(2), 115 Stat. 34, provides: ''The amendments made by paragraph (1) [amending subsec. (a)(3) of this section] shall take effect as if enacted on November 1, 2000, immediately after the enactment of the Veterans Benefits and Health Care Improvement Act of 2000 [enacted Nov. 1, 2000].''.

Effective date of Dec. 6, 2002 amendments. Act Dec. 6, 2002, P. L. 107-330, Title III, § 308(e)(2), 116 Stat. 2828, provides: ''The amendments made by this subsection [amending subsec. (a) of this section] shall take effect November 1, 2000.''.

Effective date of Dec. 16, 2003 amendment. Act Dec. 16, 2003, P. L. 108-183, Title III,

READJUSTMENT BENEFITS 38 USCS § 3524

§ 303(b), 117 Stat. 2659, provides: "The amendment made by subsection (a) [amending subsec. (h) of this section] shall take effect as of September 11, 2001.".

CODE OF FEDERAL REGULATIONS
Department of Veterans Affairs—Vocational rehabilitation and education, 38 CFR 21.1 et seq.

RESEARCH GUIDE
Am Jur:
77 Am Jur 2d, Veterans and Veterans' Laws § 137.

INTERPRETIVE NOTES AND DECISIONS

Ten-year period described in 38 USCS § 3512(b)(1) does not begin until last of three possible alternatives set forth in subsection (b)(1) has been eliminated and regulation limiting period of eligibility for dependents' educational assistance to fixed term of ten years is unlawful. Ozer v Principi (2001) 14 Vet App 257, 2001 US App Vet Claims LEXIS 69.

Board of Veterans' Appeals erred in denying veteran's wife Dependents' Education Assistance benefits under 38 USCS § 3512, on basis that she married veteran more than 10 years after he was deemed permanently and totally disabled, because 10-year period began on date wife became eligible under 38 USCS § 3501(a)(1)(D)(i), which was date she married veteran. Cypert v Peake (2008) 22 Vet App 307, 2008 US App Vet Claims LEXIS 1554.

§ 3513. Application

CODE OF FEDERAL REGULATIONS
Department of Veterans Affairs—Vocational rehabilitation and education, 38 CFR 21.1 et seq.

RESEARCH GUIDE
Am Jur:
77 Am Jur 2d, Veterans and Veterans' Laws § 137.

INTERPRETIVE NOTES AND DECISIONS

Because benefits were based on status of child as eligible person through each disabled veteran parent, and absent aggregation restrictions, under 2003 version of 38 USCS § 3511(a)(1), appellant student with two disabled parents could receive educational benefits not to exceed 45 months from status of each parent; in 38 USCS § 3513, Congress did not specifically limit number of parents making such application for benefits or number of parents under whose auspices application could be made. Osman v Peake (2008) 22 Vet App 252, 2008 US App Vet Claims LEXIS 1063.

§ 3514. Processing of applications

RESEARCH GUIDE
Am Jur:
77 Am Jur 2d, Veterans and Veterans' Laws § 137.

SUBCHAPTER III. PROGRAM OF EDUCATION

§ 3520. Educational and vocational counseling

CODE OF FEDERAL REGULATIONS
Department of Veterans Affairs—Medical, 38 CFR 17.30 et seq.
Department of Veterans Affairs—Vocational rehabilitation and education, 38 CFR 21.1 et seq.

§ 3521. Approval of application

CODE OF FEDERAL REGULATIONS
Department of Veterans Affairs—Medical, 38 CFR 17.30 et seq.
Department of Veterans Affairs—Vocational rehabilitation and education, 38 CFR 21.1 et seq.

§ 3523. Disapproval of enrollment in certain courses

CODE OF FEDERAL REGULATIONS
Department of Veterans Affairs—Vocational rehabilitation and education, 38 CFR 21.1 et seq.

§ 3524. Discontinuance for unsatisfactory progress

CODE OF FEDERAL REGULATIONS
Department of Veterans Affairs—Vocational rehabilitation and education, 38 CFR 21.1 et seq.

38 USCS § 3531

SUBCHAPTER IV. PAYMENTS TO ELIGIBLE PERSONS

§ 3531. Educational assistance allowance

CODE OF FEDERAL REGULATIONS

Department of Veterans Affairs—Nondiscrimination in federally-assisted programs of the Department of Veterans Affairs-effectuation of Title VI of the Civil Rights Act of 1964, 38 CFR 18.1 et seq.
Department of Veterans Affairs—Delegation of responsibility in connection with Title VI, Civil Rights Act of 1964, 38 CFR 18a.1 et seq.
Department of Veterans Affairs—Practice and procedure under Title VI of the Civil Rights Act of 1964 and Part 18 of this chapter, 38 CFR 18b.1 et seq.
Department of Veterans Affairs—Vocational rehabilitation and education, 38 CFR 21.1 et seq.
Department of Veterans Affairs—Loan guaranty and vocational rehabilitation and counseling programs, 48 CFR 871.100 et seq.

RESEARCH GUIDE

Am Jur:
77 Am Jur 2d, Veterans and Veterans' Laws § 137.

§ 3532. Computation of educational assistance allowance

(a)(1) The educational assistance allowance on behalf of an eligible person who is pursuing a program of education consisting of institutional courses shall be paid at the monthly rate of $788 for full-time, $592 for three-quarter-time, or $394 for half-time pursuit.

(2) The educational assistance allowance on behalf of an eligible person pursuing a program of education on less than a half-time basis shall be paid at the rate of the lesser of—

(A) the established charges for tuition and fees that the educational institution involved requires similarly circumstanced nonveterans enrolled in the same program to pay; or

(B) $788 per month for a full-time course.

(b) The educational assistance allowance to be paid on behalf of an eligible person who is pursuing a full-time program of education which consists of institutional courses and alternate phases of training in a business or industrial establishment with the training in the business or industrial establishment being strictly supplemental to the institutional portion, shall be computed at the rate of $788 per month.

(c)(1) [Unchanged]

(2) The monthly educational assistance allowance to be paid on behalf of an eligible person pursuing a farm cooperative program under this chapter [38 USCS §§ 3500 et seq.] shall be $636 for full-time, $477 for three-quarter-time, or $319 for half-time pursuit.

(d) [Unchanged]

(e) In the case of an eligible person who is pursuing a program of education under this chapter [38 USCS §§ 3500 et seq.] while incarcerated in a Federal, State, local, or other penal institution or correctional facility for conviction of a felony, the educational assistance allowance shall be paid in the same manner prescribed in section 3482(g) of this title [38 USCS § 3482(g)] for incarcerated veterans, except that the references therein to the monthly educational assistance allowance prescribed for a veteran with no dependents shall be deemed to refer to the applicable allowance payable to an eligible person under corresponding provisions of this chapter [38 USCS §§ 3500 et seq.] or chapter 36 of this title [38 USCS §§ 3670 et seq.], as determined by the Secretary.

(f)(1) Subject to paragraph (3), the amount of educational assistance payable under this chapter for a licensing or certification test described in section 3501(a)(5) of this title [38 USCS § 3501(a)(5)] is the lesser of $2,000 or the fee charged for the test.

(2) The number of months of entitlement charged in the case of any individual for such licensing or certification test is equal to the number (including any fraction) determined by dividing the total amount paid to such individual for such test by the full-time monthly institutional rate of the educational assistance allowance which, except for paragraph (1), such individual would otherwise be paid under this chapter [38 USCS §§ 3500 et seq.].

(3) In no event shall payment of educational assistance under this subsection for such a test exceed the amount of the individual's available entitlement under this chapter [38 USCS §§ 3500 et seq.].

(g)(1) Subject to paragraph (3), the amount of educational assistance payable under this chapter for a national test for admission or national test providing an opportunity for course credit at institutions of higher learning described in section 3501(a)(5) of this title [38 USCS § 3501(a)(5)] is the amount of the fee charged for the test.

(2) The number of months of entitlement charged in the case of any individual for a test described in paragraph (1) is equal to the number (including any fraction) determined by dividing the total amount of educational assistance paid such individual for such test by the full-time

monthly institutional rate of educational assistance, except for paragraph (1), such individual would otherwise be paid under this chapter [38 USCS §§ 3500 et seq.].

(3) In no event shall payment of educational assistance under this subsection for a test described in paragraph (1) exceed the amount of the individual's available entitlement under this chapter [38 USCS §§ 3500 et seq.].

(As amended June 9, 1998, P. L. 105-178, Title VIII, Subtitle B, § 8210(a), as added July 22, 1998, P. L. 105-206, Title IX, § 9014(b), 112 Stat. 866; Nov. 1, 2000, P. L. 106-419, Title I, Subtitle B, § 111(a), Subtitle C, § 122(b)(4), 114 Stat. 1830, 1834; Dec. 27, 2001, P. L. 107-103, Title I, § 102(a), 115 Stat. 978; Dec. 16, 2003, P. L. 108-183, Title III, § 302(a), 117 Stat. 2658; Dec. 10, 2004, P. L. 108-454, Title I, § 106(b)(3), 118 Stat. 3603; Dec. 22, 2006, P. L. 109-461, Title X, § 1002(e), 120 Stat. 3465.)

HISTORY; ANCILLARY LAWS AND DIRECTIVES

Amendments:

1998. Act June 9, 1998 (effective on 10/1/98 and applicable with respect to educational assistance allowances paid for months after 9/98, as provided by § 8210(e) of such Act, which appears as a note to this section), as amended July 22, 1998 (effective simultaneously with the enactment of, and as if included in, Act June 9, 1998, as provided by § 9016 of Act July 22, 1998, which appears as 23 USCS § 101 note), in subsec. (a), in para. (1), substituted "$485" for "$404", substituted "$365" for "$304", and substituted "$242" for "$202" and, in para. (2), substituted "$485" for "$404"; in subsec. (b), substituted "$485" for "$404"; and, in subsec. (c), in para. (2), substituted "$392" for "$327", substituted "$294" for "$245", and substituted "$196" for "$163".

Act July 22, 1998 (effective simultaneously with the enactment of, and as if included in, Act June 9, 1998, as provided by § 9016 of Act July 22, 1998, which appears as 23 USCS § 101 note) amended Act June 9, 1998, which amended this section.

2000. Act Nov. 1, 2000 (effective and applicable as provided by § 111(e) of such Act, which appears as a note to this section), in subsec. (a), in para. (1), substituted "$588" for "$485", substituted "$441" for "$365", and substituted "$294" for "$242" and, in para. (2), substituted "$588" for "$485"; in subsec. (b), substituted "$588" for "$485"; and, in subsec. (c)(2), substituted "$475" for "$392", substituted "$356" for "$294", and substituted "$238" for "$196".

Such Act further (effective and applicable as provided by § 122(d) of such Act, which appears as 38 USCS § 3032 note) added subsec. (f).

2001. Act Dec. 27, 2001 (effective and applicable as provided by § 102(e) of such Act, which appears as a note to this section), in subsec. (a), in para. (1), substituted "$670" for "$588", substituted "$503" for "441", and substituted "$335" for "$294", and, in para. (2), substituted "$670" for "$588"; in subsec. (b), substituted "$670" for "$588"; and, in subsec. (c)(2), substituted "$541" for "$475", substituted "$406" for "$356", and substituted "$271" for "$238".

2003. Act Dec. 16, 2003 (effective 7/1/2004 and applicable to educational assistance allowances payable under 38 USCS §§ 3500 et seq. and 3687(b)(2) for months beginning on or after that date, as provided by § 302(e) of such Act, which appears as a note to this section), in subsec. (a), in para. (1), substituted "at the monthly rate of $788 for full-time, $592 for three-quarter-time, or $394 for half-time pursuit." for "at the monthly rate of $670 for full-time, $503 for three-quarter-time, or $335 for half-time pursuit.", and, in para. (2), substituted "at the rate of the lesser of—

"(A) the established charges for tuition and fees that the educational institution involved requires similarly circumstanced nonveterans enrolled in the same program to pay; or

"(B) $788 per month for a full-time course."

for "at the rate of (A) the established charges for tuition and fees that the educational institution involved requires similarly circumstanced nonveterans enrolled in the same program to pay, or (B) $670 per month for a full-time course, whichever is the lesser."; in subsec. (b), substituted "$788" for "$670"; and, in subsec. (c)(2), substituted "shall be $636 for full-time, $477 for three-quarter-time, or $319 for half-time pursuit." for "shall be $541 for full-time, $406 for three-quarter-time, and $271 for half-time pursuit.".

2004. Act Dec. 10, 2004, added subsec. (g).

2006. Act Dec. 22, 2006, in subsec. (e), substituted "local, or other penal institution or correctional facility" for "or local penal institution".

Other provisions:

Effective date and application of June 9, 1998 amendments. Act June 9, 1998, P. L. 105-178, Title VIII, Subtitle B, § 8210(e), as added July 22, 1998, P. L. 105-206, Title IX, § 9014(b), 112 Stat. 866, provides: "The amendments made by this section [amending 38 USCS §§ 3532(a), (b), (c)(2), 3534(b), 3542(a), and 3687(b)(2)] shall take effect on October 1, 1998, and shall apply with respect to educational assistance allowances paid for months after September 1998.".

Effective date and application of Nov. 1, 2000 amendments. Act Nov. 1, 2000, P. L. 106-419, Title I, Subtitle B, § 111(e), provides: "The amendments made by subsections (a) through (d) [amending 38 USCS §§ 3532(a), (b), (c)(2), 3534(b), 3542(a), and 3687(b)(2)] shall take ef-

38 USCS § 3532

fect on November 1, 2000, and shall apply with respect to educational assistance allowances paid under chapter 35 of title 38, United States Code [38 USCS §§ 3500 et seq.], for months after October 2000.".

Effective date and application of Dec. 27, 2001 amendments. Act Dec. 27, 2001, P. L. 107-103, Title I, § 102(e), provides: "The amendments made by this section [amending 38 USCS §§ 3532(a), (b), (c)(2), 3534(b), 3542(a), and 3687(b)(2)] shall take effect as of January 1, 2002, and shall apply with respect to educational assistance allowances payable under chapter 35 and section 3687(b)(2) of title 38, United States Code [38 USCS §§ 3500 et seq. and § 3687(b)(2)], for months beginning on or after that date.".

Effective date and applicability of Dec. 16, 2003 amendments. Act Dec. 16, 2003, P. L. 108-183, Title III, § 302(e), 117 Stat. 2659, provides: "The amendments made by this section [amending 38 USCS §§ 3532(a)–(c), 3534(b), 3542(a), and 3687(b)(2)] shall take effect on July 1, 2004, and shall apply with respect to educational assistance allowances payable under chapter 35 and section 3687(b)(2) of title 38, United States Code [38 USCS §§ 3500 et seq. and § 3687(b)(2)], for months beginning on or after that date.".

CODE OF FEDERAL REGULATIONS
Department of Veterans Affairs—Vocational rehabilitation and education, 38 CFR 21.1 et seq.

RESEARCH GUIDE
Am Jur:
77 Am Jur 2d, Veterans and Veterans' Laws § 137.

INTERPRETIVE NOTES AND DECISIONS

Desire to reduce federal spending provided rational basis for enactment of § 3532(d) providing for educational assistance at institution in Philippines at rate of 50 centers per dollar. Reeves v West (1998) 11 Vet App 255.

§ 3533. Special assistance for the educationally disadvantaged

CODE OF FEDERAL REGULATIONS
Department of Veterans Affairs—Vocational rehabilitation and education, 38 CFR 21.1 et seq.

RESEARCH GUIDE
Am Jur:
77 Am Jur 2d, Veterans and Veterans' Laws § 137.

§ 3534. Apprenticeship or other on-job training; correspondence courses
(a) [Unchanged]
(b) Any eligible spouse or surviving spouse shall be entitled to pursue a program of education exclusively by correspondence and be paid an educational assistance allowance as provided in section 3686 (other than subsection (a)(2)) of this title [38 USCS § 3686] and the period of such spouse's entitlement shall be charged with one month for each $788 which is paid to the spouse as an educational assistance allowance for such course.
(As amended June 9, 1998, P. L. 105-178, Title VIII, Subtitle B, § 8210(b), as added July 22, 1998, P. L. 105-206, Title IX, § 9014(b), 112 Stat. 866; Nov. 1, 2000, P. L. 106-419, Title I, Subtitle B, § 111(b), 114 Stat. 1830; Dec. 27, 2001, P. L. 107-103, Title I, § 102(b), 115 Stat. 978; Dec. 16, 2003, P. L. 108-183, Title III, § 302(b), 117 Stat. 2659.)

HISTORY; ANCILLARY LAWS AND DIRECTIVES
Amendments:
1998. Act June 9, 1998 (effective on 10/1/98 and applicable with respect to educational assistance allowances paid for months after 9/98, as provided by § 8210(e) of such Act, which appears as 38 USCS § 3532 note), as amended July 22, 1998 (effective simultaneously with the enactment of, and as if included in, Act June 9, 1998, as provided by § 9016 of Act July 22, 1998, which appears as 23 USCS § 101 note), in subsec. (b), substituted "$485" for "$404".
Act July 22, 1998 (effective simultaneously with the enactment of, and as if included in, Act June 9, 1998, P. L. 105-178, and as provided by § 9016 of Act July 22, 1998, which appears as 23 USCS § 101 note) amended Act June 9, 1998, which amended this section.
2000. Act Nov. 1, 2000 (effective and applicable as provided by § 111(e) of such Act, which appears as 38 USCS § 3532 note), in subsec. (b), substituted "$588" for "$485".
2001. Act Dec. 27, 2001 (effective and applicable as provided by § 102(e) of such Act, which appears as 38 USCS § 3532 note), in subsec. (b), substituted "$670" for "$588".
2003. Act Dec. 16, 2003 (effective 7/1/2004 and applicable to educational assistance allowances payable under 38 USCS §§ 3500 et seq. and 3687(b)(2) for months beginning on or after that date, as provided by § 302(e) of such Act, which appears as 38 USCS § 3532 note), in subsec. (b), substituted "$788" for "$670".

CODE OF FEDERAL REGULATIONS
Department of Veterans Affairs—Vocational rehabilitation and education, 38 CFR 21.1 et seq.

READJUSTMENT BENEFITS 38 USCS § 3540

RESEARCH GUIDE
Am Jur:
77 Am Jur 2d, Veterans and Veterans' Laws § 137.

§ 3535. Approval of courses

RESEARCH GUIDE
Am Jur:
77 Am Jur 2d, Veterans and Veterans' Laws § 137.

§ 3536. Specialized vocational training courses

CODE OF FEDERAL REGULATIONS
Department of Veterans Affairs—Vocational rehabilitation and education, 38 CFR 21.1 et seq.

RESEARCH GUIDE
Am Jur:
77 Am Jur 2d, Veterans and Veterans' Laws § 137.

§ 3537. Work-study allowance

(a) Subject to subsection (b) of this section, the Secretary shall utilize, in connection with the activities described in section 3485(a) of this title [38 USCS § 3485(a)], the services of any eligible person who is pursuing, in a State, at least a three-quarter-time program of education (other than a course of special restorative training) and shall pay to such person an additional educational assistance allowance (hereinafter in this section referred to as "work-study allowance") in return for such eligible person's agreement to perform such services. The amount of the work-study allowance shall be determined in accordance with section 3485(a) of this title [38 USCS § 3485(a)].
(b) [Unchanged]
(As amended June 5, 2001, P. L. 107-14, § 8(a)(16), 115 Stat. 35.)

HISTORY; ANCILLARY LAWS AND DIRECTIVES
Amendments:
2001. Act June 5, 2001, in subsec. (a), substituted "hereinafter" for "hereafter".

RESEARCH GUIDE
Am Jur:
77 Am Jur 2d, Veterans and Veterans' Laws § 137.

SUBCHAPTER V. SPECIAL RESTORATIVE TRAINING

§ 3540. Purpose

The purpose of special restorative training is to overcome, or lessen, the effects of a manifest physical or mental disability which would handicap an eligible person (other than a person made eligible under subparagraph (C) of such section by reason of a spouse being listed in one of the categories referred to in that subparagraph) in the pursuit of a program of education.
(As amended Dec. 27, 2001, P. L. 107-103, Title I, § 109(a), 115 Stat. 986; Dec. 21, 2006, P. L. 109-444, § 3(b)(4), 120 Stat. 3307; Dec. 22, 2006, P. L. 109-461, Title III, § 301(b)(4), 120 Stat. 3427.)

HISTORY; ANCILLARY LAWS AND DIRECTIVES
Explanatory notes:
Section 3(b)(4) of Act Dec. 21, 2006, P. L. 109-444, amended this section; however, pursuant to § 1006(b) of Act Dec. 22, 2006, P. L. 109-461, which appears as 38 USCS § 101 note, as of the enactment of Act Dec. 22, 2006, P. L. 109-461, Act Dec. 21, 2006, P. L. 109-444 and the amendments made by such Act were deemed for all purposes not to have taken effect and such § 3(b)(4) ceased to be in effect.

Amendments:
2001. Act Dec. 27, 2001, substituted "subparagraphs (A), (B), and (D) of section 3501(a)(1) of this title" for "section 3501(a)(1)(A) of this title".
2006. Act Dec. 22, 2006 (applicable with respect to a payment of educational assistance for a course of education pursued after enactment, as provided by § 301(d) of such Act, which appears as 38 USCS § 3501 note), substituted "(other than a person made eligible under subparagraph (C) of such section by reason of a spouse being listed in one of the categories referred to in that subparagraph)" for "(as defined in subparagraphs (A), (B), and (D) of section 3501(a)(1) of this title)".

38 USCS § 3540 — VETERANS' BENEFITS

CODE OF FEDERAL REGULATIONS

Department of Veterans Affairs—Nondiscrimination in federally-assisted programs of the Department of Veterans Affairs-effectuation of Title VI of the Civil Rights Act of 1964, 38 CFR 18.1 et seq.
Department of Veterans Affairs—Delegation of responsibility in connection with Title VI, Civil Rights Act of 1964, 38 CFR 18a.1 et seq.
Department of Veterans Affairs—Practice and procedure under Title VI of the Civil Rights Act of 1964 and Part 18 of this chapter, 38 CFR 18b.1 et seq.
Department of Veterans Affairs—Vocational rehabilitation and education, 38 CFR 21.1 et seq.
Department of Veterans Affairs—Per diem for nursing home care of veterans in State homes, 38 CFR 51.1 et seq.
Department of Veterans Affairs—Forms, 38 CFR 58.10 et seq.
Department of Veterans Affairs—Loan guaranty and vocational rehabilitation and counseling programs, 48 CFR 871.100 et seq.

RESEARCH GUIDE

Am Jur:
77 Am Jur 2d, Veterans and Veterans' Laws § 137.

§ 3541. Entitlement to special restorative training

(a) The Secretary at the request of an eligible person is authorized—
   (1), (2) [Unchanged]
Such a course, at the discretion of the Secretary, may contain elements that would contribute toward an ultimate objective of a program of education.
(b) [Unchanged]
(As amended Dec. 27, 2001, P. L. 107-103, Title I, § 109(b)(1), 115 Stat. 986.)

HISTORY; ANCILLARY LAWS AND DIRECTIVES

Amendments:
2001. Act Dec. 27, 2001, in subsec. (a), in the introductory matter, deleted "of the parent or guardian" following "request".

CODE OF FEDERAL REGULATIONS

Department of Veterans Affairs—Per diem for nursing home care of veterans in State homes, 38 CFR 51.1 et seq.
Department of Veterans Affairs—Forms, 38 CFR 58.10 et seq.

RESEARCH GUIDE

Am Jur:
77 Am Jur 2d, Veterans and Veterans' Laws § 137.

§ 3542. Special training allowance

(a) While the eligible person is enrolled in and pursuing a full-time course of special restorative training, the eligible person shall be entitled to receive a special training allowance computed at the basic rate of $788 per month. If the charges for tuition and fees applicable to any such course are more than $247 per calendar month, the basic monthly allowance may be increased by the amount that such charges exceed $247 a month, upon election by the eligible person to have such person's period of entitlement reduced by one day for each such increased amount of allowance that is equal to one-thirtieth of the full-time basic monthly rate of special training allowance.
(b), (c) [Unchanged]
(As amended June 9, 1998, P. L. 105-178, Title VIII, Subtitle B, § 8210(c), as added July 22, 1998, P. L. 105-206, Title IX, § 9014(b), 112 Stat. 866; Nov. 1, 2000, P. L. 106-419, Title I, Subtitle B, § 111(c), 114 Stat. 1830; Dec. 27, 2001, P. L. 107-103, Title I, §§ 102(c), 109(b)(2), 115 Stat. 978, 986. Dec. 16, 2003, P. L. 108-183, Title III, § 302(c), 117 Stat. 2659.)

HISTORY; ANCILLARY LAWS AND DIRECTIVES

Amendments:
1998. Act June 9, 1998 (effective on 10/1/98 and applicable with respect to educational assistance allowances paid for months after 9/98, as provided by § 8210(e) of such Act, which appears as a note to this section), as amended July 22, 1998 (effective simultaneously with the enactment of, and as if included in, Act June 9, 1998, as provided by § 9016 of Act July 22, 1998, which appears as 23 USCS § 101 note), in subsec. (a), substituted "$485" for "$404", substituted "$152" for "$127" in two places, and substituted "$16.16" for "$13.46".

Act July 22, 1998 (effective simultaneously with the enactment of, and as if included in, Act June 9, 1998, as provided by § 9016 of Act July 22, 1998, which appears as 23 USCS § 101 note) amended Act June 9, 1998, which amended this section.

2000. Act Nov. 1, 2000 (effective and applicable as provided by § 111(e) of such Act, which appears as 38 USCS § 3532 note), in subsec. (a), substituted "$588" for "$485", substituted "$184" for "$152" in two places, and substituted "such increased amount of allowance that

READJUSTMENT BENEFITS 38 USCS § 3561

is equal to one-thirtieth of the full-time basic monthly rate of special training allowance.'' for ''$16.16 that the special training allowance paid exceeds the basic monthly allowance.''.

2001. Act Dec. 27, 2001, in subsec. (a), substituted ''the eligible person shall be entitled to receive'' for ''the parent or guardian shall be entitled to receive on behalf of such person'', and substituted ''upon election by the eligible person'' for ''upon election by the parent or guardian of the eligible person''.

Such Act further (effective and applicable as provided by § 102(e) of such Act, which appears as 38 USCS § 3532 note), in subsec. (a), substituted ''$670'' for ''$588'', and substituted ''$210'' for ''$184'' in two places.

2003. Act Dec. 16, 2003 (effective 7/1/2004 and applicable to educational assistance allowances payable under 38 USCS §§ 3500 et seq. and 3687(b)(2) for months beginning on or after that date, as provided by § 302(e) of such Act, which appears as 38 USCS § 3532 note), in subsec. (a), substituted ''$788'' for ''$670'', and substituted ''$247'' for ''$210'' in two places.

CODE OF FEDERAL REGULATIONS

Department of Veterans Affairs—Per diem for nursing home care of veterans in State homes, 38 CFR 51.1 et seq.
Department of Veterans Affairs—Forms, 38 CFR 58.10 et seq.

RESEARCH GUIDE

Am Jur:
77 Am Jur 2d, Veterans and Veterans' Laws § 137.

§ 3543. Special administrative provisions

(a) In carrying out the Secretary's responsibilities under this chapter [38 USCS §§ 3500 et seq.] the Secretary may by agreement arrange with public or private educational institutions or others to provide training arrangements as may be suitable and necessary to accomplish the purposes of this subchapter [38 USCS §§ 3540 et seq.]. In any instance where the Secretary finds that a customary tuition charge is not applicable, the Secretary may agree on the fair and reasonable amounts which may be charged for the training provided to the eligible person.

(b) [Unchanged]

(c) In a case in which the Secretary authorizes training under section 3541(a) of this title [38 USCS § 3541(a)] on behalf of an eligible person, the parent or guardian shall be entitled—

(1) to receive on behalf of the eligible person the special training allowance provided for under section 3542(a) of this title [38 USCS § 3542(a)];

(2) to elect an increase in the basic monthly allowance provided for under such section; and

(3) to agree with the Secretary on the fair and reasonable amounts which may be charged under subsection (a).

(As amended Dec. 27, 2001, P. L. 107-103, Title I, § 109(b)(3), (4), 115 Stat. 986.)

HISTORY; ANCILLARY LAWS AND DIRECTIVES

Amendments:
2001. Act Dec. 27, 2001, in subsec. (a), substituted ''for the training provided to the eligible person'' for ''the parent or guardian for the training provided to an eligible person''; and added subsec. (c)

CODE OF FEDERAL REGULATIONS

Department of Veterans Affairs—Per diem for nursing home care of veterans in State homes, 38 CFR 51.1 et seq.
Department of Veterans Affairs—Forms, 38 CFR 58.10 et seq.

RESEARCH GUIDE

Am Jur:
77 Am Jur 2d, Veterans and Veterans' Laws § 137.

SUBCHAPTER VI. MISCELLANEOUS PROVISIONS

§ 3561. Authority and duties of Secretary

CODE OF FEDERAL REGULATIONS

Department of Veterans Affairs—Nondiscrimination in federally-assisted programs of the Department of Veterans Affairs-effectuation of Title VI of the Civil Rights Act of 1964, 38 CFR 18.1 et seq.
Department of Veterans Affairs—Delegation of responsibility in connection with Title VI, Civil Rights Act of 1964, 38 CFR 18a.1 et seq.
Department of Veterans Affairs—Practice and procedure under Title VI of the Civil Rights Act of 1964 and Part 18 of this chapter, 38 CFR 18b.1 et seq.
Department of Veterans Affairs—Vocational rehabilitation and education, 38 CFR 21.1 et seq.

Department of Veterans Affairs—Loan guaranty and vocational rehabilitation and counseling programs, 48 CFR 871.100 et seq.

§ 3562. Nonduplication of benefits

INTERPRETIVE NOTES AND DECISIONS

Because benefits were based on status of child as eligible person through each disabled veteran parent, and absent aggregation restrictions, under 2003 version of 38 USCS § 3511(a)(1), appellant student with two disabled parents could receive educational benefits not to exceed 45 months from status of each parent; Congress adopted explicit language to prevent person receiving educational assistance from simultaneously receiving certain other benefits under separate program as evidenced by 38 USCS §§ 3562, 3695, but Dependents' Educational Assistance benefits to eligible child of permanently and totally disabled parent was one program, and Congress, by placing limitations on receipt of additional benefits under two or more programs, placed no limitations on amount or length of benefits for "eligible persons" under single program or benefit. Osman v Peake (2008) 22 Vet App 252, 2008 US App Vet Claims LEXIS 1063.

§ 3563. Notification of eligibility

The Secretary shall notify the parent or guardian of each eligible person whose eligibility is based on the death or disability of a parent or on a parent being listed in one of the categories referred to in section 3501(a)(1)(C) of this title [38 USCS § 3501(a)(1)(C)] of the educational assistance available to such person under this chapter [38 USCS §§ 3500 et seq.]. Such notification shall be provided not later than the month in which such eligible person attains such person's thirteenth birthday or as soon thereafter as feasible.

(As amended Dec. 21, 2006, P. L. 109-444, § 3(b)(5), 120 Stat. 3307; Dec. 22, 2006, P. L. 109-461, Title III, § 301(b)(5), 120 Stat. 3427.)

HISTORY; ANCILLARY LAWS AND DIRECTIVES

Explanatory notes:
Section 3(b)(5) of Act Dec. 21, 2006, P. L. 109-444, amended this section; however, pursuant to § 1006(b) of Act Dec. 22, 2006, P. L. 109-461, which appears as 38 USCS § 101 note, as of the enactment of Act Dec. 22, 2006, P. L. 109-461, Act Dec. 21, 2006, P. L. 109-444 and the amendments made by such Act were deemed for all purposes not to have taken effect and such § 3(b)(5) ceased to be in effect.

Amendments:
2006. Act Dec. 22, 2006 (applicable with respect to a payment of educational assistance for a course of education pursued after enactment, as provided by § 301(d) of such Act, which appears as 38 USCS § 3501 note), substituted "each eligible person whose eligibility is based on the death or disability of a parent or on a parent being listed in one of the categories referred to in section 3501(a)(1)(C) of this title" for "each eligible person defined in section 3501(a)(1)(A) of this title".

§ 3564. Annual adjustment of amounts of educational assistance

(a) With respect to any fiscal year, the Secretary shall provide a percentage increase in the rates payable under sections 3532, 3534(b), and 3542(a) of this title [38 USCS §§ 3532, 3534(b), and 3542(a)] equal to the percentage by which—

(1) the Consumer Price Index (all items, United States city average) for the 12-month period ending on the June 30 preceding the beginning of the fiscal year for which the increase is made, exceeds

(2) such Consumer Price Index for the 12-month period preceding the 12-month period described in paragraph (1).

(b) Any increase under subsection (a) in a rate with respect to a fiscal year after fiscal year 2004 and before fiscal year 2014 shall be rounded down to the next lower whole dollar amount. Any such increase with respect to a fiscal year after fiscal year 2013 shall be rounded to the nearest whole dollar amount.

(Added Nov. 1, 2000, P. L. 106-419, Title I, Subtitle B, § 111(f)(1)(A), 114 Stat. 1831; Dec. 16, 2003, P. L. 108-183, Title III, § 304(b), 117 Stat. 2660.)

HISTORY; ANCILLARY LAWS AND DIRECTIVES

Effective date of section:
This section took effect on October 1, 2001, as provided by § 111(f)(3) of Act Nov. 1, 2000, P. L. 106-419, which appears as a note to this section.

Amendments:
2003. Act Dec. 16, 2003, designated the existing provisions as subsec. (a), and, in such subsection, in the introductory matter, deleted "(rounded to the nearest dollar)" following "increase"; and added subsec. (b).

Other provisions:
Effective date of 38 USCS §§ 3564 and 3687(d). Act Nov. 1, 2000, P. L. 106-419, Title I, Subtitle B, § 111(f)(3), 114 Stat. 1831; June 5, 2001, P. L. 107-14, § 8(b)(1), 115 Stat. 36 (effective as of 11/1/00, and as if included in Act Nov. 1, 2000 as originally enacted, as provided by § 8(b) of such Act), provides: "Sections 3564 and 3687(d) of title 38, United States Code, as added by this subsection, shall take effect on October 1, 2001.".

SUBCHAPTER VII. PHILIPPINE COMMONWEALTH ARMY AND PHILIPPINE SCOUTS

§ 3565. Children of certain Philippine veterans

(a) **Basic eligibility.** The term "eligible person" as used in section 3501(a)(1) of this title [38 USCS § 3501(a)(1)] includes the children of those Commonwealth Army veterans and "New" Philippine Scouts who meet the requirements of service-connected disability or death, based on service as defined in section 3566 of this title [38 USCS § 3566].

(b) **Administrative provisions.** The provisions of this chapter [38 USCS §§ 3500 et seq.] and chapter 36 [38 USCS §§ 3670 et seq.] shall apply to the educational assistance for children of Commonwealth Army veterans and "New" Philippine Scouts, except that—

(1), (2) [Unchanged]

(c) **Delimiting dates.** In the case of any individual who is an eligible person solely by virtue of subsection (a) of this section, and who is above the age of seventeen years and below the age of twenty-three years on September 30, 1966, the period referred to in section 3512 of this title [38 USCS § 3512] shall not end until the expiration of the five-year period which begins on September 30, 1966.

(As amended June 15, 2006, P. L. 109-233, Title V, § 503(8)(A), 120 Stat. 416.)

HISTORY; ANCILLARY LAWS AND DIRECTIVES

Amendments:
2006. Act June 15, 2006, in subsecs. (a)–(c), inserted the subsection headings, which headings formerly appeared as centered headings preceding such subsections.

CODE OF FEDERAL REGULATIONS

Department of Veterans Affairs—Adjudication, 38 CFR 3.1 et seq.
Department of Veterans Affairs—Nondiscrimination in federally-assisted programs of the Department of Veterans Affairs-effectuation of Title VI of the Civil Rights Act of 1964, 38 CFR 18.1 et seq.
Department of Veterans Affairs—Delegation of responsibility in connection with Title VI, Civil Rights Act of 1964, 38 CFR 18a.1 et seq.
Department of Veterans Affairs—Practice and procedure under Title VI of the Civil Rights Act of 1964 and Part 18 of this chapter, 38 CFR 18b.1 et seq.
Department of Veterans Affairs—Vocational rehabilitation and education, 38 CFR 21.1 et seq.
Department of Veterans Affairs—Loan guaranty and vocational rehabilitation and counseling programs, 48 CFR 871.100 et seq.

CHAPTER 36. ADMINISTRATION OF EDUCATIONAL BENEFITS

Section

SUBCHAPTER I. STATE APPROVING AGENCIES

3673. Approval activities: cooperation and coordination of activities.

SUBCHAPTER II. MISCELLANEOUS PROVISIONS

3684A. Procedures relating to computer matching program.
3689. Approval requirements for licensing and certification testing.
3698. Comprehensive policy on providing education information to veterans.
[3699. Repealed]

HISTORY; ANCILLARY LAWS AND DIRECTIVES

Amendments:
2000. Act Nov. 1, 2000, P. L. 106-419, Title I, Subtitle C, § 122(c)(2), 114 Stat. 1837, amended the analysis of this chapter by adding item 3689.
2003. Act Dec. 16, 2003, P. L. 108-183, Title III, § 306(g), 117 Stat. 2661, amended the analysis of this chapter by deleting the subchapter III HEADING and items 3698 and 3699, which read:
"SUBCHAPTER III. EDUCATION LOANS
"3698. Eligibility for loans; amount and conditions of loans; interest rate on loans.
"3699. Revolving fund; insurance.".

38 USCS § 3670

2008. Act Oct. 10, 2008, P. L. 110-387, Title IX, § 901(a)(3), 122 Stat. 4142, amended the analysis of this chapter by substituting item 3684A for one which read: "3684A. Procedures relating to computer matching programs.".

Act Oct. 10, 2008, P. L. 110-389, Title III, Subtitle B, § 326(a)(2)(B), amended the analysis of this chapter by substituting item 3673 for one which read: "3673. Cooperation.".

2013. Act Jan. 10, 2013, P. L. 112-249, § 1(a)(2), 126 Stat. 2400, amended the analysis of this chapter by adding item 3698.

SUBCHAPTER I. STATE APPROVING AGENCIES

§ 3670. Scope of approval

CODE OF FEDERAL REGULATIONS

Department of Veterans Affairs—Vocational rehabilitation and education, 38 CFR 21.1 et seq.
Department of Veterans Affairs—Loan guaranty and vocational rehabilitation and counseling programs, 48 CFR 871.100 et seq.

RESEARCH GUIDE

Am Jur:
77 Am Jur 2d, Veterans and Veterans' Laws § 124.

§ 3671. Designation

(a) [Unchanged]

(b)(1) [Unchanged]

(2) Except as otherwise provided in this chapter [38 USCS §§ 3670 et seq., in the case of courses subject to approval by the Secretary under section 3672 of this title [38 USCS § 3672], the provisions of this chapter [38 USCS §§ 3670 et seq.] which refer to a State approving agency shall be deemed to refer to the Secretary.

(As amended Jan. 4, 2011, P. L. 111-377, Title II, § 203(a)(2)(B), 124 Stat. 4125.)

HISTORY; ANCILLARY LAWS AND DIRECTIVES

Amendments:
2011. Act Jan. 4, 2011 (effective on 8/1/2011, as provided by § 203(e) of such Act, which appears as 38 USCS § 3034 note), in subsec. (b)(2), substituted "Except as otherwise provided in this chapter, in the case" for "In the case".

§ 3672. Approval of courses

(a) [Unchanged]

(b)(1) The Secretary shall be responsible for the approval of courses of education offered by any agency of the Federal Government authorized under other laws to supervise such education. The Secretary may approve any course in any other educational institution in accordance with the provisions of this chapter and chapters 34 and 35 of this title [38 USCS §§ 3670 et seq., 3451 et seq., and 3500 et seq.].

(2)(A) Subject to sections 3675(b)(1) and (b)(2), 3680A, 3684, and 3696 of this title [38 USCS §§ 3675(b)(1), (2), 3680A, 3684, and 3696], the following programs are deemed to be approved for purposes of this chapter [38 USCS §§ 3670 et seq.]:

(i) An accredited standard college degree program offered at a public or not-for-profit proprietary educational institution that is accredited by an agency or association recognized for that purpose by the Secretary of Education.

(ii) A flight training course approved by the Federal Aviation Administration that is offered by a certified pilot school that possesses a valid Federal Aviation Administration pilot school certificate.

(iii) An apprenticeship program registered with the Office of Apprenticeship (OA) of the Employment Training Administration of the Department of Labor or a State apprenticeship agency recognized by the Office of Apprenticeship pursuant to the Act of August 16, 1937 (popularly known as the "National Apprenticeship Act"; 29 U.S.C. 50 et seq.).

(iv) A program leading to a secondary school diploma offered by a secondary school approved in the State in which it is operating.

(B) A licensure test offered by a Federal, State, or local government is deemed to be approved for purposes of this chapter [38 USCS §§ 3670 et seq.].

(c)(1) In the case of programs of apprenticeship where—

(A) the apprenticeship standards have been approved by the Secretary of Labor pursuant to section 2 of the Act of August 16, 1937 (popularly known as the "National Apprenticeship Act") (29 U.S.C. 50a), as a national apprenticeship program for operation in more than one State, and

(B) the training establishment is a carrier directly engaged in interstate commerce which provides such training in more than one State,

the Secretary shall act as a "State approving agency" as such term is used in section 3687(a)(1) of this title [38 USCS § 3687(a)(1)] and shall be responsible for the approval of all such programs.

(2) The period of a program of apprenticeship may be determined based upon a specific period of time (commonly referred to as a "time-based program"), based upon the demonstration of successful mastery of skills (commonly referred to as a "competency-based program"), or based upon a combination thereof.

(3)(A) In the case of a competency-based program of apprenticeship, State approving agencies shall determine the period for which payment may be made for such a program under chapters 30 and 35 of this title [38 USCS §§ 3001 et seq. and 3500 et seq.] and chapter 1606 of title 10 [10 USCS §§ 16131 et seq.]. In determining the period of such a program, State approving agencies shall take into consideration the approximate term of the program recommended in registered apprenticeship program standards recognized by the Secretary of Labor.

(B) The sponsor of a competency-based program of apprenticeship shall provide notice to the State approving agency involved of any such standards that may apply to the program and the proposed approximate period of training under the program.

(4) The sponsor of a competency-based program of apprenticeship shall notify the Secretary upon the successful completion of a program of apprenticeship by an individual under chapter 30 or 35 of this title [38 USCS §§ 3001 et seq. or 3500 et seq.], or chapter 1606 of title 10 [10 USCS §§ 16131 et seq.], as the case may be.

(d)(1) Pursuant to regulations prescribed by the Secretary in consultation with the Secretary of Labor, the Secretary and State approving agencies shall actively promote the development of apprenticeship and on the job training programs for the purposes of sections 3677 and 3687 of this title [38 USCS §§ 3677 and 3687] and shall utilize the services of disabled veterans' outreach program specialists under section 4103A of this title [38 USCS § 4103A] to promote the development of such programs. The Secretary of Labor shall provide assistance and services to the Secretary, and to State approving agencies, to increase the use of apprenticeships.

(2) In conjunction with outreach services provided by the Secretary under chapter 77 of this title [38 USCS §§ 7701 et seq.] for education and training benefits, each State approving agency shall conduct outreach programs and provide outreach services to eligible persons and veterans about education and training benefits available under applicable Federal and State law.

(e) [Unchanged]

(As amended Dec. 27, 2001, P. L. 107-103, Title III, § 303, 115 Stat. 992; Dec. 10, 2004, P. L. 108-454, Title I, §§ 104(a), (b), 110(b), 118 Stat. 3601, 3605; Jan. 4, 2011, P. L. 111-377, Title II, § 203(a)(1), 124 Stat. 4124.)

HISTORY; ANCILLARY LAWS AND DIRECTIVES

Amendments:

2001. Act Dec. 27, 2001, in subsec. (d), inserted "and State approving agencies", designated the existing provisions as para. (1), and added para. (2).

2004. Act Dec. 10, 2004, in subsec. (c), designated the existing provisions as para. (1), redesignated former paras. (1) and (2) as subparas. (A) and (B), respectively, and, in subpara. (A) as so redesignated, inserted "apprenticeship" before "standards", and added new paras. (2)–(4); and, in subsec. (d)(1), substituted "of apprenticeship and on the job training programs" for "of programs of training on the job (including programs of apprenticeship)", and added the sentence beginning "The Secretary of Labor . . .".

2011. Act Jan. 4, 2011 (effective 8/1/2011, as provided by § 203(e) of such Act, which appears as 38 USCS § 3034 note), in subsec. (b), designated the existing provisions as para. (1), and added para. (2).

INTERPRETIVE NOTES AND DECISIONS

Conclusion by Board of Veterans' Appeals that, while claimant pointed to paralegal program, he had not shown that he took any course in furtherance of gaining paralegal certificate, was not clearly erroneous; critically, certificates he submitted did not demonstrate that he enrolled in courses as part of approved program of study, such as paralegal program. Celano v Peake (2009) 22 Vet App 341, 2009 US App Vet Claims LEXIS 12.

§ 3673. Approval activities: cooperation and coordination of activities

(a) Cooperation in activities. The Secretary and each State approving agency shall take cognizance of the fact that definite duties, functions and responsibilities are conferred upon the Secretary and each State approving agency under the educational programs established under this chapter and chapters 34 and 35 of this title [38 USCS §§ 3670 et seq., 3451 et seq., and 3500 et seq.]. To assure that such programs are effectively and efficiently administered, the cooperation of the Secretary and the State approving agencies is essential. It is necessary to establish an exchange of information pertaining to activities of educational institutions, and particular attention should be given to the enforcement of approval standards, enforcement of enrollment restrictions, and fraudulent and other criminal activities on the part of persons connected with educational institutions in which eligible persons or veterans are enrolled under this chapter and chapters 34 and 35 of this title [38 USCS §§ 3670 et seq., 3451 et seq., and 3500 et seq.].

(b) **Coordination of activities.** The Secretary shall take appropriate actions to ensure the coordination of approval activities performed by State approving agencies under this chapter and chapters 34 and 35 of this title [38 USCS §§ 3670 et seq., 3451 et seq., and 3500 et seq.] and approval activities performed by the Department of Labor, the Department of Education, and other entities in order to reduce overlap and improve efficiency in the performance of such activities.

(c) **Availability of information material.** The Secretary will furnish the State approving agencies with copies of such Department of Veterans Affairs informational material as may aid them in carrying out chapters 34 and 35 of this title [38 USCS §§ 3451 et seq. and 3500 et seq.].

(d) **Use of State approving agencies for compliance and oversight activities.** The Secretary may utilize the services of a State approving agency for such compliance and oversight purposes as the Secretary considers appropriate without regard to whether the Secretary or the agency approved the courses offered in the State concerned.

(As amended Oct. 10, 2008, P. L. 110-389, Title III, Subtitle B, § 326(a)(1), (2)(A), (3), 122 Stat. 4169; Jan. 4, 2011, P. L. 111-377, Title II, § 203(b), 124 Stat. 4125.)

HISTORY; ANCILLARY LAWS AND DIRECTIVES

Amendments:
2008. Act Oct. 10, 2008, substituted the section heading for one which read: "Cooperation"; in subsec. (a), inserted the subsection heading; redesignated subsec. (b) as subsec. (c); inserted new subsec. (b); and, in subsec. (c) as redesignated, inserted the subsection heading.

2011. Act Jan. 4, 2011 (effective on 8/1/2011, as provided by § 203(e) of such Act, which appears as 38 USCS § 3034 note), added subsec. (d).

§ 3674. Reimbursement of expenses

(a)(1) [Unchanged]

(2)(A) The Secretary shall make payments to State and local agencies, out of amounts available for the payment of readjustment benefits, for the reasonable and necessary expenses of salary and travel incurred by employees of such agencies in carrying out contracts or agreements entered into under this section, for expenses approved by the Secretary that are incurred in carrying out activities described in section 3674A(a)(3) of this title [38 USCS § 3674A(a)(3)] (except for administrative overhead expenses allocated to such activities), and for the allowance for administrative expenses described in subsection (b).

(B) The Secretary shall make such a payment to an agency within a reasonable time after the agency has submitted a report pursuant to paragraph (3) of this subsection.

(C) Subject to paragraph (4) of this subsection, the amount of any such payment made to an agency for any period shall be equal to the amount of the reasonable and necessary expenses of salary and travel certified by such agency for such period in accordance with paragraph (3) of this subsection plus the allowance for administrative expenses described in subsection (b) and the amount of expenses approved by the Secretary that are incurred in carrying out activities described in section 3674A(a)(3) of this title [38 USCS § 3674A(a)(3)] for such period (except for administrative overhead expenses allocated to such activities).

(3) [Unchanged]

(4) The total amount made available under this section for any fiscal year shall be $19,000,000.

(b) [Unchanged]

(c) Each State and local agency with which the Secretary contracts or enters into an agreement under subsection (a) of this section shall report to the Secretary periodically, but not less often than annually, as determined by the Secretary, on the activities in the preceding twelve months (or the period which has elapsed since the last report under this subsection was submitted) carried out under such contract or agreement. Each such report shall describe, in such detail as the Secretary shall prescribe, services performed and determinations made in connection with ascertaining the qualifications of educational institutions in connection with this chapter and chapters 32, 34, and 35 of this title [38 USCS §§ 3670 et seq., 3201 et seq., 3450 et seq., and 3500 et seq.] and in supervising such institutions.

(As amended Nov. 1, 2000, Title I, Subtitle C, § 123, 114 Stat. 1837; June 5, 2001, P. L. 107-14, § 8(a)(7), 115 Stat. 34; Dec. 6, 2002, P. L. 107-330, Title III, § 301, 116 Stat. 2824; June 30, 2008, P. L. 110-252, Title V, § 5005, 122 Stat. 2379.)

READJUSTMENT BENEFITS 38 USCS § 3675

HISTORY; ANCILLARY LAWS AND DIRECTIVES
Amendments:
2000. Act Nov. 1, 2000, in subsec. (a)(4), inserted "or, for each of fiscal years 2001 and 2002, $14,000,000", and substituted "the amount applicable to that fiscal year under the preceding sentence" for "$13,000,000" in two places.
2001. Act June 5, 2001, in subsec. (a)(2), in subpara. (A), deleted ", effective at the beginning of fiscal year 1988," following "shall", and substituted "section 3674A(a)(3)" for "section 3674A(a)(4)", in subpara. (B), substituted "paragraph (3)" for "paragraph (3)(A)" and, in subpara. (C), substituted "section 3674A(a)(3)" for "section 3674A(a)(4)"; and, in subsec. (c), deleted "on September 30, 1978, and" preceding "periodically", and deleted "thereafter," following "annually,".
2002. Act Dec. 6, 2002, in subsec. (a)(4), inserted ", for fiscal year 2003, $14,000,000, for fiscal year 2004, $18,000,000, for fiscal year 2005, $18,000,000, for fiscal year 2006, $19,000,000, and for fiscal year 2007, $19,000,000".
2008. Act June 30, 2008, in subsec. (a)(4), substituted "shall be $19,000,000." for "may not exceed $13,000,000 or, for each of fiscal years 2001 and 2002, $14,000,000, for fiscal year 2003, $14,000,000, for fiscal year 2004, $18,000,000, for fiscal year 2005, $18,000,000, for fiscal year 2006, $19,000,000, and for fiscal year 2007, $19,000,000. For any fiscal year in which the total amount that would be made available under this section would exceed the amount applicable to that fiscal year under the preceding sentence except for the provisions of this paragraph, the Secretary shall provide that each agency shall receive the same percentage of the amount applicable to that fiscal year under the preceding sentence as the agency would have received of the total amount that would have been made available without the limitation of this paragraph.".

§ 3674A. Evaluations of agency performance; qualifications and performance of agency personnel
(a) The Secretary shall—
  (1) [Unchanged]
  (2) take into account the results of annual evaluations carried out under paragraph (1) when negotiating the terms and conditions of a contract or agreement under section 3674 of this title [38 USCS § 3674];
  (3), (4) [Unchanged]
(b)(1) Each State approving agency carrying out a contract or agreement with the Secretary under section 3674(a) of this title [38 USCS § 3674(a)] shall—
  (A), (B) [Unchanged]
  (2), (3) [Unchanged]
(As amended Nov. 11, 1998, P. L. 105-368, Title X, § 1005(b)(8), 112 Stat. 3365; June 5, 2001, P. L. 107-14, § 8(a)(8), 115 Stat. 35.)

HISTORY; ANCILLARY LAWS AND DIRECTIVES
Amendments:
1998. Act Nov. 11, 1998, in subsec. (b)(1), in the introductory matter, deleted "after the 18-month period beginning on the date of the enactment of this section" following "of this title".
2001. Act June 5, 2001, in subsec. (a)(2), substituted "paragraph (1)" for "clause (1)".

§ 3675. Approval of accredited courses
(a)(1) The Secretary or a State approving agency may approve accredited programs (including non-degree accredited programs) offered by proprietary for-profit educational institutions when—
  (A)–(D) [Unchanged]
  (2), (3) [Unchanged]
(b) As a condition of approval under this section, the Secretary or the State approving agency must find the following:
  (1) The educational institution keeps adequate records, as prescribed by the Secretary or the State approving agency, to show the progress and grades of the eligible person or veteran and to show that satisfactory standards relating to progress and conduct are enforced.
  (2), (3) [Unchanged]
(c)(1) A State approving agency may approve the entrepreneurship courses offered by a qualified provider of entrepreneurship courses.
  (2) For purposes of this subsection, the term "entrepreneurship course" means a non-degree, non-credit course of business education that enables or assists a person to start or enhance a small business concern (as defined pursuant to section 3(a) of the Small Business Act (15 U.S.C. 632(a))).
  (3) Subsection (a) and paragraphs (1) and (2) of subsection (b) shall not apply to—

(A) an entrepreneurship course offered by a qualified provider of entrepreneurship courses; and

(B) a qualified provider of entrepreneurship courses by reason of such provider offering one or more entrepreneurship courses.

(4) Notwithstanding paragraph (3), a qualified provider of entrepreneurship courses shall maintain such records as the Secretary determines to be necessary to comply with reporting requirements that apply under section 3684(a)(1) of this title [38 USCS § 3684(a)(1)] with respect to eligible persons and veterans enrolled in an entrepreneurship course offered by the provider.

(As amended Dec. 16, 2003, P. L. 108-183, Title III, § 305(a), 117 Stat. 2660; Dec. 10, 2004, P. L. 108-454, Title I, § 110(c)(1), 118 Stat. 3605; Jan. 4, 2011, P. L. 111-377, Title II, § 203(c), 124 Stat. 4125.)

HISTORY; ANCILLARY LAWS AND DIRECTIVES

Amendments:

2003. Act Dec. 16, 2003 (applicable as provided by § 305(f) of such Act, which appears as 38 USCS § 3452 note), added subsec. (c).

2004. Act Dec. 10, 2004 (effective as if included in the enactment of Act Dec. 16, 2003, as provided by § 110(c)(2) of Act Dec. 10, 2004, which appears as a note to this section), in subsec. (c), added para. (4).

2011. Act Jan. 4, 2011 (effective on 8/1/2011, as provided by § 203(e) of such Act, which appears as 38 USCS § 3034 note), in subsec. (a)(1), substituted "The Secretary or a State approving agency may approve accredited programs (including non-degree accredited programs) offered by proprietary for-profit educational institutions'" for "A State approving agency may approve the courses offered by an educational institution"; and in subsec. (b), in the introductory matter and in para. (1), inserted "the Secretary or".

Other provisions:

Effective date of Dec. 10, 2004 amendment. Act Dec. 10, 2004, P. L. 108-454, Title I, § 110(c)(2), 118 Stat. 3605, provides: "The amendment made by paragraph (1) [adding subsec. (c)(4) of this section] shall take effect as if included in the enactment of section 305(a) of the Veterans Benefits Act of 2003 (Public Law 108-183; 117 Stat. 2660) [amending this section].".

CODE OF FEDERAL REGULATIONS

Office of Postsecondary Education, Department of Education—Secretary's recognition procedures for State agencies, 34 CFR 603.20 et seq.

§ 3676. Approval of nonaccredited courses

(a), (b) [Unchanged]

(c) The appropriate State approving agency may approve the application of such institution when the institution and its nonaccredited courses are found upon investigation to have met the following criteria:

(1)–(3) [Unchanged]

(4) The institution maintains a written record of the previous education and training of the eligible person and clearly indicates that appropriate credit has been given by the institution for previous education and training, with the training period shortened proportionately and the eligible person so notified.

(5)–(12) [Unchanged]

(13) The institution has and maintains a policy for the refund of the unused portion of tuition, fees, and other charges in the event the eligible person fails to enter the course or withdraws or is discontinued therefrom at any time before completion and—

(A) in the case of an institution (other than (i) a Federal, State, or local Government institution or (ii) an institution described in subparagraph (B)), such policy provides that the amount charged to the eligible person for tuition, fees, and other charges for a portion of the course shall not exceed the approximate pro rata portion of the total charges for tuition, fees, and other charges that the length of the completed portion of the course bears to its total length; or

(B) in the case of an institution that is a nonaccredited public educational institution, the institution has and maintains a refund policy regarding the unused portion of tuition, fees, and other charges that is substantially the same as the refund policy followed by accredited public educational institutions located within the same State as such institution.

(14) [Unchanged]

(d), (e) [Unchanged]

(As amended Dec. 22, 2006, P. L. 109-461, Title III, § 303, 120 Stat. 3428; Oct. 10, 2008, P. L. 110-389, Title III, Subtitle B, § 322, 122 Stat. 4168.)

READJUSTMENT BENEFITS 38 USCS § 3679

HISTORY; ANCILLARY LAWS AND DIRECTIVES

Amendments:

2006. Act Dec. 22, 2006, in subsec. (c)(13), substituted "before completion and—" and subparas. (A) and (B) for "prior to completion and such policy must provide that the amount charged to the eligible person for tuition, fees, and other charges for a portion of the course shall not exceed the approximate pro rata portion of the total charges for tuition, fees, and other charges that the length of the completed portion of the course bears to its total length.".

2008. Act Oct. 10, 2008, in subsec. (c)(4), deleted "and the Secretary" preceding "so notified".

RESEARCH GUIDE

Other Treatises:

1 Rapp, Education Law (Matthew Bender), ch 5, Funding, Support and Finances of Education § 5.03.

§ 3677. Approval of training on the job

(a) [Unchanged]

(b)(1) The training establishment offering training which is desired to be approved for the purposes of this chapter [38 USCS §§ 3670 et seq.] must submit to the appropriate State approving agency a written application for approval which, in addition to furnishing such information as is required by the State approving agency, contains a certification that—

(A) the wages to be paid the eligible veteran or person (i) upon entrance into training, are not less than wages paid nonveterans in the same training position and are at least 50 per centum of the wages paid for the job for which the veteran or person is to be trained, and (ii) such wages will be increased in regular periodic increments until, not later than the last full month of the training period, they will be at least 85 per centum of the wages paid for the job for which such eligible veteran or person is being trained; and

(B) there is reasonable certainty that the job for which the eligible veteran or person is to be trained will be available to the veteran or person at the end of the training period.

(2) The requirement under paragraph (1)(A)(ii) shall not apply with respect to a training establishment operated by the United States or by a State or local government.

(3) The requirement for certification under paragraph (1) shall not apply to training described in section 3452(e)(2) of this title [38 USCS § 3452(e)(2)].

(c) [Unchanged]

(d)(1) The Secretary may conduct a pilot program under which the Secretary operates a program of training on the job under this section for a period (notwithstanding subsection (c)(2)) of up to three years in duration to train employees of the Department to become qualified adjudicators of claims for compensation, dependency and indemnity compensation, and pension.

(2)(A) Not later than three years after the implementation of the pilot project, the Secretary shall submit to Congress an initial report on the pilot project. The report shall include an assessment of the usefulness of the program in recruiting and retaining of personnel of the Department as well as an assessment of the value of the program as a training program.

(B) Not later than 18 months after the date on which the initial report under subparagraph (A) is submitted, the Secretary shall submit to Congress a final report on the pilot project. The final report shall include recommendations of the Secretary with respect to continuation of the pilot project and with respect to expansion of the types of claims for which the extended period of on the job training is available to train such employees.

(As amended Nov. 11, 1998, P. L. 105-368, Title II, Subtitle A, § 205(a), 112 Stat. 3327; Dec. 10, 2004, P. L. 108-454, Title I, § 108, 118 Stat. 3604; Oct. 10, 2008, P. L. 110-389, Title III, Subtitle B, § 325, 122 Stat. 4169.)

HISTORY; ANCILLARY LAWS AND DIRECTIVES

Amendments:

1998. Act Nov. 11, 1998 (applicable as provided by § 205(b) of such Act, which appears as a note to this section), in subsec. (b), designated the existing provisions as para. (1), redesignated former paras. (1) and (2) as subparas. (A) and (B), respectively, and, in subpara. (A) as redesignated, redesignated cls. (A) and (B) as cls. (i) and (ii), respectively, and added para. (2).

2004. Act Dec. 10, 2004, added subsec. (d).

2008. Act Oct. 10, 2008, added subsec. (b)(3).

Other provisions:

Application of Nov. 11, 1998 amendments. Act Nov. 11, 1998, P. L. 105-368, Title II, Subtitle A, § 205(b), 112 Stat. 3327, provides: "The amendments made by subsection (a) [amending subsec. (b) of this section] shall apply with respect to approval of programs of training on the job under section 3677 of title 38, United States Code, on or after October 1, 1998.".

§ 3679. Disapproval of courses

(a) Any course approved for the purposes of this chapter [38 USCS §§ 3670 et seq.] which fails

38 USCS § 3679 VETERANS' BENEFITS

to meet any of the requirements of this chapter [38 USCS §§ 3670 et seq.] shall be immediately disapproved by the Secretary or the appropriate State approving agency. An educational institution which has its courses disapproved by the Secretary or a State approving agency will be notified of such disapproval by a certified or registered letter of notification and a return receipt secured.

(b) [Unchanged]

(As amended Jan. 4, 2011, P. L. 111-377, Title II, § 203(d), 124 Stat. 4126.)

HISTORY; ANCILLARY LAWS AND DIRECTIVES

Amendments:

2011. Act Jan. 4, 2011 (effective on 8/1/2011, as provided by § 203(e) of such Act, which appears as 38 USCS § 3034 note), in subsec. (a), inserted "the Secretary or" in two places.

SUBCHAPTER II. MISCELLANEOUS PROVISIONS

§ 3680. Payment of educational assistance or subsistence allowances

(a) **Period for which payment may be made.** Payment of educational assistance or subsistence allowances to eligible veterans or eligible persons pursuing a program of education or training, other than a program by correspondence, in an educational institution under chapter 31, 34, or 35 of this title [38 USCS §§ 3100 et seq., 3451 et seq., or 3500 et seq.] shall be paid as provided in this section and, as applicable, in section 3108, 3482, 3491 or 3532 of this title [38 USCS § 3108, 3482, 3491 or 3532]. Such payments shall be paid only for the period of such veterans' or persons' enrollment in, and pursuit of, such program, but no amount shall be paid—

(1)–(3) [Unchanged]

Notwithstanding the foregoing, the Secretary may, subject to such regulations as the Secretary shall prescribe, continue to pay allowances to eligible veterans and eligible persons enrolled in courses set forth in clause (1) of this subsection during periods when schools are temporarily closed under an established policy based on an Executive order of the President or due to an emergency situation. However, the total number of weeks for which allowances may continue to be so payable in any 12-month period may not exceed 4 weeks.

(b) **Correspondence training certifications.** No educational assistance allowance shall be paid to an eligible veteran or spouse or surviving spouse enrolled in and pursuing a program of education exclusively by correspondence until the Secretary shall have received—

(1), (2) [Unchanged]

(c) **Apprenticeship and other on-job training.** No training assistance allowance shall be paid to an eligible veteran or eligible person enrolled in and pursuing a program of apprenticeship or other on-job training until the Secretary shall have received—

(1), (2) [Unchanged]

(d) **Advance payment of initial educational assistance or subsistence allowance.** (1)–(5) [Unchanged]

(e) **Recovery of erroneous payments.** (1), (2) [Unchanged]

(f) **Payments for less than half-time training.** Payment of educational assistance allowance in the case of any eligible veteran or eligible person pursuing a program of education on less than a half-time basis shall be made in an amount computed for the entire quarter, semester, or term not later than the last day of the month immediately following the month in which certification is received from the educational institution that such veteran or person has enrolled in and is pursuing a program at such institution. Such lump sum payment shall be computed at the rate provided in section 3482(b) or 3532(a)(2) of this title [38 USCS § 3482(b) or 3532(a)(2)], as applicable.

(g) **Determination of enrollment, pursuit, and attendance.** (1) The Secretary may, pursuant to regulations which the Secretary shall prescribe, determine and define with respect to an eligible veteran and eligible person the following:

(A) Enrollment in a course or program of education or training.

(B) Pursuit of a course or program of education or training.

(C) Attendance at a course or program of education or training.

(2) The Secretary may withhold payment of benefits to an eligible veteran or eligible person until the Secretary receives such proof as the Secretary may require of enrollment in and satisfactory pursuit of a program of education by the eligible veteran or eligible person. The Secretary shall adjust the payment withheld, when necessary, on the basis of the proof the Secretary receives.

(3) In the case of an individual other than an individual described in paragraph (4), the Secretary may accept the individual's monthly certification of enrollment in and satisfactory pursuit of a program of education as sufficient proof of the certified matters.

READJUSTMENT BENEFITS
38 USCS § 3680

(4) In the case of an individual who has received an accelerated payment of basic educational assistance under section 3014A of this title [38 USCS § 3014A] during an enrollment period for a program of education, the Secretary may accept the individual's certification of enrollment in and satisfactory pursuit of the program of education as sufficient proof of the certified matters if the certification is submitted after the enrollment period has ended.

(As amended Nov. 1, 2000, P. L. 106-419, Title I, Subtitle C, § 121, 114 Stat. 1833; Dec. 27, 2001, P. L. 107-103, Title I, § 104(b), 115 Stat. 981; June 15, 2006, P. L. 109-233, Title V, § 503(8)(A), 120 Stat. 416; Jan. 4, 2011, P. L. 111-377, Title II, § 206(a), 124 Stat. 4126.)

HISTORY; ANCILLARY LAWS AND DIRECTIVES

Amendments:

2000. Act Nov. 1, 2000 (applicable as provided by § 121(b) of such Act, which appears as a note to this section), in subsec. (a), in the undesignated paragraph following para. (3), substituted subpara. (C) for one which read: "(C) during periods between a semester, term, or quarter where the educational institution certifies the enrollment of the eligible veteran or eligible person on an individual semester, term, or quarter basis if the interval between such periods does not exceed one full calendar month.".

2001. Act Dec. 27, 2001 (effective 10/1/2002, and applicable with respect to enrollments in courses or programs of education or training beginning on or after that date, as provided by § 104(c) of such Act, which appears as 38 USCS § 3014A note), substituted subsec. (g) for one which read:

"Determination of Enrollment, Pursuit, and Attendance

"(g) The Secretary may, pursuant to regulations which the Secretary shall prescribe, determine and define enrollment in, pursuit of, and attendance at, any program of education or training or course by an eligible veteran or eligible person for any period for which the veteran or person receives an educational assistance or subsistence allowance under this chapter for pursuing such program or course. Subject to such reports and proof as the Secretary may require to show an eligible veteran's or eligible person's enrollment in and satisfactory pursuit of such person's program, the Secretary may withhold payment of benefits to such eligible veteran or eligible person until the required proof is received and the amount of the payment is appropriately adjusted. The Secretary may accept such veteran's or person's monthly certification of enrollment in and satisfactory pursuit of such veteran's or person's program as sufficient proof of the certified matters.".

2006. Act June 15, 2006, in subsecs. (a)–(g), inserted the subsection headings, which headings formerly appeared as centered headings preceding such subsections.

2011. Act Jan. 4, 2011 (effective on 8/1/2011, as provided by § 206(b) of such Act, which appears as a note to this section), in subsec. (a), in the concluding matter, substituted "of this subsection during periods when schools are temporarily closed under an established policy based on an Executive order of the President or due to an emergency situation. However, the total number of weeks for which allowances may continue to be so payable in any 12-month period may not exceed 4 weeks." for "of this subsection—

"(A) during periods when the schools are temporarily closed under an established policy based upon an Executive order of the President or due to an emergency situation;

"(B) during periods between consecutive school terms where such veterans or persons transfer from one approved educational institution to another approved educational institution for the purpose of enrolling in and pursuing a similar course at the second institution if the period between such consecutive terms does not exceed 30 days; or

"(C) during periods between school terms where the educational institution certifies the enrollment of the eligible veteran or eligible person on an individual term basis if (i) the period between those terms does not exceed eight weeks, and (ii) both the terms preceding and following the period are not shorter in length than the period.".

Other provisions:

Application of Nov. 1, 2000 amendment. Act Nov. 1, 2000, P. L. 106-419, Title I, Subtitle C, § 121(b), 114 Stat. 1833, provides: "The amendment made by subsection (a) [amending subsec. (a) of this section] shall apply with respect to payments of educational assistance under title 38, United States Code, for months beginning on or after the date of the enactment of this Act.".

Effective date of Jan. 4, 2011 amendment. Act Jan. 4, 2011, P. L. 111-377, Title II, § 206(b), 124 Stat. 4127, provides: "The amendment made by this section [amending subsec. (a) of this section] shall take effect on August 1, 2011.".

CODE OF FEDERAL REGULATIONS

Department of Veterans Affairs—Vocational rehabilitation and education, 38 CFR 21.1 et seq.
Department of Veterans Affairs—Loan guaranty and vocational rehabilitation and counseling programs, 48 CFR 871.100 et seq.

RESEARCH GUIDE

Am Jur:
45B Am Jur 2d, Job Discrimination § 772.

38 USCS § 3680

77 Am Jur 2d, Veterans and Veterans' Laws § 135.

§ 3680A. Disapproval of enrollment in certain courses

(a) The Secretary shall not approve the enrollment of an eligible veteran in—
  (1)–(3) [Unchanged]
  (4) any independent study program except an accredited independent study program (including open circuit television) leading (A) to a standard college degree, or (B) to a certificate that reflects educational attainment offered by an institution of higher learning.

(b)–(f) [Unchanged]

(g) Notwithstanding subsections (e) and (f)(1), the Secretary may approve the enrollment of an eligible veteran in a course approved under this chapter if the course is offered by an educational institution under contract with the Department of Defense or the Department of Homeland Security and is given on or immediately adjacent to a military base, Coast Guard station, National Guard facility, or facility of the Selected Reserve.

(As amended Nov. 11, 1998, P. L. 105-368, Title X, § 1005(b)(9), 112 Stat. 3365; Dec. 27, 2001, P. L. 107-103, Title I, § 111(a), 115 Stat. 986; Nov. 25, 2002, P. L. 107-296, Title XVII, § 1704(d), 116 Stat. 2315.)

HISTORY; ANCILLARY LAWS AND DIRECTIVES

Amendments:
1996. Act Oct. 9, 1996, in subsec. (c), substituted "radio." for "radio or by open circuit television, except that the Secretary may approve the enrollment of an eligible veteran in a course, to be pursued in residence, leading to a standard college degree which includes, as an integral part thereof, subjects offered through open circuit television."; in subsec. (d)(2)(C), substituted "subsection (g)" for "3689(b)(6) of this title"; and added subsecs. (e)–(g).
1998. Act Nov. 11, 1998, in subsec. (d)(2)(C), deleted "section" preceding "subsection (g)".
2001. Act Dec. 27, 2001 (applicable as provided by § 111(b) of such Act, which appears as a note to this section), in subsec. (a)(4), inserted "(A)" and ", or (B) to a certificate that reflects educational attainment offered by an institution of higher learning".
2002. Act Nov. 25, 2002 (effective on 3/1/2003 pursuant to § 1704(g) of such Act, which appears as 10 USCS § 101 note), in subsec. (g), substituted "of Homeland Security" for "of Transportation".

Other provisions:
Application of Dec. 27, 2001 amendments. Act Dec. 27, 2001, P. L. 107-103, Title I, § 111(b), provides: "The amendments made by subsection (a) [amending subsec. (a)(4) of this section] shall apply to enrollments in independent study courses beginning on or after the date of the enactment of this Act.".

RESEARCH GUIDE

Am Jur:
77 Am Jur 2d, Veterans and Veterans' Laws §§ 131, 133.

§ 3681. Limitations on educational assistance

(a) No educational assistance allowance granted under chapter 30, 34, 35, or 36 of this title [38 USCS §§ 3001 et seq., 3451 et seq., 3500 et seq., or 3670 et seq.] or 106 or 107 [106A] of title 10 [10 USCS §§ 2131 et seq. or 2141 et seq.], or subsistence allowance granted under chapter 31 of this title [38 USCS §§ 3100 et seq.] shall be paid to any eligible person (1) who is on active duty and is pursuing a course of education which is being paid for by the Armed Forces (or by the Department of Health and Human Services in the case of the Public Health Service); or (2) who is attending a course of education or training paid for under chapter 41 of title 5 [5 USCS §§ 4101 et seq.].

(b) No person may receive benefits concurrently under two or more of the provisions of law listed below:
  (1) [Unchanged]
  (2) Chapters 106 and 107 [106A] and section 510 of title 10 [10 USCS §§ 2131 et seq., 2141 et seq., and 510].
  (3)–(5) [Unchanged]

(As amended Jan. 4, 2011, P. L. 111-377, Title II, § 202(b), 124 Stat. 4124.)

HISTORY; ANCILLARY LAWS AND DIRECTIVES

Explanatory notes:
The bracketed number "106A" has been inserted in subsecs. (a) and (b)(2) to indicate the chapter number probably intended by Congress. Section 532(a) of Act Oct. 28, 2005, P. L. 108-375, redesignated chapter 107 of title 10 (10 USCS §§ 2141 et seq.) as chapter 106A and enacted a new chapter 107 (10 USCS §§ 2151 et seq.).

READJUSTMENT BENEFITS
38 USCS § 3684

Amendments:

2011. Act Jan. 4, 2011 (effective on 8/1/2011, as provided by § 202(c) of such Act, which appears as 38 USCS § 3322 note), in subsec. (b)(2), inserted "and section 510".

INTERPRETIVE NOTES AND DECISIONS

1. Generally

Because benefits were based on status of child as eligible person through each disabled veteran parent, and absent aggregation restrictions, under 2003 version of 38 USCS § 3511(a)(1), appellant student with two disabled parents could receive educational benefits not to exceed 45 months from status of each parent; Congress adopted explicit language to prevent person receiving educational assistance from simultaneously receiving certain other benefits under separate program as evidenced by 38 USCS §§ 3562, 3695, and from receiving benefits concurrently under two or more of educational provisions as evidenced by 38 USCS § 3681, but Dependents' Educational Assistance benefits to eligible child of permanently and totally disabled parent was one program, and Congress, by placing limitations on receipt of additional benefits under two or more programs, placed no limitations on amount or length of benefits for "eligible persons" under single program or benefit. Osman v Peake (2008) 22 Vet App 252, 2008 US App Vet Claims LEXIS 1063.

§ 3683. Conflicting interests

CODE OF FEDERAL REGULATIONS

Department of Veterans Affairs—Vocational rehabilitation and education, 38 CFR 21.1 et seq.

§ 3684. Reports by veterans, eligible persons, and institutions; reporting fee

(a)(1) Except as provided in paragraph (2) of this subsection, the veteran or eligible person and the educational institution offering a course in which such veteran or eligible person is enrolled under chapter 31, 34, 35, or 36 of this title [38 USCS §§ 3100 et seq. 3451 et seq., 3500 et seq., or 3670 et seq.] shall, without delay, report to the Secretary, in the form prescribed by the Secretary, such enrollment and any interruption or termination of the education of each such veteran or eligible person. The date of such interruption or termination will be the last date of pursuit, or, in the case of correspondence training, the last date a lesson was serviced by a school.

(2), (3) [Unchanged]

(b) [Unchanged]

(c) The Secretary may pay to any educational institution, or to the sponsor of a program of apprenticeship, furnishing education or training under either this chapter or chapter 31, 34 or 35 of this title [38 USCS §§ 3670 et seq. or 3100 et seq., 3451 et seq., or 3500 et seq.] a reporting fee which will be in lieu of any other compensation or reimbursement for reports or certifications which such educational institution or joint apprenticeship training committee is required to submit to the Secretary by law or regulation. Such reporting fee shall be computed for each calendar year by multiplying $12 by the number of eligible veterans or eligible persons enrolled under this chapter or chapter 31, 34 or 35 of this title [38 USCS §§ 3670 et seq. or 3100 et seq., 3451 et seq., or 3500 et seq.] or $15 in the case of those eligible veterans and eligible persons whose educational assistance checks are directed in care of each institution for temporary custody and delivery and are delivered at the time of registration as provided under section 3680(d)(4) of this title [38 USCS § 3680(d)(4)], during the calendar year. The reporting fee shall be paid to such educational institution or joint apprenticeship training committee as soon as feasible after the end of the calendar year for which it is applicable. No reporting fee payable to an educational institution under this subsection shall be subject to offset by the Secretary against any liability of such institution for any overpayment for which such institution may be administratively determined to be liable under section 3685 of this title [38 USCS § 3685] unless such liability is not contested by such institution or has been upheld by a final decree of a court of appropriate jurisdiction. Any reporting fee paid an educational institution or joint apprenticeship training committee after the date of the enactment of the Post-9/11 Veterans Educational Assistance Improvements Act of 2011 [enacted Jan. 4, 2011] shall be utilized by such institution or committee solely for the making of certifications required under this chapter or chapter 31, 34, or 35 of this title [38 USCS §§ 3670 et seq. or 3100 et seq., 3451 et seq., or 3500 et seq.] or for otherwise supporting programs for veterans. The reporting fee payable under this subsection shall be paid from amounts appropriated for readjustment benefits.

(d) Not later than 90 days after the date of the enactment of this subsection [enacted Jan. 10, 2013], the Secretary shall ensure that the Department provides personnel of educational institutions who are charged with submitting reports or certifications to the Secretary under this section with assistance in preparing and submitting such reports or certifications.

(As amended Nov. 11, 1998, P. L. 105-368, Title II, Subtitle A, § 201(a), (b), 112 Stat. 3326; Nov. 1, 2000, P. L. 106-419, Title IV, § 404(a)(7), 114 Stat. 1865; Dec. 10, 2004, P. L. 108-454, Title I, § 110(d), 118 Stat. 3605; Oct. 13, 2010, P. L. 111-275, Title X, § 1001(i), 124 Stat. 2896; Jan.

4, 2011, P. L. 111-377, Title II, § 204(a), (b), 124 Stat. 4126; Jan. 10, 2013, P. L. 112-249, § 3, 126 Stat. 2401.)

HISTORY; ANCILLARY LAWS AND DIRECTIVES

Amendments:
1998. Act Nov. 11, 1998 (applicable with respect to calendar years beginning after 12/31/98, as provided by § 201(c) of such Act, which appears as a note to this section), in subsec. (c), substituted "during the calendar year." for "on October 31 of that year; except that the Secretary may, where it is established by such educational institution or joint apprenticeship training committee that eligible veteran plus eligible person enrollment on such date varies more than 15 percent from the peak eligible veteran enrollment plus eligible person enrollment in such educational institution or joint apprenticeship training committee during such calendar year, establish such other date as representative of the peak enrollment as may be justified for such educational institution or joint apprenticeship training committee." and added the sentence beginning: "The reporting fee payable . . . .".
2000. Act Nov. 1, 2000, in subsec. (c), substituted "calendar" for "calender" following "during the".
2004. Act Dec. 10, 2004, in subsec. (c), substituted "or to the sponsor of a program of apprenticeship" for "or to any joint apprenticeship training committee acting as a training establishment".
2010. Act Oct. 13, 2010, in subsec. (a)(1), substituted "34," for "34,,".
2011. Act Jan. 4, 2011 (effective on 10/1/2011, as provided by § 204(c) of such Act, which appears as a note to this section), in subsec. (c), substituted "multiplying $12" for "multiplying $7" and "or $15" for "or $11", and inserted the sentence beginning "Any reporting fee . . . .".
2013. Act Jan. 10, 2013, added subsec. (d).

Other provisions:
Application of Nov. 11, 1998 amendments. Act Nov. 11, 1998, P. L. 105-368, Title II, Subtitle A, § 201(c), 112 Stat. 3326, provides: "The amendments made by this section [amending subsec. (c) of this section] shall apply with respect to calendar years beginning after December 31, 1998.".
Effective date of Jan. 4, 2011 amendments. Act Jan. 4, 2011, P. L. 111-377, Title II, § 204(c), 124 Stat. 4126, provides: "The amendments made by this section [amending subsec. (c) of this section] shall take effect on October 1, 2011.".

RESEARCH GUIDE

Am Jur:
77 Am Jur 2d, Veterans and Veterans' Laws § 130.

§ 3684A. Procedures relating to computer matching program

RESEARCH GUIDE

Am Jur:
37A Am Jur 2d, Freedom of Information Acts § 399.
77 Am Jur 2d, Veterans and Veterans' Laws §§ 130, 135.

§ 3685. Overpayments to eligible persons or veterans

RESEARCH GUIDE

Am Jur:
77 Am Jur 2d, Veterans and Veterans' Laws § 135.

§ 3686. Correspondence courses

(a)(1) Each eligible veteran (as defined in section 3452(a)(1) and (2) of this title [38 USCS § 3452(a)(1) and (2)]) and each eligible spouse or surviving spouse (as defined in section 3501(a)(1)(B), (C), (D), or (E) of this title [USCS § 3501(a)(1)(B), (C), (D), or (E)]) who enters into an enrollment agreement to pursue a program of education exclusively by correspondence shall be paid an educational assistance allowance computed at the rate of 55 percent of the established charge which the institution requires nonveterans to pay for the course or courses pursued by the eligible veteran or spouse or surviving spouse. The term "established charge" as used herein means the charge for the course or courses determined on the basis of the lowest extended time payment plan offered by the institution and approved by the appropriate State approving agency or the actual cost to the veteran or spouse or surviving spouse, whichever is the lesser. Such allowance shall be paid quarterly on a pro rata basis for the lessons completed by the veteran or spouse or surviving spouse and serviced by the institution.

(2), (3) [Unchanged]

(b) The enrollment agreement shall fully disclose the obligation of both the institution and the veteran or spouse or surviving spouse and shall prominently display the provisions for affirmance, termination, refunds, and the conditions under which payment of the allowance is made by the Secretary to the veteran or spouse or surviving spouse. A copy of the enrollment agreement shall be furnished to each such veteran or spouse or surviving spouse at the time such veteran or spouse or surviving spouse signs such agreement. No such agreement shall be effective unless such veteran or spouse or surviving spouse shall, after the expiration of five days after the enrollment agreement is signed, have signed and submitted to the Secretary a written statement, with a signed copy to the institution, specifically affirming the enrollment agreement. In the event the veteran or spouse or surviving spouse at any time notifies the institution of such veteran's or spouse's intention not to affirm the agreement in accordance with the preceding sentence, the institution, without imposing any penalty or charging any fee shall promptly make a full refund of all amounts paid.

(c) [Unchanged]

(As amended Dec. 21, 2006, P. L. 109-444, § 3(c)(1), 120 Stat. 3307; Dec. 22, 2006, P. L. 109-461, Title III, § 301(c)(1), 120 Stat. 3427; Oct. 10, 2008, P. L. 110-389, Title III, Subtitle B, § 323, 122 Stat. 4168.)

HISTORY; ANCILLARY LAWS AND DIRECTIVES

Explanatory notes:
Section 3(c)(1) of Act Dec. 21, 2006, P. L. 109-444, amended this section; however, pursuant to § 1006(b) of Act Dec. 22, 2006, P. L. 109-461, which appears as 38 USCS § 101 note, as of the enactment of Act Dec. 22, 2006, P. L. 109-461, Act Dec. 21, 2006, P. L. 109-444 and the amendments made by such Act were deemed for all purposes not to have taken effect and such § 3(c)(1) ceased to be in effect.

Amendments:
2006. Act Dec. 22, 2006 (applicable with respect to a payment of educational assistance for a course of education pursued after enactment, as provided by § 301(d) of such Act, which appears as 38 USCS § 3501 note), in subsec. (a)(1), substituted "(D), or (E)" for "or (D)".
2008. Act Oct. 10, 2008, in subsec. (b), substituted "five" for "ten".

RESEARCH GUIDE

Other Treatises:
1 Rapp, Education Law (Matthew Bender), ch 5, Funding, Support and Finances of Education § 5.03.

§ 3687. Apprenticeship or other on-job training

(a) [Unchanged]

(b)(1) [Unchanged]

(2) The monthly training assistance allowance of an eligible person pursuing a program described under subsection (a) shall be $574 for the first six months, $429 for the second six months, $285 for the third six months, and $144 for the fourth and any succeeding six-month period of training.

(3) [Unchanged]

(c) [Unchanged]

(d) With respect to any fiscal year, the Secretary shall provide a percentage increase (rounded to the nearest dollar) in the rates payable under subsection (b)(2) equal to the percentage by which—

(1) the Consumer Price Index (all items, United States city average) for the 12-month period ending on the June 30 preceding the beginning of the fiscal year for which the increase is made, exceeds

(2) such Consumer Price Index for the 12-month period preceding the 12-month period described in paragraph (1).

(e)(1) For each month that an individual (as defined in paragraph (3)) is paid a training assistance allowance under subsection (a), the entitlement of the individual shall be charged at a percentage rate (rounded to the nearest percent) that is equal to the ratio of—

(A) the training assistance allowance for the month involved, to

(B) the monthly educational assistance allowance otherwise payable for full-time enrollment in an educational institution.

(2) For any month in which an individual fails to complete 120 hours of training, the entitlement otherwise chargeable under paragraph (1) shall be reduced in the same proportion as the monthly training assistance allowance payable is reduced under subsection (b)(3).

(3) In this section, the term "individual" means—

(A) an eligible veteran who is entitled to monthly educational assistance allowances payable under section 3015(e) of this title [38 USCS § 3015(e)], or

(B) an eligible person who is entitled to monthly educational assistance allowances payable under section 3532(a) of this title [38 USCS § 3532(a)],

as the case may be.

38 USCS § 3687

(As amended June 9, 1998, P. L. 105-178, Title VIII, Subtitle B, § 8210(d), as added July 22, 1998, P. L. 105-206, Title IX, § 9014(b), 112 Stat. 866; Nov. 1, 2000, P. L. 106-419, Title I, Subtitle B, § 111(d), (f)(2), 114 Stat. 1830, 1831; Dec. 27, 2001, P. L. 107-103, Title I, § 102(d), 115 Stat. 978; Dec. 16, 2003, P. L. 108-183, Title III, § 302(d), 117 Stat. 2659; Dec. 10, 2004, P. L. 108-454, Title I, § 102(a), 118 Stat. 3600.)

HISTORY; ANCILLARY LAWS AND DIRECTIVES

Amendments:
1998. Act June 9, 1998 (effective on 10/1/98 and applicable with respect to educational assistance allowances paid for months after 9/98, as provided by § 8210(e) of such Act, which appears as a note to this section), as amended July 22, 1998 (effective simultaneously with the enactment of, and as if included in, Act June 9, 1998, as provided by § 9016 of Act July 22, 1998, which appears as 23 USCS § 101 note), in subsec. (b)(2), substituted "$353" for "$294", substituted "$264" for "$220", substituted "$175" for "$146", and substituted "$73" for "$88".

Act July 22, 1998 (effective simultaneously with the enactment of, and as if included in, Act June 9, 1998, as provided by § 9016 of Act July 22, 1998, which appears as 23 USCS § 101 note) amended Act June 9, 1998, which amended this section.

2000. Act Nov. 1, 2000 (effective and applicable as provided by § 111(e) of such Act, which appears as 38 USCS § 3532 note), in subsec. (b)(2), substituted "$428" for "$353", substituted "$320" for "$264", substituted "$212" for "$175", and substituted "$107" for "$88".

Such Act further (effective 10/1/01, as provided by § 111(f)(3) of such Act, which appears as 38 USCS § 3564 note), added subsec. (d).

2001. Act Dec. 27, 2001 (effective and applicable as provided by § 102(e) of such Act, which appears as 38 USCS § 3532 note), in subsec. (b)(2), substituted "$488" for "$428", substituted "$365" for "$320", substituted "$242" for "$212", and substituted "$122" for "$107".

2003. Act Dec. 16, 2003 (effective 7/1/2004 and applicable to educational assistance allowances payable under 38 USCS §§ 3500 et seq. and 3687(b)(2) for months beginning on or after that date, as provided by § 302(e) of such Act, which appears as 38 USCS § 3532 note), in subsec. (b)(2), substituted "shall be $574 for the first six months, $429 for the second six months, $285 for the third six months, and $144 for the fourth and any succeeding six-month period of training." for "shall be $488 for the first six months, $365 for the second six months, $242 for the third six months, and $122 for the fourth and any succeeding six-month periods of training.".

2004. Act Dec. 10, 2004 (applicable to months beginning after 9/30/2005, as provided by § 102(b) of such Act, which appears as a note to this section), added subsec. (e).

Other provisions:
Application of Dec. 10, 2004 amendment. Act Dec. 10, 2004, P. L. 108-454, Title I, § 102(b), 118 Stat. 3600, provides: "The amendment made by subsection (a) [adding subsec. (e) of this section] shall apply with respect to months beginning after September 30, 2005.".

Increase in benefit for individuals pursuing apprenticeship or on-job training; survivors and dependents educational assistance. Act Dec. 10, 2004, P. L. 108-454, Title I, § 103(c), 118 Stat. 3601, provides:

"(1) For months beginning on or after October 1, 2005, and before January 1, 2008, subsection (b)(2) of section 3687 of title 38, United States Code, shall be applied as if—

"(A) the reference to '$574 for the first six months' were a reference to '$650 for the first six months';

"(B) the reference to '$429 for the second six months' were a reference to '$507 for the second six months'; and

"(C) the reference to '$285 for the third six months' were a reference to '$366 for the third six months'.

"(2) Subsection (d) of such section 3687 shall not apply with respect to the provisions of paragraph (1) for months occurring during fiscal year 2006.

"(3) For months beginning on or after January 1, 2008, the Secretary shall carry out subsection (b)(2) of such section 3687 as if paragraphs (1) and (2) were not enacted into law.".

§ 3688. Measurement of courses

(a) [Unchanged]
(b) The Secretary shall define part-time training in the case of the types of courses referred to in subsection (a), and shall define full-time and part-time training in the case of all other types of courses pursued under this chapter [38 USCS §§ 3670 et seq.], chapter 30, 32, 33, or 35 of this title [38 USCS §§ 3001 et seq., 3201 et seq., 3301 et seq., or 3500 et seq.], or chapter 106 of title 10 [10 USCS §§ 2131 et seq.].

(As amended June 30, 2008, P. L. 110-252, Title V, § 5003(b)(2)(A)(ii), 122 Stat. 2375.)

HISTORY; ANCILLARY LAWS AND DIRECTIVES

Amendments:
2008. Act June 30, 2008 (effective on 8/1/2009, as provided by § 5003(d) of such Act, which appears as 10 USCS § 16163 note), in subsec. (b), inserted "33,".

INTERPRETIVE NOTES AND DECISIONS

Veteran was not entitled to educational benefits for enrollment period between August 31, 1992 and October 23, 1992, since commencing date of award was one year before VA received enrollment certification from university which occurred subsequent to enrollment period; and veteran was not entitled to benefits at full-time rate for courses taken in summer of 1993 since, under law in effect at that time, courses could not be considered full-time. Taylor v West (1998) 11 Vet App 436.

§ 3689. Approval requirements for licensing and certification testing

(a) In general. (1) No payment may be made for a licensing or certification test described in section 3452(b) or 3501(a)(5) of this title [38 USCS § 3452(b) or 3501(a)(5)] unless the test is deemed approved by section 3672(b)(2)(B) of this title [38 USCS § 3672(b)(2)(B)] or the Secretary determines that the requirements of this section have been met with respect to such test and the organization or entity offering the test. The requirements of approval for tests and organizations or entities offering tests shall be in accordance with the provisions of this chapter and chapters 30, 32, 33, 34, and 35 of this title [38 USCS §§ 3670 et seq., 3001 et seq., 3201 et seq., 3301 et seq., 3451 et seq., and 3500 et seq.] and with regulations prescribed by the Secretary to carry out this section.

(2) To the extent that the Secretary determines practicable, State approving agencies may, in lieu of the Secretary, approve licensing and certification tests, and organizations and entities offering such tests, under this section.

(b) Requirements for tests. (1) Subject to paragraph (2), a licensing or certification test is approved for purposes of this section only if—

(A) the test is required under Federal, State, or local law or regulation for an individual to enter into, maintain, or advance in employment in a predetermined and identified vocation or profession; or

(B) the Secretary determines that the test is generally accepted, in accordance with relevant government, business, or industry standards, employment policies, or hiring practices, as attesting to a level of knowledge or skill required to qualify to enter into, maintain, or advance in employment in a predetermined and identified vocation or profession.

(2) A licensing or certification test offered by a State, or a political subdivision of a State, is deemed approved by the Secretary for purposes of this section.

(c) Requirements for organizations or entities offering tests. (1) Each organization or entity that is not an entity of the United States, a State, or political subdivision of a State, that offers a licensing or certification test for which payment may be made under chapter 30, 32, 33, 34, or 35 of this title [38 USCS §§ 3001 et seq., 3201 et seq., 3301 et seq., 3451 et seq., or 3500 et seq.] and that meets the following requirements, shall be approved by the Secretary to offer such test:

(A) The organization or entity certifies to the Secretary that the licensing or certification test offered by the organization or entity is generally accepted, in accordance with relevant government, business, or industry standards, employment policies, or hiring practices, as attesting to a level of knowledge or skill required to qualify to enter into, maintain, or advance in employment in a predetermined and identified vocation or profession.

(B) The organization or entity is licensed, chartered, or incorporated in a State and has offered such test, or a test to certify or license in a similar or related occupation, for a minimum of two years before the date on which the organization or entity first submits to the Secretary an application for approval under this section.

(C) The organization or entity employs, or consults with, individuals with expertise or substantial experience with respect to all areas of knowledge or skill that are measured by the test and that are required for the license or certificate issued.

(D) The organization or entity has no direct financial interest in—

(i) the outcome of the test; or

(ii) organizations that provide the education or training of candidates for licenses or certificates required for vocations or professions.

(E) The organization or entity maintains appropriate records with respect to all candidates who take the test for a period prescribed by the Secretary, but in no case for a period of less than three years.

(F)(i) The organization or entity promptly issues notice of the results of the test to the candidate for the license or certificate.

(ii) The organization or entity has in place a process to review complaints submitted against the organization or entity with respect to the test or the process for obtaining a license or certificate required for vocations or professions.

(G) The organization or entity furnishes to the Secretary such information with respect to the test as the Secretary requires to determine whether payment may be made for the test under chapter 30, 32, 33, 34, or 35 of this title [38 USCS §§ 3001 et seq., 3201 et seq., 3301 et seq., 3451 et seq., or 3500 et seq.], including personal identifying information, fee payment, and test results. Such information shall be furnished in the form prescribed by the Secretary.

(H) The organization or entity furnishes to the Secretary the following information:

(i) A description of the licensing or certification test offered by the organization or entity, including the purpose of the test, the vocational, professional, governmental, and other entities that recognize the test, and the license or certificate issued upon successful completion of the test.

(ii) The requirements to take the test, including the amount of the fee charged for the test and any prerequisite education, training, skills, or other certification.

(iii) The period for which the license or certificate awarded upon successful completion of the test is valid, and the requirements for maintaining or renewing the license or certificate.

(I) Upon request of the Secretary, the organization or entity furnishes such information to the Secretary that the Secretary determines necessary to perform an assessment of—

(i) the test conducted by the organization or entity as compared to the level of knowledge or skills that a license or certificate attests; and

(ii) the applicability of the test over such periods of time as the Secretary determines appropriate.

(2) With respect to each organization or entity that is an entity of the United States, a State, or political subdivision of a State, that offers a licensing or certification test for which payment may be made under chapters 30, 32, 34, or 35 of this title [38 USCS §§ 3001 et seq., 3201 et seq., 3451 et seq., or 3500 et seq.], the following provisions of paragraph (1) shall apply to the entity: subparagraphs (E), (F), (G), and (H).

(d) **Administration.** Except as otherwise specifically provided in this section or chapter 30, 32, 33, 34, or 35 of this title [38 USCS §§ 3001 et seq., 3201 et seq., 3301 et seq., 3451 et seq., or 3500 et seq.], in implementing this section and making payment under any such chapter for a licensing or certification test, the test is deemed to be a "course" and the organization or entity that offers such test is deemed to be an "institution" or "educational institution", respectively, as those terms are applied under and for purposes of sections 3671, 3673, 3674, 3678, 3679, 3681, 3682, 3683, 3685, 3690, and 3696 of this title [38 USCS §§ 3671, 3673, 3674, 3678, 3679, 3681, 3682, 3683, 3685, 3690, and 3696].

(e) **Professional Certification and Licensure Advisory Committee.** (1) There is established within the Department a committee to be known as the Professional Certification and Licensure Advisory Committee (hereinafter in this section referred to as the "Committee").

(2) The Committee shall advise the Secretary with respect to the requirements of organizations or entities offering licensing and certification tests to individuals for which payment for such tests may be made under chapter 30, 32, 33, 34, or 35 of this title [38 USCS §§ 3001 et seq., 3201 et seq., 3301 et seq., 3451 et seq., or 3500 et seq.], and such other related issues as the Committee determines to be appropriate.

(3)(A) The Secretary shall appoint seven individuals with expertise in matters relating to licensing and certification tests to serve as members of the Committee.

(B) The Secretary of Labor and the Secretary of Defense shall serve as ex officio members of the Committee.

(C) A vacancy in the Committee shall be filled in the manner in which the original appointment was made.

(4)(A) The Secretary shall appoint the chairman of the Committee.

(B) The Committee shall meet at the call of the chairman.

(5) The Committee shall terminate December 31, 2006.

(Added Nov. 1, 2000, P. L. 106-419, Title I, Subtitle C, § 122(c)(1), 114 Stat. 1835; Dec. 6, 2002, P. L. 107-330, Title III, § 308(d), 116 Stat. 2828; June 30, 2008, P. L. 110-252, Title V, § 5003(b)(2)(A)(iii), 122 Stat. 2375; Jan. 4, 2011, P. L. 111-377, Title II, § 203(a)(2)(C), 124 Stat. 4125.)

HISTORY; ANCILLARY LAWS AND DIRECTIVES

Explanatory notes:

A prior § 3689 (Act Oct. 24, 1972, P. L. 92-540, Title III, § 316(2), 86 Stat. 1087; Oct. 15, 1976, P. L. 94-502, Title V, § 509(b), 90 Stat. 2401; Nov. 23, 1977, P. L. 95-202, Title III, § 305(a)(1), 91 Stat. 1442; Oct. 17, 1980, P. L. 96-466, Title VI, § 601(g), 94 Stat. 2208; Dec. 18, 1989, P. L. 101-237, Title IV, §§ 418, 423(b)(1)(A), 103 Stat. 2087, 2092; Aug. 6, 1991, P. L. 102-83, § 5(a), 105 Stat. 406) was repealed by Act Oct. 9, 1996, P. L. 104-275, Title I, § 103(a)(1)(A), 110 Stat. 3326. Such section provided for the period of operation required for approval of a course. Provisions similar to those of this section were contained in former 38

USC §§ 1675, 1725, prior to repeal by Act Oct. 24, 1972, P. L. 92-540, Title IV, §§ 401(6), 402(2), 86 Stat. 1090.

Effective date of section:
This section took effect on March 1, 2001, pursuant to § 122(d) of Act Nov. 1, 2000, P. L. 106-419, which appears as 38 USCS § 3032 note.

Amendments:
2002. Act Dec. 6, 2002, in subsec. (c)(1)(B), substituted "such test, or a test to certify or license in a similar or related occupation," for "the test".
2008. Act June 30, 2008 (effective on 8/1/2009, as provided by § 5003(d) of such Act, which appears as 10 USCS § 16163 note), in subsecs. (a)(1), (c)(1), (G), (d), and (e)(2), inserted "33,".
2011. Act Jan. 4, 2011 (effective on 8/1/2011, as provided by § 203(e) of such Act, which appears as 38 USCS § 3034 note), in subsec. (a)(1), inserted "the test is deemed approved by section 3672(b)(2)(B) of this title or".

Other provisions:
Applicability of section. This section applies with respect to licensing and certification tests approved by the Secretary of Veterans Affairs on or after March 1, 2001, pursuant to § 122(d) of Act Nov. 1, 2000, P. L. 106-419, which appears as 38 USCS § 3032 note.

§ 3690. Overcharges by educational institutions; discontinuance of allowances; examination of records; false or misleading statements

(a) Overcharges by educational institutions. If the Secretary finds that an educational institution has—

    (1), (2) [Unchanged]

the Secretary may disapprove such educational institution for the enrollment of any eligible veteran or eligible person not already enrolled therein under this chapter or chapter 31, 34, or 35 of this title [38 USCS §§ 3670 et seq. or 3101 et seq., 3451 et seq., or 3500 et seq.].

(b) Discontinuance of allowances. (1), (2) [Unchanged]

    (3)(A) The Secretary may suspend educational assistance to eligible veterans and eligible persons already enrolled, and may disapprove the enrollment or reenrollment of any eligible veteran or eligible person, in any course as to which the Secretary has evidence showing a substantial pattern of eligible veterans or eligible persons, or both, who are receiving such assistance by virtue of their enrollment in such course but who are not entitled to such assistance because (i) the course approval requirements of this chapter are not being met, or (ii) the educational institution offering such course has violated one or more of the recordkeeping or reporting requirements of this chapter [38 USCS §§ 3670 et seq.] or chapter 30, 32, 33, 34, or 35 of this title [38 USCS §§ 3001 et seq., 3201 et seq., 3301 et seq., 3451 et seq., or 3500 et seq.].

    (B) [Unchanged]

(c) Examination of records. Notwithstanding any other provision of law, the records and accounts of educational institutions pertaining to eligible veterans or eligible persons who received educational assistance under this chapter [38 USCS §§ 3670 et seq.] or chapter 31, 32, 34, or 35 of this title [38 USCS §§ 3100 et seq., 3201 et seq., 3451 et seq., or 3500 et seq.] as well as the records of other students which the Secretary determines necessary to ascertain institutional compliance with the requirements of such chapters, shall be available for examination by duly authorized representatives of the Government.

(d) False or misleading statements. Whenever the Secretary finds that an educational institution has willfully submitted a false or misleading claim, or that a veteran or person, with the complicity of an educational institution, has submitted such a claim, the Secretary shall make a complete report of the facts of the case to the appropriate State approving agency and, where deemed advisable, to the Attorney General of the United States for appropriate action.

(As amended June 15, 2006, P. L. 109-233, Title V, § 503(8)(A), 120 Stat. 416; June 30, 2008, P. L. 110-252, Title V, § 5003(b)(2)(A)(iv), 122 Stat. 2375 .)

HISTORY; ANCILLARY LAWS AND DIRECTIVES

Amendments:
2006. Act June , 2006, in subsecs. (a)–(d), inserted the subsection headings, which headings formerly appeared as centered headings preceding such subsections.
2008. Act June 30, 2008 (effective on 8/1/2009, as provided by § 5003(d) of such Act, which appears as 10 USCS § 16163 note), in subsec. (b)(3)(A), inserted "33,".

RESEARCH GUIDE

Other Treatises:
5 Rapp, Education Law (Matthew Bender), ch 13, Education Records Management and Retention § 13.04.

38 USCS § 3691

§ 3691. Change of program

(a)–(c) [Unchanged]

(d)(1) For the purposes of this section, the term "change of program of education" shall not be deemed to include a change by a veteran or eligible person from the pursuit of one program to the pursuit of another program if—

(A) the veteran or eligible person has successfully completed the former program;

(B) the program leads to a vocational, educational, or professional objective in the same general field as the former program;

(C) the former program is a prerequisite to, or generally required for, pursuit of the subsequent program;

(D) in the case of a change from the pursuit of a subsequent program to the pursuit of a former program, the veteran or eligible person resumes pursuit of the former program without loss of credit or standing in the former program; or

(E) the change from the program to another program is at the same educational institution and such educational institution determines that the new program is suitable to the aptitudes, interests, and abilities of the veteran or eligible person and certifies to the Secretary the enrollment of the veteran or eligible person in the new program.

(2) A veteran or eligible person undergoing a change from one program of education to another program of education as described in paragraph (1)(E) shall not be required to apply to the Secretary for approval of such change.

(As amended Oct. 10, 2008, P. L. 110-389, Title III, Subtitle B, § 324, 122 Stat. 4168.)

HISTORY; ANCILLARY LAWS AND DIRECTIVES

Amendments:

2008. Act Oct. 10, 2008, in subsec. (d), in the introductory matter, inserted "(1)", redesignated former paras. (1)–(4) as subparas. (A)–(D), respectively, in subpara. (C) as redesignated, deleted "or" following the concluding semicolon, in subpara. (D) as redesignated, substituted "; or" for a concluding period, added subpara. (E), and added para. (2).

RESEARCH GUIDE

Am Jur:

77 Am Jur 2d, Veterans and Veterans' Laws §§ 134, 136.

§ 3692. Advisory committee

(a) There shall be a Veterans' Advisory Committee on Education formed by the Secretary which shall be composed of persons who are eminent in their respective fields of education, labor, and management and of representatives of institutions and establishments furnishing education to eligible veterans or persons enrolled under chapter 30, 32, 33, or 35 of this title [38 USCS §§ 3001 et seq., 3201 et seq., 3301 et seq., or 3500 et seq.] and chapter 1606 of title 10 [10 USCS §§ 16131 et seq.]. The committee shall also, to the maximum extent practicable, include veterans representative of World War II, the Korean conflict era, the post-Korean conflict era, the Vietnam era, the post-Vietnam era, and the Persian Gulf War. The Assistant Secretary of Education for Postsecondary Education (or such other comparable official of the Department of Education as the Secretary of Education may designate) and the Assistant Secretary of Labor for Veterans' Employment and Training shall be ex officio members of the advisory committee.

(b) The Secretary shall consult with and seek the advice of the committee from time to time with respect to the administration of this chapter [38 USCS §§ 3670 et seq], chapters 30, 32, 33, and 35 of this title [38 USCS §§ 3001 et seq., 3201 et seq., 3301 et seq., and 3500 et seq.], and chapter 1606 of title 10 [10 USCS §§ 16131 et seq.]. The committee may make such reports and recommendations as it considers desirable to the Secretary and the Congress.

(c) The committee shall remain in existence until December 31, 2013.

(As amended Dec. 16, 2003, P. L. 108-183, Title III, § 307, 117 Stat. 2661; June 30, 2008, P. L. 110-252, Title V, § 5003(b)(2)(A)(v), 122 Stat. 2375; Oct. 13, 2010, P. L. 111-275, Title I, § 102, 124 Stat. 2866.)

HISTORY; ANCILLARY LAWS AND DIRECTIVES

Amendments:

2003. Act Dec. 16, 2003, in subsec. (a), substituted "chapter 1606" for "chapter 106", and inserted ", to the maximum extent practicable,"; in subsec. (b), substituted "chapters 30" for "chapter 30", and substituted "chapter 1606" for "chapter 106"; and, in subsec. (c), substituted "December 31, 2009" for "December 31, 2003".

2008. Act June 30, 2008 (effective on 8/1/2009, as provided by § 5003(d) of such Act, which appears as 10 USCS § 16163 note), in subsecs. (a) and (b), inserted "33,".

2010. Act Oct. 13, 2010, in subsec. (c), substituted "December 31, 2013" for "December 31, 2009".

READJUSTMENT BENEFITS   38 USCS § 3695

RESEARCH GUIDE

Am Jur:
77 Am Jur 2d, Veterans and Veterans' Laws § 124.

§ 3694. Use of other Federal agencies

(a) In general. In carrying out the Secretary's functions under this chapter or chapter 34 or 35 of this title [38 USCS §§ 3670 et seq. or 3451 et seq. or 3500 et seq.], the Secretary may utilize the facilities and services of any other Federal department or agency. Any such utilization shall be pursuant to proper agreement with the Federal department or agency concerned; and payment to cover the cost thereof shall be made either in advance or by way of reimbursement, as may be provided in such agreement.

(b) Coordination of information among the Departments of Veterans Affairs, Defense, and Labor with respect to on-job training. At the time of a servicemember's discharge or release from active duty service, the Secretary of Defense shall furnish to the Secretary such pertinent information concerning each registered apprenticeship pursued by the servicemember during the period of active duty service of the servicemember. The Secretary, in conjunction with the Secretary of Labor, shall encourage and assist States and private organizations to give credit to servicemembers for the registered apprenticeship program so pursued in the case of any related apprenticeship program the servicemember may pursue as a civilian.

(As amended Dec. 10, 2004, P. L. 108-454, Title I, § 107, 118 Stat. 3603.)

HISTORY; ANCILLARY LAWS AND DIRECTIVES

Amendments:
2004. Act Dec. 10, 2004, designated the existing provisions as subsec. (a) and inserted the subsection heading; and added subsec. (b).

§ 3695. Limitation on period of assistance under two or more programs [Caution: See prospective amendment note below.]

(a) The aggregate period for which any person may receive assistance under two or more of the provisions of law listed below may not exceed 48 months (or the part-time equivalent thereof):

(1)–(3) [Unchanged]

(4) Chapters 30, 32, 33, 34, 35, and 36 [38 USCS §§ 3001 et seq., 3201 et seq., 3301 et seq., 3451 et seq., 3500 et seq., and 3670 et seq.].

(5) Chapters 107, 1606, 1607, and 1611 of title 10 [10 USCS §§ 2141 et seq., 16131 et seq., 16161 et seq., and 16401].

(6)–(8) [Unchanged]

(b) [Unchanged]

(As amended Oct. 5, 1999, P. L. 106-65, Div A, Title V, Subtitle F, § 551(b), 113 Stat. 614; Dec. 27, 2001, P. L. 107-103, Title V, § 509(d), 115 Stat. 997; Dec. 28, 2001, P. L. 107-107, Div A, Title X, Subtitle E, § 1048(i)(8), 115 Stat. 1229; Oct. 28, 2004, P. L. 108-375, Div A, Title V, Subtitle C, § 527(b)(2), 118 Stat. 1894; June 30, 2008, P. L. 110-252, Title V, § 5003(b)(1)(B), 122 Stat. 2375; Aug. 6, 2012, P. L. 112-154, Title IV, § 401(a), 126 Stat. 1188.)

HISTORY; ANCILLARY LAWS AND DIRECTIVES

Prospective amendments:
Amendment of subsec. (a)(4) and addition of subsec. (c), effective October 1, 2013. Act Aug. 6, 2012, P. L. 112-154, Title IV, § 401(a), 126 Stat. 1188 (effective 10/1/2013 and applicable as provided by § 401(b) of such Act, which appears as a note to this section), provides:

"Section 3695 is amended—

"(1) in subsection (a)(4), by striking '35,'; and

"(2) by adding at the end the following new subsection:

" "(c) The aggregate period for which any person may receive assistance under chapter 35 of this title [38 USCS §§ 3500 et seq.], on the one hand, and any of the provisions of law referred to in subsection (a), on the other hand, may not exceed 81 months (or the part-time equivalent thereof).'.".

Amendments:
1999. Act Oct. 5, 1999, in subsec. (a)(5), substituted "Chapters 107, 1606, and 1610" for "Chapters 106 and 107".

2001. Act Dec. 27, 2001, in subsec. (a)(5), substituted "1611" for "1610".

Act Dec. 28, 2001, purported to amend subsec. (a)(5) by substituting "1611" for "1610"; however, because of a prior amendment, this amendment could not be executed.

2004. Act Oct. 28, 2004, in subsec. (a)(5), inserted "1607,".

2008. Act June 30, 2008 (effective on 8/1/2009, as provided by § 5003(d) of such Act, which appears as 10 USCS § 16163 note), in subsec. (a), substituted para. (4) for one which read: "(4) Chapters 30, 32, 34, 35, and 36 of this title, and the former chapter 33.".

38 USCS § 3695

Other provisions:
Effective date and application of Aug. 6, 2012 amendments. Act Aug. 6, 2012, P. L. 112-154, Title IV, § 401(b), 126 Stat. 1188, provides: "The amendment made by subsection (a) shall take effect on October 1, 2013, and shall not operate to revive any entitlement to assistance under chapter 35 of title 38, United States Code, or the provisions of law referred to in section 3695(a) of such title, as in effect on the day before such date, that was terminated by reason of the operation of section 3695(a) of such title, as so in effect, before such date.".

Revival of entitlement reduced by prior utilization of chapter 35 assistance. Act Aug. 6, 2012, P. L. 112-154, Title IV, § 401(c), 126 Stat. 1188, provides:

"(1) In general. Subject to paragraph (2), in the case of an individual whose period of entitlement to assistance under a provision of law referred to in section 3695(a) of title 38, United States Code (other than chapter 35 of such title [38 USCS §§ 3500 et seq.]), as in effect on September 30, 2013, was reduced under such section 3695(a), as so in effect, by reason of the utilization of entitlement to assistance under chapter 35 of such title [38 USCS §§ 3500 et seq.] before October 1, 2013, the period of entitlement to assistance of such individual under such provision shall be determined without regard to any entitlement so utilized by the individual under chapter 35 of such title [38 USCS §§ 3500 et seq.].

"(2) Limitation. The maximum period of entitlement to assistance of an individual under paragraph (1) may not exceed 81 months.".

CODE OF FEDERAL REGULATIONS
Department of Veterans Affairs—Vocational rehabilitation and education, 38 CFR 21.1 et seq.

RESEARCH GUIDE
Am Jur:
77 Am Jur 2d, Veterans and Veterans' Laws § 129.

INTERPRETIVE NOTES AND DECISIONS

Plain language of 38 USCS § 3695(a)(4), (5) prohibited any award of education benefits to veteran beyond stated maximum aggregate period, and statute did not provide for waiver of limitation or exception for veteran's non-continuous periods of both active and reserve service. Davenport v Principi (2002) 16 Vet App 522, 2002 US App Vet Claims LEXIS 997.

Because benefits were based on status of child as eligible person through each disabled veteran parent, and absent aggregation restrictions, under 2003 version of 38 USCS § 3511(a)(1), appellant student with two disabled parents could receive educational benefits not to exceed 45 months from status of each parent; Congress adopted explicit language to prevent person receiving educational assistance from simultaneously receiving certain other benefits under separate program as evidenced by 38 USCS §§ 3562, 3695, but Dependents' Educational Assistance benefits to eligible child of permanently and totally disabled parent was one program, and Congress, by placing limitations on receipt of additional benefits under two or more programs, placed no limitations on amount or length of benefits for "eligible persons" under single program or benefit. Osman v Peake (2008) 22 Vet App 252, 2008 US App Vet Claims LEXIS 1063.

§ 3696. Limitation on certain advertising, sales, and enrollment practices

(a)–(c) [Unchanged]

(d)(1) The Secretary shall not approve under this chapter any course offered by an educational institution if the educational institution provides any commission, bonus, or other incentive payment based directly or indirectly on success in securing enrollments or financial aid to any persons or entities engaged in any student recruiting or admission activities or in making decisions regarding the award of student financial assistance.

(2) To the degree practicable, the Secretary shall carry out paragraph (1) in a manner that is consistent with the Secretary of Education's enforcement of section 487(a)(20) of the Higher Education Act of 1965 (20 U.S.C. 1094(a)(20)).

(As amended Jan. 10, 2013, P. L. 112-249, § 2, 126 Stat. 2401.)

HISTORY; ANCILLARY LAWS AND DIRECTIVES
Amendments:
2013. Act Jan. 10, 2013, added subsec. (d).

CODE OF FEDERAL REGULATIONS
Department of Veterans Affairs—Vocational rehabilitation and education, 38 CFR 21.1 et seq.

RESEARCH GUIDE
Am Jur:
45B Am Jur 2d, Job Discrimination § 772.
77 Am Jur 2d, Veterans and Veterans' Laws § 130.

§ 3697. Funding of contract educational and vocational counseling

(a) Subject to subsection (b) of this section, educational or vocational counseling services obtained

READJUSTMENT BENEFITS
38 USCS § 3698

by the Department of Veterans Affairs by contract and provided to an individual under section 3697A of this title [38 USCS § 3697A] or to an individual applying for or receiving benefits under section 524 [38 USCS § 524] or chapter 30, 32, 33, 34, or 35 of this title [38 USCS §§ 3001 et seq., 3201 et seq., 3301 et seq., 3451 et seq., or 3500 et seq.] or chapter 106 of Title 10 [10 USCS §§ 2131 et seq.], shall be paid for out of funds appropriated, or otherwise available, to the Department of Veterans Affairs for payment of readjustment benefits.

(b) [Unchanged]

(As amended June 30, 2008, P. L. 110-252, Title V, § 5003(b)(2)(A)(vi), 122 Stat. 2375.)

HISTORY; ANCILLARY LAWS AND DIRECTIVES

Amendments:
2008. Act June 30, 2008 (effective on 8/1/2009, as provided by § 5033(d) of such Act, which appears as 10 USCS § 16163 note), in subsec. (a), inserted "33,".

RESEARCH GUIDE

Am Jur:
77 Am Jur 2d, Veterans and Veterans' Laws § 125.

§ 3697A. Educational and vocational counseling

(a) [Unchanged]

(b) For the purposes of this section, the term "individual" means an individual who—
  (1) is eligible for educational assistance under chapter 30, 31, 32, or 33 of this title [38 USCS §§ 3001 et seq., 3100 et seq., 3201 et seq., or 3301 et seq.] or chapter 106 or 107 [106A] of title 10 [10 USCS §§ 2131 et seq. or 2141 et seq.];
  (2), (3) [Unchanged]

(c)–(e) [Unchanged]

(As amended June 30, 2008, P. L. 110-252, Title V, § 5003(b)(2)(B), 122 Stat. 2375.)

HISTORY; ANCILLARY LAWS AND DIRECTIVES

Explanatory notes:
The bracketed number "106A" has been inserted in subsec. (b)(1) to indicate the chapter number probably intended by Congress. Section 532(a) of Act Oct. 28, 2005, P. L. 108-375, redesignated chapter 107 of title 10 (10 USCS §§ 2141 et seq.) as chapter 106A and enacted a new chapter 107 (10 USCS §§ 2151 et seq.).

Amendments:
2008. Act June 30, 2008 (effective on 8/1/2009, as provided by § 5003(d) of such Act, which appears as 10 USCS § 16163 note), in subsec. (b)(1), substituted "32, or 33" for "or 32".

RESEARCH GUIDE

Am Jur:
77 Am Jur 2d, Veterans and Veterans' Laws § 125.

§ 3698. Comprehensive policy on providing education information to veterans

(a) **Comprehensive policy required.** The Secretary shall develop a comprehensive policy to improve outreach and transparency to veterans and members of the Armed Forces through the provision of information on institutions of higher learning.

(b) **Scope.** In developing the policy required by subsection (a), the Secretary shall include each of the following elements:
  (1) Effective and efficient methods to inform individuals of the educational and vocational counseling provided under section 3697A of this title [38 USCS § 3697A].
  (2) A centralized mechanism for tracking and publishing feedback from students and State approving agencies regarding the quality of instruction, recruiting practices, and post-graduation employment placement of institutions of higher learning that—
    (A) allows institutions of higher learning to verify feedback and address issues regarding feedback before the feedback is published;
    (B) protects the privacy of students, including by not publishing the names of students; and
    (C) publishes only feedback that conforms with criteria for relevancy that the Secretary shall determine.
  (3) The merit of and the manner in which a State approving agency shares with an accrediting agency or association recognized by the Secretary of Education under subpart 2 of part H of title IV of the Higher Education Act of 1965 (20 U.S.C. 1099b) information regarding the State approving agency's evaluation of an institution of higher learning.
  (4) Description of the information provided to individuals participating in the Transition Assistance Program under section 1144 of title 10 relating to institutions of higher learning.

(5) Effective and efficient methods to provide veterans and members of the Armed Forces with information regarding postsecondary education and training opportunities available to the veteran or member.

(c) Postsecondary education information. (1) The Secretary shall ensure that the information provided pursuant to subsection (b)(5) includes—

(A) an explanation of the different types of accreditation available to educational institutions and programs of education;

(B) a description of Federal student aid programs; and

(C) for each institution of higher learning, for the most recent academic year for which information is available—

(i) whether the institution is public, private nonprofit, or proprietary for-profit;

(ii) the name of the national or regional accrediting agency that accredits the institution, including the contact information used by the agency to receive complaints from students;

(iii) information on the State approving agency, including the contact information used by the agency to receive complaints from students;

(iv) whether the institution participates in any programs under title IV of the Higher Education Act of 1965 (20 U.S.C. 1070 et seq.);

(v) the tuition and fees;

(vi) the median amount of debt from Federal student loans under title IV of the Higher Education Act of 1965 (20 U.S.C. 1070 et seq.) held by individuals upon completion of programs of education at the institution of higher learning (as determined from information collected by the Secretary of Education);

(vii) the cohort default rate, as defined in section 435(m) of the Higher Education Act of 1965 (20 U.S.C. 1085(m)), of the institution;

(viii) the total enrollment, graduation rate, and retention rate, as determined from information collected by the Integrated Postsecondary Education Data System of the Secretary of Education;

(ix) whether the institution provides students with technical support, academic support, and other support services, including career counseling and job placement; and

(x) the information regarding the institution's policies related to transfer of credit from other institutions, as required under section 485(h)(1) of the Higher Education Act of 1965 (20 U.S.C. 1092(h)(1)) and provided to the Secretary of Education under section 132(i)(1)(V)(iv) of such Act (20 U.S.C. 1015a(i)(1)(V)(iv)).

(2) To the extent practicable, the Secretary shall provide the information described in paragraph (1) by including hyperlinks on the Internet website of the Department to other Internet websites that contain such information, including the Internet website of the Department of Education, in a form that is comprehensive and easily understood by veterans, members of the Armed Forces, and other individuals.

(3)(A) If the Secretary of Veterans Affairs requires, for purposes of providing information pursuant to subsection (b)(5), information that has been reported, or information that is similar to information that has been reported, by an institution of higher learning to the Secretary of Education, the Secretary of Defense, the Secretary of Labor, or the heads of other Federal agencies under a provision of law other than under this section, the Secretary of Veterans Affairs shall obtain the information the Secretary of Veterans Affairs requires from the Secretary or head with the information rather than the institution of higher learning.

(B) If the Secretary of Veterans Affairs requires, for purposes of providing information pursuant to subsection (b)(5), information from an institution of higher learning that has not been reported to another Federal agency, the Secretary shall, to the degree practicable, obtain such information through the Secretary of Education.

(d) Consistency with existing education policy. In carrying out this section, the Secretary shall ensure that—

(1) the comprehensive policy is consistent with any requirements and initiatives resulting from Executive Order No. 13607 [38 USCS § 3301 note]; and

(2) the efforts of the Secretary to implement the comprehensive policy do not duplicate the efforts being taken by any Federal agencies.

(e) Communication with institutions of higher learning. To the extent practicable, if the Secretary considers it necessary to communicate with an institution of higher learning to carry out the comprehensive policy required by subsection (a), the Secretary shall carry out such communication through the use of a communication system of the Department of Education.

(f) Definitions. In this section:

"(1) The term "institution of higher learning" has the meaning given that term in section 3452(f) of this title [38 USCS § 3452(f)].
"(2) The term "postsecondary education and training opportunities" means any postsecondary program of education, including apprenticeships and on-job training, for which the Secretary of Veterans Affairs provides assistance to a veteran or member of the Armed Forces.
(Added Jan. 10, 2013, P. L. 112-249, § 1(a)(1), 126 Stat. 2398.)

HISTORY; ANCILLARY LAWS AND DIRECTIVES

Explanatory notes:
A prior § 3698 (Act Dec. 3, 1974, P. L. 93-508, Title III, § 301(a), 88 Stat. 1589; Oct. 15, 1976, P. L. 94-502, Title V, §§ 502(a), 513(a)(23), 90 Stat. 2399, 2403; Nov. 23, 1977, P. L. 95-202, Title I, § 104(3), Title II, § 202, 91 Stat. 1435, 1438; Oct. 18, 1978, P. L. 95-476, Title II, § 201, 92 Stat. 1502; Oct. 17, 1980, P. L. 96-466, Title II, Part A, § 203(4), Part B, § 213(4), Title VI, §§ 601(h), 603(b), Title VIII, § 801(g), 94 Stat. 2189, 2191, 2208, 2216; Aug. 13, 1981, P. L. 97-35, Title XX, § 2005(d), 95 Stat. 783; Oct. 12, 1982, P. L. 97-295, § 4(60), (61), 96 Stat. 1309; Oct. 14, 1982, P. L. 97-306, Title II, § 208, 96 Stat. 1436; Oct. 24, 1984, P. L. 98-543, Title II, Part A, § 204(3), 98 Stat. 2742; Nov. 18, 1988, P. L. 100-689, Title I, Part B, § 124(b), 102 Stat. 4174; Dec. 18, 1989, P. L. 101-237, Title IV, § 423(b)(1)(A), 103 Stat. 2092; March 22, 1991, P. L. 102-16, § 5(a), 105 Stat. 50; Aug. 6, 1991, P. L. 102-83, § 5(a), (c)(1), 105 Stat. 406) was repealed by Act Dec. 16, 2003, P. L. 108-183, Title III, § 306(e), 117 Stat. 2661, effective 90 days after enactment, as provided by § 306(h)(2) of such Act, which appears as 38 USCS § 3485 note. It related to eligibility for loans, the amount and conditions of loans, and interest rates on loans.

Other provisions:
Termination of loan program; discharge of liabilities; termination of loan fund. Act Dec. 16, 2003, P. L. 108-183, Title III, § 306(a)–(c), 117 Stat. 2661, provide:
"(a) Termination of program. The Secretary of Veterans Affairs may not make a loan under subchapter III of chapter 36 of title 38, United States Code [former 38 USCS §§ 3698 et seq.], after the date of the enactment of this Act.
"(b) Discharge of liabilities. Effective as of the date of the transfer of funds under subsection (c)—
    "(1) any liability on an education loan under subchapter III of chapter 36 of title 38, United States Code [former 38 USCS §§ 3698 et seq.], that is outstanding as of such date shall be deemed discharged; and
    "(2) the right of the United States to recover an overpayment declared under section 3698(e)(1) of such title that is outstanding as of such date shall be deemed waived.
"(c) Termination of loan fund. (1) Effective as of the day before the date of the repeal under this section of subchapter III of chapter 36 of title 38, United States Code [former 38 USCS §§ 3698 et seq.], all monies in the revolving fund of the Treasury known as the 'Department of Veterans Affairs Education Loan Fund' shall be transferred to the Department of Veterans Affairs Readjustment Benefits Account, and the revolving fund shall be closed.
    "(2) Any monies transferred to the Department of Veterans Affairs Readjustment Benefits Account under paragraph (1) shall be merged with amounts in that account and shall be available for the same purposes, and subject to the same conditions and limitations, as amounts in that account.".
Survey; report; definitions. Act Jan. 10, 2013, P. L. 112-249, § 1(b)–(d), 126 Stat. 2400, provides:
"(b) Survey. In developing the policy required by section 3698(a) of title 38, United States Code, as added by subsection (a), the Secretary of Veterans Affairs shall conduct a market survey to determine the availability of the following:
    "(1) A commercially available off-the-shelf online tool that allows a veteran or member of the Armed Forces to assess whether the veteran or member is academically ready to engage in postsecondary education and training opportunities and whether the veteran or member would need any remedial preparation before beginning such opportunities.
    "(2) A commercially available off-the-shelf online tool that provides a veteran or member of the Armed Forces with a list of providers of postsecondary education and training opportunities based on criteria selected by the veteran or member.
"(c) Report. Not later than 90 days after the date of the enactment of this Act, the Secretary of Veterans Affairs shall submit to the appropriate committees of Congress a report that includes—
    "(1) a description of the policy developed by the Secretary under section 3698(a) of title 38, United States Code, as added by subsection (a);
    "(2) a plan of the Secretary to implement such policy; and
    "(3) the results of the survey conducted under subsection (b), including whether the Secretary plans to implement the tools described in such subsection.
"(d) Definitions. In this section:
    "(1) Appropriate committees of Congress. The term 'appropriate committees of Congress' means—
        "(A) the Committee on Veterans' Affairs and the Committee on Health, Education, Labor, and Pensions of the Senate; and

"(B) the Committee on Veterans' Affairs and the Committee on Education and the Workforce of the House of Representatives.

"(2) Commercially available off-the-shelf. The term 'commercially available off-the-shelf' has the meaning given that term in section 104 of title 41, United States Code.

"(3) Postsecondary education and training opportunities. The term 'postsecondary education and training opportunities' means any postsecondary program of education, including apprenticeships and on-job training, for which the Secretary of Veterans Affairs provides assistance to a veteran or member of the Armed Forces.".

[§ 3699. Repealed]

HISTORY; ANCILLARY LAWS AND DIRECTIVES

This section (Act Dec. 3, 1974, P. L. 93-508, Title III, § 301(a), 88 Stat. 1591; Oct. 15, 1976, P. L. 94-502, Title V, § 513(a)(24), 90 Stat. 2404; Oct. 12, 1982, P. L. 97-295, § 4(61) in part, 96 Stat. 1309; Dec. 18, 1989, P. L. 101-237, Title IV, § 423(b)(1), (2) 103 Stat. 2092; Aug. 6, 1991, P. L. 102-83, § 5(a), (c)(1), 105 Stat. 406) was repealed by Act Dec. 16, 2003, P. L. 108-183, Title III, § 306(e), 117 Stat. 2661, effective 90 days after enactment, as provided by § 306(h)(2) of such Act, which appears as 38 USCS § 3485 note. It provided for a revolving fund known as the "Department of Veterans Affairs Education Loan Fund".

CHAPTER 37. HOUSING AND SMALL BUSINESS LOANS

Section

SUBCHAPTER I. GENERAL

3707A. Hybrid adjustable rate mortgages.

SUBCHAPTER III. ADMINISTRATIVE PROVISIONS

3722. Veterans Housing Benefit Program Fund.
[3723–3725. Repealed]
3734. Annual submission of information on the Veterans Housing Benefit Program Fund and housing programs.
[3735. Transferred]

SUBCHAPTER V. DIRECT HOUSING LOANS FOR NATIVE AMERICAN VETERANS

3761. Direct housing loans to Native American veterans; program authority.
3762. Direct housing loans to Native American veterans; program administration.
3763. Native American Veteran Housing Loan Program Account.
3764. Qualified non-Native American veterans.
3765. Definitions.

[SUBCHAPTER VI. TRANSFERRED]

[3771. Repealed]
[3772–3775. Transferred]

HISTORY; ANCILLARY LAWS AND DIRECTIVES

Amendments:

1998. Act Nov. 11, 1998, P. L. 105-368, Title VI, §§ 601(b), 602(e)(3)(C), 112 Stat. 3345, 3347, amended the analysis of this chapter, by adding item 3722, deleting item 3723, which read: "3723. Direct loan revolving fund.", deleting item 3724, which read: "3724. Loan Guaranty Revolving Fund.", deleting item 3725, which read: "3725. Guaranty and Indemnity Fund.", substituting item 3734 for one which read: "3734. Annual submission of information on the Loan Guaranty Revolving Fund and the Guaranty and Indemnity Fund.", substituting item 3763 for one which read: "3763. Housing loan program account.", and adding the Subchapter VI heading and items 3771–3775.

2001. Act Dec. 21, 2001, P. L. 107-95, § 5(g)(2), 115 Stat. 918, amended the analysis of this chapter by deleting item 3735, which read: "3735. Housing assistance for homeless veterans.", and deleting the Subchapter VI heading and items 3771–3775, which read:

"SUBCHAPTER VI. LOAN GUARANTEE FOR MULTIFAMILY TRANSITIONAL HOUSING FOR HOMELESS VETERANS

"3771. Definitions.
"3772. General authority.
"3773. Requirements.
"3774. Default.

READJUSTMENT BENEFITS   38 USCS § 3701

"3775. Audit.".
2002. Act Dec. 6, 2002, P. L. 107-330, Title III, § 303(b), 116 Stat. 2826, amended the analysis of this chapter by adding item 3707A.
2006. Act June 15, 2006, P. L. 109-233, Title I, §§ 103(f)(4), 104(c), 120 Stat. 401, 402, amended the analysis of this chapter by substituting the Subchapter V heading and items 3761 and 3762 for ones which read:

"SUBCHAPTER V. NATIVE AMERICAN VETERAN HOUSING LOAN PILOT PROGRAM
"3761. Pilot program.
"3762. Direct housing loans to Native American veterans.";
and substituting items 3764 and 3765 for former item 3764, which read: "3764. Definitions.".

SUBCHAPTER I. GENERAL

§ 3701. Definitions

(a) [Unchanged]

(b) For the purposes of housing loans under this chapter [38 USCS §§ 3701 et seq.]—

(1)–(5) [Unchanged]

(6) The term "veteran" also includes, for purposes of home loans, the surviving spouse of a veteran who died and who was in receipt of or entitled to receive (or but for the receipt of retired or retirement pay was entitled to receive) compensation at the time of death for a service-connected disability rated totally disabling if—

(A) the disability was continuously rated totally disabling for a period of 10 or more years immediately preceding death;

(B) the disability was continuously rated totally disabling for a period of not less than five years from the date of such veteran's discharge or other release from active duty; or

(C) the veteran was a former prisoner of war who died after September 30, 1999, and the disability was continuously rated totally disabling for a period of not less than one year immediately preceding death.

(c) [Unchanged]

(As amended Aug. 6, 2012, P. L. 112-154, Title II, § 206(a), 126 Stat. 1178.)

HISTORY; ANCILLARY LAWS AND DIRECTIVES

Amendments:

2012. Act Aug. 6, 2012 (applicable to loans guaranteed after the date of enactment, as provided by § 206(b) of such act, which appears as a note to this section), in subsec. (b), added para. (6).

Other provisions:

Application of Aug. 6, 2012 amendment. Act Aug. 6, 2012, P. L. 112-154, Title II, § 206(b), 126 Stat. 1178, provides: "The amendment made by subsection (a) [adding subsec. (b)(6) of this section] shall apply with respect to a loan guaranteed after the date of the enactment of this Act.".

Clarification with respect to certain fees. Act Aug. 6, 2012, P. L. 112-154, Title II, § 206(c), 126 Stat. 1179, provides: "Fees shall be collected under section 3729 of title 38, United States Code, from a person described in paragraph (6) of section 3701(b) of such title, as added by subsection (a) of this section, in the same manner as such fees are collected from a person described in paragraph (2) of section 3701(b) of such title.".

CODE OF FEDERAL REGULATIONS

Department of Veterans Affairs—Vocational rehabilitation and education, 38 CFR 21.1 et seq.
Department of Veterans Affairs—Loan guaranty, 38 CFR 36.4201 et seq.
Department of Veterans Affairs—Loan guaranty and vocational rehabilitation and counseling programs, 48 CFR 871.100 et seq.

RESEARCH GUIDE

Am Jur:

77 Am Jur 2d, Veterans and Veterans' Laws §§ 113, 115, 121, 161.

Commercial Law:

6 Debtor-Creditor Law (Matthew Bender), ch 51, Mortgage Foreclosure § 51.02.

Other Treatises:

2 Banking Law (Matthew Bender), ch 21, National Banks: Regulation, Supervision, and Control § 21.03.

38 USCS § 3701

INTERPRETIVE NOTES AND DECISIONS

1. Generally

Where VA, pursuant to 38 USCS § 3702(b), refused to extend full home loan guaranty amounts to veterans following veterans' discharges in bankruptcy, VA's refusal did not violate anti-discrimination provision of 11 USCS § 525(a) because veteran home loan guaranty entitlement was not "other similar grant" within meaning of § 525(a); thus, § 525(a) did not apply to veteran guaranty entitlement; veteran home loan guaranty entitlement was not similar to licenses, permits, charters, and franchises because veteran guaranty entitlement did not implicate government's gate-keeping role in determining who might pursue certain livelihoods. Ayes v United States Dep't of Veterans Affairs (2006, CA5 NC) 473 F3d 104, 47 BCD 144, CCH Bankr L Rptr ¶ 80814.

Where plaintiffs, who sought temporary restraining orders and temporary injunctions restraining defendants from executing any administrative offset against them, had been involved in class action resulting in consent decree that did not provide protection from such offsets and 31 USCS § 3711(g)(9) required that such debts be administratively offset, injunctions and temporary restraining orders were denied. Bradshaw v Veneman (2004, DC Dist Col) 338 F Supp 2d 139.

Residential programs of Department of Housing and Urban Development under 42 USCS § 1441, and Secretary of Veterans Affairs under 38 USCS §§ 3701–3764, which merely provided financial backing, but did not rise the level of "agency action," did not require environmental assessment under 42 USCS § 4332, or violate Endangered Species Act, 16 USCS § 1536(a)(2), with respect to San Pedro Riparian National Conservation Area, 16 USCS § 460xx. Ctr. for Biological Diversity v United States HUD (2008, DC Ariz) 541 F Supp 2d 1091.

§ 3702. Basic entitlement

(a)(1) [Unchanged]

(2) The veterans referred to in the first sentence of paragraph (1) of this subsection are the following:

(A)–(D) [Unchanged]

(E) Each veteran described in section 3701(b)(5) of this title [38 USCS § 3701(b)(5)].

(F) Each veteran who was discharged or released from a period of active duty of 90 days or more by reason of a sole survivorship discharge (as that term is defined in section 1174(i) of title 10).

(3), (4) [Unchanged]

(b)–(f) [Unchanged]

(As amended Nov. 11, 1998, P. L. 105-368, Title VI, § 603(a), 112 Stat. 3348; Nov. 30, 1999, P. L. 106-117, Title VII, Subtitle B, § 711, 113 Stat. 1584; Dec. 27, 2001, P. L. 107-103, Title IV, § 405(a), 115 Stat. 993; Dec. 16, 2003, P. L. 108-183, Title IV, § 403, 117 Stat. 2664; Aug. 29, 2008, P. L. 110-317, § 6(a), 122 Stat. 3528.)

HISTORY; ANCILLARY LAWS AND DIRECTIVES

Amendments:

1998. Act Nov. 11, 1998 (effective on 10/1/98, as provided by § 602(f) of such Act, which appears as 38 USCS § 2106 note), in subsec. (a)(2)(E), substituted "September 30, 2003," for "October 27, 1999,".

1999. Act Nov. 30, 1999, in subsec. (a)(2)(E), substituted "September 30, 2007," for "September 30, 2003,".

2001. Act Dec. 27, 2001, in subsec. (a)(2)(E), substituted "September 30, 2009" for "September 30, 2007".

2003. Act Dec. 16, 2003, in subsec. (a)(2)(E), substituted "Each" for "For the period beginning on October 28, 1992, and ending on September 30, 2009, each".

2008. Act Aug. 29, 2008 (applicable with respect to any sole survivorship discharge granted after 9/11/2001, as provided by § 10(a) of such Act, which appears as 5 USCS § 2108 note), in subsec. (a)(2), added subpara. (F).

CODE OF FEDERAL REGULATIONS

Department of Veterans Affairs—Adjudication, 38 CFR 3.1 et seq.
Department of Veterans Affairs—Vocational rehabilitation and education, 38 CFR 21.1 et seq.
Department of Veterans Affairs—Loan guaranty, 38 CFR 36.4201 et seq.

RESEARCH GUIDE

Am Jur:

77 Am Jur 2d, Veterans and Veterans' Laws §§ 114, 115, 161.

Other Treatises:

Cohen's Handbook of Federal Indian Law (Matthew Bender), ch 22, Government Services for Indians § 22.05.

READJUSTMENT BENEFITS 38 USCS § 3703

INTERPRETIVE NOTES AND DECISIONS

5. Scope of guaranty

Where VA, pursuant to 38 USCS § 3702(b), refused to extend full home loan guaranty amounts to veterans following veterans' discharges in bankruptcy, VA's refusal did not violate antidiscrimination provision of 11 USCS § 525(a) because veteran home loan guaranty entitlement was not "other similar grant" within meaning of § 525(a); thus, § 525(a) did not apply to veteran guaranty entitlement; veteran home loan guaranty entitlement was not similar to licenses, permits, charters, and franchises because veteran guaranty entitlement did not implicate government's gate-keeping role in determining who might pursue certain livelihoods. Ayes v United States Dep't of Veterans Affairs (2006, CA4 NC) 473 F3d 104, 47 BCD 144, CCH Bankr L Rptr ¶ 80814.

§ 3703. Basic provisions relating to loan guaranty and insurance [Caution: See prospective amendment note below.]

(a)(1)(A) Any loan to a veteran eligible for benefits under this chapter [38 USCS §§ 3701 et seq.], if made for any of the purposes specified in section 3710 of this title [38 USCS § 3710] and in compliance with the provisions of this chapter [38 USCS §§ 3701 et seq.], is automatically guaranteed by the United States in an amount not to exceed the lesser of—

    (i)(I)–(III) [Unchanged]

    (IV) in the case of any loan of more than $144,000 for a purpose specified in clause (1), (2), (3), (5), (6), or (8) of section 3710(a) of this title [38 USCS § 3710(a)], the lesser of the maximum guaranty amount (as defined in subparagraph (C)) or 25 percent of the loan; or

    (ii) [Unchanged]

(B) The maximum amount of guaranty entitlement available to a veteran for purposes specified in section 3710 of this title [38 USCS § 3710] shall be $36,000, or in the case of a loan described in subparagraph (A)(i)(IV) of this paragraph, the maximum guaranty amount (as defined in subparagraph (C)), reduced by the amount of entitlement previously used by the veteran under this chapter [38 USCS §§ 3701 et seq.] and not restored as a result of the exclusion in section 3702(b) of this title [38 USCS § 3702(b)].

(C) In this paragraph, the term "maximum guaranty amount" means the dollar amount that is equal to 25 percent of the Freddie Mac conforming loan limit limitation determined under section 305(a)(2) of the Federal Home Loan Mortgage Corporation Act (12 U.S.C. 1454(a)(2)) for a single-family residence, as adjusted for the year involved.

(2) [Unchanged]

(b), (c) [Unchanged]

(d)(1) The maturity of any housing loan at the time of origination shall not be more than thirty years and thirty-two days.

(2), (3) [Unchanged]

(e)(1) Except as provided in paragraph (2) of this subsection, an individual who pays a fee under section 3729 of this title [38 USCS § 3729], or who is exempted under section 3729(c) of this title [38 USCS § 3729(c)] from paying such fee, with respect to a housing loan guaranteed or insured under this chapter that is closed after December 31, 1989, shall have no liability to the Secretary with respect to the loan for any loss resulting from any default of such individual except in the case of fraud, misrepresentation, or bad faith by such individual in obtaining the loan or in connection with the loan default.

(2) The exemption from liability provided by paragraph (1) of this subsection shall not apply to—

    (A) an individual from whom a fee is collected (or who is exempted from such fee) under section 3729(b)(2)(I) of this title [38 USCS § 3729(b)(2)(I)]; or

    (B) [Unchanged]

(f) [Unchanged]

(As amended Nov. 11, 1998, P. L. 105-368, Title VI, § 602(e)(1)(A), 112 Stat. 3346; Dec. 27, 2001, P. L. 107-103, Title IV, § 401, 115 Stat. 993; Dec. 6, 2002, P. L. 107-330, Title III, § 308(f)(1), 116 Stat. 2828; Dec. 10, 2004, P. L. 108-454, Title IV, § 403, 118 Stat. 3616; Oct. 10, 2008, P. L. 110-389, Title V, § 504(a), 122 Stat. 4176; May 20, 2009, P. L. 111-22, Div A, Title I, § 102(a), 123 Stat. 1636; Aug. 6, 2012, P. L. 112-154, Title VII, § 701(d), 126 Stat. 1204.)

HISTORY; ANCILLARY LAWS AND DIRECTIVES

Prospective amendments:

Amendment of subsec. (d)(3), effective Aug. 6, 2013. Act Aug. 6, 2012, P. L. 112-154, Title VII, § 701(d), 126 Stat. 1204 (effective 1 year after enactment, as provided by § 701(g) of such Act, which appears as 38 USCS § 2109 note), provides that para. (3) of subsec. (d) of this section is amended to read as follows:

"(3)(A) Any real estate housing loan (other than for repairs, alterations, or improvements) shall be secured by a first lien on the realty. In determining whether a loan is so secured, the Secretary may either disregard or allow for subordination to a superior lien created by a duly recorded covenant running with the realty in favor of either of the following:

"(i) A public entity that has provided or will provide assistance in response to a major disaster as determined by the President under the Robert T. Stafford Disaster Relief and Emergency Assistance Act (42 U.S.C. 5121 et seq.).

"(ii) A private entity to secure an obligation to such entity for the homeowner's share of the costs of the management, operation, or maintenance of property, services, or programs within and for the benefit of the development or community in which the veteran's realty is located, if the Secretary determines that the interests of the veteran borrower and of the Government will not be prejudiced by the operation of such covenant.

"(B) With respect to any superior lien described in subparagraph (A) created after June 6, 1969, the Secretary's determination under clause (ii) of such subparagraph shall have been made prior to the recordation of the covenant.".

Amendments:
1998. Act Nov. 11, 1998 (effective on 10/1/98, as provided by § 602(f) of such Act, which appears as 38 USCS § 2106 note), in subsec. (e)(1), substituted "3729(c)" for "3729(c)(1)".
2001. Act Dec. 27, 2001, in subsec. (a)(1), in subparas. (A)(i)(IV) and (B), substituted "$60,000" for "$50,750".
2002. Act Dec. 6, 2002 (effective as if included in the enactment of § 402 of Act Nov. 1, 2000, as provided by § 308(f)(2) of Act Dec. 6, 2002, which appears as a note to this section), in subsec. (e)(2)(A), substituted "3729(b)(2)(I)" for "3729(b)".
2004. Act Dec. 10, 2004, in subsec. (a)(1), in subparas. (A)(i)(IV) and (B), substituted "the maximum guaranty amount (as defined in subparagraph (C))" for "$60,000", and added subpara. (C).
2008. Act Oct. 10, 2008, in subsec. (a)(1)(A)(i)(IV), inserted "(5),".
2009. Act May 20, 2009, in subsec. (d)(1), inserted "at the time of origination".

Other provisions:
Effective date of Dec. 6, 2002 amendment. Act Dec. 6, 2002, P. L. 107-330, Title III, § 308(f)(2), 116 Stat. 2828, provides: "The amendment made by paragraph (1) [amending subsec. (e)(2)(A) of this section] shall take effect as if included in the enactment of section 402 of the Veterans Benefits and Health Care Improvement Act of 2000 (Public Law 106-419; 114 Stat. 1861) [enacted Nov. 1, 2000].".
Temporary increase in maximum loan guaranty amount for certain housing loans guaranteed by Secretary of Veterans Affairs. Oct. 10, 2008, P. L. 110-389, Title V, § 501, 122 Stat. 4175; Aug. 6, 2012, P. L. 112-154, Title VII, § 702(c), 126 Stat. 1205, provides:
" Notwithstanding subparagraph (C) of section 3703(a)(1) of title 38, United States Code, for purposes of any loan described in subparagraph (A)(i)(IV) of such section that is originated during the period beginning on the date of the enactment of this Act and ending on December 31, 2014, the term "maximum guaranty amount" shall mean an amount equal to 25 percent of the higher of—

"(1) the limitation determined under section 305(a)(2) of the Federal Home Loan Mortgage Corporation Act (12 U.S.C. 1454(a)(2)) for the calendar year in which the loan is originated for a single-family residence; or

"(2) 125 percent of the area median price for a single-family residence, but in no case to exceed 175 percent of the limitation determined under such section 305(a)(2) for the calendar year in which the loan is originated for a single-family residence.".

Implementation of May 20, 2009 amendment. Act May 20, 2009, P. L. 111-22, Div A, Title I, § 102(b), 123 Stat. 1636, provides: "The Secretary of Veterans Affairs may implement the amendments made by this section [amending subsec. (d)(1) of this section] through notice, procedure notice, or administrative notice.".

CODE OF FEDERAL REGULATIONS

Department of Veterans Affairs—Nonprocurement debarment and suspension, 2 CFR 801.10 et seq.
Department of Veterans Affairs—Vocational rehabilitation and education, 38 CFR 21.1 et seq.
Department of Veterans Affairs—Loan guaranty, 38 CFR 36.4201 et seq.

RESEARCH GUIDE

Am Jur:
77 Am Jur 2d, Veterans and Veterans' Laws §§ 113, 121, 161.

Commercial Law:
1 Debtor-Creditor Law (Matthew Bender), ch 6, The Cost of Credit § 6.02.

Law Review Articles:
Hazard. Employers' obligations under the Uniformed Services Employment and Reemployment Rights Act. 31 Colo L 55, February 2002.
Beasley. Protecting America's reservists: application of state and federal law to reservists' claims of unfair labor practices. 7 Ga BJ 10, February 2002.

READJUSTMENT BENEFITS 38 USCS § 3706

Whelan. The Uniform Services Employment and Reemployment Rights Act and homeland security. 71 J Kan BA 20, January 2002.

Fernandez. The need for the expansion of military reservists' rights in furtherance of the total force policy: a comparison of the USERRA and ADA. 14 St Thomas L Rev 859, Summer 2002.

§ 3704. Restrictions on loans

(a), (b) [Unchanged]

(c)(1) [Unchanged]

(2) In any case in which a veteran is in active-duty status as a member of the Armed Forces and is unable to occupy a property because of such status, the occupancy requirements of this chapter [38 USCS §§ 3701 et seq.] shall be considered to be satisfied if—

(A) the spouse of the veteran occupies or intends to occupy the property as a home and the spouse makes the certification required by paragraph (1) of this subsection; or

(B) a dependent child of the veteran occupies or will occupy the property as a home and the veteran's attorney-in-fact or legal guardian of the dependent child makes the certification required by paragraph (1) of this subsection.

(d)–(f) [Unchanged]

(As amended Aug. 6, 2012, P. L. 112-154, Title II, § 207, 126 Stat. 1179.)

HISTORY; ANCILLARY LAWS AND DIRECTIVES

Amendments:

2012. Act Aug. 6, 2012, in subsec. (c), substituted para. (2) for one which read:

"(2) In any case in which a veteran is in active duty status as a member of the Armed Forces and is unable to occupy a property because of such status, the occupancy requirements of—

"(A) paragraph (1) of this subsection;

"(B) paragraphs (1) through (5) and paragraph (7) of section 3710(a) of this title;

"(C) section 3712(a)(5)(A)(i) of this title; and

"(D) section 3712(e)(5) of this title;

shall be considered to be satisfied if the spouse of the veteran occupies the property as the spouse's home and the spouse makes the certification required by paragraph (1) of this subsection.".

CODE OF FEDERAL REGULATIONS

Department of Veterans Affairs—Vocational rehabilitation and education, 38 CFR 21.1 et seq.

Department of Veterans Affairs—Loan guaranty, 38 CFR 36.4201 et seq.

RESEARCH GUIDE

Am Jur:

77 Am Jur 2d, Veterans and Veterans' Laws §§ 113, 115, 161.

§ 3705. Warranties

CODE OF FEDERAL REGULATIONS

Department of Veterans Affairs—Vocational rehabilitation and education, 38 CFR 21.1 et seq.

RESEARCH GUIDE

Am Jur:

77 Am Jur 2d, Veterans and Veterans' Laws §§ 116, 161.

INTERPRETIVE NOTES AND DECISIONS

Motion to compel production of nine documents withheld on claim that they were anesthesiology quality assurance control drug records was granted where from description of documents and their intended recipients, it was far from clear that those documents were drug usage evaluations subject to privilege created by 38 USCS § 5705; there was no indication that documents concerned drug dosage, routing, or schedule of use, nor that they evaluated drugs selected. Bethel v United States (2007, DC Colo) 242 FRD 580, motion to strike den, motion gr, in part, motion den, in part (2007, DC Colo) 2007 US Dist LEXIS 43395.

§ 3706. Escrow of deposits and downpayments

CODE OF FEDERAL REGULATIONS

Department of Veterans Affairs—Vocational rehabilitation and education, 38 CFR 21.1 et seq.

RESEARCH GUIDE

Am Jur:

77 Am Jur 2d, Veterans and Veterans' Laws § 161.

§ 3707. Adjustable rate mortgages

(a) The Secretary shall carry out a project under this section for the purpose of guaranteeing loans in a manner similar to the manner in which the Secretary of Housing and Urban Development insures adjustable rate mortgages under section 251 of the National Housing Act [12 USCS § 1715z-16].

(b)–(d) [Unchanged]

(As amended Dec. 10, 2004, P. L. 108-454, Title IV, § 404, 118 Stat. 3616; Oct. 10, 2008, P. L. 110-389, Title V, § 505(a), 122 Stat. 4176; Aug. 6, 2012, P. L. 112-154, Title II, § 208, 126 Stat. 1179.)

HISTORY; ANCILLARY LAWS AND DIRECTIVES

Amendments:

2004. Act Dec. 10, 2004, in subsec. (a), substituted "during fiscal years 1993 through 2008" for "during fiscal years 1993, 1994, and 1995".

2008. Act Oct. 10, 2008, in subsec. (a), substituted "2012" for "2008".

2012. Act Aug. 6, 2012, in subsec. (a), substituted "project under this section" for "demonstration project under this section during fiscal years 1993 through 2012".

CODE OF FEDERAL REGULATIONS

Department of Veterans Affairs—Adjudication, 38 CFR 3.1 et seq.
Department of Veterans Affairs—Loan guaranty, 38 CFR 36.4201 et seq.

RESEARCH GUIDE

Am Jur:
77 Am Jur 2d, Veterans and Veterans' Laws §§ 115, 161.

§ 3707A. Hybrid adjustable rate mortgages

(a) The Secretary shall carry out a project under this section for the purpose of guaranteeing loans in a manner similar to the manner in which the Secretary of Housing and Urban Development insures adjustable rate mortgages under section 251 of the National Housing Act [12 USCS § 1715z-16] in accordance with the provisions of this section with respect to hybrid adjustable rate mortgages described in subsection (b).

(b) Adjustable rate mortgages that are guaranteed under this section shall be adjustable rate mortgages (commonly referred to as "hybrid adjustable rate mortgages") having interest rate adjustment provisions that—

(1) specify an initial rate of interest that is fixed for a period of not less than the first three years of the mortgage term;

(2) provide for an initial adjustment in the rate of interest by the mortgagee at the end of the period described in paragraph (1); and

(3) comply in such initial adjustment, and any subsequent adjustment, with subsection (c).

(c) Interest rate adjustment provisions of a mortgage guaranteed under this section shall—

(1) correspond to a specified national interest rate index approved by the Secretary, information on which is readily accessible to mortgagors from generally available published sources;

(2) be made by adjusting the monthly payment on an annual basis;

(3) in the case of the initial contract interest rate adjustment—

(A) if the initial contract interest rate remained fixed for less than 5 years, be limited to a maximum increase or decrease of 1 percentage point; or

(B) if the initial contract interest rate remained fixed for 5 years or more, be limited to a maximum increase or decrease of such percentage point or points as the Secretary may prescribe;

(4) in the case of any single annual interest rate adjustment after the initial contract interest rate adjustment, be limited to a maximum increase or decrease of such percentage points as the Secretary may prescribe; and

(5) be limited, over the term of the mortgage, to a maximum increase of such number of percentage points as the Secretary shall prescribe for purposes of this section.

(d) The Secretary shall promulgate underwriting standards for loans guaranteed under this section, taking into account—

(1) the status of the interest rate index referred to in subsection (c)(1) and available at the time an underwriting decision is made, regardless of the actual initial rate offered by the lender;

(2) the maximum and likely amounts of increases in mortgage payments that the loans would require;

(3) the underwriting standards applicable to adjustable rate mortgages insured under title II of the National Housing Act [12 USCS §§ 1707 et seq.]; and

(4) such other factors as the Secretary finds appropriate.

READJUSTMENT BENEFITS   **38 USCS § 3710**

(e) The Secretary shall require that the mortgagee make available to the mortgagor, at the time of loan application, a written explanation of the features of the adjustable rate mortgage, including a hypothetical payment schedule that displays the maximum potential increases in monthly payments to the mortgagor over the first five years of the mortgage term.

(Added Dec. 6, 2002, P. L. 107-330, Title III, § 303(a), 116 Stat. 2825; Dec. 10, 2004, P. L. 108-454, Title IV, § 405(a), (b), 118 Stat. 3616; June 15, 2006, P. L. 109-233, Title I, § 102, 120 Stat. 399; Oct. 10, 2008, P. L. 110-389, Title V, § 505(b), 122 Stat. 4176; Aug. 6, 2012, P. L. 112-154, Title II, § 209, 126 Stat. 1179.)

HISTORY; ANCILLARY LAWS AND DIRECTIVES

Amendments:

2004. Act Dec. 10, 2004, in subsec. (a), substituted "during fiscal years 2004 through 2008" for "during fiscal years 2004 and 2005"; and, in subsec. (c), redesignated para. (4) as para. (5), substituted paras. (3) and (4) for former para. (3), which read: "(3) be limited, with respect to any single annual interest rate adjustment, to a maximum increase or decrease of 1 percentage point; and", and, in para. (5) as redesignated, substituted "such number of percentage points as the Secretary shall prescribe for purposes of this section." for "5 percentage points above the initial contract interest rate.".

2006. Act June 15, 2006, in subsec. (c)(4), substituted "such percentage points as the Secretary may prescribe" for "1 percentage point".

2008. Act Oct. 10, 2008, in subsec. (a), substituted "2012" for "2008".

2012. Act Aug. 6, 2012, in subsec. (a), substituted "project under this section" for "demonstration project under this section during fiscal years 2004 through 2012".

Other provisions:

Dec. 10, 2004 amendments; no effect on guarantee of loans under hybrid adjustable rate mortgage guarantee demonstration project. Act Dec. 10, 2004, P. L. 108-454, Title IV, § 405(c), 118 Stat. 3616, provides: "The amendments made by this section [amending this section] shall not be construed to affect the force or validity of any guarantee of a loan made by the Secretary of Veterans Affairs under the demonstration project for the guarantee of hybrid adjustable rate mortgages under section 3707A of title 38, United States Code, as in effect on the day before the date of the enactment of this Act.".

§ 3708. Authority to buy down interest rates: pilot program

RESEARCH GUIDE

Am Jur:

77 Am Jur 2d, Veterans and Veterans' Laws § 115.

SUBCHAPTER II. LOANS

§ 3710. Purchase or construction of homes

(a) Except as provided in section 3704(c)(2) of this title [38 USCS § 3704(c)(2)], any loan to a veteran, if made pursuant to the provisions of this chapter [38 USCS §§ 3701 et seq.], is automatically guaranteed if such loan is for one or more of the following purposes:

(1)–(11) [Unchanged]

(12) With respect to a loan guaranteed after the date of the enactment of this paragraph [enacted Dec. 22, 2006] and before the date that is five years after that date, to purchase stock or membership in a cooperative housing corporation for the purpose of entitling the veteran to occupy for dwelling purposes a single family residential unit in a development, project, or structure owned or leased by such corporation, in accordance with subsection (h).

If there is an indebtedness which is secured by a lien against land owned by the veteran, the proceeds of a loan guaranteed under this section or made under section 3711 of this title [38 USCS § 3711] for construction of a dwelling or farm residence on such land may be used also to liquidate such lien, but only if the reasonable value of the land is equal to or greater than the amount of the lien.

(b) No loan may be guaranteed under this section or made under section 3711 of this title [38 USCS § 3711] unless—

(1)–(7) [Unchanged]

(8) in the case of a loan to refinance a loan (other than a loan or installment sales contract described in clause (7) of this subsection or a loan made for a purpose specified in subsection (a)(8) of this section), the amount of the loan to be guaranteed or made does not exceed 100 percent of the reasonable value of the dwelling or farm residence securing the loan, as determined pursuant to section 3731 of this title [38 USCS § 3731].

(c)–(g) [Unchanged]

(h)(1) A loan may not be guaranteed under subsection (a)(12) unless—

38 USCS § 3710

(A) the development, project, or structure of the cooperative housing corporation complies with such criteria as the Secretary prescribes in regulations; and

(B) the dwelling unit that the purchase of stock or membership in the development, project, or structure of the cooperative housing corporation entitles the purchaser to occupy is a single family residential unit.

(2) In this subsection, the term "cooperative housing corporation" has the meaning given such term in section 216(b)(1) of the Internal Revenue Code of 1986 [26 USCS § 216(b)(1)].

(3) When applying the term "value of the property" to a loan guaranteed under subsection (a)(12), such term means the appraised value of the stock or membership entitling the purchaser to the permanent occupancy of the dwelling unit in the development, project, or structure of the cooperative housing corporation.

(As amended Dec. 22, 2006, P. L. 109-461, Title V, § 501, 120 Stat. 3431; Oct. 10, 2008, P. L. 110-389, Title V, § 504(b), 122 Stat. 4176.)

HISTORY; ANCILLARY LAWS AND DIRECTIVES

Amendments:
2006. Act Dec. 22, 2006, in subsec. (a), added para. (12); and added subsec. (h).
2008. Act Oct. 10, 2008, in subsec. (b)(8), substituted "100 percent" for "90 percent".

CODE OF FEDERAL REGULATIONS

Department of Veterans Affairs—Loan guaranty, 38 CFR 36.4201 et seq.
Department of Veterans Affairs—Loan guaranty and vocational rehabilitation and counseling programs, 48 CFR 871.100 et seq.

RESEARCH GUIDE

Am Jur:
77 Am Jur 2d, Veterans and Veterans' Laws § 115.

Other Treatises:
2 Environmental Law Practice Guide (Matthew Bender), ch 9A, Government Financing § 9A.02.

§ 3711. Direct loans to veterans

(a)–(j) [Unchanged]

(k) Without regard to any other provision of this chapter [38 USCS §§ 3701 et seq.], the Secretary may take or cause to be taken such action as in the Secretary's judgment may be necessary or appropriate for or in connection with the custody, management, protection, and realization or sale of investments under this section, may determine the Secretary's necessary expenses and expenditures, and the manner in which the same shall be incurred, allowed and paid, may make such rules, regulations, and orders as the Secretary may deem necessary or appropriate for carrying out the Secretary's functions under this section and, except as otherwise expressly provided in this chapter [38 USCS §§ 3701 et seq.], may employ, utilize, compensate, and, to the extent not inconsistent with the Secretary's basic responsibilities under this chapter [38 USCS §§ 3701 et seq.], delegate any of the Secretary's functions under this section to such persons and such corporate or other agencies, including agencies of the United States, as the Secretary may designate.

(As amended Nov. 11, 1998, P. L. 105-368, Title VI, § 602(e)(1)(B), 112 Stat. 3346.)

HISTORY; ANCILLARY LAWS AND DIRECTIVES

Amendments:
1998. Act Nov. 11, 1998 (effective on 10/1/98, as provided by § 602(f) of such Act, which appears as 38 USCS § 2106 note), in subsec. (k), deleted "and section 3723 of this title" preceding "and, except" and preceding "to such persons".

CODE OF FEDERAL REGULATIONS

Department of Veterans Affairs—Loan guaranty, 38 CFR 36.4201 et seq.

RESEARCH GUIDE

Am Jur:
77 Am Jur 2d, Veterans and Veterans' Laws § 115.

INTERPRETIVE NOTES AND DECISIONS

Where plaintiffs, who sought temporary restraining orders and temporary injunctions restraining defendants from executing any administrative offset against them, had been involved in class action resulting in consent decree that did not provide protection from such offsets and 31 USCS § 3711(g)(9) required that such debts be administratively offset, injunctions and temporary restraining orders were denied. Bradshaw v Veneman (2004, DC Dist Col) 338 F Supp 2d 139.

§ 3712. Loans to purchase manufactured homes and lots

CODE OF FEDERAL REGULATIONS
Department of Veterans Affairs—Loan guaranty, 38 CFR 36.4201 et seq.

RESEARCH GUIDE
Am Jur:
77 Am Jur 2d, Veterans and Veterans' Laws § 115.

§ 3713. Release from liability under guaranty

CODE OF FEDERAL REGULATIONS
Department of Veterans Affairs—Loan guaranty, 38 CFR 36.4201 et seq.

RESEARCH GUIDE
Am Jur:
77 Am Jur 2d, Veterans and Veterans' Laws § 117.

Commercial Law:
1A Debtor-Creditor Law (Matthew Bender), ch 8, Fair Debt Collection § 8.08.

§ 3714. Assumptions; release from liability

(a)–(c) [Unchanged]
(d) With respect to a loan guaranteed, insured, or made under this chapter, the Secretary shall provide, by regulation, that at least one instrument evidencing either the loan or the mortgage or deed of trust therefor, shall conspicuously contain, in such form as the Secretary shall specify, a notice in substantially the following form: "This loan is not assumable without the approval of the Department of Veterans Affairs or its authorized agent".
(e) [Unchanged]
(f)(1) This section shall apply—
  (A) [Unchanged]
  (B) in the case of loans to finance the purchase of such property, only to loans which are closed after January 1, 1989.
 (2) [Unchanged]
(As amended Nov. 11, 1998, P. L. 105-368, Title X, § 1005(b)(10), 112 Stat. 3365; Dec. 27, 2001, P. L. 107-103, Title IV, § 403, 115 Stat. 993.)

HISTORY; ANCILLARY LAWS AND DIRECTIVES
Amendments:
1998. Act Nov. 11, 1998, in subsec. (f)(1)(B), substituted "after January 1, 1989" for "more than 45 days after the date of the enactment of the Veterans' Benefits and Programs Improvement Act of 1988".
2001. Act Dec. 27, 2001, substituted subsec. (d) for one which read: "(d) The Secretary shall provide that the mortgage or deed of trust and any other instrument evidencing the loan entered into by a person with respect to a loan guaranteed, insured, or made under this chapter shall contain provisions, in such form as the Secretary shall specify, implementing the requirements of this section, and shall bear in conspicuous position in capital letters on the first page of the document in type at least 2 and $1/2$ times larger than the regular type on such page the following: 'This loan is not assumable without the approval of the Department of Veterans Affairs or its authorized agent.'.".

CODE OF FEDERAL REGULATIONS
Department of Veterans Affairs—Loan guaranty, 38 CFR 36.4201 et seq.

RESEARCH GUIDE
Am Jur:
77 Am Jur 2d, Veterans and Veterans' Laws § 117.

SUBCHAPTER III. ADMINISTRATIVE PROVISIONS

§ 3720. Powers of Secretary

(a) [Unchanged]
(b) The powers granted by this section may be exercised by the Secretary without regard to any other provision of law not enacted expressly in limitation of this section, which otherwise would govern the expenditure of public-funds, except that division C (except sections 3302, 3501(b), 3509, 3906, 4710, and 4711) of subtitle I of title 41 [41 USCS §§ 3101 et seq. (except 41 USCS

38 USCS § 3720
VETERANS' BENEFITS

§§ 3302, 3501(b), 3509, 3906, 4710, and 4711)] shall apply to any contract for services or supplies on account of any property acquired pursuant to this section.

(c), (d) [Unchanged]

(e) [Deleted]

(f), (g) [Unchanged]

(h)(1) [Unchanged]

(2) The Secretary may not under this subsection guarantee the payment of principal and interest on certificates or other securities issued or approved after December 31, 2016.

(As amended Nov. 11, 1998, P. L. 105-368, Title VI, §§ 602(c)(1), 604(a), 112 Stat. 3346, 3348; Nov. 1, 2000, P. L. 106-419, Title IV, § 402(a), 114 Stat. 1861; Dec. 27, 2001, P. L. 107-103, Title IV, § 405(b), 115 Stat. 994; Jan. 4, 2011, P. L. 111-350, § 5(j)(3), 124 Stat. 3850; Aug. 6, 2012, P. L. 112-154, Title VII, § 702(a), 126 Stat. 1205.)

HISTORY; ANCILLARY LAWS AND DIRECTIVES

Amendments:

1998. Act Nov. 11, 1998 (effective on 10/1/98, as provided by § 602(f) of such Act, which appears as 38 USCS § 2106 note) deleted subsec. (e), which read:

"(e)(1) The Secretary is authorized from time to time, as the Secretary determines advisable, to set aside first mortgage loans, and installment sale contracts, owned and held by the Secretary under this chapter as the basis for the sale of participation certificates as herein provided. For this purpose the Secretary may enter into agreements, including trust agreements, with the Government National Mortgage Association, and any other Federal agency, under which the Association as fiduciary may sell certificates of participation based on principal and interest collections to be received by the Secretary and the Association or any other such agency on first mortgage loans and installment sale contracts comprising mortgage pools established by them. The agreement may provide for substitution or withdrawal of mortgage loans, or installment sale contracts, or for substitution of cash for mortgages in the pool. The agreement shall provide that the Governmental National Mortgage Association shall promptly pay to the Secretary the entire proceeds of any sale of certificates of participation to the extent such certificates are based on mortgages, including installment sale contracts, set aside by the Secretary and the Secretary shall periodically pay to the Association, as fiduciary, such funds as are required for payment of interest and principal due on outstanding certificates of participation to the extent of the pro rata amount allocated to the Secretary pursuant to the agreement. The agreement shall also provide that the Secretary shall retain ownership of mortgage loans and installment sale contracts set aside by the Secretary pursuant to the agreement unless transfer of ownership to the fiduciary is required in the event of default or probable default in the payment of participation certificates. The Secretary is authorized to purchase outstanding certificates of participation to the extent of the amount of the Secretary's commitment to the fiduciary on participations outstanding and to pay the Secretary's proper share of the costs and expenses incurred by the Government National Mortgage Association as fiduciary pursuant to the agreement.

"(2) The Secretary shall proportionately allocate and deposit the entire proceeds received from the sale of participations into the funds established pursuant to sections 3723 and 3724 of this chapter, as determined on an estimated basis, and the amounts so deposited shall be available for the purposes of the funds. The Secretary may nevertheless make such allocations of that part of the proceeds of participation sales representing anticipated interest collections on mortgage loans, including installment sale contracts, on other than an estimated proportionate basis if determined necessary to assure payment of interest on advances theretofore made to the Secretary by the Secretary of the Treasury for direct loan purposes. The Secretary shall set aside and maintain necessary reserves in the funds established pursuant to sections 3723 and 3724 of this chapter to be used for meeting commitments pursuant to this subsection and, as the Secretary determines to be necessary, for meeting interest payments on advances by the Secretary of the Treasury for direct loan purposes.".

Such Act further (applicable with respect to contracts entered into under this section after the end of the 60-day period beginning on enactment, as provided by § 604(b) of such Act, which appears as a note to this section), in subsec. (b), substituted ", except that title III of the Federal Property and Administrative Services Act of 1949 (41 U.S.C. 251 et seq.) shall apply to any contract for services or supplies on account of any property acquired pursuant to this section." for "; however, section 3709 of the Revised Statutes (41 U.S.C. 5) shall apply to any contract for services or supplies on account of any property acquired pursuant to this section if the amount of such contract exceeds the amount prescribed in clause (1) of the first sentence of such section.".

2000. Act Nov. 1, 2000, in subsec. (h)(2), substituted "December 31, 2008" for "December 31, 2002".

2001. Act Dec. 27, 2001, in subsec. (h)(2), substituted "December 31, 2011" for "December 31, 2008".

2011. Act Jan. 4, 2011, in subsec. (b), substituted "division C (except sections 3302, 3501(b), 3509, 3906, 4710, and 4711) of subtitle I of title 41" for "title III of the Federal Property and Administrative Services Act of 1949 (41 U.S.C. 251 et seq.)".

2012. Act Aug. 6, 2012, in subsec. (h)(2), substituted "December 31, 2016" for "December 31, 2011".

Other provisions:
Applicability of amendment made by § 604(a) of Act Nov. 11, 1998. Act Nov. 11, 1998, P. L. 105-368, Title VI, § 604(b), 112 Stat. 3348, provides: "The amendment made by subsection (a) [amending subsec. (b) of this section] shall apply with respect to contracts entered into under section 3720 of title 38, United States Code, after the end of the 60-day period beginning on the date of the enactment of this Act.".

CODE OF FEDERAL REGULATIONS
Department of Veterans Affairs—General provisions, 38 CFR 1.9 et seq.
Department of Veterans Affairs—Loan guaranty, 38 CFR 36.4201 et seq.
Department of Veterans Affairs—Loan guaranty and vocational rehabilitation and counseling programs, 48 CFR 871.100 et seq.

RESEARCH GUIDE
Am Jur:
77 Am Jur 2d, Veterans and Veterans' Laws § 120.

§ 3721. Incontestability

RESEARCH GUIDE
Am Jur:
77 Am Jur 2d, Veterans and Veterans' Laws § 113.

§ 3722. Veterans Housing Benefit Program Fund

(a) There is hereby established in the Treasury of the United States a fund known as the Veterans Housing Benefit Program Fund (hereinafter in this section referred to as the "Fund").

(b) The Fund shall be available to the Secretary, without fiscal year limitation, for all housing loan operations under this chapter, other than administrative expenses, consistent with the Federal Credit Reform Act of 1990.

(c) There shall be deposited into the Fund the following, which shall constitute the assets of the Fund:

(1) Any amount appropriated to the Fund.

(2) Amounts paid into the Fund under section 3729 of this title [38 USCS § 3729] or any other provision of law or regulation established by the Secretary imposing fees on persons or other entities participating in the housing loan programs under this chapter [38 USCS §§ 3701 et seq.].

(3) All other amounts received by the Secretary on or after October 1, 1998, incident to housing loan operations under this chapter [38 USCS §§ 3701 et seq.], including—

(A) collections of principal and interest on housing loans made by the Secretary under this chapter [38 USCS §§ 3701 et seq.];

(B) proceeds from the sale, rental, use, or other disposition of property acquired under this chapter [38 USCS §§ 3701 et seq.];

(C) proceeds from the sale of loans pursuant to sections 3720(h) and 3733(a)(3) of this title [38 USCS §§ 3720(h) and 3733(a)(3)]; and

(D) penalties collected pursuant to section 3710(g)(4)(B) of this title [38 USCS § 3710(g)(4)(B)].

(d) Amounts deposited into the Fund under paragraphs (2) and (3) of subsection (c) shall be deposited in the appropriate financing or liquidating account of the Fund.

(e) For purposes of this section, the term "housing loan" shall not include a loan made pursuant to subchapter V of this chapter [38 USCS §§ 3761 et seq.].

(Added Nov. 11, 1998, P. L. 105-368, Title VI, § 602(a)(2), 112 Stat. 3345; June 5, 2001, P. L. 107-14, § 8(a)(16), 115 Stat. 35.)

HISTORY; ANCILLARY LAWS AND DIRECTIVES
References in text:
The "Federal Credit Reform Act of 1990", referred to in this section, is Title V of Act July 12, 1974, P. L. 93-344, as added by Act Nov. 5, 1990, P. L. 101-508, Title XIII, § 13201(a), 104 Stat. 1388-609, which appears generally as 2 USCS §§ 661 et seq. For full classification of such Act, consult USCS Tables volumes.

Explanatory notes:
A prior § 3722 (Act Sept. 2, 1958, P. L. 85-857, § 1, 72 Stat. 1214; March 3, 1966, P. L. 89-358, § 5(c), 80 Stat. 26; Oct. 4, 1966, P. L. 89-623, § 1, 80 Stat. 873; May 7, 1968, P. L. 90-301, § 2(b), 82 Stat. 113) was repealed by Act Dec. 31, 1974, P. L. 93-569, § 7(a), 88 Stat. 1866, effective Dec. 31, 1974, as provided by § 10 of Act Dec. 31, 1974. Such section provided for

recovery of treble damages in cases where sales were made to veterans of property in excess of the approved appraised value.

Effective date of section:
This section took effect on Oct. 1, 1998, pursuant to § 602(f) of Act Nov. 11, 1998, P. L. 105-368, which appears as 38 USCS § 2106 note.

Amendments:
2001. Act June 5, 2001, in subsec. (a), substituted "hereinafter" for "hereafter".

Other provisions:
Transfers of amounts into Veterans Housing Benefit Program Fund. Act Nov. 11, 1998, P. L. 105-368, Title VI, § 602(b), 112 Stat. 3346 (effective on Oct. 1, 1998, as provided by § 602(f) of such Act, which appears as 38 USCS § 2106 note), provides:

"All amounts in the following funds are hereby transferred to the Veterans Housing Benefit Program Fund:

"(1) The Direct Loan Revolving Fund, as such fund was continued under section 3723 of title 38, United States Code (as such section was in effect on the day before the effective date of this title).

"(2) The Department of Veterans Affairs Loan Guaranty Revolving Fund, as established by section 3724 of such title (as such section was in effect on the day before the effective date of this title).

"(3) The Guaranty and Indemnity Fund, as established by section 3725 of such title (as such section was in effect on the day before the effective date of this title).".

INTERPRETIVE NOTES AND DECISIONS

Where VA, which had partially guaranteed mortgage on veteran's home, purchased home at foreclosure and then resold it at profit, no law entitled veteran to return of profit; in fact, this result was contemplated in 38 USCS § 3722(c)(3)(B). Anderson v United States (2009) 85 Fed Cl 532.

[§ 3723. Repealed]

HISTORY; ANCILLARY LAWS AND DIRECTIVES

This section (Act Sept. 2, 1958, P. L. 85-857, § 1, 72 Stat. 1214; June 30, 1959, P. L. 86-73, § 4, 73 Stat. 156; July 14, 1960, P. L. 86-665, § 4, 74 Stat. 532; July 6, 1961, P. L. 87-84, § 3, 75 Stat. 202; Feb. 29, 1964, P. L. 88-274, 78 Stat. 147; Sept. 2, 1964, P. L. 88-560, Title VII, § 701(e)(2), 78 Stat. 801; June 30, 1976, P. L. 94-324, §§ 6, 7(27), 90 Stat. 721; Oct. 12, 1982, P. L. 97-295, § 4(68), 96 Stat. 1310; Jan. 12, 1983, P. L. 97-452, § 2(e)(2), 96 Stat. 2479; Oct. 28, 1986, P. L. 99-576, Title IV, Part A, § 405, 100 Stat. 3281; Dec. 18, 1989, P. L. 101-237, Title III, § 313(b)(1), (8), (9), 103 Stat. 2077; Aug. 6, 1991, P. L. 102-83, § 5(a), (c)(1), 105 Stat. 406) was repealed by Act Nov. 11, 1998, P. L. 105-368, Title VI, § 602(a)(1), 112 Stat. 3345, effective Oct. 1, 1998, as provided by § 602(f) of such Act, which appears as 38 USCS § 2106 note. It provided for a direct loan revolving fund.

[§ 3724. Repealed]

HISTORY; ANCILLARY LAWS AND DIRECTIVES

This section (Act July 14, 1960, P. L. 86-665, § 7(a), 74 Stat. 532; June 30, 1976, P. L. 94-324, § 7(28), 90 Stat. 722; Nov. 3, 1981, P. L. 97-72, Title III, § 303(j), 95 Stat. 1060; July 18, 1984, P. L. 98-369, Division B, Title V, Part B, § 2511(b), 98 Stat. 1117; May 23, 1986, P. L. 99-322, § 2(a), 100 Stat. 494; Nov. 18, 1988, P. L. 100-689, Title III, § 303, 102 Stat. 4177; Dec. 18, 1989, P. L. 101-237, Title III, §§ 302(a)(2), (3)(A), (C), 313(b)(1), (2), 103 Stat. 2070, 2077; Aug. 6, 1991, P. L. 102-83, § 5(a), (c)(1), 105 Stat. 406) was repealed by Act Nov. 11, 1998, P. L. 105-368, Title VI, § 602(a)(1), 112 Stat. 3345, effective Oct. 1, 1998, as provided by § 602(f) of such Act, which appears as 38 USCS § 2106 note. It provided for a loan guaranty revolving fund.

[§ 3725. Repealed]

HISTORY; ANCILLARY LAWS AND DIRECTIVES

This section (Act Sept. 2, 1958, P. L. 85-857, § 1, 72 Stat. 1215; July 14, 1960, P. L. 86-665, § 7(a), 74 Stat. 532; June 30, 1976, P. L. 94-324, § 7(29), 90 Stat. 722; Dec. 18, 1989, P. L. 101-237, Title III, § 302(a)(1), 103 Stat. 2069; June 13, 1991, P. L. 102-54, § 15(a)(2), 105 Stat. 289; Aug. 6, 1991, P. L. 102-83, § 5(a), (c)(1), 105 Stat. 406; Oct. 28, 1992, P. L. 102-547, § 2(b)(2), 106 Stat. 3634) was repealed by Act Nov. 11, 1998, P. L. 105-368, Title VI, § 602(a)(1), 112 Stat. 3345, effective Oct. 1, 1998, as provided by § 602(f) of such Act, which appears as 38 USCS § 2106 note. It provided for a guaranty and indemnity fund.

§ 3726. Withholding of payments, benefits, etc.

RESEARCH GUIDE

Am Jur:
77 Am Jur 2d, Veterans and Veterans' Laws § 113.

§ 3727. Expenditures to correct or compensate for structural defects in mortgaged homes

(a) The Secretary is authorized, with respect to any property improved by a one-to-four-family dwelling inspected during construction by the Department of Veterans Affairs or the Federal Housing Administration which the Secretary finds to have structural defects seriously affecting the livability of the property, to make expenditures for (1) correcting such defects, (2) paying the claims of the owner of the property arising from such defects, or (3) acquiring title to the property; except that such authority of the Secretary shall exist only (A) if the owner requests assistance under this section not later than four years (or such shorter time as the Secretary may prescribe) after the mortgage loan was made, guaranteed, or insured, and (B) if the property is encumbered by a mortgage which is made, guaranteed, or insured under this chapter [38 USCS §§ 3701 et seq.] after May 7, 1968.

(b) [Unchanged]

(c) The Secretary is authorized to make expenditures for the purposes of this section from the fund established pursuant to section 3722 of this title [38 USCS § 3722].

(As amended Nov. 11, 1998, P. L. 105-368, Title VI, § 602(e)(1)(C), Title X, § 1005(b)(11), 112 Stat. 3346, 3365.)

HISTORY; ANCILLARY LAWS AND DIRECTIVES

Amendments:

1998. Act Nov. 11, 1998, in subsec. (a), substituted "May 7, 1968" for "the date of enactment of this section.

Such Act further (effective on 10/1/98, as provided by § 602(f) of such Act, which appears as 38 USCS § 2106 note), in subsec. (c), substituted "fund established pursuant to section 3722 of this title" for "funds established pursuant to sections 3723 and 3724 of this title, as applicable".

RESEARCH GUIDE

Am Jur:

77 Am Jur 2d, Veterans and Veterans' Laws § 120.

§ 3728. Exemption from State anti-usury provisions.

RESEARCH GUIDE

Am Jur:

77 Am Jur 2d, Veterans and Veterans' Laws § 113.

Commercial Law:

1 Debtor-Creditor Law (Matthew Bender), ch 6, The Cost of Credit § 6.02.

§ 3729. Loan fee

(a) Requirement of fee. (1) Except as provided in subsection (c), a fee shall be collected from each person obtaining a housing loan guaranteed, insured, or made under this chapter [38 USCS §§ 3701 et seq.], and each person assuming a loan to which section 3714 of this title [38 USCS § 3714] applies. No such loan may be guaranteed, insured, made, or assumed until the fee payable under this section has been remitted to the Secretary.

(2) The fee may be included in the loan and paid from the proceeds thereof.

(b) Determination of fee. (1) The amount of the fee shall be determined from the loan fee table in paragraph (2). The fee is expressed as a percentage of the total amount of the loan guaranteed, insured, or made, or, in the case of a loan assumption, the unpaid principal balance of the loan on the date of the transfer of the property.

(2) The loan fee table referred to in paragraph (1) is as follows:

LOAN FEE TABLE

Type of loan	Active duty veteran	Reservist	Other obligor
(A)(i) Initial loan described in section 3710(a) to purchase or construct a dwelling with 0-down, or any other initial loan described in section 3710(a) other than with 5-down or 10-down (closed before January 1, 2004)	2.00	2.75	NA
(A)(ii) Initial loan described in section 3710(a) to purchase or construct a dwelling with 0-down, or any other initial loan described in section 3710(a) other than with 5-down or 10-down (closed on or after January 1, 2004, and before October 1, 2004)	2.20	2.40	NA

Type of loan			
(A)(iii) Initial loan described in section 3710(a) to purchase or construct a dwelling with 0-down, or any other initial loan described in section 3710(a) other than with 5-down or 10-down (closed on or after October 1, 2004, and before October 1, 2017)	2.15	2.40	NA
(A)(iv) Initial loan described in section 3710(a) to purchase or construct a dwelling with 0-down, or any other initial loan described in section 3710(a) other than with 5-down or 10-down (closed on or after October 1, 2017)	1.40	1.65	NA
(B)(i) Subsequent loan described in section 3710(a) to purchase or construct a dwelling with 0-down, or any other subsequent loan described in section 3710(a) (closed before October 1, 2017)	3.30	3.30	NA
(B)(ii) Subsequent loan described in section 3710(a) to purchase or construct a dwelling with 0-down, or any other subsequent loan described in section 3710(a) (closed on or after October 1, 2017)	1.25	1.25	NA
(C)(i) Loan described in section 3710(a) to purchase or construct a dwelling with 5-down (closed before October 1, 2017)	1.50	1.75	NA
(C)(ii) Loan described in section 3710(a) to purchase or construct a dwelling with 5-down (closed on or after October 1, 2017)	0.75	1.00	NA
(D)(i) Initial loan described in section 3710(a) to purchase or construct a dwelling with 10-down (closed before October 1, 2017)	1.25	1.50	NA
(D)(ii) Initial loan described in section 3710(a) to purchase or construct a dwelling with 10-down (closed on or after October 1, 2017)	0.50	0.75	NA
(E) Interest rate reduction refinancing loan	0.50	0.50	NA
(F) Direct loan under section 3711	1.00	1.00	NA
(G) Manufactured home loan under section 3712 (other than an interest rate reduction refinancing loan)	1.00	1.00	NA
(H) Loan to Native American veteran under section 3762 (other than an interest rate reduction refinancing loan)	1.25	1.25	NA
(I) Loan assumption under section 3714	0.50	0.50	0.50
(J) Loan under section 3733(a)	2.25	2.25	2.25

(3) Any reference to a section in the "Type of loan" column in the loan fee table in paragraph (2) refers to a section of this title.

(4) For the purposes of paragraph (2):

(A) The term "active duty veteran" means any veteran eligible for the benefits of this chapter [38 USCS §§ 3701 et seq.] other than a Reservist.

(B) The term "Reservist" means a veteran described in section 3701(b)(5)(A) of this title [38 USCS § 3701(b)(5)(A)] who is eligible under section 3702(a)(2)(E) of this title [38 USCS § 3702(a)(2)(E)].

(C) The term "other obligor" means a person who is not a veteran, as defined in section 101 of this title [38 USCS § 101] or other provision of this chapter [38 USCS §§ 3701 et seq.].

(D) The term "initial loan" means a loan to a veteran guaranteed under section 3710 [38 USCS § 3710] or made under section 3711 of this title [38 USCS § 3711] if the veteran has

READJUSTMENT BENEFITS   38 USCS § 3729

never obtained a loan guaranteed under section 3710 [38 USCS § 3710] or made under section 3711 of this title [38 USCS § 3711].

(E) The term "subsequent loan" means a loan to a veteran, other than an interest rate reduction refinancing loan, guaranteed under section 3710 [38 USCS § 3710] or made under section 3711 of this title [38 USCS § 3711] if the veteran has previously obtained a loan guaranteed under section 3710 [38 USCS § 3710] or made under section 3711 of this title [38 USCS § 3711].

(F) The term "interest rate reduction refinancing loan" means a loan described in section 3710(a)(8), 3710(a)(9)(B)(i), 3710(a)(11), 3712(a)(1)(F), or 3762(h) of this title [38 USCS § 3710(a)(8), 3710(a)(9)(B)(i), 3710(a)(11), 3712(a)(1)(F), or 3762(h)].

(G) The term "0-down" means a downpayment, if any, of less than 5 percent of the total purchase price or construction cost of the dwelling.

(H) The term "5-down" means a downpayment of at least 5 percent or more, but less than 10 percent, of the total purchase price or construction cost of the dwelling.

(I) The term "10-down" means a downpayment of 10 percent or more of the total purchase price or construction cost of the dwelling.

(c) Waiver of fee. (1) A fee may not be collected under this section from a veteran who is receiving compensation (or who, but for the receipt of retirement pay or active service pay, would be entitled to receive compensation) or from a surviving spouse of any veteran (including a person who died in the active military, naval, or air service) who died from a service-connected disability.

(2)(A) A veteran described in subparagraph (B) shall be treated as receiving compensation for purposes of this subsection as of the date of the rating described in such subparagraph without regard to whether an effective date of the award of compensation is established as of that date.

(B) A veteran described in this subparagraph is a veteran who is rated eligible to receive compensation—

(i) as the result of a pre-discharge disability examination and rating; or

(ii) based on a pre-discharge review of existing medical evidence (including service medical and treatment records) that results in the issuance of a memorandum rating.

(As amended Nov. 11, 1998, P. L. 105-368, Title VI, §§ 602(e)(1)(D), 603(b), 112 Stat. 3346, 3348; Nov. 1, 2000, P. L. 106-419, Title IV, § 402(b), 114 Stat. 1861; June 5, 2001, P. L. 107-14, § 8(b)(4), 115 Stat. 36; Dec. 27, 2001, P. L. 107-103, Title IV, §§ 405(c), 406, 115 Stat. 994; Dec. 16, 2003, P. L. 108-183, Title IV, § 405, 117 Stat. 2665; Dec. 10, 2004, P. L. 108-454, Title IV, § 406, 118 Stat. 3617; Oct. 13, 2010, P. L. 111-275, Title II, § 204, 124 Stat. 2874; Aug. 3, 2011, P. L. 112-26, § 3(a), 125 Stat. 269; Oct. 5, 2011, P. L. 112-37, § 15, 125 Stat. 398; Nov. 21, 2011, P. L. 112-56, Title II, Subtitle E, § 265(a), 125 Stat. 732; Aug. 6, 2012, P. L. 112-154, Title II, § 210, Title VII, § 702(b), 126 Stat. 1179, 1205.)

HISTORY; ANCILLARY LAWS AND DIRECTIVES

Amendments:

1998. Act Nov. 11, 1998 (effective on 10/1/98, as provided by § 602(f) of such Act, which appears as 38 USCS § 2106 note), in subsec. (a), in para. (1), substituted "(c)" for "(c)(1)" and, in para. (4), designated the existing provisions as subpara. (A) and, in such subparagraph, substituted "With respect to a loan closed during the period specified in subparagraph (B)" for "With respect to a loan closed after September 30, 1993, and before October 1, 2002,", and added subpara. (B); and, in subsec. (c), deleted the paragraph designator "(1)" preceding "A fee" and deleted paras. (2) and (3), which read:

"(2) There shall be credited to the Guaranty and Indemnity Fund (in addition to the amount required to be credited to such Fund under clause (A) or (B) of paragraph (2) of section 3725(c) of this title or paragraph (3) of that section), on behalf of a veteran or surviving spouse described in paragraph (1) of this subsection, an amount equal to the fee that, except for paragraph (1) of this subsection, would be collected from such veteran or surviving spouse.

"(3) Credits to the Guaranty and Indemnity Fund under paragraph (2) of this subsection with respect to loans guaranteed, insured, or made under this chapter that are closed during fiscal year 1990 shall be made in October 1990.".

2000. Act Nov. 1, 2000, as amended by Act June 5, 2001 (effective as of 11/1/00, and as if included in Act Nov. 1, 2000 as originally enacted, as provided by § 8(b) of the 2001 Act), substituted the text of this section for text which read:

"(a)(1) Except as provided in subsection (c) of this section, a fee shall be collected from each veteran obtaining a housing loan guaranteed, insured, or made under this chapter, and from each person obtaining a loan under section 3733(a) of this title, and no such loan may be guaranteed, insured, or made under this chapter until the fee payable under this section has been remitted to the Secretary.

"(2) Except as provided in paragraphs (4) and (5) of this of subsection, the amount of such fee shall be 1.25 percent of the total loan amount, except that—

"(A) in the case of a loan made under section 3711 of this title or for any purpose specified in section 3712 (other than section 3712(a)(1)(F)) of this title, the amount of such fee shall be one percent of the total loan amount;

"(B) in the case of a guaranteed or insured loan for a purchase (except for a purchase referred to in section 3712(a) of this title), or for construction, with respect to which the veteran has made a downpayment of 5 percent or more, but less than 10 percent, of the total purchase price or construction cost, the amount of such fee shall be 0.75 percent of the total loan amount;

"(C) in the case of a guaranteed or insured loan for a purchase (except for a purchase referred to in section 3712(a) of this title), or for construction, with respect to which the veteran has made a downpayment of 10 percent or more of the total purchase price or construction cost, the amount of such fee shall be 0.50 percent of the total loan amount;

"(D) in the case of a loan made to, or guaranteed or insured on behalf of, a veteran described in section 3701(b)(5) of this title under this chapter, the amount of such fee shall be—

"(i) two percent of the total loan amount;

"(ii) in the case of a loan for any purpose specified in section 3712 of this title, one percent of such amount; or

"(iii) in the case of a loan for a purchase (other than a purchase referred to in section 3712 of this title) or for construction with respect to which the veteran has made a downpayment of 5 percent or more of the total purchase price or construction cost—

"(I) 1.50 percent of the total loan amount if such downpayment is less than 10 percent of such price or cost; or

"(II) 1.25 percent of the total loan amount if such downpayment is 10 percent or more of such price or cost;

"(E) in the case of a loan guaranteed under section 3710(a)(8), 3710(a)(9)(B)(i), 3710(a)(11), 3712(a)(1)(F), or 3762(h) of this title, the amount of such fee shall be 0.5 percent of the total loan amount; and

"(F) in the case of a loan made under section 3733(a) of this title, the amount of such fee shall be 2.25 percent of the total loan amount.

"(3) The amount of the fee to be collected under paragraph (1) of this subsection may be included in the loan and paid from the proceeds thereof.

"(4)(A) With respect to a loan closed during the period specified in subparagraph (B) for which a fee is collected under paragraph (1), the amount of such fee, as computed under paragraph (2), shall be increased by 0.75 percent of the total loan amount other than in the case of a loan described in subparagraph (A), (D)(ii), (E), or (F) of paragraph (2).

"(B) The specified period for purposes of subparagraph (A) is the period beginning on October 1, 1993, and ending on September 30, 2002, except that in the case of a loan described in subparagraph (D) of paragraph (2), such period ends on September 30, 2003.

"(5)(A) Except as provided in subparagraph (B) of this paragraph, notwithstanding paragraphs (2) and (4) of this subsection, after a veteran has obtained an initial loan pursuant to section 3710 of this title, the amount of such fee with respect to any additional loan obtained under this chapter by such veteran shall be 3 percent of the total loan amount.

"(B) Subparagraph (A) of this paragraph does not apply with respect to (i) a loan obtained by a veteran with a downpayment described in paragraph (2)(B), (2)(C), or (2)(D)(iii) of this subsection, and (ii) loans described in paragraph (2)(E) of this subsection.

"(C) This paragraph applies with respect to a loan closed after September 30, 1993, and before October 1, 2002.

"(b) Except as provided in subsection (c) of this section, a fee shall be collected from a person assuming a loan to which section 3714 of this title applies. The amount of the fee shall be equal to 0.50 percent of the balance of the loan on the date of the transfer of the property.

"(c) A fee may not be collected under this section from a veteran who is receiving compensation (or who but for the receipt of retirement pay would be entitled to receive compensation) or from a surviving spouse of any veteran (including a person who died in the active military, naval, or air service) who died from a service-connected disability.".

2001. Act June 5, 2001 (effective as of 11/1/2000, and as if included in Act Nov. 1, 2000 as originally enacted, as provided by § 8(b) of such Act), amended § 402(b) of Act Nov. 1, 2000, which amended this section.

Act Dec. 27, 2001, in subsec. (b), in para. (2), substituted "December 31, 2011" for "December 31, 2008" wherever appearing, and, in para. (4)(B), inserted "who is eligible under section 3702(a)(2)(E) of this title".

2003. Act Dec. 16, 2003 (effective January 1, 2004, as provided by § 405 of such Act), in subsec. (b), substituted para. (2) for one which read:

"(2) The loan fee table referred to in paragraph (1) is as follows:

LOAN FEE TABLE

Type of loan	Active duty veteran	Reservist	Other obligor
(A)(i) Initial loan described in section 3710(a) to purchase or construct a dwelling with 0-down, or any other initial loan described in section 3710(a) other than with 5-down or 10-down (closed before November 18, 2011)	2.00	2.75	NA
(A)(ii) Initial loan described in section 3710(a) to purchase or construct a dwelling with 0-down, or any other initial loan described in section 3710(a) other than with 5-down or 10-down (closed on or after November 18, 2011)	1.25	2.00	NA
(B)(i) Subsequent loan described in section 3710(a) to purchase or construct a dwelling with 0-down, or any other subsequent loan described in section 3710(a) (closed before November 18, 2011)	3.00	3.00	NA
(B)(ii) Subsequent loan described in section 3710(a) to purchase or construct a dwelling with 0-down, or any other subsequent loan described in section 3710(a) (closed on or after November 18, 2011)	1.25	2.00	NA
(C)(i) Loan described in section 3710(a) to purchase or construct a dwelling with 5-down (closed before November 18, 2011)	1.50	2.25	NA
(C)(ii) Loan described in section 3710(a) to purchase or construct a dwelling with 5-down (closed on or after November 18, 2011)	0.75	1.50	NA
(D)(i) Initial loan described in section 3710(a) to purchase or construct a dwelling with 10-down (closed before November 18, 2011)	1.25	2.00	NA
(D)(ii) Initial loan described in section 3710(a) to purchase or construct a dwelling with 10-down (closed on or after November 18, 2011)	0.50	1.25	NA
(E) Interest rate reduction refinancing loan	0.50	0.50	NA
(F) Direct loan under section 3711	1.00	1.00	NA
(G) Manufactured home loan under section 3712 (other than an interest rate reduction refinancing loan)	1.00	1.00	NA
(H) Loan to Native American veteran under section 3762 (other than an interest rate reduction refinancing loan)	1.25	1.25	NA
(I) Loan assumption under section 3714	0.50	0.50	0.50
(J) Loan under section 3733(a)	2.25	2.25	2.25"

2004. Act Dec. 10, 2004, in subsec. (c), designated the existing provisions as para. (1), and added para. (2).
2010. Act Oct. 13, 2010, in subsec. (c)(1), inserted "or active service pay".
2011. Act Aug. 3, 2011 (effective 10/1/2011, pursuant to § 3(b) of such Act, which appears as a note to this section), in subsec. (b)(2)(B), in cl. (i), substituted "October 1, 2011" for "January 1, 2004", and substituted "3.30" for "3.00" in two places, in cl. (ii), substituted "October 1, 2011, and before October 1, 2012" for "January 1, 2004, and before October 1, 2011", and substituted "2.80" for "3.30" in two places, and in cl. (iii), substituted "October 1, 2012" for "October 1, 2011".
Act Oct. 5, 2011, in subsec. (b)(2), substituted "November 18, 2011" for "October 1, 2011" wherever appearing.

38 USCS § 3729   VETERANS' BENEFITS

Act Nov. 21, 2011 (effective on enactment, as provided by § 265(b) of such Act, which appears as a note to this section), in subsec. (b)(2), in subpara. (A), in cls. (iii) and (iv), substituted "October 1, 2016" for "November 18, 2011", in subpara. (B), in cl. (i), substituted "October 1, 2016" for "November 18, 2011", deleted cls. (ii) and (iii), which read:

"LOAN FEE TABLE

Type of loan	Active duty veteran	Reservist	Other obligor
(B)(ii) Subsequent loan described in section 3710(a) to purchase or construct a dwelling with 0-down, or any other subsequent loan described in section 3710(a) (closed on or after November 18, 2011, and before October 1, 2012)	2.80	2.80	NA
(B)(iii) Subsequent loan described in section 3710(a) to purchase or construct a dwelling with 0-down, or any other subsequent loan described in section 3710(a) (closed on or after October 1, 2012 and before October 1, 2013)	2.15	2.15	NA",

redesignated cl. (iv) as cl. (ii), and in such clause as redesignated, substituted "October 1, 2016" for "October 1, 2013", and in subparas. (C)(i), (C)(ii), (D)(i), and (D)(ii), substituted "October 1, 2016" for "November 18, 2011".

2012. Act Aug. 6, 2012, in subsec. (b)(2), in subparas. (A)(iii), (A)(iv), (B)(i), (B)(ii), (C)(i), (C)(ii), (D)(i), and (D)(ii), substituted "October 1, 2017" for "October 1, 2016"; and in subsec. (c), substituted para. (2) for one which read: "(2) A veteran who is rated eligible to receive compensation as a result of a pre-discharge disability examination and rating shall be treated as receiving compensation for purposes of this subsection as of the date on which the veteran is rated eligible to receive compensation as a result of the pre-discharge disability examination and rating without regard to whether an effective date of the award of compensation is established as of that date.".

Other provisions:

Fee for loan assumption; Dec. 13, 2002 through Sept. 30, 2003. Act Dec. 6, 2002, P. L. 107-330, Title III, § 307, 116 Stat. 2827, provides:

"(a) In general. For the period described in subsection (b), the Secretary of Veterans Affairs shall apply section 3729(b)(2)(I) of title 38, United States Code, by substituting '1.00' for '0.50' each place it appears.

"(b) Period described. The period referred to in subsection (a) is the period that begins on the date that is 7 days after the date of the enactment of this Act and ends on September 30, 2003.".

Effective date of Dec. 16, 2003 amendment. Act Dec. 16, 2003, P. L. 108-183, Title IV, § 405, 117 Stat. 2665, provides that the amendment made by such section to subsec. (b)(2) of this section is effective January 1, 2004.

Temporary increase in certain housing loan fees. Act June 15, 2006, P. L. 109-233, Title I, § 101(f), 120 Stat. 399, provides: "For a subsequent loan described in subsection (a) of section 3710 of title 38, United States Code, to purchase or construct a dwelling with 0-down or any other subsequent loan described in that subsection, other than a loan with 5-down or 10-down, that is closed during fiscal year 2007, the Secretary of Veterans Affairs shall apply section 3729(b)(2) of such title by substituting '3.35' for '3.30'.".

Effective date of Aug. 3, 2011 amendment. Act Aug. 3, 2011, P. L. 112-26, § 3(b), 125 Stat. 269, provides: "The amendments made by subsection (a) [amending subsec. (b)(2)(B) of this section] shall take effect on the later of October 1, 2011, or the date of the enactment of this Act.".

Effective date of Nov. 21, 2011 amendments. Act Nov. 21, 2011, P. L. 112-56, Title II, Subtitle E, § 265(b), 125 Stat. 733, provides:

"The amendments made by subsection (a) [amending subsec. (b)(2) of this section] shall take effect on the later of—

"(1) November 18, 2011; or

"(2) the date of the enactment of this Act.".

CODE OF FEDERAL REGULATIONS

Department of Veterans Affairs—Loan guaranty, 38 CFR 36.4201 et seq.

§ 3730. Use of attorneys in court

(a) The Secretary shall authorize attorneys employed by the Department of Veterans Affairs to exercise the right of the United States to bring suit in court to foreclose a loan made or acquired by the Secretary under this chapter [38 USCS §§ 3701 et seq.] and to recover possession of any property acquired by the Secretary under this chapter [38 USCS §§ 3701 et seq.]. The Secretary may acquire the services of attorneys, other than those who are employees of the Department of Veterans Affairs, to exercise that right. The activities of attorneys in bringing suit under this section shall be subject to the direction and supervision of the Attorney General and to such terms and conditions as the Attorney General may prescribe.

(b) [Unchanged]

(As amended Nov. 11, 1998, P. L. 105-368, Title X, § 1005(b)(12), 112 Stat. 3365.)

HISTORY; ANCILLARY LAWS AND DIRECTIVES

Amendments:
1998. Act Nov. 11, 1998, in subsec. (a), substituted "The Secretary shall" for "Within 180 days after the date of the enactment of this section, the Secretary shall take appropriate steps to".

RESEARCH GUIDE

Am Jur:
77 Am Jur 2d, Veterans and Veterans' Laws § 120.

§ 3731. Appraisals

RESEARCH GUIDE

Am Jur:
77 Am Jur 2d, Veterans and Veterans' Laws §§ 113, 120.

§ 3732. Procedure on default

(a)(1) [Unchanged]

(2)(A) Before suit or foreclosure the holder of the obligation shall notify the Secretary of the default, and within thirty days thereafter the Secretary may, at the Secretary's option, pay the holder of the obligation the unpaid balance of the obligation plus accrued interest and receive an assignment of the loan and security. Nothing in this section shall preclude any forbearance for the benefit of the veteran as may be agreed upon by the parties to the loan and approved by the Secretary.

(B) In the event that a housing loan guaranteed under this chapter is modified under the authority provided under section 1322(b) of title 11, the Secretary may pay the holder of the obligation the unpaid principal balance of the obligation due, plus accrued interest, as of the date of the filing of the petition under title 11, but only upon the assignment, transfer, and delivery to the Secretary (in a form and manner satisfactory to the Secretary) of all rights, interest, claims, evidence, and records with respect to the housing loan.

(3)–(5) [Unchanged]

(b) [Unchanged]

(c)(1)–(9) [Unchanged]

(10)(A)–(C) [Unchanged]

(D) For the purpose of determining the liability of the United States under a loan guaranty under paragraphs (5)(B), (6), (7)(B), and (8)(B), the amount of the total indebtedness with respect to such loan guaranty shall include, in any case in which there was an excessive delay caused by the Department of Veterans of Affairs in the liquidation sale of the property securing such loan, any interest which had accrued as of the date of such sale and which would not be included, except for this subparagraph, in the calculation of such total indebtedness as a result of the specification of an earlier date under subparagraph (C)(i) of this paragraph.

(11) This subsection shall apply to loans closed before October 1, 2013.

(As amended Nov. 1, 2000, P. L. 106-419, Title IV, § 402(c), 114 Stat. 1863; Dec. 27, 2001, P L. 107-103, Title IV, § 405(d), 115 Stat. 994; Dec. 16, 2003, P. L. 108-183, Title IV, § 406, 117 Stat. 2666; June 15, 2006, P. L. 109-233, Title V, § 503(9), 120 Stat. 416; Oct. 13, 2010, P. L. 111-275, Title VIII, § 802(a), 124 Stat. 2888; Oct. 5, 2012, P. L. 112-191, Title II, § 201, 126 Stat. 1439.)

HISTORY; ANCILLARY LAWS AND DIRECTIVES

Amendments:
2000. Act Nov. 1, 2000, in subsec. (c)(11), substituted "October 1, 2008" for "October 1, 2002".
2001. Act Dec. 27, 2001, in subsec. (c)(11), substituted "October 1, 2011" for "October 1, 2008".
2003. Act Dec. 16, 2003, in subsec. (c)(11), substituted "October 1, 2012" for "October 1, 2011".

2006. Act June 15, 2006, in subsec. (c)(10)(D), substituted "paragraphs (5)(B), (6), (7)(B), and (8)(B)" for "clause (B) of paragraphs (5), (6), (7), and (8) of this subsection".

2010. Act Oct. 13, 2010 (applicable to a housing loan guranteed after the date of enactment, as provided by § 802(b) of such Act, which appears as a note to this section), in subsec. (a)(2), designated the existing provisions as subpara. (A), and added subpara. (B).

2012. Act Oct. 5, 2012, in subsec. (c)(11), substituted "October 1, 2013" for "October 1, 2012".

Other provisions:
Application of Oct. 13, 2010 amendments. Act Oct. 13, 2010, P. L. 111-275, Title VIII, § 802(b), 124 Stat. 2889, provides: "The amendments made by subsection (a) [amending subsec. (a)(2) of this section] shall apply with respect to a housing loan guaranteed after the date of the enactment of this Act.".

RESEARCH GUIDE

Am Jur:
77 Am Jur 2d, Veterans and Veterans' Laws § 121.

INTERPRETIVE NOTES AND DECISIONS

9. Miscellaneous

VA was under no obligation to provide counseling to veteran before foreclosure pursuant to 38 USCS § 3732(a)(4) since effective date of § 3732 was prospectively set for one year after date of foreclosure on veteran's house, and argument that duty to counsel applies retroactively is without merit because duty to assist applies to development of evidence and only attaches once claim has been well grounded; in months preceding foreclosure, veteran had no claim, much less well grounded claim, for debt waiver or other VA benefit. Berotti v West (1998) 11 Vet App 194.

Where VA which had partially guaranteed mortgage on veteran's home, purchased home at foreclosure and then resold it at profit, no law entitled veteran to return of profit and thus, Court of Federal Claims jurisdiction under Tucker Act, 28 USCS § 1491; veteran's reliance on 38 USCS § 3732(a)(1) was misplaced because benefit of subrogation under 38 USCS § 3732(a)(1) was afforded to VA against borrower, not to borrower against VA. Anderson v United States (2009) 85 Fed Cl 532.

§ 3733. Property management

(a)(1)–(3) [Unchanged]

    (4)(A) Except as provided in subparagraph (B), the amount of a loan made by the Secretary to finance the purchase of real property from the Secretary described in paragraph (1) may not exceed an amount equal to 95 percent of the purchase price of such real property.

    (B)(i) The Secretary may waive the provisions of subparagraph (A) in the case of any loan described in paragraph (5).

    (ii) A loan described in subparagraph (A) may, to the extent the Secretary determines to be necessary in order to market competitively the property involved, exceed 95 percent of the purchase price.

(5) The Secretary may include, as part of a loan to finance a purchase of real property from the Secretary described in paragraph (1), an amount to be used only for the purpose of rehabilitating such property. Such amount may not exceed the amount necessary to rehabilitate the property to a habitable state, and payments shall be made available periodically as such rehabilitation is completed.

(6) The Secretary shall make a loan to finance the sale of real property described in paragraph (1) at an interest rate that is lower than the prevailing mortgage market interest rate in areas where, and to the extent, the Secretary determines, in light of prevailing conditions in the real estate market involved, that such lower interest rate is necessary in order to market the property competitively and is in the interest of the long-term stability and solvency of the Veterans Housing Benefit Program Fund established by section 3722(a) of this title [38 USCS § 3722(a)].

(7) During the period that begins on December 16, 2003, and ends on September 30, 2013, the Secretary shall carry out the provisions of this subsection as if—

    (A) the references in the first sentence of paragraph (1) to "65 percent" and "may be financed" were references to "85 percent" and "shall be financed", respectively;

    (B) the second sentence of paragraph (1) were repealed; and

    (C) the reference in paragraph (2) to "September 30, 1990," were a reference to "September 30, 2013,".

(b) [Unchanged]

(c)(1) [Unchanged]

    (2) The Secretary shall include a summary of the information compiled, and the Secretary's findings, under paragraph (1) in the annual report submitted to the Congress under section 529 of this title [38 USCS § 529]. As part of such summary and findings, the Secretary shall provide a separate analysis of the factors which contribute to foreclosures of loans which have been assumed.

READJUSTMENT BENEFITS 38 USCS § 3734

(d) [Unchanged]
(e) [Deleted]
(As amended Nov. 11, 1998, P. L. 105-368, Title VI, § 602(c)(2), (e)(1)(E), 112 Stat. 3346; Dec. 16, 2003, P. L. 108-183, Title IV, § 404, 117 Stat. 2664; June 15, 2006, P. L. 109-233, Title V, § 503(10), 120 Stat. 416; Oct. 13, 2010, P. L. 111-275, Title X, § 1001(j), 124 Stat. 2897.)

HISTORY; ANCILLARY LAWS AND DIRECTIVES

Amendments:

1998. Act Nov. 11, 1998 (effective on 10/1/98, as provided by § 602(f) of such Act, which appears as 38 USCS § 2106 note), in subsec. (a)(6), substituted "Veterans Housing Benefit Program Fund established by section 3722(a)" for "Department of Veterans Affairs Loan Guaranty Revolving Fund established by section 3724(a)"; and deleted subsec. (e), which read:

"(e) Notwithstanding any other provision of law, the amount received from the sale of any note evidencing a loan secured by real property described in subsection (a)(1) of this section, and the amount received from the sale of securities under section 3720(h) of this title, shall be credited, without any reduction and for the fiscal year in which the amount is received, as offsetting collections of—

"(1) the revolving fund for which a fee under section 3729 of this title was collected (or was exempted from being collected) at the time of the original guaranty of the loan that was secured by the same property; or

"(2) in any case in which there was no requirement of (or exemption from) a fee at the time of the original guaranty of the loan that was secured by the same property, the Loan Guaranty Revolving Fund; and

the total so credited to any revolving fund for a fiscal year shall offset outlays attributed to such revolving fund during such fiscal year.".

2003. Act Dec. 16, 2003, in subsec. (a), in para. (4), in subpara. (A), deleted "of this paragraph" following "subparagraph (B)", and deleted "of this subsection" following "paragraph (1)", and, in subpara. (B), in cl. (i), deleted "of this paragraph" following "subparagraph (A)", and deleted "of this subsection" following "paragraph (5)", and, in cl. (ii), deleted "of this paragraph" following "subparagraph (A)", in paras. (5) and (6), deleted "of this subsection" following "paragraph (1)", and added para. (7); and, in subsec. (c)(2), deleted "of this subsection" following "paragraph (1)".

2006. Act June 15, 2006, in subsec. (a)(7), in the introductory matter, substituted "December 16, 2003" for "the date of the enactment of the Veterans' Benefits Act of 2003".

2010. Act Oct. 13, 2010, in subsec. (a)(7), in the introductory matter, inserted the comma after "2003".

RESEARCH GUIDE

Am Jur:

77 Am Jur 2d, Veterans and Veterans' Laws § 121.

INTERPRETIVE NOTES AND DECISIONS

Nonjudicial foreclosure sale of VA-owned home by homeowners association owed past-due fees is void, where federal law governs determination of whether title to land owned by U.S. has passed to another party under Property and Supremacy Clauses, because purpose of VA Home Loan Guaranty Program is to permit otherwise ineligible veterans to own homes, policy under 38 USCS § 3733(d) is to sell acquired properties for highest price as quickly as possible and to return funds to Veterans Housing Benefit Program Fund, and permitting foreclosure due to unnoticed, unpaid association fees would run counter to federal law. Yunis v United States (2000, CD Cal) 118 F Supp 2d 1024.

§ 3734. Annual submission of information on the Veterans Housing Benefit Program Fund and housing programs

(a) In the documents providing detailed information on the budget for the Department of Veterans Affairs that the Secretary submits to the Congress in conjunction with the President's budget submission for each fiscal year pursuant to section 1105 of title 31 [31 USCS § 1105], the Secretary shall include—

(1) a description of the operations of the Veterans Housing Benefit Program Fund during the fiscal year preceding the fiscal year in which such budget is submitted; and

(2) the needs of such fund, if any, for appropriations for—

(A), (B) [Unchanged]

(b) The matters submitted under subsection (a) of this section shall include, with respect to the fund referred to in subsection (a), the following:

(1) [Unchanged]

(2) Estimates of the amount of revenues derived by the fund in the fiscal year preceding the fiscal year of the submission, in the fiscal year of the submission, and in the fiscal year following the fiscal year of the submission from each of the following sources:

(A) [Unchanged]

38 USCS § 3734

(B) Investment income.
(C) Sales of foreclosed properties.
(D) Loan asset sales.
(E) Each additional source of revenue.
(F), (G) [Redesignated]
(3) [Unchanged]

(c) The information submitted under subsection (a) shall include a statement that summarizes the financial activity of each of the housing programs operated under this chapter [38 USCS §§ 3701 et seq.]. The statement shall be presented in a form that is simple, concise, and readily understandable, and shall not include references to financing accounts, liquidating accounts, or program accounts.

(As amended Nov. 11, 1998, P. L. 105-368, Title VI, § 602(d), (e)(1)(F), (3)(A), 112 Stat. 3347; June 5, 2001, P. L. 107-14, § 8(a)(9), 115 Stat. 35; Dec. 6, 2002, P. L. 107-330, Title III, § 308(g)(12), 116 Stat. 2829.)

HISTORY; ANCILLARY LAWS AND DIRECTIVES

Amendments:
1998. Act Nov. 11, 1998 (effective on 10/1/98, as provided by § 602(f) of such Act, which appears as 38 USCS § 2106 note) substituted the section heading for one which read: "§ 3734. Annual submission of information on the Loan Guaranty Revolving Fund and the Guaranty and Indemnity Fund"; in subsec. (a), in para. (1), substituted "Veterans Housing Benefit Program Fund" for "Loan Guaranty Revolving Fund and the Guaranty and Indemnity Fund" and substituted "fund," for "funds,"; in subsec. (b), in the introductory matter, substituted "the fund" for "each fund", in para. (2), deleted subpara. (B), which read: "(B) Federal Government contributions made under clauses (A) and (B) of section 3725(c)(2) of this title.", redesignated subparas. (C)–(G) as subparas. (B)–(F), respectively, and, in subpara. (B) as redesignated, substituted "section 3729(a)(3)" for "subsections (a)(3) and (c)(2) of section 3729 of this title"; and added subsec. (c).

2001. Act June 5, 2001, in subsec. (a), in the introductory matter, deleted "United States Code," following "title 31," and, in para. (2), in the introductory matter, substituted "appropriations for" for "appropriations in".

2002. Act Dec. 6, 2002, in subsec. (b)(2), deleted subpara. (B) which read: "(B) Federal Government payments under section 3729(a)(3).", and redesignated subparas. (C)–(F) as subparas. (B)–(E), respectively.

RESEARCH GUIDE

Am Jur:
77 Am Jur 2d, Veterans and Veterans' Laws § 120.

[§ 3735. Transferred]

HISTORY; ANCILLARY LAWS AND DIRECTIVES

This section, relating to housing assistance for homeless veterans, was transferred to Subchapter V of Chapter 20 of this Title and redesignated 38 USCS § 2041 by Act Dec. 21, 2001, P. L. 107-95, § 5(c), 115 Stat. 918.

§ 3736. Reporting requirements

RESEARCH GUIDE

Am Jur:
77 Am Jur 2d, Veterans and Veterans' Laws § 120.

SUBCHAPTER IV. SMALL BUSINESS LOANS

§ 3741. Definitions

CODE OF FEDERAL REGULATIONS

Department of Veterans Affairs—Loan guaranty and vocational rehabilitation and counseling programs, 48 CFR 871.100 et seq.

RESEARCH GUIDE

Am Jur:
77 Am Jur 2d, Veterans and Veterans' Laws § 119.

Bankruptcy:
6 Collier on Bankruptcy (Matthew Bender 16th ed.), ch 707, Dismissal of a Case or Conversion to a Case under Chapter 11 or 50 ¶ 707.04.

§ 3742. Small business loan program

RESEARCH GUIDE
Am Jur:
77 Am Jur 2d, Veterans and Veterans' Laws § 119.

§ 3743. Liability on loans

RESEARCH GUIDE
Am Jur:
77 Am Jur 2d, Veterans and Veterans' Laws § 119.

§ 3744. Approval of loans by the Secretary

RESEARCH GUIDE
Am Jur:
77 Am Jur 2d, Veterans and Veterans' Laws § 119.

§ 3745. Interest on loans

RESEARCH GUIDE
Am Jur:
77 Am Jur 2d, Veterans and Veterans' Laws § 119.

Commercial Law:
1 Debtor-Creditor Law (Matthew Bender), ch 6, The Cost of Credit § 6.02.

§ 3746. Maturity of loans

RESEARCH GUIDE
Am Jur:
77 Am Jur 2d, Veterans and Veterans' Laws § 119.

§ 3748. Preference for disabled veterans

RESEARCH GUIDE
Am Jur:
77 Am Jur 2d, Veterans and Veterans' Laws § 119.

§ 3749. Revolving fund

RESEARCH GUIDE
Am Jur:
77 Am Jur 2d, Veterans and Veterans' Laws § 119.

§ 3751. Termination of program

RESEARCH GUIDE
Other Treatises:
Cohen's Handbook of Federal Indian Law (Matthew Bender), ch 22, Government Services for Indians § 22.05.

SUBCHAPTER V. DIRECT HOUSING LOANS FOR NATIVE AMERICAN VETERANS

HISTORY; ANCILLARY LAWS AND DIRECTIVES
Amendments:
2006. Act June 15, 2006, P. L. 109-233, Title I, § 103(f)(1), 120 Stat. 400, substituted the subchapter heading for one which read: "SUBCHAPTER V. NATIVE AMERICAN VETERAN HOUSING LOAN PILOT PROGRAM".

§ 3761. Direct housing loans to Native American veterans; program authority

(a) The Secretary shall make direct housing loans to Native American veterans. The purpose of such loans is to permit such veterans to purchase, construct, or improve dwellings on trust land. The Secretary shall make such loans in accordance with the provisions of this subchapter [38 USCS §§ 3761 et seq.].

(b) The Secretary shall, to the extent practicable, make direct housing loans to Native American veterans who are located in a variety of geographic areas and in areas experiencing a variety of economic circumstances.

(c) [Deleted]

(As amended Dec. 27, 2001, P. L. 107-103, Title IV, § 402(a), 115 Stat. 993; Dec. 10, 2004, P. L. 108-454, Title IV, § 407, 118 Stat. 3617; June 15, 2006, P. L. 109-233, Title I, § 103(a), (f)(2), 120 Stat. 399, 400.)

HISTORY; ANCILLARY LAWS AND DIRECTIVES

Amendments:

2001. Act Dec. 27, 2001, in subsec. (c), substituted "December 31, 2005" for "December 31, 2001".

2004. Act Dec. 10, 2004, in subsec. (c), substituted "December 31, 2008" for "December 31, 2005".

2006. Act June 15, 2006, substituted the section heading for one which read: "§ 3761. Pilot program"; in subsec. (a), deleted "establish and implement a pilot program under which the Secretary may" preceding "make direct housing" and substituted "shall make such loans" for "shall establish and implement the pilot program"; in subsec. (b), substituted "The" for "In carrying out the pilot program under this subchapter, the"; and deleted subsec. (c), which read: "(c) No loans may be made under this subchapter after December 31, 2008.".

Other provisions:

Repeal of provisions relating to consultation with Advisory Committee on Native-American Veterans. Act Oct. 28, 1992, P. L. 102-547, § 8(b), 106 Stat. 3640, which formerly appeared as a note to this section, was repealed by Act June 15, 2006, P. L. 109-233, Title I, § 103(c)(2), 120 Stat. 400. It required the Secretary of Veterans Affairs to consider the views and recommendations, if any, of the Advisory Committee on Native-American Veterans in carrying out the direct housing loan pilot program.

CODE OF FEDERAL REGULATIONS

Department of Veterans Affairs—Loan guaranty and vocational rehabilitation and counseling programs, 48 CFR 871.100 et seq.

RESEARCH GUIDE

Other Treatises:

Cohen's Handbook of Federal Indian Law (Matthew Bender), ch 22, Government Services for Indians § 22.05.

§ 3762. Direct housing loans to Native American veterans; program administration

(a) The Secretary may make a direct housing loan to a Native American veteran under this subchapter [38 USCS §§ 3761 et seq.] if—

(1)(A) the Secretary has entered into a memorandum of understanding with respect to such loans with the tribal organization that has jurisdiction over the veteran; or

(B) the tribal organization that has jurisdiction over the veteran has entered into a memorandum of understanding with any department or agency of the United States with respect to direct housing loans to Native Americans that the Secretary determines substantially complies with the requirements of subsection (b); and

(2) [Unchanged]

(b)(1) Subject to paragraph (2), the Secretary shall ensure that each memorandum of understanding that the Secretary enters into with a tribal organization shall provide for the following:

(A)–(D) [Unchanged]

(E) That the tribal organization agrees to such other terms and conditions with respect to the making of direct loans to Native American veterans under the jurisdiction of the tribal organization as the Secretary may require in order to ensure that loans under this subchapter [38 USCS §§ 3761 et seq.] are made in a responsible and prudent manner.

(2) [Unchanged]

(c)(1)(A) Except as provided in subparagraph (B), the principal amount of any direct housing loan made to a Native American veteran under this section may not exceed $80,000.

(B)(i) Subject to clause (ii), the Secretary may make loans exceeding the amount specified in subparagraph (A) in a geographic area if the Secretary determines that housing costs in the area are significantly higher than average housing costs nationwide. The amount of such increase shall be the amount that the Secretary determines is necessary in order to make direct housing loans under this subchapter [38 USCS §§ 3761 et seq.] to Native American veterans who are located in a variety of geographic areas and in geographic areas experiencing a variety of economic conditions.

(ii) The amount of a loan made by the Secretary under this subchapter [38 USCS §§ 3761 et seq.] may not exceed the maximum loan amount authorized for loans guaranteed under section 3703(a)(1)(C) of this title [38 USCS § 3703(a)(1)(C)].

(2), (3) [Unchanged]

(d)–(h) [Unchanged]

(i)(1) The Secretary shall, in consultation with tribal organizations (including the National Congress of American Indians and the National American Indian Housing Council), carry out an outreach program to inform and educate Native American veterans of the availability of direct housing loans for Native American veterans who live on trust lands.

(2) Activities under the outreach program shall include the following:

(A) Attending conferences and conventions conducted by the National Congress of American Indians in order to work with the National Congress in providing information and training to tribal organizations and Native American veterans regarding the availability of housing benefits under this subchapter [38 USCS §§ 3761 et seq.] and in assisting such organizations and veterans with respect to such housing benefits.

(B)–(D) [Unchanged]

(E) Assisting tribal organizations and Native American veterans with respect to such benefits.

(F) [Unchanged]

(j) The Secretary shall include as part of the annual benefits report of the Veterans Benefits Administration information concerning the cost and number of loans provided under this subchapter [38 USCS §§ 3761 et seq.] for the fiscal year covered by the report.

(As amended Dec. 27, 2001, P. L. 107-103, Title IV, § 402(b), (c), 115 Stat. 993; June 15, 2006, P. L. 109-233, Title I, § 103(b), (c)(1), (d), (e), (f)(3), 120 Stat. 400, 401.)

HISTORY; ANCILLARY LAWS AND DIRECTIVES

Amendments:

2001. Act Dec. 27, 2001, in subsec. (a)(1), designated the existing provisions as subpara. (A) and, in such subparagraph, substituted "or" for "and", and added subpara. (B); and, in subsec. (j), in the introductory matter, substituted "2006" for "2002".

2006. Act June 15, 2006, substituted the section heading for one which read: "§ 3762. Direct housing loans to Native American veterans"; in subsec. (a), in the introductory matter, inserted "under this subchapter"; in subsec. (b)(1)(E), substituted "loans under this subchapter are made" for "the pilot program established under this subchapter is implemented"; in subsec. (c)(1), in subpara. (A), inserted "veteran", and, in subpara. (B), designated the existing provisions as cl. (i) and, in such clause as so designated, substituted "Subject to clause (ii), the" for "The", and substituted "make direct housing loans under this subchapter" for "carry out the pilot program under this subchapter in a manner that demonstrates the advisability of making direct housing loans", and added cl. (ii); in subsec. (i), in para. (1), deleted "the pilot program provided for under this subchapter and" preceding "the availability", and, in para. (2), in subpara. (A), substituted "under this subchapter and in assisting such organizations and veterans with respect to such housing benefits" for "under the pilot program and in assisting such organizations and veterans in participating in the pilot program", and, in subpara. (E), substituted "with respect to such benefits" for "in participating in the pilot program"; and substituted subsec. (j) for one which read:

"(j) Not later than February 1 of each year through 2006, the Secretary shall transmit to the Committees on Veterans' Affairs of the Senate and House of Representatives a report relating to the implementation of the pilot program under this subchapter during the fiscal year preceding the date of the report. Each such report shall include the following:

"(1) The Secretary's exercise during such fiscal year of the authority provided under subsection (c)(1)(B) to make loans exceeding the maximum loan amount.

"(2) The appraisals performed for the Secretary during such fiscal year under the authority of subsection (d)(2), including a description of—

"(A) the manner in which such appraisals were performed;

"(B) the qualifications of the appraisers who performed such appraisals; and

"(C) the actions taken by the Secretary with respect to such appraisals to protect the interests of veterans and the United States.

"(3) The outreach activities undertaken under subsection (i) during such fiscal year, including—

"(A) a description of such activities on a region-by-region basis; and

"(B) an assessment of the effectiveness of such activities in encouraging the participation of Native American veterans in the pilot program.

"(4) The pool of Native American veterans who are eligible for participation in the pilot program, including—

"(A) a description and analysis of the pool, including income demographics;

"(B) a description and assessment of the impediments, if any, to full participation in the pilot program of the Native American veterans in the pool; and

38 USCS § 3762 VETERANS' BENEFITS

"(C) the impact of low-cost housing programs operated by the Department of Housing and Urban Development and other Federal or State agencies on the demand for direct loans under this section.

"(5) The Secretary's recommendations, if any, for additional legislation regarding the pilot program.".

RESEARCH GUIDE

Other Treatises:

Cohen's Handbook of Federal Indian Law (Matthew Bender), ch 22, Government Services for Indians § 22.05.

§ 3763. Native American Veteran Housing Loan Program Account

(a) There is hereby established in the Treasury of the United States an account known as the "Native American Veteran Housing Loan Program Account" (hereinafter in this subchapter [38 USCS §§ 3761 et seq.] referred to as the "Account").

(b) [Unchanged]

(As amended Nov. 11, 1998, P. L. 105-368, Title VI, § 602(e)(3)(B), 112 Stat. 3347; June 5, 2001, P. L. 107-14, § 8(a)(16), 115 Stat. 35.)

HISTORY; ANCILLARY LAWS AND DIRECTIVES

Amendments:

1998. Act Nov. 11, 1998 (effective on 10/1/98, as provided by § 602(f) of such Act, which appears as 38 USCS § 2106 note) substituted the section heading for one which read: "§ 3763. Housing loan program account".

2001. Act June 5, 2001, in subsec. (a), substituted "hereinafter" for "hereafter".

§ 3764. Qualified non-Native American veterans

(a) **Treatment of non-Native American veterans.** Subject to the succeeding provisions of this section, for purposes of this subchapter [38 USCS §§ 3761 et seq.]—

(1) a qualified non-Native American veteran is deemed to be a Native American veteran; and

(2) for purposes of applicability to a non-Native American veteran, any reference in this subchapter [38 USCS §§ 3761 et seq.] to the jurisdiction of a tribal organization over a Native American veteran is deemed to be a reference to jurisdiction of a tribal organization over the Native American spouse of the qualified non-Native American veteran.

(b) **Use of loan.** In making direct loans under this subchapter [38 USCS §§ 3761 et seq.] to a qualified non-Native American veteran by reason of eligibility under subsection (a), the Secretary shall ensure that the tribal organization permits, and the qualified non-Native American veteran actually holds, possesses, or purchases, using the proceeds of the loan, jointly with the Native American spouse of the qualified non-Native American veteran, a meaningful interest in the lot, dwelling, or both, that is located on trust land.

(c) **Restrictions imposed by tribal organizations.** Nothing in subsection (b) shall be construed as precluding a tribal organization from imposing reasonable restrictions on the right of the qualified non-Native American veteran to convey, assign, or otherwise dispose of such interest in the lot or dwelling, or both, if such restrictions are designed to ensure the continuation in trust status of the lot or dwelling, or both. Such requirements may include the termination of the interest of the qualified non-Native American veteran in the lot or dwelling, or both, upon the dissolution of the marriage of the qualified non-Native American veteran to the Native American spouse.

(Added June 15, 2006, P. L. 109-233, Title I, § 104(a)(2), 120 Stat. 401.)

HISTORY; ANCILLARY LAWS AND DIRECTIVES

Explanatory notes:

A prior 38 USCS § 3764 was redesignated 38 USCS § 3765.

RESEARCH GUIDE

Other Treatises:

Cohen's Handbook of Federal Indian Law (Matthew Bender), ch 22, Government Services for Indians § 22.05.

§ 3765. Definitions

For the purposes of this subchapter [38 USCS §§ 3761 et seq.]—

(1) The term "trust land" means any land that—

(A) is held in trust by the United States for Native Americans;

(B) is subject to restrictions on alienation imposed by the United States on Indian lands (including native Hawaiian homelands);

(C) is owned by a Regional Corporation or a Village Corporation, as such terms are defined in section 3(g) and 3(j) of the Alaska Native Claims Settlement Act, respectively (43 U.S.C. 1602(g), (j)); or

(D) is on any island in the Pacific Ocean if such land is, by cultural tradition, communally-owned land, as determined by the Secretary.

(2) The term "Native American veteran" means any veteran who is a Native American.

(3) The term "Native American" means—

(A) an Indian, as defined in section 4(d) of the Indian Self-Determination and Education Assistance Act (25 U.S.C. 450b(d));

(B) a native Hawaiian, as that term is defined in section 201(a)(7) of the Hawaiian Homes Commission Act, 1920 (Public Law 67-34; 42 Stat. 108);

(C) an Alaska Native, within the meaning provided for the term "Native" in section 3(b) of the Alaska Native Claims Settlement Act (43 U.S.C. 1602(b)); and

(D) a Pacific Islander, within the meaning of the Native American Programs Act of 1974 (42 U.S.C. 2991 et seq.).

(4) The term "tribal organization" shall have the meaning given such term in section 4(l) of the Indian Self-Determination and Education Assistance Act (25 U.S.C. 450b(l)) and shall include the Department of Hawaiian Homelands, in the case of native Hawaiians, and such other organizations as the Secretary may prescribe.

(5) The term "qualified non-Native American veteran" means a veteran who—

(A) is the spouse of a Native American, but

(B) is not a Native American.

(Added Oct. 28, 1992, P. L. 102-547, § 8(a), 106 Stat. 3639; June 15, 2006, P. L. 109-233, Title I, § 104(a)(1), (b), 120 Stat. 401, 402.)

HISTORY; ANCILLARY LAWS AND DIRECTIVES

References in text:
"Section 201(a)(7) of the Hawaiian Homes Commission Act, 1920 (Public Law 67-34; 42 Stat. 108)", referred to in this section, is § 201(a)(7) of Act July 9, 1921, ch 42, which is classified to 48 USCS § 692. Such section has been omitted from the Code as obsolete.

Explanatory notes:
This section formerly appeared as 38 USCS § 3764.

Amendments:
2006. Act June 15, 2006, redesignated this section, enacted as 38 USCS § 3764, as 38 USCS § 3765; and added para. (5).

SUBCHAPTER VI. [TRANSFERRED]

HISTORY; ANCILLARY LAWS AND DIRECTIVES

This subchapter (former 38 USCS §§ 3771 et seq.), relating to loan guarantees for multifamily transitional housing for homeless veterans, was transferred, except for § 3771, to Chapter 20 (38 USCS §§ 2051 et seq.) by Act Dec. 21, 2001, P. L. 107-95, § 5(d)(1), 115 Stat. 918.

[§ 3771. Repealed]

HISTORY; ANCILLARY LAWS AND DIRECTIVES

This section (Act Nov. 11, 1998, P. L. 105-368, Title VI, § 601(a), 112 Stat. 3342) was repealed by Act Dec. 21, 2001, P. L. 107-95, § 5(d)(3). It provided definitions for purposes of former 38 USCS §§ 3771 et seq.

[§ 3772. Transferred]

HISTORY; ANCILLARY LAWS AND DIRECTIVES

This section was transferred to Chapter 20 and redesignated 38 USCS § 2051 by Act Dec. 21, 2001, P. L. 107-95, § 5(d)(1), 115 Stat. 918.

[§ 3773. Transferred]

HISTORY; ANCILLARY LAWS AND DIRECTIVES

This section was transferred to Chapter 20 and redesignated 38 USCS § 2052 by Act Dec. 21, 2001, P. L. 107-95, § 5(d)(1), 115 Stat. 918.

38 USCS § 3774

[§ 3774. Transferred]

HISTORY; ANCILLARY LAWS AND DIRECTIVES

This section was transferred to Chapter 20 and redesignated 38 USCS § 2053 by Act Dec. 21, 2001, P. L. 107-95, § 5(d)(1), 115 Stat. 918.

[§ 3775. Transferred]

HISTORY; ANCILLARY LAWS AND DIRECTIVES

This section was transferred to Chapter 20 and redesignated 38 USCS § 2054 by Act Dec. 21, 2001, P. L. 107-95, § 5(d)(1), 115 Stat. 918.

CHAPTER 39. AUTOMOBILES AND ADAPTIVE EQUIPMENT FOR CERTAIN DISABLED VETERANS AND MEMBERS OF THE ARMED FORCES

§ 3901. Definitions

For purposes of this chapter [38 USCS §§ 3901 et seq.]:

(1) The term "eligible person" means the following:

(A) Any veteran entitled to compensation under chapter 11 of this title [38 USCS §§ 1101 et seq.] for any of the following disabilities, if the disability is the result of any injury incurred or disease contracted in or aggravated by active military, naval, or air service:

  (i) The loss or permanent loss of use of one or both feet.

  (ii) The loss or permanent loss of use of one or both hands.

  (iii) The permanent impairment of vision of both eyes of the following status: central visual acuity of 20/200 or less in the better eye, with corrective glasses, or central visual acuity of more than 20/200 if there is a field defect in which the peripheral field has contracted to such an extent that the widest diameter of visual field subtends an angular distance no greater than twenty degrees in the better eye.

  (iv) A severe burn injury (as determined pursuant to regulations prescribed by the Secretary).

(B) Any member of the Armed Forces serving on active duty who is suffering from any disability described in clause (i), (ii), (iii), or (iv) of subparagraph (A) of this paragraph if such disability is the result of an injury incurred or disease contracted in or aggravated by active military, naval, or air service.

(2) [Unchanged]

(As amended Oct. 13, 2010, P. L. 111-275, Title VIII, § 803(a), (b), 124 Stat. 2889.)

HISTORY; ANCILLARY LAWS AND DIRECTIVES

Amendments:

2010. Act Oct. 13, 2010 (effective on 10/1/2011, as provided by § 803(c) of such Act, which appears as a note to this section), in the introductory matter, substituted "chapter:" for "chapter—", in para. (1), in the introductory matter, substituted "means the following: for "means—", in subpara. (A), in the introductory matter, substituted "Any veteran" for "any veteran" and "the following disabilities" for "the disabilities described in subclause (i), (ii), or (iii) below", in cls. (i) and (ii), substituted the concluding period for a semicolon, in cl. (iii), substituted the concluding period for "; or", and added cl. (iv), and in subpara. (B), substituted "Any member" for "any member" and "clause (i), (ii), (iii), or (iv) of subparagraph (A)" for "subclause (i), (ii), or (iii) of clause (A) of this paragraph".

Other provisions:

Effective date of Oct. 13, 2010 amendments. Act Oct. 13, 2010, P. L. 111-275, Title VIII, § 803(c), 124 Stat. 2889, provides: "The amendments made by this section [amending para. (1) of this section] shall take effect on October 1, 2011.".

RESEARCH GUIDE

Am Jur:

77 Am Jur 2d, Veterans and Veterans' Laws § 75.

INTERPRETIVE NOTES AND DECISIONS

2. Adaptive equipment

Board erred by interpreting General Counsel opinion to bar section 1151 beneficiary from eligibility for either special housing adaption grant or grant for acquiring automobile and adaptive equipment as result of disability caused by VA medical care, as well as in failing to look to language of sections 3901 and 3902 in determine appellants's entitlement to such benefits and was thus deficient in terms of adequate statement of reasons or bases; GC opinion did not examine chapter 39 statutory provisions or provide any basis for determining that eligibility under it is condition on veteran's having service-connected condition. Kilpatrick v Principi (2002) 16 Vet App 1,

2002 US App Vet Claims LEXIS 79, affd (2003, CA FC) 327 F3d 1375.

§ 3902. Assistance for providing automobile and adaptive equipment

(a) The Secretary, under regulations which the Secretary shall prescribe, shall provide or assist in providing an automobile or other conveyance to each eligible person by paying the total purchase price of the automobile or other conveyance (including all State, local, and other taxes) or $18,900 (as adjusted from time to time under subsection (e)), whichever is the lesser, to the seller from whom the eligible person is purchasing under a sales agreement between the seller and the eligible person.

(b)–(d) [Unchanged]

(e) Effective on October 1 of each year (beginning in 2011), the Secretary shall increase the dollar amount in effect under subsection (a) by a percentage equal to the percentage by which the Consumer Price Index for all urban consumers (U.S. city average) increased during the 12-month period ending with the last month for which Consumer Price Index data is available. In the event that such Consumer Price Index does not increase during such period, the Secretary shall maintain the dollar amount in effect under subsection (a) during the previous fiscal year.

(As amended Dec. 27, 2001, P. L. 107-103, Title V, § 503, 115 Stat. 995; Dec. 16, 2003, P. L. 108-183, Title IV, § 402(b), 117 Stat. 2664; Oct. 13, 2010, P. L. 111-275, Title VIII, § 804(a), (b), 124 Stat. 2889.)

HISTORY; ANCILLARY LAWS AND DIRECTIVES

Amendments:

2001. Act Dec. 27, 2001, in subsec. (a), substituted "$9,000" for "$8,000".

2003. Act Dec. 16, 2003 (applicable with respect to assistance furnished on or after enactment, as provided by § 402(c) of such Act, which appears as 38 USCS § 2102 note), in subsec. (a), substituted "$11,000" for "$9,000".

2010. Act Oct. 13, 2010 (effective on 10/1/2011, as provided by § 804(c) of such Act, which appears as a note to this section), in subsec. (a), substituted "$18,900 (as adjusted from time to time under subsection (e))" for "$11,000"; and added subsec. (e).

Other provisions:

Effective date of Oct. 13, 2010 amendments. Act Oct. 13, 2010, P. L. 111-275, Title VIII, § 804(c), 124 Stat. 2890, provides: "The amendments made by this section [amending subsec. (a) and adding subsec. (e) of this section] shall take effect on October 1, 2011.".

RESEARCH GUIDE

Am Jur:

77 Am Jur 2d, Veterans and Veterans' Laws § 75.

INTERPRETIVE NOTES AND DECISIONS

Veteran's widow was not entitled to receive automobile purchase assistance as accrued benefit to which veteran was entitled before his death, since record did not show that certificate of eligibility was ever issued or that veteran entered into sales agreement to purchase automobile between time his eligibility was established and his death; 38 USCS § 5121 accrued benefits are paid to veteran's surviving spouse, children, or dependent parent, or person who bore expense of last sickness and burial, while automobile purchase assistance payment is made to seller of automobile. Gillis v West (1998) 11 Vet App 441.

Board erred by interpreting General Counsel opinion to bar section 1151 beneficiary from eligibility for either special housing adaption grant or grant for acquiring automobile and adaptive equipment as result of disability caused by VA medical care, as well as in failing to look to language of sections 3901 and 3902 in determine appellants's entitlement to such benefits and was thus deficient in terms of adequate statement of reasons or bases; GC opinion did not examine chapter 39 statutory provisions or provide any basis for determining that eligibility under it is condition on veteran's having service-connected condition. Kilpatrick v Principi (2002) 16 Vet App 1, 2002 US App Vet Claims LEXIS 79, affd (2003, CA FC) 327 F3d 1375.

§ 3903. Limitations on assistance; special training courses

(a)(1) Except as provided in paragraph (2), no eligible person shall be entitled to receive more than one automobile or other conveyance under the provisions of this chapter [38 USCS §§ 3901 et seq.], and no payment shall be made under this chapter [38 USCS §§ 3901 et seq.] for the repair, maintenance, or replacement of an automobile or other conveyance.

(2) [**Caution: This paragraph takes effect 1 year after enactment of Act Aug. 6, 2012, P. L. 112-154, as provided by § 701(g) of such Act, which appears as 38 USCS § 2109 note.**] The Secretary may provide or assist in providing an eligible person with a second automobile or other conveyance under this chapter [38 USCS §§ 3901 et seq.] if—

(A) the Secretary receives satisfactory evidence that the automobile or other conveyance previously purchased with assistance under this chapter [38 USCS §§ 3901 et seq.] was destroyed—

(i) as a result of a natural or other disaster, as determined by the Secretary; and

(ii) through no fault of the eligible person; and

(B) the eligible person does not otherwise receive from a property insurer compensation for the loss.

(b)–(d) [Unchanged]

(e)(1) [Unchanged]

(2) The Secretary is authorized to obtain insurance on automobiles and other conveyances used in conducting the special driver training courses provided under this subsection and to obtain, at Government expense, personal liability and property damage insurance for all persons taking such courses without regard to whether such persons are taking the course on an in-patient or out-patient basis.

(3) [Unchanged]

(As amended Nov. 30, 1999, P. L. 106-117, Title VIII, § 804, 113 Stat. 1586; Aug. 6, 2012, P. L. 112-154, Title VII, § 701(e), 126 Stat. 1204.)

HISTORY; ANCILLARY LAWS AND DIRECTIVES

Amendments:

1999. Act Nov. 30, 1999, in subsec. (e)(2), deleted "(not owned by the Government)" after "conveyances".

2012. Act Aug. 6, 2012 (effective 8/6/2013, as provided by § 701(g) of such Act, which appears as 38 USCS § 2109 note), in subsec. (a), designated the existing provisions as para. (1), substituted "Except as provided in paragraph (2), no" for "No", and added para. (2).

RESEARCH GUIDE

Am Jur:

77 Am Jur 2d, Veterans and Veterans' Laws § 75.

§ 3904. Research and development

(a) [Unchanged]

(b) In carrying out subsection (a) of this section, the Secretary, through the Under Secretary for Health, shall consult and cooperate with the Secretary of Health and Human Services and the Secretary of Education, in connection with programs carried out under section 204(b)(3) of the Rehabilitation Act of 1973 [29 USCS § 764(b)(3)] (relating to the establishment and support of Rehabilitation Engineering Research Centers).

(As amended Aug. 7, 1998, P. L. 105-220, Title IV, § 414(c), 112 Stat. 1242.)

HISTORY; ANCILLARY LAWS AND DIRECTIVES

Amendments:

1998. Act Aug. 7, 1998 (effective on enactment, as provided by § 507 of such Act, which appears as 20 USCS § 9201 note), in subsec. (b), substituted "section 204(b)(3) of the Rehabilitation Act of 1973 (relating to the establishment and support of Rehabilitation Engineering Research Centers)" for "section 204(b)(2) of the Rehabilitation Act of 1973 (29 U.S.C. 762(b)(2)) (relating to the establishment and support of Rehabilitation Engineering Research Centers)".

RESEARCH GUIDE

Am Jur:

77 Am Jur 2d, Veterans and Veterans' Laws § 75.

CHAPTER 41. JOB COUNSELING, TRAINING, AND PLACEMENT SERVICE FOR VETERANS

Section

4102A. Assistant Secretary of Labor for Veterans' Employment and Training; program functions; Regional Administrators.

4103. Directors and Assistant Directors for Veterans' Employment and Training; additional Federal personnel.

4104A. Collaborative veterans' training, mentoring, and placement program.

4110. Advisory Committee on Veterans Employment, Training, and Employer Outreach.

4110B. Coordination and nonduplication.

[4111. Repealed]

4112. Performance incentive awards for quality employment, training, and placement services.

4113. Transition Assistance Program personnel

4114. Credentialing and licensure of veterans: demonstration project.
[4115–4419. Repealed]
[4120. Transferred]

HISTORY; ANCILLARY LAWS AND DIRECTIVES

Amendments:
1999. Act Nov. 30, 1999, P. L. 106-117, Title IX, § 901(b), 113 Stat. 1587, amended the analysis of this chapter by adding item 4111.
2000. Act Nov. 1, 2000, P. L. 106-419, Title IV, § 404(a)(8), 114 Stat. 1865, amended the analysis of this chapter by adding item 4110B.
2001. Act Dec. 21, 2001, P. L. 107-95, § 5(g)(3), 115 Stat. 919, amended the analysis of this chapter by deleting item 4111, which read: "4111. Homeless veterans' reintegration programs.".
2002. Act Nov. 7, 2002, P. L. 107-288, §§ 3(b), 4(a)(2), (3)(A)(ii), 116 Stat. 2038, 2042, amended the analysis of this chapter by substituting items 4102A and 4103 for ones which read: "4102A. Assistant Secretary of Labor for Veterans' Employment and Training; Regional Administrators.
"4103. Directors and Assistant Directors for Veterans' Employment and Training.", deleting item 4104A, which read: "4104A. Performance of disabled veterans' outreach program specialists and local veterans' employment representatives.", and adding item 4112.
2003. Act Dec. 16, 2003, P. L. 108-183, Title III, § 309(a)(2), 117 Stat. 2663, amended the analysis of this chapter by adding item 4113.
2006. Act June 15, 2006, P. L. 109-233, Title II, § 202(a)(3), 120 Stat. 403, amended the analysis of this chapter by substituting item 4110 for one which read: "4110. Advisory Committee on Veterans Employment and Training.".
Act Dec. 22, 2006, P. L. 109-461, Title VI, § 604(a)(2), 120 Stat. 3439, amended the analysis of this chapter by adding item 4114.
2011. Act Nov. 11, 2011, P. L. 112-56, Title II, Subtitle B, § 223(a)(2), Subtitle C, § 234(c), 125 Stat. 718, 722, amended the analysis of this chapter by adding item 4104A and by substituting item 4113 for one which read: "4113. Outstationing of Transition Assistance Program personnel".

§ 4100. Findings

HISTORY; ANCILLARY LAWS AND DIRECTIVES

Other provisions:
Committee to raise employer awareness of skills of veterans and benefits of hiring veterans.
Act Nov. 7, 2002, P. L. 107-288, § 6, 116 Stat. 2046, provides:
"(a) Establishment of Committee. There is established within the Department of Labor a committee to be known as the President's National Hire Veterans Committee (hereinafter in this section referred to as the 'Committee').
"(b) Duties. The Committee shall establish and carry out a national program to do the following:
"(1) To furnish information to employers with respect to the training and skills of veterans and disabled veterans, and the advantages afforded employers by hiring veterans with such training and skills.
"(2) To facilitate employment of veterans and disabled veterans through participation in America's Career Kit national labor exchange, and other means.
"(c) Membership. (1) The Secretary of Labor shall appoint 15 individuals to serve as members of the Committee, of whom one shall be appointed from among representatives nominated by each organization described in subparagraph (A) and of whom eight shall be appointed from among representatives nominated by organizations described in subparagraph (B).
"(A) Organizations described in this subparagraph are the following:
"(i) The Ad Council.
"(ii) The National Committee for Employer Support of the Guard and Reserve.
"(iii) Veterans' service organizations that have a national employment program.
"(iv) State employment security agencies.
"(v) One-stop career centers.
"(vi) State departments of veterans affairs.
"(vii) Military service organizations.
"(B) Organizations described in this subparagraph are such businesses, small businesses, industries, companies in the private sector that furnish placement services, civic groups, workforce investment boards, and labor unions as the Secretary of Labor determines appropriate.
"(2) The following shall be ex officio, nonvoting members of the Committee:
"(A) The Secretary of Veterans Affairs.
"(B) The Secretary of Defense.
"(C) The Assistant Secretary of Labor for Veterans' Employment and Training.
"(D) The Administrator of the Small Business Administration.

"(E) The Postmaster General.

"(F) The Director of the Office of Personnel Management.

"(3) A vacancy in the Committee shall be filled in the manner in which the original appointment was made.

"(d) Administrative matters. (1) The Committee shall meet not less frequently than once each calendar quarter.

"(2) The Secretary of Labor shall appoint the chairman of the Committee.

"(3)(A) Members of the Committee shall serve without compensation.

"(B) Members of the Committee shall be allowed reasonable and necessary travel expenses, including per diem in lieu of subsistence, at rates authorized for persons serving intermittently in the Government service in accordance with the provisions of subchapter I of chapter 57 of title 5 [5 USCS §§ 5701 et seq.] while away from their homes or regular places of business in the performance of the responsibilities of the Committee.

"(4) The Secretary of Labor shall provide staff and administrative support to the Committee to assist it in carrying out its duties under this section. The Secretary shall assure positions on the staff of the Committee include positions that are filled by individuals that are now, or have ever been, employed as one of the following:

"(A) Staff of the Assistant Secretary of Labor for Veterans' Employment and Training under section 4102A of title 38, United States Code as in effect on the date of the enactment of this Act.

"(B) Directors for Veterans' Employment and Training under section 4103 of such title as in effect on such date.

"(C) Assistant Director for Veterans' Employment and Training under such section as in effect on such date.

"(D) Disabled veterans' outreach program specialists under section 4103A of such title as in effect on such date.

"(E) Local veterans' employment representatives under section 4104 of such title as in effect on such date.

"(5) Upon request of the Committee, the head of any Federal department or agency may detail, on a nonreimbursable basis, any of the personnel of that department or agency to the Committee to assist it in carrying out its duties.

"(6) The Committee may contract with and compensate government and private agencies or persons to furnish information to employers under subsection (b)(1) without regard to section 3709 of the Revised Statutes (41 U.S.C. 5) [41 USCS § 6101].

"(e) Report. Not later than December 31, 2003, 2004, and 2005, the Secretary of Labor shall submit to Congress a report on the activities of the Committee under this section during the previous fiscal year, and shall include in such report data with respect to placement and retention of veterans in jobs attributable to the activities of the Committee.

"(f) Termination. The Committee shall terminate 60 days after submitting the report that is due on December 31, 2005.

"(g) Authorization of appropriations. There are authorized to be appropriated to the Secretary of Labor from the employment security administration account (established in section 901 of the Social Security Act (42 U.S.C. 1101)) in the Unemployment Trust Fund $3,000,000 for each of fiscal years 2003 through 2005 to carry out this section.

Report on implementation of employment reforms. Act Nov. 7, 2002, P. L. 107-288, § 7, 116 Stat. 2048, provides:

"(a) Study. The Comptroller General of the United States shall conduct a study on the implementation by the Secretary of Labor of the provisions of this Act during the program years that begin during fiscal years 2003 and 2004. The study shall include an assessment of the modifications under sections 2 through 5 of this Act [for full classification, consult USCS Tables volumes] of the provisions of title 38, United States Code, and an evaluation of the impact of those modifications, and of the actions of the President's National Hire Veterans Committee under section 6 of this Act [note to this section], to the provision of employment, training, and placement services provided to veterans under that title.

"(b) Report. Not later than 6 months after the conclusion of the program year that begins during fiscal year 2004, the Comptroller General shall submit to Congress a report on the study conducted under subsection (a). The report shall include such recommendations as the Comptroller General determines appropriate, including recommendations for legislation or administrative action.".

Veterans retraining assistance program. Act Nov. 21, 2011, P. L. 112-56, Title II, Subtitle A, § 211, 125 Stat. 713, provides:

"(a) Program authorized. (1) In general. Not later than July 1, 2012, the Secretary of Veterans Affairs shall, in collaboration with the Secretary of Labor, establish and commence a program of retraining assistance for eligible veterans.

"(2) Number of eligible veterans. The number of unique eligible veterans who participate in the program established under paragraph (1) may not exceed—

"(A) 45,000 during fiscal year 2012; and

"(B) 54,000 during the period beginning October 1, 2012, and ending March 31, 2014.

"(b) Retraining assistance. Except as provided by subsection (k), each veteran who participates in the program established under subsection (a)(1) shall be entitled to up to 12 months of retraining assistance provided by the Secretary of Veterans Affairs. Such retraining assistance may only be used by the veteran to pursue a program of education (as such term is defined in section 3452(b) of title 38, United States Code) for training, on a full-time basis, that—

"(1) is approved under chapter 36 of such title [38 USCS §§ 3670 et seq.];

"(2) is offered by a community college or technical school;

"(3) leads to an associate degree or a certificate (or other similar evidence of the completion of the program of education or training);

"(4) is designed to provide training for a high-demand occupation, as determined by the Commissioner of Labor Statistics; and

"(5) begins on or after July 1, 2012.

"(c) Monthly certification. Each veteran who participates in the program established under subsection (a)(1) shall certify to the Secretary of Veterans Affairs the enrollment of the veteran in a program of education described in subsection (b) for each month in which the veteran participates in the program.

"(d) Amount of assistance. The monthly amount of the retraining assistance payable under this section is the amount in effect under section 3015(a)(1) of title 38, United States Code.

"(e) Eligibility. (1) In general. For purposes of this section, an eligible veteran is a veteran who—

"(A) as of the date of the submittal of the application for assistance under this section, is at least 35 years of age but not more than 60 years of age;

"(B) was last discharged from active duty service in the Armed Forces under conditions other than dishonorable;

"(C) as of the date of the submittal of the application for assistance under this section, is unemployed;

"(D) as of the date of the submittal of the application for assistance under this section, is not eligible to receive educational assistance under chapter 30, 31, 32, 33, or 35 of title 38, United States Code [38 USCS §§ 3001 et seq., 3100 et seq., 3201 et seq., 3301 et seq., or 3500 et seq.], or chapter 1606 or 1607 of title 10, United States Code [10 USCS §§ 16131 et seq. or 16161 et seq.];

"(E) is not in receipt of compensation for a service-connected disability rated totally disabling by reason of unemployability;

"(F) was not and is not enrolled in any Federal or State job training program at any time during the 180-day period ending on the date of the submittal of the application for assistance under this section; and

"(G) by not later than October 1, 2013, submits to the Secretary of Labor an application for assistance under this section containing such information and assurances as that Secretary may require.

"(2) Determination of eligibility. (A) Determination by Secretary of Labor. (i) In general. For each application for assistance under this section received by the Secretary of Labor from an applicant, the Secretary of Labor shall determine whether the applicant is eligible for such assistance under subparagraphs (A), (C), (F), and (G) of paragraph (1).

"(ii) Referral to Secretary of Veterans Affairs. If the Secretary of Labor determines under clause (i) that an applicant is eligible for assistance under this section, the Secretary of Labor shall forward the application of such applicant to the Secretary of Veterans Affairs in accordance with the terms of the agreement required by subsection (h).

"(B) Determination by Secretary of Veterans Affairs. For each application relating to an applicant received by the Secretary of Veterans Affairs under subparagraph (A)(ii), the Secretary of Veterans Affairs shall determine under subparagraphs (B), (D), and (E) of paragraph (1) whether such applicant is eligible for assistance under this section.

"(f) Employment assistance. For each veteran who participates in the program established under subsection (a)(1), the Secretary of Labor shall contact such veteran not later than 30 days after the date on which the veteran completes, or terminates participation in, such program to facilitate employment of such veteran and availability or provision of employment placement services to such veteran.

"(g) Charging of assistance against other entitlement. Assistance provided under this section shall be counted against the aggregate period for which section 3695 of title 38, United States Code, limits the individual's receipt of educational assistance under laws administered by the Secretary of Veterans Affairs.

"(h) Joint agreement. (1) In general. The Secretary of Veterans Affairs and the Secretary of Labor shall enter into an agreement to carry out this section.

"(2) Appeals process. The agreement required by paragraph (1) shall include establishment of a process for resolving disputes relating to and appeals of decisions of the Secretaries under subsection (e)(2).

"(i) Report. (1) In general. Not later than July 1, 2014, the Secretary of Veterans Affairs shall, in collaboration with the Secretary of Labor, submit to the appropriate committees of Congress a report on the retraining assistance provided under this section.

"(2) Elements. The report required by paragraph (1) shall include the following:
"(A) The total number of—
"(i) eligible veterans who participated; and
"(ii) associates degrees or certificates awarded (or other similar evidence of the completion of the program of education or training earned).
"(B) Data related to the employment status of eligible veterans who participated.
"(j) Funding. Payments under this section shall be made from amounts appropriated to or otherwise made available to the Department of Veterans Affairs for the payment of readjustment benefits. Not more than $2,000,000 shall be made available from such amounts for information technology expenses (not including personnel costs) associated with the administration of the program established under subsection (a)(1).
"(k) Termination of authority. The authority to make payments under this section shall terminate on March 31, 2014.
"(l) Appropriate committees of Congress defined. In this section, the term 'appropriate committees of Congress' means—
"(1) the Committee on Veterans' Affairs and the Committee on Health, Education, Labor, and Pension of the Senate; and
"(2) the Committee on Veterans' Affairs and the Committee on Education and the Workforce of the House of Representatives.".

CODE OF FEDERAL REGULATIONS

Employment and Training Administration, Department of Labor—Administrative procedure, 20 CFR 601.1 et seq.
Employment and Training Administration, Department of Labor—Establishment and functioning of State employment services, 20 CFR 652.1 et seq.
Employment and Training Administration, Department of Labor—Services of the employment service system, 20 CFR 653.100 et seq.
Employment and Training Administration, Department of Labor—Administrative provisions governing the Job Service System, 20 CFR 658.400 et seq.
Office of the Assistant Secretary for Veterans' Employment and Training, Department of Labor—Services for veterans, 20 CFR 1001.100 et seq.

RESEARCH GUIDE

Am Jur:
77 Am Jur 2d, Veterans and Veterans' Laws § 99.

§ 4101. Definitions

For the purposes of this chapter [38 USCS §§ 4101 et seq.]—
(1)–(6) [Unchanged]
(7) The term "employment service delivery system" means a service delivery system at which or through which labor exchange services, including employment, training, and placement services, are offered in accordance with the Wagner-Peyser Act.
(8) [Unchanged]
(9) The term "intensive services" means local employment and training services of the type described in section 134(d)(3) of the Workforce Investment Act of 1998 [29 USCS § 2864(d)(3)].
(As amended Nov. 7, 2002, P. L. 107-288, § 5(a)(1)(A), (c)(1), 116 Stat. 2044, 2045.)

HISTORY; ANCILLARY LAWS AND DIRECTIVES

Amendments:
2002. Act Nov. 7, 2002 (effective on enactment, as provided by § 5(c)(2) of such Act, which appears as a note to this section), substituted para. (7) for one which read: "(7) The term 'local employment service office' means a service delivery point which has an intrinsic management structure and at which employment services are offered in accordance with the Wagner-Peyser Act.".
Such Act further (effective on enactment, as provided by § 5(a)(2) of such Act, which appears as a note to this section), added para. (9).

Other provisions:
Employment assistance and services for veterans ineligible for assistance under this chapter. Act Oct. 17, 1980, P. L. 96-466, Title V, § 512, 94 Stat. 2207 (effective 10/1/80, as provided by § 802(e) of such Act); Oct. 21, 1998, P. L. 105-277, Div A, § 101(f) [Title VIII, Subtitle IV, § 405(d)(28), (f)(20)], 112 Stat. 2681-424, 2681-432 (effective as provided by § 405(g) of Subtitle IV of Title VIII of § 101(f) of Division A of such Act, which appears as 5 USCS § 3502 note), provides: "The Secretary of Labor shall assure that any veteran who is made ineligible for employment assistance under chapter 41 of title 38, United States Code [38 USCS §§ 4101 et seq.], by virtue of the amendments made by section 503(1) of this Act shall be provided with the employment assistance and services made available under the provisions of the Act entitled 'An Act to provide for the establishment of a national employment system and for cooperation with the States in the promotion of such system, and for other purposes', approved June 6, 1933 (commonly referred to as the 'Wagner-Peyser Act'), (29 U.S.C. 49–49k),

title I of the Workforce Investment Act of 1998 [29 USCS §§ 2801 et seq. generally; for full classification, consult USCS Tables volumes] and other applicable provisions of law.".

Effective date of amendments made by § 5(a) of Act Nov. 7, 2002. Act Nov. 7, 2002, P. L. 107-288, § 5(a)(2), 116 Stat. 2044, provides: "The amendments made by paragraph (1) [amending 38 USCS §§ 4101, 4102, 4106, 4107, and 4109] shall take effect on the date of the enactment of this Act.".

Effective date of amendments made by § 5(c) of Act Nov. 7, 2002. Act Nov. 7, 2002, P. L. 107-288, § 5(c)(2), 116 Stat. 2045, provides: "The amendments made by paragraph (1) [amending para. (7) of this section] shall take effect on the date of the enactment of this Act.".

CODE OF FEDERAL REGULATIONS

Employment and Training Administration, Department of Labor—Administrative procedure, 20 CFR 601.1 et seq.
Employment and Training Administration, Department of Labor—Establishment and functioning of State employment services, 20 CFR 652.1 et seq.
Employment and Training Administration, Department of Labor—Services of the employment service system, 20 CFR 653.100 et seq.
Employment and Training Administration, Department of Labor—Administrative provisions governing the Job Service System, 20 CFR 658.400 et seq.

§ 4102. Purpose

The Congress declares as its intent and purpose that there shall be an effective (1) job and job training intensive services program, (2) employment placement service program, and (3) job training placement service program for eligible veterans and eligible persons and that, to this end policies and regulations shall be promulgated and administered by an Assistant Secretary of Labor for Veterans' Employment and Training, established by section 4102A of this title [38 USCS § 4102A], through a Veterans' Employment and Training Service within the Department of Labor, so as to provide such veterans and persons the maximum of employment and training opportunities, with priority given to the needs of disabled veterans and veterans who served on active duty during a war or in a campaign or expedition for which a campaign badge has been authorized through existing programs, coordination and merger of programs and implementation of new programs, including programs carried out by the Veterans' Employment and Training Service to implement all efforts to ease the transition of servicemembers to civilian careers that are consistent with, or an outgrowth of, the military experience of the servicemembers.
(As amended Nov. 7, 2002, P. L. 107-288, § 5(a)(1)(B), (b)(1), 116 Stat. 2044, 2045.)

HISTORY; ANCILLARY LAWS AND DIRECTIVES

Amendments:

2002. Act Nov. 7, 2002 (effective on enactment, as provided by § 5(a)(2) of such Act, which appears as 38 USCS § 4101 note), substituted "job and job training intensive services program," for "job and job training counseling service program,".

Such Act further (effective on enactment, as provided by § 5(b)(2) of such Act, which appears as a note to this section), substituted "and veterans who served on active duty during a war or in a campaign or expedition for which a campaign badge has been authorized" for "and veterans of the Vietnam era", and substituted ", including programs carried out by the Veterans' Employment and Training Service to implement all efforts to ease the transition of servicemembers to civilian careers that are consistent with, or an outgrowth of, the military experience of the servicemembers." for a concluding period.

Other provisions:

Effective date of amendments made by § 5(b)(1) of Act Nov. 2, 2002. Act Nov. 2, 2002, P. L. 107-288, § 5(b)(2), 116 Stat. 2045, provides: "The amendments made by paragraph (1) [amending this section] shall take effect on the date of the enactment of this Act.".

§ 4102A. Assistant Secretary of Labor for Veterans' Employment and Training; program functions; Regional Administrators

(a) Establishment of position of Assistant Secretary of Labor for Veterans' Employment and Training. (1) There is established within the Department of Labor an Assistant Secretary of Labor for Veterans' Employment and Training, appointed by the President by and with the advice and consent of the Senate, who shall formulate and implement all departmental policies and procedures to carry out (A) the purposes of this chapter, chapter 42, and chapter 43 of this title [38 USCS §§ 4100 et seq., 4201 et seq., 4301 et seq.], and (B) all other Department of Labor employment, unemployment, and training programs to the extent they affect veterans.

(2) The employees of the Department of Labor administering chapter 43 of this title [38 USCS §§ 4301 et seq.] shall be administratively and functionally responsible to the Assistant Secretary of Labor for Veterans' Employment and Training.

(3)(A) There shall be within the Department of Labor a Deputy Assistant Secretary of Labor for Veterans' Employment and Training. The Deputy Assistant Secretary shall perform such functions as the Assistant Secretary of Labor for Veterans' Employment and Training prescribes.

(B) No individual may be appointed as a Deputy Assistant Secretary of Labor for Veterans' Employment and Training unless the individual has at least five years of service in a management position as an employee of the Federal civil service or comparable service in a management position in the Armed Forces. For purposes of determining such service of an individual, there shall be excluded any service described in subparagraphs (A), (B), and (C) of section 308(d)(2) of this title [38 USCS § 308(d)(2)].

(b) Program functions. The Secretary shall carry out the following functions:

(1) Except as expressly provided otherwise, carry out all provisions of this chapter and chapter 43 of this title [38 USCS §§ 4100 et seq., 4301 et seq.] through the Assistant Secretary of Labor for Veterans' Employment and Training and administer through such Assistant Secretary all programs under the jurisdiction of the Secretary for the provision of employment and training services designed to meet the needs of all veterans and persons eligible for services furnished under this chapter [38 USCS §§ 4100 et seq.].

(2) In order to make maximum use of available resources in meeting such needs, encourage all such programs, and all grantees and contractors under such programs to enter into cooperative arrangements with private industry and business concerns (including small business concerns owned by veterans or disabled veterans), educational institutions, trade associations, and labor unions.

(3) Ensure that maximum effectiveness and efficiency are achieved in providing services and assistance to eligible veterans under all such programs by coordinating and consulting with the Secretary of Veterans Affairs with respect to (A) programs conducted under other provisions of this title, with particular emphasis on coordination of such programs with readjustment counseling activities carried out under section 1712A of this title [38 USCS § 1712A], apprenticeship or other on-the-job training programs carried out under section 3687 of this title [38 USCS § 3687], and rehabilitation and training activities carried out under chapter 31 of this title [38 USCS §§ 3100 et seq.] and (B) determinations covering veteran population in a State.

(4) Ensure that employment, training, and placement activities are carried out in coordination and cooperation with appropriate State public employment service officials.

(5) Subject to subsection (c), make available for use in each State by grant or contract such funds as may be necessary to support—

(A) disabled veterans' outreach program specialists appointed under section 4103A(a)(1) of this title [38 USCS § 4103A(a)(1)],

(B) local veterans' employment representatives assigned under section 4104(b) of this title [38 USCS § 4104(b)], and

(C) the reasonable expenses of such specialists and representatives described in subparagraphs (A) and (B), respectively, for training, travel, supplies, and other business expenses, including travel expenses and per diem for attendance at the National Veterans' Employment and Training Services Institute established under section 4109 of this title [38 USCS § 4109].

(6) Monitor and supervise on a continuing basis the distribution and use of funds provided for use in the States under paragraph (5).

(7) Establish, and update as appropriate, a comprehensive performance accountability system (as described in subsection (f)) and carry out annual performance reviews of veterans employment, training, and placement services provided through employment service delivery systems, including through disabled veterans' outreach program specialists and through local veterans' employment representatives in States receiving grants, contracts, or awards under this chapter [38 USCS §§ 4100 et seq.].

(8) With advice and assistance from the Advisory Committee on Veterans Employment, Training, and Employer Outreach established under section 4110 of this title [38 USCS § 4110], furnish information to employers (through meetings in person with hiring executives of corporations and otherwise) with respect to the training and skills of veterans and disabled veterans, and the advantages afforded employers by hiring veterans with such training and skills, and to facilitate employment of veterans and disabled veterans through participation in labor exchanges (Internet-based and otherwise), and other means.

(c) Conditions for receipt of funds. (1) The distribution and use of funds under subsection (b)(5) in order to carry out sections 4103A(a) and 4104(a) of this title [38 USCS §§ 4103A(a) and 4104(a)] shall be subject to the continuing supervision and monitoring of the Secretary and shall not be governed by the provisions of any other law, or any regulations prescribed thereunder, that are inconsistent with this section or section 4103A or 4104 of this title [38 USCS § 4103A or 4104].

(2)(A) A State shall submit to the Secretary an application for a grant or contract under subsection (b)(5). The application shall contain the following information:

(i) A plan that describes the manner in which the State shall furnish employment, training, and placement services required under this chapter [38 USCS §§ 4100 et seq.] for the program year, including a description of—

(I) duties assigned by the State to disabled veterans' outreach program specialists and local veterans' employment representatives consistent with the requirements of sections 4103A and 4104 of this title [38 USCS §§ 4103A and 4104];

(II) the manner in which such specialists and representatives are integrated in the employment service delivery systems in the State; and

(III) the program of performance incentive awards described in section 4112 of this title [38 USCS § 4112] in the State for the program year.

(ii) The veteran population to be served.

(iii) For each employee of the State who is assigned to perform the duties of a disabled veterans' outreach program specialist or a local veterans' employment representative under this chapter [38 USCS §§ 4100 et seq.]—

(I) the date on which the employee is so assigned; and

(II) whether the employee has satisfactorily completed such training by the National Veterans' Employment and Training Services Institute as the Secretary requires for purposes of paragraph (8).

(iv) Such additional information as the Secretary may require to make a determination with respect to awarding a grant or contract to the State.

(B)(i) Subject to the succeeding provisions of this subparagraph, of the amount available under subsection (b)(5) for a fiscal year, the Secretary shall make available to each State with an application approved by the Secretary an amount of funding in proportion to the number of veterans seeking employment using such criteria as the Secretary may establish in regulation, including civilian labor force and unemployment data, for the State on an annual basis. The proportion of funding shall reflect the ratio of—

(I) the total number of veterans residing in the State that are seeking employment; to

(II) the total number of veterans seeking employment in all States.

(ii) The Secretary shall phase in over the three fiscal-year period that begins on October 1, 2003, the manner in which amounts are made available to States under subsection (b)(5) and this subsection, as amended by the Jobs for Veterans Act.

(iii) In carrying out this paragraph, the Secretary may establish minimum funding levels and hold-harmless criteria for States.

(3)(A)(i) As a condition of a grant or contract under this section for a program year, in the case of a State that the Secretary determines has an entered-employment rate for veterans that is deficient for the preceding program year, the State shall develop a corrective action plan to improve that rate for veterans in the State.

(ii) The State shall submit the corrective action plan to the Secretary for approval, and if approved, shall expeditiously implement the plan.

(iii) If the Secretary does not approve a corrective action plan submitted by the State under clause (i), the Secretary shall take such steps as may be necessary to implement corrective actions in the State to improve the entered-employment rate for veterans in that State.

(B) To carry out subparagraph (A), the Secretary shall establish in regulations a uniform national threshold entered-employment rate for veterans for a program year by which determinations of deficiency may be made under subparagraph (A).

(C) In making a determination with respect to a deficiency under subparagraph (A), the Secretary shall take into account the applicable annual unemployment data for the State and consider other factors, such as prevailing economic conditions, that affect performance of individuals providing employment, training, and placement services in the State.

(4) In determining the terms and conditions of a grant or contract under which funds are made available to a State in order to carry out section 4103A or 4104 of this title [38 USCS § 4103A or 4104], the Secretary shall take into account—

(A) the results of reviews, carried out pursuant to subsection (b)(7), of the performance of the employment, training, and placement service delivery system in the State, and

(B) the monitoring carried out under this section.

(5) Each grant or contract by which funds are made available to a State shall contain a provision requiring the recipient of the funds—

(A) to comply with the provisions of this chapter [38 USCS §§ 4100 et seq.]; and

(B) on an annual basis, to notify the Secretary of, and provide supporting rationale for, each nonveteran who is employed as a disabled veterans' outreach program specialist and local veterans' employment representative for a period in excess of 6 months.

(6) Each State shall coordinate employment, training, and placement services furnished to veterans and eligible persons under this chapter [38 USCS §§ 4100 et seq.] with such services furnished with respect to such veterans and persons under the Workforce Investment Act of 1998 and the Wagner-Peyser Act.

(7) Of the amount of a grant or contract under which funds are made available to a State in order to carry out section 4103A or 4104 of this title [38 USCS § 4103A or 4104] for any program year, one percent shall be for the purposes of making cash awards under the program of performance incentive awards described in section 4112 of this title [38 USCS § 4112] in the State.

(8)(A) As a condition of a grant or contract under which funds are made available to a State in order to carry out section 4103A or 4104 of this title [38 USCS § 4103A or 4104], the Secretary shall require the State to require each employee hired by the State who is assigned to perform the duties of a disabled veterans' outreach program specialist or a local veterans' employment representative under this chapter to satisfactorily complete training provided by the National Veterans' Employment and Training Services Institute during the 18-month period that begins on the date on which the employee is so assigned.

(B) For any employee described in subparagraph (A) who does not complete such training during such period, the Secretary may reduce by an appropriate amount the amount made available to the State employing that employee.

(C) The Secretary may establish such reasonable exceptions to the completion of training otherwise required under subparagraph (A) as the Secretary considers appropriate.

(9)(A) As a condition of a grant or contract under which funds are made available to a State in order to carry out section 4103A or 4104 of this title [38 USCS § 4103A or 4104] for any program year, the Secretary may require the State—

(i) to demonstrate that when the State approves or denies a certification or license described in subparagraph (B) for a veteran the State takes into consideration any training received or experience gained by the veteran while serving on active duty in the Armed Forces; and

(ii) to disclose to the Secretary in writing the following:

(I) Criteria applicants must satisfy to receive a certification or license described in subparagraph (B) by the State.

(II) A description of the standard practices of the State for evaluating training received by veterans while serving on active duty in the Armed Forces and evaluating the documented work experience of such veterans during such service for purposes of approving or denying a certification or license described in subparagraph (B).

(III) Identification of areas in which training and experience described in subclause (II) fails to meet criteria described in subclause (I).["]

(B) A certification or license described in this subparagraph is any of the following:

(i) A license to be a nonemergency medical professional.

(ii) A license to be an emergency medical professional.

(iii) A commercial driver's license.

(C) The Secretary shall share the information the Secretary receives under subparagraph (A)(ii) with the Secretary of Defense to help the Secretary of Defense improve training for military occupational specialties so that individuals who receive such training are able to receive a certification or license described in subparagraph (B) from a State.

(D) The Secretary shall publish on the Internet website of the Department available to the public—

(i) any guidance the Secretary gives the Secretary of Defense with respect to carrying out this section; and

(ii) any information the Secretary receives from a State pursuant to subparagraph (A).

(d) Participation in other federally funded job training programs. The Assistant Secretary of Labor for Veterans' Employment and Training shall promote and monitor participation of qualified veterans and eligible persons in employment and training opportunities under title I of the Workforce Investment Act of 1998 and other federally funded employment and training programs.

(e) Regional Administrators. (1) The Secretary shall assign to each region for which the Secretary operates a regional office a representative of the Veterans' Employment and Training Service to serve as the Regional Administrator for Veterans' Employment and Training in such region.

(2) Each such Regional Administrator shall carry out such duties as the Secretary may require to promote veterans employment and reemployment within the region that the Administrator serves.

(f) Establishment of performance standards and outcomes measures. (1) The Assistant Secretary of Labor for Veterans' Employment and Training shall establish and implement a comprehensive performance accountability system to measure the performance of employment service delivery systems, including disabled veterans' outreach program specialists and local veterans' employment representatives providing employment, training, and placement services under this chapter [38 USCS §§ 4100 et seq.] in a State to provide accountability of that State to the Secretary for purposes of subsection (c).

(2) Such standards and measures shall—

(A) be consistent with State performance measures applicable under section 136(b) of the Workforce Investment Act of 1998 [29 USCS § 2871(b)]; and

(B) be appropriately weighted to provide special consideration for placement of (i) veterans requiring intensive services (as defined in section 4101(9) of this title [38 USCS § 4101(9)]), such as special disabled veterans and disabled veterans, and (ii) veterans who enroll in readjustment counseling under section 1712A of this title [38 USCS § 1712A].

(g) Authority to provide technical assistance to States. The Secretary may provide such technical assistance as the Secretary determines appropriate to any State that the Secretary determines has, or may have, an entered-employment rate in the State that is deficient, as determined under subsection (c)(3) with respect to a program year, including assistance in the development of a corrective action plan under that subsection.

(h) Consolidation of disabled veterans' outreach program specialists and veterans' employment representatives. The Secretary may allow the Governor of a State receiving funds under subsection (b)(5) to support specialists and representatives as described in such subsection to consolidate the functions of such specialists and representatives if—

(1) the Governor determines, and the Secretary concurs, that such consolidation—

(A) promotes a more efficient administration of services to veterans with a particular emphasis on services to disabled veterans; and

(B) does not hinder the provision of services to veterans and employers; and

(2) the Governor submits to the Secretary a proposal therefor at such time, in such manner, and containing such information as the Secretary may require.

(As amended Oct. 21, 1998, P. L. 105-277, Div A, § 101(f) [Title VIII, Subtitle IV, § 405(d)(29)(A), (f)(21)(A)], 112 Stat. 2681-424, 2681-432; Nov. 11, 1998, P. L. 105-368, Title X, § 1005(b)(13), 112 Stat. 3365; Nov. 7, 2002, P. L. 107-288, § 4(a)(1), 116 Stat. 2038; Dec. 16, 2003, P. L. 108-183, Title VII, § 708(b)(1)(A), (2), 117 Stat. 2673; June 15, 2006, P. L. 109-233, Title II, § 201, Title V, § 503(11), 120 Stat. 402, 416; Dec. 22, 2006, P. L. 109-461, Title VI, § 601(a), (b), 120 Stat. 3436; Oct. 13, 2010, P. L. 111-275, Title I, § 103(a), Title X, §§ 1001(k), 124 Stat. 2866, 2897; Nov. 21, 2011, P. L. 112-56, Title II, Subtitle C, § 241(c), 125 Stat. 728; Jan. 2, 2013, P. L. 112-239, Div A, Title V, Subtitle E, § 544(a), 126 Stat. 1737.)

HISTORY; ANCILLARY LAWS AND DIRECTIVES

References in text:

The "Wagner-Peyser Act", referred to in this section, is Act June 6, 1933, ch 49, which appears generally as 29 USCS §§ 49 et seq. For full classification of such Act, consult USCS Tables volumes.

The "Workforce Investment Act of 1998", referred to in this section, is Act Aug. 7, 1998, P. L. 105-220, which appears generally as 20 USCS §§ 9201 et seq. and 29 USCS §§ 2801 et seq. For full classification of such Act, consult USCS Tables volumes.

"Title I of the Workforce Investment Act of 1998", referred to in this section, is Title I of Act Aug. 7, 1998, P. L. 105-220, which appears generally as 29 USCS §§ 2801 et seq. For full classification of such Title, consult USCS Tables volumes.

Explanatory notes:

The quotation marks have been enclosed in brackets in subsec. (c)(9)(A)(ii)(III) to indicate the probable intent of Congress to delete them.

Amendments:

1998. Act Oct. 21, 1998 (effective on enactment as provided by § 405(g)(1) of Subtitle IV of Title VIII of § 101(f) of Division A of such Act, which appears as 5 USCS § 3502 note), in subsec. (d), substituted "the Job Training Partnership Act and title I of the Workforce Investment Act of 1998" for "the Job Training Partnership Act".

Act Oct. 21, 1998 (effective on 7/1/2000, as provided by § 405(g)(2)(B) of Subtitle VIII of Title IV of § 101(f) of Division A of such Act, which appears as 5 USCS § 3502 note), in subsec. (d), deleted "the Job Training Partnership Act and" preceding "title I".

Act Nov. 11, 1998, in subsec. (e)(1), substituted the sentence beginning "A person may not be assigned . . . ." for "Each Regional Administrator appointed after the date of the enactment of the Veterans' Benefits Improvements Act of 1996 shall be a veteran.".

2002. Act Nov. 7, 2002 (effective and applicable as provided by § 4(a)(4) of such Act, which appears as a note to this section), substituted this section for one which read:

"§ 4102A. Assistant Secretary of Labor for Veterans' Employment and Training; Regional Administrators

"(a)(1) There is established within the Department of Labor an Assistant Secretary of Labor for

38 USCS § 4102A

Veterans' Employment and Training appointed by the President by and with the advice and consent of the Senate, who shall be the principal advisor to the Secretary with respect to the formulation and implementation of all departmental policies and procedures to carry out (A) the purposes of this chapter, chapter 42, and chapter 43 of this title, and (B) all other Department of Labor employment, unemployment, and training programs to the extent they affect veterans. The employees of the Department of Labor administering chapter 43 of this title shall be administratively and functionally responsible to the Assistant Secretary of Labor for Veterans' Employment and Training.

"(2) There shall be within the Department of Labor a Deputy Assistant Secretary of Labor for Veterans' Employment and Training. The Deputy Assistant Secretary shall perform such functions as the Assistant Secretary of Labor for Veterans' Employment and Training prescribes. The Deputy Assistant Secretary shall be a veteran.

"(b) The Secretary shall—

"(1) except as expressly provided otherwise, carry out all provisions of this chapter and chapter 43 of this title through the Assistant Secretary of Labor for Veterans' Employment and Training and administer through such Assistant Secretary all programs under the jurisdiction of the Secretary for the provision of employment and training services designed to meet the needs of disabled veterans, veterans of the Vietnam era, and all other eligible veterans and eligible persons;

"(2) in order to make maximum use of available resources in meeting such needs, encourage all such programs and all grantees under such programs to enter into cooperative arrangements with private industry and business concerns (including small business concerns), educational institutions, trade associations, and labor unions;

"(3) ensure that maximum effectiveness and efficiency are achieved in providing services and assistance to eligible veterans under all such programs by coordinating and consulting with the Secretary of Veterans Affairs with respect to (A) programs conducted under other provisions of this title, with particular emphasis on coordination of such programs with readjustment counseling activities carried out under section 1712A of this title, apprenticeship or other on-the-job training programs carried out under section 3687 of this title, and rehabilitation and training activities carried out under chapter 31 of this title, and (B) the Veterans' Job Training Act (29 U.S.C. 1721 note);

"(4) ensure that job placement activities are carried out in coordination and cooperation with appropriate State public employment service officials;

"(5) subject to subsection (c)(2) of this section, make available for use in each State, directly or by grant or contract, such funds as may be necessary (A) to support (i) disabled veterans' outreach program specialists appointed under section 4103A(a)(1) of this title, and (ii) local veterans' employment representatives assigned under section 4104(b) of this title, and (B) to support the reasonable expenses of such specialists and representatives for training, travel, supplies, and fringe benefits, including travel expenses and per diem for attendance at the National Veterans' Employment and Training Services Institute established under section 4109 of this title;

"(6) monitor and supervise on a continuing basis the distribution and use of funds provided for use in the States under paragraph (5) of this subsection; and

"(7) monitor the appointment of disabled veterans' outreach specialists and the assignment of local veterans' employment representatives in order to ensure compliance with the provisions of sections 4103A(a)(1) and 4104(a)(4), respectively, of this title.

"(c)(1) The distribution and use of funds under subsection (b)(5) of this section in order to carry out sections 4103A(a) and 4104(a) of this title shall be subject to the continuing supervision and monitoring of the Secretary and shall not be governed by the provisions of any other law, or any regulations prescribed thereunder, that are inconsistent with this section or section 4103A or 4104 of this title.

"(2) In determining the terms and conditions of a grant or contract under which funds are made available in a State in order to carry out section 4103A or 4104 of this title, the Secretary shall take into account (A) the results of the evaluations, carried out pursuant to section 4103(c)(15) of this title, of the performance of local employment offices in the State, and (B) the monitoring carried out under this section.

"(3) Each grant or contract by which funds are made available in a State shall contain a provision requiring the recipient of the funds to comply with the provisions of this chapter.

"(d) The Assistant Secretary of Labor for Veterans' Employment and Training shall promote and monitor participation of qualified veterans and eligible persons in employment and training opportunities under title I of the Workforce Investment Act of 1998 and other federally funded employment and training programs.

"(e)(1) The Secretary shall assign to each region for which the Secretary operates a regional office a representative of the Veterans' Employment and Training Service to serve as the Regional Administrator for Veterans' Employment and Training in such region. A person may not be assigned after October 9, 1996, as such a Regional Administrator unless the person is a veteran.

"(2) Each such Regional Administrator shall be responsible for—

"(A) ensuring the promotion, operation, and implementation of all veterans' employment and training programs and services within the region;

"(B) monitoring compliance with section 4212 of this title with respect to veterans' employment under Federal contracts within the region;

"(C) protecting and advancing veterans' reemployment rights within the region; and

"(D) coordinating, monitoring, and providing technical assistance on veterans' employment and training programs with respect to all entities receiving funds under grants from or contracts with the Department of Labor within the region.".

2003. Act Dec. 16, 2003 (effective as if included in the enactment of § 4(a) of Act Nov. 7, 2002, P. L. 107-288, as provided by § 708(b)(1)(B) of the 2003 Act, which appears as a note to this section), in subsec. (c)(2)(B)(ii), substituted "October 1, 2003" for "October 1, 2002".

Such Act further, in subsec. (f)(1), substituted "May 7, 2003," for "6 months after the date of the enactment of this section,".

2006. Act June 15, 2006, in subsec. (b), added para. (8); in subsec. (c)(7), substituted "Of" for "With respect to program years beginning during or after fiscal year 2004, one percent of" and substituted "for any program year, one percent" for "for the program year"; and, in subsec. (f)(1), substituted "The" for "By not later than May 7, 2003, the".

Act Dec. 22, 2006 (applicable as provided by § 601(c) of such Act, which appears as a note to this section), in subsec. (c), in para. (2)(A), redesignated cl. (iii) as cl. (iv), and inserted a new cl. (iii), and added para. (8).

2010. Act Oct. 13, 2010 (applicable as provided by § 103(b) of such Act, which appears as a note to this section), in subsec. (c)(8)(A), substituted "18-month period" for "three-year period".

Such Act further, in subsec. (b)(8), substituted "Employment, Training" for "Employment and Training".

2011. Act Nov. 21, 2011, added subsec. (h).

2013. Act Jan. 2, 2013 (applicable to a program year beginning on or after enactment, as provided by § 544(b) of such Act, which appears as a note to this section), added subsec. (c)(9).

Other provisions:

Effective date and applicability of Nov. 7, 2002 amendments. Act Nov. 7, 2002, P. L. 107-288, § 4(a)(4), 116 Stat. 2042, provides: "The amendments made by this subsection [amending 38 USCS §§ 4102A, 4103, 4107(b), and the chapter analysis preceding 38 USCS § 4100, and repealing 38 USCS § 4104A] shall take effect on the date of the enactment of this Act, and apply for program and fiscal years under chapter 41 of title 38, United States Code [38 USCS §§ 4100 et seq.], beginning on or after such date.".

Effective date of amendment made by § 708(b)(1) of Act Dec. 16, 2003. Act Dec. 16, 2003, P. L. 108-183, Title VII, § 708(b)(1)(B), 117 Stat. 2673, provides: "The amendment made by subparagraph (A) [amending subsec. (c)(2)(B)(ii) of this section] shall take effect as if included in the enactment of section 4(a) of the Jobs for Veterans Act (Public Law 107-288; 116 Stat. 2038).".

Application of Dec. 22, 2006 amendments. Act Dec. 22, 2006, P. L. 109-461, Title VI, § 601(c), 120 Stat. 3436, provides: "Paragraph (8) of section 4102A(c) of title 38, United States Code [subsec. (c) of this section], as added by subsection (a), and clause (iii) of section 4102A(c)(2)(A) of such title [subsec. (c)(2)(A) of this section], as added by subsection (b), shall apply with respect to a State employee assigned to perform the duties of a disabled veterans' outreach program specialist or a local veterans' employment representative under chapter 41 of such title [38 USCS §§ 4100 et seq.] who is so assigned on or after January 1, 2006.".

Application of Oct. 13, 2010 amendments. Act Oct. 13, 2010, P. L. 111-275, Title I, § 103(b), 124 Stat. 2866, provides:

"(1) Applicability to new employees. The amendment made by subsection (a) shall apply with respect to a State employee assigned to perform the duties of a disabled veterans' outreach program specialist or a local veterans' employment representative under chapter 41 of title 38, United States Code [38 USCS §§ 4101 et seq.], who is so assigned on or after the date of the enactment of this Act.

"(2) Applicability to previously-hired employees. In the case of such a State employee who is so assigned on or after January 1, 2006, and before the date of the enactment of this Act, the Secretary of Labor shall require the State to require, as a condition of a grant or contract under which funds are made available to the State in order to carry out section 4103A or 4104 of title 38, United States Code, each such employee to satisfactorily complete the training described in section 4102A(c)(8)(A) of such title [38 USCS § 4102A(c)(8)(A)] by not later than the date that is 18 months after the date of the enactment of this Act.".

Application of Jan. 2, 2013 amendment. Act Jan. 2, 2013, P. L. 112-239, Div A, Title V, Subtitle E, § 544(b), 126 Stat. 1738, provides: "The amendment made by subsection (a) [adding subsec. (c)(9) of this section] shall apply with respect to a program year beginning on or after the date of the enactment of this Act.".

RESEARCH GUIDE

Am Jur:

77 Am Jur 2d, Veterans and Veterans' Laws §§ 99, 102.

§ 4103. Directors and Assistant Directors for Veterans' Employment and Training; additional Federal personnel

(a) Directors and Assistant Directors. (1) The Secretary shall assign to each State a representative of the Veterans' Employment and Training Service to serve as the Director for Veterans' Employment and Training, and shall assign full-time Federal clerical or other support personnel to each such Director.

(2)(A) Each Director for Veterans' Employment and Training for a State shall, at the time of appointment, have been a bona fide resident of the State for at least two years.

(B) The Secretary may waive the requirement in subparagraph (A) with respect to a Director for Veterans' Employment and Training if the Secretary determines that the waiver is in the public interest. Any such waiver shall be made on a case-by-case basis.

(3) Full-time Federal clerical or other support personnel assigned to Directors for Veterans' Employment and Training shall be appointed in accordance with the provisions of title 5 governing appointments in the competitive service and shall be paid in accordance with the provisions of chapter 51 and subchapter III of chapter 53 of title 5 [5 USCS §§ 5101 et seq. and 5331 et seq.].

(b) Additional Federal personnel. The Secretary may also assign as supervisory personnel such representatives of the Veterans' Employment and Training Service as the Secretary determines appropriate to carry out the employment, training, and placement services required under this chapter [38 USCS § 4100 et seq.], including Assistant Directors for Veterans' Employment and Training.

(As amended Nov. 7, 2002, P. L. 107-288, § 4(a)(1), 116 Stat. 2042; Oct. 10, 2008, P. L. 110-389, Title III, Subtitle A, § 316, 122 Stat. 4167.)

HISTORY; ANCILLARY LAWS AND DIRECTIVES

Amendments:

2002. Act Nov. 7, 2002 (effective and applicable as provided by § 4(a)(4) of such Act, which appears as 38 USCS § 4102A note), substituted this section for one which read:

"§ 4103. Directors and Assistant Directors for Veterans' Employment and Training

"(a) The Secretary shall assign to each State a representative of the Veterans' Employment Service to serve as the Director for Veterans' Employment and Training, and shall assign full-time Federal clerical or other support personnel to each such Director. The Secretary shall also assign to each State one Assistant Director for Veterans' Employment and Training per each 250,000 veterans and eligible persons of the State veterans population and such additional Assistant Directors for Veterans' Employment and Training as the Secretary shall determine, based on the data collected pursuant to section 4107 of this title, to be necessary to assist the Director for Veterans' Employment and Training to carry out effectively in that State the purposes of this chapter. Full-time Federal clerical or other support personnel assigned to Directors for Veterans' Employment and Training shall be appointed in accordance with the provisions of title 5 governing appointments in the competitive service and shall be paid in accordance with the provisions of chapter 51 and subchapter III of chapter 53 of title 5.

"(b)(1)(A) Each Director for Veterans' Employment and Training and Assistant Director for Veterans' Employment and Training (i) shall, except as provided in subparagraph (B) of this paragraph, be a qualified veteran who at the time of appointment has been a bona fide resident of the State for at least two years, and (ii) shall be appointed in accordance with the provisions of title 5 governing appointments in the competitive service and shall be paid in accordance with the provisions of chapter 51 and subchapter III of chapter 53 of title 5.

"(B) If, in appointing a Director or Assistant Director for any State under this section, the Secretary determines that there is no qualified veteran available who meets the residency requirement in subparagraph (A)(i), the Secretary may appoint as such Director or Assistant Director any qualified veteran.

"(2) Each Director for Veterans' Employment and Training and Assistant Director for Veterans' Employment and Training shall be attached to the public employment service system of the State to which they are assigned. They shall be administratively responsible to the Secretary for the execution of the veterans' and eligible persons' counseling and placement policies of the Secretary through the public employment service system and in cooperation with other employment and training programs administered by the Secretary, by grantees of Federal or federally funded employment and training programs in the State, or directly by the State.

"(c) In cooperation with the staff of the public employment service system and the staffs of each such other program in the State, the Director for Veterans' Employment and Training and Assistant Directors for Veterans' Employment and Training shall—

"(1)(A) functionally supervise the provision of services to eligible veterans and eligible persons by such system and such program and their staffs, and (B) be functionally responsible for the supervision of the registration of eligible veterans and eligible persons in local employment offices for suitable types of employment and training and for counseling and placement of eligible veterans and eligible persons in employment and job training programs, including the program conducted under the Veterans' Job Training Act (Public Law 98-77; 29 U.S.C. 1721 note);

"(2) engage of job development and job advancement activities for eligible veterans and eligible persons, including maximum coordination with appropriate officials of the Department of Veterans Affairs in that agency's carrying out of its responsibilities under subchapter II of chapter 77 of this title and in the conduct of job affairs, job marts, and other special programs to match eligible veterans and eligible persons with appropriate job and job training opportunities and otherwise to promote the employment of eligible veterans and eligible persons;

"(3) assist in securing and maintaining current information as to the various types of available employment and training opportunities, including maximum use of electronic data processing and telecommunications systems and the matching of an eligible veteran's or an eligible person's particular qualifications with an available job or on-job training or apprenticeship opportunity which is commensurate with those qualifications;

"(4) promote the interest of employers and labor unions in employing eligible veterans and eligible persons and in conducting on-job training and apprenticeship programs for such veterans and persons;

"(5) maintain regular contact with employers, labor unions, training programs and veterans' organizations with a view to keeping them advised of eligible veterans and eligible persons available for employment and training and to keeping eligible veterans and eligible persons advised of opportunities for employment and training;

"(6) promote and facilitate the participation of veterans in Federal and federally funded employment and training programs and directly monitor the implementation and operation of such programs to ensure that eligible veterans, veterans of the Vietnam era, disabled veterans, and eligible persons receive such priority or other special consideration in the provision of services as is required by law or regulation;

"(7) assist in every possible way in improving working conditions and the advancement of employment of eligible veterans and eligible persons;

"(8) supervise the listing of jobs and subsequent referrals of qualified veterans as required by section 4212 of this title;

"(9) be responsible for ensuring that complaints of discrimination filed under such section are resolved in a timely fashion;

"(10) working closely with appropriate Department of Veterans Affairs personnel engaged in providing counseling or rehabilitation services under chapter 31 of this title, cooperate with employers to identify disabled veterans who have completed or are participating in a vocational rehabilitation training program under such chapter and who are in need of employment;

"(11) cooperate with the staff of programs operated under section 1712A of this title in identifying and assisting veterans who have readjustment problems and who may need employment placement assistance or vocational training assistance;

"(12) when requested by a Federal or State agency or a private employer, assist such agency or employer in identifying and acquiring prosthetic and sensory aids and devices which tend to enhance the employability of disabled veterans;

"(13) monitor the implementation of Federal laws requiring veterans preference in employment and job advancement opportunities within the Federal Government and report to the Office of Personnel Management or other appropriate agency, for enforcement or other remedial action, any evidence of failure to provide such preference or to provide priority or other special consideration in the provision of services to veterans as is required by law or regulation;

"(14) monitor, through disabled veterans' outreach program specialists and local veterans' employment representatives, the listing of vacant positions with State employment agencies by Federal agencies, and report to the Office of Personnel Management or other appropriate agency, for enforcement or other remedial action, any evidence of failure to provide priority or other special consideration in the provision of services to veterans as is required by law or regulation; and

"(15)(A) not less frequently than annually, conduct, subject to subclause (B) of this clause, an evaluation at each local employment office of the services provided to eligible veterans and eligible persons and make recommendations for corrective action as appropriate; and

"(B) carry out such evaluations in the following order of priority: (I) offices that demonstrated less than satisfactory performance during either of the two previous program years, (II) offices with the largest number of veterans registered during the previous program year, and (III) other offices as resources permit.".

2008. Act Oct. 10, 2008, in subsec. (a)(2), designated the existing provisions as subpara. (A), and added subpara. (B).

RESEARCH GUIDE

Am Jur:
77 Am Jur 2d, Veterans and Veterans' Laws § 102.

§ 4103A. Disabled veterans' outreach program

(a) Requirement for employment by States of a sufficient number of specialists. (1) Subject to approval by the Secretary, a State shall employ such full- or part-time disabled veterans' outreach program specialists as the State determines appropriate and efficient to carry out intensive services and facilitate placements under this chapter [38 USCS §§ 4100 et seq.] to meet the employment needs of eligible veterans with the following priority in the provision of services:

    (A) Special disabled veterans.

    (B) Other disabled veterans.

    (C) Other eligible veterans in accordance with priorities determined by the Secretary taking into account applicable rates of unemployment and the employment emphases set forth in chapter 42 of this title [38 USCS §§ 4201 et seq.].

(2) In the provision of services in accordance with this subsection, maximum emphasis in meeting the employment needs of veterans shall be placed on assisting economically or educationally disadvantaged veterans.

(3) In facilitating placement of a veteran under this program, a disabled veterans' outreach program specialist shall help to identify job opportunities that are appropriate for the veteran's employment goals and assist that veteran in developing a cover letter and resume that are targeted for those particular jobs.

(b) Requirement for qualified veterans. A State shall, to the maximum extent practicable, employ qualified veterans to carry out the services referred to in subsection (a). Preference shall be given in the appointment of such specialists to qualified disabled veterans.

(c) Part-time employees. A part-time disabled veterans' outreach program specialist shall perform the functions of a disabled veterans' outreach program specialist under this section on a half-time basis.

(d) Additional requirement for full-time employees. (1) A full-time disabled veterans' outreach program specialist shall perform only duties related to meeting the employment needs of eligible veterans, as described in subsection (a), and shall not perform other non-veteran-related duties that detract from the specialist's ability to perform the specialist's duties related to meeting the employment needs of eligible veterans.

(2) The Secretary shall conduct regular audits to ensure compliance with paragraph (1). If, on the basis of such an audit, the Secretary determines that a State is not in compliance with paragraph (1), the Secretary may reduce the amount of a grant made to the State under section 4102A(b)(5) of this title [38 USCS § 4102A(b)(5)].

(As amended Oct. 21, 1998, P. L. 105-277, Div A, § 101(f) [Title VIII, Subtitle IV, § 405(d)(29)(B), (f)(21)(B)], 112 Stat. 2681-424, 2681-432; Nov. 11, 1998, P. L. 105-368, Title X, § 1004(a), 112 Stat. 3364; Dec. 21, 2001, P. L. 107-95, § 9(a), 115 Stat. 920; Nov. 7, 2002, P. L. 107-288, § 4(b)(1), 116 Stat. 2043; Dec. 22, 2006, P. L. 109-461, Title VI, § 602(a), 120 Stat. 3437; Nov. 21, 2011, P. L. 112-56, Title II, Subtitle C, §§ 234(b), 241(a), 125 Stat. 722, 728.)

HISTORY; ANCILLARY LAWS AND DIRECTIVES

Amendments:

1998. Act Oct. 21, 1998 (effective on enactment as provided by § 405(g)(1) of Subtitle IV of Title VIII of § 101(f) of Division A of such Act, which appears as 5 USCS § 3502 note), in subsec. (c)(4), substituted "including part C of title IV of the Job Training Partnership Act and title I of the Workforce Investment Act of 1998" for "(including part C of title IV of the Job Training Partnership Act (29 U.S.C. 1501 et seq.))".

Act Oct. 21, 1998 (effective on 7/1/2000, as provided by § 405(g)(2)(B) of Subtitle VIII of Title IV of § 101(f) of Division A of such Act, which appears as 5 USCS § 3502 note), in subsec. (c)(4), deleted "part C of title IV of the Job Training Partnership Act and" preceding "title I".

Act Nov. 11, 1998, in subsec. (a)(1), substituted "for each 7,400 veterans who are between the ages of 20 and 64 residing in such State." for "for each 6,900 veterans residing in such State who are either veterans of the Vietnam era, veterans who first entered on active duty as a member of the Armed Forces after May 7, 1975, or disabled veterans.", deleted "of the Vietnam era" following "to qualified disabled veterans", and deleted "If the Secretary finds that a qualified disabled veteran of the Vietnam era is not available for any such appointment, preference for such appointment shall be given to other qualified disabled veterans." preceding "If the Secretary finds".

2001. Act Dec. 21, 2001, in subsec. (c), added para. (11).

2002. Act Nov. 7, 2002 (effective and applicable as provided by § 4(b)(3) of such Act, which appears as a note to this section), substituted the text of this section for text which read:

"(a)(1) The amount of funds made available for use in a State under section 4102A(b)(5)(A)(i) of this title shall be sufficient to support the appointment of one disabled veterans' outreach program specialist for each 7,400 veterans who are between the ages of 20 and 64 residing in such State. Each such specialist shall be a qualified veteran. Preference shall be given in the appointment of such specialists to qualified disabled veterans. If the Secretary finds that no qualified disabled veteran is available for such appointment, such appointment may be given to any qualified veteran. Each such specialist shall be compensated at rates comparable to those paid other professionals performing essentially similar duties in the State government of the State concerned.

"(2) Specialists appointed pursuant to this subsection shall be in addition to and shall not supplant employees assigned to local employment service offices pursuant to section 4104 of this title.

"(b)(1) Pursuant to regulations prescribed by the Secretary of Labor, disabled veterans' outreach program specialists shall be assigned only those duties directly related to meeting the employment needs of eligible veterans, with priority for the provision of services in the following order:

"(A) Services to special disabled veterans.

"(B) Services to other disabled veterans.

"(C) Services to other eligible veterans in accordance with priorities determined by the Secretary taking into account applicable rates of unemployment and the employment emphases set forth in chapter 42 of this title.

In the provision of services in accordance with this paragraph, maximum emphasis in meeting the employment needs of veterans shall be placed on assisting economically or educationally disadvantaged veterans.

"(2) Not more than three-fourths of the disabled veterans' outreach program specialists in each State shall be stationed at local employment service offices in such State. The Secretary, after consulting the Secretary of Veterans Affairs and the Director for Veterans' Employment and Training assigned to a State under section 4103 of this title, may waive the limitation in the preceding sentence for that State so long as the percentage of all disabled veterans' outreach program specialists that are stationed at local employment service offices in all States does not exceed 80 percent. Specialists not so stationed shall be stationed at centers established by the Department of Veterans Affairs to provide a program of readjustment counseling pursuant to section 1712A of this title, veterans assistance offices established by the Department of Veterans Affairs pursuant to section 7723 of this title, and such other sites as may be determined to be appropriate in accordance with regulations prescribed by the Secretary after consultation with the Secretary of Veterans Affairs.

"(c) Each disabled veterans' outreach program specialist shall carry out the following functions for the purpose of providing services to eligible veterans in accordance with the priorities set forth in subsection (b) of this section:

"(1) Development of job and job training opportunities for such veterans through contacts with employers, especially small- and medium-size private sector employers.

"(2) Pursuant to regulations prescribed by the Secretary after consultation with the Secretary of Veterans Affairs, promotion and development of apprenticeship and other on-job training positions pursuant to section 3787 of this title.

"(3) The carrying out of outreach activities to locate such veterans through contacts with local veterans organizations, the Department of Veterans Affairs, the State employment service agency and local employment service offices, and community-based organizations.

"(4) Provision of appropriate assistance to community-based groups and organizations and appropriate grantees under other Federal and federally funded employment and training programs including title I of the Workforce Investment Act of 1998 in providing services to such veterans.

"(5) Provision of appropriate assistance to local employment service office employees with responsibility for veterans in carrying out their responsibilities pursuant to this chapter.

"(6) Consultation and coordination with other appropriate representatives of Federal, State, and local programs (including the program conducted under the Veterans' Job Training Act (Public Law 98-77; 29 U.S.C. 1721 note)) for the purpose of developing maximum linkages to promote employment opportunities for and provide maximum employment assistance to such veterans.

"(7) The carrying out of such other duties as will promote the development of entry-level and career job opportunities for such veterans.

"(8) Development of outreach programs in cooperation with appropriate Department of Veterans Affairs personnel engaged in providing counseling or rehabilitation services under chapter 31 of this title, with educational institutions, and with employers in order to ensure maximum assistance to disabled veterans who have completed or are participating in a vocational rehabilitation program under such chapter.

"(9) Provision of vocational guidance or vocational counseling services, or both, to veterans with respect to veterans' selection of and changes in vocations and veterans' vocational adjustment.

"(10) Provision of services as a case manager under section 14(b)(1)(A) of the Veterans' Job Training Act (Public Law 98-77; 29 U.S.C. 1721 note).

"(11) Coordination of employment services with training assistance provided to veterans by entities receiving funds under section 2021 of this title.".

2006. Act Dec. 22, 2006 (applicable with respect to pay periods beginning after the date that is 180 days after enactment, as provided by § 602(c) of such Act, which appears as a note to this section), added subsec. (c).

2011. Act Nov. 21, 2011, in subsec. (a), in para. (1), in the introductory matter, inserted "and facilitate placements", and added para. (3); and added subsec. (d).

Other provisions:
Application of Nov. 11, 1998 amendments. Act Nov. 11, 1998, P. L. 105-368, Title X,

38 USCS § 4103A
VETERANS' BENEFITS

§ 1004(b), 112 Stat. 3364, provides: "The amendments made by this section [amending subsec. (a)(1) of this section] shall apply with respect to appointments of disabled veterans' outreach program specialists under section 4103A of title 38, United States Code, on or after the date of the enactment of this Act.".

Effective date and applicability of Nov. 7, 2002 amendments. Act Nov. 7, 2002, P. L. 107-288, § 4(b)(3), 116 Stat. 2044, provides: "The amendments made by this subsection [amending 38 USCS §§ 4103A, 4104] shall take effect on the date of the enactment of this Act, and apply for program years under chapter 41 of title 38, United States Code [38 USCS §§ 4100 et seq.], beginning on or after such date.".

Applicability of Dec. 22, 2006 amendments. Act Dec. 22, 2006, P. L. 109-461, Title VI, § 602(c), 120 Stat. 3437, provides: "Section 4103A(c) of title 38, United States Code [subsec. (c) of this section], as added by subsection (a), and section 4104(d) of such title [38 USCS § 4104(d)], as amended by subsection (b), shall apply with respect to pay periods beginning after the date that is 180 days after the date of the enactment of this Act.".

RESEARCH GUIDE

Am Jur:
77 Am Jur 2d, Veterans and Veterans' Laws § 103.

§ 4104. Local veterans' employment representatives

(a) Requirement for employment by States of a sufficient number of representatives. Subject to approval by the Secretary, a State shall employ such full- and part-time local veterans' employment representatives as the State determines appropriate and efficient to carry out employment, training, and placement services under this chapter [38 USCS §§ 4100 et seq.].

(b) Principal duties. As principal duties, local veterans' employment representatives shall—

(1) conduct outreach to employers in the area to assist veterans in gaining employment, including conducting seminars for employers and, in conjunction with employers, conducting job search workshops and establishing job search groups; and

(2) facilitate employment, training, and placement services furnished to veterans in a State under the applicable State employment service delivery systems.

(c) Requirement for qualified veterans and eligible persons. A State shall, to the maximum extent practicable, employ qualified veterans or eligible persons to carry out the services referred to in subsection (a). Preference shall be accorded in the following order:

(1) To qualified service-connected disabled veterans.

(2) If no veteran described in paragraph (1) is available, to qualified eligible veterans.

(3) If no veteran described in paragraph (1) or (2) is available, then to qualified eligible persons.

(d) Part-time employees. A part-time local veterans' employment representative shall perform the functions of a local veterans' employment representative under this section on a half-time basis.

(e) Additional requirements for full-time employees. (1) A full-time local veterans' employment representative shall perform only duties related to the employment, training, and placement services under this chapter [38 USCS §§ 4100 et seq.], and shall not perform other non-veteran-related duties that detract from the representative's ability to perform the representative's duties related to employment, training, and placement services under this chapter [38 USCS §§ 4100 et seq.].

(2) The Secretary shall conduct regular audits to ensure compliance with paragraph (1). If, on the basis of such an audit, the Secretary determines that a State is not in compliance with paragraph (1), the Secretary may reduce the amount of a grant made to the State under section 4102A(b)(5) of this title [38 USCS § 4102A(b)(5)].

(f) Reporting. Each local veterans' employment representative shall be administratively responsible to the manager of the employment service delivery system and shall provide reports, not less frequently than quarterly, to the manager of such office and to the Director for Veterans' Employment and Training for the State regarding compliance with Federal law and regulations with respect to special services and priorities for eligible veterans and eligible persons.

(As amended June 5, 2001, P. L. 107-14, § 8(a)(10), 115 Stat. 35; Dec. 21, 2001, P. L. 107-95, § 9(b), 115 Stat. 920; Nov. 7, 2002, P. L. 107-288, § 4(b)(2), 116 Stat. 2043; Dec. 22, 2006, P. L. 109-461, Title VI, § 602(b), 120 Stat. 3437; Nov. 21, 2011, P. L. 112-56, Title II, Subtitle C, § 241(b), 125 Stat. 728.)

HISTORY; ANCILLARY LAWS AND DIRECTIVES

Amendments:
2001. Act June 5, 2001, in subsec. (a), in para. (1), in the introductory matter, substituted "For any fiscal year," for "Beginning with fiscal year 1988,", in subpara. (B), substituted "subparagraph" for "clause", and, in subpara. (C), substituted "subparagraphs" for "clauses", and, in para. (4), deleted "on or after July 1988" following "representatives"; and, in subsec. (b), in the introductory matter, substituted "shall perform the following functions:" for "shall—", in paras. (1)–(10), capitalized the initial letter of the first word and substituted the

Readjustment Benefits

38 USCS § 4104

concluding period for a semicolon, in para. (11), capitalized the initial letter of the first word and substituted the concluding period for "; and" and, in para. (12), capitalized the initial letter of the first word.

Act Dec. 21, 2001, purported to amend subsec. (b) by deleting "and" at the end of para. (11); however, because of prior amendments, this amendment could not be executed.

Such Act further, in para. (12), substituted "; and" for a concluding period, and added para. (13).

2002. Act Nov. 7, 2002 (effective and applicable as provided by § 4(b)(3) of such Act, which appears as 38 USCS § 4103A note), substituted the text of this section for text which read:

"(a)(1) For any fiscal year, the total of the amount of funds made available for use in the States under section 4102A(b)(5)(A)(ii) of this title shall be sufficient to support the appointment of 1,600 full-time local veterans' employment representatives and the States' administrative expenses associated with the appointment of that number of such representatives and shall be allocated to the several States so that each State receives funding sufficient to support—

"(A) the number of such representatives who were assigned in such State on January 1, 1987, for which funds were provided under this chapter, plus one additional such representative;

"(B) the percentage of the 1,600 such representatives for which funding is not provided under subparagraph (A) of this paragraph which is equal to the average of (i) the percentage of all veterans residing in the United States who reside in such State, (ii) the percentage of the total of all eligible veterans and eligible persons registered for assistance with local employment service offices in the United States who are registered for assistance with local employment service offices in such State, and (iii) the percentage of all full-service local employment service offices in the United States which are located in such State; and

"(C) the State's administrative expenses associated with the appointment of the number of such representatives for which funding is allocated to the State under subparagraphs (A) and (B) of this paragraph.

"(2)(A) The local veterans' employment representatives allocated to a State pursuant to paragraph (1) of this subsection shall be assigned by the administrative head of the employment service in the State, after consultation with the Director for Veterans' Employment and Training for the State, so that as nearly as practical (i) one full-time representative is assigned to each local employment service office at which at least 1,100 eligible veterans and eligible persons are registered for assistance, (ii) one additional full-time representative is assigned to each local employment service office for each 1,500 eligible veterans and eligible persons above 1,100 who are registered at such office for assistance, and (iii) one half-time representative is assigned to each local employment service office at which at least 350 but less than 1,100 eligible veterans and eligible persons are registered for assistance.

"(B) In the case of a service delivery point (other than a local employment service office described in subparagraph (A) of this paragraph) at which employment services are offered under the Wagner-Peyser Act, the head of such service delivery point shall be responsible for ensuring compliance with the provisions of this title providing for priority services for veterans and priority referral of veterans to Federal contractors.

"(3) For the purposes of this subsection, an individual shall be considered to be registered for assistance with a local employment service office during a program year if the individual—

"(A) registered, or renewed such individual's registration, for assistance with the office during that program year; or

"(B) so registered or renewed such individual's registration during a previous program year and, in accordance with regulations which the Secretary shall prescribe, is counted as still being registered for administrative purposes.

"(4) In the appointment of local veterans' employment representatives, preference shall be given to qualified eligible veterans or eligible persons. Preference shall be accorded first to qualified service-connected disabled veterans; then, if no such disabled veteran is available, to qualified eligible veterans; and, if no such eligible veteran is available, then to qualified eligible persons.

"(b) Local veterans' employment representatives shall perform the following functions:

"(1) Functionally supervise the providing of services to eligible veterans and eligible persons by the local employment service staff.

"(2) Maintain regular contact with community leaders, employers, labor unions, training programs, and veterans' organizations for the purpose of (A) keeping them advised of eligible veterans and eligible persons available for employment and training, and (B) keeping eligible veterans and eligible persons advised of opportunities for employment and training.

"(3) Provide directly, or facilitate the provision of, labor exchange services by local employment service staff to eligible veterans and eligible persons, including intake and assessment, counseling, testing, job-search assistance, and referral and placement.

"(4) Encourage employers and labor unions to employ eligible veterans and eligible persons and conduct on-the-job training and apprenticeship programs for such veterans and persons.

"(5) Promote and monitor the participation of veterans in federally funded employment and training programs, monitor the listing of vacant positions with State employment agencies by Federal agencies, and report to the Director for Veterans' Employment and Training for the State concerned any evidence of failure to provide priority or other special consideration in the provision of services to veterans as is required by law or regulation.

"(6) Monitor the listing of jobs and subsequent referrals of qualified veterans as required by section 4212 of this title.

"(7) Work closely with appropriate Department of Veterans Affairs personnel engaged in providing counseling or rehabilitation services under chapter 31 of this title, and cooperate with employers in identifying disabled veterans who have completed or are participating in a vocational rehabilitation training program under such chapter and who are in need of employment.

"(8) Refer eligible veterans and eligible persons to training, supportive services, and educational opportunities, as appropriate.

"(9) Assist, through automated data processing, in securing and maintaining current information regarding available employment and training opportunities.

"(10) Cooperate with the staff of programs operated under section 1712A of this title in identifying and assisting veterans who have readjustment problems and who may need services available at the local employment service office.

"(11) When requested by a Federal or State agency, a private employer, or a service-connected disabled veteran, assist such agency, employer, or veteran in identifying and acquiring prosthetic and sensory aids and devices needed to enhance the employability of disabled veterans.

"(12) Facilitate the provision of guidance or counseling services, or both, to veterans who, pursuant to section 5(b)(3) of the Veterans' Job Training Act (29 U.S.C. 1721 note), are certified as eligible for participation under such Act; and

"(13) coordinate employment services with training assistance provided to veterans by entities receiving funds under section 2021 of this title.

"(c) Each local veterans' employment representative shall be administratively responsible to the manager of the local employment service office and shall provide reports, not less frequently than quarterly, to the manager of such office and to the Director for Veterans' Employment and Training for the State regarding compliance with Federal law and regulations with respect to special services and priorities for eligible veterans and eligible persons.".

2006. Act Dec. 22, 2006 (effective on the date that is 180 days after enactment, as provided by § 602(c) of such Act, which appears as 38 USCS § 4103A note), redesignated subsec. (d) as subsec. (e); and inserted a new subsec. (d).

2011. Act Nov. 21, 2011, redesignated subsec. (e) as subsec. (f); and inserted a new subsec. (e).

Other provisions:

Pilot program to integrate and streamline functions of local veterans' employment representatives. Act Oct. 9, 1996, P. L. 104-275, Title III, Subtitle A, § 303, 110 Stat. 3332; Nov. 11, 1998, P. L. 105-368, Title X, § 1005(c)(1), 112 Stat. 3366, provides:

"(a) Authority to conduct pilot program. In order to assess the effects on the timeliness and quality of services to veterans resulting from re-focusing the staff resources of local veterans' employment representatives, the Secretary of Labor may conduct a pilot program under which the primary responsibilities of local veterans' employment representatives will be case management and the provision and facilitation of direct employment and training services to veterans.

"(b) Authorities under Chapter 41. To implement the pilot program, the Secretary of Labor may suspend or limit application of those provisions of chapter 41 of title 38, United States Code [38 USCS §§ 4101 et seq.] (other than subsections (b)(1) and (c) of section 4104) that pertain to the Local Veterans' Employment Representative Program in States designated by the Secretary under subsection (d), except that the Secretary may use the authority of such chapter, as the Secretary may determine, in conjunction with the authority of this section, to carry out the pilot program. The Secretary may collect such data as the Secretary considers necessary for assessment of the pilot program. The Secretary shall measure and evaluate on a continuing basis the effectiveness of the pilot program in achieving its stated goals in general, and in achieving such goals in relation to their cost, their effect on related programs, and their structure and mechanisms for delivery of services.

"(c) Targeted veterans. Within the pilot program, eligible veterans who are among groups most in need of intensive services, including disabled veterans, economically disadvantaged veterans, and veterans separated within the previous four years from active military, naval, or air service shall be given priority for service by local veterans' employment representatives. Priority for the provision of service shall be given first to disabled veterans and then to the other categories of veterans most in need of intensive services in accordance with priorities determined by the Secretary of Labor in consultation with appropriate State labor authorities.

"(d) States designated. The pilot program shall be limited to not more than five States to be designated by the Secretary of Labor.

"(e) Reports to Congress. (1) Not later than one year after the date of the enactment of this Act, the Secretary of Labor shall submit to the Committees on Veterans' Affairs of the Senate and the House of Representatives an interim report describing in detail the development and implementation of the pilot program on a State by State basis.

"(2) Not later than 120 days after the expiration of this section under subsection (h), the Secretary of Labor shall submit to the Committees on Veterans' Affairs of the Senate and the House of Representatives a final report evaluating the results of the pilot program and make recommendations based on the evaluation, which may include legislative recommendations.

"(f) Definitions. For the purposes of this section:

"(1) The term 'veteran' has the meaning given such term by section 101(2) of title 38, United States Code.

"(2) The term 'disabled veteran' has the meaning given such term by section 4211(3) of such title.

"(3) The term 'active military, naval, or air service' has the meaning given such term by section 101(24) of such title.

"(g) Allocation of funds. Any amount otherwise available for fiscal year 1997, 1998, or 1999 to carry out section 4102A(b)(5) of title 38, United States Code, with respect to a State designated by the Secretary of Labor pursuant to subsection (d) shall be available to carry out the pilot program during that fiscal year with respect to that State.

"(h) Expiration date. The authority to carry out the pilot program under this section shall expire on October 1, 1999.".

RESEARCH GUIDE

Am Jur:
77 Am Jur 2d, Veterans and Veterans' Laws § 104.

§ 4104A. Collaborative veterans' training, mentoring, and placement program

(a) Grants. The Secretary shall award grants to eligible nonprofit organizations to provide training and mentoring for eligible veterans who seek employment. The Secretary shall award the grants to not more than three organizations, for periods of two years.

(b) Collaboration and facilitation. The Secretary shall ensure that the recipients of the grants—

(1) collaborate with—

(A) the appropriate disabled veterans' outreach specialists (in carrying out the functions described in section 4103A(a) [38 USCS § 4103A(a)]) and the appropriate local veterans' employment representatives (in carrying out the functions described in section 4104 [38 USCS § 4104]); and

(B) the appropriate State boards and local boards (as such terms are defined in section 101 of the Workforce Investment Act of 1998 (29 U.S.C. 2801)) for the areas to be served by recipients of the grants; and

(2) based on the collaboration, facilitate the placement of the veterans that complete the training in meaningful employment that leads to economic self-sufficiency.

(c) Application. To be eligible to receive a grant under this section, a nonprofit organization shall submit an application to the Secretary at such time, in such manner, and containing such information as the Secretary may require. At a minimum, the information shall include—

(1) information describing how the organization will—

(A) collaborate with disabled veterans' outreach specialists and local veterans' employment representatives and the appropriate State boards and local boards (as such terms are defined in section 101 of the Workforce Investment Act of 1998 (29 U.S.C. 2801));

(B) based on the collaboration, provide training that facilitates the placement described in subsection (b)(2); and

(C) make available, for each veteran receiving the training, a mentor to provide career advice to the veteran and assist the veteran in preparing a resume and developing job interviewing skills; and

(2) an assurance that the organization will provide the information necessary for the Secretary to prepare the reports described in subsection (d).

(d) Reports. (1) Not later than six months after the date of the enactment of the VOW to Hire Heroes Act of 2011 [enacted Nov. 21, 2011], the Secretary shall prepare and submit to the appropriate committees of Congress a report that describes the process for awarding grants under this section, the recipients of the grants, and the collaboration described in subsections (b) and (c).

(2) Not later than 18 months after the date of enactment of the VOW to Hire Heroes Act of 2011 [enacted Nov. 21, 2011], the Secretary shall—

(A) conduct an assessment of the performance of the grant recipients, disabled veterans' outreach specialists, and local veterans' employment representatives in carrying out activities under this section, which assessment shall include collecting information on the number of—

(i) veterans who applied for training under this section;

(ii) veterans who entered the training;

(iii) veterans who completed the training;
(iv) veterans who were placed in meaningful employment under this section; and
(v) veterans who remained in such employment as of the date of the assessment; and

(B) submit to the appropriate committees of Congress a report that includes—
(i) a description of how the grant recipients used the funds made available under this section;
(ii) the results of the assessment conducted under subparagraph (A); and
(iii) the recommendations of the Secretary as to whether amounts should be appropriated to carry out this section for fiscal years after 2013.

(e) Authorization of appropriations. There is authorized to be appropriated to carry out this section $4,500,000 for the period consisting of fiscal years 2012 and 2013.

(f) Definitions. In this section—
(1) the term "appropriate committees of Congress" means—
(A) the Committee on Veterans' Affairs and the Committee on Health, Education, Labor, and Pension of the Senate; and
(B) the Committee on Veterans' Affairs and the Committee on Education and Workforce of the House of Representatives; and
(2) the term "nonprofit organization" means an organization that is described in section 501(c)(3) of the Internal Revenue Code of 1986 [26 USCS § 501(c)(3)] and that is exempt from taxation under section 501(a) of such Code [26 USCS § 501(a)].

(Added Nov. 21, 2011, P. L. 112-56, Title II, Subtitle C, § 234(a), 125 Stat. 721.)

HISTORY; ANCILLARY LAWS AND DIRECTIVES

Explanatory notes:
A former § 4104A (Act May 20, 1988, P. L. 100-323, § 4(a)(1), 102 Stat. 562; Aug. 6, 1991, P. L. 102-83, § 5(a), (c)(1), 105 Stat. 406) was repealed by Act Nov. 7, 2002, P. L. 107-288, § 4(a)(3)(A)(i), 116 Stat. 2042, effective and applicable as provided by § 4(a)(4) of such Act, which appears as 38 USCS § 4102A note. It related to the performance of disabled veterans' outreach program specialists and local veterans' employment representatives.

§ 4105. Cooperation of Federal agencies

(a) [Unchanged]
(b) For the purpose of assisting the Secretary and the Secretary of Veterans Affairs in identifying employers with potential job training opportunities under the Veterans' Job Training Act (Public Law 98-77; 29 U.S.C. 1721 note) and otherwise in order to carry out this chapter [38 USCS §§ 4100 et seq.], the Secretary of Defense shall, on the 15th day of each month, provide the Secretary and the Secretary of Veterans Affairs with updated information regarding any list maintained by the Secretary of Defense of employers participating in the National Committee for Employer Support of the Guard and Reserve.

(As amended June 15, 2006, P. L. 109-233, Title V, § 503(12), 120 Stat. 417.)

HISTORY; ANCILLARY LAWS AND DIRECTIVES

Amendments:
2006. Act June 15, 2006, in subsec. (b), substituted "shall, on the 15th day of each month, provide the Secretary and the Secretary of Veterans Affairs with updated information regarding" for "shall provide, not more than 30 days after the date of the enactment of this subsection, the Secretary and the Secretary of Veterans Affairs with", and deleted "and shall provide, on the 15th day of each month thereafter, updated information regarding the list" following "Reserve".

RESEARCH GUIDE

Am Jur:
77 Am Jur 2d, Veterans and Veterans' Laws § 99.

§ 4106. Estimate of funds for administration; authorization of appropriations

(a) The Secretary shall estimate the funds necessary for the proper and efficient administration of this chapter [38 USCS §§ 4100 et seq.] and chapters 42 and 43 of this title [38 USCS §§ 4211 et seq. and [4321] 2021 et seq.]. Such estimated sums shall include the annual amounts necessary for salaries, rents, printing and binding, travel, and communications. Sums thus estimated shall be included as a special item in the annual budget for the Department of Labor. Estimated funds necessary for proper intensive services, placement, and training services to eligible veterans and eligible persons provided by the various State public employment service agencies shall each be separately identified in the budgets of those agencies as approved by the Department of Labor. Funds estimated pursuant to the first sentence of this subsection shall include amounts necessary in all of the States for the purposes specified in paragraph (5) of section 4102A(b) of this title [38

READJUSTMENT BENEFITS   38 USCS § 4107

USCS § 4102A(b)] and to fund the National Veterans' Employment and Training Services Institute under section 4109 of this title [38 USCS § 4109] and shall be approved by the Secretary only if the level of funding proposed is in compliance with such sections. Each budget submission with respect to such funds shall include a separate listing of the amount for the National Veterans' Employment and Training Services Institute together with information demonstrating the compliance of such budget submission with the funding requirements specified in the preceding sentence.
(b)–(d) [Unchanged]
(As amended Nov. 7, 2002, P. L. 107-288, §§ 4(d)(1), 5(a)(1)(C), 116 Stat. 2044.)

HISTORY; ANCILLARY LAWS AND DIRECTIVES

Amendments:
2002. Act Nov. 7, 2002 (effective on enactment and applicable to budget submissions beginning with fiscal year 2004, as provided by § 4(d)(2) of such Act, which appears as a note to this section), in subsec. (a), substituted the sentence beginning "Each budget submission . . . ." for "Each budget submission with respect to such funds shall include separate listings of the amount for the National Veterans' Employment and Training Services Institute and of the proposed numbers, by State, of disabled veterans' outreach program specialists appointed under section 4103A of this title and local veterans' employment representatives assigned under section 4104 of this title, together with information demonstrating the compliance of such budget submission with the funding requirements specified in the preceding sentence.".
Such Act further (effective on enactment, as provided by § 5(a)(2) of such Act, which appears as 38 USCS § 4101 note), in subsec. (a), substituted "proper intensive services" for "proper counseling".

Other provisions:
Effective date and applicability of amendment made by § 4(d)(1) of Act Nov. 7, 2002. Act Nov. 7, 2002, P. L. 107-288, § 4(d)(2), 116 Stat. 2044, provides: "The amendment made by paragraph (1) [amending subsec. (a) of this section] shall take effect on the date of the enactment of this Act, and apply to budget submissions for fiscal year 2004 and each subsequent fiscal year.".

RESEARCH GUIDE
Am Jur:
77 Am Jur 2d, Veterans and Veterans' Laws § 99.
45B Am Jur 2d, Job Discrimination § 772.

§ 4107. Administrative controls; annual report
(a) The Secretary shall establish administrative controls for the following purposes:
   (1) To insure that each eligible veteran, especially veterans of the Vietnam era and disabled veterans and each eligible person, who requests assistance under this chapter [38 USCS §§ 4100 et seq.] shall promptly be placed in a satisfactory job or job training opportunity or receive some other specific form of assistance designed to enhance such veteran's and eligible person's employment prospects substantially, such as individual job development or intensive services.
   (2) [Unchanged]
(b) The Secretary shall apply performance standards established under section 4102A(f) of this title [38 USCS § 4102A(f)] for determining compliance by the State public employment service agencies with the provisions of this chapter [38 USCS §§ 4100 et seq.] and chapter 42 of this title [38 USCS §§ 4211 et seq.]. Not later than February 1 of each year, the Secretary shall report to the Committees on Veterans' Affairs of the Senate and the House of Representatives on the performance of States and organizations and entities carrying out employment, training, and placement services under this chapter [38 USCS §§ 4100 et seq.], as measured under subsection (b)(7) of section 4102A of this title [38 USCS § 4102A]. In the case of a State that the Secretary determines has not met the minimum standard of performance (established by the Secretary under subsection (f) of such section), the Secretary shall include an analysis of the extent and reasons for the State's failure to meet that minimum standard, together with the State's plan for corrective action during the succeeding year.
(c) Not later than February 1 of each year, the Secretary shall report to the Committees on Veterans' Affairs of the Senate and the House of Representatives on the success during the preceding program year of the Department of Labor and its affiliated State employment service agencies in carrying out the provisions of this chapter and programs for the provision of employment and training services to meet the needs of eligible veterans and eligible persons. The report shall include—
   (1) specification, by State and by age group, of the numbers of eligible veterans, disabled veterans, special disabled veterans, eligible persons, recently separated veterans (as defined in section 4211(6) of this title [38 USCS § 4211(6)]), and servicemembers transitioning to civilian careers who registered for assistance with, or who are identified as veterans by, the public employment service system and, for each of such categories, the numbers referred to and placed

in permanent and other jobs, the numbers referred to and placed in jobs and job training programs supported by the Federal Government, the number who received intensive services, and the number who received some, and the number who received no, reportable service;

(2) a comparison of the rate of entered employment (as determined in a manner consistent with State performance measures applicable under section 136(b) of the Workforce Investment Act of 1998 [29 USCS § 2871(b)]) for each of the categories of veterans and persons described in paragraph (1) of this subsection with such rate of entered employment (as so determined) for nonveterans of the same age groups registered for assistance with the public employment system in each State;

(3) [Unchanged]

(4) a report on activities carried out during the preceding program year under section 4212(d) of this title [38 USCS § 4212(d)];

(5) a report on the operation during the preceding program year of programs for the provision of employment and training services designed to meet the needs of eligible veterans and eligible persons, including an evaluation of the effectiveness of such programs during such program year in meeting the requirements of section 4102A(b) of this title [38 USCS § 4102A(b)], the efficiency with which services were provided through such programs during such year, and such recommendations for further legislative action relating to veterans' employment and training as the Secretary considers appropriate;

(6) a report on the operation during the preceding program year of the program of performance incentive awards for quality employment services under section 4112 of this title [38 USCS § 4112]; and

(7) performance measures for the provision of assistance under this chapter [38 USCS §§ 4100 et seq.], including—

(A) the percentage of participants in programs under this chapter [38 USCS §§ 4100 et seq.] who find employment before the end of the first 90-day period following their completion of the program;

(B) the percentage of participants described in subparagraph (A) who are employed during the first 180-day period following the period described in such subparagraph;

(C) the median earnings of participants described in subparagraph (A) during the period described in such subparagraph;

(D) the median earnings of participants described in subparagraph (B) during the period described in such subparagraph; and

(E) the percentage of participants in programs under this chapter who obtain a certificate, degree, diploma, licensure, or industry-recognized credential relating to the program in which they participated under this chapter [38 USCS §§ 4100 et seq.] during the third 90-day period following their completion of the program.

(As amended Nov. 7, 2002, P. L. 107-288, §§ 4(a)(3)(B), (e)(1), 5(a)(1)(D); (E), (d)(1), 116 Stat. 2042, 2044, 2045; Nov. 21, 2011, P. L. 112-56, Title II, Subtitle C, § 238, 125 Stat. 726.)

HISTORY; ANCILLARY LAWS AND DIRECTIVES

Amendments:

2002. Act Nov. 7, 2002 (effective on enactment and applicable as provided by § 4(a)(4) of such Act, which appears as 38 USCS § 4102A note), in subsec. (b), substituted "The Secretary shall apply performance standards established under section 4102A(f) of this title" for "The Secretary shall establish definitive performance standards".

Such Act further, in subsec. (c)(5), deleted "(including the need for any changes in the formulas governing the appointment of disabled veterans' outreach program specialists under section 4103A(a)(2) of this title and the assignment of local veterans' employment representatives under section 4104(b) of this title and the allocation of funds for the support of such specialists and representatives)" following "legislative action".

Such Act further (effective on enactment, as provided by § 5(a)(2) of such Act, which appears as 38 USCS § 4101 note), in subsec. (a)(1), substituted "intensive services" for "employment counseling services"; and, in subsec. (c)(1), substituted "the number who received intensive services" for "the number counseled".

Such Act further (applicable to reports for program years beginning on or after 7/1/2003, as provided by § 5(d)(2) of such Act, which appears as a note to this section), in subsec. (b), substituted the sentences beginning "Not later than February 1 . . ." and "In the case of a State . . ." for "A full report as to the extent and reasons for any noncompliance by any such State agency during any fiscal year, together with the agency's plan for corrective action during the succeeding year, shall be included in the annual report of the Secretary required by subsection (c) of this section."; and, in subsec. (c), in para. (1), deleted "veterans of the Vietnam era" following "eligible veterans," and substituted "eligible persons, recently separated veterans (as defined in section 4211(6) of this title), and servicemembers transitioning to civilian careers who registered for assistance with, or who are identified as veterans by," for "eligible persons who registered for assistance with", in para. (2), substituted "the rate of entered employment (as determined in a manner consistent with State performance measures applicable under section 136(b) of the Workforce Investment Act of 1998)'' for "the job placement rate" and substituted "such rate of entered employment (as so determined)" for "the job placement rate", in para. (4), substituted "section 4212(d)" for "sections 4103A and 4104", and deleted "and" following the concluding semicolon, in para. (5), substituted "; and" for a concluding period, and added para. (6).

2011. Act Nov. 21, 2011, in subsec. (c), in para. (2), substituted "paragraph (1)" for "clause (1)", in para. (5), deleted "and" following the concluding semicolon, in para. (6), substituted "; and" for a concluding period, and added para. (7).

Other provisions:
Application of amendments made by § 5(d)(1) of Act Nov. 7, 2002. Act Nov. 7, 2002, P. L. 107-288, § 5(d)(2), 116 Stat. 2046, provides: "The amendments made by paragraph (1) [amending subsecs. (b) and (c) of this section] shall apply to reports for program years beginning on or after July 1, 2003.''.

RESEARCH GUIDE
Am Jur:
45B Am Jur 2d, Job Discrimination § 772.
77 Am Jur 2d, Veterans and Veterans' Laws § 99.

§ 4108. Cooperation and coordination

RESEARCH GUIDE
Am Jur:
77 Am Jur 2d, Veterans and Veterans' Laws § 99.

§ 4109. National Veterans' Employment and Training Services Institute

(a) In order to provide for such training as the Secretary considers necessary and appropriate for the efficient and effective provision of employment, job-training, intensive services, placement, job-search, and related services to veterans, the Secretary shall establish and make available such funds as may be necessary to operate a National Veterans' Employment and Training Services Institute for the training of disabled veterans' outreach program specialists, local veterans' employment representatives, Directors for Veterans' Employment and Training, and Assistant Directors for Veterans' Employment and Training, Regional Administrators for Veterans' Employment and Training, and such other personnel involved in the provision of employment, job-training, intensive services, placement, or related services to veterans as the Secretary considers appropriate, including travel expenses and per diem for attendance at the Institute.

(b) [Unchanged]

(c)(1) Nothing in this section shall be construed as preventing the Institute to enter into contracts or agreements with departments or agencies of the United States or of a State, or with other organizations, to carry out training of personnel of such departments, agencies, or organizations in the provision of services referred to in subsection (a).

(2) All proceeds collected by the Institute under a contract or agreement referred to in paragraph (1) shall be applied to the applicable appropriation.

(d)(1) The Secretary shall require that each disabled veterans' outreach program specialist and local veterans' employment representative who receives training provided by the Institute, or its successor, is given a final examination to evaluate the specialist's or representative's performance in receiving such training.

(2) The results of such final examination shall be provided to the entity that sponsored the specialist or representative who received the training.

(As amended Nov. 7, 2002, P. L. 107-288, § 5(a)(1)(F), (e), 116 Stat. 2044, 2046; Nov. 21, 2011, P. L. 112-56, Title II, Subtitle C, § 240(a), 125 Stat. 727.)

HISTORY; ANCILLARY LAWS AND DIRECTIVES
Amendments:
2002. Act Nov. 7, 2002 (effective on enactment, as provided by § 5(a)(2) of such Act, which appears as 38 USCS § 4101 note), in subsec. (a), substituted "intensive services," for "counseling," in two places.
Such Act further added subsec. (c).
2011. Act Nov. 21, 2011 (applicable to training beginning on or after the date that is 180 days after enactment as provided by § 240(b) of such Act, which appears as a note to this section), added subsec. (d).

Other provisions:
Application of Nov. 21, 2011 amendment. Act Nov. 21, 2011, P. L. 112-56, Title II, Subtitle C, § 240(b), 125 Stat. 727, provides: "Subsection (d) of section 4109 of title 38, United States Code, as added by subsection (a), shall apply with respect to training provided by the National

Veterans' Employment and Training Services Institute that begins on or after the date that is 180 days after the date of the enactment of this Act.''.

RESEARCH GUIDE

Am Jur:
77 Am Jur 2d, Veterans and Veterans' Laws § 106.

§ 4110. Advisory Committee on Veterans Employment, Training, and Employer Outreach

(a)(1) There is hereby established within the Department of Labor an advisory committee to be known as the Advisory Committee on Veterans Employment, Training, and Employer Outreach.

(2) The advisory committee shall—

(A) assess the employment and training needs of veterans and their integration into the workforce;

(B) determine the extent to which the programs and activities of the Department of Labor are meeting such needs;

(C) assist the Assistant Secretary of Labor for Veterans' Employment and Training in carrying out outreach activities to employers with respect to the training and skills of veterans and the advantages afforded employers by hiring veterans;

(D) make recommendations to the Secretary, through the Assistant Secretary of Labor for Veterans' Employment and Training, with respect to outreach activities and the employment and training of veterans; and

(E) carry out such other activities that are necessary to make the reports and recommendations referred to in subsection (f) of this section.

(b) [Unchanged]

(c)(1) The Secretary of Labor shall appoint at least 12, but no more than 16, individuals to serve as members of the advisory committee as follows:

(A) Seven individuals, one each from among representatives nominated by each of the following organizations:

(i) The National Society of Human Resource Managers.

(ii) The Business Roundtable.

(iii) The National Association of State Workforce Agencies.

(iv) The United States Chamber of Commerce.

(v) The National Federation of Independent Business.

(vi) A nationally recognized labor union or organization.

(vii) The National Governors Association.

(B) Not more than five individuals from among representatives nominated by veterans service organizations that have a national employment program.

(C) Not more than five individuals who are recognized authorities in the fields of business, employment, training, rehabilitation, or labor and who are not employees of the Department of Labor.

(2) [Unchanged]

(d) The following, or their representatives, shall be ex officio, nonvoting members of the advisory committee:

(1), (2) [Unchanged]

(3) The Director of the Office of Personnel Management.

(4) The Assistant Secretary of Labor for Veterans Employment and Training.

(5) The Assistant Secretary of Labor for Employment and Training.

(6) The Administrator of the Small Business Administration.

(7) [Redesignated]

(8) [Deleted]

(9) [Redesignated]

(10)–(12) [Deleted]

(e) [Unchanged]

(f)(1) Not later than December 31 of each year, the advisory committee shall submit to the Secretary and to the Committees on Veterans' Affairs of the Senate and House of Representatives a report on the employment and training needs of veterans, with special emphasis on disabled veterans, for the previous fiscal year. Each such report shall contain—

(A) an assessment of the employment and training needs of veterans and their integration into the workforce;

(B) an assessment of the outreach activities carried out by the Secretary of Labor to employers with respect to the training and skills of veterans and the advantages afforded employers by hiring veterans;

(C) an evaluation of the extent to which the programs and activities of the Department of Labor are meeting such needs;

(D) a description of the activities of the advisory committee during that fiscal year;

(E) a description of activities that the advisory committee proposes to undertake in the succeeding fiscal year; and

(F) any recommendations for legislation, administrative action, and other action that the advisory committee considers appropriate.

(2) [Unchanged]

(g), (h) [Unchanged]

(As amended June 15, 2006, P. L. 109-233, Title II, § 202(a)(1), (2), (b)–(d), 120 Stat. 403; Dec. 22, 2006, P. L. 109-461, Title VI, § 604(b), 120 Stat. 3439; Oct. 10, 2008, P. L. 110-387, Title IX, § 901(a)(4), 122 Stat. 4142.)

HISTORY; ANCILLARY LAWS AND DIRECTIVES

Amendments:

2006. Act June 15, 2006, substituted the section heading for one which read: "§ 4110. Advisory Committee on Veterans Employment and Training"; in subsec. (a), in para. (1), substituted "Advisory Committee on Veterans Employment, Training, and Employer Outreach" for "Advisory Committee on Veterans Employment and Training", in para. (2), in subpara. (A), inserted "and their integration into the workforce", in subpara. (B), deleted "and" after the concluding semicolon, redesignated subpara. (C) as subpara. (E), and inserted new subparas. (C) and (D); in subsec. (c), substituted para. (1) for one which read:

"(1) The Secretary of Labor shall appoint at least 12, but no more than 18, individuals to serve as members of the advisory committee consisting of—

"(A) representatives nominated by veterans' organizations that have a national employment program; and

"(B) not more than 6 individuals who are recognized authorities in the fields of business, employment, training, rehabilitation, or labor and who are not employees of the Department of Labor.";

in subsec. (d), deleted paras. (3) and (4), which read:

"(3) The Secretary of Health and Human Services.",

"(4) The Secretary of Education.",

deleted para. (8), which read: "(8) The Chairman of the Equal Employment Opportunity Commission.", and deleted paras. (10)–(12), which read:

"(10) The Postmaster General.

"(11) The Director of the United States Employment Service.

"(12) Representatives of—

"(A) other Federal departments and agencies requesting a representative on the advisory committee; and

"(B) nationally based organizations with a significant involvement in veterans employment and training programs, as determined necessary and appropriate by the Secretary of Labor.",

and redesignated paras. (5), (6), (7), and (9) as paras. (3), (4), (5), and (6), respectively; in subsec. (f)(1), in the introductory matter, substituted the sentence beginning "Not later than December 31 of each year . . ." for "Not later than July 1 of each year, the advisory committee shall submit to the Secretary of Labor a report on the employment and training needs of veterans.", in subpara. (A), inserted "and their integration into the workforce", in subpara. (B), deleted "and" following the concluding semicolon, redesignated subparas. (B) and (C) as subparas. (C) and (F), respectively, and inserted new subparas. (B), (D) and (E).

Act Dec. 22, 2006, in subsec. (c)(1)(A), in the introductory matter, substituted "Seven" for "Six", and added cl. (vii).

2008. Act Oct. 10, 2008, in subsec. (c)(1), in the introductory matter, substituted "16" for "15".

Other provisions:

Termination of reporting requirements. For termination, effective May 15, 2000, of provisions of subsec. (g) of this section relating to periodic reports to Congress, see § 3003 of Act Dec. 21, 1995, P. L. 104-66, which appears as 31 USCS § 1113 note. See also page 125 of House Document No. 103-7.

References to Advisory Committee. Act June 15, 2006, P. L. 109-233, Title II, § 202(a)(4), 120 Stat. 403, provides: "Any reference to the Advisory Committee established under section 4110 of such title [Title 38, USCS] in any law, regulation, map, document, record, or other paper of the United States shall be considered to be a reference to the Advisory Committee on Veterans Employment, Training, and Employer Outreach.".

RESEARCH GUIDE

Am Jur:

77 Am Jur 2d, Veterans and Veterans' Laws § 105.

38 USCS § 4110A

§ 4110A. Special unemployment study

(a)(1) The Secretary, through the Bureau of Labor Statistics, shall conduct an annual study of unemployment among each of the following categories of veterans:

  (A) Veterans who were called to active duty while members of the National Guard or a Reserve Component.

  (B) Veterans who served in combat or in a war zone in the Post 9/11 Global Operations theaters.

  (C) Veterans who served on active duty during the Post 9/11 Global Operations period who did not serve in the Post 9/11 Global Operations theaters.

  (D) Veterans of the Vietnam era who served in the Vietnam theater of operations during the Vietnam era.

  (E) Veterans who served on active duty during the Vietnam era who did not serve in the Vietnam theater of operations.

  (F) Veterans discharged or released from active duty within four years of the applicable study.

  (G) Special disabled veterans.

(2) [Unchanged]

(3) [Redesignated]

(b) The Secretary shall promptly submit to Congress a report on the results of each study under subsection (a).

(c) In this section:

  (1) The term "Post 9/11 Global Operations period" means the period of the Persian Gulf War beginning on September 11, 2001, and ending on the date thereafter prescribed by Presidential proclamation or law.

  (2) The term "Post 9/11 Global Operations theaters" means Afghanistan, Iraq, or any other theater in which the Global War on Terrorism Expeditionary Medal is awarded for service.

(As amended Nov. 11, 1998, P. L. 105-368, Title X, § 1005(b)(14), 112 Stat. 3365; Oct. 10, 2008, P. L. 110-389, Title III, Subtitle A, § 317, 122 Stat. 4167.)

HISTORY; ANCILLARY LAWS AND DIRECTIVES

Amendments:

1998. Act Nov. 11, 1998 deleted subsec. (b), which read: "(b) The first study under this section shall be completed not later than 180 days after the date of the enactment of this section."; redesignated subsec. (a)(3) as subsec. (b) and, in such subsection as redesignated, substituted "subsection (a)" for "paragraph (1)".

2008. Act Oct. 10, 2008, in subsec. (a)(1), in the introductory matter, substituted "an annual study" for "a study every two years", and substituted subparas. (A)–(G) for former subparas. (A)–(E), which read:

  "(A) Special disabled veterans.

  "(B) Veterans of the Vietnam era who served in the Vietnam theater of operations during the Vietnam era.

  "(C) Veterans who served on active duty during the Vietnam era who did not serve in the Vietnam theater of operations.

  "(D) Veterans who served on active duty after the Vietnam era.

  "(E) Veterans discharged or released from active duty within four years of the applicable study.";

and added subsec. (c).

Other provisions:

Termination of reporting requirements. For termination, effective May 15, 2000, of provisions of subsec. (b) of this section relating to periodic reports to Congress, see § 3003 of Act Dec. 21, 1995, P. L. 104-66, which appears as 31 USCS § 1113 note. See also page 125 of House Document No. 103-7.

RESEARCH GUIDE

Am Jur:

77 Am Jur 2d, Veterans and Veterans' Laws § 99.

§ 4110B. Coordination and nonduplication

In carrying out this chapter [38 USCS §§ 4100 et seq.], the Secretary shall require that an appropriate administrative entity in each State enter into an agreement with the Secretary regarding the implementation of the Workforce Investment Act of 1998 that includes the description and information described in paragraphs (8) and (14) of section 112(b) of the Workforce Investment Act of 1998 (29 U.S.C. 2822(b)).

(Added Aug. 7, 1998, P. L. 105-220, Title III, Subtitle B, § 322, 112 Stat. 1087; June 15, 2006, P. L. 109-233, Title V, § 503(13), 120 Stat. 417.)

HISTORY; ANCILLARY LAWS AND DIRECTIVES

References in text:
The "Workforce Investment Act of 1998", referred to in this section, is Act Aug. 7, 1998, P. L. 105-220. For full classification of such Act, consult USCS Tables volumes.

Effective date of section:
This section took effect on August 7, 1998, pursuant to § 507 of Act Aug. 7, 1998, P. L. 105-220, which appears as 20 USCS § 9201 note.

Amendments:
2006. Act June 15, 2006, substituted "the Workforce Investment Act of 1998" for "this Act" following "implementation of", and inserted "(29 U.S.C. 2822(b))".

RESEARCH GUIDE

Am Jur:
45B Am Jur 2d, Job Discrimination § 774.

[§ 4111. Repealed]

HISTORY; ANCILLARY LAWS AND DIRECTIVES

This section (Act Nov. 30, 1999, P. L. 106-117, Title IX, § 901(a), 113 Stat. 1586) was repealed by Act Dec. 21, 2001, P. L. 107-95, § 5(e)(3), 115 Stat. 918. It related to reintegration programs for homeless veterans. For similar provisions, see 38 USCS § 2021.

A prior section 4111 (Act Sept. 2, 1958, P. L. 85-857, § 1, 72 Stat. 1247; Oct. 11, 1962, P. L. 87-793, Part II, Title IV, § 804, 76 Stat. 861; Nov. 7, 1966, P. L. 89-785, Title I, § 108, 80 Stat. 1370; Nov. 21, 1983, P. L. 98-160, Title II, § 206, 97 Stat. 1001) was repealed by Act May 7, 1991, P. L. 102-40, Title IV, § 401(a)(3), 105 Stat. 210. Such section provided for appointment of additional employees.

§ 4112. Performance incentive awards for quality employment, training, and placement services

(a) Criteria for performance incentive awards. (1) For purposes of carrying out a program of performance incentive awards under section 4102A(c)(2)(A)(i)(III) of this title [38 USCS § 4102A(c)(2)(A)(i)(III)], the Secretary, acting through the Assistant Secretary of Labor for Veterans' Employment and Training, shall establish criteria for performance incentive awards programs to be administered by States to—

(A) encourage the improvement and modernization of employment, training, and placement services provided under this chapter; and

(B) recognize eligible employees and employment service offices for excellence in the provision of such services or for having made demonstrable improvements in the provision of such services.

(2) The Secretary shall establish such criteria in consultation with representatives of States, political subdivisions of States, and other providers of employment, training, and placement services under the Workforce Investment Act of 1998 consistent with the performance measures established under section 4102A(b)(7) of this title [38 USCS § 4102A(b)(7)].

(b) Form of awards. Under the criteria established by the Secretary for performance incentive awards to be administered by States, an award under such criteria may be a cash award or such other nonfinancial awards as the Secretary may specify.

(c) Administration and use of awards. Performance incentive cash awards under this section—

(1) shall be made from amounts allocated from the grant or contract amount for a State for a program year under section 4102A(c)(7) of this title [38 USCS § 4102A(c)(7)];

(2) in the case of such an award made to an eligible employee, shall be in addition to the regular pay of the recipient; and

(3) in the case of such an award made to an employment service office, may be used by that employment service office for any purpose.

(d) Eligible employee defined. In this section, the term "eligible employee" means any of the following:

(1) A disabled veterans' outreach program specialist.

(2) A local veterans' employment representative.

(3) An individual providing employment, training, and placement services to veterans under the Workforce Investment Act of 1998 or through an employment service delivery system (as defined in section 4101(7) of this title [38 USCS § 4101(7)]).

(Added Nov. 7, 2002, P. L. 107-288, § 3(a), 116 Stat. 2037; Dec. 22, 2006, P. L. 109-461, Title VI, § 603, 120 Stat. 3437.)

HISTORY; ANCILLARY LAWS AND DIRECTIVES

References in text:
The "Workforce Investment Act of 1998", referred to in this section, is Act Aug. 7, 1998, P.

38 USCS § 4112   VETERANS' BENEFITS

L. 105-220, which appears generally as 20 USCS §§ 9201 et seq. and 29 USCS §§ 2801 et seq. For full classification of such Act, consult USCS Tables volumes.

Explanatory notes:
A prior § 4112 (Act Sept. 2, 1958, P. L. 85-857, § 1, 72 Stat. 1247; Nov. 7, 1966, P. L. 89-785, Title I, § 109(a), 80 Stat. 1370; Aug. 2, 1973, P. L. 93-82, Title II, § 205(b), 87 Stat. 192; Oct. 21, 1976, P. L. 94-581, Title I, § 110(8), Title II, §§ 209(b)(3), 210(c)(6), 90 Stat. 2849, 2861, 2864; Dec. 20, 1979, P. L. 96-151, Title III, § 305, 93 Stat. 1096; Aug. 26, 1980, P. L. 96-303, Title I, Part B, § 115, 94 Stat. 1039; March 2, 1984, P. L. 98-223, Title II, § 209, 98 Stat. 44; May 20, 1988, P. L. 100-322, Title II, Part C, § 224, 102 Stat. 532) was repealed by Act May 7, 1991, P. L. 102-40, Title IV, § 401(a)(3), 105 Stat. 210. It provided for a special medical advisory group and other advisory bodies.

Amendments:
2006. Act Dec. 22, 2006, in subsec. (a)(1)(B), inserted "and employment service offices"; in subsec. (c), substituted the heading for one which read: "Relationship of award to grant program and employee compensation.", in para. (1), deleted "and" following the concluding semicolon, in para. (2), substituted "in the case of such an award made to an eligible employee, shall be" for "is", and substituted "; and" for a concluding period, and added para. (3).

RESEARCH GUIDE
Other Treatises:
1 Rapp, Education Law (Matthew Bender), ch 5, Funding, Support and Finances of Education § 5.01.

§ 4113. Transition Assistance Program personnel

(a) Requirement to contract. In accordance with section 1144 of title 10 [10 USCS § 1144], the Secretary shall enter into a contract with an appropriate private entity or entities to provide the functions described in subsection (b) at all locations where the program described in such section is carried out.

(b) Functions. Contractors under subsection (a) shall provide to members of the Armed Forces who are being separated from active duty (and the spouses of such members) the services described in section 1144(a)(1) of title 10 [10 USCS § 1144(a)(1)], including the following:

(1) Counseling.
(2) Assistance in identifying employment and training opportunities and help in obtaining such employment and training.
(3) Assessment of academic preparation for enrollment in an institution of higher learning or occupational training.
(4) Other related information and services under such section.
(5) Such other services as the Secretary considers appropriate.

(Added Dec. 16, 2003, P. L. 108-183, Title III, § 309(a)(1), 117 Stat. 2663; June 15, 2006, P. L. 109-233, Title IV, § 402(e)(2), 120 Stat. 411; Nov. 21, 2011, P. L. 112-56, Title II, Subtitle B, § 223(a)(1), 125 Stat. 717.)

HISTORY; ANCILLARY LAWS AND DIRECTIVES
Explanatory notes:
A prior § 4113 (Act Sept. 2, 1958, P. L. 85-857, § 1, 72 Stat. 1247; Nov. 7, 1966, P. L. 89-785, Title I, § 110, 80 Stat. 1371; Oct. 21, 1976, P. L. 94-581, Title I, § 110(9), Title II, § 209(a)(5), (c)(5), 90 Stat. 2849, 2860, 2862) was repealed by Act May 7, 1991, P. L. 102-40, Title IV, § 401(a)(3), 105 Stat. 210. Such section provided for travel expenses of employees.

Amendments:
2006. Act June 15, 2006, in subsec. (a)(2), substituted "section 6304(a)" for "section 7723(a)".
2011. Act Nov. 21, 2011, substituted this section for one which read:
"§ 4113. Outstationing of Transition Assistance Program personnel
"(a) Stationing of TAP personnel at overseas military installations. (1) The Secretary—
"(A) shall station employees of the Veterans' Employment and Training Service, or contractors under subsection (c), at each veterans assistance office described in paragraph (2); and
"(B) may station such employees or contractors at such other military installations outside the United States as the Secretary, after consultation with the Secretary of Defense, determines to be appropriate or desirable to carry out the purposes of this chapter.
"(2) Veterans assistance offices referred to in paragraph (1)(A) are those offices that are established by the Secretary of Veterans Affairs on military installations pursuant to the second sentence of section 6304(a) of this title.
"(b) Functions. Employees (or contractors) stationed at military installations pursuant to subsection (a) shall provide, in person, counseling, assistance in identifying employment and training opportunities, help in obtaining such employment and training, and other related information and services to members of the Armed Forces who are being separated from active duty, and

Readjustment Benefits — 38 USCS § 4114

the spouses of such members, under the Transition Assistance Program and Disabled Transition Assistance Program established in section 1144 of title 10.

"(c) Authority to contract with private entities. The Secretary, consistent with section 1144 of title 10, may enter into contracts with public or private entities to provide, in person, some or all of the counseling, assistance, information and services under the Transition Assistance Program required under subsection (a).".

Other provisions:
Deadline for implementation. Act Dec. 16, 2003, P. L. 108-183, Title III, § 309(b), 117 Stat. 2663, provides: "Not later than 90 days after the date of the enactment of this Act, the Secretary of Labor shall implement section 4113 of title 38, United States Code, as added by subsection (a), and shall have employees of the Veterans' Employment and Training Service, or contractors, to carry out that section at the military installations involved by such date.".

Deadline for implementation. Act Nov. 21, 2011, P. L. 112-56, Title II, Subtitle B, § 223(b), 125 Stat. 718, provides: "The Secretary of Labor shall enter into the contract required by section 4113 of title 38, United States Code, as added by subsection (a), not later than two years after the date of the enactment of this Act.".

§ 4114. Credentialing and licensure of veterans: demonstration project

(a) Demonstration project authorized. The Assistant Secretary for Veterans' Employment and Training shall carry out a demonstration project on credentialing in accordance with this section for the purpose of facilitating the seamless transition of members of the Armed Forces from service on active duty to civilian employment.

(b) Identification of military occupational specialties and associated credentials and licenses.
(1) The Assistant Secretary for Veterans' Employment and Training shall, in consultation with the Assistant Secretary for Employment and Training, select not more than five military occupational specialties for purposes of the demonstration project. Each specialty so selected by the Assistant Secretary for Veterans' Employment and Training shall require a skill or set of skills that is required for civilian employment in an industry with high growth or high worker demand.

(2) The Assistant Secretary shall enter into a contract with an appropriate entity representing a coalition of State governors to consult with appropriate Federal, State, and industry officials and identify requirements for credentials, certifications, and licenses that require a skill or set of skills required by a military occupational specialty selected under paragraph (1).

(3) The Assistant Secretary shall analyze the requirements identified under paragraph (2) to determine which requirements may be satisfied by the skills, training, or experience acquired by members of the Armed Forces with the military occupational specialties selected under paragraph (1).

(c) Elimination of barriers to credentialing and licensure. The Assistant Secretary shall cooperate with appropriate Federal, State, and industry officials to reduce or eliminate any barriers to providing a credential, certification, or license to a veteran who acquired any skill, training, or experience while serving as a member of the Armed Forces with a military occupational specialty selected under subsection (b)(1) that satisfies the Federal and State requirements for the credential, certification, or license.

(d) Period of project. The period during which the Assistant Secretary shall carry out the demonstration project under this section shall be the two-year period beginning on the date of the enactment of the VOW to Hire Heroes Act of 2011 [enacted Nov. 21, 2011].

(Added Dec. 22, 2006, P. L. 109-461, Title VI, § 604(a)(1), 120 Stat. 3437; Nov. 21, 2011, P. L. 112-56, § 237(a), 125 Stat. 725.)

HISTORY; ANCILLARY LAWS AND DIRECTIVES

Explanatory notes:
A prior § 4114 (Act Sept. 2, 1958, P. L. 85-857, § 1, 72 Stat. 1247; Aug. 6, 1962, P. L. 87-574, § 4(2), 76 Stat. 309; Nov. 7, 1966, P. L. 89-785, Title I, § 111(a)–(c), 80 Stat. 1371; Oct. 22, 1970, P. L. 91-496, §§ 1, 3, 84 Stat. 1092; Aug. 2, 1973, P. L. 93-82, Title II, § 206, 87 Stat. 192; Oct. 21, 1976, P. L. 94-581, Title I, §§ 109, 110(10), Title II, §§ 205(g), 209(a)(6), (c)(6), 210(c)(7), 90 Stat. 2848, 2849, 2859, 2860, 2862, 2864; Nov. 23, 1977, P. L. 95-201, § 4(a)(2), 91 Stat. 1430; Aug. 26, 1980, P. L. 96-330, Title I, Part B, § 116(b), 94 Stat. 1039; Oct. 12, 1982, P. L. 97-295, § 4(85), 96 Stat. 1312; Dec. 3, 1985, P. L. 99-166, Title II, § 203, 99 Stat. 950; Oct. 28, 1986, P. L. 99-576, Title II, Part B, § 214, 100 Stat. 3258; May 20, 1988, P. L. 100-322, Title II, Part C, § 223, 102 Stat. 531; Nov. 18, 1988, P. L. 100-687, Div B, Title XV, § 1503(a)(2), 102 Stat. 4133; Aug. 15, 1990, P. L. 101-366, Title II, § 203, 104 Stat. 439) was repealed by Act May 7, 1991, P. L. 102-40, Title IV, § 401(a)(3), 105 Stat. 210. It provided for temporary full-time, part-time, and without compensation appointments, and residencies or internships.

Amendments:
2011. Act Nov. 21, 2011, in subsec. (a), substituted "shall" for "may"; in subsec. (b), in para. (1), substituted "Assistant Secretary for Veterans' Employment and Training shall, in consulta-

tion with the Assistant Secretary for Employment and Training," for "Assistant Secretary shall", substituted "not more than five military" for "not less than 10 military", and inserted "for Veterans' Employment and Training", and in para. (2), substituted "enter into a contract with an appropriate entity representing a coalition of State governors to consult with appropriate Federal, State, and industry officials and" for "consult with appropriate Federal, State, and industry officials to"; and substituted subsec. (d) for former subsecs. (d)–(h), which read:

"(d) Task force. The Assistant Secretary may establish a task force of individuals with appropriate expertise to provide assistance to the Assistant Secretary in carrying out this section.

"(e) Consultation. In carrying out this section, the Assistant Secretary shall consult with the Secretary of Defense, the Secretary of Veterans Affairs, appropriate Federal and State officials, private-sector employers, labor organizations, and industry trade associations.

"(f) Contract authority. For purposes of carrying out any part of the demonstration project under this section, the Assistant Secretary may enter into a contract with a public or private entity with appropriate expertise.

"(g) Period of project. The period during which the Assistant Secretary may carry out the demonstration project under this section shall be the period beginning on the date that is 60 days after the date of the enactment of the Veterans Benefits, Health Care, and Information Technology Act of 2006 and ending on September 30, 2009.

"(h) Funding. The Assistant Secretary may carry out the demonstration project under this section utilizing unobligated funds that are appropriated in accordance with the authorization set forth in section 4106 of this title.".

Other provisions:
Veteran Skills to Jobs Act. Act July 23, 2012, P. L. 112-147, 126 Stat. 1138, provides:
"Section 1. Short title.
"This Act may be cited as the 'Veteran Skills to Jobs Act'.
"Sec. 2. Consideration of relevant military training for issuance of a Federal license
"(a) In General. The head of each Federal licensing authority shall consider and may accept, in the case of any individual applying for a license, any relevant training received by such individual while serving as a member of the armed forces, for the purpose of satisfying the requirements for such license.
"(b) Definitions. For purposes of this Act—
    "(1) the term 'license' means a license, certification, or other grant of permission to engage in a particular activity;
    "(2) the term 'Federal licensing authority' means a department, agency, or other entity of the Government having authority to issue a license;
    "(3) the term 'armed forces' has the meaning given such term by section 2101(2) of title 5, United States Code; and
    "(4) the term 'Government' means the Government of the United States.
"Sec. 3. Regulations.
"The head of each Federal licensing authority shall—
    "(1) with respect to any license a licensing authority grants or is empowered to grant as of the date of enactment of this Act, prescribe any regulations necessary to carry out this Act not later than 180 days after such date; and
    "(2) with respect to any license of a licensing authority not constituted or not empowered to grant the license as of the date of enactment of this Act, prescribe any regulations necessary to carry out this Act not later than 180 days after the date on which the agency is so constituted or empowered, as the case may be.".

[§§ 4115–4119. Repealed]

HISTORY; ANCILLARY LAWS AND DIRECTIVES

These sections (§ 4115—Act Sept. 2, 1958, P. L. 85-857, § 1, 72 Stat. 1248; § 4116—Act Oct. 31, 1965, P. L. 89-311, § 6(a), 79 Stat. 1156; July 18, 1966, P. L. 89-506, § 5(b), 80 Stat. 307; Aug. 2, 1973, P. L. 93-82, Title II, § 207, 87 Stat. 193; Oct. 21, 1976, P. L. 94-581, Title I, § 110(11), Title II, §§ 209(a)(7), 210(c)(8), 90 Stat. 2849, 2861, 2864; May 20, 1988, P. L. 100-322, Title II, Part A, § 203(a)(1), 102 Stat. 509; § 4117—Act Nov. 7, 1966, P. L. 89-785, Title I, § 112(a), 80 Stat. 1371; Aug. 2, 1973, P. L. 93-82, Title II, § 208, 87 Stat. 194; Oct. 21, 1976, P. L. 94-581, Titles I, § 110(12), Title II, § 209(a)(1), (8), 90 Stat. 2849, 2860, 2861; § 4118—Act Oct. 22, 1975, P. L. 94-123, § 2(d)(l), 89 Stat. 670; Nov. 23, 1977, P. L. 95-201, § 3(a), 91 Stat. 1429; Aug. 26, 1980, P. L. 96-330, Title I, Part A, §§ 102(a)(1), (b)–(d), 103(a), 104(a), Title II, § 202, 94 Stat. 1030, 1031, 1034, 1035, 1047; Oct. 12, 1982, P. L. 97-295, § 4(86), 96 Stat. 1312; Sept. 13, 1982, P. L. 97-258, § 3(k)(6), 96 Stat. 1065; Oct. 28, 1986, P. L. 99-576, Title II, Part D, § 231(a), 100 Stat. 3263; Jan. 8, 1988, P. L. 100-238, Title I, § 126, 101 Stat. 1757; § 4119—Act Aug. 26, 1980, P. L. 96-330, Title I, Part B, § 116(a)(1), 94 Stat. 1039) were repealed by Act May 7, 1991, P. L. 102-40, Title IV, § 401(a)(3), 105 Stat. 210. Section 4115 provided for the promulgation of regulations necessary to the administration of the Department of Medicine and Surgery; § 4116 provided for the defense of certain malpractice and negligence suits; § 4117 provided for contracts for scarce medical specialist services; § 4118 provided for special pay for physicians and dentists; § 4119 provided for the relationship between this subchapter [former 38 USCS §§ 4101 et seq.] and other provisions of law.

CHAPTER 42. EMPLOYMENT AND TRAINING OF VETERANS

Section
4215. Priority of service for veterans in Department of Labor job training programs.

HISTORY; ANCILLARY LAWS AND DIRECTIVES

Amendments:
2002. Act Nov. 7, 2002, P. L. 107-288, § 2(a)(2), 116 Stat. 2034, amended the analysis of this chapter by adding item 4215.

§ 4211. Definitions

As used in this chapter [38 USCS §§ 4211 et seq.]—
(1)–(3) [Unchanged]
(4) The term "eligible veteran" means a person who—
  (A) [Unchanged]
  (B) was discharged or released from active duty because of a service-connected disability;
  (C) as a member of a reserve component under an order to active duty pursuant to section 12301(a), (d), or (g), 12302, or 12304 of title 10, served on active duty during a period of war or in a campaign or expedition for which a campaign badge is authorized and was discharged or released from such duty with other than a dishonorable discharge; or
  (D) was discharged or released from active duty by reason of a sole survivorship discharge (as that term is defined in section 1174(i) of title 10).
(5) The term "department or agency" means any agency of the Federal Government or the District of Columbia, including any Executive agency as defined in section 105 of title 5 [5 USCS § 105] and the United States Postal Service and the Postal Rate Commission [Postal Regulatory Commission], and the term "department, agency, or instrumentality in the executive branch" includes the United States Postal Service and the Postal Rate Commission [Postal Regulatory Commission].
(6) The term "recently separated veteran" means any veteran during the three-year period beginning on the date of such veteran's discharge or release from active duty.
(As amended Nov. 1, 2000, P. L. 106-419, Title III, Subtitle C, § 322(c), 114 Stat. 1855; Nov. 7, 2002, P. L. 107-288, § 2(b)(2)(D), 116 Stat. 2036; Aug. 29, 2008, P. L. 110-317, § 6(b), 122 Stat. 3528.)

HISTORY; ANCILLARY LAWS AND DIRECTIVES

Explanatory notes:
"Postal Regulatory Commission" has been inserted in brackets in para. (4) pursuant to § 604(f) of Act Dec. 20, 2006, P. L. 109-435 (39 USCS § 404 note), which provides that a reference in any provision of law to the Postal Rate Commission shall be considered a reference to the Postal Regulatory Commission.

Amendments:
2000. Act Nov. 1, 2000 added para. (6).
2002. Act Nov. 7, 2002 (applicable to contracts entered into on or after 12/1/2003, as provided by § 2(b)(3) of such Act, which appears as a note to this section), in para. (6), substituted "three-year period" for "one-year period".
2008. Act Aug. 29, 2008 (applicable with respect to any sole survivorship discharge granted after 9/11/2001, as provided by § 10(a) of such Act, which appears as 5 USCS § 2108 note), in para. (4), in subpara. (B), deleted "or" following the concluding semicolon, in subpara. (C), substituted "; or" for a concluding period, and added subpara. (D).

Other provisions:
Application of Nov. 7, 2002 amendments. Act Nov. 7, 2002, P. L. 107-288, § 2(b)(3), 116 Stat. 2036, provides: "The amendments made by this subsection [amending 38 USCS §§ 4211(6) and 4212] shall apply with respect to contracts entered into on or after the first day of the first month that begins 12 months after the date of the enactment of this Act.".

CODE OF FEDERAL REGULATIONS

Employment and Training Administration, Department of Labor—Administrative provisions governing the Job Service System, 20 CFR 658.400 et seq.
Office of the Assistant Secretary for Veterans' Employment and Training, Department of Labor—Services for veterans, 20 CFR 1001.100 et seq.
Office of Federal Contract Compliance Programs, Equal Employment Opportunity, Department of Labor—Affirmative action and nondiscrimination obligations of contractors and subcontractors regarding special disabled veterans and veterans of the Vietnam era, 41 CFR 60-250.1 et seq.
Office of Federal Contract Compliance Programs, Equal Employment Opportunity, Department of Labor—Affirmative action and nondiscrimination obligations of contractors and subcontractors regard-

ing disabled veterans, recently separated veterans, other protected veterans, and Armed Forces service medal veterans, 41 CFR 60-300.1 et seq.
Office of the Assistant Secretary for Veterans' Employment and Training Service, Department of Labor—Annual report from Federal contractors, 41 CFR 61-300.1 et seq.

RESEARCH GUIDE

Am Jur:
45A Am Jur 2d, Job Discrimination § 695.
45B Am Jur 2d, Job Discrimination § 772.
77 Am Jur 2d, Veterans and Veterans' Laws § 95.

Labor and Employment:
10 Larson on Employment Discrimination, ch 173, Veterans' Preference Laws § 173.01.
4 Labor and Employment Law (Matthew Bender), ch 130, Employment Discrimination—Relation to Other Laws § 130.01.

§ 4212. Veterans' employment emphasis under Federal contracts

(a)(1) Any contract in the amount of $100,000 or more entered into by any department or agency of the United States for the procurement of personal property and nonpersonal services (including construction) for the United States, shall contain a provision requiring that the party contracting with the United States take affirmative action to employ and advance in employment qualified covered veterans. This section applies to any subcontract in the amount of $100,000 or more entered into by a prime contractor in carrying out any such contract.

(2) In addition to requiring affirmative action to employ such qualified covered veterans under such contracts and subcontracts and in order to promote the implementation of such requirement, the Secretary of Labor shall prescribe regulations requiring that—

(A) each such contractor for each such contract shall immediately list all of its employment openings with the appropriate employment service delivery system (as defined in section 4101(7) of this title [38 USCS § 4101(7)]), and may also list such openings with one-stop career centers under the Workforce Investment Act of 1998, other appropriate service delivery points, or America's Job Bank (or any additional or subsequent national electronic job bank established by the Department of Labor), except that the contractor may exclude openings for executive and senior management positions and positions which are to be filled from within the contractor's organization and positions lasting three days or less;

(B) each such employment service delivery system shall give such qualified covered veterans priority in referral to such employment openings; and

(C) each such employment service delivery system shall provide a list of such employment openings to States, political subdivisions of States, or any private entities or organizations under contract to carry out employment, training, and placement services under chapter 41 of this title [38 USCS §§ 4100 et seq.].

(3) In this section:

(A) The term "covered veteran" means any of the following veterans:

(i) Disabled veterans.

(ii) Veterans who served on active duty in the Armed Forces during a war or in a campaign or expedition for which a campaign badge has been authorized.

(iii) Veterans who, while serving on active duty in the Armed Forces, participated in a United States military operation for which an Armed Forces service medal was awarded pursuant to Executive Order No. 12985 (61 Fed. Reg. 1209) [10 USCS prec § 1121 note].

(iv) Recently separated veterans.

(B) The term "qualified", with respect to an employment position, means having the ability to perform the essential functions of the position with or without reasonable accommodation for an individual with a disability.

(b) If any veteran covered by the first sentence of subsection (a) believes any contractor of the United States has failed to comply or refuses to comply with the provisions of the contractor's contract relating to the employment of veterans, the veteran may file a complaint with the Secretary of Labor, who shall promptly investigate such complaint and take appropriate action in accordance with the terms of the contract and applicable laws and regulations.

(c) The Secretary of Labor shall include as part of the annual report required by section 4107(c) of this title [38 USCS § 4107(c)] the number of complaints filed pursuant to subsection (b) of this section, the actions taken thereon and the resolutions thereof. Such report shall also include the number of contractors listing employment openings, the nature, types, and number of positions listed and the number of veterans receiving priority pursuant to subsection (a)(2)(B).

(d)(1) Each contractor to whom subsection (a) applies shall, in accordance with regulations which the Secretary of Labor shall prescribe, report at least annually to the Secretary of Labor on—

(A) the number of employees in the workforce of such contractor, by job category and hiring location, and the number of such employees, by job category and hiring location, who are qualified covered veterans;

(B) the total number of new employees hired by the contractor during the period covered by the report and the number of such employees who are qualified covered veterans; and

(C) the maximum number and the minimum number of employees of such contractor during the period covered by the report.

(2) The Secretary of Labor shall ensure that the administration of the reporting requirement under paragraph (1) is coordinated with respect to any requirement for the contractor to make any other report to the Secretary of Labor.

(3) The Secretary of Labor shall establish and maintain an Internet website on which the Secretary of Labor shall publicly disclose the information reported to the Secretary of Labor by contractors under paragraph (1).

(As amended Oct. 31, 1998, P. L. 105-339, §§ 7(a), 8, 112 Stat. 3188, 3189; Nov. 1, 2000, P. L. 106-419, Title III, Subtitle C, § 322(a), (b), 114 Stat. 1855; Nov. 7, 2002, P. L. 107-288, § 2(b)(1), (2)(A)–(C), 116 Stat. 2034; Aug. 6, 2012, P. L. 112-154, Title VII, § 708, 126 Stat. 1207.)

HISTORY; ANCILLARY LAWS AND DIRECTIVES

References in text:
The "Workforce Investment Act of 1998", referred to in this section, is Act Aug. 7, 1998, P. L. 105-220, which appears generally as 20 USCS §§ 9201 et seq. and 29 USCS §§ 2801 et seq. For full classification of such Act, consult USCS Tables volumes.

Amendments:
1998. Act Oct. 31, 1998, in subsec. (a), substituted "$25,000" for "$10,000" and substituted "special disabled veterans, veterans of the Vietnam era, and any other veterans who served on active duty during a war or in a campaign or expedition for which a campaign badge has been authorized" for "special disabled veterans and veterans of the Vietnam era"; in subsec. (b), substituted "veteran covered by the first sentence of subsection (a)" for "special disabled veteran or veteran of the Vietnam era"; and, in subsec. (d)(1), in subpara. (A), substituted "special disabled veterans, veterans of the Vietnam era, or other veterans who served on active duty during a war or in a campaign or expedition for which a campaign badge has been authorized" for "veterans of the Vietnam era or special disabled veterans" and deleted "and" after the concluding semicolon, in subpara. (B), substituted "special disabled veterans, veterans of the Vietnam era, or other veterans who served on active duty during a war or in a campaign or expedition for which a campaign badge has been authorized" for "veterans of the Vietnam era or special disabled veterans" and substituted "; and" for a concluding period, and added subpara. (C).

2000. Act Nov. 1, 2000, in subsecs. (a) and (d)(1)(A) and (B), inserted "recently separated veterans,".

2002. Act Nov. 7, 2002 (applicable with respect to contracts entered into on or after 12/1/2003, as provided by § 2(b)(3) of such Act, which appears as 38 USCS § 4211 note), substituted subsec. (a) for one which read: "(a) Any contract in the amount of $25,000 or more entered into by any department or agency for the procurement of personal property and nonpersonal services (including construction) for the United States, shall contain a provision requiring that the party contracting with the United States shall take affirmative action to employ and advance in employment qualified special disabled veterans, veterans of the Vietnam era, recently separated veterans, and any other veterans who served on active duty during a war or in a campaign or expedition for which a campaign badge has been authorized. The provisions of this section shall apply to any subcontract entered into by a prime contractor in carrying out any contract for the procurement of personal property and non-personal services (including construction) for the United States. In addition to requiring affirmative action to employ such veterans under such contracts and subcontracts and in order to promote the implementation of such requirement, the President shall implement the provisions of this section by promulgating regulations which shall require that (1) each such contractor undertake in such contract to list immediately with the appropriate local employment service office all of its employment openings except that the contractor may exclude openings for executive and top management positions, positions which are to be filled from within the contractor's organization, and positions lasting three days or less, and (2) each such local office shall give such veterans priority in referral to such employment openings."; in subsec. (c), deleted "suitable" preceding "employment", and substituted "subsection (a)(2)(B)" for "subsection (a)(2) of this section"; and, in subsec. (d), in para. (1), in the introductory matter, deleted "of this section" following "subsection (a)", and substituted subparas. (A) and (B) for ones which read:

"(A) the number of employees in the work force of such contractor, by job category and hiring location, who are special disabled veterans, veterans of the Vietnam era, recently separated veterans, or other veterans who served on active duty during a war or in a campaign or expedition for which a campaign badge has been authorized;

"(B) the total number of new employees hired by the contractor during the period covered by the report and the number of such employees who are special disabled veterans, veterans of the Vietnam era, recently separated veterans, or other veterans who served on active duty during a war or in a campaign or expedition for which a campaign badge has been authorized; and".

and, in para. (2), deleted "of this subsection" following "paragraph (1)".

2012. Act Aug. 6, 2012, in subsec. (d), added para. (3).

CODE OF FEDERAL REGULATIONS

Employment and Training Administration, Department of Labor—Administrative provisions governing the Job Service System, 20 CFR 658.400 et seq.

Office of Federal Contract Compliance Programs, Equal Employment Opportunity, Department of Labor—Rules of practice for administrative proceedings to enforce equal opportunity under Executive Order 11246, 41 CFR 60-30.1 et seq.

Office of Federal Contract Compliance Programs, Equal Employment Opportunity, Department of Labor—Affirmative action and nondiscrimination obligations of contractors and subcontractors regarding special disabled veterans and veterans of the Vietnam era, 41 CFR 60-250.1 et seq.

Office of Federal Contract Compliance Programs, Equal Employment Opportunity, Department of Labor—Affirmative action and nondiscrimination obligations of contractors and subcontractors regarding disabled veterans, recently separated veterans, other protected veterans, and Armed Forces service medal veterans, 41 CFR 60-300.1 et seq.

Office of the Assistant Secretary for Veterans' Employment and Training Service, Department of Labor—Annual report from Federal contractors, 41 CFR 61-300.1 et seq.

RESEARCH GUIDE

Am Jur:

45A Am Jur 2d, Job Discrimination §§ 25, 98, 171, 393, 551, 583, 695.

45B Am Jur 2d, Job Discrimination §§ 772, 1380, 1384, 1389, 1671, 1753, 1802, 1825.

77 Am Jur 2d, Veterans and Veterans' Laws § 96.

Labor and Employment:

6 Larson on Employment Discrimination, ch 116, Federal Government Contracts § 116.01.

10 Larson on Employment Discrimination, ch 173, Veterans' Preference Laws § 173D.01.

4 Labor and Employment Law (Matthew Bender), ch 115, Government Contracts § 115.01.

10 Labor and Employment Law (Matthew Bender), ch 256, Recruiting, Hiring and Training § 256.03.

10 Labor and Employment Law (Matthew Bender), ch 271, Record Keeping and Agency Notice Posting § 271.14.

INTERPRETIVE NOTES AND DECISIONS

2. Application

Plaintiff's employer fire department was not party to federal procurement contract so as to make provisions of Vietnam Era Veterans' Readjustment Assistance Act applicable to it; grant agreements are not procurement contracts, including that with Federal Emergency Management Agency, whose purpose was to carry out public purpose authorized by federal statute, not to procure property or services for direct benefit of U.S. government, and separate employment relationship between government and employees in event of catastrophe does not change FEMA agreement into procurement contract. Partridge v Reich (1998, CA9 Nev) 141 F3d 920, 98 CDOS 2500, 98 Daily Journal DAR 3459, 157 BNA LRRM 3005.

One of relator's theories of liability alleged that corporation submitted false claims by seeking payment despite having filed inaccurate VETS-100 reports; however, relator failed to point to any provision of Vietnam Era Veterans Readjustment Assistance Act, 38 USCS § 4212, that required corporation to expressly attest to accuracy of reports. United States ex rel. Kirk v Schindler Elevator Corp. (2009, SD NY) 606 F Supp 2d 448.

One of relator's theories of liability, alleging that corporation falsely certified its compliance with Vietnam Era Veterans Readjustment Assistance Act, 38 USCS § 4212, by submitting claims for payment while knowing that it did not have affirmative action program for veterans or procedure to allow veterans to self-identify as required by statute, failed; relator could point to no statutory provision or implementing rule requiring corporation to expressly certify—as condition to payment—that it had affirmative action program. United States ex rel. Kirk v Schindler Elevator Corp. (2009, SD NY) 606 F Supp 2d 448.

3. Complaints

Although relator alleged that despite its noncompliance with Vietnam Era Veterans Readjustment Assistance Act, 38 USCS § 4212, corporation submitted to agencies of U.S. hundreds of requests for payment under its government contracts, each of which was false or fraudulent claim, because U.S. Department of Labor's responses to relator's Freedom of Information Act requests constituted administrative investigations and reports; those investigations and reports publicly disclosed allegations or transactions underlying relator's claims; those claims were based upon public disclosure; and relator was not original source of information, relator's claims were statutorily barred. United States ex rel. Kirk v Schindler Elevator Corp. (2009, SD NY) 606 F Supp 2d 448.

4. Private right of action

Defendant former employer's veteran employee reports, submitted to Department of Labor (DOL) under Vietnam Era Veterans Readjustment Assistance Act, 38 USCS § 4212, and produced to plaintiff former employee by DOL under Freedom of Information Act, 5 USCS § 552, requests, and letters stating no responsive records were found for certain years, were not administrative reports or investigations under 31 USCS § 3730(e)(4)(A) so as to bar employee's False Claims Act case under 31 USCS § 3729. United States ex rel. Kirk v Schindler Elevator Corp. (2010, CA2 NY) 601 F3d 94.

5. Judicial review

Secretary of Department of Labor was properly

granted summary judgment on veteran's Administrative Procedure Act, 5 USCS §§ 701 et seq., complaint, because Secretary and Office of Federal Contract Compliance Programs promptly discharged duty under 38 USCS § 4212(b) and 41 CFR § 60-250.61(d) to investigate veteran's administrative complaint under Vietnam Era Veterans' Readjustment Assistance Act of 1974 and discretionary decision not to initiate enforcement proceedings was immune from judicial review. Greer v Chao (2007, CA8 Minn) 492 F3d 962, 89 CCH EPD ¶ 42881.

6. Miscellaneous

In former employee's qui tam action alleging that former employer had violated reporting requirements under Vietnam Era Veterans' Readjustment Assistance Act of 1972, Department of Labor's three written Freedom of Information Act responses to employee's wife, along with their attached records, were "reports" within meaning of False Claims Act's, 31 USCS §§ 3279&N3733, public disclosure bar, 31 USCS § 3730(e)(4)(A), because, inter alia, broad ordinary meaning of "report" was consistent with generally broad scope of public disclosure bar. Schindler Elevator Corp. v United States ex rel. Kirk (2011, US) 131 S Ct 1885, 179 L Ed 2d 825, 32 BNA IER Cas 252, 94 CCH EPD ¶ 44175, 22 FLW Fed S 975.

Job applicant did not file administrative complaint with Department of Labor; thus, even if private right of action exists under Vietnam Era Veterans' Readjustment Assistance Act, 38 USCS § 4212, it could not be pursued here. Douris v Bucks County (2005, ED Pa) 16 AD Cas 790, app dismd (2005, CA3 Pa) 2005 US App LEXIS 17759.

§ 4213. Eligibility requirements for veterans under Federal employment and training programs

(a) Amounts and periods of time specified in subsection (b) shall be disregarded in determining eligibility under any of the following:

(1) Any public service employment program.

(2) Any emergency employment program.

(3) Any job training program assisted under the Economic Opportunity Act of 1964.

(4) Any employment or training program carried out under title I of the Workforce Investment Act of 1998 (29 U.S.C. 2801 et seq.).

(5) Any other employment or training (or related) program financed in whole or in part with Federal funds.

(b) Subsection (a) applies with respect to the following amounts and periods of time:

(1) Any amount received as pay or allowances by any person while serving on active duty.

(2) Any period of time during which such person served on active duty.

(3) Any amount received under chapters 11, 13, 30, 31, 32, and 36 of this title [38 USCS §§ 1101 et seq., 1301 et seq., 3001 et seq., 3100 et seq., 3201 et seq., 3670 et seq.] by an eligible veteran.

(4) Any amount received by an eligible person under chapters 13 and 35 of this title [38 USCS §§ 1301 et seq., 3500 et seq.].

(5) Any amount received by an eligible member under chapter 106 of title 10 [10 USCS §§ 2131 et seq.].

(As amended Oct. 21, 1998, P. L. 105-277, Div A, § 101(f) [Title VIII, Subtitle IV, § 405(d)(29)(C), (f)(21)(C)], 112 Stat. 2681-424, 2681-432; Nov. 1, 2000, Title IV, § 404(a)(9), 114 Stat. 1865.)

HISTORY; ANCILLARY LAWS AND DIRECTIVES

References in text:

"Title I of the Workforce Investment Act of 1998", referred to in this section, is Title I of Act Aug. 7, 1998, P. L. 105-220, which appears generally as 29 USCS §§ 2801 et seq. For full classification of such Title, consult USCS Tables volumes.

Amendments:

1998. Act Oct. 21, 1998 (effective on enactment as provided by § 405(g)(1) of Subtitle IV of Title VIII of § 101(f) of Division A of such Act, which appears as 5 USCS § 3502 note), substituted "program carried out under the Job Training Partnership Act or title I of the Workforce Investment Act of 1998," for "program assisted under the Job Training Partnership Act (29 U.S.C. 1501 et seq.),".

Act Oct. 21, 1998 (effective on 7/1/2000, as provided by § 405(g)(2)(B) of Subtitle VIII of Title IV of § 101(f) of Division A of such Act, which appears as 5 USCS § 3502 note), deleted "the Job Training Partnership Act or" preceding "title I".

2000. Act Nov. 1, 2000 substituted the text of this section for text which read: "Any (1) amounts received as pay or allowances by any person while serving on active duty, (2) period of time during which such person served on such active duty, and (3) amounts received under chapters 11, 13, 30, 31, 35, and 36 of this title by an eligible veteran, any amounts received by an eligible person under chapters 13 and 35 of such title, and any amounts received by an eligible person under chapter 106 of title 10, shall be disregarded in determining eligibility under any public service employment program, any emergency employment program, any job training program assisted under the Economic Opportunity Act of 1964, any employment or training program carried out under title I of the Workforce Investment Act of 1998, or any other employment or training (or related) program financed in whole or in part with Federal funds.".

38 USCS § 4213   VETERANS' BENEFITS

CODE OF FEDERAL REGULATIONS

Employment and Training Administration, Department of Labor—Administrative provisions governing the Job Service System, 20 CFR 658.400 et seq.

RESEARCH GUIDE

Am Jur:
77 Am Jur 2d, Veterans and Veterans' Laws § 107.
45A Am Jur 2d, Job Discrimination § 695.
45B Am Jur 2d, Job Discrimination § 772.

§ 4214. Employment within the Federal Government

(a)(1) The United States has an obligation to assist veterans of the Armed Forces in readjusting to civilian life. The Federal Government is also continuously concerned with building an effective work force, and veterans constitute a uniquely qualified recruiting source. It is, therefore, the policy of the United States and the purpose of this section to promote the maximum of employment and job advancement opportunities within the Federal Government for qualified covered veterans (as defined in paragraph (2)(B)) who are qualified for such employment and advancement.

(2) In this section:

  (A) The term "agency" has the meaning given the term "department or agency" in section 4211(5) of this title [38 USCS § 4211(5)].

  (B) The term "qualified covered veteran" means a veteran described in section 4212(a)(3) of this title [38 USCS § 4212(a)(3)].

(b)(1) To further the policy stated in subsection (a) of this section, veterans referred to in paragraph (2) of this subsection shall be eligible, in accordance with regulations which the Office of Personnel Management shall prescribe, for veterans recruitment appointments, and for subsequent career-conditional appointments, under the terms and conditions specified in Executive Order Numbered 11521 (March 26, 1970) [5 USCS § 3302 note], except that—

  (A)–(E) [Unchanged]

(2) This subsection applies to qualified covered veterans.

(3) A qualified covered veteran may receive such an appointment at any time.

(c), (d) [Unchanged]

(e)(1) [Unchanged]

(2) Information shown for an agency under clauses (A) through (D) of paragraph (1) of this subsection—

  (A) [Unchanged]

  (B) shall be shown separately (i) for veterans who are entitled to disability compensation under the laws administered by the Secretary whose discharge or release from active duty was for a disability incurred or aggravated in line of duty, and (ii) for other veterans.

(f) [Unchanged]

(g) To further the policy stated in subsection (a) of this section, the Secretary may give preference to qualified covered veterans for employment in the Department as veterans' benefits counselors and veterans' claims examiners and in positions to provide the outreach services required under section 6303 of this title [38 USCS § 6303], to serve as veterans' representatives at certain educational institutions as provided in section 6305 of this title [38 USCS § 6305], or to provide readjustment counseling under section 1712A of this title [38 USCS § 1712A].

(As amended Nov. 7, 2002, P. L. 107-288, § 2(c)(1)–(3), 116 Stat. 2036; June 15, 2006, P. L. 109-233, Title IV, § 402(e)(3), 120 Stat. 411.)

HISTORY; ANCILLARY LAWS AND DIRECTIVES

Amendments:

2002. Act Nov. 7, 2002 (applicable as provided by § 2(c)(4) of such Act, which appears as a note to this section), in subsec. (a), in para. (1), substituted "life." for "life since veterans, by virtue of their military service, have lost opportunities to pursue education and training oriented toward civilian careers.", substituted "uniquely qualified" for "major", and substituted "qualified covered veterans (as defined in paragraph (2)(B))" for "disabled veterans and certain veterans of the Vietnam era and of the post-Vietnam era", and substituted para. (2) for one which read: "(2) For the purposes of this section, the term 'agency' means a department, agency, or instrumentality in the executive branch."; in subsec. (b), in para. (1), in the introductory matter, substituted "recruitment" for "readjustment", in para. (2), substituted "to qualified covered veterans." for "to—

  "(A) a veteran of the Vietnam era; and

  "(B) veterans who first became a member of the Armed Forces or first entered on active duty as a member of the Armed Forces after May 7, 1975, and were discharged or released from active duty under conditions other than dishonorable.", and substituted para. (3) for one which read:

"(3)(A) Except as provided in subparagraph (C) of this paragraph, a veteran of the Vietnam era may receive an appointment under this section only during the period ending—

"(i) 10 years after the date of the veteran's last discharge or release from active duty; or

"(ii) December 31, 1995, whichever is later.

"(B) Except as provided in subparagraph (C) of this paragraph, a veteran described in paragraph (2)(B) of this subsection may receive such an appointment only within the 10-year period following the later of—

"(i) the date of the veteran's last discharge or release from active duty; or

"(ii) December 31, 1989.

"(C) The limitations of subparagraphs (A) and (B) of this paragraph shall not apply to a veteran who has a service-connected disability rated at 30 percent or more.

"(D) For purposes of clause (i) of subparagraphs (A) and (B) of this paragraph, the last discharge or release from active duty shall not include any discharge or release from active duty of less than ninety days of continuous service unless the individual involved is discharged or released for a service-connected disability, for a medical condition which preexisted such service and which the Secretary determines is not service connected, for hardship, or as a result of a reduction in force described in section 3011(a)(1)(A)(ii)(III) of this title or of an involuntary separation described in section 3018A(a)(1).";

in subsec. (e)(2)(B), deleted "of the Vietnam era" preceding "who are entitled"; and, in subsec. (g), substituted "qualified covered veterans" for "qualified special disabled veterans and qualified veterans of the Vietnam era", and substituted "under section 1712A of this title," for "under section 1712A of this title to veterans of the Vietnam era.".

2006. Act June 15, 2006, in subsec. (g), substituted "section 6303" for "section 7722" and substituted "section 6305" for "section 7724".

Other provisions:

Termination of reporting requirements. For termination, effective May 15, 2000, of provisions of subsec. (e) of this section relating to periodic reports to Congress, see § 3003 of Act Dec. 21, 1995, P. L. 104-66, which appears as 31 USCS § 1113 note. See also page 188 of House Document No. 103-7.

Application of Nov. 7, 2002 amendments. Act Nov. 7, 2002, P. L. 107-288, § 2(c)(4), 116 Stat. 2036, provides: "The amendments made by this subsection [amending this section] shall apply to qualified covered veterans without regard to any limitation relating to the date of the veteran's last discharge or release from active duty that may have otherwise applied under section 4214(b)(3) as in effect on the date before the date of the enactment of this Act.".

Employment assistance: other Federal agencies. Act Nov. 21, 2011, P. L. 112-56, Title II, Subtitle C, § 235(b), 125 Stat. 724, provides:

"(1) Definitions. In this subsection—

"(A) the term 'agency' has the meaning given the term 'Executive agency' in section 105 of title 5, United States Code; and

"(B) the term 'veteran' has the meaning given that term in section 101 of title 38, United States Code.

"(2) Responsibilities of Office of Personnel Management. The Director of the Office of Personnel Management shall—

"(A) designate agencies that shall establish a program to provide employment assistance to members of the Armed Forces who are being separated from active duty in accordance with paragraph (3); and

"(B) ensure that the programs established under this subsection are coordinated with the Transition Assistance Program (TAP) of the Department of Defense.

"(3) Elements of program. The head of each agency designated under paragraph (2)(A), in consultation with the Director of the Office of Personnel Management, and acting through the Veterans Employment Program Office of the agency established under Executive Order 13518 [5 USCS § 3301 note] (74 Fed. Reg. 58533; relating to employment of veterans in the Federal Government), or any successor thereto, shall—

"(A) establish a program to provide employment assistance to members of the Armed Forces who are being separated from active duty, including assisting such members in seeking employment with the agency;

"(B) provide such members with information regarding the program of the agency established under subparagraph (A); and

"(C) promote the recruiting, hiring, training and development, and retention of such members and veterans by the agency.

"(4) Other office. If an agency designated under paragraph (2)(A) does not have a Veterans Employment Program Office, the head of the agency, in consultation with the Director of the Office of Personnel Management, shall select an appropriate office of the agency to carry out the responsibilities of the agency under paragraph (3).".

CODE OF FEDERAL REGULATIONS

Office of Personnel Management—Veterans recruitment appointments, 5 CFR 307.101 et seq.

38 USCS § 4214

Employment and Training Administration, Department of Labor—Administrative provisions governing the Job Service System, 20 CFR 658.400 et seq.

RESEARCH GUIDE

Am Jur:
45A Am Jur 2d, Job Discrimination § 695.
45B Am Jur 2d, Job Discrimination § 1671.
77 Am Jur 2d, Veterans and Veterans' Laws §§ 95, 100.

Labor and Employment:
10 Larson on Employment Discrimination, ch 173, Veterans' Preference Laws § 173D.01.

Law Review Articles:
Hazard. Employers' obligations under the Uniformed Services Employment and Reemployment Rights Act. 31 Colo L 55, February 2002.

Beasley. Protecting America's reservists: application of state and federal law to reservists' claims of unfair labor practices. 7 Ga BJ 10, February 2002.

Whelan. The Uniform Services Employment and Reemployment Rights Act and homeland security. 71 J Kan BA 20, January 2002.

INTERPRETIVE NOTES AND DECISIONS

1. Generally

Petitioner Air Force's 5 USCS § 7117(a)(1) conflict argument, that respondent union's proposals as to dealing with reduction in force conflicted with 38 USCS § 4214(a)(1) and 5 CFR § 307.103 as to veterans recruitment appointments, and that it had no duty to negotiate over proposals, was waived under 5 USCS § 7123(c) for not being presented to Federal Labor Relations Authority. United States Dep't of Air Force v FLRA (2012, App DC) 680 F3d 826, 193 BNA LRRM 2450.

Agency did not violate veteran's preference rights since both appellant and selectee were in same preference category under 38 USCS § 4214. Whitney v Dep't of the Army (2002, MSPB) 92 MSPR 423.

2. Appointment

Merit Systems Protection Board committed legal error when it upheld administrative judge's decision that Board did not have authority to review veteran's claim that VA ("VA") violated Veterans Employment Opportunities Act when it found that he was not qualified for IT specialist position; Board had jurisdiction to determine whether VA properly afforded veteran right to compete for job and properly determined, in accordance with 5 CFR § 302.302(d), that he was not qualified for position, and remand was required so Board could decide those issues. Lazaro v Dep't of Veterans Affairs (2012, CA FC) 666 F3d 1316.

Postal employee was not veterans readjustment appointment (VRA) under 38 USCS § 4214, even though she was eligible for VRA status, and, was, thus, not exempted from requirement that she complete one year of current continuous service before she was eligible to appeal her termination to Merit System Protection Board, where she was hired by Postal Service from hiring worksheet. Howard v Henderson (2000, MD Ala) 112 F Supp 2d 1276.

3. Promotion

Pursuant to OPM regulations, 45-year-old federal employee's veteran status made him ineligible for noncompetitive promotion; therefore, fact that student intern's position was noncompetitively converted to full-time position that had not been offered to employee did not establish prima facie case of age discrimination under 29 USCS § 633a, part of Age Discrimination in Employment Act. Whitman v Mineta (2005, DC Alaska) 382 F Supp 2d 1130.

5. Private right of action

Court of Appeals did not read Rehabilitation Act as extending its private remedy to rights contained in Vietnam Era Veterans' Readjustment Assistance Act; therefore, no private remedy existed for plaintiff employee on his challenge to enforce defendant federal agency's hiring and retention policy for disabled veterans. Seay v TVA (2003, CA6 Tenn) 339 F3d 454, 92 BNA FEP Cas 577, 2003 FED App 275P.

There is no private right of action under 38 USCS § 4214. Ledbetter v City of Topeka (2000, DC Kan) 112 F Supp 2d 1239, 80 CCH EPD ¶ 40655, 48 FR Serv 3d 212, affd (2003, CA10 Kan) 61 Fed Appx 574.

38 USCS § 4214 does not provide employee with private cause of action. Fizer-Jordan v Ziglar (2003, ED Mich) 242 F Supp 2d 474, 172 BNA LRRM 2189.

§ 4215. Priority of service for veterans in Department of Labor job training programs

(a) **Definitions.** In this section:
  (1) The term "covered person" means any of the following individuals:
    (A) A veteran.
    (B) The spouse of any of the following individuals:
      (i) Any veteran who died of a service-connected disability.
      (ii) Any member of the Armed Forces serving on active duty who, at the time of application for assistance under this section, is listed, pursuant to section 556 of title 37 [37 USCS § 556] and regulations issued thereunder, by the Secretary concerned in one or more of the following categories and has been so listed for a total of more than 90 days: (I) missing in action, (II) captured in line of duty by a hostile force, or (III) forcibly detained or interned in line of duty by a foreign government or power.
      (iii) Any veteran who has a total disability resulting from a service-connected disability.
      (iv) Any veteran who died while a disability so evaluated was in existence.

(2) The term "qualified job training program" means any workforce preparation, development, or delivery program or service that is directly funded, in whole or in part, by the Department of Labor and includes the following:

    (A) Any such program or service that uses technology to assist individuals to access workforce development programs (such as job and training opportunities, labor market information, career assessment tools, and related support services).

    (B) Any such program or service under the public employment service system, one-stop career centers, the Workforce Investment Act of 1998, a demonstration or other temporary program, and those programs implemented by States or local service providers based on Federal block grants administered by the Department of Labor.

    (C) Any such program or service that is a workforce development program targeted to specific groups.

(3) The term "priority of service" means, with respect to any qualified job training program, that a covered person shall be given priority over nonveterans for the receipt of employment, training, and placement services provided under that program, notwithstanding any other provision of law. Such priority includes giving access to such services to a covered person before a non-covered person or, if resources are limited, giving access to such services to a covered person instead of a non-covered person.

(b) Entitlement to priority of service. (1) A covered person is entitled to priority of service under any qualified job training program if the person otherwise meets the eligibility requirements for participation in such program.

(2) The Secretary of Labor may establish priorities among covered persons for purposes of this section to take into account the needs of disabled veterans and special disabled veterans, and such other factors as the Secretary determines appropriate.

(c) Administration of programs at State and local Levels. An entity of a State or a political subdivision of the State that administers or delivers services under a qualified job training program shall—

(1) provide information and priority of service to covered persons regarding benefits and services that may be obtained through other entities or service providers; and

(2) ensure that each covered person who applies to or who is assisted by such a program is informed of the employment-related rights and benefits to which the person is entitled under this section.

(d) Addition to annual report. (1) In the annual report required under section 4107(c) of this title [38 USCS § 4107(c)] for the program year beginning in 2003 and each subsequent program year, the Secretary of Labor shall evaluate whether covered persons are receiving priority of service and are being fully served by qualified job training programs. Such evaluation shall include—

    (A) an analysis of the implementation of providing such priority at the local level;

    (B) whether the representation of veterans in such programs is in proportion to the incidence of representation of veterans in the labor market, including within groups that the Secretary may designate for priority under such programs, if any; and

    (C) performance measures, as determined by the Secretary, to determine whether veterans are receiving priority of service and are being fully served by qualified job training programs.

(2) The Secretary may not use the proportion of representation of veterans described in subparagraph (B) of paragraph (1) as the basis for determining under such paragraph whether veterans are receiving priority of service and are being fully served by qualified job training programs.

(Added Nov. 7, 2002, P. L. 107-288, § 2(a)(1), 116 Stat. 2033; Nov. 21, 2011, P. L. 112-56, Title II, Subtitle C, § 239, 125 Stat. 727.)

HISTORY; ANCILLARY LAWS AND DIRECTIVES

References in text:

The "Workforce Investment Act of 1998", referred to in this section, is Act Aug. 7, 1998, P. L. 105-220, which appears generally as 20 USCS §§ 9201 et seq. and 29 USCS §§ 2801 et seq. For full classification of such Act, consult USCS Tables volumes.

2011. Act Nov. 21, 2011, in subsec. (a)(3), added the sentence beginning "Such priority includes . . ."; and substituted subsec. (d) for one which read: "(d) Addition to annual report. In the annual report required under section 4107(c) of this title for the program year beginning in 2003 and each subsequent program year, the Secretary of Labor shall evaluate whether covered persons are receiving priority of service and are being fully served by qualified job training programs, and whether the representation of veterans in such programs is in proportion to the incidence of representation of veterans in the labor market, including within groups that the Secretary may designate for priority under such programs, if any.".

38 USCS § 4215 VETERANS' BENEFITS

Other provisions:
Requirement to promptly establish one-stop employment services. Act Nov. 7, 2002, P. L. 107-288, § 4(c), 116 Stat. 2044, provides: "By not later than 18 months after the date of the enactment of this Act, the Secretary of Labor shall provide one-stop services and assistance to covered persons electronically by means of the Internet, as defined in section 231(e)(3) of the Communications Act of 1934 [47 USCS § 231(e)(3)], and such other electronic means to enhance the delivery of such services and assistance.".

Department of Labor implementation of regulations for priority of service. Act Dec. 22, 2006, P. L. 109-461, Title VI, § 605, 120 Stat. 3439, provides: "Not later than two years after the date of the enactment of this Act, the Secretary of Labor shall prescribe regulations to implement section 4215 of title 38, United States Code [this section].".

CODE OF FEDERAL REGULATIONS
Office of the Assistant Secretary for Veterans' Employment and Training, Department of Labor—Application of priority of service for covered persons, 20 CFR 1010.100 et seq.

RESEARCH GUIDE
Am Jur:
45A Am Jur 2d, Job Discrimination § 695.

FOR INDEX, SEE GENERAL INDEX VOLUMES AND SUPPLEMENTS THERETO